Also by Simon Sebag Montefiore

NONFICTION
*Potemkin: Catherine the Great's Imperial Partner*
*Stalin: The Court of the Red Tsar*
*Young Stalin*
*Jerusalem: The Biography*
*Titans of History*

FICTION
*Sashenka*
*One Night in Winter*

# THE ROMANOVS

# The
# ROMANOVS
## 1613–1918

## Simon Sebag Montefiore

ALFRED A. KNOPF    NEW YORK    2016

THIS IS A BORZOI BOOK
PUBLISHED BY ALFRED A. KNOPF

www.aaknopf.com

Library of Congress Cataloging-in-Publication Data
Names: Sebag Montefiore, Simon, [date], author.
Title: The Romanovs : 1613–1918 / by Simon Sebag Montefiore.
Description: First American edition. | New York : Alfred A. Knopf, 2016. |
"This is a Borzoi Book." | Includes bibliographical references.
Identifiers: LCCN 2015046026 (print) | LCCN 2015046253 (ebook) |
ISBN 9780307266521 (hardcover) | ISBN 9781101946978 (ebook)
Subjects: LCSH: Romanov, House of. | Russia—Kings and rulers—
Biography. | Russia—History—1613–1917.
Classification: LCC DK37.8.R6 S43 2016 (print) | LCC DK37.8.R6 (ebook) |
DDC 947.09/9—dc23
LC record available at http://lccn.loc.gov/2015046026

Jacket design and lettering by Nicholas Misani

Manufactured in the United States of America
First American Edition

*To My Darling Daughter*
*Lily Bathsheba*

# CONTENTS

# ILLUSTRATIONS

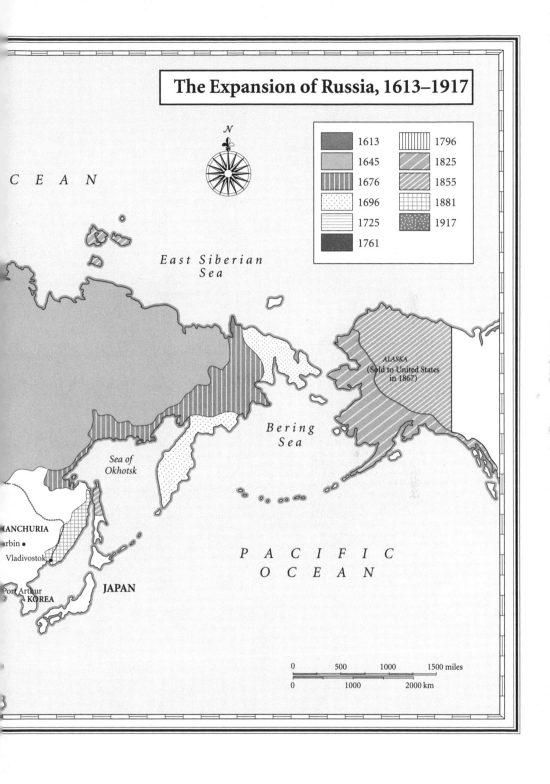

# The Expansion of Russia, 1613–1917

N

| | | | |
|---|---|---|---|
| | 1613 | | 1796 |
| | 1645 | | 1825 |
| | 1676 | | 1855 |
| | 1696 | | 1881 |
| | 1725 | | 1917 |
| | 1761 | | |

East Siberian
Sea

OCEAN

ALASKA
(Sold to United States
in 1867)

Bering
Sea

Sea of
Okhotsk

MANCHURIA

Harbin ●

Vladivostok ●

PACIFIC
OCEAN

Port Arthur

KOREA

JAPAN

| 0 | 500 | 1000 | 1500 miles |
|---|---|---|---|
| 0 | 1000 | | 2000 km |

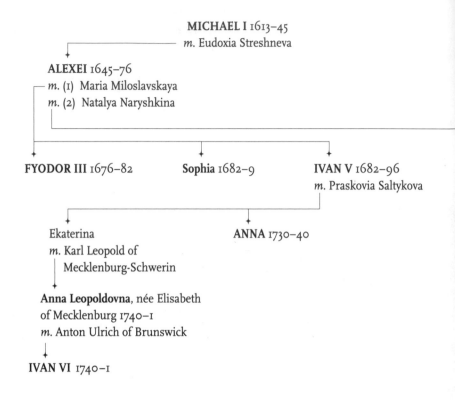

MICHAEL I 1613–45
*m.* Eudoxia Streshneva

ALEXEI 1645–76
*m.* (1) Maria Miloslavskaya
*m.* (2) Natalya Naryshkina

FYODOR III 1676–82      Sophia 1682–9      IVAN V 1682–96
*m.* Praskovia Saltykova

Ekaterina      ANNA 1730–40
*m.* Karl Leopold of
Mecklenburg-Schwerin

Anna Leopoldovna, née Elisabeth
of Mecklenburg 1740–1
*m.* Anton Ulrich of Brunswick

IVAN VI 1740–1

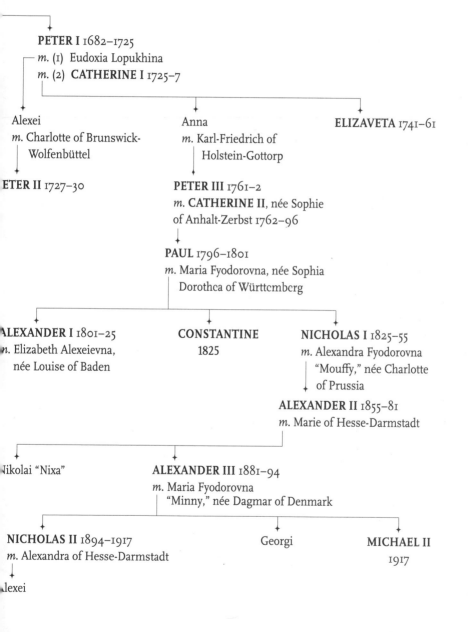

# THE HOUSE OF ROMANOV

**PETER I** 1682–1725
m. (1) Eudoxia Lopukhina
m. (2) **CATHERINE I** 1725–7

Alexei
m. Charlotte of Brunswick-
Wolfenbüttel

**ETER II** 1727–30

Anna
m. Karl-Friedrich of
Holstein-Gottorp

**PETER III** 1761–2
m. **CATHERINE II**, née Sophie
of Anhalt-Zerbst 1762–96

**ELIZAVETA** 1741–61

**PAUL** 1796–1801
m. Maria Fyodorovna, née Sophia
Dorothea of Württemberg

**ALEXANDER I** 1801–25
m. Elizabeth Alexeievna,
née Louise of Baden

**CONSTANTINE**
1825

**NICHOLAS I** 1825–55
m. Alexandra Fyodorovna
"Mouffy," née Charlotte
of Prussia

**ALEXANDER II** 1855–81
m. Marie of Hesse-Darmstadt

Nikolai "Nixa"

**ALEXANDER III** 1881–94
m. Maria Fyodorovna
"Minny," née Dagmar of Denmark

**NICHOLAS II** 1894–1917
m. Alexandra of Hesse-Darmstadt

Alexei

Georgi

**MICHAEL II**
1917

# INTRODUCTION

Heavy is the cap of Monomakh.
—Alexander Pushkin, *Boris Godunov*

The greatest empire is to be emperor of oneself.
—Seneca, *Epistle 113*

I t was hard to be a tsar. Russia is not an easy country to rule. Twenty
sovereigns of the Romanov dynasty reigned for 304 years, from 1613
until tsardom's destruction by the Revolution in 1917. Their ascent
started in the reign of Ivan the Terrible and ended in the time of
Rasputin. Romantic chroniclers of the tragedy of the last tsar like to
suggest that the family was cursed, but the Romanovs were actually
the most spectacularly successful empire-builders since the Mongols.
The Russian empire, it is estimated, grew by fifty-five square miles (142
square kilometres) per day after the Romanovs came to the throne in
1613, or 20,000 square miles a year. By the late nineteenth century, they
ruled one sixth of the earth's surface—and they were still expanding.
Empire-building was in a Romanov's blood.

In some ways, this book is a study of character and the distorting
effect of absolute power on personality. It is partly a family story of love,
marriage, adultery and children, but it is not like other such stories—
royal families are always extraordinary because power both sweetens
and contaminates the traditional familial chemistry: the allure and corruption of power so often trump the loyalty and affection of blood. This
is a history of the monarchs, their families and retinues, but it is also a
portrait of absolutism in Russia—and whatever else one believes about
Russia, its culture, its soul, its essence have always been exceptional, a
singular nature which one family aspired to personify. The Romanovs
have become the very definition not only of dynasty and magnificence
but also of despotism, a parable of the folly and arrogance of absolute
power. No other dynasty except the Caesars has such a place in the

popular imagination and culture, and both deliver universal lessons about how personal power works, then and now. It is no coincidence that the title "tsar" derives from Caesar just as the Russian for emperor is simply the Latin "imperator."

The Romanovs inhabit a world of family rivalry, imperial ambition, lurid glamour, sexual excess and depraved sadism; this is a world where obscure strangers suddenly claim to be dead monarchs reborn, brides are poisoned, fathers torture their sons to death, sons kill fathers, wives murder husbands, a holy man, poisoned and shot, arises, apparently, from the dead, barbers and peasants ascend to supremacy, giants and freaks are collected, dwarfs are tossed, beheaded heads kissed, tongues torn out, flesh knouted off bodies, rectums impaled, children slaughtered; here are fashion-mad nymphomaniacal empresses, lesbian *ménages à trois*, and an emperor who wrote the most erotic correspondence ever written by a head of state. Yet this is also the empire built by flinty conquistadors and brilliant statesmen that conquered Siberia and Ukraine, took Berlin and Paris, and produced Pushkin, Tolstoy, Tchaikovsky and Dostoevsky; a civilization of towering culture and exquisite beauty.

Out of context, these excesses seem so overblown and outlandish that ascetic academic historians find themselves bashfully toning down the truth. After all, the legends of the Romanovs—the juice of Hollywood movies and TV drama series—are as potent and popular as the facts. That is why the teller of this story has to be wary of melodrama, mythology and teleology—the danger of writing history backwards—and cautious of methodology. Scepticism is essential; scholarship demands constant verification and analysis. But one of the benefits of narrative history is that each reign appears in context to give a portrait of the evolution of Russia, its autocracy and its soul. And in these larger-than-life characters misshapen by autocracy, a distorted mirror appears, which reflects the tropes of all human character right back at us.

If the challenge of ruling Russia has always been daunting, the role of autocrat could only be truly exercised by a genius—and there are very few of those in most families. The price of failure was death. "In Russia the government is autocracy tempered by strangulation," quipped the French woman of letters Madame de Staël. It was a dangerous job. Six of the last twelve tsars were murdered—two by throttling, one by dagger, one by dynamite, two by bullet. In the final catastrophe in 1918, eighteen Romanovs were killed. Rarely was a chalice so rich and so poisonous. I particularly examine each succession, always the best test of a regime's stability. It is ironic that now, two centuries after the Romanovs finally agreed a law of succession, Russian presidents still effectively nominate their successors just as Peter the Great did. Whether a smooth handover or desperate transition, these moments of extreme tension, when existential necessity demands that every reserve of ingenuity be deployed, every intrigue explored, reveal the fundamentals of power.

The essence of tsardom was the projection of majesty and strength. Yet this had to be combined with what Otto von Bismarck, rival and ally of the Romanovs, called "the art of the possible, the attainable, the art of the next best." For the Romanovs, the craft of survival was based on the balancing of clans, interests and personalities of both a minuscule court and a gigantic empire. Emperors needed to keep the support of their army, nobility and their administration. If they lost all three, they were likely to be deposed—and, in an autocracy, that usually meant death. As well as playing the lethal game of politics, the sovereigns had to exude visceral, almost feral authority. An effective tsar could be harsh provided he was consistently harsh. Rulers are often killed not for brutality but for inconsistency. And tsars had to inspire trust and respect among their courtiers but sacred reverence among the peasantry, 90 per cent of their subjects, who saw them as "Little Fathers." They were expected to be severe to their officials but benign to their peasant "children": "the tsar is good," peasants said, "the nobles are wicked."

Power is always personal: any study of a Western democratic leader today reveals that, even in a transparent system with its short periods in office, personalities shape administrations. Democratic leaders often rule through trusted retainers instead of official ministers. In any court, power is as fluid as human personality. It flows hydraulically to and from the source, but its currents constantly change; its entire flow can be redirected, even reversed. In an autocracy, the power is always in flux, as changeable as the moods, relationships and circumstances—personal and political—of one man and his sprawling, teeming domains. All courts work in similar ways. In the twenty-first century, the new autocracies in Russia and China have much in common with that of the tsars, run by tiny, opaque cliques, amassing vast wealth, while linked together through hierarchical client–patron relationships, all at the mercy of the whims of the ruler. In this book, my aim is to follow the invisible, mysterious alchemy of power to answer the essential question of politics, laconically expressed by that maestro of powerplay, Lenin: *kto kogo?*—who controls whom?

In an autocracy, the traits of character are magnified, everything personal is political, and any proximity to the sovereign is transformed into power, woven into a golden thread extending from the crown to anyone it touches. There were sure ways to gain the intimate confidence of a tsar. The first was to serve in court, army or government and especially to deliver military victory; the second was to guarantee security—every ruler, not only those in Russia, needs an indispensable hatchetman; the third was mystical—to ease divine access for the imperial soul; and the fourth and oldest way was amorous or sexual, particularly in the case of female empresses. In return, the tsars could shower these servitors with cash, serfs and titles. Tsars who turned their back on the court's brokering arrangement or who performed dramatic reversals of foreign policy against the wishes of their potentates, particularly the generals, were liable to be murdered—assassination being one of the few ways for the elite to protest in an autocracy without formal opposition. (The people's way to protest was urban riot and peasant uprising, but for a tsar his nearby courtiers were far more deadly than distant peasants—and only one, Nicholas II, was ever overthrown by popular revolt.)

Intelligent tsars understood that there was no division between their public and private lives. Their personal life, played out at court, was inevitably an extension of politics: "Your destiny," wrote the Roman historian Cassius Dio about Augustus, "is to live as in a theatre where your audience is the whole world." Yet even on such a stage, the real decision-making was always shadowy, arcane and moulded by the ruler's intimate caprice (as it is in today's Kremlin). It is impossible to understand Peter the Great without analysing his naked dwarfs and dildo-waving mock-popes as much as his government reforms and foreign policy. However eccentric, the system worked and talent rose to the top. It may be surprising that two of the ablest ministers, Shuvalov and Potemkin, started as imperial lovers. Emperor Paul's Turkish barber, Kutaisov, became as influential as a born-prince. So, a historian of the Romanovs must examine not just official decrees and statistics on steel production but also the amorous arrangements of Catherine the Great and the mystical lechery of Rasputin. The more powerful official ministers became, the more the autocrats asserted their power by bypassing them to use personal retainers. In gifted emperors, this made their deeds mysterious, startling and awesome, but in the case of incompetent ones, it muddled government hopelessly.

The success of autocracy depends mainly on the quality of the individual. "The secret of nobility," wrote Karl Marx, "is zoology"—breeding. In the seventeenth century, the Romanovs used brideshows—beauty contests—to select their Russian brides, but by the early nineteenth century, they were choosing wives from "the studfarm of Europe"—the German principalities, thereby joining the wider family of European royalty. But breeding politicians is not a science. How many families produce one outstanding leader, let alone twenty generations of monarchs, mostly selected by the lottery of biology and the tricks of palace intrigue, with the acumen to be an autocrat? Very few politicians, who have chosen a political career, can fulfil the aspirations and survive the strains of an elevated office that, in a monarchy, was filled so randomly. Yet each tsar had to be simultaneously dictator and generalissimus, high priest and "Little Father," and to pull this off, they needed all the qualities listed by the sociologist Max Weber: the "personal gift of grace," the "virtue of legality" and the "authority of the eternal yesterday," in other words, magnetism, legitimacy and tradition. And after all that, they had to be efficient and wise too. Fearsome respect was essential: in politics, ridicule is almost as dangerous as defeat.

The Romanovs did produce two political geniuses—the "Greats," Peter and Catherine—and several of talent and magnetism. After Emperor Paul's brutal murder in 1801, all the monarchs were dutiful and hard-working, and most were charismatic, intelligent and competent, yet the position was so daunting for the normal mortal that no one sought the throne any more: it was a burden that had ceased to be enjoyable. "How can a single man manage to govern [Russia] and correct its abuses?" asked the future Alexander I. "This would be impossible not only for a man of ordinary abilities like me but even for a genius . . ." He fantasized about running off to live on a farm by the Rhine. His successors were all terrified of the crown and avoided it if they could; yet when they were handed the throne, they had to fight to stay alive.

Peter the Great understood that autocracy required tireless checking and threatening. Such were—and are—the perils of ruling this colossal state while presiding over a personal despotism without clear rules or limits, that it is often futile to accuse Russian rulers of paranoia: extreme vigilance, backed by sudden violence, was and is their natural and essential state. If anything, they suffer from Emperor Domitian's witty complaint (shortly before his own assassination) that "the lot of princes is most unhappy since when they denounced a conspiracy, no one believed them until they had been assassinated." But fear alone was not enough: even after killing millions, Stalin grumbled that still, no one obeyed him. Autocracy "is not as easy as you think," said the supremely intelligent Catherine: "unlimited power" was a chimera.

The decision of individuals often redirected Russia, though rarely in the way intended. To paraphrase the Prussian field-marshal Helmuth von Moltke, political "plans rarely survive the first contact with the enemy." Accidents, friction, personalities and luck, all bounded by the practicalities of guns and butter, are the real landscape of politics. As the Romanovs' greatest minister Potemkin reflected, the politician of any state must not just react to contingencies, he must "improve on events." Or, as Bismarck put it, "the statesman's task is to hear God's footsteps marching through history, and to try and catch on to His coattails as He marches past." So often the last Romanovs found themselves forlornly and obstinately trying to defy the march of history.

The believers in Russian autocracy were convinced that only an all-powerful individual blessed by God could project the effulgent majesty necessary to direct and overawe this multinational empire and manage the intricate interests of such a vast state. At the same time, the sovereign had to personify the sacred mission of Orthodox Christianity and give meaning to the special place of the Russian nation in world history. Since no man or woman could fulfil such duties alone, the art of delegation was an essential skill. The most tyrannical of the Romanovs, Peter the Great, was superb at finding and appointing talented retainers from all over Europe regardless of class or race, and it is no accident that Catherine the Great promoted not only Potemkin but also Suvorov, the outstanding commander of the Romanov era. Stalin, himself an adept chooser of subordinates, reflected that this was Catherine's superlative gift. The tsars sought ministers with the aptitude to rule and yet the autocrat was always expected to rule in his or her own right: a Romanov could never appoint a masterful Richelieu or Bismarck. Emperors had to be above politics—and be astute politicians too. If power was wisely delegated and broad advice considered, even a moderately gifted ruler could achieve much, though modern autocracy demanded as delicate a handling of complex issues as democratic politics today.

The tsar's contract with the people was peculiar to a primitive Russia of peasants and nobles, but it does bear some similarity to that of the twenty-first century Kremlin—glory abroad and security at home in return for the rule of one man and his court and their near-limitless enrichment. The contract had four components—religious, imperial, national and military. In the twentieth century, the last tsar still saw himself as the patrimonial lord of a personal estate—blessed by divine sanction. This had evolved: during the seventeenth century, patriarchs (the prelates of the Orthodox Church) could challenge the supremacy of tsars. After Peter the Great had dissolved the patriarchate, the dynasty could present itself as almost a theocracy. The autocracy was consecrated at the moment of anointment during coronations that presented the tsars as transcendent links between God and man. Only in Russia did the state, made up of dreary petty functionaries, become almost sacred in itself. But this also developed over time. Though much is made of the legacy of Byzantine emperors and Genghizid khans, there was nothing special in the sixteenth century about the status of tsars, who drew their charisma from the medieval royal Christology much like other European monarchs. But, unlike the rest of Europe, Russia did not develop independent assemblies and civil institutions, so its medieval status lasted much longer—right into the twentieth century, by which time it looked weirdly obsolete even in comparison to the court of the German kaisers. This mystical mission, which justified Romanov rule right up until 1917, explains much about the intransigent convictions of the last tsar Nicholas and his wife Alexandra.

The autocracy was legitimized by its ever-expanding multi-faith, multi-ethnic empire, yet the later emperors regarded themselves as the leaders first of the Russian nation but then of the entire Slavic community. The more they embraced Russian nationalism, the more they excluded (and often persecuted) their huge non-Russian populations, such as Poles, Georgians, Finns, and especially Jews. As the Jewish dairyman Tevye in *Fiddler on the Roof* joked, "God bless the tsar and keep him . . . far away from us." This contradiction between empire and nation was the source of many difficulties. The court of the Romanovs was a mixture of family estate office, Orthodox crusading order and military headquarters—characteristics that, in very different ways, explain some of the zeal and aggression of the Romanov successor-regimes, the Soviet Union and today's Russian Federation.

Even in the pre-industrial age, the tsar's schedule was overfilled with holy ceremonies and military reviews, not to speak of factional strife and family rows, leaving precious little time to think deeply about how to solve complex problems. It was a punishing job for a born politician to hold for five years, let alone a lifetime—and many tsars ruled for over twenty-five years. Given that most elected leaders in our democracies tend to be close to madness before ten years in office have elapsed, it is hardly surprising that tsars who reigned for many decades became exhausted and deluded. The tsar's ability to make the right decisions was also limited by the information he was given by his entourage: all the monarchs claimed they were enveloped in lies, yet the longer they ruled, the more they believed what they wished to hear. "Take care not to be Caesarofied, dyed in the purple," warned Marcus Aurelius, but it was easier said than done. The demands intensified as centuries passed. It was harder to be the director of an empire of trains, telephones and dreadnoughts than of horses, cannon and blunderbusses. Although this is a study of personal power, too much emphasis on the personal obscures the sweep of historical forces, the potency of ideas and the impact of steel, dynamite and steam. Technical advances intensified the challenges for a medieval autocracy.

When one reads of the chaotic drift and capricious decadence of the weak tsars of the late seventeenth century and the hedonistic empresses of the eighteenth, the historian (and the reader of this book) has to ask:

How was Russia so successful when it seemed to be so poorly ruled by such grotesques? Yet, even when a child or an idiot was on the throne the autocracy could still function. "God is in heaven and the tsar is far away," said the peasants and in their remote villages they cared little and knew less of what was happening in Petersburg—as long as the centre held. And the centre did hold because the Romanov dynasty was always the apex and façade of a political system of family and personal connections, working sometimes in rivalry, oftentimes in cooperation, to govern the realm as junior partners to the throne. The system was flexible. Whenever a tsar married, the bride's family joined the core of power, and tsars promoted talented favourites, victorious generals and competent foreigners, particularly Tatar princelings, Baltic Germans and Scottish Jacobites, who refreshed this sanctum of connections, providing the social base that helped make Russia such a successful pre-modern empire.

Its heart was the alliance between the Romanovs and the nobility who needed royal support to control their estates. Serfdom was the foundation of this partnership. The ideal of autocracy was in practice a deal whereby the Romanovs enjoyed absolute power and delivered imperial glory while the nobility ruled their estates unchallenged. The crown was the greatest of the landowners so that the monarchy never became the plaything of the nobility as happened in England and France. Yet the noble network of interrelated clans served in government, at court and above all in the classic dynastic-aristocratic army which rarely challenged the tsars and instead became an effective machine of imperial expansion and state cohesion, binding gentry and peasantry under the potent ideology of tsar, God and nation. Since the Romanovs came to power in a desperate civil war, the Time of Troubles (1603–13), the regime was on a military footing from the start. Constant wars against Poles, Swedes, Ottomans, British, French, Germans meant that the autocracy developed as a command centre, mobilizing its nobility and constantly recruiting Western technology. Crown and nobility milked the resources of the serfs, who paid taxes, provided grain and served as soldiers, much cheaper to put in the field than those in other parts of Europe. The Romanovs' success in unifying the country, and the deep fear of any further mayhem, meant that even if individual tsars might be liquidated, the monarchy was generally secure, always supported by their nobility—with rare exceptions in 1730, 1825 and 1916/17. For most of the time, the Romanovs and their retainers could cooperate in the sacred, prestigious and profitable enterprise of repelling foreign aggression and building an empire. Hence this book is a story not just of the Romanovs but of other families too, Golitsyns, Tolstoys and Orlovs.

The nexus for this alliance was the court, an entrepôt of prizes, a club of glamour and majesty, where supposedly lightweight empresses, such as Anna and Elizaveta, proved especially adept at finessing the relationship with their swaggering magnates. This partnership thrived until the Crimean War in the 1850s when the old regime somehow had to be converted into a viable modern state. The struggle abroad required the Romanov empire to compete in a relentless geopolitical tournament of power with Britain, Germany, Japan and America, whose wealth and technology far outstripped those of Russia. Russia's potential could be unlocked only by reforming peasant landownership, by breakneck industrialization based on Western credit and by broadening political participation and dismantling the corrupt, repressive autocracy, something the last two Romanovs, Alexander III and Nicholas II, were ideologically incapable of doing. They faced a conundrum: how to maintain their vast borders, while projecting a power proportionate to their imperial pretensions from a backward society. If they failed abroad, they lost their legitimacy at home. The more they failed at home, the less they could afford to play the empire abroad. If they bluffed and were exposed, they either had to retreat humiliatingly, or fight and risk revolutionary catastrophe.

It is unlikely that even Peter or Catherine could have solved the predicaments of revolution and world war faced by Nicholas II in the early twentieth century, but it was unfortunate that the Romanov who faced the darkest crises was the least capable and most narrow-minded, as well as the unluckiest. Nicholas was both a poor judge of men and unwilling to delegate. While he could not fill the role of autocrat himself, he used his power to make sure no one else did either.

The very success of the old ways until the 1850s made it all the harder to change. Just as the radical and murderous culture of the Soviet Union can be understood only through Marxist-Leninist-Stalinist ideology, so the often bizarre, daft and self-defeating trajectory of the last Romanovs can be understood only through their ideology: sacred autocracy. This ultimately distorted the monarchy, becoming an end in itself, an obstacle to the running of a modern state: the impossible conundrum here was to attract able politicians and to widen participation in the regime without losing its outdated pillars, nobility and church—what Trotsky called the world of "icons and cockroaches."

After all, the epochs of the Great Dictators of the 1920s and 1930s, and the new autocracies of the early twenty-first century, show that there is nothing incompatible about modernity and authoritarianism— even in today's world of the internet and twenty-four-hour news. It was the character of tsarist monarchy and Russian society that made it unworkable. The solutions were not as simple as they now appear with the aid of hindsight, magnified by smug Western superiority. As the reformer Alexander II learned, "a king's lot," in the words of Marcus Aurelius, was "to do good and be damned." Western historians scold the last two tsars for failing to institute immediate democracy. This could be a delusion: such radical surgery might simply have killed the patient much earlier.

The fate of the Romanov family was unbearably cruel and is often presented as inevitable, but it is worth remembering that such was the strength of the monarchy that Nicholas II ruled for twenty-two years—his first ten moderately successfully—and he survived defeat, revolutionary ferment and three years of world war. The February Revolution of 1917 destroyed the monarchy but the family were not doomed until October when they fell into the hands of the Bolsheviks, seven months after the abdication. Even then, Lenin contemplated different scenarios before presiding over that atrocious crime: the slaughter of parents and innocent children. Nothing in history is inevitable.

The massacre marks the end of the dynasty and our narrative but not the end of the story. Today's Russia throbs with the reverberations of its history. The very bones of the Romanovs are the subject of intense political and religious controversy while their imperial interests—from Ukraine to the Baltics, Caucasus to Crimea, Syria and Jerusalem to the Far East—continue to define Russia and the world as we know it. Blood-spattered, gold-plated, diamond-studded, swash-buckled, bodice-ripping and star-crossed, the rise and fall of the Romanovs remains as fascinating as it is relevant, as human as it is strategic, a chronicle of fathers and sons, megalomaniacs, monsters and saints.[1]

# ACKNOWLEDGEMENTS AND SOURCES

This book is not meant to be a full history of Russia nor an economic, diplomatic or military survey, nor a full biography of Peter the Great or Nicholas II, nor an anatomy of Revolution, nor a genealogical study. Other historians have covered these subjects much better than I. Only two great historians, one American, one British, have written on the entire dynasty: both have done so brilliantly. Professor Bruce Lincoln, expert on the Great Reforms and much else, wrote the magisterial *The Romanovs: Autocrats of All the Russias* in which he divides his narrative into alternating domestic and foreign policy chapters. The late Professor Lindsey Hughes wrote *The Romanovs: Ruling Russia 1613–1917*, a masterful, scholarly analysis. I recommend both, but this is the first Romanov history to blend together the personal and political into a single narrative, using archives and published works.

Some of the world's outstanding scholars have read and commented on this entire book or the section on their speciality: Dr. Sergei Bogatyrev, scholar of the sixteenth- and seventeenth-century monarchy, author of *The Sovereign and His Counsellers* on Ivan the Terrible, now writing a history of the Rurikids, read and corrected the seventeenth-century section from Michael to Peter the Great. Simon Dixon, Professor of Russian History at University College London, author of *Catherine the Great*, checked the eighteenth-century section from Peter the Great to Paul. Professor Dominic Lieven, author of *Russia against Napoleon* and more recently *Towards the Flame: Empire, War and the End of Tsarist Russia*, commented on the nineteenth- and twentieth-century section from Alexander I to Nicholas II. Professor Geoffrey Hosking, author of *Russia and the Russians* and *Russia: People and Empire*, read and corrected the entire book as did Professor Robert Service, author of the *History of Modern Russia*. Dr. John Casey of my old college Gonville and Caius, Cambridge, also brought his meticulous stylistic and editorial eye to my manuscript. I hope that the advice of this galaxy of scholarship has helped me avoid mistakes, but any that survive are my own responsibility.

I have drawn on much neglected material on all the tsars' reigns, mostly primary documents, some unpublished, many published in historical journals in the nineteenth century. I have also used many secondary works throughout, so the book is overall a work of synthesis.

The official materials are vast, not to speak of the personal ones. Each tsar wrote to ministers, lovers, relatives, simultaneously running foreign, domestic and cultural policies. This is a study of the dynasty, the interrelation of monarchy, family, court and, as it developed, the state—a survey of Russian political power from the seventeenth to the twentieth centuries. By the late nineteenth century, in addition to the colossal official correspondence of each tsar, most Romanovs and most ministers also kept diaries, wrote memoirs and of course many letters, and the family itself was enormous.

Memoirs must be treated with scepticism but letters and diaries are invaluable. Five priceless correspondences stand out: those between Peter the Great and his mistress-empress Catherine I; between Catherine the Great and her partner Potemkin; between Alexander I and his sister Catiche; between Alexander II and his mistress-wife Katya Dolgorukaya; and between Nicholas II and Alexandra. Some of these letters are already famous, such as a number of those of Catherine and Potemkin, and of Nicholas and Alexandra, yet both these couples wrote several thousand letters, varying from perfume-drenched love notes to long political discussions. Naturally most of them are little known. The correspondence of Alexander II and Katya Dolgorukaya numbers around 3,000 letters: it is overwhelmingly unpublished. Few historians have worked on this extraordinary trove and none has read it all, partly because the letters were for a long time in private hands and returned to the Russian archives relatively recently.

I follow twenty monarchs and several regents over three centuries. Out of the twenty tsars, three—Peter I, Catherine II and Nicholas II—are household names, while Rasputin has long since graduated from history to myth. But the less famous monarchs are just as fascinating. I aim to treat all the tsars equally, though the increasing volume of material along with the size of the family means that there is much more to cover in the last decades.

The greatest weight of pre-judgement and legend, martyrdom and romance hangs over Nicholas and Alexandra. Thousands of books have been written on every aspect of the last imperial couple, who have become a publishing-internet industry. The atrocious killing of the family both overshadows and over-illuminates their lives. After all, Nicholas and his family are now saints. Generations of biographers and bloggers portray Nicholas as a loving family man and, with his wife, as the definition of a romantic couple, but this study treats them and Rasputin as both intimate and political figures in a fresh, unvarnished way without the burden of plangent romance, Soviet disgust or liberal contempt.

In this titanic enterprise, I have been helped by many generous scholars and experts whose knowledge and judgement far outstrip mine. In the course of my researches into Catherine the Great, Potemkin and now the entire Romanov dynasty, over fifteen years, I have visited the great majority of Romanov palaces, many key sites, and state archives, from Moscow and Petersburg to Peterhof and Tsarskoe Selo to Odessa, Tbilisi, Borzhomi, Baku, Sebastopol, Bakhtiserai, Yalta, Livadia, Dnieperpetrovsk, Nikolaev and Kherson, and have also accessed archives in foreign cities, London, Warsaw and Paris—too many to mention every curator, director and guide. But I must thank above all the Director of the State Hermitage Museum, Dr. Mikhail Piotrovsky, the Director of the State Kremlin Museums, Dr. Elena Gagarina, and the Director of the State Archive of the Russian Federation, GARF, Dr. Sergei Mironenko.

I would also like to thank HRH the Prince of Wales, who has warmly and generously helped and encouraged my work in Russia and shared materials on the restoration of Romanov palaces; HRH the duke of Edinburgh, who kindly met me to discuss his family connections; HRH Prince Michael of Kent, who shared his experiences of the burial of Nicholas II and family; Princess Olga Romanoff, granddaughter of Grand Duke Alexander Mikhailovich (Sandro) and Xenia Alexandrovna, who indulged my questions on the family; Princess Elizabeth of Yugoslavia and her son Nick Balfour, who shared family photographs and letters; Princess Katya Galitzine; Countess Stefania Calice for her research into her family collection of letters and her sharing of unpublished Romanov letters including Grand Duchess Alexandra Iosifovna's account of Nicholas I's death; Professor Catherine Merridale for advice and encouragement; Lars Tharp for Rasputin's sea-cucumber; Adam Zamoyski for sharing gems of research on Nicholas I; Dr. Mark Donen for researching the Comte de Langeron's account of Paul's murder in the Sorbonne archives; Ben Judah for sharing his research on Vladimir Putin's reflections on Nicholas II; Helen Rappaport, author of *Four Sisters*, who warned me about the pitfalls of Romanov research; my dear friend Musa Klebnikov who shared the unpublished manuscript of her late, much-missed husband, Paul, on Stolypin; Galina Oleksiuk, who taught me Russian when I embarked on *Catherine the Great and Potemkin*, and her daughter Olesya Nova, who helped me with research, as well as the excellent young historian Lucy Morgan who did research for me in England. Above all I am enormously grateful to Dr. Galina Babkova, who helped me research all my earlier books and who introduced me to the indispensable Daulet Zhandaryev, a most talented young historian, who

xxxii      ACKNOWLEDGEMENTS AND SOURCES

helped me with the huge research. Thanks to the superb Peter James for his immaculate copyediting. I am lucky to have the support of a super-agent, Georgina Capel, and her outstanding colleagues Rachel Conway, Romily Withington and Valeria Huerta; and to have such fine publishers in my editors Bea Hemming and Holly Harley at Weidenfeld and Sonny Mehta at Knopf.

I thank the great Isabel de Madariaga, who, though she died before she could read this book, taught me, with the charming but stern rigour of Catherine the Great whom she resembled, how to write history and how to analyse Russia.

My father, Dr. Stephen Sebag-Montefiore, died during the writing of this book. I deeply miss his wisdom and warmth in all matters—and his skill as an editor. Thanks to my mother April Sebag-Montefiore for her golden advice, literary gifts, and wonderful company. My parents-in-law Charles and Patty Palmer Tomkinson have as always been generous supporters. I am deeply grateful for the serenity, kindness, beauty, love and indulgence of my wife, Santa, who, having survived Stalin and Jerusalem, has now endured the Romanovs. I owe her everything: she is truly my tsarina. My inspirations are of course my darling children. Thank you, Lily and Sasha, for your delightful charm, mischief, irreverence and affection that has kept me going. My books are dedicated alternately to Santa and the children. This one is for Lily.

This book has unexpectedly touched my family history: my ancestor Sir Moses Montefiore met Emperors Nicholas I and Alexander II. My very existence is owed, if that is the word, to two of the tragedies of Russian-Jewish history. The family of my maternal grandmother, the Woolfs, fought for Poland against the Romanovs in 1863 then escaped to Britain. The family of my maternal grandfather, the Jaffes, fled Russia after the Kishinev pogrom in 1904. They bought tickets from Lithuania to New York then were surprised to be disembarked in Ireland. They had been tricked! When they protested, the people-smugglers explained they had promised to deliver them to "New Cork," not New York. They settled in Limerick, where they were then driven out of their homes in a pogrom that took place in the British Isles in 1904. As I wrote about Gallipoli, I could not forget that my great-grandfather, Major Cecil Sebag-Montefiore, was left for dead there in a heap of bodies and never really recovered from his head wound, nor as I wrote about the Western intervention against the Bolsheviks in 1918 that his son, my grandfather, Colonel Eric Sebag-Montefiore, was a member of the British expedition that occupied Batumi. Such connections are of course commonplace—but somehow they help to add grit to the oyster.

Simon Sebag Montefiore

# NOTE

For all Russian dates, I use the Julian Old Style calendar which in the seventeenth century was ten days behind the Gregorian New Style calendar used in the West; in the eighteenth century it was eleven days behind, in the nineteenth twelve days behind and in the twentieth thirteen days behind. For a small number of well-known dates, I use both.

On titles, I variously call the ruler by the titles tsar, autocrat, sovereign and grand prince until Peter the Great's assumption of the title emperor. After that I use all of them interchangeably, though there was increasingly a Slavophile tone in using the Russian "tsar" rather than the European–Roman "emperor."

A tsar's son was a tsarevich ("son of the tsar"); a daughter was a tsarevna. Later all the children (and grandchildren) of monarchs were grand prince (*veliki kniaz*) and grand princess. These titles were traditionally translated as grand duke and grand duchess.

The crown prince was known as the heir (*naslednik*) but also more simply as grand duke and tsarevich ("son of the tsar"). In 1721, Peter the Great, adopting the Roman title emperor, styled his children caesarevich ("son of the Caesar") or tsesarevich. I use the spelling caesarevich so that the reader can easily differentiate from tsarevich. In 1762, Catherine the Great styled her son Paul caesarevich and it became the title of the heir though the last tsar preferred the more Russian "tsarevich."

To avoid long discussions of the changing meaning of the terms Slavophile and Pan-Slav, I use Slavophile generically to describe those who wished to use Russia's Slavic identity to guide policy at home and abroad.

I use Constantinople not Istanbul for the Ottoman capital because that is what most contemporaries including Ottoman diplomats called it; I also used the Russian Tsargrad.

Russians are generally given a first name and their father's name as patronymic. Thus the Grand Duke Konstantin Konstantinovich is Constantine son of Constantine. The Romanov names were often repeated so the family becomes increasingly complicated—even Nicholas II complained, "there are too many Constantines and Nicholases," and there were also numerous Mikhails and Alexeis. I have tried to make this easier for the reader by using nicknames or different spellings, and including lists of characters with nicknames.

On Russian spelling, I use the most familiar version, so Tsar Michael instead of Mikhail, Peter instead of Piotr, Paul instead of Pavel. But I also at times use Nikolai and Mikhail. My decisions on all these questions are solely designed to make this puzzle comprehensible and to make characters recognizable. This leads to all sorts of linguistic inconsistencies to which I plead guilty.

# THE ROMANOVS

# PROLOGUE

# Two Boys in a Time of Troubles

Two teenaged boys, both fragile, innocent and ailing, open and close the story of the dynasty. Both were heirs to a political family destined to rule Russia as autocrats, both raised in times of revolution, war and slaughter. Both were chosen by others for a sacred but daunting role that they were not suited to perform. Separated by 305 years, they played out their destinies in extraordinary and terrible scenarios that took place far from Moscow in edifices named Ipatiev.

At 1:30 a.m. on 17 July 1918, in the Ipatiev House in Ekaterinburg, in the Urals, 800 miles east of Moscow, Alexei, aged thirteen, a sufferer from haemophilia, son of the former tsar Nicholas II, was awakened with his parents, four sisters, three family retainers and three dogs, and told that the family must urgently prepare to move to a safer place.

At night on 13 March 1613, in the Ipatiev Monastery outside the half-ruined little town of Kostroma on the Volga River 200 miles northeast of Moscow, Michael Romanov, aged sixteen, a sufferer from weak legs and a tic in his eye, the only one of his parents' five sons to survive, was awakened with his mother to be told that a delegation had arrived. He must prepare urgently to return with them to the capital.

Both boys were startled by the exceptional occasion that they would now confront. Their own parents had sought the paramount prize of the crown on their behalf—yet hoped to protect them from its perils. But they could not be protected because their family had, for better or worse, enrolled in the cruel game of hereditary power in Russia, and their weak shoulders were selected to bear the terrible burden of ruling. But for all the parallels between these transcendent moments in the lives of Alexei and Michael, they were, as we shall see, travelling in very different directions. One was the beginning and one was the end.

*

Alexei, a prisoner of the Bolsheviks, in a Russia shattered by savage civil war and foreign invasion, got dressed with his parents and sisters. Their clothes were woven with the famous jewels of the dynasty, secreted for a future escape into a new freedom. The boy and his father, the ex-tsar Nicholas II, both donned plain military shirts, breeches and peaked caps. Ex-tsarina Alexandra and her teenaged daughters all wore white blouses and black skirts, no jackets or hats. They were told to bring little with them, but they naturally tried to collect pillows, purses and keepsakes, unsure if they would return or where they were going. The parents knew they themselves were unlikely to emerge from this trauma with their lives, but even in that flint-hearted age, it would surely be unthinkable to harm innocent children. For now, befuddled by sleep, exhausted by living in despair and uncertainty, they suspected nothing.[1]

Michael Romanov and his mother, the Nun Martha, had recently been prisoners but were now almost fugitives, lying low, seeking sanctuary in a monastery amid a land also shattered by civil war and foreign invasion, not unlike the Russia of 1918. They too were accustomed to living in mortal danger. They were right to be afraid for the boy was being hunted by death squads.

In her mid-fifties, the Nun Martha, the boy's mother, had suffered much in the brutal reversals of this, the Time of Troubles, which had seen their family fall from splendour and power to prison and death and back: the boy's father, Filaret, was even now in Polish captivity; several uncles had been murdered. Michael was scarcely literate, decidedly unmasterful and chronically sick. He and his mother presumably just hoped to survive until his father returned. But would he ever return?

Mother and son, torn between dread and anticipation, told the delegation of grandees from Moscow to meet the boy outside the Ipatiev in the morning, unsure what the dawn would bring.[2]

The guards in the Ipatiev House of Ekaterinburg watched as the Romanovs came down the stairs, crossing themselves as they passed a stuffed female bear with two cubs on the landing. Nicholas carried his ailing son.

The commandant, a Bolshevik commissar named Yakov Yurovsky, led the family outside, across a courtyard and down into a basement, lit by a single electric bulb. Alexandra asked for a chair and Yurovsky had two brought for the two weakest members of the family: the ex-tsarina and Alexei. She sat on one chair and Nicholas set his son on the other. Then he stood in front of him. The four grand duchesses, Olga, Tatiana, Maria and Anastasia—whose collective nickname was the acronym

OTMA—stood behind Alexandra. Yurovsky hurried out of the room. There were many arrangements to make. For days, coded telegrams had clicked between Ekaterinburg and Moscow on the future of the imperial family as anti-Bolshevik forces, known as the Whites, advanced on Ekaterinburg. Time was running out. A death squad waited in the neighbouring room, some of its members drunk, all heavily armed. The family, serene and quiet, were still tousled and bemused with sleep, perhaps hoping that somehow during this rushed perambulation they would fall into the hands of the rescuing Whites who were so close. They sat facing the door calmly and expectantly as if they were waiting for a group photograph to be taken.

At dawn on 14 March, Michael, dressed in formal fur-lined robes and sable-trimmed hat, accompanied by his mother, emerged to watch a procession, led by Muscovite potentates, known as boyars, and Orthodox bishops, known as metropolitans. It was freezing cold. The delegates approached. The boyars wore kaftans and furs; the metropolitan bore the Miraculous Icon of the Dormition Cathedral, which Michael would have immediately recognized from the Kremlin where he had recently been a prisoner. As an additional persuasion, they held aloft the Fyodorov Mother of God, the Romanovs' revered icon, the family's protectress.

When they reached Michael and his mother, they bowed low, and their astonishing news was delivered in their first words to him. "Sovereign Lord, Lord of Vladimir and Moscow, and Tsar and Grand Prince of All Russia," said their leader Metropolitan Feodorit of Riazan. "Muscovy couldn't survive without a sovereign . . . and Muscovy was in ruins," so an Assembly of the Land had chosen him to be their sovereign who would "shine for the Russian Tsardom like the sun," and they asked him to "show them his favour and not disdain to accept their entreaties" and "deign to come to Moscow as quickly as possible." Michael and his mother were not pleased. "They told us," reported the delegates, "with great fury and crying that *He* did not wish to be Sovereign and *She* wouldn't bless him to be Sovereign either and they walked off into the church." One can almost hear the magnificent anger of the mother and the sobbing confusion of the boy. In 1613, the crown of Russia was not a tempting proposition.

At 2:15 a.m., Alexei and family were still waiting in sleepy silence when Comrade Yurovsky and ten armed myrmidons entered the ever more crowded room. One of them noticed Alexei, "sickly and waxy," staring "with wide curious eyes." Yurovsky ordered Alexei and the family to stand and, turning to Nicholas, declared: "In view of the fact that your

relatives continue their offensive against Soviet Russia, the Presidium
of the Urals Regional Council has decided to sentence you to death."

"Lord oh my God!" said the ex-tsar. "Oh my God, what is this?" One
of the girls cried out, "Oh my Lord, no!" Nicholas turned back: "I can't
understand you. Read it again, please."

The Moscow magnates were not discouraged by Michael's refusal. The
Assembly had written out the specific answers that the delegates were to
give to each of Michael's objections. After much praying, the grandees
"almost begged" Michael. They "kissed the Cross and humbly asked" the
boy they called "our Sovereign" if he would be the tsar. The Romanovs
were wounded after years of persecution and humiliation. They were
lucky to be alive. Michael again "refused with a plaintive cry and rage."

Yurovsky read out the death sentence again and now Alexei and the
others crossed themselves while Nicholas kept saying, "What? What?"

"THIS!" shouted Yurovsky. He fired at the ex-tsar. The execution
squad raised their guns, levelled them at the family and fired wildly in
a deafening pandemonium of shots, "women's screams and moans,"
shouted orders of Yurovsky, panic and smoke. "No one could hear anything," recalled Yurovsky. But as the shots slowed, they realized that
Tsarevich Alexei and the women were almost untouched. Wide-eyed,
terrified, stunned and still seated on his chair, Alexei stared out at them
through the smoke of gunpowder and plaster dust that almost extin-
guished the light amid a diabolic scene of upturned chairs, waving legs,
blood and "moans, screams, low sobs . . ."

In Kostroma, after six hours of argument, the grandees knelt and wept
and pleaded that, if Michael didn't accept the crown, God would visit
utter ruin on Russia. Finally Michael agreed, kissing the Cross, and
accepted the steel-tipped staff of tsardom. The grandees crossed themselves and rushed to prostrate themselves and kiss the feet of their new
tsar. A ruined capital, a shattered kingdom, a desperate people awaited
him at the end of the dangerous road to Moscow.

ACT I

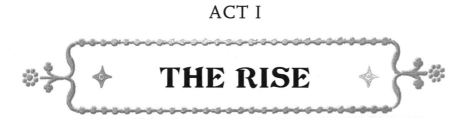

THE RISE

# THE ROMANOVS

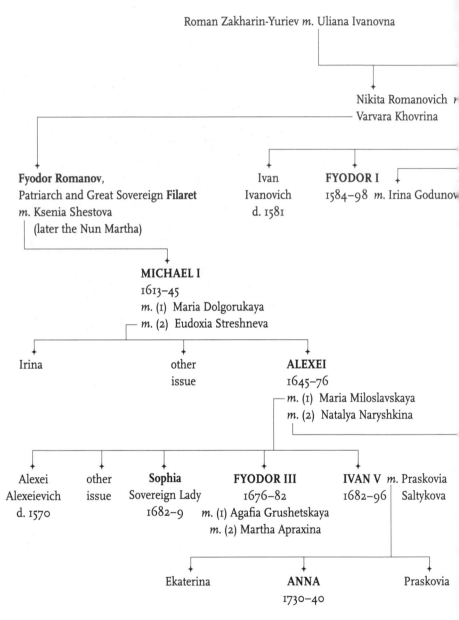

Roman Zakharin-Yuriev *m.* Uliana Ivanovna

Nikita Romanovich *m*
Varvara Khovrina

**Fyodor Romanov,**
Patriarch and Great Sovereign **Filaret**
*m.* Ksenia Shestova
(later the Nun Martha)

Ivan
Ivanovich
d. 1581

**FYODOR I**
1584–98 *m.* Irina Godunov

**MICHAEL I**
1613–45
*m.* (1) Maria Dolgorukaya
*m.* (2) Eudoxia Streshneva

Irina

other
issue

**ALEXEI**
1645–76
*m.* (1) Maria Miloslavskaya
*m.* (2) Natalya Naryshkina

Alexei
Alexeievich
d. 1570

other
issue

**Sophia**
Sovereign Lady
1682–9

**FYODOR III**
1676–82
*m.* (1) Agafia Grushetskaya
*m.* (2) Martha Apraxina

**IVAN V** *m.* Praskovia
1682–96 Saltykova

Ekaterina

**ANNA**
1730–40

Praskovia

* Ivan the Terrible was the first of the Grand Princes of Muscovy to be crowned tsar. He was married
as many as seven times. Maria Nagaya was his last wife.

# THE RURIKIDS

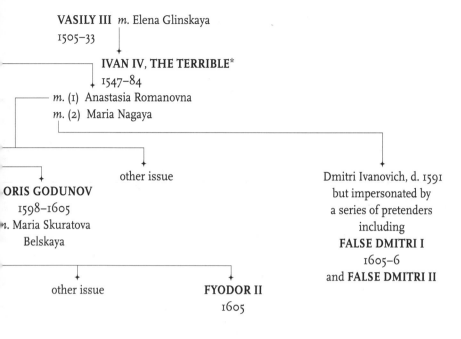

**VASILY III** *m.* Elena Glinskaya
1505–33

**IVAN IV, THE TERRIBLE***
1547–84
*m.* (1)  Anastasia Romanovna
*m.* (2)  Maria Nagaya

other issue

Dmitri Ivanovich, d. 1591
but impersonated by
a series of pretenders
including
**FALSE DMITRI I**
1605–6
and **FALSE DMITRI II**

**ORIS GODUNOV**
1598–1605
*m.* Maria Skuratova
Belskaya

other issue          **FYODOR II**
1605

**PETER I, THE GREAT**          Natalya
1682–1725
*m.* (1)  Eudoxia Lopukhina

Alexei Petrovich

# THE RURIKIDS
# AND ROMANOVS
### c. 1500–1700

## SCENE 1

# The Brideshows

# CAST

## THE LAST OF THE RURIKID TSARS

IVAN THE TERRIBLE 1547–84
Anastasia Romanovna Zakharina-Yurieva, his first tsarina
Ivan Ivanovich, their eldest son and heir, murdered by his father
FYODOR I, their second son, tsar 1584–98
Dmitri Ivanovich, Ivan the Terrible's last son, mysteriously killed. Identity assumed by three impostors, the False Dmitris

## THE TIME OF TROUBLES: tsars and pretenders

BORIS GODUNOV, tsar 1598–1605
THE FALSE DMITRI, tsar 1605–6
VASILY SHUISKY, tsar 1606–10
Second False Dmitri, known as the "Brigand of Tushino"
Ivan Dmitrievich, the "Baby Brigand"
Marina Mniszech, daughter of a Polish nobleman, wife of the First False Dmitri, Second False Dmitri and Ivan Zarutsky, mother of the Baby Brigand, known as "Marinka the Witch"

### Warlords

Prince Dmitri Pozharsky, hero of the resistance
Kuzma Minin, merchant of Nizhny Novgorod, leader of the resistance
Prince Dmitri Trubetskoi, aristocrat and leader of Cossacks

### Foreign invaders

King Sigismund III of Poland
Prince Władysław of Poland, later king
Gustavus Adolphus, king of Sweden

## THE FIRST OF THE ROMANOVS

Nikita Romanovich Zakharin-Yuriev, brother of Anastasia, first wife of
    Ivan the Terrible
His son Fyodor Nikitich Romanov, later the priest Filaret
Ksenia Shestova, later the Nun Martha, Fyodor's wife
Their son, MICHAEL, the first Romanov tsar, 1613–45
Ivan Romanov, Fyodor's brother, Michael's uncle, boyar
Anna Khlopova, Michael's first fiancée
Maria Dolgorukaya, his first wife
Eudoxia Streshneva, his second wife
Irina, tsarevna, daughter of Michael and Eudoxia
ALEXEI, son and heir of Michael and Eudoxia, tsar 1645–76


## COURTIERS: ministers etc.

Fyodor Sheremetev, Romanov cousin, boyar and chief minister
Mikhail Saltykov, Romanov cousin, royal cupbearer and armsbearer
Prince Ivan Cherkassky, Romanov cousin of Circassian descent, boyar
Prince Dmitri Cherkassky, Romanov cousin of Circassian descent, boyar
Prince Dmitri Pozharsky, patriotic warlord, later boyar and chief
    commander
Prince Dmitri Trubetskoi, aristocrat and Cossack warlord, candidate for
    tsar

Michael was in no rush to proceed to Moscow, but Moscow was desperate for him to arrive. In the civil war, the contestants for supremacy—aristocratic magnates, foreign kings, Cossack chieftains, impostors and adventurers—had fought their way towards Moscow, hungry to seize the crown. But Michael Romanov and the Nun Martha were unenthusiastic. There has never been a more miserable, whining and melancholic procession to a throne. But the plight of Russia early in 1613 was dire, its trauma dystopian. The territory between Kostroma and Moscow was dangerous; Michael would pass through villages where dead bodies lay strewn in the streets. Russia was far smaller than the Russian Federation today; its border with Sweden in the north was close to Novgorod, that with Poland–Lithuania close to Smolensk, much of Siberia in the east was unconquered, and most of the south was still the territory of the khanate of the Tatars. But it was still a vast territory with around 14 million people, compared to about 4 million in England at the time. Yet Russia had almost disintegrated; famine and war had culled its population; the Poles were still hunting the boy-tsar; Swedish and Polish–Lithuanian armies were massing to advance into Russia; Cossack warlords ruled swathes of the south, harbouring pretenders to the throne; there was no money, the crown jewels had been looted; the Kremlin palaces were ruined.

The transformation of Michael's life must have been convulsive: the court of a tsar had to be reconstructed, courtier by courtier, silver spoon by silver spoon, diamond by diamond. He and his mother were undoubtedly terrified of what awaited them in the capital and they had every reason to be anxious. Yet now this teenager of an untitled noble family, whose father was lost in a foreign prison, found greatness thrust upon him, a greatness that he owed, above all, to the family's first patron, Ivan the Terrible.[1]

Thirty years after his death, Ivan still cast his dread shadow over Russia and the boy Michael. Ivan had expanded the Russian empire—and almost destroyed it from within. He had first boosted its splendour and then poisoned it—a fifty-year reign of triumph and madness. But his first and favourite wife, the mother of his first brood of sons, was a Romanov—and the founder of the family's fortunes.

Ivan himself was the scion of a royal family descended from Rurik, a semi-mythical Scandinavian prince who, in 862, was invited by Slavs and other local tribes to rule them, becoming the founder of the first Russian dynasty. In 988, Rurik's descendant Vladimir, grand prince of Rus, converted to Orthodoxy in Crimea under the authority of the Byzantine emperor and patriarch. His loose confederation of principalities, known as Kievan Rus, bound together by the Rurik dynasty, would ultimately extend almost from the Baltic to the Black Sea. But between 1238 and 1240 it was shattered by the Mongol armies of Genghis Khan and his family who, during their two centuries of Russian dominion, allowed Rurikid princes to rule small principalities as vassals. The Mongols' view of a single universal emperor under God and their brutally arbitrary judicial decisions may have contributed to the Russian idea of autocracy. There was much mingling and marriage with the Mongols; many famous Russian families were descended from them. Gradually the Russian princes started to challenge Mongol authority: Ivan III the Great, grand prince of Moscow, had collected many of the Russian cities, particularly the republic of Great Novgorod in the north and Rostov in the south, under the Muscovite crown and in 1480 he decisively confronted the Mongol khans. After the fall of Byzantium to the Islamic Ottomans, he claimed the mantle of leadership of Orthodoxy. Ivan married the last Byzantine emperor's niece, Sophia Paleologue, which allowed him to present himself as heir to the emperors. Ivan the Great started to style himself "Caesar," which was russianized into "Tsar," his new imperial status allowing his monkish propagandists to assert that he was regathering the territories of Rus.* His son Vasily III continued his work, but Vasily's son predeceased him so it was his grandson Ivan IV, Ivan the Terrible as he became, who succeeded to the throne as a toddler. His mother may have been poisoned and the child was traumatized when the rivalries of courtiers erupted into violence, growing up to be as magnetic, dynamic and imaginative as he was volatile and unpredictable.

At his coronation in 1547, when he was sixteen, Ivan was the first grand prince to be crowned tsar. The young autocrat had already launched his ritual search for a wife. In a tradition that derived from both of the precursors of tsardom—Mongol khans and the Byzantine emperors—he called a brideshow. Every choice of royal bride raised new clans to power and destroyed others. The brideshow was designed to diminish such turbulence by virtue of the tsar's deliberate choice of

* The double-headed eagle was probably adopted as the grand princes aspired to the status of the Habsburg dynasty. It was probably later that monks claimed that the double-headed eagle represented Rome and Constantinople, capital of the eastern Roman or Byzantine empire—with Moscow as the Third Rome.

a girl from the middle gentry. Five hundred virgins were summoned from throughout his realm for this Renaissance beauty-contest, which was won by a girl named Anastasia Romanovna Zakharina-Yurieva, the great-aunt of the boy Michael.

The daughter of the minor branch of a clan that was already at court, Anastasia was ideal, thanks to her combining a safe distance from influential potentates with a comforting familiarity. Ivan knew her already since her uncle had been one of his guardians. She was descended from Andrei Kobyla, whom the grand prince had promoted to the rank of boyar* in 1346–7, but her branch of the family stemmed from his fourth son, the boyar Fyodor, who was called Koshka—"the Cat." Each generation was known by the name of the male in the generation before, so the Cat's children were dubbed the Koshkins, an appropriate designation given the Romanov family's feline gifts for survival. Anastasia's great-grandfather, Zakhar, and her grandfather, Yuri, were boyars, but her father Roman died young. However, he gave his name to the Romanovichi, who would become known as the Romanovs.[2]

Soon after the coronation, on 2 February 1547, Ivan married Anastasia. The marriage was a success. She gave him six children of whom two male heirs survived, Ivan and Fyodor, and she had the gift of being able to calm his manic temperament. Yet he still exhausted her with his unpredictable frenzies and constant travels. At first his reign prospered: he marched south-eastwards on a Christian Orthodox crusade to defeat the Islamic Tatars, the descendants of Genghis Khan who were now divided into smaller khanates. First he conquered the khanates of Kazan and Astrakhan—triumphs he celebrated by building St. Basil's Cathedral on Red Square; he despatched merchant adventurers and Cossack buccaneers to begin the conquest of vast, rich Siberia; he brought in European experts and merchants to modernize Muscovy and fought the Commonwealth of Poland–Lithuania to control the rich cities of the Baltic. But it was to be a long war which undermined the sanity of the tsar and the loyalty of his overmighty grandees, many of whom had their own links to the Poles. At the same time, he was often at war with the other regional power, the khanate of the Crimean Tatars† to the south.[3]

---

* Boyars were the top echelon of the nobility and were appointed by the tsar. This had nothing to do with the hereditary title of prince, which the tsar by tradition could not grant. Princes were descendants of the rulers of the cities that Moscow had conquered, often the obscure scions of the uncountable lineage of Rurik, grand prince of Kiev, or of Gedimin, founding grand duke of Lithuania, or of Tatar khans. Some princes were super-rich magnates who owned over 100,000 acres; but many princes were neither rich nor boyars. Titles did not always matter: the Romanovs had been boyars but they were never princes.
† The Crimean khanate, ruled by the Giray family, descendants of Genghis Khan, was for

In 1553, Ivan fell ill. His wife's brother Nikita Romanovich tried to persuade the courtiers to swear allegiance to the tsar's baby son—but they refused, because they favoured his adult cousin, Prince Vladimir of Staritsa. The tsar recovered but emerged fixated on the treachery of his nobles and the independent allegiances of Prince Vladimir and the other magnates. In 1560, Anastasia died at the age of twenty-nine. Ivan was distraught, convinced she had been poisoned by hostile grandees.* She may indeed have been poisoned, but she may just as easily have died of a disease or well-intentioned medicine. Either way, the defections and intrigues of his own magnates now sent Ivan into a spiral of violence: he suddenly withdrew from Moscow to a provincial stronghold whence he divided the realm between his private fief, the Separateness—*Oprichnina*—and the rest of the country. He unleashed a fearsome corps of black-clad upstart henchmen, the *oprichniki*, who astride black horses decorated with brooms and dog's heads, to symbolize incorruptibility and ferocious loyalty, launched a reign of terror. As Ivan lurched between spasms of killing, praying and fornication, no one was safe. His instability was exacerbated by the fragility of his dynasty: only his son Ivan seemed likely to survive to adulthood since the youngest Fyodor was not strong. It was essential to marry again—which became an obsession like that of his contemporary Henry VIII. While he sought foreign brides, a princess from the dynasty ruling Sweden and Poland in the hope of winning the Polish throne, and an Englishwoman, possibly even Elizabeth I herself, Ivan worked his way through as many as eight wives, three of whom may have been poisoned, and some of whom may have been murdered on his own orders. When his second wife, a Tatar princess, died in 1569, another suspected victim of poisoning, he went berserk, purging his own ministers, cutting off noses and genitals, then descending with a posse of dog-headed *oprichniki* on to the cities of Tver and Novgorod, killing virtually their entire populations, treating victims with boiling then frozen water, hanging them from hooks inserted through their ribs, roping women and children together and pushing them under the ice. Taking advantage of Ivan's demented distractions, the Tatar khan captured and burned Moscow.

After the *oprichniki* had done his bidding, Ivan reunited the tsardom but then abdicated and appointed a Tatar khan's son, converted to

---

three centuries a middling European power, extending from southern Ukraine to northern Caucasus and based at Baktiserai in Crimea. Its army of 50,000 mounted archers was so formidable that for a long time the tsars paid it tribute. Its khans were closely allied with the Ottoman sultans whom they helped to control the Black Sea.

* When her body was analysed in the twentieth century, it was found to contain dangerous levels of mercury—but then so were other sixteenth-century bodies tested at the same time. Mercury was often used as a medicine.

Christianity, as grand prince of Russia before taking back the throne. There was some method in the madness: Ivan's cruelties broke the power of the territorial magnates—even though they were garnished with the personal sadism of his diabolical idiosyncrasy. Anastasia's brother Nikita Romanovich remained the uncle of the heirs to the throne, but the Romanovs were no safer than anyone else from the tsar. In 1575, at least one Romanov was killed and Nikita's lands ravaged.

At a brideshow in September 1580, Ivan chose a new wife, Maria Nagaya, who gave him the son, Dmitri, that he craved. Yet, in 1581, in a rage he killed his own eldest son by Anastasia, Ivan, driving his iron-tipped staff into the boy's head, the awful climax of his reign. He had already debased Russia, but now he condemned it to chaos for the heirs to the throne were his other son by Anastasia, the weak and simple-minded Fyodor—and the baby Dmitri.

On Ivan the Terrible's death in 1584, Nikita Romanovich helped ensure the succession of his nephew Fyodor I. But Nikita died soon afterwards and his influence was inherited by his son Fyodor Nikitich Romanov, future father of Michael.

Tsar Fyodor left the ruling to his able minister Boris Godunov, who had risen as one of Ivan's *oprichniki* and now consolidated his power by marrying his sister to the tsar. The last Rurikid heir was Ivan's youngest son, the eight-year-old Dmitri, who now vanished from the scene. He officially died from a knife wound to the throat, self-inflicted during an epileptic fit. This would have been such a freak accident it may actually have happened, but inevitably many believed he had either been assassinated by Godunov—or been spirited away to safety.

When Tsar Fyodor died childless in 1598, the Muscovite line of the Rurikid dynasty was extinct.[4]

There were two candidates for the throne—Fyodor's minister and brother-in-law Boris Godunov, and Fyodor Romanov, eldest nephew of the late Tsarina Anastasia, and son of Nikita Romanovich, who was known as the best-dressed boyar at court. Fyodor Romanov married Ksenia Shestova, but of their six children, including four sons, only one daughter and one son survived: the future Tsar Michael was born in 1596 and was probably raised in a mansion near Red Square on Varvarka Street.* He was showered with gifts but his childhood was not stable for long.

* In 1856, their descendant Emperor Alexander II bought the building on this site from its neighbouring monastery to celebrate his coronation. Most of it dates from much later, but its foundations are fifteenth century. It is likely that Michael Romanov was brought up here.

Godunov was elected tsar by an Assembly of the Land, so he was the nearest thing to a legitimate ruler after the extinction of the rightful dynasty, and he was initially backed by Fyodor Romanov. Godunov was gifted, but luck is essential in politics and he was unlucky. His enduring achievement took place on his eastern borders, where his Cossack adventurers managed to conquer the khanate of Sibr, opening up the vastness of Siberia. But Russia herself suffered famine and disease, while Boris's own illness undermined his tenuous authority.

Fyodor Romanov, whose intrigues and escapes displayed all the agility of his cat-like ancestors, helped spread the fatal rumours that Ivan the Terrible's late son Dmitri had escaped and was still alive. A showdown was nearing, and the Romanovs brought military retainers into Moscow. When Michael Romanov was only five, his world was destroyed.

In 1600, Godunov pounced on Fyodor and his four brothers, who were accused of treason and sorcery; their servants testified under torture to their practice of witchcraft and stashes of "poisonous herbs." Tsar Boris burned down one of their palaces, confiscated their estates and exiled them to the Arctic. To ensure that Fyodor Romanov could never be tsar, he was forced to take holy orders, under a new priestly name Filaret, while his wife became the Nun Martha. Michael was sent to live with his aunt, the wife of his uncle Alexander Romanov, in the remote village of Belozersk. He remained there for fifteen frightening months before he and his aunt were allowed to move to a Romanov estate fifty miles from Moscow. Three of the five Romanov brothers were liquidated or died mysteriously. "Tsar Boris got rid of us all," Filaret remembered later. "He had me tonsured, killed three of my brothers, ordering them strangled. I now only had one brother Ivan left." Godunov could not kill all of the Romanovs, with their special connections to the Rurikid tsars, not after the murky demise of Tsarevich Dmitri. The vanishing of royal children at the hands of power-hungry relatives has a fitting way of destroying the very power they seek.

The whispering campaign percolated through the land and convinced many that the real Rurikid heir, Tsarevich Dmitri, had been raised in Poland and was now ready to claim his throne; this unleashed the mayhem that became known as the Time of Troubles.

This first pretender to the throne was almost certainly not the real Dmitri but, even now, no one is sure of his real identity—hence he is usually known as the False Dmitri. He may have been a renegade monk who had lived in the Kremlin, where he learned about court life. Dmitri was probably brought up to believe he was the real prince and that gave him an unshakeable belief in his destiny. In October 1604, as power leeched away from Godunov, the False Dmitri, backed by the Poles, his army swelled by Cossack* freebooters, marched on Moscow. Given the feverish popular reverence for Russia's sacred monarchs, the resurrection or survival of the rightful tsar seemed a Christ-like miracle. Godunov died of a brain haemorrhage and was succeeded by his son, Fyodor II. But the boy's throat was cut before the mysterious pretender took the city.[5]

On 20 June 1605, the False Dmitri triumphantly entered Moscow. Ivan the Terrible's last wife, the mother of the real Dmitri, accepted him as her long-lost son. This brazen showman was crowned tsar, but as he desperately tried to reconcile his different backers, Polish and Russian, Orthodox and Catholic, boyar and Cossack, he summoned back the Romanov brothers and appointed Filaret metropolitan of Rostov, a promotion that would keep him out of Moscow. Michael, now ten, and his mother moved with Filaret to Rostov.

The tsar fell in love with the daughter of his Polish backer, Marina Mniszech, whom he married and crowned in the Dormition Cathedral. The fact that she was a Catholic Pole shattered his mystique and she soon became loathed as "Marinka the Witch." Nine days later, at four in the morning, the boyars rang the bells and blockaded the palace. Dmitri leapt from a window but broke his leg and was shot and stabbed at least twenty-one times. Deciding who should be tsar next, the boyars weighed the claims of the Romanovs, taking account of their link to the rightful dynasty. One brother, Ivan, was unpopular, the other, Filaret, was a monk, so that left Filaret's son, Michael. But he was too young. Finally, the leader of the coup, Vasily Shuisky, a member of another branch of the Rurikid dynasty and a feckless conspirator, was chosen as Tsar Vasily IV while Filaret became the patriarch of the Orthodox Church.

False Dmitri's disembowelled body was exhibited naked: "his skull had been stove in and his brain lay beside him," a minstrel's bagpipes were stuffed in his mouth to suggest he played the devil's tune and his genitals were laid alongside the rest of these giblets. Filaret Romanov plotted against Vasily IV until he was sacked and ordered to his see of Rostov.

* The Cossacks, their name derived from the Turkish and Arabic word *Kazak* for adventurer or freebooter, were originally Tatar warriors, but by the sixteenth century they were mainly Slavic communities that settled in the borderlands of Muscovy, Tatary and Poland, living by hunting, fishing and banditry. The wars between the Tatars, Russians and Poles gave them plenty of opportunity to fight as mercenaries and independent raiders (initially infantrymen, then fighting on fleets of *chaika*—seagull—boats, later they became cavalry). In the Time of Troubles, the Cossacks, some fighting for the Poles, others for the different sides in the civil war, became arbiters of power. Indeed they were instrumental in electing Michael Romanov. The increasing oppression of peasants, forced by tsars and landowners into the slavery known as serfdom, drove thousands to flee to Cossack communities, brotherhoods of proud freemen, "hosts," which elected leaders, known as hetman (Ukrainian) or ataman (Russian).

The genie of the undead Tsarevich Dmitri now stalked the land. The reservoir of popular faith in the extinct dynasty of Ivan the Terrible was deep: more than ten different adventurers led armies claiming to be sons or grandsons of Ivan the Terrible. But one pretender, a second False Dmitri, even more mysterious than the first, became a real threat.

A former teacher, fluent in Polish and Russian, possibly a converted Jew, advanced to Tushino outside Moscow where he was joined by Marinka the Witch, widow of the First False Dmitri. When she met the coarse Second False Dmitri, nicknamed the "Brigand," she shuddered. She had no choice but to recognize him as her husband. They then married—in secrecy, since if the Brigand really was the False Dmitri they were already married. She was soon pregnant.

Meanwhile Filaret was reunited with his ex-wife Martha and his son Michael in Rostov—but their trials were not over. In Moscow, Tsar Vasily Shuisky was losing the war against the Brigand, so he called in the help of the king of Sweden who advanced into Russia and occupied Novgorod.

The Brigand's Cossacks conquered the south and advanced on Rostov, where Filaret rallied the defence until October 1608 when he was captured. The Brigand appointed him patriarch. The disintegration of Russia was irresistibly tempting to the neighbouring Poles and Swedes who were rivals for power around the Baltic and were both closely linked to Russian boyars and merchants. Ivan the Terrible had fought a twenty-four-year war against both kingdoms for control of the Baltic and Poland itself. The kingdom of Poland and the grand duchy of Lithuania had recently merged into a huge new state, which included most of today's Poland, Ukraine, Belarus and the Baltic states. Ivan's demoniac sacking of Novgorod had no doubt persuaded that trading city that it might be happier under Swedish rule. So it was inevitable that these rising powers would be tempted to feast on the carcass of Russia.

As the Swedes swallowed Novgorod and the north, the king of Poland, Sigismund III, was reluctantly drawn into the war by the intrigues of his own magnates and the need to restrain Sweden. The Brigand fled to the south, while Vasily IV was overthrown in a coup by the seven key boyars, who included Ivan Romanov: the ex-tsar was made a monk and later died in a Polish jail. They met to choose a new tsar. Filaret proposed Michael. But when news arrived that the Brigand had raised a new Cossack army in the south, the boyars decided they needed an adult with an army and elected Władysław, son of the Polish king, as tsar.

Moscow itself was occupied by Polish mercenaries who looted the royal treasures of the Kremlin. Filaret was sent to negotiate with the Polish king, leaving Michael behind in the Polish-occupied Kremlin with his uncle Ivan.

Filaret, who seems to have been genuinely committed to a Polish tsar, met King Sigismund outside Smolensk and demanded that Władysław convert to Orthodoxy, but the Poles saw no reason for their prince to forsake Catholicism. Filaret was arrested and imprisoned in Poland while, to counteract the Polish candidate, Novgorod proposed that the Swedish king, Gustavus Adolphus, become tsar of Russia. Russia seemed doomed until December 1610, when, in the absence of a tsar, it was the head of the Orthodox Church, the Patriarch Hermogen, who dared to speak out and call for a holy national war against the foreign invaders. Hermogen, captured by the Poles, paid for his courage with his life, but out of this uprising came the election of the Romanov tsar.

The call was answered in Nizhny Novgorod by a coalition of patriots and adventurers. The Brigand had been murdered by his own bodyguard in revenge for one of his many atrocities, but the pretence was not quite over. Marinka the Witch, Polish tsarina of two False Dmitris, now gave birth to a son. Under the banner of her toddling pretender known as the "Baby Brigand," she and her Cossacks rode to join the militia in Nizhny Novgorod. In March 1611 this unlikely alliance marched on Moscow. In vicious fighting, the Poles set light to Moscow and retreated to the Kremlin, where they held Michael and the boyars as prisoners. But the militia failed to defeat the Poles and fell apart.

Finally in the autumn of 1611, back in Nizhny Novgorod, a capable soldier but middle-ranking nobleman, Prince Dmitri Pozharsky, and a local merchant, Kuzma Minin, gathered an army of national liberation and advanced on Moscow, backed by an aristocratic warlord and former supporter of the Brigand, Prince Dmitri Trubetskoi—while Marinka the Witch and the Baby Brigand fled south.

The patriots defeated the Poles, cut off their supply lines and then besieged the Kremlin, where the Poles and boyars started to starve. Bodies lay around the fortress; a merchant found a sack of human heads and limbs near the walls. Michael Romanov remained within this charnel-house with his mother. Finally, on 26 October 1612, the boyars including young Michael Romanov emerged from the Kremlin—and the Poles surrendered: most were slaughtered. Apart from the Baby Brigand in the south, the civil war was over.

The patriots immediately called an Assembly of the Land to elect a new tsar to save the motherland. But the boyars, who had only narrowly escaped being butchered by the Cossacks, were warned that as punishment for their treason they were not to appear at the Assembly. Lucky to be alive, Michael Romanov and his mother vanished into the countryside, seeking sanctuary at the Ipatiev Monastery. No one knew where they had gone—and initially no one cared. The Romanovs, tainted collaborators, were surely finished for ever.[6]

Eight hundred delegates arrived at the dilapidated Kremlin in the freezing month of January 1613: they camped in roofless halls and met sometimes in the Riverside Palace, at other times in the Dormition Cathedral. They fasted in the hope of receiving divine guidance but remained divided: the magnates supported the Swedish prince Karl-Filip, the king's brother, while the gentry and Cossacks insisted on a Russian tsar. Prince Pozharsky was the hero of the hour but he was not a boyar, his family neither rich nor eminent. The Cossacks proposed their leader Prince Dmitri Trubetskoi, who was a scion of Lithuanian royalty and successful freebooter, but for everyone else he was tainted by his closeness to the Brigand.

When these had all been rejected, the ataman of the Don Cossacks proposed Michael Romanov. Voices shouted that he was too young. The Assembly voted him down. Then a petition was submitted proposing Michael, who gained supporters as the everyman candidate—he appealed to conservative boyars as cousin of the last rightful tsars, to the Cossacks because his father had been the Brigand's patriarch. He was too young to have any personal enemies or to be blamed for his uncle's Polish collaboration—and the absence of his father meant that no one controlled him. He was an immaculate pawn.

On 7 February, Cossacks won the vote for "our lawful Tsar Michael Fyodorovich," but some of the boyars, who had joined the Assembly, favoured the Swede. The Cossacks surrounded their palaces, accusing them of selling out to foreigners. The crowds backed the innocent boy. The boyars put up Ivan Romanov as a stop-Michael candidate, but he himself proposed the grandest and richest of the boyars, owner of 134,000 acres, Prince Dmitri Mstislavsky, who refused.[*] Michael's cousins Fyodor Sheremetev and Prince Dmitri Cherkassky canvassed for him, but even they were not delighted by their candidate. He was barely literate, sickly and unintelligent, but at least his domineering father Filaret was in captivity and the overweening Trubetskoi was bought off with the gift of vast estates and semi-royal titles. "Let us have Misha Romanov," wrote Sheremetev, "for he is still young and not yet wise; he

---

* Two of the most obvious candidates were absent: Michael's father, Filaret Romanov, and Prince Vasily Golitsyn were both prisoners in Poland. Filaret was ruled out because he was a priest, but Golitsyn's credentials—royal descent from Gedemin, the founding grand duke of Lithuania, boyar rank, stupendous wealth and personal prestige—were impeccable. Had he been present, this might be a history of the Golitsyn dynasty—except that such a paragon of breeding might not have appealed to the Cossacks who dominated the voting.

will suit our purposes." But the Cossacks took the decision out of their hands as one of the Polish nobles told the prisoner Filaret: "The Don Cossacks made your son sovereign."

The decision had to be unanimous. After two weeks, the Assembly fasted for two days and then, on 21 February, voted rank by rank for Michael. Outside the Kremlin in Red Square the crowd waited until the metropolitan of Riazan Fyodorit stood on the platform and cried: "Michael Fyodorovich Romanov!" Thus by popular acclaim, and by election, like a Cossack chieftain, Michael was chosen. But everyone understood that these shoddy wheeler-dealings had to be forgotten and effaced: only God's blessing could make a true tsar. And then there was another problem: where was the new tsar? No one knew exactly.

As soon the rumours about Michael reached the Poles, they despatched Cossacks to kill him. He was somewhere around Kostroma. They scoured the area, learning that a peasant called Ivan Susanin knew where he was. "While we the Great Sovereign were in Kostroma," wrote Michael later, "the Poles and Lithuanians came into the region and Susanin misled them and they tortured him with great and immeasurable torments to get him to reveal where the Great Sovereign was. But Ivan, though he knew all about us, suffered but did not tell them so they tortured him to death."*

Yet Michael was still oblivious. On 2 March 1613, the delegation set off from Moscow to find their tsar but, as we saw in the Prologue, when they did offer him the throne, his mother cried out that "they had never wanted to be tsar. Michael wasn't old enough, and all ranks of people had sinfully betrayed earlier sovereigns, and that was why these sins had lost Muscovy the blessing of God! And seeing all this treachery, lies, shame and murders and outrages to earlier sovereigns how would even a true tsar be treated after such duplicity and betrayal?"

As the negotiations developed, the Nun Martha's argument became a little more practical and focused: "the boy's father Filaret was oppressed" in a Polish jail. Would the king of Poland punish the boy's father? And how could the boy accept the throne without his father's permission?

The delegates had been instructed that, if Michael baulked, they were

---

* The truth of the Ivan Susanin story is attested by Tsar Michael's rescript just six years later. This was the beginning of an official Romanov myth. Nicholas I took a special role in its embellishment. When the composer Glinka created his opera *Ivan Susanin*, Nicholas I changed its title to *A Life for the Tsar*, which made its significance very clear and turned it into the semi-official Romanov anthem. (The opera became one of Stalin's favourites.) The descendants of the heroically loyal peasant were invited to all Romanov coronations right up until that of Nicholas II in 1896, and they were specially honoured at the tercentenary of the dynasty in 1913.

"to plead with him in every way to take pity and be our tsar because by this election God had chosen him." Martha wondered how they would fund an army in a ruined country. How could he be crowned when the crowns had been pillaged? How would they reach Moscow across bandit-infested badlands?

The grandees replied that no one would betray Michael Romanov because he was the heir of the last true tsar Fyodor whose mother was a Romanov. All ranks had unanimously elected him. And they would arrange to free his father. This convinced the Romanovs. Michael accepted.

In faraway Poland, his father Filaret was informed that his son had been elected tsar. He was infuriated by his son's acceptance without his permission. "When I left him, he was so young and without family." He shrugged: "What was my son to do?"[7]

As he processed towards Moscow, Michael complained every step of the way. On 19 April he stopped at Yaroslavl, where he again panicked: "It had never even entered our thoughts that we could reign over so many great realms—we aren't even of mature age. The Muscovite realm is in ruins and the Muscovite people so feeble-minded on account of their sins . . . How will a lawful hereditary ruler fare in Moscow, let alone myself?"

"Have mercy on us orphans, Great Sovereign," replied the grandees, pleading with the tsar to hurry. Michael lingered in Yaroslavl where the "Cossacks incessantly importune us and we have nothing—how are we to pay our soldiers? We can expect the Lithuanians and Swedes very soon!" And he needed royal regalia: without this, he would be an emperor with no clothes.

On 17 April he finally started to travel. "We're coming slowly with little transport and our servicemen in poor condition with many of our musketeers and Cossacks having to travel on foot," he grumbled to the Assembly—and "not many of my courtiers have even arrived." When he reached the Trinity Monastery near Moscow, he specified which Kremlin apartments he wanted repaired for himself and his mother. On 28 April, he and his mother had a very public tantrum. Metropolitan Fyodorit and boyar Fyodor Sheremetev wrote urgently to Moscow that "the Sovereign and his mother spoke angrily and tearfully to all the ranks assembled at the monastery."

"You did us obeisance and said you'd come to your senses and give up banditry, but you spoke falsely," cried the mother.

"We, your slaves," replied the warlords Pozharsky and Trubetskoi, "have endured hunger and hardship and harsh sieges. Now there are many with us waiting outside Moscow who petition you Our Sovereign to be graced by your presence." In other words, it was time to stop whining.

On 2 May Michael entered the holy city as bells rang from all the churches. Moscow was regarded by Russians as their sacred capital, a new Jerusalem. Even in this age of religious fervour, foreigners were amazed by the ritualistic piety of the Russians and their severe code of behaviour. Russian men wore long beards, as sacred tribute to God, and long robes, kaftans, with pleated sleeves that hung almost to the floor, on their heads sable or black-fox hats. Musical instruments and smoking were banned and noblewomen, whether virgins or wives, were restricted to their family *terem*, the separate living quarters of Muscovite women, where they were veiled and hidden. Yet none of this stopped the practice of the national pastime, drinking. Ordinary women were to be seeing lying around the streets, blind drunk.

Michael processed into the sixty-four-acre Kremlin, the fortress, palace and sacred esplanade of this New Jerusalem—now a pitiful sight. There was rubble heaped in the squares; chairs and beds had been used as firewood; the palaces had served as charnel-houses, full of bodies that had been piled up during the long sieges. The rambling complex of royal residences—the three-storey wooden Terem Palace with its gilded, frescoed throne room, the Golden Chamber and the connected Palace of Facets—were being hurriedly repaired to be ready for the coronation. (The new tsar's alterations, adding two stone storeys where the royal family would live, would take three years to complete.) In the first months, Michael stayed in the palaces of his nobles, who traditionally had their own residences within the Kremlin.

The Kremlin had been founded on this hill between the Moskva and Neglinnaya rivers as the prince's residence in the mid-twelfth century at a time when Moscow was a minor town compared to the chief Russian principalities, Vladimir and Rostov, and to the republic of Great Novgorod. In 1326, Ivan I, known as Moneybags, built the Dormition Cathedral, where grand princes were crowned, and the Cathedral of the Archangel Michael, where they were buried. Ivan had promoted Moscow as the centre of religious and royal authority, but Ivan the Great was the real creator of the Kremlin as Michael would have known it. Advised by his Italian-educated wife, the Byzantine princess, Ivan hired Italian Renaissance masters to rebuild both the cathedrals, raise his Ivan the Great Tower, craft his Palace of Facets, and fortify this acropolis with the crenellated red walls and battlements that now seem so Russian, and were then seen as exotically Italian.

Michael paraded through the Temple Mount of this holy precinct to pray in the five-domed Dormition Cathedral, where he received the oaths of allegiance. The boy had to assume the sacred charisma of monarchy and there was only one way to do this—via the rituals of coronation. The monarchy had ceased to exist: the coronation must transform Michael into the personification of its restoration. Yet this mystical moment started with an unholy row.[8]

On the morning of 11 July 1613, the day before his seventeenth birthday, the boy tsar met the boyars in the Golden Chamber, but the meeting soon degenerated into a dispute about precedence, the combination of family pedigree and length of service that in this restored court assumed paramount importance. Michael commanded that the rules of precedence were in abeyance during the coronation, but when his secretary announced that his uncle Ivan Romanov would bear the crown rather than the swaggering warlord Prince Trubetskoi (who had wanted to be tsar himself), the latter refused to allow this because his ancestry was superior. "It is true your ancestry is superior to Ivan Romanov's," replied Michael. "But he must now be accorded higher rank because he is my uncle." Trubetskoi reluctantly agreed to carry the sceptre instead.

At two o'clock that afternoon, Michael, clad in the Byzantine-style golden robes that had earlier been blessed by Metropolitan Efrem (the senior clergyman—there was no patriarch because the tsar's father Filaret was still in prison), entered the Palace of Facets. The boyars prostrated themselves before the frail boy.

As thirty-three Kremlin bells pealed, the courtiers and boyars, bearing on scarlet cushions the crown, orb (held by Pozharsky), sceptre and golden salver of the newly crafted royal regalia, emerged out of the Red Porch to bow thrice then process down the Red Staircase and across Cathedral Square towards the Dormition Cathedral. Then came the cathedral's archpriest sprinkling holy water, so ensuring that Michael would step only on sanctified ground. The tsar entered the cathedral to the chanting of the hymn "Many Years" rendered without musical instruments as none were used in Orthodox services. When he stood in the church before the icons of the golden iconostasis, Efrem asked for God's blessing. Then it was Michael's turn and the boy, who had never before taken part in such a ceremony let alone spoken formally in public, declared that Russia had suffered terrible trials in the fifteen years since the death of the last rightful tsar, his cousin Fyodor, son of Ivan the Terrible. Now Russians must restore peace and order.

Efrem tied a reliquary of a splinter of the True Cross around the boy's neck, then blessed his head and pronounced the benediction as if ordaining a priest, an act of consecration. Next he placed on his head the fur-rimmed Crown (or Cap) of Monomakh, embellished with rubies and emeralds, and handed him the orb and sceptre. Michael sat on the throne of Monomakh. The Cap had never been owned by the Byzantine emperor Constantine Monomakh who gave it his name, but was a royal Mongol helmet, adapted in the fourteenth century, while the wooden throne, carved with lions and Byzantine scenes, had actually been built for Ivan the Terrible. Efrem declared Michael to be grand prince, tsar and sovereign autocrat of Russia. Afterwards, Michael took off the crown, placed it on the golden salver and passed it to his uncle Ivan Romanov, handing the sceptre to Trubetskoi (who had grumbled about this order of things) and the orb to his cousin Sheremetev. His head was then anointed with the holy oil that bestowed his sacred charisma. Then, in the ritual followed by every tsar until 1896, he emerged to walk to the Archangel Cathedral next door to pray at the graves of Ivan the Terrible and Fyodor, while Prince Mstislavsky thrice threw coins over the tsar to celebrate the prosperity of Russia's bridegroom. In fact he was in dire straits.[9]

Michael was surrounded by fractious boyars, some of whom had aspired to be tsar themselves. The kings of Sweden and Poland were gathering armies to crush him; the Tatar khan ravaged the south and the Baby Brigand, the false grandson of Ivan the Terrible, held court in Astrakhan. The country was ruined. The chances of success must have seemed no better than even.

Michael was inexperienced politically and even his supporters described him as dim and placid. Foreigners noticed his genial smile, but during his long reign there are only a couple of occasions when he became angry enough to make any impression. He was ill much of the time. His eye twitched and his legs were unsteady, but it is hard to tell whether he was simply a weak nonentity or whether his frailties were the symptoms of traumas experienced in the Troubles. He was punctiliously pious—as was expected of a true tsar. He liked new technology, collected clocks and enjoyed Western entertainments, employing a troupe of acrobats, clowns and dwarfs in his Poteshnye (Amusement) Palace. Dwarfs and freaks were regarded as lucky mascots, but they were also expressions of the exceptionalism of royalty: Michael's favourite companion was the dwarf Mosiaga. There was dancing, drums were played and tightropes walked. The tsar was an avid gardener and hunter. Everything suggests a passive, good-natured and cheerful boy who lived for routine and order. We have no lifelike portraits: his image as sweet-natured tsar was more important than his ability to make decisions.[10]

The boy tsar initially shared power with the boyars and the Assembly. He agreed that he would not "execute anyone without fair trial and in

conjunction with the boyars." The Assembly remained almost permanently in session. The Kremlin was dominated by Pozharsky and the
heroes of the uprising, who were despatched in every direction to fight
the regime's enemies. Michael's election was an act of patriotic defiance,
his mission to co-ordinate the rout of foreign invaders, and thus from
the very start the Romanovs had to provide military leadership.

First his generals defeated the army of the Baby Brigand and Marinka
the Witch, both of whom were captured. Her latest husband, the Cossack ataman Zarutsky was impaled with a spike up his rectum on Red
Square; Marinka was starved to death; the four-year-old Baby Brigand
was hanged from the Kremlin walls. This was no time to take chances.
Tatars, Poles and Swedes were at least bloodied. On 15 October 1615, the
Swedes agreed the Peace of Stolbovo. Novgorod was returned, but Gustavus Adolphus laid the foundations of a Swedish empire in Livonia;
Russia was cut off from the Baltic.

Michael could now concentrate on the chief enemy, the Poles, with
Pozharsky as his best commander. Yet no one could forget that Michael's father, Filaret, was still a Polish prisoner. The tsar's first letter to
Filaret made clear that the old man was potentially the real force in the
government: "to the most venerable and exalted Metropolitan, father of
fathers, Great Sovereign Filaret, worthy of sacred and divinely adorned
rank, diligent seeker of lost sheep: your son, scion of your eminently
illustrious stem, Michael, Tsar and Grand Prince, Autocrat of all Russia,
bows his head zealously to the ground . . ."

In Polish captivity, meeting his son's first envoy under the eyes of his
captors, Filaret had to square his former allegiance to the Poles with the
election of his son as tsar: "I've acted in good faith until now, but now
my own son has been elected sovereign. In this way, you committed an
injustice to me. You could have elected someone else but now you did
this without my knowledge . . ." And here was the crux: "He became
sovereign not through his wish but by the Grace of God." While the
Poles were determined to destroy Michael, they were unlikely to release
his father—and at some point the tsar would have to call a brideshow to
choose a wife.[11]

Michael and the people who had elected him desperately wanted a real
sacred tsar with the splendour of a royal court—to make it seem as if
the atrocities of the last ten years had never happened. Ritual had to be
performed, antiquity restored, but the court had to be created afresh—
and everything new had to seem traditional. The disintegration that
followed the death of Ivan the Terrible had shown what could happen
when the autocrat had destroyed all opposition but left the autocracy

without a base. From the very start, the Romanovs ruled with a core of great families whom they rewarded with grants of land, *pomestia*, held temporarily in return for military service.

First Michael's retainers restored the ceremony of sacred monarchy. In the vaulted audience chamber, illustrated with biblical scenes, the young tsar, wearing robes set with diamonds and a diamond-studded sable-trimmed hat, the gold sceptre in his hand, sat on a raised throne with four gilded pillars each surmounted with a golden eagle. Beside the throne was a gold imperial apple as large as a skittle ball on a silver pyramid and a gold basin and ewer and towel. On each side stood boyars and officials in white damask robes, lynx-fur hats and white boots with gold chains around their necks, gleaming silver axes over their shoulders.

Michael's life was dominated by religious services that could often last from dawn till dusk, and strict observation of all festivals—which covered nearly all the days of the year. On the Feast of Epiphany, 6 January, the tsar, surrounded by courtiers and his musketeers, the *streltsy*, an elite regiment founded by Ivan the Terrible, gathered around a hole broken in the ice of the Moskva River to "bless the waters of the Jordan," a ritual that promoted Moscow as Jerusalem, Russia the Holy Land.

The calibrated hierarchy of court was re-created. In all autocracies, favour is measured by proximity to the ruler. In Moscow this was expressed as "beholding the bright eyes of the Sovereign." The court was the entrepôt of power where the nobles offered their recognition and service to the monarch, who in response distributed jobs, land, power, titles and marriages and in turn expected them to help command his armies and organize the mobilization of his resources. The court brokered power, enabled participants to amass wealth, bonded them in their shared loyalty to the monarchy—but it also allowed them to compete without resorting to civil war or revolution. Here they played out their conflicts—political rivalries, sexual intrigues—which were adjudicated by the monarch and his trusted henchmen. No one could forget the Troubles, and the autocracy was regarded as essential not just to unite the country and reconquer lost lands but also to prevent any slide back to mayhem. Once established, the Romanovs were rarely challenged as the rightful dynasty.

Every morning the boyars and courtiers* approached the Red Stair-

---

* Ten or so boyars were appointed by the tsar to sit on his Council. He raised a few to the rank of privy boyar. However rich and grand boyars were, they wrote to the tsar signing off with childish diminutives like "Your submissive slaves Mitka and Sashka." Beneath them were the lords-in-waiting, *okolnichii*, then council nobles, *dumnyi dvorianie*. Low-born clerks, *dyaki*, actually ran the departments of state and the most important of these became *dumnyi dyaki*, council secretaries. These top four layers sat in the Council and from them were chosen ministers and courtiers. The chairmen of the fifty or so offices, *prikazi*, the

case that led from Cathedral Square up to the private apartments in the
Terem Palace. The junior officials, "the people of the square," waited at
the bottom, but the lucky few, "the people of the apartments," could go
on up. The royal suite was a line of rooms of increasing and impenetrable sanctity. Only the very highest could reach the Golden Chamber, the
third chamber next to the royal bedchamber. The tsar was so sacred that
no one was allowed to look him in the eye, and he was greeted by his
subjects with total prostration. If he was bled by doctors, the blood was
blessed and buried in a special blood pit to prevent sorcery.

As ever in the Kremlin, security was paramount. Just in case his much
promoted, sweet-natured sanctity was not enough, Michael ordered that
anyone hearing "the tsar's word or deed"—a fearsome phrase which
meant that someone suspected treason—was to inform his enforcer,
Prince Yuri Suleshov, a converted princeling of the Tatar Golden Horde,
who ran the Office of Investigations. Even now, the court had a strong
Tatar flavour with many converted princelings, none more powerful
than Michael's half-Tatar cousins, the princes Cherkassky.[12] The court
was restored, but Michael could no longer afford to wait for his father to
return. He had to find a wife, a magnificent but perilous role in a court
where poison was just another political tool. In late 1615, he called a
brideshow.

Courtiers fanned out across the kingdom to select teenaged virgins,
mostly from middling gentry families, who were despatched to Moscow
where they lived with relatives or in a specially chosen mansion. These
candidates, perhaps as many as 500 of them, were reduced to around
sixty girls, primped and groomed by their families.

The contestants first appeared before a jury of courtiers and doctors
who weeded out the weakest. Descriptions were sent to the tsar and his
advisers, but apart from beauty and health, the essential details were
any kinship ties to Kremlin clans. As they waited nervously, their family
trees were researched in detail.

This ancient tradition fascinated foreign visitors who regarded it as
the most exotic of Muscovite customs. It projected the mysterious but

---

government departments, ran the court and the country—some political like the Foreign
Office or Great Treasury, some regional like the Kazan Office, others personal, the Great
Court Office. In a court where poisoning was a frequent occurrence, the Royal Pharmacy, in
charge of the tsar's own medicines, was so important that it was virtually always controlled
by the chief minister. But the tsar's life was run by courtiers such as the keeper of the seal,
master of the horse and most intimately, the *postelnichi*, gentlemen of the bedchamber.
Pozharsky, the warlord who had actually established the Romanovs, was promoted to boyar
and showered with lands yet the absurdity of precedence made him the constant object of
violent complaints by boyars of more senior families.

wholesome majesty of autocracy but was really a practical response to the tsars' difficulty in attracting foreign wives to their isolated and far-away court. The shows were designed to calm the brutal competition between court factions by using an open ritual to choose a respectable maiden from the provincial gentry. The tsars wished to marry beneath themselves to avoid any links to boyar factions who did not want the bride to be connected to their rivals. Yet they each secretly hoped to promote a girl related (however distantly) to themselves.

The best girls were selected for the next stage, the viewing (smotriny), at which the tsar himself whittled down the contestants, who were now examined by the head of the Great Court Office and by royal doctors to assess their fecundity, the point of the entire exercise. The rejected were given presents and sent home, but the lucky six or so finalists moved into a special Kremlin mansion, then were presented to the tsar who signalled his choice by giving his handkerchief and gold ring to the chosen maiden.

The brideshows were not as fair as they looked: they could not be rigged but they could be manipulated. The last girls presented to the tsar were the result of the very intense politicking that the ritual was designed to avoid. The art of winning brideshows was to get more than one suitable candidate into the viewing. More than that the courtiers could not do. The tsar did not control the finalists, but no one could control whom he chose at the final viewing.

The winner and her father changed their names to signify their new status as royal in-laws; the girl assumed the title of tsarevna, and she and her mother moved into the Terem Palace to be trained—but also to be guarded because, as Michael's bride was about to discover, the winner was in danger.[13]

Just before Christmas 1615, the girls arrived to be inspected by Michael who chose Maria Khlopova, of middling gentry, by giving her the ring and kerchief. Changing her name to Anastasia, and receiving the higher title "tsarina," she, her grandmother and her aunt were installed in the top storey of the Terem Palace while her uncle Gavril Khlopov joined the royal retinue. But this threatened the most powerful of Michael's courtiers. Fyodor Sheremetev, the cousin who had travelled to Kostroma to offer him the throne, ran much of the government, but Mikhail Saltykov, nephew of the tsar's mother Martha, who had been with them in Kostroma, had the most to lose. Saltykov and Martha opposed Khlopova.

About six weeks after the betrothal, the tsar, Saltykov and the fiancée's uncle Khlopov were inspecting Turkish sabres in the Armoury. "Such sabres could be made in Moscow," boasted Saltykov, who as royal armsbearer ran the Armoury. The tsar handed a sabre to his prospective uncle-in-law asking if he really thought the Armoury could match the workmanship.

"Not as good," replied Khlopov. Saltykov grabbed the sword back and the two men argued in front of the tsar.

Soon afterwards, the bride vomited and fainted before the whole court. She had eaten too many sweets, her uncle later testified, but this case of possible food poisoning raised fatal questions: was she healthy enough to bear children and had her family hidden a secret disease? The tsar, or his mother, ordered Saltykov to supervise the girl's health—with breathtaking naivety or malevolence. Saltykov started dosing her with potions from the Pharmacy, after which she began suffering convulsions and vomiting. Everyone was horrified—as they were meant to be. Probably backed by the tsar's mother, the mastermind behind this malign intrigue, Saltykov suborned the doctors to say the girl was concealing an incurable disease and was incapable of having children. The poor girl along with her family were exiled to Siberia, her father appointed governor of faraway Vologda. After six weeks of royalty, the girl and her family were ruined. Michael loved the girl, yet he did not investigate further: he did not feel strong enough to overrule his mother. But this was not the end of the story.[14]

In October 1617 Prince Władysław of Poland advanced with his army to Viazma, 150 miles to the east, and dug in. On 9 September the following year, Michael summoned the Assembly to mobilize the nation, his appeal reeking of panic. On 1 October, the Poles attacked Moscow and reached the Arbat Gates, but as winter set in, mutinies and famine broke the Polish army in this last battle of the Troubles. On 2 February 1619, Michael agreed to the fourteen-year Truce of Deulino that gave Poland possession of Smolensk. It was a humiliation, but Michael had held the kingdom together, no small feat—and he got something back that was almost as important.[15]

On 14 June 1619, Michael, now aged twenty-three, accompanied by excited crowds, travelled to the Pryesna River five miles outside the city, and waited. A carriage with its own escort was approaching. When it was close, his father, Filaret, grey-bearded, and almost seventy, climbed out. After nine years' separation, son and father were both so moved that they hugged and prostrated themselves on the ground for a long time, weeping with joy. When they set off home, Filaret rode in a sleigh while Michael walked alongside back to Moscow, which welcomed them to the sound of bells and cheers. A week later, in the Golden Chamber, Filaret was nominated patriarch by the visiting Theophanes, patriarch of Jerusalem.

Filaret, masterful and cantankerous survivor of Ivan the Terrible and Fyodor, of exile and tonsure, of two False Dmitris and Polish captivity, was never going to be a mere clergyman. Michael appointed him grand sovereign, effectively co-tsar—they ruled together in a diarchy. The patriarch, who had only a "fair knowledge of the Scriptures," had waited too long for power. He was "irascible, suspicious and so imperious that even the tsar was afraid of him"—and his political skills have led some to compare him to his contemporary, Cardinal Richelieu.

The letters of tsar and patriarch show how father and son addressed each other formally. "We pray Almighty God that we shall see your holy fair and angelic face and kiss your Holiness's head and bow down to do obeisance," wrote Michael. Filaret went through the motions of advising—"And how will you, Sovereign, command on the Crimean business?"—but then he answered his own question: "To me, the Sovereign, I think that . . ." They received ambassadors sitting side by side on identical thrones, sometimes diplomatically playing different roles. "Don't declare it is written by me," Filaret instructed Michael in one case.

There was respect but not intimacy. "The natural affections of the son," noticed a Dutch envoy, were "directed much more towards his mother than towards his father on account of the long separation." Yet they worked things out together. "It's written, O Sovereign," wrote the tsar to his father, "that you Great Sovereign and our father and pilgrim, wish to be in Moscow for the Feast of the Trinity but that's not convenient for you because the roads will be impassable in your carriage. Perhaps it would be better if you came on the Monday . . . But let it be as our Great Sovereign wishes."

Filaret was the strongman of the Kremlin, and no one did more to establish the Romanovs. He was the impresario behind an array of ostentatious ceremonies and architectural improvements to project the prestige of the crown.* He ruled through a trusted coterie—his much younger brother Ivan, and his cousins, Sheremetev and the half-Tatar Prince Ivan Cherkassky. If any boyar stepped out of line, he was liable to be imprisoned. Nine of them were exiled. Filaret spent much time ad-

---

* Filaret hired a Scottish architect, Christopher Galloway, to refashion the Kremlin's Saviour Tower, adding a clock which delighted father and son. He relished the theatricality of this super-patriarchate: every Palm Sunday, Michael re-enacted Christ's entry into Jerusalem—but it was the patriarch not he who rode the ass. Wearing Monomakh's Crown and full royal robes, the tsar prayed with the boyars in the Kremlin then walked out with the patriarch, followed by the entire court. At the platform in Red Square, which served as Golgotha, the tsar held the horse (picturesquely dressed up as a donkey with false ears) as the patriarch mounted it and then processed back into the Kremlin to the Dormition Cathedral. Afterwards the patriarch thanked the tsar for this service with a payment of 200 roubles.

judicating between boyars, who feuded constantly over precedence and frequently resorted to physical violence. Many boyars remembered him as one of them: the gruff but loyal Prince Lykov-Obolensky once swore at Filaret in church. Now it was lonely at the top: Filaret grumbled to his son that his only friends were Cherkassky, Lykov and his brother Ivan.

Yet Filaret's purpose, the Romanov mission, was to mobilize Russia. He "administered everything concerning tsardom and army," and he saw his most urgent task as preparing for vengeance against Poland. Tax collecting was reformed; the Church disciplined and its lands co-opted by the dynasty, laying the foundations for its wealth. The landowners were given greater control over their serfs in return for their readiness to fight. As border clashes with Poland intensified, Filaret knew that his Polish and Swedish enemies were technically far ahead of Russia, but with Europe now being ravaged by the Thirty Years War, experienced mercenaries were plentiful and he hired English and Scottish officers to modernize the army. But the dynasty needed an heir: the tsar must marry.[16]

Michael refused to consider any other candidates for four years, still dreaming of the poisoned Maria Khlopova. But in 1621 Filaret offered his son's hand to two foreign princesses, only for the Western monarchs to rebuff these uncouth parvenus—surely to Michael's relief because he now persuaded his father to return to the case of Maria. Filaret ordered his doctors Bills and Bathser to examine the exiled girl, now in Nizhny Novgorod, and they returned with the news that she was entirely healthy. Filaret then turned on Armsbearer Saltykov: why had he claimed that she suffered from an incurable illness?

Filaret and Michael, sitting in judgement with Ivan Romanov, Ivan Cherkassky and Sheremetev, tried Saltykov and his brother. Sheremetev was sent to Nizhny Novgorod to interview Maria, who explained that she had vomited only once—until Saltykov had given her a tincture from the Royal Pharmacy.

Michael was enraged. Saltykov was dismissed and banished for "hindering the Tsar's pleasure and marriage treasonably. The Sovereign's favour to you . . . was greater than you deserved, but you acted solely for own enrichment to make sure that no one but you enjoyed the Sovereign's favour." Saltykov escaped with his head only because he was protected by the tsar's mother, who ensured the Saltykovs were not destroyed—and could one day return.

Now Michael presumed he could marry Maria Khlopova, but the Nun Martha refused to bless the match: the girl was spoilt goods. The tsar's mother had a better candidate, her relative Princess Maria Dolgorukaya.

The tsar remained close to his mother, and she presided over the bride-show in which Michael selected her choice. On 19 September 1624, he married Dolgorukaya, a triumph for his mother's intrigues. But, four months later, the bride died.*

There was no time to mourn: Michael had to marry again, and fast. At the brideshow viewing, Michael presented Eudoxia Streshneva, daughter of poor gentry, with the ring and kerchief. Filaret had her closely guarded in the Terem Palace during the engagement. On 5 February 1626, they were married and spent their first night with the traditional kernels of wheat between their sheets, sheaves of rye beneath the bed and the icons over it.

Eudoxia suffered the constant interference of her mother-in-law, the Nun Martha, but even without that, the life of a tsarina was stiflingly puritanical and limited. Households were supposedly run according to the joyless *Domostroi*, household rules written by a sixteenth-century monk, which specified that "disobedient wives should be severely whipped" while virtuous wives should be thrashed "from time to time but nicely in secret, avoiding blows from the fist that cause bruises."

Royal women were secluded in the *terem*, not unlike an Islamic harem. Heavily veiled, they watched church services through a grille; their carriages were hung with taffeta curtains so that they could not look out or be seen; and when they walked in church processions, they were concealed from public gaze by screens borne by servants. In the Terem Palace, they sewed all day, and would kneel before the Red Corner of icons when entering or leaving a room. They wore sarafans, long gowns with pleated sleeves, and headdresses called kokoshniks, while make-up and even mirrors were banned as demonic. The rules were more relaxed lower down the social ladder. Merchants' wives blackened their teeth, wore white make-up, daubs of rouge, and had their eyebrows and eyelashes dyed black, "so they look as if someone has thrown a handful of flour at their faces and coloured their cheeks with a paintbrush." The lower classes had more fun, bathing nude in mixed bathhouses, carousing in the streets, but it was precisely to avoid this lairy wassailing that the piety of the *terem* was so rigidly enforced.

Yet Tsarina Eudoxia thrived there. The first of their ten children, Irina, was born exactly nine months after the wedding: tsarinas gave

---

* The Dolgorukys claimed descent from Yuri Long-Arm (Dolgo-ruky), grand prince of Kiev, who founded Moscow in 1156. But this was mythical. They were actually descended much later from the fifteenth-century ruler of Obolensk, Prince Ivan Obolensky the Long-Arm. This was not the last Romanov marriage to a Dolgorukaya, though it was said any Romanov marriage to a Dolgorukaya was cursed. The Dolgorukys were one of the families, like the Sheremetevs, Saltykovs and Golitsyns, who helped govern up to 1917. Nicholas II's last prime minister was a Golitsyn, and he went into Siberian exile with a Dolgoruky.

birth in the bathhouse of the Terem Palace. Each child was celebrated with a banquet in the Golden Chamber. After another daughter, an heir, Alexei, was born in 1629, followed by two more sons.[17]

Filaret, the ex-prisoner of the Poles, was spoiling for a fight with Poland even though few boyars felt that Russia was ready. In April 1632, he got his chance: King Sigismund III died. The Commonwealth of Poland–Lithuania was a huge country, stretching from the Baltic to near the Black Sea, but it was an awkward union of two separate realms, a constitutional contradiction with two governments and one parliament, which was elected by the entire nobility and in which every delegate had a veto. This parliament, the Sejm, chose its kings, leaving royal elections open to foreign machinations. Poland's idiosyncratic rules, overmighty magnates and widespread bribery often left the country languishing in anarchic limbo. After the Polish occupation of Moscow during the Troubles, Poland would remain Russia's ancestral enemy.

Filaret's war began in farce and ended in tragedy. He amassed an impressive 60,000 men but this antiquarian Muscovite army led by bickering boyars was obsolete. Only his 8,000 mercenaries under the Scotsman Colonel Leslie and the Englishman Colonel Sanderson could compare to the modern armies in the Thirty Years War.* When he sent two boyars to take Smolensk, they argued over precedence and had to be dismissed.

The new commanders, the boyar Mikhail Shein, who had shared Filaret's Polish imprisonment, and the lord-in-waiting Artemii Izmailov, started to besiege Smolensk in August 1633, but the fortress was re-inforced by Władysław IV, the newly elected Polish king who still claimed the Russian throne. By October, the Russians had lost 2,000 men in one skirmish and were facing food shortages. Shein was a blowhard who on his departure had boasted to the tsar that "when most of the boyars were sitting by their firesides" he alone was fighting—"no one was equal to him." But he was soon in a panic. Michael tried to calm Shein with the pious reflection that "many things happen in war and still God's mercy exists," but the situation in the camp deteriorated.

Leslie and Sanderson hated each other so bitterly that the Scotsman accused the Englishman of treason. As they brawled in front of the army, Leslie shot Sanderson dead. Shein started negotiating with the

---

* Traditional Muscovite armies were raised by noble servitors, the *pomestchiki*, who in return for *pomestia*, grants of land from the tsar, supplied soldiers. In this way, Filaret raised 26,000 men, but many of them were armed with bows and arrows. He recruited 11,000 undisciplined Cossack cavalry and 18,000 Tatars and Chuvash horsemen armed with crossbows. The 20,000 musketeers were more impressive.

Poles and on 19 February 1634 he surrendered, marching out past King Władysław who finally saw his chance to take Moscow. As the Poles advanced, Shein and Izmailov were arrested, tried for treason and for kissing the Catholic cross, and beheaded. But the Polish advance was abruptly stopped by news that Murad IV, the Ottoman sultan,* was invading Poland. On 17 May, Poland and Russia signed the Perpetual Peace. Władysław kept Smolensk—but finally recognized Michael as tsar.[18]

In October 1633, at the height of the crisis, Filaret died aged eighty, followed by Martha. Michael, thirty-five, ruled through his relatives Cherkassky and Sheremetev, while his heir, Alexei, as exuberant as his father was docile, was growing up in the cosy gloom of the Terem Palace.

When Alexei was five, Michael appointed a well-born if penurious nobleman, Boris Morozov, as his tutor. Traditionally princes were given only an elementary education, but Morozov taught him about the technology of the West, introduced him to Latin, Greek and Polish and helped him build up a library. His father, who loved gardens and gadgets, gave him a market garden and showed him his latest toy, a gilded organ with mechanical cuckoos and nightingales. Father and son also shared a taste for entertainments, employing sixteen dwarfs dressed in red and yellow outfits.

Morozov was an excellent choice and unusually for princes growing up in the fissiparous Kremlin, Alexei had a happy childhood. Morozov arranged that Alexei should be taught with twenty other boys, and when he was nine he was joined by a boy four years older named Arteem Matveev. As Michael himself reflected later, Morozov—who spent thirteen years "living constantly with us"—had almost become one of the family.[19]

Then, in 1639, two of Michael's sons died almost simultaneously, one aged five, the other just after being born. The family tragedies took their toll on the tsar. In April 1645 he fell ill with scurvy, dropsy and probably

---

* Murad IV combined the military gifts of Caesar with the demented sadism of Caligula but he was the last great Ottoman sultan, succeeded by his brother Ibrahim the Mad, who was an erotomaniac obsessed with furs, scent and enormously fat women. Ruling from Constantinople, the Ottoman sultan-caliphs had conquered a colossal empire that stretched from the borders of Iraq to the Aegean, including the Balkans (present-day Greece, Bulgaria, Romania and former Yugoslavia), north Africa, present-day Turkey and the entire Middle East, including Jerusalem and Mecca. Their European subjects were mainly Orthodox Christian Slavs who, bought as slaves and converted to Islam as children, provided their finest generals, officials and concubines. They had reached their height a century earlier under Suleiman the Magnificent but until the end of the eighteenth century, they remained a formidable empire of vast military resources. In 1637, independent Cossacks stormed the Ottoman fortress of Azov and offered it to Michael but, after consulting an Assembly, he conceded he was not yet strong enough to challenge the Ottomans.

depression. Three doctors analysed the tsar's urine. He wept so much that the doctors seriously diagnosed a deluge of tears in his stomach, liver and spleen, which deprived his organs of natural warmth and chilled his blood. They prescribed Rhenish wine laced with herbs and a purgative, with no supper. On 14 May they ordered another purgative. On the 26th they found the royal urine to be colourless because his stomach and liver were not working "due to too much sitting, cold drinks and melancholy caused by grief," the seventeenth-century diagnosis of depression. But he didn't improve. Sheremetev, who had offered him the throne thirty years earlier, personally nursed Michael but to no avail.

On 12 July, he fainted in church. "My insides," he groaned, "are being torn apart." His belly was massaged with balsam as his court realized that the tsar, forty-nine years old, was dying. Amid a stench of sweat and urine, the chanting of priests, the flickering of candles and the swinging of censers, royal deathbeds were theatres of dignity and sanctity—he who had lived like a king was expected to know how to die like one. Monarchs do not die like the rest of us: the tsar passed away but the power was passed on very much alive. Their deathbeds were public and practical transactions. Courtiers mourned a beloved master, but they also participated in the end of one reign and beginning of another. The transfer of power is always the ultimate test of a regime's stability—but until 1796 there was no law of succession in Russia so deathbeds were dangerous political crises which often deteriorated into lethal tournaments. Whispered last words were regarded as sacred, but a moment after the last breath only the whims of the new tsar really mattered. Such fraught setpieces were simultaneously family occasions and state ceremonies. Last-minute death-chamber intrigues could change everything.

The tsarina and heir were summoned along with Morozov and the patriarch. Michael said goodbye to his wife, blessed the heir with the kingdom and told Morozov: "To my boyar I entrust my son and implore you, even as you've served us joyfully, living with us for thirteen years, so keep serving him now!"

At 2 a.m. he took confession. Alexei noticed that his father's belly "stirred and rumbled," the rattle of death. As Michael died, Nikita Romanov, son of Ivan and therefore Alexei's second cousin, emerged into the antechamber to be the first to take the oath of loyalty to the new tsar, repeating that no foreigners be recognized as tsar and that every citizen was obliged to report any "evil designs"—while a single bell tolled and the widow and daughters howled in grief. There would be no Assembly to confirm the succession. The Romanovs no longer needed one. Alexei was tsar by God's will and none other.[20]

SCENE 2

# The Young Monk

# CAST

ALEXEI Mikhailovich, tsar 1645–76, "Young Monk"
Maria Miloslavskaya, tsarina, his first wife
Sophia, their daughter, later sovereign lady
Alexei Alexeievich, their eldest surviving son and heir
FYODOR III, their third son, tsar 1676–82
IVAN V, their fifth son, tsar 1682–96
Natalya Naryshkina, tsarina, Alexei's second wife
PETER I (THE GREAT), their son, tsar 1682–1725
Irina Mikhailovna, tsarevna, sister of Tsar Alexei
Nikita Ivanovich Romanov, the tsar's cousin, son of Ivan Romanov


## COURTIERS: ministers etc.

Boris Morozov, Alexei's tutor and chief minister
Ilya Miloslavsky, his father-in-law and minister
Nikon, patriarch
Bogdan Khitrovo, courtier, "Whispering Favourite"
Afanasy Ordyn-Nashchokin, minister
Arteem Matveev, Alexei's childhood friend and chief minister
Prince Ivan Khovansky, general, "Windbag"

Tsars were buried simply and quickly. The next day, 14 July 1645, Alexei, clad in black as he received condolences around the open coffin, led the simple procession from the Terem Palace to the Archangel Michael Cathedral where tsars were laid to rest, before eating the honeyed porridge of the funeral banquet. Moscow was tense: there had not been a peaceful handover of power for sixty years. The coronation must be arranged urgently. The Tatar khan was attacking in the south and the Polish king harboured one of the three new pretenders on the loose. Even thirty years after the Troubles, no one could ignore Russia's so-called "three plagues—typhus, Tatars and Poles."

On 18 August, the tsar's mother Eudoxia died—the teenager had lost both parents within five weeks. Alexei went on pilgrimage to Zagorsk, then fasted and prayed to purify himself. On 28 September, wearing the blessed red, gold and white robes, the tsar processed down lines of musketeers to be crowned in the Dormition Cathedral, and afterwards his cousin Nikita Romanov threw the coins.

The new tsar looked the part and lived it too: six feet tall, burly, energetic and healthy, with a lustrous red beard, he enjoyed falconry and hunting. At first, it was said he passed much of his time with the women in the *terem*, where he had spent his childhood, yet he swiftly imposed himself on his court in a way his father had never managed.[1]

Alexei was the one of the best-prepared heirs. His personal papers reveal an intelligent, restless and sharp-tongued reformer who did not suffer fools gladly. He wrote poems, made sketches and constantly wrote down ideas on every possible subject; he always sought foreign technology to improve his army and palaces—foreshadowing the approach of his son Peter the Great.* His rages were dangerous and he was quite capable of thumping a minister in the middle of a Council meeting. When the steward of his monasteries got drunk, he wrote him a letter calling him "a God-hater, Christ-seller, singleminded little Satan, damned scoffing enemy, wicked sly evildoer"; but, typically, the man's punishment was merely to have this read out in public and to atone sincerely.

---

* The real Alexei thus bears little resemblance to his reputation as "the meek one," the good, all-Russian saintly nonentity who became fashionable with Slavophiles in the nineteenth century as a contrast to the Westernized military emperors personified by Peter the Great. Alexei became the hero of the last tsar Nicholas II, who identified with his simple Slavic piety and named his son after him.

He could be as tender as he was cruel. After his top boyar Prince Nikita Odoevsky lost his son, Alexei comforted him: "Don't grieve too much. Of course you must grieve and shed tears but not too much . . ." But he was always the God-blessed autocrat, a playful tormentor of his courtiers. When he felt better after being bled, he forced all his courtiers to be bled too, even his old uncle who protested he was too weak. "Perhaps you think your blood more precious than mine?" said Alexei, who then struck him and watched as he was bled.

Alexei awoke at 4 a.m. each day, prayed in his private chapel for twenty minutes, before receiving those retainers privileged to see "the bright eyes," until at 9 a.m. he heard a two-hour mass. At Easter, he would pray standing for six hours, prostrating himself more than a thousand times.

At dinner at noon, he ate alone while the boyars ate at nearby tables: sometimes to reward a victory, he invited one of them to join him or sent them one of his dishes. Formal banquets were marathons of gourmandizing—seventy dishes of bear meat, beef, pigeon, sturgeon, accompanied by vodka, beer or kvass, a traditional Slavic drink of low alcoholic content.

After a siesta, Alexei was back in church for vespers before more meetings, games of chess and backgammon and further prayers. He was known as the "Young Monk," and his religiosity was so all-consuming that even visiting churchmen were physically exhausted by a few days in the Kremlin. A coterie of Zealots of Piety, protégés of the tsar's confessor, encouraged him to launch a campaign of puritanical moral regeneration to reform the vices of Muscovites. Adam Olearius, a German visitor, noted voluptuous dances, bare-bottomed mooning, drunken naked women splayed outside taverns and of course "lusts of the flesh," and added that Muscovites were "addicted to sodomy, not only with boys but with horses." It is unlikely that equine sodomy was really popular in the backstreets of Moscow, but binge-drinking women were then as now a sign of a rotten society. Alexei enforced the ban on musical instruments, smoking, swearing and drinking, denounced sexual immorality and pensioned off his dwarfs and replaced them with an irreproachably respectable retinue of cripples and monks. Diabolical mandolins were burned in a bonfire of the instruments in Red Square. "Take care that nowhere should there be shameful spectacles and games," he ordered, "and no wandering minstrels with tambourines and flutes." He noted his own act of charity: "Gave six roubles, ten kopeks each, to sixty people."[2]

Straight after the coronation, he retired his father's minister Sheremetev, now aged sixty-nine, and promoted his ex-tutor Boris Morozov, whom he called his "father-substitute," to be chief minister with a constellation of offices—Treasury, Musketeers and Pharmacy—and a luxurious palace within the Kremlin. In one of his first decisions, Morozov organized a brideshow.[3]

Six maidens reached the final to be viewed by the tsar. On 4 February 1648, he selected Efemia Vsevolozhskaya. The wedding was quickly scheduled for the 14th to avoid poisoning or maleficence but at a public ceremony the girl fainted as the crown was set on her head, sparking fears of witchcraft or epilepsy. Whether she had been poisoned or was just unlucky, Morozov, who had favoured another candidate, exploited her misfortune. She was given the fine linens prepared for her wedding as a parting present, expelled from the *terem* and exiled with her family. Alexei found consolation in bear-hunting.

When the bride-search was resumed, Morozov favoured the two daughters of a protégé. They were ideal because, if the tsar married one sister, Morozov could marry the other. Morozov had probably placed one of the girls among the final six beauties—but at the viewing the tsar had foiled his plan by choosing Vsevolozhskaya, who then conveniently fainted. Now Morozov arranged for the tsar to encounter the intended girl in his sister's apartments.

She was Maria, daughter of Ilya Miloslavsky, nephew of the long-serving secretary of the Foreign Office. Well-travelled by Muscovite standards, Miloslavsky had started as a wine-server to an English merchant and had travelled to Holland to hire Western experts.

On 16 January 1647, Alexei rode through a frozen Moscow alongside the sleigh bearing his fiancée Maria. Prince Yakov Cherkassky, the third richest boyar, was best man. Afterwards, the couple held court, sharing a throne in the Hall of Facets. Alexei banqueted on swan stuffed with saffron, she on goose, suckling pig and chicken. The tsar's Zealots persuaded the groom to ban any dancing or carousing. They drank just *kvass*, no vodka, and observed none of the traditional pagan fertility rituals. Nonetheless Maria swiftly fell pregnant and their partnership lasted twenty-one years, producing five sons and eight daughters. Maria would be the quintessential Muscovite wife, a paragon of pious modesty closeted in the *terem*.

Ten days later, Morozov, fifty-seven, married the teenaged Anna Miloslavskaya, making him the tsar's brother-in-law. While her sister Maria was marrying a strapping young monarch, it must have been a miserable match for Anna. According to the tsar's English doctor, Anna was a "succulent black young lass" who preferred young flirtations rather than her old husband, "so that, instead of children, jealousies were got." The marriage soon proved its value to Morozov: it saved his life.

Morozov had raised the salt tax four times yet, while he promoted austerity, his own nose was deep in the trough. Within a couple of years, though he had inherited just 100 serf households, he was the second richest boyar, while his cousin, the chief of investigations Ivan Morozov, was the fifth richest. Soon he was the most hated man in Moscow, where the discontent reflected a concurrence of war, revolution and famine across Europe.[4]

On 1 June 1648, when Alexei was returning from one of his many pilgrimages, he suddenly found himself surrounded by an angry crowd, who seized his bridle but also offered him the welcoming gifts of blood and salt: the mob denounced the bloodsuckers of Alexei's own government, particularly Morozov's ally Leonid Pleshcheev who ran Moscow. Alexei promised to investigate and rode on. The protesters closed more menacingly on Pleshcheev's retainers, who galloped their horses into the crowd, striking out with their whips and arresting ringleaders. As Alexei came down the Red Staircase next morning on his way to church, a crowd demanded the release of the prisoners. When they saw Morozov, they chanted: "Yes and we'll have you too!" The crowd beat up boyars and demanded the head of Pleshcheev.

The mob rampaged towards Morozov's palace, beat his steward to death, threw one of his servants out of a window, pillaged his treasures and raided his wine cellars, drinking so manically that they literally bathed in alcohol. They caught his terrified young wife Anna but let her go with the consolation: "Were you not the sister of the Grand Princess, we'd hack you to bits!" They also raided the palaces of the loathed ministers. The tax collector Chisyi was sick in bed but managed to hide under a birch broom until a servant betrayed him by pointing at it. They beat him, dragged him outside "like a dog" and, stripping him naked, finished him off on a dungheap: "That's for the salt [tax], you traitor!" The mob then surrounded the Terem Palace.

Morozov and his ally Peter Trakhaniotov secretly escaped from the Kremlin. The popular Nikita Romanov, the tsar's cousin, came out to promise the crowd that abuses would be punished; in response they blessed the tsar but demanded Morozov and his henchmen at once. Nikita swore that Morozov had fled; only Pleshcheev remained. They bayed for blood. Alexei reluctantly gave him up. As Pleshcheev appeared, they cudgelled him to "such a pulp that his brains splattered over his face, his clothing torn off and the naked body dragged through the dirt around the marketplace. Finally a monk came and chopped the remnants of the head off the trunk." In the chaos, Morozov, unable to get out of the city, slipped back into the Kremlin. Alexei announced that he was dismissing Morozov, and in his stead appointed Nikita Romanov and Prince Yakov Cherkassky.

Gangs got drunk on barrels of looted liquor, quaffing out of shoes, hats and boots, and lighting fires until, suddenly, the whole wooden city caught alight. The crowd found Pleshcheev's head, trampled on it, soaked it in vodka and lit it before throwing his mangled torso into the flames along with the disinterred bodies of his allies. Trakhaniotov, who had taken refuge at the Trinity Monastery, was brought back and beheaded on Red Square.

When a smouldering calm finally descended upon Moscow, Alexei, accompanied by Nikita Romanov, addressed the crowd in Red Square, apologized for the crimes of his ministers and promised lower prices, but then, speaking with dignity, he added: "I've sworn to give Morozov to you and I cannot completely justify him but I cannot give him up. This person is dear to me, the husband of the tsarina's sister. It would be hard to hand him over to death." Tears ran down his face. "Long live the tsar," cried the crowd. On 12 June, guarded by musketeers, Morozov left for imprisonment in a monastery on the White Sea in the Arctic north—though Alexei wrote by hand to the abbot: "Believe this letter. See to it you protect him from harm . . . and I shall reward you."

On 12 July, Alexei made another concession, calling an Assembly of the Land to draft a new law code that was meant to protect the people and reassure the nobles. "The time of confusion is receding," wrote Alexei to Morozov's keepers on the White Sea, ordering them to send his "father-substitute" southwards in stages for his discreet return to Moscow. On 1 September, as the Assembly gathered in the Kremlin, Prince Nikita Odoevsky presented the new Code that promised "justice equal for all from greatest to least," but at a time when the English Parliament was about to try an anointed king for his life, there was nothing populist about Alexei's laws. During a period of instability and fear, the tsar consolidated his legitimacy by agreeing an alliance with the nobles that would be the foundation of Romanov rule until 1861. He confirmed noble grants of land which were gradually being transformed into permanent holdings. Justice would be dispensed by landowners to their peasants, who were now serfs totally owned by their masters and prohibited from leaving the estates. If they escaped, they could be hunted down.*

---

* Serfdom, which was common to much of eastern and central Europe, had been tightening its grip on Russia since Ivan the Terrible. Tsar Boris Godunov, keen to win the loyalty of military servitors and provincial gentry, had consolidated the ownership of peasants. Alexei's laws completed the process. The name is sometimes confusing to Westerners: the serfs were bound to the land and initially it was the land, not the serfs themselves, that was

The death penalty, including new delicacies such as burying alive and burning, was imposed for sixty-three crimes. The punishments were savage—but probably no more so than those in England. The essential tool was the knout, mentioned 141 times in Alexei's Code: a rawhide whip, often with metal rings or wires attached like a cat-o'-nine-tails, that ripped off the skin and cut to the bone. Ten strokes could kill and anything over forty was close to a death sentence. In return for Romanov autocracy and military mobilization at the top, Alexei granted noble tyranny over the peasantry, 90 per cent of the population. Nobility would be defined by the privilege of owning other human beings, setting a Russian pattern of behaviour: servility to those above, tyranny to those below.

Alexei felt confident enough to sack his new ministers and promote his father-in-law Miloslavsky, a coarse rapscallion with "limbs and muscles like Hercules" who was "covetous, unjust and immoral," a sex pest and peculator who soon built himself a Kremlin mansion on the spoils of office. Alexei was so irritated by him that he actually slapped him during a Council meeting. When he grumbled about a minister "with every sort of evil, sly Muscovite trait," he was surely thinking of his father-in-law. But he granted real power to an altogether more impressive character.[5]

Nikon, who resembled a biblical prophet, was the son of a peasant. After the death of his three children, he had persuaded his wife to take the veil so that he could become a monk in the freezing far north. Six feet six, brawny, wild-eyed, haughty with an abrasive and dogmatic style, he performed a thousand genuflections a day and his fasts were so stringent that he saw visions. As a member of the Zealots, he encouraged the austerities of Alexei, who appointed him metropolitan of Novgorod where he proved himself by suppressing the 1648 riots.

Alexei called Nikon "my special friend" and "the Great Shining Sun,"

---

owned. Many were crown serfs owned by the tsar: they could be given as gifts to favourites. But they were different from the black slaves who would later toil in the Caribbean and American plantations: they paid taxes, owned small plots of land and had to serve in the army. Serfs provided both the tsar's income through taxes and manpower through military service. Wealth was now measured not in acres but in "souls"—and that referred only to male souls or households owned, since female serfs were much less valuable. At this time, the tsar owned the most serfs with 27,000 households, followed by Nikita Romanov with 7,000 and Cherkassky with 5,000, while the two Morozov cousins owned 10,000. As the centuries passed, in return for their support the Romanovs allowed the nobles to tighten their control over the serfs. By the eighteenth century, the serfs were physically owned by masters, who could sell and buy them, punish them at will and decide who they married. In 1861, Alexander II was referring to Alexei and his Code when he said: "The Autocracy established serfdom and it's up to the Autocracy to abolish it."

and they shared a worldview of sacred monarchy. When Charles I of England was beheaded, Alexei was disgusted: he expelled the English from Russia. Meanwhile the Polish borderlands of Ukraine were degenerating into ferocious civil war as the Orthodox people rebelled against the Polish Catholic nobility. If the world was tilting in a dangerous way, Nikon preached that the Orthodox mission of the Russian tsar must be purified, ready for a crusade against the Catholic Poles and the Islamic Tatars.

Patriarch Paisos of Jerusalem, visiting Moscow, encouraged this imperial-sacred mission by hailing Alexei as "King David and Constantine the Great, the new Moses." Nikon took up the mission as Alexei prepared his army for the crusade. On 25 July 1652, Nikon was enthroned as patriarch, processing around the Kremlin walls with Alexei himself holding his bridle, one of the rituals of his installation. "In you," wrote Alexei, "I've found someone to lead the Church and advise me in governing the realm." Nikon started to sign most of the tsar's decrees.

Nikon, obsessed with Moscow's role as the New Jerusalem,* believed that the corruption of the realm was equalled only by the deviations of the Church: he first turned on foreigners, forbidding them to wear Russian dress and confining them to a so-called Foreigners' or German Quarter where they could pray in their infidel Protestant churches, smoke their tobacco and party with their whores. Despite this, Russia continued to hire ever more foreign military experts. As for the church, its pure Byzantine services had been tainted with innovations sanctioned under Ivan the Terrible that must be purged: henceforth the sign of the cross must be made only with three fingers instead of two. Nikon claimed that he was returning to the correct Byzantine usage, but traditionalists known as the Old Believers were prepared to die unspeakable deaths rather than make a cross with three fingers. As Nikon repressed these dissidents, a dystopic hell was descending on Ukraine—and the Orthodox rebels appealed to the tsar, offering him an irresistible opportunity to expand his empire and redeem the lost lands of Kievan Rus.[6]

The Orthodox leader in Ukraine was Bogdan Khmelnitsky, a Cossack officer who had served the Ottoman sultans and Polish kings, learning Turkish and French before retiring to farm—until his ten-year-old son was gravely wounded by a Catholic nobleman. Khmelnitsky launched a

---

* Nikon was the seventh patriarch, an office only established in 1589—but as Filaret had shown, a patriarch could challenge the secular power of the tsar. Nikon celebrated his growing power by building a new palace in the Kremlin and promoted this vision of Moscow as Jerusalem by starting his New Jerusalem Monastery in which the cathedral was exactly based on the Holy Sepulchre in the Holy City.

Great Revolt, fired by Cossack hatred for Polish Catholic lords. But he and his rebels also resented the Jews who often served as the agents for Polish magnates. They exercised this loathing on the large communities of Jews who had found refuge in tolerant Poland after the persecutions that had expelled them from Spain and much of western Europe. Elected hetman of the Zaparozhian Cossacks, Khmelnitsky unleashed his apocalyptic horsemen in a savage purge of Catholics and Jews. Somewhere between 20,000 and 100,000 Jews were massacred in such gleefully ingenious atrocities—disembowelled, dismembered, decapitated; children were cutleted, roasted and eaten in front of raped mothers—that nothing like this would be seen in the bloodlands of eastern Europe until the Holocaust of the twentieth century.

Khmelnitsky won the backing of the khan of the Crimea, whose superb Tatar horsemen enabled him to defeat a series of Polish armies. In December 1648, he rode a white horse into Kiev and declared himself not just the hetman of a new Cossack state but the grand prince of Rus. This astonishing ascendancy did not last long: when his Crimean allies deserted him and the Poles defeated him, he turned in desperation to a new protector. In January 1654, he swore fidelity to Tsar Alexei, who in return recognized Khmelnitsky's hetmanate. For Russians, this was the moment Ukraine became theirs; for Ukrainians, the occasion when Russia recognized their independence.* In fact, it was just an expedient military alliance in a war sponsored by Alexei to attack Poland and to conquer Ukraine.[7]

Once Khmelnitsky had agreed to contribute 20,000 Cossacks against Poland, Alexei declared war. On 23 April 1654, in a state of religious exaltation, thousands of troops assembled in the Kremlin to be blessed by Nikon. "When battle commences you and your men must go forward singing on God's mission. Go into battle joyfully!" wrote Alexei to his general, Prince Nikita Trubetskoi, sounding like his contemporary Oliver Cromwell. Alexei was going to war too: he therefore bestowed on Nikon the title "great sovereign" that had been held by his grandfather: perhaps their relationship resembled that of Michael and Filaret.

On 18 May, accompanied by Morozov and Miloslavsky, the tsar, still just twenty-five years old, led his Great Regiment out of Moscow

---

* It was to celebrate the 300th anniversary of Khmelnitsky's oath to Alexei that Stalin, just before his death, decided to give Crimea, by then the headquarters of the Russian Black Sea fleet and favourite resort of the Russian elite, to the Soviet republic of Ukraine, a decision upheld by his successor Nikita Khrushchev in 1954. Neither foresaw that the USSR would break up and that Ukraine would become an independent country, alienating Crimea from Russia.

towards Smolensk. Dressed in a pearl-encrusted robe and bearing orb and sceptre, he rode in a gilded carriage lined in crimson satin and drawn by horses with pearl-set hooves, escorted by twenty-four hussars and twenty-five standards, his personal ensign the golden eagle fluttering overhead. He laid siege to Smolensk and started to bombard the fortifications, Alexei directing the guns with a ballistic talent that would be shared by his son Peter the Great. On 16 August, he tried to storm the walls, but the Poles detonated a mine under a tower filled with Russian troops—"Don't grieve about the assault—we gave them a beating," Alexei reassured his sisters in Moscow. On 23 September, Smolensk fell, followed by thirty other towns, and his experience allowed the tsar to assess his entourage more rigorously: he still loved Morozov but he despised Miloslavsky. "Two spirits are riding with us," he complained; "one exudes cheer, reliability and hope, the other is sultry, stormy and vile: how can one trust two-faced men?"

In February 1657, the Muscovites, who had just recovered from an outbreak of plague, welcomed Alexei as he paraded sixty Polish standards—the first tsar since Ivan the Terrible to celebrate such a victory. He now found Nikon ever more domineering, but the patriarch remained as great sovereign when Alexei went back to war and captured Minsk and swathes of today's Ukraine, Belarus and Lithuania. He proudly added White Russia to his list of domains. But, alarmed by his victories, Sweden invaded to spoil the party.

It made sense to negotiate with Poland and turn his guns on Sweden, but, at Nikon's insistence, Alexei went to war against the Swedes before he had secured peace with the Poles. Sweden was a sophisticated European power, tempered by the Thirty Years War—and Alexei found himself in a quagmire. Then there was the problem of Nikon, who now asserted the superiority of the patriarch over the tsar.

The glowering priest and the young autocrat openly clashed during a service. "You're a quarrelsome peasant," said the tsar.

"Why do you revile me?" answered the patriarch.

Alexei had to back Nikon's suppression of all resistance to his religious reforms, but his entourage must have grumbled to him about the patriarch's intolerable self-righteousness. Alexei ceased to consult him, half revering, half loathing this "son of a bitch." The military situation was deteriorating. On the death of Khmelnitsky, the Poles offered the Cossacks a better deal than the Russians and they switched sides with disastrous consequences. Yet Nikon, who had promoted the war, now revelled in the plenitude of the great sovereign, lecturing the tsar as if he were a neophyte. He lived magnificently amid his own quasi-royal court, and his 30,000-rouble robes were so jewel-encrusted that he struggled to stand in them. There were rumours of lissom nuns cavorting in his cloisters.[8]

The courtier must not only obey the monarch's orders but anticipate his unspoken wishes, wishes that the monarch may not even recognize himself. Sensing Alexei's resentment, the boyars suddenly united in hostility to Nikon. Alexei's mother's family, the Streshnevs, loathed him—Simon Streshnev named a lolloping mastiff "Nikon" and taught it to make the patriarchal blessing with its paw—a sign of the way the patriarch was regarded in the tsar's intimate circle.

On 4 July 1658, Alexei did not invite Nikon to a banquet for the visiting Georgian king Teimuraz.* Nikon sent one of his courtiers, Prince Dmitri Meshchersky, to inquire—surely it was an oversight. Meshchersky found the chief armourer Bogdan Khitrovo, nicknamed the "Whispering Favourite," guarding the Red Staircase, brandishing his jewel-encrusted staff of office to hold back importuning crowds. He punched Meshchersky.

"You shouldn't strike me—I'm here on duty."

"Who are you?" asked Khitrovo, who knew perfectly well.

"The patriarch's servitor."

"Don't make so much of yourself. Why should we respect the patriarch?" and with that he smashed him on the head with his baton, sending him bleeding back to Nikon. The patriarch was next confronted by the boyar Prince Yuri Romodanovsky who told him, "You insult the tsar's majesty. You call yourself Great Sovereign."

"The tsar gave me that title . . ."

"Yes," retorted Romodanovsky, "and now the Tsarish Majesty forbids it."

The old showman tried to call the tsar's bluff in public, a gambit that could have cost him his life. In the middle of his service in the Dormition Cathedral, he declared, "I can no longer be your shepherd . . . The Great Sovereign has violated his oath . . . I have to leave this temple and this city." Before a scandalized congregation, he then changed into a monk's cowl and waited for the tsar to change his

---

* Teimuraz was the exiled poet-warrior king of Kakheti and Kartli, two of the principalities that made up Georgia, once a powerful kingdom under the Bagrationi dynasty that had ruled the entire Caucasus in the twelfth century. Georgia was one of the most ancient Christian nations with a strong culture of poetry and honour and its own totally distinctive alphabet, but both its lands and dynasty were now fragmented into fiefdoms, torn between voracious Islamic empires, the Shiite Persians and the Sunni Ottomans—later rivalled by the Russians. When Teimuraz was exiled by Shah Abbas the Great, he came to beg Alexei's help in vain. Muscovy was not yet powerful enough to intervene but it was the beginning of Georgia's long, bitter and needy relationship with Russia that continues today.

mind. But Alexei did not. Nikon left for New Jerusalem. But he had one more card to play.[9]

Alexei was a different man from the one who had launched the crusade in 1654. He returned a confident warlord who had seen how the Polish lords lived. He commissioned an English agent to buy tapestries, trees, lace, singing parrots and royal carriages to embellish his newly sumptuous palaces and hired mineralogists, alchemists, glassmakers and an English doctor, Samuel Collins, who soon noticed that "he begins to make his court and edifices more stately, to furnish his rooms with tapestries and contrive a house of pleasure." Engaging 2,000 new foreign officers, he reformed the army and studied ballistics technology.

Rid of Nikon, he realized that every ruler needs a chancellery to enforce his orders, creating a new Office of Secret Affairs. When boyars missed his dawn church services he registered their names and had them collected with hands bound behind their backs and, wearing their robes, tossed into the river where they might easily have drowned or died of the cold. "This is your reward," he laughed, "for preferring to sleep with your wives instead of celebrating the lustre of this blessed day." He relished this despotic bullying, writing to his friends, "I have made it my custom to duck courtiers every morning in a pond. The baptism in the Jordan is well done. I duck four or five, sometimes a dozen, whoever fails to report on time for my inspection."

But these games were deadly serious. He put the old boyars in their place. When he had to promote a military bungler like Prince Ivan Khovansky, nicknamed the "Windbag," the tsar did so "even though everyone called you a fool." He indulgently reprimanded the Whispering Favourite Khitrovo for keeping a harem of Polish sex slaves and he was infuriated by the whoremongering of his own father-in-law Miloslavsky: Alexei told him either to give up sex or to marry fast.

Now the war lurched towards disaster. The Poles and Swedes made peace with each other, so that Poland and its Cossack and Tatar allies could turn on Russia. In June 1659, Alexei's army was routed by a Polish–Cossack–Tatar coalition, losing as many as 40,000 men, and his gains in Ukraine and Livonia. But the tsar had found a brilliant new minister to guide him out of this crisis: Afanasy Ordyn-Nashchokin, son of a poor noble from Pskov, secured peace with the Swedes at Kardis. Alexei consulted the Council. There the bovine Miloslavsky suggested that if he were appointed to supreme command he'd bring back the king of Poland in chains.

"What!" Alexei shouted. "You have the effrontery, you boor, to boast of your skills? When have you ever borne arms? Pray tell us the fine actions you have fought! You old fool ... Or do you presume to mock me impertinently?" Seizing him by the beard, he slapped him across the face, dragged him out of the Golden Chamber and slammed the doors behind him.

Nashchokin* recommended not just peace with Poland but a real alliance if not a union under Alexei as king of Poland. But meanwhile his general Prince Grigory Romodanovsky struggled to hold on to eastern Ukraine. When he did well, Alexei praised him, but when he failed he received a furious epistle that must have made his hair stand on end: "May the Lord God reward you for your satanic service ... thrice-damned and shameful hater of Christians, true son of Satan and friend of devils, you shall fall into the bottomless pit for failing to send those troops. Remember, traitor, by whom you were promoted and rewarded and on whom you depend! Where can you hide? Where can you flee?"

The people too were feeling the strain.[10]

On 25 July 1662, Alexei and his family were attending church at his favourite Kolomenskoe Palace outside Moscow when a huge crowd started calling for the head of his father-in-law Miloslavsky, who as Treasury boss was hated for devaluing the coinage with copper. Sending his family to hide in the tsarina's apartments, Alexei emerged to reason with the crowd while he summoned reinforcements from Moscow, not realizing the capital was in the hands of the rioters and that more protesters were approaching.

Alexei was on his horse ready to ride back to Moscow when this furious sea of humanity washed over him. He was manhandled, the tsarina insulted, and his retainers were about to draw their swords when his troops charged the crowd from behind. "Save me from these dogs!" cried Alexei and spurred his horse. The mob was driven into the river and many were arrested. Alexei attended the torture chambers and specified the punishments: "ten or twenty thieves" hanged at once, eighteen left to rot on gibbets along the roads into Moscow and a hundred at Kolomenskoe; tongues were ripped out, bodies dismembered.

When he was riding through Moscow, he wielded the tsar's traditional steel-pointed staff, the very one with which Ivan the Terrible had mur-

---

* When, at this vital moment, Nashchokin's son defected to the enemy and the shamed father sent in his resignation, Alexei refused to accept it. His response sounds tolerant and rather modern. "We learned your son has absconded, causing you terrible grief. We the Sovereign Tsar were affronted by the bitter affliction, this evil dagger that has pierced your soul ... we grieve also on account of your wife ... but you should rise up again, become strong, have trust. As to your son's treachery we know he acted against your will. He's a young man and so like a bird he flits here and there, but like a bird he will get tired of flying and return to his nest."

dered his son. When a man rushed through his guards, Alexei killed him with the staff. It turned out that the man had not been paid. "I killed an innocent man," but the commander who didn't pay him "is guilty of his blood" and was dismissed.

The Copper Riot shook the tsar, who suffered palpitations, nose-bleeds and indigestion which his doctors Collins and Engelhardt treated with laxatives, opium and hellebore to slow the heart. Yet his boisterous activity shows an astonishingly tough constitution, as his brood of sons proved. His eldest was also named Alexei and now Maria gave birth to another son, Fyodor. When the carefully educated eldest turned thir-teen, he was presented as the heir.[11]

On the night of 18 December 1664, a convoy of ten sleighs swept into the snow-covered Kremlin, halting outside the Dormition Cathedral. Out stepped Nikon. Alexei ordered his immediate departure, but this mysterious visitation exposed the seething conflicts around the tsar.*

Alexei ordered that everyone must obey the new rules of Orthodox ritual—or die. He tried conciliating the leader of the Old Believers, Avvakum, but he remained defiant. Two well-connected female courti-ers, Feodosia Morozova, sister-in-law of his late minister, and Princess Eudoxia Urusova, were obdurate. They were banned from court, then ar-rested and offered liberty if they just crossed themselves in the new way, but when Alexei visited them in the dungeons Morozova defiantly gave him the two fingers. Alexei was determined not to create martyrs, so he had them tortured then starved to death. Avvakum had his wife and chil-dren buried alive in front of him; he himself was just exiled. But across Russia, Old Believers were burned alive. Many fled to Siberia and to the Cossack badlands; some fortified the Arctic island monastery of Solovki.

In December 1666, Nikon was tried and found guilty, deposed as patriarch and exiled. The destruction of Nikon removed any rival to the tsar, who became the sacred vicegerent of God on earth, while the Church became simply the religious arm of the monarchy. As this prob-lem was solved, in January 1667, Nashchokin negotiated peace with Poland, winning Smolensk and (for an initial period of two years) Kiev. The Cossack hetmanate was divided between Poland and Russia, and, four centuries after the fall of Kievan Rus, the reconquest of Ukraine

---

* As he left, Nikon surrendered letters from a boyar who claimed that the tsar himself had secretly invited the patriarch. This was probably half-true since Alexei was toying with the options of how to deal with the problems of Nikon and the Old Believers. But the boyar was arrested and, in the presence of Alexei, tortured with red-hot prongs, until he changed his testimony and protected the tsar. But if this was a court provocation to expose the patriarch's megalomania, it worked. If it was designed to discredit his reforms, it failed.

had begun. Nashchokin was promoted to chief minister. Just as Alexei added Little Russia to his titles, tragedy swooped on the new-minted "tsar of all the Russias."*12

On 3 March 1669, the forty-three-year-old Tsarina Maria, after twenty-one years of marriage, gave birth to her thirteenth child, but the child and the mother died soon afterwards. The tsar's elder sons, Alexei Alexeievich, thirteen, his heir, and the frail Fyodor attended the funeral. There were also two sickly toddlers, Simon and Ivan. In June, Simon died. Alexei had earlier taken a mistress, Ariana, who bore him a son, Ivan Musin-Pushkin. But he needed more legitimate heirs.

In November, Khitrovo, chief of the Great Court Office, organized a brideshow. Alexei viewed thirteen maidens in small groups of two to eight girls. Then on 17 January 1670, the tsarevich Alexei died of an illness, leaving Fyodor as heir (followed by the handicapped baby Ivan). A new marriage was imperative. An air of panic pervaded the brideshows. In April, the tsar narrowed his choice to Ovdotia Beliaeva and Natalya Naryshkina. Beliaeva was backed by the tsar's eldest sister, the spinster Irina, now aged forty-two, while Naryshkina was the ward and niece by marriage of Alexei's boyhood friend and courtier Arteem Matveev.

Beliaeva was still the front runner, though Khitrovo wondered if her "skinny arms" implied a lack of fecundity. Her uncle tried to persuade the official doctor to attest to her healthiness while accusing Khitrovo of witchcraft. Just as the tsar seemed about to choose Beliaeva, two anonymous letters were found in the Hall of Facets and the Tower Hall of the Kremlin accusing Naryshkina of unknown but diabolical machinations probably involving the bewitchment of the tsar—and alleging she had flirted with a Polish nobleman before she came to Moscow.

The tsar ordered the arrest of Beliaeva's uncle and female servants and relatives who were all tortured but revealed nothing. The letter-writer was never discovered, but the perpetrator was surely the tsar's sister and her two Miloslavsky cousins. Instead of destroying Naryshkina, they destroyed their own candidate. Alexei saw Naryshkina again, possibly at Matveev's house, where he may have held some of the viewings.

Matveev, who had been educated with Alexei then had commanded his bodyguard and run his intelligence service, lived differently from the other Muscovites—and his protégée seemed different too. Matveev was married to Mary Hamilton, daughter of a Scottish Catholic refugee

---

* The Romanovs claimed "all the Russias" once ruled by Kievan Rus: Muscovy was Great Russia, Belorussia was White Russia, Ukraine was Little Russia. The territories of the Crimean khanate and Ottoman sultanate in today's south Ukraine were later called New Russia. Galicia, then ruled by Poland and later by Habsburg Austria, was Red Russia.

from Puritan England, who was not hidden in a *terem* but was educated, well dressed and free spoken in a house that was a treasure trove of Western sophistication, inhabited by actors and musicians, decorated with paintings, and even mirrors, usually banned in the *terem*.

The eighteen-year-old Natalya Naryshkina, who had "dark wide eyes, rounded sweet face, high forehead, whole figure beautiful, and limbs well proportioned," was the daughter of a colonel from Smolensk related to Matveev's wife. "I've found a suitable mate in you, Little Pigeon," said the tsar. Encouraged by Tsarevna Irina and the Miloslavskys, the families of the other girls now accused Matveev and Khitrovo of enchanting the tsar and bewitching the doctors with sorcery to reject their daughters. Sorcery was often a symptom of political conspiracy. Alexei personally ran the investigation, writing on one of the accusations: "Save me Lord from the sly, the iniquitous!" A reference to his sister? If so, she failed again. In spring 1670, as Alexei prepared to marry Natalya, a Cossack freebooter named Stenka Razin led an army of runaway serfs and Old Believers up the Volga towards Moscow.[13]

At the tsar's wedding on 22 January 1671, Natalya Naryshkina was "blooming with youth and beauty," but his eldest daughter was older than the bride. His six surviving daughters were kept in monastic splendour and teeth-gnashing boredom in the Terem Palace, but Alexei had had them educated. The most intelligent of them, the thirteen-year-old Sophia, especially hated the bride and her Naryshkins, who threatened to displace the Miloslavskys as the leading family at court.

On 16 June, Alexei celebrated the defeat of the Cossack uprising of Stenka Razin in a very different ceremony. Razin was tortured on the platform in Red Square, to Alexei's gruesome specifications: he was knouted, his limbs were dislocated and forced back into their sockets, he was burned with a red-hot iron and cold water was dripped on to his head, drop by drop, before he was dismembered, quartered alive, beheaded and his innards fed to dogs. But the legend of Razin would long haunt the Romanovs.

The wedding changed everything. The new tsarina's patron, Matveev, took over the government* while the two Miloslavskys were despatched to govern distant provinces. On 30 May 1672, Natalya gave birth to

---

* Matveev headed the Foreign Office and the Royal Pharmacy. Nashchokin, who had been "Keeper of the Great Seal and Protector of the Sovereign's Great Ambassadorial Affairs" as well as president of the Foreign and Ukraine Offices, was sacked. "You promoted me," Nashchokin grumbled to Alexei, "so it's shameful of you not to support me and so give joy to my enemies." But this bumptious minister of humble origins had staked his career on the failed alliance with Poland.

a sturdy son, Peter. Alexei celebrated by promoting her father and Matveev to lords-in-waiting. The Ottomans, suddenly resurgent after decades of harem intrigues, invaded Poland where Cossacks acclaimed a new impostor as the tsar's dead son Simon, a frightening echo of the Troubles. Alexei dreamed of being "an all-conquering emperor to drive the Turks out of Christian lands" and sent troops into Ukraine. The Cossacks surrendered the False Simon, who in September 1674 was tortured by Alexei's ministers to reveal his backers. In Red Square, his limbs were sliced off and the twitching trunk was impaled up his rectum—a warning to all False Simons.[14]

As he negotiated with the West in the face of the new Ottoman threat, Alexei started to remodel his palaces, probably inspired by the magnificence of Louis XIV, the Sun King. He commissioned the first play ever performed for a tsar and at Preobrazhenskoe, one of his constellation of suburban palaces around Moscow, he built the first tsarist theatre and watched a play artfully based on his own romance with Natalya, *The Comedy of Artaxerxes* (which the tsarina and the children could enjoy through the grilles of a partition). This was such a success that he built a Kremlin theatre and a new Palace of Amusements* on the site of old Miloslavsky's mansion, and gave Natalya twenty-two more dwarfs.

The tsarina started to open the curtain of her carriage and show her face to the public, then she went out unveiled in an open carriage and emerged from behind the screen at church, while Alexei held parties at which he "drank them all drunk." Amid the fun, there was a flash of future glory: as Alexei held a diplomatic reception, there was a scuffling outside the hall and the door was kicked open by the irrepressible little Peter who ran in—pursued by his mother.

While the tsar and his young wife visited their pleasure palaces, Peter followed in a "small carriage all encrusted with gold," while "four dwarfs rode alongside and another behind, all riding miniature horses." But Peter was four and the heir was now the sickly teenager Fyodor. As the Miloslavskys plotted against the Naryshkins, it seemed unlikely Fyodor would outlive the energetic tsar.

When the tsar enjoyed his young family, he directed a small war

---

* The Poteshnye Palace has a special place in modern history: Stalin and many of the top Bolsheviks had their apartments there in the late 1920s. In 1932, this was where Stalin's wife Nadezhda committed suicide. The exquisite pink palace still stands, occupied by Kremlin security agencies. Outside Moscow, Alexei was also rebuilding the Kolomenskoe Palace that he transformed into an eclectic domed, gabled wooden fantasia that combined elements of Ivan the Terrible, Byzantium and Versailles. In the throne room, two copper mechanical lions rolled their eyes and roared just like the ones that had dazzled visitors in Constantinople.

against the 500 armed Old Believers who had fortified the Solovki island monastery in the Arctic. On 22 January 1676, he received the news that his troops had stormed it. During a comedy that night in his new theatre, Alexei, still only forty-seven, fell ill, his body swelling up alarmingly. Matveev, head of the Pharmacy, supervised the medicines. The drugs were made up by the doctors, then in front of everyone each potion was tasted first by the doctors, next by Matveev, then by the gentlemen of the bedchamber, and if all showed no signs of poison, the tsar himself drank—and Matveev finished the draught. But nothing could save the tsar from dying of renal and cardiac failure.

"When I ruled the empire," he reflected, "millions served me as slaves and thought me immortal," but now "I smell no sweet odours and am overcome by sorrow for I am nailed to my bed by cruel disease . . . Alas I'm a great emperor, yet I hold the smallest worms in dread." Fyodor was so ill, he was stretchered into the death chamber, where his father placed the sceptre in his hands and advised him to follow the advice of the Whispering Favourite Khitrovo.

"I'd never have married," said Alexei to the sobbing Natalya, "if I'd known our time was to be so short," for he could no longer protect her. The new tsar Fyodor would be a Miloslavsky.

At night on 29 January, Alexei died. His chaplain Savinov was just preparing his valedictory charter when the patriarch beat him to it and placed his own version in the hands of the still-warm tsar. As widow and children mourned, the tournament for power started over the body. Savinov shouted, "I'll kill the patriarch—I've already raised 500 men!" The daggers were out.[15]

SCENE 3

# The Musketeers

# CAST

FYODOR III, tsar 1676–82, son of Tsar Alexei and Maria Miloslavskaya
Agafia Grushetskaya, tsarina, Fyodor's first wife
Martha Apraxina, tsarina, his second wife
Sophia, sovereign lady, daughter of Tsar Alexei and Maria Miloslavskaya,
    sister of Fyodor III, Ivan V and half-sister of Peter the Great
IVAN V, son of Tsar Alexei and Maria Miloslavskaya, tsar 1682–96
Praskovia Saltykova, tsarina, Ivan V's wife
Ekaterina, their daughter, later married Karl Leopold, duke of
    Mecklenburg-Schwerin
ANNA, their daughter, later married Friedrich Wilhelm, duke of Cour-
    land, empress of Russia 1730–40
Natalya Naryshkina, tsarina, widow of Tsar Alexei, mother of Peter
PETER I (THE GREAT), son of Tsar Alexei and Natalya Naryshkina, tsar
    1682–1725
Eudoxia Lopukhina, Peter's first wife


COURTIERS: ministers etc.

Ivan Iazykov, chief courtier of Fyodor
Mikhail Likhachev, chief courtier of Fyodor
Arteem Matveev, Alexei's chief minister
Prince Yuri Dolgoruky, old general and head of the Musketeers Office
Prince Ivan Khovansky, leader of the mutinous Musketeers, "Windbag"
Ivan Miloslavsky, leader of the Miloslavsky faction, "Scorpion"
Prince Vasily Golitsyn, Sophia's lover, chief minister, field marshal
Fyodor Shaklovity, Sophia's henchman, head of the Musketeers Office
Patrick Gordon, Scottish mercenary, "Cock of the East"
Franz Lefort, Swiss mercenary

A lexei was buried in the Archangel Cathedral, but his successor Tsar Fyodor III had to be borne behind the coffin on a stretcher. Natalya followed on a sleigh, her sobbing head on the knee of one of her ladies.

The new tsar, aged fourteen, was breathless, wheezing and beardless, thin as a reed, cadaverously pale and chronically ill with scurvy. He was so weak that he had fallen off a horse and broken his legs. Yet he was intelligent and well educated, fluent in Polish and Latin, and he turned out to be enlightened and determined—when his health allowed.

As Fyodor lay ill in bed, tended by his aunts and six sisters, he watched helplessly as his courtiers unleashed their vendettas. Everyone turned on Matveev. The Miloslavskys were back. The chief of the Musketeers and a relative of Michael's first wife, Prince Yuri Dolgoruky, backed by Khitrovo and the Miloslavskys, accused Matveev of embezzlement. Behind them, emerging blinking into the light, came the malevolent Irina, spinster daughter of Tsar Michael, who had schemed to stop the Naryshkin marriage five years earlier. Now they would all have their vengeance.

On 3 February 1676 Matveev was dismissed. But this was only the start. A new Investigations Office was created to build the case against him, while the old Muscovite ways were reimposed: "Plays and ballets will cease for ever."

The tsar's cousin, Ivan Miloslavsky, nicknamed the "Scorpion," as-sumed the role of inquisitor in alliance with Irina. On 3 July, Matveev was arrested for trying to murder Fyodor through his control of the Phar-macy. One of the doctors claimed that Matveev's house serfs, Ivashka the Jew and Zakharka the Dwarf, were poisoning—or bewitching—Tsar Fyodor. Ivashka the Jew was tortured to death. Miloslavsky was framing Matveev, but the invalid tsar refused to execute him and he was instead despatched into faraway exile.

The Scorpion and the spinster turned on the Naryshkins. As they watched, their servants were tortured by the bluff general Yuri Dolgo-ruky himself with tears in his eyes, asking if this was not enough. When Natalya bravely confronted Miloslavsky as "the persecutor of widows and orphans," Irina halted the torture. The Naryshkins were exiled, Natalya and Peter sent to the estate of Preobrazhenskoe.

Tsar Fyodor tried to assert himself. On 4 April, Palm Sunday, 1680, the tsar unusually made a public appearance in the Palm Sunday procession where he noticed a girl named Agafia Grushetskaya, who was "beautiful as an angel." He soon discovered that she spoke four languages and played the harpsichord, and he fell in love with her. Fyodor told the court he was going to marry her. But his uncle Miloslavsky bullied the tsar into finding his bride the traditional way: through a brideshow. Eighteen semi-finalists were reduced to six for royal viewing. Fyodor chose none. Miloslavsky then framed Agafia and her mother, accusing them of prostitution. Fyodor was so depressed that he retired to bed and refused to eat, but his two favourites, Ivan Iazykov and Mikhail Likhachev, interrogated mother and daughter to prove their innocence.

On 18 July, the tsar married Agafia in a small private wedding. Iazykov, who had encouraged and may have orchestrated the entire match, was promoted to lord-in-waiting and armourer. The Scorpion was exiled. On 18 July 1681, Agafia gave birth to a boy. Three days later, she and the baby died. Fyodor's health collapsed.

Meanwhile the Ottomans were marching on Kiev. Their first advance was turned back by a rising boyar Prince Vasily Golitsyn, whom Fyodor had appointed commander of the southern armies, but when they returned, a precedence row between generals almost lost the war. On 24 November 1681, Fyodor, advised by Golitsyn, announced to an Assembly that "the Devil had implanted the idea of precedence." The records were burned in a bonfire. Ignoring the Miloslavskys, he rehabilitated the Naryshkins.

Fyodor was determined to father an heir. At a new brideshow, he chose Martha Apraxina, goddaughter of Matveev and cousin of Iazykov who keenly promoted their candidate. On 15 February 1682, the sovereign married Martha, who persuaded Fyodor to recall Matveev. In the unforgiving sport of royal splicing, the losing candidate, Praskovia Saltykova, and her father were exiled to Siberia.

Fyodor did not enjoy his bride for long. He was dying. The court was no longer fulfilling its role as intermediary and adjudicator between monarch, factions and military, just as a synchronicity of crises now threatened to tear the state apart. On 23 April 1682, a regiment of musketeers protested that their wages were being stolen by their colonel. When they complained to Dolgoruky, chief of the Musketeers Office, he ordered them knouted. Instead the regiment mutinied—not knowing that in the Terem Palace, Tsar Fyodor, at the age of twenty-one, had just died.[1]

Next day, the boyars met in the Golden Chamber to decide between the two tsareviches. "Which of the two princes shall be tsar?" asked the patriarch. Ivan, fifteen, was the mentally and physically handicapped scion of the Miloslavskys. Peter, ten, was the healthy hope of the Naryshkins. The boyars and the swiftly convened Assembly chose Peter, and his five Naryshkin uncles were promoted to high posts. But Sophia, the late tsar's sister, protested that the interests of Ivan had been overlooked. At Fyodor's funeral, she appeared in the procession without the usual moving screens and suggested that Tsar Fyodor had been poisoned.

On 29 April, the musketeers, a fearsome sight with their pikes, muskets, fur-rimmed hats and long scarlet robes, poured into the Kremlin to demand the whipping of their corrupt colonels. This hereditary corps of infantry had been founded by Ivan the Terrible to guard tsar and Kremlin with the latest musketry, but over time their weapons had become outdated just as they had become deeply entrenched as praetorian power-players and rich merchants. Faced with 25,000 enraged musketeers, the authorities buckled. Their colonels were whipped, but the covin of Tsarevna Sophia and the Miloslavskys spread the story that Tsarevich Ivan, the rightful elder tsar, was in danger from the Naryshkins. The rumour metastasized through the musketeer ranks.

On 7 May, the tsar's twenty-three-year-old uncle Ivan Naryshkin was unwisely over-promoted to boyar and armourer. Rumours spread that this popinjay had sat on the tsar's throne and tried on the crown. Ivan was in peril. Soon the musketeers came to believe that Ivan had been murdered. Sophia and Miloslavsky sent round their henchman Peter Tolstoy to inflame the musketeers, encouraged by Prince Ivan Khovansky, a brave if blowhard general nicknamed the Windbag, who convinced them that they must rescue Ivan. They rushed to the palace.

By noon, thousands of them had massed beneath the Red Staircase demanding to see Ivan, alive or dead. Tsarina Natalya, supported by the patriarch, brought the two boys, Ivan and little Peter, out on to the porch. The mass of shaggy musketeers went silent. Windbag Khovansky called for calm as a few soldiers came up to examine the boys. Then the musketeers shouted that they wanted Ivan as tsar—and the heads of all the Naryshkins. The musketeers surrounded the little group, at which the white-bearded Matveev came out and suggested that they ask forgiveness of the little boys and then disperse. They went quiet. Matveev returned inside. Then Mikhail Dolgoruky, son of the general, threatened them for their impertinence. "Death to the traitors," they screamed, storming up the Red Staircase. They tossed Dolgoruky off the balcony to be impaled on the raised pikes. "Cut him to pieces!" While he was sliced into sections, they burst into the palace, and found Matveev in the banqueting hall talking to Natalya, who was holding the hands of Peter and Ivan. She tried to hold on to Matveev but, as the boys watched, the ruffians impaled him too on the raised pikes below. Peter never forgot these atrocious sights, which may have triggered his epilepsy. "The thought of the musketeers made me quake," he said later, "and kept me from sleeping." As Peter and Ivan were escorted back inside, the musketeers ran amok.

The marauders searched the Kremlin, building by building. They had a death list of twenty targets—not just Naryshkins but also Fyodor's favourites. One of the Naryshkin brothers hid in a church but was betrayed by a dwarf: he was tossed off the Red Staircase on to the pikes. They bore each victim to Red Square, which they converted into an alfresco abattoir where pieces of Matveev were already on display. Their chief prize of the day was the haughty Yuri Dolgoruky. A delegation of musketeers visited him at home to apologize for tossing his son on to the pikes. The father gave them vodka but, just as they were leaving, his son's widow emerged in tears. "Don't cry, daughter," he consoled her. "My son is dead but his teeth live on!" Hearing this threat of vengeance, the musketeers hacked the general into pieces, which joined the giblets heaped up in Red Square where the crowds, brandishing arms, guts or heads, cried, "Here's Boyar Matveev! Make way for him!" Later Matveev's manservant was allowed to collect his body parts on a pillow and take them for burial.

By morning, the musketeers were convinced that Tsarevich Ivan was in danger of poisoning from a doctors' plot by converted Jews who had supposedly poisoned Tsar Fyodor. The musketeers killed the suspect Jews—but so far they had culled only one Naryshkin and they really wanted Ivan Naryshkin. Massing at the Red Staircase, they demanded his head: "We know you've got him in there." Inside the palace, the huddled but divided family faced unbearable decisions. The Naryshkins hid in the nursery of Peter's little sister. Only Sophia, who had her own direct line to the musketeers through Khovansky, kept her head. She was already giving orders. She came out with Tsarinas Natalya and Martha to beg for Ivan Naryshkin's life on their knees, but the musketeers threatened, "Hand him over or we'll search—then things will turn out badly!"

"Your brother won't escape the musketeers," Sophia told Natalya. "Don't let us all be murdered on his account. You have to give up your brother." Ivan Naryshkin agreed. Peter, aged ten, must have seen his weeping mother and the departure of his uncle: Natalya and her brother prayed in the Church of the Saviour and then, holding an icon, Ivan went bravely out to the baying musketeers. The young man was tortured for hours but never admitted trying to murder the tsar even when his joints were snapped. Finally, his legs and arms hanging wrongwise, he was impaled on pikes then dismembered, before the musketeers stomped him to pulp.

Sophia now emerged from the shadows. This fierce girl was just twenty-five, yet after a life spent in seclusion she had the confidence to deal with an all-male cast of gore-stained musketeers and scheming boyars. She is usually depicted as dark, round-faced and plain but this may just be the fruit of chauvinism and political malice.* Perhaps the best description is by someone who really knew her well. She was "a princess endowed with all the accomplishments of body and mind to perfection, had it not been for her boundless ambition and insatiable desire for governing," wrote her half-brother Peter, who would have every reason to loathe her but admitted she was talented. She was certainly opportunistic, articulate and politically supple, a deadly opponent. For now, she too was trying to survive amid an unpredictable orgy of bloodletting.

Overnight on 16/17 May, the musketeers approved their champion Khovansky as their commander and forced the execution of Iazykov and Likhachev, but Sophia, accompanied by Natalya, persuaded them to spare the other Naryshkins. Khovansky, speaking as the "father" of the musketeers, hailed Sophia as "Sovereign Lady Tsarevna" and asked her to place both tsars on the throne. On 26 May, Ivan and Peter were declared co-tsars with Sophia as "the Great Sovereign Lady"—Russia's first female ruler.[2]

Khovansky disdained his young puppet Sophia, believing that he should rule Russia. He and many of the musketeers were Old Believers. Now he demanded that Sophia hold a public meeting to reverse her father's reforms. Sophia agreed. First she had to arrange a novelty: a double coronation. New crowns and jewels had to be crafted.

On 25 June, the two boys were crowned as "double tsars," Ivan wearing the original Cap of Monomakh while Peter, as the younger, wore a copy.† As a woman, the sovereign lady could not take part, watching through a grille as Vasily Golitsyn, now chief of the Foreign Office, carried the sceptre.

Golitsyn, thirty-nine years old, a scion of that numerous clan descended from Grand Duke Gedimin of Lithuania, and married with

---

* The only written description of her was recorded seven years later by a French visitor who had never met her: "She was of monstrous size with a head as big as a bushel with hair on her face, growths on her legs, but although her stature is broad, short and coarse, her mind is subtle, nimble and shrewd."
† Both crowns (and their double throne) can be seen in the Kremlin Armoury today. Peter I and Ivan V were the last tsars to be crowned with this Mongol headdress, which was becoming too modest.

children to a Streshneva, the family of Tsar Michael's second wife, was an urbane grandee whose blue eyes, pointed moustaches, trimmed beard and "Polish clothes" make him look more like a French marquis than a Russian boyar. His palace was well known for its gallery of Gobelin tapestries, Venetian china, German engravings, Dutch carriages, Persian rugs. Now Sophia came to depend on him. In her coded letters, she calls him "my lord, my light, my dear, my joy, my soul." She longed to tell him "what's been happening" and could scarcely wait "until I see you in my embrace." She had found not just a lover but a statesman— and she was going to need him.

On 5 July 1682, in the Palace of Facets, Sophia, accompanied by her old aunts as well as by Tsarinas Natalya and Martha but without either tsar, faced Khovansky's Old Believer musketeers. Khovansky tried to bully her into agreeing to Old Believer's demands, but she leapt to her feet and warned them that it was unthinkable that she should reverse her father's reforms, for then "tsars wouldn't be tsars." She threatened that "We shall leave the country."

"It's high time you went to a convent, lady," muttered the musketeers. "We can do without you." But she faced them down, denouncing the "rebellious blockheads" who had brought "rebellion and chaos" to Moscow. To make herself quite clear, she had them executed and Avvakum burned at the stake along with 20,000 other Old Believers.

She had to escape Khovansky and the suffocating Kremlin. Accompanied by the two tsars, Sophia set off on a three-month tour of the country palaces and monasteries, leaving Khovansky in charge of the government—or so he thought.

Sophia probed his weakness, demanding that he send the royal bodyguard out to Kolomenskoe, but Khovansky prevaricated, trying to avoid giving her any troops. Sophia launched her own counter-coup. On 2 September, a denunciation of his treason appeared on the gates of Kolomenskoe, and Khovansky was summoned and then surprised and arrested. Sophia and the boyars condemned Windbag for his "attempt to take over the Muscovite state." Khovansky was beheaded in front of Sophia. The musketeers begged her forgiveness. Sophia had for the moment restored the court as the broker of balanced power and merited prizes. The tsars and tsarevna returned to the Kremlin.[3]

In July 1683, the Ottomans launched a bid to conquer the West: they besieged Vienna. The city was close to falling until rescued by King John Sobieski of Poland. As the Ottomans retreated, Sophia agreed with Poland to join Christendom's Holy League and attack the sultan's ally, the Crimean khan—in return for perpetual ownership of Kiev and much of Ukraine.

The Russians had long been terrorized by the Tatar khans; now for the first time, they were going to take the war to Islam. Planning this challenging expedition, Golitsyn, promoted by Sophia to "Guardian of the Great Royal Seal and the State's Great Ambassadorial Affairs," consulted his chief mercenary, Patrick Gordon. Nicknamed the "Cock of the East," this rambunctious forty-nine-year-old Scottish nobleman, a Catholic refugee from Calvinism, had fought for Poland and Sweden, been wounded four times, captured six times, escaped twice. Hired by Alexei, he almost returned to serve Charles II of England but could not resist his lucrative Russian adventure. The Cock believed that the Russians could take Crimea, that lush peninsula hanging like a jewel over the Black Sea, which no tsar had so far attempted.

On 26 April 1684, Sophia received her new Polish allies as she sat sable-clad on her throne while the treaty was read to the two tsars. Their double throne had a curtained window in the back so that Golitsyn could whisper instructions. Tsar Ivan was now seventeen, old enough to rule, but he "babbled when he spoke." He was half blind and his eyes flickered and darted so unnervingly that he had to wear a green taffeta blindfold so as not to alarm visitors. He was also mentally handicapped. On the other side of the double throne was his half-brother Peter, so "nimble and eager to ask questions and to stand up that he had to be restrained by his attendant until the older tsar was ready." As Sophia and Golitsyn prepared for their Crimean war, Peter was almost twelve, and soon it would be hard for Sophia to deny him a role in government.[4]

Peter was already extraordinary. He was a peculiar but striking physical specimen: though most of his portraits give the impression of a gigantic solidity, he was freakishly tall—he would soon reach six feet eight— and jerky in his movements. His face twitched in a constant flicker of strange tics and he was beginning to suffer from epileptic fits. He had lost his father at four, and seen trusted ministers tossed on to the lances of the musketeers, uncles given up for slaughter, at the age of ten. His beloved cousin, Tikhon Streshnev, related to Tsar Michael's wife, stood in as a paternal figure: Peter always called him "father." Although he impressed everyone with his intelligence and strength, he had shown little interest in formal education. Tsar Fyodor and his mother had appointed as tutor a courtier named Nikita Zotov, who proved unable to persuade the young tsar to study books. Instead the jovial Zotov told him stories of his father's wars, stimulated his interest in artillery—and taught him to drink. Peter adored him as the butt of jokes—and later as his trusted secretary—for the rest of his life. While he learned some German and enjoyed Greek mythology and Roman history, he never mastered languages, grammar or philosophy. Instead Zotov let him learn carpentry, tinker with cannons, and parade soldiers.

As soon as he was old enough, Peter absented himself from the ceremonies of court. The boy swiftly made himself chief of the staff of stableboys and falconers of Preobrazhenskoe, the palace to which his mother had been banished. First he asked for carpentry tools, chisels and hammers, then for a lathe, and throughout his life he found relaxation in crafting ivory and wood. In January 1683, he demanded uniforms and a couple of horse-drawn wooden cannon for his games, and by the summer he was ordering real cannon and real gunpowder. He was starting his lifelong affair with explosives, proud to assume the lowly rank of "bombardier." Playing the drums, lighting the fuses of his cannons and drilling his pals, he formed his first play unit out of 300 friends, foreigners and servants which became the Preobrazhensky Guards Regiment. He turned Preobrazhenskoe into his own military encampment and when it was full he commandeered the next village, Semyonovskoe, where he based a second regiment, the Semyonovsky.

One of the first to enrol in the play regiments was Alexander "Aleshka" Menshikov, a stableboy of obscure origins—his father was variously described as a pie-seller, a worker on barges or a non-commissioned officer. Almost the same age as Peter, he enrolled in the artillery, ensuring that he was close to Bombardier Peter. He was lean and tough, and in his intelligent pragmatism, vaulting ambition and vicious temper he resembled Peter himself. He also matched the tsar in his love of the bottle. Years later, he mocked his own origins by hosting a party in his palace wearing an apron and pretending to sell pies. Yet this was done to please Peter: woe betide anyone except the tsar who derided his low birth. This vindictive hater beat up anyone who insulted him and pursued his enemies to the gallows with untiring malignity. He would outlive Peter—and rule Russia.

Peter's other early retainer was Menshikov's opposite: Prince Fyodor Romodanovsky was a saturnine soldier-courtier who was already fifty years old, "with the appearance of a monster and character of a wicked tyrant, drunk day in day out but more faithful to His Majesty than anyone." He was devoted to Peter, who appointed him the first commander of his play regiment. Later he became Peter's secret policeman and arch-torturer, regarded by foreigners as the second man of the regime. These two would be Peter's chief lieutenants for the next twenty years. But it was technology, not men, that changed Peter's life.

In 1688 a boyar, Prince Yakov Dolgoruky, brought Peter a present from

Paris: a sextant, an instrument for navigation. Peter was fascinated. No Russian knew how to use it until he showed it to a middle-aged Dutch trader named Franz Timmerman from the German Quarter. Together they explored the outhouses on his father's estate at Izmailovo outside Moscow, where they found an old boat that the Dutchman recognized as English. Learning about ships from Timmerman, Peter recruited more foreigners with whom he repaired and relaunched the boat.

Timmerman showed him round the redbrick Dutch houses and plain Lutheran churches of the German Quarter near Preobrazhenskoe where Russia's foreign mercenaries and experts had been confined since 1652. After the dour rituals of the Kremlin, Peter fell in love with this new world of Dutch technology, Scotch whisky and German girls—and it mattered because his new friends were also Russia's best soldiers. Patrick Gordon became Peter's "loyal and brave" mentor while a younger foreigner, Franz Lefort, a Swiss mercenary, became his "heart-friend." Lefort, married to a cousin of Gordon's, taught his young friend about Western artillery and tactics. He introduced him to Western girls and they shared the taste and the constitution for long nights of drinking in Lefort's house. Their drunken coterie became known as his Jolly Company. Age never figured in Peter's friendships: Lefort was thirty-four, but Peter was maturing fast.

Peter's carousing with Lefort worried his mother: it was time for him to marry. While she (advised by Streshnev) looked for a modest Russian girl to save him from the German wenches, Peter was learning the Western art of war, training 10,000 soldiers, decked out in German-style uniforms, green for the Preobrazhensky, sky-blue for the Semyonovsky. In 1685, he himself helped dig Pressburg, a small fortress for his war games on Moscow's River Iauza. In his manoeuvres, he appointed General Ivan Buturlin as "King of Poland" and Romodanovsky as "King of Pressburg."

If Peter's regiments appeared playful, that was an illusion. Now he had his own little army to serve as his praetorians. Sophia was threatened not so much by the numbers—she herself commanded 25,000 musketeers—as by Peter's vigorous maturity. Soon he was bound to demand power for himself.[5]

On 22 February 1687, the two tsars saw off Field Marshal Golitsyn and his army after a mass in the Dormition Cathedral. Sophia watched her lover from the tsarina's throne and accompanied him to the gates of the Kremlin. Golitsyn was "a greater statesman than soldier" and was reluctant to leave Moscow—but, pressed by Peter's allies, he had to accept the poisoned chalice of this Tatar expedition.

Accompanied by Gordon and Lefort, Golitsyn marched south, meeting up with 50,000 Cossacks, but the path to Crimea passed through a wilderness. When he was 130 miles from Perekop, the narrow isthmus into Crimea, Golitsyn found himself in "a dreadful predicament," as General Gordon put it, horses dying, soldiers sick. Golitsyn "was beside himself," wrote Lefort, "and he wept most bitterly." Golitsyn retreated. No sooner had he left than the Tatar cavalry reappeared to raid Poland. Golitsyn returned to Moscow, knowing that he would have to go back to Tatary.

Peter was a problem and Sophia started to look for solutions. One was to find a wife for the other tsar, Ivan—but who would marry this babbling invalid with the flitting eyes? Could he actually father a child? In January 1684, Sophia and Miloslavsky the Scorpion held a brideshow that was merely a cloak for the selection of their candidate: Praskovia Saltykova, the runner-up in Tsar Fyodor's last brideshow. But understandably this outspoken girl was not keen: she said she would rather die than marry Tsar Ivan, but that very month she did marry him. No one was surprised when there was no sign of children.

A better idea was for Sophia to become tsarina in her own right. She asked her most loyal henchman, Fyodor Shaklovity, to canvass support. Rising from peasant stock to become a secretary in Alexei's Secret Office, she promoted him to chief of the Musketeers Office. But the musketeers were not keen to crown a woman.

During 1688, as Golitsyn prepared his second expedition, Peter approached his sixteenth birthday and started to show his power: he had his Naryshkin uncles promoted, attended the Council and borrowed foreign troops for his regiments. He started to build a small play fleet on a nearby lake.

Meanwhile the two tsars were in a fecundity race, encouraged by their backers. After five years, Ivan V and Praskovia had produced no children. Peter's mother Natalya held the traditional but now obsolete brideshow for him to "select" the bride of her choice, Eudoxia Lopukhina, daughter of a family close to the Naryshkins. On 27 January 1689, Peter and Eudoxia were married. On 21 March, to general amazement, Tsar Ivan's first child, a girl, was born. Three daughters survived to adulthood—and the middle one, Anna, would become empress of Russia. Sometimes necessity is the father of invention: cynics assigned this late harvest of children to Praskovia's lover Vasily Yushkov.

If Ivan V produced a boy, Sophia might be able to hold off Peter. In the meantime, a victory would justify her rule. In May, when Golitsyn and his army reached Perekop, he was constantly harassed by the mounted Tatar archers whom he was unable to bring to battle. Some 20,000 men died of disease and starvation. Forced to retreat, he fought off the Tatar cavalry in skirmishes that he claimed as victories—to the delight of his mistress. "My joy, my light," she praised him.

Her future would be decided either in the deserts of Perekop or in the beds of the tsars: both their wives were now pregnant. When Golitsyn's despatches arrived, she was walking towards the gates of St. Sergius Monastery on a pilgrimage. "I can't remember how I entered," she replied breathlessly. "I read as I walked . . . I can hardly believe I'll ever see you again. Great indeed will be the day when I have you with me again. If possible, I'd set you before me in a single day . . . I shall tell you all that's happened." Soon everyone learned the real story—and Peter prepared to make his move.

On 8 July as Golitsyn prepared to make his triumphant entry, Sophia and both tsars heard mass in St. Basil's Cathedral. As Sophia accompanied the icons, Peter strode up. "It was not fitting that her shameful person should be present at the ceremony," he said. She refused to leave. Peter galloped away. Sophia and Tsar Ivan welcomed Golitsyn, but Peter did not turn up. He criticized the bestowal of victory laurels after such a defeat and refused to receive Golitsyn. Both sides were suspicious. Sophia feared that Peter would march on Moscow with his play regiments and kill her; Peter, tormented by the vision of Matveev on a pike, feared that she had commanded Shaklovity to attack with the musketeers. On 4 August Peter ordered his arrest. On the 7th Sophia summoned Shaklovity, saying that she had intelligence that that very night Peter planned to "kill all the sovercigns," Ivan and herself. Shaklovity mustered the musketeers.

Just before midnight, Peter got a message that Shaklovity was on his way to kill him. He leapt on to a horse in his nightgown and galloped into the woods, where his boots and clothes were brought to him. He rode all night to hide in the fortified Trinity Monastery, "where he threw himself on a bed weeping bitterly." The play regiments and his mother and wife joined him there. For a moment, the two sides waited. Then Peter ordered the musketeers to report to him at the monastery. It was hard for them to resist the orders of a crowned tsar.

When Sophia heard of this, Shaklovity waved it aside: "Let him go. He's mad." Instead she set out to confront Peter personally, but when she got close, he ordered her not to proceed another step. She returned to the Kremlin.

On 1 September he commanded her to surrender Shaklovity for "gathering troops to murder us"—and insisted that Golitsyn must be exiled. Sophia was so outraged by this that she ordered Peter's courier to be beheaded, but there was no executioner on duty, itself a sign of her disintegrating authority. Instead she fiercely rallied musketeers and courtiers, reminding them that she "had taken the government upon her in a very troublesome time" and won victories, but now their "enemies sought not Shaklovity but the life of her and her brother." Once again, she was playing the card: Tsar Ivan was in danger! But this time it didn't work.

Three days later, Peter summoned Gordon and his foreign mercenaries. The canny Cock marched to Peter's side: this was "the decisive moment," he wrote in his diary. The musketeers, afraid of finding themselves on the losing side, demanded the arrest of Shaklovity. Sophia refused, but she had to give him up just as she had forced Natalya to give up her brother. In chains, he was carted off to Peter at the Trinity where he was tortured until he confessed a plot to crown Sophia and murder Peter. Shaklovity was beheaded; Golitsyn surrendered to Peter; and Sophia was arrested.

Peter went on manoeuvres with the play regiments, telling his brother tsar Ivan that the "shameful third person, our sister," was finished and the two brothers would rule on together—as they did, formally at least, until Ivan's early death six years later. But on 18 February 1690 Tsarina Eudoxia gave birth to a son, whom Peter named after his father—Alexei. The Miloslavskys had lost the biological as well as the political race.

Sophia was confined in luxury in the Novodevichy Monastery. Golitsyn was sentenced to death but was spared because Peter's chief adviser was his first cousin, Prince Boris Golitsyn. He spent twenty-four years in Arctic exile. At Peter's court, the tournament of power would be still more vicious. The prizes were glittering, the ascent vertiginous, the descent sudden and the end often lethal.[6]

SCENE 4

# The All-Drunken Synod

# CAST

PETER I (THE GREAT), tsar and emperor 1682–1725
Natalya Naryshkina, tsarina, his mother, widow of Tsar Alexei
Eudoxia (née Lopukhina), tsarina, his first wife
Alexei Petrovich, his son and heir
IVAN V, tsar 1682–96, Peter's half-brother
Praskovia (née Saltykova), tsarina, Ivan's wife
Anna Mons, Peter's German mistress
Martha Scavronskaya (CATHERINE I), his Livonian mistress, later his
    second wife and empress of Russia 1725–7
Sophia, ex-sovereign lady, Peter's half-sister


## COURTIERS: ministers etc.

Patrick Gordon, Scottish general and Peter's adviser, "Cock of the
    East"
Franz Lefort, Peter's Swiss adviser, field marshal and general-admiral
Prince Fyodor Romodanovsky, prince-caesar, head of the Preobrazhen-
    sky Office, chief of the secret police
Nikita Zotov, tutor, prince-pope, secretary, count
Tikhon Streshnev, Peter's "father," chief of military supplies
Alexander Menshikov, Peter's courtier and friend, later prince, field
    marshal, "Aleshka," "Prince from the Dirt"
Prince Boris Golitsyn, Peter's adviser during the 1690s
Fyodor Golovin, the first chancellor of Russia, general-admiral, field
    marshal
Gavril Golovkin, ambassador, chancellor, count
Boris Sheremetev, the first Russian count, Peter's commander, field
    marshal

## ENEMIES

Charles XII, king of Sweden, Peter's chief enemy, "Last of the Vikings,"
 "Ironhead"
Adam Löwenhaupt, Swedish general
Carl Gustav Rehnskiöld, Swedish marshal
Ivan Mazeppa, Cossack hetman

P eter, by temperament and talent, saw himself first as a warlord—and he was already preparing for war against the Ottomans. He left his handicapped brother Ivan to stagger through the interminably solemn rituals of the Muscovite court while his boozy uncle Ivan Naryshkin formally ran the government. Real power was wherever Peter was, and the peripatetic tsar was usually at Preobrazhenskoe where he drilled his army and created a rough mock court. He appointed no more boyars. Only his retainers mattered now, whether they were the Swiss or Scottish mercenaries, the sons of pie-sellers or hereditary princes. The most trusted was the fearsome Fyodor Romodanovsky, chief of a new all-purpose agency, the Preobrazhensky Office, whom Peter now promoted to a new title, "prince-caesar," a surrogate tsar. Peter called him "Your Majesty," signing himself "Your eternal slave." This freed the tsar from the tedious formality of elaborate rituals "which I hate." Peter ruled mainly through a tiny coterie of relatives, predominantly connected to the wives of his grandfather, father and brother—Dolgorukys, Saltykovs, Naryshkins, Apraxins—but including Ivan Musin-Pushkin, whom he called "brother": he was Tsar Alexei's illegitimate son. His surrogate "father," old Streshnev, became his indispensable organizer of military supplies.

By the autumn of 1691, Peter was ready to try out his Guards, commanded by the prince-caesar and Lefort with Peter serving as a humble bombardier, in manoeuvres against the musketeers. The Guards performed well, and afterwards, the tsar convened his new All-Mad All-Jesting All-Drunken Synod (or Assembly), an inebriated dining society that was, in part, the government of Russia in brutally raucous disguise. It had started as the Jolly Company but Peter made it ever more elaborate. Between 80 and 300 guests, including a circus of dwarfs, giants, foreign jesters, Siberian Kalmyks, black Nubians, obese freaks and louche girls,* started carousing at noon and went on to the following dawn. The prince-caesar headed its secular arm along with Buturlin, the so-called "king of Poland," but Peter could not resist

* Among an ever-changing cast of freaks, he always sought giants: his French giant (known in Russian as Nikolai Zhigant, who was later displayed—first alive and then dead and stuffed—in Peter's Cabinet of Curiosities) and Finnish giantess were usually dressed as babies while dwarfs often appeared made-up as old men—or totally naked jumping out of pies. He was very fond of his favourite dwarfs who travelled in his entourage.

mocking the mummery of the Orthodox church. He appointed his old tutor, Nikita Zotov, as a drunken prelate—Patriarch Bacchus—but in order not to offend his solemnly Orthodox subjects he mocked the Catholics instead. Zotov became the prince-pope. Dressed in a high tin hat and a coat half made of gambling cards and astride a ceremonial beer barrel, the prince-pope presided over a conclave of twelve soused cardinals with Peter as "proto-deacon."

The regulations for these "sacred services" were drawn up by the despotic carouser himself: the first was that "Bacchus be worshipped with strong and honourable drinking." All the officials of the Drunken Synod bore obscene titles (often connected to the Russian word for the male genitalia—*khui*)—so the prince-pope was attended by Archdeacons Thrust-the-Prick, Go-to-the-Prick, and Fuck-Off, and a hierarchy of penile courtiers bearing phallic sausages on cushions.

Prince-Pope Zotov, often stark naked except for his mitre, started the dinners by blessing the kneeling, berobed guests with a pair of Dutch pipes instead of a cross. Since Peter could never be still, he would jump up and play the drums or order the blowing of trumpets and lead the company outside to fire artillery or light fireworks. Then he would come back to the table to eat yet another course of food before once again leading the party out to jump into a convoy of sleighs.

At Christmas, the prince-pope led 200 of Peter's "Jolly Company" on sleighs through the streets of Moscow to sing carols outside some of the grander houses; during Lent, Zotov led the cavalcade on a carriage pulled by goats, pigs and bears while his cardinals rode on donkeys and bullocks. Peter always delighted in the reversal of identities. But woe betide anyone who thought this was voluntary fun. "All goblets were to be emptied promptly," he ordered in his club rules, "and members were to get drunk daily and never go to bed sober." Any breaking of rules or avoidance of toasts was to be punished by a bumpering of the dreaded and capacious Eagle Goblet brimming with brandy.

A steely capacity for alcohol (which he usually called Ivashka, the Russian version of John Barleycorn) was essential to rise at Peter's court. Peter was blessed with an iron metabolism for alcohol, rising at dawn to work even after these marathon wassails. Menshikov could keep up, though he often subsided under the tables. The old Cock, Patrick Gordon, spent much of the next day in bed.

Peter's friend Franz Lefort was a tireless debauchee—"Alcohol never overcomes him." Since Peter was bored by etiquette, he built Lefort a stone palace with an enormous banqueting hall which became Jolly Company clubhouse and royal reception-room. Peter dined with Lefort two or three times a week, and it was the Swiss who introduced

him to the open-thighed nuns of the Synod's female branch whose enthusiastic brassiness was such a contrast to his joyless marriage.

Anna Mons, aged seventeen, the "exceedingly beautiful" daughter of
a German merchant, was already one of Lefort's many mistresses when
she met Peter. But the tsar was tolerant of the sexual histories of his girl-
friends and she became his chief mistress in a circle that was essentially
macho and military. His inseparable companion, though, was not Anna
but Aleshka Menshikov, now his favourite among the *denshchiki*, the
courtiers who slept at the foot of his bed or outside his door.

When the highly strung Peter suffered insomnia, he called for a
*denshchik* and rested his head on his stomach. Sometimes during this
strenuous life, the left side of Peter's face would start to twitch which
could lead to a full eye-rolling fit. Then his aides would summon someone soothing, often his girlfriend, to calm him, saying tactfully, "Peter
Alexeievich, here's the person you wanted to talk to."

This bacchanal was not just an adolescent phase—Peter's profane
parodies continued with enthusiastic frequency right up to his death. He
might seem like a terrifying circus master presiding over a seventeenth-
century version of a decadent rock band on tour, yet there was no division
between business and bacchanalia. However eccentric, prince-popes,
prince-caesars and Archdeacon Fuck-Off were influential appointments
at his court that was half-military headquarters, half-drunken carnival.
While official members of the Synod tended to be older retainers like
Zotov, membership of the mock-court, Jolly Company and Synod overlapped haphazardly with his top generals, secretaries, admirals and
fools. Nor was it as sacrilegious as it seemed: Peter was a believer in
God and his own holy monarchy. In part, these outrageous revels helped
exalt his exceptional authority, blessed with sacred grace, to remake his
realm as he saw fit, free of any restraints.

The Jolly Company reflected Peter's personal sense of fun, but it is
easy to forget that the young tsar had been raised amid the most savage
political strife. Whether organizing a party of naked female dwarfs or
planning provisions for an army, Peter was a born autocrat, as visionary
as he was meticulous and industrious, compulsively regulating every
detail of every enterprise, scrawling orders in numbered lists. This
enforced carousing was tyranny by feasting—just the colourful side of
Peter's restless, daily drive, dynamic but grinding, joyful but violent,
to modernize Russia, to build up its armed forces, to compel its elites
to serve his vision, to find gifted retainers to direct his monumental
projects.

The masquerade of the prince-caesar was no joke either: however
informal and spontaneous Peter appeared, security always came first.

Romodanovsky was his secret police chief, and Peter usually participated in his investigations and tortures. Even his absurd pantomimes
served political purposes. Here he was able to balance his henchmen,
whether they were parvenus or Rurikid princes; he could play them off
against each other to ensure they never plotted against him. Here he
policed their corruption in his own rough way while he assigned duties,
prizes and punishments. The horseplay was often more like hazing,
humiliating his grandees, keeping them close under his paranoid
eye, promoting his own power as they competed for favour and for
proximity to the tsar. His games of inversion simply underlined his
own absolute supremacy. More than that, he had seen young tsars like
Fyodor III and Ivan V as pathetic prisoners of rigid religious ritual: his
boisterous play-acting, appointing a mock-tsar as well as mock-bishops,
while he himself served as a mere bombardier, deacon or sailor, was
liberating, giving him a personal and political flexibility never before
enjoyed by a Russian monarch. His ability to be both sacred autocrat
and plain bombardier somehow added to the dangerous mystique of
this life force, and his physical strength and size meant that whatever
rank he held he would always exude a terrible power.

At any moment, Peter might switch from jollity to menace. He frequently punched his henchmen, either out of over-exuberance or out of
fury. Once when Peter noticed Menshikov dancing while wearing his
sword, against the rules of civilized society, he smashed him in the nose
and later punched him again so hard that he knocked him out. In February 1692, Boris Golitsyn persuaded a servant to tease his rival Yakov
Dolgoruky by ruffling his hair. Dolgoruky stabbed the boy to death with
a fork. Both had to appear before Peter the next day and walk to prison
on foot, though they were soon forgiven. But the lifestyle was deadly:
several of his ministers died of alcoholism.

No wonder Peter's traditional subjects believed that the tsar might be
the anti-Christ. As he capered and drilled his Guards, his wife Eudoxia
was neglected and her brothers gradually became the focus of opposition to the tsar. Peter had the prince-caesar torture to death one of his
wife's uncles (hardly the sign of a happy marriage). Only his mother
dared restrain him. "Why do you trouble yourself about me?" he teased
her benignly. Then, in January 1694, she died. "You've no idea how sad
and bereft I am," admitted the tsar—just as he prepared for his first war.[1]

In spring 1695, Peter, now twenty-three years old, marched south to
attack the Ottoman fortress of Azov that stood where the Don flowed
into the Sea of Azov. Gordon and Lefort, accompanied by Bombardier
Peter, sailed down the Volga and Don to start their siege but he divided

the command and lacked the correct equipment. After four months, Peter listened to Gordon's advice: he needed siege artillery, a fleet and a single commander. He called off the siege, losing thousands on the march back to Moscow, but in the spring he moved to Voronezh where, sleeping in a loghouse next to his shipyard, he rose at dawn each day to build a fleet, Russia's first. While he was working, his brother Ivan died: Peter returned to Moscow and gave him a traditional funeral. The old Muscovite court was buried with him—though he was survived by his formidable wife Praskovia (Saltykova), much liked by Peter despite her old-fashioned style, and by his daughters, who would provide some of Peter's successors.

In May 1696, Peter was back at Azov with an army of 46,000. Naval Captain Peter shared his tent with Menshikov, whom he called "my heart," to whom he wrote affectionately "I really need to see you, I only want to see you." A gay aspect to the friendship, however, seems far-fetched. The siege was masterminded by Gordon, who devised "a moving rampart" to tighten the encirclement under fire. When it surrendered, Peter thanked the Cock for giving him "the whole expanse of Azov" and promoted him to full general. Peter refortified Azov, but founded the new port of Taganrog, Russia's first naval base, on the Sea of Azov—the first challenges to Ottoman mastery of the Black Sea.

On 10 October 1696, Peter treated Moscow to a Roman triumph, parading statues of Mars and Hercules: if his technology was German or Dutch, he was lauded as a victorious Roman commander—*imperator*. The prince-pope, armour-clad in a six-horsed carriage, led the procession followed by Gordon and Lefort, promoted to general-admiral. Much further back, Peter himself strode jovially with the naval captains, wearing a black German coat and breeches. The Muscovites were bewildered.[2]

Two weeks later, the Foreign Office announced: "The Sovereign had directed for his great affairs of state that to the neighbouring nations . . . shall be sent his great ambassadors," led by General-Admiral Lefort and his minister Fyodor Golovin, also general-admiral. It did not announce that Peter himself, travelling incognito (which meant without diplomatic formality—but everyone knew who he was) as "Peter Mikhailov," would be with them. Whenever Peter left Moscow, he would confer *all* power upon several men, leaving them in a state of paralysing rivalry; in this case he left the prince-caesar, the Cock, his uncle Ivan Naryshkin and Boris Golitsyn to vie for power. He was determined to learn the trade of shipbuilding and to return with the technologies of the West—"I am a pupil and need to be taught," he declared. His father had been fascinated by technology, but Peter had decided to do something utterly extraordinary: to leave his realm and his court behind and, in order to catch up on his own lacklustre education, to force-feed himself with a crash course in Western technology, an act of autodidactic will unparalleled in world history, let alone in Russia's. It was a mix of hedonistic junket, diplomatic offensive, military reconnaissance and educational sabbatical. No other tsar had ever left Russia. It was too risky and his absence would end in carnage.

The Jolly Company were toasting the trip at Lefort's palace when, as General Gordon wrote, "a merry night" was ruined by "the accident of discovering treason against His Majesty." A musketeer officer and two boyars had been denounced for criticizing Peter's lifestyle and policies, and the tsar reacted with macabre ingenuity: he could not afford to leave the 50,000 musketeers in any doubt that treason would not be tolerated—but naturally the case channelled the trauma of his childhood. He ordered the coffin of the long-dead Miloslavsky, whom he had called Scorpion, to be exhumed and placed on a cart pulled by swine until it stood beneath the gallows and its lid removed. The victims were dismembered and beheaded so that their fresh blood spattered Miloslavsky's putrefied carcass.

On 20 March 1697, Lefort and Golovin set off with their embassy of 250 ministers, friends, priests, trumpeters, cooks, soldiers, dwarfs, Menshikov—and "Peter Mikhailov." Wherever he went, Peter was dazzled by the technical sophistication of the West, while the West was horrified by his uncouth ebullience and barbaric rages: few royal trips have had so many diplomatic incidents. The first stop was Riga in the Swedish province of Livonia, where he sketched the fortifications. When the Swedes ordered him to stop, Peter was enraged by their insolence and at once conceived a loathing for this "accursed place." Travelling through the Holy Roman Empire, the patchwork of German principalities, he met Sophia, electress of Hanover, the mother of the future George I of England. Faced with a crowd of elegant German women, Peter, who had no small talk, became bashful: "I don't know what to say!" Sophia admired his "great vivacity of mind, he was very gay, very talkative and he told us he was working himself building ships and showed us his hands and made us touch the callouses." Afterwards he danced with dwarfs and ladies, amazed to feel the latter's whalebone corsets: "These German women have devilish hard bones!" he cried. The electress recognized "a very extraordinary man . . . at once very good and very bad."

On 18 August 1697, Peter reached the Zaandam shipyard in Holland where he enrolled as "shipwright Mikhailov." "And so that the monarch might not be shamefully behind his subjects in that trade," he later explained in the royal third person, "he himself undertook a journey to

Holland and in Amsterdam giving himself up with other volunteers to the learning of naval architecture." He hired Dutch and Venetian shipwrights and ordered each of his grandees to fund a ship in his new navy. But he soon realized that Russia needed its own know-how and he later despatched fifty noblemen to train in the Dutch shipyards. Here, among sailors, merchants and fixers, he sought and recruited gifted men, regardless of class, age or nationality. Holland formed his tastes, sartorial, architectural and necrophilic. In Amsterdam Peter loved attending the post-mortems of a famous anatomist. When one of his courtiers was repulsed by the bodies, Peter made him lean over and bite a mouthful of flesh. Fascinated by the deconstruction of the human body, he bought a set of surgical instruments that always travelled with him. If his retainers needed an operation or a tooth pulled, he insisted on doing it himself. Fearing his probings, his staff kept their toothaches to themselves.

On 11 January 1698, Peter arrived in London where he visited King William III at Kensington Palace, watched Parliament in session and picked up an English actress, Laetitia Cross, who became his courtesan for the rest of the trip. Renting Sayes Court, John Evelyn's immaculate house in Deptford, he treated it like a Jolly Company clubhouse. He had never seen a wheelbarrow, so he organized wheelbarrow races that soon destroyed the garden's trimmed topiary, while indoors the Russians used the paintings for target practice, the furniture for firewood and the curtains as lavatory paper. Feather beds and sheets "were ripped apart as if by wild animals."

The "wild animals" moved on to meet the Holy Roman Emperor in Vienna, where Peter received news from Romodanovsky that the musketeers in Azov had mutinied and marched on Moscow until defeated by General Gordon. "I have received your letter in which your grace writes that seed of Ivan Mikhailovich [Miloslavsky] is sprouting," he replied to the prince-caesar. "I beg you to be severe . . ." The rebels were knouted and tortured. A total of 130 were executed, and 2,000 prisoners awaited Peter's return.

On 19 July, the tsar met up with the newly elected king of Poland, Augustus the Strong, who was also elector of Saxony. Blue-eyed, brawny and priapic, Augustus, then aged twenty-eight, would father 354 bastards and, as he got older, his erotomania became so incontinent that he supposedly seduced his own daughter without realizing it. He specialized in shocking uptight visitors by opening the curtains around a bed to reveal a nude beauty as a gift but nothing surprised Peter. The monarchs drank, reviewed armies and planned the seminal project of Peter's reign: the demolition of the Swedish empire, vulnerable after the death of its king had left the throne to a fifteen-year-old boy, Charles XII. Here was an opportunity to avenge the Troubles and open a window on to the Baltic.

Peter ordered the 2,000 rebel musketeers imprisoned at Preobrazhenskoe, where Romodanovsky built fourteen bespoke torture chambers.[3]

On the night of 4 September 1698, Peter arrived back in Moscow with Lefort and Golovin but galloped straight on to Preobrazhenskoe where he was reunited with Anna Mons. In the morning, the boyars flocked to greet and prostrate themselves before their returned sovereign. But Peter, clean-shaven except for a moustache and wearing Western clothes, raised them and embraced them before producing a barber's razor to shave off their Muscovite beards, symbols of Orthodox sanctity and respect. Romodanovsky and the others submitted to their sovereign-barber. At a banquet, Peter sent his fool, Jacob Turgenev, round the tables shaving boyars, while at Lefort's home he sheared off the long sleeves of boyars' robes. As he resculpted his boyars into Western nobles, he created the Order of St. Andrei, the blue ribbon, and awarded it to his minister Golovin and his trusted general Boris Sheremetev, a descendant of Tsar Michael's minister. Everything was done fast. "You need to work and have everything prepared ahead of time," he once wrote, "because wasted time, like death, cannot be reversed."

Then he turned to dark matters. "Around my royal city I shall have gibbets and gallows set up on walls and ramparts, and each and every one of the rebels I will put to direful death."

First, there was the problem of Tsarina Eudoxia: during a four-hour confrontation, he demanded that she become a nun but she refused. She said it was her duty to raise their eight-year-old son Alexei. Peter simply kidnapped Alexei, and his mother was put in a monastery. One of Eudoxia's uncles must have protested because he was tortured to death by Romodanovsky (as his brother had been). The fourteen torture chambers were working day and night, except Sundays, to force his musketeer prisoners to reveal their plot to depose Peter and restore Sophia. The musketeers showed astonishing fortitude. When prisoners passed out, the tsar's doctor revived them to be tortured anew. Peter attended many of the tortures and insisted that all his entourage join in. When one of them survived first the "horrible cracking" as his limbs were dislocated on the rack and then twenty lashes of the knout without uttering a word, Peter, "tired at last, raised the stick in his hand and thrust it so violently into his jaws as to break them open," growling: "Confess, beast, confess."

After a month of this, Peter ordered the executions to start. Two hundred musketeers were hanged from the walls in Moscow, six at each gate, 144 in Red Square. Beheading hundreds more at Preobrazhenskoe, Peter ordered his magnates to wield the axes themselves, implicating them—and checking their loyalty though some were inept headsmen. One boyar hit his victim so low that he almost sliced him in half while Romodanovsky beheaded four and Menshikov, who had much to prove, claimed to have done twenty. Our source for this, Johann-Georg Korb, an Austrian diplomat, claimed that Peter himself beheaded five musketeers, but he did not see it personally.* Peter was transfixed by decapitation as biological experiment and regularly recounted how one of the victims remained sitting up for some time after his head had been removed.

The executions were accompanied by drunken dinners at Lefort's palace which often ended in government ministers brawling with each other to the amazement of foreigners. When one diplomat criticized conditions in Moscow, Peter told him, "If you were a subject of mine, I'd add you as a companion to the those hanging from the gibbet." His suspicion that a boyar was selling commissions sent the intoxicated Peter berserk: he drew his sword and tried to kill the man until Romodanovsky and Zotov defended his innocence, which only provoked him to cut Zotov on the head and Romodanovsky on the finger. Lefort disarmed him but was tossed on to his back; then Menshikov, throwing himself into the path of the rampaging giant, tackled him. When on another occasion Naryshkin and Golitsyn got into a fight, Peter threatened to behead whoever was in the wrong.

The musketeers were finished but their confessions almost incriminated Sophia. Peter had 196 rebels hanged just outside her windows, their bodies left to rot all winter. When Peter travelled down to Voronezh to toil on his new fleet, he received terrible news. His best friend Lefort had died of a fever. "Now I'm alone without a trusted man," he said. "He alone was faithful to me." Peter rushed back and forced his boyars, always jealous of Lefort, to mourn the Swiss adventurer at a state funeral. He wept as he kissed the corpse. Soon afterwards, Gordon also died. Peter was there to close his eyes and acclaim the "loyal and brave" Cock: "I can only give him a handful of earth; he gave me Azov." It was a long time—and high praise—before Peter could say after a party

---

* A German "sword of justice," designed to be displayed at judicial sittings as well as to remove heads, was said to be the weapon used by Peter to behead musketeers. It is impossible to prove this, but the sword can be seen today in the Kremlin Armoury. When a musketeer named Orlov kicked away the head of the victim before him and stepped forward to die, Peter acclaimed his courage and freed him. He was the grandfather of Catherine the Great's lover, Grigory Orlov.

at Menshikov's: "This is the first time I've really enjoyed myself since Lefort's death."

Peter started the new century with a new foreign policy and a new government:* fortifying Azov, he turned his beloved cannons northwards.⁴

On 19 August 1700, Peter, backed by allies Poland and Denmark, attacked Sweden. But the young King Charles XII repelled the Poles and then knocked Denmark out of the war. On 1 October just as the Russians besieged Narva, Charles XII amazed everyone by landing in Estonia and leading his small army of 10,000 towards the 40,000 Russians.

On 17 November, outside Narva, Peter appointed a French mercenary, the duc de Croy, as commander before himself departing. Peter did not expect the Swedes to attack, but the next day Charles XII stormed his fortified camp. Three horses were shot from beneath the Swedish king. "I see the enemy want me to practise riding," he joked. The Russians were routed, Croy and 145 cannon captured. Peter did not panic and never lost his buoyant optimism, but the genius of Charles demanded that he himself take supreme command and create a standing army, with modern artillery. The Romanovs had come to power to lead resistance to foreign invaders; now Peter intensified the militarization of the state, mobilizing his nobility for twenty years of warfare and sacrifice. He was not surprised that "our untried pupils got the worst of it against such a disciplined army—it was child's play" for the Swedes. "We mustn't lose our heads in misfortune," he told Sheremetev. He learned his lesson to avoid divided command and appointed Sheremetev his commander-in-chief. Twenty years older than he, this super-rich boyar who was related to the Romanovs had served as a page to Tsar Alexei, but he straddled old and new worlds having travelled in the West and cut off his own beard as a young man. This cautious if safe general, never a drinking crony, had a touchy relationship with Peter.

The Swedish king had to choose whether to hit Russia or Poland first. Ten years younger than Peter, Charles was just eighteen, tall, round-faced, blue-eyed, already balding. He had tempered himself with relentless riding to be a Spartan warrior-king: he could pick up a glove from the ground at a gallop. Possibly homosexual, he disdained any

---

* As he travelled through Russia, Peter ruled through a tiny chancellery made up of Fyodor Golovin, the calm, overworked, omnicompetent minister who was field marshal, admiral-general and foreign secretary; a couple of trusted chefs de cabinet including Prince-Pope Zotov; and the indispensable, half-literate Menshikov whom he now appointed to his first post: governor to the Tsarevich Alexei. Peter's last decree of the old century was to change the Byzantine calendar which dated the world from the creation. At the end of Byzantine year 7208, Peter adopted the Western style of dating from the birth of Christ: it was now 1 January 1700.

interest in women ("I am married to the army") and preferred to read his Bible—and drill his infantry until they were the best in Europe. They worshipped him as "the Last of the Vikings." An impetuous practitioner of attack at all times, he possessed a grim messianic self-belief: when he later faced setbacks, he struck a coin inscribed: "What worries you? God and I still live!" Charles, known to some as "Ironhead," would pursue his war to the end: "I resolved never to start an unjust war but never to end a just one." His acumen as warlord matched Peter's—and their duel to the death would last eighteen years.[5]

Luckily for Peter, who needed time to mobilize and rebuild after the debacle of Narva, Charles first marched into Poland, deposing Augustus the Strong in favour of his own puppet king, while Peter attacked Swedish garrisons around the Baltic. On 30 December 1701, Sheremetev defeated a Swedish army. Elated, Peter sent Menshikov to present Sheremetev with his field marshal's baton and the *cordon bleu* of his new Order of St. Andrei. Spending much of his time with the armies or organizing supplies, Peter started to roll up Swedish strongholds in Livonia, a campaign eased by the outbreak of a European conflict, the War of the Spanish Succession, which complicated Charles's position. On 14 October 1702, advancing in Ingria (the south-eastern shore of the Gulf of Finland), the Russians took the Swedish fortress of Nöteborg. Peter renamed it Shlisselburg ("Key-Fortress")—because it was the "key" to the River Neva—and appointed Menshikov as its governor.

On 1 May 1703, Peter and Menshikov captured Nyenskans. On the 16th, on the nearby Hare Island the foundations were laid for a fortress that Peter was to call St. Peter and Paul—but it is possible he was not himself present for this moment, which was later mythologized with the tsar choosing the place with the aid of an eagle. Yet within a year, when this stronghold was finished, Peter had started to see it as the foundation of a new city that would be both symbol and catalyst of his ambitions for Russia—a monument to his victories over the Swedes, a port for a naval tsar, and a Western metropolis for a modernized Russia: he named it St. Petersburg. Opposite the fortress (and close to the future Winter Palace), he built a little *domik*, a three-room cabin in Dutch baroque style, his home for the next five years while he created a shipyard and admiralty. Petersburg became "my Eden . . . my darling," shared above all with Menshikov: "I can't help writing to you from this paradise; truly here we live in heaven."[6]

Peter rushed back to Moscow where he celebrated a Roman triumph and awarded both Menshikov and himself the *cordon bleu*. On 23 November 1703, he threw a revel on the nameday of Menshikov, whom he now awarded the title of count of Hungary, procured from the Holy Roman Emperor.* Peter's itinerant court was joined by Menshikov's new gaggle of female admirers.

Menshikov was courting a teenaged girl of noble family, Daria Arseneva, who served as a maid-of-honour to Peter's sister. Daria and her sister joined Menshikov's household. It was there, in October 1703, that Peter, now aged thirty-one, met a girl who had already led a turbulent life. She was to be as formidable in her way as Peter himself and her rise was the most meteoric of any individual in the eighteenth century.

Martha Scavronskaya, nineteen years old, black-eyed, voluptuous, fair-haired, was the daughter of a peasant, probably Lithuanian or Scandinavian by nationality, who was orphaned and adopted by a Lutheran pastor who in turn married her off to a Swedish soldier. On her husband's death, she was captured and marched into a Russian camp naked but for a blanket. After an affair with a Russian cavalryman, she was passed on to Sheremetev, who employed her as laundrywoman (and probably mistress), before presenting her to Menshikov, who likewise employed her as a laundress (and probably mistress).

Peter and Anna Mons had drifted apart after he discovered that she was romancing two foreign ambassadors simultaneously. Peter merely confiscated her mansion and jewels—and her family remained at court. Now he became fond of Martha the Lithuanian laundress, converting her to Orthodoxy and giving her the name "Catherine." "Hello mister captain," Catherine wrote in one of her first letters to him. "Your rowing-boat is ready: should it be sent to Your Worship?" She knew that the way to his heart was through his boats.

Just over nine months later, Catherine gave birth to the first of their children, a daughter. "Congratulations on your new-born," she wrote. She would spend most of the next twenty years pregnant. But the child soon died, the first of many. Of their twelve children, only two grew to adulthood and he ascribed their loss to God's will—though he treasured boys (whom he called his "recruits") more than girls. "Thank God the mother's healthy" was how he consoled himself. As he and Menshikov, now commanding the cavalry, mopped up Swedish forces in Livonia, capturing Narva, they travelled in a foursome with Catherine and Daria.

Peter's relationship with Catherine was based not only on her physical attractions and their shared parenthood and grief but also on her irrepressible cheerfulness, and on the unflappable serenity that allowed

---

* Russian tsars, unlike most other monarchs in Europe, did not by tradition award titles. The Holy Roman Emperor, a title usually held by the Habsburg archduke of Austria, could create princes and counts of the Holy Roman Empire and happily would provide them at the tsar's request.

her to handle Peter deftly. When he was struck by one of his fits, she would cradle his head on her knee and soothe him. She could carry her drink and was physically strong, once raising a sceptre that Peter himself struggled to lift: she liked to dress as an Amazon at sittings of the All-Drunken Synod.

Even years later, they still flirted. "If you were here," she wrote in one letter, "there'd soon be another little Shishenka [child]," and joshed about his new mistresses, while he in turn teased her about her admirers: "It's quite evident you've found someone better than me," and joked that it was revenge for his own infidelities. Since she never learned to write, her letters were dictated. Peter usually called her "Mother" or "Katerinushka my friend" and missed her when they were apart: "Mother, I am bored without you and you I think are the same." He shared tales of his escapades—"we drink like horses." Unlike the traditional Muscovite royal brides, Catherine did not come to court with a lineage and a faction of ambitious relatives who would change the balance of power. Instead she made her own alliances, particularly with Menshikov—and created her own persona with such aplomb that ultimately she became a plausible candidate for the throne in her own right. "The chief reason why the tsar was so fond of her," recalled Alexander Gordon, son of the Scottish general, "was her exceeding good temper." She always cheerfully told him that while he might find other "laundresses," he should not forget his old one.

In July 1706, Peter's minister-marshal-admiral, Golovin, died aged fifty-six of alcoholic excess. After Lefort, Peter realized he had "lost two admirals" to "that disease." This loss increased the power of Menshikov,* whom Peter promoted to the Russian title of prince of Ingria—the first princely title ever awarded by a tsar. His enemies nicknamed him "the Prince from the Dirt."[7]

In January 1708, Charles, deploying 44,000 of Europe's finest troops, invaded Russia. Peter said that he would not give up any territory even if he lost ten or twenty battles—but the war concentrated his mind on his mortality. In November, he secretly married Catherine. The stress frayed his tolerance of any failure. "I am surprised at you," he wrote to his half-brother Musin-Pushkin when he failed in a task during the war,

---

* No one inherited all of Golovin's power. The punctilious and stingy Gavril Golovkin, a relative of Peter's mother who had accompanied him to the Dutch shipyards, took over the Foreign Office while the jovial and able Fyodor Apraxin, brother-in-law of Fyodor III who had joined the play regiments as a boy, became general-admiral of the fleet. Meanwhile Marshal Sheremetev was rewarded for crushing a Cossack revolt in Astrakhan with the title count, the first ever given by a tsar. Golovkin and Apraxin were soon counts too.

"as I thought you had a brain but now I see you're stupider than a dumb beast." When the news came that Charles was advancing, he wrote to tell Catherine that "The enemy is coming and we don't know where he's going next," adding that he was sending presents for her ("Mama") and their new baby. As he anxiously rode between Petersburg, Moscow and Kiev, adjudicating rows between his commanders and allocating resources, Peter watched and waited. He had ordered a scorched-earth policy across Poland and Lithuania where Charles was wintering with his army, but he told Catherine that he had "so little time, don't expect regular letters."

Charles advanced, but the Russians would not give him the setpiece battle he craved that would allow him to deliver a knockout blow. Shadowing, harassing and drawing in the Swedes, Sheremetev commanded the main army, Menshikov the cavalry, while the Russian ally, the Cossack hetman Ivan Mazeppa, covered the south. Peter was exhilarated by Russian successes: "I've never seen such orderly conduct in our troops!" Catherine shared in good news and bad. "We did a fine dance right under the nose of the fiery Charles," he told her in August. By September, low on supplies, Charles faced the big decision, whether to push for Moscow or swerve southwards to the fecund steppes of Ukraine. He waited for his general Adam Löwenhaupt to march down from Livonia with 12,000 men, but finally, on 15 September 1708, Charles turned south into Ukraine, confident that Löwenhaupt, just ninety miles away, would catch up. But Peter and Menshikov saw their chance. On 28 September, they pounced on Löwenhaupt at the Lesnaya River. "All day it was impossible to see where victory would lie," wrote Peter, but by morning Löwenhaupt had lost his supplies and half his men. Charles received 6,000 men and nothing to feed them with. "This victory," wrote Peter, "may be called our first."

Then, on 27 October, Peter received desperate news from Menshikov: his Cossack ally Mazeppa had switched sides and betrayed Ukraine to Charles. Now sixty-three years old, Mazeppa had ruled his hetmanate for over twenty years, skilfully playing off Tatars, Ottomans, Russians and Poles, but the Swedish advance placed him in a dilemma.* Charles

---

* A highly educated nobleman, Mazeppa had studied in the West and served at the Polish court until he had a rash love affair with the wife of a Polish grandee. The cuckolded husband had him seized, stripped naked and tied to a wild horse, and then unleashed into the steppes where—it was said—he happened to be rescued by the Zaparozhian Cossacks. It was not the last time his love life almost destroyed him. Months earlier in mid-1708, the old seducer had fallen in love with Matrena Kochubey, aged twenty, whose father, a Cossack judge, denounced his treason to Peter. But the tsar did not believe him, handing over Kochubey to Mazeppa, who swiftly beheaded him. The minister of Alexander I and Nicholas I, Prince Kochubey, was the judge's great-grandson.

offered him an independent Ukraine. Mazeppa had backed Peter against his sister in 1682 but the hetman sensed the tsar would reduce his independence and that Menshikov wanted to be hetman himself. Staying with Peter he could end with nothing. Waiting at his capital, he secretly negotiated with Charles.

Now, as Charles approached, Mazeppa ignored Peter's summons. The tsar despatched Menshikov—and Mazeppa made his decision and galloped north with his Cossack host to join Charles. Menshikov found Mazeppa had gone. "We received your letter of the hetman's totally un-expected and evil treason," wrote Peter, "with great astonishment."

Charles and Peter realized simultaneously that the hetman's capital Baturin was the key to Ukraine. Swedish king and Russian favourite raced towards the Cossack capital. Menshikov won. He stormed Baturin but, unable to fortify it, burned it and slaughtered its 10,000 inhabitants. Even today, archaeologists in Baturin continue to unearth skeletons.[8]

Winter withered the Swedish army, now down to 24,000 men. Charles must either fight or retreat. Peter, building ships in Azov and reforming his government to ease his mobilization of troops and supplies,* waited; Sheremetev and Menshikov watched. Then, in April 1709, Charles laid siege to the small town of Poltava to win a base—or provoke a battle.

"As regards Poltava, it would be best to attack the enemy," Peter wrote to Menshikov. "We need the field marshal [Sheremetev] too. It is clear this is of prime importance but I leave everything to your good judge-ment." On 27 May, Menshikov summoned him. "I'll travel as fast as I can." He galloped up from Azov. On 4 June, Peter joined Sheremetev and Menshikov, along with Catherine, his favourite blackamoor Hanni-bal† and his dwarf Iakim Volkov.

"With God's help," he felt sure, "by the end of this month, we shall do the main business with them." Assuming supreme command, the un-surpassed incarnation of autocratic warlord, Peter ordered the advance,

---

* Between 1707 and 1709, Peter divided Russia into nine *gubernii*—governorships—with Menshikov as governor of St. Petersburg, his surrogate "father" Streshnev in Moscow and all the other posts held by the tsar's relatives. The governors were responsible directly to Peter, bypassing the formal central government, the old administrative offices (*prikazy*) still based on Moscow.

† In 1703, Gavril Golovkin had ordered the purchase in Constantinople of a black slave-boy, "Abram the blackamoor," probably seized by slave traders from Chad or Ethiopia. Peter stood godfather at the christening of this Muslim boy—who was henceforth Abram Petrovich Hannibal. He served as one of Peter's black pages, known as Nubians, Arabs or Abyssinians who became an exotic feature of the Romanov court up until 1917. Hannibal was exceptionally talented. Spotting that the boy had a gift for languages and mathematics, Peter had him educated in France. He rose to become the first black general in Europe and great-grandfather of the poet Pushkin, who wrote his life-story as *The Negro of Peter the Great*.

halting half a mile from Poltava and consolidating a rectangular camp for his 40,000 men, bounded on one side by the steep banks of the river and defended on the other three by ramparts and spikes. Cossacks guarded a camp for baggage in the rear where Catherine waited. The Russians fortified their position, which was accessible only by a corridor through the woods which Peter ordered to be blocked by six redoubts crossed by another four, garrisoned by 4,000 men: an obstacle that would break any Swedish advance.

As Charles observed the Russian works, he was wounded in the foot. On Sunday 26 June, lying on his bed in his headquarters in a nearby monastery, his foot seeping blood, he called a council of war. True to form, he decided on a pre-emptive attack to counter Peter's overwhelming superiority. At dawn the Swedes would creep through the redoubts, then surprise the Russians by storming the camp. It was a risky scheme, with many possibilities for confusion in the darkness. For speed and surprise, the artillery was left behind. The wounded king could not command himself. Yet co-ordination was essential—and the Swedish generals loathed each other.

On 27 June, in the greyness before dawn, the Swedish army, 8,000 infantry and 9,000 cavalry, took up their positions while Charles, borne into battle slung on a camp bed suspended between two horses, surrounded by a chosen guard of body-blockers, plus his minister Count Piper, joined the commander Carl Gustav Rehnskiöld on the left while Löwenhaupt commanded the right. At 4 a.m., as the sun rose over the horizon, the Swedes advanced, but the necessary surprise was swiftly blown as the Russian redoubts opened fire. Almost immediately the Swedish plan went awry. Instead of bypassing the Russian redoubts, the Swedish centre stopped to assault them repeatedly, an irrelevant but bloody mini-battle, never arriving at the rendezvous to fight the real battle on the other side. Instead they were attacked by Menshikov's cavalry until Peter ordered him to withdraw and divide his men into two units on either flank. One Swedish column was lost in the gloom and never arrived, while Löwenhaupt's infantry on the right became separated, emerging from the woods to face the Russian camp on their own. When Rehnskiöld and Charles finally arrived to join him, they found half their small army missing.

At 9 p.m., Peter, standing on the ramparts of his camp, wearing a black tricorn hat, high boots, the green coat with red sleeves of a Preobrazhensky colonel and the cordon bleu of St. Andrei across his chest, spotted the gap between the Swedish formations and sent Menshikov, flashily wearing white, and his cavalry to attack the corps adrift in the centre. Lost and isolated, the Swedish troops surrendered.

Rehnskiöld and Charles waited for two hours, looking for their missing forces.

It was a momentous opportunity: Peter held a council of war in his tent and then emerged to order the army to position itself for battle—just as Rehnskiöld decided to withdraw. The Swedish lines turned and formed up to retreat, but it was too late. To Rehnskiöld's horror, the gates of the Russian camp were opened and out marched the entire army to form a crescent, with Peter directing the left and Sheremetev the centre. Peter reminded the men that they fought "for the state . . . not for Peter," who "sets no value on his own life if only Russia and Russian piety and glory may live!" In this address, the monarch shared his majestic dream of Russian greatness that made him for all his coarseness and violence such an inspiring leader for his long-suffering nobility.

Rehnskiöld hesitated, then halted his retreat and gave the order for the Swedes to wheel around and form up for battle: the weary but superbly trained Swedes wheeled perfectly under fire, then waited for the order to advance. They marched slowly forward, not breaking step as Russian cannonades scythed them down. Their right smashed into the Russians, forcing them back, but their left had been decimated by the Russian salvoes. Given the Russian superiority, the very momentum of Swedish success on the right rendered the shattered left ever more vulnerable. A musketball knocked off Peter's hat. He ordered his infantry to advance into the gap opening up between the Swedish left and right. Peter's saddle was hit and a bullet was deflected from his chest by an icon he wore round his neck. As Charles's Royal Guards fought to the last man, the Swedes broke. Charles himself was almost captured. Twenty-one of his twenty-four bearers were killed, and he had to be lifted on to a horse, pouring blood. Now he had to ride for his life.

Some 6,900 Swedes lay dead or wounded, while 2,700 were prisoners. Peter was exhilarated, riding through his men, embracing his generals. A field chapel was erected for a Te Deum, then the tsar awaited his prisoners. Menshikov shepherded them in to kneel and hand over their swords to their victor. After this ritual obeisance, Peter moved to a resplendent Persian tent for a banquet. Every toast was greeted with the thunder of a cannonade. After Marshal Rehnskiöld and Count Piper had been brought in, Peter toasted them before asking, "Where is my brother Charles?" But the king was making his escape to the south.* Peter returned Rehnskiöld's sword and toasted his "teachers" in the art of war.

---

* Pursued by Menshikov, Charles, accompanied by Mazeppa, his Cossacks (who as traitors could not surrender) and a small retinue, just made it to the Bug River where he abandoned his army and escaped to Ottoman territory, whence he continued to direct the war against Peter.

"Who are your teachers?" asked Rehnskiöld.

"You are, gentlemen," replied Peter.

"Well then, the pupils have returned their thanks to their teachers," said the defeated marshal.

That evening, Peter wrote fourteen notes "from the camp at Poltava," including this one to the nearby Catherine:

> Matushka, good day. All-merciful God has this day granted us an
> unprecedented victory over the enemy.
> Peter
> PS Come here and congratulate us!

Peter reported playfully to Romodanovsky in Moscow: "The whole enemy army has ended up like Phaeton.* I congratulate Your Majesty," he added, jokingly raising the prince-caesar to a new mock-title: emperor. Two days later, Peter promoted Menshikov to marshal, Golovkin to the new post of chancellor and rained serfs on Sheremetev. Colonel Peter thanked the prince-caesar for his own promotion to lieutenant-general and rear admiral, though "I haven't deserved so much, Your Majesty."

Peter was convinced that the victory had won the Baltic—"Now, with God's help, the final stone in the foundation of St. Petersburg has been laid"—and marked the end of the Swedish empire and the resurgence of Russia. Writing to Catherine, he called it "our Russian resurrection."

Yet the war was far from over. As Sheremetev marched north to seize the Baltic and Menshikov galloped to secure Poland, Peter and Catherine headed to Kiev where, "for my sins, I've been struck down by bouts of chills and heat nausea and fatigue." When he recovered, he renewed his alliance with Augustus the Strong and restored him to the throne of Poland. "I'm bored without you," he told Catherine. "The Poles are constantly in conference about Ivashka Khmelnitsky [alcohol]. You joke about my flirtations; we have none; for we are old and not that sort of people. The bridegroom [Menshikov had just married Daria] had an interview the day before yesterday with Ivashka and had a bad fall and still lies powerless."

"Please come soon," replied Catherine. "Oh my dear, I miss you . . . It seems like a year since we saw each other." On 14 November, Peter joined Sheremetev at the siege of Riga: "I launched the first three bombs with my own hands—vengeance on that accursed place."

On 18 December, Catherine gave birth to a daughter, Elizaveta. Peter visited mother and child. Two days later, flanked by two favourites, Menshikov and Prince Vasily Dolgoruky, colonel of the Preobrazhensky

---

* In Greek mythology, Phaeton drove his chariot so fast and high that it exploded in flames—a metaphor for the dangers of excessive ambition.

Guards, he rode through seven arches into Moscow with thousands of Swedish prisoners. After a Te Deum at the Dormition Cathedral, he climbed the Red Staircase, where he had seen such atrocities as a boy, and entered the Palace of Facets, where Rehnskiöld and Piper were presented to the "tsar" on his throne. But when they made their obeisance before him, they were puzzled to see not the giant they had met at Poltava but the beetle-browed prince-caesar, enthroned on a dais and served dinner by Menshikov, Sheremetev and the real tsar.

During the summer and winter of 1710, the Russians took the Baltic ports of Riga, Reval and Vyborg. "Good news," Peter exulted to Catherine. "We win a strong cushion for St. Petersburg."

Yet Charles, recuperating on Ottoman territory, was encouraging the sultan to join the war. When Peter forcefully demanded that Charles be handed over, he offended Ottoman pride. As the sultan plotted war, Peter planned two weddings—one for the royals, one for the dwarfs.9

ACT II

THE APOGEE

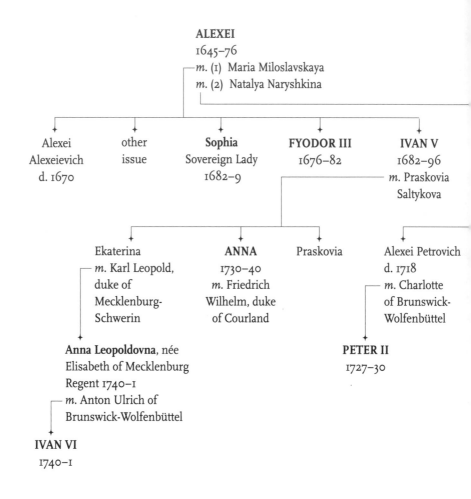

**ALEXEI**
1645–76
— *m.* (1) Maria Miloslavskaya
*m.* (2) Natalya Naryshkina

| Alexei Alexeievich d. 1670 | other issue | **Sophia** Sovereign Lady 1682–9 | **FYODOR III** 1676–82 | **IVAN V** 1682–96 *m.* Praskovia Saltykova |

Ekaterina
— *m.* Karl Leopold, duke of Mecklenburg-Schwerin

**ANNA**
1730–40
*m.* Friedrich Wilhelm, duke of Courland

Praskovia

Alexei Petrovich
d. 1718
— *m.* Charlotte of Brunswick-Wolfenbüttel

**Anna Leopoldovna**, née Elisabeth of Mecklenburg
Regent 1740–1
— *m.* Anton Ulrich of Brunswick-Wolfenbüttel

**PETER II**
1727–30

**IVAN VI**
1740–1

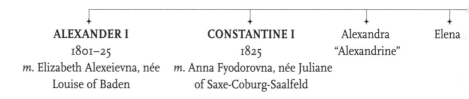

| **ALEXANDER I** 1801–25 *m.* Elizabeth Alexeievna, née Louise of Baden | **CONSTANTINE I** 1825 *m.* Anna Fyodorovna, née Juliane of Saxe-Coburg-Saalfeld | Alexandra "Alexandrine" | Elena |

* Peter the Great was the first emperor of Russia. All of his successors were both emperors and tsars.

# THE
# ROMANOVS
## c. 1700–1800

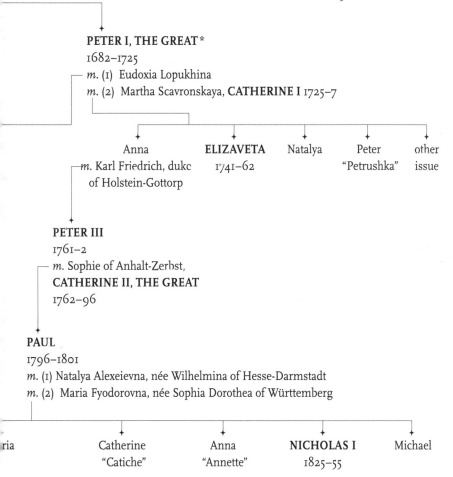

**PETER I, THE GREAT** *
1682–1725
*m.* (1) Eudoxia Lopukhina
*m.* (2) Martha Scavronskaya, **CATHERINE I** 1725–7

Anna      **ELIZAVETA**    Natalya     Peter     other
*m.* Karl Friedrich, duke    1741–62           "Petrushka"   issue
of Holstein-Gottorp

**PETER III**
1761–2
*m.* Sophie of Anhalt-Zerbst,
**CATHERINE II, THE GREAT**
1762–96

**PAUL**
1796–1801
*m.* (1) Natalya Alexeievna, née Wilhelmina of Hesse-Darmstadt
*m.* (2) Maria Fyodorovna, née Sophia Dorothea of Württemberg

ria        Catherine       Anna       **NICHOLAS I**     Michael
"Catiche"      "Annette"      1825–55

## SCENE 1

# The Emperor

# CAST

PETER THE GREAT, tsar and emperor 1682–1725
Eudoxia (née Lopukhina), tsarina, his first wife, now a nun
Alexei, tsarevich, his eldest son by Eudoxia
Charlotte, princess of Brunswick, Alexei's wife
PETER II, son of Alexei and Charlotte, Peter the Great's grandson, tsar
  1727–30
CATHERINE I (formerly Martha Scavronskaya), tsarina, Peter the Great's
  second wife, empress of Russia 1725–7
Anna, their daughter, later wife of Karl Friedrich, duke of Holstein-
  Gottorp, "Annushka"
ELIZAVETA, their daughter, empress of Russia 1741–62
Peter Petrovich, their baby son, "Petrushka"
Praskovia (née Saltykova), tsarina, widow of Tsar Ivan V
Ekaterina, daughter of Ivan V and Praskovia, married Karl Leopold,
  duke of Mecklenburg-Schwerin, "Wild Duchess"
ANNA, daughter of Ivan V and Praskovia, married Friedrich Wilhelm,
  duke of Courland, empress of Russia 1730–40
Afrosina Fyodorova, Alexei's Finnish mistress


## COURTIERS: ministers etc.

Prince Fyodor Romodanovsky, prince-caesar, head of Preobrazhensky
  Office
Prince Ivan Romodanovsky, his son, prince-caesar, head of the
  Preobrazhensky Office
Alexander Menshikov, first prince, field marshal and Peter's best friend,
  "Aleshka," "Prince from the Dirt"
Boris Sheremetev, field marshal, count
Gavril Golovkin, chancellor, count
Fyodor Apraxin, general-admiral, count, brother of Tsarina Martha,
  Fyodor III's wife
Prince Vasily Dolgoruky, commander of the Preobrazhensky Guards
Peter Tolstoy, henchman of Miloslavskys, secret police chief

Peter Shafirov, vice chancellor, first baron
Anton Devier, police chief of Petersburg
Pavel Iaguzhinsky, procurator-general


## ENEMIES

Charles XII, King of Sweden, "Last of the Vikings," "Ironhead"
Baltacı Mehmet Pasha, Ottoman grand vizier

P oltava changed Russia's status in Europe. From now on, it was a
  great power and the Romanovs were no longer Muscovite barbarians
from the borderlands of Europe. Tsars Michael and Alexei had aspired
to marry into European royalty but had always been snubbed; now it
was different, and Peter moved swiftly to marry Romanovs to European
princes. He negotiated the marriage of his niece, Anna, to Friedrich
Wilhelm, duke of Courland, a small Baltic principality in today's Latvia.
The first Russian royal wedding to a foreigner for 200 years was to be
held not in Moscow but in Petersburg, where Peter decided to lay on a
royal-and-dwarf spectacular to launch the city as his new capital.

Its embellishment had already started. Grandees had been ordered
to build stone palaces in the city; government departments were moved
there; and Peter hired Italian and German architects to design a great
European metropolis.*

When Anna's bridegroom arrived, Peter proudly showed him around
the city himself. The duke was distinguished only by his appetite for
drink. Peter was bored by the bovine Friedrich and found the bride
Anna, daughter of Tsar Ivan V, charmless. She was broad-shouldered
and sour-faced, regularly bullied by her mother, Tsarina Praskovia,
whom she hated. Praskovia was a dragon who ruled her court at the
Izmailovo Palace outside Moscow with capricious ferocity. When a
sacked servant tried to denounce her to Peter for criticizing his reforms,
Praskovia had him arrested, then beat him with a cane in his cell and,
dousing him in vodka, set him alight. With such a mother, no wonder
Anna was a gloomy bride.

On 31 October 1710, at Menshikov's palace, Peter, unusually sporting a majestic Frenchified costume, a red cloak lined in sable with a
white perruque, and brandishing a ribboned baton, held the crown over
the groom, while Menshikov did the same over the bride. But the tsar
got restless, asked someone else to take over and ordered the priest to
shorten the service, impatient to begin his firework display.

---

* Menshikov showed the way by ordering the Italian architect Giovanni Fontana to build
the city's first stone palace on Vasilevsky Island, which became the tsar's own headquarters.
Meanwhile a Swiss-Italian, Domenico Trezzini, was building the Peter and Paul Cathedral
beside the fortress, while across the Neva he created Peter's Summer Palace, a small,
two-storey villa in Dutch baroque style. Not far from his cabin, Peter built a two-storey
wooden Winter Palace.

After three days of feasting, Anna and Friedrich were the star guests at the marriage of Peter's favourite dwarf, Iakim Volkov. Peter had specified to the prince-caesar that "dwarfs male and female residing in boyar homes in Moscow are to be collected and sent to St. Petersburg." When they arrived they were cooped up "like cattle" before being distributed to grandees who were to dress them for the weddings.

First a dwarfish master of ceremonies, struggling to hold his full-sized staff of office, led a procession of seventy-two dwarfs, tsar and court that ended at the Peter and Paul Cathedral where Peter held the crown over the bride's head as the congregation and even the priest tried without success to stifle giggles. At the wedding banquet in Menshikov's palace, Peter and Catherine, accompanied by the duke and duchess of Courland, sniggered as the dwarfs feasted at a table overseen by the dwarf-marshal and bumpered full-sized goblets of vodka. When the music began, the drunken dwarfs started to dance and fall over, to the amusement of the tsar and the foreign ambassadors who now roared with laughter at "the comical capers, strange grimaces and odd postures of this medley of pygmies," some of whom "had huge hunchbacks and little legs, others big bellies and short crooked legs like a badger's." Afterwards Peter put the dwarf couple to bed in his room in the palace. The bacchanalia ended only when Anna and her husband departed for Courland, but the duke had drunk so much that he died soon after leaving.

The teenaged widow Anna returned to her uncle, who forbade her to remarry and despatched her back to rule Courland. In its capital, Mitau, Anna was neglected, disdained and always starved of funds by the tsar, who nonetheless dictated her every move to ensure that the duchy remained a Russian satellite.

Peter was sobered by Sultan Ahmet III's declaration of war, and rushed southwards to raise troops and head off the Ottoman invasion. Peter may have expected an easy victory. In fact, he was marching into a trap.[1]

On 25 February 1711, Peter held a religious-military parade in Cathedral Square in the Kremlin to bless his crusade to liberate the Orthodox under Ottoman rule, in alliance with the Moldavian hospodar, Dmitri Cantemir, and destroy the "enemies of Christ." He emblazoned his banners with Constantine the Great's motto: "By this sign shall you conquer!"

However, Peter was surprised by the swift Ottoman advance towards Ukraine and Poland. He had to get to the Danube first. He urged Sheremetev to move faster. "I'm not an angel," grumbled the marshal, "but I'm ordered to do the work of an angel rather than a human being." Short of men and munitions, Peter blamed his officials who acted "without regard for the troubles and grief in which your leader finds himself." He threatened to prosecute them as "traitors of the fatherland." Peter felt alone in his mission. "It's hard to live," he later told Catherine, "because I have to keep both sword and pen in my hand—and you know yourself I've no helpers."

Peter aspired to be the first servant of a rational state, which he tried to create in a series of administrative and hierarchical reforms. Now he founded a new institution, the Senate, a nine-member cabinet, filled with his trusted relatives and including Menshikov of course, to run the country in his absence. Yet Peter distrusted his own nobles and officials, knowing that many opposed his aggressive reforms: in turn he called them "dogs." Whenever he was distracted, chaos reigned as his henchmen, unrestrained by the decorum of his new Senate, wrestled (often literally) for money and power. While state-building with his new institutions, he undermined his own rational ideas with his tyrannical, idiosyncratic style. He dictated everything, soon grousing that the senators were incapable of decision-making. This is the complaint of autocrats, from Peter to Stalin and Putin, who concentrate fearsome power in one man and then reprimand their assistants for not thinking for themselves. "They imitate the crab in the course of their work," wrote Peter, "so I'll deal with them not with words but with my fists." Peter warned that if they did not get to work "It will be the worse for you!" Only fear worked. He frequently punched or beat his grandees with his cane. Many understandably resented his menacing hyperactivity.

Now he was starting to realize that Menshikov was avaricious and brutal as his depredations ravaged allied Poland. "Mend your ways," Peter warned him, "or you'll answer with your head." Peter began to transfer his favour to the fearless, haughty Vasily Dolgoruky, who frequently denounced Menshikov's corruption and violent extortions. "Inform me where the money's gone . . . I know nothing of your province," Peter warned Menshikov, "as if it's another country." Autocrats have assistants, advisers and interests, but they do not have—or should not have—friends. Peter loved his "heart's child" Menshikov, but he promoted and protected him because he was the most effective and the most committed in carrying out his projects, to which most of the aristocrats were indifferent.

Now, knowing that he might never return from "this hazardous journey," he left both Menshikov and the rival Fyodor Apraxin in charge, telling both that "All the country is entrusted to you," thereby once more ensuring plenipotentiary paralysis. Worrying about his illegitimate daughters, he decided he should marry Catherine formally so that, he explained to Menshikov, if "they were left orphans they will be more protected." He married her privately, announcing that she was the "true and lawful Sovereign Lady."

On 6 March, he and Catherine went off to war in a race "to reach the Danube before the Turks." As they headed south, Peter again fell ill, suffering "two weeks of paroxysms so severe I didn't expect to survive but sweats and urination began to relieve me." Catherine soothed her epileptic husband, while trying to protect her ally Menshikov. "I beg Your Highness not to be troubled by believing any stupid gossip from here," she wrote to the Prince from the Dirt, "for the Rear Admiral [Peter] keeps you in love."

The Ottomans under Grand Vizier Baltacı Mehmet Pasha easily beat Peter to the Danube. "I'm amazed at your slow progress," he reprimanded Marshal Sheremetev, advancing with the main army. "Ten days are lost. Had you done as ordered, you'd have reached the Danube before the Turks," and now he wondered, "Will there be anything to eat?" He was running out of supplies. He should have called off the campaign. On 24 June, Peter rendezvoused with Sheremetev. Their 38,000 men were systematically enveloped by the vizier's 150,000 plus 50,000 horsemen under the Crimean Khan Devlet Giray. Suddenly, in "burning heat day and night," lacking provisions, Peter found himself in extreme jeopardy. "Never since I started to serve," he wrote, "have I been in such a deep position." He ordered the building of a fortified camp—just in time. On 9 July, Baltacı surrounded Peter, who built a deep pit protected by a circle of carts to shelter Catherine and her ladies from sun and missiles: there the tsarina waited serenely as the battle raged and her ladies sobbed loudly. The elite Ottoman janissaries attacked; Peter's Moldavian allies were useless but his artillery proved its worth. "Lord God emboldened our men to the extent that though they outnumbered us by 100,000 they were constantly beaten back" until they were in a stand-off. Peter called this "a banquet of death." He faced death or capture: he is said to have written to the Senate to say that, if he was indeed seized, they should "cease to regard me as your tsar" and should choose "the most worthy" successor.

Peter offered to negotiate, but Baltacı thought he had him like "a bird in the hand," as the tsar later put it; annihilation was imminent. Catherine won Peter's undying admiration by keeping her nerve, facing danger "not as a woman but as a man" and advising that he should again approach Baltacı.

Her instincts were sound. The janissaries had been mauled by Peter's artillery and wanted peace. In the lull, Peter sent one of his brilliant new men to negotiate: Peter Shafirov, son of a Polish Jew with a gift for languages, had started as the tsar's diplomatic translator but he had made himself so indispensable that Peter promoted him to vice-chancellor and the first Russian baron.* Peter offered Baltacı 150,000 roubles, and Catherine was said to have added all her jewellery to the bribe. "I deduce that the Turks are disposed to peace," Peter wrote to Shafirov on 11 July, revealing his desperation, "but are slow to get there. If they genuinely want peace, agree with them on everything they want except enslavement and let us know by the end of the day so we can begin our desperate march."

Shafirov negotiated superbly from a position of ignominious weakness, surrendering Peter's first prize, Azov, and its flotilla—but otherwise Peter got off lightly. In his sanctuary across the Ottoman border, Charles of Sweden, hearing of Peter's predicament, tried to get the sultan to stop the treaty that would save Peter. Finally he galloped for Baltacı's camp, but on 12 July Peter and Baltacı signed. Next day Charles arrived to watch his nemesis escape.†

"My good fortune," mused Peter, "consisted in receiving only fifty lashes when I was condemned to receive a hundred."²

Peter, weary and sickening, travelled with Catherine through Poland to rally his Polish and Danish allies in the Swedish war—and to marry off his eldest son Alexei. He left Catherine at Thorn while he took the waters at Carlsbad, though the wholesomeness of spas bored him. "Katerinushka, my friend, how are you?" he wrote to Catherine. "Tomorrow we begin our cure. The place is so merry you might call it an honourable dungeon . . . Worst of all there is no good beer!" When she told him to relax, he joshed that she wanted revenge for one of his infidelities: "It is quite evident you've found someone better than me . . . Is it one of ours or a man of Thorn? I rather think . . . you want to be avenged for what I did two years ago. That's the way you daughters of Eve act with us old fellows!"

In October, the purified tsar arrived at Torgau castle in Saxony to marry Alexei to Charlotte, daughter of the duke of Brunswick-Lüneburg-Wolfenbüttel, one of those German principalities that would become

---

* Peter the Great had not been keen to attract Jews to Russia—"I'd rather see the best Mahommedans than Jews, rascals and cheats"—yet he was happy to promote converted Jews such as Baron Shafirov and General Devier, later police chief of Petersburg.

† Shafirov, left behind as a hostage, negotiated the Treaty of Adrianople in Constantinople, which now made it impossible for Charles XII to remain in the Ottoman empire. In a swashbuckling ride across Europe, Ironhead took just thirteen days to travel from Wallachia to Stralsund, the last Swedish stronghold on the Baltic, without changing boots or clothes. On arrival, his boots had to be cut from his feet. But he made sure: the war went on.

Russia's marriage-agency and link the dynasty into the wider royal family of Europe. But Peter was already worried about and displeased by Alexei.

At the age of eight, Alexei had been forcibly removed from his mother when she was confined to a monastery, surely a trauma for any child. Worse, Peter had placed him under the governorship of the harsh Menshikov, who had both bullied the boy and taught him to drink heavily. Half ignored, half intimidated, Alexei grew up fearing Peter's implacable energy, his pursuit of Western culture and expertise, of Dutch ships and of German uniforms, his brutal wars and his menacing reforms: he cleaved to his mother's Muscovite Orthodoxy. Now twenty-two, dark, long faced and sad eyed, all he had in common with his father was his height and his taste for drink, but he lacked his iron constitution.

Peter tried to train Alexei in war. When in March 1708 Alexei had grumbled that he had not been summoned to Petersburg—"I'm very sad to be left here"—Peter replied, "You write that you're sad and bored . . . but you should be able to work out for yourself that time requires it thus." The traditionalist Alexei did not approve of Russian marriages to foreigners. "So now I know he wishes to marry me not to a Russian but to one of these people [Westerners]," he complained to his confessor. "What he wishes will happen." Peter arranged for him to meet Charlotte but Alexei found her poxy and made no comment. "Why," asked Peter, "haven't you written to tell me what you think of her?"

On 14 October 1711, Peter watched Alexei marry Charlotte, who remained Lutheran though any children would be Orthodox. "I congratulate you on a new daughter-in-law," he told Catherine. "Please announce it to the All-Joking Prince-Pope!" Peter knew that Alexei was dangerous. Charles XII had planned to replace Peter with his son. To protect his new family and father a new heir, the tsar arranged another marriage: his own.[3]

At 7 a.m. on 19 February 1712, Peter, dressed as a rear admiral with one of his Dutch sailors, Admiral Cruys, as best man, formally married Catherine in Petersburg at the Church of St. Isaac of Dalmatia. Peter had promised to Menshikov that if he survived the Turkish war, "We'll complete this in St. Petersburg," and he had kept his word.

Peter and Catherine's two surviving daughters were bridesmaids along with their aunts and cousins, including the widowed duchess of Courland—so that the chapel contained three future empresses of Russia: Catherine, Elizaveta and Anna. Only Tsarevich Alexei was not there, apparently sulking in honour of his mother. Peter's attendant at the wedding was a new upstart favourite, Pavel Iaguzhinsky, who now emerged for the first time as his inseparable companion.[*]

After the naval wedding, the couple rode in sleighs through rows of trumpeters and drummers to the Winter Palace where in the dining hall he hung his own present to his wife—an ebony and ivory candelabra he had crafted himself—suspended over the guests for the banquet. At the hard-drinking party, Peter joked to the ambassadors that it was "a fecund marriage for they already had five children."

The Swedish war was far from over. Charles was defiant, convinced that he would prevail, so that even after Poltava, Petersburg was not yet secure. The tsar methodically rolled up the Swedish empire, fighting on several fronts simultaneously, by land and sea, an effort, driven by his merciless acumen, that stretched Russian resources to their limit. He conquered enemy territory around the Baltic then marched into Swedish Pomerania in Germany. Catherine accompanied him during the German campaign, before he left Menshikov in command and returned to Petersburg. That year, Peter and General-Admiral Apraxin managed to conquer Finland, and on 27 July 1714 they defeated the Swedish navy[†]—but the tsar's pleasure was blighted by revelations of Menshikov's greed and insubordination, gleefully reported by Dolgoruky.

On 23 November, Peter celebrated Menshikov's nameday, then went on from the prince's palace to the house of an English shipbuilder. There Peter suddenly turned on his friend: "Well, Alexander, today I saw signs of your disloyalty. I raised you from nothing, but you're raising yourself above me. I knew well you were robbing me and I permitted it, but now I'm well informed you've stolen millions." Catherine tried to intercede, but Peter retorted: "Madame, this isn't your business."

"Father," the prince wept. "Everything is yours!"

"You're getting rich," answered Peter. "I'm getting poor. You're a thief."

Two days later, Peter arrested Menshikov's henchmen, senators, governors and the secretary of the Admiralty Alexander Kikin, and appointed Dolgoruky, who had served so well at Poltava and the Pruth, to torture them and indict the prince. Apraxin and Golovkin admitted

---

[*] Strikingly handsome, sternly efficient in war, government and diplomacy, unusually incorruptible and an invincible carouser, Iaguzhinsky, the Polish-born son of a church organist, had started as the tsar's *denshchik*, been promoted to a new rank in the tsarist entourage, adjutant-general, for his courage at Pruth and now accompanied Peter everywhere, usually riding in his carriage on his trips. He was appointed master of ceremonies at the Jolly Company. In some ways, he was a new, more honest Menshikov.

[†] As a result, Apraxin proposed that the tsar should be promoted to full general, which delighted Peter. "As the general's mistress you should congratulate me!" he told Catherine. "As general and general's wife, let's congratulate each other mutually," she teased. "But I don't recognize this rank until I can see you personally here. I wish you'd at least been a full admiral!"

their corruption but were forgiven. On 6 April 1715, three of Menshi-kov's associates were executed. Menshikov himself was colossally fined. Dolgoruky and the aristocrats now dominated government. Just when it seemed that his favourite could lose his head, the tsar was distracted by the tragedy of his own son.[4]

Alexei was no better a husband to his wife Charlotte than Peter had been to Eudoxia. But this was partly Peter's fault: he demanded Alexei accompany him to war, leaving Charlotte behind alone and miserable. Peter ordered her back to Petersburg, but the teenager, terrified of the tsar, panicked and ran back to her parental home, where Peter him-self came to find her. "We would never have thwarted your wish to see your family," he soothed her, "if only you'd informed us beforehand." Peter settled the couple in Petersburg where Alexei indulged in furious drunken bouts then abandoned Charlotte so that he could recover in Carlsbad. When she gave birth to his daughter, he never wrote to her. "No one knows where he is," Charlotte wept. On his return, Alexei fell in love with a teenaged Finnish serfgirl, Afrosina Fyodorova, captured in the war, and moved the buxom redhead into his marital palace. Yet, despite Alexei's alcoholic collapses, Charlotte became pregnant again. She was not the only one: Peter's wife Catherine was also expecting a child. If she gave birth to a son, that would make Peter less dependent on the tsarevich.

As Peter waited for the births,* he fell ill and brooded over Alexei, suspecting that his son was opposed to his entire vision for Russia. In Petersburg, on 11 October, he wrote a letter to Alexei commanding him to mend his "obstinacy and ill-nature" or "I will deprive you of the suc-cession as one cuts off a useless member." Peter would have preferred to leave Russia to a "worthy stranger than to my own unworthy son." On 12 October in Petersburg, Charlotte gave birth to Alexei's son, whom she named Peter—but she fell ill with fever. Sick himself, Peter visited her in his wheelchair—just before she died. On the 27th, the day of Charlotte's funeral, Peter delivered his ultimatum to Alexei, and the very next day Catherine gave birth to a son who was also named Peter, known as Petrushka—finally, an heir to replace Alexei. "God grant we may see him grow up," Peter wrote to Catherine, "rewarding us for our

---

* In January 1715, Peter presided over the wedding in Moscow of the seventy-year-old Prince-Pope Zotov, the ultimate topsy-turvy spectacular of the Drunken Synod. The bride-groom arrived in a carriage pulled by bears; the heralds were the "greatest stammerers in all Russia," the stewards and waiters "were old decrepit men," the running footmen were "so fat and bulky they had to be led" and the couple were married by a centenarian priest who had "lost eyesight and memory."

former grief about his brothers." In a matter of days, Peter had gone from having one unsatisfactory heir to three.

Peter ordered artillery salvoes and placed casks of beer on the streets where tsar and people got "inhumanly drunk" for days. Alexei consulted Dolgoruky about how to react to his father's ultimatum. Peter was feeling old (he was forty-four)—Catherine sent him spectacles "to help me with my old age"—and suffered from fevers and fits so grave that he was given the Last Sacraments. "I am a man," Peter warned Alexei, "and I must die." Peter's favourites resented his tyranny but even more they feared that, when he died, the ferocious Menshikov would rule as regent. They insured themselves by cultivating the heir.

Dolgoruky interceded with Peter to let the boy retire to an estate and afterwards boasted to Alexei, "I've saved you from the block by speaking to your father." But Alexei's chief adviser was Alexander Kikin, who had managed the navy and was so close to the tsar that he called him "Dedushka"—grandpa—until he was temporarily dismissed for corruption. Positioning himself to be Alexei's future minister, Kikin advised him to flee to Germany: "I'll find you somewhere to hide." Alexei started to boast to his mistress Afrosina that a revolt against Peter would break out soon, supported by much of the Senate and by others who backed him or hated Menshikov.

Father and son brooded. At a party, Peter opened up to the Danish ambassador: if a monarch had risked his life to create a respected state, should he leave it to "a fool who would begin the destruction" of all his achievements? "If gangrene starts in his finger," said Peter, offering his thumb to the ambassador, "would I not be obliged to have it cut off?"

Alexei, the gangrenous thumb, wrote back asking to be disinherited. "You rather hate my tasks which I perform for my people," Peter replied bitterly on 19 January 1716, "and you will be the destroyer of them . . . Either change your ways or be a monk. Give immediately your decision . . . And if you don't, I will treat you as a malefactor."

Peter departed for his second tour of Europe to form a coalition to destroy Sweden* and plan the ultimate dream—to marry his daughter to the greatest monarch in Europe.

Peter was away for more than year, but the demands of his ever more

* In another strategic marriage, on 8 April 1716, Peter married his niece, Ekaterina Ivanovna, eldest daughter of his late brother Tsar Ivan V and Tsarina Praskovia, to Karl Leopold, duke of Mecklenburg-Schwerin, who allowed his duchy to be garrisoned with a Russian army. Later the outrages perpetrated by this alcoholic and sadistic clod would lose him his duchy—but this marriage matters because the Mecklenburgs' daughter, Princess Elizabeth, born in December 1718, later converted to Orthodoxy as Anna Leopoldovna and ruled Russia as regent for her infant son.

ambitious wars placed yet more pressure on the Senate to raise supplies at home. Finally Menshikov, who had been left in charge of Peter's daughters and baby son, tore a shred off the senators and, displaying the energy that made him Peter's indispensable servitor, himself supplied the army.

On 26 August, Peter told Alexei to either join him at war or enter a monastery, an order that forced the boy into a secret decision to defy his father, seek foreign help and escape the monastery. He must flee—but where?

On 26 September, Alexei, telling Menshikov that he was joining his father, borrowed cash and then left in disguise, adopting the incognito of "Kokhansky," an officer, with just four retainers—one of whom was his mistress Afrosina in disguise as a pageboy. On the road near Libau, he bumped into his aunt, Peter's half-sister Maria, to whom he tearfully admitted he was going to escape. "Your father will find you no matter where," she said—but she did not inform the tsar.

At Libau, the tsarevich met Kikin, who suggested that he flee to Vienna, where Emperor Karl VI, married to his late wife Charlotte's sister, would help him. But in throwing himself on to the mercy of strangers, Alexei betrayed Peter. As they parted, Kikin warned: "Remember, if your father sends someone to persuade you to return, don't do it. He'll have you publicly beheaded."

As Alexei escaped, Peter was in Copenhagen organizing his most ambitious campaign so far: he assumed command of an Anglo-Danish-Russian fleet to storm mainland Sweden, but the coalition fell apart and Peter travelled towards Amsterdam on his way to Paris.

In October, Peter realized that his heir had vanished. He tried to trace Alexei, fearing that he was lurking among the Russian armies where he could plan a coup. But no one had seen him.

On 10 November, the imperial vice-chancellor in Vienna was awoken in the middle of the night by the arrival of a visitor who claimed to be Tsarevich Alexei. When the lachrymose traveller turned out to be the real thing, Emperor Karl found himself in possession of a useful but dangerous diplomatic pawn which, played clumsily, could lead to war with Peter. In conversations with the Austrian ministers and in private with his "pageboy" Afrosina, Alexei expressed the hope that the Russian army in Mecklenburg would revolt and march into Russia, and that, once he had seized the throne, he would move the capital back to Moscow, abandon the fleet and launch no more wars. He bragged that the emperor would back him. Meanwhile the Austrians secretly moved Alexei to Ehrenberg Castle, in the Tyrol, a few days away from Vienna.

*

In December 1716, Peter, who was in Amsterdam confined to bed with a fever, learned that Alexei was in Vienna; he wrote to the emperor to demand his return and ordered his ambassador to find him. Catherine, pregnant again, had stopped near the Dutch border. On 2 January 1717, Peter celebrated the birth of a son: "God has blessed us by giving us another recruit." Sons were always "recruits" for the military tsar. "As soon as possible I'll come to you," but the next day Peter heard that the baby had died. "How suddenly our joy has changed to grief . . . What answer can I give you except that of the long-suffering Job? The Lord has given and the Lord has taken away."

In May, Peter, accompanied by Dolgoruky and his blackamoor Hannibal, arrived in Paris, where a regent, Philippe duc d'Orléans, ruled on behalf of the seven-year-old Louis XV. Peter offered an alliance sealed by the marriage of his seven-year-old daughter Elizaveta to the king. The French were respectful but privately untempted by a child born out of wedlock to a peasant girl. When the tsar met the little king ("who is only a finger or two taller than our Luke [a dwarf]," he told Catherine), he lifted him up and threw him in the air, shocking the French courtiers. He stayed at Versailles—where he was underwhelmed by the palace but overwhelmed by the fountains which he would soon emulate. But his entourage entertained him by inviting a troupe of whores for an orgiastic rout. Catherine teased him about the girls. "I got your letter full of jokes," Peter replied with heavy-footed humour. "You say I'll be looking about for a lady but that wouldn't be at all becoming to my old age."

"I think Your Worship is distracted by a multitude of fountains and other amusements and forgets us," she joked in a cascade of double entendres. "Though I think you have found new laundresses, your old laundress hasn't forgotten you!"

"As for laundresses," he replied, "I'm not that type and besides I'm old."

In June, Peter departed France, leaving Hannibal to study artillery and mathematics, and took the waters at Spa, but he was "already bored drinking just water and a bit of wine" though he was accompanied by a French courtesan who may have been responsible for the fact that the tsar was suffering from venereal disease. "The doctors ban domestic fun," complained Peter to his wife. "I've sent my mistress back for I wouldn't be able to resist the temptation if I kept her here." Catherine reminded him that he had sent away his mistress because she had venereal disease: "I hope the mistress's admirer [that is, Peter] will not arrive in the same state of health as she did! From which God preserve us!"

Catherine missed him: "If the old man was here, we'd soon have another kid!" she wrote. "How lonely I am without you," he replied—and soon after they were reunited she fell pregnant again.[*]

All this time, the humiliating treachery of his son gnawed at Peter. He had despatched a tough officer of giant stature Alexander Rumiantsev to hunt down Alexei and bring him home. As the Austrians moved Alexei towards Naples, Rumiantsev followed. Soon Peter heard the news that Alexei was now hidden in the Castle of St. Elmo in Naples.

In July he sent his trusted factotum Peter Tolstoy to join Rumiantsev and secure Alexei, whatever it took. Tolstoy, now seventy-two, a vulpine master of the black arts of politics, had been ambassador in Constantinople, but in 1682, as a young man, he had served the Miloslavskys raising the musketeers against Peter's family. When Tolstoy redeemed himself by enrolling as the oldest student of shipbuilding, Peter forgave but never forgot, taking Tolstoy's head in his hands: "Oh head, head!" he teased menacingly. "You wouldn't be on your shoulders if you were not so wise."

In Vienna, Tolstoy convinced Emperor Karl to encourage a family reconciliation.

On 26 September 1717, at the Neapolitan viceroy's palace, Alexei was horrified to meet the cadaverous Tolstoy and the lugubrious Rumiantsev, who handed him a letter: "Your disobedience and contempt are known throughout the world," Peter wrote. If Alexei returned, "I assure you and promise to God I won't punish you . . . If you refuse, I as a father give my everlasting curse and, as a sovereign, declare you traitor."

Alexei hesitated. Tolstoy understood that Alexei's fragile confidence rested on his love for Afrosina. The viceroy placed the redhead in Tolstoy's clutches. He suborned her with promises and presents until she agreed to advise Alexei to return. On 3 October, Alexei consented, providing he could retire to a country estate and marry her.

Peter, back in Petersburg, accepted these terms, but he was alarmed to find that his baby son Petrushka was sickly. While he waited for Alexei to arrive, Peter investigated his corrupt magnates Menshikov and Sheremetev. To show that no one was above the law, he had a Guards officer and prince executed in public. Meanwhile, scrapping the old

---

[*] Peter had recently learned of the disaster that had befallen his forces in Central Asia, which was ruled by several independent khanates and emirates. Hearing reports of the wealth in the khanate of Khiva (in today's Uzbekistan), he commissioned a converted Circassian princeling, Alexander Bekovich-Cherkassky, to lead a small expedition to persuade Khiva to accept Russian suzerainty. Bekovich managed to defeat the khan, who then tricked and captured him. Bekovich was beheaded, his body stuffed and displayed in the khan's palace.

Muscovite offices and copying the Swedish administration, he reorganized the government into "collegia,"* but, without a local system beneath them, his Senate and collegia continued to host pugilistic squabbles between his magnates. Infuriated, Peter compared them to "fishwives." The courtiers were amazed that Alexei was returning: "Did you hear that the fool tsarevich is coming home and they're bringing Afrosina?" muttered Dolgoruky. "He'll get a coffin not a wedding!"

On 21 January 1718, Alexei, guarded by Tolstoy and Rumiantsev, crossed the Russian border. Furious father and anxious son converged on Moscow for their grim showdown.[5]

On 3 February 1718, Peter and his grandees, guarded by three battalions of loyal Preobrazhensky Guards, muskets armed, watched as the prisoner Alexei was escorted by Tolstoy into the Kremlin's Grand Dining Hall. The son fell to his knees, confessed his guilt and begged for mercy. Peter offered it—if he renounced the throne and named traitors. Father and son retired to a side room where the latter denounced his associates and renounced the succession. Then Peter declared his baby Petrushka as the heir, while Shafirov read out Alexei's pardon.

The next day, appointing Tolstoy as chief of a new Secret Chancellery of Investigations, Peter launched a case against his son whom he surely saw as an existential threat. But he must also have personally hated him. Questioned by Tolstoy, Alexei named Kikin and Dolgoruky as his supporters. Only Afrosina knew nothing. Peter launched a purge of his disloyal retainers. In Petersburg, Menshikov arrested Kikin and Dolgoruky. Kikin and Alexei's servants were tortured by Tolstoy and his assistant Andrei Ushakov while Peter watched.

The tsar struggled to understand how Kikin had betrayed him: "How could a clever man like you go against me?" he asked during the torture session.

"The mind needs space if you restrict it," answered Kikin.

Dolgoruky's betrayal must have stung Peter: this hero of Poltava and Pruth, godfather of his daughter Elizaveta, resented the tsar's despotism. "If it weren't for the tsarina's [Catherine's] influence on the sovereign's cruel character," he had told Alexei, "our life would be impossible." Dolgoruky confessed to sympathy for the tsarevich without torture. Here we get a hint of just how much Peter's Jolly Company of

---

* These new departments (initially eight then nine) took the place of the old offices (*prikazy*). The collegia presidents initially were also senators. Golovkin was president of the Foreign Collegium; Menshikov of the Collegium of War. The whole point of the collegia was that they were *not* ministries, being (in theory at least) under collective boards rather than individual control as part of an attempt to limit corruption.

henchmen secretly resented his tyranny. Yet even within the sanctum of
ruling families, the price of betraying the tsar was death.

Peter suspected that his ex-wife Eudoxia had known of her son's
plans. Now forty-four, she had been a nun for nineteen years—or so
Peter thought. When she was investigated, he discovered that Dosifei,
bishop of Rostov, had told her that when Alexei was tsar she would be
tsarina again. Eudoxia had stopped wearing the veil long before and had
taken a lover, an officer named Stepan Glebov who, under torture, refused to admit treason. The bishop of Rostov was arrested and accused
of wishing for the tsar's death. Once again, Eudoxia's Lopukhin family
was at the centre of the opposition: her brother Avraam was implicated.

On 14 March, before a vast crowd in Red Square, the bishop and
three of the servants were broken with hammers and left to die on the
wheel. Two noblewomen, including one of Catherine's ladies, Princess
Anastasia Golitsyna, were flogged. Glebov, Eudoxia's lover, was knouted,
burned with red-hot irons and nailed on to a spiked plank for two days.
Kikin was shattered on the wheel, revived, broken again and left to
suffer until the second day when Peter arrived to inspect his victims.
Kikin begged Peter for mercy. The tsar had him put out of his misery
by beheading, but Glebov refused to confess and Peter allowed the next
stage of his punishment to go ahead: impalement with a sharpened
stake up his anus. Peter ordered that he be dressed in furs to make
sure he lived longer and suffered more. Avraam Lopukhin was executed
too; Dolgoruky escaped the axe but, exiled to Kazan, his downfall was
absolute. In fact he would return, only to fall again, enjoying one of the
most dramatic careers of this rollercoaster century.

On 19 March, Peter, travelling with his son and Tolstoy, returned
to Petersburg where Alexei was confined to the next-door mansion,
guarded twenty-four hours a day by soldiers with lit fuses over loaded
cannon.

Alexei begged Catherine to persuade Peter to let him marry Afrosina.
Instead she was arrested. Alexei and the girl were separately interrogated by Peter. Afrosina damned her lover with revelations of his hopes
for an army rebellion, his plans to overturn all of Peter's achievements
and his letters to the emperor denouncing his father. Struggling now
for his life, Alexei admitted writing letters while drunk but insisted that,
though he expected Peter to die within two years, he would not have rebelled in his lifetime. But on 16 May Alexei broke, naming Sheremetev
and even the prince-caesar as sympathizers. Peter took both Afrosina
and Alexei out to his cottage, Mon Plaisir, on his new estate Peterhof,
outside Petersburg, and interrogated them again. Peter focused on
whether Alexei was planning to rebel while his father was still alive: if

the army had mutinied, Alexei admitted, "and if they'd called me, even in your lifetime, I would have joined the rebels."

Alexei was thrown into the Trubetskoi Bastion of the Peter and Paul Fortress. Next he was tried for treason. Faced with reams of Alexei's confessions, the bishops showed caution, recommending Old Testament severity and New Testament mercy, but the senators, their minds concentrated by the knowledge that many had been implicated by Alexei, agreed to any "necessary examination": torture.

On 19 June, Alexei received twenty-five blows of the knout which failed to generate any more revelations. On the 24th, he received fifteen more, then another twenty-five lashes and then a further nine. Peter had all Alexei's courtiers tortured and his confessor's testimony was as damning as that of Afrosina. Alexei admitted, "I wished for my father's death." Now convinced that Alexei had planned his assassination, Peter was satisfied. After so many blows, Alexei was broken. Just to be sure, Peter sent Tolstoy with a last couple of questions. Alexei confessed that he would have paid the emperor to raise an army against the tsar.

That night, Menshikov, Golovkin, Apraxin, Tolstoy and others, sitting as a tribunal, sentenced Alexei to death for "horrid double parricide, against the Father of his country and his Father by nature." The next day, Peter sent an official to tell Alexei of the sentence—but he was dying anyway.

At 8 a.m. on 26 June, Peter and his entourage visited Alexei "for a session in the torture chamber." Menshikov's schedule records that he himself stayed half an hour, but the fortress log reveals that some of them stayed for three hours, leaving Alexei at 11 a.m. utterly broken. "At 6 p.m.," reads the log, "Tsarevich Alexei Petrovich died." Did Peter kill him personally, did he send over Rumiantsev to strangle him or did he expire of apoplexy? Most likely he died of shock, blood loss or infection after knouting, which would have flayed and shredded his back to the bone. Forty lashes of the knout could kill a strong man and Alexei suffered many more. (An expert executioner could kill a man with a few lashes by breaking the backbone or keep him alive for weeks.) The body lay in the Holy Trinity Church for four days but on 27 and 29 June Peter held parties to celebrate Poltava and his nameday. On the 30th, Peter wept at the funeral as Alexei was buried in the family's new Peter and Paul tomb. On 9 December Alexei's confessor and servants were beheaded while others had their tongues cut out and nostrils clipped. Peter's real view was expressed in the inscription on a medal he had struck at the end of the year: "The horizon has cleared."

Peter had thickened with age; he was burly and husky now but also wearier and more distrustful. The inquisition into corruption cost more heads. Menshikov survived. "Menshikov will always be Menshikov," Peter told Catherine, but "unless he reforms he will lose his head."* Yet none of this restrained Peter's driving ambition to change Russia and build Petersburg.[6]

During summer, Peter lived simply in his small Summer Palace, waking up at 4 a.m. and starting work still wearing a nightshirt and a Chinese dressing-gown, standing at an upright desk to scrawl out his orders. The palace, on the mainland, had just fourteen rooms; he lived upstairs, Catherine downstairs. When he was relaxing, he worked on his lathe in the Turning Room or in his Laboratory where he experimented with fireworks. Then in his plain green coat of the Preobrazhensky Guards, high black boots (in the Kremlin Armoury, remarkable for their size—and the smallness of the feet) and brandishing his cane, he headed off early to meetings at the Admiralty and Senate—the government had been moved to Petersburg in 1713. Unlike Menshikov, who proceeded through the city in a fan-shaped carriage with postilions and outriders, Peter often toured the city at mid-afternoon in a plain two-wheeled two-seater carriage with the city's police commissioner (a post that resembled a modern mayor), Anton Devier, born Antonio de Vieira, a Portuguese Jew whom he had hired as a cabinboy in Holland. In the evenings, he relaxed at the Four Frigates tavern, smoking Dutch pipes and drinking German beer or pepper vodka with Dutch sailors.

Assisted by Menshikov and Devier,[†] Peter drove the creation of Petersburg by sheer will. No detail, from public buildings to road grids, was too small for him. "No one defecates except in the appointed places,"

---

* Afrosina escaped punishment: she later married and lived for many years in Petersburg; Eudoxia returned to her monastery. Meanwhile the older generation of Peter's retainers was dying out: Prince-Caesar Romodanovsky died in 1717. Peter mourned the old monster to Romodanovsky's son Ivan: "There goes everyone one way or another by God's will. Bear this in mind and don't give in to grief. And please don't imagine I have abandoned you or forgotten your father's good deeds." Peter appointed Ivan Romodanovsky as new prince-caesar and chief of the Preobrazhensky Office, even though he more often used Tolstoy's Secret Chancellery for sensitive matters. Prince-Pope Zotov died in December 1717: Peter oversaw the election of a new prince-pope in a ritual involving the kissing of the bare breasts of the arch-abbess of the Female Synod, Daria Rzhevskaya, and voting with coloured eggs. Peter Buturlin, a veteran crony ("Peter-Prick" in Synod jargon) was chosen just before Alexei's return.

† The parvenu loathes no one so much as another upstart. Hence Menshikov's hatred for both Devier and Shafirov was visceral. When Devier fell in love with his unmarried sister Anna Menshikova, the prince rejected his suit. But Anna fell pregnant. Devier asked Menshikov to allow the marriage to legitimize the child, only for the prince to kick him downstairs. Devier appealed to Peter, who ordered the marriage. Later Menshikov got his revenge.

he specified in his decree creating the Admiralty. "If anyone defecates in other than the appointed places, he is to be beaten with a cat-o'-nine-tails and ordered to clean it up." The city was expanding from its original buildings on Petrograd Island and around the fortress. Even while he was destroying his son, Peter was directing a multinational team of architects on a variety of projects.*

Social life still revolved around the frequent meetings of the Drunken Synod and raucous revels at Menshikov's palace and sailors' taverns, but Peter wanted to foster civilization of the sort he had admired in Paris and Amsterdam. He ordered Devier to hold polite tea-and-drinks parties for both sexes, drafting his *Regulations for Holding Assemblies* to lay down the rules. The girls must dress in Western fashions, with French rouge and no more blackened teeth; the men in German or Dutch coats. Dancing, card games and pipe-smoking had to be conducted with decorum—no vomiting or fighting! No one should be forced to drink or do anything "on pain of emptying the Great Eagle" goblet of brandy. Those who did not attend were fined—and no one could leave early because Peter placed soldiers at the door. He also drafted *The Honourable Mirror of Youth*—his guide to civilized behaviour—and anyone who spat, talked with their mouth full or vomited was likely to receive a whack from the tsarist cane.

Peter's creativity came at a terrible price: his new city was effectively built by slave workers, criminals sentenced to suffer his new punishment, forced hard labour—known as *katorga*, meaning "galley," and indeed many of these convicts rowed his Baltic fleet while others extracted gold and silver in the Far Eastern mines of Altai and Nerchinsk. Untold numbers toiled in the icy waters of the Neva building Petersburg and nameless legions of them perished to create Peter's dream.[7]

"Our people are like children who never get down to learning their alphabet unless their master forces them" was how Peter justified his pursuit of progress by terror. "How compulsion is needed in our country," he exclaimed on another occasion, "where the people are novices at everything." He regularly beat his beloved Saxon chef with his cane

---

* He had Trezzini create new buildings for the collegia on Vasilevsky Island near where his German architect Georg Johann Mattarnovi designed the Kunstkammer to house his collection of curiosities and live exhibits including a hermaphrodite who later escaped. Dwarfs and giants appeared alive (and later embalmed) along with the genitalia of a hermaphrodite, Siamese twins and two-headed babies and (soon) the preserved heads of ill-fated courtiers. His new French architect-general Alexandre LeBlond laid out Nevsky Prospect, the main boulevard of the city that ran for two and a half miles from the Winter Palace and Admiralty out to Trezzini's St. Alexander Nevsky Monastery—it remains the artery of today's city.

and when he noticed a broken bridge on one of his inspections of the city with Devier, he smacked him with his cane and then invited him back into the carriage: "Get in, brother." His 1716 Military Code was draconian, applying the death penalty to 122 charges (double that of the previous Code of 1649) and specifying barbarous new delicacies such as breaking on the wheel and quartering, borrowed like many of his new ideas from the West. He knew that "they call me a savage ruler and tyrant," but he did not apologize for it. "Who says this? People who don't know . . . that many of my subjects placed most foul hindrances to carrying out my best plans for the benefit of the fatherland and therefore it was essential to treat them with great severity."

His menacing hyperactivity was always for the "common good," and though he was happiest living in his small villas, wearing plain clothes and disdaining court ritual, after visiting Versailles he realized that a European potentate needed the panoply as well as the plenitude of power.[8] Catherine, the peasant-tsarina who now dyed her hair black to downplay her tanned skin and brassy blondeness, was happy to enjoy the splendour and provide the court that an empire required. Peter knocked down the first wooden Winter Palace and had Mattarnovi build a slightly larger version with a hall for receptions while he created a galaxy of rural palaces around the city.*

Soon after Alexei's death, in August 1718, Catherine gave birth to a daughter, Natalya. Peter loved his daughters, often asking after "Annushka," "Lizetta" (Elizaveta, after whom he named one of his ships) and "our big girl Natalya." Elizaveta recalled that her father "often required an account of what I learned in the course of the day. When he was satisfied he gave recommendations accompanied by a kiss and sometimes a present." Nonetheless Peter hoped to exploit them to make useful marriages in Europe. Meanwhile his only surviving son Petrushka had barely teethed before he started to display military prowess. "He's drilling his soldiers and firing cannon," reported Catherine to Peter about the three-year-old "recruit," who missed his father: "He has

---

* His favourite was Peterhof, nineteen miles west of Petersburg. Set on the seaside, he first built a one-storey villa, Mon Plaisir, where he could enjoy views of his Kronstadt naval base. He designed it in Dutch Colonial style with a study devoted to his naval hobbies and a Chinese lacquer room. Then after his Parisian visit, he decided to emulate Versailles and the Château de Marly with their fountains. LeBlond built a palace and the sculptor Carlo Rastrelli helped design the first waterworks. When the tsar and tsarina were there, Peter stayed in Mon Plaisir and Catherine in the big palace whence she would come down and cook for him in the Dutch-tiled pantry. They also developed another suburban palace. Much earlier Peter had given Catherine an estate fifteen miles south of the city that they named Tsarskoe Selo (Tsar Village). She surprised him by commissioning the German architect Johann Friedrich Braunstein to build her a palace there which was later vastly expanded by her daughter Elizaveta into the baroque wedding cake that we see today.

a bone to pick with you: when I remind him Papa's away, he doesn't like it. He likes it better when Papa's here."

After her pregnancy, Catherine returned to her own boisterous coterie, made up of the same ladies as fifteen years before, whom she ruled with the same despotic whim as her husband. After being flogged publicly for sympathizing with Alexei, Anastasia Golitsyna was welcomed back as Catherine's mistress of revels. After the death of Daria Rzhevskaya, Peter appointed her princess-abbess of the Drunken Female Synod, once rewarding her for her canine "howling." Matrena Balk, Catherine's mistress of robes, was the sister of Anna Mons, Peter's original mistress; Catherine's chamberlain was their flashy brother, Willem.

Catherine shared Peter's iron party endurance which exhausted her courtiers. "Sire, the Tsarina is never willing to go to sleep before 3 a.m.," complained Golitsyna to Peter, "and I have to be constantly by her." Whenever the other ladies-in-waiting fell asleep, "The Lady Tsarina deigns to say, 'Auntie are you dozing?' while Mary Hamilton walks around the room with a mattress which she spreads on the floor and Matrena Balk strides around reprimanding everyone. With your presence I shall get freedom from bedroom service."

Peter casually and impulsively chose mistresses from Catherine's retinue.* "I hear you also have a mistress?" Frederick IV of Denmark once asked Peter. "My brother," replied Peter, unsmiling, "my harlots don't cost me much but yours cost you thousands which could be better spent." His "harlots" received no privileges—and a few rolls with the tsar were not enough to save a girl's head, however beautiful.[9]

In the autumn of 1718, Peter launched an investigation into one of Catherine's maids-of-honour who was his ex-mistress: Mary Hamilton, descendant of Scottish royalists. "Much addicted to gallantry," she managed to become pregnant three times by her lover Ivan Orlov, one of Peter's adjutants who, summoned urgently by the tsar, was so terrified

---

* His most beautiful mistress was Princess Maria Cherkasskaya, but his favourite was said to be the well-educated Maria Matveeva. She was the granddaughter of Tsar Alexei's minister Matveev, who had been thrown on to the musketeers' pikes in 1682. Peter married her off to Rumiantsev as a reward for his delivering Tsarevich Alexei. Maria outlived her husband and everyone else to become the doyenne of the courts of the Empresses Elizaveta and Catherine the Great; raised to countess, she dined out (with much innuendo) on her memories of Peter. Her son Peter, born in 1720 and said to be the tsar's son, became one of Catherine the Great's best generals. Peter started an affair with a true child of his carnival-court, Princess Avdotia Rzhevskaya, the fifteen-year-old daughter of Daria, the arch-abbess of the female branch of the Drunken Synod, which went on for many years. She was notoriously wanton and untameable—Peter nicknamed her Virago. Even after he had married her off to General Grigory Chernyshev, she was said to have given the tsar VD, for which he told her husband to whip her. Her son Zakhar, who later ran Catherine the Great's army, may have been Peter's.

that he fell to his knees and accidentally blurted out a confession of his affair with Mary—and how she had aborted three babies. In the debauched round of court promiscuity, her lover was also sleeping with Peter's mistress Avdotia Rzevskaya. Mary tried to win Orlov back by stealing Catherine's jewellery and giving it to him. Fearing her infidelity to the tsar would be exposed and she too would be tortured, Avdotia accused Mary of claiming that Catherine lightened her skin using beeswax. In this bonfire of the mistresses, Catherine furiously searched Mary's room and found her jewels, and Peter recalled that a dead baby had been found near the palace. Hamilton was arrested, tortured in front of Peter, and confessed to killing three babies. Peter had her sentenced to death. Two tsarinas, Catherine and Praskovia, begged for mercy. He refused to "be either Saul or Ahab nor violate divine law by excess of kindness." On 14 March 1719, Mary appeared gorgeous on the scaffold in a white silk dress with black ribbons, but she expected a pardon, particularly when Peter mounted the gibbet. He kissed her but then said quietly: "I can't violate the law to save your life. Endure your punishment courageously and address your prayers to God with a heart full of faith." She fainted, and he nodded at the executioner, who brought down his sword. Peter lifted up the beautiful head and began to lecture the crowd on anatomy, pointing out the sliced vertebrae, open windpipe and dripping arteries, before kissing the bloody lips and dropping the head. He crossed himself and strode off. Peter, that connoisseur of decapitation who had found the beheadings of his musketeers so curious, had the head embalmed and placed in his Cabinet of Curiosities, where an English visitor inspecting it "in a crystal vessel" noted that "The face is the most beautifulest my eyes ever beheld."

Soon afterwards, Peter learned of a more welcome death. Charles XII was inspecting his siege of a Danish fortress when his aides heard a sound like "a stone thrown into mud." A bullet had hit Ironhead in one temple and passed out of the other.

A third death delivered a cruel blow. On 25 April 1719, Menshikov visited the bedside of little Petrushka. Peter had arranged the marriage of his French giant, Nicholai Zhigant, to a giantess.* He and Catherine were celebrating at the gigantist wedding when they heard the news that

---

* A new jester had recently joined his court and he quickly became a favourite: he was a Portuguese Jew called Jan la Costa. He was an intelligent, multilingual failed merchant who combined coruscating wit with biblical learning. Peter liked to debate religion with him. When the Samoyeds, a tribe of Siberian reindeer herders, arrived to put on shows in Petersburg, Peter declared La Costa their king and made them swear allegiance to him and gave him an island as his realm. Peter's doctor Lestocq tried to seduce La Costa's daughter, at which the jester appealed to the tsar. Lestocq was reprimanded. Costa long outlived Peter, still a fixture at court in the 1730s.

Petrushka had died. Catherine was heartbroken: her court records show that she kept the baby's toys with her until her own death. As for Peter, he suffered an epileptic fit and locked himself in his room for days until his henchmen begged him to end his "useless and excessive sorrow." The child's death ruined his plan for the succession. But before solving it in his own eccentric way, he had to end the war with Sweden.

Peter launched an assault on the coasts of Sweden, even raiding Stockholm itself, persisting until the new king sued for peace, agreeing a treaty at Nystadt. On 4 September 1721, five days after the peace had been signed,* a euphoric Peter disembarked at the Peter and Paul Fortress, prayed in church, reported to Prince-Caesar Ivan Romodanovsky and then, mounting a dais, toasted the weeping and cheering crowd, who were offered pails of free alcohol as his cannon fired salvoes. "Rejoice and thank God!" he shouted. This was the start of two months of partying. At the wild wedding of the new prince-pope, "Peter-Prick" Buturlin, to the young widow of the old one, toasts were drunk out of giant goblets shaped like male and female genitalia, the groom was tipped into a vat of beer and their wedding night was spent in an al fresco bed on Senate Square.

On 22 October, to the blare of trumpets and the thunder of cannonades, Petersburg celebrated a Roman triumph. After a sermon by Archbishop Feofan Prokopovich,† Chancellor Golovkin hailed the tsar as "Father of the Fatherland," an epithet awarded to Roman Caesars, and "Peter the Great, Emperor of all Russia," effectively making an offer that had been agreed by the Senate a few days earlier—and which was accepted by the tsar with a nod. From now on, Muscovy became Russia and the tsar was also an emperor (Peter simply adopted the Roman word *imperator*) while any sons would be "caesarovichi"—sons of Caesar. Then the real party started, with giants dressed as babies, the prince-pope's and cardinals' carriages pulled by pigs, bears and dogs.

---

* Nystadt was negotiated by two of Peter's most talented aides: Count James—Yakov—Bruce, a Scotsman, superb organizer and chief of artillery who was a bibliophile, alchemist, astronomer and magus known as the Russian Faust for his esoteric experiments. Andrei Osterman was the multilingual son of a Westphalian pastor who had become one of Peter's secretaries and senior diplomats. "Osterman never makes a mistake," said Peter, who now raised Bruce to count and Osterman first to baron then to vice-president of the Foreign Collegium. Peter married Osterman brilliantly to his own relative, Martha Streshneva.

† Peter appointed Prokopovich as procurator of the Holy Synod in charge of the Church, a role that evolved into the post of ober-procurator, always held by a layman, effectively the tsar's church minister. There would be no more patriarchs under the Romanovs. After the February 1917 Revolution a patriarch was appointed, but the post was abolished by the Bolsheviks. It took a militant atheist-Marxist, trained as a boy for the priesthood, to restore the patriarchate in 1943 to rally nationalist spirit in the Great Patriotic War: Stalin.

Yet "time is death," said Peter, who did not rest. Now that Russia was finally at peace in Europe, the overthrow of the Shah of Persia and Persian persecution of Christians in the eastern Caucasus offered the opportunity to fight Muslims and expand the empire along the coastline of the Caspian Sea. Peter could not resist a new exotic war which accelerated a frenzy of reforms and concentrated his mind on the succession.

In January 1722, Peter, inspired by his belief that universal state service should be the only condition for eminence in society, created the Table of Ranks, a hierarchy to encourage competition for honours and attract new talent. Articulating the militarization of the high nobility, Peter declared that the military were superior to civilians. He ordered the nobility to serve as officers or administrators for life, but at the same time rising men, even the sons of peasants, could achieve nobility just by reaching a certain rank.* But war and splendour are expensive: Peter funded the Russian court and war machine by creating a new head tax to be paid by each male peasant instead of each household, increasing the strain on the serfs, some 93 per cent of the population, who already had to serve almost a lifetime—twenty-five years—in the army. Knowing he might die in the south, Peter declared, "It will always be for the ruling monarch to appoint whom he wishes to the succession." As he set off, he promoted his forceful favourite Pavel Iaguzhinsky, to the new post of procurator-general of the Senate. "He knows my intentions," he told the senators. "What he deems necessary, that do!" The procurator-general was meant to supervise the government. "Here is my eye," Peter said to the senators, "with which I shall see everything."[10]

In May 1722 Peter and 60,000 troops, accompanied by Catherine (as well as his current mistress, a pretty Greek, Princess Maria Cantemir), marched down the Caspian coast, which was then the territory of Persia. Defeating Persian troops, he managed to take the ancient port

---

* Henceforth nobility was a reward for service, and the state in the person of the tsar would decide a man's position, helping to ensure that the Russian nobility was so interlinked with the autocracy that it never developed the independence truly to challenge the throne (except for spasms of regicidal strangling), but it was a circular dependence as the Romanovs never developed an alternative support either. Peter divided his servitors into three services—military, civil and court—each divided into fourteen classes. All officers became nobles, while a man reaching Grade 8 in the civil service automatically became a hereditary nobleman. But Peter still looked to his traditional nobles, Saltykovs and Golitsyns, to fill the top grades. A tiny web of families, around 5,000 individuals, continued to dominate army, court and countryside: about 8 per cent of the population owned 58.9 per cent. This was their privilege in return for serving in the army and government. But the nobles hated this enforced service and as soon as Peter was gone, they undermined his rules, with noble children joining the Guards at the age of seven. Soon nobles were allowed to avoid service altogether. Yet the Table of Ranks, symbol of the militarization of Russia, endured until 1917.

of Derbent,* but disease, lack of provisions and destruction of ships in a storm paralysed the expedition. The heat was so punishing that Peter and the ever game Catherine shaved their heads, he sporting a wide-brimmed fedora, she a bombardier's cap. Peter, suffering from a bladder infection possibly caused by VD, retreated to Astrakhan, but his troops later took the key port of Baku.

Peter, exhausted, returned to Moscow where he found Menshikov at war with Shafirov, brawling at senatorial meetings. Menshikov's protégé Prince Matvei Gagarin had embezzled large sums while he governed Siberia (it was said he was so rich that he shod his horses in gold). When Peter had Gagarin hanged outside the Senate, he forced his grandees to watch.

"Heads will fly," Peter warned. "I don't know who I can trust. I have only traitors around me." He had all of them investigated, but the charges stuck to both Menshikov and Shafirov, whom he sentenced to death. As Shafirov laid his head on the block, the axe was raised and at the last minute, Peter's adjutant announced the sentence was commuted to Siberian exile. Menshikov was seriously rattled. "I recognize my guilt and realize I can't justify my actions," he told Peter. "I tearfully and in utter humility beseech Your Majesty's forgiveness." Peter beat him with his cane. When Catherine interceded, Peter warned her: "Menshikov was conceived in lawlessness and he'll end his life in knavery. If he doesn't mend his ways, he'll end up shorter by a head." Menshikov was fined and sacked from the War Collegium. Peter sentenced more officials to death, insisting "Don't bury the body—let it stay on top of the ground for all to see," and told Iaguzhinsky to hang anyone who stole so much as a rope. Iaguzhinsky advised against such severity, "unless Your Majesty wishes to be left alone without servitors or subjects. We all steal, only some more and more visibly than others."[11]

On 5 March 1723, back in Petersburg, Peter inspected his buildings, launched ships and organized his Drunken Synod, now calling himself "Archdeacon Pachomius Crams-with-his-Prick." When he travelled down the coast to check his new Reval palace he missed Catherine: "All's merry here but when I come to the country house and you're not there, I feel so sad!" Plagued by his bladder, Peter needed to name his successor. Grandson, daughters, nieces? Who was it to be?

A young prince, Karl Friedrich, duke of Holstein-Gottorp, arrived in Petersburg hoping to win Russian help against Denmark—and to marry one of the emperor's daughters. Peter designated Annushka,

---

* In Islamic Daghestan, Peter ordered women to be unveiled, and Catherine invited the soldiers to file through her tent so the men could admire them: no wonder she was so popular with the troops. In Derbent, Peter built a *domik*, a cottage, to live in.

then vacillated about an actual betrothal. Holstein stayed for more than two years in Petersburg, becoming one of the family almost by osmosis.

Meanwhile Peter was irked by his two nieces, the morose Anna of Courland and the frivolous Ekaterina of Mecklenburg, who both had excellent claims to the throne since they were the daughters of Tsar Ivan V. Their mother Tsarina Praskovia loved the attractive Ekaterina, nicknamed the "Wild Duchess," and persuaded Peter to let her leave the violent Leopold of Mecklenburg and come home with her newborn daughter. When diplomats visited mother and daughter, tsarina and duchess resided in a filthy bedroom with a "half-blind dirty mandora-player reeking of garlic and sweat," who sang filthy songs, and "an old dirty blind wretched stupid woman who wandered wearing nothing more than a blouse." They made "this hag dance and she would imme-diately lift her stinking old rags in front and back and show all she had beneath."

Yet Tsarina Praskovia was disgusted by the conduct of her sulky daughter Anna, the widowed duchess of Courland. Peter had made Anna stay in the Courlandian capital. Lonely, poor and desperate to marry again, she wrote over thirty letters begging Peter for help. When he ignored them, Anna beseeched Catherine "my dear Sovereign to ask our dear uncle to have mercy on me to settle the matter of my marriage" and to ask also for money: "I have nothing more than the damask you ordered and I have neither suitable diamonds nor laces nor linens nor a fine dress and I can hardly maintain my home and put food on the table."

Peter despatched a courtier, Peter Bestuzhev-Riumin, to run Courland—and Anna, whom he soon seduced. He was nineteen years her senior. This appalled Tsarina Praskovia, who appealed to Peter. But "I am entirely pleased with Bestuzhev," Anna told Catherine, "and he conducts my business here very well." As for her mother, she stole her daughter's paltry allowance. "I shan't live in the misery and suffering caused by this feud with my mother," declared Anna. Praskovia cursed her daughter.

Mother and daughter both appealed to Catherine, who managed to impose peace. "I've heard from our Sovereign Catherine that you con-sider yourself under my curse," Praskovia wrote grudgingly to Anna. "I forgive you everything for the sake of Her Majesty and I absolve you of every sin committed before me."

When Praskovia, last link to old Muscovy, died, Peter gave her a mag-nificent funeral, but her daughters would not succeed him. Suddenly he announced that "since Our best beloved Spouse Consort and Empress Catherine has been a great support to us, we have decided she shall be crowned."[12]

\*

On 7 May 1724, Peter, in a blue tunic with red stockings, and Catherine, wearing a crimson dress sewn with gold, with five ladies to bear her train, flanked by pageboys in green outfits and white wigs and Guardsmen in bright green with gold braid, boots and spurs, emerged from the Kremlin's Terem Palace, nodded thrice at the crowd and then came down the Red Staircase, processing to the Dormition Cathedral.\* In this new-model ceremony, Peter, not the clergy, was the source of all power. He placed the crown on Catherine's head, handing her the orb—but keeping the sceptre. As she knelt, tears streamed down her face, but when she tried to kiss his hand, Peter raised her.

When Peter returned to Petersburg in June, his bladder infection, known as stone and strangury, flared up again. He could no longer pass urine. Surgery was the only answer. Peter had to lie on a table holding his doctor's hands as his Dutch surgeon passed a catheter into his bladder to relieve the pressure of the urine. Blood and pus seeped out, which suggests there was already a raging infection. Finally he was able to pass a stone. Yet his illness did not stop Peter sailing on the Gulf of Finland and even plunging into the sea to rescue some sailors. Catherine kept an eye on his health: when he was partying on a new frigate, she sailed past on her own boat and called in through the porthole: "Time to go home, old man."

Then on 8 November, he swooped on Catherine's court.[13]

---

\* The retinue was a snapshot of who was in favour: Peter was attended by Menshikov, Catherine by the Duke of Holstein and Apraxin with Chancellor Golovkin and his deputy Osterman bearing her train. At Catherine's request, Prince Vasily Dolgoruky, who had been close to execution six years earlier, was pardoned and invited to carry the orb. Bruce bore the new imperial crown with a ruby "as large as a pigeon's egg"—and 2,562 diamonds. Tolstoy, who carried the mace, was afterwards promoted to count. Menshikov scattered the coins. Soon afterwards, more of his crimes were exposed. Peter lost patience and refused even to see Menshikov.

SCENE 2

# The Empresses

# CAST

PETER THE GREAT, tsar and emperor 1682–1725

CATHERINE I (née Scavronskaya), empress 1725–7, widow of Peter the Great

Alexander Menshikov, prince, her former lover, generalissimus

Peter Tolstoy, count, chief of the Secret Chancellery

Andrei Ushakov, chief of the Secret Chancellery, baron

Andrei Osterman, count, vice-chancellor, general-admiral, "Oracle"

PETER II, emperor 1727–30, son of Tsarevich Alexei, grandson of Peter the Great

Prince Ivan Dolgoruky, Peter II's grand chamberlain and best friend

Princess Ekaterina Dolgorukaya, Peter II's fiancée

Prince Alexei Lukich Dolgoruky, father of Ivan and Ekaterina

Prince Vasily Lukich Dolgoruky, uncle of Ivan and Ekaterina, brother of Alexei

Prince Dmitri Golitsyn, member of Supreme Privy Council and architect of offer of throne to Anna

Prince Vasily Vladimirovich Dolgoruky, Peter the Great's favourite, veteran of battles of Poltava and Pruth, exiled in the Alexei case, pardoned 1724, promoted by Peter II to field marshal, member of Supreme Privy Council

ANNA, empress 1730–40, daughter of Tsar Ivan V and Tsarina Praskovia (née Saltykova), duchess of Courland

Ekaterina, Anna's elder sister, duchess of Mecklenburg, married Karl Leopold, duke of Mecklenburg, "Wild Duchess"

Ernst Biron, ex-groom, Anna's lover and later duke of Courland, briefly regent

Prince Alexei Cherkassky, member of the Council, later chancellor

Semyon Saltykov, Anna's first cousin, governor of Moscow

Artemii Volynsky, member of the Council

Christoph von Münnich, count, field marshal, head of the War Collegium, later premier minister

Ernst von Münnich, the marshal's son, chamberlain, later grand marshal of court

Anna Leopoldovna (née Elisabeth of Mecklenburg), regent 1740–1, daughter of Ekaterina and Leopold of Mecklenburg, Anna's niece and heiress, princess of Brunswick

Prince Anton Ulrich of Brunswick, husband of Anna Leopoldovna, later generalissimus

IVAN VI, emperor 1740–1, the Brunswicks' eldest son

Baroness Julie von Mengden, friend of Anna of Brunswick, "Julka"

Count Maurice Lynar, Anna of Brunswick's lover, Julie's fiancé, Saxon ambassador

ELIZAVETA, empress 1741–62, daughter of Peter the Great and Catherine I, first cousin of Ivan V's daughter Anna

Anna, her elder sister, married the duke of Holstein, "Annushka"

C atherine's golden boy was her chamberlain Willem Mons, aged thirty, the brother of Peter's early mistress. Mons, who had served at Poltava, was "one of the most handsome men I've ever seen," according to a Danish envoy, but also one of the most ostentatious. At her glittering new court,* he liked to dress in plumed cap, velvet suit and silver cummerbund and was mocked for ennobling his name to Moens de la Croix—but his splendour was paid for in bribes, which he charged for access to Catherine. Worse, it was rumoured that he was her lover. "Her relations with M. Mons were public knowledge," wrote Jean-Jacques Campredon, the French envoy. "I am Your Grace's slave," read a letter found among his papers, "and true only to you, ruler of my heart." Was the empress too clever to risk an affair? Did she fall in love?

On 27 October 1724, when Peter returned to St. Petersburg after his tour, he was informed of Mons's bribe-taking. On 8 November, he dined with Catherine, coolly greeted the omnipresent Mons, then retired. When Mons was smoking a pipe before bed, General Ushakov, deputy chief of the Secret Chancellery, arrested him. Next day, Peter attended the interrogations, but before the torture had started, Mons fainted and confessed to embezzlement.

Catherine may have appealed for Mons. "I made you and I can unmake you as easily as this," Peter supposedly screamed at Catherine as he smashed a Venetian mirror in the palace.

"Do you think that will improve the beauty of the palace?" replied Catherine calmly. But a wounded tiger is always the most dangerous and Mons was doomed. While he awaited execution, he wrote love poetry in German:

I know how I will die
I dared to love the one
I should have only respected,
I burn with passion for her.

\*

* Peter had devised Russia's first Westernized court for Catherine with a Germanic hierarchy of courtiers from *Oberhofmarschall* (grand marshal of court) down to *Kammerherr* (chamberlain) and *Kammerjunker* (gentleman of the bedchamber), rigged out in green, gold and scarlet-trimmed tunics and white wigs, with equally flamboyant uniforms for his blackamoors—all designed of course by the supreme control freak.

On 16 November, in freezing weather, Mons was beheaded on Trinity Square; his sister Matrena was flogged and exiled. Mons's head was preserved in a jar and presented to Catherine.*[1]

On the day of the execution, Peter ordered the betrothal of his daughter Annushka to the duke of Holstein and, in a display of grace under pressure, Catherine practised dancing the minuet with her daughters. It was agreed that Annushka would renounce the succession herself, but their children would ultimately succeed to the throne.

A cheerful Peter drafted decrees, despatched the Danish navigator Vitus Bering to explore the borders of America,[†] and on 3 January 1725 wrote a note to his Moscow governor which catches his fearsome tone: "I've no idea if you're alive or dead or have forsaken your duty or turned to crime, but since we left Moscow I've seen no reports from you. If you haven't arrived here by 10 February, you will be the cause of your own ruin!" But, long before that, Peter was contemplating his own.

On 6 January, the ailing emperor presided over the Blessing of the Waters on the frozen Neva—one of the few Muscovite religious rituals transferred to Petersburg. After ten days, doctors diagnosed inflammation of the bladder and probably gangrene, but Peter, in agony and unable to urinate, retired to bed in Catherine's apartments upstairs at the Winter Palace in a small room off the Grand Hall. Nursed devotedly by Catherine, who scarcely left him, he kept working from bed, but on 23 January he realized he was dying. He told Prokopovich, his chief churchman, that he was "apprehensive of his coming fate," observing that "mortal man is a wretched creature." Two days later, the panicking doctors, all Germans and Dutch, managed to extract almost two pints of putrid urine from the feverish emperor, who then rallied. The next day, he felt well enough to eat porridge, which brought on violent spasms.

---

* This head too was later placed in the Chamber of Curiosities (where it remains today). After Peter's death Catherine I could have buried it quietly. She did not—whatever that signifies. Catherine was especially afraid that, after the Mons case, Peter could jettison her in favour of his young mistress, the semi-royal Princess Maria Cantemir. She was the daughter of Dmitri, the hospodar of Moldavia who was one of the Constantinople Greeks appointed by the sultans to rule Moldavia and Wallachia. After a short reign as a Russian ally during the Pruth campaign, Peter welcomed this philosopher, composer and historian to Petersburg where his daughter's position made him influential. Accompanying Peter to Astrakhan, Maria became pregnant, alarming Catherine at a time when the succession was wide open. The baby died but back in Petersburg she resumed her place as Peter's favourite. Rumours spread that she had given Peter VD. After his death, Catherine temporarily sent her away from court. Under Empress Anna she held a literary salon in Petersburg.
† "Sail on vessels to the north and, based on current expectations," Peter wrote to Captain Bering on 23 December 1724, "because no one knows where it ends, see if it appears this land is part of America . . . You are to seek where Asia and America split." The expedition resulted in the discovery of the Bering Strait—and later in the Russian colonization of Alaska.

Gangrene putrefied him from within. Complaining of a "burning sen-sation," he cried in agony.

Once again, the deathbed of a tsar was a theatre of the public and the private. Amid the sweat, the groaning, the stench of infection and the weeping of his henchmen, all leaned in to hear to whom Peter had decided to leave the throne. At one point, Catherine left the deathbed to consult with Tolstoy—and with Menshikov, whom Peter had rejected. She and her daughters would be vulnerable if Peter died. On 27 Jan-uary, the last rites were administered twice by Prokopovich. "Lord I believe," Peter gasped. "I hope . . . I hope God will forgive me my many sins because of the good I tried to do." Catherine asked him to pardon Menshikov, who, lurking outside, was brought in and forgiven—just in time. At 2 p.m., Peter supposedly requested pen and paper, wrote "Give all to . . ." and, since he could write no more, asked for his daughter An-nushka so that he could dictate his wishes. Instead he sank into a coma.[2]

While Catherine and his daughters knelt praying by the emperor, Men-shikov and Tolstoy canvassed the Guards. At 6 a.m. on 28 January, Peter, aged fifty-two, in the forty-third year of his reign, died. The grandees gathered down the corridor in the Great Hall to fight it out. As no one seriously considered Peter's nieces, there were three candidates for the throne: the obvious one by male primogeniture was Peter Alexeievich, aged nine, Peter's grandson, supported by the aristocracy of Dolgorukys and Golitsyns. But that would surely mean the destruction of those who had tortured his father Alexei to death. The second was Annushka, Pe-ter's eldest daughter, and her fiancé Holstein—but they were not yet married. The other daughters Elizaveta and Natalya were too young.

The third option was Empress Catherine, already crowned, and supported by Peter's henchmen. Catherine had no hunger for power; Menshikov had it in spades. He summoned the Guards, who had shared the rigours of Peter's wars with Catherine, their praetorian mood sweet-ened with bonus pay in her name. Some officers of the Guards crept into the room to listen at the back as Prince Dmitri Golitsyn, an experi-enced official, proposed that Peter Alexeievich succeed with the widow as regent. Tolstoy warned against the rule of a child and proposed the Empress Catherine, "who has learned the art of ruling from her hus-band." The Guards, on parade in the courtyard below, shouted their approval; drums started to roll. "Who dared bring troops here without my orders?" shouted Prince Nikita Repnin, chief of the War Collegium. "Aren't I field marshal?"

"I did it, Your Excellency," answered the Guards commander Ivan Buturlin, "on the express command of our Sovereign Lady Empress

Catherine to whom you and I owe immediate obedience." As the ordinary Guardsmen wept—"Our Father is dead; Our Mother lives"—Apraxin and Menshikov proposed that "Her Majesty be proclaimed Autocrat."

Catherine had remained on her knees by her husband's bed, but now she emerged, leaning on Holstein's arm, to face the grandees, sobbing that she was "widow and orphan." Apraxin fell to his knees and hailed her to the roar of the Guards outside. Her accession was announced by the Senate and the Generalitet, the fifty generals of the high command. She promised to rule in Peter's spirit. No woman had ever ruled Russia in her own right. Now Russia was entering an age dominated by the rule of women.[3]

Peter was embalmed and lay in state. While she mourned Peter, the empress lost another child, Natalya, aged six, who died of measles, and her little coffin was placed in the Great Hall next to the giant one of her father. On 8 March, Catherine walked behind two coffins, one huge and one tiny, to the beat of kettledrums, the thunder of cannonades and the chant of sacred choirs. At the funeral, Prokopovich, standing beside the coffin in the unfinished Peter and Paul Cathedral,* compared Peter to Moses, Solomon, David and Constantine the Great. "He left us in body but his spirit remains." That spirit was personified by Catherine, who had to be prised weeping off the coffin. Peter remained unburied and on display in the Peter and Paul Cathedral until it was completed eight years later.[4]

Between sobbing visits to his body, Catherine embraced Petrine debauchery even before the end of official mourning. "Those amusements were almost daily drinking bouts," observed the French envoy Campredon, "which last the entire night and into the next day." At dinners, where most of the company ended up unconscious under the table, the empress partied with Menshikov and Princess Anastasia Golitsyna, who won 100 roubles by bumpering two goblets of vodka. Catherine dictated her own ironic instructions: "No ladies are to get drunk upon any pretence whatever nor shall gentlemen, before 9 p.m." Yet she combined this with homeliness, cooking for her coterie.†

---

* James Bruce created a new style of funeral—with its formal lying-in-state, slow martial marches, military grandeur—which now seems quintessentially Russian, serving not just the tsars but the secretary-generals of the Soviet Communist Party.

† She did not forget her family, ordering her two brothers and two sisters, Livonian cattle-herders who spoke no Russian, to be set up in the splendour of Tsarskoe Selo. They were all raised to the rank of count and enriched beyond their dreams: their descendants, the counts Scavronsky and Hendrikov among others, remained at the apex of Russian aristocracy until the Revolution.

Menshikov took over the planning of Annushka's wedding to the duke of Holstein and, to make sure the special pavilion was ready, he slept in it to supervise the workers. Annushka's marriage on 21 May to the small, unprepossessing German would ultimately decide the succession until 1917.

Catherine aspired to rule herself, rather than through ministers and commanded the Senate to report to her every Friday, planning to ease the taxes on the peasantry, yet she lacked both the discipline to wade through papers and the force to stop the brawls of Peter's pugnacious henchmen. So, on 8 February 1726, she created a Supreme Privy Council, made up of six of Peter's henchmen (Chancellor Golovkin was now sixty-six; Apraxin sixty-seven; Tolstoy* eighty), with the traditional aristocrats represented by Prince Dmitri Golitsyn. Although Menshikov was the fifth member, much of the real work was done by the sixth and youngest, the industrious Baron Andrei Osterman, aged forty, nicknamed the Oracle. This German clergyman's son, recruited by Peter at the age of seventeen, managed foreign policy as vice-chancellor, but Catherine also appointed him to the vital role of governor—or *oberhof-meister* in court rank—of young Grand Duke Peter.

Catherine hoped these old retainers would balance Menshikov while confining their fissiparous feuds to the Council chamber. Instead Menshikov, still just fifty-three, dominated them while bombarding Catherine with demands for more money, souls, titles. Menshikov's "lust for power, arrogance, greed, neglect of friends and relations" was now so boundless that he became by far the richest magnate, owning 3,000 villages, seven towns, building up the domain he had always wanted in Ukraine. Soon he owned 300,000 serfs. (In 1700, the richest grandee, Prince Mikhail Cherkassky, had owned just 33,000.) Since there were other marshals, he persuaded Catherine to appoint him generalissimus, a title held by a select few—culminating in Stalin. Like the shark that can clean its gills only by eating more, Menshikov could survive only by consuming more to safeguard what he already had. If he stopped, he would be destroyed—the dilemma of Russian power, then and now, when the retirement of a leader is impossible without insurance that he will not be prosecuted nor his fortune confiscated. His rapacity soon aroused "general hatred."

Catherine attended the Council's first sessions but soon started roistering at all hours. On 1 April 1726, during a drinking marathon, she ordered the alarms to be sounded throughout the city, but when the

---

* Catherine abolished the Secret Chancellery, transferring its torturers back to the Preo-brazhensky Office: the abolition of the secret police, while re-creating it with a new name, would become a ritual of new leaders, royal, Soviet and presidential.

inhabitants of Petersburg and the denizens of the palaces rushed out of their beds and into the streets in fear of fire or flood, they learned that it was an April Fool's Day joke. When courtiers wore the wrong clothes to her balls, she imposed bumpers of the dreaded vodka goblet. Released from her husband's despotism, she thoroughly enjoyed the young men now available to her, taking a young lover, flaxen-haired chamberlain Count Reinhold von Löwenwolde (who closely resembled the decapitated Mons). But she played so hard that Löwenwolde collapsed, either from sexual exhaustion or alcohol poisoning.[5]

She almost immediately faced a near-war with Britain, the beginning of a long rivalry. That naval power, reliant on supplies of timber and tar from the Baltic, had been alarmed by Peter's successes there and George I, who as elector of Hanover also resented Russian influence in Germany, had tried to organize a coalition against him. In spring 1726, George tried again, this time blockading the Baltic. In the panic that Petersburg might come under attack, Catherine promised to command the fleet in person. It did not come to war, but the crisis increased her dependence on Menshikov, who took charge on the Baltic, travelling to Courland where he tried to make himself duke. His brutality so alienated the Courlanders that Tolstoy persuaded Catherine to dismiss him. But Menshikov did not break. He bounced.[6]

During Petersburg's White Nights, that phenomenon of northern climes when the sun is visible all night and it is never dark, the court register records that for days on end, Catherine banqueted at 3 a.m., rising at 5 p.m. to party until dawn again. She sometimes held parades at night. After these wassails, she suffered fevers, asthma, coughs, nosebleeds and swollen limbs, which concentrated the minds of her ministers.

Grand Duke Peter, son of the murdered Alexei, was the sole male heir. How to reconcile Petrine parvenus with the aristocrats? While Menshikov was out of favour after his Courlandish atrocities, the wily Osterman noticed that the adolescent Peter was attracted to his curvaceous blonde sixteen-year-old aunt, Elizaveta, and proposed that they marry, thereby merging the factions.

Since the Church forbade such consanguinity, Menshikov suggested that his own daughter Maria should marry Peter. Maria was already engaged to a Lithuanian, Prince Peter Sapieha, but it happened that Catherine took a fancy to him. Menshikov seized the opportunity, offering Sapieha to the empress. "The empress has literally snatched Sapieha away from the princess [Maria]," noticed the Dutch envoy, "and made him her favourite." She was so happy with her conquest that she agreed to Menshikov's suggestion. The granddaughter of a pie-seller was marrying the grandson of an emperor. Menshikov would be father-in-law and controller of the next tsar. Tolstoy mobilized his allies to stop him, backing Peter the Great's daughters Annushka (or Elizaveta) for the succession. The girls fell to their knees and tearfully begged their mother not to back Menshikov and the son of Tsarevich Alexei. Catherine sobbed too but backed Menshikov. In November 1726, she collapsed with a chill, bleeding from the nose, her limbs swollen. But she recovered to Bless the Waters on Epiphany, arriving in a golden carriage, wearing a silvery dress trimmed with gilded Spanish lace, a white-feathered hat and a field marshal's baton. That night she fell ill.

Taking command of the palace, Menshikov realized that only "the very cunning" Tolstoy could stop him. "In dealing with him," he mused, "it doesn't hurt to keep a good stone in one's pocket to break his teeth if he decides to bite."

Catherine was dying—and one of Tolstoy's allies, Anton Devier, blunderingly blabbed about Tolstoy's scheming. On 26 April, Menshikov struck against his enemies. He arrested Tolstoy, Police Commissioner Devier and secret policeman Ushakov, uncovering a "conspiracy" against the empress. Now she signed her will.* On 6 May, Menshikov brought the sinking empress the evidence against Tolstoy, who was exiled to Solovetsky Island in the Northern White Sea. He never returned. At 9 p.m. that evening, Catherine died. This time there was no crisis. Menshikov had terrorized all opposition. Peter II, aged eleven, was declared *imperator*.[7]

The embalming was flawed. Such was the heat that Catherine's body started to decompose. After her funeral, she joined her husband, unburied in the Peter and Paul Fortress. The Supreme Privy Councillors, who now included Peter the Great's daughters Elizaveta and Annushka and the latter's husband Holstein, were meant to act as joint regents but Menshikov took control with "perfect despotism."

The boy-emperor, "who had great vivacity and an excellent memory," was "very tall and large-made, fair but much tanned from hunting, young and handsome." He trusted his governor, Osterman the Oracle, and adored his aunt Elizaveta, but his best friend was his hunting pal, the nineteen-year-old Prince Ivan Dolgoruky. At first he was probably

---

* She made Menshikov promise to ensure that her unmarried daughter Elizaveta wed Holstein's cousin the prince-bishop of Lübeck, Karl August of Holstein, who had just arrived in Petersburg. Elizaveta was at times meant to marry virtually everyone from Louis XV to the shah of Persia, but the prince-bishop was the one she really loved. He soon died but his influence outlived him: when Empress Elizaveta later chose a girl to marry her heir, she selected the prince-bishop's niece, Sophie of Anhalt-Zerbst—who became Catherine the Great.

afraid of the abrasive Menshikov, who dictated his every move. Determined that Peter should marry his daughter Maria, Menshikov moved the emperor into his own palace to control him better. The prince played the role of trying to balance the factions beneath him, promoting the Dolgorukys and Golitsyns who privately despised him.

Menshikov had not completely given up the ambition of procuring the dukedom of Courland, as princely domain and potential sanctuary. There, Anna was again ensconced with her older lover Bestuzhev. After Bestuzhev had been denounced for turning Anna's palace "into a dishonourable whorehouse," he was arrested. Anna was crushed and in twenty-five letters to Petersburg she begged Menshikov "not to take Bestuzhev away from me" and beseeched Osterman "to intervene for me, a poor woman, with His Serene Highness [Menshikov]. Don't let me spend the rest of my life in tears." She ended with a pathetic testament to her love for Bestuzhev: "I have grown accustomed to him." No penurious provincial widow could have more prostrated herself before the paramount pie-seller—yet Anna was a tsar's daughter. She consoled herself with male lovers and then enjoyed a "particular friendship," a lesbian crush on a pretty Lithuanian, Princess Oginski: "The two were continually together and they very often lay in the same bed."

No one would have guessed her imminent destiny, but however hopeless her prospects for the throne, however plain her looks, she was not bereft of male company for long.[8]

When Tsar Peter fell ill with pleurisy, Aunt Elizaveta rushed to his bedside in the Menshikov Palace and nursed him. The doctors ordered Peter to take the air in the countryside. At Peterhof, the emperor hunted with Ivan Dolgoruky, consulted with Osterman and flirted with Elizaveta, an alliance united by nothing except hatred of Menshikov.

Peter decided to send Elizaveta 9,000 ducats for her expenses, but Menshikov intercepted the courier: "The emperor's too young to know how to dispose of the money. Carry it to my apartments." When Peter discovered what had happened, he summoned Menshikov "in a great rage." Menshikov was "perfectly thunderstruck," but the tsar, "stamping his foot," said, "I will make you know that I am the emperor and I will be obeyed." In June, Menshikov invited the emperor to celebrate his birthday at the prince's Oranienbaum estate, but Elizaveta persuaded him that he should go hunting instead. Then, aided by Elizaveta, he moved out of Menshikov's house and into the Summer Palace.

On 26 August, Menshikov fell ill, coughing blood—but he still dictated instructions to the tsar from his sickbed: "I ask you to fulfil my request that until you reach adulthood you be obedient to Baron

Osterman and the honourable ministers and do nothing without their advice"—by which Menshikov meant his own advice, to "be a just Sovereign, take care of your health and, knowing what earnest care I took with your upbringing, deign to protect my family and be merciful to your bride to whom at the appointed time you will be married." But this dictation from the dying dictator did not work any more: "I shall not marry before the age of twenty-five," the tsar announced. The Supreme Privy Council, terrified of Menshikov, advised caution.

"I will show you who is emperor," shouted the boy. "Menshikov or me!"

Menshikov had now "alienated all those close to him—a man with whom it was intolerable to live. Everyone conspired against him." On 7 September Menshikov arose from his deathbed. But he was too late: as he lay sick, power, that mysterious, invisible alchemy of personality, fear and authority, had leached away. The following day, Peter signed the order to arrest him. Menshikov was awoken at dawn by General Semyon Saltykov and sent into comfortable exile. "The vain and empty glory of the arrogant Goliath has perished," wrote one official, "everyone is ecstatic and I now live without fear." But when the Menshikovs reached Tver, the prince was arrested and accused of spying for Sweden. Tried and sentenced, "this colossus of a pygmy, raised almost to royal status, this arrogant man who showed us an example of ingratitude of spirit," departed for Berezov in Siberia with just his family. The winter was so cruel that his wife, his daughter Maria then he himself soon perished, the end of an extraordinary ride.⁹

Peter decided he wanted to rule without a minister like Menshikov, but he was too young and feckless and his government immediately sank into a "terrible state of chaos." He promoted Ivan Dolgoruky to the pivotal court position of grand chamberlain, and after claiming that he would decide everything himself, the tsar spent every minute in the company of his young mentor whose father and uncles he promoted to the Supreme Privy Council along with the veteran Marshal Dolgoruky. They joined Osterman and Dmitri Golitsyn in a cabinet where power see-sawed dizzily between these three factions, proving that autocracy needed an autocrat to function at all. "The tsar doesn't deal with business," wrote a foreign diplomat. "No one is paid; everyone steals as much as he can," while an epidemic of diplomatic illnesses paralysed the state. "All the members of the Council are 'unwell' and do not attend meetings."

Ivan Dolgoruky was alarmed that Peter was falling in love with Aunt Elizaveta. "She's a beauty the like of which I've never seen," wrote the Spanish envoy, the duke of Liria. "An amazing complexion, glowing eyes, perfect mouth, a throat and bosom of rare whiteness. She's tall, exceptionally lively, dances well, rides fearlessly, is very flirtatious and doesn't lack brains." Her nickname was Russian Venus. For once this was not just royal hyperbole.

Osterman revived his plan of marrying the two, but the Golitsyns deployed a good-looking young Guards officer of a family much favoured by Peter the Great, Alexander Buturlin, to provide better guidance than Peter was receiving from that dissipated jackanapes Dolgoruky. Buturlin became Peter's new mentor and for a while he seemed to be in charge of policy. Then Ivan Dolgoruky fell (genuinely) ill. Peter rallied to his companion, keeping vigil at his bedside. As he recovered so did the fortunes of the Dolgorukys, while outside the sickroom Elizaveta waited with Buturlin, who became her first lover.[10]

After Peter II had been crowned in Moscow in February 1728, he did not return to Petersburg, a decision that was both recreational and political.* The hunting was better around Moscow, and he was rejecting Peter the Great's work, surely in honour of the father killed by his grandfather, for he also pardoned all the conspirators exiled in the Tsarevich Alexei case—and recalled his grandmother, Tsarina Eudoxia, long since discarded. Peter II declared that he loathed his grandfather's navy—"I don't intend to sail the seas as did my grandfather"—and he abolished the Preobrazhensky Office. The boy became popular for his moderation, his Russianness—and his inactivity, after his grandfather's hyperactive tyranny.

He was jealous of Buturlin's affair with Elizaveta and posted the officer to Ukraine. Elizaveta was heartbroken, yet this short crisis between boy and aunt gave the Dolgorukys their chance to bid for the supreme prize. "There is no court in Europe," complained Liria, "that is so volatile as this one."

In September 1729, Peter went hunting with Ivan Dolgoruky and 620 hounds at Gorenki near Moscow. The Dolgoruky kennels became the chancellery of Russia; all business was at a standstill. "There is no tsar here," wrote Liria from Moscow, "nor any ministers. We can accomplish nothing." Ivan Dolgoruky's father, Alexei, introduced the fourteen-year-old tsar to his daughter Ekaterina, who was three years older. "Without being a beauty, she had a very pretty face" and "languishing big blue eyes." His wiser cousin, Marshal Vasily Dolgoruky, who had narrowly survived Peter the Great's terror, advised strongly against the entire

---

* Peter II lived between the Kremlin and Lefort's palace, which survives as the rather dilapidated archive of the Collegium and Ministry of War. Some of the research used in this book was conducted there by the author, who once fell through the rickety stairs. It stands near the dreaded Lefortovo Prison, scene of many executions during Stalin's Terror.

stratagem, but the family could not resist trying to divert the plenitude of autocracy to themselves. As so often in such a scheme, the pawn, Ekaterina, wanted nothing of it—she was in love with an Austrian diplomat, Count Melissimo—but Peter fell in love with her and agreed to marry her. The Dolgorukys tried to tighten their grip by marrying their debauched booby, Ivan, to the luminous Elizaveta, who refused such a *mésalliance.*

In Moscow, the Dolgorukys triumphantly announced the betrothal of their daughter to the tsar. The couple sat on a dais in the Lefortovo Palace receiving congratulations. When Elizaveta kissed his hand, Peter looked forlorn, while "the pretty victim" Ekaterina, "dressed in a stiffened bodied gown of silver tissue with a coronet on her head," was "very melancholy and pale," noticed the English ambassador's wife. Suddenly the "forsaken swain" Melissimo approached, "to everyone's surprise." Ekaterina "snatched her hand out of the emperor's and gave it to the other to kiss, ten thousand different passions on her face."

The marriage was set for 18 January 1730. Peter presided over the Blessing of the Waters on the 6th, but when he reviewed the troops in the freezing cold and walked behind the gilded sleigh of his fiancée Dolgorukaya, he complained of a headache. The next day, spots revealed smallpox. Osterman stayed at the bedside of his pupil in the Lefortovo Palace. At 3 a.m. on 18 January, the day set for his marriage to Ekaterina, Peter died.* So close yet so far, the Dolgorukys came up with a desperate plan.[11]

"Scarce had Peter II closed his eyes than his friend Prince Ivan Dolgoruky came out of the chamber flourishing his drawn sword and cried out 'Long live Empress Ekaterina'," by which he meant his sister, Ekaterina Dolgorukaya. No one joined in his acclamation, but the Dolgorukys had falsified Peter's will to nominate his fiancée. Faced with a near-extinct dynasty, they were effectively launching a coup to subvert and replace the Romanovs.

Osterman claimed to be ill and retired to his sickbed. Gathering in the Lefortovo Palace near the tsar's body, the seven remaining members of the Supreme Privy Council—four Dolgorukys and two Golitsyns plus old Golovkin—met to decide on a new monarch. Peter was the

---

* The tsar's other aunt, Peter the Great's daughter Annushka, duchess of Holstein, was absent in Kiel, giving birth to a son, Karl-Peter Ulrich, who thanks to the interwoven marriage alliances of Europe was potentially heir to the duchy of Holstein, the kingdom of Sweden and the Russian empire. This birth of a grandson of Peter the Great, a rare male heir, was celebrated by a ball in Moscow, but his mother caught a chill at the celebrations in Kiel. Annushka died in May aged just twenty-six. Her baby would reign—and marry Catherine the Great.

last of the male Romanovs, which gave the councillors the first real opportunity since 1613 to change the very nature of autocracy. First Alexei Dolgoruky produced the forged will leaving the empire to his own daughter. Even his cousin Marshal Vasily Dolgoruky refused to support this preposterous chicanery. Prince Dmitri Golitsyn brushed aside the Dolgorukys: "We must choose from the illustrious Romanov family and no other." There were five female candidates. The rightful empress by Empress Catherine's will was Elizaveta, but Golitsyn reminded his peers that she was born illegitimate. In any case, she refused to bid for the throne, later musing, "I'm glad I didn't. I was too young . . ." Amazingly Tsarina Eudoxia, Peter the Great's rejected first wife, now restored to her rank, proposed herself as successor to her grandson—but she had no following. Golitsyn proposed "to choose one of the [three] daughters of Tsar Ivan [V]," Peter the Great's handicapped brother. The eldest girl, the Wild Duchess Ekaterina, was ruled out for being married to the oafish duke of Mecklenburg, so Golitsyn chose the next: Anna, the downtrodden widow of Courland. "She was born in our midst from a Russian mother and a good old family," he said—in other words, she was no upstart Empress Catherine and she had neither faction, nor known views, and she was single. Golitsyn* suggested that "to make our lives easier and provide ourselves with more freedoms," Anna would be a figurehead, forced to accept only limited powers.

"Although we might achieve this," mused one of the Dolgorukys, "we might not hold on to power."

"We'll hold on to it all right," replied Golitsyn, dictating the terms to be offered to Anna, ending with the words: "Should I not fulfil any part of this promise, I shall be deprived of the Russian throne." This plan has been compared to the monarchy dominated by a landed oligarchy that developed in England after the Glorious Revolution forty years earlier, but really it was a brazen Dolgoruky power-grab, meagrely camouflaged by highfalutin ideals. To pull it off, they had to get to Anna before she discovered that this was just the scheme of six old aristocrats. So they closed the gates of Moscow and despatched a Golitsyn and a Dolgoruky to offer her their conditions: the tsar would no longer be able to marry, appoint an heir, declare war, levy taxes or spend revenues—without the permission of the Council. This would have constituted the greatest change in Russian government between 1613 and 1905.

---

* Golitsyn, now sixty-five, had suffered under Petrine tyranny: head of the Commerce Collegium, he had been entangled in the fall of Shafirov and was only saved by the mediation of Catherine. This grandest of Russian aristocrats had to thank the peasant-empress by prostrating himself at her feet and touching his forehead to the ground.

As soon as this news spread through the Lefortovo Palace, the race was on to beat the cabal to Anna. Karl Gustav von Löwenwolde, a Baltic courtier who had been one of Anna's lovers, despatched a courier to reach her first.

That night, on 18 January, Anna went to bed in the dreary town of Mitau not knowing that she was already empress of Russia.

She learned the astonishing news from Löwenwolde. So on the 25th, when Princes Vasily Lukich Dolgoruky (uncle of Ivan and Ekaterina) and Mikhail Golitsyn (brother of Dmitri) arrived to offer her the throne, she knew what to expect. Now thirty-seven years old, a swarthy, deep-voiced scowler, she had cheeks "as big as a Westphalian ham" and a face that her mother's fool had compared to a bearded Muscovite: "Ding-dong here comes Ivan the Terrible!" After twenty years of humiliation, this tsar's daughter would have agreed to anything to get out of Courland. "I promise to observe the conditions without exception," she wrote—and prepared to leave for Moscow, where the Guards were now seething with outrage at the aristocratic coup.

As soon as she arrived outside Moscow, Anna was joined by her Saltykov cousins, by her sister Ekaterina—and, secretly, by her lover, a former groom named Ernst Biron. On 15 February 1730, Anna entered Moscow in a carriage to the boom of 156 cannon. While she was carefully watched by the cabal, Osterman cunningly arranged that her ladies-in-waiting were the wives of its enemies. These women handled the messages from Osterman—hidden in clocks, sewn into shirts and wrapped in baby's swaddling-clothes—that informed her that the aristocrats had few supporters. Peter the Great's henchmen had been created by the autocracy, so had the Guards; many officers believed that autocracy was the only system that could govern Russia; and all resented this machination of Dolgorukys and Golitsyns. The senior officers—the Generalitet—were organized by Osterman to sign a petition. Meanwhile Anna cultivated the Preobrazhensky Guards, served them vodka with her own hand and declared herself their colonel.

On 25 February in the Kremlin, when Anna majestically greeted the elite in the company of the Golitsyns and Dolgorukys, Prince Alexei Cherkassky, Russia's richest man and figurehead of the Generalitet, presented the petition asking her to rule as autocrat.

"What right have you got, prince, to presume to make law?" asked Vasily Lukich Dolgoruky.

"As much as a Dolgoruky. You've deceived the empress!" insisted Cherkassky, supported by the Guards, who offered to kill Anna's enemies. Instead, the empress invited the Golitsyns and Dolgorukys to a dinner. Afterwards, they returned to the hall where the Generalitet asked her to assume absolute power—but she feigned confusion: "The conditions I signed in Mitau weren't the wish of the people?"

"*Nyet!*" roared the Guards.

Turning on the cabal, Anna said, "That must mean you deceived me!" She sent for the signed conditions. "So this isn't necessary," she declared, as she slowly tore the paper in half.[12]

On 28 April 1730, Anna was crowned by Archbishop Prokopovich with a new crown made up of over 2,500 precious stones and 28 diamonds. As she processed out of the cathedral, she stopped at a specially built loge to greet that other woman summoned from the distant past: Peter the Great's ex-wife Eudoxia—who had wanted to be empress herself.[13]

Anna promoted her lover Biron to grand chamberlain and count of the Holy Roman Empire—quite a rise. Three years her senior, Biron, the "extremely handsome" son of a Courlandian huntsman of minor nobility, had been a groom who then charmed his way into the favour of Anna's lover Bestuzhev. When Bestuzhev was exiled, Biron replaced him as Anna's paramour. Biron was coarse and uneducated—he had once killed someone in a fight. The groom had such a "great fancy for horses" that "he talked to men as horses and horses as men." "Haughty and ambitious, abrupt and even brutal, avaricious, he was an implacable enemy." Biron "exercised a total authority" over Anna. "She couldn't bear to be separated from him for a minute," and "if he had a sombre expression the empress would look worried. If he was cheerful, her joy was obvious." They often walked around holding hands and fell ill at the same times. "Never was there an intimate couple who so completely shared both their joys and sorrows."

Osterman staged a Lazarus-like recovery, returned to his post as vice-chancellor and was promoted to count by the grateful empress, who now abolished the Supreme Privy Council and ran most of her domestic and foreign affairs through Osterman the Oracle. He was no fashion-plate: notorious for the "filth" of his "disgusting clothes," stinking soiled wig, brimming spittoon, "servants dressed like beggars," he was mocked for the ugliness and reek of his mistresses. Nonetheless he was a "master of subtlety and dissimulation" with "so strange a way of talking that few persons could ever boast of understanding him. Everything he said or wrote could be taken two ways."

Mocking Osterman's hypochondria, Biron laughed that "He complains of earache and his face and head are bandaged . . . and he has not shaved or washed for weeks." Yet Anna needed Osterman. "For God's sake take heart and come see me tomorrow," she wrote to him. "I need very much to talk to you and I shall never let you down. Fear nothing and everything shall come right!"

Anna did not feel safe in Moscow—and she wished to channel some of her uncle Peter's glory—so she returned to Petersburg. On arrival, she was impressed by the fireworks and triumphal arches prepared by General Burkhard Christoph von Münnich, a German military engineer hired by Peter the Great who rose to become Peter II's chief of artillery and "one of the best generals of his age." Anna took a liking to this "handsome-faced, very fair, tall and slender" general. He fancied himself as a gallant, but the ladies laughed at "his German stiffness": when he flirted "with all the ladies . . . suddenly snatching your hand and kissing it in raptures," his efforts resembled "a frolicsome cow." This showman had already curried favour with Anna by denouncing two officials for hesitating to support her in the first days of her reign. Behind the courtly manners seethed "devouring ambition." Anna promoted him to head the War Collegium and to the rank of field marshal. It seemed as if three Germans now ran Russia—Biron, Osterman and Münnich.[14]

Anna disliked the poky Winter Palace so she commissioned the Italian architect Carlo Rastrelli to demolish the old edifice and build a new one to befit her imperial aspirations—and meanwhile moved into the late Admiral Apraxin's house next door. Biron, his wife and his son joined her. Living between there and Peterhof, she rose daily between 6 and 7 a.m., breakfasted with the Birons, met her ministers at nine, then at noon dined with the Birons. She and Biron craved magnificence with all the excitement of a tsar's poor relative and a provincial groom arrived in power. But despite the vast sums now spent on clothes, carriages, palaces, games of pharo and Italian theatre, "the richest coat would sometimes be worn with the vilest wig," observed a German visitor, "or a splendidly dressed man would appear in the wretchedest carriage. You see gold and silver plate in heaps on one side, grossest filth on the other. For one well-dressed woman, you see ten frightfully disfigured. The union of finery and meanness is universal."

The empress "is a very large made woman, very well shaped for her size," observed Jane Rondeau, the wife of the British envoy who was much favoured by her, and whose letters give the only positive portrait of the empress, with her "brown complexion, black hair, dark blue eyes. She has an awefulness in her countenance at first sight but when she speaks, she has an inexpressibly sweet smile and she talks a good deal to everybody." Anna was kind to Münnich's son Ernst, who found her "gentle and compassionate but had the fault of allowing evil done in her name" by a "vindictive" Biron.

Actually there was no end to her cruel games. "Find out what baby she bore," she instructed one of her governors, ordering him to investigate a mother just delivered of a child. Childless herself and unmarried, she wished to torment this couple, by pretending to the father that the baby had been born handicapped. "A person or a monster, a son or daughter? Write it all. If she recovers, send her and baby here. And when you report, write one letter with the truth and another letter which is fake with something funny especially if you describe the baby as not a normal human!"

She made up for her lack of drinking by presiding over a circus of grotesques, including Beznoika the Legless Mama, Tall Daryushka the Handless and Garbuchka the Hunchback.

Like an omnipotent schoolgirl bully, Anna arranged female hair-pulling fights between crippled crones that had to draw blood, and dwarf-tossing. "She spent entire days chattering and listening to fools," recalled Ernst Münnich. Her favourite dwarf was Pedrillo, a Neapolitan violinist who, after Biron had asked if his pregnant wife was as ugly as a goat, invited empress and court to visit his home where they found him in bed with a lactating goat in a nightdress.

Peter the Great's Jewish jester da Costa was now entertaining his fourth tsar but Anna preferred reducing aristocrats to the status of fools, forcing Prince Mikhail Golitsyn and Count Alexei Apraxin to serve in her circus. Golitsyn, the grandson of Regent Sophia's minister, had secretly converted to Catholicism to marry an Italian girl and, as a punishment, Anna ordered him to abandon the wife and serve as her cupbearer for *kvass*, renaming him Prince Kvassky. Anna was delighted when he arrived in the first consignment of tomfoolery sent by her cousin the Moscow governor, Semyon Saltykov. "We're grateful to you for sending Golitsyn, Miliutin* and Bakhirev's wife," she wrote, "but Golitsyn's the best and outdoes all the fools here. If you find another like him do let me know." Golitsyn's speciality was to dress as a hen and sit on a straw-basket nest for hours clucking in front of the court. After mass on Sundays, Golitsyn and the other fools sat in rows cackling and clucking in chicken outfits. Yet she also cared for her entertainers. She had her veteran dwarf Bakhirev thrashed for asking not to be tossed—then funded his medical treatment and supply of wine. She was incensed when she discovered that laundresses were mixing up "the empress's blouses and linen" with those of ordinary courtiers. "Henceforth there shall be a separate chamber for our linen. This rule

* Miliutin the fool who specialized in tickling Anna's feet was the ancestor of Count Dmitri Miliutin, war minister of Alexander II, and his brother Nikolai, architect of the liberation of the serfs in 1861.

to be enforced most strictly. Only the laundry of Legless Mama may be washed with our laundry."

She bombarded Saltykov with requests for novelties and gossip. Her interest in other people's secrets was occasionally positive—she loved matchmaking—but usually sinister: "As soon as you get this letter, go to Vlasov's sister's home and get the love letters from the chest and send them to me." She spent a lot of time investigating her fools: "Go to Apraxin's storeroom and look for a portrait of his father and send it to us—if he hides anything, the Apraxins will be sorry." She often requested more chatty ladies: "Find a girl in Pereslavl who resembles Tatiana who will die soon to replace her . . . You know our tastes—girls around forty who are talkative." If the performers failed she slapped their faces. One such girl, Nastasia Shestakova, remembered how on arrival she was taken to secret police chief Ushakov, who sent her to the empress. "Spend the night with me," said the empress. Shestakova was delivered to the bedroom where the empress gave a hand to kiss and then "She grasped me so strongly by the shoulders that she seized my whole body and it was painful." But Anna was not pleased: "You've aged, you've become yellow. You must touch up your eyebrows . . . Have I aged?"

"Not at all, dear Matushka, there's not a trace of old age in Your Imperial Highness," answered the girl.

"How do I compare in weight with Avdotya Ivanovna?"

"She is twice as heavy."

"Come closer to me." Anna's kindness "became simultaneously terrifying and pleasing," recalled the girl, who threw herself on her knees. "Pick yourself up," said the empress. "Now speak. Tell me stories of robbers."

"But I've never lived with robbers."

"Speak now!" This was a dictatorship of loquacity. She required constant chatter, the imperial eighteenth-century version of talk radio, yet these accounts, like that of Princess Oginski earlier, suggest that she herself was bisexual.

She was as politically vigilant as she was personally curious. She recalled Ushakov, who had helped kill Tsarevich Alexei, and promoted him to baron and head of her new Secret Chancellery. She so enjoyed his revelations that she would break off her beloved hunting to hear gossip and conspiracies. She founded her own Guards regiment, named after her mother's estate, the Izmailovsky, filled with German officers whom she trusted after her many years in Germanic Courland. No hint of conspiracy was too small for her. "We heard that the bishop of Voronezh didn't immediately order prayers for my accession and said something suspicious," she told a governor. "Report immediately and tell no one!"

Anna declared that she would rule in the spirit of Peter the Great, something no one else could really do. She has been condemned for her caprices, her cruelties and her German favourites—her reign is known as the *Bironovchina*, the time of Biron. Yet there is some sexism in this as her shenanigans were no more grotesque than those of Great Peter himself. And her henchmen were not quite as German as they seemed. She appointed Peter's able, experienced lieutenants, creating a three-man cabinet "attached to Our Court," consisting of Chancellor Golovkin, Cherkassky (co-organizer of the coup on her behalf) and of course the indispensable Osterman. Lazy, vicious and weak, distracted by hunting, spying and dwarf-baiting, Anna allowed this troika to issue imperial orders signed by all three. Since Golovkin and Cherkassky were often ill or absent, Osterman was chief minister. He was born in Germany but he had served in Russia for thirty years and was married to a Streshneva.

Anna built on the pact between the autocrat and her serf-owning nobility who were keen to avoid Peter the Great's universal service. Faced with peasant unrest, Anna allowed nobles to keep at least one son at home to run the estate—the first step back from Peter's rules—while she permitted masters to hunt down and reclaim escaping serfs. She used her magnificent court to impress foreigners—and reward her officials. In this sense, she was no fool. And even her bullying games probably had a political use: the nobility had tried to neuter the autocrat. Now Anna's games reminded them of their place.

She took her time to destroy the Dolgorukys and Golitsyns. Peter II's friend Ivan Dolgoruky, his unfortunate sister Ekaterina and his family were arrested and despatched to Berezov in Siberia, where they remained for eight years—when a more terrible vengeance awaited them. "Confiscate all diamonds, gold and silver from Prince Alexei Dolgoruky," she ordered Saltykov, "and send it to us."

Anna knew that it was an autocrat's duty to ensure a smooth succession, but she was determined that it would not be the popular Elizaveta.[15]

Now twenty-one, Elizaveta was often described as the "most beautiful girl in Russia," much to the irritation of the empress, who watched her cousin's little court for any hint of treason, ordering Marshal Münnich to "find out who goes to Elizaveta's house" since "she drives out at night and people call out to her, showing their devotion." Cabmen were hired "to observe Her Imperial Highness." Anna was surely jealous of the Russian Venus.

When two young Guardsmen connected to Elizaveta were denounced for treasonable talk, Anna had them beheaded—but she also exiled the tsarevna's new lover, her page Alexei Shubin. Anna's vigilance was understandable, but at this time Elizaveta's court was more interested in sex than power: presiding over her own Ukrainian choir, Elizaveta ran several lovers in tandem. One of the choristers, Alexei Razumovsky, was to last for the rest of her life, but she was constantly looking for new ones. "Little Mother Tsarevna, how fine that Prince Ordov is," lady-in-waiting Mavra Shepeleva wrote to Elizaveta, catching the tone of their coterie. "As tall as Buturlin, just as slim, such eyes just like yours in colour, slim legs, wears his own hair down to his waist, arms as lovely as Buturlin's. I can also report I bought a snuffbox and the picture on it really resembles you when you're naked." Apart from a few eighteenth-century touches, their chatter was as saucy as that of texting teenagers today.

Instead of Elizaveta, Anna nominated her niece as heir: the thirteen-year-old Anna Leopoldovna, the daughter of her late sister Ekaterina and Karl Leopold, duke of Mecklenburg. Mrs. Rondeau, the English ambassador's wife, observed that the heiress was "neither handsome nor genteel. She is grave, seldom speaks, never laughs," a gravity deriving "rather from stupidity than judgement." To father an heir, the empress summoned a fourteen-year-old German, Anton Ulrich, prince of Brunswick-Wolfenbüttel-Bevern, as the girl's future husband. But the heiress hated him on sight and was soon embroiled in her own murky scandal.[16]

Once the succession had been decided, Anna wanted to enjoy her freaks and her hunting. "We are not to be disturbed with minor matters," she told the cabinet, but the less interested a monarch was in politics, the more savage the competition. She let Osterman run her foreign policy, which, with astonishing flexibility, he directed under Catherine I, Peter II and now Anna, disentangling Russia from war with Persia (at the cost of abandoning Peter the Great's conquests in today's Daghestan and Azerbaijan), while maintaining an alliance with Austria to limit the continent's dominant power, France.

While Osterman dominated abroad, Biron looked for ways to remove Münnich from court. When, in February 1733, Augustus the Strong, king of Poland, died, Anna backed his son as his successor, but Louis XV's policy was to construct an "Eastern Barrier" of Poland, Sweden and the Ottomans to prevent Russian expansion. He backed his own candidate and sent French troops. Then as now, Russia abhorred Western advances up to its borders—and ever since the Time of Troubles, when the Poles had taken Moscow, it feared a strong Poland. Anna intervened in this War of the Polish Succession, but when her generals became bogged down, Biron proposed that Münnich take command, removing him from Petersburg and hopefully embroiling him in an inglorious quagmire. Instead Münnich defeated the French—and returned with a grandiose plan to win further glory.

During the Polish war, the Crimean Tatars raided Ukraine, sparking a joint Russian and Austrian war against the Ottomans, promoted by Münnich who promised to capture Constantinople within four years. Osterman warned against this, but the flashy Münnich got his way.

In early 1736, Münnich stormed the fortress of Azov, while Anna's Irish general, Peter Lacey, burned the Crimean capital, Bachtiserai. But the war was costly, Russia's system of provisioning was inept and Münnich's brazen egotism offended his generals, who were quickly on the verge of mutiny, appealing to Anna and Biron. When he tried to resign in a huff, Anna reprimanded him, complaining to Osterman, "The behaviour of these generals causes great sorrow. We bestowed not only high rank but great fortunes and their behaviour doesn't accord with my generosity." But her analysis reveals her common sense: "We can't destroy the Turkish state on our own . . . What do we do with this discord among our generals? If we can find a way to destroy the Treaty of Pruth [forced on Peter the Great], wouldn't it be better to end the war? We depend on your skill and loyalty and you and your family will be in my favour." But even Oracle Osterman could not get her out of the war yet.[17]

Prince Anton of Brunswick, the stammering fiancé of the heiress, was serving under Münnich, who admired the boy's courage but thought him sexually ambiguous. So did his fiancée. Anna Leopoldovna's governess was a Baltic German noblewoman named Madame d'Aderkass who became inseparable from her charge, sparking lesbian rumours while simultaneously both governess and princess became enamoured of Count Maurice Lynar, the young Saxon ambassador. When the empress heard rumours that "accused this girl of sharing the tastes of the famous Sappho," Anna expelled the governess and had Lynar recalled.

"What her crime is, is yet a great secret," wrote Jane Rondeau, the English ambassador's wife, adding that the heiress had been "examined" to check her virginity and for "semblance de hommesse." The Englishwoman concluded that "Most people think it must be something very notorious or Her Majesty would never have sent her away in such a hurry." Anna Leopoldovna did enjoy intimate relationships with girls because she became ever closer to her maid-of-honour, Baroness Julie von Mengden. The heiress's marriage was now urgent.[18]

As an autocrat becomes older, the struggle for influence intensifies, which in turn makes the sovereign more suspicious and therefore more dangerous. Biron promoted a new minister, the energetic Artemii Volynsky, to the Council. Volynsky had been Peter the Great's adviser on Persia, though the first emperor had beaten him with his cane for embezzlement. Anna found the confrontational and innovative Volynsky refreshing, but her favour encouraged him to overthrow Biron himself.

Though Biron was at the height of his powers, he suffered from the perennial fear of all favourites: that after the death of his patroness, he would be destroyed. So, like Menshikov, he dreamed of becoming duke of Courland. The old dynasty there had just become extinct and he begged Anna to procure him the throne. She had him elected duke, but, back in Petersburg, he spotted an opportunity in the matter of the heiress's marriage to rise even higher.

Now that Prince Anton of Brunswick was back from the war, the empress arranged the heiress's betrothal, but the girl did not want to marry that "milksop." "Nobody wants to consider that I have a princess on my hands who has to be married," the empress told Biron. As for Prince Anton, "neither I nor the princess like the prince," and Biron too thought him "ordained to produce children in Russia but lacking the intelligence even for that." Even if the choice of Anton was a mistake, "Time's passing; she's in her prime," said the empress. "Ladies of our status don't always marry out of love," and there were diplomatic implications for Anton was the candidate of Russia's ally, Austria. When the heiress said she would prefer anyone else, Biron suggested his own son, irritating the empress. But it was his own protégé, Volynsky, who led the canvassing against Biron. Finally the heiress declared that she would prefer to marry Anton, nephew of the Holy Roman Emperor, than the son of a groom. Biron was furious.

On 3 July 1739, Biron processed to the wedding in a coach attended by twenty-four footmen, eight running footmen, four heyducks, four pages, and two gentlemen-in-waiting. The empress, in a hooped silver gown and her hair speckled with diamonds, accompanied the heiress in a golden carriage, the latter wearing "a stiffened bodied gown of silver, a stomacher of diamonds and her black hair curled with four tresses twisted with diamonds and a coronet of diamonds." The carriages were accompanied by running "negroes dressed in black velvet so exactly fitted to their bodies that they appeared naked" except for white feathers in their hair.

Afterwards, the empress helped dress the bride while Biron brought the nightshirted bridegroom to bed. "All this," mused Jane Rondeau, "to tie together two people who heartily hated each other." The heiress, now Anna of Brunswick, "showed it throughout the feasting—and continues to treat him with the utmost contempt." Yet they had to conceive a son.[19]

Now in the fourth year of the war against the Ottomans, Russia was restless* as Münnich invaded the principalities of Moldavia and Wallachia on the lower Danube (present-day Romania). In September at Stavuchany Münnich finally defeated the Ottomans and negotiated peace, winning back Azov and a part of the Caucasus, but he did not win the right to build a fleet on the Black Sea. The war had cost Russia much in blood and treasure—and the gains were meagre.

Anna watched her old enemies: Vasily Dolgoruky and Dmitri Golitsyn were denounced and arrested for privately disparaging the empress. Far away in Siberian exile, Ekaterina Dolgorukaya, once Peter II's fiancée, had been courted by a presumptuous clerk who was thrashed by her brother. The clerk denounced them for treasonable talk and the empress arrested the family and had them concentrated in Shlisselburg. Under torture, Ivan, Peter II's favourite, confessed to falsifying the tsar's will and to sedition. None of these fallen bunglers was a threat, but Anna ordered a judicial massacre: Golitsyn was sentenced to death but died in prison. Marshal Dolgoruky was sentenced to death, commuted to life imprisonment on Solovetsky Island, while his cousins Ivan and three others were beheaded, the innocent pawn Ekaterina Dolgorukaya locked in a monastery. Meanwhile a luckier bride had better news: the princess of Brunswick was pregnant.[20]

The empress, who amused herself by inventing new torments for her chicken-clucking fool Golitsyn, decided to marry him to a fat and ugly middle-aged Kalmyk servant nicknamed Buzhenina—Pork 'n' Onions— after the empress's favourite dish. Her minister Volynsky pandered to her playful sadism and devised a spectacular of freakish whimsy: the empress and a cavalcade of women in national dress from each of the "barbarous races" processed to the new Winter Palace in carriages pulled by dogs, reindeer, swine and camels followed by an elephant with a cage on its back containing Golitsyn and Pork 'n' Onions. The empress led the couple on to the frozen Neva to reveal an ice palace thirty-three feet high amid a fair of wonders including an ice cannon that fired real shells and an elephant that projected water jets into the air. Inside their bridal

---

* Anna expelled all Jews to soothe popular discontent. After Peter I's death, Catherine I had expelled all Jews in 1727. Now Anna reissued that decree. A Jew was burned alive for building a synagogue opposite a church in his village and for converting a Christian, who was executed with him. Yet Biron was the patron of a "court Jew," Isaac Libman from Riga, who was appointed "Ober-Hof-Kommissar" at Anna's court in 1734 where he handled and earned vast sums as supplier to the armies and as middleman in artistic and jewellery commissions such as the bejewelled sword awarded to Münnich. Libman unusually remained a practising Jew who continued to serve Anna. One of the empress's doctors was the converted Portuguese Jew Antonio Sanchez.

palace, Anna showed the "bridal fools" a lavatory commode and (the big joke) a four-poster bed with mattress and pillows all carved out of ice—but, to the empress's glee, lacking any soft linen or bedclothes. The log fire too was a trick—lit by naphtha. Leaving the frozen couple, guarded by soldiers, Anna retired to the Winter Palace. They survived their wedding night, and Pork 'n' Onions later produced two sons.[21]

The impresario of the Ice Wedding, Volynsky, started to plot against Biron. At his salon, he discussed reform and criticized Anna's grotesque ineptitude. "Our sovereign is a fool," he told his coterie. "When you report, you get no decision from her at all." Reading a description of Joanna II, queen of Naples, as "weak, foolish and dissolute," the minister exclaimed, "SHE! This is she!"

Anna celebrated the Turkish peace—but there was little to show for it since by the Treaty of Belgrade the resurgent French forced Russia to abandon all its gains except Azov, which was not to be fortified. Anna gave Münnich a diamond-studded sword, but it was not enough: aspiring to royalty like Biron, he asked to be prince of Ukraine. "The marshal is really too modest," Anna replied tartly. "I would have thought he'd be satisfied with nothing less than Grand Duke of Muscovy." Volynsky got 20,000 roubles.

"Extremely impetuous, a man of boundless ambition, vanity and indiscretion," Volynsky felt confident enough to pitch his ideas on reform and on reduction of German influence to Empress Anna because she had resented Biron's attempt to marry his son to the heiress. Volynsky suggested dismissing her favourite. Biron struck back: "Either he or I must go," he told Anna. She wept, but on 12 April Volynsky and his circle were arrested and tortured by Ushakov until his comments on Anna herself and his plans for a coup were revealed.

Volynsky was found guilty of plotting to murder Biron, Münnich and Osterman, and was sentenced to death by impalement. On 27 June, the physical ruin of the once vigorous Volynsky, many of his joints dislocated by torture, was dragged out in bandages. Spared the impalement, his tongue was cut out—then, his mouth gagged to stop the bleeding, his right hand and head were sliced off.

The flustered empress, now extremely anxious about rumours that Sweden was about to attack but grateful that "our trustee" Münnich was in charge, retreated from this spectacle of butchery to go hunting.[22]

On 12 August, the empress returned from Peterhof in time to see Anna of Brunswick deliver a male heir named Ivan after the empress's father. Anna effectively kidnapped the baby from the exhausted mother. But the heir had arrived just in time, for on 5 October the empress fainted after a dinner with the Birons and was carried to her bed.

Fearing what would happen if the princess of Brunswick became regent, Biron insinuated that someone else must be found to "keep the unruly people quiet"—namely himself. The British ambassador Edward Finch reported the empress's symptoms "strong vomitings attended with vast quantities of putrid blood."

Lying in the Summer Palace the empress had not specified whether the princess of Brunswick or her baby Ivan was now the heir nor, if it was to be the baby, who would be regent. Osterman retired to bed, until Anna summoned him. Arriving in a sedan-chair, he backed the baby to be tsar. But Anna prevaricated about the regency. Biron begged on his knees.

Osterman advised Anna against a Biron regency, and she herself feared that it would endanger the already hated Biron. "I warn you, duke, you will be unhappy," she said, but if he lost power, his enemies would destroy him; his only choice was to amass more. Biron summoned the grandees and charmed, threatened and bribed them into acquiescence. But Anna did not sign the decree. On 10 October she was well enough to present the baby to the courtiers: "Here's your future ruler!"

On the 15th, Anna sickened, unable to pass urine. She still had not signed the regency decree. Now she called in an old servant, signed the document in front of her, told her to conceal it in a jewellery box, keep the key and not reveal it until she was dead. On the 17th, Anna was paralysed on her left side and in agony in her loins as the infection spread—but she remained awake. At around 7 p.m. she bid goodbye to the princess of Brunswick and Elizaveta. "Never fear, never fear," she murmured. At 10 p.m., Anna died at the age of forty-six.

As the doors of the death chamber swung open, the princess of Brunswick wept over the body. Biron was distraught. Procurator-General Prince Nikita Trubetskoi, newly appointed to that long-vacant office, announced the accession of the baby-emperor Ivan VI. The prince of Brunswick stood frozen behind the chair of his wife until Biron asked, "Don't you wish to hear the last commands of the empress?" Osterman read out the regency decree: Biron was the ruler of Russia. Afterwards the triumphant regent went to his rooms—and the Brunswicks went to nurse the new tsar, aged six weeks.[23]

The body of the empress lay in state* in the Summer Palace, where the regent chose to live until she was buried. Next morning the baby-emperor

---

* On 9 October the other emperor in Europe, Holy Roman Emperor Karl VI, archduke of Austria, had died in Vienna, leaving only a female heir, his daughter Maria Theresa.

and his parents moved to the Winter Palace. Biron had noticed the passive-aggressive discontent of the Brunswicks and he immediately started to court Tsarevna Elizaveta, raising her allowance. Anna's body was barely cold before the hatred for Biron started to bubble over. Osterman, sensing danger, retired to bed, painting his face with lemon juice and staging fake fits, but a group of noblemen were denounced for insulting Biron, who had them tortured. They implicated Prince Anton himself. On 23 October, Biron staged a humiliating public interrogation of Anton of Brunswick during which he admitted that "he wanted to rebel a little." Biron threatened to send the tsar's parents back to Germany. Agonizing over his own unpopularity, he kept Marshal Münnich close. They had dinner every night. Münnich expected to be promoted to supreme commander—but nothing happened. Biron used him to harass the Brunswicks, but this meant that the marshal was constantly visiting them in the Winter Palace. On 8 November, when he was alone with Anna of Brunswick, he told her that she was in danger from Biron and sought her permission to arrest him. He asked her to march with him. She agreed, and Münnich recruited one of his colonels, Hermann von Manstein, as chief hatchetman—then went to dinner with the regent, who, "moody and restless, often changed the discourse like an absent man."

"Tell me, marshal," Biron asked him, "in your military ventures, did you ever undertake an affair of consequence by night?"

Did the duke know what was planned that night? Was Münnich himself about to be arrested? He had to answer with his usual elan that "he didn't remember but that his maxim was—'Always seize the favourable moment!'"

That moment was now. At 11 p.m., as Münnich was saying goodnight, Biron revealed that after the tsarina's funeral he was going to place Elizaveta or Holstein on the throne and destroy his enemies. Münnich was even more "determined to strike his blow without delay."

At 2 a.m., the marshal met Manstein and thirty trusted Guardsmen and together they headed to the Winter Palace. Leaving Manstein to explain the mission to the palace sentries, Münnich used a back entrance to enter the apartment of Julie von Mengden, maid-of-honour, who led him along the corridors to the apartment of the Brunswicks. Julie woke them up: the marshal was waiting. Anton asked what it was all about, but his wife told him it was nothing. She sent him to bed.

---

He had canvassed Europe to agree what became known as the Pragmatic Sanction—that a female could succeed him—though the imperial title would have to be held by her husband. But her accession provided an opportunity for a young monarch who had also just succeeded to his throne: the Prussian Frederick II the Great.

Münnich invited Anna of Brunswick to lead the troops. Instead she addressed the officers. When they filed in, the young princess told them that she "hoped they wouldn't refuse the greatest mission for the young tsar and his parents—to arrest the regent whose atrocities were known to everyone, and they were to do whatever the marshal ordered." Then she embraced Münnich and the officers kissed her hand. They set off into the night towards the Summer Palace—and Anna and her friend Julie went to see the little emperor.

Münnich told the men to load their muskets. Two hundred yards from the Summer Palace, Münnich halted his men and ordered Manstein to approach the regent's guards, who instantly agreed to join the revolution. Münnich, "who liked all his enterprises to have something striking about them," turned to Manstein: "Gather twenty men, enter the palace, seize the duke and, if he resists, slaughter him without mercy!"

Manstein crept inside the palace with his twenty men following silently—but he got lost in the corridors. He could not ask the servants, so he just kept going until, "after going through two chambers," he came to a locked sliding door that he forced open. "In the chamber," he remembered, he "found a great bed in which the duke and duchess [the Birons] were lying buried in so profound a sleep that not even the forcing of the door had woken them." Getting close to the bed, he drew the curtains, finding himself on the duchess's side, and "desired to speak to the regent." Both the Birons sat up, and "began to scream with all their might, rightly judging," as Manstein put it, "that he had not come to bring them any good news." Stark naked, Biron threw himself to the ground, hoping to hide under the bed. At this Manstein ran round and, "springing" on to his prey, "held him fast until the Guards arrived." The duke got to his feet "distributing blows with his fists left and right" which the soldiers answered with their rifle butts. They threw him to the ground and stuffed a handkerchief in his mouth, tied his hands and then carried him "naked as he was" into the guardroom. Having borne him struggling and kicking through the Great Hall past the open coffin of Empress Anna, they loaded him into Münnich's carriage. Biron had ruled for three weeks.

The shrieking duchess chased after them in her nightdress until a soldier tossed her into a snowdrift. Back at the Winter Palace, Anna of Brunswick addressed the gathered Guards and declared herself "Grand Duchess of Russia and the Regent of the Empire." Münnich, imagining "that no one would dare to undertake the least thing against him," demanded that the new regent promote him to generalissimus, but she replied, "This [rank] would suit no one better than the father of the emperor." Münnich could not restrain his "outrageous ambition" and then wanted to be duke of Ukraine. Days later, the regent promoted her husband to generalissimus, Münnich to "premier ministre" and Osterman to general-admiral—all Germans. To satisfy the Russians she appointed Cherkassky as chancellor. She most trusted Ivan Brilkin, one of her chamberlains who had been exiled by Empress Anna for facilitating her affair with Lynar. She promoted him to procurator-general. On 23 December, Empress Anna was buried—and so far, Ivan VI had reigned for just six weeks.[24]

The baby tsar's throne was a high-backed chair on wheels, a pram imperial. When he was driven from the Summer to the Winter Palace, he sat on a cot on his nurse's knee in the royal carriage escorted by a detachment of the Guards and chamberlains walking on foot and preceded by the grand marshal of the court while his young mother the regent, Anna of Brunswick, followed in her carriage.

Just twenty-two years old, "handsome, with a very pretty figure, extremely capricious, passionate and indolent," Anna loved just two people in a highly unusual *ménage à trois*, a girl and a man. Her tiny coterie met all day for cards, sewing and chat. "Frank, sincere, intelligent . . . her cold exterior concealed an affable, loving and loyal heart," wrote her friend Ernst Münnich, the marshal's son.

The regent now did exactly what she liked, lazing around with her hair *distrait*, wearing just a louche "petticoat and short cloak—a very simple state of undress," while reading romantic novels. "Nothing was more delightful for her than to read about an unhappy imprisoned princess, expressing herself with noble pride."

Her darling girlfriend was Julie von Mengden, daughter of a Baltic German courtier. Her confidante during the coup, Julie—or Julka—olive-skinned, dark and beautiful, received one of Biron's estates worth 140,000 roubles and all his gilded regalia and costumes. Anna's lover was Count Lynar, whom she met in Julie's suite while Julie kept guard outside, barring her husband from entering. But Lynar, still Saxon ambassador, had returned to Dresden to resign so that Anna could appoint him grand chamberlain.

The British ambassador, Edward Finch, with whom the regent played cards every night, observed this *ménage à trois* and reported to London that Anna of Brunswick "loved Julia as passionately as only a man loves a woman." Indeed "I should give your lordship but a faint idea of it by adding that the passion of a lover for a new mistress is but a jest to it." Another intimate observer noticed that the girls slept together in the same bed "without any other dress than a petticoat." Yet Anna's love letters to Lynar prove that she loved him—"my soul, yours till death"—and Julie was in love with him too—"her heart is far away." Their letters, which have not been published, show that this was that unusual thing—a truly circular *ménage à trois*—because when she wrote about "her" Julie's love for Lynar, she also wrote "my" immediately above each "her." Lynar was always in her thoughts: "I won't be happy until I know you're on your way here."

This was the *ménage* or something like it that had so alarmed Empress Anna five years earlier. The regent evidently wanted both Julie and Lynar, yet she was married. So they planned that Julie should marry Lynar. This meant that the Saxon lover could regularly visit the regent. Needless to say, this upset her husband and led to "misunderstandings which last whole weeks," encouraged by the minxy Julie "who inflamed the grand duchess even more against her husband." But, to complicate matters further, when she wasn't sleeping with Julie or Lynar, she shared a bed with Prince Anton and was soon pregnant again.

Regent Anna was a clement ruler, yet totally out of her depth. "She loved to do good," remarked Manstein, "but didn't know how to do it properly." Münnich was unimpressed: "She was naturally lazy and never appeared at Cabinet." When he presented her with business, she often told him, "I wish my son was already of age to rule by himself." But she did not trust the slippery marshal. "I don't know who to believe," she wrote naively to Lynar, "but I've never had so many friends since I took the regency. Better not to know everything." No autocrat could ever afford to think such a thing.[25]

Meanwhile Biron, under interrogation in Shlisselburg Fortress, revealed that he would never have accepted the regency without the encouragement of Münnich, "the most dangerous man in the empire." When he returned from sick leave early in 1741, Münnich discovered that he was premier only in name. Rising to the apogee of his power, in a career that had started with Peter the Great in 1703, Osterman cleverly exposed Münnich's ignorance of foreign policy. When the marshal threatened to resign, the regent accepted it and placed him under house arrest. Osterman was supreme.

In July 1741, sensing Petersburg was adrift and encouraged by France, Sweden, keen to win back its lost territories, seized the moment. Citing Russian aggression, the rule of German interlopers and the exclusion of Elizaveta, the Swedes attacked Russia. Here they touched on the regent's most sensitive nerve: Elizaveta, thirty-two years old, popular for her earthy sensuality and common touch, was a charismatic contrast to German regent, baby and minister. The Guards loved her: on New Year's Eve, her palace at Tsaritsyn Lug beside the Field of Tsaritsyn parade ground was "packed with Guardsmen unceremoniously calling the princess their godmother."

The Brunswicks tried to marry her to Anton's brother Ludwig. Elizaveta began to consider launching a coup, encouraged by the conspiratorial French ambassador, the marquis de La Chétardie, whose mission was to break the Austrian alliance. The mastermind of her intrigues was Jean Armand de Lestocq, a French doctor hired by Peter the Great and trusted by Catherine. This Lestocq, whom Manstein called "the most giddy man alive and least capable of keeping a secret," fancied himself an international man of mystery. Elizaveta became the centre of a web of coded notes, signals given at balls and masked meetings "on dark nights during thunderstorms, heavy downpours, and snowstorms, at places people used to dump rubbish." Lestocq, that maestro of clandestinity, liaised with the French and the Swedes. But Elizaveta was pleasure-loving and a coup was a perilous enterprise. She prevaricated.

On 23 August, the army defeated the Swedes, a victory that should have fortified the regent, yet her adviser Lynar was still abroad. As her authority leached away, Osterman advised Anna to become empress. She set her coronation for 7 December.

On 20 October, the shah of Persia, Nadir Shah,* sent a magnificent embassy, riding on fourteen elephants to Petersburg, that showered the regent with Mughal jewels, which Anna enjoyed showing to Julie. "The Persian ambassador had an audience with his elephants," the regent wrote to her lover Lynar in Germany. "But asks for the hand of Princess Elizaveta: what is to be done? Don't take this as a Persian fairytale: I'm not joking . . ." The shah was indeed deadly serious. "He asks for her hand or threatens to go to war." Osterman refused to let the Persians meet Elizaveta. Elizaveta was never going to retire to the harem of this monster but, craving his jewels, she warned Osterman not to forget that she was the daughter of his master Peter the Great.

The poor regent was ever more "fretful" and, at one of her court days, she tripped on her dress and fell at Elizaveta's feet. Only Lynar could rescue her: "I won't be happy until you're on your way here," she wrote to him on 13 October. He feared that Julie was overtaking him in her affections. "How could you even for a moment doubt her/my love after

---

* Nadir Shah was an extraordinary Persian warlord, a herdsman's son who had raised himself to the throne. An eighteenth-century, Near Eastern version of Napoleon with a touch of Tamerlane, he conquered Iraq and then the Caucasus where the Russians were forced to retreat. In 1739 he defeated the Mughals and captured Delhi, where he looted the Peacock Throne. These elephants and jewels were Mughal booty. The conqueror was assassinated in 1747. The elephants were presented to the regent who kept them in a special yard.

all the signs given by her/me?" She reassured him. Meanwhile, she dreaded the court masquerades: "I won't be able to enjoy entertaining (without you my soul) because I foresee my dear Julia, whose heart and soul is far away, won't be fun. It's true what the song says: nothing looks like you but everything reminds me of you. I kiss you—yours till death."

Osterman's spies warned Anna that Elizaveta's coup was imminent. "There's so many things I want to hear your opinion about," Anna told Lynar about the visit of a French agent to Elizaveta. "Everyone gives me so much advice, I don't know who to believe . . . Half is surely lies."

On 23 November, the regent, holding her court day, took Elizaveta aside: "What's this, Matushka—I hear that Your Highness corresponds with the army of the enemy and your doctor visits the French envoy?" Elizaveta "shed abundance of tears" and protested her innocence so sincerely that the regent believed her. That night at their card game, the marquis de Botta, the Austrian envoy, warned Anna: "Don't neglect taking care of yourself. You're on the brink of a precipice. Save yourself! Save the emperor!"

As soon as Elizaveta got home, she "returned to the game"—as the French ambassador Chétardie put it—consulting Dr. Lestocq and her coterie. The Guards were being sent off to the war, Lestocq was about to be arrested and the regent was about to be crowned empress. It was now or never. "This requires daring," said her most trusted courtier Mikhail Vorontsov, "but where is such daring to be found but in the child of Peter the Great?" The next morning Lestocq supposedly offered her a card with a crown on one side and the nun's veil with gallows on the other. "Take your choice, My Lady," he said.[26]

SCENE 3

# Russian Venus

# CAST

Anna of Brunswick, regent and grand duchess 1740–1
Prince Anton of Brunswick, her husband, generalissimus
IVAN VI, emperor 1740–1, their son
Baroness Julie von Mengden, their friend, "Julka"
ELIZAVETA, empress 1741–61, daughter of Peter the Great and Catherine I
PETER III, emperor 1761–2, duke of Holstein, grand duke, son of Annushka, grandson of Peter the Great, Elizaveta's nephew and heir, "Little Holstein Devil"
CATHERINE II (THE GREAT), empress 1762–96 (née Sophie of Anhalt-Zerbst), grand duchess, wife of Peter III
PAUL I, emperor 1796–1801, son of Peter III and Catherine II


COURTIERS: ministers etc. of Elizaveta

Jean Armand de Lestocq, court doctor and Prussian agent, later count
Alexei Razumovsky, count, Elizaveta's lover, "Night Emperor"
Kyril Razumovsky, his brother, count, hetman of Cossacks
Mikhail Vorontsov, count, vice-chancellor, later chancellor
Andrei Ushakov, secret police chief, general, count
Alexei Bestuzhev-Riumin, count, vice-chancellor, later chancellor
Prince Vasily Dolgoruky, field marshal, head of War Collegium
Prince Nikita Trubetskoi, procurator-general, field marshal
Nikita Panin, Paul's oberhofmeister
Peter Shuvalov, count, master of ordnance, field marshal, "Mughal"
Alexander Shuvalov, his brother, count, secret police chief, field marshal, "Terror"
Ivan Shuvalov, cousin of Peter and Alexander, Elizaveta's lover

## SEVEN YEARS WAR

Stepan Apraxin, field marshal, count, head of War Collegium
Alexander Buturlin, count, field marshal
Frederick the Great, king of Prussia
Count Wilhelm von der Goltz, Prussian emissary


## COURTIERS: ministers etc. of Peter III

Elizabeth Vorontsova, mistress of Peter III, niece of Mikhail Vorontsov
Andrei Gudovich, Peter's favourite, adjutant-general
Baron Karl von Ungern-Sternberg, his other favourite, adjutant-general
Alexander Glebov, procurator-general
Dmitri Volkov, state secretary
Lev Naryshkin, master of the horse


## SUPPORTERS OF CATHERINE

Grigory Orlov, Guards officer, Catherine's lover
Alexei Orlov, his brother, "Scarface," Guards officer
Grigory Potemkin, sergeant of the Horse Guards, "Alcibiades"

After midnight on 25 November 1741, Elizaveta donned a breastplate and, accompanied by Dr. Lestocq, music master Schwartz and courtier Vorontsov, emerged from her palace and drove in a sleigh through a blizzard across Petersburg to the Preobrazhensky Guards barracks where she rallied her supporters, 300 in total. "My friends," she said, holding a pike, "just as you served my father, now loyally serve me!" This Venus in a cuirassier must have been a stirring sight for any Guardsman. "We'll die for Your Majesty and the Motherland!" they cried.

At 2 a.m., they sped off on sleighs through the snow. They halted at Admiralty Square and proceeding on foot advanced silently towards the Winter Palace. A French diplomat "caught sight of 400 grenadiers at the head of whom stood the most beautiful" Elizaveta. As they hurried through the grey light, Elizaveta struggled to walk in the snow with her gown and breastplate, so the Guards picked her up and bore her on their shoulders, her gold locks flowing.

Entering the palace, Elizaveta addressed the sentries in their guardroom: "Wake up, children, you know who I am. Will you follow me?" They immediately joined her, allowing Vorontsov and Lestocq to lead a detachment up to the apartments of the regent, while others fanned out around the city to arrest Münnich and Osterman.

Regent Anna of Brunswick was awoken by soldiers and arrested by Vorontsov and Lestocq. "Ach, we're finished," she sighed. She dressed and climbed into the sleigh that was to convey her to Elizaveta's palace; her husband was tossed in after her, half naked. "Will we see the princess [Elizaveta]?" she asked, but in fact she never saw her again. She begged for Julie to be allowed to stay with her, and this was permitted.

The Guards waited for the deposed baby Ivan VI to awaken in his crib, and he was then arrested (in so far as a Guardsman can "arrest" a baby) and brought to Elizaveta, who held the ex-tsar in her arms. "You're not guilty of anything," she said. As dawn broke, soldiers celebrated; courtiers rushed to worship the rising sun.[1]

At her palace, Elizaveta first embraced her Cossack lover Alexei Razumovsky and then received the submission of the grandees, while in another chamber, under guard, the fallen Brunswicks and Julie von Mengden awaited their fate with their two babies, one of them a deposed tsar. She immediately promoted Razumovsky and courtiers Vorontsov and the Shuvalov brothers, Peter and Alexander—all to be counts and chamberlains.*

Elizaveta disdained to appoint a cabinet like Anna, and was keen to rule directly as her father had done. Actually, she ruled through two men. Since she had no experience of politics, she allowed the French ambassador Chétardie to propose that Biron's fallen sidekick, Alexei Bestuzhev-Riumin, should be vice-chancellor. But Elizaveta must have known him well anyway as he was the son of Peter's retainer who became Empress Anna's lover. Bestuzhev, now forty-eight, was ungainly, sloppy-lipped, "more feared than loved, exceedingly scheming, suspicious, wilful and daring, tyrannical in his principles, an implacable enemy but a friend to his friends." This diplomatic hypochondriac was an amateur chemist who had invented his own nerve-calming medicine. Her other potentate was Prince Nikita Trubetskoi, aged forty-two, who had helped organize Anna's counter-coup in 1730. He possessed aptitude and connections, a Naryshkin relative married to one of Chancellor Golovkin's many daughters. Restored to his old office of procurator-general, he ran most of her domestic government.

The new Prussian king, later known as Frederick the Great, had recently launched an unprovoked attack on Austria to seize the rich province of Silesia, encouraged by the death of Tsarina Anna because he knew the rule of the baby Ivan VI would prevent Russia intervening. He was exploiting the questionable succession of a female heir, the young Maria Theresa, to the Austrian throne; his attack† sparked dec-

---

* Vorontsov came from an old boyar family; the Shuvalov brothers were a new family from Kostroma but both were connected to the Scavronskys, the family of Elizaveta's mother. Peter Shuvalov consolidated his position by marrying Elizaveta's confidante Mavra Shepeleva. The empress remembered her father's favourites too: Hannibal had only just survived the intrigues of Menshikov, Anna and the regency, but on 12 January 1742 Elizaveta promoted him to major-general and awarded him the 6,000-acre estate of Mikhailovskoe, later famous as the home of his great-grandson, the poet Pushkin. And in the last act of a rollercoaster career, she recalled her godfather, Marshal Vasily Dolgoruky, from the frozen hell of Solovetsky Island, to become head of the War Collegium. In 1746, he died in office.
† Son of that repellent maniac Frederick William, who had beheaded his son's best friend outside his window, Frederick inherited the throne of a small northern kingdom with a full treasury and a fine army. An aesthete who played the flute and wrote music, an intellectual who debated with the *philosophes*, and a wit whose acidic bons mots are still funny today, he despised Christianity which he saw as a superstition "spawned in the fevered imaginations of the Hebrews." His Silesian war was the exploit of a reckless political gambler: "Take first; negotiate after," said this cynical diplomat. He was also an enlightened visionary who regarded himself as "servant of the state" and a brilliant general. He despised female power and was uninterested in women, completely ignoring his unfortunate wife, and created an openly homoerotic court, favouring a series of male minions including the Italian Count Agarotti to whom he addressed a poem entitled "The Orgasm." The paragon of a warrior-king, he was hero-worshipped by many. When Napoleon visited his tomb after defeating Prussia he said, "Hats off, gentlemen. If he was alive we wouldn't be here."

ades of European wars—and a competition between Austria, Prussia and France to win over Elizaveta. The empress agreed with Bestuzhev that Russia should follow Osterman's longstanding policy of alliance with Austria to contain France and the newly aggressive Prussia. But her intimates Vorontsov and Lestocq, encouraged by a golden shower of bribes, supported Prussia and France. Lestocq, whose "black and evil heart" was addicted to intrigue, lobbied and spied for his paymasters—even though he knew he would go too far: "I'll be banished in the end!"

On 28 November Elizaveta generously allowed the Brunswicks, Julie and the baby tsar to leave for Riga—and probably Germany. But a day later she ordered their imprisonment in a Baltic fortress. She had dealt with the past. Now for the future.*

She summoned her thirteen-year-old nephew, Karl Peter Ulrich, duke of Holstein, who, as both grandson of Peter the Great and great-nephew of Charles XII, was potential heir to both Russia and Sweden. By the will of Catherine I, he actually ranked above Elizaveta in the Russian succession. "I'm waiting with friendly impatience, my dearest nephew," she declared, "your benevolent and supportive aunt Elizaveta." On 5 February 1742, he arrived and began his Orthodox instruction: Peter Fyodorovich, as he was now known, was proclaimed heir and grand duke.

Peter arrived just in time for the coronation: Elizaveta travelled to Moscow with Razumovsky in Empress Anna's giant sleigh (now in the Kremlin Armoury), the size of a Hollywood Winnebago, pulled by twenty-three horses, and containing tables, beds and even a stove. On 27 February, Elizaveta and her nephew processed into Moscow in a cavalcade of carriages, embarking on two months of prayers and balls that climaxed on 25 April when the empress, wearing a gold brocade dress, entered the Dormition Cathedral. But here there was a change: just as her father had himself crowned her mother in 1724, now Elizaveta placed Anna's crown on her own head, a ritual repeated by all the Romanovs down to 1896.[2]

On Elizaveta's return to Petersburg, her generals advanced into Swedish Finland while Frederick of Prussia was winning his war against Austria. Chétardie, keen to save the French ally Sweden and reduce Russian

---

* Osterman and Münnich were sentenced to death, a penalty that was demanded particularly by Marshal Dolgoruky, who had been exiled and almost executed while Osterman was in power. On 18 January 1742, as Osterman laid his head on the block before an avid crowd, a voice rang out: "God and the empress grant you life!" The reprieved prisoners set out for Siberia where, somewhere on the road, Münnich passed his victim Biron, whom Elizaveta had allowed to settle on a provincial estate. Osterman died in Siberia in 1747.

power, aided by his agent Lestocq, tried to undermine Bestuzhev. But the Russian conquest of Finland left him so exposed that he resigned and returned to Paris. Just when Bestuzhev had signed the peace with Sweden and moved closer to Austria, a conspiracy against Elizaveta threatened to change everything.

One night at a Petersburg tavern, Colonel Ivan Lopukhin, son of that prominent court family, grumbled to a friend about female rule and base origins—criticisms of Elizaveta. The friend denounced him. Under torture, Lopukhin implicated his mother, Countess Natalya Lopukhina, daughter of Matrena Balk, sister of Willem Mons, executed in the last days of Peter the Great. As the "brightest flower" of Anna's and Ivan VI's court, she had indulged in a bitchy rivalry with its other beauty, Elizaveta. After her accession, Elizaveta banned ladies from wearing pink, her favourite colour, but Lopukhina had flouted her order, adding a pink rose to her hair. Elizaveta ordered Lopukhina to kneel before her, cut off the offending lock of hair—and slapped her. Now she was arrested. But this was about much more than fashion policing: the suspects were a cabal that had flourished under Ivan VI. As suspects were tortured by secret police chief Ushakov, now raised to count, Elizaveta directed the interrogations almost as ruthlessly as her father.* She learned that the Lopukhins had been in contact with one of the guards of Ivan VI, whom they wished to reinstate—and simultaneously that Frederick of Prussia was hoping to restore the baby-tsar.

All were sentenced to death by quartering or beheading. At a ball, Elizaveta dramatically pardoned the capital sentences to the cheers of the guests. Instead the women were simply to have their tongues ripped out—those organs of female loose talk; the men to be broken on the wheel. On 31 May, Countess Lopukhina and Anna Bestuzheva were stripped naked and whipped with birches and knouts. Bestuzheva had managed to bribe the executioner who merely clipped her tongue but Lopukhina had failed to do so and when she struggled and bit his hand, he ripped the tongue out with such violence that she passed out. "Who'll take the tongue of the beautiful Madame Lopukhina?" he asked, holding it up. Then her men's bones were hammered to smithereens on the wheel.[3]

No one flouted Elizaveta's fashion rules again, but the revelations of

* When two minor plotters, Sophie Liliënfeld and her husband, were arrested, the girl was pregnant but Elizaveta insisted that "Notwithstanding her condition, as they disregarded the Sovereign's health, there's no reason to spare the rogues, it's better not to hear from them for a century than to expect any fruits from them." Apart from Lopukhina, the main victim was Anna Bestuzheva, whose connections reveal the tiny world of the court: daughter of Chancellor Golovkin, ex-wife of procurator-general Iaguzhinsky, now married to vice-chancellor Bestuzhev's brother.

Prussian plans to rescue the infant tsar Ivan VI rebounded on his family in Voronezh. Elizaveta had them moved at once to Solovetsky in the Arctic. Winter delayed the family at Kholmogory near Archangel in the far north, where Ivan was kept in a special cell while the family settled in the bishop's house. Elizaveta ordered the four-year-old ex-tsar to be kept in solitary confinement, known only as "Grigory," never seeing his parents again.

Anna was now pregnant for the second time since her downfall. The childless Elizaveta was motivated by greed as well as jealousy: she wanted Biron's jewels and was happy to use Anna's love for Julie to get them. "Ask Anna to whom she gave the diamonds which were not found," Elizaveta ordered her officer in Kholmogory. "If Anna says she didn't give the diamonds to anyone, tell her I'll be forced to torture Julka and if she pities her, she shouldn't expose her to such suffering." When little Ivan was ill, Elizaveta banned medical treatment. But he lived on.[4]

After the Lopukhin conspiracy, Vice-Chancellor Bestuzhev was under a cloud, the Austrian alliance in doubt, and the French and Prussians saw their chance. King Frederick proposed a wife for Elizaveta's heir: Sophie, princess of Anhalt-Zerbst, was the daughter of a poor prince in Prussian service but her mother, Joanna, was the sister of the prince-bishop of Lübeck, the only man Elizaveta herself had wanted to marry. "No one," remarked Frederick, "better suited the intentions of Russia and the interests of Prussia." Elizaveta agreed and Frederick commissioned Princess Joanna to help overthrow the pro-Austrian Bestuzhev. Sophie, the future Catherine the Great, set off for Petersburg.

On 9 February 1744, Catherine, as Sophie was renamed on her conversion to Orthodoxy, and her busybody mother arrived at Moscow's Golovin Palace to meet Empress Elizaveta. Then Catherine was presented to Peter, who was excited to meet her. These second cousins had a lot in common as Germans at the Russian court. Catherine's mother had ordered her to charm empress and grand duke, and she succeeded with both. She dutifully listened to Peter's long stories and did all she could to please the empress. Aged fourteen, she at once started instruction in Russian and Orthodoxy, swiftly mastering both—but the marriage nearly did not happen at all.

First Peter fell ill with measles: afterwards he never returned to his studies and his Russian was barely intelligible. Next Catherine suffered a lung infection. When her mother tried to stop her being bled, the empress, sweeping in with her doctors Lestocq and Sanchez, cradled her and took over her treatment, unimpressed by the mother's heartless interventions. Catherine soon learned that her mother was already out of her depth in this turbulent court.

Bestuzhev, the pro-Austrian, had been opposed to the Prussian-arranged marriage, so Frederick's agent Princess Joanna threw herself into intrigues against the vice-chancellor while he was bombarded with offers of Prussian bribes. Elizaveta ordered Bestuzhev and Vorontsov to "open all her letters and see what she's scheming." Chétardie, recently returned to court, plotted with Joanna and reported to Versailles that the empress wasted time on "the most trifling things, enjoying her toilette five times daily, carousing in her apartments with the most vulgar riff-raff." Bestuzhev opened the letters and broke the French code. On 6 June 1744, he confronted Chétardie—and showed the empress these insults.

Outraged by his betrayal, Elizaveta expelled the Frenchman and threatened to throw out Princess Joanna, yet that incorrigible meddler continued to conspire with Lestocq and Frederick the Great. Elizaveta promoted Bestuzhev to chancellor and backed his consistent, traditional alliance with Austria—though the pro-French Vorontsov became his deputy. For the first time in decades, Russian ministers were directing Russian policy—but the heir's Prussian-backed marriage went ahead. In August, Peter came down with smallpox, from which he emerged strangely different, and heavily pockmarked. He recovered in time for his wedding, but the illness may have left him sterile.

At 7 a.m. on 21 August 1745, Catherine was dressed in a silver-brocade wedding dress with a wince-making eighteen-inch waist and a cascade of jewels topped with a diamond tiara. At ten o'clock, rouged and sleekly glowing, she joined Peter and Elizaveta in the eight-horse imperial carriage so big it resembled "a little castle," focus of a procession of 120 carriages that trundled slowly through Petersburg to the Cathedral of Our Lady of Kazan. After the three-hour ceremony, which was followed by a ball at the palace, Catherine was put to bed by giggling ladies. But her husband Peter, drinking with his German cronies, did not appear for hours and, when he did, nothing happened. The marriage would end in murder, but even in its first hours, it precipitated a deadly showdown. Bestuzhev sprang his traps. First he showed Elizaveta the treacherous letters of Catherine's mother. She was sent home. Mother and daughter never met again. Then Bestuzhev entrapped Lestocq taking Prussian bribes.

On 11 November, the empress attended Lestocq's marriage. On the 13th she ordered his arrest. The doctor was tortured and sentenced to death, which Elizaveta commuted to life imprisonment. Frederick had completely failed to win over Elizaveta who, to him, personified all the faults of female power: her rule was simply the "rule of cunt," and he mocked her as an oriental sultana, a power-mad nymphomaniac, like Emperor Claudius's wife—the "Messalina of the North"—insults that earned him her undying hatred.[5]

After Frederick the Great's intrigues, Elizaveta was extremely touchy on the subject of children. On 27 February 1746, the fallen regent Anna of Brunswick gave birth to a third son, but died a week later.* The body was pickled and brought to Petersburg where Elizaveta, accompanied by Catherine, sobbed throughout the funeral of a woman whom she had destroyed—and whose bounty of royal heirs illustrated the apathy of the unconsummated grand ducal marriage.

Peter was already making himself unpopular. Just on brattish reputation, Empress Anna had nicknamed him the Little Holstein Devil, and when Elizaveta got to know him, she agreed. The eighteen-year-old paraded his Holsteiners, mocking the Russian military, giggled as he spilt wine at dinner and made faces at mass "whereby all those in church have been outraged"—and ignored Catherine. Meanwhile his adjutants, Zakhar Chernyshev and his brothers, flirted with Catherine.

Then, while recuperating from an illness, Peter arranged a puppet theatre next to the empress's apartments. Hearing voices through a wooden partition, he drilled holes and invited his sidekicks to join him. He even brought in benches so that the audience could watch the peepshow. When Catherine looked through the hole, she was frightened—but it was too late. Elizaveta heard sniggering and caught them red-handed. "She showered furious condemnation and gross words upon him," recalled Catherine, "betraying as much contempt for him as anger."

"My nephew's a monster," Elizaveta wrote to Razumovsky. "The devil take him." She threatened to treat him as Peter the Great had treated Alexei—and then stormed out.[6]

*

* Anna's husband Anton lived on in Kholmogory with four of his children for over twenty years until his death in 1776. Their two sons and two daughters remained imprisoned in the house there, humble and yet contented for almost forty years. During the 1770s, one daughter, then aged thirty-seven, asked Catherine the Great that "we be allowed to leave the house and go for walks in the meadow; we have heard that flowers grow there," and also that "someone be sent to us who could teach us to dress properly" as "neither we nor our servants know" how to wear corsets or toques. These notes were so poignant that in 1780 Catherine the Great allowed the four to move to Denmark, but they were unaccustomed to normal life. In 1803, Princess Catherine Antonovna of Brunswick asked Alexander I if she could return to Kholmogory "because for me that was paradise." The last of the family died aged sixty-six in Denmark in 1807. As for Julie von Mengden, after twenty years in confinement, she was released aged forty-three by Peter III in 1762 and died in 1786.

The hole in the wall was a window into Elizaveta's world of intimidating frivolity. The teenagers had stared into the apartment where the empress dined informally with her lover Razumovsky. The table, a grand version of a dumb waiter, was hitched up from a lower floor so that the empress and her favourites could talk and play freely—without the eavesdropping servants.

Elizaveta and Razumovsky had been together for thirteen years. Even young Catherine was dazzled, calling him "the most handsome man" she had ever seen. Born just Razum, a Cossack villager hired for his looks and voice to sing in Elizaveta's choir, he was her enduring love. There were rumours that they had secretly married in 1742 in the village of Perovo near Moscow. There is no proof of this, though this paragon of manhood never married anyone else. Both highly religious, it is more likely this ceremony was some sort of blessing.

In 1744, the empress set off on pilgrimage to Kiev, accompanied by Catherine, Peter and Razumovsky. Elizaveta deigned to visit his village— the homecoming of the Cossack boy who had done well. Razumovsky forbade his uncles "to boast in my name and preen themselves as my relatives." But Elizaveta enjoyed his earthy family and so adored his sixteen-year-old brother Kyril, a goatherd in rags, that she invited him to Petersburg and then played Pygmalion to turn him into a cultured aristocrat.

Back in the capital, Elizaveta gave Alexei Razumovsky an apartment in the Winter Palace connected to her own. While the "Night Emperor"—as diplomats called him—was not interested in power, he became fabulously rich. When he was later joined by his brother, they were powerful because of their proximity to the autocrat, yet both shepherds-turned-counts remained surprisingly easy-going. Elizaveta was always in charge, even though she worked as little as possible and partied relentlessly. Time is so often the first victim of autocracy. She often partied until 6 a.m., sleeping till midday and sending for jewellers and ministers in the middle of the night. "Nobody ever knew the hour Her Imperial Majesty would deign to have dinner," recalled Catherine, "and it often happened that the courtiers having waited playing cards till 2 a.m. and gone to sleep were awakened to attend Her Majesty's supper." If they were too sleepy to speak, they were likely to get a slap.

"One could not see her for the first time without being struck by her beauty and majestic bearing," wrote Catherine. "She was a large woman but, though she was stout," her frame could bear it: "she was not disfigured by it and her head was also very beautiful." In dress, morals and taste, she personified the saucy, frothy excess of rococo, the age of the fake beauty spot and the towering wig.* Elizaveta "danced with perfection and had a particular grace in all she did." According to Catherine, "one only regretfully turned one's gaze away from her because no object could replace her." Yet no one admired Elizaveta's beauty more than she herself, and she believed she looked best in male costume. Hence she frequently held what she called Metamorphoses, transvestite balls in which, channelling the topsy-turvy games of her father, she would metamorphose into a very pretty man.

Elizaveta herself specified every detail: "Ladies are to be in gentlemen's clothes the gentlemen in ladies' clothes whatever they have, dresses with full skirts, caftans or negligées." The men "wore hoop skirts and were coiffed like ladies." Catherine hated the Metamorphoses because "most of the women resembled stunted little boys," and men disliked them too as they "felt they were hideous" in drag. "No women looked good except the empress since she was very tall with a powerful build. She had more beautiful legs than I've ever seen on a man."

The autocrat was a fashion despot, issuing decrees like this: "Ladies to wear white caftans of taffeta; cuff-edgings and skirts to be green, lapels trimmed with gold braid: they must have on their heads a papillon-like embellishment with green ribbons, hair drawn up smoothly. Gentlemen: wear white kaftans, camisoles with small slit cuffs, green collars, gold-braided buttonholes."

She always got what she wanted. "I am told a French ship has arrived with ladies' clothes, men's hats and for women beauty spots and gold taffeta," she wrote. "Have all this and the merchant brought here immediately!" When she learned that she had not got there first, one can hear the menace in her response: "Summon the merchant and ask why he was lying when he said he'd sent all the lapels and collars which I'd chosen . . . Now I demand them so order him to find them and not keep them for someone else. And if anyone holds them back, tell him from me he will regret it (ladies included). Whoever I see wearing them will share this punishment!"

* She commissioned a new Winter Palace from Bartolomeo Rastrelli (Carlo Rastrelli's son), but his rococo masterpiece was the Catherine Palace, named after her mother, at Tsarskoe Selo. Everything was done in a rush and Elizaveta interfered in every detail. "It was the work of Penelope," joked Catherine. "What was done today, was destroyed tomorrow. That house was pulled down six times and rebuilt again." But the result, finished in 1756, was stupendous—the façade 1,000 feet long with some 220 pounds of gold; its Great Hall was 8,600 to 10,700 square feet in size. Its Amber Room featured amber panels (given to Peter the Great by the Prussian King Frederick William) set in gold. Elizaveta even travelled rococo: her favourite carriage, ordered from Paris by Kyril Razumovsky (now in the Kremlin Armoury), was so big its wheels are taller than a man; its doors and sides are painted with mythologically sensual scenes by François Boucher.

On her death, there were 15,000 dresses in her wardrobe plus "two chests filled with silk stockings, several thousand pairs of shoes and more than 100 untouched lengths of French fabric."*

But Petersburg's sophistication was a façade: there was so little furniture that the contents of each palace had to be moved every time the empress changed residence. Often her own palaces were so badly built they fell down. When Catherine and Peter were staying in one of Razumovsky's new wooden palaces, the building suddenly started to sink. The grand ducal couple just got out alive; sixteen servants were killed, and a weeping Razumovsky threatened to commit suicide. In Moscow, Elizaveta's Golovin Palace, where seventeen maids-of-honour had to sleep in a cupboard, caught fire. The empress lost 4,000 dresses, and she, Peter and Catherine only just escaped. "It's not rare," marvelled Catherine, "to see coming from an immense courtyard full of mire and filth that belongs to a hovel of rotten wood, a lady covered in jewels and superbly dressed, in a magnificent carriage, pulled by six old nags, and with badly combed valets."

No wonder Peter and Catherine were dazzled by what they saw through the spyhole. But their youthful hijinks ended in mortification and they were obliged to kneel before Elizaveta. "We beg your pardon, Matushka," they said. Even the self-absorbed Elizaveta realized that if Catherine was to get pregnant, she herself had to take control.[7]

She drew up new rules: Peter's German cronies were sent home. She reprimanded the jackanapes for his juvenile games and told Catherine that her sole purpose was to produce an heir. The flirtatious Chernyshevs were despatched abroad. Elizaveta placed her relative, Maria Choglokova, and her husband in charge of the household. Catherine loathed her and burst into tears, a tantrum that brought the empress charging into their apartments. Once again, Catherine knelt and said: "Pardon, Matushka!"

Now more carefully supervised, Catherine suffered from the loneliness of her position. Her first consolation was reading: unlike her husband, who read romantic novels, she was seriously intellectual,

---

* Keeping up with Elizaveta was so expensive that even her ministers were constantly on the verge of impoverishment—and were always begging for more cash. "I've been compelled to buy and furnish households, servants, carriages, and for ceremonies and festivities to make uniforms, rich clothes, fireworks and feasts," Vorontsov told Elizaveta, asking for money for a "poor man" because "the maintenance of a house has begun to exceed my daily income. My duties force me to live like a minister not like a philosopher." Bestuzhev begged Vorontsov to intercede with the empress in respect of his own debts, "or I'll be forced to live in my old wooden kennel and hold meetings with ambassadors in there!" Catherine herself, living on a generous allowance, was soon deeply in debt.

consuming the masterpieces of the Enlightenment. But she suffered depression and headaches. "I lived a life for eighteen years," she said, "from which ten others would have gone crazy and twenty would have died of melancholy."

That pale beanpole was developing into a buxom woman who, she later recalled, loved to ride a horse wildly for as long as thirteen hours at a stretch. Both the depression and the riding may well have been symptoms of sexual frustration and certainly were signs of a girl starved of affection. "I never believed myself to be beautiful," wrote Catherine, "but I was pleasant and that I suppose was my strength." She was not beautiful, but she was comely, blue-eyed and blessed with an acute political intelligence, sexual magnetism and invincible charm.

"There is a woman for whom an honest man would suffer a few blows of the knout without regret," said a courtier as he watched her dance. While Catherine started to attract suitors, Elizaveta had fallen in love again.[8]

In 1748 Elizaveta, now thirty-nine, fell seriously ill, producing conspiracies at court as nervous grandees planned for the future. Catherine told Peter that if in danger they could count on the Chernyshevs and the Guards, but when a huntsman fell to his knees and told the grand duke that he would help him win the throne, Peter panicked and rode off. "From that day, he showed interest in gaining power," Catherine noticed—but lacked the ability to manipulate it.

When the empress recovered, she embarked on one of her many pilgrimages, this time to St. Sabbas near Moscow, where her long-serving retainer Peter Shuvalov introduced her to his orphaned first cousin Ivan Shuvalov. He charmed her so much that she recruited him as companion in prayers at the New Jerusalem Monastery. Sexual indulgence blended naturally with Elizaveta's passionate piety.*

Appointed gentleman of the bedchamber, Shuvalov moved into the Night Emperor's apartments next to Elizaveta, and she gave Razumovsky the Anichkov Palace as a present. Shuvalov was sweet-looking and sweet-natured, but his elevation brought his less sweet relatives to power. The Shuvalovs threatened Bestuzhev and Razumovsky, who

---

* She ordered crackdowns on Old Believers. There had been ineffective decrees to expel the Jews in 1727 and 1740. Elizaveta ordered these decrees to be applied. When a minister pointed to the utility of Jewish trade, she wrote: "I'm not interested in earning profit from the enemies of Christ." Even when Bestuzhev asked if he could employ a Jew in Vienna, she "refused, not wanting a single Jew in her service." Anti-semites are often willing to overlook the Jewishness of their doctors: Elizaveta had inherited Anna's Jewish-born Dr. Sanchez.

devised a counter-seduction—in the person of a young actor who starred in the cadet corps theatre. "She took pleasure in dressing the actors," noted a diplomat, "had superb costumes made for them, and they were covered in her jewels. Above all we noticed that the leading man, a handsome boy of eighteen, was the most adorned." This was Nikita Beketov. At a performance of the playwright Alexander Sumarokov's latest tragedy, Elizaveta fell in love with Beketov. "Outside the theatre he was seen wearing exquisite diamond buckles, rings, watches and lace." The Shuvalovs struck back by lending Beketov an ointment that gave him a rash; then they told Elizaveta the boy was homosexual and afflicted with VD. The empress was horrified.

Ivan Shuvalov, her last great love, eighteen years her junior, had triumphed. "At this time, he was just eighteen and had a very nice face, respectful, polite, attentive and very sweet," wrote Catherine. "I found him in the antechamber, a book in hand. I also liked to read so I remarked upon this." There was something impressive in this delicate connoisseur who was "mild and generous to all." Even as favourite, he was mostly regarded as "beautiful and noble." He turned down titles. "I can say I was born without the desire to attain wealth, honours or titles," he explained later to Vorontsov. "And if, dear sir, I didn't succumb to these temptations throughout the years when passion and vanity possess people, then today, all the more so, I see no reason to do so." His patrons and cousins, the Shuvalov brothers, long-serving courtiers in Elizaveta's entourage, became her chief ministers.*

Yet her young lover, a cut above all of them, grew up quickly, becoming a Russian Maecenas. He was the founder of Moscow University, a newspaper and the Academy of Arts (which met in his delicately elegant palace), backing Russian talent from the peasant-born sculptor Fyodor Shubin to Sumarokov and the poet-scientist Mikhail Lomonosov. He corresponded with Voltaire and built an extraordinary library and art collection of works by Rembrandt and Rubens, which became the seed of the Hermitage Museum.

Titles or no titles, he gradually became the real power in Russia, creating policy privately with the empress, enjoying "all the privileges of a minister without being one." Like Razumovsky, but even more so, he did the empress credit.

---

* Peter Shuvalov, married to the empress's confidante Mavra, was a creative and innovative minister in charge of domestic affairs, and was later chief of artillery, reforming taxes and ordnance. He was notorious for his pomposity and greed, sucking up monopolies of tallow and whale so that he could live with "Asiatic luxury, covered with diamonds like the Mughal," said the French diplomat Jean-Louis Favier. His brother Alexander, whose spasmodic nervous twitch gave him a "hideous grimace," succeeded the late Ushakov as secret police chief—"the Terror of the court, city, the whole empire."

She remains notorious for her fashion addiction and social tyranny, and suffers from the comparison with her brilliant successor but one, Catherine the Great. Yet she restored Russian pride and imperial authority, and clarified the succession. She enjoyed many lovers but none of them became overmighty, and all were surprisingly popular; and she chose well in her ministers Trubetskoi and Bestuzhev.

Yet the cost of her armies, palaces and dresses fell heavily on the millions of serfs, source of all wealth. Hundreds of thousands fled while thousands of others rose up in armed rebellions that had to be crushed. As she eased her father's system of compulsory service for nobles, who increasingly avoided serving for life, she intensified their control over their serfs who, as mere chattels, no longer even took the oath of allegiance and could now be sold and bought, and their masters could now exile them to Siberia for "insolence" without any state permission. Altogether, the "Elizabethan Age" of this spoilt but intelligent and well-meaning empress was a frivolous sequel to the rule of her father—and a rehearsal for that of Catherine the Great.[9]

Elizaveta became more dangerous as she aged. "Never did a woman reconcile herself with greater difficulty to the loss of youth and beauty," observed Favier. When she was angry with what she saw in the mirror, she "locks herself in her chambers." She tried to beat ageing by appearing in gold brocade, "her hair loaded with diamonds, combed back and gathered on top," and no one else was allowed to attempt this coiffeur. Once her hair-dyeing went wrong and, since the blunder obliged her to shave off her hair, she forced every girl at court to do the same. "The ladies wept but obeyed. The empress sent them black perukes to wear till it grew out again." She forbade any mention of illness, beautiful women or her enemy Frederick the Great. "Through her kindness and humanity," wrote Favier, "one sees frequently her pride, arrogance, sometimes even cruelty, but most of all her paranoia." She was always on the move, "she rarely slept two nights in a row in the same place," changed palaces in the middle of the night, altered the positions of doors in her houses—and closely followed any investigations by Alexander Shuvalov, the Terror.[10] Her own ageing concentrated her mind on the sex life of Catherine and Peter: "The empress was very angry that we had no children and wanted to know whose fault it was."

Their principal lady-in-waiting, Choglokova, procured a "pretty painter's widow" Madame Groot to seduce Peter, but whether he was impotent, infertile or just inept, someone else would have to impregnate the grand duchess. Catherine implied that there were moments of closeness between her and Peter. She admits that their marriage was consummated after five years—at this time—and she boasts that Peter asked her advice on political matters and nicknamed her "Madame Resource" for her ingenuity. But the good times were fleeting. She could have loved him, she claimed, if only he had loved her. Having clearly lost his virginity to Madame Groot, he started affairs with Biron's daughter and an actress, followed by a relationship with Madame Teplova, wife of an official. "Imagine, she writes me four-page letters," this charmless unromantic bragged to his wife, showing her Teplova's love letters, "and claims that I should read it and what's more answer it, while I have to go and drill [the Holsteiners]?" Catherine's memoirs are thoroughly prejudiced, written much later in different versions, and she had every reason to libel Peter. But, judging by the reactions of everyone else at court, he was as rebarbative as she claimed.

Catherine found herself the object of much flirtation from Zakhar Chernyshev, now back at court, and from the "truly handsome" (and married) Kyril Razumovsky, who was genial "with an original mind." She asked why he kept visiting.

"Love," he said.

"For whom?"

"For you," he replied. Delighted, she burst out laughing.*

Yet she was most taken with her chamberlain, the twenty-six-year-old Sergei Saltykov, "handsome as the dawn," who, she noticed, kept turning up. Choglokova, with the empress as puppet mistress, was facilitating the access to Catherine of two courtiers: Lev Naryshkin and Saltykov. It was surely no coincidence that the Naryshkins and the Saltykovs were the two families that had married into the Romanovs.

In a clumsy conversation about sex that Catherine thought suspicious (was it a trick?), Choglokova, declaring "how much I love my country," offered: "You are free to choose 'LN' or 'SS.'" Catherine chose SS who, as she later put it, "told me he loved me passionately" and explained to her the mystery of "the happiness that could come from such things"— the joys of sex.

By December 1752, as the court moved to Moscow, Catherine was pregnant, yet her marriage was miserable. Peter captured a rat which he sentenced to death in a military tribunal and hanged in her bedroom.

---

* Elizaveta had sent Kyril on a Grand Tour of Europe to make a Cossack goatherd into a grand seigneur. He studied at Göttingen University. On his return, aged eighteen, she appointed him president of the Academy of Sciences; when he was twenty-two, she made him hetman of Ukraine and a count, and he remained a favourite throughout Elizaveta's and Catherine the Great's reigns. In the Cossack capital Baturin, he built a neo-classical palace. Later, when his sons behaved like aristocrats, Kyril reminded them of their origins by calling for his valet: "Here, bring me my peasant's rags in which I came to Petersburg. I want to recall the happy time when I drove my cattle, crying 'Tsop! Tsop!'"

When she laughed, he was offended. Even though she miscarried twice, Choglokova allowed the lovers to meet, while in a significant gambit, Chancellor Bestuzhev, once Catherine's enemy, encouraged the affair and started to cultivate her: she was the future. She needed little encouragement, either politically or sexually, and soon was pregnant again. Elizaveta appointed Alexander Shuvalov—the Terror—as ober-hofmeister of the young household.

On 20 September 1754, in the Summer Palace in Petersburg, Catherine gave birth to a son, whom she named Paul. The baby was immediately swept up and kidnapped by the empress, thrilled to have an heir. Catherine was left exhausted and bloodied on dirty sheets. While the grand duke boozed with his lackeys, she recovered by reading Voltaire and Montesquieu. When she was given 100,000 roubles as a reward for producing an heir, Peter complained that he had not received a prize, so Elizaveta borrowed the money back and gave it to him. Saltykov, his work done, was sent abroad.

Was Paul the son of Saltykov or of Peter? Catherine, radiating unforgivable malice towards Paul, insisted in her private writings that he was her lover's son—which would make the entire dynasty down to 1917 Saltykov, not Romanov. It is impossible to know, but even in the eighteenth century some babies were the children of their official parents. It is a miracle of genetics that traits of parents appear in children who have never known either of them. Paul grew up hideous so Catherine deliberately muddied the waters by emphasizing the ugliness of Saltykov's brother. Certainly Paul did not look anything like *le beau* Saltykov, but he did look and behave like Peter.[11]

Now the countdown to a new European war intensified the deadly rivalries that Peter and Catherine could not avoid.

On 12 June 1755 a new British ambassador, Sir Charles Hanbury-Williams, arrived in Petersburg charged with winning over Elizaveta to an alliance against France and Prussia, a policy supported by Bestuzhev. When Catherine sat next to the "merry and pleasant" Hanbury at dinner, they hit it off and he became her elder mentor—and she even wrote her first memoirs for him. Afterwards they watched his twenty-two-year-old Polish secretary, Stanisław Poniatowski, as he danced. The Pole, romantic and cultured child of the Enlightenment, flirted with her. "Endowed with very great sensitivity and an appearance that was at least interesting and pleasing at first sight," Catherine knew she was attractive, "and therefore halfway along the road to temptation . . . for to tempt and be tempted are very close." Catherine and Poniatowski became lovers—but their affair was soon overtaken by the baroque drama that was European power politics.*

On 19 September, Bestuzhev and Hanbury persuaded Elizaveta to agree an alliance with Britain—designed to stop Frederick's aggression and specifically protect George II's German kingdom, Hanover. Hanbury "was overjoyed with his success" and Frederick was rattled—but Elizaveta delayed signing the treaty for so long that on 16 January 1756, Frederick of Prussia dramatically pulled off his own alliance with Britain. This Anglo-Prussian axis made a confusing mess of Elizaveta's own Anglo-Russian treaty aimed at Prussia—and it threw Frederick's old ally France into the arms of its traditional enemy Austria, which was already allied with Russia. Elizaveta was incensed and blamed Bestuzhev but these poisonous contradictions were unsustainable and could only be resolved by a diplomatic revolution: in May, France and Austria signed the Treaty of Versailles.

On 18 August 1756, Frederick, funded by London, invaded Saxony, a strike that Russia could not tolerate. Elizaveta joined France and Austria in the Seven Years War, to crush Frederick who now faced the greatest powers in Europe.† Elizaveta created a war cabinet called the Conference of the Imperial Court. Behind the scenes, it was Ivan Shuvalov, now aged twenty-nine, who, while refusing to join the Conference, read despatches and sent orders to generals.

Yet the future was uncertain: Peter, who spent his time drilling a small detachment of Holstein soldiers in Prussian style, often wearing a Prussian general's uniform, had always hero-worshipped Frederick.

---

* Its serpentine twists were personified by a transvestite French diplomat, the Chevalier d'Eon, who now arrived in Petersburg as an agent of "Le Secret de Roi," the covert personal policy of Louis XV that aimed to secure the Polish throne for the king's brother and a French alliance with Russia. D'Eon, who was apparently born with hermaphroditic genitals that were more male than female, was unsure of his transgender sexuality—a rather twenty-first-century phenomenon. In Petersburg, he claimed that he had assumed the identity of a woman, Mademoiselle Auguste, to communicate with Elizaveta whose transvestite balls made such sexual transformation quite natural. But it seems he invented his crossdressing in Petersburg. His transgender crisis came later when he was sent on to London in 1763. There he embarrassed his king by unconsciously revealing plans to invade Britain. Rumours spread that d'Eon was really a woman. In 1777, Louis XVI disowned but pardoned him provided he assumed his female identity, which he did for the rest of his life, asserting that he had been born a woman. Yet when he died in 1810, doctors found him male.

† When Elizaveta learned of Frederick the Great's plans to overthrow her in favour of Ivan VI she tightened the already draconian security around the fifteen-year-old prisoner who was moved to the Shlisselburg Fortress. He was once brought into Petersburg where at Peter Shuvalov's house, Elizaveta inspected this wreck of a boy, hollow-eyed, stuttering and half mad, though he knew who he was. He was returned to his place of secret, solitary confinement—a Russian version of the man in the iron mask. "If he talks obscenely, put him in chains," ordered Alexander Shuvalov. "If he pays no attention, beat him with a stick." In the event of any attempt to liberate him, he was to be killed.

Now that Russia was at war with his hero, he greeted news of Russian successes with incredulity: "All this is a lie; my sources speak quite differently." He did not conceal from Catherine that he "felt he hadn't been born for Russia and he didn't suit the Russians nor the Russians him."

Worried about what would happen when the empress died, Bestuzhev made desperate contingency plans—always a risky activity. Using the society jeweller Bernardi as covert courier to Catherine, the old chancellor proposed that Peter should rule in tandem with his wife while he himself ran the government. Catherine did not commit herself.

Elizaveta appointed as commander-in-chief the head of the War Collegium, Stepan Apraxin, son of Peter the Great's admiral, who was an ally of Bestuzhev and a friend of Catherine. But travelling with a personal baggage train that took 500 horses to bear his luxuries, he advanced slowly, nervous of the brilliance of his enemy Frederick and the instability of his own court. On 19 August 1757 at Gross-Jägersdorf, Apraxin defeated the Prussians.

Elizaveta was ecstatic, yet Russian supply and command were both woeful. Apraxin did not advance—instead, learning the empress was ill, he "retreated as if vanquished," wrote an amazed Frederick. Bestuzhev became uneasy and encouraged Catherine to write to Apraxin telling him "to turn his march around."

Peter had come to hate Catherine so much that she feared his accession. She was superb with male potentates and spent hours talking with old countesses: "I sat down with them, inquired about their health, offered advice on what to take in case of illness . . . I learned the names of pugdogs, parrots, fools. In this simple and innocent fashion I accumulated great goodwill." She promoted herself as "an honest and loyal knight" in whom "the charms of a very attractive woman" were "joined to the mind of a man . . . Thus I disarmed my enemies." But she had to be careful: she fell pregnant by Poniatowski.

"God knows where my wife gets her pregnancies," shouted Peter. "I don't know if the child is mine." She realized she faced three possible paths: "1. to share the Grand Duke's fortune; 2. to be exposed constantly to everything it pleased him to devise against me; 3. to take a path independently. A question of perishing with him or by him or saving myself, my children and perhaps the state."

Elizaveta attended the birth of the grand duchess's daughter. Soon Catherine was in real jeopardy.[12]

On 8 September 1757, as Elizaveta came out of mass in Tsarskoe Selo, she fell in a dead faint and did not wake up for two hours. As she recovered, the empress, encouraged by Shuvalov and vice-chancellor Vorontsov, mulled over the fishy manoeuvrings of Apraxin and Bestuzhev. It smelt like treason. On 14 February 1758, Bestuzhev was arrested and interrogated by the Terror; Vorontsov was promoted to chancellor; and the procurator-general Trubetskoi, somehow implicated, fell under a cloud.

Next morning, Poniatowski sent Catherine a note of warning: Bernardi the jeweller, her go-between with Bestuzhev, was under interrogation. Assailed by "a flood of ideas each more unpleasant than the last," Catherine felt "a dagger in my heart." She knew that the spotlight of the Secret Chancellery had been turned on her and Peter, but she was greatly reassured when Bestuzhev sent this message: "Nothing to fear; there was time to burn everything."

If there was no evidence of Bestuzhev's plans for the succession, Catherine was still vulnerable thanks to her letters to Apraxin and the denunciations of her husband. But she knew that the empress preferred her to Peter. "Today my damned nephew irritated me as never before," Elizaveta wrote to Ivan Shuvalov. At 1:30 a.m. on 13 April, the nocturnal tsarina had Catherine woken up and brought to her: Peter and the Terror joined them, while Ivan Shuvalov listened from behind a screen. Catherine threw herself on her knees before Elizaveta, begging to be sent home to Zerbst because "I've incurred your disfavour and the hatred of the grand duke."

"Why do you want to be sent back? Remember you have children," replied the empress.

"My children are in your hands," answered Catherine cleverly.

"You're extremely proud," said Elizaveta. "You imagine no one's cleverer than you."

"If I did believe this, nothing would disabuse me more than my present state."

Catherine "was terribly wicked and very stubborn," Peter told the Terror. The empress wheeled round to silence him.

"How did you dare send orders to Marshal Apraxin?" Elizaveta asked Catherine. "How can you deny it? Your letters are right here."

"Bestuzhev's lying," asserted Catherine.

"Well then, if he's lying, I'll have to have him tortured," said the empress.

Catherine had survived the showdown. When Peter left, Elizaveta held her back. "I'll have many more things to tell you," she said quietly—and later their mutual loathing for Peter brought them back together. Secretly Catherine was no longer impressed by the bullying empress. "Oh that log of a woman," she quoted Poniatowski as saying, "she drives us mad. If only she would die!"

The war strained Elizaveta's nerves. The coalition of Russia, Austria,

France and Sweden should have been able to crush Frederick, but he knew that "unity of command is the most important thing in war" and he outwitted the clumsy allies. Elizaveta ordered Apraxin's arrest. After his first interrogation by Alexander Shuvalov, he perished from a stroke. Catherine now lost Poniatowski, banished to Poland. She distracted herself by reading Diderot, but in March 1759 her baby died.[13]

On 12 April, a lieutenant of the Izmailovsky Guards, Grigory Orlov, aged twenty-five, wounded thrice at the Battle of Zorndorf the previous August, arrived in Petersburg escorting a prisoner, Count Kurt von Schwerin, an adjutant of Frederick. With ironic symmetry, Peter's head was completely turned by the Prussian, while Catherine fell in love with his dashing escort, Orlov.

Gigantic in stature, angelic of face, Orlov deployed heroic derring-do on the battlefield and legendary sexual equipment in the bedroom. He was "blessed with every advantage of figure, countenance and manner." He was soon appointed adjutant to Peter Shuvalov, but quickly offended the Mughal by seducing his mistress, Princess Elena Kurakina.

Meanwhile Peter was thrilled to hobnob with Schwerin, his link to Frederick the Great. "If I were sovereign," he told the count, "you would not be a prisoner of war." This was the sort of foolish comment that outraged Orlov and his fellow Guardsmen, who had shed so much blood at Zorndorf.

Catherine surely arranged to meet Orlov whenever Schwerin talked to her husband. Their affair did not start immediately, but by late 1760 they were in love and Catherine was pregnant. Orlov was "very handsome," wrote the French ambassador, the baron de Breteuil, and "very stupid." The sort of bluff soldier everyone loves, son of a provincial governor, "he was a simple and straightforward man without pretensions, affable, popular, good humoured and honest. He never did an unkindness." He and his four brothers were popular in the Guards, particularly Alexei Orlov, known as "Scarface," who was all "brute force and no heart," precisely the sort of cut-throat a princess in distress might require.[14]

The war was bleeding Russia—and Elizaveta. The new Winter Palace was nearly ready, but she could not afford to finish her apartments. "I fight on," she declared, "even if I have to sell half my clothes and all my diamonds." Frederick outmanoeuvred his cumbersome opponents, but in the spring the Russians, now under General Peter Saltykov, took Frankfurt, then in August 1759 routed Frederick himself at Kunersdorf. "I believe all is lost," wrote Frederick who wore a suicide pack around his neck containing eighteen opium pills. "Farewell for ever."

Elizaveta celebrated but Peter did not believe it: "I know Russians can never beat Prussians." The empress appointed her first lover, Alexander Buturlin, promoted to count and field marshal, to take command, but his leaden slowness outraged her. "The news of your retreat," she wrote, "has caused us more sorrow than a lost battle. We command you to move directly on Berlin and occupy it. If anyone says our army is not fit to storm fortresses, he'll be arrested and brought here in chains!"

In July 1761, Elizaveta, now fifty, collapsed with "an attack of hysterical vapours and convulsions that left her unconscious for some hours." Ignoring her accession-day and birthday, she recuperated alone with Ivan Shuvalov and her grandson Paul, her legs so swollen she could scarcely walk. In August, her cavalry took Berlin for four days—but Frederick fought on. She was dying and Ivan Shuvalov felt the power haemorrhaging away as courtiers looked to the future, to Peter. "I see cunning which I don't understand," Shuvalov wrote to Vorontsov, "and danger which comes from people for whom I have only done good services. My inability to continue providing these has resulted in a loss of respect for me . . . I was never so naive as to think they loved me rather than the benefit they obtained from me." In August, Elizaveta sacked Trubetskoi as procurator-general—after twenty years, leading to a purge of 153 of his protégés in top posts. As the government shook, several conspiracies were hatching. Catherine was encouraged in her plans by Kyril Razumovsky and was backed by Orlov. While Peter was now in love with the unprepossessing Elizabeth Vorontsova, the chancellor's niece, her sister Princess Ekaterina Dashkova, the sparky wife of a Guards officer, represented another group keen to overthrow Peter as soon as Elizaveta was dead. All the factions visited Catherine by night.

"Trust me," Dashkova said to her.

"No one trusted her," thought Catherine.

"You have only to give the order," said Dashkova, "and we will enthrone you."

"I've made no plans," replied Catherine, who was very pregnant by Orlov. "Only one thing to do: meet events bravely."[15]

Elizaveta ordered Ivan Shuvalov to approach Nikita Panin, the governor of Catherine's baby son Paul, to discuss bypassing Peter. Paul would be tsar with Catherine as regent. Panin discouraged him. On 23 December Elizaveta suffered a stroke. In a bedroom in an old wing of the Winter Palace, the Razumovskys and a weeping Ivan Shuvalov stood around the deathbed. Catherine, pregnancy artfully hidden, sat by the bed while Peter drank outside. On the 24th, news of victories against Prussia arrived—Frederick was on the verge of destruction—but the empress was unconscious. At 4 p.m. on Christmas Day she died—then the sobbing courtiers fell to their knees and kissed Peter's hand. The doors were thrown open: Marshal Trubetskoi, with tears running down his face, announced the accession of Peter III.[16]

The crapulent emperor stood at the doorway of the death chamber while Vorontsov set up his government in neighbouring rooms.* Peter radiated magnanimity to Ivan Shuvalov. On the first night of the new reign, Shuvalov stood behind the gloating emperor's chair, jesting and serving him, even though "his cheeks showed his despair," according to Catherine, "for his skin was scratched with all five fingers." Real power, however, resided with the tsar's intimates, his adjutant-generals, the Ukrainian Andrei Gudovich and the Baltic baron Karl von Ungern-Sternberg. The most important friend was far away at Breslau in desperate straits: Frederick the Great.

Peter was determined to make peace at once with his hero and then go to war against Denmark on behalf of his own duchy of Holstein with the aim of winning back the duchy of Schleswig. Even his own chancellor Vorontsov could not believe that the emperor would actually execute such an anti-Russian programme. Peter meant every word.

"We have the most excellent opinion of Your Highness," he wrote to Frederick, "and would be pleased to prove it in every way."

"Thank God," Frederick exclaimed, "on the brink of ruin. . . yet one woman dies and the nation revives . . . Such are the sports of fortune!" He wrote gushingly to Peter: "I'm so glad Your Imperial Majesty received his throne which long belonged to him not so much by heredity but by virtue and to which he adds a new lustre.

"You do of course jest when you praise my reign," replied Peter, "whereas I see you as one of the world's greatest heroes."

A truce was immediately agreed. The letters exchanged between them reveal an emperor infatuated with the king of Prussia, and Frederick for his part incredulously thankful for a miracle of providence.† The Russian army was ordered to withdraw, but Frederick, fearing that it

---

* Peter recalled from exile the victims of the 1740s—Julie von Mengden, the tongueless Lopukhina, Biron and the seventy-nine-year-old Marshal Münnich. The head of the War Collegium, Alexander Glebov, was promoted to procurator-general, Dmitri Volkov became state secretary. Government effectively moved to Glebov's house. Peter's uncles Prince Georg of Holstein and Prince August Friedrich of Holstein-Beck joined his Council with the latter in the key security role, governor-general of Petersburg.

† This was the Miracle of the House of Brandenburg. In April 1945, Hitler, trapped in his Berlin bunker as the allies closed in, hoped that the death of US President F. D. Roosevelt would break up the alliance and save him—just as the death of Elizaveta had done for his hero Frederick the Great. The king's portrait hung optimistically in the bunker.

was all too good to be true, sent his twenty-six-year-old adjutant, Count Wilhelm von der Goltz, to clinch the deal in Petersburg.

Empress Catherine, her pregnancy draped in voluminous black mourning clothes, prayed for three days almost constantly beside the swelling imperial cadaver, which lay in state in a virginal white dress. She followed punctiliously all the mourning rites. When Elizaveta's head became too swollen for the crown to fit on it, Catherine helped the jeweller squeeze it on to the skull.

The contrast between empress and emperor was acute: Peter was soon to be thirty-four but he behaved like a teenager, and a wayward teenager with supreme power has always been a frightening thing. He saw Catherine most mornings and, when the new Winter Palace was ready, they inspected the new apartments together. They were civil to each other, but no more. Peter detested Catherine so much he refused to utter her name: Catherine was just "She."

On 25 January 1762, the body of Elizaveta, now in her signature gold brocade, was processed through the streets on an eight-horse carriage, followed by Peter and Catherine. Clearly soused, Peter mocked the ceremonial procession by stopping, letting the cortège continue and then running to catch up, causing chaos behind him as his courtiers hung on to his train or ended up standing on it.

In the first weeks of his reign, he rose at 7 a.m., gave orders while dressing, received ministers at eight, then inspected the Senate, then at eleven held the parade. His first measures were liberal and popular. On 17 January, Peter and his entourage had crossed the ice-covered Neva to the collegia to sign a decree cancelling Peter the Great's obligatory noble service, a measure that had been discussed for some time and anyway reflected the reality that over the last forty years the nobles had found ways to evade what they regarded as Petrine servitude unfitting for European grandees. Peter reduced the salt tax and sensibly refused to present the nobility with a gold statue for their service. "Gold can be better used," he said. But it was the army that really mattered: Peter loathed the overmighty Guards, whom he described as "janissaries." Plausible rumours spread that he would disband them, and they naturally loathed him back. In private, the Orlovs nicknamed him "the ugly freak."

Peter ordered women to use the French curtsey (normal at the Prussian court) instead of the Russian bow—then mocked their first attempts. He stuck out his tongue at priests in church. Smoking a Holsteiner pipe, quaffing with "the sons of German shoemakers," he was always "tossing off several bottles of beer" at Gudovich's house, where he and his cohorts acted "just like children, hopping on one leg while their friends pushed them over. You may judge what it is like to see all our government leaders in decorations, stars and orders jumping around," playing hopscotch.

The emperor prided himself on his simple retainers, boasting to Dashkova that "It's better to deal with crude people who are honest like your sister [Vorontsova] than you clever ones who suck the juice out of an orange and throw away the peel." He did not hide his intention of marrying Vorontsova. "Be a little more understanding to us," Peter threatened Dashkova. "The time will come when you'll lament that you treated your sister disdainfully. You should learn your sister's thoughts and seek her favour." He meant that he would divorce Catherine. Vorontsova would be empress.

"Deep sorrow is etched in the Empress Catherine's face," reported Breteuil. "She'll have no importance, and is treated with contempt, but she is held in general affection and neglects nothing in cultivating the love of all." As for Peter, he "doubled his attention on Countess Vorontsova ... He has strange tastes. In appearance it's hard to find anyone uglier. She looks like a scullery-maid." Observing these three players, "It's hard to imagine Catherine won't take extreme measures." Meanwhile, Frederick of Prussia seemed to be running Petersburg.[17]

On 21 February, his envoy, Goltz, accompanied by a ruffian named Captain Steuben, arrived in Petersburg, met Peter and assumed command of Russian foreign policy. State Secretary Volkov, drafting the Prussian treaty and threats of war to Denmark, tried to delay both. He got his draft agreed by Peter until denounced by Captain Steuben and temporarily arrested. Goltz himself wrote the treaty. On 29 April, Peter signed it. He warned Denmark that if Schleswig was not returned, it faced "extreme calamity" and planned to command the war in person.

Peter agreed to recognize all Frederick's conquests, and in return the Prussian agreed to any gains from Denmark. The love-in was as hot as ever: "Make use of Stettin and all else I possess as if it was your own," Frederick told Peter. "Tell me how many Prussian troops you need. Though I'm old and broken, I myself would march against your enemies."

Goltz was the real minister, while Chancellor Vorontsov was ignored.* The emperor lacked the essential quality of the Russian autocrat: implacable vigilance. When Goltz warned against conspiring courtiers,

---

* The tsar promoted the fallen (and dying) Peter Shuvalov to field marshal (along with the Terror) and offered Ivan the vice-chancellorship, but the former favourite asked to retire. Alexei Razumovsky also retired from court. (On her deathbed, Elizaveta had made Peter promise to honour the Razumovskys and Shuvalovs.)

he naively replied that "he knew of their disloyalty. He feels he's given them so much work they have no leisure to think of conspiracy and are harmless." To offend the Church was unwise, to mock old courtiers and women imprudent, to insult Catherine foolish and to outrage the Guards simply insane—to do all of these was suicidal. Frederick advised him to get crowned fast "as I don't trust the Russians . . . Any other nation would thank heaven for having a sovereign with such outstanding and admirable qualities"—and it was a bad idea to leave Petersburg. "Recall what happened during Peter the Great's absence. What if there is a plot to enthrone Ivan VI?"

"Since the war's about to begin, I see no time for a coronation in the splendour the Russians expect," boasted the emperor on 15 May. "If Russians wished me harm, they'd have done something long ago as I walk the streets without protection."

In a popular but unwise measure, Peter abolished the Secret Chancellery: "The hated phrase 'tsar's word and deed' hereby signifies nothing. I forbid it." It was only in June that he instituted the Secret Expedition under the aegis of the Senate, ordering Alexander Shuvalov to hand secret police work to Volkov, who was of dubious loyalty, and to Grand Master of the Horse Lev Naryshkin, who was a witty raconteur unsuited for secret policing. Yet he did order Ivan VI to be killed "if anyone unexpectedly tries to seize the prisoner." Ungern-Sternberg was placed in charge of the ex-tsar, who was brought into town to be inspected by the emperor.

"Who are you?" Peter asked him.

"The emperor."

"How do you know?"

"The Virgin and angels told me."

Peter gave him a dressing-gown, whereupon he danced "like a savage." "Prince Ivan is strongly guarded," Peter reassured Frederick. As for the Russians, "I can assure you that when you know how to handle them, you can rely on them."[18]

Showing remarkable nerve, Catherine kept her advanced pregnancy secret. On 11 April, she gave birth to a son, Alexei, surnamed Bobrinsky, who was hidden in the house of her valet. As she recovered, she discussed action separately with Orlov and his brothers, and with Kyril Razumovsky (who knew that Peter planned to replace him as hetman with Gudovich) and Dashkova. Panin, little Paul's oberhofmeister, suave, plump and worldly (he had probably had a short affair with Elizaveta), was also a reformer who favoured a more Westernized noble oligarchy. While he would serve Catherine, he was never devoted to her: he knew that Peter's real heir was Paul—but he too backed the coup.

Like Elizaveta before her, Catherine hesitated. The costs of failure were terrifyingly high. Then Peter went too far.

On 9 June, one of the "white nights," the tsar held a dinner for 400 guests to celebrate peace with Prussia—and the coming war with Denmark. It was the first gala at Rastrelli's new baroque Winter Palace: the evening started with a fireworks display.* Peter III, sitting with his Germans, toasted the imperial family, Frederick the Great and peace, but Catherine, down the table, did not stand. The tsar sent Gudovich to ask why not. Catherine replied that she was one of the three members of the family. Peter sent Gudovich back to say that his two uncles were also members—and then he cursed her aloud. "*Durok!*" he shouted. "Fool!" Catherine burst into tears, but then, gathering herself, turned to her sympathetic neighbour, Prince Fyodor Bariatinsky, and managed to engage him in normal conversation.

That night, Peter ordered his adjutant Bariatinsky to arrest her. Bariatinsky, devoted to Catherine, friends with Orlov, informed the tsar's uncle Prince Georg of Holstein, who prevailed on Peter to cancel the order. Bariatinsky next warned Orlov and Catherine. After a holiday at Oranienbaum, the emperor planned to go to war with the Guards. The conspirators decided to arrest him as he left.[19]

On 12 June, Peter travelled to the suburban palace Oranienbaum, leaving Catherine in the city. Her conspiracy took shape. On the 17th she left for Peterhof, staying in Peter the Great's villa, Mon Plaisir— but in the city the conspiracy was now spreading almost too fast. A twenty-two-year-old sergeant in the Horse Guards, Grigory Potemkin, heard about the plot and, presenting himself to one of Orlov's allies, demanded to join. "I have no fear," Peter III told Frederick, but his new Secret Expedition heard rumours that Orlov was conspiring, so he assigned one of his adjutants to watch him closely. But it was his brother Scarface who organized the coup.

Meanwhile a minor conspirator was arrested who implicated Captain Passek, friend of the Orlovs. On 27 June, Passek was arrested. Under torture he would reveal the conspiracy. Alexei Orlov prepared to start the revolution while another brother, Fyodor, called on Dashkova, perhaps to check on her. It was the first she had heard of the coup, but when Orlov hesitated over whether to upset Catherine by awakening

---

* The fireworks were organized by General Abram Hannibal, Peter the Great's black godson. As a favourite of Elizaveta, he was hated by Peter III. At the start of the dinner, Hannibal was handed an imperial order by Prince Georg of Holstein dismissing him. "Sacked after fifty-seven years of loyal service," said Hannibal who "retired to his estates."

her that night, Dashkova told him, "You've lost time already. As for your fears of alarming the empress, better she be conveyed to Petersburg in a fainting fit than share the scaffold with us!" Fyodor Orlov disclosed the plans to Kyril Razumovsky, who promised to raise his Izmailovsky Guards and as president of the Academy of Sciences to print the manifestos. That evening, Scarface jumped into a carriage, to be joined by Bariatinsky—and, on the running-board, by Sergeant Potemkin—and galloped for Peterhof.[20]

At 6 a.m. on 28 June, the carriage halted outside Mon Plaisir and Scarface ran inside and burst into Catherine's bedroom, waking up his brother's mistress.

"All's ready," said Scarface. "You must get up. Passek's been arrested." Catherine needed to hear no more but dressed swiftly in black and mounted the carriage. The postilions whipped up the horses, Potemkin rode on the shafts to guard the empress, who was covered with a blanket, and they rushed towards Petersburg. Suddenly Catherine reached for her head—she was still wearing her nightcap—and, throwing it off, she laughed. Scarface rendezvoused with a carriage coming the other way, bearing, always important in a coup, a French hairdresser named Michel who arranged Catherine's hair on the way to the revolution. Nearer the city, Catherine and Scarface switched to a carriage bearing Grigory Orlov, and together they arrived at the barracks of the Izmailovsky Guards, where they found just "twelve soldiers and a drummer." From such small beginnings, empires are taken. Razumovsky rallied the Izmailovskys and soon "soldiers rushed to kiss my hands, feet, the hem of the dress," recalled Catherine. Hetman Razumovsky kissed hands on bended knee. The other regiments followed, young Potemkin leading out his Horse Guards.

The empress alighted at the Winter Palace where senators and generals were assembling to issue the manifesto hailing "Catherine II." Panin arrived with her son, Grand Duke Paul, in nightshirt and cap. The doors were opened; soldiers, priests, women milled in the corridors to gawp or take the oath. When Catherine appeared at a balcony, she was cheered.

Peter still controlled the armies, in Germany and Livonia, massed for the Danish war, and the navy out at Kronstadt. Legates were sent to secure their support, but now Catherine had to seize Peter himself. Perhaps recalling how male costume had become Elizaveta, Catherine demanded a uniform. Outside the soldiers were shedding their hated new Prussian uniforms and donning their old tunics. Catherine sported the red-chased green coat of the Preobrazhensky Guards. She ordered the Guards to mass in Palace Square for the march to Peterhof.

*

Oblivious to all this, Peter III, accompanied by Chancellor Vorontsov, Goltz, his mistress and the seventy-nine-year-old Marshal Münnich, back in favour, inspected a parade of Holsteiners. Then he left Oranienbaum and arrived at Peterhof to celebrate the Feast of St. Peter and Paul with Catherine. But Mon Plaisir was deserted. Peter panicked and, rushing in, he saw Catherine's gala dress abandoned on the bed, a ghostly omen— for she had changed her clothes in every sense. "Didn't I tell you she was capable of anything?" he cried. He started to weep and drink and dither.

The only courtier not to lose his head was that veteran of coups Münnich who, invoking Peter's grandfather, gave the correct advice: "Take command of the Russian army in Pomerania then lead them to Russia and, I guarantee Your Majesty, Petersburg will be at your feet in six weeks!" But this Peter was no Peter the Great. The tsar sent emissaries to negotiate with Catherine. First he despatched Vorontsov, who had ridden on the board of Elizaveta's sleigh in *her* coup, but when he reached Petersburg, he simply threw himself on his knees before Catherine and then resigned. Peter's dwindling entourage trundled back to Oranienbaum, where Münnich persuaded him to seize Kronstadt.

On this silvery night, Peter embarked on a schooner, but he was totally drunk and had to be helped on board by his mistress and the old marshal. Three hours later, outside Kronstadt, Münnich announced the emperor, but the sailors called back: "There's no longer an emperor. Vivat Catherine II!" Peter fainted. He had predicted this to Catherine, saying, "I'll die in Russia." He just wanted to abdicate and retire to Holstein. He decided to negotiate.

Catherine, dressed raffishly in her Guards uniform, holding a naked sabre, emerged into Palace Square, mounted her grey thoroughbred Brilliant and reviewed the 12,000 Guards waiting for her. Not all of them were sober. The streets were filled with tipsy soldiers who had raided the taverns and all around were their discarded uniforms like the morning after a fancy-dress party. Catherine, now thirty-three, her hair auburn, her eyes blue, eyelashes black, small and full-figured, rode through the ranks, but she realized that her sabre was missing the *dragonne*, the sword-knot, and in an age when such things matter, that sharp young Horse Guards sergeant, who had ridden on her carriage earlier, galloped up and offered her his. Potemkin had brought himself to her attention in a daring way, and she noticed his giant stature, splendid head of auburn hair and long sensitive face with a cleft chin, looks that, with his intellect, had won him the nickname "Alcibiades."

When he tried to ride back into the ranks, his horse, trained to ride in squadron, refused to leave her side: "This made her laugh . . . she talked to him," and "by this happy chance," Potemkin later recalled, he would later become her partner in power and the love of her life—"all thanks to a fresh horse."

Catherine and the Guards marched through the blue incandescence of the undarkening night, sleeping for a few hours on the way, while the two Orlov brothers, Grigory and Alexei, galloped ahead to Oranienbaum where they arrested Peter III, forcing him to sign his abdication, which Grigory brought back to his empress. Peter was guided into his carriage accompanied by his mistress and Gudovich, while the Guards shouted "Vivat Catherine II!" At Peterhof, he was visited by Catherine's adviser, Panin. He begged not to be separated from Vorontsova. When this was refused, he asked just to take his fiddle, his black servant Narcissus and his dog Mopsy. Panin agreed. Catherine planned to imprison this husk of an emperor in Shlisselburg near ex-tsar Ivan VI, but that evening Scarface escorted Peter to the nearby estate of Ropsha. Catherine returned to Petersburg.[21] She never saw Peter again.[*]

When Princess Dashkova entered Catherine's study, she was "astonished" to find Grigory Orlov "stretched out at full length on a sofa" going through state papers. "I asked what he was about. 'The empress has ordered that I open them,' he replied."

Catherine rewarded her friends but did not punish her enemies. The Petersburg garrison got a bonus of half a year's salary. Razumovsky and Panin received 5,000 roubles annually, Grigory and Alexei Orlov got 800 souls and 24,000 roubles each, with the lover himself getting a further 50,000. Potemkin could choose between 600 souls and 18,000 roubles: Catherine insisted he be promoted and threw in another 10,000 roubles. But Catherine was kind if patronizing to her husband's mistress, Elizabeth Vorontsova, sending her to the country "or she'll traipse into the Palace."

Nikita Panin became the senior member of Catherine's Foreign Collegium though never its chief—she could never forget that he wanted Paul to rule as soon as he was of age. She appointed Zakhar Chernyshev, her suitor of the 1740s, to head the War Collegium, and found a skilful and honest politician in Prince Alexander Viazemsky, who as procurator-general ran her entire domestic government, from finance

---

[*] Frederick was unsurprised by the fall of his protégé but underestimated his successor: "He allowed himself to be removed like a child sent off to bed," he said. "Catherine was young, weak, alone and foreign and on the verge of prison. The Orlovs did everything. Catherine is unable to rule anything. She leapt into the arms of those who wished to save her. Peter III's lack of courage and refusal to take Münnich's advice ruined him."

to law, for a remarkable twenty-eight years. In an illustration of the tiny world of the political clans, he was married to the daughter of Trubetskoi, who had served as procurator for twenty years before him. She did not over-promote Grigory Orlov, placing him in charge of artillery and of attracting colonists to the new lands of southern Ukraine. After the initial excitement of reading state papers, the lazy, pleasure-loving Orlov did not exert himself to exercise power. Panin hated the upstart Orlovs, while the Chernyshevs and Razumovsky oscillated between the two. But the Orlovs had a plan to ensure their priceless position of intimate proximity: Grigory must marry Catherine. Unfortunately, she already had a husband.[22]

Peter, now guarded at Ropsha by Scarface, Bariatinsky and twelve others, including Potemkin, bombarded Catherine with requests: "Your Majesty, if you don't want to kill someone already quite wretched, then take pity and leave me Elizabeth [Vorontsova] as my only consolation . . . If you wanted to see me for a moment, that would be the height of my wishes." When she did not answer, he pitifully asked to live in a bigger room and to be allowed to retire to Germany: "I ask Your Majesty not to treat me as the greatest criminal; I don't know if I ever offended you?"

Closeted with Scarface, Peter had every reason to be frightened. The guards and the prisoner drank copiously in this *danse macabre*: "Our ugly freak," Scarface wrote to Catherine on 2 July, "is seriously ill with cholic. I fear he might die tonight, but I fear even more he might survive. The first fear is that he talks gibberish all the time which amuses us and the second fear is that he is really a danger to all of us." The menace was blood-chilling, but Catherine did not replace the jailers.

On 6 July, Scarface reported that Peter was so ill he was almost unconscious: "I don't think he'll last till evening." This sinister diagnosis sounded more like a death sentence, and the atmosphere at Ropsha was like a tightening garrotte—but neither Catherine nor the Orlovs could be safe while Peter lived.

That evening, Scarface reported that there had been a most unfortunate accident: "Matushka, how can I explain!" The "dying" man had miraculously recovered by evening to join his jailers in a drinking bout. During a brawl with Bariatinsky at the table, "we had no time to separate them. He is no more. I don't remember what we did but all of us are guilty. Have mercy on me for my brother's sake. I've confessed everything . . . Forgive us and order an end quickly. Life is not worth living. We have angered you and lost our souls for ever." The letters suggest that the killing was premeditated but lubricated with alcohol. The strangling was a necessity and a convenience for Catherine, but she believed that she would be tainted for ever with a matricide and regicide: "My glory is spoilt, Posterity will never forgive me." But it did.

The emperor's body lay in state in a plain coffin at the Nevsky Monastery. A cravat concealed his livid throat, a lowered hat the blackened face. Catherine issued a statement that Peter had died of "haemorrhoidal colic," an absurd diagnosis that was to become a humorous euphemism for political murder. When Catherine invited the *philosophe* Jean d'Alembert to visit, he joked he did not dare go, since he was "prone to piles, a very dangerous condition in Russia."

Peter had delayed his coronation; Catherine was not going to make the same mistake.[23]

SCENE 4

# The Golden Age

# CAST

CATHERINE II THE GREAT, empress 1762–96 (née Sophie of Anhalt-Zerbst), widow of Peter III

PAUL I, emperor 1796–1801, son of Peter and Catherine

Natalya Alexeievna (née Princess Wilhelmina of Hesse-Darmstadt), Paul's first wife

Maria Fyodorovna (née Princess Sophia Dorothea of Württemberg), Paul's second wife

ALEXANDER I, emperor 1801–25, first son of Paul and Maria

Elizabeth Alexeievna, Alexander's wife (née Princess Louise of Baden)

CONSTANTINE I, emperor 1825, second son of Paul and Maria

Anna Fyodorovna (née Princess Juliane of Saxe-Coburg-Saalfeld), Constantine's wife

### CATHERINE'S FAVOURITES: adjutant-generals

Grigory Orlov, grand master of ordnance, count, later prince

Alexander Vasilchikov, "Iced Soup"

Grigory Potemkin-Tavrichesky, prince, "Alcibiades," "Cyclops," "Serenissimus"

Peter Zavadovsky, imperial secretary, later count, member of the Council, "Petrusa"

Semyon Zorich, "Savage"

Ivan Rimsky-Korsakov, "King of Epirus"

Alexander Lanskoy, "Sasha"

Alexander Yermolov, "White Negro"

Alexander Dmitriev-Mamonov, count, "Mr. Redcoat"

Platon Zubov, count, later prince, "Blackie," "Tooth," "Zodiac"

### COURTIERS: ministers etc.

Nikita Panin, oberhofmeister of Grand Duke Paul, member of the Foreign Collegium, count

Zakhar Chernyshev, president of the War Collegium, count

Kyril Razumovsky, count, hetman of Ukraine, then field marshal

Peter Rumiantsev-Zadunaisky, count, field marshal

Alexei Orlov-Chesmensky, admiral, count, brother of Grigory, "Scarface"

Alexander Bezborodko, secretary for foreign affairs, later count, prince, chancellor

Nikolai Saltykov, oberhofmeister of Paul then Alexander, later count and prince, president of War Collegium

Valerian Zubov, count, "Child," brother of Platon

Fyodor Rostopchin, Paul's retainer

Countess Praskovia Bruce, lady-in-waiting to Catherine

Alexandra Branitska (née Engelhardt), Potemkin's niece, countess, "Sashenka"

Ekaterina Scavronskaya (née Engelhardt), Potemkin's niece, countess, "Katinka," "Kitten," "Angel," "Venus"

Ekaterina Nelidova, Paul's mistress, "Little Monster"

Countess Varvara Golovina, courtier and friend of Grand Duchess Elizabeth

In mid-September 1762, Catherine, along with her son Paul, aged eight, and his governor Panin, entered Moscow in procession. On the 22nd, she crowned herself as empress in the Dormition Cathedral. Afterwards in the coronation honours, Grigory Orlov was named adjutant-general, a title that came to mean the same as grand chamberlain under Empress Anna—imperial *inamorato*. All five Orlov brothers and Panin were raised to count. Potemkin received another 400 souls and the court rank of gentleman of the bedchamber.

Straight after the ceremony, little Paul came down with a fever. Catherine, who already hated Moscow where she had almost died as a teenager, was frantic that he should not die: he was the only legitimate pillar of her regime for she herself had not the slightest claim to the throne—unless Paul pulled through. Mercifully he recovered.

Returning to Petersburg, Catherine was only too aware of the fragility of her position. Carefully watching everyone through her Secret Expedition and deftly stroking all factions and offending few, she presented a reassuring picture of smiling intelligence and imperturbable confidence. Almost immediately there was a plot among a few Guardsmen to enthrone Ivan VI but it was swiftly foiled. Tirelessly hard working— "Time belongs not to me but to the empire" she said, like Peter the Great—Catherine rose each morning at six, made her own coffee before her servants got up, and started work. Knowing what suited her figure, and her Russian constituency, she wore rich but never gaudy long Russian-style dresses for every day. Now in her mid-thirties, "she may still be called beautiful," in the view of the British ambassador Sir George Macartney, while the prince de Ligne, who knew her later, thought her "more handsome than beautiful": all cited her pretty colouring, good teeth and bright blue eyes.

She wrote numerous letters every day, suffering she admitted from a "graphomania" that matched her other compulsive hobbies— "Anglomania," her taste for English painting and gardens, also "plantomania," neo-classical building and what she called her "gluttonous greed" for art-collecting, all of which were also ways of projecting her majesty. She added a pavilion on to the Winter Palace, which she called the Little Hermitage, to store her art and entertain her friends in private at her soirées. In the tradition of Peter the Great, she wrote ten rules for her guests:

1. All ranks to be left at the doors along with swords and hats.
2. Parochialism and ambitions shall likewise be left at the doors.

And lastly:

10. One shall not wash dirty linen in public and shall mind one's own business until one leaves.

Like Elizaveta, she used *tables volants*, raised by pulleys, to avoid the eavesdropping of servants. She later added a further extension, known as the Old Hermitage, to show off her art.* She wrote decrees, letters, satirical plays and instructions as well as constantly reworking her secret memoirs. Catherine was a tireless self-promoter: her letters to Voltaire and the *philosophes* were designed to be copied.

This born politician was utterly realistic about the limits of her own autocracy: "One must do things in such a way that people think they themselves want it to be done this way." When her secretary cited her boundless power, she laughed. "It's not as easy as you think. First, my orders would not be carried out unless they were the kind of orders that could be carried out . . . I take advice, I consult and when I am convinced of general approval, I issue my orders and have the pleasure of observing what you call blind obedience. And that is the foundation of unlimited power." But when her power was challenged, she was ruthless though never cruel: "It's necessary to have a wolf's teeth and a fox's tail." When she heard of a nobleman who was repeatedly criticizing her, she advised him to cease "or get himself transferred to a place where even the ravens wouldn't be able to find his bones."

She received ministers in the morning and drafted her decrees. At 11 a.m., she performed her toilette, entertained Orlov and often went on a walk with just him, her beloved greyhounds and a couple of ladies-in-waiting. After lunch at one, she worked in her apartments until six, the "lover's hour" when she received Orlov before dressing for a gala, a court day (Sundays), the theatre (Mondays and Thursdays) or a masquerade ball (Saturdays). On these occasions, Catherine, who understood the power of splendour, projected her grandeur to Europe. She retired with Orlov and liked to be in bed by eleven.

"My position," wrote Catherine to her former lover Poniatowski, "is such that I have to observe the greatest caution. The least soldier of the Guard thinks when he sees me: 'That is the work of my hands.' "

---

* Her letters show the glee she took in the chase, in the deal and in the possession of art. She immediately started collecting for her Hermitage, later buying the vast collections of the Saxon minister Count von Brühl and the British premier Sir Robert Walpole—while privately she collected ivory cameos and engraved jewels that still remain in her specially constructed wooden cabinets in the Hermitage Museum, though they are not displayed.

Poniatowski, still in love with her, dreamed of marrying her. Catherine found this naivety irritating: "Since I have to speak plainly, and you have resolved to ignore what I have been telling you, the fact is that if you come here you are likely to get us both slaughtered." But the disappointed Pole was to be royally consoled.[1]

"I am sending Count Keyserling to Poland immediately to make you king after the death of the present one," wrote Catherine to Poniatowski a month after the coup. Augustus III died in September and the Orlovs and Chernyshevs wanted his son to succeed but she decided on Poniatowski. Far from an imperial caprice to repay sexual services, Catherine was a dispassionate paragon of *raison d'état*, pursuing the Petrine policy of controlling Poland as a satellite through a client king. Poniatowski, related through his Czartoryski mother to the Polish magnates, would be utterly submissive, but he still fantasized: "If I desired the throne, it was because I saw you on it." When she put him in his place, he whined gallantly: "Don't make me king but bring me to your side."

Frederick the Great was happy to back this policy in return for Russian support, and an alliance was signed on 31 March 1764. On 26 August, Poland's Election Sejm (assembly), surrounded by Russian troops, elected Poniatowski as King Stanislas-Augustus. "Nikita Ivanovich! I congratulate you on the king we have made," Catherine exulted to Panin. "This event greatly increases my trust in you."* Panin saw the Prussian alliance as the first step in a new "Northern System" of Protestant–Scandinavian powers to fortify Russian control of the Baltic and restrain the "Catholic Block" of Austria and France. Meanwhile, having made her ex-lover a king, would she now marry her present love and make Orlov an emperor?[2]

If bringing Poniatowski to Russia would have been a quick way to get slaughtered, so was marrying Orlov. But all through her life, Catherine longed for the intimacy of family, which she had to find in her friends and lovers.

Her parents were dead. Her son Paul was still little, but, as with so many royal families, their relationship was poisoned by the inevitable sequence of heredity that reversed the benign nature of motherhood. His maturity could herald her destruction. If Paul showed ability, his

---

* At the same time, in one of those very Russian reversals of fortune, she restored the duchy of Courland to Ernst Biron, Empress Anna's favourite who had been in exile for twenty-two years until pardoned by Peter III. He ruled as a Russian puppet until his death, when he was succeeded by his son Peter Biron.

interests could become undeniable. Fortunately, his erratic character ruined their relationship but justified her rule.

In the place of family, Catherine created an intimate coterie. Her closest friend was her long-serving lady-in-waiting, Countess Praskovia Bruce, the daughter of Countess Rumiantseva, once Peter the Great's mistress. Bruce was an ally in all matters amorous—"the person to whom I can say everything, without fear of the consequences." They shared the same taste in men and the same sexual enthusiasm which led to Praskovia's reputation as *l'éprouveuse*, "trying out" the empress's lovers. It turned out to be a bit more complicated than that, but every monarch needs a confidant for such matters who combines the loyalty of a friend, the tact of a diplomat and the earthiness of a pimp.

Catherine forgave her "born comic" Lev Naryshkin for supporting Peter III and reappointed him master of the horse, though he was so unathletic she joked that he should be "master of the donkey." But, for Catherine, her lover would always be the centre of her life. Far from being the nymphomaniac of legend, she was an obsessional serial monogamist who adored sharing card games in her cosy apartments and discussing her literary and artistic interests with her beloved: she gave Adjutant-General Orlov the apartment above hers. Whenever he liked, he descended the green staircase directly into her rooms. She played cards, pharo and bezique, every evening with Orlov, to whom she was committed, yet she had another admirer in the palace. Potemkin, whom she had met on the night of the coup, was famous for his good looks ("his hair is more beautiful than mine," she said), brilliant intellect, interest in theology, and mimicry. When Orlov was struggling to entertain the empress, he invited Potemkin to amuse her. When she asked him to show off his mimicry, he denied any such talents but did so in a slight German accent that was identical to that of the empress herself. After a short silence while the company waited to see if this would amuse her, she laughed uproariously. At some point, when she encountered Potemkin in the palace corridors, he fell to this knees and, taking her hand, declared his love.

She did not encourage him—and yet Catherine carefully promoted Potemkin's career. His love life was legendary and there are hints that he may have had an affair with her confidante Countess Bruce. Then he suddenly disappeared from court. It is said that he had been beaten up with billiard cues by the Orlovs for flirting with Catherine. More likely it was an infection. Either way he lost his left eye and his confidence, sinking into depression. Catherine asked what had become of Potemkin, sending a message via Countess Bruce: "It's a great pity when a person of such rare merits is lost from society, the Motherland and those who value him." When he returned to court, the man once known as Alcibiades for his wit and beauty was re-nicknamed "Cyclops."

She needed and loved Orlov, who was a central part of her life: she was openly warm with him, a man who loved music and singing. "After dinner," the Court Journal recorded one evening, "Her Imperial Majesty graciously returned to her inner apartments and the gentlemen in the card room sang songs; then the court singers and servants and, on the orders of Count G. G. Orlov, the soldiers of the Guard, sang gay songs in another room." For now, Catherine had to balance the aspirational Orlovs with the old aristocracy. Like every favourite, Grigory sought to perpetuate the brothers' position through marriage.

The rumours disturbed the sensitive balance of the court. "The empress can do as she wishes," Panin warned her, "but Madame Orlov will never be empress of Russia." In May 1763, while Catherine was on a pilgrimage from Moscow to Rostov, a gentleman of the bedchamber Khitrovo was arrested for planning to kill the Orlovs and marry Catherine to Ivan VI. The case made an Orlov marriage impossible.

On 5 July 1764, while Catherine was touring her Baltic provinces, the second of her big tours, an unhinged officer, Vasily Mirovich, tried to liberate Prisoner Number One—once known as Ivan VI—from the bowels of Shlisselburg in order to make him emperor. Unaware that Catherine had confirmed the orders of Elizaveta and Peter that he should be killed if anyone attempted access, Mirovich and his friends seized the gatehouse and headed for the cell. After a shoot-out, he found the ex-emperor bleeding from multiple stab wounds. He kissed the body and surrendered. Catherine rushed back to the capital. Mirovich was beheaded while his cohorts suffered the dreaded *Spitsruten*, in which victims stripped to the waist ran the gauntlet down a line of 1,000 men who beat them with rods. A sentence of ten or twelve such runs could be fatal.

Two ex-tsars had died messily, yet their vanishing, and the youth of her son Paul, left a clear path for her to work her magic. Amazingly the regicidal, uxoricidal German usurper recovered her reputation not just as Russian tsar and successful imperialist but also as an enlightened despot, the darling of the *philosophes*.[3]

On 30 July 1767, Catherine, in a coach drawn by eight horses and followed by sixteen carriages of courtiers who included two Orlovs, two Chernyshevs and Potemkin, as well as her son Paul, processed from Moscow's Golovin Palace into the Kremlin to open her enlightened project, the Legislative Commission. Five hundred elected delegates, from nobility and townsfolk to peasants and non-Russians, first joined her for a blessing in the Dormition Cathedral (Muslims waiting outside), and then walked into the Palace of Facets to launch Catherine's Great Instruction. It was a mark of her commitment that all her favourites were involved: just returned from eighteen months of mysterious absence, her now one-eyed protégé Potemkin was appointed one of the "Guardians of Exotic Peoples," while Grigory Orlov read out the Great Instruction, which she had written herself, in a ceremony based on the opening of Parliament by the British monarch.

The Instruction digested the works of Montesquieu, Beccaria and the *philosophes* such as Diderot's *Encyclopaedia*. The *philosophes* were not modern democratic liberals, but they were enemies of superstition and tyranny and advocates of justice, order and reason. Like all vain intellectuals, their heads were easily turned by the favour of potentates and they had a weakness for showy, enlightened despots. Catherine sincerely shared their ideas and abhorred slavery. Behind the façades of baroque palaces, particularly in Moscow, she remembered how serfs were imprisoned in stinking dungeons—"There's not a house there without iron collars, chains and instruments of torture for those who commit the least infraction." At its most extreme, this had led to a case of serial murder when Daria Saltykova, a young widow and member of the family of Empress Anna's mother, tortured and killed hundreds of serfs.* But Catherine's decency did not stop her giving away tens of thousands of souls to her favourites. She was extremely wary of challenging the privileges of her nobility, particularly that of owning serfs. Indeed as owner of the millions of serfs on crown lands, she was herself the biggest serf-owner, and she knew that this partnership of tsar and nobility, based on their convergence of interests—service in government and army on one hand and suppression and ownership of millions of human chattels on the other—was the foundation of the empire. She missed few opportunities to reinforce it.

If the Commission was partly designed as an advertisement of her enlightened philosophy and philanthropy, it was to prove a very long-winded

---

* Saltykova, wounded when her lover got married, avenged herself on her serf girls, organizing a house of horrors. Apart from two or three men, her victims were all women, tortured for minor failures in their tasks, thrashed and tormented with boiling water, hammers, nails, "logs, boards and rolling pins." Nicknamed Saltychikha she repeatedly bribed the local police, who frequently punished anyone who complained because she was the relative of the governor of Moscow, a Saltykov. She was finally arrested in 1762. Catherine ordered a full investigation that revealed 138 probable murders, including ten-year-olds and pregnant women, and found her guilty of 38. But, given that cruelty towards serfs was so common among the nobility and indeed was one of their privileges, the empress was remarkably lenient. Saltychikha was publicly chained with a plaque around her neck reading "This woman has tortured and murdered," and was then imprisoned for life.

one. The delegates were keener to discuss the petitions, pleading local and social issues instead of imperial ones—though they did also coin the soubriquet "Catherine the Great" that was echoed around Europe by Voltaire. The talking-shop soon started to irk Catherine. She returned to Petersburg where she was rescued from its ponderous deliberations by the turbulence of war and love.[4]

In June 1768 Russian Cossacks, in a bid to defeat Polish rebels who had risen against King Stanislas, pursued a number of them over the border into Ottoman territory, only to run amok in a massacre of Jews and Tatars. On 25 September, Sultan Mustafa III threw the Russian ambassador into the Fortress of Seven Towers, thereby declaring war. Deploying 80,000 troops, Catherine's two armies, one under her commander-in-chief Prince Alexander Golitsyn and the other under the gifted Peter Rumiantsev, thrust down the Dniester River with orders to win control of southern Ukraine. If all went well, they could fight their way round the Black Sea and attack Crimea while crossing the Pruth and the Danube into today's Bulgaria to threaten Constantinople itself.

"My soldiers are off to fight the Turks as if off to a wedding," enthused the over-confident Catherine to her correspondent Voltaire. But warmongering politicians soon discover that war is never a wedding. The army was made up of conscripted peasants, stolen from village and family, often ill treated by serfmaster-officers and serving for twenty-five years. But in some ways service allowed them to escape the dreary poverty of rural life. They could become officers and, despite savage discipline, they found a unique national and Orthodox esprit in military communes known as *artels*, one of the peculiarities that made the Russian army formidable in morale (and cheaper to run than any Western equivalent). "The Turks are tumbling like ninepins," went the Russian saying, "but our men stand firm—though headless."

When the first Ottoman fortress fell, Catherine was exhilarated, but the gains came slowly. Alexei "Scarface" Orlov suggested "a cruise" to the Mediterranean and Catherine ordered the Baltic Fleet to sail via Gibraltar to attack the Ottomans and rally Orthodox and Arab rebellions. Orlov, who had never been to sea, was in command—though he left the sailing to his Scottish admiral, Samuel Greig. On 24 June 1770, Scarface sailed fireships into the Ottoman fleet moored in Chesme harbour. The sultan's fleet was destroyed, 11,000 Ottoman sailors drowned. Catherine celebrated and awarded Scarface a new surname: Chesmensky. The Russians found themselves temporary masters of the eastern Mediterranean and for the first time embarked on a military adventure

in the Arab world, bombarding Syrian ports and, for six months, occupying Beirut.*

On the same day as Chesme, Rumiantsev led 25,000 Russians to
defeat 150,000 Turks at the River Larga in today's Romania, and in
August, he pulled off another victory on the Kagul River. A frosty and
flinty grand seigneur who had learned his craft from Frederick the
Great during the Seven Years War, Rumiantsev, brother of Countess
Bruce, supposedly the natural son of Peter the Great, earned his marshal's baton.

Catherine immortalized her victories by creating a Russian triumphal
theme park at Tsarskoe Selo with obelisks for the land battles and a lake
and column for Chesme.† But all was not quite well either in the empire
or in the empress's apartments: that November, the heroic general who
brought back Rumiantsev's despatches was Potemkin.[5]

Privately, Catherine's relationship with Orlov was becoming strained.
Politically there was a fault in the design of the Orlovs: the brains,
the brawn, the taste and the charm were not united in one man but
distributed with admirable fairness among the five brothers: Scarface
had the ruthlessness, Fyodor the culture, while Grigory had only his
courage, charm and looks. "All his good qualities were overshadowed
by licentiousness." Diderot, who met him in Paris, described him as "a
boiler always boiling but never cooking anything." His low tastes were
notorious. "Anything is good enough for him," observed Durand de
Distroff, a French diplomat. "He loves like he eats—he's as happy with a

---

* Orlov was approached by the Arab strongmen of Egypt and the area of northern Israel
and southern Syria/Lebanon, who were rebelling against the Ottoman sultan and had
managed for a short time to take Damascus. When Catherine approved, Orlov sent a
squadron that bombarded the Syrian coast, then in June 1772 stormed Beirut, returning to
occupy it the next year. The Arab leaders promised Russia possession of Jerusalem but the
Russians were soon overtaken by the broiling ethnic-factional turmoil of Middle Eastern
politics. They had a chance to set up an Arab client state but Catherine withdrew from
Syrian politics when she made peace with the Ottomans in 1774.
† Catherine had never liked the rococo glitz of Elizaveta's Catherine Palace, which she
called "whipped cream." Though experimenting in hugely wasteful projects with other
styles (including Tsaritsyno near Moscow which she had pulled down and then rebuilt
in neo-Gothic style), she adored the simplicity of neo-classicism. Her favourite architect
was the neo-classicist Charles Cameron, who arrived in 1779: "At present I am very taken
with Mr. Cameron, a Scot by nationality and a Jacobite, a great draughtsman, well versed
in antique monuments and well known for his book on the *Baths of Rome*. At the moment
we are making a garden with him on a terrace . . ." Starting with the Chinese Village at
Tsarskoe Selo, Cameron remodelled Elizaveta's rococo interiors at the Catherine Palace,
added her new private apartments, the Agate Rooms, created the new village and cathedral
of Sophia, inspired by Constantinople and Hagia Sophia, and erected an array of commem-
orative columns and follies in the park there. But his masterpiece was the Cameron Gallery
that still seems to hang in the air.

Kalmyk or a Finnish peasant girl as with the prettiest girl at court. That's the sort of oaf he is."

Catherine was tiring of his limited intellect and clumsy manners—but she later told Potemkin that Orlov would have "remained for ever had he not been the first to tire." She was corresponding in secret with Potemkin, whose career she watched so carefully. At the start of the war, Potemkin received the ceremonial key of court chamberlain, a signal of high favour. But at the same time he wrote to Catherine chivalrously: "The only way I can express my gratitude to Your Majesty is to shed my blood for Your glory. The best way to achieve success is fervent service to the Sovereign and scorn for one's own life." Catherine sent a note to Zakhar Chernyshev, president of the War Collegium: "Chamberlain Potemkin must be appointed to the war." Potemkin performed brilliantly as a cavalry general. "He was the hero of the victory," reported his commander, Rumiantsev, after one battle. It was unlikely that he returned to court without some encouragement from the empress, and the Court Journal reveals that Potemkin dined with her eleven times during his short stay. He then returned to the front, pulling off more victories. While Rumiantsev besieged Silistria and another general invaded Crimea, fever ravaged the armies; harvests failed; and then terrible news arrived.

Bubonic plague raged in Moscow. By August 1770, some 500 were dying a day. As the governor fled, the city spun out of control and a mob murdered the bishop. On 21 September 1771 Grigory Orlov rushed to Moscow where, courageously facing down mobs, he efficiently restored order. Catherine built him a triumphal arch at Tsarskoe Selo. "Count Orlov," she told one of her Western correspondents, "is the handsomest man of his generation."

The Orlovs seemed safe—but Catherine was privately consulting Potemkin, back in Petersburg. The empress later regretted not starting a relationship with Potemkin in 1772. At the same time, Catherine sent Orlov to open talks with the Turks at Fokshany. Watched by Rumiantsev and Potemkin, Orlov floundered, storming out of the negotiations. Catherine was demanding that the Ottomans recognize the independence of Crimea, a first step towards Russian control. But Austria and Prussia had a price for their acquiescence: a carve-up of Poland. Catherine agreed the so-called First Partition in which Russia, Prussia and Austria annexed slices of Poland. But just when it seemed peace was close, Sweden encouraged the Ottomans to fight on.

On 30 August 1772 Catherine appointed Alexander Vasilchikov, a good-looking but stolid Guards officer, as her new adjutant-general and moved him into a Winter Palace apartment near her own. While Orlov was ruining the negotiations, Catherine had taken a new lover. Orlov galloped back but was stopped—for "quarantine"—at the city gates and ordered to wait at his nearby estate. Catherine had to tread carefully with the Orlovs. In sensitive negotiations, she promised Grigory to consign "all that has passed to oblivion." She would never forget "how much I owe your clan." She settled their break-up with a generosity that was to be her signature. Orlov received an annual pension of 150,000 roubles, a sum of 100,000 roubles to set up his household, 10,000 serfs, the neo-classical Marble Palace that she was already building for him, and the right to use the title of prince of the Holy Roman Empire. Prince Orlov went travelling for a while, later returning with honour to court; Potemkin was promoted to lieutenant-general while Catherine tried to settle down with Vasilchikov. Presumably she had chosen Vasilchikov because she knew that Potemkin would be dominant, eccentric and all-consuming. But she found Vasilchikov corrosively dull. She admitted later to Potemkin that "his caresses made me cry." She nicknamed him "soupe à la glace"—"Iced Soup."[6]

She was keen to get out of the war. Rumiantsev's army, ravaged by disease, was stuck besieging Silistria, where Potemkin distinguished himself with lightning cavalry raids. In July 1773, Catherine mentioned his name for the first time to Voltaire. Then on 17 September the Cossacks, Tatars and runaways serfs of Yaiksk in the south-eastern borderlands rose in rebellion, under the leadership of a Don Cossack claiming to be the undead Peter III. The pretender was actually Emelian Pugachev, a deserter who declared that his scrofula scars were signs of royalty. His revolt unleashed a powder keg. Towns fell, nobles were dismembered, women raped and added to the "emperor's harem," while Pugachev's army swelled—and marched northwards.

As if this was not enough, Catherine now faced a challenge from her own son: on 20 September 1772, Paul turned eighteen. He could expect marriage, his own court and a political role. Paul and his adviser Panin believed that the rightful tsar should actually reign. That would spell disaster for Catherine.[7]

Paul needed a wife. As a boy, Catherine had teased him about love, while Orlov and Panin took him to visit the maids-of-honour. When he reached puberty, Catherine had introduced him to a young Polish widow who bore him a son.* Unsurprisingly, growing up in this louche

---

* Simon Veliki, who later joined the Royal Navy and died in the Antilles in 1794.

milieu, Paul feared a cuckold's horns when he was married. Culturally he was steeped in the Enlightenment and had been taught by Panin that vainglorious war, unfettered absolutism and immoral female rule—all implicit criticisms of his mother—endangered good government and orderly society. Yet these ideas were completely contradicted by his belief in limitless sacred autocracy, Prussian militarism and medieval chivalry.

Catherine started to look for wives among the minor princesses of the Holy Roman Empire, whence she herself had come. She selected Princess Wilhelmina of Hesse-Darmstadt and invited her to Petersburg. Paul liked her, but just as she converted to Orthodoxy under the name Natalya, he was embroiled in an intrigue, hatched by an ambitious Holsteiner diplomat, Caspar von Saldern, to make him joint tsar with Catherine. Panin discouraged it, but Catherine was alarmed. She avoided giving him a full separate court.

On 29 September 1773, Paul married Natalya in a blaze of festivities and fireworks. At times mother and son had been close, particularly when she had nursed him during an illness two years earlier, but even before the Saldern affair Catherine found Paul narrowminded, sour and charmless. Now he was dangerous too. Rivalry would gradually destroy their meagre familial ties.[8]

As Russia became bogged down in this interminable war, and the southern Volga region exploded in the Pugachev revolt, Petersburg and Europe watched in fascination as Prince Orlov cheerfully returned to court, where Catherine was now ensconced with Iced Soup. That expert analyst of Russia, Frederick the Great, noted that Orlov was performing all duties "except fucking," but the fastidiously homoerotic warlord was disgusted by Catherine's earthy sexuality: "It's a terrible business when the prick and the cunt decide the interests of Europe." Her very throne in jeopardy, Catherine picked up her pen and wrote a letter to an officer besieging a faraway Ottoman fortress:

> Sir! Lieutenant-General and Chevalier, you are probably so absorbed with staring at Silistria that you have no time to read letters . . . But since I am most anxious to preserve for ever brave, clever and talented individuals, I beg you to keep out of danger. When you read this letter you may well ask yourself why I have written it. To this I reply: so that you have confirmation of my way of thinking about you because I have always been
>     Your most benevolent, Catherine

As soon as the army had fought its way back across the Danube, with Potemkin the last to cross, covering the rear, he galloped for Petersburg, where he hurried to present himself at court. He bumped into Orlov on the stairs of the Winter Palace.

"Any news?" he asked.

"No," replied Prince Orlov, "except I'm on the way down and you're on the way up." But nothing happened. Vasilchikov remained in position. Catherine vacillated. Always mercurial, swinging between coenobite and sybarite, Potemkin confronted her and then stormed off to the Nevsky Monastery where he declared that he would become a monk. Countess Bruce rushed between the monastic cell and the imperial palace, bearing the words of Potemkin's love song—he was very musical: "As soon as I saw you, I thought of you alone. But O heavens, why did you destine me to love her and her alone?"

Finally Catherine surrendered—as she remembered in a letter to Potemkin:

> Then came a certain hero [*bogatry*, a Russian mythical knight] who, through his valour and demeanour, was already very close to our heart: on hearing of his arrival, people began to talk, not knowing we had written to him already on the quiet with the secret intention of trying to discover whether he really had the intention Countess Bruce suspected, the inclination I wanted him to have.

Potemkin joined her in Tsarskoe Selo, then at the Winter Palace. When he became her lover, Catherine was captivated by this flamboyant force of nature, their sexual affinity equalled only by their shared intellectual and political enthusiasms.

"My darling," she wrote to Potemkin, "the time I spend with you is so happy. We passed four hours together, boredom vanishes and I don't want to part. My dear, my friend, I love you so much: you're so handsome, so clever, so playful, so witty. When I'm with you, I attach no importance to the world. I've never been so happy." They planned their trysts in the palace *banya*, the bathhouse.

"Yes or no?" asked Count Alexei Orlov-Chesmensky.

"About what?" replied the empress.

"Is it love?" asked Scarface.

"I can't lie."

"Yes or no?"

"Yes!"

Scarface started to laugh. "You meet in the *banya*?"

"Why do you think so?"

"Because for four days we've seen the light in the window later than usual. It was clear yesterday you'd made an assignation later so you've agreed not to display affection—to put others off the scent. Good move!"

Only Scarface could talk to her like this—but his chat, repeated by her to Potemkin, showed how the court was electrified. The bathhouse echoed with the laughter and love-making of these two sensualists. "My darling friend," she scribbled in a note, "I fear you might be angry with me. If not all the better. Come quickly to my bedroom and prove it."

Poor Iced Soup was miserable. "I was merely a sort of kept woman," he later recalled, "I was scarcely allowed to go out or see anyone. When I was anxious for the Order of St. Anna, I mentioned it to the empress and next day found 30,000 roubles in my pocket. As for Potemkin, he gets what he wants. He is the master." Vasilchikov moved out of the palace; Potemkin moved in.

Catherine was still in crisis, but now she had a fearless and intelligent partner. "I've withdrawn from a certain good-natured but extremely dull character," she wrote, "who has immediately been replaced by one of the greatest, wittiest and most original eccentrics of this iron century."9

"A woman is always a woman," wrote an aghast Frederick the Great, who coined his own vaginal principle of philosophical misogyny. "In feminine government, the cunt has more influence than a firm policy guided by reason."

This would be the great love affair and the supreme political partnership of her life. Potemkin and Catherine were opposites in terms of their style of living: she was orderly, Germanic, measured and cool; Potemkin was wild, disorganized, Slavic, emotional and larger than life, panache personified. She was ten years older, born royal; he was the son of minor Smolensk gentry, brought up spoiled among five sisters. In religion, she was a rationalist, almost an atheist, while he combined Orthodox mysticism with a rare Enlightened tolerance. He was a wit; she liked to laugh; he sang and wrote music; she was tone deaf but loved to listen. He was nocturnal; she went to bed at eleven every night. She was practical in foreign policy; he was imaginative and visionary. While she was always in love with one person, he was a voracious and animalistic enthusiast who could not stop seducing and making love to the most beautiful aristocratic women and European adventuresses of his time—as well as to at least three of his gorgeous nieces.

Yet they shared many passions—both were sexual creatures, earthy and unshockable. They adored literature, neo-classicist architecture and English gardens (Potemkin travelled with a garden, borne by serfs, that was planted wherever he stopped for the night). Both were obsessional collectors of art and jewels and both relished splendour—though his tastes were sultanic, if not pharaonic. But above all they lived for power.

Potemkin was the only man she ever loved who was as intelligent as she was—Grigory Orlov said Potemkin was "clever as the devil." For all his flights of poetical fancy he possessed the energy and acumen to make vast projects into reality, a master of the art of the possible: "our duty is to improve on events" was how he defined the politician's challenge. "She is crazy about him," said her friend Senator Ivan Yelagin. "They may well be in love because they are exactly the same." That is why Catherine called him "my twin soul."

Catherine was already teaching Potemkin, who she later boasted she had raised from "sergeant to marshal," the theatre of politics: "Behave cleverly in public and that way no one will know what we're really thinking." Even in their early letters, sexual play alternates with power play. "The doors will be open," she writes in one note. "I'm going to bed. Darling I will do whatever you command. Shall I come to you or will you come to me?"

She called him "my Cossack" and "Bijou" as well as "Golden Cockerel," "Lion of the Jungle" and "Tiger"; he always called her "Matushka." During her Hermitage card parties, attended by favoured ambassadors, Potemkin often burst in, unannounced and wearing Turkish dressing-gowns or even pantaloons, chewing on a radish and walking moodily through the room, an Oriental personification of a Slavic hero, sometimes the sparkling life and soul, at other times brooding and silent. Catherine had to rewrite her list of Hermitage regulations: "Rule Three: You are requested to be cheerful without however destroying, breaking or biting anything."

As with all his eccentricities there was a point to this: he was a unique phenomenon not dependent on the rules of ordinary men. Even though his tantrums and hypochondria exhausted her, her own desire for him amazed her:

> I woke at five . . . I have given strict rules to the whole of my body to the last hair to stop showing you the slightest sign of love . . . Oh Monsieur Potemkin! What a trick you have played to unbalance a mind, previously thought to be one of the best in Europe . . . What a shame! Catherine II the victim of this crazy passion . . . one more proof of your supreme power over me. Well, mad letter, go to where my hero dwells . . .

The empress was so in love with him that she crept to his room and waited outside in the cold for his aides to leave. Their letters resemble modern emails, and we can imagine the messengers scampering back and forth between their apartments.

He: "Dear Matushka I've just got back but I'm frozen . . . First I want to know how you're feeling."

Michael (*left*), the first Romanov tsar. His son and successor Alexei (*right*) was boisterous, innovative and passionate, but his temper could be dangerous.

Alexei's daughter, Sophia, was the first woman to rule Russia.

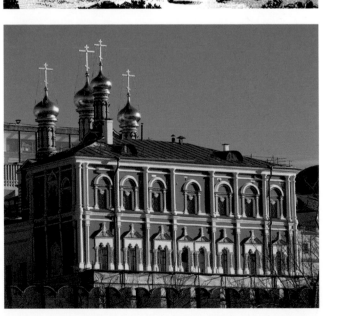

*Above right* The Terem Palace, where royal princesses lived in sumptuous but pious and gloomy seclusion in the upper floors.

*Right* Alexei kept his dwarfs and actors in the exquisite Poteshnye (Amusements) Palace. It was later Stalin's home, where his wife Nadya committed suicide.

*Opposite page* The creator of modern Russia, Peter was exceptional in every way. A born autocrat who enjoyed drunken orgies, he combined menacing hyperactivity and ferocious violence with visionary genius.

*Right* Peter was even more terrifying and impatient in middle age. As he built Petersburg, he forced Russia to modernize so that he could finally defeat the Swedes.

*Below* Peter's wife and successor, Catherine I, enjoyed an extraordinary rise from promiscuous Lithuanian peasant-girl to crowned empress of Russia in her own right.

Alexei, Peter the Great's son and heir—until the tsar realized that he threatened to destroy everything he had created. When the boy fled to Vienna, Peter had him hunted down and lured back to Petersburg.

Menshikov—"the Prince from the Dirt"—Peter's vicious, ambitious and talented henchman, rose to vast wealth and became ruler of Russia, but ultimately reached too far.

Peter II, Peter the Great's grandson, hoped to reverse all his reforms and move the capital back to Moscow. Half in love with his aunt Elizaveta, he was even keener on hunting, but on the day of his planned marriage he fell ill.

Anna (*above left*), with cheeks "as big as a Westphalian ham," was cruel and suspicious, embittered by a bullying mother and a long exile in Courland. She favoured dwarf-tossing, collecting limbless freaks and forcing her fools to pretend to be chickens. Her lover, Ernst Biron (*above right*), who rose from groom to become the duke of Courland, "talked to men as horses and to horses as men."

Ivan VI became emperor at eight weeks old. His good-natured and sensual mother, Anna Leopoldovna (*above*), ruled while enjoying a *ménage à trois* with her lovers Julie von Mengden (*right*, with Ivan) and Count Lynar.

*Above* Elizaveta, Russian Venus: blonde, Amazonian and wanton, she kept several lovers simultaneously and enforced her fashion tastes on her court. But when it came to power, she was very much Peter the Great's daughter.

*Left* Newlyweds, the future Peter III and Catherine. This obscure German princess of supreme intelligence was brought to Russia by Elizaveta to marry her heir. Their marriage ended in murder.

*Opposite page* Blue-eyed and curvaceous, charming, majestic and industrious, Catherine the Great conquered Ukraine, Crimea and Poland, built a famed art collection and projected Russian power—but she always had to be in love.

Catherine fell in love with the handsome war hero Grigory Orlov (*left*), who helped her seize power. She found her real partner in the brilliant and sultanic Grigory Potemkin, her "twin soul"—*right*, in the uniform of Grand Admiral of the Black Sea Fleet (with Catherine's diamond-set portrait pinned to his chest).

*Left* Catherine in her late fifties, wearing her travelling costume for Potemkin's 1787 tour of Crimea. Her last lover Platon Zubov (*above*)—forty years her junior—was arrogant, inept and overpromoted. He was no Potemkin.

She: "I rejoice you're back, my dear. I'm well. To get warm: go to the *banya*."

He replies that he has now had his bath.

She: "My beauty, my darling, whom nothing resembles, I am full of warmth and tenderness for you and you will have my protection as long as you live. You must be, I guess, more handsome than ever after the bath."

Yet she needed him in her crisis of power: "I have masses of things to tell you and in particular on the subject we spoke about yesterday." On 5 March 1774, she used him to give orders to Chernyshev on military matters and he was promoted to lieutenant-colonel of the Preobrazhensky Guards, but he concentrated first on organizing the defeat of Pugachev. As for the war, he was already checking through the peace terms with the Ottomans, but he suggested that one more offensive was needed: he persuaded her "to empower Rumiantsev and thus peace was achieved," as she put it. On 31 March, Potemkin was appointed governor-general of New Russia, the newly conquered regions of southern Ukraine. Catherine gave him regular gifts of 100,000 roubles, but it was power that interested him. He demanded to join her council running the war: "Sweetheart, as you asked me to send you with something to the Council today, I wrote a note . . . so if you want to go, be ready at midday." On 30 May, he was promoted to general-en-chef and vice-president of the War Collegium. This upset the old balance of her entourage: Chernyshev resigned, but the couple revelled in partnership. "General loves me?" she wrote to him. "Me loves general."[10]

On 9 June, Rumiantsev crossed the Danube and thrust into Ottoman territory—but on 21 July news arrived that the Cossack rebel, Pugachev, had raised a new army and stormed Kazan. The Volga region was aflame, unleashing a savage class war, a serf uprising and slaughter of landowners. Would he march on Moscow? A rattled Catherine held an emergency Council at Peterhof. The Orlovs, Chernyshevs and Razumovsky, all upset by the rise of Potemkin and terrified by Pugachev, barely uttered a word, until afterwards Panin suggested to Potemkin that they send his aggressive brother General Peter Panin with dictatorial powers to suppress the revolt. Catherine loathed Peter Panin, "a first-class liar," but she agreed, backed by Potemkin.

The stress was alleviated two days later by the news that Rumiantsev, armed with Catherine's articles corrected by Potemkin, had signed the Peace of Kuchuk-Kainardzhi. "I think today is the happiest day of my life," Catherine rejoiced, for she had won a toehold on the Black Sea, a strip of southern Ukraine, an independent khanate of Crimea, the right to build a Black Sea fleet—and, vaguely, the role as protector of Ottoman Christians, a right that would become important in the next century.

On 13 July, her generals had managed finally to defeat Pugachev, who fled back towards his home, the Don, where he was betrayed. General Panin decimated villages, hung thousands from their ribs and floated gallows down the Volga. Pugachev was sentenced to quartering then beheading, but Catherine humanely ordered that he be first beheaded.[11] There died the ghost of Peter III.*

After Pugachev, Catherine was in no mood to take any risks with pretenders and now she faced a very different case: "Princess Elizabeth," a slender twenty-year-old with an Italianate profile, alabaster skin and grey eyes, claimed to be the daughter of Empress Elizaveta and the Night Emperor. No one ever discovered her true identity—maybe the daughter of a Nuremberg baker—but she was adept at hooking credulous older aristocrats. Scarface monitored her progress around Italy. Catherine demanded in gangsterish tones that the Ragusans hand Elizabeth over. If not, "one can toss a few bombs into the town." Even better, Scarface should just "capture her without noise."

Orlov-Chesmensky courted the ersatz princess. She believed she was gulling him, but when she came on board his flagship, greeted as the "empress," the "villain" was arrested and sent to Petersburg where she was imprisoned in the Peter and Paul Fortress. She appealed to Catherine, signing her letters "Elizabeth," only for the empress to show how a real autocrat behaved: "Send someone to tell the notorious woman that if she wishes to lighten her petty fate, she should stop playing comedy."†

Catherine and Paul headed to Moscow to celebrate the victory with triumphal arches, parades and fireworks—the first of her spectacles stage-managed by her impresario of international magnificence, Potemkin. On 10 July, the empress and tsarevich proceeded through lines of troops in the Kremlin, she wearing a small crown and ermine-lined purple cloak, to a Te Deum in the Dormition, flanked by Marshal Rumiantsev and General Potemkin, while twelve generals held a purple

---

* Almost. Pugachev was not the only Peter III at large. The first of these impostors was Stephen the Small, a mysterious diminutive salesman in the tiny Balkan principality of Montenegro who in 1767 announced that he was Peter III and seized power. Liquidating any opponents, the miniature tyrant reformed Montenegrin government and defeated both Ottomans and Venetians. Fighting the Ottomans herself, Catherine sent an envoy to offer aid provided the Montenegrins remove Stephen. But in 1773, just as Catherine had finally destroyed Pugachev, Stephen was assassinated by his barber.

† The legend of this girl is that she perished in her cell when the Neva flooded—the famous painting of Flavitsky. But actually she died, aged twenty-three, of consumption on 4 December 1775. She was known as Tarakanova—the princess of the cockroaches (perhaps after the sole companions of her last days).

canopy over her. Afterwards, surrounded by her four marshals, she handed out the prizes of victory: Rumiantsev received the surname "Zadunaisky"—"Over the Danube"—plus 5,000 souls and 100,000 roubles, while Potemkin became a count and was told by the empress, "I'll give you my portrait [a miniature set in diamonds] on the day of peace, my jewel, my heart, dear husband."

Their relationship was so all-consuming that it started to burn them both. Catherine had found her political partner in Potemkin, but he drove her mad with his mood swings and wild jealousy. Even though she claimed that "For you, I'd do the impossible—I'll be your humble maid or lowly servant or both," it was hard for an eighteenth-century Russian man to maintain an equal relationship with a powerful, sexually independent woman. "No, Grishenka," she reassured him, "it's impossible for me to change towards you. Can one love anybody after having loved you?" She warned him that it was bad for his health, called him a "cruel Tatar," threatened to lock herself in her room for ever and then tried affection—"I'll love you for ever in spite of yourself"—and more sweetly: "Batinka, come to see me so I can calm you with my endless caresses." But she too was demanding and needy: when he threatened to kill any rivals, claiming that she had had fifteen lovers before him, she wrote him "a sincere confession," surely the most extraordinary document ever written by a monarch. She admitted her four lovers before him, denied wantonness but explained the essence of her nature: "The trouble is that my heart can't be without love for even an hour." She understood his dilemma and decided to put his mind at rest: "My dear soul, cher Epoux, darling husband, come and snuggle up, if you please. Your caress is sweet and lovely to me. Beloved husband."

She had probably gone through some form of marriage or blessing with Potemkin, whom she henceforth often called her husband and herself "your wife." If she was "Matushka," he became "Batinka"— "Papa."* But now she complained that he often did not speak to her. He seemed to be withdrawing from the relationship. His behaviour was appalling, ignoring her at her own dinners. They sometimes made up their fights in the form of letters that went back and forth between them:

---

* The most likely date is 4 June 1774, probably in St. Sampsonovsky Church, but there is no proof. Apart from Catherine's letters, the best evidence is the way she treated Potemkin and how he behaved. She ordered that he was to be greeted with the same ceremony as the imperial family and allowed him almost unlimited access to government funds. She virtually adopted his nieces and expected them and her lovers to call her and Potemkin mother and father.

| Potemkin | Catherine |
|---|---|
| Let me my love say this | I allow it. |
| Which will, I hope, end our | |
| argument. | The sooner the better. |
| Don't be surprised I am | |
| Disturbed by our love. | Don't be disturbed. |
| Not only have you showered me | |
| With good deeds, | So have you on me. |
| You have placed me in your | |
| Heart. I want to be | You are there firmly |
| There alone, and above everyone else | & strongly and will remain there. |
| Because no one has ever loved you so | I see it and believe it. |
| much | |
| And as I have been made by your hands | Happy to do so. |
| That you should be happy in being good | |
| To me; | It will be my greatest pleasure |
| That you should find rest from the | |
| Great labours arising from your high | |
| Station in thinking of my comfort. | Of course. |
| Amen. | Give rest to our thoughts and let |
| | our feelings act freely. They are |
| | most tender and will find the best |
| | way. |
| | End of quarrel. Amen. |

She began to tire of these tempers, slow to understand the pressures on a favourite which were even greater for one so ambitious. Both she and Potemkin were human furnaces who demanded an endless supply of praise, love and attention in private, and glory and power in public. It was these gargantuan appetites that made this relationship at once so painful and so productive. It would take a delicate arrangement to keep Potemkin as partner and husband yet liberate both of them to love others. "The essence of our disagreement," she reflected, "is always the question of power and never that of love."

Catherine was now working on local government reforms, with Potemkin correcting the documents, but the drafting was done by a pair of secretaries commandeered from Rumiantsev's staff: Alexander Bezborodko, an ungainly but canny and industrious Ukrainian with a superb memory, was the cleverer of the two, while Peter Zavadovsky was more methodical and better looking. Sheltering from Potemkin's volcanic tantrums, Catherine and the reliable Zavadovsky fell in love over these drafts—with Potemkin's acquiescence mixed with jealousy. On 2 January 1776, Zavadovsky was appointed adjutant-general.

"150 kisses shall I joyfully give you every hour. I love your smile," she wrote to her "Petrusa," relishing the holistic powers of her breasts and their love-making. "Petrushinka, I rejoice you've been healed by my little pillows and if my caress eases your health then you'll never be sick."

Catherine constantly reassured the emotional Potemkin of his unique and impregnable position in her heart and regime:

> My Lord and Cher Epoux,
> Why do you want to cry? Why do you prefer to believe your unhealthy imagination rather than the real facts, all of which confirm your wife. Was she not attached to you two years ago by holy ties? I love you and am bound to you by all possible ties.

She gave him the Anichkov Palace (while he set up house in the Shepilev Mansion adjoining the Winter Palace on Millionnaya Street so that he could enter Catherine's apartments through a covered passageway) and procured the title prince of the Holy Roman Empire for him. From now on, always known as "Serenissimus," Potemkin would be her partner and husband while each enjoyed relationships with younger partners.

Now, just as Catherine and Potemkin changed the direction of foreign policy, scandal and tragedy hit the marriage of Paul.[12]

On 10 April 1776, Grand Duchess Natalya Alexeievna went into labour, attended by Catherine in an apron. Natalya was already a disappointment to the empress, who knew she was extravagant and suspected she was unfaithful. For two days, Catherine rushed repeatedly to the bedside, but it became apparent that Natalya was unable to give birth due to a deformation of the spine. After two days of agony the dead foetus infected the mother. On 15 April she died.

Paul, half mad with grief, was understandably reluctant to consider a new wife—but the empire needed its heir. Catherine callously showed him his wife's love letters to his best friend, Andrei Razumovsky, son of Kyril.

Frederick the Great suggested a new candidate, the sixteen-year-old Princess Sophia Dorothea of Württemberg, passed over the first time because she had been too young. Inheriting his father's Prussophilia, Paul travelled to Berlin to meet her. Frederick the Great was not impressed by Paul, whom he predicted would suffer "a fate like his unfortunate father." Nonetheless the grand duke returned with a fiancée, soon renamed Maria Fyodorovna, "tall, fair, inclined to embonpoint," dutiful and prudish. When they married on 26 September, Prince Orlov held the crown over Paul's head. Obsessed with rules and inspections, Paul wrote an instruction on how he expected his wife to behave, yet the marriage was splendidly fecund: Maria would be the mother of two, if not three, emperors.

Catherine was quite affectionate to Paul at this time. "My dear son," she wrote from Tsarskoe Selo, her favourite suburban residence, "yesterday I came here and it's quite desolate without you . . . Tsarskoe Selo is bereft of its embellishment when you're not here." She was delighted with "this delicious creature" Maria—"my princess"—and celebrated by giving "the Seconds," as she grandly called them, an estate near Tsarskoe Selo. There, Catherine's architect Cameron built Pavlovsk, a palace of Palladian perfection, which Paul resented as a manifestation of his mother's control. He sacked Cameron as fast as he could. His struggle with his mother would be fought architecturally in a battle of the palaces, as well as personally and politically.

On 12 December 1777, Catherine was beside herself with excitement when Maria gave birth to a son whom the empress named Alexander. Kidnapping him from the maternal bedchamber, she told the parents, "Your children belong to you, to me and to the state." As he grew, she raved about Alexander's "rare beauty" and brilliant mind, ordering his toys, designing him the world's first romper suit and writing an ABC textbook for his education. She soon called him "the monarch in training"—as if Paul did not exist.[13]

Just when the succession had been settled, Catherine discovered that Zavadovsky was not finding it easy to be her lover. Her Petrusa wanted to spend all his time with her, yet she told him firmly that she belonged "to the empire." Zavadovsky, frightened of Potemkin, started to sulk. When Potemkin was made a prince, she coaxed Zavadovsky, "If you went to congratulate His Highness, the Highness will receive you affectionately. If you lock yourself up, neither I nor anyone will be accustomed to see you." Zavadovsky wept, knowing he was losing her, but this irked the empress: "I can't understand why you can't see me without tears in your eyes." But even their break-up was directed by Potemkin. "Both of us need spiritual peace," wrote Catherine. "I'll talk to Prince Grigory Alexandrovich [Potemkin]." Zavadovsky confided in the other big man of the court: "Prince Orlov told me you want to go," she wrote in May 1777. "I agree. After dinner I can meet you." In a new tradition, the outgoing lover nominated an intermediary, something between a literary agent and a divorce lawyer, to negotiate his golden goodbye. "He tearfully chose Count Kyril Razumovsky," Catherine told Potemkin, sending him a present. "Bye bye, dear, enjoy the books!" Zavadovsky was showered with bounty—"three or four thousand souls . . . 50,000 roubles and 30,000 in future years"—but left distraught. "I advise you to translate Tacitus or practise Russian history," she lectured him briskly. If only studying history could really cure heartbreak—but her real advice was: "In order that Prince Potemkin be friendly with you, make the effort."

It goes without saying that Catherine had found someone new. Potemkin held an opulent dinner at his new estate at Ozerki for the empress, his nieces—and Semyon Zorich, thirty-one years old, a Serbian major in the Hussars, one of the prince's aides, nicknamed "le vrai sauvage." Catherine fell in love with this macho cockatoo who was soon strutting around the court in his bejewelled clothes. The Serbian savage was resentful that her real relationship was still with Potemkin. "Give Senyusha the attached letters," she wrote to Potemkin. "It's so dull without you." Instead of weeping like Zavadovsky, Zorich challenged Potemkin to a duel. The Savage would have to go.

Potemkin was now spending much of his time in New Russia, planning new cities, reforming the Cossacks, constructing the new Black Sea fleet and plotting to annex the Crimea, but he kept a close eye on Catherine's happiness, rushing back to console the empress whenever there was a crisis. She ended it with Zorich, who received an estate with 7,000 souls. "The child's gone," Catherine reported to Potemkin. "As for the rest, we'll discuss it together." Far from being glib switches from lover to lover, these upheavals were agonizing for Catherine—but she had already met Zorich's successor. A few days later she was recovering at a Potemkin estate with his nieces—and another Potemkin aide-de-camp, the twenty-four-year-old Major Ivan Rimsky-Korsakov, vain, "good natured but silly." Catherine's confidante, Countess Bruce, was there too, however, and she was attracted to Rimsky-Korsakov herself.

"I'm afraid of burning my fingers," Catherine confided to Potemkin, asking for his "clever guidance." Two days after the house party, on 1 June 1778, Korsakov, whose "Grecian beauty" inspired Catherine to nickname him "King of Epirus," was appointed adjutant-general. "Adieu mon bijou," Catherine wrote to Potemkin. "Thanks to you and the King of Epirus, I'm happy as a chaffinch." Catherine, now aged forty-nine, was gratefully hungry for Korsakov, writing to him: "Thank you for loving me!" But ominously he started to avoid her. "When will I see you?" she asked. "If he doesn't come back soon, I'll go looking for him in town." When she went looking, she surprised Korsakov *in flagrante delicto* with Countess Bruce. In the resulting uproar, Korsakov had the impertinence to boast of his sexual antics with both women while demanding munificent gifts. Furious, humiliated but still maternally indulgent, Catherine told the boy to "calm yourself . . . I've demonstrated I'm taking care of you." Korsakov's affair ruined Catherine's friendship with Countess Bruce.

She recovered for six months, flirting with various candidates but probably returning to Potemkin until she settled down with one of Potemkin's aides, Alexander Lanskoy—twenty-one to her fifty-one—who was her ideal placid pupil, fitting perfectly into the Catherine–Potemkin family. Her relationships were always as pedagogic as they were sexual: she and Lanskoy enjoyed studying Greek and Latin classics, artistic studies and theatrical–literary criticism. She liked to claim that her boudoir was an academy for training servants of the state.

It was family she craved: she wanted Lanskoy and others to regard her and Potemkin as parents. To Potemkin, she usually referred to Lanskoy as "the child," while the favourites were expected to call her "Matushka" and him "Batushka"—Mama and Papa. When Potemkin was unwell, Lanskoy had to write, "I've heard from Matushka that you, Batushka Prince Grigory Alexandrovich, are ill which troubles me greatly: get better!" and he too told Potemkin: "You can't imagine how dull it is without you, Batushka, come immediately."

Meanwhile Potemkin was successively in love with his three nieces, who became the reigning court belles. First Alexandra, known as "Sashenka" who became Catherine's surrogate daughter and devoted friend. Then he moved on to Varvara (whom he called "Sweet Lips" and who signed herself "Grishenkin's Pussycat"—the sexual tone is unmissable) and Ekaterina (whom both Catherine and Potemkin called "Katinka the Kitten," "Angel" or just "Venus"). Catherine treated "our nieces" like daughters and he the favourites like sons whom he governed to protect her feelings—and his power. Together they were the children of this weird, unconventional marriage that allowed Catherine and Potemkin the serenity in which to embark on their greatest project. "One mind is good," Catherine told Marshal Rumiantsev about her partnership with Potemkin, "but two is better."[14]

On 27 April 1779, Grand Duchess Maria Fyodorovna gave birth to a second son whom Catherine, prompted by Potemkin, named Constantine and designated to become emperor of Constantinople after the fall of the Ottomans. Potemkin persuaded the empress that Russia's future lay southwards around the Black Sea. Peter the Great's work around the Baltic was finished; Poland was a secure Russian client state; but the lands of Ukraine that they now called New Russia were a wilderness waiting to be developed. On the Black Sea, Potemkin planned cities with universities and attracted foreign colonists to settle them. In 1778, he built his first naval city, Kherson, named after the ancient Khersones, and started to create the fleet that would be his legacy. To complete his plan, he needed Crimea. In 1780, Bezborodko, Catherine's secretary and all-round "factotum," who grumbled that Potemkin was good at "thinking up ideas that someone else has to carry out," drafted the "Note on Political Affairs" that laid out the so-called Greek Project.

As Potemkin took over foreign policy, Britain and France were distracted by the American War of Independence. The seizure of Crimea and the Ottoman carve-up required a new alliance with Austria—and this brought Potemkin into conflict with Panin, who was snoozing astride foreign policy like a somnolent, sickly sloth. His Northern System, based around a Prussian alliance, had delivered a partition of Poland, but it was obsolete.

Empress Maria Theresa had long regarded Catherine as a regicidal nymphomaniac, but her son, her co-ruler Emperor Joseph II, was more pragmatic and ambitious, if no less snobbish. Keen to expand his own territories, he needed Russian help. As the tension rose, Potemkin grew irritable with young Lanskoy. "Please let me know if Alexander [Lanskoy] has annoyed you somehow," Catherine interceded, "and if you're angry with him and why exactly."

Potemkin met Joseph at the border. On 9 May 1780, Catherine, accompanied by Potemkin's nieces and Bezborodko, but leaving Panin behind, set off to meet the Holy Roman Emperor at Mogilev. They got on well with Joseph, an obsessional reformer whose military-command measures to rationalize his complicated inheritance from Belgium to Italy and the Balkans, in the spirit of the Enlightenment, would end by offending everyone. His friend Charles-Joseph, prince de Ligne, described his reign as a "continual crection that will never be satisfied." He lacked all charm and empathy, but Catherine and Potemkin were delighted by his effervescent envoy, the prince de Ligne, the soi-disant "jockey diplomatique."* On 18 May 1781, Catherine signed a secret alliance with Joseph to share the Ottoman empire.[15]

"The system with Austria's court," Catherine congratulated Potemkin, "is your achievement." Panin retired angrily to his estates, while Catherine and Potemkin worried about the Prussophile Paul's reaction.

The awkward heir, now twenty-nine, balding and pug-nosed, was

* "I'd like to be a pretty girl until thirty, a general till sixty, and a cardinal till eighty," joked Ligne, who personified the decadent cosmopolitanism of his time. His charm was such that he was friends with Frederick the Great, Marie Antoinette and Catherine the Great, as well as with Rousseau, Voltaire and Casanova. Catherine called him "the most pleasant and easy person who plays all sorts of tricks like a child." "I like to be a foreigner everywhere, a Frenchman in Austria, an Austrian in France, both a Frenchman and an Austrian in Russia." His letters were copied, his bons mots repeated across Europe.

unlikely ever to forgive Potemkin for usurping his place as the second man of the state—and doing it so well.* Now they devised a plan to win over Paul: a Grand Tour including Austria. Since Paul was suspicious of anything connected to his mother and Potemkin, they persuaded one of his retainers to suggest it and then agreed when Paul begged to go. But the malicious Panin came up from the country and warned Paul that this could be a trick to destroy him as Peter the Great had destroyed his son Alexei. He could lose the succession and his children.

Paul collapsed in panic, "terrified of the empress as sovereign and mother." While capable of rational political plans, aesthetic taste and chivalrous generosity, he was also morose and hysterical, prone to foam-flecked rages, and tormented by the memory of his murdered father. He had nightmares about Peter the Great in which his great-grandfather warned "poor Paul" that he would die young.

When they were due to leave on 13 September, the grand duke and duchess suddenly refused to depart. Finally on the 19th, the Seconds, travelling in the fairytale incognito of "Count and Countess of the North," kissed their children tearfully. The grand duchess fainted and had to be carried to the carriage, while Paul followed in abject terror. The next morning, Panin was dismissed.

Paul was welcomed to Vienna by Joseph, to whom he soon denounced the new alliance, threatening to throw Potemkin into prison. Catherine had his entourage's letters opened and, reading those of Paul's courtier Prince Alexander Kurakin, she discovered that her son hated "the horrible situation in the Motherland" and discussed "breaking the neck" of Potemkin. Kurakin was banished.

Catherine never forgave the Seconds, whom she more often nicknamed "the Heavy Baggage," but she tried to get on with her son even when he lost control of his own household.[16]

Catherine soon afterwards presented Paul with Orlov's former estate Gatchina.† While Maria embellished Pavlovsk with Roman busts and

---

* Potemkin planned to become duke of Courland, king of Poland or monarch of a new improvised kingdom of Dacia to insure himself after Catherine's death. As part of his strategy, he married off his nieces: Sashenka married the Polish grand hetman Ksawery Branicki, but raised her children in the Winter Palace. Katinka the Kitten married Count Paul Scavronsky, descendant of the brother of Catherine I, a zany eccentric who so loved opera he addressed everyone, including servants, in operatic recitative. Varvara married Prince Sergei Golitsyn, while the youngest, Tatiana, married Prince Nikolai Yusupov. Rasputin's murderer was descended from them.
† Prince Grigory Orlov died insane. Much to Catherine's chagrin—the happiness of an ex-lover is often both welcome and unbearable—Orlov had unexpectedly married his nineteen-year-old niece and gone travelling. Her sudden death in Switzerland possibly drove him to madness, but it was more likely a symptom of tertiary syphilis.

a chalet to remind her of Württemberg, he made Gatchina a cross between a neo-classical palace with follies like his "Isle of Love"—and a
Germanic barracks. Like his father, he worshipped Frederick the Great.
"It was like a visit to a foreign country," wrote Nikolai Sablukov, a Guards
officer. "Like a small German town." There this martinet attracted a
cadre of harsh German and cashiered Russian officers.* In charge of the
army, Potemkin had designed a loose-fitting military uniform for ease
of movement. Paul hated "the Potemkin Army," insisting that everyone
at Gatchina wear Prussian uniform, including stockings, a pointed hat,
a waxed hairdo and a pigtail, which took hours to prepare. Paul punished any infringement according to Prussian rules.

Paul's marriage appeared ideal: Maria was "loved for her high virtues
and finds happiness only in her children." Despite being sorely tried
by Paul's behaviour, she was devoted to him—and constantly pregnant,
producing four sons and six daughters.

Yet Paul's household was in turmoil: soon after his return from
abroad, Paul fell in love with one of Maria's ladies-in-waiting, Ekaterina
Nelidova, an unmarried and pious twenty-seven-year-old, who was,
noted a courtier, "small, exceedingly plain, swarthy, tiny-eyed, with a
mouth that stretched from ear to ear and legs as short as a dachshund's."
But this "petite brunette with dark and sparkling black eyes" was "astonishingly quick and clever and a most elegant dancer."

Paul never slept with Nelidova, who called herself his "sister" and
would have preferred to live in a monastery. Her chastity appealed to
Paul's sentimental chivalry, which was a reaction to his mother's lu-
bricity. Although he enjoyed fleeting sexual escapades with low-born
mistresses, he valued Nelidova's faith in him—and her slapstick
humour. "The little enchantress" arranged for guests to fall into baths
or sleep in beds that fell apart, much to Paul's honking delight.

Maria was so unhappy that she appealed to Catherine, who was bemused by her son's lack of taste, telling Maria: "Look how beautiful you
are; your rival is a little monster; stop torturing yourself and be sure of
your charms." Paul sanctimoniously explained to his mother that his
relationship with Nelidova was "a friendship holy and gentle but innocent and pure." Given his other affairs, Catherine must have snorted at
the humbug.

* The exception was the discerning and contrary young nobleman Fyodor Rostopchin,
descendant of Tatar princelings, who, out of old-fashioned sanctimony, despised Potemkin
and the favourites: when he gave the grand duke the present of a set of toy soldiers, Paul
embraced him. "Now it turns out that I've become a favourite of the grand duke," worried
Rostopchin. "You know what unpleasant consequences result from blatant signs of his
favour." Rostopchin, famous as the man who burned Moscow in 1812, recorded his times
in his acerbic memoirs and letters to his friend Count Simon Vorontsov.

This only convinced Catherine even more that the future lay with her grandson Alexander. She appointed an experienced soldier-courtier Nikolai Saltykov (a great-nephew of Empress Anna) as his governor and hired a young Swiss tutor of Enlightened views, Frédéric-César Laharpe to teach him French. Laharpe became, Alexander later wrote, "a man to whom I owe everything except life itself." When the child was ten, Catherine praised him as "a person of rare beauty, goodness and understanding" who showed precocious knowledge, as happy discussing history as playing blind man's buff. She even started to build the child the biggest palace in Russia, which she called Pella after the birthplace of Alexander the Great. She was tempted to skip the Heavy Baggage and make Alexander heir.[17]

As Britain and France fought and the Americans won their independence, Potemkin persuaded Catherine to annex Crimea. "Imagine Crimea is yours," he wrote to Catherine, "and the wart on your nose is no more . . . This deed will win you immortal glory greater than any Russian Sovereign. Crimea assures dominance of the Black Sea . . . Russia needs paradise!"

"We could decide it all in half an hour together but now I don't know where to find you," wrote Catherine. Potemkin bounded into town in a state of febrile ebullience: they now proposed the entire Greek Project to Joseph, who agreed to the annexation of Crimea.

"Keep your resolution, Matushka," said Serenissimus as he left in April 1783. But, once in the south, he toiled so hard that he forgot to write to Catherine, who grumbled, "Neither I nor anyone knows where you are!" On 10 July Potemkin wrote that "In three days, I will congratulate you with Crimea."

A few days later, Serenissimus pulled another rabbit out of the hat, when the indomitable old warrior-king Hercules (or Erakle) of Kartli-Kakhetia placed the largest of the Georgian kingdoms under Catherine's protection. "The Georgian business is concluded," he wrote. "Has any other Sovereign so illuminated an epoch? You've acquired territories that Pompey and Alexander just glanced at." Crimea was where St. Vladimir had converted to Orthodoxy, "the source of our Christianity and thus our humanity," wrote Serenissimus to the empress. "You've destroyed the Tatar Horde—the tyrant of Russia in olden times. Order your historians to prepare much ink and paper!" Catherine was thrilled and disdained the complaints of Europe: "Let them jest while we do business!"

Exhausted in bed after a quick journey back to Petersburg, Serenissimus awoke to find a sealed message from Catherine on his bedside table: Potemkin was promoted to field marshal, appointed president of the War Collegium and given 100,000 roubles to build the Taurida Palace; Kuban and Crimea were added to his viceroyalty and he received the surname "Tavrichesky": prince of Taurida. "I'm committed to you for a century!" Catherine told him.

Now spending most of his life in the south, in constant dynamic motion, living in Sardanapalian extravagance,* Potemkin's first act was to found a naval base on the site of the Turkish village of Akhtiar—"the best harbour in the world," he told Catherine. He called it the "August City"—Sebastopol.[18]

Potemkin's work required tranquillity in Catherine's bedroom, but on 25 June 1784 Lanskoy, at the age of twenty-six, died of diphtheria.

"I've been plunged into the most acute sorrow," she told Potemkin, "and my happiness is no more." She spent three weeks in bed, desperately ill. Her Scottish doctor John Rogerson feared for her life, which he further endangered by bleeding and laxatives; Bezborodko, recently raised to count, summoned Potemkin.

On 10 July, Serenissimus arrived from Sebastopol. The courtiers heard the two of them "howling" together. Tsarskoe Selo was sweltering, but Catherine had delayed the burial. She was too ill to attend the funeral. Potemkin lived with her day and night, like an old husband and wife, until, as she put it, "he awakened us from the sleep of the dead." For a year, Catherine had no lover. When she went to church, young Guardsmen preened in their best uniforms and tightest breeches to catch her attention.

Now fifty-seven, Catherine flirted with two aides of Potemkin. Serenissimus held a ball at his Anichkov Palace where Alexander Yermolov stood behind the empress's chair as she played cards. The new lover was straw-haired and almond-eyed with a flat nose: Potemkin nicknamed him "the White Negro." Catherine still decided everything with Potemkin. "Without you I feel as if I'm without hands," she wrote. Yermolov intrigued against Potemkin.

---

* He travelled with his own court of aristocrats and adventurers, English, American, French, a harem of mistresses, an Italian composer, English gardeners, his own orchestra and a synod of bishops, mullahs and a Jewish rabbi and army supplier, Joshua Zeitlin, whom Potemkin promoted to "court adviser," giving him noble rank and the right to own estates. When Zeitlin petitioned Catherine against calling Jews zhidi—Yids—Potemkin backed him and advised calling them evrei—Hebrews—which is how they still appear in official Russian documents. His enemies muttered that he liked anyone "with a big snout." As well as Kherson, he founded new towns Nikolaev and Mariupol. Inland he created a capital on the Dnieper, Ekaterinoslav—Glory of Catherine (today's Dnieperpetrovsk)—where he planned a university and a church based on St. Paul's-outside-the-Walls in Rome.

On 15 July 1786, the White Negro departed with 4,000 souls and 130,000 roubles. That very evening, Serenissimus arrived with his aide-de-camp Alexander Dmitriev-Mamonov, whom he supposedly sent to Catherine with a watercolour and a saucy question: what did she think of the painting? "The contours are fine," she replied, "but the choice of colours less fortunate." But Mamonov, twenty-six, a cultured Francophile who always wore a red coat, was much better liked. "Mr. Redcoat," as she called him, was soon a count, owner of 27,000 serfs and a much loved member of her improvised family. Catherine was ready to celebrate the climax of her reign and the rise of Russia as a Black Sea power in a spectacular southern junket.[19]

At 11 a.m. on 7 January 1787, Catherine left Tsarskoe Selo in a convoy of fourteen carriages and 124 sleighs with an entourage of twenty-two including her lover Mr. Redcoat and Ivan Shuvalov (Empress Elizaveta's favourite, recently returned to Russia and appointed grand chamberlain), along with the ambassadors of France, Austria and England (whom she called her "Pocket Ministers"). On 22 April, after the ice had melted on the Dnieper, Catherine and Potemkin embarked on a flotilla of seven luxurious barges, each with its own orchestra, library and drawing room, painted in gold and scarlet, decorated in gold and silk, manned by 3,000 oarsmen, crew and guards and serviced by eighty boats. The dining barge seated seventy and Catherine's *Dnieper* had a boudoir with twin beds for her and Mr. Redcoat. "It was like Cleopatra's fleet," observed Ligne. "Never was there a more brilliant and agreeable voyage." The French minister, the comte de Ségur, likewise thought "it was like a fairytale."

On 7 May, disembarking at Kremenchuk, Catherine rendezvoused with Emperor Joseph II. They laid the foundation stones for the prince's new city Ekaterinoslav, then travelled on to his port of Kherson through an arch that read: "The Road to Byzantium." The monarchs were escorted by Tatar horsemen into Crimea. On 22 May, they dined in a palace on the Heights of Inkerman on a spit that jutted out over the sea. When Serenissimus gave a sign, the curtains were drawn to unveil twenty-four ships-of-the-line in the natural amphitheatre of the new naval base of Sebastopol. "Madame," declared Ségur, "by creating Sebastopol, you have finished in the south what Peter the Great started in the north." Catherine, noted Joseph, was "totally ecstatic." She kept saying, "It's Prince Potemkin to whom I owe everything." Joseph squirmed with jealous astonishment at the fleet: "The truth is it is necessary to be here to believe what I see."

Back in Petersburg, Grand Duke Paul summoned the ambassadors to question Potemkin's achievements.* When they insisted that the cities and the ships-of-the-line were real, Paul exploded, "This bitch of a nation doesn't want to be governed only by women!"[20]

After the party came the hangover: on 5 August, when Catherine and Potemkin were recovering from the trip, Sultan Abdul Hamid declared war. While she mobilized her armies, under Potemkin and Rumiantsev, Catherine had to hold her nerve until the spring. Potemkin was shivering and sick in Kremenchuk. Catherine encouraged him: "I'm afraid you have no more nails on your fingers," she wrote. But when a freak storm scattered his beloved new fleet, Potemkin offered to resign: "I can't stand it any more." Catherine rallied Serenissimus: "In these moments, my dear friend, you're not just a private person who does what he likes. You belong to the state, you belong to me." Only one ship had been lost. Potemkin advanced to protect his new cities by besieging the Ottoman stronghold of Ochakov. After defeating the Ottomans in the estuary overlooked by Ochakov,† he declared: "I've gone mad with joy." But just when things were finally improving, Sweden attacked Russia.

Now it was Catherine's turn to panic: Petersburg was almost undefended. On 9 July, Greig defeated the Swedish fleet—to Catherine's delight: "Petersburg has the look of an armed camp . . . so, my friend, I too have smelled gunpowder."

"Nothing in the world do I desire as much as that, on taking Ochakov, you come here for an hour," Catherine wrote to Potemkin, "so

* The Black Sea Fleet, added to the thirty-seven ships-of-the-line in the Baltic, placed Russia instantly equal to Spain and France, though far behind the 174 of Britain. Potemkin, Grand Admiral of the Black Sea Fleet and Grand Hetman of the Black Sea Cossacks, was at his height yet the journey would be for ever overshadowed by the accusation that Potemkin had falsified his achievements by painting façades of villages—"Potemkin Villages." In fact, the witnesses confirmed the reality; the accusations were invented by men who had never been to the south and started before Catherine had even left Petersburg, but Paul was determined to prove that Potemkin was an inept dreamer, while Russia's European enemies hoped that the new Russian power was illusory. The achievements were solid, but the prince was an impresario of political spectacle. At Balaclava, in a very Potemkinish touch, the monarchs were met by a regiment of Amazon cavalry: 200 girls in crimson velvet skirts and gleaming breastplates with long plaited hair, carrying muskets and sabres. There was no pretence that they were real but nowadays we are more used to presidents watching choreographed dancing on state visits. As for the phrase "Potemkin Village," it unfairly came to mean a sham though it remains ideally suited to political fraud in despotic regimes, including Russia.
† Catherine hired an American admiral, John Paul Jones, whom she sent down to Potemkin. Jones commanded some of the early victories, but Potemkin preferred his other foreign admiral, Prince Karl de Nassau-Siegen, a penniless German soldier of fortune who had once been the lover of the queen of Tahiti. Nassau and Jones soon hated each other. Potemkin sent Jones back to Catherine in Petersburg where he was accused by a procuress of raping her twelve-year-old daughter. Probably framed by Nassau, Jones left for Paris where he died, his body lost until 1906 when it was reburied at the US naval base of Annapolis.

that I might first have the satisfaction of seeing you after such a long separation and second that I might talk over so many things with you in person." The Western powers were suspicious of Russia's Crimean annexation and naval power. In August, England, Prussia and Holland signed an alliance aimed at Russia, while in Poland "a great hatred has risen against us," Catherine informed Serenissimus. "Take Ochakov," she begged him. At 4 a.m. on 6 December, Potemkin stormed Ochakov. Mr. Redcoat woke Catherine with the news: "I was poorly but you cured me!"

She celebrated with Te Deums. On 4 February 1789, Potemkin returned to Petersburg. Catherine left the ball she was at and surprised him while he was changing. Britain and Prussia were encouraging the new Sultan Selim III and Sweden to stay in the war; Russia's ally Joseph was dying in Vienna. Potemkin advised appeasement until he had won the Ottoman war; Catherine wanted peace from the Ottomans to face Prussia.

Her lover, Mamonov, was neglecting her, often either ill or absent. Potemkin kept warning her: "Haven't you been jealous of [maid-of-honour] Princess Shcherbatova?" he asked her. "Isn't there an affaire d'amour?" Catherine was frequently in tears. "Matushka, spit on him!" said Potemkin. In May he left for the front. They would not meet for another two years during which Paris turned the world upside down.[21]

As Potemkin advanced into Wallachia and Moldavia, by now often known as the Danubian Principalities, the Parisian mob stormed the Bastille. Louis XVI had lost control of Paris. Soon afterwards, the National Assembly passed the Declaration of the Rights of Man, which in turn encouraged the Poles in their own revolution against Russia. Catherine was horrified by both. Then Redcoat confessed he had fallen in love with maid-of-honour Daria Shcherbatova "a year and a half earlier" and asked to marry her. Catherine collapsed at this betrayal.

"I've never been a tyrant to anybody," she told Potemkin, "and I hate compulsion. Is it possible you forgot my generosity of character and considered me a wretched egotist? You could have healed me by telling me the truth." Potemkin replied that "I hinted, I felt sorry for you." Catherine granted Redcoat 2,250 serfs and 100,000 roubles.

"A sacred place," joked Zavadovsky ruefully, "is never empty for long."

Catherine had already found Redcoat's replacement—or two. In her letter to Potemkin, she mentioned that she had met Platon Zubov, a twenty-two-year-old cornet in the Guards whom she called "le Noiraud"

("Blackie,") and his younger brother Valerian, "the Child," aged eighteen: "both innocent souls and sincerely attached to me."[22] As the court had long known about Redcoat's infidelity, Nikolai Saltykov, oberhofmeister of Paul's household and an enemy of Potemkin, had time to push the Zubov boys forward—because Potemkin was away at war.

Zubov was probably the handsomest of her favourites. Now sixty-one, stout with swollen legs, dyspepsia and wind, tormented by crises of war and revolution, Catherine could not resist. She took because she could. One of four brothers of minor nobility related to Saltykov, Zubov was pretty, dark and musical—he played the violin. Catherine fell in love with Blackie. "I'm fat and merry," she told Potemkin, "come back to life like a fly in summer." She praised Zubov's "beautiful eyes," yet she rationalized her sexual fever. "By educating young men," she told Potemkin, "I do a lot of good for the state." It was certainly an unusual form of civil service training.

On 3 July, the day the Bastille fell, Blackie was promoted to adjutant-general. Catherine nervously awaited Potemkin's approval. "Your peace of mind is most necessary," she insisted to Potemkin. "Comfort us, caress us." She made Zubov write flattering letters to Potemkin: "I enclose for you an admiring letter from the most innocent soul . . . Think what a fatal situation it would be for my health without this man. Adieu, mon ami, be nice to us!"

"My dear Matushka, how can I not sincerely love the man who makes you happy?" Potemkin replied finally. Zubov was a pinprick. He had important news: "a multitude of victories." On 20 July, the superb general and irrepressible eccentric Alexander Suvorov* defeated the Turks at Fokshany; and just a few weeks later he, together with the Austrians, vanquished the grand vizier at the River Rimnik. Three days later Potemkin took the fortress of Hadji-Bey where he decided to build a new city—Odessa—and then accepted the surrender of Bender. Catherine raised Suvorov to count with the surname "Rymniksky" and lectured Potemkin on the dangers of stardom: "Show the world your greatness of character."

Catherine was still attracted to the younger Zubov brother Valerian: "I'm terribly fond of the child and he's attached to me too and cries like a baby when barred from seeing me." It is most likely it was his elder

---

* Notorious for his idiosyncrasies, Suvorov, probably Russia's greatest ever commander, resembled a shabby, wiry, bristlingly alert scarecrow who liked to do calisthenical exercises stark naked in front of the army. He was relentlessly aggressive ("death is better than defence") and never defeated: "one minute decides the battle; one day the fate of empires." His colloquial instructions in his *Art of Victory* could be taught to ordinary soldiers: "The bullet is a bitch; only the bayonet knows its stuff!"; "Train hard; fight easy" and "No battle is won in the study."

brother Blackie who stood in his way, for ten days later the Child was sent off to the army.

A nation's enemies multiply in proportion to its successes. Just as the Ottomans were about to collapse, Prussia put together a coalition of Ottomans, Poles and Swedes against Russia while threatening Austria with attack if it did not withdraw from the war. On 31 January 1790, Prussia signed an alliance with Constantinople. Nine days later, Joseph II, Catherine's ally, died. Prussia tightened its ring by signing an alliance with revolutionary Poland. On 16 July, the Austrian monarch, Leopold, king of the Romans, withdrew from the war. "Now we're in a crisis," said Catherine, facing the "danger of triple war" while "the French madness" spread to Russia.*

In Tsarskoe Selo, Catherine could hear the thunder of cannonades from the sea battles won by Nassau-Siegen—until that reckless adventurer was defeated on 28 June. But the rout enabled the Swedes to make peace with honour. "We pulled one paw out of the mud," Catherine celebrated to Potemkin. "As soon as you pull out the other one, we'll sing hallelujah!" That autumn, Potemkin delivered a series of victories from the Caucasus to the Danube and finally besieged the fortress of Ismail with its garrison of 35,000 men and 265 cannon. On 11 December, Suvorov stormed it: almost 40,000 perished in one of the bloodiest days of the century that should have vanquished Constantinople. Instead William Pitt, the British prime minister, demanded that Catherine give up all her gains—or face war against Britain and Prussia.

Catherine and Potemkin, who had just arrived in Petersburg, argued about what to do. Potemkin wanted a deal with Prussia, while Catherine vacillated. At the same time, Poland adopted a new constitution under the slogan "The King with the Nation." Catherine chose to regard this as an extension of French Jacobinism and tended towards backing Potemkin's plans for Poland, where he was considering hiving off the Orthodox provinces as his own private kingdom. She cried, he banged the doors and bit his nails, she went to bed with spasms in her bowels. Finally she agreed to let Potemkin appease Prussia. But the coalition had already fallen apart when Charles James Fox scuppered Pitt in Parliament. Once again, their paws were almost out of the mud.[23]

---

* In June 1790, a young nobleman Alexander Radishchev published *A Journey from St. Petersburg to Moscow* which, adopting the Enlightened ideals Catherine had once embraced, attacked Russian absolutism, serfdom and favouritism in the shape of Potemkinian extravagance—all signs of what she called "the French infection . . . the French venom" of a "rabble-rouser worse than Pugachev." On 26 July he was sentenced to be beheaded, but Catherine commuted it to exile to Siberia. Later she arrested Nikolai Novikov, whose journalism she had previously patronized. But he was connected to Paul and the Prussians. He was imprisoned in Shlisselburg.

*

At 7 a.m. on 28 April 1791, Catherine slowly dismounted from her carriage at the neo-classical colonnade of Potemkin's Taurida Palace, wearing a full-length long-sleeved Russian dress with a rich diadem. Potemkin, in a scarlet tailcoat and diamond-spangled cloak, knelt before her and then led her into the gigantic Colonnade Hall (the biggest in Europe) where 3,000 guests (but not the uninvited Blackie) awaited them. The party was a wild extravagance, costing more than 150,000 roubles. As the climax, forty-eight boys and girls, led by Alexander and Constantine, danced the first quadrille, then a bejewelled elephant was unveiled, its rider ringing a bell that heralded the emergence of an entire theatre with boxes. Potemkin invited Catherine to stay in the cosy apartments decorated in her style and had prepared one overture if she stayed and another if she went home. When the empress left at 2 a.m., Serenissimus fell to his knees and then gave a sign to the orchestra which played a love song he had written long before: "The only thing that matters in the world is you." Both Catherine and Potemkin burst into tears.

During the next two months, they worked out a plan for peace with Warsaw, Berlin and Constantinople. Yet throughout July news of more victories arrived from the Caucasus, the Danube and the Black Sea, all celebrated by dinners for Potemkin. He wanted to "pull the Tooth" (*zub* means tooth) but failed to dislodge Zubov. Nonetheless Potemkin remained the indispensable statesman. As Blackie himself admitted later, "I couldn't remove him from my path" because "The Empress always met his wishes halfway and simply feared him as though he was an exacting husband." In a revealing aside, Zubov added: "It's his fault I'm not twice as rich as I am."

On 24 July, Potemkin left Petersburg, pursued by a note from Catherine: "Bye, my friend, I kiss you." When he reported on the preliminary peace with the Ottomans, she wrote, "Everybody here is thrilled." But then came the terrifying news that Potemkin was ill. She burst into tears and prayed for him. Catherine sent doctors to him with Sashenka. Travelling to Jassy, he fell ill again.

"My sincere friend, Prince Grigory Alexandrovich," she wrote on 30 September, the day he turned fifty-two. "Your sickness upsets me utterly; for love of Christ, take whatever the doctors recommend!" Now desperately ill, finding it hard to breathe and fainting, he wrote this letter with a shaking hand: "Matushka, Most Merciful Lady! In my present condition, so tired by illness, I pray to the Most High to preserve your precious health and I throw myself at your sacred feet. Your Imperial Majesty's most faithful and grateful subject. Prince Potemkin of Taurida. Oh Matushka, how ill I am!"

Catherine was just reading his earlier letters. "Your doctors assure me you're better," she wrote back, ordering Sashenka: "Stay with him." When he awoke next morning, he insisted on leaving for the Black Sea, dictating her a note: "No more strength to bear my torment. Salvation alone remains to leave this town. I don't know what will become of me." Then he managed to scrawl to Catherine: "The only escape is to leave." On a track amid the Bessarabian steppe, Potemkin cried out: "That's enough." Sashenka had him carried out on to the steppe where his Cossacks laid him down, his head on her knee, sighing "forgive me, merciful Matushka-Sovereign." As Potemkin, probably the dynasty's greatest minister, died on the steppe, a watching Cossack muttered: "Lived on gold, died on grass."

Seven days later, on 12 October, when the news arrived in Petersburg, Catherine fainted and her courtiers feared she had suffered a stroke. "Tears and desperation," recorded her secretary. "At 8 they let blood, at ten to bed."

"A sudden deathblow has just fallen on my head," she wrote in praise of Potemkin. "My pupil, my friend, almost my idol, Prince Potemkin of Taurida has died. You can't imagine how broken I am . . ."

Catherine appointed Bezborodko to finalize the Ottoman peace, securing the territories of New Russia and the protection of the Orthodox Christians. When Potemkin's entourage returned, she sobbed with them. She frequently moved into Potemkin's Taurida Palace. "How can I replace Potemkin?" she asked her secretary. "Now everybody, like snails, will start to stick their necks out," she said. "So, I too am old." She constantly reflected that "No one came close to Potemkin."

Zubov's moment had come. "Without feeling triumphant," he could finally "breathe at the end of a long and hard subordination."[24]

"The Tooth outrageously shows off his power," reported Fyodor Rostopchin, Paul's retainer, but he "isn't clever, concealing his lack of talent with technical phrases." Worse, "he displays a coarse, excessive arrogance, and visiting him is totally humiliating. Each morning, crowds of sycophants besieged the doors of his apartments, filling the anteroom and reception halls." When the egregious Zubov was ready to receive visitors, the folding doors of his reception room were opened. Then "Zubov slowly entered in a dressing-gown" as "servants approached him to dress his hair and powder it, curled and brushed up into a tuft." Everyone "remained standing and no one dared talk." Once dressed, "this young man sprawled on an armchair picking his nose and staring at the ceiling, a puffed-up and lifeless expression on his face," smirking as his monkey "jumped over the head of those lickspittles or he talked to his jesters." Zubov was educated and had a good memory but, concluded Rostopchin, "He's just negligent and incapable."[25]

Yet this popinjay was now "the head of everything." The French Revolution had tilted the world. Russia, Austria and Prussia were keen to suppress it. On 10 January 1793 Louis XVI was guillotined and Catherine retired to bed, depressed. On 8 March, she fell downstairs but suffered only bruising. She turned to Zubov, now raised to count, to arrange the Second Partition of Poland. "Now I'm taking Ukraine in recompense for my expenses and loss of people," she said—and Prussia shared the spoils.

Catherine heaped rewards on Blackie: her portrait in diamonds (only ever received by Orlov and Potemkin), and some of Potemkin's old posts—though Saltykov was rewarded with the War Collegium.

Catherine felt her age. She noticed how hardly anyone could remember her own accession over thirty years earlier. One of the few was Ivan Shuvalov. He was touchingly shy with her, and courtiers laughed at his antique manners. Catherine told them, "Gentlemen, the Grand Chamberlain and I have been friends for forty years and I'm entitled to jest with him." But the old empress had lost none of her charm. "Still fresh, rather short and stout, her whole person was marked by dignity and grace, grave and noble," noted a young Pole, Prince Adam Czartoryski, who was at court as a hostage for Polish good behaviour and to seek restitution of his confiscated estates. He hated her for destroying Poland yet could not help but admire her. "She was like a mountain stream which carries everything with it. Her face, already wrinkled but full of expression, showed haughtiness and the spirit of domination, on her lips a perpetual smile." Countess Varvara Golovina remembered a hearty dinner with the other ladies-in-waiting when a hand offered them some more food. They were helping themselves before they noticed the iceberg-sized solitaire diamond on the finger: it was the empress.

If she was to bypass Paul in the succession, she would have to find a wife for Alexander. Catherine was in a hurry. Even when he was nine Catherine admitted, "I fear one danger for him: that of women, for he will be chased ... for he is a figure who sets everyone alight." When he was twelve and his governor reported the boy's "nocturnal dreams," Catherine deputed a court lady to initiate Alexander into "the mysteries of all transports engendered by sensual delight." Now, after reviewing the available German princesses, she invited the daughters of the prince of Baden to Petersburg, where they were welcomed by Catherine, Zubov and Sashenka. The fifteen-year-old Alexander chose Princess Louise, aged fourteen, as his future wife. "Everyone said it was two angels getting betrothed," gushed Catherine. "They're quite in love."

On 9 October 1793, Catherine presided over Alexander's marriage to the Baden princess who, converted to Orthodoxy, was renamed Elizabeth Alexeievna. Shuvalov and Bezborodko held the crowns over "these beautiful children" before a sobbing empress.

Elizabeth was pretty, with blue eyes and flowing flaxen locks. "She united indescribable grace and attraction of face and form with quick understanding and clearness of thought," recalled Varvara Golovina. Alexander looked like his tall fair mother. "His soul," considered Rostopchin, "is even more beautiful than his body: never in one person has such moral and physical perfection been combined." Elizabeth thought him "very tall and well formed, especially the legs, light-brown hair, blue eyes, very pretty teeth, charming skin colour, rather handsome."

"You ask me if the Grand Duke *truly* pleases me," Elizabeth wrote to her mother. "Yes, Mama . . . for some time he has pleased me like mad." But there were problems: "One notices little nothings which are not to my taste." Meanwhile Alexander was touchingly answering his mother's awkward questions about sex: "You ask me my dear Mama if my little Lisa is pregnant. No not yet for the thing is not accomplished. It must be agreed that we are big children and very maladroit ones since we take all the trouble imaginable to do so but don't succeed."

Alexander "has fine qualities" but "he's lazy, never touches a book," complained Rostopchin, who admired Elizabeth. "Her husband adores her and together they're like children when there's nobody there." As one of his courtiers complained, "he is spoiled in every sense." But the youngsters were corrupted by the sexual and political intrigues of the court, ground between the forces of Catherine and Paul.[26]

Alexander navigated between his father and grandmother with a permanent mask of inscrutability, advised by his "crafty and intriguing" oberhofmeister, Nikolai Saltykov, descendant of Tsarina Praskovia's family, a meagre, limping weasel with a pomaded toupee and the habit of constantly hitching up his breeches. "Wishing to conciliate both the empress and her son, he used to involve the Grand Duke in perpetual dissimulation . . . to inspire in him a dislike for the empress and dread for his father." Alexander and his brother Constantine simultaneously lived two lives—one at Tsarskoe Selo with the empress where they dressed in French-style court dress, and another at Gatchina with the grand duke where they wore Prussian military uniform.

Now living in the Alexander Palace built for them by Catherine, Alexander and Elizabeth's relationship suffered under this pressure. "He had the feelings of a brother for his wife but she wanted from him the love she would have given him." Ignored by her husband, "She's dying of boredom," observed Rostopchin. Her "angelic face, slight and elegant figure and graceful movements," wrote Varvara Golovina, "attracted universal attention . . ." Catherine tried to amuse them and herself with constant parties: "we're constantly doing nothing," said Elizabeth, "we spend all week dancing."

"One evening in the midst of the entertainments," wrote Golovina, sensitive wife of the couple's grand marshal and niece of Ivan Shuvalov, "Grand Duke Alexander came up to me and said, 'Zubov is in love with my wife.'" Golovina soon noticed that Platon Zubov was looking "dreamy" and "casting languishing looks at the Grand Duchess." Zubov was indeed in love with Elizabeth: "Soon all Tsarskoe Selo was in on the secret of this unfortunate folly." Zubov was now "everything here. There's no power but his," so the couple's courtiers tried to corrupt her to promote Zubov's "crazy passion." "Count Zubov is in love with my wife—what an embarrassing situation," Alexander kept telling his friends. "If you treat him well, it's as if you approve and if coldly to discourage him, the empress will be offended." It was usually after dinner that Zubov "was seized with a love fit," noticed Czartoryski, "and he then did nothing but sigh, lie on a sofa with a sad air and the appearance of a man seriously in love."

Confiding her agonizing situation to her mother in Baden and to her friend Varvara Golovina, she codenamed Zubov "the Zodiac." The attentions of the Zodiac did turn her head: "I could beat myself when I think of the follies of that time . . . there is no longer any question of them; I care no more for the Zodiac than for the wind," she told Golovina.

While the bride fended off Zodiac, Catherine was eager for her to become pregnant, and her lupine courtiers spied on the girl constantly: when her period was late, her governess told Catherine. "Even more embarrassing," Elizabeth confessed to Golovina, "the empress told Zodiac and if I tell the empress it's not so, she will tell him that too," but when her "red bird" arrived, Zubov knew all about it.

Elizabeth unsurprisingly sought feminine consolation, which she found in the person of the twenty-eight-year-old Varvara Golovina. One day out hunting, fetching in their riding-habits, they surreptitiously swapped beaver hats "without a word being spoken" and later "She gave me a little paper with her portrait and a locket of her hair," wrote Golovina. One day at Mon Plaisir at Peterhof, "She suddenly took me into the little palace and unreservedly laid bare her most intimate feelings." On 30 May 1794, the two girls went on a drive through Tsarskoe Selo at which something happened between them: "one of my dearest recollections." On an idyllic spring night, alone in the gardens, "The Grand Duchess leaned against me while I drank in every word from her lips," recalled Golovina. On another occasion, she "took me by the hand, pulled me into my bedroom, locked the door and flinging herself into my arms burst into tears." Elated by their love affair, whether or not it was consummated, Elizabeth bombarded the countess with love letters. "Oh it is cruel to be here at the Taurida Palace," she wrote on 11 August. "I don't enjoy life when I am separated from you . . . You're constantly in my mind and you agitate me till I can do nothing. Oh I have lost the sweet thought that occurred to me this morning . . ." Alexander seemed to approve this lesbian crush. "They cannot *forbid* me to love you and I am in a manner authorized by *someone else* who has quite as much right if not more to *order* me to love you," Elizabeth told Golovina. "You occupy my thoughts all day and until I go to sleep; if I wake in the night, you come immediately into my mind."

In the spring of 1795, Elizabeth sent her most enigmatic letter remembering their passion of 30 May: "My God, all the sensations that merely the memories of those sweet moments bring back to me." But Alexander had read Golovina's latest letter and, Elizabeth explained, he "asked me for an explanation. I partly told him."

Alexander and the courtiers now demanded that the two girls be parted. "I'm separated from you and cannot see you . . . Oh heavens, if you only knew my torments," wrote Elizabeth. "Oh God, how dearly I love you. You make my life bearable here . . . You really are mine. Even my husband doesn't know me as well as you." Meanwhile Catherine finally noticed Zubov's infatuation—there was a row and his attentions ceased. These intrigues brought Elizabeth and Alexander together. They shared their disgust with this degenerate and suffocating court. Alexander sought to escape the crown altogether.[27]

"It's unbelievable," Alexander wrote a little later to his tutor Laharpe. "Everyone is stealing; there's scarcely a single honest man," and he insisted that "I'd willingly give up my rank for a farm next to yours. My wife shares my feelings and I am enchanted to find such feelings in her."

Catherine might have been equally horrified by his sympathies for his father Paul, who now commanded 130 officers and 2,000 men in his private army at his fiefdom of Gatchina. There Alexander and Constantine shared their father's pain and found consolation in the simple military life at Gatchina. "That's our manner, in the Gatchina style," Alexander said, delighted that they "do us the honour of fearing us." Yet they themselves were often victims of Paul's demented military drilling.

"The Grand Duke invents ways to make himself hated by everyone," wrote Rostopchin. "He punishes indiscriminately without distinction." Drilling his mini-army, he "imagines himself to be the late King of Prussia. The slightest delay or contradiction unhinges him and inflames him with fury." In one of the few things that united him with his mother, Paul was obsessed with the French Revolution. "He sees Jacobins everywhere and the other day he arrested four officers whose plaits were too short, a sure sign of revolutionary sympathy," noted Rostopchin. Paul tyrannized his court and even his wife and sons, infuriated that at forty-one "I have nothing to do." When he lost his temper with his sons, Maria and his mistress Nelidova tried to soothe him. Meanwhile an artillery blast deafened Alexander in one ear, which Rostopchin explained, "Makes chatting unpleasant because you have to shout."

Catherine could hear the artillery booming over at Gatchina as she walked her greyhounds at Tsarskoe Selo. She loathed Paul's militarism and saw in him Peter III redux. He was so bitter that she compared him to "mustard after dinner."* After Alexander's marriage, she wrote that he would in time be "crowned with all the ceremonies"—no mention of Paul at all. She remembered Peter the Great and Tsarevich Alexei: "Peter's wisdom here is unquestionable" in "dethroning his ungrateful, disobedient and incapable son" who was filled with "hatred for his father, malice and singular jealousy."

Now she decided to leave the empire to Alexander. First Catherine invited his tutor Laharpe to help her convince the boy. Laharpe "made every effort to dissuade her" at which, remembering his revolutionary sympathies, she sent him back to Switzerland. Paul seemed to flaunt his instability. In a temper, he warned a courtier that when he came to the throne he would behead him. When reported to Catherine she said: "He's mad." When the heir agreed with something Zubov said, the favourite sneered: "Did I say something stupid then?" Zubov thought Paul insane. "I know it as you do," replied Catherine, "but unfortunately he's not mad enough." But she did not give up.[28]

In the spring of 1794, a new, more radical revolution had broken out in Poland where Russians and their allies were killed and arrested. Catherine and Zubov ordered a full invasion, with the Prussians attacking from the west, the double carve-up that would be replayed by Stalin and Hitler in 1939.

---

* Paul himself was so angered by the whims of female rule that he and Maria secretly signed a sensible law of succession to be issued when he became tsar, based on male primogeniture.

On 18 October, Suvorov stormed Praga, killing 7,000 and, when Warsaw surrendered, he wrote to Catherine: "Hurrah! Warsaw is yours!"

"Hurrah, field marshal!" she replied, thereby promoting him. Poland ceased to exist until 1918.* Catherine, turning sixty-seven, celebrated this tarnished victory by showering positions and gifts on Platon Zubov— 13,199 souls, prince of the Holy Roman Empire, 100,000 roubles.

Meanwhile to the south, the Persian shah Aga Mohammed Khan, who was, unusually for a fierce warrior and founder of a dynasty, a eunuch, invaded and conquered the Caucasus, annihilated Hercules' army and sacked the Georgian capital, Tiflis (today's Tbilisi), building Tamurlanian towers of bodies of massacred women and children. This gave the Zubovs the chance to propose their own Oriental Project to liberate the Christians of the Caucasus. Catherine appointed Valerian Zubov, who had lost a leg in Poland, to command the army that took Derbent and Baku.

At Tsarskoe Selo on 29 June 1796, as the empress watched anxiously, Maria Fyodorovna gave birth to yet another future emperor, Nicholas. Catherine proposed to Maria that they persuade Paul to renounce the throne. Dreaming of locking him in a Baltic fortress, Catherine asked the grand duchess to sign a document agreeing. Maria indignantly refused; Catherine was "very irritated."

Yet at almost the same time Alexander was writing to a trusted friend that "I'm in no way satisfied with my position, it's much too brilliant for my character. How can a single man manage to govern it and correct its abuses? This would be impossible not only for a man of ordinary abilities like me but even for a genius . . . My plan is once I've renounced this scabrous place, I will settle with my wife on the banks of the Rhine."

Catherine's other hope, Constantine, destined for the Byzantine throne, was even more of a worry. She married him off to a German princess,† but the grotesque Constantine, "unstable and obstinate, begins to

---

* Catherine was as appalled by the Polish lords as by their Jewish stewards—"venal corrupt liars, braggarts, oppressors, dreamers, they lease their estates to be run by Jews who suck blood from their subjects and give the lords little. Here in a word is the Poles' spitting image."

† This time she invited the prince and princess of Saxe-Coburg-Saalfeld to bring their three daughters to Petersburg. It was said that when Catherine and Constantine watched them arrive at the Winter Palace, the elder two princesses tripped as they dismounted from the carriage but the third, Juliane, stepped down without mishap. "All right," said Constantine, "If it must be so, I'll have the little monkey. It dances prettily." On 15 February 1796, Constantine married Juliane, now Grand Duchess Anna. Later Coburg became what Bismarck called "the studfarm of Europe." Anna's brother Leopold married Princess Charlotte, heir to the British throne, and after her early death he became the first king of Belgium and promoted the marriage of his nephew Prince Albert of Saxe-Coburg to Queen Victoria.

resemble his father, indulging in spasms of anger," wrote Rostopchin. His outrages included firing live rats out of cannons, playing drums at breakfast and beating up girls. He managed to infect his wife, Anna, with VD. "She was attacked by a complaint without knowing its cause," noted Countess Golovina. His "violent temper and savage caprices," as Czartoryski put it, were hushed up until finally Charlotte Lieven, the governess of Paul's small children, reported that Constantine had ferociously beaten a hussar in his regiment. Catherine had him arrested but was so shaken she almost had a stroke. Worse was to follow when Zubov delivered his final bungle.[29]

That summer, Catherine welcomed the young Swedish king, Gustavus IV Adolphus, who had come to finalize his betrothal to her eldest granddaughter, Alexandrine. Zubov oversaw the deal in which Paul's daughter would be allowed to practise her Orthodoxy in Lutheran Sweden—but he had not nailed it down.

At 6 p.m. on 11 September, the empress, watched by the entire court, ascended her throne at the Winter Palace to announce the betrothal, but the king never arrived. After three and a half excruciating hours, Catherine learned that the deal was off. She lunged at Zubov's official with her stick. Five days later, she asked Alexander directly about the succession and showed him her decree to disinherit Paul. On 24 September, he replied politely committing to nothing. She needed time, time she no longer had.[30]

SCENE 5

# The Conspiracy

# CAST

PAUL I, emperor 1796–1801, son of Peter III and Catherine the Great

Maria Fyodorovna, empress (née Princess Sophia Dorothea of Württemberg), Paul's second wife

ALEXANDER I, emperor 1801–25, first son of Paul and Maria

Elizabeth Alexeievna, empress (née Princess Louise of Baden), Alexander's wife

CONSTANTINE I, emperor 1825, second son of Paul and Maria

Anna Fyodorovna (née Princess Juliane of Saxe-Coburg-Saalfeld), Constantine's wife

## COURTIERS, ministers etc.

Alexander Bezborodko, chancellor, prince

Alexander Suvorov, count, prince, field marshal, generalissimus

Fyodor Rostopchin, count, adjutant-general, president of Foreign Collegium, postmaster

Alexei Arakcheev, count, co-commandant of Petersburg, quartermaster-general, "Corporal of Gatchina," "Ape in Uniform"

Prince Alexander Kurakin, vice-chancellor

Prince Alexei Kurakin, procurator-general

Nikita Panin, vice-chancellor, nephew of Catherine the Great's minister

Peter von der Pahlen, governor of Petersburg, chief minister, "Professor of Cunning"

Peter Obolyaninov, procurator-general

Prince Platon Zubov, Catherine the Great's former lover

Count Nikolai Zubov, master of the horse, "Colossus," Platon's brother

Ekaterina Nelidova, Paul's mistress, "Little Monster"

Anna Lopukhina, later Princess Gagarina, Paul's mistress

Ivan Kutaisov, count, Paul's barber, fixer, gentleman of the bedchamber, master of the robes, "Figaro"

Count Fyodor Golovkin, master of ceremonies

Countess Varvara Golovina, friend of Empress Elizabeth

On 5 November 1796, Catherine rose at 6 a.m., made her own coffee as usual and started to write. When she visited her water closet, she suffered a stroke and fell to the floor where she remained until nine when her chamberlain found her, breathless, purple-faced, speechless. She opened her eyes but then sank into a coma. It took six men to carry her into the bedroom but, unable to lift her on to the bed, they laid her on a mattress on the floor. "First to be warned, Prince Zubov was the first to lose his head." Alexander, weeping, and Constantine, both in "Potemkin" uniforms, arrived with their wives. At 3:45, Dr. Rogerson realized that she had suffered a massive stroke. Count Nikolai Zubov, master of the horse, the giant of the four brothers, known as "the Colossus," galloped to Gatchina.

A soldier reported to Paul that Zubov had arrived. Remembering his father, Paul grabbed Maria's hand: "My dear, we're lost." How many Zubovs were there? he asked. "Well, we can cope with one!" Zubov fell to his knees and Paul understood.

On the road to Petersburg, Paul encountered Rostopchin. "What a moment for you, Monseigneur," Rostopchin said.

"Wait, my dear, wait," replied Paul. "God has sustained me for forty-two years"—and they travelled on together. At 8:30 they arrived at the Winter Palace. Catherine's panting form lay on a mattress attended by tearful retainers, past and present: the octogenarian Scarface, Bezborodko and Prince Zubov. When the latter asked for a glass of water, no one bothered to fetch it. "The empress," observed Czartoryski, "was lifeless, like a machine whose movement has ceased."

Paul swept through the death chamber with scarcely a glance at his mother to set up headquarters in the inner chamber. There he summoned Zubov, ordering him to surrender all Catherine's papers. He soon found Scarface's letter confessing to the murder of his father Peter III and his son Alexander's refusal of Catherine's plan to change the succession. Paul summoned Alexander and Constantine.

A gangly, scowling officer in Gatchina uniform passed the dying empress to report to Paul: Alexei Arakcheev, aged twenty-eight, born of poor gentry, known as "the Corporal of Gatchina," was devoted to Paul and a brutal stickler for discipline. When Paul saw that his shirt was stained from the journey, he gave Arakcheev one of his own shirts. He turned to Alexander and, joining his hand to that of Arakcheev, he said, "Be friends for ever." Then Paul and Maria had an improvised dinner in the corridor outside the death chamber.

Elizabeth spent the night sobbing, until Alexander returned to change into his Prussian uniform. "His mother still breathed and the emperor had nothing better to do than make his sons put on uniforms. The pettiness!" she wrote. "When I saw him wearing it I burst into tears." Outside, Paul's courtiers—the coarse Gatchina officers in their outdated Prussian uniforms—were arriving. "The grand duke," wrote Rostopchin, "is surrounded by such people that the most honest would deserve to be hanged." The courtiers "asked in amazement who were these Ostrogoths?" The "Ostrogoths" were the future.

In the afternoon, Alexander brought his wife to the deathbed. "At 5 a.m. the breaths of the empress grew weaker. Several times the doctors thought the last moment had come . . . The rattle was so loud one could hear it in the corridor . . . Blood went to her face, alternately red, then violet in colour." Zubov sat alone in a corner: the courtiers, noticed Rostopchin, "avoided him like the plague." Bezborodko is said to have shown Paul the unsigned letter from his wife Maria—and Catherine's decree removing him from the succession. Bezborodko tore these into shreds and was rewarded for this loyalty.

At 9 p.m., Dr. Rogerson announced the last moments: Paul and Maria, Alexander, Constantine and their wives stood on the right, the doctors, Charlotte Lieven, governess of the imperial children, the intimate courtiers and Zubov, Bezborodko and Paul's man Rostopchin, on the left. Catherine's breathing ceased at 9:45 p.m., in her sixty-eighth year and the thirty-fifth of her reign. Everyone sobbed. The procurator-general threw open the door and proclaimed the new emperor. Alexander and Elizabeth and the courtiers dropped to their knees. Zubov, "his hair wild, his eyes rolling hideously," according to Elizabeth, "wept with horrible grimaces. The poor Zodiac has fallen on hard times." Zubov retreated to the house of his sister, expecting the worst, while Empress Maria returned to the death chamber to supervise the body.[1]

The death of Peter III preyed on Paul's mind. After the church service, he noticed that old Scarface, exhausted by the long vigil, had gone home. Summoning Rostopchin and another Gatchina henchman, General Nikita Akharov, he said, "I know you're tired but go to Count Orlov's house and make him take the oath; I don't want him to forget 29 June." He was referring to the overthrow of Peter III in

1762. Awoken at 3 a.m., the startled octogenarian swore allegiance in his nightshirt.*

Next day, 7 November, Paul sported the new Prussian uniform of the Guards. He was accompanied by Alexander and Constantine, who "appeared in their new costumes looking like old portraits of German officers walking out of their frames."

Paul changed everything that was connected to his mother.† Catherine lay in the Great Hall guarded by the Chevalier-Gardes, tears running down their cheeks. When Countess Golovina cried, Arakcheev, "the instrument of the emperor's rigorous severities, gave me a violent push and told me to be quiet." Elizabeth then "came up gently to me and gently squeezed my hand from behind." But Catherine did not lie alone for long.

On 9 November, Paul announced that his father Peter III and his mother Catherine II would be buried together. "My mother having been called to the throne by the voice of the people was too busy to arrange for my father's last rites," he explained sarcastically. "I'm just remedying that oversight."

Eleven days later, Paul attended the exhumation of his father at the Nevsky Monastery. He kissed the shroud. Next he summoned the regicides Orlov-Chesmensky and Bariatinsky to play their roles. Orlov claimed he was too old, but Paul pointed at the crown and shouted: "Carry it and march!" When Bariatinsky's daughter appealed for a pardon, Paul replied: "I too had a father."

On 1 December Paul followed the cortège on foot down Nevsky Prospect. Bariatinsky led the coffin while Orlov-Chesmensky carried the crown behind it. Peter III lay in state next to Catherine. Orlov-Chesmensky and Bariatinsky were fortunate just to be banished. Catherine and Peter were buried together.[2]

*

* Orlov-Chesmensky's fellow regicide Prince Fyodor Bariatinsky was sacked as marshal of the court, while Peter III's favourite Gudovich, and Captain Peter Izmailov, the Guardsman who had denounced Catherine's conspiracy in June 1762, were returned from exile and promoted.
† Paul confirmed Zubov in his offices and even visited and toasted him at the house of his sister. But then he sent Constantine to dismiss him. Zubov retired to his baroque Rundale Palace in Courland, formerly belonging to Biron. But he would return to Paul's life with a vengeance. Potemkin was anathema to Paul: his Taurida Palace was turned into a cavalry barracks. Later Paul ordered Potemkin's tomb in Kherson to be smashed and his bones scattered. Some 12,000 Polish prisoners were released; King Stanisław-Augustus was rehabilitated and invited to the coronation; the radical Radishchev was returned from exile; Bobrinsky, Paul's illegitimate half-brother, son of Prince Orlov, was summoned and raised to count; Catherine's colossal Pella Palace, built for Alexander, was totally demolished. Valerian Zubov's Persian expedition was immediately recalled.

On 8 November, the Gatchina regiments marched towards the Winter Palace like an invasion of Ostrogoths in the old-fashioned Prussian uniforms. "In spite of our grief for the empress, we split our sides laughing" at the new uniforms, wrote Guards officer Colonel Sablukov. But the Guards were still in their Potemkin uniforms. The emperor "bowed, puffed and blew as the guard marched past, shrugged his shoulders to show his displeasure." Then suddenly "the army of Gatchina was approaching."

Paul "galloped off to meet them and returned in raptures with these troops," wrote Sablukov. "What officers! What strange-looking faces! What manners!" Paul's Gatchina Guards joined the old Guards. He ordered his adjutant-general Rostopchin to reform and Prussianize the army—starting with the uniforms. He regarded the waxed Prussian plaits as the expression of the ancien régime against the tousled locks of French freedom. "Never was there any change of scene at a theatre so sudden and so complete as the change of affairs at the accession of Paul," recalled Czartoryski. "In less than a day, costumes, manners, occupations, all were altered." Anything French, new and fashionable was banned: breeches, stockings, buckled shoes, powdered hair in a queue were all allowed, but trousers, frockcoats, round hats, top boots, laced shoes were banned, on pain of arrest. Scissors were used to cut the tails off the "revolutionary" frockcoats. "Nothing was so odious for the upper classes" as the banning of the frockcoat, recalled the courtier Fyodor Golovkin, putting the nobilities back in their place.

Paul's gleeful pedantry was directed by the new governor of Petersburg, Akharov, known as "the minister of terror." At the sight of the tsar or his family or just passing a palace, "all those seated inside carriages had to step out and make their bow," recalled Sablukov. If Akharov spotted anyone wearing the "liberal" round hat, they were chased through the streets by adjutants, and if caught, bastinadoed. Spotting a nanny pushing a pram, Paul himself absurdly scolded her for lèse-majesté for not doffing the baby's bonnet which he then removed: the baby was the future poet Alexander Pushkin. Petersburg, "under Catherine the most fashionable metropolis in Europe" in Sablukov's view, "ceased to look like a modern town, becoming more like a German one two centuries back."

The "chief occupation of each day" was now the daily military parade, the Wachtparade. The emperor, immaculate in high boots and Prussian uniform, his bald head bare to the elements and wielding a whip or cane, would be surrounded by the dazzling staff of His Imperial Majesty's Mobile Military Chancellery and his Suite, with its ninety-three adjutants and aides-de-camp. Here he concentrated power. He promoted his veteran courtiers, Prince Alexei Kurakin, to procurator-general, and his brother Prince Alexander, to vice-chancellor to run foreign policy with Bezborodko. "I'm just a soldier, I don't get involved in administration," he boasted, "that's what I pay Kurakin and Bezborodko to do." Actually, Paul revelled in power, bursting with pride that a male Romanov was again *imperator*. Decrees poured out of him—more than 2,000 just in his first year.

His decisions were then published in the official gazette, where they inspired both fear and ridicule. "Paul's petulance and extravagant strictness and severity made service very unpleasant," wrote Colonel Sablukov. When the emperor took a fancy to one of Elizabeth's maids-of-honour, he inserted this in the Orders of the Day: "Thanks to Grand Duke Alexander for having such a pretty maid-of-honour." At the parades he asserted his power in remarks worthy of Caligula: "Do you know that the only *grand seigneur* in Russia is the man I am talking to at that instant—and only while I am talking to him?" He was reversing the compact between the *seigneurs* and the monarch which had been the foundation of Russian greatness since Tsar Alexei and which had been consolidated by his mother. By such slights, he reminded his entourage that his entire reign was a living imperial coup against the pretensions of these ruling magnates and families. Walking with Prince Repnin he said, "Marshal, you see this guard of 400 men? At one word, I could promote every one of them to marshal." Paul frequently thumped his chest and declared: "Here is the law!" The tsar revoked the law banning the physical punishment of nobles, a direct challenge to their privileges and pride as a ruling class, based on their right to own and whip their serfs. Soon nobles were being chastised. A staff captain was sentenced to 1,000 strokes; a priest was knouted for owning radical books; an officer had his tongue cut out. Instant sentences of exile were so common that "When we mounted guard, we used to put a few hundred roubles in banknotes into our coat pockets so as not to be left penniless if suddenly sent away." At one parade, Paul lost his cool completely and "struck three officers with his cane." As we will see, they would not forget the humiliation. Paul actually quoted Caligula's dictum—"Let them hate so long as they fear me." They feared him, but they laughed too. And nothing saps authority like laughter.

Behind the military punctilio, this enemy of female power was dominated by women. It was Maria and Paul's mistress Nelidova who had promoted their allies, the Kurakins. "As for the empress," wrote Elizabeth, "she's good, incapable of doing wrong, but I can't bear her abasement before Nelidova, the abominable little passion of the emperor." Every wife knows that the best way to save a marriage is to befriend the husband's mistress. Nelidova, Elizabeth explained to her mother, "is the only person who can influence the emperor so the empress makes obeisance to her and thus wins the favour of the emperor." The emperor persuaded Nelidova to return to court, where she dominated*—along with an even more unlikely potentate: his barber.

The "chief arbiter of everything" was the "once Turkish now Christian first valet" Kutaisov. During the first Ottoman war, Catherine gave Paul a Turkish slaveboy, captured at Kutais in Georgia. Paul stood as god-father when he was converted to Orthodoxy as Ivan Kutaisov and sent him to be trained at Versailles. On his return he served as Paul's *valet de chambre*. Kutaisov now became Paul's confidant, fixer and pimp—"he looked like a sort of Figaro."

Yet "Paul was sincerely pious, really benevolent, generous, a lover of truth and hater of falsehood, ever anxious to promote justice," wrote Sablukov. He "was of a very romantic disposition and delighted in everything *chevalresque*"; and he sometimes had a sense of humour, even about himself. When he heard that Sablukov drew caricatures, he asked: "Have you made mine?" and "laughed heartily" at the likeness. "But these praiseworthy qualities were rendered useless by a total want of moderation, extreme irritability and irrational, impatient expectation of obedience."

Only one man stood up to him. "Sire, there is powder and powder; curls are not cannon, a pigtail is not a bayonet and I'm not a Prussian but a pure-blooded Russian," Suvorov told the emperor, who dismissed him with one of his idiosyncratic parade-ground orders: "Marshal Suvorov, having declared to His Imperial Highness that since there is no war he had nothing to do, is to remain without service for making such a remark." Arakcheev, the Corporal of Gatchina, harassed and exiled Russia's invincible hero.

"Never was there a sovereign more terrible in his severity or more liberal when he was in generous mood," noted Czartoryski. "Amid all that was eccentric and ridiculous, there was an element of seriousness and justice. The Emperor wished to be just."[3]

On 18 March 1797, Paul and the family arrived at Catherine's neo-Gothic Petrovsky Palace outside Moscow, where he insisted on the first of many *baise-mains à genoux* (hand-kissing on bended knee) for the entire court. At noon on the 28th, the day before Palm Sunday, Paul accompanied by his sons on horseback rode into the Kremlin, with the empress and

---

* Nelidova was probably genuinely alarmed by Paul and was certainly pious, but she also knew that the more virtuous she seemed to Paul, the greater her power over him. She begged him to reduce his gift of 2,000 serfs to her mother: "For God's sake, Sire, as a favour please reduce this gift . . . to 500 souls."

Elizabeth and Anna following in carriages. Paul so enjoyed this that he rode as slowly as possible: the procession took five hours. "Everything was repeated," complained his master of ceremonies Count Fyodor Golovkin wearily. "The emperor was as excited as a child."

At 5 a.m. on 5 April, the courtiers gathered for the coronation of the emperor and empress. Ladies were ready at seven and the procession set off at eight. Unusually Paul wore a *dalmatique*, a vestment like a bishop's cope, to symbolize the tsar as high priest of Orthodoxy, plus boots, uniform and sword, which Metropolitan Gabriel, archbishop of Novgorod, who was officiating, asked him to remove. Paul obeyed before entering the Dormition Cathedral where the ex-king of Poland, in another blow aimed at Catherine, watched from the balcony. Maria was the first tsarist wife to be crowned with her husband, who placed the crown on her head.

Afterwards, Paul read out the decree, signed by Maria and himself in 1788, that regulated the succession by male primogeniture, starting with his heir Alexander—a sensible plan to avoid the instability that had bedevilled Russia throughout the eighteenth century. Then he promulgated his Family Law, turning the dynasty into a political institution, laying out titles (the heirs to be known as caesareviches), precedence, property, income (run by a Ministry of the Imperial Apanages) and rules for living—no grand duke could marry a commoner.

Afterwards at the Kremlin Palace Paul and Maria received more *baise-mains-à-genoux* before bestowing promotions and gifts—a total of 82,000 souls.* "The ceremony was long but it was followed by a hundred others invented by emperor and master of ceremonies to please him . . . Paul's passion for ceremonies equalled his passion for the military," recalled Golovkin. Paul and Maria, both Germanic sticklers for punctilio, insisted that "It was essential that the emperor hear the knee hit the floor and feel the kiss on the hand." All ceremonies had to take place in silence in order to check that the kneelings made the sound of a rifle butt; and if anyone chattered, as they used to during Catherine's reign, Paul shouted: "Silence!" When Elizabeth entwined her tiara with flowers, Empress Maria ripped them off shouting, "That's improper!"

---

* Bezborodko was made a prince (the first made by a tsar since Menshikov), received 16,000 souls and was then promoted to chancellor. Arakcheev became a baron. The rising Turkish valet Kutaisov was only promoted to gentleman of the bedchamber 4th class and grumbled to Paul himself who was so enraged that he hit him and drove him out of the room, threatening exile. Nelidova saved him, a kindness she would soon regret. He was then promoted to a new role, master of the robes. Finally Paul announced new protections for the serfs, a gesture that sparked a flurry of peasant revolts in the countryside which had to be repressed. It was typical of Paul's inconsistency to pose as protector of the serfs while handing thousands out as chattels to his henchmen.

And when the tsar saw that his two daughters-in-law were wearing cloaks, he shrieked, "Take off those cloaks and never put them on again!" Yet "when people were not trembling, they rushed into a mad delirious gaiety—never was there so much laughter," noted Countess Golovina, "a sarcastic laugh often changing into a grimace of terror." The women "were dying of fatigue."

Paul "was so angry when the ceremonies came to an end" that he added an extra four days of them—and even at parades he could not resist wearing his *dalmatique*, "one of the most curious sights imaginable," mused Golovkin, resembling as it did a bejewelled tea-cosy, combined with high Prussian boots, a tunic and a three-cornered hat. Amid this compulsive flummery, a sexual intrigue was hatched by the Turkish barber. Knowing that there was no sex with Nelidova, Kutaisov planned to "give the monarch a mistress in the full extent of the word." Selecting a teenaged nubile, Figaro "placed her ceaselessly under the nose of His Majesty and it was obvious enough to worry the empress." Paul soon noticed "the lively black eyes" of Anna Lopukhina.[4]

In any marriage, one should not underestimate the power of nagging, but in an absolute monarchy that power can be absolute and Paul was harassed by a nagging coalition of wife and mistress.

"I'd feel happy and relaxed if I was allowed to plead for unfortunates without arousing your rage against me or them," Nelidova wrote to Paul, adding in another letter: "But you know how you love the nagger?" Once Paul "entered the guardroom in a great hurry as simultaneously a lady's shoe flew over His Majesty's head and just missed it," recalled Colonel Sablukov, who was on duty at the time. Then "Mademoiselle Nelidova came out of the corridor, picked up the shoe, put it on" and left. The next day, Paul confided in Sablukov, "My dear, we had a bit of a ruckus yesterday," and ordered him to ask Nelidova to dance to the orchestra. "Charming, superb, delicious!" cried the emperor as he watched his Little Monster dance a minuet. Wife and mistress nagged Paul into dismissing the terror of Petersburg, Akharov, but their importuning infuriated him, and he blamed Maria. She appealed to Nelidova to bring Paul back to her. "The empress says without you Pavlovsk isn't beautiful," Nelidova told Paul. "Her heart is sad at parting from you." Paul and Maria often needed Nelidova, as in this joint letter from Gatchina in August 1797: "You are our good, our true friend and always will be . . ." (Maria); "Only you are lacking for my happiness . . ." (Paul).

After one outburst of rage, Paul apologized to Nelidova: "Forgive a man who loves you more than he loves himself." Nelidova was trying to save Paul from himself: "Sovereigns more than others have to exercise patience and moderation," she wrote to him. But the women overreached themselves.

As an alliance of European powers failed to contain revolutionary France, Paul found himself too short of cash to wage war. Manipulated by a dubious Dutch banker, Maria and Nelidova supported the Kurakins in the creation of a Bank of Assistance for the Nobility, which turned into a scandal from which the brothers made fortunes. Paul blamed the women. When Maria (whose homeland Württemberg had been seized by the French) and Nelidova canvassed Paul to join Austria and Britain against France, Paul had had enough—and Figaro Kutaisov set up his honeytrap.[5]

Once Paul noticed his wife Maria whispering to Alexander Kurakin. "Madame," Paul called out, "I see you want to make friends and prepare the role for yourself of Catherine, but you won't find me a Peter III."

In January 1798, Maria gave birth to a fourth son, Michael. But the birth was so dangerous that the doctors ordered her to abstain from sex. "The instigator and prime mover of this plot" was Rostopchin, who hated Kurakin and Nelidova, while Bezborodko was keen to avoid war and keep Maria out of politics.

While on a visit to Moscow, Paul asked Figaro why he was so loved there but not in Petersburg.

"Sire, it happens that here [in Moscow] you are seen as you truly are, good, magnanimous and sensitive," explained the barber, "while in Petersburg it is said if some grace is extended that it's the empress or Fräulein Nelidova or the Kurakins who've extracted it from you—but if you punish, it is you alone."

"Thus it's said I'm governed by those women?" asked Paul.

"Even so, Sire."

At a ball, Kutaisov pointed out Anna Lopukhina.

"Your Majesty, you've turned a head."

"Isn't she a child?" murmured Paul.

Hardly, replied Kutaisov, she was sixteen.

Paul was infatuated, but Lopukhina, a virgin related to Peter the Great's first wife, could not be procured like a showgirl. Figaro negotiated with her parents.

Returning to Pavlovsk in late June, the tsar rejected Maria and Nelidova. "On 25 July, the storm broke when the Emperor ordered Monseigneur [Alexander] to tell the Empress never again to interfere in politics," but the son took his mother's side: "I see I have lost not only my wife but my son."

Paul screamed at Nelidova to get out for ever—then tested Alexander by offering him the crown to hold: "It's amazingly heavy. Here hold it. Judge for yourself." Alexander turned pale.

"The emperor exhibited all the symptoms," wrote Countess Golovina, "of a young man of twenty," even confiding in his son Alexander: "Just fancy how much in love I must be!" The new mistress, observed Golovina, "had a pretty head, pretty eyes, well-marked black eyebrows and black hair, beautiful teeth, an attractive mouth, a little retroussé nose—but a very poor figure, ill made and narrow chested! But she was kind and incapable of doing harm to anyone."

Lopukhina resisted the advances of "the ugliest man in the empire" for a long time until, suffocating from the imperial attentions, she "burst into tears and begged to be unmolested, confessing her love for Prince Pavel Gagarin," a young army officer. Paul had the two married at once and congratulated himself on his virtue. But Gagarin ill-treated his tainted wife and, in collusion with Kutaisov, "worked up Paul's evil passions" so that Lopukhina, now known as Princess Gagarina, succumbed dutifully to the emperor's seduction.

Paul sacked the Kurakins and appointed Gagarina's father, Peter Lopukhin, ex-police chief of Moscow, as procurator-general. But the real winner was Figaro, now raised to count. The emperor's domestic maestro, "despite his crass ignorance," wrote Golovkin, "aspired to be a minister. In the meantime, the ministers consulted him daily." Yet Figaro never became arrogant, wrote Sablukov—"He was always ready to help people and was never known to injure anyone." But only in Russia, thought Czartoryski, could "the autocratic wand of Tsarism accomplish this metamorphosis" of a slave into an aristocrat.

Paul and Figaro now shared boyish erotic escapades. "Middle-sized, a little stout, but alert and quick in his movements, very dark, always smiling with Eastern eyes and a countenance displaying a sensual joviality," Figaro took as his own mistress the French actress Madame Chevalier, for whom he bought a house next to that of Gagarina. "They used to drive together incognito on these expeditions."

Paul was "so excited" by his conquest of Gagarina "that the poor man was quite beside himself" and "thought he could never be generous enough." Gagarina received a palace while her complaisant husband was promoted at one point to run the War Collegium. Gagarina's favourite colour was scarlet. Paul changed the colours of Guards regiments' uniforms for her* and when he went to visit Gagarina with Kutaisov, his

---

* These changes of uniform caused uproar at the Collegium of Manufactures, where Sablukov's father was in charge. When Paul found out that the latest change had been delayed, he immediately wrote a note ordering: "Banish Privy Councillor Sablukov and

carriage and footmen were all accoutred in crimson. Paul had forbidden waltzes as "licentious," but Gagarina adored waltzing; so, in a classic Pauline reversal, waltzing went from being banned to obligatory. Just as Paul changed mistress and ministry in June 1798, a French general, who had made his name conquering Italy, departed to attack Egypt.[6]

On his way, General Napoleon Bonaparte occupied Malta, seat of the Knights of Malta, which outraged their new grand master—Paul himself. This religious-military order had originally been known as the Knights of St. John of Jerusalem, whose crusading history appealed to Paul. A suave Italian count and Knight of Malta* arrived in Petersburg to invite Paul to become the Order's protector and then grand master. He embraced the Order's rituals with all the excitement of a schoolboy and made Kutaisov its master of the horse. Paul saw himself as the leader not just of Orthodoxy but of all Christendom in a crusade with Austria and Britain against atheistic France, whose conquests he abhorred and whose ideals he feared.

This new coalition agreed to attack the French in Holland, along the Rhine, in Switzerland and in Italy before invading France itself. Paul signed a treaty with London, but naively placed Russian armies at the disposal of Austria. The timing, however, was perfect: the French government, the Directory, was corrupt and divided. Its best general was in Egypt while Paul's best general was languishing on his estates. When he renegotiated with the Austrians, they fondly remembered their joint victories against the Ottomans under Suvorov and suggested him as an acceptable commander. Paul recalled him to Petersburg.

At a ball in February 1799, the sixty-nine-year-old Marshal Suvorov reappeared at court, bathing in Paul's favour. "No contrast could have been more striking," noted Countess Golovina, "than the austere soldier, in the turmoil of a ball, with his white hair and gaunt face, and the Emperor dividing his attentions between Suvorov and a simple girl [Princess Gagarina] whose pretty face would hardly have been noticeable had it not happened to win the favour of the Emperor."

Paul ordered two Russian corps to march towards Italy and Switzerland to join up with the Austrians, while another joined the British to attack Holland. On 17 February, Suvorov set off to take command of

---

dismiss from service." Poor old Sablukov was banished, only to be recalled by the emperor who "with tears in his eyes apologized for his petulance."

* This was Count Giulio Litta. The Knights were meant to be celibate warriors, but Litta fell in love with the rich "kitten" Katinka Scavronskaya, Potemkin's niece-mistress. Paul, an avid matchmaker, sponsored the happy marriage and Litta served as a marshal of the Russian court for the next thirty years.

Austro-Russian forces in Italy, and there he drubbed the French. But the Austrian ministers undermined their Russian allies. Suvorov offered to resign, but Paul, who sent his son Constantine to serve with him, encouraged him to fight on. Paul even challenged General Bonaparte to a duel, with his plump sybaritic Figaro as his second. When Prussia hesitated to join the coalition, Paul published "a challenge to any sovereign who differed from him to settle the difference in single combat," but as Czartoryski joked, "Paul would have been in great difficulty if the challenge had been accepted as he was very timid on horseback." In August, Suvorov won the Battle of Novi and took northern Italy.

Yet the Russian and Austrian armies in Switzerland were floundering. Suvorov marched over the Alps, but the Austrians now abandoned their allies. Only Suvorov could have fought his way out. Paul, exasperated by Austria's betrayals, recalled the marshal.* Meanwhile in Holland the Anglo-Russian expedition was also a debacle, since the British were as inept as the Austrians. Faced with personal insults and military disasters, Paul reversed his entire policy, contemplated war against Britain and decided Bonaparte was his hero. [7]

"The emperor is literally not in his senses," the British ambassador, Charles Whitworth, confided to London. Whitworth's mistress was the sister of Prince Zubov, the thirty-three-year-old Olga Zherebtsova, who fostered a conspiracy to murder Paul. First she put together Whitworth with the chief champion of the pro-British policy in the Russian government, Count Nikita Panin, nephew of Catherine's minister. Now that old Bezborodko had died, Paul appointed Rostopchin as president of the Foreign Collegium and postmaster†—but he also made Panin his vice-chancellor. Rostopchin had argued for a new pro-French policy and dismemberment of the Ottoman empire, Panin for a British alliance. Paul had then rudely rejected Panin who decided the tsar was insane and should be murdered. Two other Zubov allies were brought in: Admiral José Ribas, a Latino ruffian who had helped found Odessa, and Count Peter von der Pahlen, new governor-general of Petersburg, who arranged a farcical meeting with the heir to the throne.

---

* Suvorov was greeted with promotion to the rank of generalissimus (held before by Menshikov and Anton of Brunswick and afterwards only by Stalin) and the romantic title prince of Italy. But Paul became jealous. Citing his contravention of "all my instructions, [and] being surprised by this, I order you to tell me what possessed you to do it." Suvorov-Italiisky died soon afterwards. Paul made Constantine, who had served courageously, caesarevich, the title of the heir—in this case Alexander. For a while Russia had two caesareviches.
† The postmaster was also a spymaster since he ran the *cabinets noirs* that perlustrated the mail, secretly opening private and diplomatic letters, copying them, breaking codes and resealing them.

Panin secretly met Alexander and proposed that Paul should allow his son to rule as regent. Both were terrified, Panin nervously gripping a dagger. When Panin wondered aloud if they were being followed, Alexander shrieked. He did not commit to the plan, but nor did he report the conspiracy. Whitworth was recalled when Paul turned against Britain, Ribas died early, and Paul exiled Panin to Moscow. Only Pahlen remained of the conspirators—and he was sent to defend the frontiers.

Rostopchin, promoted to count, helped Paul prepare for war against Austria and friendship with France. Bonaparte abandoned his army in Egypt and returned to France, where, in November 1799, he seized power as the semi-monarchical first consul. He dynamically restored French fortunes, retaking Italy and in June 1800 defeating the Austrians at Marengo. Paul was now captivated by Bonaparte. "I'm full of respect for the First Consul and his military talent," he wrote. "He acts. He is a man with whom one can do business." His infatuation with Napoleon resembled his father's crush on Frederick the Great, a passion that only intensified when France presented Malta to Grand Master Paul, despite the fact that the island soon fell to the British. Paul recognized the new borders of France and put together a Northern System of Denmark, Sweden and Prussia to act in armed neutrality against Britain.

Within months, Napoleon and Paul were planning a fantastical scheme to send the French General Masséna with 35,000 men to rendezvous in Astrakhan with a Russian army of 35,000 infantry and 50,000 Cossacks. Together they would cross the Caspian, capture Kandahar, then invade British India.[8]

Paul, "more suspicious than ever," now launched what Czartoryski called a "reign of terror: all who belonged to the court or came before the emperor were in a state of continual fear. In going to bed, it was quite uncertain whether during the night some policeman would not come with a *kibitka* [wagon] to drive you off at once to Siberia." Paul's paranoia was justified—but it was also self-fulfilling.

Paul's plan for dealing with Alexander (and his brother Constantine) was to burden them with so many duties that the boys would scarcely have time to visit their wives let alone plan a coup. "The Grand Dukes," explained Golovina, "were nothing better than corporals: their duties carried absolutely no power." "Tied as I am to the trivialities of military service," complained Alexander, "I find myself carrying out the duties of an under-officer." Sablukov noticed that "both Grand Dukes had a terror of their father. If he looked in the least angry, they would tremble like aspen leaves."

Alexander was watched by Baron Arakcheev, a grisly and implacable myrmidon with a "convulsively twitching neck, large ears, a big ill-shaped head and sallow face with hollow cheeks, bulging forehead and deep grey eyes." Nicknamed the "Ape in Uniform," Arakcheev was co-commandant of Petersburg alongside Alexander himself. The emperor gave him the estate of Gruzino—and Zubov's apartments in the Winter Palace. "The terror of everyone," an incorruptible organizer of "superior cleverness, severity and indefatigable vigilance," he was the opposite of the liberal Alexander.

Yet the Ape and the angel formed a surprising partnership: when Alexander was expected to present his report at 5 a.m., Arakcheev entered his room with the report completed and got his signature (while Elizabeth hid under the bedclothes) to present to his father. "Do me a favour," reads a typical note to Arakcheev, "and be here when my guard is mounted so they get nothing wrong." Alexander needed Arakcheev: "Forgive me for troubling you, my friend, but I'm young and badly need your advice."

Elizabeth hated Paul. "This man is repugnant to me; anyone who displeases His Majesty may expect a coarse rebuke," Elizabeth told her mother. "Oh mama, it's painful and frightful to see daily injustices and brutalities. It's all the same to him if he is loved or loathed provided he's feared . . . He is hated and feared at least by everyone . . . His humour more changeable than a weathervane."

The couple's relationship with the emperor was not improved when Paul encouraged Alexander to have an affair with the sister of his mistress Gagarina by locking them in a room together. When Alexander had a few moments off parade, he chose his own mistress, sharing Madame Chevalier with Figaro.

"Everything is turned upside down at once," he wrote to one of his best friends. "Absolute power disrupts everything. It is impossible for me to enumerate all the madness" in a country that had become "a plaything for the insane." He believed that the "army wastes all its time on the parade ground . . . Power is unlimited and exercised perversely. You can judge how I am suffering."

Alexander confided in his four best friends, a coterie of liberal aristocrats,* led by Prince Adam Czartoryski, a Polish patriot in Russian service, who was a study in ambiguity. He asked Czartoryski to draft a constitution and a manifesto that denounced "the evils of the regime, the blessings of liberty and justice" and his "resolution to abdicate" after

* Apart from Czartoryski the others were Count Pavel Stroganov, scion of the merchant-princes of Siberia who had spent time in revolutionary France, Victor Kochubey (Cossack nobleman, nephew of Bezborodko, and Paul's vice-chancellor for a short time) and Nikolai Novosiltsev.

reforming Russia. To complicate matters, Elizabeth fell in love with Czartoryski, though she found Alexander complaisant. When she gave birth to a daughter, the child's hair was black. Paul rightly suspected that Czartoryski was the father. The Pole narrowly avoided Siberia. Instead Paul appointed him minister to Sardinia.

Paul sensed danger all around him and started to build a new, more secure palace in Petersburg, the Gothic-style Mikhailovsky Castle. When there was a fire alarm at Pavlovsk, Paul panicked, convinced it was a revolution, and ran for his life, while the hearts of Grand Duchess Elizabeth and her sister-in-law Anna "beat with *hope* that it was something." The emperor rushed at a group of hussars with sword drawn crying, "Get back, you scum!" He ordered two soldiers to be whipped in front of him—for starting the panic. He treated Alexander as a threat. "They are really bad together now," reported Elizabeth, and Alexander told his ex-tutor Laharpe: "I've become the unhappiest being."[9]

Yet at the start of 1800 no conspiracy existed and the throne was guarded by devoted henchmen, Rostopchin as minister and spymaster, Arakcheev, now count and quartermaster-general, as military strongman, and a new procurator-general, Peter Obolyaninov, ex-steward of Gatchina. Yet one by one Paul himself destroyed the very men devoted to his protection and promoted the ones set on his destruction.

When Arakcheev covered up a theft perpetrated under his brother's watch, Paul dismissed him. "These appointments are a real lottery," reflected Alexander, who wrote secretly to the Ape in Uniform: "My friend, I don't need to send renewed assurances of my unshakeable friendship ... Believe me, it will never change." But it took just one man of action to change everything: Pahlen had been sacked twice and reappointed twice to the key post of governor-general of Petersburg. Earlier Paul had dismissed him as governor of Livonia for entertaining Zubov.* But somehow, Pahlen had befriended Kutaisov who kept advising Paul to reappoint him. After suffering from Paul's whims so frequently, Pahlen decided the emperor must go. "The weak man talks," he said. "The brave man acts." Pahlen cultivated an image of easy-going bonhomie, offering his visitors a glass of champagne, which concealed a vulpine gift for conspiracy—his nickname was "Professor of Cunning."

Pahlen, as governor-general, had access to Alexander, who was commandant, and he started to probe "lightly, vaguely." Alexander "listened but didn't answer." When Pahlen told him that Paul must be removed,

---

* On 26 February 1797, Pahlen received this note from the emperor: "To my surprise I found out about the disreputable services provided by you to Prince Zubov in Riga, from which I draw my own conclusions about your character and about which my behaviour to you will be proportionate."

Alexander said he was "resigned to go on suffering." But in late December or January 1801 Pahlen coaxed the heir into agreeing to a vague plan to be regent or to rule if his father abdicated—but only after extracting "the sacred promise that Paul's life be assured." Alexander planned to "establish his father in the Mikhailovsky Palace" where "he'd have the whole winter garden to walk and ride in." He decided to add a theatre and riding school "so to bring together everything that could have made Emperor Paul's life happy."

"I promised," recalled Pahlen, "but I knew it was impossible—if Paul had not ceased to live, the blood of innocents would soon flood the capital . . . My liaisons with Alexander raised the suspicions of the emperor." They cut back their meetings, communicating with unsigned notes immediately destroyed.

Pahlen sought men who knew how to drown kittens. "I needed the Zubovs and Bennigsen," a tough German officer exiled by Paul. Understanding Paul's chivalry, Pahlen appealed to his generosity: should he not recall the Zubovs? Pahlen needed Figaro's backing and that was simply won. Olga Zherebtsova, the Zubovs' sister, hinted to the barber that Prince Zubov wished to marry his daughter. On 1 November, Paul pardoned the Zubovs, appointing them to minor jobs but he offered nothing to General Leo Bennigsen, who hated him all the more.

In the first weeks of 1801, Paul exiled twenty-six officers. "A crescendo was approaching that would be bloody," claimed Pahlen later. "There wasn't one of us who was sure of a day of his existence! Raised to such a delicate and important position, I was one of the most in danger!" Czartoryski put it best: Paul "was too fantastic and capricious. No one could ever rely on him."

Pahlen worked to undermine Rostopchin. Simultaneously the Professor of Cunning played an even deeper game: having gradually drawn the heir into his conspiracy, he then effectively betrayed him to Paul, implying that Alexander, Constantine and their mother were plotting against him. Paul brooded on how to punish his family. Pahlen next reported to Alexander on Paul's plans to destroy him.* Two hundred officers flocked to join the plot.

On 1 February, Paul moved into his forbidding new Mikhailovsky Palace, complete with moat, drawbridges and many of the paintings

---

* This account of the conspiracy is based on a variety of unpublished and published sources that allow us to tell the story from several points of view: the unpublished notes (now in the Sorbonne) of a French émigré, the comte de Langeron, who interviewed Pahlen, Bennigsen and Grand Duke Constantine; Grand Duchess Elizabeth's letters to her mother and her memoirs as told to Countess Golovina; Bennigsen's anonymous memoirs; Czartoryski's memoirs probably contain Alexander's own version of events; Sablukov's memoirs are priceless because he was present on the night but not in the conspiracy.

from the Hermitage. Figaro and Gagarina lived downstairs while the emperor's young children were above his bedroom. Yet a fortress is only as safe as the men who guard it. Pahlen, responsible for security, knew the daily codes, and most of the emperor's adjutants were conspirators. The Professor of Cunning found that the best place to meet was the salon of the secret police chief Obolyaninov, who was "unsuspicious of any evil design," while Paul "never suspected intimates of Obolyaninov."*

Meanwhile Paul was enthusiastically launching his quixotic war against Britain in alliance with Napoleon. In January 1801, he ordered the ataman of the Don Cossacks, Vasily Orlov (no relation to Prince Orlov), to lead 20,000 men against India.†

In mid-February, Pahlen managed to get Rostopchin exiled to his estates, and he himself replaced him as president of the Foreign Collegium and postmaster with the power to open letters. But, as the conspiracy spread, Sablukov noticed that "The whole appearance of society showed something extraordinary was going on." Pahlen himself was in danger of exposure. Once he was carrying a secret note when Paul, seeing his pockets bulging with letters, asked to see them, teasing him: "Are those love letters?" Paul reached for them and Pahlen's blood froze. Just in time he said, "Sire, leave it—you hate tobacco and my handkerchief is full of it."

"Ugh, what piggery!" cried Paul, desisting. On another occasion, when Pahlen was hiding a list of the conspirators and Paul's order of the day, Paul demanded that he hand over the latter. Facing a 50–50 chance of destruction, Pahlen reached into his pocket and luckily brought out the right piece of paper.

Riding in the gardens, Paul suddenly gripped his own throat: "I felt suffocated. I felt as if I was going to die. Won't they strangle me?" His courtiers reassured him. He had talked of dying of "a sore throat"—his euphemism for strangulation.

At 7 a.m. on 7 March, Pahlen, making his report, found the tsar "preoccupied and serious. He looked at me for two minutes without saying a word." Someone had given Paul a list of conspirators.

"You were here in 1762?" he asked Pahlen.

* Yet Paul was certainly watching the original conspirator, Panin, telling his Moscow governor, "I opened his letter in which he writes about an imaginary aunt (who doesn't exist) who is the only one in the world with soul and heart and other nonsense. I see from all this that he is the same so please send him away but tell him to stop lying either by tongue or pen."
† This was not Paul's only expansionist policy: Georgia's kingdoms, Kartli-Kakhetia and Imeretia, still ruled by kings of the Bagration dynasty, Giorgi XII and Solomon II, had never recovered from the recent depredations of the eunuch-shah of Persia. In December 1800, the Russians claimed that the dying Giorgi XII of Kartli-Kakhetia had left his realm to Russia: Paul's troops took control. Around the same time, Paul officially sponsored the Russian-American Company to colonize Alaska, the start of Russia's American empire that lasted until 1867.

"Yes, Sire."

"You were in the revolution which deprived my father of his throne and his life?"

"I was a young cornet in the Guards, but why does Your Majesty ask?"

"They're planning to replay 1762."

Pahlen trembled but collecting himself replied: "Yes, Sire, they want to. I know it and I am in the plot."

"What are you saying?"

"You have nothing to fear. I hold all the threads of the conspiracy and you'll soon know all." He reassured Paul that he had been crowned, unlike his father, who "was a foreigner and you a Russian," while Empress Maria "had neither the genius nor the energy of your mother," Catherine the Great.

The emperor threatened arrests and hangings—at which Pahlen solemnly replied that he would be shocked when he learned who the conspirators were. He presented a list confirming Paul's nightmare: Maria, Alexander and Constantine were its leaders. Paul and Pahlen planned a counter-coup to arrest them all. Paul confided to Kutaisov that after his counter-strike, "We'll live without constraint like brothers," and he told Princess Gagarina, "I see it's time to carry out my coup." She innocently repeated his words to Pahlen: "I don't know what he means by the great coup he plans."

Pahlen frightened Alexander by revealing Paul's plans. He set the date as the Ides of March, the 15th, but Caesar was becoming too suspicious. Alexander proposed the 11th when his own Semyonovsky Guards were on duty.

Yet someone had clearly denounced the conspiracy to Paul. Around 9 March, without telling Pahlen, he secretly summoned Arakcheev and Rostopchin to return at once to Petersburg—clearly to take command of the counter-coup. But Pahlen, in charge of the posts, opened the letters and showed them to Paul, asking if they were forgeries. Paul asserted that they were genuine. When Arakcheev received Paul's note—"I need you. Come at once"—he galloped for Petersburg.

On 10 March, Paul was tetchy. After the afternoon concert, he brooded in his apartments, then before dinner he confronted Maria and his elder sons with the charge of treason. It is said that he found Voltaire's *Brutus* on Alexander's desk and sent Kutaisov to him with a copy of Voltaire's *Peter the Great*, the account of the torture of Tsarevich Alexei underlined. At dinner, the pug-snouted emperor sat, arms crossed, staring at his wife and sons. He placed the boys under house arrest and ordered Obolyaninov to readminister the oath of allegiance. As he stalked out of the dinner, Maria burst into tears.[10]

*

The next day, the 11th, Paul was more relaxed. The family were joined at dinner by the one-eyed General Mikhail Kutuzov, who would achieve immortality as the hero of 1812. "There were twenty of us at dinner," recalled Kutuzov, and Paul "was very gay, cheerful and affectionate to his wife and sons." But the general may have misunderstood when Paul asked Alexander why he looked so anxious, advising him to take good care of his health.

Afterwards Paul played with his children upstairs. "When Father visited us," recalled Nicholas, who was then aged four, "he was extremely fun," and in the huge hallways "we all played on sleighs indoors. Even Mother joined in." But that night, after Paul had gone, little Michael was asked what game he was playing. "Burying Father!" he replied. Had the child somehow overheard something? The nannies silenced him.

Late at night Pahlen made a second report of the day to the emperor and noticed that, while Alexander's Semyonovskys were on duty around the palace, Sablukov's Horse Guards patrolled the royal apartments. Pahlen informed Paul that the loyal Horse Guards were Jacobins and recommended dismissing them; and, as a sensible precaution given his wife's disloyalty, he advised him to lock the door to his wife's rooms.

Some time during the day, Figaro received a letter warning of the plot. "Business Tomorrow" was Kutaisov's "favourite saying." The letter was found in his pocket the next day, unopened.

At 8 p.m. Colonel Sablukov, reporting to his colonel-in-chief Constantine, found both the boys "very much excited." "You all seem to be mad here," muttered Sablukov. Alexander "crept about like a frightened hare" and, when Paul appeared, he flitted away "like a lamplighter." Only when the emperor had gone did Alexander open his door and peep into the room. "He sneaked again towards us like a crouching pointer." Having been warned of the fate of Tsarevich Alexei, Alexander was jumpy.

"You know nothing," explained Alexander. "We are both under house arrest. We've both been brought by Obolyaninov to the chapel to take the oath of allegiance." But as soon as he got home Sablukov was summoned by the emperor again. Accompanied by his little dog Spitz and his aide-de-camp Uvarov, one of the conspirators, Paul declared: "You're Jacobins." As Uvarov was "making silly faces and smiling behind the emperor," the tsar dismissed the Horse Guards, leaving two unarmed valets on guard. After visiting his mistress downstairs, Paul, wearing as usual his "drawers, a white linen waistcoat" and a nightcap, went to bed with his sword, cane and sash hanging over his military cot.

Across town, the conspirators were attending several dinner parties held by different officers—but all of them, more than sixty, including three Zubov brothers, converged on the apartment of Colonel Talyzin at the Winter Palace. Wearing their Catherinian uniforms and medals, they excitedly quaffed goblets of Pahlen's champagne. Bennigsen recalled "terrible joy" and "extreme drunkenness" among princes and senators, Georgians, Germans and a French valet. Most were young; some were romantic constitutionalists, some were drunken thugs itching for a fight—and three were the officers who had been personally thrashed by Paul. All discussed the new reign and a constitution, and Nikolai Bibikov, colonel of the Izmailovskys, suggested massacring the entire dynasty.

Just before midnight, Pahlen arrived from court—while Count Arakcheev galloped up to the gates of Petersburg to save the emperor. On Pahlen's orders he was denied entry and sent back to his estate.

Pahlen and Bennigsen, both Germans, both ruthless and calm, both aged fifty-six, were the only two who had not been drinking. Pahlen toasted the new tsar before dividing the conspirators into two squads. The first under Prince Zubov, still only thirty-four, and Bennigsen was to enter the palace through a prearranged postern-gate and penetrate straight to the bedchamber of the emperor, while he himself with the other squad was to surround the palace, cutting off any escape routes. What if Paul resisted? "As everybody knows," replied Pahlen, "you can't make an omelette without breaking eggs."

Just after midnight, Pahlen led his posse towards the front of the Mikhailovsky, while Bennigsen and Zubov hurried round the back of the palace, guided by Paul's adjutant Argamakov across a bridge over the moat and into the royal apartments. On the way half of them got lost in the dark, so it was twelve, including Platon and Nikolai Zubov, who followed Bennigsen into the fortress.

They drew their swords as the adjutant led them right up to the antechamber, but the valet would not open the door.

"I've come to submit the report," said Argamakov.

"Are you crazy? It's after midnight."

"It's actually 6 a.m. and if you don't open it, you'll get me into trouble with the emperor." The door opened and they burst in. One of the valets shouted a warning until "I slashed him dangerously on the head with my sabre," recalled Bennigsen. Platon Zubov lost his nerve and wanted to flee. Bennigsen gripped his arm: "What? Now you want to withdraw? We're too advanced to follow your advice which would ruin us all. The wine is poured and must be drunk." The twelve crowded through the unlocked door into the staircase just as another twenty or more drunken, bloodthirsty bravos poured up the stairs, but the glacially cool Bennigsen and the excitable Zubov strode towards the imperial chamber.

The valet's cry* had awoken Paul. He rushed to escape, but his other exit, leading to Maria's chamber, had been locked on his own orders. There was a trapdoor leading to a tunnel out of the palace under his desk, but before he could open it, Bennigsen and Zubov, bearing swords and candles, burst into the chamber. They hurried to the bed. It was empty. "He's got away!" cried Zubov, but Bennigsen felt the bedclothes: "The nest is still warm." Holding up candles they peered around the room. Nothing. Moonlight broke through the clouds. Bennigsen saw bare feet beneath a screen: "Voilà," he said.

They dragged Paul out in his nightcap and bare feet to face Bennigsen, whose "long, thin, pale, angular form with his hat on his head and sword drawn must have seemed a terrible spectre."

"Sire, you have ceased to reign. Alexander is emperor. We've arrested you on his orders. You must abdicate," said Bennigsen in French. "Your life is not in danger, but if you resist, I can't protect you!" Prince Zubov accused him of intolerable despotism. As Bennigsen checked the other doors, Nikolai "Colossus" Zubov and more conspirators barged their way into the bedchamber.

"Arrested?" asked Paul in his nightshirt. "What does this mean? Arrested?" Zubov repeated Bennigsen's speech in Russian at which Paul, regaining some imperious pride, started to argue with the drunken Colossus who growled at Paul: "Why do you shout so?" He slapped the emperor. Paul pushed him away. "What have I done to you?" he cried.

"You've tortured us for four years," shouted a lairy ruffian. The conspirators and the emperor stared at each other breathlessly, then there was a tumult as another posse of shouting officers, led by Prince Iashvili, a Georgian bravo once caned by the emperor himself, forced their way into the bedchamber. Prince Zubov, fearing that Paul was being rescued by loyal troops, panicked and fled downstairs. Then Iashvili and his cohorts rushed at the tsar, knocking over screen, lamp and emperor.

---

* Princess Gagarina heard nothing, but the cry had roused Kutaisov, "the dexterous Figaro," who without even shoes or stockings, in a dressing-gown and nightcap, slipped away down the stairs and ran through the town to hide in a friend's house, not to the mansion of his mistress Madame Chevalier where troops were sent to arrest him. Figaro was not arrested but retired, founding a noble family: one of his grandsons was killed at Borodino and a Kutaisov count was in the suite of Nicholas II. As for Princess Gagarina, still only twenty-three, she and her mean-spirited husband were sent to Italy. "One can't criticize her conduct in her wasted life," wrote Empress Elizabeth when she died young in 1805. "A good woman." She finally found love with a young Pole, Prince Boris Czetvertinsky (brother of Alexander's future mistress)—but died in childbirth at twenty-seven. It turned out that Gagarina was not Paul's only lover: three months after his death, a mistress gave birth to a daughter who was surnamed Musin-Yuriev (Yuriev being one of the early Romanov surnames) and endowed with the estate of Ropsha (where Peter III had been murdered). Paul's widow Maria took over the upbringing of the girl, who died at eighteen months.

"For heaven's sake, Sire, don't attempt to escape or you'll be murdered," cried Bennigsen, who claimed he rushed out to find a lamp. It was no coincidence that Prince Zubov and Bennigsen should have left the room at the moment the hit squad arrived (if they left at all). It is more likely they were stepping aside as they handed over to the assigned killers who threw themselves on to the tsar. Paul struggled in the mêlée until Nikolai "Colossus" Zubov, the man who had brought Paul news of his accession, seized a massive golden snuffbox and smashed it into his face, crushing his cheek and knocking in his eye. Paul went down, probably hitting the corner of his desk. Lieutenant Ivan Tatarinov and Captain Yakov Skariatin, assisted by Iashvili, threw themselves on to the fighting emperor. It took several big men to break him. Sablukov says these were the three officers whom Paul had beaten—"He paid dearly for this at the hour of his death." They frenziedly beat and choked him. Colonel Bibikov held his thinning hair and banged his head on the floor; Skariatin seized Paul's sash from over the bed and, aided probably by Iashvili and Tatarinov, got it round the tsar's neck. Zubov's French valet sat on his feet. Paul got his fingers between the sash and his throat, begging to be spared, to be allowed to pray. Then, staring up wild-eyed into the faces of his killers, he thought he recognized his son Constantine and in a tragic moment resembling Caesar's "Et tu, Brute?" he spluttered: "What? Your Highness is here?" He resumed his pleas. "Mercy, Your Highness, mercy! Some air, for God's sake."

The stranglers tightened the sash until Paul was still—at which more of the conspirators "avenged themselves of personal insults by kicking and trampling on the body, mangling the unfortunate corpse." They "tightened the knot and dragged along the dead body, striking it." Bennigsen reappeared with a lamp, halted the stomping and took command. Examining the "mangled body" for life, he placed thirty Guards on the doors and dumped the corpse on the bed.[11]

Alexander I was obliviously waiting downstairs. "Without undressing, he threw himself on his bed full of anxiety and doubt," until there was "a knock on his door" and he saw his father's murderer "Count Nikolai Zubov, his dress in disorder, face flushed with wine and the excitement of the murder who cried hoarsely: 'All is over!'"

"What is over?" asked Alexander, but Colossus did not answer clearly until the grand duke noticed that he addressed him as "Your Majesty while Alexander thought he was merely Regent." He was "prostrate with grief and despair." Pahlen now arrived, conveniently late: if the plot had failed, he could have arrested the plotters.

"People will say I'm murderer of my father," sobbed Alexander.

"I was promised his life would be spared. I'm the most unfortunate creature!"

"That's enough childishness." Pahlen shook him briskly by the arms. "Go and start your reign. Show yourself to the Guards."

"And my mother?"

"I'll go to her."

Pahlen woke up Charlotte Lieven, mistress of the robes, "a lady of great strength and power of mind," and ordered her to rouse Maria. At first the empress thought her eldest daughter Alexandrine had died but then she understood. "Oh it's the emperor!" she cried, jumping out of the bed in her nightgown.

"He's had a stroke," said Lieven.

"No, he's been murdered!" insisted Maria, but the Guards refused to let the empress through the anteroom to Paul's bedchamber. "How dare you! Let me pass!" she shrieked. The Grenadiers crossed their muskets. Tended by Madame Lieven and her two daughters Maria and Catherine, the empress "lost her head" and overcome with "ambition and sadness" suddenly "declared that in consequence of her coronation, she was the ruling empress and allegiance should be sworn to her. She must reign now." Catherines I and II had both succeeded their husbands as sovereign. Was she deluded or bidding for power? She turned to the Grenadiers on guard: "As your emperor has died a victim to treason, I am your empress. I alone am your legitimate sovereign. Follow me and protect me!"

Alexander woke up his wife Elizabeth, who was shocked by "the horrible crime." He was "annihilated—his sensitive soul will forever be damaged," she told her mother. Outside she could hear hurrahs acclaiming the new emperor. She and Alexander wept together. "I don't know what I am!" he told her.

Constantine, who knew nothing, was "sleeping like a twenty-year-old" when he was loudly awoken by a drunken Prince Zubov who "brutally pulled off my blankets and roughly told me, 'Get up, go to Emperor Alexander, he awaits you!'"

Constantine was "astonished—I stared at Zubov still half asleep. I thought I was dreaming." So Zubov pulled him out of bed. He ran to his brother's salon, where "I found him stretched on a sofa in floods of tears with Empress Elizabeth. That's when I learned of the assassination of my father. I believed it was a plot to kill all of us!" But just at that moment an officer warned Alexander that their mother was claiming the throne for herself.

"My God! Yet more embarrassment!" wailed Alexander, sending Pahlen off to reason with her. Outside, troops were massing but some worried that Paul was still alive—despite the shrill acclamations of Zubov. "But that's impossible," replied Bennigsen. "He's damaged, smashed. He's got to be painted and arranged." The soldiers refused to swear allegiance to Alexander without seeing the body, so Bennigsen let them in and they reported that the emperor was "very dead." They took the oath.

Pahlen "forced the tsar to hurry away fast" to the Winter Palace. As he left with Constantine, with Pahlen and Zubov riding triumphantly on the running boards, Alexander asked Elizabeth to go to his mother and persuade her to join them at the Winter Palace.

Back in the Mikhailovsky Palace, that night was "like a vague dream" to Paul's young son Nicholas: "I was awakened and saw in front of me Countess Lieven. I noticed the Semyonovsky Guards on duty and I was taken to Mother." Soon afterwards, an adjutant arrived from the Winter Palace asking Maria to come "in the name of the emperor and empress."

"Tell my son," Maria replied, "that until I see my husband dead, I shall not acknowledge him as my sovereign."

Elizabeth found that her mother-in-law "had gone totally crazy. The officers wouldn't let her see the body but she wouldn't go until she'd seen him."

"But Emperor Alexander is at the Winter Palace," explained Elizabeth.

"I know no Emperor Alexander," cried Maria with "appalling shrieks." "I want to see my emperor." Elizabeth herself collapsed, later telling Countess Golovina that it was "the most terrible night of her life." She spent the horrendous early hours with the hysterical dowager empress. Once the Scottish doctor James Wylie had cleaned up the body with varnish and paint, Bennigsen let her in. That calmed her.

Elizabeth went to join Alexander at the Winter Palace. The tsar told her, "I'm not sure I can fulfil my duties. I resign my power to whoever will take it. Let those who committed this crime be responsible." Then Maria arrived with all her children. Nicholas only remembered that "Alexander threw himself before Mother and I can still hear him sobbing. I was glad when I was allowed to play with my wooden horses again." The new emperor endured a "heart-rending interview" with his mother, who shouted at him: "Alexander, are you guilty?" He denied it and they embraced. Outside the city celebrated. "After Paul's excess of despotism," Elizabeth noticed, "a mad joy reigns," and she admitted to her mother: "At last I can breathe."

Next morning, at the ten o'clock parade, Emperor Alexander I reviewed the Guards who had cut off their hair plaits, burned their Prussian hats and redonned their Russian uniforms. "The conspirators were very arrogant," particularly Prince Zubov, who was "looking very unsoldierly with all his smiles and foppery." Alexander was a broken man, noticed Sablukov. "He walked slowly, as if his knees were giving way, hair distrait, eyes tearful, his regard fixed ahead of him as if to say 'They abused my youth, they tricked me!'" Alexander issued a manifesto promising to rule "according to the heart of Our Very August Grandmother, Empress Catherine the Second."

Alexander and his mother returned to the Mikhailovsky. When he saw Paul's smashed face, "he was horrified and stood transfixed." Constantine was shocked too. "Well, my friend," he said when Sablukov reported to him, "my brother may reign if he pleases, but if the throne were ever to come to me, I should certainly not accept it."

The assassins surrounded Alexander. "I have seen the young prince," reported a French diplomat, "walking . . . preceded by the assassins of his ancestor, surrounded by those of his father and by all appearances followed by his own." Pahlen dominated everything, spending most of his time with Alexander, who "found affairs absolutely neglected and disordered," he later told his brother Nicholas. "Our parent changed everything but didn't replace it by anything."

The tsar reversed his father's works.* He amnestied Paul's exiles, dissolved the secret police, prohibited torture, restored the rights of the nobility (particularly the ban on corporal punishment) and, recalling the Cossacks galloping towards British India, gradually restored warm relations with Britain.

Yet Pahlen "treated him like a child." Alexander despised "that treacherous immoral man and his crimes." He summoned his liberal friends led by Czartoryski (Empress Elizabeth's lover), to whom he confessed the moral nightmare of patricide: "If you had been here, things wouldn't have turned out as they did." Alexander complained about Pahlen's "dictatorial ways" until a courtier replied, "When flies annoy me, I drive them away."

After Paul's death, peasants, moved by the martyrdom of a sacred tsar, sent icons to the dowager empress with the inscription from the Second Book of Kings—"Had Zimri peace, who slew his master?" Pahlen demanded their removal; Alexander refused. At 10 a.m. on 17 June, at the parade, Pahlen arrived as usual in his carriage, but one of Alexander's

---

* Closing down the Mikhailovsky Palace, which became the military engineers' school, he resided officially at the Winter Palace but liked to live at Kamenny Ostrov, an ochre palace, built by Catherine the Great, on a small island in the Neva. Paul had lent it to Poniatowski, the last king of Poland. Here Alexander created a "court of exaggerated simplicity totally devoid of etiquette and he met his courtiers only on intimate familiar terms." Now a nod was the only bow required, no longer Paul's prostrations. The emperor himself relished walking around Petersburg on his own or with a single companion—his regular route becoming known as *le tour imperial*.

adjutants told him to remount and go into exile on his Baltic estates. Soon afterwards, Prince Zubov, Bennigsen and the stranglers Iashvili, Skariatin and Tatarinov were ordered out of Petersburg.*

None of the assassins was prosecuted. Yet, as Czartoryski understood, "Alexander punished himself with more severity than the others." His father's murder hovered over him "like a vulture," and he often "saw in imagination Paul's mutilated bloodstained body on the steps of the throne." He remained "alone for hours sitting in silence."[12]

---

* The dowager empress's suffering was not over: a few days later, her eldest daughter Alexandrine, who had failed to marry the king of Sweden and then had married the Habsburg Archduke Joseph, also died. Maria moved Paul's blood-spattered blouse and bed to Pavlovsk where she kept them in a bedchamber shrine. Of the chief conspirators, Panin succeeded Pahlen as president of the Foreign Collegium for a short time, then was exiled. Zubov returned to his Courland estate where he married a young Polish girl. But Alexander did forgive some conspirators: the one-legged Lothario Valerian Zubov remained in Petersburg and sat on the Council because Alexander was fond of him and he had played no direct role in the killing, while Prince Peter Volkonsky, who was a conspirator, became his constant companion. Bennigsen commanded against Napoleon, but Alexander treated him with distaste. "The ingrate!" murmured Bennigsen. But Maria made sure he would never receive his marshal's baton. Iashvili wrote an insolent and insensitive letter to Alexander, who almost arrested him. He and the other stranglers did not return to Petersburg for twenty-five years. In 1834, the poet Pushkin was fascinated to see Skariatin at balls in Petersburg, pointed out as the man who had strangled an emperor. The 11th of March remained "that day of horror" (as Alexander II called it), and the tsars always attended mass for Paul that day until 1917.

## SCENE 6

# The Duel

# CAST

Maria Fyodorovna, dowager empress, widow of Paul I
ALEXANDER I, emperor 1801–25, son of Paul and Maria
Elizabeth, empress, his wife
CONSTANTINE I, emperor 1825, Alexander's brother, caesarevich, later commander of the Polish army
Anna Fyodorovna (née Princess Juliane of Saxe-Coburg-Saalfeld), his first wife
Joanna Grudzińska, Princess Lowicza, his second wife
Catherine, his sister, married Prince Georg of Oldenburg, then King Wilhelm of Württemberg, "Catiche"
Anna, his sister, later queen of Holland, "Annette"
NICHOLAS I, emperor 1825–55, his brother
Alexandra Fyodorovna (née Princess Charlotte of Prussia), Nicholas's wife, "Mouffy"
Michael, Alexander's youngest brother
Elena Pavlovna (née Princess Charlotte of Württemberg), his wife


## COURTIERS: ministers etc.

Prince Adam Czartoryski, Polish patriot, lover of Empress Elizabeth, foreign minister
Victor Kochubey, count, later prince, vice-chancellor, interior minister, president of State Council
Count Pavel Stroganov, deputy interior minister
Nikolai Novosiltsev, deputy justice minister, after 1815 Alexander's representative in Poland, later count
Alexei Arakcheev, inspector-general of artillery, war minister, count, "Ape in Uniform," "Vampire"
Count Nikolai Rumiantsev, foreign minister, chancellor, later prince
Prince Alexander Golitsyn, mystic, ober-procurator of Holy Synod, postmaster, education minister
Karl von Nesselrode, count, envoy to Paris, foreign minister, later chancellor

Ioannis Capo d'Istria, born in Corfu, count, foreign minister, first head of state of Greece

Mikhail Speransky, state secretary, later count, governor-general of Siberia

Fyodor Rostopchin, count, governor-general of Moscow

Maria Naryshkina, mistress and mother of Alexander's children, "Aspasia of the North"

Princess Zinaida Volkonskaya, Alexander's mistress

Wilhelmina, duchesse de Sagan, Biron's granddaughter, mistress of Metternich and probably of Alexander

Princess Ekaterina "Katya" Bagration, daughter of Countess Katinka Scavronskaya, wife of General Peter Bagration, mistress of Metternich and probably of Alexander, "Naked Angel," "White Pussycat"

## NAPOLEONIC WARS

Count Levin Bennigsen, murderer of Paul I, commander 1806–7, chief of staff 1812

Mikhail Barclay de Tolly, prince, marshal, war minister, commander 1812 and 1813–15

Mikhail Kutuzov, prince, marshal, commander against Turks and at Austerlitz 1805, commander-in-chief 1812

Prince Peter Bagration, commander of army 1812 and hero of Borodino

Prince Peter Volkonsky, chief of staff, Nicholas I's court minister

Alexander Chernyshev, envoy to Paris, cavalry commander 1812, Nicholas I's war minister and prince, "Northern Lovelace"

Russia enjoyed a carnival of hope as Alexander unleashed his liberal tendencies—yet the new tsar remained a study of inscrutability. His dazzling looks were inherited from his tall, fair German mother, his charm from Catherine the Great, but his invincible geniality was a screen that concealed his real thoughts. If he was an adept actor, a master of dissembling, the man who had lived through Catherine's decline and Paul's terror and assassination, could be forgiven a taste for clandestinity and a talent for serpentine manoeuvre. But there turned out to be more steeliness there than even his friends had expected.

In 1801, Alexander created a new Council and replaced Peter the Great's collegia with eight Western-style ministries, reforms that completed Peter's vision of a simplified central government. But his ministers were still the same grandees who had run Russia since Tsar Michael, and he wanted to find his own way so he appointed Adam Czartoryski and his friends as their deputies.* And then secretly he created an Intimate Committee made up of his friends. "We had the privilege of coming to dine with the emperor without a prior appointment," recalled Czartoryski. "Our confabs took place two or three times a week," then after official dinner and coffee, Alexander would disappear and the four liberals would be led through corridors to reappear in the emperor's salon to discuss a constitution, a semi-elected senate and the abolition of serfdom.

The fate of his father always reminded Alexander of the danger of challenging the clans of nobility and the autocracy of his grandmother and the militarism of his father ran much deeper in him than the liberalism of his education and coterie. Besides, the only way to impose his reforms was by his own despotism. He prevaricated on most of these measures (though he did repeal the law that allowed landowners to exile

---

* Three of the new ministries—interior, justice and finance—were the result of the break-up of the old office of procurator-general. Alexander's friend Kochubey (raised to count, then exiled by Paul) became his long-serving interior minister with Stroganov as his deputy. The Anglophile veteran Count Alexander Vorontsov, who had served Catherine the Great, became foreign minister with Czartoryski as his deputy. Novosiltsev was deputy justice minister. In August, Laharpe arrived too, hoping to promote his liberal agenda.

serfs for "insolence"), let the Intimate Committee lapse*—and became distracted by foreign affairs.

At first Alexander pursued a policy of neutrality but then, keen to strut the international stage (and admire the famed beauty of the queen of Prussia), he organized his first royal summit. At Memel, on 29 May 1802, he met King Frederick William III and his charming queen Louise, with whom he fell a little in love. The emperor flirted with Louise and fought off her vampish sister. As his room adjoined their apartment, Alexander told Czartoryski that "he carefully locked his bedroom door to prevent his being surprised and led into dangerous temptations he wished to avoid." This friendship with the Hohenzollerns connected him with the rising European resistance against French hegemony.

Napoleon Bonaparte, first consul for life, who combined the rationalism of the Enlightenment and the liberties of the French Revolution with the monarchical conservatism of a born autocrat and the boundless ambitions of a condottiere, had mobilized the resources of France in the face of repeated coalitions designed to destroy him, organized by Britain and the powers of the ancien régime. Now he annexed much of Italy, took control of Switzerland and started to rearrange Germany. He probed Alexander, asking for his mediation with the British. But Napoleon's domination of Germany challenged Russian interests there, while his treaty with the Ottomans gradually convinced Alexander that Bonaparte was "one of the most infamous tyrants in history." Moving closer to Britain, Austria and his new Prussian friends, Alexander contemplated war against an overweening France. In April 1803, he summoned the Ape in Uniform, Paul's drear henchman Arakcheev, whom he appointed inspector-general of artillery. Much more than that, the general was Alexander's devoted enforcer, considerably more important than his liberal friends, and it was he who created the superb artillery that would hold its own against Napoleon.† As the tsar became

---

* The Russian possession of the Ionian Islands, taken from the French in 1799, allowed Alexander, advised by a Corfiote nobleman Ioannis Capo d'Istria, to experiment with the liberal constitution of his so-called Septinsular Republic which he favoured for everywhere—except Russia itself. Within Russia, the enduring achievements of his liberal experiment were in education where he created a new Ministry of Public Instruction under the ancient Zavadovsky (Catherine the Great's lover of 1774–6), reorganized Moscow University, opened new universities in Vilnius, Tartu, Kharkov, Kazan and later Petersburg and lycées for the civil service, most famously the Tsarskoe Selo school where Pushkin was one of the first pupils.

† After failing to rescue Paul, Arakcheev had retired to his estate at Gruzino, where he erected a memorial portrait of the late tsar with the legend in gold: "My heart is pure and my spirit without reproach vis-à-vis You." Arakcheev's dogged loyalty to Paul and his harsh militarism and personal devotion to Alexander (his motto was "Devoted without Flattery") explain his rise to power as much as do his discipline and efficiency.

increasingly involved in European politics, he was finally creating a family. But not with his wife.[1]

Empress Elizabeth suffered from Alexander's neglect and their lack of children. It was not all Alexander's fault for there was something self-centred in Elizabeth's sensibility—as her lady-in-waiting observed: "A burning, passionate imagination was combined in her with a cold heart incapable of real affection." When Czartoryski returned to Petersburg, he and Elizabeth were temporarily reunited, while the emperor had affairs with French actresses, international adventuresses and the wives of his courtiers. But he was so voraciously hunted by women that he resisted the more aggressive. Hence his nickname "le Don Juan Platonique." Czartoryski bitchily implied that he preferred "Platonic coquetry—it seldom happened that the virtue of the ladies to whom Alexander paid his attentions was really in danger." But by then the two men had ceased to be friends.

In 1801, the ruling court beauty was the Polish Maria Naryshkina, née Princess Chetvertinska, whose father had been hanged as a traitor by the Polish revolutionaries in 1794. Famed for looks "found only in the paintings of Raphael," "her beauty," noted the memoirist Filipp Vigel, "was so perfect it seemed unnatural, impossible." At sixteen, she had married the older Dmitri Naryshkin, master of the horse, but he could not control "the Aspasia of the North," who always dressed with chic simplicity in a Grecian dress of white crêpe. She was the mistress of Valerian Zubov when Alexander fell in love with her. After two years, she succumbed to him.

He never mentioned Naryshkina to his straitlaced mother but felt no guilt towards poor Elizabeth because, as he later admitted, "I imagined wrongly no doubt that the appearances that united my wife and I were without our participation . . . My rank obliged me to respect these appearances, but I thought I could dispose of my own heart and for fifteen years I was faithful to Madame Naryshkina."

Naryshkina kept out of politics, otherwise, Alexander explained, "everything would have been finished." But she still tormented his discarded empress. Elizabeth longed for a child. When she saw "the Lady" at a ball and asked after her health, Naryshkina "had the impudence to tell me of her first pregnancy which was so little advanced that I wouldn't have been aware of it . . . Don't you think, Mama, this is the height of effrontery? She knew very well I was not ignorant of how she got pregnant." This baby died, as Elizabeth reported to her mother: "the death of that baby, that caused me so much pain, shows Providence doesn't want to suffer an illegitimate child in this family," but "I felt sorry for the emperor from the bottom of my heart." She noted that Alexander was heartbroken, while "the mother consoled herself quickly. She lost another baby last winter and danced three weeks later!"

Naryshkina gave Alexander several children. Two survived to adulthood. Alexander visited them daily, spending *gemütlich* evenings with them. He said his only real happiness was "my little family."

Yet the woman who was closest to Alexander was his sister Catherine—"Catiche," snub-nosed but thick-haired, full-lipped and energetic. Calling her his "Absurd Little Mad Thing" and for her Turkish looks, "Bisiam," he told her, "If you are a mad thing, you are the most delicious one that ever existed. I adore you!" She was eleven years younger and brought up after Alexander had long since left home. She was both familiar and stranger. "You've made a conquest of me and I am mad about you!" he wrote to her in September 1805. "I love few things in the world like my Bisiam. Farewell light of my eyes, adored of my heart, pole-star of the age, wonder of Nature or better than all these, Bisiam Bisiamovna with the snub nose . . . on which I press the tenderest of kisses."

Alexander was happiest among women—yet his life would be dominated by a man who inspired admiration, hatred and fear: Napoleon Bonaparte, whom he saw as both "the transcendent talent" and "the infernal" genius of his time.[2]

In March 1804, Bonaparte executed the duc d'Enghien, an act of terrorism that finally ruptured relations with Alexander, particularly since the Bourbon prince was kidnapped from Baden, the home of Empress Elizabeth, who was "totally overcome by the news."

At the Council on 5 April, Czartoryski declared that "this atrocious assassination" proved France was a "brigands' lair." Soon afterwards, Bonaparte crowned himself emperor of the French. Alexander did not recognize his title—and demanded the evacuation of Bonaparte's Italian and German conquests. On 30 March 1805, Russia and Britain, the latter pledging £1.25 million per 100,000 Russian soldiers, agreed to fight France just as Napoleon declared himself king of Italy. On 28 July, Austria joined the coalition.

On 9 September, as two Russian armies took up position, covering neutral Prussia in the north and joining forces with the Austrians in the south, Alexander set off from Petersburg, surrounded by a golden suite including Czartoryski.* On the way he stopped at the Czartoryski estate

---

* Now formally promoted to foreign minister, Czartoryski was widely distrusted at court, but he himself appreciated his increasingly contradictory role as a Polish patriot serving the Russian tsar, as a liberal serving an autocrat: "I had no inclination to serve Russia" but "I was there merely by accident like an exotic plant in a foreign land."

at Pulaway where, exhilarated by expectation of victory, the "affable monarch" as he called himself flirted with or had an affair with Potemkin's niece. This was the forty-four-year-old Katinka Scavronskaya, now Countess Litta, whose "attractive adiposity has excited my imagination." He basked in the admiration of the Poles who believed that this idyll signalled the re-creation of the Polish kingdom under Czartoryski. But, as Napoleon headed across Germany, Alexander was playing a double game.

Alexander secretly despatched his favourite Prince Peter Dolgoruky, aged twenty-seven, to negotiate with Frederick William III of Prussia, who would never contemplate a Polish kingdom, to tempt him into the war against Napoleon. At the end of September, Alexander travelled to seal the deal in Berlin, sworn by torchlight at the tomb of Frederick the Great. This was a betrayal of Czartoryski, who never forgave the tsar—though he remained foreign minister. Napoleon had already outwitted the allies, forcing an Austrian army into surrender at Ulm. The Russians withdrew to combine with the main Austrian army.

When Alexander arrived, his troops received him "in coldness and mournful silence"—for they had been outmanoeuvred and undersupplied. His general was the fat, one-eyed, and extremely experienced Mikhail Kutuzov. "One couldn't be wittier than Kutuzov," noted the French émigré in Russian service, comte de Langeron, "nor less forceful" nor "smarter and more cunning." The general was blessed with "prodigious memory, well-educated amiability, good nature," but this was combined with "the great violence and crudeness of a peasant, insurmountable laziness, and egotism"—and a "villainous and disgusting libertinage."

Kutuzov withdrew, skilfully avoiding the battle Napoleon sought, but the inexperienced emperor now assumed the command against the world's greatest general, ignoring Kutuzov in favour of "five or six young favourites" who mocked that eighteenth-century relic. The general "was treated," noted Langeron, "without respect."

Napoleon sent an envoy, General René Savary, to offer terms. Faced with "thirty popinjays who under various titles surround the emperor of Russia," he informed Napoleon that "presumption, imprudence and thoughtlessness" reigned in Alexander's retinue. Alexander prepared for battle but sent Dolgoruky to demand that Napoleon renounce Italy. Napoleon's sense of his own prospects was encouraged by this "excessively arrogant whippersnapper who spoke to me as one would speak to a boyar being sent to Siberia." Napoleon laughed that the prince took "my extreme moderation as a mark of great terror."

"Tomorrow," he told his foreign minister Charles Maurice de

Talleyrand, prince de Benevento, on 18 November, "there will probably be a very serious battle with the Russians . . . blood spilled uselessly . . ." Alexander was a "brave and worthy man led astray by those around him who are sold to the English." Massing near the village of Austerlitz, the coalition's 85,000 men were numerically superior to Napoleon's 65,000, but the emperor of the French was preparing for a battle he was sure he could win.

"Whippersnapper" Dolgoruky duly reported that "our success is beyond doubt." The Holy Roman Emperor Francis joined the armies. Napoleon was unimpressed by his opponents: the thirty-seven-year-old Francis was "a blockhead occupied only in botany and gardening," who "was so moral he never made love to anyone except his wife," while Alexander was "too fickle and too weak." The tsar, who had a tendency to disdain his own Russians and respect the higher civilization of Germans, accepted an Austrian plan that called for a complicated, reckless manoeuvre to abandon the high ground of the Pratzen Heights in an attempt to turn the French right flank. When Kutuzov queried the plan in his old-fashioned courtly manner, Alexander snapped: "None of your business."

At 7:30 next morning, 20 November, Napoleon calmly yielded his right flank to draw in the Russian–Austrian forces, who abandoned the Pratzen Heights and exposed their centre. This accomplished, the French emperor achieved surprise by appearing behind them to seize the very high ground they were just abandoning. Alexander galloped excitedly around the battlefield with Dolgoruky. "Instead of continually going to advance posts or exposing yourself, where the presence of Your Majesty only upset and hindered the generals," wrote Czartoryski in a devastating letter to Alexander afterwards, "it would be better to remain more distant." At 9 a.m., Kutuzov tried to stall the withdrawal, until Alexander and his suite of "thirty popinjays" galloped up to almost accuse the old general of cowardice. "Mikhail Ilarionovich, why aren't you advancing?" asked Alexander. "We're not in manoeuvres at Tsaritsyno . . ."

"Sire," replied Kutuzov, "if I don't start, it's precisely because we're not in the field of Tsaritsyno. But if you order it . . ." Alexander overruled Kutuzov; the French occupied the heights that the Russians had just left, and at 10:15 a.m. Napoleon said, "Let's finish this war with a thunderclap." A warlord at the pinnacle of his genius, he launched his attack on the exposed centre, precisely concentrating overwhelming force at the weakest point and most opportune time.

Alexander, confused by the "horribly majestic spectacle" opening up before him, was obliviously standing close to the fulcrum of this slaughter—28,000 Russians were killed or wounded. Moments later he was almost run down by his own men as they fled for their lives. "It was precisely at the place where you were located that the rout was immediate and complete," added Czartoryski. Left with only Czartoryski, his friend Prince Peter Volkonsky and Dr. Wylie, Alexander was bundled to safety in the countryside, in danger from his own fever, the risk of battle and capture by the French. "Seeking refuge in a peasant hut," Empress Elizabeth wrote, "whether from exhaustion or chagrin, not having eaten for twenty-four hours, he suffered such stomach cramp that Wylie feared he wouldn't last the night." Dr. Wylie sedated the shivering emperor with wine and opium.[3]

"The Russian army is not merely beaten," Napoleon wrote to his wife Josephine, "it's destroyed." Alexander was effectively abandoned by the Austrian emperor, who sued for peace, losing territories and the title of Holy Roman Emperor. Arriving in Petersburg on 26 November, Alexander was recognized as "the real cause of our defeat. Now all the misfortune is attributed to him alone," admitted Novosiltsev, who had been at Austerlitz with him. Even the tsar's mother warned him that "lured and deceived by Prussia and betrayed by Austria, the glory of armies has suffered the most regrettable failure—the aura of invincibility is destroyed."

Alexander did not collapse but tried to coax Prussia back into the war. He removed Czartoryski in July 1806 and henceforth conducted his own foreign policy, with increasing skill. He declared a holy crusade against that "Beast of the Apocalypse" Napoleon, diabolical enemy of Orthodoxy and champion of the Jews (the Romanovs' first resort to official anti-semitism). That July, Frederick William agreed to return to the war against France. But Napoleon was not resting either: he opened a second front behind Alexander, encouraging the Ottomans to retake control of Wallachia and Moldavia. In October, long before the Russians and Prussians could combine forces, Napoleon destroyed the Prussians at Jena. Alexander should now have made peace, but he still sought glory on behalf of Russia and his stricken (but duplicitous) Prussian friends—and, as commander, turned to Count Bennigsen, murderer of his father.

On 26 January 1807, Bennigsen fought Napoleon himself to a grinding bloody draw at Eylau, losing 26,000 men; the French lost 20,000. But the Russian army was intact until 2 June, when Napoleon defeated Bennigsen at Friedland, where the Russians lost 20,000 dead, over 40 per cent of their men. Alexander needed immediate peace.[4]

"I desire that a close union between our two nations may repair past evils," Alexander instructed Prince Dmitri Lobanov-Rostovsky, his envoy to Napoleon. "An entirely new system . . . and I flatter myself Emperor Napoleon and I will understand each other easily provided we deal without intermediaries." They agreed to meet at Tilsit, where their engineers erected a white pavilion on a specially constructed raft in the middle of the Niemen River, the border between their empires. "Few sights will be more interesting," wrote Napoleon. He was right. The division of Europe between two emperors, based on an expedient friendship, made this one of the most famous summits in history.

As Alexander prepared to meet his vanquisher, accompanied by Constantine, he was under no illusions. "Bonaparte claims I'm only an idiot," he soon afterwards wrote to his sister Catiche. "He who laughs last laughs best! And I put all my hope in God." After his disastrous rush for glory, Alexander was entering a long game. He could hardly believe what was about to happen, as he told Catiche: "Me, spending my days with Bonaparte! Whole hours in tête-à-tête with him!" Alexander's practice in duplicity qualified him well for the seduction of Napoleon. "He possessed to a high degree," wrote his courtier Baron Korff, "the facility to subordinate men to himself and penetrate their souls while hiding all his own feelings and thoughts."

On 13 June, Napoleon was rowed across to the raft so that he was there to meet Alexander when he disembarked from his side. The two men embraced, then Alexander said, "I will be your second against the English." Napoleon was delighted: "Those words changed everything." They turned together and disappeared through the pavilion door surmounted with Russian and French eagles and elaborate "A"s and "N"s, to talk for two hours in French without interpreters. Alexander pleaded for Prussia, which he wished to save not only out of chivalry for its queen but as an essential ally.

The younger emperor, still only twenty-nine, was "not dazzled by false confidence" but was happy to learn from "this extraordinary man" who "liked to show me his superiority in imaginative sallies." For his part, Napoleon, the elder at thirty-eight, could not help but be a little patronizing, yet he was utterly charmed. "My dear, I've just seen Emperor Alexander and I'm very pleased with him, a very handsome, good and young emperor," he told Empress Josephine. "More intelligent than is commonly thought," he later decided, "it would be hard to have more wit than Alexander, but there's a piece missing and I can't discover which." Alexander was somewhat seduced by the genius of his era. Napoleon's "light-grey eyes," he later recalled, "gaze at you so piercingly that you cannot withstand them."

On the second day, Frederick William was allowed to sit in silently on their discussions, when he no doubt learned that Prussia was to be harshly diminished. After the meeting, a hundred guns saluted and Alexander joined Napoleon in Tilsit. Each night, the three monarchs dined together, with Napoleon and Alexander bored to tears by the lumpish Prussian; they would say good night—and then, like a secret assignation, Alexander would steal back to join Napoleon for long talks into the night.

Alexander sought peace without losing honour or territory. Napoleon sought mastery over Europe with a junior partner. These sons of the Enlightenment were dreamers as well as pragmatists. War, Napoleon explained, was not "a difficult art" but "a matter of hiding fear as long as possible. Only by this means is one's enemy intimidated and success not in doubt." Alexander praised elective republics and criticized hereditary monarchy which he regarded as irrational—except in Russia, where local conditions made it essential. Napoleon, the parvenu emperor who had been elected by plebiscite to the throne of a guillotined king, defended heredity to the dynastic autocrat who had acquiesced in paternal regicide. "Who is fit to be elected?" asked Napoleon. "A Caesar, an Alexander only comes along once a century, so that election must be a matter of chance."

"At Tilsit, I chattered away," admitted Napoleon. As the two of them bargained over new kingdoms and spheres, Alexander asked for Constantinople. "Constantinople is the empire of the world," replied Napoleon gnomically. "I called the Turks barbarians and said they ought to be turned out of Europe," he recalled. He played on Alexander's fantasies, suggesting a joint march eastwards to take Constantinople and then attack British India. "But I never intended to do so," Napoleon admitted later. Alexander, who understood the game, later called this "the language of Tilsit."

On 25 June, Lobanov, Paul's minister Kurakin and Talleyrand signed the Treaty of Tilsit. Alexander lost no territory but relinquished the Ionian Islands and Wallachia and Moldavia, recognized Napoleon's brothers as kings of Westphalia and Naples, and promised to blockade England. Prussia suffered grievously, but Alexander refused to annex Prussian Poland. Instead Napoleon created a grand duchy of Warsaw, a possible Polish base against Russia.

"God has saved us," Alexander boasted to Catiche.

"As long as I live, I shan't get used to knowing you pass your days with Bonaparte," Catiche replied. "It seems like a bad joke." A worse joke was mooted. Napoleon's marriage with Josephine was childless so, keen to found his own dynasty, he contemplated divorce. Talleyrand sounded out Alexander about a marriage to Catiche, who was already considering matrimony with another suitor, Emperor Francis of Austria, but the tsar thought him dull—and dirty. "Then I can wash him," replied Catiche, who added that he certainly would not be dull after marrying her. When Napoleon was mentioned, "I wept hot tears like a calf," she admitted. "Princes are of two kinds—worthy people with scant brains and clever ones but of hateful character." The former were preferable but "if the divorce came about" and Napoleon asked for her, she "owed that sacrifice to the State." Napoleon was not yet single—but Catiche, to avoid him, had to marry fast.

As they parted, Alexander invited Napoleon to Petersburg: "I'll order his quarters warmed to Egyptian heat." The summit resembled one of those short love affairs in which both lovers promise eternal love even though both know they will ultimately return to their real lives. Looking back at the end of his life, Napoleon reflected that "Perhaps I was happiest at Tilsit." As for Alexander, his days with Napoleon seemed "like a dream," he told Catiche. "It's past midnight and he's just left. Oh I wish you could have witnessed all that happened." But given his appalling hand, "Instead of sacrifices, we got out of the struggle with a sort of lustre."

His mother and his brother Constantine led the opposition to the new French alliance, much to Elizabeth's outrage: the family had "betrayed and sold the emperor." After her affair with Czartoryski, the twenty-eight-year-old Elizabeth had fallen in love with a Guards captain, Alexis Okhotnikov, aged twenty-three, and become pregnant. This infuriated the unstable Constantine, who, devoted to Alexander, almost certainly ordered the captain's murder (without the tsar's knowledge): Okhotnikov was stabbed coming out of the theatre. The empress visited him before he died and afterwards gave birth to a daughter Lisinka, her delight. But Lisinka died at the age of two, leaving Elizabeth poleaxed.[5]

As Petersburg seethed against the French, Alexander promoted* Arakcheev to war minister to reform the army. Arakcheev served as his "guard-dog with his obtuse ferocity and unconditional loyalty." Utterly trusted and universally loathed as "the Vampire," he ran Alexander's chancellery, able to sign on the emperor's behalf. Simultaneously, Alexander promoted the Ape's opposite, Mikhail Speransky, son of a village priest, who had himself studied for the priesthood. This liberal

---

* Alexander appointed the Francophile Count Nikolai Rumiantsev as foreign minister and later chancellor. Rumiantsev, fifty-four years old, had argued against an British alliance and for a French alliance back in 1804. The son of Catherine the Great's marshal (and possibly grandson of Peter the Great), he was a polymathic book-collector and naturalist (orchids and butterflies are named after him) who had sponsored the first Russian world circumnavigation, so that Bodega Bay in California was originally Rumiantsev Bay.

humanist was made deputy justice minister, but he quickly became Alexander's state secretary. He proposed an almost American system with a presidential tsar, semi-elected legislature and independent judiciary, linked together by a council of state. He openly criticized serfdom and his measures implied that nobles needed some qualifications to take part in government. Speransky's humble origins, dynamic reforms and Francophile culture created enemies. There had been many favourites before—and all had been co-opted by marriage and interest into the clans of nobility, but Speransky's ideas were a threat to their privilege of being born to govern, command and own serfs. "With just a third of Speransky's brain," sneered his rival Arakcheev, "I'd be a very great man."

While society plotted against his French policy, Alexander welcomed Napoleon's ambassadors, first Savary, duc de Rovigo, and then Armand de Caulaincourt, duc de Vicenza, as if these Bonapartist henchmen were his friends. Then, as chinks started to show in French invincibility, Napoleon invited Alexander as his star guest at a new summit.

"My Alexander," wrote his mother, begging him not to go, "you're guilty of criminal self-deception."

"We will do everything to prove the sincerity" of Russia's "tight alliance with France, this fearful colossus," replied Alexander to his mother—until "the moment when we will calmly observe his fall. The wisest policy is to await the right moment to take measures." He could only follow "the indications of my conscience, my essential conviction, the desire that has never left me to be useful to my country."

On 17 September 1808, Alexander (accompanied by Speransky) was greeted by Napoleon five miles outside Erfurt. As well as the two emperors, there were four kings and a constellation of other German princes attending this three-week demonstration of the panoply of Napoleonic power—but it was all about Russia and France. During their eighteen days together, the two emperors banqueted, hunted, danced and attended illuminations and the theatre: when one of the actors onstage in the play *Oedipus* declaimed "A great man's friendship is the gift of the gods," Alexander turned and presented his hand to Napoleon to the applause of the entire audience. Napoleon, a born actor himself, half admired Alexander's thespian talents, calling him the "Talma of the North" after the top French actor.

But Napoleon grumbled because Alexander had become "stubborn as a mule." Alexander was treated to his first Napoleonic tantrum, with the imperial foot stamping on the imperial hat. "You're violent and I am stubborn," said Alexander. "Let us talk and be reasonable—or I leave." Napoleon noticed that "he plays deaf when things are said he is reluctant to hear." Alexander was slightly deaf, but there was plenty he did not wish to hear. The Russians disliked the grand duchy of Warsaw and Napoleon's Continental System, a blockade of British trade which was damaging the Russian economy. Alexander took the opportunity to demand rewards. Napoleon offered Russia the very same tidbits offered by Hitler to Stalin in similar circumstances in 1939: Moldavia and Wallachia "as part of the Russian empire" and Finland, then a Swedish duchy. "It's not right that the beauties of Petersburg should be interrupted by Swedish cannon," Napoleon generously reflected. In return, Alexander promised to uphold the Continental System against Britain and support Napoleon if attacked by Austria.

Yet Alexander's vision of himself as a European crusader was encouraged by a traitor at the heart of Napoleon's court. Napoleon had recently sacked his foreign minister, the lame and reptilian Talleyrand. He still admired "the man with the most ideas, the most flair," though he had recently called him "shit in a silk stocking" to his face. Now appointed to the sinecure office of vice-grand-elector, Talleyrand secretly betrayed him to the tsar—for cash. "Sire, it is up to you to save Europe," he told Alexander, "and you won't manage unless you resist Napoleon. The French people are civilized, their sovereign is not; the sovereign of Russia is civilized, but his people are not. Thus it is up to the sovereign of Russia to be the ally of the French people."

Napoleon had one more demand. "I tell you of one of the most grievous plights in which I ever found myself," Alexander told Catiche.* "Napoleon is obtaining a divorce and casting an eye on Anne." Their youngest sister Annette was just fourteen. "Mother," wrote Alexander "showed more calm over it than I should have believed." Maria concluded, "How wretched would the child's existence be united to a man of villainous character to whom nothing is sacred and without restraint since he does not believe in God? And would this sacrifice profit Russia? All of that makes me shudder." Alexander thought "the right course is hard to choose." Napoleon did not realize the Russians regarded him

---

* Catiche was no longer available, having married one of those stupid but sweet princes she preferred: Prince George of Oldenburg. She had previously been in love with the married Prince Peter Bagration, a Russified Georgian and impetuous general who had been Suvorov's protégé. Bagration was married to Katya, the daughter of Katinka Scavronskaya, now Countess Litta. During Paul's reign, Bagration had fallen in love with Katya, but she was in love with Peter von der Pahlen. When Paul heard about Bagration's infatuation, he insisted on sponsoring the marriage. "Bagration married the young [great] niece of the great Prince Potemkin," reported Langeron. "This rich and lustrous partner did not suit him. Bagration was a mere soldier, with the tone and manners of one, and he was extremely ugly. His wife was as white as he was black, and she would not be happy with such a husband for long . . ." Soon Bagration was in love with Grand Duchess Catiche—and Princess Bagration would be one of the most notorious women in Europe.

as a fiend. "I'm happy with Alexander; I think he is with me," he told Josephine. "Were he a woman, I think I'd make him my lover."[6]

That love was soon to be tested. After his return, Alexander was more interested in promoting reform at home and seizing his own prizes abroad to rescue his damaged prestige. He launched his Swedish war to gobble up the Swedes' province of Finland which would safeguard the approaches to Petersburg. By February 1808, the Russian troops were floundering, so Alexander sent in Arakcheev. The Vampire reorganized the armies, enabling Alexander's best generals, the dependable Mikhail Barclay de Tolly and the ferocious Prince Bagration, to cross the ice and assault Stockholm. The Swedes agreed to cede Finland, which became a Russian grand duchy until 1917. "The peace is perfect," Alexander boasted to Catiche, "and absolutely the one I wanted. I cannot thank the Supreme Being enough."[7]

Napoleon now discovered the limits of his Russian alliance. In April 1809, Emperor Francis again went to war against Napoleon. Alexander fulfilled his promises by despatching 70,000 troops but with instructions not to help the French in the slightest. "It's not an alliance I have here," fulminated Napoleon. "I've been duped." At Wagram, Napoleon defeated the Austrians.

In November, Napoleon offered Alexander a settlement of the Polish question—in return for his own betrothal to Annette. "My sister could not do better," lied the tsar to Caulaincourt. Alexander started negotiating a "reciprocal agreement never to permit the re-establishment of Poland." The French agreed, but when Alexander insisted that Annette could not marry for two years, Napoleon reneged on the Polish deal, and instead married Emperor Francis's daughter Archduchess Marie-Louise. Annette was saved from the Corsican ogre, but the Romanovs had been insulted.

As for Napoleon, he started to despise Alexander with that special hatred reserved for the beloved mistress who ends a cherished affair. Napoleon insulted him as "a shifty Byzantine" and "a Greek of the lower empire, fake as a coin," comments that have defined Alexander ever since. Yet every ruler in Europe had to dissemble their real views and compromise with Napoleon: it was Napoleon's Icaran vanity that deluded him into believing that any of them meant their diplomatic expressions of loyalty. Alexander was a pragmatist living (and trying to stay alive and on his throne) in dangerous times who survived because of that same versatility which others might called dissembling. "His personality is by nature well meaning, sincere and loyal, and his sentiments and principles are elevated," observed Caulaincourt, "but beneath all this there exists an acquired royal dissimulation and a dogged persistence that nothing will overcome."[8]

Alexander and Napoleon were now preparing for war: there was no time to waste.

As Arakcheev toiled to improve the army, Speransky had proposed his reform of autocracy, so radical that nothing even approaching it would be conceded until 1905. Alexander half accepted it, creating a new Council of State and a nominal committee of ministers but, under attack from all sides, he continued to rule autocratically, as he had always done. Yet even this limited reform was a triumph for Speransky.

Vampire Arakcheev, a strangely thin-skinned melodramatist, jealously resigned as war minister in a disingenuous letter: "Sire, don't be angry with a man who's lived half his life without using flattery . . . You know the limits of my education which is why I feel I'm nothing more than a good officer . . ."

"I cannot hide from you my great surprise . . . Allow me to leave aside the title I bear and speak to you as a man to whom I am personally attached," replied an irritated Alexander, who needed Arakcheev. "At a time when I expect ardent and zealous help from all honest people, you abandon me, preferring your personal vanity."

They were reconciled when Alexander visited Arakcheev's estate, Gruzino. "It's a truly charming place," Alexander told Catiche. "The order that reigns here is unique . . . I'm sure there's nothing like it in the empire . . . The village streets have just that sort of tidiness that pleases me so much." But its bleak militaristic perfection came at a price.

Arakcheev ruled his serfs cruelly, grading his punishments: a whipping for a first offence but, for a second, a thrashing by his soldiers using clubs known as "Arakcheev sticks." Each serf carried a punishment book in which Arakcheev wrote comments such as: "If she doesn't know her prayers by Lent, I'll have her soundly whipped." The estate was really run by the extraordinary figure of Anastasia Minkina, a jet-haired serf girl who had been bought by Arakcheev and then manumitted. "Plump, with a grenadier's figure and fiery black eyes," she became housekeeper, mistress and then the mother of an illegitimate son. Afterwards Arakcheev married a young noble girl in Petersburg who was so horrified by his tyranny that she quickly left him. Afterwards he stuck to collecting pornography, while in Gruzino Minkina was allowed to terrorize his serfs with all the sadistic zeal of someone who had escaped their ranks.

Arakcheev refused to return as war minister but agreed to supervise his successor, Barclay de Tolly, from the Council of State as they prepared the army for war. In July 1810, Queen Louise of Prussia died, supposedly weakened by Napoleon's defeat of her nation. Alexander declared, "I swear to avenge her death." He considered an offensive against Napoleon. In December 1810, their relationship deteriorated further when Napoleon annexed Oldenburg, the duchy of Catiche's father-in-law. While neither wanted war, Alexander told him, if it came, "I will know how to fight." Napoleon hectored him about infringements of the British blockade—and started to plan an invasion of Russia.

Alexander sought Prussian support and obtained a promise from the Austrians that if they fielded a corps against Russia it would not actually fight. To the north, he allied himself with Sweden,* but to the south his troops struggled to defeat the Ottomans. That December, Alexander discussed with Czartoryski the creation of a Polish kingdom (with himself as king) to fight the French, but the prince shot down the tsar's plan: "the French and Poles are brothers" while the Russians were Poland's "bitterest enemies."

Napoleon and Alexander now learned of each other's offensive plans. "Everything is assuming a dark hue here," Alexander told Catiche in January 1811. "It seems blood will flow but I have done all humanly possible to avoid it."9

"What can reasonably be hoped of Napoleon?" Alexander asked Catiche on 5 July 1811. "Is he the man to relinquish a gain unless by force of arms? And have we the means to compel him?" The pressure was punishing. "Never have I led such a dog's life," he told his sister on 10 November. "Often in the week I get out of bed to sit at my desk and leave it only to eat a morsel alone and then go back until I go to bed." Arakcheev and Barclay increased the army's size, adopting the corps and division systems, ordered munitions, built fortifications, modernized the artillery, while Alexander, aided by Speransky, weighed the intelligence sent by his spymasters in Paris.† "We're on continual alert," he told Catiche. "Hostilities may start at any moment."

---

* Since the Vasa dynasty had no heirs, the Swedes chose a French revolutionary general, Marshal Jean-Baptiste Bernadotte, prince de Pontecorvo, as their crown prince: he became King Charles XIV. He ruled Sweden until 1844 and his dynasty still rules Sweden today.
† At the Paris embassy, Alexander's factotum Karl von Nesselrode processed Talleyrand's gossipy but expensive reports in which the tsar was codenamed "Louise" and Talleyrand himself was "Handsome Leander." Nesselrode was joined by Alexander's aide-de-camp Alexander Chernyshev, twenty-seven-year-old nephew of Catherine the Great's lover Lanskoy; Chernyshev ran a mole in Napoleon's War Ministry. He also gathered intelligence by dazzling Parisian salons and penetrating the boudoirs of the well-informed Parisiennes who "looked at each other like wild cats when the Northern Lovelace appeared," excited by "his attire, that waspish way of being enclosed in his suit, his hat with its plume, hair thrown in big tufts, that Tatar face, his almost perpendicular eyes . . ." according to Laure Junot, duchesse d'Abrantès, probably one of his conquests.

"I will not be the first to draw the sword," he told Caulaincourt, "but I will be the last to put it back in its sheath. If the fortune of war runs against me, I'd rather withdraw to Kamchatka [in eastern Siberia] than cede provinces." Caulaincourt was impressed: "People believe him to be weak but they are wrong," he informed Paris. "His amenable personality has limits and he won't go beyond them: these limits are as strong as iron." When Caulaincourt returned to Paris, he spent five hours trying to convince Napoleon not to attack Russia. "One good battle," retorted Napoleon, "will see the end of all your friend Alexander's fine resolutions."

Catiche, who now lived in Tver where her husband was governor, was one of the few with whom the tsar could discuss how to face the coming invasion. "I am here on sentry duty," Alexander told her on 21 November 1811. "Alas, I cannot use my ancient rights (it's your feet in question do you hear) to imprint most tender kisses in your bedroom at Tver." Incestuous foot-kissing aside, they discussed how to confront such an enemy, considering all outcomes—even losing Petersburg and Moscow. "You will recall I often foresaw" such sacrifices, he later wrote. "The actual loss of the two capitals was believed to be possible."

Alexander created a police ministry (another idea copied from Napoleon) under Alexander Balashov, whose spies reported discontent on every side. Catiche presided over a patriotic salon at her palace in Tver. She extended her patronage to the historian Nikolai Karamzin whose *Memoir on Ancient and Modern Russia* provided the intellectual ballast in her campaign against all things French, liberal—or connected to Speransky. Catiche's ally, once Paul's minister, Rostopchin told Alexander that "Even if unfortunate circumstances forced us to retreat, the Russian emperor would still be menacing in Moscow, terrifying in Kazan and invincible in Tobolsk."[10]

As for love, Alexander's relationship with Naryshkina was fracturing: their daughter Zinaida died. "I have lost my child and with her a part of the happiness I enjoyed in this world," he told Catiche. He was unfaithful with one of his sister's ladies-in-waiting, while Naryshkina too started affairs so that when she gave birth to her son Emmanuel the only certain thing about his paternity was that it could not be attributed to his father.* Yet their "little family" remained the most cherished part of his life. A letter from their daughter Sophie, aged five, catches their intimacy: "My dear papa, I'm so sorry you hurt yourself. I hope you will

* Emmanuel Naryshkin was distinguished only by his longevity: amazingly he served as a court chamberlain at the court of the last tsar, dying only in 1901. His mother Maria Naryshkina also lived a long life, remarrying after her husband's death and dying in 1854.

soon be well for I long to see you. I think of you every day. I send you my love and a kiss. Your little affectionate Sophie."

"The horizon grows darker and darker," Alexander told Catiche on 24 December. Napoleon, "the curse of the human race, becomes daily more abominable." In February 1812, Napoleon told Alexander: "I cannot disguise from myself that Your Majesty no longer has any friendship for me."

"Neither my feelings nor my politics have changed," replied Alexander. "Am I not allowed to suppose it is Your Majesty who has changed to me?" But he ended ominously: "If war must begin, I will know how to sell my life dearly."

In early 1812, War Minister Barclay warned him that he must wind up the Ottoman war: Napoleon was coming. Kutuzov forced the surrender of the Ottoman army in March, then negotiated the Peace of Bucharest, in which Russia gained Bessarabia and returned Wallachia.* Alexander hated Kutuzov for being correct at Austerlitz—but he rewarded him with the title of prince.

Catiche, aided by much of noble society, intensified her campaign against Speransky. Alexander appointed Rostopchin as governor-general of Moscow; while, inspired by Catiche and Arakcheev, his inquisitor Balashov fabricated a case against the loyal Speransky, who, in a bon mot true enough to hurt, had described Alexander as "too weak to govern and too strong to be governed." They discovered that Speransky had failed to share intelligence reports from Paris.

At 8 p.m. on 17 March, Alexander summoned Speransky for an agonizing two-hour confrontation at which the servitor, unjustly accused of treason, was sacked. Speransky found his wife in tears and Balashov waiting for him at his house, where he was arrested and exiled that very night. Alexander suffered: he admitted that "If someone cuts off your arm, you would shout and cry in pain," and he was full of resentment

---

* Bessarabia, the part of Moldavia between the Dnieper and Pruth rivers, was not his only southern conquest: after Paul's death, Alexander had formally annexed the main kingdom of Georgia, Kartli-Kakhetia. When Alexander's governor General Lazarev arrested the Dowager Queen Mariam, she stabbed him to death. She was brought to Petersburg, and it was feared she might assassinate Alexander. But, treated well, the murderous queen of Georgia became an exotic ornament of the Russian court, where she attended all the coronations and lived until 1850. In 1803, the Dadiani princes of Mingrelia on the Black Sea coast were taken under Russian protection. In 1809, King Solomon II of Imeretia, now allied to the Ottomans, fought Russian troops until in 1810, with Solomon surrounded, Alexander deposed him and annexed the kingdom. The Russians needed a port to link the Caucasus with Odessa: the best port was Soukhoumi, ruled by the princes of Abkhazia. These princes often changed their religion and names as power swung between the Ottomans and Russians, depending on who was winning. Now the prince of Abkhazia, Sefer Bey, converted to Orthodoxy and, as a Russian ally, changed his name to Prince Giorgi Shervashidze. He gave Russia access to Soukhoumi.

that the grandees had forced him to sacrifice his favourite. "*They* took away Speransky, who was my right hand," he complained pathetically—though he mused that Speransky "was really guilty only towards me alone having paid back my confidence with the blackest and most abominable ingratitude." Alexander knew he was "no traitor," but "the situation didn't allow a strict rigorous examination of the denunciations . . . ," he told Novosiltsev. "The enemy was knocking at the door of the empire" so "it was important to me not to seem guilty in the eyes of my subjects."

The sacrifice was for a higher cause. "I am playing the great game," Alexander said, adding that "The war about to break out is one for the independence of nations," for Napoleon now ruled a multinational empire of 45 million. If anything, Napoleon's Grande Armée was an army of nations, including a large Polish contingent, as well as Spaniards, Germans, Dutch, Italians, Austrians and even a squadron of Egyptian Mamluks.

On 14 April, as Napoleon prepared to leave his young wife and new baby son, the king of Rome, in Paris to take command of the largest invasion force so far in history, Alexander arrived in Vilna.[11]

On the night of 11 June, Alexander, now thirty-five, plump and balding, still dashing in his Semyonovsky uniform, was attending a ball at Bennigsen's estate near Vilna when Balashov whispered in his ear that Napoleon had crossed the Niemen. The invasion of Russia had started. He left the party to consult with his staff. Since Napoleon had gathered 615,000 men in total, with 415,000 in his initial force, he far outnumbered the Russians, who fielded roughly 250,000 in three armies. The First Army of the West of 136,000 was under the uninspiring war minister Barclay de Tolly. The Second Army of the West, deployed further south, numbering 57,000, was commanded by Prince Bagration, while the Third Army of 48,000 covered the south. Alexander agonized between the stolid Barclay, the leader of a "German" faction who favoured a staged withdrawal to lure the enemy into the interior, and the reckless Bagration, backed by the Russian faction who favoured immediate battle. If Alexander had appointed Bagration, the Russians would probably have been defeated somewhere around Vilna. But Alexander did not rate Bagration, so "I had no one better" than Barclay. Arakcheev became his indispensable henchman, running the rear as secretary for the empire for military affairs. "The entire French war," boasted Arakcheev, "passed through my hands."

Alexander—no tactician and always afraid of his father's fate—lacked the advantages possessed by Napoleon, who united in his person absolute command of politics and war. The invasion now looks like a supreme gamble, but Napoleon had thrice defeated Russian armies and, having studied Charles XII's invasion, he had no intention of conquering Russia nor of penetrating the interior. In a short three-week campaign, he would briskly destroy the Russian army in "one good battle" and force the weak tsar to accept terms. Alexander's advantages all depended on the unglamorous tactics of retreat, patience, endurance.

Alexander sent Balashov to offer Napoleon the choice of withdrawal or war "until Russian soil is entirely purged of the enemy." Napoleon advanced, but wrote back to claim that "The private feelings I bear for you are not in the least affected by these events." As Balashov left with his letter, Napoleon jokingly asked which was the best road to Moscow. "Sire, one can take whichever one wants," replied Balashov. "Charles XII went by way of Poltava." Napoleon had still not computed that this would be a different sort of war with a different species of enemy.

On 15 June, hours ahead of Napoleon himself, Alexander withdrew from Vilna as Barclay with the main army headed towards the fortified military camp at Drissa, the brainchild of a Prussian general. On 5 July, Barclay swiftly retired from the ill-chosen camp, aiming to meet up with Bagration's army. Some of Alexander's advisers realized that his presence with the army was not an advantage. Deference to the emperor inhibited frank expression of opinion. Arakcheev, Balashov and his new state secretary Admiral Shishkov, prompted by Catiche, signed a petition, left among his papers, asking him to leave the army. "You must be enduring a martyrdom," Catiche wrote, "but the more you can conquer yourself and be emperor, the more you will do your sheer duty. I believe you quite as able as your generals but you have to play the role not only of captain but of ruler. If you make mistakes it all falls on your head." Next day, Alexander told Arakcheev: "I've read your paper."

Alexander agreed to sacrifice my "pride on the altar of utility because I . . . inspired no trust in the troops" and would leave the army, telling his soldiers: "I shall never abandon you." But the strategy had not changed. "Our entire goal," he wrote to Bagration, who was crying out for battle, "must be directed towards gaining time and drawing out the war as long as possible." As he left, to everyone's relief, he told Barclay: "Goodbye, general, goodbye again. I entrust to you my army; don't forget I have no other."

On 11 July Alexander rallied the home front in Moscow, where he was moved by a crowd whose size and fervour "brought tears to my eyes." But Empress Elizabeth put it best: "From the moment Napoleon crossed our borders it was as if an electric spark burst over Russia."[12]

\*

As Napoleon pursued Barclay in search of his decisive victory, the war minister withdrew eastwards and joined up with Bagration close to Smolensk. The Russians stalwartly defended the city and Napoleon thought that finally he would get his battle: "At last I have them." Again Napoleon was disappointed. He had planned to spend the winter in Smolensk; instead he occupied a ruined city. He should have withdrawn; disease was already ravaging the Grand Armée—but pride drew him on.

The fighting allowed Barclay to retreat once again. His withdrawals and vacillations drove Bagration, Suvorov's fierce protégé, into a rage. "Russians are not made to flee," he protested to Arakcheev, his way of informing the emperor. "We've become worse than Prussians!"

When Napoleon took Smolensk, Bagration was "ashamed to wear the uniform. What an imbecile. Minister Barclay is running away . . . This disgusts me so much I'll go crazy!" Catiche later admitted, "The thing I most regret in life is not having been a man in 1812," and she blamed Alexander for his generals' disagreements: "You've left them in perfect indecision."

Back in Petersburg, where he spent the summer, Alexander recognized the "great ferocity against the war minister due to the irresolution of his conduct and the disorder with which he does his duties," which had not been helped by "the feud between him and Bagration." Serfs were restive, nobles panicking, the Motherland in jeopardy. Russia had to give battle—or the tsar would lose his throne.

Alexander was tempted to take command of the army himself, but Catiche warned him starkly that though "the enemy will be in Moscow in ten days, in God's name do not command in person for we need without delay a leader in whom the troops have confidence and on that score, you inspire none!" Alexander wanted anyone except the popular Kutuzov, who was in Petersburg in charge of the militia, while Catiche's husband urged, "Bagration is adored, the army longs for him. You don't like him but your glory is at stake. Trust the prince with the command!"

Alexander called an Extraordinary Committee of veteran retainers and new favourites to choose a commander. "Everyone wanted Kutuzov," whom "we chose as being the oldest," Alexander reported to Catiche, and "in great favour among the public." Bennigsen became his chief of staff. "I find it necessary to appoint one general-in-chief for all the active armies," Alexander wrote to Kutuzov on 8 August, "and your distinguished military rank, patriotism and long record of great deeds wins my confidence."

The sixty-six-year-old Kutuzov possessed the Slavic charisma lacked by Barclay and the world-weary caution lacked by Bagration. In the 1860s, Leo Tolstoy's novel *War and Peace* presented him as an oracular

personification of the soul of the Russian nation; in 1941, Stalin promoted him as a genius; he was neither. But this protégé of Potemkin and
Suvorov had vast experience, having served as a governor-general and
as ambassador to the sultan. He was wise, unflappable and sly, a nature
symbolized by his eye wound: bullets had (not once but twice, in 1773
and 1787) passed fortuitously through his right temple and out through
his right eye without affecting his judgement or shaking his sangfroid.
If he could no longer stay awake during a war council nor mount a horse,
this priapic antique concealed two peasant-girl mistresses disguised as
Cossack boys among his staff. Kutuzov promised the tsar that he would
rather die than surrender Moscow. He was to fight a battle yet preserve
the army, two contradictory promises that could not possibly be fulfilled.

Far from the fray, Alexander, almost alone at Kamenny Ostrov, had
to watch impotently as Kutuzov made the decisions. So instead he concentrated on diplomacy and logistics, ruling through Arakcheev, their
intimacy revealed by this note from the tsar insisting that the general
change his plans for dinner: "The simplest thing is to say you're ill or
that I've invited you to dinner. My dinner will certainly be better!"

Alexander opened relations with Britain and signed an alliance with
Bernadotte of Sweden, freeing up his Finnish corps to fight the French.
But he found consolation in mysticism inspired by a childhood friend,
Prince Alexander Golitsyn. Until 1803 Golitsyn had been a notorious Lo-
thario, but after Alexander unexpectedly appointed him ober-procurator
of the Holy Synod, he underwent a Damascene conversion to mysticism.

"In moments such as those in which we find ourselves," Alexander
wrote to Golitsyn, "even the most hardened person feels a return towards
his Creator . . . I surrender myself to this feeling . . . I find there my only
consolation, my sole support. This sentiment alone sustains me." Golitsyn was not only his spiritual brother and minister for religion—but
also one of his secret policemen: as postmaster, he perlustrated private
letters and reported on their contents to the tsar.

Alexander started to see the war against Napoleon as a way to create
a new Christian fraternity of kings that would bring about the reign of
peace on earth. Golitsyn advised reading the Bible. "My dear, it seems
to me a whole new world is revealed to my eyes," Alexander wrote,
thanking him for his suggestions. His new beliefs, however, a univer-
salist Christianity, with elements of freemasonry and pantheism based
on a mixture of biblical reading and evangelical fervour, had more in
common with Protestantism than with Orthodoxy.

Far to the south, as Kutuzov took command of the army, he faced
a cruel dilemma, telling Rostopchin, governor-general of Moscow: "I
haven't yet resolved what is more important: to lose the army or to lose

Moscow. In my opinion, the loss of Moscow would entail the loss of Russia."[13]

On 26 August, Kutuzov chose to make his stand near the village of Borodino, ninety miles from Moscow, in a battle between 125,000 Russians with 624 guns, who were packed into a salient defended by newly built redoubts, and 130,000 men of the Grande Armée with 587 guns. Kutuzov planned for a defensive battle. The redoubts were to bleed the French. In his earlier battles, Napoleon had prided himself on devising an ingenious flanking manoeuvre, but at Borodino he ordered repeated frontal assaults against the dug-in Russians and particularly their Grand Redoubt. The fighting, often hand to hand, bayonet to bayonet, was primal in its savagery, and the firing-power of the cannonades of a thousand guns on a tiny battlefield, packed with men and animals, in the flamboyant uniforms of its time, turned it into the most gorgeously dressed abattoir in history; the redoubts changed hands repeatedly, taking an atrocious toll on both sides. The slaughter was astonishingly intense, "the bloodiest single day in the history of warfare" until the First World War: the French lost 35,000 wounded or dead, the Russians 45,000, with Bagration fatally wounded. Just as the battle might possibly have been won, Napoleon was asked to throw in his reserves. He refused to commit his elite Imperial Guards. As night fell, both dazed commanders believed uneasily that they had just won; Kutuzov felt sure that the battle would extend into a second day—but it was Napoleon who had failed to win a clear victory out of a lack of both imagination and boldness, two qualities which he had never lacked before.

"The battle was the bloodiest of recent times," Kutuzov reported to Alexander, declaring that the Russians had kept possession of the battlefield, definition of victory. "I defeated Napoleon," he boasted to his wife. The tsar promoted Kutuzov to marshal and awarded him 100,000 roubles. As the news of the butcher's bill came in, Kutuzov realized that his plan to fight on the next day was impossible: "Our extraordinary losses, especially the wounding of key generals, forced me to withdraw down the Moscow road." During the night—and contrary to his report to Alexander—Kutuzov pulled back several miles. Napoleon claimed victory: the road to Moscow was open, and he dubbed Borodino "the battle of Moscow." Ultimately both Napoleon and Kutuzov saw that Borodino had been a ghastly draw. "I ought to have died at the battle of Moscow," Napoleon later admitted in exile, but it did decide the fate of the city.

On 1 September, Kutuzov held a war council in a peasant hut in Fili, where the old general understood that, now facing the choice of losing the army or Moscow, he must save the army: "Napoleon is a torrent but

Moscow is the sponge that will soak him up." Kutuzov took the decision but this was exactly the choice that Alexander had avoided by leaving the army, and it would have been an impossible one for a monarch to make. Kutuzov marched his army through the streets of Moscow and out the other side; he abandoned the ancient capital, without fully informing the governor-general, Count Rostopchin, who ordered the evacuation of the entire population. Captured capitals, from Vienna to Berlin, had usually greeted Napoleon with cowed aristocratic politeness. This was a sign that this was a new national war *à l'outrance*. In scenes of dystopic exodus, the roads teemed and seethed with the long-suffering, trudging masses, carts heaped with a lifetime's belongings, as multitudes, half a million people, the entire Muscovite population, fled the city, heading eastwards. Rostopchin opened the jails and, as the city emptied, he decided that "If I am asked, I won't hesitate to say, 'Burn the capital rather than deliver it to the enemy.'" Kutuzov and his generals had already blown up ammunition stores as they left. At a secret meeting in the governor's house, Rostopchin and Police Minister Balashov ordered the burning of further buildings, which started an unstoppable conflagration that tore through the wooden structures. Embarrassingly, Rostopchin's two city mansions were among the few buildings that did not catch fire. Afterwards, when the French approached his estate at Voronovo, a palace packed with French luxuries and Roman antiquities, Rostopchin ordered it burned, leaving a sign that read: "Frenchmen, I abandon to you my two houses in Moscow . . . with their contents worth half a million roubles. Here you will find only ashes."

On 3 September, as Kutuzov headed south-westwards and set up a well-placed camp on the Old Kaluga Road, no one greeted Napoleon at the gates of Moscow. Only a few French tutors, actresses and lethiferous bands of looters haunted the streets as Moscow burned for six days. Napoleon was spooked by what he saw. He should have withdrawn at once; his presence in Moscow broke his cardinal rule that he must conquer armies, not cities—but he had not been able to resist the storied city of golden domes. He moved into the Kremlin and waited to negotiate from within a city of ashes.[14]

"Moscow is taken," Catiche informed Alexander on 6 September in a scrawled note. "Some things are beyond comprehension. Don't forget your resolution: no peace and you have hope of recovery of your honour!" Alexander was devastated by this news, exasperated by Kutuzov and his own helplessness. "Kutuzov had not warned me he had decided to retreat four miles to recover," he told Catiche, and "Those fatal four miles poisoned all the delight I had in victory." Alexander protested: "From

29 August, I've had no reports from you," he told Kutuzov. "Then on 1 September, I heard the sad news that you've decided to leave Moscow with the army. You can imagine the effect of this news and your silence torments my astonishment!"

A week later the émigré French colonel Alexandre Michaud, one of the tsar's favourite adjutants, arrived from Kutuzov. "My God—what sad news you bring me, colonel," sighed Alexander as he read the marshal's report: "The occupation of Moscow is not the conquest of Russia. I move with the army in the direction of Tula to preserve the immense resources prepared in our central provinces."

Petersburg was bewildered. Revolution seemed possible. When Alexander entered Kazan Cathedral, he was received in sepulchral silence. Two days later, after no word from Kutuzov, he wrote: "Not receiving any news from you about the accidents befalling the armies entrusted to you, I can't hide my own anxiety and the depression caused in St. Petersburg. I want you to set yourself a rule: send reports to me every two days!"

His brother Constantine, whom Catiche called a "hopeless" master of hysterical hindsight, now joined his mother and Chancellor Rumiantsev in a demand for peace talks, but Alexander refused, stiffened by the sister who longed to fight herself: "My dear, no peace and even if you were at Kazan, no peace!"

"Be persuaded," he replied, "my resolution to fight is more unshakeable than ever: I would prefer to cease to be than compromise with the monster who is the scourge of mankind." Then even Catiche wavered: "You are loudly accused of your empire's misfortune."

Alexander kept his nerve but painfully admitted that "As to talent, I may be lacking it but it cannot be acquired . . . Napoleon who blends the most terrible roguery with the most transcendent talent is backed by the whole of Europe," so "it's hardly astonishing if I meet with reverses." He warned Catiche that Napoleon plotted to turn her against him: family loyalty was essential. "I am more determined than ever to fight to the end."*

Sending Michaud back to Kutuzov, Alexander made clear he would achieve victory and, even if he lost his throne, he would happily live as a peasant eating potatoes before he signed a peace: "Napoleon or me. Me or him! We cannot reign simultaneously. I've learned to understand this, he won't deceive me!"

---

* At this supreme moment, Catiche needed his help. Her ex-lover "Bagration died yesterday: I told you he holds documents that might cruelly compromise me if they fell into strange hands." These were her love letters of course. Alexander reported back that he had got the papers.

To everyone, the destruction of Moscow seemed an apocalyptic moment, and it stimulated Alexander's growing mysticism. "The burning of Moscow illuminated my soul and the judgement of God on the frozen battlefield filled my heart with the warmth of faith." It was a stronger Alexander who now emerged, despatching his adjutant Alexander Chernyshev to plan the counter-offensive. Chernyshev led cavalry raids against the French, the beginning of a partisan war against the invaders.

As Kutuzov rested his infantry and allowed his cavalry to harass French lines while winter approached, Napoleon wasted over a month in the Kremlin: "I considered the business done." He expected Alexander, whom he still regarded as weak, to negotiate terms. Instead he was now discovering that the Russians were fighting a patriotic war such as he had experienced only in Spain. "This is a war of extermination," he explained. "To burn their own cities! A demon has got into them. What a people!" The demon was the spark of the Russian nation, the war was its crucible. Kutuzov mocked Napoleon for failing "to spot a trap visible to the whole world" and his "absurd cheek in offering peace when he could no longer make war." But Alexander berated Kutuzov, "Nothing's been done to take action against the enemy," and warned him: "Remember you still have to account to the offended nation for the loss of Moscow."

On 6 October, Kutuzov managed to bloody the French at Tarutino— just as Napoleon finally realized that he had fatally misjudged Russia and Alexander. Winter was coming and he had to retreat fast. He left the Kremlin with the Grande Armée. In pique, he ordered the Kremlin to be destroyed. When he heard the distant crump of explosives he announced that the "ancient citadel of tsars no longer exists." But the charges, like the campaign, never ignited.[15]

Kutuzov wept when he heard that Napoleon was retreating, but he was in danger of being outflanked when the Grande Armée headed for Maloyaroslavets. On 11–12 October, at the closely fought Battle of Maloyaroslavets, Kutuzov ruined Napoleon's hope of an orderly retreat. The old marshal followed in a parallel march, harassing the French but keeping his distance.

Napoleon sent a peace offer to Alexander. "Peace?" replied Alexander. "But as yet we've not made war. My campaign is only just beginning." He was frustrated by Kutuzov's slow pursuit. On 3–6 November, Kutuzov bruised the passing French at Krasnyi in a rolling skirmish in which he took over 20,000 prisoners and killed a further 10,000. "Yet another victory," Kutuzov told his wife, but he was keen to avoid more battles. "I'm by no means sure," said Kutuzov, "the total destruction of Napoleon would be of such benefit."

His forces were down to fewer than 60,000 men and he let the other armies, under the German-born general, Prince Peter Sayn-Wittgenstein from the north and Admiral Chichagov from the south, take over the pursuit. Kutuzov had let Napoleon escape. "It is with extreme sadness that I realize that the hope of wiping away the dishonour of Moscow's loss by cutting off the enemy's retreat has been lost," wrote Alexander, thanks to Kutuzov's "inexplicable inactivity." Kutuzov offered to resign. When he reoccupied Smolensk, Alexander bit his lip and awarded him a resounding new title: prince of Smolensk.

As two Russian armies converged on him, Napoleon and the remnants of his army, harried by Cossacks and facing total destruction, raced to cross the Berezina River. In a feat of French engineering, luck, courage and Russian incompetence, Napoleon crossed the Berezina and then, abandoning his men to Russian winter and revenge, he raced for Paris. "It seems the All-Powerful has brought on the head of this monster all the miseries he intended for us," Alexander wrote with grim satisfaction to both Arakcheev and Catiche as Napoleon's retreat turned to rout in the first week of November.

"The delight is general," replied Catiche, though she reflected her brother's view that Prince Kutuzov-Smolensky "shines with splendour he doesn't deserve." On 11 December,* Alexander arrived back in Vilna to retake supreme command from the ailing Kutuzov, appointing as chief of staff his intimate Prince Peter Volkonsky who became, along with Arakcheev, his omnipresent lieutenant. The two men loathed each other. Vilna with its 30,000 corpses resembled a vast refrigerated mortuary. Entering a gruesome warehouse where "they'd stacked corpses as high as the walls," he saw something moving. "I suddenly spotted, amid those inanimate bodies, living beings." The emperor finally got the chance to reflect on the fall of Napoleon, telling his pretty courtier Sophie de Tisenhaus about the irresistible gaze of those "light-grey eyes . . . What a career he's ruined! The spell is broken."

Kutuzov had no intention of pursuing Napoleon into Europe, in which he was supported by the dowager empress and Catiche. Russia had lost 150,000 men; the army was down to 100,000. But Alexander had a different vision of a personal and national mission, one that was now decisive in European history. He left Nikolai Saltykov, that relic of the reigns of Elizaveta and Catherine, in charge in Petersburg, and

---

* On 15 December 1812, Catiche lost her beloved husband George of Oldenburg, aged only twenty-four.

advanced into Europe to destroy Napoleon. "You have saved not just Russia," he told his soldiers, "but all of Europe."[16]

On 1 January 1813, Alexander and his army crossed the Niemen into Napoleon's empire, immediately reaching out to the Prussian king, who by late February had joined this new alliance against France, fielding 150,000 Russians and 80,000 Prussians, all to be funded by Britain.

This newly confident Alexander summoned the seven attractive wives of his generals—but not his own empress—to join him in "a small feminine court." The first to arrive was Princess Zinaida Volkonskaya, twenty-three years old, sensitive, cultured and a sublime singer, unhappily married to a ne'er-do-well adjutant who was also accompanying the emperor. As they travelled, Alexander often called on the ladies, but he visited Zinaida alone. "You alone have the rare talent of making all those around you more lovable since you yourself are full of indulgent kindness."

Germany was the new battleground. Napoleon astonished Europe with the speed with which he rebuilt his army. Now Alexander had recruited Prussia to his coalition, he needed Austria, whose foreign minister, the thirty-nine-year-old Count Clemens von Metternich, hoped to restore Austrian status by escaping the French alliance and mediating with Russia. Son of a minor aristocrat from the Rhineland, he had risen fast to become Emperor Francis's leading adviser, a wealthy magnate and a prolific lover. Metternich's "blue-eyed benevolent gaze," wrote the novelist Stendhal, "would fool God himself." Metternich's letters to his many mistresses were filled with vain boasts and emotional neediness, but in the service of Austria he played his hand skilfully. If he was smug, he had much to be smug about. This was the man Alexander had to coax away from Napoleon.

In early March, Alexander's army, co-operating with the Prussians, advanced into Saxony. On 16 April, Kutuzov died, freeing Alexander of his *bête noire*. In Dresden for Easter, Alexander was now convinced he was doing "a sacred duty." He wrote to Golitsyn: "Since Petersburg, not a day passes without my reading the Holy Scripture." He celebrated with his troops: "At midnight we sang the Pascal hymn on the banks of the Elbe. It would be difficult to express to you the emotion I felt penetrate me as I looked back on this year and reflected where Divine Providence has brought us." But his piety did not get in the way of his affair with the married Zinaida. Meanwhile Napoleon, fielding a new army, was advancing.

In late April and early May, the allies, facing Napoleon at Lützen and Bautzen, commanded by the mediocre Wittgenstein and Alexander, were narrowly defeated, though their armies remained intact. The Prussians despaired, but Alexander's cool optimism reassured them. He sacked Wittgenstein and reappointed Barclay, who bought time by defeating the French in smaller engagements while Alexander worked on the Austrians.

"We are all in the best possible spirits," the tsar wrote to Zinaida on 14 May. "Our troops distinguished themselves even if the final result was not quite as successful as we had hoped," but "to all the hopes I have for military success, I must add the sincerest one for the joy of seeing you as soon as possible!" Then he declared his feelings for her. His love was accepted.

"I've often said I was afraid of disturbing you when I expressed my sentiments to you," he wrote, because "I wanted to be sure you yourself were sure too and had not misunderstood. It's my heart that now dictates these words to you!" The tsar added that the love letter was being delivered to her by her own husband, Prince Nikita Volkonsky, whom Alexander mocked as "the ordinary post." On 4 June, Napoleon, exhausted and short of cavalry, agreed to an armistice. Alexander "much to my regret had to agree to this." It turned out to be Napoleon's mistake.

Setting up headquarters at Reichenbach, Emperor Francis and Metternich arrived to negotiate with both Alexander and Napoleon. Fearing that the fall of Napoleon would herald Russian domination, Metternich offered him the chance to keep most of his conquests, including much of Germany, in return for making concessions to Russia, Austria and Prussia, a balance-of-power compromise. Metternich found himself close to Ratiborschitz, the palace of his new mistress, Wilhelmina de Biron, duchesse de Sagan, who, as granddaughter of Empress Anna's favourite, was a semi-detached Russian. At exhausting meetings at Sagan's chateau, Alexander tried to persuade Metternich to declare war on France.

Alexander's affair with Zinaida was at its height and he anticipated the "reward"—sexual, presumably—that he hoped to receive: "I await the moment of our meeting with the liveliest impatience . . . Forever yours heart and soul. A." Days later he joined her at Teplitz where the coalition leaders were gathered. "I am impatient to be at your feet," he told Zinaida. "May I come to you between 7 and 8?" Afterwards he wrote, "I'm so grateful for the indulgence with which you received me. These moments will never be erased from my mind." The erotic and the mystical were combined in him. After one enjoyable assignation, he declared that "My only ambition is to give peace to the universe."

Sweden, under its crown prince and ex-Napoleonic marshal

Bernadotte, had already joined the alliance, which was now boosted by £2 million of British cash. Napoleon agreed to extend the armistice and negotiate a compromise in Prague. Metternich was delighted, Alexander furious, but the breathing space had its advantages. "It gives me hope of seeing you," Alexander wrote to Catiche, who was in Prague to canvass the Austrians. "I can't thank you enough for all you've already done," said the tsar. "I regret you've said nothing yet about Metternich and what's needed to have him wholly ours: I have the necessary funds so don't be shy!" The tactics of bribery, Alexander confided, "are the safest of all."

In July, when the negotiations opened, Napoleon went back on his word, offering only a return to the status quo before 1812. On 1 August, Austria declared war, throwing another 130,000 men into the field against France, its last condition being that Prince Karl von Schwarzenberg be appointed commander-in-chief. Alexander "kissed and pummelled me as if I was his long-lost brother," wrote the modest Schwarzenberg, who complained bitterly to his wife about Alexander's entourage: "I have to put up with weaklings, fops, pedlars of crackpot schemes, intriguers, blockheads, gasbags, nit-pickers, in a word, innumerable vermin."

On 5 August, the armies set off towards Dresden which they could have taken. Instead the clumsiness and procrastination of multinational command, exacerbated by "Tsar Alexander's unfortunate compulsion to meddle in decision-making," allowed Napoleon to take Dresden. The allies retreated, but two days later the Russians redeemed themselves. Commanded by Barclay and spearheaded by Alexander's Guards, they defeated the French at a savage little battle at Kulm, watched by the tsar. Those days would provide his favourite memories, for at last Alexander, the joke of Austerlitz and liability of 1812, had won military laurels. The tide had turned.[17]

As he wrangled his allies towards France, Alexander and the monarchs were accompanied by a bedraggled caravan of courtiers, *grandes dames* and *grandes horizontales*—among them Prussians, Corsicans, Frenchmen, even Laharpe, the tsar's boyhood tutor. The ministers lolloped along in mud-spattered formal dress with swords and decorations as they spent their boring days soaked in the rain, stranded on marshy roads until suddenly terrified by the roar of cannon and the sight of shattered bodies, sharing hovels at night and, if not too fastidious, raddled tavern whores. Alexander the soldier kept up with his troops, so that Metternich and his own ministers were always trying to catch up with him. "Throughout military operations," Metternich told his mistress Wilhelmina, "I'd spend evenings with His Imperial Majesty from 8/9 p.m. to midnight."

"I lead a dog's life," Alexander told Catiche on 5 October, "and can scarcely cope with the terrible pressure of work on my hands." Alexander thanked the Supreme Being. "My belief that God reserves for himself alone the power to conduct everything and my confidence in him has grown stronger," he wrote to his mystical brother, Golitsyn. "With us, everything goes brilliantly."

After abandoning Dresden, Napoleon massed 203,000 men at Leipzig where the allies, with 326,000, challenged his hold on Germany. On 4 October 1813, Alexander, accompanied by Francis, Frederick William and Bernadotte of Sweden, presided over the Battle of Nations, where 500,000 men with 2,000 guns slashed and blasted each other for three days. For once, Alexander's heated protest at Schwarzenberg's plan saved the allies from disaster. When enemy cavalry threatened the tsar's own position, he directed a charge by Cossack Guards that scattered them.

Only Arakcheev shamed himself by fleeing when a shell landed near by. Alexander was ebullient. "Almighty God has granted us a striking victory over the famous Napoleon," he told Golitsyn. "And here we are two days' march from Frankfurt!"*

Alexander was in a hurry to invade France, but Metternich saw Austria balancing Russia and France. "I argued at least three hours with your fine emperor. I told him off as I do my son," he boasted to Wilhelmina. "I dashed over to Meiningen to arrange a few points in the destiny of the world with Emperor Alexander." By the end of October, they were in Frankfurt where Alexander found a new mistress, Madame Bethmann, a bosomy Dutch banker's wife whom Metternich mocked as "a Dutch cow."

At Basel on Russian New Year's Day, Alexander, Francis, Frederick William and 200,000 men crossed the Rhine into France. The tsar pushed for a quick advance on Paris, which horrified Metternich. The Austrians wanted only a partial invasion to force Napoleon to compromise and possibly leave his son on the throne.

A new civilian now joined the caravan. Viscount Castlereagh, the

---

* The fortunes of war delayed some lovers, facilitated others. "It was in the midst of great strategic movements, princess, that I received your delightful letter," wrote Alexander to Zinaida from Leipzig, apologizing that her latest love letter had been lost for two days during the excitement of battle in the pockets of Peter Volkonsky's "innumerable wardrobe before I could have it, making the excuse he'd left it in a third coat, though he was already wearing two." During a rare romantic moment on the field of Leipzig heaped with bodies, Prince Peter Volkonsky found a nineteen-year-old French girl weeping for her fallen French husband. Though his wife was near by in Alexander's retinue, Volkonsky picked her up and made her his mistress. No wonder he forgot that he was carrying the emperor's love letters in his pocket! Later he took his mistress to the Congress of Vienna, where she visited him nightly in the Hofburg Palace dressed as a boy.

tall, laconic British foreign secretary and paymaster of the coalition, distrusted Alexander's overbearing swagger and mystical rapture, both moods alien to British phlegm. "The most dangerous for us," Castlereagh told his prime minister, the Earl of Liverpool, on 6 January 1814, "is the *chevaleresque* tone of Emperor Alexander. He has a *personal* feeling about Paris, distinct from political-military considerations," a keenness to parade his Guards through Paris to avenge Moscow. Yet Castlereagh agreed with the tsar that Napoleon had to go.

Alexander now ordered Schwarzenberg to march on Paris. Schwarzenberg refused. When Metternich and Castlereagh caught up with them at Langres on 13 January, they found the tsar in a frenzy. "Tsar Alexander has had another of those fits of buffoonery that often seize him," wrote Schwarzenberg. "Heaven protect us!" Castlereagh wished the tsar would be "more measured in his projects . . . more intelligible in his own views." But it was easy to misunderstand Alexander. He did see the fall of Napoleon as his own personal apotheosis and millenarian triumph, but this shrewd analyst understood the Corsican monster better than the others: lasting peace could be made only in Paris. Castlereagh wanted the Bourbons restored to the throne. Alexander entertained a farrago of schemes oscillating between a regency for Napoleon's son under Empress Marie-Louise and a constitutional monarchy or a progressive republic with Bernadotte as consul or king. Napoleon, recapturing his old flair, won a series of battles but success made him more intransigent. On 26 February at Chaumont, the allies agreed not to make a separate peace and to fight Napoleon to the end.

"I had in my heart an invincible desire to place all at the discretion of God," Alexander told Golitsyn. "While the council met I left for a moment, fell to my knees in my bedroom and there before the Lord made an effusion of my heart." The Lord answered with "a hard resolution of will and a kind of blazing clarity of purpose: take Paris!" Then the Prussian General Blücher, a gnarled cavalryman who shared Alexander's bellicosity, defeated Napoleon and was ready to advance— until he suffered a nervous breakdown and went blind, convinced he was pregnant with an elephant (fathered by a Frenchman). The advance faltered. Had a septuagenarian cavalryman pregnant with an elephant saved Napoleon?[18]

Napoleon, seeking death in battle and refusing to contemplate a last stand in Paris, veered east, hoping to divert the allies. But Cossacks captured a note from him to his wife Marie-Louise revealing his plans. Talleyrand was treacherously encouraging Alexander, who discovered from intercepted letters of Paris's governor to Napoleon that the capital was ill defended. Here the tsar was again decisive: on 11 March the allies refused the bait and turned on Paris.

On 12 March, the Russians defeated Marshal Marmont outside Paris. Napoleon had ordered Empress Marie-Louise, his three-year-old son the king of Rome and her councillors to leave the city, but Talleyrand, seeing himself as a regent for the baby king, begged her to stay. Instead she abandoned Paris and ruined her son's prospect of keeping the throne. On 18 March, the city surrendered. At 2 a.m., in bed at the Château de Bondy on the outskirts, Alexander was brought the act of capitulation; insouciantly he put it under his pillow and went to sleep. At dawn, he despatched his adjutant Mikhail Orlov* and then Nesselrode to Paris to seek out Talleyrand, whom Napoleon rightly described as "gold mixed with shit." Defying Napoleon's orders, he had artfully remained in Paris. He warned Alexander against assassins in the Elysée Palace and invited him to stay with him instead. When some of his German courtiers suggested destroying Paris, Alexander retorted that God had made him powerful "to secure peace in the world." He added: "whether in the palaces or the ruins, 'Europe will sleep tonight in Paris.'"[19]

"The imagination can hardly take in the idea of the Russians in Paris!" exclaimed Catiche. At 11 a.m., Alexander, sporting the undress uniform of his Chevalier-Gardes, escorted by the Cossack Life Guards in scarlet tunics and blue baggy trousers, astride his horse *Eclipse*, a gift from Napoleon, rode into Paris, Frederick William on his left, Schwarzenberg on his right, followed by Constantine and (the newly promoted) Marshal Barclay and his Guards. The tsar exchanged banter with Paris ladies in the crowd: "I don't come as an enemy," he said.

"We've been awaiting you," they cried.

"If I didn't come sooner, it was due to French bravery," he replied. Then he reviewed the Guards on the Champs-Elysées.

At 6 p.m., Alexander rode up to the Hôtel Talleyrand on rue Saint-Florentin, where he took over the first floor, Nesselrode the second, Talleyrand the entresol, while the Cossack and Preobrazhensky Guards protected the mansion, which was now the headquarters of the Russian empire. When Napoleon offered to abdicate in favour of his son, Talleyrand and Alexander entertained the idea, but the absence of Marie-Louise and the king of Rome undermined it. At a meeting on 19 March, Alexander "cast a glance at Prince Schwarzenberg who agreed with a nod as did the King of Prussia": no more Bonapartes! "France

---

* The brothers Mikhail and Alexei Orlov, both Guards officers and adjutants to the tsar, were the illegitimate sons of Count Fyodor Orlov, brother of Catherine the Great's lover Grigory.

must be strong and great," he said, finally agreeing to the restoration of Louis XVIII if limited by a constitution. Alexander "speaks much less nonsense than I'd have believed," Metternich reported to Francis. Next day, Talleyrand summoned the Senate, which elected him as premier and deposed the Bonapartes.

At 3 a.m. on 24 March, Marshals Marmont, Ney and Macdonald, accompanied by Caulaincourt, arrived to persuade the tsar to back a regency for the king of Rome. Alexander distrusted the Bourbons and, if the army was still Bonapartist, he was tempted to back the king of Rome as Napoleon II. But, overnight, Marmont's troops surrendered to the Austrians. When the marshals returned in the morning, Alexander learned that their troops were not as Bonapartist as they claimed—and reluctantly turned back to the Bourbons. "The emperor," he said, "must abdicate unconditionally." As the four disappointed Bonapartists left, Alexander called Caulaincourt back to discuss what territory Napoleon should receive—Corsica, Sardinia, Corfu? Caulaincourt suggested Elba. Napoleon abdicated.

Alexander realized that the Bourbons would not survive without respecting "the past 25 years of glory," but on 18 May 1814 he signed a treaty with the newly arrived Louis XVIII that was foolishly generous to Napoleon, whom he insisted become the emperor of Elba. He sent his general-aide-de-camp Count Pavel Shuvalov to accompany the fallen ruler to his minuscule empire. "At last the great aim is achieved," Alexander told Catiche on 20 April. "Napoleon no longer tyrannizes France and Europe." This gigantic and triumphant enterprise of war, diplomacy and logistics—the supply of Russian armies from Moscow to Paris—was overwhelmingly Alexander's achievement, unequalled by any Russian ruler.

"Paris," as Metternich told Wilhelmina, "was a vast beautiful madhouse" in which Alexander much preferred the flashy glamour of the Bonapartes to the prudish sanctimony of the Bourbons. The tsar visited the two ex-empresses Marie-Louise and Josephine, from whom he bought Canova statues and Caravaggio paintings for the Hermitage.

The most powerful man in Europe was magnanimous, but there was nothing modest in the conviction that he was God's chosen. "The feeling that prompts me," he explained to Catiche, "is the purest desire to grow morally perfect." He celebrated Easter with Orthodox and Catholic priests on the Place de la Concorde: "our spiritual triumph has reached its goal" but "I was amused to see the French marshals jostle each other to kiss the Russian cross!"[20]

*

Catiche, who was revelling in her brother's kudos—"to be your sister is the best passport"—planned to meet Alexander in London. Their junket there turned out to be a comedy of Russian insolence and British boorishness. Waiting for her boat at Rotterdam, she was accosted by the duke of Clarence (the future William IV), a coarse sailor who lived with an actress. "The handsome sailor," she joked, "is still at his tricks. I submit myself to the Creator but this only I know for sure: I shall not become Mrs. Clarence."

Catiche stirred up trouble from the moment she arrived: her harassed minders were the Russian ambassador Christoph Lieven and his clever but meddlesome wife Dorothea. Catiche, recalled Countess Lieven,* "was a remarkable person" with "an excessive thirst for authority and a very high opinion of herself . . . who startled and astonished the English." In the streets of London, "I hear people say, Let me see the sister of Emperor Alexander the saviour of the world," Catiche reported to Alexander.

When the prince regent arrived to call on her at the Pulteney Hotel, Piccadilly, the meeting was frosty. Countess Lieven was berated both by the regent—"Your Grand Duchess is not good-looking"—and by the grand duchess—"Your Prince is ill-bred." The regent's "boasted affability is the most licentious, the most obscene I ever heard, and I am far from being puritanical or prudish, but I vow that with him and his brothers I have often not only to get stiffly on my stiffs, but not to know what to do with ears and eyes. A brazen way of looking where eyes should never go!"

Catiche baited the regent by befriending his estranged wife Caroline. "The Absurd Little Mad Thing" was so rude that even the Lievens found her "unbearable." If Catiche was demonstrating the arrogance of Romanov majesty, the British seemed keen to parade the porcine lechery of the Hanoverians, for Catiche now attracted a third of these gruesome brothers, the duke of Sussex, who sent her a proposal. "As she turned down husbands," noted Countess Lieven, "our Duchess took delight in taking them from others." She was "very seductive in glance and manners, an assured gait, a proud look, a bright eye and the most beautiful

---

* The Lievens were at the heart of the Baltic German cousinhood. Christoph's mother was the redoubtable Countess Charlotte Lieven, mistress of the robes, governess of Emperor Paul's younger children. His wife Dorothea was a Benckendorff, daughter of Empress Maria's late best friend. As a girl she had a romance with Grand Duke Constantine and Empress Maria had considered marrying Dorothea to Arakcheev, so she was lucky to marry Lieven. Sharp-faced, incisive and self-obsessed, Countess Lieven became a one-woman diplomatic-amorous whirlwind whose lovers included Metternich of Austria, Earl Grey of Britain and François Guizot of France, living proof of Henry Kissinger's dictum: "power is the greatest aphrodisiac."

*Left* "Let them hate so long as they fear me," Paul declared, but he was both tyrant and laughing-stock: he reviewed his troops wearing Prussian uniform, tricorn hat and a sacred *dalmatique* that made him resemble a teapot with boots.

*Below* Maria Fyodorovna, the pretty Württemberg-born empress, struggled to manage Paul, making an alliance with his powerful mistress Nelidova.

Kutaisov (*below left*) rose from Turkish slaveboy to Paul's barber, pimp and then count, earning the nickname Figaro. He arranged Paul's affair with Anna Lopukhina (*below*).

Tormented by his role in his father's murder, mocked by Napoleon, Alexander I was inscrutable and mystical, but he developed a will of steel that changed Europe. Underrated by history, he fought his way to Paris.

Alexander was fascinated and disgusted by Napoleon: at their meeting on a raft at Tilsit in 1807, they divided up Europe. "If he was a woman I'd make him my mistress," raved Napoleon.

The burning of Moscow, 1812: the climax of Napoleon's invasion of Russia and the greatest humiliation of Alexander's life.

Alexei Arakcheev, "The Vampire," organized the war for Alexander and ended up running Russia. He was loathed for his grotesque tyranny.

One-eyed, lazy and wise, Mikhail Kutuzov was hated by Alexander, who was forced to appoint him commander-in-chief. He fought Napoleon to a draw at Borodino.

Alexander ignored his wife Elizabeth (*above left*), who sought consolation in love affairs with a female courtier and the tsar's best friend; he built a family with Maria Naryshkina (*above right*), the reigning court beauty; and, among many mistresses at the Congress of Vienna, he enjoyed the favours of Princess Katya Bagration (*right*), known as "Naked Angel" and "White Pussycat."

Alexander learns of the victory at the Battle of Leipzig in October 1813, with Austrian Emperor Francis and Prussian King Frederick William—this accelerated the fall of Napoleon.

A rare happy marriage: Nicholas I (*top left*) loved his Prussian wife Mouffy (*above*, with the future Alexander II and Maria). Their favourite home was the Cottage, Peterhof (*above left*), but the Great Kremlin Palace (*left*) better reflected Nicholas's vision of Russia.

*Far left* Varenka Nelidova, the beauty of Nicholas's court, was his favourite mistress whom he visited twice daily.

*Left* Nicholas regarded the poet Pushkin as a troublesome if disreputable talent: he censored his poetry, fancied his wife and banned him from fighting his fatal duel—but to no avail.

Alexander II was the most endearing and attractive of the Romanovs. His liberation of the serfs was wildly popular, but it raised expectations that could not be satisfied.

After the disaster of the Crimean War, Alexander's best friend and swashbuckling paladin Prince Bariatinsky finally defeated the jihadi insurgency in the Caucasus: here Bariatinsky (*seated*) accepts the surrender of the legendary leader Shamyl.

Nixa (*above left*), eldest son of Alexander II, was the perfect heir, who fell in love with the perfect consort, Minny of Denmark. His early death ruined his parents' marriage. Minny later became engaged to his brother, the galumphing giant Sasha, later Alexander III (*above right*).

Alexander II with his dull, ailing empress, Marie (*far right*), who gave him a bounty of male heirs. *From left* Paul, Sergei, Maria, Alexis, Sasha (leaning proudly over Minny, holding the future Nicholas II) and Vladimir.

Alexander II fell in love with Katya Dolgorukaya (*above left*), when she was a schoolgirl. They finally became lovers at Belvedere (*top right*); Alexander praised Katya's capacity for sexual pleasure and her luxurious golden hair and body, which he himself sketched (*above right*).

Alexander II's brother, Kostia (*above, far right*), helped push through his reforms, but his eldest son Nikola (*standing*), was a decadent erotomaniac who stole his parents' diamonds for his American courtesan Fanny Lear (*above left*), while the second son, KR (*above, far left*), became a poet-playwright with a secret sexual life.

After Alexander II's hedonistic sailor son Alexis impregnated his mistress, he was sent on an American tour (*left*, with General Custer), where he hunted buffalo and showgirls.

hair in the world." She played havoc with the regent's plans to marry his heiress Princess Charlotte to the prince of Orange. Catiche flirted brazenly with him and then introduced Charlotte to one of her Russian officers, Prince Leopold of Saxe-Coburg, whom she would ultimately marry.

At the end of May, Alexander* arrived in Piccadilly to be mobbed by an admiring crowd. He was not impressed by the regent. "A poor prince," he commented, and outraged him by consorting with the Whig opposition. In society, "he was the full young man, a fine waltzer, gallant to women though confining himself to young ones. Surrounded and flattered, his conquests were as manifold as his gallantries."[21]

On his way back to Russia, he was met by delegates from Petersburg who offered him the title "Alexander the Blessed," which he refused. Arriving in Petersburg on 13 July, he prayed at Kazan Cathedral—"penetrated by humility," observed Golitsyn, "he attributed everything, the victory to the Lord." After a year and a half away from Russia, he appointed a German and a Greek, Nesselrode and Capo d'Istria, as joint foreign ministers,[†] but he was now exhausted. He delegated power at home to the despised Arakcheev.

Alexander was estranged from his wife Elizabeth, while his "adored marriage" with Maria Naryshkina was ending bitterly for moral reasons because, as Alexander explained to Catiche, "people think she's the obstacle to a rapprochement with my wife" and "she doesn't want my nation to have a wrong to reproach me with. I love her too much to

---

* In Paris, Alexander offered Arakcheev his marshal's baton. Arakcheev had been crucial in managing the war, though he had played no role in strategy—but he refused. However when the tsar sent him home to run Petersburg, the Vampire sulked. Alexander pacified him with a revealing tribute: "It's with true chagrin that I am separated from you. Receive again the expression of my recognition of your numerous services which will always be engraved in my heart. I am susceptible to boredom and affliction. After fourteen years of hard government, ruinous war and two dangerous years, I see myself deprived of the man in whom I always have unlimited confidence. There's no one in whom I've had the same confidence . . . Your devoted friend for life, Alexander."

† He sacked Chancellor Rumiantsev, State Secretary Shishkov and Moscow Governor-General Rostopchin. Arakcheev became rapporteur of the Committee of Ministers and director of Alexander's chancellery, which he ran from his own house—his rule known as *Arakcheevschina*—the time of Arakcheev. As for the foreign ministers, Karl von Nesselrode had a German father and a Jewish mother but was raised as an Anglican at the British embassy in Lisbon. Dreary, colourless, submissive, he looked like a small-town clerk. "I'm called when I'm needed," he boasted to his wife. "I am completely passive." His rival Ioannis Capo d'Istria, now thirty-one, was a fascinating meteor, a liberal reformer, born in Corfu, trained as a doctor, promoted by Alexander to chief minister of the Septinsular Republic of the Ionian Islands. As the tsar's foreign minister he was the champion of progressive causes—or, as Metternich saw it, "a complete and thorough fool, a perfect miracle of wrong-headedness."

make her act against her conviction." Alexander was sorry that "the happiness of fourteen years of union will be sacrificed to our duties." When he discovered that she was actually in love with someone else, he was hurt by "this person after all she has done." Signing off to Catiche at the end of "the relationship where I put my life's happiness," he declared, "I'm about to depart for Vienna."

On 13 September 1814, Alexander was greeted by Emperor Francis outside Vienna, where in perhaps the most self-indulgent international junket of all history, a congress of two emperors, five kings, 209 reigning princes, about 20,000 officials, from marshals and ministers to clerks and spies, and just about every gold-digger, mountebank and prostitute in Europe, maybe 100,000 in all, bargained, blackmailed and fornicated their way through banquets and balls, to reshape a continent after twenty years of war.

Alexander moved into the Hofburg Palace, while two ambitious women manoeuvred themselves into the centre of the action by renting neighbouring apartments in the Palm Palace.

Wilhelmina de Sagan, already Metternich's mistress, possessed "noble and regular features, a superb figure, the bearing of a goddess"—and a mind trained in history and philosophy. Corrupted by "the frightening immorality" of her childhood, seduced by her mother's lover, her promiscuity now drove Metternich to distraction. "She sins seven times a day," he groused, "and loves as often as others dine."*

Across a corridor in the Palm Palace lived Princess Katya Bagration, daughter of Potemkin's niece Katinka and widow of the hero of Borodino. Settling in Vienna, she had hooked Metternich, who fathered her daughter Clementine. "She was as beautiful as an angel, bright, the liveliest of the beauties of Petersburg," recalled Langeron. Katya showed off her figure in diaphanous dresses—hence her nickname "the Naked Angel." In Vienna, her alabaster skin and erotic specialities won her the soubriquet "the White Pussycat." Naturally the two vamps loathed each other. Metternich's police chief Baron Hager called Bagration's side of the Palm Palace "the Russian Camp," Wilhelmina's "the Austrian Camp."

---

* Her youngest sister, Dorothea, aged twenty, was on the other side—as partner of Talleyrand. Their mother, the duchess of Courland, had once been his mistress. Dorothea was first engaged to Czartoryski until, at Erfurt, Talleyrand had asked Alexander to marry her to Talleyrand's ne'er-do-well nephew, by whom she dutifully had two sons. Talleyrand arranged for his duchy of Dino to be ceded to his nephew so that she could be duchesse de Dino. Thirty-nine years younger than the cadaverous prince, Dorothea became his last mistress—though he had to share her with a young Austrian, Count Karl Clam-Martinitz. In 1820, Dorothea gave birth to a daughter whom Talleyrand treated as his own.

As soon as he arrived, Alexander summoned Castlereagh and Metternich. The latter exulted that "He knows nothing of what I want and I know exactly what he wants." While Talleyrand exploited the bickering to restore French prestige, Metternich retreated every night to Wilhelmina's apartment. Across the landing, there was a commotion when Princess Bagration's bell was rung in the middle of the night. Opening her door in a state of undress, the White Pussycat welcomed the tsar, who stayed, the secret police reported, three hours.

Alexander aimed to create a larger Polish kingdom* with himself as king that the other powers rightly saw as a Russian satellite, a fear happily exploited by Talleyrand. "I conquered the Duchy [of Warsaw]," Alexander bragged, arguing that Russia had suffered more than anyone. He hoped to repay Prussia by demolishing Napoleon's ally, Saxony. When Talleyrand argued, Alexander warned, "If the King of Saxony won't abdicate he'll be packed off to Russia—he'll die there!" His sinister threats, sounding more like Stalin than Alexander the Blessed, perturbed his allies.

The tsar himself was determined to play the lead in the pageant of Vienna. Slapping marshals' backs saying "we soldiers" and mocking Metternich as a civilian, he was never out of high-collared, embroidered uniform. But the fashion for skin-tight breeches was now a challenge for the fattening imperial buttocks, which led to tantrums. "I found him today trying on eight or nine pairs of hussars' breeches," wrote one of his ministers, "and inconsolable to find them all too tight or too short." He was so cross, he sent to Petersburg for a pair of breeches that would fit. To tighten his skin, this metrosexual thirty-five-year-old rubbed his face daily with a block of ice. He flirted compulsively with the beauties of Vienna: his chat-up routine started with mournful reflections on the end of his relationship with Maria Naryshkina who "had broken my heart and still makes it bleed every day." But Alexander was often crudely direct: at a ball, he told Countess Szechenyi, whose husband had gone off to dance, "Your husband seems to have left you. It would be a great pleasure to occupy his place for a while."

"Does Your Majesty take me for a province?" replied the countess in the best bon mot of the Congress. At a public masked ball, an outraged

---

* Alexander had travelled via Czartoryski's estate to show the Poles that "revenge is not in my nature"—and Czartoryski joined his delegation, which included the German Nesselrode, the Greek Capo d'Istria and the Corsican Pozzo di Borgo, with only one Russian, his ambassador to Vienna, Count Andrei Razumovsky (who in Catherine the Great's reign had had an affair with Paul's first wife); his wife Elizabeth, his brother Constantine and his sister Catiche formed the Romanov contingent. His ex-mistresses Maria Naryshkina and Zinaida Volkonskaya were there too, much to his irritation. He sent Naryshkina home and cut Volkonskaya.

girl told the unmasked but pesky emperor that he was an oaf. "Alexander was thunderstruck."

"What are politics, if not women?" reflected Talleyrand. At Princess Bagration's, informers reported how Alexander jealously cross-examined her about her feelings for Metternich, who was tormented by the possibility that his mistress across the landing, Wilhelmina, would return to her favourite lover Prince Alfred Windischgrätz—or, much worse, succumb to Alexander. First Windischgrätz turned up. "With friends, one counts the days," Wilhelmina told him. "With you, I count the nights and I don't want to miss a single one." She dumped Metternich.

The partying was so excessive that the prince de Ligne, that relentless socialite now seventy-nine years old, punned that "*Le Congrès ne marche pas, il danse.*" Alexander "dances almost continually," wrote Friedrich Gentz, Metternich's secretary, "a magnet for women." His whores were procured by the Northern Lovelace, Chernyshev, who also handled his affair with Madame Bethmann of Frankfurt. The police agents reported that he was making regular calls on a Petersburg banker's wife Madame Schwartz, who told one informer that, sexually, Alexander preferred bourgeois ladies to aristocrats. It may be that he simply found them more discreet than *grandes dames*. Meanwhile the thirty-five-year-old Empress Elizabeth rekindled with her ex-lover Czartoryski, who begged her to divorce and marry him. Elizabeth already longed to go home to Baden, but Alexander refused. Meanwhile Catiche fought off suitors and fell for the married Crown Prince Wilhelm of Württemberg.

After years of war, Vienna became an erotic *Ronde*. Like his brother, Constantine, who had imported a French mistress, called on Princess Bagration. The police reported that the White Pussycat accepted not just Constantine but Catiche's Württemberger. Metternich's agents could barely keep up with her assignations—they said her apartment was becoming a royal bordello. Rarely have police files been so entertaining.

The Russians were said to be the worst-behaved visitors. On 9 November, Police Agent D reported that Alexander's courtiers, "not content with treating the Hofburg like a pigsty, are behaving very badly and constantly bringing in harlots." Vienna overflowed with such an embarrassing bounty of easily available sex that the streets seemed to swim with eager peasant-girls. One of Alexander's officers blamed the girls: "It is impossible not to mention the unbelievable depravity of the female sex of the lower orders." The police agents reported that the *maladies galantes*—VD—were raging.

The Congress was getting bad-tempered. Alexander's petulance was tormenting his courtiers. While the tsar "was endlessly charming to all foreigners," recalled one of his entourage, he "was not the same towards us, giving the impression our manners lagged those of Europeans. He was curt with us."* He danced so much at one ball that he fainted and retired to bed for a few days.

Frustrated that he was not getting his way on Poland, Alexander was driving the coalition apart. On 11 October, after a row with Metternich, he went to visit Princess Bagration in the Palm Palace, but at the top of the stairs, instead of turning left, he turned right and called on Wilhelmina with whom he spent several hours. Vienna was agog, Princess Bagration indignant, Metternich heartbroken. Wilhelmina longed to get her daughter Vava out of Russia. Alexander used this to humiliate Metternich. Then, through an anonymous note, Alexander offered Metternich £100,000 and the restoration of Wilhelmina's favours—in return for Poland. "I'm not surprised at anything any more when it comes to that man," Metternich wrote to Wilhelmina. "I'm quite ill. My body has been affected."

Castlereagh feared nothing less than an exchange of Napoleonic hegemony for that of Romanov imperium and advised Liverpool, again sounding very like twenty-first-century statesmen dealing with modern Russia, that only strength not appeasement would work with Alexander: "Acquiescence will not keep him back nor will opposition accelerate his march." It was necessary "to watch him and resist him if necessary as another Bonaparte."

Alexander's bullying played into the hands of Talleyrand, who persuaded Britain and Austria to join France in a secret anti-Russian entente, signed on 9 December. Two days later, an oblivious emperor gave a ball for his birthday at the Razumovsky Palace, where Beethoven played for the last time. Finally the Polish issue was agreed: Alexander became the constitutional king of Poland under the crown of Russia. But the Saxon question became so embittered that there was talk of war with Russia, until Alexander finally agreed to leave a rump of Saxony. The danger of a new conflagration was symbolically manifested on New Year's Eve when the Razumovsky Palace caught fire. As his priceless paintings were consumed by the flames, Razumovsky, wearing a sable dressing-gown, wept under a tree, comforted by Alexander.

The Congress has a bad reputation for its dissolute behaviour and conservative diplomacy, but its peace, however aristocratic and monarchical, was a sensible, pragmatic settlement, much more enduring than its twentieth-century equivalent, the unrealistic and idealistic Treaty of

---

* Constantine lived up to his reputation as the Angry Hyena: when Wilhelmina de Sagan's lover Windischgrätz challenged him to a duel, he struck him with a riding crop. Vienna was relieved when Alexander sent him off to command his Polish army.

Versailles of 1919. Nonetheless the tsar was so disgusted by the cynical horsetrading (in other words, the resistance to his own sacred wishes) that he conceived a Holy Alliance, a Christian brotherhood of monarchs—and he was just about to propose this when amazing news arrived.

"An unexpected event, Mama, that will astonish you as much as it has us, has just given a different direction to all ideas," he reported to his mother. "Napoleon left his island of Elba on 26 February." He was once again emperor of the French.

It was Metternich who had rushed to break the news to Alexander. The tsar, ready to face Napoleon in battle, offered himself as dictator of the alliance with the king of Prussia, Schwarzenberg and the duke of Wellington as his deputies. But Wellington, who had now replaced Castlereagh in Vienna, said he would "prefer to carry a musket" himself rather than serve under the tsar.

As Russian, Prussian, Austrian and British troops massed on French borders and the final Congress treaty was signed,* the odds were against the Corsican monster. "A mass of 850,000 men," the tsar told his mother, "are ready to crush the evil genius."[22]

As Alexander mustered his armies at Heilbronn in Germany, Catiche arranged for him to meet the priestess of his new sphere of mysticism. On 4 June 1815, he received Baroness Juliana Krüdener, a fifty-year-old Baltic German noblewoman (great-granddaughter of Marshal Münnich) and wife of a Russian diplomat who claimed mystical powers to contact God directly and foresee the imminent Apocalypse. Such chiliastic cults were fashionable and Alexander, already steeped in mysticism, had heard of Krüdener's prophecy that the downfall of the anti-Christ Napoleon would, directed by a certain angelic monarch, herald the Second Coming. Krüdener's sly millenarian flattery, expressed in biblical gobbledegook, dovetailed with Alexander's self-righteous egomania. "My obeisances to Virginia [his nickname for Krüdener]," Alexander wrote to Catiche. "Tell her my devotion to her is undying."

On 6 June (18 June New Style), Wellington defeated Napoleon at Waterloo. This time, Alexander would take no chances with Napoleon. "We shall insist," he told Barclay, "on having him turned over to us."

---

* The septuagenarian prince de Ligne, friend of Frederick the Great, Catherine the Great and Marie Antoinette, died in the last days of the Congress. As for Princess Bagration, out of favour and with debts of 300,000 francs, she was placed under house arrest until she fled Vienna, following Alexander to beg him to pay off her creditors. She set up a salon in Paris attended by Stendhal and Balzac, finally marrying a British diplomat, Lord Howden. Wilhelmina de Sagan moved on to become the mistress of Lord Stewart, Castlereagh's brother, before marrying a third husband, Count Karl Schulenberg. She never got her daughter back from Russia but remained friends with Metternich and died in 1839.

But having earlier learned of the secret anti-Russian alliance, he was repelled by Paris—"this accursed place."

Staying at the Elysée Palace, he invited Baroness Krüdener to come to Paris as his spiritual guide. She arrived with a Cossack escort and lodged at the Hôtel Montchenu next door to facilitate their nightly prayer sessions. "I saw only a desire to beat poor France and a wish to give rein to that passion of vengeance which I despise," he told Catiche. "My only consolations flow from the Supreme Being." Alexander insisted that France should not be penalized by the allies* and he proposed the Holy Alliance, guaranteed by the monarchs living together as Christian brethren—"to apply," Alexander explained to one of his diplomats, "the principles of peace, concord and love which are the fruit of Christian religion and morality to the political relationships of states."

On 29 August, Alexander presided over his Review of Virtues, a parade of 150,000 Russians, attended by the monarchs of Austria and Prussia as well as by Wellington, the comte d'Artois (Louis XVIII's brother) and Krüdener, grey-haired and plainly dressed. Next day his entire army sang Slavonic hymns, then prostrated themselves before seven altars. "This," he told the baroness, "has been the most beautiful day of my life."

"The emperor's mind is not quite sound," Castlereagh told Liverpool. When Alexander showed the treaty to him and Wellington, "it was not without difficulty we went through the interview with becoming gravity." It was a "piece of sublime mysticism and nonsense." Britain resisted, but most of Europe signed.[23]

In October 1815, Alexander, the new king of Poland, entered Warsaw in Polish uniform and granted his new kingdom a constitution, giving Poles the sort of liberties that he never offered the Russians. The pupil of Laharpe saw the Polish constitution as a test, confiding in the Prussian General von Borstell, "Poland is necessary to me for the civilization of my empire." The weary Alexander, swinging between fluffy liberalism and irascible autocracy, returned to Petersburg in time for Christmas.

The tsar had always recognized the evil of serfdom. Now his prestige was so high that he was tempted to abolish it. The next year, he actually liberated the serfs of Livonia, a bold move, and commissioned

---

* Louis XVIII returned to power and dismissed Talleyrand, letting Alexander propose the new prime minister: Armand du Plessis, duc de Richelieu, governor-general of New Russia and the Crimea for over ten years—and the real creator of Odessa. Talleyrand mocked the appointment of "the Frenchman who best knows Crimea." In New Russia, Alexander replaced Richelieu with another worldly Frenchman, Langeron, who continued to foster the cosmopolitan rise of Odessa.

Novosiltsev, Kochubey and even Arakcheev to present plans for Russia proper, which was a much more complicated and sensitive matter.

When some liberal nobles submitted plans to free their own serfs after the Livonian reform Alexander asked: "To whom does legislative power belong?"

"Without doubt to Your Imperial Majesty."

"In that case," snapped Alexander, "recognize my right to legislate as I consider most useful for the good of my subjects." Reform could come only from the autocrat, and even then it had its limits.

Metternich complained that the tsar "is incapable of persevering in the same system of ideas," having "left Jacobinism to embrace mysticism," while "the Rights of Man are replaced by Bible-reading." But actually he had already tired of Baroness Krüdener. She had boasted unwisely of her powers over him. He never saw her again.

Instead it was the militaristic autocrat who now promoted a vast new project at home—to settle soldiers and their families in military colonies, inspired partly by Arakcheev's estate, where they could support themselves by farming which would reduce the colossal expense of Europe's biggest army and reduce the cruelties of the existing conscription system. It was an excellent idea in principle—but not in execution. "The emperor had the idea," recalled the wife of his brother Nicholas, "but the execution was entrusted to Arakcheev." Soon a third of soldiers in the Russian army and their families lived in these colonies. Arakcheev and his thuggish martinets "did not do it gently," wrote Nicholas's wife, "but on the contrary with hard and cruel measures that made the peasants discontented." The Vampire became the project's fanatical administrator, reporting every detail to the grateful emperor.

The restless Alexander set off on a tour of the empire, the first of many. Overall, he would travel an astonishing 160,000 miles, inspecting provinces or attending foreign congresses.* These congresses were summit meetings held frequently by the Concert of Europe, the victors of the war, led by Alexander himself, to maintain peace. Loathing ceremony, bored by Petersburg rigmarole, spoiled by success, no longer

---

* On 27 August 1818 Alexander set off for Aix-la-Chappelle, the first of the post-Waterloo congresses, to meet Emperor Francis and King Frederick William III, as well as Metternich, Richelieu, Castlereagh and Wellington. Here Countess Lieven took up again with Constantine and then embarked on a great affair with Metternich, complicating the tsar's diplomacy. Alexander was keen to promote his Holy Alliance to guarantee conservative stability across Europe and help Spain recover its rebellious colonies in South America, even suggesting to the Spanish that, in return for old Russian warships to crush the South Americans, Russia would receive Minorca as a naval base, an echo of a similar idea of Catherine and Potemkin. At Aix, Metternich and Castlereagh vetoed this idea, but the powers agreed to end their occupation of France. The others feared the size of the Russian army, but Alexander insisted: "I consider my Army as the Army of Europe."

consoled by sex, glory or mysticism, tormented by the memory of his father and suffering from a niggling, paranoiac uneasiness that sometimes approached frenzy, he travelled with a tiny entourage of just Dr. Wylie and Volkonsky.* His first tour to the ruins of Moscow was probably the most effective of his reign for he ordered his architect, Joseph Bove, to rebuild the city centre: the Bolshoi, Theatre Square, the University and Red Square that we see today are Alexander's most enduring legacy.

Then, in 1819, some 28,000 military colonists rebelled, only to be brutally repressed by Arakcheev. "I saw decisiveness and prompt action is needed," he reported to his tsar, by which he meant draconian Prussian-style military punishments. Two thousand were arrested; 275 sentenced to death, commuted to running the atrocious *Spitsruten*. These unfortunates ran twelve times down the so-called "green street" of a thousand beaters; 160 perished. "You could only tell by their heads," wrote a witness, "that these were men and not slaughtered meat."

"I understand what your sensitive soul must have undergone," Alexander reassured Arakcheev, "but I appreciate your good judgement." Alexander approved Arakcheev's brutality, supposedly saying, "These colonies will be created, whatever they cost, even if it's necessary to cover with bodies the road from Petersburg to Choudova." But he insisted, "I've mastered harder problems and I mean to be obeyed on this one."

Across Europe, in Spain, Portugal, Germany and France, revolutionary ideas, disseminated by secret societies, threatened the Holy Alliance. Even Britain experienced radical unrest and the Peterloo Massacre. The assassination of the French heir, the duc de Berry, alarmed Alexander so much that he now demanded a concert of European monarchs to enforce a "general system." The British and Austrians still resisted a doctrine of intervention, both fearing Russian power, until a revolution broke out in Naples.

In October 1820, Alexander, accompanied by his brother Nicholas, met Francis and Frederick William at Troppau, where it was Metternich who now proposed a doctrine of conservative intervention to crush the revolutions across Europe. In a last flaring of his liberalism, it was now Alexander who opposed this until, on 28 October, he received disturbing news that changed his entire attitude. His beloved Semyonovsky Guards had mutinied. Revolution threatened Russia.[24]

*

* He did at least correct an injustice from seven years earlier. On 30 August 1817, Alexander rehabilitated Speransky, appointing him governor of Penza, issuing a decree that admitted the dubious case against his former "right hand." Soon afterwards, in a letter totally absolving Speransky, he promoted him to governor-general of Siberia.

The mutiny was a reaction to the brutality of an oafish German colonel, a protégé of Arakcheev, but Alexander saw it as the tentacle of an octopus-like revolutionary conspiracy—"the Empire of Evil which spreads swiftly using all the occultish means of the satanic genius who directs it." Still at Troppau, Alexander, working through Arakcheev, ordered harsh punishments: "The emperor has deigned to spare these men the knout [but] he orders the infliction of 6,000 blows of the birch to each, after which they will be sent to forced labour in the mines." Many died on "green street."

As Alexander and Metternich moved their congress southwards to Laibach, so that the king of Naples could join them, the tsar embraced the Austrian's plan to crush "the empire of evil" in Naples—and anywhere else. "Isn't it our duty as Christians to struggle against this enemy and his infernal work with all our power and all the means that Divine Providence has placed in our hands?" he wrote to Golitsyn in a multi-paged rant. "I would say the real evil is more dangerous still than the devastating despotism even of Napoleon." Alexander was convinced that there was a dastardly international conspiracy directed from Paris by a revolutionary organization called the Comité Central. Alexander did not yet know that there were indeed secret societies even within his own Guards, made up of liberal nobles who had returned from Paris determined to overthrow the autocracy.

In 1816, thirty well-connected officers formed the Union of Salvation. This then divided into a Northern Society, which planned a constitutional monarchy based on the US presidency, and a more radical Southern Society, established in the Ukrainian army, which decided to assassinate the emperor. The membership of these cells overlapped with that of the Arzamas Society, a self-congratulatory literary club of dilettantes, some liberal, some conservative. One of its founders, the romantic poet Vasily Zhukovsky, spotted real poetic talent: he proposed the election of a boy who had just left Alexander's lycée at Tsarskoe Selo. Alexander Pushkin's mother was the granddaughter of Hannibal, "the Negro of Peter the Great," while his father was the scion of an old boyar family. Blessed with exotic looks, black curly hair and a lithe figure, Pushkin made his name with the romantic poem *Ruslan and Ludmilla*. Dreaming of freedom, the boy mingled with the bewhiskered heroes of the Napoleonic Wars, some of whom were planning revolution. The irreverent Pushkin entertained the salons with his many seductions and outrageous satires. He vilified the vampiric Arakcheev*

---

* Pushkin's verse on Arakcheev was devastating: "Oppressor of all Russia / Persecutor of governors / And tutor to the Council / To the tsar he is friend and brother / Full of malice and vengeance / Without wit, without feeling, without honour / Who is he? Loyal

and dared mock Alexander, "the wandering despot" with a "plump posterior."

In 1819, Alexander, on first hearing about this prodigy, asked the Guards commander Prince Ilarion Vasilchikov for a Pushkin poem. He liked what he read, thanking Pushkin for his "noble sentiments"—but the next year an informer denounced the poet to Kochubey, who informed the fat-bottomed tsar. General Miloradovich, governor-general of Petersburg in charge of one branch of the secret police, was ordered to confiscate the verses, but Pushkin burned them first. Yet with fearless honesty the poet agreed to write them out again. "Pushkin must be exiled to Siberia," said the emperor; "he's flooded Russia with seditious verse." The poet Zhukovsky and historian Karamzin—the two court intellectuals—and even the dowager empress appealed on Pushkin's behalf. Instead Alexander exiled Pushkin to New Russia.

Pushkin was the least of his problems: now a Guards officer close to the family named Alexander Benckendorff denounced a skein of conspiracies to the tsar. Finally returning to Tsarskoe in May 1821, Alexander was greeted by Guards commander Vasilchikov, chief of another security agency, who confirmed the conspiracies. Surprisingly Alexander did not order hangings. "My dear Vasilchikov, you know I have shared and encouraged these illusions and mistakes. So it's not for me to crush them."

That would be left to his successor. But who would that be?[25]

On the very night of his father's assassination, the official heir, Constantine, had said that he did not want the throne—and he had not changed his mind since. He was still a sadistic martinet and volatile hellion, unsuited to be tsar. While showing off his troops to foreigners, he pierced the foot of a general standing at attention with his sword to prove his discipline. True, he seemed to have improved. He quoted Molière in letters to his sisters, laughed at his own pug-nosed ugliness and enjoyed his life as commander-in-chief of the army of Poland. It was in Poland that in 1815 he fell in love with a sweet-natured Polish countess, Joanna Grudzińska. She seems to have made him gentler. If he divorced his estranged wife and married his Catholic mistress, it would further encourage Alexander to alter the succession.[26]

The next in line was the much younger Nicholas, who looked like an emperor. When he was born, Catherine the Great hailed him as a

---

without flattery / The penny soldier of a whore." Here is his more good-natured verse on the war-hero Alexei Orlov, his mistress and his small penis: "Orlov in bed with Istomina / Lay in squalid nudity / In the heated affair the inconstant general / Had not distinguished himself. / Not intending to insult her dear one / Lais took a microscope / And says: 'Let me see, my sweet, what you fucked me with.' "

"colossus" with "a basso voice and hands almost as big as mine" and he grew up into a gigantic, blue-eyed, fair-haired man, regularly described as "beautiful." The younger brothers and sisters were brought up by their distant mother Maria, who left Nicholas feeling starved of love. Instead he found affection with his stalwart governesses, both the wives of Germanic officers, "la Générale" Lieven (whom he called "Mutterkins") and her junior, "la Colonelle" Julia Adlerberg, but above all with his beloved Scottish nanny Jane Lyon. It was Lyon who taught Nicholas to hate Jews and Poles, whom she had come to loathe during the revolutionary tumult in Warsaw in 1794. As he got older, Nicholas was bullied by his governor General Gustav Lamsdorf whose "fear and coercion," he wrote, "undermined my filial trust in my mother to whom we were rarely admitted alone." Nicholas consoled himself in a secret society he formed with his favourite sister Annette and youngest brother Michael called the Triolathy in which they used codewords and wore special rings. "We rarely saw Emperor Alexander," recalled Nicholas, but "our guardian angel was especially affectionate to us." On Alexander's visits to his young brothers, the tsar drilled them with rifles—truly the sons of Paul.

When Nicholas reached puberty, Lamsdorf had him shown the syphilis ward of a hospital as a warning against promiscuity, a vision that "so horrified me that I knew no woman until my marriage." After 1812, Nicholas longed to serve, but he and Michael were not allowed to join the tsar until the fall of Paris, setting off with instructions from their mother who hoped the "military regime will not cause you to become crude, coarse and severe."

The brothers paraded through Paris with "mad joy," but on his way back Nicholas passed through Berlin, where he met Princess Charlotte of Prussia, daughter of Frederick William and the late Louise. "There I saw," he reminisced, "the one who, by my own choice, from first glance, excited in me a desire to give myself to her for life." The giant fell in love with this dainty but delicate flower, whom he always called "Mouffy." Romance in a family of paradomaniacs meant their love letters were filled with regimental details, and Nicholas confided to Mouffy that the military was his ideal for society: "the Army is order . . . I regard all human life as nothing more than service." He got the tsar's permission to pursue the match. In Paris after Waterloo, Alexander was already considering Nicholas for the throne. Baroness Krüdener hailed the teenaged grand duke: "Monseigneur, you will be emperor."

"Emperor?" replied Nicholas. "A crown bought by the loss of brother Constantine would be a crown of thorns."

In October 1816, Nicholas and Mouffy were engaged: as she converted to Orthodoxy, and was taught Russian by the poet Zhukovsky, Nicholas trained for the throne. First, he was sent on a European tour. In London, hosted by Wellington and the prince regent, he was ogled by British ladies who exclaimed: "Devilish handsome! The handsomest man in Europe." But he was unimpressed by Parliament: "I have never thought any system could be better than that by which kings were delegated by providence to govern the masses." Then followed a Russian tour on which he recorded his anti-semitic and anti-Polish sentiments in his diary.

On 1 July 1817, Nicholas and Mouffy were married. "A huge number of jewels were hung on me," recalled the frail Mouffy, who formally became Alexandra Fyodorovna, "so heavy I thought I'd die." "I felt very happy when our hands were joined," she wrote. "I placed my life in the keeping of my Nicholas and he has never betrayed that trust."

Yet Nicholas, now commander of the Izmailovsky Guards, was a pompous stickler for rules, hated for his humourless severity. He worshipped Alexander as "The Angel," but was less cosmopolitan and genial than he, more of a Russian disciplinarian. "Order had collapsed after the return from France," he recalled. "Officers wore tailcoats and even went on exercises in evening dress! Service was just a word, and no rules," he added. "I had a fiery zeal which turned superiors and subordinates against me." Mouffy charmed everyone. "I was very weak, very pale and (they claimed) very interesting-looking," she reflected later. "A few faces welcomed me with kind looks among them [Alexei] Orlov and Benckendorff," two of the most lady-killing bravoes. "It's true my Nicholas's appearance was too serious for his twenty-one years," she admitted, but in private "he was very tender and loving." Yet "absolutely no one liked him," noted the memoirist Vigel—except the ladies. At a masquerade, a masked lady propositioned him: "Do you know you're the most beautiful man in Russia?"

"My good madame," he replied sanctimoniously, "that is a matter that concerns my wife alone."

In 1818, Mouffy, pregnant for the first time, travelled to Moscow. "I heard the first cry of my first child," she wrote. "Nikki kissed me and burst into tears and thanked God."

"It's a boy," announced Maria, who presided over the accouchement.

"Our happiness redoubled," recalled Mouffy, "and yet I remember feeling something grave and melancholy in the thought that this creature would one day be emperor." The "delightful child, white, plump with big deep blue eyes" would be Alexander II. Then in January 1819, their sister Catiche, queen of Württemberg, just thirty years old, died of erysipelas. The loss shook Alexander. At a dinner with Nicholas and Mouffy that summer, the tsar, whom they idolized with "an adoration going as far as exaltation," suddenly declared that he was delighted by their marital bliss, which he himself so lacked, adding that the birth of a son was "a sign of God's grace." To Mouffy's shocked surprise, he went on to say that "he was doubly pleased to see Nicholas fulfil his duties well, since one day a great weight would rest on him, that he regarded him as his replacement—and much earlier than presumed since it would happen while he was still alive."

"We were seated like two statues," she remembered. "Eyes wide!"

"We were struck like a thunderbolt," declared Nicholas, who felt "an abyss opening up beneath his feet into which an irresistible force throws him."

"You seem surprised," said the tsar, explaining that Constantine was determined to renounce the throne. "For myself, I am decided to leave my functions and retire from the world." Nicholas and Mouffy wept.

Constantine set the ball in motion by asking Alexander for a divorce so that he could marry his Polish love. That September, Alexander, accompanied by Nicholas, visited Constantine and agreed. In the summer of 1820, Constantine married his new wife. Now Alexander told his brothers, "I want to abdicate."

"Never had the shadow of such an idea come into our heads!" claimed Mouffy. Both protested too much since they knew this was likely. Empress Elizabeth noticed Nicholas's ambition: "Nicholas has only one idea in his head—to reign."

In early 1821, Constantine wrote to Alexander renouncing the throne. On 16 August 1823, Alexander signed a manifesto appointing "our second brother Nicholas" as successor.* "The emperor hinted about it to us," wrote Nicholas, "but did not expand any more and we made every effort to avoid [the subject]." Unwisely, and fatally, this was never made public.[27]

In February 1821, Prince Alexander Ypsilantis, a Greek ex-adjutant of the tsar, led a ragtag detachment of adventurers into Ottoman Moldavia, hoping to spark an Orthodox rebellion against the sultan and force Russian intervention. The invasion was easily foiled and Ypsilantis was soon fleeing for his life, but it was embarrassing for Alexander, who had not sanctioned it. He was sure it had been ordered by the diabolical revolutionary Comité Central of Paris to divert the allies, "preventing us from destroying other synagogues of Satan." But Greeks across Ottoman territories rebelled, Mahmud II hanged the patriarch of Constantinople and the cause mobilized Russians on behalf of their brethren.

---

* Their youngest brother Michael, a jovial soldier and practical joker but an oafish husband, married Elena Pavlovna (the former Princess Charlotte of Württemberg) in February 1824.

Alexander's co-foreign minister, Capo d'Istria, believed that Russia should back the Greeks, but Metternich, fearing Russian influence in the East and revolutionary liberalism in the West, urged Alexander to treat them as "a criminal enterprise." It was a "trap," grumbled the tsar, who finally sacked Capo d'Istria and backed Metternich. "The Russian cabinet has ruined in one blow the great achievement of Peter the Great and all his successors," crowed Metternich.*

The "huge burden" of reigning† was wearing down Alexander. "He imagined seeing things that nobody would have thought of doing: that people were making fun of him, comically imitating him, making signs," wrote Mouffy. His increasing deafness isolated him more and he turned on Mouffy, his "remarks and reproaches" making her cry— though he soon returned to his affectionate ways.

The all-powerful Vampire, Arakcheev, exploited Alexander's long absences and weary paranoia to destroy the emperor's two closest retainers. As he departed for Verona, the tsar ordered the dissolution of "secret societies of all denominations," but while he was away Arakcheev used this to attack Golitsyn, unleashing an Orthodox firebrand, Archimandrite Photius, to accuse him of revolutionary apostasy and reveal "the plan of revolution." The emperor sacked his friend as education minister. He also sacked Volkonsky as chief of staff and replaced him with Baron Hans-Karl Dibich, a German who had long served in Russia. "God only knows," said Volkonsky, but "the one thing I regret is that one day the emperor will surely learn the infamies of the villain [Arakcheev] who has caused the fall of many honest men."

On 6 June 1824, Alexander's beloved daughter Sophia Naryshkina died just before her wedding. He heard the news during the morning parade. He paled and said, "I receive punishment for all the errors of my ways," and continued with the parade.

---

* In October 1822, Alexander travelled to a congress in Verona where he proposed sending 150,000 Russian troops to the West to eliminate any revolutions, starting with that in Spain. Britain, represented by Wellington (as Castlereagh had just committed suicide), disapproved and instead France invaded Spain. Alexander spent the congress pursuing Lady Londonderry while Wellington (according to the French foreign minister) looked for sex on the streets of Verona. As for Capo d'Istria, he became the first head of state of independent Greece but was assassinated in 1831.

† He revealed his mentality to his ex-mistress Zinaida Volkonskaya, thanking her for treating "me with such kindness when you could well have thought me ungrateful and insensitive when I am neither." It was the "huge burden which weighs on me which makes me seem so." He looked forward to seeing her to "express in person how touched I am by the friendly way you treat me in spite of my sins." Zinaida later held a salon in her Moscow mansion which is now Yelisev's Foodstore, attended by Pushkin, but her liberal sympathies later displeased Tsar Nicholas I and she moved to Italy where she lived in the Villa Volkonsky, today's British embassy.

"God has miraculously torn you from sin," agreed Golitsyn unforgivingly. "He takes back to Himself the fruit of this tie which should not have seen the light of day."

"Don't worry about me," Alexander wrote to Arakcheev. "It's God who wished it and I know how to submit myself. I support my pain with resignation and I pray God will fortify my soul." He travelled to Arakcheev's estate Gruzino to grieve.

On 7 November, the Neva flooded, submerging entire neighbourhoods, killing many, as the emperor, back in the Winter Palace, organized the relief effort. Then Elizabeth fell seriously ill. These blows brought him closer to his wronged wife, to whom he proposed a long stay in the south, for his rest and her health. Relations with the Ottomans were tense and he also needed to inspect the armies—and purge them of revolutionaries. "I know I am surrounded by assassins," he mused. Just before he left, he received a young captain from the Second Army in Ukraine named John Sherwood, born in Kent, who warned him, via Dr. Wylie, that conspirators planned a coup.

At this darkening moment, on 1 September 1825, Alexander, followed by Elizabeth, embarked on the honeymoon they had never had.

On 23 September, the emperor arrived first in Taganrog on the Sea of Azov, accompanied only by Dr. Wylie, Volkonsky (who had rejoined his entourage) and Chief of Staff Dibich. Alexander oversaw the decoration of a small one-storey villa. Ten days later, Elizabeth arrived. When she asked him when he planned to return to Petersburg "so I could prepare myself for his departure, he answered, 'As late as possible . . . not before the new year.' That put me in a good mood all day."

After a month, Count Michael Vorontsov, newly appointed governor-general of New Russia, invited the tsar to inspect Crimea. Alexander agreed, but first he received the confirmation that there was indeed a conspiracy against him. Then he heard of the tragedy that had befallen Arakcheev.[28]


The Vampire's common-law wife with the black eyes and grenadier's figure, Anastasia Minkina, had long terrorized the Gruzino peasants to enforce the discipline that so impressed the tsar. On 6 September Minkina had her maid thrashed and locked up two other girls in her jail. The next day, the beaten maid and her brother crept into Minkina's bedroom and cut her throat so savagely she was almost beheaded.

Arakcheev abandoned the government and galloped for Gruzino, where he threw himself on the ground crying out to whoever would listen: "You have killed her. Kill me too. Kill me quickly!" Many of the serfs were arrested and tortured.

"The throbbing of my heart, a daily fever, three weeks without a night's rest, grief and depression have all made me so weak, I've lost my memory," he told the emperor. "You wouldn't recognize your faithful servant."

"You say you don't know where to go," Alexander replied, seeking to comfort Arakcheev. "Come to me. You don't possess a friend whose affection is more sincere." But he also urged him to return to his duties. Twenty-five of Arakcheev's servants were knouted; many died.[29]

While Arakcheev's serfs were being tortured, Sherwood, who had been ordered by Alexander to investigate, exposed both secret societies. The more radical Southern Society, strengthened by alliances with other groups, the Polish Secret Patriotic Society and the United Slavs, planned to assassinate Alexander while he stayed at the palace of Sashenka Branitska, Potemkin's niece. Great names were implicated. Sherwood was meant to hand over this evidence at a meeting with Arakcheev, who, neglecting the emperor's safety "because of a drunken, fat, pockmarked and loose woman," as Sherwood put it, never turned up. But the reports finally reached Alexander in Taganrog.

Alexander now had no choice but to act. As he ordered the arrest of the southern conspirators, he left Taganrog to ride happily along the Crimean shoreline, telling Volkonsky, "I'm going to move to Crimea . . . to live like a simple mortal. I've served twenty-five years and soldiers are given leave after this time . . . And you too will resign and be my librarian."

On 27 October, the tsar caught a chill then a fever. On 4 November, he fell seriously ill, though he made it back to Taganrog where Elizabeth and his doctors nursed him. Wylie offered medicines, but Alexander refused, supposedly telling his suite, "Why should I be cautious? I have two saints praying for me, Queen Louise of Prussia and my dear sister," Catiche. If that story is true, those two queens were the loves of his life. For several days he improved but then the fever got worse. Dr. Wylie started to worry.

On 14 November Alexander felt better, but when he got up to shave, he fainted. Prompted by Volkonsky, Elizabeth begged the emperor to take the Last Sacraments.

"In what condition am I really?" he asked Wylie. "Am I near my end?"

"Yes, Sire," replied the Scot. "Your Imperial Majesty has rejected my prescriptions. I speak not as a physician but an honest man. It's my duty as a Christian to tell you—there is no time to lose." Alexander took communion, drifting in and out of consciousness. Dibich wrote to the dowager empress in Petersburg and to Constantine, the apparent heir in Warsaw; the family prayed. Early on the 17th, Alexander rallied. "Today there's a very decided amendment in the state of the emperor," Elizabeth wrote to Maria. "Even Sir James Wylie considers the case more satisfactory." But that night, the tsar became comatose and Wylie knew he was dying, probably of typhoid. At 10:50 a.m. on 19 November, Alexander, forty-seven years old, died. "Our Angel is in Heaven," wrote Elizabeth, "and I sadly am on earth." The empress reflected on their lives as "friends since childhood. Together we traversed all the stages of life. Often distant we always found each other again. Finally on the true path, we only tasted the sweetness of our union. It was at this moment he was taken away from me." Attended by his tiny entourage, this seaside death in a bijou villa in a small town lacked the traditional drama of imperial deathbeds—but the very absence of official witnesses made this one of the great Romanov mysteries: had Alexander really died or had the mystic tsar falsified his own death?*

The body was embalmed by the doctors, but they lacked the facilities of Petersburg, and the job was botched. Soon, the stench was eye-watering, the face unrecognizably blackened.[30]

In the perilous confusion of the next few days, the empire would in theory have two emperors—and yet, in practice, none.

---

* The distance from Petersburg, the putrefaction that made the body unrecognizable, and inconsistencies in the reports of Elizabeth and the doctors, all helped spawn the legend that Alexander was still alive. Had he become a travelling hermit? In 1836, police in Perm, in the Urals, arrested a holy elder—a *starets*—named Fyodor Kuzmich, aged sixtyish, blue-eyed, deaf in one ear and fluent in French with knowledge of the Russian court. After a whipping and exile for refusing to reveal his past, he wandered as a hermit, teaching scripture and history until he retired to Tomsk. By the time he died in 1864, many believed him to be Alexander. It is said that Alexander III ordered Alexander I's tomb to be opened and found it empty. This is a myth that plays into three traditions: the sacred tsar who escapes the wicked nobles to do good works and wander as a holy man, itself connected to chiliastic Byzantine legends of the Final Emperor who appears in Jerusalem at the End of Days (Alexander the hermit is said to have made the pilgrimage to Jerusalem); the tradition of dead tsars who reappeared as pretenders; and the ideal of the *starets*, that type made most famous by Rasputin.

ACT III

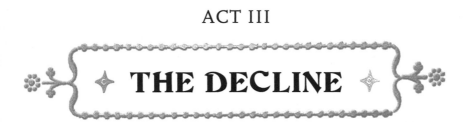

THE DECLINE

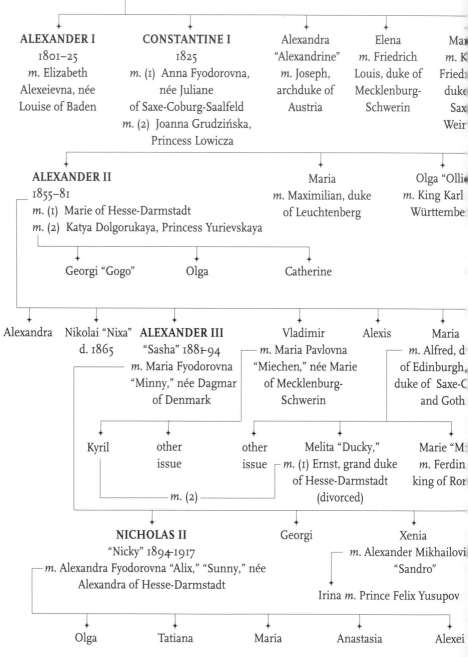

**PAUL I**
1796–1801
*m.* (1)  Natalya Alexeievna, née Wilhelmine of Hesse-Darmstadt
*m.* (2)  Maria Fyodorovna, née Sophia Dorothea of Württemberg

**ALEXANDER I**
1801–25
*m.* Elizabeth
Alexeievna, née
Louise of Baden

**CONSTANTINE I**
1825
*m.* (1)  Anna Fyodorovna,
née Juliane
of Saxe-Coburg-Saalfeld
*m.* (2)  Joanna Grudzińska,
Princess Lowicza

Alexandra
"Alexandrine"
*m.* Joseph,
archduke of
Austria

Elena
*m.* Friedrich
Louis, duke of
Mecklenburg-
Schwerin

Ma
*m.* K
Fried
duke
Sax
Wein

**ALEXANDER II**
1855–81
*m.* (1)  Marie of Hesse-Darmstadt
*m.* (2)  Katya Dolgorukaya, Princess Yurievskaya

Maria
*m.* Maximilian, duke
of Leuchtenberg

Olga "Olli
*m.* King Karl
Württembe

Georgi "Gogo"          Olga          Catherine

Alexandra      Nikolai "Nixa"      **ALEXANDER III**          Vladimir          Alexis          Maria
                  d. 1865          "Sasha" 1881–94          *m.* Maria Pavlovna          *m.* Alfred, d
                                   *m.* Maria Fyodorovna          "Miechen," née Marie          of Edinburgh,
                                   "Minny," née Dagmar          of Mecklenburg-          duke of  Saxe-C
                                   of Denmark          Schwerin          and Goth

Kyril          other          other          Melita "Ducky,"          Marie "M
               issue          issue      *m.* (1)  Ernst, grand duke          *m.* Ferdin
                                         of Hesse-Darmstadt          king of Ror
                                         (divorced)

—— *m.* (2) ——

**NICHOLAS II**          Georgi          Xenia
"Nicky" 1894–1917          *m.* Alexander Mikhailovi
*m.* Alexandra Fyodorovna "Alix," "Sunny," née          "Sandro"
Alexandra of Hesse-Darmstadt
          Irina *m.* Prince Felix Yusupov

Olga          Tatiana          Maria          Anastasia          Alexei

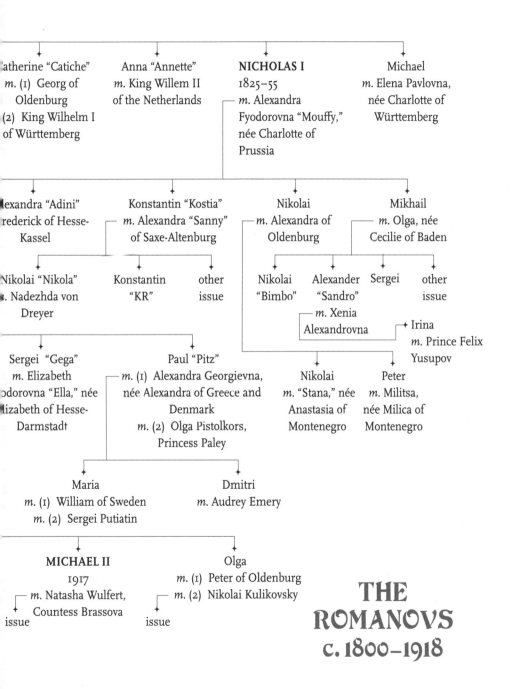

Catherine "Catiche"
*m.* (1) Georg of
Oldenburg
(2) King Wilhelm I
of Württemberg

Anna "Annette"
*m.* King Willem II
of the Netherlands

**NICHOLAS I**
1825–55
*m.* Alexandra
Fyodorovna "Mouffy,"
née Charlotte of
Prussia

Michael
*m.* Elena Pavlovna,
née Charlotte of
Württemberg

Alexandra "Adini"
Frederick of Hesse-
Kassel

Konstantin "Kostia"
*m.* Alexandra "Sanny"
of Saxe-Altenburg

Nikolai
*m.* Alexandra of
Oldenburg

Mikhail
*m.* Olga, née
Cecilie of Baden

Nikolai "Nikola"
*m.* Nadezhda von
Dreyer

Konstantin
"KR"

other
issue

Nikolai
"Bimbo"

Alexander
"Sandro"
— *m.* Xenia
Alexandrovna

Sergei

other
issue

Irina
*m.* Prince Felix
Yusupov

Sergei "Gega"
*m.* Elizabeth
Fyodorovna "Ella," née
Elizabeth of Hesse-
Darmstadt

Paul "Pitz"
*m.* (1) Alexandra Georgievna,
née Alexandra of Greece and
Denmark
*m.* (2) Olga Pistolkors,
Princess Paley

Nikolai
*m.* "Stana," née
Anastasia of
Montenegro

Peter
*m.* Militsa,
née Milica of
Montenegro

Maria
*m.* (1) William of Sweden
*m.* (2) Sergei Putiatin

Dmitri
*m.* Audrey Emery

**MICHAEL II**
1917
— *m.* Natasha Wulfert,
Countess Brassova
issue

Olga
*m.* (1) Peter of Oldenburg
— *m.* (2) Nikolai Kulikovsky
issue

# THE
# ROMANOVS
## c. 1800–1918

# Jupiter

# CAST

Maria Fyodorovna, dowager empress, widow of Paul I

NICHOLAS I, emperor 1825–55, son of Paul I and Maria

Alexandra Fyodorovna (née Princess Charlotte of Prussia), empress, Nicholas's wife, "Mouffy"

ALEXANDER II, emperor 1855–81, their eldest son, caesarevich, married Princess Marie of Hesse-Darmstadt

Maria, their eldest daughter, married Max de Beauharnais, duke of Leuchtenberg

Olga, their second daughter, "Ollie," married Karl I, king of Württemberg

Alexandra, their third daughter, "Adini," married Prince Frederick of Hesse-Kassel

Konstantin, their second son, "Kostia," "Aesop," married Princess Alexandra of Saxe-Altenburg, "Sanny"

Nikolai Nikolaievich, their third son, married Princess Alexandra of Oldenburg

Mikhail, their fourth son, married Olga, née Princess Cecilie of Baden

CONSTANTINE I, emperor, 1825, second son of Paul I and Maria, elder brother of Nicholas I, caesarevich, briefly emperor, married Princess Lowicza

Anna, "Annette," sixth daughter of Paul and Maria, married King William II of the Netherlands

Michael, youngest son of Paul and Maria, married Elena Pavlovna (née Princess Charlotte of Württemberg), "Family Intellectual"


COURTIERS, ministers etc.

Mikhail Miloradovich, count, general, governor-general of Petersburg, "Bayard"

Alexander Benckendorff, count, chief of the Third Section

Prince Peter Volkonsky, court minister

Vladimir Adlerberg, court minister, count

Ivan Paskevich, general, count of Yerevan, prince of Warsaw, field marshal

Karl von Nesselrode, foreign minister, chancellor, count
Alexander Chernyshev, war minister, count, prince, "Northern Lovelace"
Hans-Karl Dibich, German general, count, chief of staff, "Samovar"
Alexei Orlov, soldier-diplomat, chief of the Third Section, count, prince
Prince Vasily Dolgoruky, war minister, chief of the Third Section
Count Michael Vorontsov, governor-general of New Russia and Caucasus, prince, "Milord"
Prince Alexander Menshikov, chief of admiralty, governor of Finland, commander in Crimea

Varvara Nelidova, Nicholas's mistress, "Varenka"
Vasily Zhukovsky, poet, tutor to Mouffy, then to Alexander II
Alexander Pushkin, poet

As Dibich sent news of the tsar's death to both Petersburg and Warsaw and made the arrangements for the body to return to the capital, Alexander's widow and all the courtiers swore allegiance to Emperor Constantine I—but the chief of staff also accelerated the investigation into the conspiracies.

The couriers took six days to reach Warsaw but eight days to gallop the 1,400 miles to Petersburg. In Warsaw, on 25 November 1825, Constantine's entourage did not know that he had renounced the throne. Naturally they all wanted to take the oath, but Constantine made frenzied efforts to prevent their submissions. When Novosiltsev, Alexander's Polish representative, fell to his knees and hailed "Your Imperial Majesty," Constantine revealed that he had renounced the throne. The confused Novosiltsev tried again, prompting the caesarevich to bellow, "Desist and remember our one and only emperor is Nicholas!" Moments later, his adjutant fell to his knees, at which Constantine went berserk, shaking him by his lapels: "Silence! How can you dare speak such words? Do you realize you can be put in chains and sent to Siberia?"

On 27 November, Nicholas and his mother Maria were celebrating Alexander's recovery in the Winter Palace chapel when the dowager empress's valet brought Dibich's letter. "I saw that all was lost. Our Angel was no longer on the earth." Their mother collapsed. Nicholas prayed before the altar and, upon leaving his mother in his wife's hands, declared, "I will go to do my duty." But what was his duty?

Nicholas immediately took the oath of allegiance to Emperor Constantine and made sure everyone else did too. When he returned to tend to his mother, she was horrified: "Nicholas, what have you done? Didn't you know there is another manifesto naming you heir apparent?"

"If there is such a manifesto," replied Nicholas, "it's unknown to me . . . but we all know our master, our legitimate sovereign, is my brother Constantine, come what may!" He wrote to inform Constantine that "I've sworn the oath to you. Could I forget my honour and conscience have placed our beloved motherland in such a difficult position . . . All is in order [but] hasten here for the love of God."

"My resolve is unshakeable," Constantine replied. "I can't accept your invitation to come more quickly to you and I will go even further away if everything is not arranged in conformity with the will of our late emperor."

As the letters of the brothers crossed each other for over a week, Constantine insisted in Warsaw that he was not tsar, and Nicholas refused in Petersburg to accept that *he* was. Nicholas's sense of chivalry and Romanov fraternity meant he could not grab the crown, which had to be freely given to him by his brother, but this the unhinged Constantine could not do.

The only man in Petersburg who knew the secret of Alexander's manifesto, the mystical Alexander Golitsyn, hastened to Prince Lopukhin, ageing president of the State Council (father of Paul's mistress), urging him to summon the councillors.* Many insisted that Constantine was the heir, particularly the powerbroker during these strange days: General Mikhail Miloradovich, governor-general of Petersburg, was best friends with Constantine whom he argued was the rightful tsar, whatever Alexander had decreed. Miloradovich, one of the heroes of Borodino, was an eccentric playboy, nicknamed "Bayard," after the romantic French knight, for his womanizing in the city's theatres which he treated as a personal harem. Now he continued seducing ballerinas and assured Nicholas: "Everything is quiet."

For Nicholas, there was only one solution: Constantine must come to the capital—or at least publicly renounce the throne. So on 3 December, Nicholas begged him to do either or both. "So passed eight or nine days," recalled Nicholas. "How could we explain our silence to society? Impatience and discontent were widespread."

"Count on my feelings if you become sovereign," wrote Annette, now in The Hague, married to William, prince of Orange, to her brother Constantine, reflecting, "It will perhaps be a unique example to see two brothers fighting over who will *not* have the throne." But Empress Maria was torn between sons. "Oh my children, what a dreadful position I'm in," she wrote to Annette, adding that her youngest son "Michael is leaving today to go to our dear Emperor Constantine . . . may he soon be here with us." Michael rushed back and forth with the letters, but even when the dowager empress beseeched him, Constantine refused to leave Warsaw, terrified that a progress towards Petersburg could become an unstoppable procession to power. The Angry Hyena explained this to Nicholas—yet without the required public renunciation.

Suddenly on 12 December letters from Dibich and Chernyshev arrived from the south, addressed with "utmost urgency for the emperor's

---

* Copies of Alexander's decree of succession were conserved in the Dormition Cathedral, the Council of the Empire, the Synod and the Senate, and its contents were confided only to the two empresses (one of whom was far away in Taganrog), Golitsyn and Arakcheev, who was in Gruzino having a breakdown.

hands only!" warning of "the new plot with its branches throughout the empire."

"Just then I felt the full burden of my fate," wrote Nicholas, "and recognized with horror the situation I found myself in." He summoned Miloradovich and Golitsyn, and together they opened the note from Chernyshev naming the conspirators of the Northern Society. Nicholas realized that "I had to act without wasting a moment." He ordered Miloradovich to arrest them—but the governor-general did little except dally in bed with his latest ballerina. Nicholas commissioned his brother's minister Speransky, assisted by the historian Karamzin, who had visited the dowager empress every day since Alexander's death, to draft the accession manifesto. He then went to the private apartments where, as his wife wrote, "My Nikolai returned and knelt before me to be the first to greet me as empress," even though "Constantine does not want to issue a manifesto and holds firmly to his former decision."

That evening, a young Guards lieutenant, Yakov Rostovtsev, called on Nicholas and warned him that the coup was set for 14 December—the "fatal day."

Next morning, on the 13th, Nicholas signed his manifesto as emperor and ordered Lopukhin and the foreign minister Nesselrode to assemble the State Council that night. Grand Duke Michael, on his way back from Warsaw, would testify that Constantine had refused the throne. At 8 p.m., the twenty-three members of the Council gathered in the Winter Palace, but Michael never arrived. Finally, after midnight, Nicholas appeared alone: everyone stood as he read the manifesto. "Today I request you to take the oath," he declared in the portentously grandiloquent style that he made his own. "Tomorrow I shall command you." They bowed and took the oath.

Nicholas went to join his mother and wife, accepting the bows of their courtiers. The conspirators spent the night organizing the revolt, electing its grandest name Prince Sergei Trubetskoi as "dictator." But only a few units agreed to rebel. The "dictator" dithered, fearing that it was "a hopeless undertaking." As for Nicholas, he told Alexander Benckendorff that "By tonight, perhaps both of us will no longer be among the living but at least we'll die doing our duty." He "slept quietly, all conscience clear."

On the "fatal day" of the 14th, the emperor was up at 4 a.m. and addressed the Guards colonels at five: "You will answer to me with your heads for the tranquillity of the capital. Even if I shall be emperor for only one hour, I shall show myself worthy of the honour." The officers then rushed off to their units. At 7 a.m., Miloradovich, the Senate and the Synod gathered at the Winter Palace as soldiers took the oath to their second emperor in two weeks. At eleven, Miloradovich again reported that the city was "perfectly quiet" and supposedly returned to his mistress. But moments later, just as Michael finally arrived from Warsaw, officers burst in to report: "Sire, the Moscow Regiment is in full revolt," its commanders badly wounded. "The rebels are heading for the Senate. Order the Preobrazhensky and Household Cavalry to move against them."

Nicholas was "thunderstruck."

The new emperor prayed privately and then, telling his mother and wife "There's a bit of trouble in the Moscow Regiment, I'll head over there," he "decided to go where the danger threatened." Alexei Orlov, commander of the Horse Guards, was the first to report for action.* Nicholas ordered him to surround rebel positions. Orlov departed at a gallop. As Nicholas emerged on to Palace Square, crowded with onlookers, he found the Preobrazhensky Guards at attention in all their glory. "Form attack columns!" he ordered. As they set off, Miloradovich rode up: "This is bad. They're heading for the Senate. But I'll talk to them." Nicholas marched out with the Preobrazhensky towards the Senate—"an unparalleled moment in my life!" He ordered rifles loaded—and he sent back an adjutant to move his children from the Anichkov to the well-guarded Winter Palace. The tsar spotted Prince Sergei Trubetskoi watching from the General Staff headquarters—not knowing that he was the rebel "dictator." Miloradovich galloped up to the rebels to harangue them, but one of them shot him in the heart, another bayoneted him. He died that night. Now Nicholas, accompanied by his closest retainers Alexander Benckendorff and Vladimir Adlerberg (son of his governess), rendezvoused with Orlov and posted his loyal forces around the insurgents in Senate Square. He sent Adlerberg back to the Winter Palace to escort his family to the safety of Tsarskoe Selo—just in time. The empresses refused to leave Petersburg, but as the loyalist guards took up positions, a unit of rebel Grenadiers arrived at the palace. Disappointed, the rebels almost bumped into Nicholas himself, who barked the order: "Halt!"

"We are for Constantine!" they cried, not recognizing Nicholas. They could have assassinated him then and changed everything.

"Very well," answered the emperor, pointing towards the Senate. "Your place is over there."

---

* The careers of many grandees of Nicholas's court, including Benckendorff and Alexei Orlov were made that day. As the rebellion began, Nicholas asked an adjutant, Vasily Dolgoruky, if he was loyal. "Your Majesty, I am a Dolgoruky," he replied, saluting. Dolgoruky later rose to war minister.

When Nicholas and Benckendorff inspected their positions, the 3,000 rebels, surrounded by 9,000 loyal troops, fired on them. Grand Duke Michael marched up to demand their surrender, but they almost shot him. Nicholas noticed that the rebels were no longer shouting "Hurrah for Constantine" but instead "Hurrah for Constitution," a slogan repeated by peasant-soldiers who, noted Nicholas, "thought *Constitutsia* was the wife of Constantine."

It was 3 p.m.; soon it would be dark; the workers who were starting on St. Isaac's Cathedral were pelting his troops with debris. As for the rebels, "they fired a volley at me," but Nicholas longed to end the stand-off without bloodshed. He ordered Orlov's Horse Guards, in their white tunics with scarlet collars and brass helmets, then the Chevalier-Gardes in their breastplates, to charge, but as the rebels fired at them, both of these gorgeously accoutred squadrons of horsemen slipped on the ice. "Sire, there's not a moment to lose; there's nothing else to be done; we need case-shot!" said Prince Vasilchikov.

"Would you have me spill blood on the first day of my reign?"

"Yes sire," answered Vasilchikov, "to save your empire."

"Guns to fire in order starting from right flank!" barked Nicholas. The rebels broke; their leaders tried to rally them for an assault across the ice to secure the Peter and Paul Fortress. Strafed by cannonfire, the ice cracked, the rebels scattered. Ordering Benckendorff and Vasilchikov to round up the fleeing revolutionaries, the tsar returned to the Winter Palace.

Nicholas reviewed the troops of the Sapper Regiment, who had saved the family, in Palace Square. From the moment the shooting stopped, he consciously converted the crushing of the rebellion into a blood oath of loyalty to the dynasty, a sacrament of Russianness and rejection of Western liberalism. "I ordered my son to be brought."

Blue-eyed Alexander, eight, was in uniform. "Here is my son," Nicholas said. "Serve him faithfully." He placed the boy in the arms of soldiers, who kissed his hands and feet.

In the palace, "my rooms were much like a general headquarters during campaign . . . as despatches poured in from Vasilchikov and Benckendorff." Prisoners were delivered, including the "dictator" Trubetskoi, who claimed innocence until, faced with written evidence, "he fell to my feet shamefully."

"Take him away, everything is finished with you!" said Nicholas. "These interrogations took place all night . . . Not only did I not have time to lie down, I didn't even have time to change my clothes."

"Dear dear Constantine, your will has been done," he scribbled to his brother. "I am emperor but my God at what a price!"

"It cuts one to the heart," exclaimed the baffled Grand Duke Michael. "Are we low fellows and these honourable gentlemen or is it the other way round?"

Scarcely had Nicholas appointed an Investigation Commission* to get to the bottom of the conspiracies than revolution flared in Ukraine. On 3 January 1826, the group of 800 rebel soldiers were suppressed, the leaders sent to Petersburg. Before Nicholas could truly begin his reign, he had to punish the rebels, bury his brother and crown himself.[1]

While Benckendorff and the Investigation Commission interrogated their 579 suspects, the cortège of the late emperor Alexander was wending its way to Petersburg, directed by the tsar's beloved coachman Ilya who had never left his side, even driving him round Paris. But when it arrived, the body was so grotesquely distorted that there was no open coffin, which fuelled the rumours that there was no body inside.

As international royalty arrived for the funeral, Nicholas took control of foreign policy, using Nesselrode as his factotum. His first challenge was the fate of the ailing Ottoman empire, the so-called Eastern Question—"the most important of all"—that would culminate in war: the Orthodox Greeks and Slavs were already in revolt against the sultan. "I will give you my word of honour," Nicholas told the French ambassador, "that I don't want, don't desire and don't plan to add a single inch of territory to the holdings of Russia," but "neither will I allow that any other shall have an inch of it." As for the rebels, "I abhor the Greeks," yet he was determined to enforce the treaties of Catherine the Great and Alexander which proclaimed that Russia was the protector of the Orthodox. He dreamed of a Russian Constantinople. "I know very well that in view of the fact that I'm only twenty-nine," foreign statesmen "impute to me military leanings and desire for military victories, but they misjudge me, I love peace."

"The Duke of Wellington arrived this evening," reported the dowager

---

* "I have a firm suspicion," he confided in Constantine, "all this reaches to the State Council itself." He suspected Speransky, who would become a trusted adviser—and General Alexei Yermolov, a hero of 1812 and commander of the Caucasus. But his witchhunt was complicated by the involvement of many prominent families: Sergei Volkonsky was an ex-ADC to Tsar Alexander and the son of one of Empress Maria's ladies-in-waiting. "There are some very decent women in the families of the conspirators," wrote Maria. The hardest blow was Mikhail Orlov, Tsar Alexander's adjutant in Paris and brother of Nicholas's most loyal henchman. In his interrogation, he was welcomed by the tsar "as an old friend" but claimed to know nothing. "Until now you've talked to your old friend," growled Nicholas. "Now your Sovereign orders you!" Orlov refused. "It's all over between us," said Nicholas.

empress to Annette. "I think he's lost weight, but he still has his beautiful features and he made me very happy with what he said about Nicholas whose conduct on 14 December he much admired." When Wellington dined with the Romanovs, "his conversation is so interesting, his manner so natural he puts everyone at ease. The more one sees of him, the more one would like to see of him." But Wellington had also come to mediate between Nicholas and Sultan Mahmud II, who, angered by Russian interference, had revoked earlier agreements and refused to withdraw his troops from Wallachia and Moldavia. Wellington encouraged Nicholas, whom he thought more reasonable than Alexander, to avoid war. They agreed a deal whereby Britain would force the Ottomans to grant limited Greek independence while recognizing Russian interests in Wallachia and Moldavia. Yet Nicholas was less reasonable than he seemed: he had already sent the sultan an ultimatum.

On 13 March, Nicholas presided over the burial of Alexander* in the Peter and Paul Cathedral. "A Greek funeral is certainly calculated to rouse one's feelings," wrote Wellington, but with a stinking corpse and endless chanting, it was a "terrible ceremony." He could not wait to get home.[2]

As Nicholas awaited the outcome of his Ottoman ultimatum, he oversaw the destruction of the Decembrists. "We must seek revenge for Russia and for our national honour," he told Constantine. "There can be no mercy!"

After the Investigation Commission had delivered its report, a Special Supreme Court met on 3 June and sentenced five of the rebels to quartering, thirty-one to beheading and eighty-five to imprisonment. There was no trial and the sentences were specified by the tsar. But on 12 July, when they were brought before the court, Nicholas commuted the sentences to five hangings and the rest to imprisonment, hard labour in the mines or Siberian exile.[†]

The tsar devised every detail of the executions as a "lesson to Europe."

---

* Alexander's widow Empress Elizabeth did not long survive him, dying in May 1826, just over six months after the tsar.
† Trubetskoi received hard labour for life, Sergei Volkonsky hard labour then exile, accompanied by his young wife who became known as the "princess of Siberia." Two writers had lucky escapes. Pushkin was friends with eleven of the conspirators and sympathized with their plans. But on 14 December he was in exile on his estate. Though his name appeared frequently in the interrogations, the conspirators had refused to share their secrets with him because of his youthful indiscretion and literary genius: he had recently become even more famous thanks to his poem *The Fountain of Bakhchisaray* and the early cantos of his masterpiece *Eugene Onegin*. Alexander Griboyedov, author of *Woe from Wit*, was close to the conspirators, but on 14 December he was serving as a secretary to General Yermolov on an expedition against the Chechens. Arrested and interrogated, he was released.

On 13 July, the imperial couple attended a plangent ceremony on Senate Square to remember "a purifying sacrifice for Russian blood shed for the faith, tsar and fatherland on this spot." At three o'clock that afternoon in the fortress, five rebels had their swords broken over their heads, their insignia ripped from their uniforms; then, dressed in robes, they were led up to the scaffold. The hangings were bungled. The ropes broke, breaking the legs of the victims, who cried, "Poor Russia, we don't even know how to hang a man properly." They were simply hanged again.

"It's over; the widows remain!" Nicholas told Golitsyn. While he showed mercy to the rebel wives, he was suspicious of them too: "What's the news of poor Ryleeva, I hope she'll let me know what she needs; find what Trubetskoi and Muravev's wives are doing." He wrote of one of the widows, "Madame Konovnitsyna almost burst into my bedroom. Out of all these women I fear her the most." Bizarrely he recruited his father's pious mistress, Nelidova, to make visits to the Decembrist families. "However painful to be forced to measures that immersed families in despair," he wrote to her, "I have no less reason to complain than them." Seeing the Decembrists as a symptom of a European plot against monarchy and religion, he saw his life's work as essentially defensive. Nicholas kept the report of the Investigation Commission on his desk for the rest of his life—its "testimony so diverse, voluminous and complex that I need a firmness of mind to avoid getting lost in the chaos of it." It was his moral lodestar, his guide to ruling.

"I know I've been a disagreeable brigade commander, but now I'll change," he declared. But during the early days he talked a lot with the historian Karamzin who advised that "One of the worst political evils of our time is the absence of fear," adding that tsars should pay "more attention to men than forms." Nicholas put both maxims into action.

Nicholas is usually portrayed as a cardboard cut-out of a hubristically arrogant martinet, but he was a rare mixture: he possessed the acumen and the will to rule and control every detail of policy—and a strong sense of duty. He was a natural autocrat, perhaps the perfect model, yet he knew that autocracy was flawed. In January 1826, he created His Majesty's Own Chancellery* as his engine of autocracy. He saw "all life as service," his government as a military headquarters and ministers as officers who were simply required to obey orders, not analyse them. He was not looking for brilliance, prizing retainers who were "not wise, but service-orientated." As for the Council, it existed "only to give me its

---

* It was divided into five sections that had expanded to six by the 1840s. The First prepared his own decrees. The Second under Speransky codified the laws. The Third would be the secret police. The Fourth ran family charities, the Fifth the state serfs and the Sixth the Caucasus.

view on questions about which I seek such opinions, no more and no less." He used generals as all-purpose troubleshooters. This coterie had mostly served his brother, and had distinguished themselves in the Napoleonic wars, not to mention December 1825, so they had experienced politics at the highest level. Some were rigid pettifoggers but a few were imaginative and talented.* Using his personal authority to control his ministers and his Chancellery as a sort of government inspectorate to avoid arbitrary authoritarianism, his so-called "system" was in fact a haphazard personal arrangement of random autocratic interference.

On 25 June 1826, Nicholas appointed Alexander Benckendorff to head the Third Section of his Chancellery, a political police whose role was to "collect information concerning all events" and "dangerous and suspicious persons." Benckendorff, inspired by the police in Austria, had canvassed Nicholas for the creation of this secret police and he also took control of the small Gendarmerie, which already existed under the War Ministry. He became its commander, expanding it into a political police force to become "the moral physician of the people." He hoped that its reassuring officers in their bright-blue uniforms would "embrace the whole empire, be feared and respected and inspired by the moral authority of its chief"—himself.

Benckendorff set up his office at 16 Fontanka, employing just sixteen staff plus 300 Gendarmes, but the revolt had transformed denunciation and surveillance into acts of patriotism. He collected informers and zealously perlustrated mail until his deputy, Maxim von Fock, could rightly boast, "It is impossible to sneeze in one's house without it being reported to the Sovereign within an hour."

Benckendorff was an unlikely secret policeman. This once dissolute Baltic German aristocrat, son of Empress Maria's dearest friend and brother of Dorothea Lieven, was so vague that he sometimes forgot his own name and had to consult his own business card. When the empress, Mouffy, first arrived in Petersburg, Benckendorff had danced and flirted with her. "I had been told a lot about him," she recalled, "and heard his courage in war extolled and his wild way of living deplored though everyone laughed over it," but his "composure of manner struck me as it corresponded in no way to his reputation as a rake."†

---

* He appointed the first Court Minister to run the court with its thousands of courtiers and servants, the Romanov family, estates and palaces, as well as the chivalric orders. For the rest of the dynasty, this was one of the positions closest to the throne: he chose Alexander I's inseparable companion Prince Peter Volkonsky for the job.

† In 1811 he had been seconded to the Paris embassy where he seduced a French actress whom he shared for a while with Napoleon himself. Leaving the embassy under a cloud he smuggled the actress back into Russia before scandal forced him to send her home. Only his heroic war record redeemed him.

Though he was fifteen years older than Nicholas, Benckendorff regularly dined *en famille* with the emperor and believed that "Russia's past was admirable, its present is more than magnificent and as for its future—it is beyond anything that the boldest mind can imagine." He boasted that he alone told truth to power and had a licence to say the unsayable, proposing at various times, religious toleration, the urgent building of railways and the abolition of serfdom.

The tsar must always be awesome and move in mysterious ways: on his lightning tours, he and his secret police chief would share a *drozhky*, travelling at high speed and warning no one, as he told Benckendorff, "in order to keep my route in complete secrecy, all the more to astound Moscow." But, for all his feyness, Benckendorff's menacingly pompous harassment of artists, orchestrated by the tsar, made him the first of Russia's long line of bullying secret policemen.[3]

On 25 July 1826, the emperor rode into Moscow flanked by his brother Michael, but his little son Alexander was the real star. On 30 July "There was a great review," Nicholas's mother told his sister. "Sasha [Alexander] was with his regiment and went past his father, riding his fat horse at a gallop . . . a little angel, perfectly at ease, noticing everything without any false embarrassment. His father is so thrilled and everyone was enchanted with this child." When Constantine arrived, the three brothers and little Alexander prayed at the Dormition Cathedral. "You can't imagine the enthusiasm which Constantine's arrival causes here," wrote Maria. "People make the sign of the cross, and now say all the lies that plagued us are put to rest."

On 22 August, Nicholas crowned himself, with Constantine acting as his "assistant just as he was at Alexander's coronation," wrote their delighted mother. Afterwards, the heroes of 14 December, Orlov and Chernyshev, were raised to count, while the imperial nanny-virago, Charlotte Lieven, became a princess. Nicholas's manifesto promised gradual reform "not by daring and rash dreams, which are always destructive, but gradually and from above"—and he made a signal of reconciliation.

On Wednesday 8 September, Nicholas received the poet Pushkin, worn down by six years of provincial exile.* Their relationship was so

---

* Alexander I had exiled Pushkin, working for the Foreign Ministry, to New Russia where he caused lascivious scandal wherever he went. Seconded to the court of Count Michael Vorontsov, governor-general, Pushkin had an affair with Vorontsov's wife, Elise, daughter of Potemkin's niece Sashenka. He probably wrote *The Talisman* in her honour—and he boasted that he was the father of the Vorontsovs' daughter Sophia, breaking the code of discretion. Vorontsov sent him to inspect a plague of locusts. Pushkin avenged himself with this verse on Vorontsov: "Half an English lord, half a merchant / Half a sage, half an ignoramus / Half a scoundrel, but there's hope / That he'll be whole in the end."

unequal that one forgets they were almost the same age—the tsar was thirty, Pushkin now twenty-seven—but the contrast between the strapping pewter-eyed emperor and the tiny, simian poet with wild whiskers could not have been greater. Nicholas noticed that Pushkin had sores. Having heard of the poet's promiscuity, he suspected they were "from a notorious disease." Benckendorff had suggested to Nicholas that the poet "is undoubtedly pretty much of a good-for-nothing but if one is successful in directing his pen, then this will be advantageous." Anyway this pardoning of young talent suited Nicholas's notions of chivalry. "The emperor received me," wrote Pushkin, "in the kindest way possible."

"What would you have done had you been in Petersburg on 14 December?" asked Nicholas.

"I would have been in the ranks of the rebels," replied Pushkin.

Nicholas asked "would he give me his word to think and act differently if I released him?"

Pushkin "stretched out his hand with a promise to become different," and the tsar offered to become Pushkin's personal patron. "The tsar has freed me from censorship," wrote the poet. "He himself is my censor."

Afterwards Nicholas introduced Pushkin to his courtiers: "Here is my Pushkin!" That night at a ball, the tsar declared: "Today I had a long conversation with the cleverest man in Russia."

Encouraged by Benckendorff, Nicholas secretly contemplated fundamental reforms, even the abolition of serfdom, which he regarded as "an obvious evil," appointing a secret committee to consider them. But the committee, stacked with diehard reactionaries, proposed only minor changes and Nicholas never found the will or the moment to be more radical.[4] Besides, it required the committed will of the tsar—and he was repeatedly distracted by the more glorious urgencies of diplomacy and war.

Amid the coronation ceremonies, he learned that the Shah of Persia's crown prince Abbas Mirza had invaded the Caucasus. "I am just crowned," Nicholas exclaimed, "and here are the Persians occupying some of our provinces." Blaming the negligence of his Caucasian commander,* Nicholas promoted his favourite paladin. Ivan Paskevich, son

---

* General Alexei Yermolov, proudly descended from Genghiz Khan, was a hero of 1812. Pushkin described him as having "the head of a tiger on the torso of Hercules." Appointed by Alexander I in 1816, Yermolov's brutal repression of the defiant Chechen and Daghestan tribes sparked a full-scale jihadist insurgency. When Alexander challenged his methods, he boasted, "I desire that the terror of my name shall guard our frontiers more potently than chains or fortresses." But Benckendorff hated him, informing Nicholas that he had ruled the Caucasus "for ten years like a Turkish pasha"—he kept a harem of three Muslim concubines. More seriously, they suspected him of Decembrism. Mentioned as a sympathizer

of Ukrainian gentry, was a valiant veteran who in 1816 became young Nicholas's commander. Nicholas admired the general, fifteen years his senior, as "my father, my commanding officer." Others were less impressed: "an unbearable ass gifted only with the cunning of a Ukrainian," wrote his secretary, the poet Griboyedov, and "an idiot." He was touchy, arrogant, dull and scarcely literate, but aggressive and efficient. Paskevich stormed Persian strongholds. "Yerevan lies at the feet of Your Imperial Majesty," he reported in a chivalrous formula that appealed to Nicholas. When he took Tabriz, the Persians sued for peace, ceding Russia much of modern Armenia and Azerbaijan. Paskevich, granted a million roubles and raised to count with the surname Yerevansky, was promoted to commander-in-chief of the Caucasus. His victories were perfectly timed—another war was starting.[5]

Sultan Mahmud II had bowed before Nicholas's ultimatum but then called in the dynamic semi-independent ruler of Egypt, Mehmet Ali, to crush his Greek rebels. Nicholas agreed that a joint Anglo-French and Russian squadron should enforce a European solution. When the Egyptian–Ottoman fleet remained defiant, Admiral Codrington destroyed it at Navarino, which forced the sultan to agree to Greek independence. But as soon as London and Paris were satisfied, the sultan repudiated his promises to Nicholas and declared jihad.

In May 1828, as his troops advanced into present-day Romania, Nicholas enjoyed the exciting jaunt of war against Oriental inferiors. "Gaiety and good health are the order of the day," he boasted heartily to Constantine. "If Petersburg doesn't know where to gather in the evenings," wrote Nesselrode, "we don't suffer that dilemma here. We have several open houses . . . It is from morning to night an uninterrupted running fire of witticisms, bons mots and pranks."

On 27 May, Nicholas and his army crossed the Danube—but the Ottomans, though erratic in open battle, were formidable defenders of fortresses. Nicholas ordered three strongholds to be besieged simultaneously by overpromoted courtiers.* Nicholas's brother Michael repeatedly failed to storm Brailov. "Cheer up, my dear Michael, you did well, the army showed courage, do we have power over the will of Heaven?" he

---

in some interrogations, he had been slow to take the oath to Nicholas. Sending General Dibich down to dismiss the popular Yermolov without provoking "any fuss or trouble," Nicholas told him to investigate "the evil intentions of Yermolov, past and present; who's behind the evil in that nest of intrigues?" Yermolov was quietly and shabbily sacked.

* Nicholas demanded the storming of Varna, but there his commander, his friend Prince Alexander Menshikov, almost paid for his failure with his life: as he dismounted his horse, a cannonball flew between his legs, castrating him. Nicholas arrived at Varna himself and summoned the more competent Michael Vorontsov, governor-general of New Russia, who won its surrender.

chivvied him. "If Brailov won't surrender, I urge you to repeat the assault." Then he added, "If my opinion interests you, then let me tell you as a brother: 'I'm pleased with you!'"

The tsar fell ill with dysentery. Benckendorff told him he was no general and reported discontent in the empire. As the army withdrew back across the Danube, Nicholas returned to Petersburg* and appointed Dibich, who, in May 1829, recrossed the Danube and defeated the Ottomans. In the Caucasus, Paskevich captured Erzurum. The sultan sued for peace—Nicholas's second victory.[6]

"Russia dominates the world today," Lord Aberdeen, British foreign secretary, told Princess Lieven, "omnipotent everywhere." But on 29 July 1830, Charles X was overthrown in Paris, replaced by his cousin Louis-Philippe, whom Nicholas called "a vile usurper." But the tsar was confident: "Russia has nothing to fear." Danger was closer than he knew, however: in 1815 Poland had been given a constitution, but in the witchhunt for revolutionary societies, Alexander and Nicholas had cracked down on Polish freedoms. Constantine, commander-in-chief of the Polish army, was now loathed as a Russian tyrant.

On 17 November, Polish rebels attacked the Belvedere Palace in Warsaw hoping to capture Constantine. The Poles failed to seize him and he withdrew to his residence outside the city. Constantine could have put down the "riot" but not wishing to spoil his immaculate army, he hesitated and lost Warsaw. Nicholas brushed aside negotiations with moderates. "Well, now it's war," he told Dibich (now glorying in the surname Across-the-Balkans—Zabalkansky). But the Poles fought back. Dibich retreated.

"All this is truly inexplicable," Nicholas berated Dibich. "For God's sake be firm in your decisions, stop beating around the bush all the time and try, through some brilliant daring attack, to prove to Europe that the Russian army is still the same as twice marched to Paris." Nicholas sent in Paskevich. Cholera was spreading through the empire and it ravaged the army too, killing first Dibich, then Constantine. Nonetheless, Paskevich crushed Poland.

"Warsaw is at the feet of Your Imperial Majesty," he reported on 26 August 1831 to Nicholas, who rewarded him with the title prince of Warsaw and the governorship of Poland where he abolished the constitution and the kingdom. Nicholas earned the undying hatred of Poles:

---

* Just after his return in October 1828, his mother, Maria Fyodorovna, died. "Nicholas loved her, adored her," Mouffy wrote to Annette. "He's completely undone." Nicholas recounted Maria's death to his brother: "It's all over, my Michael, and we are orphans . . . She smiled one more time, hugging Lily, Adine, Kitty [Nicholas's daughters]. I can hardly write, no more strength!"

"I know they want to kill me, but if God doesn't will it, nothing will happen so I am quite calm."

In the east, the aggressive Egyptian strongman Mehmet Ali conquered Palestine and Syria and advanced towards Constantinople. Nicholas preferred a weak sultan to a strong Mehmet Ali. Sending ships and soldiers to save Constantinople, he persuaded the sultan to accept his protection. Persians,* Poles and Ottomans were at his feet, Austria and Prussia bowed before him, and within Russia his awesome majesty seemed Olympian.[7]

As Poland's rebellion was crushed, a cholera outbreak sparked rioting on the Haymarket in Petersburg. Hastening there with just two adjutants, Nicholas faced down the mob, then ordered them to their knees. "I have to ask God's mercy for your sins," thundered God's own emperor. "You have offended Him deeply. You've forgotten your duty of obedience to me and I must answer to God for your behaviour! Remember you're not Poles, you're not Frenchmen, you're Russians. I order you to disperse immediately." The rioters obeyed. No wonder Nicholas believed he was the sacred personification of Russia. "I am only here," he told his children preciously, "to carry out her orders and her intentions." Nicholas was convinced that "Our Russia was entrusted to us by God," once praying aloud at a parade: "O God, I thank Thee for having made me so powerful."

"No one was better created for the role," wrote Anna Tyutcheva, a young maid-of-honour who later wrote a superbly indiscreet diary. "His impressive handsomeness, regal bearing and severe Olympian profile—everything, down to the smile of a condescending Jupiter, breathed earthly deity." He played the role perfectly: "There is nothing more terrible on earth than the gaze of his colourless pewter eyes."

Nicholas worked late in his study. Minutely managing virtually everything, it was a tiring thing to be an autocrat. The tsar, noted his mother soon after his accession, "is overwhelmed with business. He's never in bed before 2 or 3 and doesn't even have time to have dinner in peace." He slept on a metal army cot under an army cloak and rose at dawn, dressed in his Horse Guards uniform with its skintight breeches;

---

* The poet-playwright Griboyedov was appointed Russian minister in Teheran, where he was hated for enforcing the peace treaty. He was lynched and torn to pieces: only a scar on his hand allowed the dismembered, headless carcass to be identified. Pushkin, travelling in the Caucasus, famously claimed to have seen his coffin on a cart returning to Tiflis. The dates do not match, so it is most probable that Pushkin invented this story. Griboyedov was buried in Tiflis, where his grave can still be seen. His young widow had it engraved: "Your spirit and works remain eternally in the memory of Russians. Why did my love for you outlive you?"

then he received ministers, usually Benckendorff, Chernyshev and Volkonsky, until ten when he joined the empress for an hour's breakfast.

Mouffy was the centre of his life. "Her tender nature and shallow mind replaced principles with sensitivity. Nicholas had a passionate adoration for this frail exquisite creature," placing her "in a golden cage of palaces, brilliant balls and handsome courtiers. She adored him and saw only the beautiful and happy." Even Pushkin was touched by her warm effervescence. "I love the empress terribly," he wrote, "despite the fact she's already thirty-five." Her graceful dancing was "like a winged lily" who "quietly weaves and glides." Nicholas appreciated her nature: "God has bestowed upon you such a happy character that it's no merit to love you." Only she could melt the despotic iceberg. When the Winter Palace caught fire, he ordered the firemen to rescue their love letters before anything else.* Even after decades of marriage, Nicholas wept when his doctors sent the frail Mouffy to take the sun in Palermo: "Happiness, joy and repose that is what I seek and find in my old Mouffy."[8]

Nicholas called this family breakfast *la revue de la famille* as if it was a military parade; yet family life, he told Annette, "is dearer to me than any conquest." Each of his children, four boys and three girls, was expected to keep a diary which the "father-commander," as he called himself, inspected along with their schoolwork. But Nicholas was most concerned to train his eldest son.

Alexander possessed the blue-eyed good looks of the Württembergs along with the blazing sensuality of Catherine the Great. But he was easy-going and emotional. Nicholas tried to avoid the brutal boredom of his own education by providing Alexander with teachers like the reformer Speransky, who advised him that in Russia's "pure monarchy" a tsar needed morality more than laws—and that he must always balance political factions and never place all his faith in one. His tutor was Vasily Zhukovsky, the romantic poet who had taught his mother Russian. "Learn to read the book that belongs to you from birth," he told the boy. "That book is Russia." Zhukovsky brought out the sensitivity of

* Nicholas loved to relax with his wife at "our paradise" at Peterhof. "At the Cottage, I am really happy," wrote Mouffy, to escape the "massive gilt" of the big palaces. Mouffy's estate Alexandria at Peterhof was given to her by Alexander. Nicholas celebrated his Ottoman victory by building their Gothic "Cottage," in fact a chunky mansion, with "For faith, tsar and fatherland" engraved over the door. Jokingly dubbing himself "Lord of the Cottage," he regarded this as "our favourite corner on earth." There they lived in "informal" bourgeois wholesomeness, later adding other ugly, mock-Gothic houses there for the children. (Under the last tsars, these expanded dachas became favourite summer residences.) Even there, Nicholas's family were meant to display their Romanov morality. The court and diplomatic corps were invited to watch the family taking tea.

the boy, whom he adored, and dared criticize the emperor himself for too much militarism. The tsar carefully balanced Mouffy's sweetness and Zhukovsky's sentimentality with a governor, General Karl Merder, a hero of 1812, who encouraged the family's pervasive militarism. Alexander grew up in his Life Guards uniform. When Merder recorded the boy's decent impulses but a lack of willpower and military ardour, Nicholas boomed, "I want him to know I won't be pleased by a lack of enthusiasm. He must be a soldier in his soul!" The balance worked.

Nicholas constantly analysed the heir. "My children are delightful," he told Annette, "the little fellow is definitely a soldier . . . my boy shoots with a big rifle and rides horseback with me," but he worried that he was "angelic but very absent minded"—like his soft-hearted mother. Alexander wept a lot. "30 March. Wrote badly and cried for no reason," he wrote in the diary that was inspected by his father.

Nicholas believed he could shape the boy: "What would you have done with the Decembrist rebels?"

"I would have forgiven them," replied little Alexander in Christian spirit.

"This is how you rule," replied Nicholas. "Remember this: die on the steps of the throne but don't give up power!" Duty and obedience ranked above all else. If Alexander had to be punished, Nicholas explained that "it's for the Motherland that you do your duty. It's not I but the Motherland who punishes and rewards you." But there was fun too: at Peterhof, Nicholas drilled the boys in their "play regiments" with real uniforms and rifles, in the Petrine tradition, and presided over character-building games in which the children and their friends had to race up the astonishingly beautiful cascade of fountains beneath the Great Palace.

Surprisingly it all worked: Alexander was the best-prepared heir in Romanov history. In April 1834, when he turned sixteen, Nicholas devised a solemn ceremony, held in the Great Church of the Winter Palace, at which Alexander took an oath, written by Speransky, to obey the autocrat and defend autocracy. Not just Alexander and his mother but even Nicholas ended up in tears. Henceforth all Romanov grand dukes celebrated their sixteenth birthdays in the same way.

Nicholas's second son was not a crybaby. Konstantin, always known as "Kostia," was "a big fat handsome fellow so quick I can't hold him," Nicholas told Annette. "He seems to belong to the family as the only thing he hears with pleasure is the drum." Another recruit!

Kostia, nicknamed "Aesop" for his clever sarcasm, was as awkward as he was ambitious, as caustic as Alexander was affable. He was naughty: only he dared pull a chair from under a minister, Count Ivan Tolstoy, who fell on the floor—in front of his father. "Madame, arise," Nicholas said to Mouffy. "We shall apologize to Ivan Matveievich for having brought up our son so badly." And Kostia had a will to power like his father: "Sasha [Alexander]," he complained in his tactless way, "was born before our father became emperor and I was born after. I am the son of an emperor and he is the son of a grand duke. It's unfair Sasha is the heir." As a boy, Alexander had agreed with him. "I wish I'd never been born a tsarevich," he told his tutor. This was all reported to Nicholas, who lectured Alexander on duty and destiny and Kostia on family unity.

Somehow both sons grew up not just revering but loving their father—though it was easier to be one of Jupiter's daughters. "Mary is in the giraffe stage . . . Ollie is getting thin," he told Annette, while the youngest Adini, whom he described as "very small and very mischievous," was his favourite: "a moppet—so sweet."

The emperor then returned to work, emerging much later for the frequent balls—public at the Winter Palace, private at his old home as grand duke, the Anichkov—at which his aquiline eye instantly noticed any infringements of the dress code. "I like people having fun," he said. "It keeps them from saying silly things."

His court was designed to be an awe-inspiring expression of his view of the world as a military hierarchy. Attended by a suite of 540 adjutants (more than doubled since Alexander), he regulated every detail of its Germanic ranks, the Great Processions on important holidays, the *baise-mains* on the imperial namedays, and the sartorial specifications, designing uniforms for men, dresses for women and servants, including the baggy red trousers, gold-braided, gold-epauletted black jackets, yellow shoes and white turbans of his twenty black guards, many of whom were now Americans.* At the Anichkov Palace, Mouffy loved to dance—and the tsar loved to flirt.[9]

Everyone in the family, even his mother, knew that Nicholas was highly sexed. When Mouffy was unable to have sex due to her frequent pregnancies, the empress dowager Maria had told Annette that "she needs to strengthen her health" as "Nicholas is already distracted at the abstinence he must observe." The courtiers encouraged the myth that the emperor looked elsewhere only after 1842 when Mouffy became ill but, however happy his marriage, his courtiers ran a well-oiled but discreet

---

* From Peter the Great to Catherine the Great, the black guards had been slaves from the markets of Constantinople. In 1810, the black valet of the US ambassador was recruited by the court. When the news spread, American slaves started to "defect" from American ships to enrol as "Nubians." Darker skins were sought to highlight the costumes. They were allowed to bring their families and visit America during the holidays. Under Nicholas, the best known was Alexander Gabriel, a US Navy cook who had deserted in a Russian port. But in 1851 Nicholas economized by cutting the number of Nubians from twenty to eight.

system of seduction, as well as a worldly coterie of married aristocratic beauties who were his mistresses.

For a while, the ruling favourite was the gold-curled "beautiful, amusing but cunning" Baroness Amalia Krüdener. One evening she had supped with Nicholas who then went on to flirt with another of his favourite beauties, Countess Elizaveta Buturlina. "You supped with him," an inquisitive courtier asked Amalia, "but last honours are for her?"

"He is a strange man," replied Amalia. "These things have to have a result but with him there is never an end, he hasn't the courage for it, he has a peculiar idea of fidelity."

When he saw a girl in the street or at a theatre who took his fancy, his adjutants approached her to arrange an assignation. "The tsar never met resistance to his lust," noted the French travel-writer the marquis de Custine. "I grew up feeling not only love but reverence," wrote a nineteen-year-old girl at court. "I regarded the tsar as an earthly god." When she was presented to him, "my heart fluttered. I felt my knees buckling." The tsar, observed Pushkin, ran "a harem of budding actresses."*

In 1832, he met a girl at a masque ball. As they danced, the masked beauty told him details of his own children which amazed him. At the end of the night, she revealed herself as Varvara Nelidova, a penniless orphan who knew so much because she was the niece of Emperor Paul's mistress. The emperor invited her to court where she charmed not only the empress but their daughter Olga, known as Ollie. Appointed maid-of-honour to his wife, "Varenka" as she was known "looked Italian and had lovely dark eyes and eyebrows," with marble shoulders, high breasts, tiny waist. She was "such fun," wrote Olga, "that she saw the comic side in everything. Papa often drank tea with her. She told him immodest stories that made Papa cry with laughter. Once he laughed so much his chair went over backwards." But the daughter insisted, as daughters do, that this was only an "innocent flirtation—Papa was faithful to his wife."

---

* The novelist Lev Tolstoy later described the emperor's seductions, probably based on the stories of his cousin Countess Alexandra Tolstoya, a lady-in-waiting. Nicholas meets a young girl at a masquerade at the theatre, noting "her whiteness, her beautiful figure, her tender voice," and leads her to a private box: "she proved to be a pretty twenty-year-old virgin, daughter of a Swedish governess" who tells Nicholas "how when quite a child, she had fallen in love with him from his portraits and made up her mind to attract his attention . . . Now she had succeeded and wanted nothing more—so she said. The girl was taken to the place where Nicholas usually had rendezvous with women and there he spent more than an hour with her . . ." This appears in the novella *Hadji Murat*, one of Tolstoy's last works. Even though it was written long afterwards in the reign of Nicholas II, there was no question of publishing it under the Romanovs. As for Mouffy, during the balls she enjoyed the innocent attentions of her own *cavaliere servente*, her favourite Chevalier-Garde, Prince Alexander Trubetskoi. But no one doubted her virtue.

The courtiers knew better. "Although the object of his affair lived in the Palace, no one ever drew attention to it," recalled lady-in-waiting Maria Frederiks. "It was done so subtly, so decently, so well. I saw them every day and never suspected anything, he held himself so respectfully in front of his wife and children. As for the lady, she never sought special privileges."

Nicholas's erotic life was organized with military punctilio: he visited Varenka twice daily, first at 9 a.m., then he joined the empress, before visiting her again at 1:30 p.m. Varenka devoted her life to the emperor. When she gave birth to children, they were said to have been adopted by his trusted retainer General Peter Kleinmikhel, who brought them up as his own—the ultimate service to his emperor.

Always on the lookout for new favourites, the emperor noticed Pushkin's new wife and devised a neat way to supervise him and flirt with her.[10]

In February 1831, the poet, thirty-one years old, married Natalya Goncharova, aged eighteen, a girl from a good family fallen on hard times. Even his proposal of marriage to Natalya had to be approved by the emperor. "His Imperial Majesty deigned to observe that he was pleased to believe . . . you had discovered within yourself those qualities of heart and character necessary for a woman's happiness, especially a woman as amiable and interesting as Mademoiselle Goncharova," wrote Benckendorff with fustian pomposity. Before they married, the bride wanted to check that the tsar still favoured her fiancé: "As for your individual position," Benckendorff lectured Pushkin, "His Imperial Majesty, in wholly paternal solicitude for you, sir, deigned to charge me, General Benckendorff, not as head of the gendarmerie but as the person in whom he pleases to place his confidence, to observe you and guide you by my counsel."

On 30 December 1833, "I had the title 'Gentleman of the Bedchamber' conferred on me (somewhat unbecoming for my years)," Pushkin complained. "But the court [meaning the tsar] wanted Natalya to dance at the Anichkov."

Pushkin soon felt the icy grip of autocracy. On 23 January he and Natalya attended their first imperial ball at the Anichkov. "I arrived in [court] uniform. I was told the guests were in tailcoats. I left. The Sovereign was displeased." Nicholas noticed immediately, telling Natalya: "He might have given himself the trouble to go and put on a tailcoat and return. Reproach him for it!"

Nicholas flirted with Natalya whenever he could, "dangling after her like some stripling officer," wrote Pushkin. He danced the French quadrille with her and sat next to her all supper. "Of a morning, he purposefully drives past her windows several times and in the evening, at a ball, asks why her blinds are always down." At first Pushkin enjoyed the court entertainments and was charmed by the empress who, laughing, greeted him—"Oh it's you!" Whenever they met at court, Nicholas talked to Pushkin and, when Natalya's dressmaker's invoices threatened to bankrupt him, lent him money, but the supervision was suffocating and, worse still, he found that not only did he have Nicholas and Benckendorff on his back but the minister of education, Sergei Uvarov, started to censor the poet too.

Uvarov, the son of a bandura-playing Guards officer who had flirted with Catherine the Great, was a classical scholar, Middle Eastern expert, pioneering geologist and visionary minister. Jealous of Pushkin, Uvarov orchestrated a campaign to undermine his reputation (and income) by attacking his history of the Pugachev Rebellion and his masterpiece, *Onegin*, the novel in poetry of heartbreak and duelling that, in many ways, created modern Russian literature. Nicholas tried to protect Pushkin,* but Uvarov was his chief ideologist, much more important to him than a penniless poet.

Pushkin loathed Uvarov, whose sycophancy, social-climbing and secret homosexuality he mocked in verse, but he soon learned that Benckendorff's spies were worse. In a letter to his wife about the coming of age of Caesarevich Alexander, he reflected, "I don't intend to present myself to the Heir with congratulations . . . I've seen three tsars. The first [Paul] ordered my cap to be taken off and scolded my nurse; the second [Alexander] was not gracious to me and the third drafted me as a page of the bedchamber." When Benckendorff's agents opened the letter, Nicholas was furious. The poet was disgusted: "What profound immorality there is in the usages of our government! The police unseal a husband's letters to his wife and take them to the tsar (a well-brought-up and honourable man) and the tsar is not ashamed to admit this and put in motion an intrigue worthy of Vidocq [the French criminal who became a secret police chief]."

* The tsar himself intervened in these games of literary malice on Pushkin's behalf. "My dear friend," Nicholas wrote to Benckendorff. "I forgot to tell you that in today's *Bee* [literary journal] there's a most unjust vulgar article directed against Pushkin," and he suggested that Benckendorff summon the critic "and forbid him to publish any criticism whatever." Every writer suffering bad reviews might wish for such a protector, but the critic in question was not only Uvarov's creature but Benckendorff's informer and Nicholas did not insist. Pushkin's experience typified the stifling control by the Third Section over intellectual life. The intellectuals reacted in different ways. In 1836, Peter Chadaev published his *Letters on the Philosophy of History* attacking Russia for living "entirely within the narrowest confines of the present without a past or future, amid dead calm," which he blamed on the backwardness of Orthodoxy. Nicholas had Chadaev declared insane.

Pushkin resigned from court which Nicholas regarded as ingratitude. "I never detain anybody," the tsar told Zhukovsky. "But in that case, everything will be finished between us," a threat that made Pushkin withdraw his resignation. "I pardon him," Nicholas told Benckendorff, "but summon him to explain the senselessness of his behaviour."

Pushkin had to endure watching the attentions that his wife enjoyed as a court beauty, attentions that would now lead to tragedy. At a ball, a guest watched Natalya surrounded by flirting Guards officers—while "a little to the side, stood a pensive Alexander Sergeievich [Pushkin] taking not the slightest part in the conversation."[11]

A young Guardsman fell obsessively in love with Natalya. Baron Georges d'Anthes was a French exile who had arrived in Petersburg with his older patron, Baron Jakob van Heeckeren, the Dutch ambassador. Heeckeren was homosexual, and clearly in love with d'Anthes, whom he adopted as his son. The ambassador had him enrolled in the gorgeously kitted Chevalier-Gardes who patrolled the palace. Whether d'Anthes "lived with Heeckeren or Heeckeren with him," wrote his fellow Chevalier-Garde Prince Alexander Trubetskoi, who shared rooms with him, "buggery at that time was widespread in high society. To judge by the fact that d'Anthes continually pursued ladies, it must be assumed his relations with Heeckeren were passive."

"I am madly in love," d'Anthes told Heeckeren in January 1836, with "the most delicious creature in Petersburg . . . and she loves me," but "the husband is revoltingly jealous." Delighted momentarily by the Frenchman, Natalya flirted too, but d'Anthes' obsession became that of a stalker who deluded himself into believing that they had had an affair and then could not accept that he had been rejected. In the autumn, he started again, cynically pursuing Natalya's plainer unmarried sister Ekaterina to get closer to her. Meanwhile the tsar himself, meeting Natalya at the Razumovskys', warned her to guard her spotless reputation.

On 4 November, Pushkin received an anonymous letter nominating him as "coadjutor to the Grand Master of the Order of Cuckolds." The poet was troubled even though he was not the only one to receive such a letter. Natalya confessed her flirtations with d'Anthes to Pushkin, who never doubted her innocence but believed (wrongly) that Heeckeren had sent the letters.* Pushkin challenged d'Anthes to a duel. Heeckeren tried to avoid the challenge by pushing d'Anthes to marry Natalya's

---

* The sender has never been identified but the ambassador was an unlikely culprit for there was no upside for him in a public scandal. Probably the sender was a malicious prankster, the crippled civil servant and social gadfly Prince Peter Dolgoruky, aged twenty, who had a proven taste for sending anonymous letters.

sister, Ekaterina, whom he had seduced in order to force Pushkin to call off the duel. Finally Pushkin agreed. The emperor summoned Pushkin and made him promise not to fight. When d'Anthes went through with the marriage to Natalya's sister, even the empress was fascinated: "is it devotion or diversion?" But now that d'Anthes was Natalya's brother-in-law, he could publicly flirt with her.

On 21 January 1837, the emperor, along with the Pushkins and the newly married d'Anthes, met at a ball where Nicholas reassured the poet of his wife's chastity. Pushkin, bursting with indignation, had to thank him.

"But could you have expected aught else from me?" replied Nicholas smugly.

"Not only could, Sire, but to speak frankly, I suspected you too of paying court to my wife." Across the ballroom, Pushkin watched furiously as d'Anthes praised her with outrageous double entendres which Natalya later reported to her husband.

Next morning, Pushkin wrote a deliberately insulting letter to Ambassador van Heeckeren—"the pimp of your son." D'Anthes challenged Pushkin to a duel. On the afternoon of 27 January, Pushkin and d'Anthes met, each accompanied by seconds, on the outskirts of Petersburg. They were placed twenty paces apart and handed their pistols. Pushkin was taking aim when d'Anthes fired. Pushkin was hit in the side and fell, but he got up to take his shot which passed through the fleshy part of d'Anthes' arm, bouncing off a button, to do him no more harm than a scratch. But d'Anthes' bullet had travelled through Pushkin's stomach to smash his sacrum. Called urgently to Pushkin's apartment, the imperial doctor Nikolai Arendt reported to the tsar that he was dying. "If God ordains we are not to meet again in this world," the tsar, just back from the theatre, wrote to Pushkin, "then accept my forgiveness and my advice to die in a Christian manner, and do not worry about your wife and children. They will be my children and I will take them into my care." Ordering the doctor to deliver this, Nicholas added, "I won't go to bed, I'll wait."

Pushkin kissed the letter. He took communion. His pain intensified as gangrene inflamed his intestines. Dr. Arendt eased his suffering with opium, while Natalya had hysterics. The tsar summoned Zhukovsky. "Tell him from me I congratulate him on fulfilling his Christian duty," said Nicholas sanctimoniously. On the afternoon of 29 January, Pushkin died. Nicholas ordered Zhukovsky to inspect his papers for treason. Instead Zhukovsky was disgusted to see how Pushkin had been harassed, scolding Benckendorff: "These reprimands of such little account to you coloured his whole life. You turned this protection into police control."

Ten thousand mourners passed the body in his apartment. The outpouring of grief was policed by Uvarov and Benckendorff who banned press articles reporting the funeral. Nonetheless huge crowds attended St. Isaac's Cathedral, after which the coffin was despatched to be buried near Pushkin's Mikhailskoe estate. Nicholas would have been amazed to learn that his own triumphs have been overshadowed in historical memory by this mere poet who would be revered as Russia's true royalty.[*12]

Yet Nicholas was not getting his way everywhere. He was losing a war against jihadists led by Imam Shamyl in Chechnya and Daghestan, in the eastern Caucasus. But when Russia's fortunes improved and he heard that victory was finally imminent, Nicholas decided to receive the surrender in person.

On 8 October, as the emperor, accompanied by Adlerberg, rode in his carriage down the precipitous road towards his Georgian capital Tiflis, "The horses bolted," he reported to Paskevich, "and we would certainly have plunged into the abyss as the horses headed over the parapet if the hand of God had not intervened. The horses hung by their necks over the edge until the traces broke and they fell, releasing us with a small injury. I thought I would die." Afterwards, escorted by twenty-four Georgian princes, the shaken Nicholas entered Tiflis to a jubilant welcome. To the north-east, his generals had trapped Shamyl, whom Nicholas expected to come to Tiflis and submit.

The mountain tribes had been resisting the Christian advance into the Caucasus ever since the 1780s, but Russia's clumsy brute force had sparked a full-scale jihadist insurgency. In 1834, Shamyl had murdered his predecessor and declared himself the imam of the black-bannered Murids, a movement of Sufi Islam. When his stronghold was stormed, Shamyl, though wounded, had leapt over the walls into an abyss and escaped, the only warrior to survive.

Now in 1837, he had been forced to agree an armistice which had been broken by the Russians themselves. He refused to submit and, fortifying a new stronghold, Akhulgo, Shamyl returned to war. The Russian victory was spoiled as much by Nicholas's meddling and the bureaucratic

* Nicholas had d'Anthes court-martialled and escorted to the border. "Heeckeren," the tsar wrote to his brother Michael, "behaved like a vile blackguard. He pimped for d'Anthes in Pushkin's absence." Heeckeren was recalled, but later became Dutch ambassador in Vienna. D'Anthes, who had three daughters with Ekaterina, thrived in France and lived until 1895. Nicholas kept his word to Pushkin, awarding a generous settlement to Natalya and the children. When she returned to Petersburg, the empress made her a maid-of-honour, while Nicholas's courtier Baron Korff noted that she "belongs to that group of privileged young women whom the emperor occasionally favours with his visits." Giving her 25,000 roubles, he sponsored her second marriage to a general. This looks like the aftermath of an affair, but there is no evidence that one took place. Natalya died in 1863.

rivalries of different committees and ministers as by Shamyl's genius for asymmetrical warfare.

In Tiflis, Nicholas's adjutants tried to entertain him with anything from celebrations of mass to girls, but the emperor replied, "I have no eyes but for my army." Before he left, he appointed new generals to crush Shamyl. "Now," he declared with preposterous magniloquence, as he climbed into his carriage, "I know the meaning of the words in Genesis—'let there be light and there was light.' "*[13]

On 21 October, at Novocherkask, Nicholas met up with his son Alexander and together they rode in Cossack uniform through the ranks of the Don Cossacks who then gathered in a circle around the cathedral. There the ataman gave the mace of office to Nicholas, who then handed it to a thrilled Alexander. "May this serve as proof of how close you are to my heart," boomed Nicholas, before turning to the Cossacks and crying, "When he replaces me, serve him as loyally as you serve me!"

In fact, Nicholas was worried about his son's indiscipline and erotic adventures. Alexander, now nineteen, had been on a tour of the empire, accompanied by his poet-tutor Zhukovsky. Alexander was mobbed by crowds, who described him as a "beauty," but he was pursued by his father's lecturing letters. "I try to find in you," wrote Nicholas, "the promise of future happiness for our beloved Mother Russia, the one for which I live, to which you were dedicated even before you were born!"

Alexander tried to live up to his paternal Jupiter, whom he saw as "the personification of our Fatherland, more than a father." He coped by developing a "powerful secretiveness," that essential armour of heirs to the throne. He also inherited his father's libido—without his glacial control. At fourteen, he fell in love with his mother's maid-of-honour Natalya Borzdina: after one of Nicholas's masquerade balls in medieval dress at Tsarskoe Selo, Alexander rendezvoused with her in the park,

---

* Back in Petersburg, there was light of a different and destructive sort. On 17 December 1837, Nicholas was at the theatre when Volkonsky, court minister, informed him that the Winter Palace was on fire, burning "like a volcano in the midst of Petersburg." Thirty Guardsmen were killed. Nicholas directed the fire-fighting, despatching Alexander to extinguish another fire at the docks. Most of the Hermitage's treasures were saved, heaped up in the snow. It was now that Nicholas touchingly ordered the saving of his love letters from Mouffy before anything else. The empress, aided by her ladies-in-waiting, packed her things until the heat was unbearable and he ordered her out. The family moved to the Anichkov. The palace burned for three days as crowds watched in dead silence. Nicholas ordered it rebuilt in a year, a seemingly impossible schedule, but the task was achieved by his harshest henchman Kleinmikhel and 6,000 workers at a terrible cost in lives. Nicholas's truly sumptuous Winter Palace, today's Hermitage Museum, was built to impress. With its 1,050 rooms and 177 staircases, it is so vast that it was said a peasant servant brought not only his entire family but a cow to provide milk for his children, and no one noticed until the stench of cow dung became unbearable.

a tryst at which he lost his virginity. Nicholas dealt with this like a true Victorian paterfamilias, taking his son to visit a syphilis hospital. But this did not discourage Alexander, who now fell in love with another of Mouffy's maids-of-honour, a Polish girl, Olga Kalinovskaya. Alexander told everyone, even his mother, about his love for Olga. Nicholas read his son's diary with some amusement. But, alarmed by hints of marriage, he removed the girl and gave Alexander some guidance: "I explained that fondness for one female is natural but no need to surrender to dreams if they aren't appropriate in rank or status. I think his taste is decent"—even if he did have an attraction for Polish girls.

Alexander "needs a stronger personality," Mouffy told her lady-in-waiting Baroness Frederiks. "Otherwise he will perish. He falls in love too easily. He must be removed from Petersburg." Hence his tour of Russia—but on his return, he missed Kalinovskaya and moped. Observing this "tendency to reverie," the emperor ordered him to find a wife and despatched him on a European tour.

After Berlin, Vienna, Milan, he passed through Hesse-Darmstadt where he was attracted by Princess Marie, modest, pretty and slight. "I like her terribly at first sight," he wrote to Nicholas, who had heard, like the rest of Europe, that there was a problem with Marie, who was possibly the daughter not of the duke but of a French stablemaster. Travelling on to London, he was enamoured by the single twenty-year-old Queen Victoria. "I'm really quite in love with the Grand Duke, a dear delightful young man," she gushed in her diary on 27 May 1839. "The Grand Duke is so very strong, you are whisked around like in a waltz which is very pleasant . . . I never enjoyed myself more. I got to bed at ¼ to 3 but I couldn't sleep till 5!" Nicholas warned Alexander that such a marriage was impossible, but he could return to Darmstadt.

On his last evening with Victoria, Alexander "took my hand and pressed it warmly; he looked pale and his voice faltered as he said, 'Words fail me to express what I feel.'" He kissed her hand and cheek. "I felt so sad to take leave of this dear amiable young man. He is so frank, so really young and merry" with "such a nice open countenance, sweet smile," wrote Victoria, "and such a manly figure."

Back in Darmstadt, Alexander and mournful Marie exchanged long love letters. Alexander sent his favourite adjutant, Prince Alexander Bariatinsky, to ask his father's permission. "Our joy, the joy of the whole family is indescribable, this sweet Marie is the fulfilment of our hopes," enthused the tsar. "How I envy those who met her before me."

Once home again, Alexander returned to Kalinovskaya. Nicholas was infuriated, threatening to disinherit him like Peter the Great and make Kostia the heir. But Alexander corrected himself. His Hessian princess was brought to Petersburg at sixteen, and converted to Ortho-doxy as Maria Alexandrovna—though she was always known as Marie. Her early married life was dominated by her parents-in-law. After the wedding in April 1841, they lived in the Winter Palace right next to Alexander's parents, while at weekends they were given the Farm at Peterhof, another mock-Gothic house beside the Cottage. Within two years, Marie gave birth to a daughter, the first of many children, but she suffered at court. Anxiety caused her to break out in rashes that she covered with a veil. "I lived like a voluntary fireman, ready to jump at the alarm" but not sure "where to run or what to do." Her role was simple: to please the emperor, deliver children—and turn a blind eye to Alexander's adventures. She succeeded at all three, becoming beloved by the courtiers. Alexander was kind and solicitous, but she was hardly the lubricious partner for this breezy Lothario: he was probably still in love with Kalinovskaya, now Princess Oginski: her son Bogdan, born in 1848, was widely believed to be his.

Meanwhile Alexander was groomed for power. He attended the State Council, commanded the Guards, served on the Caucasus Committees, but like every fashionable officer, he longed to serve in the war against Shamyl. Finally Nicholas let him go. In the forests, the heir led a charge against the Chechens. The Russians were closing in on Shamyl.[14]

In June 1839, Nicholas's generals besieged Shamyl in his strong-hold Akhulgo for eighty days and forced him to give up his eldest son Jemal-Eddin as a hostage for his good behaviour. On 29 August Akhulgo fell—but Shamyl had vanished. "Excellent," Nicholas wrote on the despatches. "So far so good. But a pity Shamyl escaped." He had Jemal-Eddin brought to Petersburg, where he welcomed the boy whom he hoped to train to become his puppet ruler of the northern Caucasus. The tsar set him up in a townhouse with his own Russian nanny. Prince Jemal-Eddin Shamyl was enrolled in the Corps de Pages. The empress took him for walks. He became russified but was tortured by memories of his indestructible father.

Shamyl, bitter at losing his son, rebuilt his armies until, by 1844, Nicholas realized that his campaign had failed. So he turned to the most sophisticated of his grandees, Count Michael Vorontsov, governor-general of New Russia and Crimea. Even though Vorontsov was sixty-two and afflicted with eye-trouble, Nicholas appointed him viceroy of the Caucasus with powers unknown since Potemkin.*

---

* Vorontsov, nicknamed "Milord," was brought up in London, where his father Simon was ambassador, and at Wilton, the seat of his sister who married the earl of Pembroke. A hero of the Napoleonic wars, he had commanded the Russian occupation forces in France then

Moving to Tiflis, Vorontsov meticulously planned his war, but the emperor ordered him to begin before he was ready. In June 1845, Vorontsov marched into Daghestan; Shamyl withdrew. "God has crowned you with success," Nicholas told Vorontsov, "and shown nothing can ever stop the Orthodox Russians when they go where their tsar bids them." But when the Russian forces reached Shamyl's capital, Dargo, they found it abandoned and themselves surrounded. Vorontsov barely escaped, losing 4,000 men. The chastened tsar praised Milord and raised him to prince, letting him pursue his undramatic strategy of cutting off Shamyl's supplies.

Shamyl now found support in Britain. He wrote to Queen Victoria. The British lionized the plucky Islamic warriors, raised funds and sent rifles, while Nicholas was increasingly regarded as a dictator* who aspired to swallow the Ottoman empire—and threaten British India. Nicholas decided that only his own charm could conquer the British.[15]

On 21 June 1844 a traveller named "Count Orlov" disembarked at Woolwich on a Dutch steamer. When he arrived at the Russian embassy in London (turning down an invitation to stay at Buckingham Palace) it was already after midnight, but the mysterious count wrote to Prince Albert, the Coburg who had recently married Queen Victoria, asking to meet her immediately. Albert was not impressed with such autocratic caprice: Nicholas, he told Victoria, "is a man inclined too much to impulse and feeling which makes him act wrongly often."

The very pregnant Victoria received Nicholas the next morning and invited him to Windsor. Arriving by train on 23 June, he refused the decadent comforts of a soft democratic bed and insisted on sleeping

---

helped make Odessa a thriving cosmopolitan city attracting Jewish and Italian settlers. With his Polish wife, Italian valet, French cook, Hungarian mistress and English groom, Vorontsov was a European who favoured Anglophile liberalism and modern technology. His coolness was no myth. When he caught his mistress, Irma Csesenyi, young Hungarian wife of his vintner, *in flagrante* with an adjutant, Vorontsov did not turn a hair. "Cornet," he said, "you are not in your uniform"—and went on to the verandah to smoke a cigar. His wife Elise was a daughter of Potemkin's niece Sashenka Branitska. She was raised in the Winter Palace, dandled by Catherine the Great. "One of the most attractive women of her time," observed a visitor. "I've never seen anything comparable to the smile on her lips which seemed to demand a kiss." In Crimea, the Vorontsovs built the Alupka Palace, in a style combining Scottish baronial with Moorish fantasia, that first made the Crimean Riviera fashionable. During the Yalta Conference of 1945, Churchill and the British delegation stayed at Alupka.

* Nicholas's image was damaged by a gossipy bestseller, *Russia in 1839*, by the camp French travel-writer the marquis de Custine. Benckendorff, spin-doctor as well as a secret policeman, suggested that Nicholas give Custine an interview, but the marquis sketched Nicholas as the brutish, megalomaniacal and adulterous tyrant of a barbarically aggressive empire that "is itself a prison, whose vast size only makes it more formidable."

on the steel cot and straw-filled leather pallet that he had brought with him.

"I highly prize England," he told Victoria and Albert, "but for what the French say about me, I care not at all! I spit on it!" The British were disturbed by this giant dogmatic Jupiter who told Sir Robert Peel, the prime minister, "I am taken for an actor but I'm not. I am thoroughly straightforward." Perhaps too straightforward. Peel asked him to talk more quietly as everyone could hear his booming pronouncements. "Turkey is a dying man," he thundered. "He will, he must die! A critical moment. I shall have to put my armies in motion; Austria must do the same . . . and the English and her maritime forces. Thus a Russian army, an Austrian army, a great English fleet will all be congregated." Now he came to the point of his trip—an understanding with Britain to plan for Ottoman disintegration without a war yet with the flexibility to express Russia's messianic mission to influence Constantinople and to have access through the Straits, a strategic necessity: "So many powderkegs close to the fire, how to prevent sparks from catching? I don't claim one inch of Turkish soil but neither will I allow any other to have an inch of it." So he proposed maintaining the status quo—and a "straightforward understanding" in case the Ottomans collapsed.

The louder he talked, the less the British believed him and the more anxious they became about his aggressive designs. After nine days, the prince consort travelled to Woolwich to see off the emperor. Victoria was not impressed by him. "He seldom smiles and when he does, the expression is not a happy one," wrote Victoria in an astute judgement. Her visitor was "stern and severe . . . his mind is an uncivilized one . . . Politics and military are the only things he takes an interest in." His autocracy was even worse, she thought, because "he is sincere, even in his most dogmatic acts," convinced "that's the only way to govern. Very clever I don't think him."[16]

She was right. Behind the bombast, he was jittery—and the risks of European revolution increased throughout his reign. Russia desperately needed reform, but the more it needed modernization in a changing Europe, the higher the risks in a revolutionary age. Nicholas sought comfort in his army as the perfect expression of his love of order where "no one commands before he himself has learned to obey . . . everything is subordinated to one goal, everything has its purpose." He was always the officer of 1815: that glory was the apogee of the Russian experience, expressed for him through the military uniforms that he meticulously designed, down to the buttons and the colour of moustaches (dyed black, he insisted, whatever the officer's hair colour), and the balletic perfection of his endless parades which reassured him that Russia was still at the height of its glory. In preserving this army as a museum of Napoleonic magnificence, he damned the very institution he most loved. But like the enlightened despots of the eighteenth century, great systemizers who avoided any reform that would impinge on their power, he respected Russia's laws and ordered Speransky to codify them: forty-five volumes were published during the 1830s. He promoted education for his civil servants, founding a school of jurisprudence. He despised serfdom—"Serfdom is an evil obvious to all"—and repeatedly returned to plans to reform or abolish it. He appointed his most gifted reformer, Count Paul Kiselev, to his Imperial Chancellery to clarify the status of the millions of crown peasants, declaring them "free inhabitants"—yet they were not freed. Nicholas finally decided that reforming serfdom was dangerous: "to touch it now would be even more destructive."

Meanwhile he sought an ideology to counteract the rising fervours of liberalism and nationalism that threatened his world. The idea of the nation as a political-cultural expression had been propagated by the French Revolution, yet ironically it was the war of liberation against Napoleon that had really legitimized nationalism as the authentic spirit of a people. In Russia, where politics was banned, literature offered a new, often coded, language to express forbidden aspirations. The literary salons of Moscow became the battlefield of a debate on the nature of Russia itself between so-called "Westerners" and "Slavophiles." The Westerners were split between liberals and socialists. The liberals, of whom there were never many, wanted Russia to become a constitutional monarchy, like, say, Britain. The socialists, espousing ideas that were just beginning to strike a chord in Russia, believed a class revolution must liberate the peasantry to achieve universal equality.

The Slavophiles espoused a nationalist cult of Russia's exceptional identity as a guide both to its role in the world and to the nature of its government at home, a vision they believed had been undermined by the Western reforms of Peter the Great. They idealized the "Russian World" of peasantry, villages, rituals and Orthodoxy, while disdaining the flaccid, decadent West. But Nicholas did not recognize that these insolent scribblers had any right to discuss matters best left to their tsar.

While he was horrified by such emotional populism anywhere in Europe and believed in Russia as empire as much as nation, even he was cautiously influenced by the zeitgeist. Nationalism, under his imperial aegis and in the right context, could strengthen the foundations of the autocracy. His brilliant long-serving education minister, Uvarov, a conservative romantic, provided the intellectual framework to defend sacred autocracy and Russian exceptionalism. "Our duty," declared Uvarov in 1833, "is to see that, in accordance with the supreme intention of our August Monarch, the education of the people is carried out in the united spirit of Orthodoxy, Autocracy and Nationality." In Nicholas's mind, only he would decide what Russian nationhood meant, in parallel with his conception of a multi-ethnic empire, but there were flaws in this. After all, this was a tsar who was by birth almost totally Germanic and had promoted more Baltic Germans to high positions than anyone since Empress Anna. When one of his officials, Yuri Samarin, proposed the russification of the Baltics, Nicholas imprisoned him briefly and reprimanded him: "What you really meant is that since Emperor Paul we have been surrounded by Germans and have ourselves been Germanized." Yet his own policy promoted Orthodox Russians as the leading people of the empire and implicitly excluded Catholic Poles, Protestant Balts, Muslim Tatars and of course Jews, who were the first to suffer.[17]

Nicholas had been taught to hate the Jews by his Scottish nanny Jane Lyon and as a youngster travelling through Russia described them as "absolute leeches, fastening themselves everywhere and completely exhausting these unfortunate provinces." He admitted to the British ambassador that "I have no great feeling for the Jews." Now promoting his new ideology, he regarded his several million Jews as an insult to Orthodoxy and devised restrictions and taxes to break them. In 1827, he ordered conscription into the army of Jewish boys from the age of twelve for twenty-five years "to move them most effectively to change their religion." Since 1804, Jews had technically had to live in the Pale, parts of Poland and Ukraine, but enforcement of this requirement was uneven. In 1835, Nicholas tightened and enforced the regulations, banning Jews from all major cities and limiting their freedoms in many ways, including their rights to own land. He planned to abolish Jewish communities, outlaw traditional dress and deploy a combination of education and harassment to persuade them to convert.

Nicholas's anti-semitism was "the most ludicrous policy since the pharaohs," in Vorontsov's opinion. "We are persecuting, hindering from living, a million citizens . . . a peaceful, submissive, industrious people, the only active people in our Polish provinces," though he added that personally "I find their customs repellent."

The British, already uneasy about Russia, were disgusted by this growing anti-semitism, which now became a European issue for the first time. In April 1846, Sir Moses Montefiore, then aged sixty-one, a wealthy baronet and brother-in-law of the banker N. M. Rothschild,

arrived in Petersburg. His mission was backed by Prime Minister Peel.*
At 1 p.m. on 28 May, the tsar himself received Montefiore, telling him
that the guard outside the palace that day was composed of Jewish soldiers: "They were always brave—the Maccabees!" But when Montefiore
insisted that all Russian Jews were loyal and industrious, Nicholas pa-
tronizingly replied: "If they were like you." Montefiore later admitted
that the tsar's remarks "against the Jews made every hair on my head
stand on end." As for Nicholas, he thought the Englishman was "kind
and honest yet a Jew and a lawyer—and for this it is forgivable for him
to wish many things." On his way home, Montefiore was mobbed by
the Jews of Vilna, the Jerusalem of the North. The Third Section secret
policemen reported the excitement of the "greedy Yids" who flocked to
"the English Messiah." He achieved little, but he kept the white gloves
he had worn that day for the rest of his life.[18] Yet the real threat to Russia
came not from home but from abroad.

"We must be ready," Nicholas told his "father-commander" Paskevich
soon after returning from England. "No mercy with these people."
While the tsar was anxiously watching Russia for signs of impending
revolution, he suffered a series of blows in his personal life. His children were growing up and, as his daughters married, he celebrated and
yet missed them.† He allowed his youngest and favourite, Adini—"the
little moppet"—to marry a Hessian prince, but she was already showing
signs of TB. On 30 July 1844, Adini died aged nineteen and pregnant.
"Our grief is lifelong," he told Annette. "An open wound we shall carry
to the grave." He consoled himself that "this dear Angel was so excellent, so pure, her end so sublime and edifying she belonged more [in
heaven] than on earth."

Then Benckendorff, whose later years were embarrassed by an

---

* Montefiore had become famous for his intervention during the 1840 Damascus "blood-
libel" case when innocent Jews including many children were tortured. Montefiore rushed
to Alexandria where he won their release from Mehmet Ali and on to Constantinople where
he persuaded Sultan Abdul Mecid to ban the libel throughout Ottoman lands. The "blood
libel," starting in 1144 in Norwich, England, then spreading across Europe and the Middle
East, framed innocent Jews who were accused of murdering Christians, often children,
in order to bake Passover cakes with their blood. It was widely believed by anti-semites
including Nicholas. Faced with a case, he knew it might be an "outrageous lie" but sensed
that "the crime was committed by Jews. Numerous examples prove that there are fiends or
sectarians among the Jews who consider Christian blood necessary for their rites." As we
will see, he was not the last Romanov to believe in this.
† First in 1839, he allowed Maria to marry into the wider Bonaparte family when she fell
in love with Max de Beauharnais, duke of Leuchtenberg, who was descended from Empress Josephine—provided that her husband moved to Petersburg. The couple agreed; the
Leuchtenbergs were often visited by Nicholas.

obsessive love affair with one of the emperor's discarded mistresses,* died. "I've been deprived of my trusty Benckendorff," he told Paskevich, "whose service and friendship of nineteen years I won't forget or replace. This year has been a heavy one." So there was a new vulnerability in his letters to his daughter Olga as she wondered whether to marry Crown Prince Karl of Württemberg: "How will you with God's help decide your fate? It's totally up to you . . . Your heart, your feelings are the guarantee that your decision will be the best . . . That's why I'm calm awaiting your decision. God be with you, my angel. Love your Papa as he loves you. Your old friend Papa." When Olga accepted the prince's proposal,† he confessed that "the emptiness it leaves with us is quite painful." Contemplating mortality after the death of Adini, the emperor planned a pilgrimage to Jerusalem.

But there was good news from Alexander and Marie, who gave birth to an heir, Nikolai, always known in the family as "Nixa": "a wonderful happiness for us," wrote the tsar. Marie was to produce two daughters and six sons—a glut of heirs.[19]

On 20 February 1848, at a court ball, Nicholas heard the shocking news that Paris had risen and that King Louis-Philippe had abdicated and fled. "We were all thunderstruck!" wrote the twenty-year-old Kostia in his diary. "Only blood is visible on the horizon. Mama too is frightened." The ferment had started in Palermo but spread rapidly across Europe.

A day later, Kostia heard that France was "a republic governed by a committee of journalists and a worker. This is what we've come to!" he exclaimed, adding a few days later: "The young officers rejoice because there is hope of war!"

"When Paris sneezes," said Metternich, "Europe catches cold." In Austria, Chancellor Metternich himself was overthrown, fleeing for his own safety, and Emperor Ferdinand abdicated in favour of his young nephew Franz Josef. Revolution infected Berlin, Frankfurt,

---

* This was Baroness Amalia Krüdener: Nicholas gave Krüdener the gift of an estate, but she was too brazen, noted the tsar's daughter, Olga: the empress "saw through her disguise." Amalia turned her attention to Benckendorff, who fell so in love with her that she "used him coldly, managing his person, money, relationships." When it seemed that Amalia was converting Benckendorff to Catholicism, Nicholas decided to remove her and appointed her husband as Swedish ambassador—but she was pregnant. The son was adopted by Count Nikolai Adlerberg, son of the tsar's best friend, now governor-general of Finland, who was also in love with her. He gave his name to her son—providing she married him after the death of her husband, which she did, holding court in Helsingfors for many years.
† Kostia escorted her to Württemberg: while in Germany, he fell in love with Princess Alexandra of Saxe-Altenburg, known as "Sanny," writing to her: "Just one thought moves me, just one image fills my eyes: forever and only she, my angel, my universe."

Budapest—and Wallachia and Moldavia, technically Ottoman-ruled but Orthodox in religion.

"This insolence threatens in its madness even Our Russia, entrusted to us by God," declared Nicholas. "But it will not succeed." In a panic of fear and outrage, he crushed the revolution in Wallachia and Moldavia, forcing the sultan to concede greater Russian control. In Paris and Vienna, the revolutions were suppressed but, right next to Poland, in Hungary, the revolutionaries declared independence. On 29 May, Franz Josef requested Russian intervention. Eight days later, Paskevich with forces totalling 350,000 invaded Hungary. But while another Russian army immediately defeated the Hungarians, Paskevich bungled his offensive, driving Nicholas to distraction: "I very much regret that [rebel general] Gorgei with his entire army escaped you! I will only understand when you personally explain it to me." On 18 July, the rebels surrendered. "Hungary lies at the feet of Your Imperial Majesty," wrote Paskevich, who was praised by the tsar: "Thou art the glory of my twenty-five-year reign."

Nicholas's power had reached its peak,* but his hegemony was fragile. He was resented almost as much by his allies Austria and Prussia as by his enemies Britain and France. Worse, Russia itself was sclerotic. The emperor's fatigue and rigidity had become potentially catastrophic problems. Nicholas had failed to realize that the world had changed. His Olympian isolation blinded him to what the country needed to compete with the West.†

His swelling bureaucracy, staffed by thousands of clerks, awaiting automatic promotions—witheringly satirized by Gogol's play *The Inspector-General*—vomited forth millions of documents that monarch and ministers could scarcely absorb, and further divided the tsar and Petersburg from the country. His army was antiquated, its arsenal of rifles obsolete, yet Chernyshev, war minister since 1827, now prince and president of the State Council, reported that the army "needed no changes whatsoever." His ministers were decrepit—Nesselrode had been foreign minister since 1814. His brother Michael dropped dead;

---

* His version of Russian supremacy was expressed in the Kremlin where he commissioned his architect Konstantin Thon to create his Great Kremlin Palace, which incorporated the nine old Muscovite chapels and Terem Palace while adding new apartments and five immense reception halls, all in his favourite Russian-Byzantine Revival style. Nicholas's gigantist monolithic vision has perfectly suited the greater Russian nationalism of modern leaders. Stalin held his banquet to celebrate victory in 1945 in the white Georgievsky Hall. Putin has renovated the throne room, the Andreevsky, with Byzantine gilded magnificence.
† His scepticism about railways (particularly their military potential) allowed Russia to fall behind the West, its first line opening from Petersburg to Tsarskoe Selo in 1837. Only in 1851 did a second passenger line open, between Moscow and Petersburg.

Mouffy was ill; Nicholas himself suffered gout. "The theatre is our only pastime," he told Annette. "We're leading a very peaceful life."[20]

Nicholas tightened censorship which, soon under twelve different committees, became suffocating: the word "republic" was removed from Greek and Roman history books while Shakespeare's *Richard III* was banned. Alexei Orlov, who had succeeded Benckendorff as head of the secret police, started to monitor an eccentric civil servant, Mikhail Butashevich-Petrashevsky, whose circle discussed socialism and atheism. Nicholas ordered its immediate dissolution. At 4 a.m. on 23 April 1849, the twenty-seven-year-old Fyodor Dostoevsky, a doctor's son and trained engineer who had won praise for his first novel *Poor Folk*, awoke to find two Gendarmes in his bedroom. Taken to 16 Fontanka, Dostoevsky and fifty others were inspected by Orlov, then despatched to the Peter and Paul Fortress where they were interrogated for months until Nicholas had Dostoevsky, Petrashevsky and fourteen others condemned to death by firing squad.

On 22 December 1849, Alexander, as commander of the Guards, supervised the spectacle as Dostoevsky and his comrades were led out to the scaffold in Semyonovsky Square where "the sentence of death was read to us, we all were made to kiss the cross, a sword was broken over our heads and we were told to don our white execution shirts." The first three were tied to stakes as the firing squad raised their rifles. "Aim!" cried the commanding officer.

"For me," wrote Dostoevsky, "only one minute of life remained . . . Then the drums sounded 'retreat' . . . and an order from His Imperial Majesty granted us our lives." Nicholas had himself devised this sadistic trick, which drove at least one of the youths to madness. "There was no joy at returning to living," wrote Dostoevsky. "People around me were shouting, but I didn't care. I had already lived through the worst." Dostoevsky departed for four years of hard labour in Siberia. Nicholas had overreacted and the crisis that would lead to the humbling of Nicholas started not in Petersburg but in Jerusalem.[21]

On Good Friday, 26 March 1846, forty monks were killed in a battle between Orthodox and Catholics in the Church of the Holy Sepulchre in Jerusalem which had been ruled by the Ottomans since 1517. The Sepulchre had long been run by the Orthodox and indeed Jerusalem was dominated by the Russians, who regarded the pilgrimage there as an essential preparation for death. Nicholas himself planned to go that year, though his own pilgrimage had been cancelled due to the revolutions. Now the Catholics threatened Orthodox rights guaranteed in Catherine the Great's treaties.

A year later, the silver star, donated by French kings, set in the marble floor of Bethlehem's Church of the Nativity was stolen. The Catholics blamed the Orthodox. Once again, the monks fought. In Constantinople, the French insisted on their right to replace the star; Nicholas disagreed.

In December 1851, the French president, Louis-Napoleon Bonaparte, the politically agile nephew of the great Napoleon, overthrew the Second Republic before crowning himself Emperor Napoleon III.* His glistening but flimsy empire needed Catholic prestige and military glory abroad—and revenge for 1815: the Holy Land was a useful pretext. But, for Nicholas, predominance in Constantinople was the real issue. Both emperors were determined to force their will on Sultan Abdul Mecid. In February 1852, Nicholas got his way, until Napoleon threatened the sultan who buckled and granted paramountcy over the Holy Sepulchre to the Catholics. Nicholas could not let this stand.

"I cannot recede from a sacred duty," Nicholas told the British ambassador. He claimed he might abandon Catherine the Great's claims to Constantinople, but then he went on to propose "reckless" schemes for reducing the Ottomans to a rump protectorate or temporarily occupying Constantinople.

The emperor had always taken most decisions on his own, but now he had become exactly what Marcus Aurelius warned against: hopelessly "over-Caesarified, dyed in the purple." "This sovereign," wrote the French ambassador the marquis de Castelbajac, "has been spoiled by adulation, success and the religious prejudices of the Muscovite nation." His Caesarian grandiloquence was now not merely absurdly portentous† but alarmingly messianic: he saw himself as an Orthodox Crusader—his father after all had been grand master of the Hospitaller Order of Jerusalem. If he had "something of Peter the Great, Paul I and a medieval knight," noted Castelbajac, "now the qualities of Paul rise to the fore." Observing him for the first time, after arriving at court, a maid-of-honour, Anna Tyutcheva, noted his "arrogant and cruel expression."

Nicholas decided to bully the sultan into the restoration of Orthodox paramountcy and an "alliance" that would turn the empire into a Russian protectorate—or face war. His calculations were not just sacred: he was risking a gamble to take a step closer to settling the Eastern

---

* Bizarrely the envoy sent by Napoleon to inform Nicholas, then visiting Berlin, of his coup was none other than d'Anthes, the Guards officer who had killed Pushkin. Napoleon III raised him to senator.

† His manifesto in 1849 had declared: "We all shall as one cry out: God is with us! Take heed O nations and submit for God is with us!" But he was just as preposterous in private: when a committee gave a dinner to thank Vorontsov for his service, Nicholas commented: "Absolutely improper. Only I can thank someone; no one else."

Question on terms advantageous to Russia—without Britain going to war for the Ottomans. His confidence was delusional. To enforce his plans, he appointed Alexander Menshikov as commander-in-chief of his southern armies and his negotiator in Constantinople.

Castrated by the Turkish cannonball in 1828, Menshikov, now sixty-five, the great-grandson of Peter the Great's favourite, was Nicholas's model of an all-purpose martinet, having governed Finland, served as ambassador to Persia, run the Admiralty for decades and most recently directed censorship. Haughty, inept and sarcastic, he was exhausted and hoped "this will be the last official action in my life which demands repose." But now he was the "envoy-plenipotentiary of peace and war."

On 16 February 1853, Prince Menshikov arrived in Constantinople, forced the dismissal of the grand vizier, then demanded a Russian protectorate. But the castrated paladin had left his maps behind, which gave the forceful British ambassador time to ruin his negotiations. Menshikov himself counselled moderation, but Nicholas replied that "without a crisis of compulsion it would be difficult" to dominate Constantinople.

In May, Menshikov presented his ultimatum, but the sultan, knowing that the British and French were sailing to his rescue, rejected it. On the 14th Menshikov broke off relations and returned to Sebastopol to take command of the armies. "War is imminent," Nicholas told Annette. "I still don't know what the English are preparing for us." A month later, Nicholas invaded the Danubian Principalities—Moldavia and Wallachia. "I must go by my own path," he told Paskevich. "You can't imagine how much all this saddens me. I've grown old . . ." Nicholas was tempted to seize Constantinople in a *coup de main*, but Paskevich advised a more cautious approach.

That summer, Austria offered a peace plan, the Vienna Note, that was too generous to Nicholas, who accepted it, but too humiliating for the sultan, who proposed alterations—dismissed by the tsar. When Napoleon offered Western withdrawal in return for Russian withdrawal, Nicholas rejected it. His intransigence threw away his last chance of peace, yet he congratulated himself on "waging war neither for worldly advantages nor conquests but for a solely Christian purpose," as he explained it to Frederick William of Prussia, "under the banner of the Holy Cross." Russia would lead the Orthodox Slavs of the Balkans in a crusade against the sultan.

"Nothing is left to me but to fight, to win or perish with honour." He was haunted by death. "I am stricken with worries," he told Annette, "and I've already paid by my first attack of gout—the sad privilege of my fifty-eight years which is truly too many—and place myself in the hands of divine will."[22]

On 4 October 1853, the sultan declared war on Russia, joined on 28 March 1854 by Britain and France. Nicholas was flabbergasted when the Austrian emperor (whose throne he had just saved) not only refused to back him but instead threatened war. Nicholas turned Franz Josef's painting to the wall and wrote "Ingrate" on the back. "Time to prepare to fight not against the Turks but against treacherous Austria," he told Paskevich, "to punish severely its shameful ingratitude."

Russia possessed a million soldiers, but the so-called Crimean War was fought on many fronts. In the Far East Anglo-French ships bombarded Kamchatka. In the Black Sea[*] the Russian fleet destroyed the Ottomans. In the Baltic, the Royal Navy fired at Kronstadt. "Our peaceful Peterhof was so calm," Alexander reported jauntily to his aunt Annette, "now the enemy is at the door. For several days the entire enemy fleet was visible from the Cottage." Yet the main Russian army had to be ready on the western border to fight the Austrians—and Paskevich got bogged down at Silistria and resigned. Since the allies threatened to relieve the Ottomans, Nicholas withdrew from the Principalities, the cause of the war—but now it was too late. "The main and real object of the war," declared Viscount Palmerston, the Russophobic British home secretary, "was to curb the aggressive ambition of Russia" and destroy Russian power in the Black Sea. Thinly stretched, badly commanded, under-supplied, Russia faced Europe's two richest, most modern powers—alone.

Nicholas and Mouffy retired to Gatchina, "dark and silent," where the maid-of-honour Anna Tyutcheva observed the emperor. In July, his face was "furrowed with suffering, his extreme pallor gave the appearance of an antique marble statue."

On 1 September 1854, an armada of 400 ships landed 60,000 French and British troops at Eupatoria in Crimea. The most vulnerable moment of a sea invasion is the landing, but Menshikov, who had never commanded more than a regiment, was taken by surprise, not expecting an attack till spring. Nonetheless he did nothing, waiting with his 35,000

---

* The viceroy of the Caucasus, the Anglophile Vorontsov (whose nephew Sidney Herbert was British war secretary), disapproved of the war but was semi-retired. In July 1854, Shamyl, who had long brooded on the surrender of his son Jemal-Eddin, now a Russian officer in Warsaw, attacked Georgia. A younger son, Gazi Muhammed, raided a country house and captured two young Georgian sisters, Princess Anna Chavchavadze and Princess Varvara Orbeliani, granddaughters of the last king, Giorgi XII, ladies-in-waiting to the empress. They were spirited away into the mountains. In desperate negotiations for over a year, Shamyl demanded the return of Jemal-Eddin.

men and 100 guns at the Alma Heights to block the road to Sebastopol. On 7 September, the allies advanced towards their prize. Menshikov was so confident that he invited the ladies of Sebastopol to spectate, but the Russians broke and fled, hampered by their old flintlock muskets, shattered by the Anglo-French Minié rifle, bad morale and the prince's bungled command. Five thousand died, and the French overran Menshikov's carriage, which was found to contain a kitchen, letters from Nicholas, his boots, ladies' underwear—and French pornography. Menshikov, bereft of military talents, tried to hide his defeats from Nicholas.

Right at the start the fighting revealed the fundamental changes in Europe since 1815: whatever the limitations of their own inept generals, the French and British fought, communicated and manoeuvred with the technology and wealth of the industrial revolution, far exceeding those of Russia, which was left behind in the age of the first Emperor Napoleon. This would decide the war's outcome, but the tsar was bewildered by Menshikov's defeat, encouraging the wavering prince: "Don't give up, I repeat, we should prove to everyone, we're the same Russians who defended Russia in 1812!" But he was soon infuriated by his commander: "Newspapers are full of reports about the battle and I got nothing. I require detailed, truthful reports . . . It's time for this to end!"

Fortunately for the Russians, the allied armies, in which the French provided the largest contingent, were almost as badly organized. If they had stormed Sebastopol now, it might have fallen, but by October the Russians had turned it into a fortress.

"I hope you find the chance to strike a blow at the enemy to maintain the honour of our arms," Nicholas urged Menshikov. On 13 October, Menshikov's reinforced army, 60,000 infantry and thirty-four squadrons of cavalry, almost overwhelmed the British at the drawn Battle of Balaclava, after which Raglan gave his preposterous order for the 661 men of the Light Brigade to charge the Russian guns in "the valley of death."

Nicholas, at Gatchina, rushed in to share the news of Balaclava with Mouffy, "so overcome with emotion that in front of all of us," wrote Tyutcheva, "he threw himself on to his knees before the icons and burst into tears." The ill empress, thinking Sebastopol had fallen, joined him—until Nicholas claimed Balaclava as a victory. But some trace of the old Jupiter remained: he now ordered Menshikov to attack again, despatching his younger sons Nikolai and Mikhail to encourage him. The Russians were superior in numbers, but Menshikov's offensive against the British at Inkerman was over-complicated: Menshikov and the grand dukes watched the massacre of 12,000 Russian troops. "The men were disordered because they were badly directed," Nikolai reported to Alexander. "The disorder came from Menshikov." The prince collapsed. "Cheer up, dear Menshikov!" wrote the emperor, though he concluded that "This defeat has so depressed Prince Menshikov that I fear the worst. He sees no more hope to attack the allies and predicts the fall of Sebastopol. Such a thought horrifies me!"

The defeats broke Jupiter. By 24 November, the courtiers "were dejected, none dared speak," while Nicholas was "not sleeping or eating, he spends the night in the empress's room, wearing only socks" so that his steps did not wake her: Jupiter in socks! The "sovereign gets more depressed every day . . . his beautiful majestic figure" like "the oak that never knew how to bend and can only perish in the storm."

The allies besieged Sebastopol. Nicholas sent Alexander down to raise morale, but on his return he told his father that Sebastopol would fall. "That giant, so intolerant of men's tears, now often wept," observed Anna Tyutcheva. Every evening, he gave his granddaughter her soup: "I come to feed this little cherub—the only good moment of the day, the only time I forget my anxieties." The tsar saw that his autocracy had in some ways been futile: "Ascending the throne, I passionately wanted to know the truth, but after listening to lies and flattery daily for thirty years, I've lost the ability to tell truth from lies."

As winter inflicted suffering on all three armies,* Menshikov proposed the abandonment of Sebastopol. "For what was the heroism of the troops, such heavy losses, if we accept defeat?" replied Nicholas. "I cannot agree with your opinion. Do not submit, I say, and don't encourage others to do so . . . We have God on our side."†

"The sight of the sovereign is enough to break your heart," reported Tyutcheva. "He's become more and more morose." Nicholas ordered Menshikov to recapture Eupatoria in case the allies landed more troops, but here too the Russians were crushed.[23]

On 31 January 1855, Nicholas caught a cold at the wedding of Count Kleinmikhel's daughter, Alexandra. "The influenza that you had is the same that has taken hold here," he told Annette. "I've been near it a few days and my wife was seriously ill with it. She is spending a very

---

* Dr. Nikolai Pirogov was the first to use anaesthetic on a battlefield and devised the modern five-state system of triage field surgery, later adopted by all the combatants of the First World War. His patroness was Grand Duchess Elena Pavlovna, sister-in-law of the emperor, widow of Grand Duke Michael, whom the tsar nicknamed "the Family Intellectual." She bought quinine in England and imported it, and she persuaded the tsar to back Pirogov, triage and female nursing, creating her own order of nurses.

† The Georgian princesses had been Shamyl's prisoners for over a year. Now Nicholas agreed to swap them for Prince Jemal-Eddin, who was summoned from Warsaw. "Sire," said the prince, "I will go back at once." Jemal was duly swapped for the princesses.

sad winter." So was he. "Nothing is happening to gladden us." While "my younger sons are at Sebastopol," he now revealed that if Austria continued to threaten him, "I should shortly be joining the army. God will do the rest." God had other plans.

On 13 February, he reviewed troops in temperatures of minus 23 degrees. As he lay in his study on his army cot, his wheezing cold worsened. On the 15th, handing over some duties to Alexander, he dismissed Menshikov, replacing him with the abler general Prince Mikhail Gorchakov.

"There's nothing dangerous about His Majesty's condition," insisted Dr. Martin Mandt the next day, but suddenly pneumonia gripped the emperor's lungs. Late on the 17th, Mandt summoned a priest.

"We were called on the 17th," wrote Grand Duke Kostia's wife, always known as "Sanny," "and spent the entire night outside the room where he took Communion."

"Am I dying?" Nicholas asked Dr. Mandt.

"Your Majesty, you have only hours to live."

"Thank you for your courage in telling me."

Nicholas directed his own deathbed, ordering the Guards brought to the palace to take the oath to Alexander. When his family sat around the bed, "He blessed us," recalled Sanny, "and kissed us telling us, 'Stay united as during my time.' "

He saw each of them alone and made Elena, the "Family Intellectual," promise to help Alexander abolish serfdom.

Then the family and retainers retired: just Mouffy, Alexander and Marie remained. Nicholas blessed Mouffy and then Marie: "Remember: remain friends!" He told Mouffy to "say goodbye to his beautiful dear Peterhof." When an aide-de-camp arrived from Sebastopol with letters from his sons Nikolai and Mikhail, he refused: "No, these things aren't my concern any more. That could hold me to life. Give the messages to my son."

As the courtiers, including our diarist Anna Tyutcheva, gathered sobbing quietly to the rattle of the tsar's lungs, "In the corridors, on the stairs, everywhere there were faces, frightened, anxious, upset, people rushed somewhere, not knowing where or why." As they "watched the drama of the night of agony," Tyutcheva "suddenly saw that unhappy Nelidova appear in the lobby, an expression of horror and deep despair reflected in her confused eyes and beautiful features, frozen and white as marble. Passing, she hurt me, grabbed my arm. 'Lovely night, Mademoiselle Tyutcheva, beautiful night,' she said in a hoarse voice. Only now did I understand the vague rumours of the relationship between the emperor and this beautiful woman."

Just then, Mouffy, empress of the "angelic kindness," remembered the mistress wandering the corridors. She told her husband, "They wish to say goodbye to you," naming her ladies-in-waiting, a list that ended, "and Varenka Nelidova."

"No my dear, I must not see her any more," he said. "Tell her I ask her forgiveness and ask her to pray for me." Nelidova went on wandering the palace, hair dishevelled, whispering "Lovely night, beautiful night."*

The emperor was overcome with shame for failing his army. "I've always tried to do what I can for them," he told Alexander, "and where I failed, it was due not to lack of goodwill but to lack of knowledge and intelligence. I ask them to forgive me." He supposedly added: "I loved war too much." As the night passed, Nicholas "thanked all his servants and called in his ministers, gave meticulous orders for his burial and warned the governor-generals of Moscow and Warsaw of his imminent death." Dr. Mandt thought there was "something superhuman" in this death. But the patient started to suffocate. "If this is the beginning of the end, it's painful," he said, telling the heir: "I want to take everything difficult, serious, upon my shoulders and leave you a peaceful, well-ordered, happy realm." Peering up at his family, he added, "I've loved you more than anything." To Alexander, he said: "Serve Russia!" Then in the ultimate masterclass of autocracy, he raised his hand to Alexander and clenched his fist—"Hold everything like this!" His three successors tried to live by this dictum.

The rasping breath was so loud that Nicholas asked Mandt: "Will this disgusting music go on long?" He told Mouffy: "You were my guardian angel." Then: "I'm cold."

"Shall we light a fire?"

"There's no point." The priest prayed; Mouffy coughed; the breathing slowed, the death rattle deepening; the family fell to their knees—and the caesarevich arose as Alexander II. The war could not be won—but could it be ended with honour?[24]

---

* Nicholas left Nelidova 200,000 roubles which she gave to charity. She left the palace until Mouffy insisted she return—and stay. She often prayed piously in the Palace Church and sometimes she read to the widowed empress. She lived until 1897.

# SCENE 2

# Liberator

# CAST

ALEXANDER II, emperor 1855–81, son of Nicholas I and Alexandra Fyodorovna

Maria Alexandrovna (née Princess Marie of Hesse-Darmstadt), empress, "Marie"

Alexandra, their eldest daughter, "Lina"

Nikolai, caesarevich, their eldest son, "Nixa"

ALEXANDER III, emperor 1881–94, caesarevich, their second son, "Sasha"

Maria Fyodorovna (née Princess Dagmar of Denmark), Sasha's wife, "Minny"

NICHOLAS II, emperor 1894–1917, their son, "Nicky"

Vladimir, third son of Alexander II and Marie

Alexis, their fourth son

Maria, their second daughter, married Prince Alfred, duke of Edinburgh

Sergei, their fifth son

Paul, their sixth son

Princess Ekaterina Dolgorukaya, Alexander II's mistress and second wife, later Princess Yurievskaya, "Katya," "Odalisque"

Prince Georgi Yurievsky, their son, "Gogo"

Princess Olga Yurievskaya, their eldest daughter

Princess Catherine Yurievskaya, their youngest daughter

Konstantin, brother of Alexander II, general-admiral, "Kostia," married Alexandra (née Princess Alexandra of Saxe-Altenburg), "Sanny"

Nikolai, their son, "Nikola"

Nikolai Nikolaievich, brother of Alexander II, commander-in-chief of army, "Nizi," married Alexandra (née Princess Alexandra of Oldenburg)

Mikhail, brother of Alexander II, viceroy of Caucasus, married Olga (née Princess Cecilie of Baden)

Alexander, their son, "Sandro"

Elena Pavlovna (née Princess Charlotte of Württemberg), aunt of Alexander II, "Family Intellectual"

## COURTIERS: ministers etc.

Count Vladimir Adlerberg, court minister

Count Sasha Adlerberg, his son, emperor's friend, court minister

Prince Alexander Gorchakov, foreign minister, later chancellor, "Old Dandy"

Prince Mikhail Gorchakov, his cousin, commander in Crimea

Prince Alexander Bariatinsky, viceroy of Caucasus

Count Alexei Orlov, secret police chief and envoy to Paris, prince

Prince Vasily Dolgoruky, war minister, secret police chief

Count Peter Shuvalov, secret police chief, minister, later ambassador to London

Yakov Rostovtsev, general, president of Editing Committee of serf reform

Nikolai Miliutin, vice-minister of interior and architect of serf reform

Dmitri Miliutin, his brother, war minister, count, later field marshal

Mikhail Loris-Melikov, general, emergency chief minister, count

Konstantin Pobedonostsev, tutor to Nixa and Sasha, ober-procurator of the Synod, "Torquemada"

Princess Alexandra Dolgorukaya, Alexander II's mistress, "Tigress"

Fanny Lear, American courtesan, lover of Grand Duke Nikolai

"The world has come tumbling down," wrote Anna Tyutcheva. Her father was no less stricken: "It is as if a god had died." No Romanov since the first, Michael, had inherited such desperate straits as Alexander II—but no autocrat was better prepared. The day after his father died, Alexander praised his "unforgettable parent" and wept before the State Council. When he saw the diplomats, he declared, "I want peace," but added, "I'll fight on and perish rather than cede."

His father lay in state for two weeks, and after the funeral Alexander sat with his wife and his brother, Kostia, the general-admiral, to take stock. Both brothers understood that the Crimean debacle proved that serfdom must be reformed because the peasant-dominated army could never compete with the armies of the industrialized West; but only Kostia demanded immediate reform. Alexander, backed by Marie, proposed "quiet for now."

The dire situation was about to get worse. Napoleon III planned to arrive in Crimea to take command, the kingdom of Piedmont-Sardinia joined the allies, and Austria threatened to attack. In June the allies attempted to storm Sebastopol, failing with heavy losses. "I am convinced we must go on the offensive," Alexander told General Mikhail Gorchakov on 30 July 1855, admitting, "I want a battle." This was his last chance to save Sebastopol—before the Austrians entered the war. In mid-August, 57,000 Russian troops attacked the French and Sardinians on the Chernaia River but were smashed. On 27 August, the French took the Russian redoubts. As the Russians withdrew, an inferno blazed in Sebastopol. On 7 September the tsar visited his armies. "Don't lose heart! Remember 1812," he wrote to General Gorchakov. "Sebastopol is not Moscow. Crimea is not Russia. Two years after the burning of Moscow our victorious troops were in Paris. We are still the same Russians!" But they weren't. It was a different world.

In mid-November, Alexander probed the intentions of the Austrians and the French but left out the British, whose new prime minister Palmerston favoured dismantling the Russian empire. Alexander declared, "We've reached the utmost limit of what's compatible with Russian honour. I'll never accept humiliating concessions." But then he received an Austrian ultimatum and the news that Sweden was about to join the allies.

On 3 January 1856, Alexander's ministers and his wise men,

Nesselrode and Vorontsov, advised him to accept the terms. Only Kostia wanted to fight on.[1]

Alexander sent the seventy-year-old Count Alexei Orlov, who had fought his way to Paris in 1814, back to the peace talks in the French capital. The swashbuckling old bravo—his hair bouffant, eyes twinkling under bristling eyebrows, his grey moustaches luxuriant, and sporting a green tunic decorated with the portraits set in diamonds of three tsars— knew how to charm the French. "So are you bringing us peace?" asked Napoleon.

"Sire," answered Orlov, "I've come to find it for it is in Paris that all things are to be found." Nonetheless the peace, signed on 18 March 1856, was the Romanovs' worst setback since the Time of Troubles: Russia lost Bessarabia, and worse, its fortifications on the Black Sea, its right to have a navy there, leaving its coastline and its vast commercial interests vulnerable to the British. Orlov, raised to prince, signed on Alexander's behalf in Paris. "It was a lasting nightmare," reflected Alexander. "I signed," he later shouted, banging the table. "An act of cowardice."

He had had little choice, but he set about reversing Paris with the help of his new foreign minister, Prince Alexander Gorchakov,* who tested the resolve of the allies. "The emperor wishes to live in good harmony with all governments," declared Gorchakov. "Russia does not sulk. Russia is collecting herself." Their policy was based on a familial alliance with Prussia, while they set out to lure France away from Britain.

Alexander sent his brother Kostia to see Napoleon, a trip on which the grand duke negotiated a Russian base at Villefranche and started the Russian relationship with Nice, while Napoleon sent to Petersburg his debonair half-brother Auguste, comte de Morny, who had opened secret negotiations with the Russians during the war.† "I rejoice to see you here," Alexander said on greeting him.

"It's impossible," Morny told Napoleon, "not to be friends with him."

---

* He was a cousin of the commander in the Crimea. A friend of Pushkin, then Nesselrode's aide at the congresses of the 1820s, Gorchakov, an intellectual owl in round spectacles, old-fashioned velvet waistcoat and long jacket, described by Pushkin as a "disciple of fashion, friend of high society, observer of dazzling customs," could quote whole stanzas of Schiller and Byron. As the tsar promoted Gorchakov, he retired Chancellor Nesselrode, moved War Minister Dolgoruky to head the secret police and appointed Orlov president of the State Council.

† Sugar nabob, racehorse-owner, bourse-speculator, art-collector, political manipulator and connoisseur of courtesans, Morny was himself a piece of Napoleonic legend—the grandson of both Talleyrand and Empress Josephine. He had organized the coup that made his half-brother emperor. Morny was the fruit of the affair between the comte de Flahaut, son of Talleyrand, and Hortense de Beauharnais, queen of Holland, daughter of Josephine, wife of Napoleon's younger brother Louis—and mother of Napoleon III.

Alexander launched a charm offensive abroad and at home. The emperor was not just the best looking and most sensitive of the Romanovs, he was also the most endearing. Now he toured Europe to visit his Coburg, Württemberg and Hessian cousins in the wider European royal family. In Stuttgart, he met Napoleon. The two got on well, but "Let's await the facts," said the tsar, "to see if we can count on him in the future."

At home, he toured the country, relaxing court rules and university restrictions, easing censorship, signalling a new openness, the smiling tsar so different from his glowering father. But behind the smiles he knew that change was essential, and he secretly planned his moves. First he turned to his best friend to restore some prestige to Russian arms in the war against Shamyl.[2]

Alexander offered Alexander Bariatinsky his choice of ministries—but he chose to be viceroy of the Caucasus with the task of destroying Shamyl. Bariatinsky, a *grand seigneur* related to the Romanovs, was an ingenious soldier, an imaginative politician and an irresistible seducer. When he flirted with Nicholas I's daughter, Ollie, who was in love with him, Jupiter was furious. But Bariatinsky redeemed himself in fighting Shamyl. He was famed for his courage and his style. When he captured some Chechens, he left them their weapons and asked them to guard him while he went to sleep. His seduction of his officers' wives was as lethal as his battle plans. "The mere thought of Bariatinsky," one of his generals told Leo Tolstoy, "shatters all my dreams of marital happiness. This man is so brilliant that I can't imagine my wife won't one day prefer him to myself."

Alexander, who was highly secretive, trusted Bariatinsky, signing his letters: "Be sure, dear friend, I embrace you from the bottom of my heart." The viceroy* advised on all matters. When Alexander was in crisis, "The only thing that gives me pleasure is the thought of seeing you soon and being able to discuss with you all the trouble in which we find ourselves."

As Bariatinsky tightened his grip on Shamyl, shortening the blockade lines to force him out of the Chechen highlands, the emperor prepared for his coronation.[3]

On 17 August 1856, the tsar rode into the ancient capital in a green tunic and cape at the front of a "golden river" of horsemen, his brothers, sons

---

* Among his achievements, Bariatinsky gradually swallowed the last Georgian principalities. First was Abkhazia, ruled for forty years by the ex-Muslim Hamud Bey, who became Prince Mikheil Shervashidze; then Mingrelia was annexed from the Dadiani dynasty.

and grandees. The coronation was always a test of endurance. As he entered the stifling cathedral his father's retainers bore the regalia—Menshikov held the orb and General Gorchakov the sword—until the latter fainted and dropped it. "It's all right to fall here," Alexander reassured him, "the important thing is that you stood firm on the battlefield."

After Alexander had crowned himself, he placed a small crown on his kneeling empress, but as she rose, it clattered off her head. The tsar calmly replaced it, but the mistakes reflected the laxness at court: Anna Tyutcheva noticed that "no one prayed, they laughed, chatted," and "some even brought food in to eat during the long service." Afterwards there were banquets—the people were traditionally invited to a vast picnic on the Khodynsky Field for spit-roasts with wine-spurting fountains, but the crowds stampeded. It was an accident waiting to happen. Morny gave the last, most sumptuous ball, at which Alexander appeared wearing the white uniform of the Chevalier-Gardes with a Légion d'Honneur sent by Napoleon III. "The words 'sympathetic to France' are repeated so often, they're getting on my nerves," boasted the suave Morny. His job was done.* Now Alexander turned to reform, which was to be at least partly a family affair.4

Kostia was the abrasive champion of reform and scourge of the rigid conservatives whom he called "the Retrogrades." He was both asset and liability: this choleric shouter was an intellectual, a cellist and a musical connoisseur—a breath of fresh air. Even under his father, Kostia had used his presidency of the Russian Geographical Society and his general-admiralship to promote young reformers, new technology and a spirit of *glasnost*. He persuaded Alexander: "No weakness, no reaction." But Alexander was well aware of Kostia's faults, warning him on his trip to Paris "to listen, don't compromise yourself, pushing your own ideas." He also recognized his brother's dynamism: "If others don't know how to appreciate you, I appreciate your diligence and your devotion."

The reformers were backed by the emperor's delightful aunt Elena. "The Family Intellectual" was the most exceptional woman in the family since Catherine the Great, an innovator in everything from nursing to music. She founded the Russian Musical Society and then the Conservatoire (in which Peter Tchaikovsky was among the students).† Naturally

---

* Morny returned home—with a wife. In his late forties, the roué fell in love with a Smolny schoolgirl, Princess Sophie Trubetskoi, possibly an illegitimate daughter of Nicholas I. After their marriage, Alexander and Marie called on the Mornys before he returned to Paris to be president of the Corps Legislatif. Rewarded with a dukedom, Morny's early death in 1865 removed the one man who might have saved Napoleon III.

† Elena was the patroness of Anton Rubinstein and his brother Nikolai, both Jewish-born pianists and composers. Anton Rubinstein played at her soirées in Petersburg and before

she was a liberal on serfdom. Alexander was unsure how to reach his end, but he started on 30 March 1856 when he surprised the Moscow nobility by declaring that serfdom was an evil, its abolition inevitable— and it would be better if the liberation "came from above rather than below." He created the Secret Committee on Peasant Reform but, always playing the game of two steps forward, one step back, to carry his courtiers with him, he appointed the reactionary Prince Orlov to head it. Orlov blocked the reforms.

In the summer of 1857, Alexander holidayed in Germany where he met up with Aunt Elena, who revealed Nicholas's last wishes that she should help him liberate the peasants. She commissioned a young official in the Interior Ministry, Nikolai Miliutin,* to devise a plan to free the serfs on her own huge estates. At her suggestion, Alexander replaced Orlov with Kostia. "Here," Alexander told Bariatinsky, "everyone's preoccupied with the emancipation of the peasants, but unfortunately our way of chattering and inventing things have created a feverish anxiety."

Alexander prodded his governor-general of Vilna, Nazimov, into persuading local nobility to request reform—then allowed them to form provincial committees to deliberate on the terms. But the nobles offered the peasants freedom—without any land. The tsar stepped in: the peasants needed land.

"The great question has just made its first step," Alexander told Bariatinsky. In the summer of 1858, the emperor toured the country, encouraging and scolding the "obstinate nobles." Alexander and Marie were cheered wildly. "We're received everywhere," the sovereign told Kostia, "with ineffable cordiality sometimes rising to madness."

"Thank God," replied Kostia, "our people haven't changed their attachment to their White Tsar, and in You, dear Sasha, they still see the one who conceived the great deed of reform of serfdom."

Bypassing the Retrogrades, Alexander pushed the Committee to produce the proposals while promoting Elena's protégé Miliutin to deputy interior minister. But vicious infighting broke out between Kostia and the Retrogrades. The brains behind the reform, Miliutin feared that "a reaction has begun to set in." When Alexander was walking in the park at Tsarskoe Selo, a clerk on the Committee thrust a petition complaining of the slowness of reform into the tsar's own hands. Days later, the

---

the Romanovs in Nice. Together they founded the Russian Musical Society in 1859 and the Conservatoire in 1862. They patronised the young Tchaikovsky, who, aged nineteen, attended musical theory classes in Elena's Mikhailovsky Palace.

* Miliutin and his brother, Dmitri, a soldier, were the nephews of Count Pavel Kiselev, Nicholas I's chief of staff for peasant affairs who had achieved limited reforms in relation to state peasants. While Miliutin planned serf emancipation, his brother Dmitri was Bariatinsky's chief of staff in the Caucasus—and would soon become war minister.

clerk was summoned to see Prince Orlov who warned him, with threatening glee, that Nicholas "would have banished you to a place so remote they'd never even have found your bones." However, Orlov added, "Our present Sovereign is so kind he's ordered me to kiss you. Here! Embrace me!" Alexander was determined to push the reform through. "We began the peasant matter together," he told an aide, "and we'll take it to the end hand in hand . . ."[5]

The news from Chechnya was "brilliant!," exclaimed Alexander on 19 May 1858. "The submission of the people of little Chechnya delights me." Bariatinsky's forces surrounded Shamyl, who in August managed a last counter-attack. Alexander admired his enemy. "Shamyl is a famous fellow for having dared this diversion even as he's almost surrounded."* Then suddenly, a Murid horseman despatched by Shamyl arrived at Russian headquarters to ask for a doctor: Jemal-Eddin, the eldest son he had lost and won back, was sick. Bariatinsky allowed a doctor to be sent. The young man was dying of sorrow. Father and son had found it impossible to reconcile, the father still a jihadist; the boy now an ex-Russian officer depressed and alone. In July, the boy duly died. Alexander waited for the endgame "with impatience."[6]

Alexander did not trust the young reformers, so he turned to an unlikely champion. Yakov Rostovtsev was the young Guardsman who on 12 December 1825 had warned Nicholas of the revolt. Now thirty years later, General Rostovtsev, beloved by the tsar, was one of the members of the Committee to oppose the reforms. Miliutin, seeing him as chief Retrograde, recruited the exiled socialist and journalist Alexander Herzen to blacken Rostovtsev for his role in 1825. Alexander was furious, calling Miliutin "a Red," and Elena had to intervene. In fact Rostovtsev had just become a convert to freeing the serfs and at the same time giving them the right to redeem their land. Again Elena was decisive. She realized that Alexander, "jealous of his power," could take her female advice and that he needed Rostovtsev. At her Thursday salon, she reconciled old Rostovtsev and "Red" Miliutin.

On 17 February 1859, Alexander made Rostovtsev chairman of the Editing Commission for the reform and he ordered Miliutin to draft

---

* And this was not the only good news from the empire. "In Asia, we've just pulled off two immense successes," Alexander told Bariatinsky. The irrepressible governor-general of eastern Siberia, Nikolai Muraviev, had agreed a new border on the Amur River with China, which had opened its cities to Russian trade. "Our position in Asia becomes much more powerful!" Alexander raised Muraviev to count with the surname "Amursky." The decaying empire of China gave Russia, checkmated in Europe, the chance to expand.

the decree. Elena had done her work well. As the prize got closer, noble "ignorance and selfish interests," Alexander told Bariatinsky, tried to sabotage the reform but "with perseverance and firmness, I hope to succeed. In my position, one needs a good dose of calm and philosophy to endure the daily stresses and feuds."

Meanwhile abroad, his relationship with Napoleon III was tested as the French and Piedmontese challenged the Austrians to unify Italy. Alexander was thrilled to threaten Franz Josef: "We're playing the same role to them as they played to us in the [Crimean] war." This was the key result of the Crimean War—the estrangement of Russia from Austria which eased the rise of Prussia. At the Battle of Solferino, the French defeated the Austrians. Most of Italy was united under the king of Piedmont.

Every day Alexander awaited news from Bariatinsky—the viceroy and the imam were negotiating surrender. "Promise him a pardon for all his past ill-deeds and an independent household—though far from the Caucasus."

On 16 August 1859, Bariatinsky sat on a rock, his staff all around him, high in the misty mountains of Daghestan near the last Murid stronghold of Gounib, which had been surrounded by the Russians. At dawn, out of its gates, rode Shamyl himself, with fifty ragged Murids. As the Russian soldiers cheered, Shamyl dismounted and walked towards the prince. Refusing to surrender his sword to anyone else, he offered it to Bariatinsky.

"Glory to Thee, O Lord!" wrote Alexander to Bariatinsky on 11 September. "These are the sentiments that filled my heart. I couldn't have hoped for or desired a more complete success." He added that the victory "belonged to you, dear friend." Alexander was heading south to inspect his armies, but "I hope to meet Shamyl."

At a parade in Kharkov, the Great Imam rode out to meet the Great White Sultan. "I am happy you are here in Russia," said Alexander. "I wish it could have happened sooner. You won't regret it"—and he embraced him.* Just as the first draft of the serfdom decree was ready, Rostovtsev fell ill with gangrene.[7]

---

* Shamyl was exiled to Kaluga where he lived with his wives, sons and retinue until he was allowed to go on *haj* to Mecca, dying in 1871. Alexander sent Bariatinsky the St. George's Cross and field marshal's baton. After Shamyl's defeat in the north-east Caucasus, the Circassian—or Cherkess—tribes in the north-west continued their less-organised resistance until Bariatinsky defeated them, cleansing their villages and driving them into Ottoman exile, a tragedy in which 400,000 were deported and thousands perished. The Circassians had long been a warrior-nation, producing the Mamluk military slave-sultans of thirteenth-century Egypt. In modern times, they still provide the bodyguards of the Assad dictators of Syria and Hashemite kings of Jordan. After twenty years of Caucasian

*

The tsar wept when he visited the dying general and wondered how to continue. Always ready to ease the path to reform, Aunt Elena introduced the tsar to "Red" Miliutin, and the two got on well. Then to the horror of the liberals and the delight of the Retrogrades, Alexander appointed a conservative, Count Vladimir Panin, to head the Commission. But Panin was an old-fashioned servitor who reassured Kostia, "If the emperor has a view different from me, I consider it my duty to abandon my convictions immediately." He did so now.

"The great matter of the emancipation is almost done," Alexander told Bariatinsky, "and to be completed has only to go through the State Council." On 27 January 1861, Alexander addressed the Council: "You can change details but the fundamental must remain unaltered . . . The autocracy established serfdom and it's up to the autocracy to abolish it." The decree was approved.

On the night of 18 February, twenty-four cannon stood primed outside the Winter Palace, and cavalry patrolled the streets; Alexander spent the night at his sister's palace with horse and carriage ready to gallop in case revolution struck. Next morning, the tsar, accompanied by his eldest sons Nikolai ("Nixa") and Alexander ("Sasha"), and joined by Kostia and Sanny with their naughty eldest son Nikolai ("Nikola") led a procession to the Great Church of the Winter Palace. After what Kostia called "marvellous prayers," the tsar presided over a jovial family breakfast. Then Alexander invited the heir Nixa, as well as Kostia, to enter his study. "First he read it out loud," wrote Kostia in his diary, "and after crossing himself he signed. I poured sand on the ink. He gave the pen to Nixa. A new era has begun. They predicted revolution." Twenty-two million serfs were freed. "In spite of all the fears of alarmists," his "great work" passed "in perfect calm," the tsar wrote to Bariatinsky. It was a grand compromise,* but it was also probably the greatest achievement of Russian autocracy. "God knows where we would have ended up on the matter of squires and peasants if the authority of the tsar had not been powerful enough," Alexander told the Prussian ambassador Otto von Bismarck soon afterwards.

---

wars, Bariatinsky's health failed and he was replaced as Caucasus viceroy by the tsar's brother, Grand Duke Mikhail, who continued the cleansing of the Circassians. Bariatinsky remained Alexander's confidant and suggested his chief of staff, Miliutin, as war minister.
* The peasants could no longer be bought and sold like chattels, no longer whipped, but they still faced arbitrary justice. They could acquire property, marry and trade, yet the liberation was not complete: they still owed their ancient labour obligations to their former masters. After seven years to work out the details of the settlement, the government would pay around 80 per cent of the value of peasant lands to the landowners. The peasants had to pay the rest. Other land could be owned by peasant communes.

This was the first of Alexander's reforms. In 1864, he gave Russia an independent judiciary with jury trial as well as a new local body—an assembly at both the provincial and district levels called the *zemstvo*, which would be partly elected and would contain peasants as well as nobles and merchants. The repression of Jews was eased: the Pale was relaxed so that top merchants and artisans could now live in Petersburg and Moscow, where Jewish financiers such as Baron Joseph Ginzburg (whose barony was granted by the duke of Hesse-Darmstadt but recognized by the tsar) started to canvass for the repeal of Nicholas I's harsh military draft.

Yet there were limits: when the Moscow Assembly proposed a constitution, he dissolved it. His aim, like the *perestroika* unleashed by Mikhail Gorbachev to reinvigorate Communism, was not to destroy autocracy but to fortify it. Soon after the liberation, Bismarck asked if he would grant a constitution. "The common people see the monarch as a paternal all-powerful lord, emissary of God," replied Alexander. "This has the force of religious sentiment . . . inseparable from personal dependence on me. If the people lost this feeling, for the power my crown imparts to me, the nimbus that the nation possesses would be ruptured . . . I'd reduce the authority of the government without compensation if I included in it representatives from nobility or nation." Alexander was a reforming autocrat, but an autocrat nonetheless.

"The tsar showed such unshakeable firmness in the great undertaking that he could ignore the murmuring of opponents of innovation," wrote General Dmitri Miliutin, the brother of the liberator of the serfs. "In this sense, the soft, humane Alexander II displayed greater decisiveness and a truer idea of his own power than his father [who was] noted for his iron will."* Yet the abolition of serfdom broke asunder the pact between ruler and nobility that had made Russia, leaving the tsar to base his power on the rifles of his army and the carapace of his unloved bureaucracy. Unmoored by this anchor, the Romanovs and society started to drift apart.

Weary from these efforts, the tsar probably hoped now to enjoy his pleasures—hunting, family holidays in Germany, and his mistresses.[8]

\*

* On 10 September 1863, US President Abraham Lincoln signed his own Emancipation Proclamation, freeing 6 million black slaves. Russia and America, the tsar told the US minister to Petersburg, Cassius Clay, "were bound together by a common sympathy in the common cause of emancipation." During the Crimean War, America had supported Russia, sharing the same foe, Britain. During the American Civil War, Britain and France leaned towards the Confederacy, but Alexander backed the Unionists, sending his Baltic Fleet to New York and his Pacific Fleet to San Francisco for seven months. The autocracy and the democracy remained allies.

On 22 November 1861, Kostia was riding into Tsarskoe Selo when he encountered the emperor "on horseback and behind him Alexandra Dolgorukaya, also on horseback and completely alone. The conclusion," Kostia confided to his diary, "is not difficult."

Princess Alexandra Dolgorukaya, one of Empress Marie's maids-of-honour, known as "the Tigress," was the first mistress of the reign. It was "painful," thought Kostia, not for moral reasons (he himself had mistresses), but because Alexandra had a reputation as a vamp.

"At first glance, this tall girl, long limbed, flat chest, bony shoulders, zinc-white face," did not seem at all attractive, observed Tyutcheva, sharing a room with her in the palace. Yet as soon as she sensed "an interesting man's gaze, she acquired the magnificent pure feline grace of a young tigress, face flushed, eyes and smile sly and tender, suffused with a mysterious charm which subjugated not only men but women . . . There was something predatory, not like a cat with its little deceits but the tigress, proud and regal in its depravity."

The Tigress made sure everyone knew it: on 20 November 1855, while the empress was earnestly reading *The Dictionary of History and Geography*, a choice that catches the tedium of Marie, surrounded by her girls, including Alexandra Dolgorukaya, the emperor came in. Suddenly the Tigress fell in a faint. Too quickly, the emperor rushed to check her pulse. "The empress continued to flick through the magazine with complete peace of mind that noted the over-eager interest shown by the Sovereign." Such are the delicate games of love at the court of autocrats. The Tigress was not Alexander's only mistress. Later when he surveyed a Winter Palace ball, he remarked that "Several of my former *pupilles* are here." Bismarck, who was so close he was almost adopted into the family, enjoyed Alexander's glamorous court—"dinners with His Majesty, evening theatre, good ballet, boxes full of pretty women"—but he noticed too that he is "constantly in love." "Every new passion is written on his face," observed lady-in-waiting Alexandra Tolstoya.

Yet the emperor and empress remained good friends. Marie had been pregnant seven times and, a few years earlier, they had been bound together by the loss of a daughter Alexandra, known as Lina, who was six when she died from meningitis. They had even tried to contact Lina with the help of a table-turning, internationally famous spiritualist.* Just

* Daniel Dunglas Home was a Scottish medium, the illegitimate son of the earl of Home, who, in the early 1850s, had become an American celebrity with his ability to levitate and contact the dead who would then communicate with cries (from the entranced Home), pinchings, bangings and knockings. He won many followers but also aroused much scepticism especially since his séances were always in darkened rooms. When observed, he was seen to deploy false limbs and take off his shoes using his naked feet. Returning to Europe, he held séances for aristocrats, writers and royalty, including Napoleon III and Eugenie

before the liberation of the serfs, Marie had given birth to a sixth son, Paul. At the age of thirty-seven, Empress Marie was prematurely aged, a pale, pinched, feverish Victorian saint in a headscarf with a hacking cough. "She was so thin and fragile," wrote Tyutcheva, "but she was unusually elegant" with "a deeply religious soul which like its physical shell seemed to come straight out of the frame of a medieval painting." She was so inhibited that when the tsar's doctor, Sergei Botkin, arrived to examine her, she refused to undress, explaining, "I'm a very private person." Botkin replied, "But, Your Majesty, I can't examine you through your robes." Botkin diagnosed TB and prescribed a warm climate, which encouraged Alexander to buy the Livadia estate in Crimea.* Yet she had a sense of humour. Alexander always told her she looked wonderful until one day she replied: "The only thing I'm wonderful for is the anatomical theatre—a teaching skeleton, covered with a thick layer of rouge and powder."

After breakfast each day, Alexander would return to his study on the second floor of the Winter Palace and receive his ministers.† He adored his family, particularly his heir, Nixa. No emperor could wish for a more perfect caesarevich than Nixa. The future, at least, was assured.[9]

Alexander had warned the Poles against any resistance on his accession—"gentlemen, let us have no dreams"—but encouraged by the

---

who, touched by his naked foot, thought it was the hand of a dead child. Arriving in Petersburg in 1858, still in his mid-twenties, Home met Kostia's mystical wife Sanny who, that July, arranged the first of three séances attended by Alexander and Marie, the dowager empress Mouffy and Kostia (Elena the Family Intellectual refused to attend) plus the tsar's mistress Alexandra "Tigress" Dolgorukaya and courtier Anna Tyutcheva who recorded all in her diary. Sitting around a table in the dark, "an inner fire seemed to radiate from" Home. The table levitated, Mouffy's ring was pulled off her finger, everyone was pinched: "this elicited cries of fear, terror and surprise . . . The Sovereign received a revelation . . . the spirit of Emperor Nicholas and the young grand duchess (Lina). They both responded to questions from the Sovereign by knocking the letters of the alphabet, but the company was struck by the "inappropriate and empty" answers. Home thrived in Russia, marrying a noble Russian girl with the novelist Alexander Dumas as best man. He returned twice. After the death of his wife, he married a second Russian. He died in 1886.

* In 1860, when the tsar asked his architect if he could have the same marble as the Vorontsovs at Alupka, he was told he could not afford it. Instead he built a two-storyed, cramped and gloomy stone Great Palace at Livadia with a smaller wooden Little Palace for his heir. Crimea became a favourite Romanov—and aristocratic—holiday resort.

† "My rule," as he later explained to his mistress, "is only to talk to my entourage about the things for which they are responsible. But I never prevent anyone, neither my brothers nor others, from talking to me frankly if they need to share something with me. As for all the grave questions for which I can't be responsible on my own, I let them be discussed in my presence in the Council so that when I approve my decisions, everyone shares in them and if they don't, they can either submit or resign." Alexander warned Bariatinsky, "The minister is responsible to me for his sphere and you for yours, and it's my duty to make sure neither of you goes beyond it."

age of reform and nationalism, and infuriated by Russian domination, the Poles and Lithuanians decided dreams were not enough. Poland seethed with discontent. "We must expect attempts at revolution" in Poland, Alexander informed Bariatinsky, "though thanks to energetic measures, I hope they'll be nipped in the bud." But instead of being nipped, they blossomed. His governor-general in Warsaw, the semi-senile General Gorchakov, responded with "lamentable weakness."

Alexander tried concessions and offered the viceroyship to Kostia. The day after he arrived in Warsaw, Kostia appeared in the royal box at the theatre where he was shot at and wounded by a tailor's apprentice, who was hanged afterwards. Kostia did not lose his nerve and followed his policy of reconciliation. But in January 1863, when he tried to remove radical youth by conscripting them into the army, the Poles rose in a full-scale rebellion, fielding 30,000 irregulars, nobles, peasants, even Jews (including a Jewish general) who fought 300,000 Russian troops in over a thousand skirmishes.

The revolt soured Alexander's *perestroika*. The Retrogrades thought too much freedom had been granted, the liberals too little. Alexander understood that "The most dangerous moment for a bad government is when it begins to reform," as Alexis de Tocqueville had recently put it. Alexander's relaxation of controls over universities and censorship of the press had created a heady expectation that led to student riots which had to be suppressed. "Here everything's quiet, thank God," the tsar informed Bariatinsky, "but a severe vigilance is more necessary than ever, given the thoughtless tendencies of so-called progress."

The 1860s were an exciting but disturbing time. Newspapers mushroomed. "I've never been greatly enamoured of writers in general," Alexander confided to Bariatinsky, "and I've sadly concluded that they are a class of individuals with hidden motives and dangerous biases." But if Kostia's generation were satisfied with the reforms, their sons, the children of the 1860s, were quickly frustrated and disillusioned, like the character Bazarov in Ivan Turgenev's novel *Fathers and Sons*, published in 1862. These Nihilists—Turgenev coined the neologism—impatiently cast aside tsarist reform to embrace atheism, modernity and revolution.

Pulling back fast, the tsar dismissed liberals like Nikolai Miliutin, who had become the bogeyman of the nobility, and promoted generals to chastise the students. Many were arrested. On 16 May 1862, fires started to break out in Petersburg. "The red rooster took on such scope," wrote the new war minister General Dmitri Miliutin, "there could be no doubt it was arson." On the 28th, Alexander rushed back from Tsarskoe Selo to fight the fires. The arsonists were never caught, but Alexander ordered the secret police to close journals and arrest radicals.* Even now he toyed with taking a step towards wider representation by converting the State Council into a partly elected advisory institution, but the riots and Polish revolution delayed his reforms.

Alexander ordered the governor-general of Vilna, General Mikhail Muraviev, who had the face of a bulldog and a figure squat as a cannon, to crush the Poles. Muraviev demanded the recall of Kostia. He liked to boast that "The only good Pole is a hanged Pole." He hanged hundreds of Poles, but thousands were shot and 18,000 were deported to Siberia.

"The Hangman" disgusted the tsar, who raised him to count but retired him. Prussia backed Alexander, but the rest of Europe, particularly the French, were appalled (though Muraviev's conduct was a good deal less savage than the British repression of the Indian Mutiny, as Russia pointed out when Britain protested at its treatment of the Poles). Meanwhile, within the family, Alexander and Marie celebrated the engagement of their son Nixa.[10]

Nixa, now nineteen years old, was the shared joy of his parents. He was more refined than his burly brothers. Slight with wavy brown hair, he was aesthetic and intelligent, and he liked drawing, but he was bold too: as a boy, he had told his awesome grandfather Nicholas that he did not wish to study French.

"And how will you converse with ambassadors, Your Highness?" asked his father.

"I'll have an interpreter," answered the boy.

"Bravo," said his father. "All Europe will laugh at you!"

"Then I'll declare war on Europe!" cried the boy, to his grandfather's amusement. When his father succeeded to the throne, Nixa sincerely told Tyutcheva: "Papa is now so busy, he's ill with fatigue—and I'm still too young to help him."

"It's not that you're too young," answered his brother Sasha. "You're too stupid."

"It's not true I'm stupid," answered the caesarevich. "Just too small."

"Too stupid," chanted Sasha and his brothers—at which Nixa threw a pillow at them.

As he grew up, Alexander was keen to ensure that Nixa was masculine

---

* Yet the repression was so soft that an arrested socialist, Nikolai Chernyshevsky, was able not only to write in his prison cell but also to publish the first work of the Revolution, *What is to be Done?*, an ideological novel whose hero Rakhmetov was a new type—the "Special Man," so ruthlessly dedicated to revolution that it was worth any human suffering: "the worse, the better." If the first radicals had been well-off noblemen, this new generation were educated lower-born members of a new class, the *intelligentsia*, many of whom started to form the first revolutionary cells, dreaming of assassinations and uprisings. (Lenin, not yet born, would read the book five times—"an overwhelming influence.")

enough to wear the crown, encouraging him to engage in military pursuits. Nixa was the best educated of heirs—"the crown of perfection," Kostia called him. "If I succeeded in forming a student equal to Nikolai Alexandrovich once in ten years, I'd think I'd have fulfilled my duties," said his history teacher. Alexander chose as his legal tutor one of the creators of his law reforms, Konstantin Pobedonostsev, who accompanied his charge on a tour of Russia. "Darling Maman," wrote the boy from his travels, "1000 thanks for your most charming letter. In reading I felt I was next to you. I could hear you talking. Here at Libau the heart rejoices to find how attached they are to our family and the principle it represents. I'm doing well in my studies. Not a minute wasted . . . Bye bye, Maman."

Years earlier, he had seen a photograph of a gamine Danish princess. "You know, dear Mama," he wrote to Marie on 3 August 1863, "I haven't fallen in love with anyone for a long time . . . You may laugh but the main reason for this is Dagmar whom I fell in love with long ago without even seeing her. I think only about her." Dagmar, always known as "Minny," was the daughter of King Christian IX of Denmark. Her sister Alexandra had just married Bertie, the prince of Wales. In mid-1864, Alexander sent Nixa off on a European tour through Italy, Germany and, most importantly, Denmark. But Denmark was at war.[11]

The tsar's uncle, King Wilhelm of Prussia, had appointed the ex-ambassador to Petersburg, Bismarck, as minister-president, to defeat the liberals and defend the monarchy. Bismarck, colossal in stature and walrus-moustached, looked like a diehard *Junker*—a conservative squire from Brandenburg and the hard-drinking veteran of duels. But he turned out to be a brilliantly ruthless and modern practitioner of the new *Realpolitik* in the ever more intensely fought tournament between the great powers, which he explained thus: "the only sound basis for a large state is egoism not romanticism." Highly strung, grotesquely malicious and hypochondriacal, thin-skinned yet tough as a rhinoceros, this instinctive risk-taker, ingenious improviser and cunning conspirator saw a solution to Prussia's domestic problems in an aggressive foreign policy that would use the kingdom's superb army to unite Germany, challenge the France of Napoleon III and harness nationalism in the service of the monarchy. As envoy to Alexander II, he had realised all this was possible because of Russian hatred of Austria after the defeat of the Crimean War.* As his first step, Bismarck instigated war against

* "Only since I arrived here [in Petersburg] have I believed in war," Bismarck explained. After the Austrian betrayals, Russia would always help Prussia "to find a way to get even with Austria." Indeed "the calm and gentle emperor spits fire and rage when he talks about

Denmark over Schleswig-Holstein, that question so complex that "Only three people," joked Palmerston, "have ever really understood the Schleswig-Holstein business—the Prince Consort, who is dead—a German professor, who has gone mad—and I, who have forgotten all about it." But Bismarck had not. In the summer of 1864, Prussia, in alliance with Austria, defeated Denmark—days before Nixa arrived in Copenhagen.[12]

"If only you knew how happy I was: I've fallen in love with Dagmar," the caesarevich told his mother. "How can I not be happy when my heart tells me I love her, love her dearly?. . . How can I describe her? Pretty, direct, intelligent, lively yet shy."

Afterwards Nixa met his parents in Darmstadt, then he hurried back to Copenhagen. On family promenades, "the two of us lagged behind," he reported to his mother. "I wanted the earth to swallow me up. I was building up to say I love you but she understood clearly: a heartfelt YES was finally said and we kissed." Nixa continued with his tour down to Italy, but there was something amiss.

He found riding painful. By the time he reached Florence he was in agony. The doctors discovered a swelling on his spine, but prescribed rest, sunshine and various treatments that kept him in bed for six weeks. He did not get better. He and Minny wrote each other love letters daily. In late December, he sailed in a Russian warship to join his mother in Nice. The love letters slowed until Minny asked if he had fallen in love with a black-eyed Italian. Nixa admitted he loved her so much that he could not control his emotions. Lying helpless in the seaside Villa Diesbach, he deteriorated until, in April 1865, an Austrian doctor diagnosed cerebrospinal meningitis. Over-sensitive to the sound of the waves, he was moved inland to the Villa Bermond,* where he suffered a stroke that paralysed him on one side.

The tsar was informed. Minny was telegraphed: "Nicholas has received the Last Rites. Pray for us and come if you can."

---

it." He was so close to the Romanovs that he enjoyed "the status of an envoy to the family." But his dearest friend there was the dowager empress, Mouffy (the favourite sister of Wilhelm), with whom he almost fell platonically in love: "for me she has something in her kindness that is maternal and I can talk to her as if I had known her from childhood . . . I could listen to her deep voice and honest laughter and even her scolding for hours . . ." When he saw her off on a holiday, "it was so enchanting . . . I had the urge . . . to leap onto the ship to travel with her."

* As the boy was deteriorating, on 2 April, just after the surrender of the Confederacy, Abraham Lincoln was assassinated at a theatre in Washington, DC, as part of a concerted conspiracy to liquidate the Unionist leadership. When the news arrived, the highly emotional emperor wept, ordered prayers chanted at the Kazan Cathedral and wrote to Mary Lincoln that the President "was the noblest and greatest Christian of our generation—a beacon to the whole world—nothing but courage, steadfastness and desire to do good."

Nixa asked Marie, "Poor ma, what will you do without your Nicky?" Joined by his brother Sasha who worshipped him, he held out his arms: "Sasha, Sasha, what are you doing here! Come quickly and kiss me!"

The emperor, accompanied by his sons Vladimir and Alexis, dashed across Europe—"with one thought, would God allow us to find him alive?" In Berlin, Wilhelm embraced him at the station and a Danish carriage, bearing Princess Minny and her mother, was attached to the train; in Paris, Napoleon III hugged Alexander on his way to Nice, where on 10 April he was met at the station by sobbing courtiers.

At the bedside, Alexander threw himself on his knees, kissing the boy's hand. Then Nixa turned to Minny. Her mother recalled, "His look—as the tsar led her by the hand up to his bed—it was of the purest happiness." Nixa smiled at her: "Isn't she wonderfully sweet, Father?"

Minny thanked God "that I reached him in time, my darling treasure. I will never forget the look he gave me when I approached him. No never!" she wrote to her father. Soon afterwards he became delirious, chattering about oppressed Slavs. Even his delirium was intelligent. Minny and the others frequently fled the room, unable to control themselves. "The poor emperor and empress!" wrote Minny. "They were so attentive to me in my and their sorrow." She stayed by the bed, "kneeling by him day and night." Nixa now longed for death. At dawn on 12 April, his governor ran across the street to the Villa Verdie to awaken the family. The boy was vomiting up his medication. As his parents and brothers surrounded him, Minny knelt beside him and wiped the vomit from his chin. "He recognized me in his final minute," she remembered. Nixa held Minny's hand, but then looked at Sasha: "Papa, take care of Sasha, he is such an honest, good man." He "raised his right hand and took Sasha's head," recorded his governor, "and seemed to be reaching for Princess Dagmar's head with his left"—a moment that would swiftly become significant. "His tongue weakened, he said his last words. Taking the empress by the hand he nodded at the doctor and said, "Take good care of her!" Then Minny kissed him and he died.

Even as the body began its journey back to Petersburg, Minny noticed the suffering of the eldest surviving brother—"Sasha who loved him so nobly—not only as a brother but as his only and best friend. It's very difficult for him, poor thing, because he must now take his beloved brother's place."

Counterfactual history is futile, but the death of this heir diverted the succession from a boy hailed by everyone for his sensitive intellect to two tsars distinguished by their narrowmindedness.

When the emperor saw Minny soon afterwards, a relative suggested that she might still join the family. "She would be very welcome," replied Alexander.[13]

"No one had such an impact on my life as my dear brother and friend Nixa," wrote Sasha as tsar twenty years later. His life had been spent in the shadow of his perfect brother: "What a change occurred in those hours and a terrible responsibility fell on my shoulders."

Sasha, twenty years old, a bearded giant, Guards officer, heroic drinker, poor linguist and bad speller with no cultural interests, was so strong that he could bend horseshoes with his bare hands. Nixa had nicknamed him "the Pug," but in the family he was regarded as an oaf: "Modelled on the pattern of a Hercules or rather a peasant, he was always wrestling with something, always knocking against something, always upsetting chairs." His stupidity was so notorious that his great-aunt Elena supposedly suggested that Alexander leave the throne to the next brother, Vladimir, who was only marginally more impressive. Visiting his irascible uncle Kostia in Warsaw, Sasha spilt the wine at dinner. "Look at the piglet they've sent from Petersburg!" shouted Kostia. When a German princess thanked him after a cloddish dance at a ball, Sasha replied, "Why can't you be honest? I've ruined your slippers and you've nearly made me sick with your scent."

Now he was the heir. "All the courtiers have horribly changed in attitude to me," wrote Sasha, "and have started to woo me." He was bewildered. "I know there are good honest people but not a few bad ones," he wrote to a friend. "How will I distinguish and how will I rule?"

Almost immediately, Alexander and Marie, who had loved Minny, started to consider her as Sasha's wife, just as the queen of Denmark gently suggested it to the tsar. Minny, who had been studying Russian and Orthodoxy, was still mourning. Sasha found her attractive and saw the sense in the match. But there was a problem.

Sasha was in love with Princess Maria Efimovna ("M.E.") Meshcherskaya, one of his mother's maids-of-honour, "a great beauty" with "something Oriental about her whole person, especially her dark velvety eyes which fascinated everyone." Minny was already writing to Sasha as "your sister and friend," but within a month of Nixa's death she heard about the plan hatched between Copenhagen and Petersburg. She wrote to the emperor—"Papa"—that Sasha must be certain in his feelings.

Sasha was in torment. He stopped seeing Meshcherskaya: "I still miss M.E.," he wrote in his diary on 25 June, yet "I have thought more about Dagmar and pray to God daily to arrange this matter which could mean my happiness for the rest of my life." Over the coming months, he

decided, "I will say goodbye to M.E. whom I loved like no one before."
Plans were made for him to visit Minny in Denmark.

But he and M.E. could not stay away from each other: M.E. became
engaged to a German prince but then Sasha went back to her: "I want to
refuse to marry Dagmar whom I can't love and don't want. I don't want
any wife except M.E." The emperor was incensed. Sasha must obey.
Sasha replied that he had never been as worthy as Nixa. He renounced
the throne. While the heir was refusing the succession, their socialist
enemies were planning to accelerate his inheritance—by assassination.
It was easily planned because everyone knew that Alexander walked
daily in the Summer Garden—even if they did not know the beautiful
reason that he was there so often.[14]

On 4 April 1866, the day planned for the assassination, the emperor met
a girl of eighteen in the Summer Garden. "The emperor talked to me
as usual," she recalled. "He asked me if I was going to visit my younger
sister at Smolny. When I told him I was going there that night, he said
he would meet me there with that boyish air of his that sometimes made
me angry." Then they parted and he walked towards his carriage.

They had first met seven years earlier. In 1859, the tsar, then aged
forty, staying at the estate of her father for the manoeuvres to mark the
150th anniversary of Poltava, had encountered a doll-like girl of ten, in
a pink cape with braided gold-auburn hair, when her mother sent her
down to greet him.

"And who are you, my child?" he asked.

"I am Ekaterina Mikhailovna," replied Princess Ekaterina "Katya"
Dolgorukaya.

"What are you doing here?"

"Looking for the emperor." Years later he reminisced that "I made
your acquaintance when you weren't even eleven but you've only got
more beautiful every year since." As for the girl, "I would never forget
my ecstasy in catching sight of this superb face, full of kindness."

The emperor heard no more of her until her feckless father spent his
fortune, then died leaving the family penniless. Her mother appealed
to Court Minister Adlerberg, who arranged for the tsar to pay for the
children's education: Katya went to the Smolny Institute, the Petersburg boarding school. When in 1864 the emperor and empress visited
Smolny, the girls each curtseyed and greeted the visitors in French.

Katya was still a child and his interest was "like a father." Yet "The
more I grew up," she recalled in her memoirs, "the more my love for
him increased." But when she left the school, she was unlikely to see
him again.

Then by "happy chance, I bumped into the emperor on 24 December 1865 walking in the Summer Garden." Alexander walked there daily with just an adjutant, or a couple of nephews—and his English red setter, Milord, watched by a crowd held back by one Gendarme. The tall and fit emperor, in his mid-forties, was still "very good looking," noted a foreign visitor at this time, "his smile enchanting; the blue eyes all the brighter for the deep tan of his face, his mouth reminding me of a Greek statue." When he spotted a pretty girl, she noticed how his "big beautiful light blue eyes gave me an acute look."

Katya was now sixteen and a half, a young woman with thick, ash-blonde hair, alabaster skin and a curvaceous figure. "At first he didn't recognize me and then he came back and asked if it was me!"

Alexander felt a true *coup de foudre*. A trusted courtier mentioned this to her ex-headmistress, who deputed her worldly cousin Vera Shebeko to approach Katya's mother. Shebeko, daughter of a civil service family, was an ex-mistress of the tsar, and even though she remained attracted to him herself, she became Katya's companion—and, some would say, the tsar's pander.

For four months, the tsar and Katya met every day in the Summer Garden. The tsar became ever more smitten by the serious girl who found young men tedious, dreaded marriage, was bored by balls and liked solitary reading. As a child of the reforms, she enjoyed sincerely discussing the blossoming of literature with her platonic walking companion.

At 3 p.m. on 4 April 1866, leaving Katya, Alexander was about to climb into his carriage by the gates where a brooding provincial no-bleman named Dmitri Karakozov stood among the usual small crowd. Expelled from Moscow University, he had joined Hell, a revolutionary faction, inspired by Chernyshevsky's novel, which wished to overthrow tsarism and create a workers' commune. Hell chose Karakozov to kill Alexander.

As the tsar passed him, the young terrorist pulled out a revolver and raised it, but just as he was pressing the trigger, the man next to him, Osip Komissarov from Kostroma, jogged him. The revolver fired too high. In the tsar's laconic diary entry: "Pistol shot missed. Killer caught." "General sympathy," added the emperor. "I went home then to Kazan Cathedral. Hurrah! The entire Guards in the White Hall." Sasha recorded "groups of people singing God Save the Tsar. General delight and thunderous hurrahs!"

Back at the Winter Palace, Alexander received the shabby Komissarov whose jog had saved his life. Naturally he was hailed as a new Ivan Su-sanin, the peasant who had protected Michael, the first Romanov tsar.

Weren't they both from Kostroma? A performance of Glinka's opera *A Life for the Tsar* was arranged. After the bemused Komissarov had been led through the ranks of the Guards in the White Hall, Alexander heaped him with prizes—money and nobility as Komissarov-Kostromsky—an accidental hero.* Yet privately the emperor attributed his survival to the love of an entirely different, much prettier saviour.

When Katya heard the shots after parting from Alexander, "I was so shocked and ill, I cried . . . and wanted to express my joy to him. I was sure he felt the same need to see me." She was right. That night, the emperor, despite escaping assassination, appeared at the Smolny Institute as he had promised. "This meeting was the best proof that we loved each other," she wrote later. "I decided that my heart belonged to him."

The following day, 5 April, "I announced to my parents that I'd prefer to die than to get married." Then she set off for the Summer Garden, where she found courtiers erecting an outdoor chapel for a Te Deum to thank God for Alexander's escape. The emperor soon arrived with his entire suite. "I will never forget," she wrote, "with what love he looked at me." When he saw her there, "I had no doubt you were my guardian angel." Their love would only intensify with each terrorist attack.[15]

If he was consoled by his "guardian angel," Alexander blamed the liberals for unleashing assassins against him and sacked any official who could be blamed, even intimates.† Removing the liberal education

---

* Soon afterwards, US President Andrew Johnson sent a delegation to congratulate Alexander on his survival: "We thank God a grief was spared to the Russian people, the peril averted by Providence cannot but make us remember our own deep sorrow at the murder of our Head, our Leader and Father." This amity brought forward the question of Russian America. Fort Ross (originally Fort Russia), the Russian port in California, had been founded by the Russian-American Company in 1812, but it had been sold privately in 1841. Emperor Paul had granted the company a trade monopoly in Alaska, ruled from New Archangel (today's Sitka), but American and British commerce undermined Russian profits, while Vladivostok became a more important port. Kostia believed that Alaska was a financial liability and militarily indefensible—as well as a potential source of friction with America. On 16 December 1866 Alexander, Kostia and Gorchakov agreed to order Baron von Stoeckl, Russian minister in Washington, to negotiate with US Secretary of State William Seward to sell Alaska for a minimum of $5 million. On 18 March 1867, Alaska was sold for $7.2 million. American newspapers mocked the transaction as "Seward's folly."
† He sacked two of his personal friends in charge of security, the arch-liberal Petersburg governor-general Prince Alexander Suvorov-Italiisky, who had studied at the Sorbonne (grandson of the generalissimus), and the secret police chief Vasily Dolgoruky (his father's last war minister). The Hangman of Poland, Muraviev, was commissioned to investigate the conspiracy. Meanwhile, the crushing of Poland intensified. Even the most liberal Russians, confronted with a Polish rebellion, turned into oppressive nationalists. Alexander tried to ban the use of Polish, Ukrainian or Lithuanian languages—yet simultaneously he was promoting not just Finnish language but a parliament in Helsinki, where a statue of "Good Alexander" still stands. Such are the inconsistencies of multinational empire.

minister "for letting young people get out of control," he appointed a gifted arch-conservative, Count Dmitri Tolstoy, to suppress the universities. But he really needed an attack dog and he found one in Count Peter Shuvalov, who became head of the Third Section and informal chief minister.

Son of Prince Zubov's Polish widow and thus the heir to that colossal fortune, Shuvalov, aged just thirty-four, had flirted with Alexander's widowed sister Maria, duchess of Leuchtenberg, until the tsar reprimanded him. But now Alexander needed Shuvalov's unscrupulous cunning. Kostia called him "the dog on a chain," and he was so powerful he was nicknamed "Peter IV."

Shuvalov created the first bodyguard of forty men for the tsar and reformed the Gendarmes. Privately he knew that reform was essential, preparing a radical plan to expand participation in government, but this champion of the nobility had venomously fought the emancipation of the serfs and now he undermined the liberal reforms, crushing the *perestroika* of the 1860s. "Everything is done under the exclusive influence of Count Shuvalov who bullies the Sovereign with daily reports about the terrible dangers," wrote the only remaining liberal in power, Dmitri Miliutin, war minister. "Now all are pulling back. Now the emperor has lost confidence in everything he created, even in himself."[16]

Sasha bowed before his father's orders to marry Minny. Twice brokenhearted, once for M.E. and once for Nixa, Sasha wrote desperately: "Oh God, what a life, is it worthwhile after everything? Why was I born and why aren't I already dead?"*

Arriving in Copenhagen on 2 June 1866, escorted by Alexis, his jovial younger brother, Sasha spent two weeks edging towards Minny. Bismarck's latest war had just broken out: when Austria challenged Prussia over their joint administration of Schleswig-Holstein, Bismarck secured the neutrality of Alexander, estranged from Austria after the Crimean War. Prussia then defeated Austria, annexed swathes of northern territory and became the hegemon of Germany.

As the Germanic powers fought, the two youngsters talked endlessly about Nixa until on 11 June, looking at photographs of the dead boy, Sasha plucked up the courage to ask Minny if she could ever love another, at which she virtually leapt on the amazed heir and kissed him. When they told the family, both burst into morbid tears for Nixa, until they were cheered up by Alexis.

On 28 October 1866, Minny, now Maria Fyodorovna, married Sasha,

---

* M.E. was married off to the rich Paul Demidov, whose family had procured the Napoleonic title prince of San Donato, but within two years she had died in childbirth.

moving into the Anichkov Palace. Empress Marie could not quite forgive Minny for moving on from Nixa. When the couple took over the
Crimean Little Palace, the empress wrote, "It's so sad to think what
might have been, and one's heart bleeds for poor Minny who must feel it
so, stepping over the threshold of a home she'd planned so delightfully
with another." Sasha struggled to get used to his new life: sometimes
he got drunk and violent. Yet out of this awkwardness, Sasha fell in love
with Minny and, when he was on manoeuvres, he wrote of his fantasies
of being naked with her "like Adam and Eve." She was soon pregnant.

On the night of 6 May 1868, at the Alexander Palace at Tsarskoe Selo,
Minny's accouchement was one of those awkward public–private occasions endured by princesses. The emperor and empress joined Sasha
for the delivery, "which bothered me intensely!" Minny told her mother.
"The emperor held me by my hand, my Sasha by the other while every
so often the empress kissed me." Sasha was in tears: "Minny suffered
very much. Papa . . . helped me hold my darling . . . At 2:30 God sent
us a son . . . I sprang to embrace my darling wife." The son became
Nicholas II.[17]

Shuvalov's crackdown infuriated the radicals and drove them deeper
into their cult of violence. A student Nihilist named Sergei Nechaev, a
charismatic psychopath, had been inspired by Chernyshevsky's "Special
Man" to believe that only the assassination of the entire Romanov dynasty could free Russia. In August 1869, after travelling around Europe
meeting the many Russian émigrés who now filled the cafés of Geneva
and London, plotting revolution, Nechaev returned to Russia where he
helped orchestrate student riots.

Escaping to Geneva, he wrote his *Revolutionary Catechism*, which
stated that "The revolutionary is a doomed man . . . subsumed by one
single interest, single thought, single passion: revolution. All tender
feelings of family, friendship, love, gratitude and even honour must be
squashed . . . Day and night he must have only one thought, one goal—
ruthless destruction." Ultimately "we must join with the swashbuckling
robber world, the true and only revolutionary in Russia." This was Len-
inism before Lenin.

Yet simultaneously the autocracy was under attack from the Slavophile right too. The talented editor-proprietor of *Moscow News*, Mikhail
Katkov, a conservative radical, was embarking on a career that saw him
become as influential as the grandees of old. Now he argued that the
tsar should bypass the nobility to forge a nation-state, the monarchy
buttressed by Russian nationalism. Meanwhile Katkov was publishing
instalments of the two novels that defined this decade: *War and Peace* by

Leo Tolstoy and *Crime and Punishment* by Fyodor Dostoevsky—surely the greatest literary scoops in media history. Tolstoy concentrated on realistic portraits of Russian characters and families in 1812, that seminal moment of Russian history—and for the moment stayed out of politics. Dostoevsky had returned from his exile a believer in the exceptional Orthodox destiny of the Russian nation and became an unlikely supporter of the Romanovs. As an ex-prisoner once sentenced to death, he was horrified but fascinated by the Nihilists, whom he alone understood: Raskolnikov, the hero of *Crime and Punishment*, dreamed of "making humanity happy and saving the poor through murder." Now Dostoevsky's predictions started to come true.

By November 1869, Nechaev had groomed a covin of susceptible disciples into a semi-mythical organization, People's Reprisal. As a test of nihilistic loyalty, he ordered his cohorts to kill an innocent student. When he was arrested and tried, Russia was shocked and Dostoevsky was inspired to write *The Devils*. Nechaev died in jail.

The spasm of youthful violence seemed to have passed. Alexander ruled through Shuvalov, who prided himself on knowing everything about the court and the radicals. He was better at palace intrigue than secret police work—yet he did not know that Alexander was wildly in love.[18]

"I always felt," Alexander wrote to Katya Dolgorukaya, "there was something that attracted us to each other, an irresistible draw." But the teenaged virgin was reserved. She did not succumb to the emperor. Whispering observers watched them walking in the Summer Gardens every day, so they moved their strolls to the shore at Peterhof and the park at Tsarskoe Selo, where her mother took a house for the summer.

On 1 July 1866, "I met you," he later reminisced with her, "on horseback near Mon Plaisir and you suggested we meet later under the pretext of giving me your portrait." They met at the Belvedere, an exquisite villa used by Alexander I and Nicholas I for meeting mistresses, on Babigon Hill. "We sat on a bench waiting for it to be opened," the tsar wrote ten years later, always relishing his memories.

"It was our first tête-à-tête," she wrote simply in her memoirs.

"I'll never forget what happened on the sofa in the mirrored room when we kissed on the mouth for the first time," he told her later, "and you made me go out while you removed your crinoline which was in our way and I was surprised to find you without your pantaloons. *Oh, oh quel horreur?* I was almost mad at this dream but it was real and I felt HE was bursting. I felt a frenzy. That's when I encountered my treasure . . . I would have given everything to dip inside again . . . I was electrified that your saucy crinoline let me see your legs that only I had ever seen"—and also by her unexpected capacity for pleasure which made her his sexual equal: "We fell on each other like wild cats."

She was grateful for his kindness: "Knowing nothing of life, innocent in my soul, I didn't appreciate that another man might have taken advantage of my innocence while he conducted himself towards me with the honesty and nobility of a man who loves and esteems a woman like a sacred object." They were both religious and believed this was, as she put it, "a passion inspired by God."

Afterwards she told him that she "dedicated her life to love him . . . I could no longer struggle with this feeling that devoured me." The emperor solemnly swore, "Now you are my secret wife. I swear if ever I am free, I will marry you." It was, he later wrote, "the happiest day of my life" and "the start of a honeymoon that has never ceased!"

The emperor insisted on appointing her a maid-of-honour to the empress. But Katya had no interest in preening her feathers at court. Nonetheless the courtiers chattered. Katya hated the gossip but she hated to be parted more. She met him to make love in his study in the Winter Palace. They saw each other every day, "mad with happiness to love each other," as she put it. But when his duties parted them, she found "the nightmare of leaving him was torture."

She and a companion set off on a European tour to ease her nerves. The courtiers presumed that this was the end of yet another minor fling—and forgot the Smolny schoolgirl. Perhaps this was meant to be the end. Madame Shebeko produced Katya's pretty sister Maria, who loved him too.[19]

The Prussians had vanquished Austria and expelled it for ever from Germany. Ever since Napoleon I, the Romanovs had treated the Hohenzollerns as their trustiest allies but also as poor relations—"the weakest of the weak," thought Gorchakov with an astonishing lack of foresight. But they were not weak any more. Now Prussia challenged France, the last obstacle to Prussian mastery of Germany. Alexander revered his uncle King Wilhelm and despised Napoleon III, but he agreed to attend the World Fair in Paris which Napoleon had promoted.

He believed that Napoleon III had "caused the premature death of my father," he wrote in his diary. "I confess I certainly didn't go to Paris for his sake!" Really he went for the sake of someone else entirely.

On 20 May 1867 at the Gare du Nord, Napoleon met Alexander, accompanied by his sons Sasha and Vladimir, and escorted them to the Elysée. Unfriendly crowds shouted "Long live Poland!" At around midnight, the emperor awoke Adlerberg, the old court minister. "I'll go for a walk," said Alexander.

Adlerberg was flabbergasted: the tsar must be accompanied.

"No need to accompany me. I'll manage on my own but please, dear, give me a little money."

"How much does His Majesty require?"

"No idea; how about 100,000 francs?"

As the tsar disappeared into the Parisian night, Adlerberg awoke Shuvalov, who explained that Alexander would be followed by both Russian and French detectives. But the two counts waited up anxiously for Alexander's return.

Out in the street, the tsar hailed a taxi and headed out to the rue de la Paix, where he was dropped off. Consulting a note under a gaslight, he entered a house but the gates shut and he could not get out of the courtyard. He tried to open the gates until a Russian agent came over and pointed to the bellrope. The emperor entered the next-door house where Katya Dolgorukaya was waiting.

"I'll never forget our first meeting in rue de la Paix, Paris!" he wrote later. "We were mad for each other"—and when he was with her, "nothing else existed for us!" The secretive tsar had said nothing to his entourage about Katya.

Back at the Elysée, "terrible possibilities flashed in our minds," recalled Shuvalov. "The idea of the tsar alone in Paris streets in the middle of the night, with 100,000 in his pocket, gave us nightmares. The idea that he could be in someone's house never occurred to us!"

Finally, at 3 a.m., he returned. Shuvalov wept with relief, eagerly listening to the reports of his agents on the tsar's adventure. Only in hindsight did Shuvalov work out that the entire trip had really been arranged around Katya. Paris, Katya herself recalled, "was only charming because we had each other, and his obligation to see the Exhibition and other duties bored him because his only aim was me and he only came for that!"

After the military show at Longchamp, Alexander shared his open carriage home with Napoleon, while Sasha and Vladimir sat behind them.

As they trotted through the Bois de Boulogne, a young man fired twice at Alexander. The shots missed and the assassin was captured. The tsar and his sons considered cutting the trip short but Empress Eugénie beseeched Alexander to stay, while Napoleon informed him that the assassin was a Polish émigré. The pro-Polish French newspapers applauded the deed; tsar and heir could not wait to get home.

The tsar attributed this second escape to Katya: "each time, my guardian angel."[20]

*

Alexander himself regarded Napoleon III's upstart empire as doomed. Napoleon could not allow a unified Germany and that now brought him into conflict with Prussia. At Alexander's frequent meetings with his uncle Wilhelm and Bismarck, the latter suggested that Prussia would support Russia's release from the treaty that ended the Crimean War—if Russia would protect Prussia's eastern flank against Austria. Alexander was happy to help.

In July 1870 Bismarck got his opportunity. Wilhelm's cousin was offered the throne of Spain. France objected and the offer was refused but the French foreign minister demanded that Wilhelm promise that the Spanish offer would never be accepted. Playing on the king's wounded sense of honour, Bismarck persuaded Wilhelm to provoke France to declare war on Germany. The Franco-Prussian War changed the shape of Europe. Unexpectedly, the Prussians decisively defeated the much vaunted French army in a modern, swift and efficient campaign. At the Battle of Sedan, Napoleon himself was captured. The people of Paris revolted and Napoleon abdicated, going into English exile. The Prussians proceeded to besiege Paris and force a humiliating peace on France, annexing the provinces of Alsace and Lorraine.

In the Hall of Mirrors at Versailles, Bismarck declared a German empire, a federation of kingdoms with Wilhelm as kaiser, creating an ingenious hybrid constitution that combined absolute monarchy with parliamentary democracy. He conceded universal suffrage and workers' welfare to disarm liberals and socialists, and deployed glorious nationalism to win popular support for his kaiser. This was so delicately balanced that it could be controlled only by the imperial chancellor, Bismarck himself.

Alexander was naturally on the side of Uncle Wilhelm. Initially he was so thrilled by the victory of his "best friend" that he sent medals to the German generals. And he noted: "I've just tried on my new Prussian uniform which suits me well."

"Prussia will never forget she is beholden to you that the war didn't take a regrettable turn," wrote the kaiser to the tsar. "Your friend until death. Wilhelm." Bismarck delivered on his promise, enabling Gorchakov in November 1870 to revoke the ban on Black Sea fortifications. "The stone that oppressed my heart for fifteen years has just been lifted," wrote Alexander, but "the future lies in union with our powerful neighbour." The Russians had not expected Germany to win such a dazzling victory over France and Gorchakov had sensibly advised the French not to be provoked. The German empire became a power-house that now directly bordered Russia; its industrial wealth, technical sophistication and modern army exposed Russian weakness and, however friendly the Romanovs and Hohenzollerns, there was bound to be some friction between Germany's fresh ambitions and Russia's traditional aspirations.

Sasha, influenced by his Danish wife Minny, criticized the "short-sighted government" (meaning his father) for helping these "Prussian pigs." Alexander perhaps missed a chance to join in with Prussia and destroy Austrian power. That was not Bismarck's plan, for he now needed Austria to limit Russia. He brought together Alexander and Franz Josef in his League of Three Emperors which, for now at least, gave Russia security and neutralized Balkan rivalries with Austria. The tsar celebrated with the kaiser and the "Iron Chancellor" in Berlin and Petersburg, where, at the theatre, the old Hohenzollern was enraptured by the legs of the ballerinas. "Wilhelm certainly likes skirts," Alexander recorded in his diary. "He followed the scene without detaching his lorgnette from his eyes. Oh what an uncle!"[21]

Every day, Alexander met Katya "my naughty minx" at the townhouse he had rented for her on the English Quay which they called "our nest." They wrote several times a day even after they had just seen each other, perhaps the most explicit correspondence ever written by a head of state, using their pet names to describe their love-making:* *Les bingerles* was sex itself. They both had uninhibited and exuberant libidos, but their unique circumstances meant they never lost the frenzied passion of new lovers. "I confess these memories reawaken my rage to plunge inside your delirious *coquillage* again," he would write. "Oh oh oh I'm smiling about it, I'm not ashamed, it's natural!"

He was delighted when she took the initiative. "I enjoyed until delirium," wrote the emperor, "lying still on the sofa while you moved on me yourself . . . we're made for each other and I see you before my eyes, now in bed, now without knickers." He praised her intense capacity for pleasure: "I joyfully felt your fountain [*ta fontaine*] watering me several times which redoubled my pleasure," he wrote. On another day, he praised her *coquille* that "went crazy attaching herself to me like

---

* Their letters and diaries have scarcely been used by historians and most of them are unpublished because they have only recently been placed in the Russian archives. After Alexander's death, Katya smuggled most of the letters to Paris. A few letters were somehow sold to private buyers, but the great majority lay forgotten until collected by the French Rothschilds who, in return for banking archives captured by the Soviets in the Second World War, restored them to the Russian archives, where they remain uncatalogued. During the reign of Nicholas II, some of Alexander's diaries and letters to Katya were collected within the archives but judged too shocking to publish. Katya's memoirs, also used here, were written after Alexander's death and are unpublished too.

a leech" and frequently sent "compliments from *mon bingerle* which is fully armed."

She relished the love-making as much as he, writing, "You know I want you. I received immense pleasure and feel overwhelmed by it, pleasure incomparable to anything else." She confessed, "I took pleasure like a mad thing under our dear blanket. This pleasure has no name, as we are the only ones who feel it." She counted the hours till they met: "My sleep was restless and short, I'm filled with seething and can't wait 2.¼ hours to see you, don't be late, I kiss you my angel, cuckoo, my everything!"

The tsar thought "your body is so appetizing" that he sketched her naked: the drawing shows her voluptuous figure and her thick tresses, usually tied up in a bun, down to her waist.

They devoured each other across court receptions: "Our eyes couldn't help searching each other out . . . I found your outfit astounding and in my eyes you were the most beautiful of the pretty girls. But you were a little pale." He wanted to waltz with her "but I think you understood I decided to dance with others only so I could dance with you. I could sense we wanted *bingerle*."

They plotted each day "so tomorrow we will be able to see each other during the morning walk," he wrote. "Our meeting on Sadovaya Street was a ray of sunshine," she enthused. "You looked so wonderful in your hussar helmet that I was proud of my dream husband." They regarded themselves as already married in "a cult of us": "I admit," she wrote, "nothing compares to the joy of taking pleasure in a frenzy of feeling as we belong to each other only before God and our bond is for ever."

His doctors tried to limit their lovemaking sessions. After Alexander had talked of "four times," "on every piece of furniture" and "in every room," she suggested that "If you think we overtire ourselves, let's rest a few days." That was at 11 a.m.; by midnight, she was adding, "This evening, I want you," and by eleven o'clock next morning, "I slept restlessly, everything inside me trembles, I can't wait till 4:45."

"He had no one who really thought of him," she wrote. "I worried for him all the time." Finding he was sleeping on "a bed as hard as stone," his father's army cot, "I replaced it with soft bedsprings." Noticing that he was reviewing troops during winter wearing a summer tunic, "I introduced uniforms of impermeable materials." Truth is always a rare commodity in an autocracy, but when ministers lied to him, "I was a lioness to stop him being tricked—his glory was my life."

Yet this life was hard for her; it is the mistress's destiny always to be waiting. "I saw no one. I followed him everywhere, lodging in shacks and attics, experiencing terrible privations but with happiness (the essential thing was to see him)." Courtiers gossiped maliciously. "Oh how sad," the tsar wrote sympathetically, "that you face unpleasantness." He thought sex was the answer: "What a pity I can't fly to you to cheer you and have *bingerle* to forget the world."

Yet she could be forceful, obstinate and sharp tongued, calling herself "this darling special despot who wants to be loved by her adored husband." She was insecure. "I arrived full of love," he complained on 5 February 1871, "you received me like a dog and only became sweet when you saw that you'd pushed me to the edge!" She believed gossip, but he reassured her: "I beg you not to believe everything you hear which mostly exists only in the imagination."*

The stress made her ill. Alexander sent her to "famous doctors" who "announced to him that the only thing that could save me was to have children." Soon she was pregnant, and she asked him to be faithful: "I know what you are capable of in one moment when you want to make it, to forget that you desire only me, and to go and make it with another woman." But pregnancy saved her.

"We were created to bring forth his sacred conception before which everything else pales ... I hope God doesn't forsake me during the childbirth," she wrote on 12 November 1871, "which frightens me terribly." On 30 April 1872, Katya gave birth to a son, Georgi, on the couch in Alexander's study at the Winter Palace. Afterwards she and the child returned to her townhouse. Ultimately they also had two daughters together.

The poor empress realized that Alexander was in love with the mistress. When her ladies discussed how Mouffy had known about Nicholas's mistress, she warned that if anyone mentioned such a thing to her, she would never see them again. Nixa's death had reduced their marriage to a morbid cult of remembrance, celebrating his birthday and deathday together. "I ask you to respect the woman in me," she told Alexander, "even if you won't be able to respect the empress." But wracked by her TB, she was often away, sent by the doctors to Livadia or Nice. The lovers longed for the empress's death. At a wedding, Alexander's

---

* In her little circle, she was subjected to the chatter of her sister Maria and her trusted companion Vera "Vava" Shebeko, both of whom were his exes, more or less in love with the tsar, which complicated matters. Shebeko was often a go-between and flirted heavily with him. At least once, she walked in on him when he was stark naked—much to his amusement: "She saw everything!" In his letters, Alexander sometimes called Katya's vagina "Vava." Since Shebeko had been his mistress before Katya, it is unclear where one Vava started and the other ended: "My compliments to Vava from *mon bingerle* which is suddenly fully armed!" A *ménage à trois* was unlikely given Katya's jealousy, so possibly they just enjoyed teasing Shebeko.

eyes met Katya's. "Our glances reflect our innermost feelings," Alexander wrote. "Because we would wish ourselves to be in place of the newly-weds."[22]

Alexander was not alone in his sinning. Grand-ducal carriages queued every night on Rossi Street outside the Imperial Ballet, which the Romanovs treated as an escort agency. The tsar's brothers Kostia and Nizi (Nikolai) both had children with ballerinas. Only the youngest brother, Mikhail, was happily married.* But it was the young generation who provoked Alexander's next crisis.

"Returning from my walk, I had a disagreeable surprise from Alexis," wrote the tsar on 18 August 1871, "who announced his affair with a girl who's now pregnant and he asked my consent to marry her and I lost an hour of my time for work."

Alexis, a lovable but shameless rogue, twenty-one years old, had joined the navy (he became a midshipman at the age of seven) and had already served long stints at sea. His girlfriend was a maid-of-honour, Alexandra Zhukovskaya, daughter of the poet, with whom Alexis had a son. "The intrigues of this demoiselle Zhukovskaya are beyond belief!" grumbled Alexander, who despatched the prodigal sailor on a world tour that included an American visit to consolidate their alliance.

Ten years earlier, Bertie, the prince of Wales, had been fêted by the Americans who liked royalty providing they were breezy, mischievous and ebullient—and Alexis was all of these. He met President Ulysses S. Grant at the White House, enjoyed assignations with a burlesque dancer in St. Louis and an actress in New Orleans and then embarked on what the newspapers called "The Great Royal Buffalo Hunt" in Nebraska. The grand duke's companions were the finest of the Old West: General George Custer, Buffalo Bill Cody and Native American chief Spotted Tail. "Regarding my success with American ladies about which so much is written in the newspapers," Alexis claimed to his prudish mother, "I can honestly say it's complete nonsense." Like many naughty princes since, he blamed media harassment for his own escapades:

---

* Kostia was tired of "my government-issue wife" Sanny. "My father has only two passions," said his son Nikola, "ambition and his dancer." Kostia resided at the Marble Palace but spent most of his time with his ballerina, Anna Kuznetsova, and their children in their house on English Prospect. Mikhail was a paragon of virility: when he met the French empress Eugénie, she exclaimed, "That's not a man, that's a horse!" The viceroy of the Caucasus was married to Olga (Cecilie of Baden) who was believed to be the natural daughter of her mother's affair with a Jewish banker named Haber. Their seven children were brought up in exotic Tiflis and a 100,000-acre estate at Borzhomi where Mikhail built the mock-Gothic Likani Palace (Stalin later "honeymooned" there with his wife Nadya and sometimes holidayed there; it still survives as a Georgian presidential villa).

"They looked on me like a wild animal, like a crocodile!"[23] But the tsar soon had family problems closer to home: a courtesan known as "the American" had just arrived in Petersburg.

"Anything that glitters captivates me," wrote Harriet Blackford, a saucy and bold-eyed blonde girl from Philadelphia who, after adventures under her new name "Fanny Lear" with French millionaires and British royalty, arrived in pursuit of more glitter in Petersburg. "I soon found myself introduced to counts, barons and princes." Fanny expanded her clientele from elderly princes ("the silver old age") to "the golden youth." At a masquerade at the Mariinsky Theatre, she noticed "a young man of 22, 6 feet tall, magnificently built, tall and slender" with a dimpled chin, "lips, red, full, sensual and passionate" and an expression of "mockery and scepticism . . . I was certain I had a Grand Duke in front of me."

"Do you know who I am, little one?" he asked her. She took him home to her room at the Hôtel de France.

Nikola, Kostia's son and the tsar's nephew, fell obsessively in love with her, making her sign an agreement of total possession: "I swear not to speak to nor to see anyone, never anywhere without permission of my august master as a well-brought-up American and I declare myself a slave in body and soul of a Grand Duke of Russia." In return, he promised her 100,000 roubles.

Nikola commissioned a nude statue of Fanny that reveals her allure. (It still stands in his Tashkent palace.) He was jealous, an occupational hazard with a courtesan, and flew into rages. She was insecure and demanded jewels. At first his father was intrigued by his son's mistress. "Nikola, I think it's the American," laughed Kostia when Nikola hid the giggling *grande horizontale* in the Marble Palace, "and I wish to see her because they say she's very pretty." Soon Kostia and Alexander were worried about the hold the American had gained over Nikola. In February 1873, Kostia reprimanded his son; then the emperor resorted to the Romanov equivalent of a British father despatching a reprobate to the colonies: he sent him to fight in Central Asia.[24]

"We are in Asia!" Nikola wrote to Fanny on his way to fight the khan of Khiva. "Goodbye Europe! Goodbye Fanny Lear, my love!"

Nikola arrived on the steppe to join the new Great Game, the struggle for Central Asia and the borderlands of India waged between Russia and Britain. "Here I am a staff officer of the Russian army of Central Asia, the same army that one beautiful day will cross Afghanistan to occupy British India!" Nikola told Fanny on 8 March 1873.

After the disaster of the Crimean War, Russia was scarcely strong enough to project power against modern industrialized powers, but Alexander and Bariatinsky saw the three main kingdoms of Central Asia as a way to reinvigorate Russian arms, promote trade and threaten British India. Here, Bariatinsky told Alexander, a British army could be lured "to the edge of the world" and annihilated. Gorchakov justified this imperialism, arguing that "all civilized nations" were forced to expand their empires to defend their frontiers from "half-savage nomads." The officers who had once flocked to the Caucasus became the conquistadors of Central Asia.

In 1864, General Mikhail Chernyaev exceeded his orders and seized Tashkent in the khanate of Kokand, which became a client state of Russia. "General Chernyaev has taken Tashkent and nobody knows why," observed Interior Minister Peter Valuev. "There's something erotic in everything that happens on the distant frontiers."

In 1868, the new governor-general of Turkestan, Konstantin von Kaufman, defeated the emir of Bukhara and annexed Samarkand, Tamerlane's old capital. The khan of neighbouring Khiva, Mohammed Rahmin II, attempted to save his independence by turning to the British, who were trying to secure nearby Afghanistan.

"We've got to finish with the British antagonism in Central Asia," decided Alexander on 11 February 1873. "I'll throw them a bone." London was offered a free hand in Afghanistan in return for Russia having one in Khiva. "If God permits," mused Alexander, "we'll get our hands on Khiva. In spite of secret British aid, we've got to teach these Asiatics a lesson."

Now the tsar's reprobate nephew commanded the advance guard in Kaufman's army. "For ten days," Nikola wrote on 18 March, "we've seen nothing but the steppes, only sand." Then the Khivans "threw themselves at our riflemen with ferocious screams. I saw them fall dead"—and "I commanded: charge! My heart beat faster as the bullets hissed around us."

On 29 May, Khiva fell,* and there is no aphrodisiac like victory. "I kiss you like a fool, like a Spaniard. I want you. I must see you. I burn with impatience," Nikola told Fanny.

Nikola was decorated by the emperor, then he and Fanny set off on a European spending spree which soon exhausted even a grand duke's budget. Back in Petersburg, they made wild love in his parents' bed

---

* The British, who had agreed that Khiva was within the Russian sphere, felt betrayed when the Russians took the city and the khan became a Russian client: his crown outlived the Romanovs, surviving until 1920. Then, in 1875, Kokand, beset with civil war, was annexed. This alarmed the British: Prime Minister Benjamin Disraeli and his Indian secretary, the marquess of Salisbury, decided to turn Afghanistan into their own client state to stop the Russians—with disastrous consequences.

and he handed Fanny diamonds, saying, "Mama gave them to me" or "It's something old I found in the palace." He sensed that his behaviour would land him in serious trouble and advised Fanny to store her valuables at the American embassy.

Alexander was about to celebrate the British marriage of his adored only daughter Maria—and Nikola gave Fanny Lear a ticket to the ceremony in the Winter Palace. The scandal was about to break.[25]

Peering down at the emperors and princes at the royal wedding from her seat in the gallery of the great Winter Palace church, Fanny observed that Alexander "had a serious and sad look—very emotional with the traces of tears on his face."

Alexander was not happy about his daughter's marriage. No Russian princess had ever married an Englishman, Alexander had not forgiven Victoria for the Crimean War, and the empires were bitter rivals. Maria, short-haired, dark and plump, was no beauty but she was clever and intellectual, serving as her father's assistant, helping him decipher letters, and she was sympathetic to his restlessness with her mother. But Maria had gone on holiday in Denmark with Sasha, Minny and Minny's sister Alexandra, married to Bertie, prince of Wales. There she had met Bertie's brother Prince Alfred, duke of Edinburgh, who, his mother the queen complained, was so irascible that he was "not a pleasant inmate in a house." Maria disagreed and they fell in love.

The queen and the tsar tried to prevent the match, but "The fate of my daughter has been decided," Alexander wrote in Germany on 29 June 1873. "God give her happiness. After a tête-à-tête with Prince Alfred, she came to ask me to bless them. I did but with a heavy heart I confess." Queen Victoria was cross. "The murder is out!" she exclaimed. The couple were married in both Orthodox and Anglican ceremonies. "During the ceremony of our darling Marie, all my thoughts," the tsar wrote to Katya, "were prayers for them—and for us."

Fanny was naturally most interested in the diamonds: "The bride was wearing a silver gown with velvet crimson train, trimmed in ermine with the most beautiful diamond crown I've ever seen."* Fanny noticed

---

* Afterwards, Alexander visited his daughter and her mother-in-law at Windsor. Thirty-five years after they almost fell in love, Queen Victoria found him "very kind but terribly altered, so thin, so old, so sad, so careworn," while he thought her "an old fool." With tears in his eyes, Alexander thanked Victoria for welcoming his daughter, and even the queen was moved as "I put my hand across the emperor and took Marie's, she herself upset." Living at Clarence House in London, the Romanov offended the British court by showing off her intellectual tastes and claiming imperial precedence over everyone except the Queen who also disapproved of Maria's jewels, once owned by Catherine the Great, that were "too good" for a girl of twenty. After Petersburg, Maria "thinks London hideous, English

Bertie, prince of Wales, and probably made sure that he spotted her: they were old acquaintances. Afterwards Nikola was so jealous that he hit her—then promised her more diamonds.

On 10 April, his mother Sanny noticed that something priceless had been stolen. "Sanny called me over," wrote Kostia, "to show me that one of our wedding icons had been broken and the diamonds stolen . . . Just awful!" They called the police. On the 12th, General Fyodor Trepov, the city governor, "told me that the diamonds from Sanny's icon have been found pawned. Delightful news!"

His anxious father was at the opera when General Trepov came into his box and told him that Nikola's adjutant was the pawner of the diamonds. "My heart was beating so hard, I was barely myself for the rest of the opera."

At 9 a.m., Trepov interrogated the adjutant in the presence of Kostia and Nikola—and the truth was revealed. "The most terrible day of my life," wrote Kostia, "when I learned my son was a thief and crook." At 11:30, Kostia reported to the tsar, who talked to Shuvalov, secret police chief, and Sasha Adlerberg, who had just succeeded his father as court minister. At the ballet, Kostia got a message from Shuvalov: "I scented evil!" The secret police chief had discovered that Nikola had stolen the diamonds "to give money to The American."

After midnight, Shuvalov and Kostia interrogated the prodigal son for three hours. "It was absolute hell for me to see the spiritual decline and corruption of Nikola," wrote Kostia. "No remorse. A wretched creature. I took his sword and placed him under guard so he wouldn't kill himself. I went to bed at 4 a.m., morally and physically destroyed."

The next morning, Alexander received his brother Kostia with "tears and tender love," but "this affection horrifies me." Kostia wanted Nikola declared mad.

Fanny, hearing nothing from her paramour, went to the Marble Palace, using her secret key, but a servant told her that Nikola had been arrested. Back at her house, a note arrived: "Don't be afraid, they'll search your house, be calm. Your unfortunate N."

Moments later, fifteen Gendarmes burst in and arrested Fanny, taking her to a cell in Trepov's house. Her servants rushed to Marshall Jewell, the American ambassador, who demanded to know where she was held. Shuvalov sent an official to negotiate with her. This turned out to be Count Levashov, "a very distinguished member of the silver old

---

food abominable, the visits to Windsor and Osborne [in other words, the Queen] boring beyond belief," noted her mother. Later, Alfred succeeded as duke of Saxe-Coburg-Gotha. After Alfred's death, she remained in Germany, the only Romanov there during the First World War.

age" who, unsurprisingly in this farce, already knew Fanny. "It was the first time I'd ever seen him sober"—and possibly with his clothes on. Fanny expected 100,000 roubles. Levashov offered 50,000 in return for jewels, papers, discretion—and instant departure. She accepted the deal. "The mismanagement," reported US diplomat Eugene Schuyler to Secretary of State Hamilton Fish, "was due to Count Shuvalov wishing to revenge himself" on the liberal Kostia. That "dog on a chain" had played politics with the Romanovs' reputation.

Alexander was mortified. "I could see clear signs of how upset he was," noticed Miliutin on 18 April. "He could not speak without tears of the shame brought on the family [by Nikola's] abominable behaviour." He dismissed Nikola from the army and declared him mentally ill— though he kept his allowance.

"Thank God," wrote Kostia. "However hard it is to be the father of a lunatic son, it would be unbearable to be the father of a criminal, which would make my position [as general-admiral and chairman of the State Council] untenable." The doctors reported that Nikola was mentally abnormal but not insane, which his father "had to accept with gratitude! I weep constantly." But Nikola's journey was just beginning. In many ways, this cultured, radical erotomaniac* turned out to be the most gifted of the later Romanovs.[26]

Alexander took the waters at Ems and visited his German cousins. But now Katya and the children followed him on his holiday: "Our *bingerles* were delicious," he wrote, "we were crazy experiencing the frenzy of dipping into each other in every imaginable position. How can I forget how I lay on my back and you rode me like a horse." When Alexander holidayed in Crimea, tsar and tsarina stayed in the big Livadia Palace, Sasha and Minny with Nicholas and the other children in the small one—and the mistress stayed nearby in her own villa, Byuk-Sarai. "At four, I'll fly to you on horseback," he wrote, to play with "Darling Gogo [the nickname of their son George] . . . a veritable angel!").

Shuvalov was undermined by his own mistakes. After the Prussian victory, Alexander realized the army had to modernize. War Minister

* Fanny wrote her memoirs, *The Romance of an American in Russia*. Shuvalov halted publication. Expelled from France, travelling with profitable peripatetic promiscuity through Monaco, Austria and Italy, she hooked Count Mirafiori, natural son of King Victor Emmanuel II. In April 1886, she died in obscurity in Nice. As for Nikola, during his first exile in Crimea, he had two children with a young noblewoman, Alexandra Abaza (she later married an aristocrat who brought up the children as his own). Moved to Orenburg, Nikola married police chief's daughter Nadezhda von Dreyer. The emperor annulled the marriage and sent him to Samara, whence he started to organize scientific expeditions to investigate the route of a Turkestan railway and irrigation of the steppes.

Miliutin proposed sensible reforms: German victories proved that only a short-service army with a big reserve of trained troops could hope to compete in a European war. His measures included equality of service for Jews. On the State Council, Shuvalov and the Retrogrades resisted any concessions to the Jews, who increasingly got the blame for all the problems of the empire, but the measure was passed.* Then, in March 1874, thousands of students, inspired by a mixture of utopian egalitarianism and a sentimental faith in the soul of the peasantry, set off to the countryside to lead the Russian people, the *narod*—to revolution. Yet Shuvalov had missed these Narodniki—Populists—completely. It was the last straw for Alexander. "You prefer it in London, don't you?" he said languidly, appointing Shuvalov ambassador. Miliutin had triumphed. "The hostile party was tamed," he wrote. "I can step calmly into the Winter Palace."

The peasants themselves were bewildered by these earnest Populists. Alexander ordered Shuvalov's successor at the Third Section, Alexander Potapov, to round up 4,000 Populists, who were brutally treated, often in solitary confinement: thirty-eight went mad and forty-eight died in prison, including twelve suicides. The combination of the failure of their "going to the people" tactic and police repression turned some sentimental revolutionaries into terrorists.[27]

Just as the radicals swerved back towards violence, the Orthodox Slavs of Bosnia-Herzogovina rebelled against the Ottoman sultan, sparking Balkan uprisings—and a Slavophile clamour for war.

The princes of Serbia and Montenegro, autonomous Orthodox principalities within the Ottoman empire, backed their Bosnian brethren and declared war on the sultan. Some 3,500 Russian officers rushed to fight for the Serbs, and General Chernyaev, conqueror of Tashkent and Slavophile hero, took command of the Serbian army—though he had to resign from the tsar's service.

The tsar demanded Western backing to force the Ottomans to protect the Orthodox, promising Queen Victoria, "We cannot and don't wish to quarrel with England. On our part it would be madness to think of Constantinople and India." But the British feared Russian power more than

---

* Miliutin brought in universal conscription without noble privileges, a reduction in the time of military service, and repealed Nicholas I's anti-semitic recruitment, giving the Jews equality at least in theory. Miliutin's old patron, Prince Bariatinsky, had hoped to become a powerful chief of staff on the model of Prussia's von Moltke—and chief minister too. Disappointed, he resisted the reforms until finally slapped down by Alexander himself. But when they met for dinner, they laughed uproariously about old times. Later Alexander could have used Bariatinsky's ingenuity. When his paladin died on 26 February 1879, Alexander reflected, "I've lost a real friend."

Ottoman atrocities. Prime Minister Benjamin Disraeli was convinced that this was a Russian power-grab, while Queen Victoria suspected that Petersburg had "instigated the insurrection in the Balkans." The tsar asked his English son-in-law, Alfred, to restrain his mother—an impossible task, of course.

At home, Alexander was overwhelmed by a wave of enthusiasm that united all parties from Slavophiles to Populists in a fever for war and Constantinople.* "It's nauseating," Sasha ranted to Minny. "All these bastards of officials who think of their own bellies not as ministers of the Russian Empire. Papa doesn't have a single decent one!"

Encouraged by his ex-tutor Pobedonostsev, who believed that "This government must either take this popular movement in hand and lead it or it will inundate the authorities," Sasha blamed his father's "absence of intelligence, strength, will." Even Empress Marie criticized "our apologetic and cautious policy." Miliutin reported that Russia could defeat the Ottomans but not the British. Alexander was balancing two foreign policies: the half gaga Gorchakov was tentative while the rabidly Slavophile ambassador in Constantinople, Nikolai Ignatiev, was keen for war, threatening and provoking the Ottomans.

"Things are going badly for the Serbs," recorded Miliutin. "Russian public opinion is displeased by our inactive diplomacy," and the talk of war concentrated the tsar's mind on the future.† He was at Livadia with the family, half fearful of war, half tempted by victory. Every afternoon he rode over to Katya. "In spite of my best efforts to avoid it, this could lead to war." He hoped that "Turkey has no allies unlike in 1856, and it's not impossible Austria and Prussia will join us." Alexander agreed with Austria that he would limit Russian gains to a small Bulgaria and compensate Vienna with Bosnia. But Ignatiev did not believe that the Pan-Slavic tsar should be bound by any limits.

The Bulgarians rebelled, only to be massacred by Ottoman irregulars. "Alas!" the tsar confided to Katya, "war plays on my nerves terribly! But may God help the Good Cause triumph!" He was consoled "by the joy of

---

* In the years since the Crimean War, Alexander had rechannelled the Russian appetite for Jerusalem into a cultural conquest: he sponsored the Palestine Society, underwrote the annual pilgrimage of tens of thousands of Russians and built an entire Russian Compound in Jerusalem to house them in massive dormitories. Placing his pious son Sergei in charge, he sent him on pilgrimage to Jerusalem.

† On 30 July 1876, Alexander reminisced to Miliutin about how he had ridden fifty years earlier, aged eight, at his father's coronation. "That's why at the age of eight, he'd promoted his own grandson," the future Nicholas II. "It's time to take this child out of female hands," said Alexander, appointing a military tutor for the boy. The tsar always called Nicky "Sunbeam." During summers at Peterhof, Nicky and his brother George liked to visit Alexander at his Farm Palace daily, playing in his study as he worked. During crises or even a violent thunderstorm, Nicky recalled his grandfather's "face was calm and unperturbed."

being with my pretty wife and children who daily make our happiness," while "I feel the delicious sex in my depths."

"Serbia is in dire straits," recorded Miliutin on 16 November. "Without strong aid from Russia, Serbia can't fight on." Disraeli's support for the cruel Ottomans backfired badly when his rival William Gladstone published his pamphlet *The Bulgarian Horrors* and the British turned against war, while Bismarck told the Reichstag that the entire Ottoman empire was "not worth the bones of one Pomeranian grenadier."

Given this breathing-space, Alexander issued an ultimatum to the sultan, and called for a conference of the powers. The diplomats met in Constantinople, where a revolution now forced a new sultan, Abdul Hamid II, to concede a constitution. His resistance to Russian demands was encouraged by Disraeli, just raised to the earldom of Beaconsfield.

"What does the new year hold for us?" Alexander asked on 1 January 1877. "I see no other end but war." But "if we prevent a coalition against Germany, Bismarck guarantees us freedom in the East" and Austria promised neutrality. Miliutin observed "the tsar's impatience to take up arms." "Just after midnight 11/12 April," wrote Alexander, "I signed the declaration of war."[28]

As the armies massed in Bessarabia, Alexander was mobbed by crowds: "I confess I'm profoundly moved." He longed to command in person, heading with a gilded entourage towards the front, but instead he over-promoted his younger brother Nikolai as commander-in-chief—a bungling general of six feet five known as "Nizi," who also happened to be a raging sex-addict.*

"The panorama is magnificent," the tsar wrote on 14 June as he reviewed some of the 200,000 troops, "and I had the feeling of being at the manoeuvres rather than a serious affair. My brother even had them put up a little tent and served an excellent breakfast." Miliutin knew that Alexander "was not as calm as he seemed," he wrote on 15 June. "The

---

* The "family soldier" Nizi "liked all women except his wife." He fell in love with a teen-aged ballerina, Ekaterina Chislova, who was venal and promiscuous but gave him four illegitimate children. For convenience, he set Chislova up in a mansion across the square from his palace. When Chislova offered sex, she put a candle in her window, an opportunity for which Nizi would interrupt any event. If it was during family dinner, an aide-de-camp would announce, "Your Imperial Highness, there's a fire in the city," until finally his wife, a frumpy and mystical Oldenburg princess, snapped, "Don't distress yourselves, it's only a candle on fire!" When the grand duchess complained about the mistress, the emperor replied, "Your husband is in his prime and needs a woman. Look at yourself! Look how you dress!" She left Nizi to live in Kiev with a dubious priest. Meanwhile, outraged by Chislova's greed which was bankrupting his foolish brother, Alexander had her arrested for corruption by General Trepov, an embarrassing mission since the governor had slept with her himself. Nizi later got her released.

emperor admitted he dreamed of his father on the eve of important events—he dreamed of him last night. He wept and we left the room to give him time to recover."

"It would have been unbearable," Alexander told Katya on 22 June, "if I'd stayed far from the theatre of war, an ordeal that would have reminded me of the pitiful state of my father that cost him his life." It was not just Russia that was mobilized: "My *bingerle* sends compliments!" he wrote to Katya on 17 June at 11 p.m. "He is suddenly armed!"

The plan was bold: first to cross the Danube in the face of the Ottoman river fleet, passing through allied Romania* into Ottoman territory; then a smaller force would seal the main Ottoman fortresses while the main army of 112,000 stormed the Shipka Pass to race through Bulgaria towards Constantinople. On 27 June, the Russians skilfully crossed the Danube, mining both sides of the river to stymie the Ottoman flotilla. Nizi, who did not grasp the implications of his own plan, split his forces into three, sending one to besiege Rustchuk to the east, another to take Plevna in the west, underestimating both fortresses. Most fatally, he reduced the vital Shipka corps to just 12,000. Yet, in an extraordinary feat, General Josef Gurko stormed the pass and held it—even when the Ottomans counter-attacked and placed the Russian forces under siege. Meanwhile, monitoring Russian progress, Beaconsfield ordered the Royal Navy's Mediterranean fleet to wait at the mouth of the Dardanelles.

At first all went well, but the sultan's best general, Osman Pasha, garrisoned the stronghold of Plevna with 36,000 men. On 9 July, the name "Plevna" appears in Alexander's diary for the first time. "I heard the disagreeable news of the first failure" at Plevna. "I realize all depends not on force but on art," he wrote on 18 July, but trying to storm fortresses and trenches manned by infantry with modern firearms was bound to be very costly.

He should have sacked Nizi. "Hello, angel of my soul," he wrote to Katya, who was awaiting news of Plevna, "to you, I tell the truth! Alas, my brother refuses to believe in the superiority of enemy forces there." All day, he visited hospitals where the casualties haunted him: "I find it hard not to weep in front of them."

At night he unwound by reminiscing to Katya about their open-air sex a year earlier: "I confess these memories give me the frenzy to be inside your delirious *coquille!*" The old harem of his little Turkish house made him long "to plunge inside you again but instead I go to bed sadly all alone."[29]

---

* Created after the Crimean War out of Wallachia and Moldavia, the new state of Romania had appointed a Catholic cousin of the Prussian king, Karl von Hohenzollern-Sigmaringen as its ruling prince and later king, Carol I.

The next attack was "defeated again by the great superiority of enemy forces," he wrote on 19 July, adding again, "in which alas my brother refuses to believe." The Russians needed their best troops and Alexander summoned the Guards. Journalists flocked to Plevna to chronicle the drama. The pressure was wearing down the emperor, who "fainted during mass in the camp church."

Nizi ordered another assault, aided by his Romanian allies. Mikhail Skobelev, a ferocious conquistador of Central Asia, known as "the White General" because of his white uniform, led constant attacks, but the Ottomans counter-attacked, inflicting 7,000 casualties.

On 26 August,* the tsar rode to "take our places on a mountain where one could see the batteries as well as those of the Turks without the least danger." Alexander spectated under a canopy as guns softened up the Turks. "My God, my God," he wrote on 29 August, "what a frightful fusillade, what blood, what innocent victims!" Three thousand Russians were killed. Then on the 31st came the great assault of 84,000 troops. Skobelev seized several bastions. When the Turks retook them, Skobelev stormed them all over again.

"The entire time, the emperor sat there next to the commander-in-chief, a pity to see him like that," wrote Miliutin. The war minister himself felt so ill "that I had to lie on the grass" as the assault again failed. "The emperor was bitter—I've never seen him like that." At an impromptu council of war under the canopy, the Russians panicked. "We've got to abandon Plevna," whispered Alexander. Nizi called for retreat. Miliutin disagreed, at which Nizi shouted, "If you think this is possible, you take command and sack me!" The emperor decided to stay and "reinforce our positions." Nizi was out of ideas. Sasha remarked that Nizi "was always stupid—we need to find some kind of genie to turn a stupid man into a wise one" and demanded his dismissal. Alexander, losing patience with "the silliness and incompetence" of the "stupid Nikolai" and "infuriated by his unpardonable defeatism," almost dismissed him. "My brother no longer inspires confidence." The dynasty was built on its military competence, yet the expectation that Romanovs should be superb generals was a flaw in a family that had

---

* The emperor moved up to a house closer to Nizi at Gorny Stoudene. The government was now based in a cottage beside the Danube, where the tsar was accompanied by War Minister Miliutin, Court Minister Sasha Adlerberg, Dr. Sergei Botkin and ex-governor-general of Petersburg Prince Suvorov-Italiisky. Here he wrote nightly letters to Katya, entertained his sons and cousins for teas, chatted to his younger friend the artillery officer Emmanuel Meshchersky, husband of Katya's sister, and went on walks and rides with Suvorov. Here he met his overmighty ally, Carol of Romania, "who thinks he's a great power," while regularly denouncing the intrigues of "that pig Beaconsfield who decides everything according to his own bonce!"

produced generations of paradomaniacs but no great captains since Poltava.*

The British enjoyed these Russian defeats, whipped up by that "old madwoman the Queen, that tramp!" spluttered Alexander on 15 September. Finally, on 23 September, Alexander appointed General Eduard Totleben "to impose a total blockade." To Katya he wrote:

> I hear the cannons of Plevna . . . On the advice of Totleben, we've given up trying to storm it and hope to force the garrison to surrender by famine . . . But all my thoughts are with you more than ever, my adored angel . . . May God keep you, give you happiness and not refuse the one thing we lack . . . I hope you won't have your period when I return as I long to have you, which is forgivable after five months of abstinence.

They would "fall on each other like cats."

On 6 November, good news arrived from the Caucasus: the fortress of Kars then the town of Batumi fell.† On the 28th, an adjutant burst in with another message for Alexander. "Osman Pasha has surrendered. I couldn't believe my ears," the elated tsar told Katya. "I hear Hurrahs endlessly." Alexander rode straight to Plevna. "The tsar seemed younger," wrote Miliutin. "The emperor held out his hand to me, asking 'To whom do we owe the taking of Plevna and not retreating? We owe this success to you!'" Awarding the St. George's Cross to Miliutin, he joked, "Does the war minister think I deserve one too?"

Yet it was now winter. The Shipka Pass, where Gurko still held out, was shrouded in snow. It seemed unlikely that the Russians could push through in such conditions. Instead of waiting, Miliutin's reformed army marched to relieve Gurko. In a remarkable exploit, Gurko stormed back through the pass, helping to take 30,000 prisoners, and on 8 December the Russians broke into Bulgaria. The tsar arrived back in Petersburg for a Te Deum and *bingerles* with Katya. Would Alexander finally take

---

* The Russians again tried to storm the Shipka Pass where Katya's brother-in-law Emmanuel Meshchersky was killed. "I'm saddened to the bottom of my heart—what a noble character and I lose in him a real friend," wrote the emperor. Soon afterwards (12 October) his nephew Serge Leuchtenberg was killed by a cannonball to the head, "a beautiful death that proves the family serve like others." Alexander wept when he saw the list of dead Guardsmen whom he knew personally. "I spent a restless night," he wrote on 5 September, "inconsolable about Emmanuel." And his baby Gogo was sick. Alexander suffered asthma and fell ill with fever.

† The war had another front in the Caucasus where Alexander had appointd his youngest brother Mikhail as commander-in-chief. A kind man and magnificent specimen of manhood, he was no general, admitting to his staff "In wartime it's better to be a coachman than a commander-in-chief." His top general, the Armenian, Mikhail Loris-Melikov was not impressed: the grand duke was "as frightened as a rabbit on the battlefield," wrote Loris-Melikov. "Masked by his handsome appearance and good manners, he's an ignoramus." But Loris possessed all the aptitude Mikhail lacked and delivered a series of victories.

Constantinople—known as "Tsargrad," Caesar's city—the longed-for prize of the Romanovs?[30]

On the day before Christmas, Sofia fell. Alexander spent much of New Year with Katya—soon pregnant again. As for Gogo, six, and Olga, five, the tsar recorded that "They missed their Papasha and they're more tender to me than ever."

Nizi was racing towards Constantinople. "The news of our armies makes me very happy," Alexander wrote to Katya on 9 January 1878. "God grant us a peace worthy of Russia." Beaconsfield was alarmed that the Russians might take Constantinople and sent in the Royal Navy, backed by a belligerent Victoria and a jingoistic public.* The tsar recorded, "[Nizi] has just told me that he could occupy this city without any difficulty," though "The English fleet is sailing towards the Bosphorus." Alexander shared every detail with Katya, mixing sex and war: "Oh how I enjoyed our *bingerles*," he wrote on 14 January. "If the Turks accept our conditions, the armistice can be announced sooner and I hope our cavalry is headed for Constantinople."

Europe teetered on the edge of war. The dreams of the Romanovs were so close to being realized, but as "I'd heard often from the intelligent prescient Bismarck," victory could be self-defeating. The brothers bickered. Nizi acted "in a haphazard manner," complained Alexander on 11 January. "It's easy to take Constantinople; the challenge is how to keep it." He told his brother that if the Ottomans did not accept his terms within forty-eight hours, "we'll only talk again under the walls of Tsargrad." Nizi reported that "The occupation of Constantinople is inevitable." If the Russians entered the city, Britain would fight.

On 12 January, Alexander ordered Ignatiev, whom he had just raised to count, to make a deal. After his earlier hesitations, Nizi was now desperate to grab the city. "Success has gone to Nikolai's head," wrote Alexander next day. "Constantinople, Tsargrad—but now it involves risks and dangers that are my responsibility." The emperor hesitated: "May God enlighten me and inform me!" he wrote on 15 January. Next day,

---

* The popular song of the day coined the neologism "jingoism": "We don't want to fight but by Jingo if we do / We've got the ships, we've got the men, we've got the money too / We've fought the Bear before, and while we're Britons true / The Russians shall not have Constantinople." But one sailor on board HMS *Sultan* in the Bosphorus was uneasy: the tsar's son-in-law and Queen Victoria's son Prince Alfred. Earlier in the crisis, the Belgian king Leopold II had suggested him as the ideal Anglo-Russian candidate to be emperor of Byzantium. "I'd sooner end the remainder of my days in China to such a fearful prospect," he replied. Now he feared orders to fire on his father-in-law's soldiers. Queen Victoria bombarded him with anti-Russian letters, which he showed to his wife and she to her parents. "The insulting things the Queen says in her letters to Alfred," Empress Marie wrote, "about the tsar and the Russian people are worthy of a fishwife."

"We are four versts from Tsargrad," but the "sultan accepts everything!" Alexander halted his armies. "I imagine how Bismarck will laugh . . . History will condemn me for my hesitation."

"My greatest enemy Beaconsfield arranges all sorts of intrigues" but "if they won't listen to reason . . . I'll force him to respect me and Russia." The tsar could not sleep, yet he still managed heroic amounts of sex: "What delicious *bingerles* before dinner," he wrote on 27 January. But, he went on, "The English conduct is infamous and our honour can't support it. I'm glad you understand everything that's happening," he told Katya. The Royal Navy sailed into the Bosphorus.

On 28 January, Alexander "in high excitement" ordered Nizi to take Constantinople, but this time the grand duke, who could see the British ships, hesitated. Alexander warned Abdul Hamid that if "a single Englishman landed, Nikolai would occupy Tsargrad." Now the tsar bombarded his brother with orders to conquer: "I'd be more calm if we had Constantinople." The sultan appealed to London. Nizi advanced to San Stefano just outside Constantinople. "The capital is in our hands," wrote Alexander excitedly on 12 February.

Not quite. Alexander allowed Ignatiev to negotiate a Slavophile peace. On 19 February, Abdul Hamid signed the Treaty of San Stefano, which created a large Russian client-state, Bulgaria, dominating the Balkans, almost the size of the medieval Bulgar empire, recognized the full independence of Serbia, Montenegro and Romania, and granted Russia Bessarabia and conquests from Kars to Batumi plus territory in Anatolia and right of passage through the Straits. On 21 February, the emperor celebrated with Katya: "You saw how my *bingerle* was glad of your invitation, how he wanted it and how he was ready crying 'Yes! Yes'—*quel horreur!*"

"The British are furious," wrote Alexander. "Jubilation!" wrote Miliutin.[31]

The triumph was short-lived. Ignatiev had overridden the informal deal with Austria. Britain and Austria demanded a European conference—or war. Bismarck offered to mediate at a congress in Berlin. Alexander and Miliutin planned a (delusional) attack on British India.* But the tsar

---

* The war minister envisaged a three-pronged attack, then considered an action on the Afghan border. But this too was cancelled. Beaconsfield reacted by establishing an Afghan protectorate under a client king until the Russians sent in a pretender to contest the Afghan throne. The British, who had not learned from their catastrophic Afghan expedition in 1842, had invaded Afghanistan and imposed British control. But their minister and staff were massacred. "It's what they deserve," Alexander told Empress Marie on 26 August 1878. Once London had disentangled itself from the Afghan quagmire, Britain was happy to withdraw provided Kabul did not become a Russian protectorate.

could not risk war against Britain and Austria. Trusting the dynastic link with Uncle Wilhelm, he hoped Bismarck would help him. "If I'd had a Bismarck," he wrote on 5 March, "I'd surely have told Nikolai at the vital moment: 'Take it; talk afterwards!' "

"Berlin promises nothing good," he told Katya on 11 March. "I'm in terrible anguish. I fear another bad night."

Nizi was sacked but promoted to marshal—and replaced by Totleben. In June, "All Europe gathered in Berlin under the presidency of the great genius Bismarck," Alexander bitterly told Katya. Beaconsfield triumphantly recounted every Russian mistake in his comical letters to Queen Victoria. As the Congress opened, "Prince Gorchakov, a shrivelled old man, was leaning on the arm of his gigantic rival" Bismarck, when the latter, "seized with a sudden fit of rheumatism, both fell to the ground and unhappily Prince Bismarck's dog, seeing his master apparently struggling with an opponent, sprang to the rescue."

Gorchakov's mauling set the tone. The senile Gorchakov blundered, mistakenly showing Beaconsfield a map of Russia's maximum concessions which he immediately accepted. When the British insisted that Jewish rights be protected in Romania, Gorchakov held forth about the backwardness of Russian "Yids." Beaconsfield, despite being wheezy himself, played a brilliant hand. "That old Jew," said Bismarck, "he's the man" while Gorchakov was just "the old fop." But it was the acute Shuvalov who took over the actual negotiations and saved Russia from a disastrous European war. Alexander was forced to accept a diminished Bulgaria divided between an Ottoman province in the south and an autonomous principality in the north which, he decided, should be ruled by his nephew, Prince Alexander of Battenberg. Serbia and Montenegro gained full independence. Russia regained Bessarabia at the mouth of the Danube and Batumi on the Black Sea. These gains were substantial—but to the bellicose Slavophiles they seemed paltry compared to the prizes of San Stefano, a disappointment made more bitter by Austria winning the administration of Bosnia and Britain gobbling Cyprus—all won with Russian blood.

Bismarck hoped to settle the Balkans, fearing, as he put it prophetically, that "One day the great European War will come out of some damned foolish thing in the Balkans." Alexander realized that Bismarck "is plotting against us with Austria," the start of their secret alliance aimed at Russia. "The alliance of the Three Emperors," he wrote, "no longer exists"—though it endured for want of an alternative.

"The emperor is in a bad mood," observed Miliutin, "and feels humiliated." Alexander was tired, his asthma and eyesight had deteriorated: Katya read him his despatches. The treaty "makes my heart bleed" but "our *bingerles* before dinner were delicious—you're so tasty, Moushka!"

The wasted victory sapped the invisible authority that is essential to every regime. It outraged the Slavophiles—and empowered the terrorists. Soon the tsar would be hunted in the streets.[32]

A new terrorist group called Land and Freedom planned to assassinate the tsar, launching a murderous assault on the wounded regime—just as 193 Populists were tried by jury in Petersburg. But most were acquitted. Alexander ordered their rearrests. On 24 January 1878, General Trepov, governor of Petersburg, was shot in his office by the twenty-eight-year-old Vera Zasulich after he had ordered radicals whipped in prison. Trepov was only wounded and the girl was arrested. Yet this would-be assassin won widespread sympathy. On 31 March, Zasulich faced jury trial but was acquitted after a brilliant defence attacked Trepov for the whippings. "It's inexplicable!" protested Alexander. "Does it mean that Trepov should be condemned to death? I ordered the arrest of Zasulich," but she was spirited out of Russia. Suddenly the terrorists struck everywhere: an official was assassinated in Kiev. A radical in Odessa, who had shot a policeman, was executed.

The head of the Third Section, General Nikolai Mezentsov, was stabbed to death in the street. "This horrible assassination has completely upset me," Alexander told Katya on 4 August. "I miss him and don't know yet with whom to replace him . . ." He worried that Katya would miscarry. "What a charming century we live in!" His new secret police chief, General Alexander Drenteln, was almost shot in his carriage. On 3 September 1878, "nine months after the day of his return," Katya wrote, "God gave us a daughter"—Catherine, born in Crimea. Back in Petersburg, they walked together and made love—"It's good to cry out," he said, "but I'm worried blood has shown. I hope it's not our *bingerles* of yesterday!" He was determined not to impregnate her again: "I wouldn't forgive myself." The emperor, sixty and weary,* celebrated New Year with Katya. "I'm still steeped in our delicious *bingerles* last night," he wrote on 1 January 1879. Even under pressure, Alexander managed to keep what Miliutin admiringly called his "happy character." The emperor recognized his own "serenity of personality which I hope

---

* Their letters give a good idea of what it was like to be a tsar. When she grumbled about his work, he explained on 13 May 1872 that he had "to fulfil the obligations of my position which impose duties on me which I cannot neglect." The Council "kept me for 2.1/2 hours this afternoon"; a ball lasted until midnight: "I was colossally bored"; the visiting shah of Persia was "an imbecile" and "getting home at 11:30 p.m. I find a heap of papers to read." In an age of telegrams, trains and howitzers, the demands of autocracy were becoming too much for one man. "Oh I love my tranquillity."

to keep in spite of everything as I work to do my duty according to my conscience without either genius or perfection."

"Today was assassinated the governor-general of Kharkov, Prince Dmitri Kropotkin," wrote Alexander on 22 February 1879. "The masked killer disappeared without trace." In fact he came to Petersburg to kill the tsar.[33]

On 2 April 1879, just after 8 a.m., the tsar, followed at a distance by Captain Kokh, his bodyguard, was strolling home across Palace Square when a young man saluted him. As he passed him, Alexander looked back into the barrel of a raised pistol. The tsar ran across the square, dodging a shot to the left and another to the right. A bullet grazed his greatcoat, another ricocheted around his legs, as Kokh tackled the assassin with his sabre. Hearing the shooting, Shuvalov, who had kept his Winter Palace apartment, rushed out and helped Alexander into a carriage.

"It's the third time God has miraculously saved me from death," wrote Alexander, rushing to Katya. "God has saved me for you!" But "he cried a long time in my arms," she recalled. When he told Empress Marie, she sensed the death of an epoch. "There's no reason to live," she told her lady-in-waiting Alexandra Tolstoya. "This is killing me. Today the killer hunted him like a hare!" Marie, "broken, desperate, her eyes feverishly bright," went into a decline.* When her ladies tried to cheer her up, she just said, "Why picnic around a bier?"

Alexander appointed governor-generals with emergency powers.† "Three were executed today," he told Marie. "Sad but what can you do?" "Dissatisfaction grips everyone," wrote Valuev, now president of the Committee of Ministers. Alexander "looks tired and speaks of nervous irritation which he tried to hide," added Valuev after a visit to Tsarskoe Selo, shocked to see "a half-ruined sovereign" surrounded by policemen and Cossacks. "The earth is quaking, the building threatens to fall, the proprietor has a dim presentiment of danger but conceals his anxiety."

After the shooting, the tsar "received an anonymous letter" that so upset him that even at midnight "I don't feel like sleeping . . ." This may have been a terrorist threat against Katya Dolgorukaya and the children, who lived in their townhouse on English Quay. Just after the war, on

---

* Alexander still wrote tender if short letters to the TB-ravaged tsarina, "my dear friend," saying, "Sorry to hear you're feeling unwell." They shared the anniversaries of Nixa's death, looked forward to meeting up again ("I kiss you tenderly. I rejoice we'll be reunited together soon"). He reported on "manoeuvres with the boys" and wrote: "May you enjoy complete calm and new resources of health" even though he secretly longed to marry Katya.
† The governor-generals were mostly successful generals in the war: Gurko governed Petersburg, Totleben, Odessa and Loris-Melikov, Kharkov.

24 April 1878, the emperor had secretly legitimized his children with the princely title Yurievsky—one of the original Romanov names—and, as Katya emphasized, that of the founder of Moscow, Yuri Dolgoruky.

Alexander could not protect Katya. After worrying for weeks, he quietly moved her and the children into the third floor of the Winter Palace close to the courtiers' quarters, far from where his wife was dying on the second floor. The tsar revelled in being "all together": "I love it that I got to wake up with you," he told Katya, "and you in bed next to me, eyes closed, prettier than ever in our sunlit room."

But Adlerberg, court minister, disapproved. "Out of some sense of decency, refined tact," recalled Adlerberg, "the tsar said nothing to me about that awkward subject and I pretended to know nothing."

On 10 May 1879, down in Crimea, thinking of his plight by the seaside, Alexander felt like a lover in a novel:

> If I was a real writer, I'd start my journal: what a beautiful May day in this natural paradise but what hell in my soul. My God, my God, how pitiful to live outside one's heart and in a marriage which is only political. My ideas, my feelings, my passions, all are far from my imperial cage. Everyone closes their eyes but they'll get a brusque wake-up the day when . . .

Days later, the eleven leaders of Land and Freedom met secretly in a forest near Lipetsk to found a terrorist faction, People's Will, electing a twenty-five-member Executive Committee that included a mousy-haired girl, Sofia Perovskaya, descended from the Razumovskys, niece of Nicholas I's interior minister and daughter of a Petersburg governor. She was the mistress of Andrei Zhelyabov, the terrorist mastermind. "The emperor has destroyed in the second half of his reign almost all the good he did in the first," they agreed. "The Executive Committee passed a death sentence on Alexander II."

Alexander soon heard about it. "I find myself," he wrote on 30 August, "like a wolf tracked by hunters."[34]

On 17 November 1879, Alexander left Crimea by train. There were two trains and two possible routes. The first train always conveyed the retinue and baggage, with the tsar in the fourth wagon of the second imperial train half an hour behind. As the second train passed through Rogashska Zastava, a colossal explosion blew it into the air. The terrorists, led by Sofia Perovskaya, knew his movements. But unusually he had travelled in the first train because the retinue train had broken down. The amateurish Third Section struggled to cope with an ingenious organization of suicide-killers—but they arrested two terrorists who were carrying dynamite; one revealed the identities of its leaders while the other, as Alexander noted on 4 December 1879, "had a plan of the Winter Palace; the dining room marked with a cross which is surely not without significance. Below the dining room are my guards. My God, are they even among them?"

Yet security in the Winter Palace, observed one of the servants, a carpenter named Stepan Khalturin, was astonishingly lax: "While most high-ranking people couldn't pass through the main entrances of the Palace, the back doors were open all day and night for any tavern acquaintance of the lowliest servant."

Khalturin was surprised because he was a People's Will assassin who was daily smuggling nitroglycerine into the palace which he stored under his pillow. "There were frequent searches but they were so superficial no one ever thought to lift my pillow (my luck!) which would have destroyed me." At one point, the carpenter was called in to mend something in Alexander's own study; the tsar was there but he could not bring himself to kill a man from behind. Khalturin accumulated so much dynamite that it was poisoning him. He had to store it in a trunk in the cellar, underneath the dining room marked with a cross. They planned to kill not just the tsar but the entire family.

On 1 January 1880, "The tsar told me," explained Kostia, "he would like to show Russia a sign of trust for the 25th anniversary of his reign*—he'd like to give society more participation in the discussion of important affairs." He ordered Valuev to draw up the plan.

That evening, Alexander heard "the news from Cannes. *She* won't live long." "She" was the empress. On 9 January, he sent Adlerberg to fetch the dying tsarina. "No one asked my opinion," Marie said. "They'd treat a sick housemaid better."

On 23 January, Kostia chaired a meeting at the Marble Palace where Sasha "was so aggressively critical that I was several times obliged to restrain him . . ." Sasha managed to crush the plan—"It's the beginning of a constitution which is no benefit to us!" Elections would just empower "windbag lawyers!" The tsar did not give up, but "I see more and more [that Sasha] and I are totally different men."

*

* The upcoming jubilee has an enduring legacy. Nikolai Rubinstein commissioned his friend Tchaikovsky to produce a symphony that would be performed at the opening of the new Cathedral of Christ the Saviour in Moscow: the result was the *1812 Overture*, so flamboyant, spectacular and almost cinematic with its booming cannons that it made Tchaikovsky internationally famous—and also embarrassed him for the rest of his life.

In the palace, "Strange things happened all the time," recalled Alexandra Tolstoya. "The carelessness was incomprehensible." The commandant General Delsal received the warning about the diagram of the palace but "regarded it as a tale." One person sensed the danger, however. "The idea of a new attack pursued me ceaselessly," recalled Katya. "On our arrival, I ordered our servants to ask the commandant to examine the rooms of the workers." He promised that "all measures had been taken but my heart wasn't reassured . . . As the days passed with terrible rapidity, I was particularly worried and I spent hours reflecting on security measures. Alas I could see the authorities were half asleep and lacking energy." Once she smelt the acridity of nitroglycerine, but everyone insisted it was just leaking gas.

Deep in the cellar, Carpenter Khalturin had 250 pounds of nitroglycerine. Every day, he passed Zhelyabov in Palace Square and said: "No."

Just after 6 p.m. on 5 February, he calmly greeted Zhelyabov in a blizzard and said: "It's ready." He had 300 pounds of nitroglycerine. The wires were connected. Fifteen minutes to get out. The two terrorists looked towards the illuminated palace. Family dinner was ready.

The snow had delayed the emperor's guest, Prince Alexander of Hesse, brother of the empress and father of the new prince of Bulgaria. The tsar sent his sons Sasha and Vladimir to meet his train. At 6:15, a servant announced that the prince had arrived and, as always, Katya accompanied the tsar along the corridors before returning to their apartment. Alexander met his brother-in-law in the Marshals' Hall and embraced him. They were about to proceed to the Yellow Dining Room when, at 6:20 p.m., suddenly "The floor rose as if it was an earthquake. The gaslights in the gallery went out, there was total darkness," wrote the Hessian prince, "and the air was filled with the disgusting odour of gunpowder." The grand dukes ran "towards the Yellow Dining Room," recalled Sasha, "whence the noise had come and we found all the windows burst open, the walls showing cracks, almost all the chandeliers out and everything covered with dust and plaster."

Two black "Nubian" guards, faces and scarlet garb whitened by plaster like mummies, stood to attention. Firebells rang. The two terrorists on the Square, satisfied that the tsar was dead, headed to a safehouse. "There was total darkness in the big courtyard and terrible screams," wrote Sasha. "Vladimir and I immediately ran to the guardhouse which wasn't easy since all the lights were out and the smoke so thick it was hard to breathe."

The emperor rushed towards his mistress's apartment, calling "Katya!," and encountered a servant with a candelabra which he commandeered.

"I couldn't feel my legs, my heart ceased to beat and I was almost mad," said Katya. She started ringing the bell to Alexander's study—no reply. Then she heard "that cherished voice crying, 'I'm coming, my adored angel.'" They embraced, then fell to their knees before the icons in her bedroom. He smilingly said: "So this is what they call a 'gas' explosion. Oh God, the victims break my heart, I'm going to the place of the blast."

Sasha got there first. "We found a terrible scene: the entire guards room was blown up and everything had collapsed six feet deep and in that pile of brick, plaster, slabs and mounds of wall lay more than fifty soldiers covered with dust and blood." Twelve were dead; sixty-nine wounded. "A heartbreaking picture!" remembered the heir. "I'll never forget that horror as long as I live." The tsar arrived: "I wept . . . the sentries are all buried at their posts!"

"On the stairs, hallways, there was bustle, chaos, dust, the smell of gas," noted Miliutin, "and in the hallway, I found the imperial family. The emperor called me into his study. As before, he showed total composure, seeing a new manifestation of God's hand saving him for the fifth time." But he was less impressed with his police: "I've started to doubt the security. In spite of the plan of the Palace uncovered by us, no one had understood anything. As always they searched with the same negligence and reported that all was well!"

Miliutin was amazed: "Everyone's thinking—where can one find peace and safety if the villains can lay mines in the royal palace itself?"

Sasha was hysterical, saying, "The sovereign must leave the evil Winter Palace." All "nerves are so taut you expect to be blown up at any moment," noted Kostia, who sensed the terrorists all around him but "We don't see them or know them; we don't even have the slightest idea of their numbers." The Romanovs "lived in a besieged fortress," mused the tsar's young nephew Sandro, Mikhail's son. "The footman serving coffee could be working for the nihilists; every chimneysweep could be the bearer of an infernal machine."

Only the dying empress was oblivious. She slept through it. The sleepless emperor understood the need for a new order: "The night will bring me counsel."[35]

"The panic continues," wrote Kostia, "wild rumours spread." Yet there was sympathy for the bombers. "No one supports the government now," realized Miliutin. Every day Alexander consulted generals Drenteln and Gurko but "both behave as if they're observers of what's going on. Yet one is Gendarme commander, the other governor-general. Halfwits!" decided Valuev. On 8 February, Sasha proposed a wartime dictator, adding menacingly, "If your life is dear to you, you should accept my project."

"I flatly refused," said Alexander, but the next day he gathered ministers and governor-generals Gurko of Petersburg and Loris-Melikov of Kharkov. "All agreed with my son. So the Supreme Commission will be named. All agreed enthusiastically." But who was to be the dictator? Then the emperor "surprised everyone."

"I gave total power to Loris-Melikov—powers so extensive that Loris will perhaps be considered a dictator." His choice was inspired.

Mikhail Loris-Melikov, aged fifty-four, was not Russian and he did not even have a home in Petersburg, but he possessed political suppleness and emotional intelligence. Scion of ancient Armenian nobility, a charmer with luxuriant black whiskers, twinkling brown eyes and a lean figure, he had made his name in 180 battles against Ottomans and Murids. In Kharkov, he had tamed terrorism by repression combined with conciliation, his trademark: his soldiers nicknamed him Fox-Tail Wolf-Fang. As he was Armenian, courtiers judged him "Eastern, flexible, sly," an image he played on teasing them, "They say the Armenian Loris is not fit to be dictator." The heir's adviser Pobedonostsev thought him a "a juggler, a manipulator—able, intelligent and crafty." Now he was so powerful that his rival Valuev nicknamed him "Michael II."

Sasha "is enchanted with his victory," wrote Alexander but he knew Sasha's Anichkov Palace was the headquarters of opposition. Loris flattered Sasha: "From the first day of my appointment, I vowed to act only in the same direction as Your Highness, finding the success of the work entrusted to me depends on it." At first, Loris and Sasha were close. "With great speed, he created for himself two patrons—Winter Palace [the tsar] and Anichkov [Sasha]," commented Pobedonostsev bitterly. "For His Majesty he became a necessity, a screen against danger. He eased the Tsarevich's approaches to His Majesty and offered ready answers—an Ariadne's thread out of the labyrinth."

"God grant Loris success in uncovering the revolutionary nest so I can have a bit of security," wrote Alexander. "If not it's better that I retire . . . to avoid a catastrophe. Let them try my indomitable son!"

Loris set to work energetically, not just "to crush sedition but the cause of sedition and its support": he clarified judicial process, abolished the salt tax, liberalized the press and universities, gleefully appeasing the students: "I've finally achieved the sacking of [education minister Dmitri] Tolstoy, the evil genius of the Russian land," crowed Loris.

He abolished the Third Section and reformed the secret police, appalled by its ineptitude. His imaginative ingenuity was remarkable for a soldier. Yet this agency remained unfit for purpose: to chase the terrorists, and to appease the heir, Loris promoted Sasha's henchman, the policeman Peter Cherevin, to the Commission. But astonishingly, instead of infiltrating the terrorists, General Cherevin pursued a mythical Jewish conspiracy, reporting on 6 April 1880, "All Jewish capitalists have entered the universal Jewish cabal with goals hostile to the entire Christian population." Then, at 2 p.m. on 20 April, as Loris stepped out of his carriage, a young man shot at him; the count ducked down but then threw himself at the assassin and subdued him—an admirable exploit—handing him over to his Cossacks. "Poor poor liberty, what crimes are committed in your name!" wrote the tsar, impressed by Loris's cool under fire. Fifty thousand spectators including Dostoevsky watched the terrorist's hanging on Semyonovsky Square. But society was ambivalent: afterwards the novelist met the publisher Alexei Suvorin. Both agreed that, though they abhorred terrorists, they would never inform the police of a plot.

Back in the palace, little Gogo was fascinated by the details of the execution as Alexander and Katya discussed it.[36]

Katya talked more and more about politics. "She pushes me towards more extreme measures against the nihilists," Alexander noted on 16 March, "and says it's necessary to hang, ceaselessly hang to extinguish this infamous revolt." But "I detest it when she gets mixed up in politics." She also nagged Alexander to make more arrangements for his children. The empress was close to death. Alexander was agonized by guilt. On 21 May he visited her. Dr. Botkin said she would survive another night, so the tsar travelled out to Tsarskoe Selo where Katya was staying with the children.

In the morning, Empress Marie was found dead: "My God, welcome her soul and forgive me my sins," Alexander wrote on 22 May. "My double life ends today. I am sorry but She [Katya] doesn't hide her joy. She talks immediately about legalizing our situation; this mistrust kills me. I'll do all for her but not against the national interest."

On the 23rd the emperor decided to marry Katya after a shortened mourning period of just forty days. "If we hadn't expected more attacks, it would never have occurred to us to marry" so quickly, she explained. On the 24th, he shared an even greater secret with her: "I will give the people a complete constitution." But Katya, "as overexcited as a child," was already dreaming of their marriage. "Katya has never so aggravated me." He promised he would crown her on 1 August 1881. Then having determined to crown a new empress and give Russia the beginnings of a constitution, he decided on 4 July, "I shall retire"—to the south of France. At Marie's funeral, on 28 May, "A blinding fork of lightning crossed the darkened sky." The tsar shivered.

The courtiers heard he was going to marry the scarlet woman they now called "Odalisque," an Ottoman concubine. On 30 May, Sasha went to see him about it but the tsar, choosing his words carefully, said that the "gossip was ill founded," at which the heir presumed there would be no marriage. Alexander tried to clarify: "I shall live as I wish and my union with Princess Dolgorukaya is definite," but "Your rights will be safeguarded." They parted in tears—and locked in an awkward misunderstanding.

Father Bazhenov, who had married the tsar to Marie, refused to marry them. On 5 July, his childhood friend Adlerberg made a last-ditch attempt to "dissuade him by citing the unpleasant impression it would make unless he waited a year after the empress's death." But Alexander might be dead by then. He could be murdered any moment, any day. "He wasn't wrong on every point," admitted the tsar, "but I've given my word." Adlerberg noticed that he was "silent, pale, confused, his hands trembled. Suddenly he stood up and left the room. The door opened and in came a woman." The count and the Odalisque rowed. She accused him of disloyalty. When Alexander peeped round the door, she snapped, "No, let us finish." Afterwards, Katya stormed out.

"I was wrong about that man," the tsar reflected. "He's a total nonentity and an intolerable blackmailer." But Alexander was supported by his younger brother Mikhail: "We have no right to criticize his decisions."

At 3 p.m. on 6 July, at Alexander I's field church in Tsarskoe Selo, the tsar, in pale-blue Hussars uniform, and Katya, in a wedding gown, were married by Father Ksenophont Nikolsky.* Adlerberg signed the certificate, though "his presence astonished me." After a small supper the couple took a carriage ride around the park. Then Alexander signed a decree: "Having entered . . . into lawful marriage with Princess Ekaterina Dolgorukaya, we command her to be named Most Serene Princess Yurievskaya" with "the same name given to the children." He feared that "Russia and History will never forgive me," yet "The stone that oppressed his heart had been lifted," wrote Katya "and [he was] as happy as a being could ever be."

Next morning, he told Count Loris: "I know how loyal you are to me. Now you must be loyal to my wife and children." Loris started to consult Katya, who afterwards reflected, "The outstanding minister understood what a valuable ally the princess was as wife of the tsar."

As the family learned of the secret marriage, he justified himself to his sister, Ollie, queen of Württemberg: Katya "preferred to renounce all

---

* The marriage was morganatic, meaning the monarch's titles could not be inherited by children of this union.

the social amusements and pleasures desired by young ladies and has devoted her entire life to me," but "without interfering in any affairs, she lives only for me, dedicated to bringing up the children." Sasha thought the marriage "forever ruined all the dear good memories of family life." As he later wrote to Minny, it was "The start of these troubled times, this living nightmare." Sasha seethed malevolently.[37]

The tsar was "a pitiful and unfortunate man" and "God's fates sent him to the misfortune of Russia; the only instincts left are dull love of power and sensuality." This description of Alexander was written not by a Nihilist but by his son Sasha's closest adviser, Konstantin Pobedonostsev, the ex-tutor who now visited the heir every day at the Anichkov Palace.

Tall, gangly and fusty with thin lips, beaky nose and thick spectacles, Pobedonostsev looked as if he had never been young, had never smiled and had never seen sunlight—indeed he loved attending funerals. Once he had drafted Alexander's legal reforms and had tutored Nixa, but he was now passionately convinced that the reforms were a disaster. Spitting hatred to his confidante, Ekaterina Tyutcheva, ex-lady-in-waiting, he declared that the tsar was "the abomination of desolation" who "only wants to live by the mindless will of the belly." But there was principle behind his venom. Nicknamed Torquemada, he was disgusted by the modern world of newspapers, stock markets, democracies and Jews, and wanted Russia frozen in the age of Nicholas I. "Here," he said, "I pay my coachman to drive slowly." A fanatical believer in the autocracy and Russia's Slavophile mission to civilization, for him there was no place for Jews ("our great ulcer") or Poles.* Even his patron, Count Sergei Stroganov, said, "He knew exactly what shouldn't be done but never what should be done instead." The tsar called Pobedonostsev a "desperate fanatic" and "a Pharisee," but to please Sasha, he and Loris appointed Torquemada to the Supreme Commission.

---

* Pobedonostsev cultivated a network of reactionary allies through the nationalist newspaper barons Mikhail Katkov and Prince Vladimir Meshchersky, who had hired Dostoevsky to edit his newspaper the *Citizen* which the heir secretly funded. The prince introduced Dostoevsky to Pobedonostsev, and they became best friends, meeting on Saturday nights for hours of discussion. "I shall run again to you as I came to you on other days for instructions," wrote the novelist as he developed *The Brothers Karamazov*. Dostoevsky best expressed their Slavophile instincts: "the Russian nation is an extraordinary phenomenon in the history of human genius." He was an avid monarchist, seeing the tsars as "a mystery, a sacrament, an anointment . . . the primary fact of our history." Delighted that one of the titans of Russian literature had decent views, Pobedonostsev introduced Dostoevsky to Sasha who had read and admired *Crime and Punishment*. The meeting was awkward—Dostoevsky could not play the courtier but it did not matter. Alexander II invited him to give lectures to the younger grand dukes, Sergei and Paul and their cousin KR. Dostoevsky, once sentenced to death by one tsar, had become the confidant of the Romanovs. He died in early 1881.

At court the ladies-in-waiting muttered against the Odalisque. Daria Tyutcheva, another of that courtier family, dared to write to the emperor: "Could you and will you promise that I'll never be put in the position of offending my feelings for our beloved empress?" Alexander was incensed but replied via Adlerberg: "If this situation does not suit you, you may do what you wish." She then resigned because, she confided to Alexandra Tolstoya, "I can't promise not to make a public scene and even spit in the face of Princess Yurievskaya at the first opportunity." But she left with a terrible prediction: "I have a good feeling that everything will change. In three or four months, all the dirt will be swept out of the Winter Palace!"[38]

On 6 August, Loris reported that order had been restored. Alexander appointed him interior minister in charge of the police, and as a sop to Sasha they brought in his two henchmen, Cherevin as his deputy minister and Pobedonostsev, as ober-procurator of the Synod.

Loris advised the tsar not to take the train to Crimea for "fear of an infernal machine." When the tsar insisted, he asked Katya and the children to travel on a different train. "A woman wouldn't miss the chance to show her devotion," noted Miliutin. Indeed "I left with him so we could die together," recalled Katya. The tsar introduced her to the ministers and she grew closer to Loris, sharing his liberalism.

At Livadia, Alexander and Loris agreed a radical reform—the election of representatives from the local assemblies to sit in the State Council where they could advise but not legislate.

The emperor wanted to introduce Sasha and Minny to his wife. Loris contrived to lure them to Crimea, only informing them when they were already approaching Yalta on the boat, with little Nicky and the other children, that Princess Yurievskaya would be there. "Just think of it," Minny complained. "He waited till we were on the boat. Here we were— trapped!" The emperor was waiting on the quay—and they found Katya living in the late empress's rooms. Sasha was polite, Minny icy.

Sasha's hostility accelerated the emperor's signing of a secret decree. "These 3,302,910 roubles are the absolute property of my wife, Serene Princess Yurievskaya née Princess Dolgorukaya, and our children," he wrote on 11 September, transferring the money from the Court Ministry to the State Bank. He sent courtiers to research Peter the Great's coronation of a peasant (Catherine I) with whom he already had several children and signed this attachment to his will:

Dear Sasha, In the event of my death, I entrust my wife and children to your care. Your friendly disposition towards them, which you displayed from the very first and which was a true joy for us, makes me believe you will not abandon them. Don't forget me and pray for your Pa who loves you tenderly.

The day of their return, the tsar held "a family dinner . . . I begged not to be present," recalled Katya, but Alexander insisted: "You're the wife I'm proud of and my family should bow before the object of their father's happiness." Katya did not seek their approval: "I never gave myself an air of importance, but I knew how to hold myself with the emperor's daughters-in-law . . . I ceded them the honours, but they shouldn't forget I was the wife of their Sovereign."

Alexander was "horrified by the mass of spitefulness" and praised Katya's "charm and your beauty which enrages the other women, furious at all the [male] looks directed at you." Besides, "your family is older than the Romanovs" and Russian—"which infuriated his family, above all the Germans." She was in her prime. "This beauty," observed a courtier, "was still well preserved and in fact had become more splendid."

Minny encouraged Sasha's fury on his mother's behalf. He confronted his father and told him he was decamping to Denmark. Alexander's response was to say that if Sasha disobeyed him, "you will no longer be heir." Sasha retreated. But when Yurievskaya presented herself to Minny at a Winter Palace reception, "To comply with court etiquette, the grand duchess gave her hand but did not kiss her as the tsar had evidently expected," noted a courtier. "The emperor broke into a torrent of impassioned language," exclaiming, "Sasha is a good son, but you—you have no heart." Katya fumed that his "heart of gold" should tolerate "the monsters in his family" who were as "heartless as they were uneducated."*

He was in a race against time, against the terrorists and his son. "If I had a capable replacement on whom I could depend," he told Katya, he would have abdicated already. The emperor fought back tears when he kissed the children good night: "When I'm no longer around, think and pray for your Papachka and don't forget his love for you."[39]

*

* The tsar's youngest sons, Sergei and Paul, were in Florence on a Grand Tour. "The coming winter seemed to me a terrible nightmare," Sergei wrote to Sasha, who now told him that "there are so many, new shocking things. Thank God you're not spending winter in Petersburg . . . I can't give you details until we meet . . . I'll add one thing: we can't go against the fait accompli. One thing remains: to obey and fulfil the wishes and will of Papa . . ." But Sergei and Paul still did not know about the marriage. "We've just received a letter from Papa talking about his wedding," Sergei wrote to Minny. "It hit me like a thunderbolt." Paul "cried a lot. The future is a black cloud," but "Tell Sasha we know our duty and all Papa's orders will be sorrowfully obeyed." When their sister Maria of Edinburgh visited, she too was appalled by the presence of a new stepmother. Only the naughty Alexis understood.

On 4 January 1881 in his study at the Winter Palace, Alexander and Loris approved the plan of reform that "would be special and strong but would have nothing in common with . . . Europe." This timid measure did not establish an instant liberal democracy but it certainly marked the beginning of a changed path for Russia. The Romanovs could no longer "rest on a thousand bayonets," said Alexander Abaza, the liberal finance minister, "and an army of officials." Autocracy had to evolve and widen participation. Alexander recorded Miliutin's advice: "These reforms are the only way to get me out of my grave political position and consolidate the Romanov dynasty." But they might as easily have accelerated the dynasty's collapse, as Mikhail Gorbachev's reforms destroyed the Soviet Union. Combined with the bad idea of crowning Katya, this could have led to a reactionary coup, like that of August 1991 against Gorbachev.* More likely it would have broadened support for the autocracy—but its real nature depended on the attitude of the tsar, and his diaries prove that he saw this as a step towards a constitution.

Loris was rounding up the terrorists. On 25 January 1881, a denunciation exposed a terrorist cell in a cheese shop on Malaya Sadova Street which Alexander travelled past every Sunday to review troops at the Mikhailovsky Manège. But there were two ways to get there and no one knew which he would choose. The police raided the house but found nothing.

The emperor was rejuvenated† by reform and by Katya—he was breezy, acting at "sixty-four like an eighteen-year-old." He even introduced her to Pobedonostsev but the sexless Torquemada was repulsed by her wanton appeal—"Just a wench!" he spat.

At a family supper, the grand master of ceremonies thrice tapped the floor with his ivory-handled staff and announced: "His Majesty the Emperor and Princess Yurievskaya." Grand Duke Sandro, the tsar's fifteen-year-old nephew, was rapt as "The emperor walked in briskly with a strikingly attractive woman on his arm" and "gave a gay wink to my father [Mikhail]" before glancing at "the massive figure of the Heir." Sandro recorded that "[I] couldn't take my eyes off her—I liked the sad

---

* "The realization of the project might have been a step toward a constitution but might not: everything depended on what would be stronger: the revolutionary party and liberal society or the resistance of the very powerful, coherent and unscrupulous party of adherents of autocracy." This was the later judgement of one of Russia's shrewdest analysts of power, Vladimir Ulyanov, then an eleven-year-old schoolboy. Later he would become known as Lenin.

† Alexander's good mood was heightened by General Skobolev's conquest of the lands across the Caspian, today's Turkmenistan, though he massacred 25,000 civilians in the storming of Geog-Teop. Massacring helpless natives was gradually becoming less fashionable and Skobolev was recalled.

expression of her beautiful face and the radiance of her rich blonde hair." But "she knew she was hated" and "frequently turned to the emperor," who "whispered words of encouragement in her small ear." Then at the end of dinner, a governess led in the children. "Ah there's my Gogo," cried Alexander as the seven-year-old started to "rearrange his whiskers. 'Tell us, Gogo, what's your full name?'"

"Prince Georgi Alexandrovich Yurievsky."

"Glad to make your acquaintance, Prince Yurievsky," said the emperor. "By the way, prince, how would you like to be a grand duke?"

Sasha's teenage son, the future Nicholas II, "seemed to enjoy immensely the idea of having acquired a seven-year-old uncle at the age of thirteen." Minny was horrified that her children were cavorting with the spawn of the Odalisque. Sandro thought that Katya "would have succeeded in winning over the men had they not been watched by the women." Afterwards his mother Olga declared: "I shall never recognize that scheming adventuress. I hate her!"

"Whether good, bad or indifferent," replied Mikhail, "she is married to the tsar."

At meetings at the Winter Palace then at the Anichkov, the tsar's Commission, chaired by Valuev, approved the reform plan—and Sasha acquiesced. On 17 February, "I signed with great joy," wrote Alexander, "and decided to reread it before the Council on 4 March." Loris planned to publish the decree on the reforms on the same day as the one on Katya's coronation. Alexander was amused by this "Armenian ruse, though I confess it's tactful and intelligent."

Sasha had turned against the liberal Loris, "angry because he is courting Princess Yurievskaya." Pobedonostsev observed how "this master-manipulator-charmer became even stronger because he untangled an even more confused knot in the stricken family," finding himself a new patron "in a certain woman." Then this minister let rip, in a letter to his confidante, against his emperor: "Forgive this man, O Lord, for he knows not what he does . . . it sickens me to look at him!" As for the emperor, he sensed Sasha's disloyalty: "I look forward to living quietly without feeling that someone close to me is calculating the number of days left for me to live."[40]

"Are the Palace guards completely safe?" Loris asked Alexander on 22 February.

"Are there traitors in my own house? If so," replied the emperor, "a poor peasant must be happier than me, the tsar of Russia." Loris reassured him. The police had not yet caught Perovskaya, who the tsar wrote on 20 February was "a real terrorist capable of killing anyone who stands in her way." They had found nothing at the shop on Sadova, yet on 23 February an unknown person delivered a warning to Katya via her brother that "I am in great danger and I should be very prudent." But four days later, Loris arrested the "famous Zhelyabov." Perhaps this relieved the "great danger"?

On the 28th, the police, this time led by a general, again searched the house on Malaya Sadova, after being warned that the terrorists had dynamited a tunnel under the road. They found nothing again. At the very least, the police were negligent and clueless. At worst, they were traitors. Their boss was Sasha's friend Cherevin, deputy interior minister, who later admitted, "I owe my career to Alexander II, but it's good they got rid of him or he'd have led Russia to disaster."

Loris warned Katya that the assassins were still out there. "Every Sunday," she wrote, "I beseeched [Alexander] not to go to the parade because it tormented me, but he was frustrated not to see his adored troops."

Adlerberg begged the tsar not to go the next day.

"Listen, Adlerberg," shouted Alexander, "I've told you before and I command you now: don't dare tell me anything about attempts on my life. Take whatever measures you and [city governor Adrian] Dvorzhitsky think necessary but leave me in peace!" That night, "I felt nervous." Dr. Botkin gave him valerian drops.

The next morning was Sunday 1 March. On Sundays, the tsar loved to review the Guards at the Mikhailovsky Manège. "Although a pessimist, Loris is in good humour this morning." Alexander approved the announcement of the reforms, which would be signed off at the Council on the 4th. Katya begged him not to attend the parade but Alexander did not want to disappoint Kostia's son Dmitri—it was his first time as aide-de-camp.

The tsar did two things that always comforted him: he wrote his diary and then, pulling up Katya's skirts, he "toppled her on to a table and took her," before, at 12:45, heading out in his bullet-proof carriage, a gift from Napoleon III, escorted by six Cossacks on horseback with another beside the coachman, followed by two sleighs, one conveying Colonel Dvorzhitsky, and the other the imperial bodyguards under Captain Kokh. "To the Manège," he ordered the coachman, via Catherine Canal.

"The parade went very well," recalled Miliutin, who was with him, "the tsar was pleased by everything and in a good mood, joking." Afterwards Sasha returned to the Anichkov Palace for lunch, while the tsar ordered the coachman: "To the Winter Palace by the same route." He was returning by the Catherine Canal.

The intelligence warnings about the cheese shop on Sadova were entirely accurate. For months, Zhelyabov's terrorists had been excavating
under the street to blow the tsar to smithereens after his Sunday parade.
If he took the other route, they trained to abandon the tunnel and rush to
kill him on the Catherine Canal. Zhelyabov's arrest would have aborted
the plan were it not for the ruthless drive of Sofia Perovskaya.

Outside the cheese store, Perovskaya saw the Gendarmes vanish—
which meant the tsar was taking the other route. She waved her
handkerchief, which ordered her four terrorists to the Canal.

The tsar stopped at the Mikhailovsky Palace, where he and his brother
Mikhail took tea for thirty minutes with their cousin, Elena's daughter
Maria.

At 2:15, the tsar mounted his armoured Napoleonic carriage and
headed down Catherine Canal. As the convoy approached Konyushenny
Bridge, a young man, Nikolai Rysakov, tossed a bomb under the carriage. When the smoke cleared, the carriage was intact, with just its rear
end damaged, but one of the mounted Cossacks and a young passer-by
lay dying on the street, while a policeman and another passer-by stood
wounded. As the guards caught the bomb-thrower, finding a pistol and
knife in his coat, the emperor dismounted and crossed himself. He had
miraculously survived a sixth time, but "He was unsteady and understandably upset," recalled Dvorzhitsky, who asked if he was okay.

"Thank God, I'm not wounded," replied Alexander. Dvorzhitsky offered him a ride home in his sleigh just as he heard the arrested terrorist
addressing someone in the crowd and simultaneously understood that
there was another bomber. He asked the tsar to leave at once; the coachman begged him to get back into the carriage. "But His Majesty, without
a word in response to the coachman's request, turned and headed towards the pavement on the canal side," walking alone, followed by the
colonel and four dismounted Cossacks leading their horses. "They surrounded the tsar," who almost slipped and was steadied by Dvorzhitsky.
Alexander wanted to talk to the terrorist, Rysakov, held by four soldiers.
"How's the tsar?" asked an officer, not recognizing him.

"Thank God, I'm fine," answered Alexander. He gestured at the dead
and wounded. "But look . . ."

"Don't thank God yet!" cried out the terrorist.

Alexander asked him his class, and was relieved to learn that he was
not a nobleman. "A fine one, you are!" he reprimanded him, then turned
back towards the carriage. Dvorzhitsky again begged the tsar to get into
the sleigh. He hesitated.

"All right, but first show me the site of the explosion." Some soldiers
from the parade had arrived and flanked the tsar with the Cossacks and

bodyguards, and he was inspecting the hole in the road, deciding what to do next, when a young man, Ignacy Hryniewiecki, leaning on the canal railings, suddenly turned and threw a bomb at Alexander's feet. The blast knocked everyone down—the tsar, Dvorzhitsky, Cossacks. Twenty lay on the street, some crawling, some dead, some stirring. Amid the snow and debris "you could see epaulettes, sabres, and bloody chunks of human flesh." The suicide-bomber himself lay dying.

The explosions reverberated across the city. At the Anichkov Palace, Sasha and Minny, who was getting her son Nicholas ready for ice-skating with his cousin Sandro, heard them. They looked at each other ominously.

On the Catherine Canal, the tsar lay near the "deafened, burned, wounded" Dvorzhitsky. But as the smoke cleared "I heard His Majesty's weak voice: 'Help!' Gathering what strength I had," wrote Dvorzhitsky, "I rushed to the tsar, half-lying, half-sitting, leaning on his right arm. Thinking that he was merely wounded heavily, I tried to lift him but the tsar's legs were shattered and blood poured out of them."

Alexander's cap had fallen off, his coat was shredded, his face bloodied, one eye half closed, the other staring into space. "Cold, I'm cold," he murmured, just as Mikhail, wearing parade uniform, arrived in his carriage and knelt beside him. "Take me to the Palace . . . there . . . to . . . die!" gasped the emperor. Nearby a third terrorist, Ivan Yemelyanov, saw that his bomb would not be needed. The blood throbbed out of the tsar's body.*

Alexander lost consciousness. Instead of bandaging his legs with a tourniquet or taking him to a hospital, the crowd, who included the terrorist Yemelyanov, lifted him on to the sleigh where he continued to bleed as it raced towards the Winter Palace. He was carried up the marble staircase to his study, leaving a trail of blood. They pulled his camp bed out of the alcove and laid him there, "completely unconscious," half sitting up, his face towards the window, shirt open, a Prussian medal round his neck, still wearing one bloodied glove. Mikhail sent an aide to the Anichkov Palace. There Minny was holding Nicholas's ice-skates and anxiously discussing the crump of the two explosions when they saw a sleigh speeding down Nevsky Prospect with an officer standing up in it. They sensed what it meant. Sasha ran down the steps. Seconds later he and Minny, accompanied by little Nicholas and his ice-skates, were racing by sleigh towards the Winter Palace, where the first doctor had just arrived.

* Sasha later commissioned the Church of the Saviour of Spilled Blood that stands on the site.

"The first thing I noticed," recalled Dr. Markus, "was the terrible dis-figurement of the lower limbs, especially the left leg, which, below the knee, was a shattered bloody mass; the right leg was also damaged. Both shattered legs were cold." The doctor tried to press the arteries to staunch the bleeding. Dr. Botkin and the other doctors arrived. At the foot of the bed, Mikhail stood sobbing, while back at his own palace a servant was announcing to his wife Olga and son Sandro that both the tsar and Mikhail had been killed. They too raced towards the Winter Palace along with some Preobrazhensky Guards rushing to defend the family.

When he arrived, Sandro followed "the big spots of black blood on the marble steps and then along the corridor to the tsar's study" where he found his father unharmed, which was such a relief that his mother, hastening after him, fainted. The emperor "looked horrible, one eye shut, the other staring." Sasha cried, "This is what we've come to," while his wife Minny still held Nicholas's ice-skates. Sandro "clung to the arm of Nicky, deathly pale in his blue sailor's suit," and started to cry.

"Steady, my boy, steady," said the towering Sasha, squeezing his shoulders.

The courtier Alexandra Tolstoya was in her room when Varenka Nelidova—Nicholas I's ex-mistress, now in her sixties—burst in: "The emperor's just been brought in wounded on a sleigh . . ." Tolstoya ran through the entire palace to reach the study, where she heard Grand Duke Vladimir order troops to secure Palace Square. The entire family and the chief ministers Loris and Miliutin had arrived. The room was packed. Tolstoya was shocked to see the emperor "lying in a shirt on his camp bed, which had been brought out into the middle of the room, covered with a drape that left his smashed legs open—a horrible sight. I looked away."

Suddenly there was a commotion. Perhaps an officious grand duke had tried to stop her entering, but then Katya, "half-dressed, ran in, fell on top of the tsar's body kissing his hands" and crying out his name. She ordered the doctors "to bring pillows, to bring oxygen, to try to revive the emperor."

The grand duchesses started to sob. Alexander was given oxygen, but his breathing rattled. He did not move, noticed Tolstoya—except for his little finger. "I didn't take my eyes off him." Father Bazhenov adminis-tered communion and extreme unction—and the tsar swallowed the wine.

Katya and Sasha held his head. Sasha asked Botkin how long his father would live. "Fifteen minutes," replied the doctor. "A hoarse voice called out: 'Silence please; the end is near!' " A deep silence reigned in the crowded room. "Everyone held their breath," recalled Tolstoya.

"The emperor is dead," said Dr. Botkin at 3:30, releasing the tsar's bloodied wrist to the cries of his widow. A "terrible sob burst from all chests," while "Princess Yurievskaya shrieked and dropped to the floor like a felled tree," noted Sandro, "her pink and white peignoir soaked in blood." Sasha, "now our young sovereign, lay before the body of his father, shedding floods of tears." Then, "standing up, he noticed Princess Yurievskaya, walked up to her and hugged her." Next he embraced Tolstoya.

The family knelt as one around the body; "looking to my right," wrote Sandro, "I saw the new ruler of Russia," Alexander III. "A strange change came over him in an instant," no longer the bovine joker.

"I saw the illegitimate children of the emperor come in, led by Madame Shebeko," wrote Tolstoya. "The poor babies looked frightened and didn't understand." Then "two Guards carried Princess Yurievskaya to her suite, doctors dressed the body of the late emperor and Gogo cried in tormented bewilderment." All of this, the death, the shrieking, was witnessed by Nicholas.

The new tsar, Alexander III, was convinced that this tragedy had started with his mother's death and his father's remarriage. "All the scum burst out and swallowed all that was holy," he later wrote to Minny. "The guardian angel flew away and everything turned to ashes, finally culminating in the dreadful incomprehensible 1 March." Now he would restore sanctity to Russia.

"A fire burned in his tranquil eyes," noticed Sandro. "A look of sacred determination had suddenly appeared in his cold sharp eyes. He rose. His relatives stood at attention."

"Have you orders, Your Majesty?" asked the city's police chief.

"Of course," replied Alexander III. "The police have lost their heads. The army will take charge. I'll confer with my ministers immediately at the Anichkov Palace." Sasha left with Minny—"Her miniature figure highlighted the mighty build of the new emperor." A crowd had gathered outside and now they cheered "this bearded giant with the shoulders of Hercules." Surrounded by a phalanx of 100 Don Cossacks in attack formation, "red lances shining in the last rays of a crimson March sunset," they rode home to Anichkov.

Vladimir emerged to address the crowd with the traditional words at the demise of a tsar, carefully chosen not to mention the word "death": "The emperor has bidden you to live long!"[41]

More assassinations were expected at any moment. "When you decide to sleep, lock the doors behind you, not only in your bedroom but all the adjoining rooms," Pobedonostsev wrote to the young tsar. "Check alarm bells before sleep since a lead wire might have been cut. Check the tsar's apartments to see no one has got in during the day."

Loris proposed pushing ahead with the constitutional reforms, but Pobedonostsev warned the tsar, "If they sing You the old sirens' song that You should continue the liberal course, for God's sake, Your Majesty, don't believe them! This would be disastrous for You and Russia! The mindless malefactors who killed Your father won't be satisfied by more concessions, they'll become crueller." As for Loris, "Pardon my frankness. Don't keep Loris. I don't trust him. He's a trickster. Not a Russian patriot." Sasha was "lost in indecision."

Pobedonostsev searched for a hard man to crush the terrorists. "May I remind you about Baranov," he wrote to the emperor. "A man devoted to You and he knows how to act when it is necessary." Alexander III appointed the naval captain Nikolai Baranov as city governor, a truculent fantasist, who had been demoted by Kostia for inventing naval heroics during the war. Baranov only intensified the panic, lurching around drunk, having trenches dug before the Winter Palace (and somehow finding time to seduce Pobedonostsev's young wife). His new Commission of Public Order included an aristocratic bodyguard called the Sacred Retinue. "The drama," noted Valuev, "is turning into comedy."

On 8 March, Alexander called a Council of Ministers at which Pobedonostsev launched a jeremiad, warning of "the end of Russia. I find myself not only in confusion but in despair . . . When do they propose a new parliament based on foreign models? Now only a few days after the nefarious deed when the remains of the benevolent tsar are not yet buried." Denouncing all Alexander II's liberal reforms, he warned that "Constitutions are the weapons of all untruth and the source of all intrigue!"

A few days later, Count Nikolai Ignatiev, the unscrupulous ex-ambassador to Constantinople who had been becalmed in a provincial governorship, wrote to the tsar to denounce "the Polish-Yiddish yelps" of "the large Polish-Yiddish group that controls the stock market, much of the press" and had drowned out true Russian voices. The tsar declared that Ignatiev was "a real native Russian" and appointed him a minister.

Baranov uncovered yet another conspiracy and advised the emperor to abandon the capital. On 29 March, Alexander and his family rushed out to Gatchina, which became their main home. "To think after having faced Turkish guns, I have to retreat now before these skunks," the tsar grumbled to his family. But Pobedonostsev now regretted promoting the manic charlatan Baranov. "Baranov is enshrouded by fog. I don't know what he's doing but in my soul I don't trust him. I am afraid there is something going on here." He suspected that Baranov's plan was "to frighten a young tsar and put him in his power." At least Loris had captured the assassins. On 3 April, Zhelyabov, Perovskaya and three others were hanged.

Meanwhile, the tsar ordered Loris to deal with his father's widow, still living with her children in the Winter Palace. On 10 April, Loris persuaded her to give up her apartments. Sasha gave her a new Petersburg home, the Pink Palace.* She hated him.

The liberals were at war with Torquemada. "I'm living with madmen," said Pobedonostsev, "and they think I'm an idiot from the sixteenth century!" He ranted at Loris: "I'm a believer . . . You idolators worship idols of freedom, all idols, idols!"

On 21 April, the tsar met them again at Gatchina. This time, Pobedonostsev was conciliatory, Alexander positive, and Loris and Miliutin left in triumph. But things were not as they seemed. "They want to lead us to representative government," the tsar wrote to Pobedonostsev. "I won't permit it." The ober-procurator saw his chance, sending the tsar a draft manifesto: "You must speak out."

"I approve wholeheartedly," wrote the tsar on 26 April. "Meet tomorrow at 2 to talk." Pobedonostsev hurried to Gatchina. The next evening, at a meeting in Loris's home, the imminent publication of an imperial manifesto was suddenly revealed. "Such unexpected news struck us like lightning," recalled Miliutin. "What manifesto? Who prepared it?" Pobedonostsev admitted that it was he. The ministers screamed at him. Pobedonostsev, sure that "TRUTH is with me," fled lest "the frenzied Asiatic Loris" should try some Armenian ruse.

The liberals resigned.† "They wanted to take me into their clutches

* But he had forgotten about Crimea. On his first visit to Livadia, he and Minny were distressed to find Yurievskaya and her children in his mother's apartments. They had a very awkward holiday together. To honour their father, Grand Dukes Sergei and Paul visited her: "You can't imagine how hard it was for us. At Peterhof she was even more tactless and disgusting than ever." Afterwards, she left for France, taking much of her royal correspondence. Living in luxury, with residences in Paris and the Riviera and a private railway car, she brought up her children abroad, only occasionally returning to the Pink Palace in Petersburg. She lived only for the memory of Alexander, preserving his bloody uniform and creating a replica of his study while writing memoirs denouncing "the incapacity" of Alexander III. When they were in Paris, Alexis and Vladimir dutifully called on her. She was friendly with Alexis, who helped her spoilt son Gogo join the Russian navy, but his abysmal conduct led to his dismissal. Nicholas II let him join the Guards instead. The three children married well. When Katya returned in the next reign, Nicholas II refused to meet her or to witness her daughter Olga's marriage to Count Merenberg, a grandson of Pushkin. Katya died in 1922. Gogo died in 1913. The youngest daughter Catherine became a nightclub singer in England, living on Hayling Island on a pension from George V's widow Queen Mary until her death in 1959.
† Kostia was sacked as general-admiral and president of the State Council (replaced by the tsar's younger uncle Mikhail, who complained, "They just want me to sit here powerless

and enslave me," Alexander told his younger brother Sergei, "but they failed and I'm especially happy to get away from Count Loris who, with just a bit more of his liberal tricks, would have brought the eve of revolution." Alexander appointed Ignatiev as interior minister (sacking the fantasist Baranov).

The era of reform was over. "In the midst of Our great grief," announced Alexander III, "the voice of God bids Us to stand staunchly for government relying on God's design with faith in the truth of autocratic power."[42] The tsar would rule like a curmudgeonly landowner.

---

like a turkey"). "They throw me away like an old glove," Kostia wrote. While his wife Sanny remained in Petersburg, Kostia retired with his ballerina and family to Crimea. When the third uncle, Nizi, was dismissed from all positions, he tearfully asked the tsar to ennoble his illegitimate brood, to which he agreed. The death of his mistress Chislova drove him mad, his priapic sexuality now metamorphosed into hypersexual insanity: "suffering from delusions," he "molested every woman he met" and, after a ballet, he "became so aroused he went backstage and tried to seduce everyone he saw," even male dancers. This was probably tertiary syphilis. He was confined to his Crimean palace. His brother Mikhail wittily expressed his "astonishment that a man of such excessive stupidity could still lose his mind."

# SCENE 3

# Colossus

# CAST

ALEXANDER III, emperor 1881–94, son of Alexander II and Marie, "Sasha," "Colossus"

Maria Fyodorovna (née Princess Dagmar of Denmark), empress, "Minny"

NICHOLAS II, emperor 1894–1917, their son, the heir, "Nicky"

Alexandra Fyodorovna (née Princess Alexandra of Hesse), Nicky's fiancée, "Alix," "Sunny"

Georgi, second son of Alexander III and Minny, "Georgy"

Xenia, their elder daughter, married Grand Duke Alexander Mikhailovich, "Sandro"

Michael, their third son, "Misha"

Olga, their younger daughter

## THE EMPEROR's SIBLINGS

Vladimir, commander of the Guards, married Maria Pavlovna, "Miechen" (née Princess Marie of Mecklenburg-Schwerin)

Alexis, general-admiral, "Beau"

Sergei, "Gega," governor-general of Moscow, married Ella (née Princess Elizabeth of Hesse)

Paul, married Princess Alexandra of Greece, "Pitz"

Maria, married to Prince Alfred, duke of Edinburgh and Saxe-Coburg-Gotha

Marie, their daughter, later queen of Romania, "Missy"

Melita, "Ducky," their daughter, later grand duchess of Hesse-Darmstadt, married to Ernst

## COURTIERS: ministers etc.

General Peter Cherevin, adjutant-general and security chief

Count Ilarion Vorontsov-Dashkov, court minister

Prince Vladimir Meshchersky, newspaper editor and adviser, "Prince of Sodom"

Konstantin Pobedonostsev, ober-procurator of the Holy Synod, "Torquemada"

Count Nikolai Ignatiev, interior minister, "Lord Liar"

Count Dmitri Tolstoy, interior minister

Sergei Witte, finance minister

Mathilde Kshessinskaya, ballerina, mistress of Nicky, "Little K"

N ow thirty-six years old, Alexander III was six feet three inches tall, and still so strong that his party-trick was to bend pokers and tear up packs of cards. Nicknamed "the Colossus," he was the sort of tsar who always knew who he was and what he wanted—no small qualities in a leader.

The Colossus was not sorry to retire to that hulking barracks-like palace of Gatchina, for he was deeply shy and hated social frippery and court balls. Ursine, husky and stout, he seemed, wrote one of his ministers, "an absolute lout like a big Russian peasant," and relished hunting, practical jokes, rough-housing and drinking. He made his own coarseness into a nationalistic virtue and prided himself on his gruff plain Russianness, dressing in boots and blouse and sporting a full beard, the first tsar to do so since Alexei.

The empress, Minny, was his opposite—she "loved to preside at solemn ceremonies" with "a radiant smile for everyone"; she adored dresses, diamonds* and balls. When they attended his brother Alexis's ball, "the emperor as always appeared and hid," noticed Admiral Shestakov, while "the empress as always danced tirelessly."

If she went away, he missed her bitterly: "My sweet darling Minny, for five years we've never been apart and Gatchina is empty and sad without you." She replied, "I'm so pleased you missed me. I thought you didn't care and wouldn't even notice . . . I terribly miss you and the idea that you're lonely and sad at Gatchina tears me apart!"

Sasha was no Lothario, but once, meeting the Austrian and German kaisers, he was so dazzled by the Austrian actress Katharina Schratt (soon to be Franz Josef's mistress) that he embarrassed everyone by paying her court and sending her flowers. Minny flirted heavily with at least one courtier, who signed his notes: "I kiss your dainty teeth." But theirs was that rare thing: a happy and faithful royal marriage. The emperor was most content presiding over horseplay with his three sons and two daughters, the last of whom, Olga, was born soon after his

---

* The tsar found the ideal presents for a wife who already had everything: in 1885, he commissioned Peter-Carl Fabergé, a Baltic German jeweller in Petersburg, to make the Hen Egg, a bejewelled egg that opens to reveal a yoke that opens to reveal a hen that opens to reveal a nest of diamonds. Altogether under Alexander and his son Nicholas II, the Romanovs commissioned fifty Fabergé eggs, usually with the only rule that they must contain a surprise.

succession. Sasha felled trees, roasted apples, rowed on the lake and indulged in food fights with bread-balls. He was not interested in books. Instead "He wanted us to read the book of nature as easily as he read it himself," recalled Olga, who was allowed to sit under his desk while he worked. "Papa turned on the hose, then we ran through the jet and got terribly wet," the sixteen-year-old Nicky recorded on 7 June 1884. "The children of course are our great consolation," the tsar told Minny; "only with them can I relax mentally, enjoy them and rejoice, looking at them." But the Colossus was so dominating that his sons were crushed. The second son Georgy was "the cleverest" and, according to General Cherevin, "the favourite of both parents," but the youngest, Michael— "Misha"—enjoyed special rights: only Misha dared to avenge the tsar's hosing by pouring a bucket of water over his head.

In the summer, the family stayed at the Cottage at Peterhof and often travelled to stay with Minny's family in Copenhagen where, "out of prison" as the tsar put it, he could live with much less security. Minny loved to spend time with her sister, the princess of Wales. Alexander bought a house where he behaved "just like a schoolboy," squirting King Christian of Denmark or King Oscar of Sweden with hosepipes, his favourite means of social expression. In a family story that is told today by Prince Philip, the duke of Edinburgh, he loved to walk in the park with his brother-in-law the prince of Wales and other relatives, where they once encountered a lost tourist who obliviously asked the way to the town centre and then asked their names so he could thank them. "The emperor of Russia, the king of Denmark, the king of Greece and the prince of Wales," came the answer. "And I'm the Queen of Sheba," replied the tourist.*

Minny had little political influence, trying in vain to rid herself of the emperor's brutish adjutant-general Cherevin. A cross between "a primeval savage, an ignoramus royal batman and a refined courtier," Cherevin "idolized Alexander III" and explained that "he divided the world into two halves: at the top, Alexander III with him, Cherevin, on guard and beneath them, the rabble" of ministers and other Romanovs. "Nothing matters but the tsar's will," he explained to a friend. "I'm not evil and I like you, but if the emperor ordered 'hang him,' I wouldn't question the order!" "The terror of the palace" sat at a desk outside the tsar's study

---

* Behind the family bonhomie, the prudish Sasha was scandalized by the decadence of his English brother-in-law, the prince of Wales. When Bertie was implicated in a sleazy baccarat scandal, the tsar was disgusted: "Stupid Bertie implicated in this filth! How nice it must be for poor Alix [Alexandra, princess of Wales] and the children to see their father mixed up in this abomination! Thank God such scandals with the Heir can only happen in England! What poor Alix must go through thanks to her feckless, depraved husband!"

and would not let anyone, especially importuning Romanovs, interrupt him. "How dare you disturb me. I'm serving the state protecting the sovereign," he shouted drunkenly. Cherevin enjoyed insulting the tsar's pompous brother Vladimir, who complained of his rudeness. "If you're pissed off," replied Alexander, "challenge him to a duel."

The tsar and Cherevin loved to drink, "but the emperor drank at the right time," the general remembered. "Not in the morning or afternoon in order to keep a clear head nor at the Wednesday-evening receptions—until only his pals remained. Then he started to frolic and play"—getting so drunk that the tsar "lay on his back and waved his arms and legs about, behaving like a child, trying to get to his feet and then falling down, grabbing the legs of anyone who walked past."

But "in the late 1880s, the doctors forbade him to drink so the worried tsarina began to follow us and check there was no drinking at the receptions. But when at the end of the evening, His Majesty was lying on his back, kicking legs and squealing, the tsarina couldn't understand how!" They defied Minny's drinking bans like this: "The emperor and myself managed to get by! We ordered jackboots with special compartments in which we could carry a flask holding the equivalent of a bottle of cognac. When the tsarina was beside us we played like good children," but when she left, "we'd exchange glances. Then: 1-2-3! We'd pull out our flasks, take a swig and then it would be again as if nothing had happened." The tsar "was very pleased with this amusement. We named it Necessity is the Mother of Invention."

"1-2-3. Necessity, Cherevin?" said the tsar.

"Invention, Your Majesty," replied Cherevin.

" '1-2-3!'—and then we'd swig!"[1]

Alexander found his self-indulgent, extravagant and over-extended family exasperating.* When the wider family got too big for their boots, the emperor smacked them down. "Stop playing the tsar," he once telegraphed to his second-youngest brother Sergei.† He "repeated that grand

---

* The Romanovs' fundamental laws were becoming untenable in such a huge family. The family was also too expensive: each grand duke received an annual salary of 250,000 roubles and each grand duchess received a dowry of a million. Sasha changed the rules to limit the number of grand-ducal "Imperial Highnesses" to the children and grandchildren of emperors; the rest would be princely "serene highnesses" who could with permission marry commoners, but he also banned morganatic and non-Orthodox marriages.

† In June 1881, he exiled Fanny Lear's lover Grand Duke Nikola permanently to Tashkent where he came into his own: he built an arabesque palace which housed his art collection (including the nude life-sized statue of Fanny) and published scientific works, irrigated the deserts, built a sixty-mile canal, towns for workers, cotton factories, bakeries and a zoo; he even paved the streets of Tashkent. The emperor was no less harsh to the rest of the family. When the eldest of Uncle Mikhail's sons Nikolai, nicknamed "Bimbo," ambled

dukes should not head departments. . . ." But "on a sudden impulse" he entrusted the navy to his brother, the buffalo-hunting sailor Alexis, who had spent 1,722 days at sea and now devoted himself to pleasure.

"Our Beau Brummel," as Sandro called Alexis, "was the best looking of the family." His niece Missy (daughter of their sister the duchess of Edinburgh) thought him a "Viking type, and would have made a perfect Lohengrin . . . fair beard, blue eyes, enormous, a superb specimen of humanity," with "a sailor's love for all good things and beautiful women in particular." His New Orleans tour had given him a taste for zoot suits. "His handsome figure was accoutred in a strange garb of his own choosing and invention which gave him the appearance of a real show-man," remembered his nephew Kyril. His favourite was "a red-striped flannel suit, a Mephistophelian affair, of which he alone among all men on earth was the proud possessor. 'I'm better dressed than any of you fellows,' he'd say." He was also extremely kind and cheerful.

As for the serious question of the navy in the age of the Dreadnought arms race, "My grand duke seems indifferent not only to the Navy but to all matters," Admiral Shestakov noted in his diary. "He drives me mad with his laziness and indifference." He lived for "love-making, food and liquor," wrote his cousin Sandro, "fast women and slow ships."

Alexis and his brothers now spent much of their time in Paris—their hangouts were known as *la tournée des grands ducs*, their fashion *le style grand duc*. There Alexis once had a French actress wheeled into dinner on a silver tray nude except for rose petals. Daydreaming in the State Council, this libertine "can think only about how he could escape to Zina's bed," observed State Secretary Alexander Polovtsov. Zina was General Skobolev's sister and the wife of his cousin Eugene of Leuchtenberg, glorying in the Napoleonic-Romanov title of duchesse de Beauharnais. "When I say Zina was 'beautiful,'" explained Sandro, "I've never seen anyone like her in all my travels which is fortunate because women of her maddening pagan appeal shouldn't really be permitted to roam at large." She was "naughty," recalled Missy, "and would have made her fortune on the screen as a vamp."

When the duke found his own bedroom locked and heard Zina's orgasmic cries, he banged on the door at which Alexis threw him down-stairs. Leuchtenberg appealed to Alexander III, who replied that if he

---

around Petersburg with unbuttoned coat and a cigar clenched in his teeth, the tsar had him arrested. When Bimbo's brother Michael (known as "Miche-Miche") married a commoner, Sophie von Merenburg, a granddaughter of Pushkin, Alexander exiled him to London where he spent the rest of his life: through his children's marriages, the duchesses of Abercorn and Westminster are descended from the unique combination of Nicholas I and Pushkin.

could not manage his own life, how could he expect others to help? But Beau's naval post would prove to be Alexander's worst decision.[2]

In April, as the tsar organized his government, murderous anti-semitic riots known as pogroms (from *gromit*, "to destroy") broke out, starting in Kherson and spreading to Odessa and Warsaw. Forty Jews were murdered and women gang-raped. Even though scarcely any of Alexander II's assassins were Jews, rumours spread that Jews had killed God's tsar. The rumours were stoked by an economic depression also blamed on Jewish merchants. Alexander ordered his interior minister Ignatiev to restore order but blamed the Jews for their own plight.

"Deep in my soul," he told the Warsaw governor General Josef Gurko, "I am very glad when they beat up Jews, but nevertheless it can't be allowed." The tsar believed that "on the soul of the Jews, a sin is burning." He had "a fierce hatred of the Jews," according to his State Secretary Polovtsov, and always opposed any improvement in their lives. "Their condition is lamentable," he wrote, "but it was forecast in the Gospel." They deserved their suffering, he explained, as they themselves had wanted the blood of Christ to remain "upon us and our children."

When asked why he had refused to promote an officer, he replied "he is a rotten, lousy Jew." Just about anything could be blamed on the Jews: when his train ran too slowly, the tsar blamed "the Yids." In the family, he called Mikhail's wife Olga "Auntie Haber" after her supposedly American Jewish father, and he encouraged an almost fetishistic anti-semitism among his entourage. "What you write about the Yids is completely just," Pobedonostsev had written to Dostoevsky. "They have coarsened everything, but the spirit of the century supports them. They are at the root of the revolutionary socialist movement and of regicide, they own the periodic press, they have the financial markets." He believed "one faith is the true faith" and all the others must be subject "to non-recognition or outright persecution."

Cherevin boasted to a dinner party that he had arrested and destroyed an innocent Jewish lawyer, explaining that "the dirty Jew" may not be guilty today "but would be yesterday and tomorrow." The pogroms were not ordered from Petersburg, but they thrived in this atmosphere.

Troops were deployed to restore order, and in September Alexander signed Emergency Laws to "preserve state security," followed, in May 1882, by Temporary Regulations on Jews, which banned pogroms but were more concerned with protecting "the interests of the local populace" by banning Jews from living in the countryside or outside the Pale.

Not all the entourage agreed with this repression: the court minister

Count Vorontsov-Dashkov* warned Alexander against "Count Ignatiev's policy of lies which reflect on you, Sire! I'm amazed how negligent Count Ignatiev is ... to stir up hostility against the Germans, smash the Jews, persecute the Poles—these are the fundamentals of his internal ethnic policy—that will end in streams of blood." He was right. This ruined Russia's image in Europe. Most Jews were loyal, but tsarist repression drove many to become revolutionaries—or emigrate. After 1881, over 60,000 Jews left annually for America.[3]

The emperor and Pobedonostsev were already dissatisfied with Ignatiev, the intelligent intriguer who was so well known for his lies that he was nicknamed "Lord Liar" and may have suffered from Munchausen Syndrome. Once order had been restored, Alexander planned his coronation. Ignatiev proposed to call an Assembly of the Land, like the one that had elected the first Romanov tsar. "I was stricken by horror," wrote Pobedonostsev to Alexander, "[fearing] the consequences should Count Ignatiev's project be executed. There will be a revolution, the destruction of Russia!"

Ignatiev resigned, replaced by the very personification of reactionary repression, Count Dmitri Tolstoy, the cultured, wealthy ex-liberal who as education minister had become loathed by liberal society. Tolstoy was Alexander's ideal minister. He soon tired of the creepy Pobedonostsev. To the tsar, Tolstoy was "the last of the Mohicans." He promoted the battered gentry, undermined the *zemstvos* and jury trials, created the new post of land captain—government-appointed officials to replace justices of the peace—and tightened censorship.[†] Then Tol-

---

* Ilarion Vorontsov-Dashkov, who had led the Sacred Retinue, the secret chivalric order of counter-terrorist tsarist knights after Alexander II's murder, now ran court/family matters. He was married to Elizaveta Shuvalova, daughter of Andrei Shuvalov and Sophia Vorontsova, the natural child of the affair between Pushkin and Elisa Vorontsova. The Vorontsov-Dashkovs, uniting three of the greatest clans of tsarist Russia and that of Potemkin, were thus vastly rich, inheriting the Alupka Palace among other treasures.

† The novelist Leo Tolstoy was the interior minister's cousin. The emperor regarded Tolstoy's *War and Peace* as a masterpiece but saw him as a "godless nihilist" and banned his later socialistic works such as *What I Believe*. After Dostoevsky's death in 1881, Tolstoy was the most famous man in Russia with huge moral authority, but he was increasingly hostile to the regime, embracing a puritanical Christian socialism with sanctimonious dogmatism. Tolstoy's appeal (citing Christ's mercy) to spare the assassins of Alexander II convinced the tsar and Pobedonostsev that he was a dangerous lunatic. "Your Christ is not our Christ," replied Pobedonostsev. Alexander forbade publication of Tolstoy's *Kreutzer Sonata* "because it's written on a completely false theme and with great cynicism." Tolstoy's wife Countess Sophia appealed to the tsar who gave her an audience at which he declared "he himself would censor the works of her husband." He was sounder on music, appointing the best ever Director of Imperial Theatres, Prince Ivan Vsevolozhsky, a refined diplomat who, backed by the ballet-loving tsar, became friend and patron of Tchaikovsky (depressed after the initial failure of *Swan Lake*), whom he encouraged to create works such as *Sleeping Beauty* and *The Nutcracker*. Vsevolozhsky was the impresario of the flowering of Russian ballet itself. The tsar received and decorated Tchaikovsky.

stoy created a secret police that was at last qualified to take on the terrorists.[4]

After Alexander II's assassination a cabal of aristocrats led by Sasha's cronies Cherevin and Vorontsov had founded a clandestine counter-revolutionary hit and espionage squad, the Sacred Retinue, to protect the new tsar and "respond to terror with terror." After a series of amateurish capers to assassinate revolutionaries, Dmitri Tolstoy closed the Retinue but hired its best agents. He turned perlustration into a science, organizing such efficient "black offices" that soon only the tsar and the interior minister himself could be certain that their mail was not being read. He set up a new organization, the Okhrannye Otdeleniia—Security Bureaux—nicknamed the "Okhrana" (the Little Security Bureau), in Moscow and Petersburg dedicated not just to stopping terrorist attacks but to penetrating the movements. Grigory Sudeikin, chief of the Petersburg Okhrana with the title inspector of the secret police, pursued the terrorists "not out of obligation but out of conviction, enthusiastically, not unlike a hunt, an art, cunning and risky with pleasure derived from success."

When he turned a People's Will leader, Sergei Degaev, he was able to arrest many of the terrorists until they became suspicious, sentencing Degaev to death unless he proved his loyalty. On 16 December 1883, Degaev arranged to meet his controller and then shot Sudeikin dead.[*] Despite this setback, the Okhrana became increasingly effective. Yet Alexander regarded his secret policemen as disreputable but necessary, not unlike the plumber who unblocks one's cesspit. And he did not think much more of his own ministers.[5]

The emperor "despised the bureaucracy and drank champagne to its obliteration." He ran the government by divine appointment and his ministers had to know their place. When a minister impertinently threatened to resign, he seized him by the collar and shouted, "Shut up! When I choose to kick you out, you will hear of it in no uncertain terms!" Politicians were "scoundrels," on whose reports he would write comments like "what a beast!" He often shouted, "as for the ministers, the devil take them." His foreign minister Nikolai Giers was a "dummy" who, he said, acted as his "clerk." He tried to find a way around the ministers, and, as he struggled to absorb complex issues, he asked his three henchmen, Cherevin, Vorontsov and head of the court chancellery, General Otto Richter, to form an all-powerful triumvirate, reducing ministerial reports to short digests. But they shied away from this responsibility.

* Astonishingly Degaev escaped from Russia and vanished, changing his name to become Alexander Pell, professor of mathematics at the University of South Dakota, dying in 1921 in Pennsylvania.

Ultimately the ministers respected Alexander because he was a plain-dealing manager. "His words never differed from his actions." His rages were short but sudden—and he was charming when he wanted to be. When, in an early case of press intrusion, a journalist published an account of Alexander barking at his family on holiday at his Polish shooting lodge Spała, the tsar exploded, tearing a shred off Vorontsov who, as court minister, had approved it: "I haven't read anything more foolish, hurtful and wrong in the newspapers, what stupid details!"

"I'm responsible for all this," Vorontsov replied, resigning his ministry. "I'd give anything for this not to have happened." But the gruff emperor soothed him with this note: "Dear Ilarion Ivanovich, will we actually split up over such trivia? If this miserable occasion gives you the idea to resign, knowing how difficult if not impossible I'd find it to replace you, I'm sure you'll give up your intention and remain in your high position as my assistant and friend."

Rough and unlettered as he was, Alexander had, recalled a minister, the clarity of a "great administrator," possessing "enormous character, good nature, firmness" and "a remarkable intuition, a kind of intelligence more important than reason." This was combined with "straightforward, childlike naivety and simple-mindedness."

He could be brutal. When a female political prisoner insulted a Gendarme, Alexander ordered: "Flog her." His minister asked for a lesser sentence than the maximum 100 strokes since she was fragile, but the tsar insisted, "Give her the hundred strokes." They killed her. "He is not wicked," wrote the diplomat Vladimir Lamsdorf, "but he's drunk with power." His war minister General Vannovsky joked that he was like "Peter the Great with his cudgel"—except "here is only the cudgel without the great Peter."

Alexander's contempt for his own ministers was a futile attitude in the modern world. In his reverence for his autocracy, he failed to see that his own arbitrariness was a flaw. "Sire," explained Richter, "we have a terrible evil. Lack of law."

"But I always stand for compliance with the laws."

"I'm not talking about you but about your administration, which abuses its power. Today Russia is like a colossal boiler in which pressure is building; when it gets a hole, people with hammers rivet them; but one day the gases will blow out a hole that can't be filled and we'll suffocate."[6]

It was time to crown the tsar—if the terrorists did not kill him first.

At 10 a.m. on 12 May 1883, escorted by the Horse Guards, the emperor rode alone into Moscow at the head of a procession of grand dukes followed by a long file of golden carriages with the empress and her little daughter Olga in the first. Three days later, the tsar crowned himself and Minny in the Dormition Cathedral. Afterwards, they attended the public feast at Khodynka Field for which Sasha "supervised every detail personally." This was "the happiest day" of his life and he treated the ritual as a credo for autocracy. This "great event," he explained afterwards to Minny, "amazed and showed morally tainted Europe that Russia is the most holy Orthodox Russia as it was under the Muscovite tsar and will be for ever."[7] Alexander believed in Russia's Slavophile mission, but after 1877 he was determined to avoid war.

"We have only two allies in this world," Alexander liked to say. "Our army and our navy." But neither was powerful enough to project Russia's imperial pretensions in competition with the industrialized Western powers. The tsar was faced with an impossible dilemma: to maintain the façade of imperial power, that prerequisite of Romanov autocracy, while coping with the reality of a backward peasant-dominated economy, an ill-organized army and a navy that was no match for Britain in the Baltic and smaller than the Ottomans' fleet in the Black Sea. The emotional demands of Slavophile opinion, made up of a section of the educated classes, were as dangerous for the dynasty as foreign defeat. "If we lose the confidence of public opinion in our foreign policy," Alexander said with his ability to get to the heart of the matter, "all is lost."

He may have been a primordial throwback, but now Alexander had to operate in the world of public opinion, stock markets and newspapers in which he found some of his most unlikely advisers*—none more so than Prince Vladimir Meshchersky, known by enemies at court as "the Prince of Sodom" and among the intelligentsia as "Prince Full-stop" after he demanded all reform must come to that punctuation mark. Meshchersky had been Sasha's go-between with his first love, ME, who was his cousin. When they married, the empress tried to ban her husband from seeing his friend, but Sasha kept up a secret correspondence with him. In the 1870s, Meshchersky founded a conservative newspaper called the *Citizen*, which Sasha funded: as tsar he made payments as large as 100,000 roubles. "We want to have a conservative press," he explained. "Just look what Bismarck spends."

Meshchersky was an ultra-reactionary but original and gifted. Although he disapproved of female education and believed that "there is nothing people fear except the birch," he was a surprising opponent of the regime's short-sighted persecution of minorities, even that of Jews.

---

* The proprietor of the *Moscow News*, Mikhail Katkov, son of poor parents, not only helped get Dmitri Tolstoy appointed to the Interior Ministry but became the brains behind many of his policies. He was almost a "shadow government," received by the tsar, whom he bluntly told, "My newspaper is not simply a newspaper: many decisions were reached within it."

His was the only newspaper that Alexander read, and Meshchersky, who sometimes met the tsar secretly, started to send him his acerbic "diary." Yet all the time he was living an openly gay life* under an emperor who prided himself on his straitlaced Orthodox morals. When Meshchersky tried to get his young lover, a bugle-boy, a job at the palace, his enemies caught the pair *in flagrante*. Pobedonostsev muttered that this was "the man who was caught with a trumpet-player of the Guards." Anyone else would have been destroyed. Yet the tsar made his own rules.

All the tsar's nationalist advisers were highly suspicious of Germany but the only solution for now was to maintain the League of Three Emperors and run an ersatz great-power policy that looked strong and hope it was not tested. Alexander was convinced that Russia would one day have to fight Germany. As for Austrians, he once bent a silver fork into a parabola to warn their ambassador: "That's what I'm going to do to your two or three army corps."†

Six months later, the League was put to the test when Alexander's cousin Alexander Battenberg, prince of Bulgaria, united his independent state with the Ottoman province. Even though this was exactly what Russia had wanted in 1878, the tsar was incensed. Battenberg had exposed Russia's failure to control its own client state and was forced to abdicate. The tsar hoped to replace him with his Georgian courtier Prince Mingrelsky. But at a melodramatic meeting in a box at the Viennese opera house, the Bulgarians offered the throne to the half-French, half-German Prince Ferdinand of Saxe-Coburg-Gotha, an officer in the Austrian army, a perfumed, bejewelled, wasp-waisted dandy with a high-pitched voice and a Bourbon nose who enjoyed courtesans and rentboys with equal relish. "This candidature is as ridiculous as the individual," Alexander boomed. But, over the next twenty-five years, "Foxy" Ferdinand successfully established Bulgaria and defied Russia at will.

The tsar considered war against Austria to remove this jackanapes, but in 1879 Bismarck had signed a defensive treaty with Austria, forming a Germanic bloc in central Europe which was soon joined by Italy to become the Triple Alliance. Alexander refused to renew the League of

* Meshchersky was friends with Tchaikovsky who, after a disastrous marriage and years of torment about his sexuality, lived a discreet gay life until his death from cholera in 1893. There was nothing discreet about Meshchersky.

† Britain remained the real enemy. In the remote mountains of Central Asia, British and Russian adventurers duelled for influence in the Great Game which brought Alexander's first crisis. In 1884, an enterprising officer seized Merv, bringing the Romanovs to the Afghan border but alarming the British. In March 1885 an Afghan force, acting as British proxies, faced a Russian unit in a stand-off at Panjdeh. "Drive them back and give them a sound thrashing," ordered Alexander. Forty Afghans were killed. The British threatened war but Prime Minister Gladstone and the tsar controlled the crisis, setting up a commission to work out the border.

Three Emperors. As the German and Russian press raised the tension between the countries with talk of a coming Teutonic–Slavic struggle, Bismarck proposed a Reinsurance Treaty ensuring neutrality in the event of war against a third party, with a secret clause giving Russia undefined rights to Constantinople. Alexander accepted Bismarck's ingenious plan, yet it contradicted Germany's alliance with Austria. Secretly Alexander was convinced that "We must break up Germany as soon as we get the chance."

Public opinion demanded that Russia play the Slav champion. But Bulgaria was ungrateful and Serbia cleaved to Austria, so Alexander sought more dependable Slavs. The tiny principality of Montenegro was ruled by the Petrović dynasty of bishop-princes. Its prince Nikola, who liked to sit all day in a gold-braided uniform smoking cigarettes on a bench in front of his minuscule "palace" and would risk anything to take over a greater Serbia, had placed four of his nine daughters in the Smolny Institute. In 1889, during a visit to Petersburg, the tsar proposed the marriage of Princess Militsa to Grand Duke Peter Nikolaievich (younger son of Nizi, the commander of the 1877 war) and another daughter, Stana, to Georgi, duke of Leuchtenberg.* These sisters would later introduce Rasputin to the Romanovs. At the betrothal banquet, Sasha toasted Prince Nikola as "the only sincere and faithful friend of Russia." The Balkan states were unreliable but unavoidable. Alexander decided that the only essential interest was, one day, winning the Straits. He realized he needed a new alliance—and a new economy. At this dangerous moment, he reached out in surprising directions to deliver both.[8]

On 17 October 1888, the tsar and his family were on the train back from Crimea when he received the director of the South-Western Railway, Sergei Witte, to whom he complained that the train was going too slowly. "Is this railway run by Yids?" asked the tsar. Witte, a brash engineer, contradicted the tsar, explaining that the trains were being driven too fast. But Alexander ordered his train to accelerate.

At midday, "we were just finishing breakfast" near Borki, reported young Nicholas to his uncle Sergei,

> when suddenly we felt a strong jolt then another much stronger and everything started to crash and we were thrown out of our chairs, the table just flew over my head and was gone. I'll never forget the smash . . . I closed my eyes and lay expecting to die . . . I saw a light and climbed out and pulled out [his sister] Xenia . . . I thought with horror about

---

* Not a success: when the tsar heard that Leuchtenberg had abandoned Stana for a French mistress in Biarritz, he thundered that "the prince is washing his filthy body in the waves of the ocean!"

Mama and Papa and what divine joy when I saw them standing on the
roof of the former dining wagon . . .

Twenty-three were dead, and the Herculean tsar helped rescue the
wounded by lifting up the roof of the carriage. A child was screaming:
"Now they'll murder us all"*—it was his youngest daughter, Olga, who
had been thrown clear of the train. Afterwards the emperor joked:
"Imagine [his next-eldest brother] Vladimir's disappointment when he
hears we've survived."†

Borki was not a bomb, but the tsar remembered the blunt railwayman
Witte, who was first promoted to run the railways. Then, summoned to
Petersburg where Alexander, wary of the Jewish railway moguls, asked
him, "Are you a friend of Jews?," Witte replied that if it was not possible
to drown them all in the Black Sea, they should at least be treated as
humans. Satisfied, the tsar appointed him communications minister,
the start of an astonishing rise.

Bombastic and barrel-chested, the thirty-nine-year-old Witte was a
new species of minister—the provincial technocrat. Son of a civil servant of Lutheran Scandinavian origins and a Dolgoruky princess, raised
in Tiflis and qualified as an engineer in Odessa, this artful intriguer
was abrasively confident yet thin-skinned, mendacious, manipula-
tive and overweeningly narcissistic. He made a virtue of "the lack of
restraint and brazenness of speech that are part of my character"—
qualities appreciated by the tsar. When it came to safeguarding a unique
asset like Witte, Sasha changed his own rules: soon after arriving in
the capital, Witte offered to resign because he had fallen in love with
a divorced Jewess. The tsar admired Witte's chivalry in marrying the
woman. As Minny later told Witte, "You were my husband's favourite
minister."

* Her reaction demonstrated the family's entirely understandable fears. The terrorists
were still hunting the tsar. On 1 March 1887, for the first time since his retreat to Gatchina,
Alexander and his family rode through the streets of Petersburg to commemorate the sixth
anniversary of his father's murder—but, as he approached, the police arrested three young
People's Will terrorists carrying bombs to perpetrate a second 1 March outrage. Five terrorists were hanged, including their bomb-maker, Alexander Ulyanov, aged nineteen, whose
execution had a decisive influence on his younger brother, Vladimir, the future Lenin.
† Vladimir, cultured but grandiloquent, was convinced he would have made a better tsar,
but his only real achievements were to collect his favourite Parisian recipes, to hold spectacular parties with his haughty wife Miechen (née Marie of Mecklenburg) and to patronize
the singer Chaliapin, pianist Rachmaniov, painter Repin and Diaghilev's Ballets Russes.
But Miechen foolishly corresponded with Bismarck, and she was denounced to the emperor who harshly reprimanded her. He was even crosser when the Vladimirs cavorted at
Cubat restaurant with a French actor and his mistress. When Vladimir kissed the mistress,
the actor kissed the grand duchess and the grand duke threatened to kill him. The tsar
ordered the French pair and the Vladimirs (temporarily) to leave Russia at once.

Russia was still mired in depression. In 1891, thousands died in a famine, exacerbated by the policy to finance industrialization by borrowing, which in turn had to be paid for by selling grain abroad. Yet Sasha denied its very existence, claiming that it was Nihilist propaganda. Only Vorontsov's intervention alerted the tsar.

Just as Russia emerged from this crisis, in 1892, Alexander promoted Witte to finance minister. As a monarchist and patriot, Witte believed that only a breakneck industrialization programme, funded by foreign borrowing, would overcome "two hundred years of economic sleep" and give Russia the power to compete with the European powers in the geopolitical tournament—or as he later put it "the fulfilment of the great political tasks of the monarchy." Ukraine was now the breadbasket of Europe, much of its grain sold through Odessa's bourses and thence by ship through the Straits. As Russia became Europe's top agricultural producer, Witte injected the economy with foreign and government investment to produce a boom. Between 1890 and 1900, the production of pig iron, steel and coal all tripled, railway tracks doubled in length while textiles made Russia one of the world's top five industrial powers. Oil was discovered in Baku, which soon produced half of the world's supply.

Nothing so symbolized Witte's dynamism as the Trans-Siberian Railway. Although already commissioned by Alexander, Witte made it his showcase. As the railway edged its way across Siberia, Witte was dizzy with the possibilities. "From the shores of the Pacific and the heights of the Himalayas," he told Alexander III, "Russia will dominate not only the affairs of Asia but Europe as well."

While Russia surged towards industrialized modernity, the emperor tried to hold the state together by mobilizing Russian nationalism and repressing the empire's minorities. In this multinational empire of 104 nationalities speaking 146 languages, according to the 1897 census, pure Russians (excluding Ukrainians) were a minority of 44 per cent. Now the emperor ordered that in addition to anti-semitic policies, only Russian was to be taught in Polish, Armenian and Georgian schools: an own-goal for the regime, unnecessarily converting millions of these people into enemies.[9]

In 1889, Dmitri Tolstoy died, mourned by Alexander. No one could replace "the last of the Mohicans" but the new interior minister, Ivan Durnovo, was an anti-semitic bigot with a preposterous fork-shaped beard, who found an ally in Alexander's strange younger brother, Sergei. In March 1891, Alexander appointed Sergei governor-general of Moscow. But "my brother doesn't want to go to Moscow," explained Alexander, "unless it's cleared of Jews," who had moved out of the Pale of Settlement as its restrictions were relaxed. The tsar ordered the police to "expel the Jews of Moscow." On 28 April, Alexander signed the first of a series of laws allowing Sergei to deport whole categories—"Jewish artisans, distillers, brewers, general craftsmen and workmen" and even "discharged Jewish soldiers." In Moscow, Sergei closed the Great Synagogue, sent Cossacks to raid Jewish homes and allowed Jewish women to remain only if they were registered as prostitutes. Twenty thousand Jews were expelled. This crackdown encouraged Jewish emigration to America to reach 137,000 a year. Sergei had mixed feelings about his post, telling his nephew Nicky, "Here I am as governor-general of Moscow, funny but also sad, I miss my regiment . . . my circle of old comrades . . . I confess leaving Petersburg, I just cried like a baby." But Sergei was ambitious: "The job doesn't scare me, it interests me very much."

Sergei was "obstinate, arrogant, disagreeable, [and] he flaunted his many peculiarities," in Sandro's view. "I can't find a single redeeming feature." Sergei was "the most frightening of the uncles," wrote Missy. "Abrupt and severe . . . his lips thin and in a firm line almost cruel . . . his eyes steely grey, his pupils narrow like a cat . . . There was something menacing about him, something in his face of the fanatic he was in his heart."

"Introspective, his spirit imprisoned within him, he hid private impulses of exceeding sensitiveness," thought his niece Maria Pavlovna, that were "almost feminine." Happiest as the commander of the Preobrazhensky Guards, he was, recalled Witte, "always surrounded by comparatively young men who were excessively affectionate towards him," revealing his own "marked liking for young men."

Aged eight, he had been affected by the death of his eldest brother Nixa and the sufferings of his mother that led her to spend many months at her ancestral home in Hesse-Darmstadt. There Sergei met his cousin Princess Elizabeth of Hesse, who was growing up with her tragic mother, Queen Victoria's daughter Alice, and wanted to become a nun. "A ravishing beauty" of "rare intelligence, delightful sense of humour, infinite patience and generous heart," blonde with grey eyes and alabaster skin, she was the "first love" of the German crown prince, Willy. But Sergei was determined to marry her and, though she refused to convert to Orthodoxy, in 1884 he succeeded. (Willy, later the kaiser, never forgave him, spreading the story that Sergei "was buggering his handsome young domestic chaplain.") Their childless marriage was possibly never consummated yet "Serge worshipped her in spite of his scoldings," noticed Missy and "Ella," as she was known, understood him: "He loved order." He may have suited Ella, who was as coldly vain as she was beautifully virtuous—"her purity was absolute," thought Missy who worshipped "this vision, a joy for the eyes."

Sergei's marriage to Ella led to Nicky's first meeting with Ella's sister, Alexandra of Hesse ("Alix"), and their relationship developed—just as Russia's relationship with the new Germany deteriorated.[10]

The accession and new policies of the twenty-nine-year-old kaiser Wilhelm II, inconsistent, impulsive and unstable, made up Alexander's mind for him. Straight after his accession in 1888, Willy set off to visit Alexander, who loathed "the rascally young fop who throws his weight about, thinks too much of himself and fancies that others worship him." Cherevin remembered that the tsar "was literally nauseated by Wilhelm who physically disgusted him." He regarded him as a sort of infantile monkey. When the tsar paid his return visit, Willy suddenly suggested the division of Europe between Germany and Russia, at which Alexander growled: "Stop whirling around like a dervish, Willy, just look at yourself in the mirror!"

Alexander felt Russia was isolated. He grasped long before most of his ministers that Bismarck was "ignoring the kinship of Romanovs and Hohenzollerns." It was a new era. "I desire to establish the principle of protecting the rights of peoples as well as dynasties," he told Giers. "I suggest you maintain a friendly attitude to France . . . at the proper time . . . to negotiate a formal alliance." But the French were immoral revolutionaries! "Such is impossible," replied a shocked Giers. Not so, answered Alexander, this was his order. But he moved with glacial slowness. In 1890, the kaiser suddenly sacked old Bismarck, and the new chancellor General von Caprivi urged him not to renew the Russian treaty—to avoid its contradictions with the Triple Alliance into which he hoped to tempt Britain. This made a French alliance inevitable. In July 1891, Alexander invited the French fleet to Kronstadt and the autocrat took off his hat for the republican (and previously illegal) "Marseillaise." When he visited the French Exhibition in Moscow, a courtier was covering a nude statue with a blanket when the emperor bellowed: "Leave it alone! I know that costume is the one the French most admire!" Both nations were threatened by Germany—and Britain. In 1894, the tsar signed the alliance with France.

The kaiser desperately tried to win back the tsar. Alexander, accompanied by Nicky, finally met him at the naval review at Kiel. There Alexander "was in the best of spirits," noted the kaiser, while Nicky "has greatly developed and is a charming, well-bred boy with agreeable manners."[11]

*

The boisterous tsar was only forty-six, so it was unlikely that Nicky would inherit for a long time. Five feet seven inches tall, timid, childlike and inscrutably passive, Nicky was fit, loving exercise and hunting, sported a clipped auburn beard and possessed velvety, radiant blue eyes, his best feature, inherited from his mother.

"The heir, now twenty-four," wrote the deputy foreign minister, Lamsdorf, "makes a strange impression, half-boy, half-man, small of stature, thin and undistinguished," yet also "obstinate" and "thoughtless." His mother had tended to infantilize her boys. "He wore his little sailor suits longer than most boys do," noted Countess "Zizi" Naryshkina. "He was a man with a small horizon and a narrow outlook and for years had barely gone beyond the wall" of the Anichkov and then Gatchina palace gardens. Even when Nicky was a Guards colonel, his mother still addressed him as "my dear little soul, my boy." His diary tells of hide-and-seek, drinking games and contests with conkers and fir cones well into his twenties.

Nicky was educated at home, both for security and out of parental inclination. This gave him that rarest of things in royal families, a warm, happy childhood—but it also made him isolated and naive. His education was deliberately easy-going, his tutor General Danilovich believing that "Mysterious forces emanating during the sacrament of coronation provided all the practical data required by a ruler." His other tutors were impressive, but Nicky was too immature to benefit. His legal and history tutor, old Pobedonostsev complained, "I could only observe he was completely absorbed picking his nose." But his favourite was his English teacher, Charles Heath. While hating English arrogance and liberalism, Nicky became the personification of Anglo-Saxon self-control, a highly unRussian quality. Perhaps his phlegm was a reaction against the unbuttoned sentimentality of his flawed grandfather. He had spent much time with Alexander II, whose serenity in the face of danger he emulated: "I set myself the task of always following Grandfather's example of calm." If so, he took it to such an extent that when faced with catastrophes his courtiers wondered if he felt anything at all. "He never laughed, and rarely cried," noted his cousin Sandro. This was partly a means of controlling the uncontrollable world around him and playing a role for which he felt inadequate, but it was linked to his profound mystical belief in fate. "He would often put his arm around me," recalled his sister Olga, "and say, 'I was born on Job's day—I'm ready to accept my fate.'" Behind his manners and shyness lurked a strong strain of cunning and determination—both useful qualities in politics. Inscrutability and unflappability are assets in anyone watched so carefully, but there is a thin line between placidity and paralysis. His first cousin Missy loved his charm, "his eyes kind, there was something gentle about his voice, low-pitched and soft," but something was missing: "one never felt estranged but neither did one get any closer."

Nicky was averagely intelligent: he learned quickly, his memory was impressive, he avidly read history, enjoyed Tolstoy and Tchaikovsky, and was a superb linguist, fluent in German and French. His English was so perfect that the tsar asked him to write his letters to Queen Victoria. Yet his capabilities were limited by the tremendous parochialism of his education and outlook.

His mother fostered his immaculate manners with traditional maternal advice for young heirs such as "Don't listen to flatterers," yet it was his father who formed his political views. Tutored by Pobedonostsev and mentored by Meshchersky, Nicky embraced his father's Muscovite vision of the throne founded on the mystical union of tsar and peasants whose devout loyalty was pure and sacred, compared to the filthy decadence of Petersburg, liberal Europe and Jewish modernity. Like his father, indeed like most of the royal and aristocratic families of *fin de siècle* Europe, he eschewed intellectual pursuits, which he would have regarded as middle class and unRussian, and he embraced Alexander's distrust of politicians and society. While he should have been raised to see himself as a political figure, as his grandfather had been, he instead regarded himself as outside and above politics.

Nicky was overwhelmed by his colossal father, who "could not tolerate weakness." Once when Nicky allowed a playmate to take the blame for his own fault, Alexander roared: "You're a girlie!" Since the tsar favoured Georgy, Cherevin implied that he did not rate Nicky. Even so, Nicky declared, "Papa is always so dear and kind to me."

Yet he could not avoid his future. When he was thirteen, the sight of his shattered grandfather dying before him must have traumatized him, just as he was thrilled by the cheers of the Moscow crowds on his father's first visit as tsar to Moscow: "What a majestic and touching picture. When Papa and Mama came through the doors and when Papa bowed to the people, such a deafening Hurrah resounded that I shuddered."

His father wished to shelter him, but he was also worried by Nicky's personality. When Witte suggested involving Nicky more in the Trans-Siberian Committee, his father barked: "Have you ever tried to discuss anything of consequence with His Imperial Highness the Grand Duke? Don't tell me you never noticed the Grand Duke is . . . an absolute child. His opinions are utterly childish. How could he preside over such a committee?" Yet he put him on that committee and, among others, the Council of State. Nicky tried to avoid any responsibilities, but his father insisted.

After his coming of age and induction as Cossack ataman, he served in the Preobrazhensky and Hussars, soon promoted to colonel, the happiest time in his life when he revelled in the routine, the camaraderie and the pranks.

Even as a Guardsman, his closest friends were his Romanov commanding officers. His world was his family, in which his uncle Sergei—known as "Gega"—was specially influential: they constantly corresponded and their relationship would become closer still when at Sergei's wedding to Ella of Hesse, he met her younger sister.

"I sat next to little twelve-year-old Alix whom I really liked a lot," Nicky wrote on 27 May 1884, though he fancied Sergei's bride Ella even more. On 31 May at Peterhof, "Alix and I wrote our names on the rear window of the Italian house [which as tsar he would convert into their home, the Lower Dacha] (we love each other)." But by November his passion had eased. "The desire to marry lasted until breakfast," he wrote on the 19th, "and then went away . . ."[12]

Alix's life had been formed by tragic death, English phlegm, obsessive piety, sanctimonious prudery and a blend of male weakness and female will. One of the many daughters of Duke Ludwig of Hesse and Princess Alice of England, she was brought up in Darmstadt.

Alix's doom-laden world was rocked by a series of tragedies. Her mother Alice was depressive and sickly. Her little brother "Frittie" suffered from the "English disease"—haemophilia—and died of bleeding after falling from a window. At six, she lost her mother and her favourite sister to diphtheria. When she grew up she acted as her father's hostess until he too died, after which she helped her weak brother Ernst ("Ernie") in the same role. "Tall, slender, graceful, with a wealth of golden hair," with blue eyes and high cheekbones, she had crystalline beauty, touching vulnerability and neurotic intensity that won her the special favour of her grandmother Queen Victoria, who "most anxiously and carefully" watched over "my sweet Alicky" while noting her hysterical nature and appalling health. "As she has no parents, I am the only person who can really be answerable for her," Victoria explained later. The tensions "have tried her nerves very much." As an orphan, "poor dear Alicky has no one but me at all." Victoria taught her how to nurse and make a bed without disturbing the patient and other "useful things." The grief-stricken (Prince Albert had died in 1861) and reclusive Queen Victoria was the biggest influence on the girl, the personification of female power.

Brought up by an English governess under Victoria's wing, Alix was fascinated by her Lutheran faith and by international politics, growing up into a solemn, inhibited and highly strung English lady who blushed in company, broke out in rashes and was frequently incapacitated by agonizing sciatica and stomach cramps. Beneath the crippling shyness and royal chilliness, she concealed a surprising combination of dogmatism, obstinacy and a tendency utterly to misread people and situations. Neither intelligent nor well-educated, she possessed an "iron will." As her brother Ernie put it, "she's splendid" but "what she needs is a superior will which can dominate her and which can bridle her."

She was a tangle of sensibility, a passionate believer who talked of "her big heart." As her son's tutor put it later, "She was nothing if not sincere." Her thin, tight lips rarely smiled.

Five years after their first meeting, Nicky met Alix again on one of her visits to Sergei and Ella. Nicky and Alix talked and danced. In their letters, they codenamed each other "Pelly I" and "Pelly II." Ella and Sergei escorted her and encouraged their romance. On 29 January 1890, Alix came out at her first ball at the Winter Palace, dressed in "white diamonds, white flowers and sash"; her cotillion dance was with Nicky. She stayed at Sergei's estate, Illinskoe.

"Oh God, I want to go to Illinskoe," wrote Nicky on 20 August. "If I don't see her now, I shall have to wait a whole year."

When she left, Nicky told the tsar of "my dream—one day to marry Alix of Hesse." But there was a problem. Her grandmother Queen Victoria wanted her to marry the heir to the British empire, Prince Eddy, the duke of Clarence. Minny wanted Nicholas to marry Hélène, the daughter of the French Bourbon, the comte de Paris. The tsar and his wife did not approve of Alix, wondering if this sombre girl was suited to be empress. Queen Victoria, who loved her, agreed: "It would not do on account of the religion and I know moreover that Minny doesn't wish it." As Nicky enjoyed partying with wild Guards officers, Cherevin had already prompted the tsar to find him a ballerina.

On 23 March 1890, the tsar and tsarina took the twenty-one-year-old Nicky to the graduation ceremony of the Imperial School of Theatrical Dance. There Nicky noticed the teenaged Polish ballerina Mathilde Kshessinskaya, who had already been selected by the tsar. At the informal supper afterwards, Alexander III ordered Mathilde to sit next to him and then placed Nicky on her other side. "Careful!" he boomed. "Not too much flirting." Mathilde noted in her diary: "He will be mine."

That summer, the tsar and Nicky attended the Krasnoe Selo manoeuvres where the grand dukes stayed in wooden cottages, parading by day, attending the theatre by night. "I positively like Kshessinskaya very much," wrote Nicky on 17 July. Once backstage she bumped into the tsar who bellowed, "Ah you must be flirting!" But Nicky was no ladykiller, and the two had not managed to meet up before Nicky was sent away on his tour. Instead of the traditional visits to the West, the heir turned East.[13]

Nicky set off with his brother Georgy, his cousin George of Greece and a diminutive Buddhism expert, Prince Esper Ukhtomsky, who believed that Russia's destiny lay in the Far East. His adventures were eagerly observed by the courts of Europe, particularly those with belly-dancers and geishas; as Kaiser Wilhelm noted, such encounters "would be a blessing for, up to now, he's refused to go near any woman."

"How intolerable to be once again surrounded by Englishmen and their scarlet uniforms," wrote Nicky in India and he was delighted by any hint of British senescence, noting the rusty Royal Navy ships in Singapore: "This makes me happier, dear Papa, since we must be stronger than the British in the Pacific Ocean." His petulance earned a gentle rebuke from his mother: "I'd like to think you're very courteous to all the English . . . You have to set your personal comfort aside; be doubly polite and never show you are bored."

But two events cast a shadow. His adored brother Georgy had to return home with a mysterious lung illness that turned out to be TB. "You can't imagine what anguish I've passed the last few days," wrote Minny.

Then in Otsu in Japan, a lunatic policeman attacked him with a sword which was adeptly deflected by George of Greece with a walking-stick. When the news reached them, Minny and Sasha "suffered agonies—at the end of our strength," but it was the "second time God has saved you" after the Borki railway crash. The tsar recalled him. On the way home, he turned the turf on the eastern end of the Trans-Siberian Railway in Vladivostok, then passed through the small town of Tomsk. Among the cheering crowds there, he was seen by a young boy, Yakov Yurovsky, who as a man, in a very different world, was to meet him again, twenty-eight years later, at the very end of his life.[14]

On his return, the caesarevich met up with Mathilde Kshessinskaya. "Since our meeting, I've been in the clouds! I shall try to come back as soon as possible." Yet he had not forgotten Alix. "I have loved her a long time," he wrote on 21 December 1891. He spent evenings at Uncle Alexis's louche palace where, on 4 January 1892, the mistress "Zina amused us with singing."

"I never thought two loves could coexist," he wrote, analysing himself on 1 April 1892. "I've already loved Alix for three years and hope to marry her . . . Since camp of 1890 I've been madly (platonically) in love with little K," yet "I never stop thinking about Alix. Would it be right to conclude from this that I am very amorous?"

Nicky and his cousin Sandro visited the ballerinas so often that the tsar grumbled to Minny that the boy had vanished: "Nicky is still in Petersburg. I don't know what he does, he doesn't telegraph, doesn't write."

On 25 January 1893, he lost his virginity: "This evening flew to my MK and spent the very best evening with her up to now. I am still under her spell—the pen is shaking in my hand." Setting her up in a mansion, 18 English Prospect, which had been the love nest of his great-uncle Kostia, he "spent the night ideally" with "Little K."

Nicky had not forgotten Alix and when he crisscrossed Europe to attend the many weddings of the royal cousinhood he hoped she would be there. He probed to see if Alix would convert to Orthodoxy, but still she stuck to her Lutheran faith. Nonetheless, the tsar changed his view, swayed by Nicky's declaration that he would not marry anyone else. Besides, the tsar's own mother was a Hessian princess. He gave his permission for Nicky to investigate Alix's own feelings. Ella and Sergei were the go-betweens. In agonizing negotiations, coded so that "he" meant "she" and vice versa, Nicky's waverings and Alix's obstinacy exasperated the intermediaries. When Nicky first asked Ella to invite Alix to Russia and then turned cold, Sergei lost his temper. "My wife [Ella] was so disappointed and outraged by your letter that she asks me to tell you she considers this case decisively finished . . . You have to go to her . . . If you have no strong character, no will or your feelings have changed," the uncle wrote to the future tsar on 14 October 1893, "it's deplorable you haven't told me or my wife . . . You empowered her to ask this question and when everything is ready, your strange answer appears. I repeat: everything is over and my wife asks you not to mention this again. It grieves my heart to have to write this to you!"

Of course it was not over. Yet Alix steadfastly refused to convert. "I cannot do it against my conscience," she wrote on 8 November 1893. "You Nicky who also have such a strong belief will understand me."* Now Nicky claimed that "everything is over between us"—"you hardly know the depth of our religion." But he did not give up: "Do you think there can exist any happiness in the whole world without you?"

His disappointment was all the more intense when on 12 January 1894 his cousin Sandro (Grand Duke Alexander Mikhailovich) got engaged to

---

* Alix did have the example of her sister. In 1888, the emperor sent Sergei, president of the Palestine Society, to Jerusalem to dedicate the gold-domed Church of St. Mary on the Mount of Olives to their mother. He was accompanied by Ella who, having refused to convert, experienced an epiphany in Jerusalem and embraced Orthodoxy passionately.

his sister Xenia. "I am thrilled," wrote Nicky. "Uncle Vladimir dragged me to supper in a new club where I got rather tipsy." He was still seeing Little K and enjoying "four-day binges," nine-hour dancing bouts, games of macao with Uncle Alexis, and "the cavalry gala suppers" with gypsies and his commanding officer, his cousin Konstantin—"KR."*

At a party at the Obolenskys', on 24 January, Nicky and his cousins "played hide and seek like little children." Hide-and-seek, reflected State Secretary Polovtsov, was "a peculiar pastime for a 24-year-old Heir." Later that month, Little K was waiting for Nicky when she received a note that the caesarevich had been "detained by the illness of his father." It was unthinkable that the tsar could be seriously ill. "My father," noted Nicky's sister Olga, "had always enjoyed an athlete's health."

Minny begged the tsar to drink less but, as Cherevin recalled, "he ignored doctors." The two pals drank on, using their cognac-equipped boots: "1-2-3 swig!" But the emperor recovered.

On 2 April, Nicky set off by train to meet virtually the entire royal cousinhood of Europe in Coburg—"the Royal Mob," as Victoria called them, and some of "the Club," Nicky's posse of royal friends—for the marriage of Ernie, brother of Alix and Ella to "Ducky" Melita of Edinburgh, granddaughter of both Queen Victoria and Alexander II. Alix awaited him there.

"My God, what a day," wrote Nicky in Coburg on 5 April. "Alix came to Aunt Ella's rooms. Noticeably prettier but extremely sad. They left us alone but she is still against changing her religion." He told her she had to agree. "No I cannot," she whispered.

"Queen Victoria arrived in great pomp, a squadron of her dragoon guards in front and a whole battalion behind the carriage." Next day, after another painful discussion with Alix, "Having changed into Prussian uniforms, we went to the station to meet Wilhelm." The British queen and German kaiser, along with the rest of the cousinhood, worked on Alix. Victoria was informed of every twist, while at Gatchina the tsar and tsarina were "waiting with an almost febrile impatience," in Minny's words. "You can't imagine how painful to be separated from you at a moment like this." Perhaps Ernie's marriage was decisive: the arrival of a duchess in Hesse ended Alix's role in Darmstadt.

On 7 April, after the wedding, the kaiser "even had a talk with Alix" and then next morning "brought her to us at home," recorded Nicky.

---

* KR was the nom de plume, "Konstantin Romanov," of Grand Duke Konstantin Konstantinovich, the second son of Kostia and hence the next brother after the wild Nikola, Fanny Lear's lover. His superb diary is one of our best sources—though it also contained the details of KR's secret life.

"She then went to Aunt Miechen and soon afterwards came into the room where I was sitting with the uncles, Aunt Ella and Wilhelm. They left us alone." Kaiser Willy "sat in the next room with the uncles and aunts waiting for the outcome of our talk," and "the first thing she said was . . . she agreed!" exulted Nicky. "I started to cry like a child and so did she!" Alix immediately became "gay, talkative, tender." After enduring the embraces of Willy, Nicky and Alix rushed to Queen Victoria, whom "I must now call 'Granny,'" before the caesarevich wrote to his mother Minny. She replied on 10 April: "My dear sweet Nicky! I was so happy and ran to announce this news to Papa." She sent a Fabergé egg and jewels: "Does she like sapphires or emeralds?" The tsar was thrilled but surprised: "I was sure your attempt would fail completely," but "everything that happened will surely have been useful in showing that not everything is so easy." He still saw Nicky as a child: "I can't imagine you as a fiancé—how strange and unusual!"

As Nicky headed back home, Little K was heartbroken to hear the news of his engagement. Before he left, he had negotiated the end of their affair, borrowing 400,000 roubles from Sandro and his brothers to buy her the house on English Prospect. "Whatever happens to my life," he wrote, "my days spent with you will ever remain the happiest memories of my youth." But Little K made a last attempt to destroy the engagement.

Alix stayed with Victoria in Windsor where she began studying Russian, but she almost collapsed from neurotic tension: "yes darling Grandmama, the new position will be full of trials and difficulties," she told Victoria. The queen in turn explained to Nicky: "she requires a great deal of rest and quiet—she had to lie down a great deal. Her dear father's death, her anxiety about her brother, and the struggle about her future have all tried her nerves very much." Crippled by sciatica, Alix travelled to Harrogate to take sulphur baths, where "rude people stand at the corner and stare: I shall stick out my tongue at them another time," she reported to Nicky,* who arrived in England on the imperial yacht *Polar Star*.

They spent a month in England, staying at Windsor with the queen and at Sandringham with Bertie, whose "houseparty was rather strange," Nicky told his mother. "Most of them were horsedealers, among others a

---

* Yet the family's joy was tinged with sadness: the doctors advised that Nicky's TB-stricken brother Georgy had to live in the warn climate of the Caucasus, far from the family. He settled in Abbas Tuman where he was protected by exotic Caucasian bodyguards but his was a lonely existence. "It is so terribly hard to see one's child suffer," wrote his broken-hearted mother. The brothers were so close that Nicky regularly reported on the progress of his romance.

Baron Hirsch"—in other words, a Jew. Maurice Hirsch was supposedly the richest man in Europe and a campaigner against Russian anti-semitism, so perhaps Bertie was making a point. "The cousins [George, duke of York, and his sisters] rather enjoyed the situation and kept teasing me about it." But Nicky, eager to avoid any infection by the Jewish bacillus, boasted piously to his mother: "I tried to keep away as much as I could and not to talk."

At Windsor, "I have become part of the English family," he told Georgy, "as indispensable to my future grandmother as her two Indians and her Scotsman"—though sometimes he called her "the old queen (belly woman)." While they were staying at Osborne on the Isle of Wight, Alix received anonymous letters (clearly written by Little K herself) revealing the story of her romance with Nicky who confirmed the details with Alix. She was touched. "Have confidence in your girly dear," she wrote in his diary, "who loves you more deeply and devotedly than she can ever say. What is past is past and we can look at it with calm—we are all tempted in this world but as long as we repent, God forgives us."*

As Nicky sailed home, Queen Victoria reflected, "The more I think of sweet Alicky's marriage the more unhappy I am. Not as to the personality for I like him very much but on account of the country and the awful insecurity to which that poor child will be exposed."[15]

On 25 July, Nicky was back in Petersburg to watch the emperor preside over the marriage of Xenia and Sandro,† but the heir noticed that the Colossus was exhausted by the end of the marriage banquet. By 10 August, Alexander III, who had "only been ill twice in his life," was ill, losing weight, suffering headaches; his feet were swelling, his skin sallow. At

---

* Little K did not vanish. The effervescent dancer became the mistress simultaneously of two grand dukes, Sergei Mikhailovich (Bimbo and Sandro's brother) and Andrei Vladimirovich (son of Vladimir and Miechen). Exploiting their power and her own ability to appeal to Nicholas II, she came to dominate the Mariinsky Ballet while amassing a fortune. When she had a child, she was unable to say who was the grand-ducal father. Asked how it felt to have two grand dukes at her feet, she replied: "Why not? I have two feet."

† The tsar and tsarina had been against this match, believing that Xenia was too young. Sandro, one of the brash Mikhailovichs with their Caucasian exoticism and dubious Jewish blood, was regarded as arrogant and demanding. Finally his father Grand Duke Mikhail intervened. The tsar agreed. "They spend the whole day kissing, embracing and lying around on the furniture in the most improper manner," Nicky told Georgy. "I was indeed amazed at the gymnastics," replied Georgy. "They almost broke the ottoman and behaved in the most improper way, for instance they would lie on top of each other, in what you might call an attempt to play Papa and Mama." Sandro recorded how the Romanov marriage regulations dictated even the costumes worn by the couple on their wedding night—in his case, a heavy silver dressing-gown and silver slippers. Intelligent, ambitious and innovative, Sandro was Nicky's close friend until 1905, but after the Revolution, his beautifully written (if self-serving) memoirs mercilessly exposed the flaws of Nicholas II.

manoeuvres he fainted. Dr. Zakharin examined him but "couldn't find anything seriously wrong," wrote Nicky on 11 August. "He needs rest." So the family set off for his Polish shooting lodges, first Białowieża, with its herd of rare European bison, then Spała, accompanied by both Nicky and Georgy. But there was little bison-hunting, and Georgy was so ill in the damp Polish forests that the emperor had to sit by his bed for entire nights until he was sent to the warmer south.

Nicky wrote to "my own darling Sunny," his new nickname for Alix, longing "to cover your sweet face with greedy, burning, loving kisses." Alix wrote that her passion was "burning and consuming me."

"Everything is yours, yours, I'd like to scream it out loud!" replied Nicky.

"What joy when I can clasp you in my arms and gaze into your precious face and beautiful tender eyes," she wrote, teasing him that "I felt so funny putting on such smart undergarments and nightgowns, don't be shocked. I suppose I ought to be shyer and primmer with you, but I can't."

The emperor was deteriorating. Finally the German specialist Professor Ernst Leyden diagnosed nephritis, inflammation of the kidneys. It would be fatal.

On 21 September, Alexander, accompanied by the empress and Nicky, arrived at the Little Palace at Livadia where Georgy was waiting. That night "we dined alone with Papa and Mama upstairs in their rooms," wrote Nicky. "I am terribly sad." Minny nursed him so sweetly that the emperor said, "Even before my death, I have got to know an angel," kissing her hand. "Poor dear Minny." By 5 October, the family was summoned. "I was overcome with emotion when we went in to the dear parents," recalled Nicky. "Papa was weaker." The prince and princess of Wales, Minny's sister, were called from Vienna. Remembering how Minny had nursed his brother Nixa, the tsar had once told Bertie that "There are no better nurses in Europe than the king of Denmark's daughters."

"Tell me the truth," Alexander asked his doctor. "How long do I have to live?"

"That is in God's hands, but I have seen marvellous cures," replied Leyden.

"Can I still live for a fortnight?"

When the doctor nodded, Sasha told Nicholas to summon Alix at once. The tsar insisted that Nicky must marry properly in Petersburg, not in Livadia, but "Papa and Mama have permitted me to send for Alix," Nicky wrote. "Ella and Uncle Sergei will bring her here."

When Alix arrived, the tsar spent much energy dressing up in full uniform and medals, so that he could receive her properly, but he was barely able to rise and kiss her when she knelt at his feet and the effort "strongly excited the patient despite the joy it caused him." "Every moment became an agony," remembered his twelve-year-old daughter Olga. "He couldn't even lie in bed."

As the Colossus made his confession, Father Yanishev asked if the tsar had briefed Nicky, but Alexander replied: "No, he himself knows everything." Yet, even now, Nicky was scarcely consulted by the courtiers. Alix resented his mother Minny. "Be firm," Alix urged Nicky, "and make the doctors come to you alone every day and tell you how they find him so that you are always the first to know." She at least felt the sacred burden of the crown hovering over his self-deprecating head. "Show your own mind," she exhorted him on 15 October, "and don't let others forget who you are."

Late on the 19th, the tsar coughed up blood and groaned that he could not breathe, he had to get out of bed. Dressed in a grey tunic, he was moved to his armchair where he waited for the dawn. When Minny came in, he sighed. "I feel the end approaching," he said. "Be calm; I am calm." He was given oxygen. The priest held his head and Minny sat beside him, around them a "crowd of relatives, physicians, courtiers and servants." Nicky and Sandro paced the verandah, "watching the death of the Colossus." At 3:30 p.m., Father Ioann of Kronstadt administered the Last Sacraments and heard his confession—"then he started to have slight convulsions." The family knelt as Father Ioann prayed. Just as a doctor gave him a glass of water, Alexander III "muttered a short prayer and kissed his wife," then sighed, and his head fell on to Minny's chest. "The end came quickly," wrote Nicholas. "It was the death of a saint." The Colossus "died as he had lived," wrote Sandro, "a bitter enemy of resounding phrases, a confirmed hater of melodrama."*

"Nobody sobbed," recalled his daughter Olga. "My mother still held him in her arms."

The family kissed the late tsar's forehead, then the new tsar's hand. "My head is spinning, I don't want to believe it!" wrote Nicholas II.

"For the first and only time in my life I saw tears in Nicky's blue eyes," recalled Sandro. "He took me by the arm and led me downstairs to his room. We embraced and cried together," then he exclaimed: "Sandro, what am I going to do? What's going to happen to me, to you, to Xenia, to Alix, to mother, to all of Russia? I'm not ready to be tsar. I never wanted to become one. I've no idea of even how to talk to the ministers. Will you help me, Sandro?" This was not in itself evidence of his lack of

---

* As the revolutionary Leon Trotsky put it, adapting the Cleopatra's Nose theory, if Alexander III had not drunk so much, history would be different. If he had lived, he would have been sixty-nine in 1914. But would he have acted any differently from his son?

acumen. Every heir since Paul had had such understandable moments of doubt.[16]

At 4 p.m., at a field altar in the garden, the late emperor's confessor Father Yanishev administered the oath to Nicholas II as the battleships of Sebastopol fired a salute. Next morning, at ten o'clock, Alix was received into Orthodoxy with the name Alexandra Fyodorovna—"a quiet radiant joy," noted Nicky—before more prayers around the body: "the expression on Papa's face was wonderful, smiling." But the body was rotting. First it was lifted from the chair and laid on a camp bed. Then after prayers at 9 p.m., "We had to carry the body downstairs," wrote Nicky, "as it has rapidly begun to decompose."

On 22 October, the prince of Wales arrived. Finding Nicky incapable of making decisions, he took control of funeral arrangements. "I wonder what his tiresome old mother [Queen Victoria] would have said," mused Olga, "if she'd seen everybody accept Uncle Bertie's authority! In Russia of all places!"

The doctors embalmed the body—but the job was botched. Soon the imperial cadaver was stinking. The family debated when the new tsar should marry. Minny and Nicky himself wanted to marry Alix there and then "while Papa is still under the same roof," but the uncles and Bertie insisted that the ceremony be held in Petersburg. On the 27th, the little tsar, Georgy and their uncles carried the coffin out of the Little Palace, handing it to a Cossack guard of honour, who bore it to the pier at Yalta, thousands of peasants falling to their knees as it passed, and on to a battleship where it lay under a canopy. At 10 a.m. on 1 November, Nicholas II arrived by train in Petersburg with the body.[17]

SCENE 4

# Master of the Land

# CAST

NICHOLAS II, emperor 1894–1917, son of Alexander III and Minny, "Nicky"

Alexandra Fyodorovna (née Princess Alexandra of Hesse), empress, "Alix," "Sunny"

Olga, their eldest daughter

Tatiana, their second daughter

Maria, their third daughter

Anastasia, their youngest daughter

Alexei, caesarevich, tsarevich, their son, "Tiny," "Baby"

## THE ROMANOVS

Maria Fyodorovna, dowager empress, widow of Alexander III, "Minny"

Uncle Vladimir, commander of Guards, military governor of Petersburg, married Miechen

Uncle Alexis, general-admiral of the Russian Imperial Fleet, "Beau"

Uncle Sergei, governor-general of Moscow, "Gega," married Ella (née Princess Elizabeth of Hesse, sister of Empress Alexandra)

Uncle Paul, "Pitz," widower of Princess Alexandra of Greece, married Olga Pistolkors

Georgy, caesarevich, second brother of the tsar

MICHAEL II, emperor, third brother of the tsar, "Misha," "Floppy"

Xenia, the tsar's sister, married Alexander Mikhailovich, "Sandro"

Olga, his other sister, married Peter, duke of Oldenburg

Nikolai Nikolaievich, commander-in-chief, "Nikolasha the Terrible," married Stana, daughter of King Nikola of Montenegro, one of the "Black Women," "the Crows"

Peter Nikolaievich, his brother, married Militsa, daughter of King Nikola of Montenegro, one of the "Black Women," "the Crows"

Konstantin Konstantinovich, son of Kostia, friend of the tsar, playwright, poet, writing under name of "KR," married "Mavra" (née Princess Elizabeth of Saxe-Altenburg)

Nikolai Mikhailovich, eldest son of Mikhail, brother of Sandro, "Bimbo," "White Crow"

Alexander Mikhailovich, son of Mikhail, brother of Bimbo, Minister of Merchant Marine, married Xenia Alexandrovna, "Sandro"

Marie, "Missy," crown princess of Romania, married to Prince Ferdinand, daughter of duke and duchess of Edinburgh, Nicky's first cousin

Melita, her sister, "Ducky," grand duchess of Hesse-Darmstadt, married to Ernst, brother of Alix, later married to Grand Duke Kyril

## COURTIERS: ministers etc.

Count Ilarion Vorontsov-Dashkov, court minister, then viceroy of Caucasus

Baron Vladimir Frederiks, court minister

Count Paul Benckendorff, grand marshal of court

Serge Witte, finance minister, later first prime minister and count

General Alexei Kuropatkin, war minister, commander in Far East

Count Vladimir Lamsdorf, foreign minister, "Madame"

Alexander Bezobrazov, state secretary, adjutant-general and secret adviser

Admiral Yevgeny Alexeev, viceroy of the Far East

Dmitri Sipiagin, interior minister

Vyacheslav Plehve, interior minister

Peter Durnovo, interior minister

General Dmitri Trepov, governor-general of Petersburg, deputy interior minister, later palace commandant

Prince Vladimir Orlov, chief of tsar's military chancellery, "Fat Orlov"

Alexander Orlov, general and friend of the tsar, "Thin Orlov"

Admiral Zinovy Rozhdestvensky, commander Second Pacific Squadron

Ivan Goremykin, prime minister, "Old Fur Coat"

Peter Stolypin, interior minister, prime minister

Alexander Izvolsky, foreign minister

Vladimir Kokovtsov, prime minister, count, "Gramophone"

General Vladimir Sukhomlinov, war minister

Sergei Sazonov, foreign minister, "Wobbler"

Alexei Khvostov, interior minister, "Tail"

Nikolai Maklakov, interior minister

General Alexander Spiridovich, commander of the tsar's bodyguard

Alexander Guchkov, president of the Duma

Mikhail Rodzianko, president of the Duma, "Fatso"

Anna Vyrubova (née Taneeva), Alexandra's friend, "Ania," "Lovesick Creature," "Cow"
Countess Elizabeth Kurakina-Naryshkina, mistress of the robes, "Zizi"

## THE HIEROPHANTS

Monsieur Nizier Anthelme Philippe, French hierophant, "Our Friend"
Grigory Rasputin, Siberian holy man, "Our Friend"

The face now rotting and black, the remains of Alexander III lay in state in the Peter and Paul Cathedral. Meanwhile at the Anichkov Palace, the new tsar—"My head was spinning"—was receiving his fellow monarchs. "The King of Serbia paid me a visit then Ferdinand of Romania—they deprived me of those few free moments when I am able to see Alix." At the burial on 7 November 1894, Minny broke down, shrieking, "Enough! Enough!" and falling into the arms of her sister the princess of Wales. Nicky presided over audience after audience in a daze. He missed his brother and closest friend Georgy, who was now his heir, the Caesarovich, but was confined to the Caucasus. And then there was his fiancée: "It's a trial to see so little of Alix," wrote Nicky. "I can't wait to be married."[1]

At 11:30 a.m. on 14 November, Nicky, accompanied by his second brother, sixteen-year-old Misha, left the Anichkov in an open carriage and headed for the Winter Palace, just as his mother departed the same palace in a carriage to collect Alexandra from the Sergeievsky Palace of Sergei and Ella, where the bride had spent her last single night. Alexandra, not yet in her wedding dress but draped in furs, accompanied the dowager empress to the Winter Palace. There, the tsar paced the Arabian Hall smoking while his bride, assisted by her sister Ella and his mother Minny, was dressed in the Malachite Hall, her hair done by a French hairdresser who then fitted the Romanov Nuptial Crown and a tiara of diamonds set in platinum. She wore Catherine the Great's Rivière necklace of 475 carats with matching earrings so heavy that they were supported with wires looped round her ears. Her dress—silver brocade, with an underskirt of silver tissue, trimmed with ermine and gold-threaded, with a diamond-studded bodice and a fifteen-foot train—required eight pages and a chamberlain to manoeuvre. When KR saw her, "She looked even paler and more delicate than usual, like a victim destined for a sacrifice." As she and Minny processed through the palace, "Dear Alicky looked quite lovely. Nicky is a very lucky man," the duke of York (the future King George V) reported to Queen Victoria.

The emperor, in scarlet Hussars tunic, holding a beaver-fur hat with an ostrich plume, was followed by the kings of Denmark and Greece and the Waleses until they reached the palace cathedral for the ceremony where his brother Misha and cousin Kyril, Uncle Vladimir's eldest, held the crowns. "I couldn't get rid of the thought that beloved unforgettable

Papa was not among us," the emperor wrote to Georgy, "and you were far away and alone. I had to summon all my strength not to break down in church—in front of everyone."* Since they were still mourning, there was no reception. While the princes were crowding around the emperor to congratulate him, Ernie of Hesse noticed that his sister had vanished: he found Alix alone in tears, saying the dress was so heavy she could not move.

Afterwards, the emperor and empress rode back to the Anichkov Palace. "We dined at 8," wrote Nicky, "and went to bed early as Alix had a bad headache." To Alix, it "seemed a mere continuation of the masses for the dead, with this difference, I now wore a white dress instead of a black one." But the passion was a success. "I'm unbelievably happy with Alix," wrote Nicky, "it's only a pity that my work takes up so much time I'd like to spend with her."[2]

"A completely new life has started for me," the tsar confided to Georgy. "I can't thank God enough for the treasure he's sent me in my wife . . . But the Lord has given me a heavy cross to bear." The cumbersome machine of Russian bureaucracy had instantly come to rest on Nicky's frail shoulders.

The tsar and tsarina immediately adopted the routine that they would follow until 1905. They started the year at the Winter Palace, with the Great Procession, the Blessing of the Waters and the social season, until Easter when they moved to Tsarskoe Selo, then spent the summer at Peterhof, followed by a cruise on the new imperial yacht *Shtandart* (built in Denmark and launched in 1895) before heading down to Livadia for the early autumn, followed by hunting at their Polish lodges.

Every day Nicky rose at eight and worked punctiliously. His "study was a perfect model of orderliness," his desk so tidy he boasted that he could "go into his study in the dark and put his hand at once on any object he knew to be there." He used a blue pencil to comment on his "unbearable papers," often leaving just a blue dot. He had no personal secretary. He "was so jealous of his prerogatives that he himself would seal the envelope containing his decisions," noted a trusted courtier. The powerful Chancellery of Nicholas I had become so enormous it had been broken up and distributed among the ministries at the end of Alexander II's reign, leaving the last tsars with little support from their petitions secretariat, the remnants of the First Section. Refusing to delegate, Nicky signed off on trivialities such as every change of name

---

* "I am so sad not to be at your wedding," wrote Georgy. "It's hard always to be away and even more so to be completely alone . . . The whole visit to Livadia seems like a dream which began pleasantly and ended up an awful nightmare."

and divorce in the empire, and lists of staff to receive Easter eggs—as well as sentences of exile and death.

He told his cousins that "he now wishes to investigate everything, to instigate changes slowly but persistently," but his immediate challenge was his uncles—and his mother. "It's better to sacrifice one man, even an uncle," he declared, "than risk the good of the realm." Yet none was sacrificed—so "Nicky spent the first ten years of his reign sitting behind a massive desk," wrote Sandro, "listening with near awe to the bellowing of his towering uncles," especially "250 pounds of Uncle Alexis packed into his resplendent uniform . . . He dreaded being alone with them." Sandro, a naval officer, regularly tried to have Alexis sacked as general-admiral but Nicky simply replied: "Sack my father's favourite brother? I believe they're right you did turn Socialist in America!" Minny refused to give her jewellery to Alix, the trivial start of the bitter schism between Nicholas's mother and wife. He was no happier with the ministers. "It is as if my gentlemen ministers have decided to wear me out, they are so persistent and tiresome," he told his mother on 27 April 1896. "I'm amazed my head doesn't burst with all the rubbish being stuffed into it."[3]

Kaiser Willy immediately started to bombard Nicky with cloying yet meddlesome letters, hoping somehow to bully him into breaking the French alliance. As for the expectations of a return to the reforms of his grandfather, Willy told him that "We Christian Kings and Emperors have only one duty imposed on us by Heaven—to uphold the principle: By the Grace of God."

The Tver local assembly now asked for the right to discuss reform. These *zemstvos*—introduced in 1864—were run by loyal liberal aristocrats, but Nicky, advised by Uncle Sergei (governor-general of Moscow) and the ghost of his father, closed down the Tver assembly. On 17 January 1895, "I was in a terrible state about having to go into the Nikolaievsky Hall and address the representatives of the nobility, the *zemstvos* and town committees." Holding his speech in his hat as a cue, he declared that "I will retain the principles of autocracy as unbendingly as my unforgettable late father" without "the senseless dreams of taking part in the business of government." The phrase "senseless dreams" was a quotation from Nicholas I. Afterwards, he "strolled in the garden with Uncle Sergei."

Nicholas confided in his friend KR* that "his father had never once

* KR's elder brother Nikola, the eccentric who had loved the American courtesan Fanny Lear, was now living like the tsar of Tashkent in his new art-filled palace, and set up a new business: his own cinema, the first in Central Asia. But he had not lost his sexual

mentioned the responsibilities that awaited him." But if he was not the best prepared of heirs, he was far from the worst. Nothing could prepare a man for autocracy—except living it.[4]

His consolation was happiness with Alix, who now started to decorate their main homes: their apartments in the Winter Palace, where no one had lived since Alexander II (whose blood still marked the bed and whose last cigarette was still in his ashtray), and the Alexander Palace at Tsarskoe where Nicky had been born. She decorated both palaces in the art nouveau style with a strong English flavour—all bric-a-brac, palms, clutter and plain furniture ordered from the catalogue of Maples of Tottenham Court Road—and as much of her favourite colour, mauve, as possible, particularly in her boudoir. Their taste was totally unRussian: the drawing rooms and Nicky's studies, with much leather and wood panelling, belonged in an unpretentious English country house or gentleman's club—except for Nicky's weights and bars, on which he liked to hang upside down, his special pool that he used for fashionable hydrotherapy, and of course the resplendent Nubians on silent watch outside his study. The tsar took some interest in the interior design: "Please warn Gonov he shouldn't order the fabric selected by me yesterday, it's only for the curtains," he told Count Paul von Benckendorff, marshal of the court. When he moved into their homes out of the Anichkov he was so happy with Alix that "my bliss is without bounds," he wrote on 26 November. "For the first time since the wedding we've been able to be alone and live truly soul-to-soul."

"Never did I believe there could be such utter happiness in this world. I love you!" she added in his diary. "No more separations." Then she wrote: "Darling it's hard to be happier than we have been." But there was also a sense of fate: "We're all placed in God's hands. Life is a riddle, the future hidden behind a curtain . . . At last united for life," she wrote in his diary, "and when this life is ended, we meet again in the other world to remain together for all eternity." They combined Victorian prudishness with private passion: "I burn with impatience to see you as soon as possible," she wrote, "to feel myself in your arms. I long for you terribly." When he was away, "Nobody to kiss and caress you," she told him. "In thoughts I am always doing it, my Angel." Like every passionate couple, they created a secret sexual vernacular with nicknames for their intimate

---

incontinence. In 1895, while his wife Nadya von Dreyer was away, he bought a Cossack girl of sixteen for 100 roubles who became his mistress, bearing him three children. Nadya always forgave him. In 1900, he wrote, "My attention was drawn to a beautiful schoolgirl, Valeria Khlemnitskaya," whom he married but Nicholas II had the marriage annulled. Of the family, only KR was allowed to visit him.

parts: his was "boysy," hers was "lady." We do not have letters from this time, but those from the Great War give us an idea of their intimacy: "Tell boysy that lady sends him her tenderest love and kisses and often thinks of him in lonely sleepless nights," she wrote. Her periods were, for reasons unknown, "Madame Beker" or the "military engineer."

Even years later, Nicky would give a "clear musical whistle like a bird call" when he wanted to summon Alix, who would jump up like a young bride, blushing, and say: "That's him calling." He often reflected that "I wouldn't have endured the burden had God not given you to me as wife and friend," but in his stiffly English way he told her, "It's difficult to say such truths, easier for me to write out on paper due to foolish shyness." She laughed that "silly old boy you are shy—except in the dark."

Yet Alexandra was not quite happy as empress. "I feel myself completely alone," she wrote to a German friend. There is a great loneliness inherent in monarchy—in autocracy, even more so. This could be helped by the presence of trusted friends. Alexandra had none and made few and, instead of being able to prepare while crown princess, she was simply dumped straight into the carnivorous world of Petersburg and court, which exacerbated her already fragile nature. She was so overwhelmed by the rigidities of the court that even after years as empress, she still did not dare change the biscuits served at tea, let alone remove her cantankerous mistress of robes. "I am in despair that those who surround my husband are apparently false . . . I weep and worry all day long because I feel my husband is so young and inexperienced. I am alone most of the time. My husband is occupied all day and spends his evenings with his mother." She was only too aware of her dynastic duties.

"The young empress fell faint in church," noticed KR. "If this is for the reason the whole of Russia longs for then praise be to God."[5]

On 2 November 1895 she went into labour in the Alexander Palace. The dowager empress and Ella massaged her back and legs during a twenty-hour labour that culminated in a forceps delivery: "a baby's voice was heard and we all breathed a sigh of relief." A girl! It was "a great joy," wrote the tsar's sister Xenia, "although it's a pity it's not a son." They named the infant Olga. Nicky comforted himself by saying, "I'm glad the child is a girl. Had it been a boy he would have belonged to the people. Being a girl she belongs to us."

The preparations for the coronation were almost complete. "Here the town is topsy-turvy with the preparations," Ella wrote to Nicky on 20 April 1896 from Moscow. "Dust, noise and Sergei works hard daily with all the affairs." Sergei boasted to his brother Paul that "all sorts of business, of course mostly coronation, exhaust me and there is so much nonsense . . . Everyone bothers me all day, no time for myself."[6]

On 9 May, the emperor rode into Moscow in a simple uniform on a white horse. "It was joyful and triumphant as it can only be in Moscow," wrote Nicholas. On the 14th, Nicholas and Alexandra rose at dawn to dress for the coronation, he in Preobrazhensky colonel's uniform with white breeches, she in a gown of silver brocade. As they prepared, Nicky paced up and down smoking while Alexandra and her ladies practised his placing of the crown on her head.

At 10:30, cannon thundered, bells tolled, Tchaikovsky's *Fanfare* rang out and the crowds cheered as tsar and tsarina appeared atop the Red Staircase and then processed down to the square and into the Dormition Cathedral, escorted by the swaggering uncles and his grandfather's old minister Miliutin bearing the crown, all sheltered under a cloth-of-gold baldachin. As he was invested with the ermine-lined Imperial Mantle by Uncle Vladimir and Misha, his St. Andrei chain with diamonds broke, the only accident during the ceremony. A chamberlain picked the pieces up and Vorontsov put them in his pocket. As Alexandra was crowned, "no joy seemed to unlift her," noticed Missy, "not even pride; aloof, enigmatic, all dignity but no warmth." Afterwards the mantles and crowns were removed for the anointing by holy oil before Nicholas celebrated the eucharist as a priest—the expression of the tsar's sacred link between God and man. "In the sight of my Maker," he later told his mother, "I have to carry the burden of a terrible responsibility, ready to render an account to Him of my actions." Now he had no doubt that he was chosen by God to rule.

On 17 May, as the tsar watched his ex-love Little K dance for his new tsarina, hundreds of thousands of peasants were massing at the Khodynka Field. "Every visitor to the field stalls will receive a kerchief containing sweets, gingerbread, sausage, an enamel mug, a breadroll," promised the posters around Moscow. "Special stalls are set up around the edge of the field for dispensing beer and mead." Some 400,000 packages had been prepared, but nearly 700,000 people turned up, their arrival eased by the new railways.

"Are you certain Uncle Sergei realizes the difficulty of the task?" Sandro asked Nicky. "I remember how concerned your father was on this occasion."

Sergei, who was embroiled in a bitter rivalry with the court minister Vorontsov over the organization of the coronation, deployed a meagre cadre of policemen to control the 700,000 peasants on an expanse that was pitted with trenches and pits, left over from military exercises.

As the masses arrived during the hot summer night, they queued for their packages, but the pressure became so intense that the crowds pushed those ahead of them into the pits and on to the ground, piling on to those who had already fallen. By the dawn, around 3,000 bodies covered the meadows, their faces "dark-purple, blue-black and crimson, dried blood filling nostrils." The police heaped some of the bodies on to wagons, "lumbering along with a quivering load of the dead, poor crushed peasants still in their gaudy festal clothes, driven through the city." The rest of the bodies were pushed under the pavilion.

Later that morning, at ten o'clock, Sergei arrived to tell Nicholas, who noted that "Today a great sin occurred." He should have cancelled the schedule, replacing magnificent ceremony with a public display of grief for the dead, but Sergei tried to suppress the news. Vorontsov, however, advised the tsar to issue a statement. Nicholas was persuaded by Sergei that the tragedy "must not be permitted to cast a shadow over the joyous occasion." As the family headed out to Khodynka, Nicky's sister Olga saw carts filled with vigorously waving peasants: "At first I thought that people were waving at us. Then my blood froze. I felt sick. Those carts carried the dead—mangled out of all recognition."

At two o'clock, the tsar and tsarina, "quiet and very pale," arrived at the Khodynka pavilion, where, welcomed by Sergei, they reviewed the peasants. The tsar's other sister Xenia, married to Sandro, was appalled: "The orchestra and band played the anthem endless times! It was painful and sad. While we were there, they were still carrying out bodies." That night, the emperor was due to appear at the ball of the French ambassador, the marquis de Montebello. The tsar sensed that it would be right to cancel, but Sergei insisted that any retreat would signify surrender to a "bleeding heart." As Alix wept, Nicky compromised: they would go for half an hour.

At 10:30 p.m. in the Sheremetev Palace, the tsars opened the dancing with the Montebellos. When they made to leave as planned, Uncles Sergei and Vladimir buttonholed them, criticizing such "useless sentimentality" that would make "a bad impression." Their cousin Bimbo,* backed up by Sandro and their brothers, intervened forcefully: Sergei must be dismissed and the festivities cancelled. Uncle Alexis piled in, accusing the Mikhailovichs of playing "to the radical grandstand, siding

---

* Bimbo—Nikolai Mikhailovich—was a sarcastic and outspoken historian. After he had fallen in love with first cousins whom he was not allowed to marry, he resolved not to wed. He and his Mikhailovich brothers loathed Vladimir and his children. Fascinated by history from an early age, he started to research in the archives, producing biographies of Alexander I and his wife Elizabeth. Thanks to him, swathes of Romanov correspondence were published and this author has used much of his research in this book.

with the revolution, trying to get the Moscow governorship." At this "infantile remark," Bimbo evoked Louis XVI and Marie Antoinette. "Remember, Nicky," he said, "the blood of those 5,000 will remain for ever a blot on your reign." Nicky and Alix returned miserably to the dance floor while Bimbo and his brothers stormed out.

"There go the four imperial followers of Robespierre," Alexis remarked to Sergei, whose "broad smile led foreigners to believe the Romanovs had lost their minds." Nicky and Alix stayed until 2 a.m. The next day they visited the injured at a hospital. Sergei did not cancel his own ball either. He "washed his hands of everything, saying it's nothing to do with him and Vorontsov is to blame," wrote Xenia. Sergei's wife Ella was in even greater denial, insisting, "Thank God, Sergei has nothing to do with this."

Sandro and Bimbo continued to demand Sergei's head and called for a formal investigation. "In three days," noted KR, "the emperor changed his mind three times." Sergei won. Vorontsov resigned, to be replaced by Baron Vladimir Frederiks.*

"Our dear uncles have behaved in a thoroughly improper manner," Georgy told the tsar. "I am amazed at their effrontery and even more by your patience."

"I don't want to talk about Moscow," Nicky replied. "It makes me sick to remember. It's not particularly comforting to think about the sad side of the coronation. This seems to be a year of hard labour with Alix and me as the martyrs." The thousands of mangled men, women and children might have disagreed.[7]

Afterwards, "the martyrs," as Nicky complained to Georgy, "are going to Austria, Germany, Denmark, England, France and finally Darmstadt," and "on top of it we have to drag our poor little daughter with us." Nicholas, like most other monarchs of his day, regarded foreign policy as

---

* Frederiks was a genial bewhiskered Guards officer of Finnish descent who called Nicky and Alix "the children" and the tsar "my boy," and was so absent-minded he once mistook the tsar for someone waiting for an audience. He headed the huge machine of the court with 500 courtiers; the imperial suite and entourage; plus 15,000 servants; and 1,300 bureaucrats of the court ministry administering the imperial theatres, palaces, hunts and estates. He led the team that ran the tsar's life: his deputy was the head of the chancellery and secretariat of petitions, Alexander III's friend Otto Richter, then (after 1900) Frederiks's son-in-law General Alexander Mossolov; Alexander Taneev managed his office; Prince Alexander Dolgoruky then Count Paul Benckendorff organized their daily lives as grand marshals of court. Prince Vladimir Orlov, known as "Fat Orlov," ran the tsar's military chancellery. As his name suggests, he was so porcine he could not sit on a horse, while his wife was so chic and slim they were known as "Flesh and Bone." Alexandra had her own chancellery; the most powerful of her ladies was the mistress of robes, the overbearing Princess Maria Golitsyna, until her death in 1909 when the tsarina finally appointed a friend, Zizi Naryshkina.

his personal responsibility but he admitted to his first foreign minister, Nikolai Giers: "I know nothing."

Faced with limited opportunities in a Europe now dominated by Germany, Nicholas saw the East as ripe for Russian expansion in the race for empire. China was disintegrating—though, locally, a resurgent Japan was keen to win its own empire. Just after Nicky's accession, Japan had defeated China in the First Sino-Japanese War. In one of his earliest decisions, Nicky, advised by Prince Alexei Lobanov-Rostovsky, the elderly grand seigneur who became foreign minister after Giers died, helped force Japan to give up some of its gains.

Kaiser Wilhelm encouraged Nicky "to cultivate the Asian Continent and defend Europe from the inroads of the Great Yellow Race," while both powers would seize Chinese ports. Soon afterwards, Willy sent Nicky his sketch showing Christian warriors fighting "the Yellow Peril."

Finance Minister Witte, already the maestro of the Trans-Siberian Railway, planned to expand into Manchuria in northern China through his policy of *pénétration pacifique*: he persuaded and bribed the Chinese to let Russia build an Eastern Chinese Railway into Manchuria. At almost the same time, Lobanov agreed with Japan to share influence in Korea. These successes gave Nicholas some confidence as he, Alix and little Olga set off on their tour.

At Breslau, the kaiser was eager to co-opt the tsar in a manic skein of ill-conceived ideas, but above all he was desperate to seduce Russia from the embrace of France. "I arranged his marriage, I have priority with him," he declared, though describing him as "small, weakly, timid with hardly a word to say." Willy jabbered at the tsar "about everything with a great desire to make himself agreeable and captivate me." But his tactile over-familiarity irritated Nicky, who complained that "he would poke him in the ribs and slap him on the back like a schoolboy."* In September 1896, Nicky and Alix arrived on the *Shtandart* at Leith to visit Grandmama at Balmoral: "the baby is magnificent," declared Queen Victoria. But behind the baby-dandling, Nicky and Grandmama were the emperor and queen-empress of empires locked in a Eurasian cold war. Britain was still Russia's chief rival though they shared growing suspicion of Germany. Nicky confided in Lord Salisbury, now British prime minister, that Willy "was a very nervous man," while he himself "was a very quiet man and he could not stand nervous

---

* At least he only poked the tsar. When he spanked the bottoms of Grand Duke Vladimir and King Ferdinand of Bulgaria, he caused diplomatic incidents.

men. He could not endure a long conversation with Kaiser Wilhelm as he never knew what he would do or say."

Afterwards, the emperor was delighted by the Parisian welcome of Russia's new allies: "Our daughter made a great impression everywhere," Nicky told his mother. "The first thing in the morning [President Félix] Faure asked Alix about was the health of 'the little grand duchess.'" Everyone in the street greeted her with "Vive la Grand Duchesse!" But, as they headed home, Lobanov-Rostovsky died suddenly on the imperial train—just when Nicholas needed his wisdom.

An Ottoman massacre of somewhere between 13,000 and 30,000 Armenians almost led to war: the Russian ambassador to Constantinople urged an immediate assault to seize the Straits and safeguard the 50 per cent of Russian exports that passed through them. Nicky approved this expedition by five battleships and 30,000 men until Witte, backed by Uncle Vladimir, warned that it would "lead to European war." This may have been one of those elusive moments when Russia could have made a deal with Austria—the Straits in return for influence in the western Balkans—that might have prevented the First World War, but the will was lacking, the prizes too tempting.

On 29 May 1897 Alix gave birth to her second daughter, Tatiana, in the Farm at Peterhof. "I was already preparing to go into retirement," Caesarevich Georgy joked to Nicky, "but it was not to be."

"My God, what will the nation say?" cried Alexandra, who retired to her icon-filled boudoir. Her isolation was a vicious circle. She already sensed her unpopularity in Petersburg society, but this frigidly haughty Englishwoman made it quite obvious she did not care. Nicky's cousin Missy sensed "nothing seemed to give her pleasure; she seldom smiled and when she did it was grudging . . . This of course damped every impulse towards her."

Just as Nicky's politeness masked his cunning, so her shyness concealed a surprising arrogance. "There's no harder craft than our craft of ruling," Queen Victoria wrote to Alicky. "I've ruled more than 50 years . . . and nevertheless every day I think about what I need to do to retain and strengthen the love of my subjects . . . It is your first duty to win their love and respect." Alexandra's reply explains much of what happened later: "You are mistaken my dear grandmamma; Russia is not England. Here we do not need to earn the love of the people. The Russian people revere their Tsars as divine beings . . . As far as Petersburg society is concerned, that is something which one may wholly disregard."

Indeed "Petersburg society" was not as important as it liked to think it was. This was the beginning of the Silver Age of poetry and art (following the Golden Age earlier in the century) in which, dissatisfied by

Orthodox religion, Victorian morality and scientific rationalism, and exhilarated by the rush of the modern, the avant-garde tested the meaning of art, faith and pleasure by experimenting with imagery, language and dance, as well as sexual adventurism, necromancy and narcotics. While a powerful mercantile class of textile and railway tycoons emerged in the cities, the nobility was mortgaging its estates, a retreat before the energy of the merchants as played out in Anton Chekhov's *Cherry Orchard*. The tsar could have made these vibrant bourgeois a pillar of monarchy as in Germany and Britain. Instead the new tycoons were excluded from all government and consoled themselves with collecting Impressionist and Cubist art. In the meantime, society was the tsar's only link to the modern world, but Alexandra was irredeemably priggish. When cousin KR performed his translation of *Hamlet* for the sovereigns, Alix was scandalized by the obscenity of Shakespeare. To Petersburg, this meant that she refused to receive anyone where there was a whiff of scandal, crossing so many names off the court-lists that there was no one left. Instead the couple only socialized with Romanovs, mainly Sandro and Xenia, while politically they looked towards the traditional mystical union with their hundred million peasants, with whom they had no contact except on public occasions. While Alix hoped for a son, Nicholas gambled for an Eastern empire.[8]

In August 1898 Kaiser Willy arrived in Petersburg. "I'm sorry to tell you," Nicky informed his mother, "we'll have to give Wilhelm the rank of Admiral in our navy. Uncle Alexis reminded me and no matter how disagreeable we're obliged. It makes me vomit!" Riding in a carriage at Peterhof, Willy suddenly asked Nicky if Germany could annex the Chinese port of Kiaochow which had earlier been offered to Russia. The tsar avoided answering. Soon afterwards, the murder of two German missionaries in China gave Willy his pretext and he wrote to ask Nicky's permission. "Can neither give nor withhold consent," replied Nicky. This persuaded his new foreign minister, Count Mikhail Muraviev (grandson of Alexander II's Hangman), that "it might be advantageous to seize another port at the earliest opportunity"—Port Arthur. As for the Chinese, "History teaches us that the Oriental respects strength and might above all."

"Absolutely correct," agreed the tsar.

On 14 November, he invited his ministers to Tsarskoe Selo where the navy argued against the Port Arthur plan because they wanted a better port in Korea, while Witte warned that these annexations threatened his Chinese alliance and railway—as well as disturbing relations with Japan. "The emperor refused to sanction the occupation," wrote Witte, but Muraviev worked on Nicky, telling him (falsely) that the British were about to seize Port Arthur. "I have decided to occupy Port Arthur," he told Witte. "Our ships with troops are on their way." He revealed his excitement to few. "You already know, dear Mama, of the occupation of Port Arthur which will be the terminus of the Siberian railway," he wrote to Minny. "At last we have a real port that doesn't freeze. I'm thankful the occupation was peaceful. This gives me real joy! Now we can feel safe out there for a long time." "This fatal step," Witte said, "will have disastrous results!"9

If Witte saw the East in terms of railways and markets, Nicholas saw a mystical Buddhist Shangri-la as well as a new empire in Manchuria, Korea and Tibet. His companion on his world tour, Prince Esper Ukhtomsky, told him that Tibet would welcome him as the Great White Tsar of myth who could rescue them from the British. Nicholas's "soft haze of mysticism," thought Witte, "refracts everything he beholds and magnifies his own person."

Now these two strands united in Nicholas's imagination. "The emperor is getting restless," noticed his new war minister, General Alexei Kuropatkin. "One of his more dangerous traits is his love for mysterious lands and individuals such as the Buriat Badmaev and Prince Ukhtomsky" who "inspire him with fantasies about the Russian tsar's greatness as ruler over all Asia."* Kuropatkin was convinced that Russia should concentrate on Europe and that there was a colossal practical flaw in all Far Eastern adventures: even with the railway, it took far too long to send troops to the East and, worse, it was almost impossible to deploy the main Baltic fleet there. Yet the tsar was not alone in his ambitions: Britain, France and Germany were racing to seize new colonies in Africa and the East, and Nicholas knew that Russia could never outrace the sophisticated arsenals of Europe. Prompted by Kuropatkin, he proposed a conference in The Hague to promote disarmament—much to the kaiser's contempt. But then events in China provided Nicky with an opportunity.10

*

* "Little Ukhtomsky is such a jolly fellow," wrote Nicky during their world tour. Unusually tolerant for a Russian nobleman, an advocate for Buddhists but also for Muslims, Poles and Jews, Ukhtomsky was a gentle eccentric who, though he remained a Christian, revered Buddhism. He introduced Nicholas first to a Buriat herbal apothecary, Peter Badmaev, whose potions soon anaesthetized half of fashionable Petersburg in their purple haze. Badmaev had met Witte and been introduced to Alexander III whom he liked to claim stood godfather when he converted to Orthodoxy. As influence-pedlar and espionage entrepreneur he backed Russian advances into the Far East. Now he met Nicholas. Then Ukhtomsky introduced Agvan Dorzhiev, a Buddhist priest who was the Dalai Lama's secret envoy, who on several visits asked Nicholas to protect Tibet from British aggression.

On 14 June 1899 at Peterhof, where they had moved into their new "Italian Renaissance"-style Lower Dacha, one of their favourite homes, Alix went into labour. "A happy day," Nicky noted. "The Lord sent us a third daughter Maria." Minny and the family celebrated with a Te Deum. "And so there's no Heir. The whole of Russia will be disappointed!" wrote KR. But Nicky reassured Alix: "I dare not complain the least having such happiness on earth, having a treasure like you my beloved Alix and already three cherubs." Heartbreaking congratulations came from Georgy: "Unfortunately I'm no longer fit for any kind of service. I'm no longer able to walk."

A few days later, Georgy went bicycling on his own and suffered a lung haemorrhage, and was found lying in the dust. He was twenty-eight. On 14 July, Georgy was buried in a "nightmare" service during which "Mama suddenly staggered, collapsed on me (with wide-open eyes yet seeing nothing) and said loudly, 'Home, let's go home, I can't stand any more!'" She snatched Georgy's hat from the coffin and tottered out.[11]

In 1900, the Boxer Rebellion, an insurrection of "Righteous and Harmonious Fists" against Western imperialism, soon backed by Chinese troops, besieged the embassies in Peking and then spread along Russia's Manchurian Railway. Nicky joined Germany, Britain, America and Japan in sending an expeditionary force to relieve the embassies, but he was quick to withdraw. "The happiest day of my life will be when we leave Peking and get out of that mess." Yet it was just starting: he had to protect "Witte's kingdom" and railway in Manchuria. Now the Boxers attacked the Russian headquarters in Harbin. In June, Nicholas sent 170,000 troops into Manchuria—the end of Witte's *pénétration pacifique*. "I'm glad," wrote Kuropatkin, "this will give us an excuse for seizing Manchuria."

This run of opportunistic successes—intervention against Japan in 1895, annexation of Port Arthur and now expansion into Manchuria—encouraged the imperial ambitions of Nicholas, who forced the Chinese to sign over Manchuria for many years and planned to seize Korea as well. "I don't want Korea for myself," he explained, "but neither can I countenance the Japanese setting foot there. Were they to try, that would be a *casus belli*."

These adventures, Witte rudely told the tsar, were "child's play which will end disastrously." Nicholas resented him and made his own private plans. As he told his secret adviser, his father's friend Prince Meshchersky: "I'm coming to believe in myself."[12]

*

On 26 October 1900, the emperor came down with a temperature, a blinding headache and pain in his legs while on holiday in Crimea. The pregnant empress nursed him like "a sister of mercy" and guarded him "like Cerberus." The doctors diagnosed typhoid. As rumours spread, Alexandra banned any bulletins, even though it was possible Nicky would die. His brother Misha was the heir, but the empress was pregnant again and believed she was bearing a tsarevich and, if the tsar died, she insisted she must serve as regent until her accouchement and, if it really was a son, up to the baby's majority.

Grand dukes, who all had their own Crimean palaces, consulted with the ministers, who always stayed at hotels in Yalta. Witte discussed "what to do if disaster struck and the emperor died. What to do about the Heir to the throne?" Misha would automatically succeed, but the empress refused to countenance this. "No," answered Alexandra, "Misha will get everything into a mess, he's so easily imposed on." It was Alexandra's first political move. "The empress began the practice of giving orders on affairs of state," noted the courtier Mossolov, "and we began to realize the empress's inadequacy for the task." The tsar recovered, but Alexandra was convinced that only her will could save Nicky and their unborn heir.*

"Alix is looking very beautiful despite her pregnancy," wrote KR. "Everyone is anxiously hoping for a son." On 5 June, at Peterhof, Alexandra gave birth to her fourth daughter, Anastasia. "Forgive us, Lord," confessed KR, "if we all felt disappointment instead of joy."

Just over a month after the birth, on 10 July, the two Montenegrin princesses who had married into the Romanovs invited Nicholas and Alexandra to consult a French healer who became "Our Friend."

Their rapture had already begun: in Easter 1900, when they stayed at the Kremlin with Sergei and Ella, "The services in those ancient churches produce a feeling of enchantment," wrote Nicky to his mother. "I never knew I could reach such heights of religious ecstasy . . . Alix shares my feelings completely which is a great joy for me." Their journey reflected Nicholas's concept of sacred monarchy. The couple "believed it was possible outside church and without regularly ordained bishops and priests to hold communion with God," wrote a close friend. "They believed

---

* A few weeks later, Alix lost her maternal figure. On 9 January 1901 (22 January New Style), Queen Victoria died. While he wrote warmly to Uncle Bertie, now Edward VII, Nicky had relished the humiliation of Britain in the Boer War. "I wish all success to these poor people in this unequal and unjust war," he told his mother. He also wrote as "your loving nephew" to reprimand Bertie for Britain's "war of extermination," a sign of his growing confidence.

prophecy in the biblical sense of the word still existed through certain highly gifted and spiritually minded persons."

The Montenegrin sisters Militsa and Stana—later known as "the Black Women" or just "the Crows"*—were enthusiastic explorers of a more esoteric road. When Stana was ill treated by her husband, Alexandra consoled her; when the empress fell ill, the sisters nursed her—but "the strongest bond between these women was their religious ecstasy."

First the Crows introduced Nicky and Alix to the epileptic holy idiot Mitka Kolyaba. But when Militsa's son fell ill, she consulted a Frenchman, Nizier Anthelme Philippe, a peasant boy who, working in his uncle's Lyons butcher shop, had experienced an epiphany and set himself up as a hierophant, specializing in the power of "psychic fluids and astral forces" to heal sickness and cure female sterility. Philippe "was about fifty, small with black hair and black moustache," wrote KR. "Very unsightly in appearance, with an ugly southern French accent." As Nicky and Alix struggled to conceive a boy, Philippe visited Petersburg. At the palace of Militsa and her husband Grand Duke Peter, noted Nicky, "This evening we met the amazing Frenchman." After the birth of Anastasia, Nicky and Alix started visiting Militsa every evening at her nearby estate, Znamenka, to meet the hierophant.

"We spent the whole evening at Renella," wrote Nicky. "M. Philippe talked and instructed us. What a wonderful few hours." The next day, Philippe came to see Alix at Peterhof: "We showed him our daughters and prayed together with him in the bedroom." They were already calling Philippe "Our Friend." On 13 July 1901, they were so rapt by him that they went to Znamenka twice, and when they reviewed a military parade in Petersburg, "Our Friend was present. After dinner we spent the whole evening at Znamenka."

"Our Friend," Alix wrote to Nicky, was the "one comfort to me . . . How rich life is since we know him and everything seems easier to bear." When Philippe told them he was praying for them in Lyons, she noted, "Don't forget Saturday evening towards 10:30." The emperor not only granted Philippe (who had scarcely attended high school let alone medical school) a medical licence but appointed him a court doctor. Soon Philippe was giving political advice: when Nicky met Kaiser Wilhelm, Alix told her husband, "Our Dear Friend will be near you and help you answering William's questions," giving him the toughness to "be friendly and severe, so that he realizes he dare not joke with you—that

---

* The elder sister Militsa was married to the sickly Peter, son of Nizi, commander-in-chief in 1877; the younger, Stana, had married Georgi, duke of Leuchtenberg, who had run off with his French mistress, leaving her to her spiritual adventures.

he learns to be afraid of you." As for reform, Philippe advised Nicky that a constitution "would be the ruin of Russia."

In the spring of 1902, Alix fell pregnant—and Our Friend was prophesying, "Russia was chosen to dominate the Far East."[13]

Nicky was introduced, by Sandro and Vorontsov, to a well-connected Chevalier-Gardes officer turned merchant adventurer, Captain Alexander Bezobrazov, who dazzled him in private conversations "twice a week and for hours on end." Bezobrazov told Nicholas that it was his "historic destiny" to conquer Manchuria and Korea. He himself wanted to be Russia's version of Cecil Rhodes. "This incoherent and pretentious braggart" told Nicky that "sooner or later we'll have to contend with the Japanese. Better to lay our cards on the table now." If Russia had to fight, "Only the bayonet can guarantee the success of our activities in Manchuria." Promises did not matter: "As for treaties and agreements we should never let them stand in the way."

"I was inspired by him," admitted the emperor later, "and I was pleased to listen to Bezobrazov when he explained that we'd chosen the wrong policy in the Far East. I realized he was right." Revelling in the cloak-and-dagger intrigue behind the backs of Witte and his ministers,* he and his secret adviser communicated through their batmen. In early 1903 the emperor granted Bezobrazov 2 million roubles "for purposes known only to His Majesty," and promoted him to state secretary and adjutant-general. Bezobrazov toured Manchuria secretly, setting up a secret paramilitary force. Witte and the other ministers realized that "Two policies have arisen in the Far East—the imperial and the Bezobrazovian." A "half-mad preposterous adventurer" was running Russia's Far Eastern policy.[14]

The Eastern adventure dovetailed with Nicholas's dreams at home of a return to a Muscovite monarchy, which were encouraged by an eccentric fogey who was a most unusual interior minister. Dmitri Sipiagin was not like a minister at all. Sporting a full-length Muscovite beard, he decorated the dining room in his mansion like the Palace of Facets and gave dinners in boyarish robes. Sipiagin addressed Nicholas as "Most Tranquil Tsar," playing into Nicholas's patrimonial view of himself as

---

* Nicholas was unlucky in his foreign ministers. Giers and Lobanov had already died. Now Muraviev, the architect of the forward China policy, dropped dead after a row with Witte at the age of fifty-five. His new foreign minister, Count Vladimir Lamsdorf, was a "strange-looking" recluse, "very pale," "exquisitely perfumed" and secretly gay. The emperor nicknamed him "Madame." Lamsdorf disapproved of the Eastern policy but was a submissive courtier from a vanished era. "I ask for nothing," he wrote in his diary. "Just decide everything and I will follow my assignment."

a Muscovite tsar (not a European emperor). "I conceive of Russia as a landed estate of which the proprietor is the tsar," Nicky explained, "the administrator is the nobility and the workers are the peasantry." When he filled in the 1897 census, he described his own profession as "Master of the Russian Land" and Alexandra's as "Mistress of the Russian Land."

The tsar called Sipiagin "my dear friend." While they were enjoying these boyarish fantasies, Sipiagin's Okhrana were charting the creation of a terrifying new terrorist threat.

The boom and then recession had created a worrying instability. During the boom, a million peasants had moved from the villages to work in the textile factories and oil refineries of Petersburg, Moscow and Baku. Their conditions were appalling, but the regime had to find a way to manage the new proletariat. In Moscow, Sergei was backing a brilliant secret policeman Sergei Zubatov, chief of the Moscow Okhrana, who was sponsoring and guiding his own unions in the new labour movement—so-called "police socialism."

Yet Russia was beset not just by the struggle of the classes but by the awakening of nations too. In this age of nationalism which seemed to doom multinational empires, the tsar chose to link his throne to the Russian nation, who made up less than half of his citizens while alienating his non-Russian citizens by aggressively following his father's russification policies from the Caucasus to Finland. Young Finns, Georgians, Jews, Poles and Armenians flocked to join nationalistic parties. But two factions ominously crossed ethnic boundaries.

The Socialist Revolutionary Party, known as the SRs, the heir of the old Populists and the People's Will, promoted peasant revolution, backed by terrorism. The writings of Karl Marx had become popular in Russia. Marx had argued that history inevitably led, by means of class struggle, through rigid stages of feudalism, capitalism and socialism, to the paradise of Communism, the common ownership of wealth. Now thanks to the success of Witte's industrial revolution, Russia possessed its own proletariat.

In March 1898, nine delegates gathered in a wooden house near Minsk to found the Russian Social-Democratic Workers' Party, the future rulers of the Soviet Union. The Okhrana arrested most of them, but Vladimir Lenin, who was in Siberian exile before leaving for Europe, and Julius Martov (né Tsederbaum) quickly became its leaders. Young people across Russia were convinced by Marx's certainty that the old order of tsars, priest, landowners and factory masters would be destroyed. This "was not only a theory," wrote Josef Djugashvili, the future Stalin, then a young seminarist, "it's an entire worldview, a philosophical system."

The SR Battle Group was, for now, the greater threat. When Sipiagin crushed student protests, his Cossacks killed thirteen demonstrators, and the SRs took their first scalp, assassinating the education minister. Sipiagin worried he was not suited to directing repression, warning, "We're standing on a volcano."

On 2 April 1902, he was approached by a man with a package in the lobby of the government offices, in the Mariinsky Palace. As he took it, the SR terrorist shot him dead. He bled to death in the arms of his friend Witte. The emperor confided in Meshchersky, "I feel fit and strong in spirit but with a deep wound in my heart from the loss of my friend Sipiagin." Meshchersky advised repression. "We need not only hardness but harshness," believed Nicholas—and the Prince of Sodom proposed the man to deliver it.[15]

"It's time to crack down," the tsar told his new interior minister, Vyacheslav Plehve, ruthless lawyer-turned-policeman who had drafted Alexander III's anti-Jewish laws and shared his views on most matters. "Now one more thing," wrote Nicholas in a friendly tone, "I forgot to mention during our audience," going on to dismiss one official "as a cunning humbug . . . I don't like him very much . . ." and denounce another "as a smug, arrogant scoundrel." Here was the tsar's authentic voice with a trusted minister. Plehve turned the Okhrana into the world's most sophisticated secret police, launching a concerted policy to lure the top revolutionaries into becoming super-informers.* Their star double-agent was the chief terrorist of the SR Battle Group, Evno Azev. This was as risky as the CIA recruiting Osama bin Laden. In return for a vast salary, Azev gave the Okhrana useful information—yet remained a committed terrorist.

As a Jew from Rostov, Azev seemed a typical revolutionary to Plehve. "Jews are much more dangerous than any constitutionalist," he said. He believed that controlled anti-semitism was a lightning-conductor for discontent and a banner to rally the masses.

In Kishinev, the capital of Bessarabia, at Easter 1903, the murder of a

---

* Plehve promoted Zubatov to head of the Okhrana in Petersburg. He expanded the agency from three bureaux to eighteen. Like many of the new generation of secret policemen, he had been a young Populist terrorist who converted to monarchism. A master of *conspiratsia*, he believed that double-agents were to be paid, groomed, intellectually engaged and almost seduced like "a beloved woman with whom you have illicit relations. Look after her like the apple of your eye. One careless move and you will dishonour her." Zubatov was precisely the sort of secret policeman that the tsar found distasteful. Plehve sent Nicholas a capacious weekly "tsar's briefing," cataloguing everything from mining accidents to opposition intelligence, but the emperor rarely met the Okhrana leaders, sharing his father's haughty view that the Okhrana organization was necessary but repellent, and that it interfered with his authentic communion with his people. But any Russian leader needs to master his own security organs.

Russian man and the death of a Russian girl in the local Jewish hospital unleashed mobs who killed forty-six Jews, wounded 600 and burned 700 homes, while the local governor did almost nothing. The pogrom appalled the world. Plehve sacked the governor but his anti-semitism was so well-known that he became hated in liberal society. He backed Nicholas's Eastern policy. "Bayonets not diplomats," said Plehve, "made Russia, and the Far Eastern problems must be solved by bayonets not pens."[16]

Meanwhile Alix was pregnant again. The tsar wrote from manoeuvres to tell her about "the ladies, some rather good looking with fatal eyes . . . [who] kept looking at Misha and me." But he only wanted "my sweet Wify. I kiss you. I love you and want you. Oh! So naughty!"

"Sweetest lovey mine," she replied, praising "the adorable expression of shyness that creeps over you and makes your sweet eyes all the more dangerous . . . You old sinner!"

When Philippe Our Friend returned, "we listened to him over supper and for the rest of the evening until 1 a.m.," wrote Nicholas. "We could go on listening to him for ever." But the family were getting nervous about this infatuation and resolved to intervene. When the emperor was away at manoeuvres, Alexandra was challenged by her sister Ella, who "assailed me about our Friend . . . I explained it all came from jealousy and inquisitiveness." As for what they were really up to, Alix congratulated herself on lying to her sister. "I stuck to the story of the remedy," concealing the "spiritism . . . which might have been difficult to explain to her." The dowager empress asked the secret agent Rachkovsky, the Okhrana *rezident* in Paris who had guarded Alexander III on his foreign trips, to investigate Philippe: he exposed Our Friend as a charlatan who had been prosecuted for practising medicine without a licence. When he saw this insolent report, the tsar sacked Rachkovsky.

Philippe ordered Alexandra not to be examined by doctors, but though she had put on weight, by the end of the summer the pregnancy was not advancing. Where was the baby? In early August she moved to Peterhof for her accouchement.

When the doctor arrived for the delivery, Alexandra finally let him examine her: she was not pregnant and never had been. Her symptoms of pregnancy were either the result of Philippe's powers of suggestion or a "molar pregnancy," the growth of a non-viable egg that causes the womb to swell as in a pregnancy. "Poor things," wrote KR. Alexandra was understandably hysterical, writing to her courtier Countess "Zizi" Naryshkina: "Dear friend, don't come! There will be no christening—there's no child—there's nothing! It's a catastrophe."

Minny and Nicky's sisters persuaded Nicky that Philippe had to go.* Before he left, laden with presents including a Serpollet motor car, he gave the empress a little bell that would ring if dark forces lurked. Philippe died soon afterwards, but not before he had warned that he would merely vanish and then reappear: "Some time you will have another friend like me who will speak to you of God."[17]

On 7 February 1903, Nicky held the first—and as it happened—the last social spectacular of his reign. The guests were in costumes of the time of the Tsar Alexei, and the "magnificent pageant" was an expression of Nicky's wish (in the words of Sandro) "to be back in the glorious past of our family," inspired by the late Sipiagin's idea of restoring Muscovite dress to court, in place of Peter the Great's Germanic ranks. Nicky, who came in the gold-brocaded robes and fur-trimmed crown of Tsar Alexei, and Alexandra, who dressed as Tsarina Maria Miloslavskaya in a silver-brocaded sarafan, bearing a mitre set with emeralds and diamonds, presided over a hall "filled with ancient Russian people" at the Hermitage Theatre. But "while we danced," wrote Sandro, "the workers were striking and the clouds in the Far East hanging dangerously low."[18]

In January 1902, Japan had isolated Russia by signing a defensive treaty with Britain which forced Nicholas to agree a phased withdrawal from Manchuria—but the emperor was more confident than ever. "Our sovereign has grandiose plans in his head," wrote Kuropatkin on 16 February 1903, "to absorb Manchuria into Russia, to begin to annex Korea. He also dreams of taking Tibet under his orb. He wants to rule Persia, to seize the Bosphorus and Dardanelles." If this outraged Britain, he felt he could depend on the kaiser who, at Reval in August, offered support. "In 1904 I shall declare war on Japan," said Nicky according to Willy, who shouted: "From now on Emperor Nicholas is called Admiral of the Pacific and I call myself Admiral of the Atlantic." "He's raving mad," whispered the tsar.

"Witte, Lamsdorf and I anxiously watch Bezobrazov," wrote General

---

* The meddling and indulgence of the family was already infuriating Nicky. Now he exiled Uncle Paul to Paris for breaking the Family Law. Paul had been married to Alexandra of Greece with whom he had a daughter. But she died in childbirth, producing a son, Dmitri. Much later, Paul fell for the married Olga Pistolkors, whom he married in Paris without permission. "The nearer the relative who refuses to submit to our family statutes the graver must be his punishment," Nicky told his mother. "I fear a whole colony of the Russian imperial family will be established in Paris with their semi-legitimate and illegitimate wives. God knows, what times we're living in when undisguised selfishness stifles all conscience, duty and ordinary decency." Paul's children Dmitri and Maria were raised by Sergei and Ella.

Kuropatkin, "and especially worry about the emperor's private correspondence with this dreamer and adventurer."*

The tsar trusted the favourite Bezobrazov over his ministers, and this entire episode fits into the long tradition of autocrats, and explains much about Nicholas. "The distrust of ministers is common to all sovereigns, starting with Alexander I," explained Plehve, who understood autocracy better than anyone. "Autocrats listen to their ministers, outwardly agree with them but always turn to outsiders who appeal to their hearts and inspire suspicion of their ministers, accusing them of encroaching on the autocratic law." Kuropatkin realized that Nicholas thought "we ministers hold back the sovereign from the realization of his dreams—he still thinks he's right and better understands the glory of Russia." Kuropatkin gently teased the emperor, suggesting he would trust him more if he was *not* a minister. "It's strange," mused Nicholas, "but perhaps that's psychologically accurate." He continued to consult Prince Meshchersky, whom he called "my secret and reliable friend."

Bezobrazov called the ministers "the mangy triumvirate," using code in his telegrams: Witte was "Nostril," Kuropatkin "Grouse" and Lamsdorf "Tadpole." But the adventurer had gone too far: "It's essential to avoid a quarrel with Japan," said Nicholas several times. "War is completely undesirable." On 7 May, he met his Eastern committee still dominated by Bezobrazov, whose project he now recognized as part of the imperial effort to win Korea. The ministers tried to resign and the tsar sacrificed Bezobrazov who had been like a "mustard plaster," he admitted. Now "I have to pull it off." But he was even more committed to winning "exclusive influence over Manchuria." The Japanese offered the only sensible solution: Russian Manchuria in return for Japanese Korea. But Nicholas rejected it. He would get both.

On 1 August, Nicholas showed the ministers he was the master, appointing Admiral Yevgeny Alexeev, more courtier than warrior (and supposedly a natural son of Alexander II much favoured by Uncle Alexis for his non-naval exploits), as viceroy of the East—"commander of all military forces and political chief." Alexeev was an aggressive champion of the new Eastern empire, but Nicholas's indecision was already undermining Japanese trust in his negotiations. Alexeev's appointment

---

* To be fair to Nicholas, it is worth remembering that not just Russia but liberal Britain was also pursuing reckless adventures in the East. In April 1903, the viceroy of India, George Curzon, despatched Colonel Francis Younghusband and a small British army to invade Tibet—partly to stop the Russians getting there first. Younghusband massacred hundreds if not thousands of Tibetans and took Lhasa for a short time, enforcing a treaty that made the country a British protectorate. But China protected Tibet. Britain was embarrassed and the Tibetans rejected the treaty.

delayed diplomacy even more. Then the emperor summoned Witte: "He shook my hand, embraced me . . . I returned home beside myself with happiness and found a written order for my dismissal on my desk." Witte, kicked upstairs to the sinecure presidency of the Council of Ministers, started to hate Nicholas, who was "100% Byzantine."

The Japanese were outraged when Russia broke its agreement to leave Manchuria. Bezobrazov had taught the emperor that treaties could be broken, and Nicholas was convinced that Russia could defeat those "macaques" because Japan was "a barbarian country" and Kuropatkin told Nicholas that "the Japanese army was a colossal joke" but he did not want a war. The emperor blithely ordered the viceroy: "I don't want war between Russia and Japan and will not permit this war. Take all measures so there is no war." Japan made further offers to Russia for a compromise but wondered if the inconsistent tsar was capable of negotiating a treaty yet alone honouring it.

If his careless arrogance was astonishing, Nicholas knew that Russia was shaking. In July 1903, Plehve crushed a strike in Odessa that led to the fall of his most gifted secret policeman, Zubatov. "If I'd been told twenty years ago that a revolution was possible in Russia," said Plehve, "I'd have laughed, and here we are on the eve of a revolution." War would be a gamble, but Plehve explained to Witte and Kuropatkin that "to avert a revolution, we need a small victorious war" to "distract the attention of the masses."[19]

As Nicholas was mishandling the Japanese negotiations, Alexandra was following Philippe's last advice: if the tsar canonized an obscure elder, Seraphim of Sarov, who had died in 1833, and if the tsarina bathed in his spring, she would conceive a boy. Nicholas ordered Pobedonostsev, the by now doddery ober-procurator of the Holy Synod, to canonize Seraphim immediately, but he objected: the tsar could not canonize anyone. "The emperor can do anything," snapped Alexandra. Nicholas overruled the Church and on 17 July 1903, the tsar and tsarina, accompanied by the entire family, joined 150,000 pilgrims in Sarov where a spectacular event had been organized by Plehve to rally the peasants to sacred tsardom.

The next day, in searing summer heat, Nicholas helped carry the saintly relics to Sarov Cathedral. "It was an incredible spectacle," Nicky felt, "to see how the crowd and especially invalids, cripples and unfortunates reacted to the holy procession." Following a service, "the elevation of the spirit was enormous." After dinner, Nicky, Alix and Ella "went down to the source where we bathed with particular emotion in the stream of icy water. In the darkness no one recognized us," wrote Nicky.

"God is miraculous through his saints." Soon afterwards, Alexandra became pregnant. Was she bearing the heir?

At this tense moment with Japan, in September 1903, Nicholas and Alexandra travelled to Germany for the wedding of Prince Andrew of Greece and Princess Alice of Battenberg (future parents of Prince Philip, duke of Edinburgh), then they went hunting. While waiting eight weeks for a reply to its final offers, Japan made other plans.

"People claim, Nicky, war is at hand," Sandro said to Nicky back in Petersburg.

"There's no question of war," Nicky replied. "The Japanese aren't going to declare war on Russia."

"Who will stop them?"

"They won't dare."[20]

After the annual Great Procession through the Winter Palace on New Year's Day 1904, the emperor sent a note to Plehve: "It is time to crack down suddenly and hard. I wish you good strength and health this year." At the reception in the Winter Palace, he told the Japanese ambassador that "Russia was not just a country but a part of the world—in order to avoid a war, it was better not to try her patience or else it could end badly." It was probably too late to negotiate, but he spurned a last-ditch offer of a Russian Manchuria and a Japanese Korea, telegraphing Viceroy Alexeev that if the Japanese landed in southern Korea, "it would not be a cause of war." As tensions rose, Kaiser Wilhelm cabled Nicky that war was "unavoidable . . . I hope the Admiral of the Pacific will not be angry with the Admiral of the Atlantic. Ta-ta!" Nicky replied with a happy birthday telegram signed: "Nicky Admiral of the Pacific."

On 24 January, Japan broke off diplomatic relations. "War, so be it, peace so be it, but the current uncertainty is really bothersome," reflected Nicholas. "All day I was in an excited mood," he reflected after he met his ministers. Petersburg held its breath—as a Japanese fleet under Admiral Togo steamed towards Port Arthur.

Next day, the emperor attended *Rusalka* at the Mariinsky Theatre. Nicholas had ruled for almost ten years, longer than most democratic leaders. His reputation as a weak but noble man, along with the tragedies of his family, lay ahead. It was true he never sought power and might have preferred the life of a Guards officer. But he now believed in his holy mission with a righteousness that justified any intrigue.

"I had rarely come across a better-mannered young man," wrote his enemy Witte. "His good breeding conceals all his shortcomings." He was unknowable and inscrutable: "he seemed to live in an imperial mist," noticed cousin Missy. But stealth and guile are essential skills in any leader, and the emperor's ability to choose his own advisers was, as Plehve understood, "connected with the basic principle of autocracy," and he prided himself on it. "You have no idea how sly I can be," he boasted to Alix. But Nicholas took his Byzantine duplicity so far that no one could trust him. He was "incapable of playing fair" or, as another minister noted, "incapable of supporting anyone over anything." Faced with bickering advisers, his attitude—"Why are you always quarrelling? I always agree with everyone about everything and then do things my own way"—became corrosive. In his private notes, Witte catalogued the tsar's "petty craftiness, stupid childlike cunning, timid dishonesty." These were the judgements of ministers whom he sacked, but even a loyal one such as Ivan Durnovo warned, "Mark my words, Nicholas II will prove a modernized version of Paul." Yet, if this had been his last night on the throne, historians might today reflect that the reign of Nicholas II, who had held the line of autocracy and laid the foundations for new conquests, had been successful, even lucky.[21]

The tsar and the audience did not know that the shooting had already started: ten Japanese warships had ambushed the fleet in Port Arthur, a Russian Pearl Harbor. Three capital ships had been damaged. Port Arthur was in chaos; the inept Viceroy Alexeev did not believe the attack had actually happened and then convinced himself it was a victory. It took him many hours to inform Nicholas.

After *Rusalka* which he thought was "very good," the tsar received a telegram: "Around midnight . . . Japanese torpedo boats launched sudden attack on our squadron at Port Arthur. Adjutant-General Alexeev."

"Is this undeclared war?" he asked himself, copying the telegram to his mother: "This has just arrived. So the war has begun. May God be with us. Nicky." Next day, the tsar prayed for victory in the Winter Palace chapel; crowds cried "God Save the Tsar." Nicky and Alix bowed from the window.

Viceroy Alexeev had only 60,000 men to defend a vast span of territory, so everything depended on how quickly Russia could get troops to the Far East, but the Trans-Siberian Railway was the only route and it took a minimum of fifty days to deploy a regiment there. The day after their surprise attack, the Japanese landed in Korea with scarcely any Russian resistance and started to advance. Nicholas, who toyed with the idea of taking command himself, appointed Kuropatkin to command the Manchurian army under the viceroy. Meanwhile at sea, on 1 April, the Far Eastern flagship the *Petropavlovsk* hit a mine and sank with the loss of 635 men including its admiral. At the Winter Palace, "Poor Alix is in bed!" wrote Xenia. "I found Mama there—she and Nicky are terribly upset and depressed."

On 17 April, Kuropatkin tried to stop the Japanese at the Battle of the Yalu River but, for the first time in recent history, Occidentals were defeated by Orientals. When the Japanese swiftly landed at Nanshan in the north of the Kwangtung Peninsula, Alexeev did not dare oppose their bridgehead. As the Japanese marched south to besiege Port Arthur, the commanders started to squabble and appealed to the tsar: the squabbling of generals was to be a fixture in the Russian command. At one point, two even indulged in a public brawl. For now, Port Arthur was too prestigious to abandon yet too exposed to defend. When an attempt to relieve it failed, the city was doomed.[22]

As the Russians fought their Eastern war, the most respected Romanov was "at war with my conscience." "My predilection has always been for simple men," admitted KR in his diary on 19 April 1904. "I dream of going to the bathhouse on the Moika . . . I can picture the familiar attendants Alexei, Frolov and particularly Sergei." The tsar's beloved cousin, KR, forty-five years old,* happily married with nine children and known as "the best man in Russia," found himself in a struggle between his public virtue and private homosexuality.

"I am overwhelmed by sinful thoughts during the committee meeting," he wrote on 21 May. "I dismissed my coachman on the Morskaya. I walked up and down twice past the bathhouse doors; on the third time I went in. And so once again, I have sinned. My mood is foul."

KR had had his first homosexual encounter in the Guards, but when he married he managed to overcome his tendencies until the new century when suddenly he threw himself into the bathhouses of Petersburg. "How appalled all these people who love and respect me would be if they knew of my depravity," he wrote. "I am loved, praised and promoted beyond what I deserve, my life is happy, I have a beautiful wife, delightful children, I've received a special mark of favour from the throne. How is it I can't deal with it?"

"Bad thoughts keep coming into my head . . . particularly in church," he wrote on 15 December 1903. On 23 June the following year, as the

---

* KR was a contradiction. On one hand he was a tall, handsome Guards officer of impeccable wholesomeness and vast wealth since he had inherited the Marble Palace and Pavlovsk among other estates, and a close friend to Nicky. Married to Mavra (formerly Princess Elizabeth of Saxe-Altenburg), he was an adoring father to his huge brood. On the other hand, he was an amateur poet, playwright and actor; he had been friends with the late Dostoevsky and Tchaikovsky, the latter impressed enough to set his poems to music. He regularly performed his plays for the imperial family. But his diaries are his masterpiece: KR specified that they could not be read for ninety-nine years after his death, and his wife Mavra often joked about what they might contain. In fact, they were preserved in the archives after the Revolution, forgotten for decades—and their astonishing revelations emerged only after the fall of Communism.

Russians fought the Japanese, KR's attendant Sergei brought his twenty-year-old brother Kondraty, "and I led the lad astray. Perhaps I caused him to sin for the first time." He let himself go: "in the morning in the bathhouse. Once again I find myself like a squirrel on a wheel . . ."[23]

The Japanese were now besieging Port Arthur, at the same time turning their guns on the main Russian army of Manchuria. The Russian generals feuded while the Japanese won every engagement. Morale was even lower at home.

On 3 June, Bobrikov, the hated governor-general of Finland, was assassinated. Plehve, protected by eight guards and travelling in an iron-windowed carriage, moved into the secret police headquarters at 16 Fontanka, but he was reassured by his super-agent Azev that assassinations were temporarily suspended. In fact Azev blamed Plehve for the Kishinev pogrom. On 15 July, Plehve was riding in his carriage to the station on his way to report to the tsar at Tsarskoe Selo when an SR terrorist tossed in a "pomegranate" (as the terrorists nicknamed their bombs) that killed the minister instantly.

As Nicholas mourned "my friend," Alexandra gave birth to a son on 30 July: "a great and unforgettable day for us . . . there are no words to thank God enough for sending us this comfort in a time of sore trials." KR noticed Misha "radiant with happiness at no longer being heir."

A 301-gun salute marked the birth of a boy. Nicholas and Alix credited Philippe. "Please somehow or other pass on our gratitude and joy to Him," the tsar told Militsa. Nicky thought Russia had had "enough Alexanders and Nicholases," so he named the boy Alexei after his favourite tsar. But after the cutting of the umbilical cord, the doctors noticed blood in Alexei's swaddling clothes. His navel bled for two days.

On the day of the birth, when Militsa and her husband drove over to Peterhof, she immediately realized that the baby might have haemophilia. Afterwards she called the tsar, suggesting he ask the doctors "if there is any sign of haemophilia." The tsar "fell silent on the phone for a long time," then started to question her and "ended by quietly repeating the word that staggered him: haemophilia." The family were only too aware of what Xenia called "the terrible disease of the English family," carried by women, suffered by men, and caused by a genetic mutation. It had appeared for the first time in the British royal family only with Queen Victoria who, through her well-married nine children, passed it to the wider cousinhood of Europe. Her son Leopold, duke of Albany, had died of it, so had Alexandra's brother. Her sister Irene, married to the kaiser's brother Heinrich, had just lost a child to it. Life expectancy would be roughly thirteen years but many sufferers lived longer.

Alexandra tearfully told the nurse, "If only you knew how fervently I've prayed for God to protect my son from our inherited curse." The doctors explained, Nicky wrote to Militsa on 1 August, "that approximate loss of blood in 48 hours was from 1/8th to 1/9th of the total quantity."

Nicholas and Alexandra made the decision to keep the disease a secret, which as the boy grew up placed the fatalistic tsar and the hysterical tsarina, still only thirty-two, under extraordinary pressure. Very few—Sergei, Ella and the Crows—would ever know. After the invalid Georgy, this second ailing caesarevich would have made the Romanovs seem weak and unlucky. But the alternatives were not tempting—feckless Misha then Uncle Vladimir's sons—unless Nicholas changed Paul's laws to make his eldest daughter Olga his heir, an option which he considered. Instead the couple were determined that "Tiny" (or "Baby," their nicknames for Alexei) must succeed to the plenitude of autocracy, which could only intensify the stress. Their suffering has formed their sympathetic modern image, yet it is worth remembering that Queen Victoria also lived in fear of Leopold's bleeds and she too kept his illness secret, though he was not her heir, and a British monarch endured far fewer responsibilities.

Six weeks after the birth, "little Alexei started to bleed from the navel," noted Nicky. The doctors rushed to bandage the wound, but "How painful it is to live through such moments of anxiety." Alix wrote to Nicky that Philippe "our dear Friend is watching over you as He did over Tiny last week—oh what anguish it was. Thank God he is well now . . ."

The tsar agonized over who to appoint interior minister. His mother persuaded him, supposedly on her knees in tears, to conciliate the opposition by appointing a wealthy liberal, Prince Peter Sviatopolk-Mirsky, who immediately loosened Plehve's repression and made overtures to society. Nicky knew that "it is always dangerous to stop halfway," but this swerve intensified expectations. When Alexei was christened, his godparents included the kaiser, Uncle Alexis, and the entire army in Manchuria.[24]

The morale among Alexei's godparents was deteriorating. The Japanese bombarded desperate Port Arthur and shattered the Pacific fleet. On 10 August, 158,000 Russians faced 125,000 Japanese in a two-week battle for Manchuria which ended in another retreat and then a further defeat. Finally the emperor recalled the incompetent viceroy and reshuffled the generals, though he longed to take command himself. "I asked Uncle Alexis—he thinks my presence with the army in this war is not necessary."

In August, Nicholas wondered whether to send his Baltic fleet around the world to fight the Japanese. His naval chief, Uncle Alexis, "had nothing to say and the courage to admit it," recalled Sandro, but he expected "our eagles to give a sound beating to the yellow-faced monkeys." Sandro, now minister of the merchant navy, urged Nicholas not to send the fleet; and its designated admiral, the fifty-five-year-old Zinovy Rozhdestvensky, a gruff disciplinarian who had risen from the ranks, begged for more modern battleships. But there was no supply of new ships. After the meeting that decided the destiny of the forty-two ships and 12,000 sailors of this so-called Second Pacific Squadron, the erotomaniac Uncle Alexis cheerfully appraised girls in conversation with Sandro asking, "Had I seen Mrs. X and how did I find Mrs. Y?"

On 2 October, the fleet sailed. "Bless its path, Lord, let it reach its destination whole," wrote Nicky in his diary, "to fulfil its hard mission for Russia." Next to his diary entry, he drew a cross.

As he entered the North Sea, Rozhdestvensky feared that the Japanese—or their British allies—would attack him. Just after midnight on 8/9 October, he spotted shadowy silhouetted boats, surely Japanese, around him on the Dogger Bank. "Open fire!" he shouted. In the panic, his flagship *Suvorov* fired on a British trawler, beheading two fishermen. "All this is very awkward," Nicky told his mother. "The English are very angry and near boiling point . . . getting their squadrons ready for action." He sent regrets to Edward VII, "but I did not apologize." Later the Russians paid £65,000 to the bereaved of Hull. The challenge was now to coal the huge fleet around the world in the face of British hostility. The kaiser, spotting a chance to prise Russia away from France, reassured the tsar—"sorry for the mishap in the North Sea"—and helped provision the fleet. If this quixotic adventure succeeded, Nicholas would be celebrated for ever for seizing victory from defeat.[25]

"Authority is shaking and all our misfortunes stem from the emperor's lack of will," wrote KR on 18 November. As the siege of Port Arthur neared its end, back home students and workers demonstrated; liberals ran a campaign to demand constitutional reform. The new minister, Mirsky, advised the tsar to concede an elected legislature: "If you don't, then change will come in the form of revolution."

"You know I don't hold autocracy for my own pleasure," the emperor lectured Mirsky. "I act in this sense only because it's necessary for Russia." Buttressed by Uncle Sergei, Nicky declared, "I'll never agree to a representative form of government because I consider it harmful to the people whom God has entrusted to me." He turned against his minister, who despaired: "Everything has failed. Let us build jails." Mirsky's wife called Nicholas "the most false man in the world."

On 22 December, Port Arthur surrendered. "Do Russians surren-der?" KR asked his diary. "Revolution," he felt, "is banging on the door. How terrifying." But "I was plagued all day by bad thoughts." He longed to see his young lover in the bathhouse, yet revolution restored KR's self-control. "What will the new year bring?"

The front scarcely moved, yet Kuropatkin finally had numerical supe-riority: 275,000 infantry and 16,000 cavalry against a total of 207,000 Japanese. On 6 January 1905, Kuropatkin ordered a massive offensive. But time was running out.[26]

That day, when the tsar attended the Blessing of the Waters on the frozen Neva, a salvo from the guns of the Peter and Paul Fortress shattered the windows of the Winter Palace: they contained real shot. Nicholas was unharmed, but the accident added to the unease as 160,000 workers went on strike in Petersburg's factories. On 8 January, Nicholas heard that "There is some priest at the head of the workers' union—the socialist Gapon." Gapon was a police agent but, tricking his Okhrana controllers, he organized a demonstration to present a petition to the tsar listing most of the demands in the revolutionary socialist agenda, from improved workers' conditions, elections to a constituent assembly and peace. Mirsky and the police panicked. Instead of using Cossacks, whose charges were terrifying and whips painful but rarely fatal, the garrison's infantry, under Uncle Vladimir, untrained for crowd control, guarded the Winter Palace and the bridges. That night the tsar secretly moved to Tsarskoe Selo.[27]

The next morning, Sunday 9 January, just as the army launched its offensive in Manchuria, Gapon led thousands of workers towards the palace. At checkpoints they were called on to halt and turn back. When they did not, the troops opened fire and cavalry charged the crowds. Over a thousand were killed, 2,000 seriously wounded. "A terrible day! Lord how painful and sad!" wrote Nicholas. "Mama arrived from town. Lunched with everyone. Went for a walk with Misha. Mama stayed the night." Faced with revolution and defeat, "My poor Nicky's cross is a heavy one to bear," Alix wrote to her sister Victoria of Battenberg, "all the more as he has nobody on whom he can thoroughly rely. He has had so many bitter disappointments but through it all he remains brave and full of faith in God's mercy . . ." Bloody Sunday inflamed the discontent on all sides. "How I wish I were clever and could be of real use . . ." the empress went on. "But the lack of what I call 'real' men is great . . . Had his father seen more men, drawn them around him, we should have lots to fill the necessary posts; now only old men and quite young ones, no one to turn to. The uncles, no good; Misha a darling child still."[28]

The emperor summoned Uncle Sergei's police chief General Dmitri Trepov* to govern Petersburg. Sergei grumbled, but he already disapproved of the reforms. Resigning as governor-general, he remained in Moscow—as an SR hit squad, disguised as cabbies, stalked their prey.

On 2 February 1905 the hit squad was ready as the grand duke's carriage arrived at the Bolshoi Theatre. The terrorist was about to give the signal to the bombers when he saw that Ella and the children were with the grand duke. On the 4th, the terrorists observed Sergei's coachman waiting outside his palace. As the carriage rolled through the Kremlin, an assassin tossed his bomb from four feet away. Nothing was left except the back wheels of the carriage. Sergei's head, shoulders, one leg and one arm were vaporized and never found. Fingers, one leg and a foot were sprinkled on to the square and roofs of surrounding buildings. A naked, one-armed, one-legged half-torso lay in the smoking debris. The coachman was alive but dying. Ella ran outside. Throwing herself to her knees in the bloody charred snow, she started to collect the "fragments of mangled flesh and placed them on an ordinary army stretcher," rummaging in the snow for pieces of Sergei because, as she explained, "he loved order." Two days later Ella went to see the arrested murderer to give him an icon: "The grand duke forgives you and I will pray for you."

At Tsarskoe Selo, the family gathered around the beleaguered emperor, who banned anyone even attending a church service and warned Uncle Alexis that he "was being tracked like a wild beast to be killed." Alexis "sobbed like a child, crying 'What a disgrace!' " Ella became a nun, founding her own holy order, while their niece and nephew, Dmitri and Marie, who had lived with them, joined the emperor at Tsarskoe Selo.

As authority drained away from the government and the harvest failed, the peasants rose up. The revolutionary parties, from Social-Democrats to Georgian Federalists and Armenian Dashnaks, assassinated over a thousand officials in a year. In Baku, Muslim Azeri mobs slaughtered 2,000 Armenians. In Petersburg, the tsar swung between repression and concession. When his new interior minister suggested radical reforms, he reprimanded him: "One would think you are afraid a revolution will break out."

"Your Majesty," replied the minister, "the Revolution has already begun."[29]

---

* Formerly in the Horse Guards, ultra-reactionary and devoted, Trepov was one of the four sons of Fyodor Trepov, the governor of Petersburg under Alexander II who had investigated Fanny Lear, had dissidents whipped and been shot and wounded by a female Nihilist. All four sons held high posts under Nicholas II and one became prime minister. For now, Trepov became the emperor's essential henchman.

*

The autocrat desperately needed good news from the East—but on 24 February, Kuropatkin had lost the Battle of Mukden. "It is painful and distressing," wrote Nicholas, who dismissed Kuropatkin. Meanwhile the Baltic fleet disappeared into the Indian Ocean, ready for battle. Admiral Togo's Japanese fleet steamed to cut it off. On 14 May, the fleets met in the Tsushima Strait in the greatest naval battle since Trafalgar, the only full-scale clash in the Dreadnought era. The Russians were annihilated, losing 4,380 dead, 5,971 prisoners (including a wounded Rozhdestven-sky), and twenty-one ships sunk including six battleships, while the Japanese lost just 117 killed and three torpedo boats. "Our picnic party at Gatchina was interrupted by a messenger: our fleet had been anni-hilated," recalled Sandro. The emperor "said nothing. As usual. Went deathly pale and lit a cigarette." Nicholas kept "admirable composure," but wrote, "Terrible news" in his diary—and told his mother: "I fear we shall have to drain the bitter cup to the dregs."

The disaster was mostly due to the fundamental challenges of deploy-ing Russian naval power in the Pacific, but if any individual could be blamed it was Uncle Alexis. The windows at his palace were shattered by the stones of rioters. When his ballerina mistress, Eliza Baletta, whom the director of imperial theatres described as "a worthless wench who ruins the repertoire," attended the ballet, the audience pointed at her jewellery and shouted: "You're wearing our battleships!"

Alexis resigned, admitting to his nephew that he "didn't believe in human beings." Nicky was sorry for him: "Poor soul." Alexis retired to Paris where he died three years later. "My favourite uncle," wrote Nicky, "noble, honourable, courageous."

A way out of the war now presented itself. The US president Teddy Roosevelt offered to mediate with Japan, inviting envoys to Portsmouth, New Hampshire. The battleship *Potemkin* mutinied in Odessa.

On 29 June, Nicky summoned Witte and asked him to represent Russia at the talks, adding that "he wouldn't pay a kopek or cede an inch of territory." Witte decided to "act as befitted the representative of a great empire." He did more than that—he behaved "with demo-cratic simplicity" while in the United States, giving interviews to the press, meeting Jewish leaders. Witte was lucky: Japan was almost bankrupt and he won an amazingly lenient treaty signed on 23 August, that gave up half Sakhalin Island but paid no indemnities. "I began to accustom myself to the thought that this is probably good," reflected the emperor who received Witte on board *Shtandart* in the Gulf of Fin-land, the only safe place for the family to go on holiday. He raised him to count.

"Your Majesty, will you now cease to doubt my loyalty and believe I'm not a revolutionary?" asked Witte.

"I entirely trust you," lied the tsar, who still resented him, "and pay no attention to all these calumnies."

Bruised by defeat, embittered by British hostility and Gallic chilliness, Nicky received an invitation from his loyal friend Kaiser Willy.[30]

As their yachts, *Hohenzollern* and *Shtandart*, met off the island of Björkö, the kaiser, who declared, "I come as a simple tourist without ceremony," had never been a more welcome sight. Both emperors were thrilled to exercise the ancient prerogatives of autocracy. "The tsar embraced me and pressed me to him as if I were his own brother," Willy told his chancellor, "and looked at me constantly with gratitude and joy." At breakfast next morning, 11 July 1905, on the *Shtandart*, Nicky denounced Anglo-French intrigues, particularly those of his wicked Uncle Bertie, "the arch-intriguer," at which Willy produced a copy of a Russo-German treaty "that I happen to have in my pocket." "His dreaming eyes sparkled with light," wrote Willy. "I pulled out the envelope, unfolded the paper on Alexander III's desk."

"Excellent! I quite agree," said the tsar.

The kaiser, "my heart beating so hard, I could hear it; my forehead and back running with moisture," then asked, "Will you sign it?"

"Yes, I will."

Afterwards, they embraced emotionally. The kaiser celebrated this "turning point in the history of Europe," breaking the encirclement of Germany and the Franco-Russian alliance. This is usually given as evidence of Nicky's ineptitude but, in some ways, he was pushing a policy that would have avoided the First World War by breaking up the two power blocs dividing Europe. Unfortunately such total reversals of policy have to be well prepared.

The tsar enjoyed his coup for over a month before he deigned or dared inform his foreign minister "Madame" Lamsdorf, who insisted that Björkö was a betrayal of France on which Russia depended for its finance. Nicholas excruciatingly had to explain to the kaiser that the treaty "will not be applicable"—it was null and void. The emperor had ended the war—but the Revolution rolled on.[31]

On 3 August, Nicholas's ministers announced a compromise—a limited consultative assembly. Nicholas had agonized and consulted about this but now it was too little, too late. Workers went on strike, peasants attacked landowners, students rioted, swathes of the Baltics and Caucasus became independent revolutionary fiefdoms.

General Trepov, just promoted to deputy interior minister, urged Nicholas to create a dictatorship. On 8 October Count Witte came to Peterhof with the opposite advice. Next day, Witte was invited back to talk to Nicky and the empress. "The basic motto of the societal movement is freedom!" he told them. Offering his help, he boomed that "A government that follows events and doesn't direct them leads the state to disaster—such is an axiom of history . . . Either stand at the head of the movement that has seized the country or proceed firmly in the opposite direction"—dictatorship. Nicky and Alix listened in near silence.

Witte heard nothing for three days. "I assure you," Nicky told his mother, "we have lived *years* in these days, such torments, doubts and indecisions." But the dowager empress,* who competed with Alexandra to influence Nicky, gave her blessing to Witte, "the only man who can help you now—a man of genius, energetic and clear-sighted."

"Petersburg and Moscow are entirely cut off from the interior," he told his mother. "The only way to get to town is by sea. How convenient for this time of year . . . It makes me sick to read the telegraphic despatches. Nothing but new strikes in schools and factories, murdered policemen, Cossacks and soldiers, riots, disorder, mutinies. But the ministers, instead of acting with quick decision, gather like frightened hens and cackle."

In Petersburg and Moscow, the revolutionaries planned armed uprisings. "I immediately gave command of all troops in Petersburg to Trepov," wrote Nicholas, who "made it plain that any disorder would be ruthlessly put down." Trepov ordered his soldiers "not to use blanks and not to spare bullets." In Peterhof, the emperor waited: "Everybody knew something was going to happen . . . like before a thunderstorm in summer." The choice was dictator "and rivers of blood," or parliament.

Nicholas blinked. On 14 October Witte steamed out to Peterhof; they talked all day. At the same time, the tsar's courtiers Frederiks and Fat Orlov advised dictatorship. The emperor laconically telegraphed the prospective dictator, his cousin Nikolasha: "Come. Nicholas."

---

* The Romanovs aggravated Nicholas even during this supreme crisis. In 1894, Nicky and Alix had got engaged at the marriage of Ducky (Melita, daughter of the duke of Edinburgh, and sister of Missy) to Alix's brother Ernst of Hesse. But the marriage had failed and Ducky fell in love with Kyril, Uncle Vladimir's son who had almost died in the sinking of the *Petropavlosk* by the Japanese. On 25 September 1905, Kyril and his first cousin Ducky married—without the tsar's permission. Nicky and Alix were furious; Nicky stripped Kyril of his title and income at which his father, Uncle Vladimir, resigned all posts, throwing his medals on Nicky's desk. "I am having doubts about punishing a man publicly at a time when people are generally ill-disposed towards the family," Nicky told his mother, so he restored Kyril's title and rights. "Ouf! What tiresome unpleasant days." Vladimir died in 1908, but his widow Miechen became Alexandra's chief enemy. "How she must have hated us," reflected Nicky.

Nikolasha—Nikolai Nikolaievich, son of Nizi, known in the family as "the Terrible" for his fearsome temper—rushed to Peterhof. A rigorous inspector of cavalry, Nikolasha fancied himself as a medieval knight, still keeping a court of dwarfs, and once demonstrating the sharpness of his sword by cutting one of his borzoi dogs in half before appalled guests. Revering "the divine origin of Tsarist power," he believed that the autocrat possessed "some special secret strength through his anointing." If the tsar ordered him to jump out of a window, "I'd do so without hesitation." Minny thought him "a good soldier at heart," but she supposedly said, "He suffers from an incurable disease. He's stupid." If not brilliant, Nikolasha was certainly commonsensical, and he was the only Romanov with the stature to become dictator. But he was not quite the strongman he seemed. A porcelain-collector, this excitable giant—he was six feet five—was now in love with the married Stana, with whom he shared fluffy beliefs in spiritism, table-turning and Philippe. Recently Nikolasha had discovered a new healer, a peasant from Siberia named Rasputin.

At Peterhof, Witte proposed his constitution to the tsar and Nikolasha, but left without an answer. Deep into the night, Nicholas discussed what to do. The tsar tried to persuade Nikolasha to become dictator. Nikolasha left the room and "ran to Frederiks, ran like a madman around his room with tears in his eyes," yelling, "We must save the Sovereign." Then he "pulled out his revolver" and, holding it against his head, shouted, "If the Sovereign doesn't accept Witte's programme and wants to nominate me dictator I will shoot myself in front of his eyes with this very revolver. We must go to the Sovereign . . . We must do this for our own sake and Russia's!" Alexandra never forgave Nikolasha for this hysterical blackmail and called the constitution "Nikolasha's fault." But, surprisingly, the ultra-reactionary Trepov advised accepting and the tsar trusted only Trepov: "You are the only one of my servants on whom I can completely rely." But he now had little choice: "Yes, Russia is being granted a constitution."

The tsar, still trying to avoid Witte, sent Frederiks and Fat Orlov to Witte's home to negotiate terms while feeling out other candidates and by the time they left at 2 a.m. Witte, now aged fifty-nine, was close to breakdown "after all this evasion, these unworthy games, secret meetings." Witte cursed "this interlaced body of cowardice, blindness craftiness and stupidity"—a description of the tsar himself. Next day, his doctors prescribed cocaine to pep him up and he set off for Peterhof.

At 5 p.m. on 17 October, in the presence of Witte and Nikolasha, Nicholas signed a document that conceded—or "imposed," in imperial jargon—civil rights for all, a bicameral parliament with the lower house, the Duma, elected with (almost) universal suffrage, a half-appointed, half-elected upper house (the State Council, not unlike Alexander II's plan in 1881), and a government co-ordinated by a prime minister: Witte.

The emperor and Nikolasha noticed that it was the anniversary of the Borki railway crash. "Twice on this day," agreed Nikolasha, "the imperial family has been saved."[32]

As Russia's first ever prime minister returned to the capital to publish the *Manifesto on the Improvement of State Order*, the tsar thought of his mother who had travelled to Denmark: "My dear Mama, you can't imagine how I suffered," but "we are in the midst of a revolution. I know you are praying for your poor Nicky." The tsar never forgot these "evil days" when, as he confided in Zizi Naryshkina, "this person" (Witte) whose name he could not bear to utter "was trying to lead me on a wrong path but I hadn't the strength to oppose him."

Witte forced his new cabinet on the emperor. "I shan't forget his insolence," seethed Nicholas. On 23 October, they appointed Peter Durnovo as interior minister, who turned out to be the indispensable strongman of 1905. "Small, all muscle and nerves," an ex-naval officer and enthusiastic womanizer, Durnovo had served Alexander III as director of police. He ordered his agents to open letters from his own mistress, a Petersburg courtesan, to a Brazilian diplomat. Discovering that she was two-timing him, he had the police raid her love nest and steal the rest of her letters. The mistress complained to the diplomat, who informed the emperor. "Get rid of this swine [Durnovo] in twenty-four hours," boomed Alexander III—but he died a year later, allowing Durnovo to rebuild his career.

This shady policeman was a quick, ruthless and astute decision-maker. Three days after his appointment, the Baltic sailors, stationed close to Petersburg, rebelled. Within five days, Durnovo had crushed them.

"When we depart the shore, we will begin to be tossed about," Witte warned Nicholas. Sure enough, instead of bringing order, the *Manifesto* aggravated the Revolution. The momentum seemed unstoppable. In Petersburg, a Soviet—a council of workers and peasants—chaired by the preening showman of revolution Leon Trotsky, directed the disorders. Lenin, now the leader of the Bolshevik faction of the Social-Democrats, secretly arrived from Geneva.* Siberia, the Caucasus and the Baltics

* The Social-Democrats were divided into two factions with some overlap but increasingly different styles. In 1902, in his essay *What is to be Done?*, Lenin demanded a revolution organized by "a few professionals as highly trained and experienced as the imperial security police." At the Party's second congress held in August 1903 in London and Brussels, Martov and most Social-Democrats outvoted Lenin, who then formed his own Majority

passed out of government control. In Baku, the Armenians avenged themselves in a slaughter of Azeris as the oilfields burned.

Nicholas blamed Witte. "It's strange such a clever man should be wrong in his forecast of an easy pacification," he told his mother. He appointed his stalwart Trepov as the commandant of Imperial Palaces, where he became "an indispensable secretary, experienced, clever and cautious. I give him Witte's bulky memoranda to read and he reports concisely."

On 1 November, at the lowest ebb of the emperor's life so far, the Crows invited Nicky and Alix to come over from Peterhof to the neighbouring Sergeevka estate. "We had tea with Militsa and Stana," wrote the tsar. "We made the acquaintance of a man of God—Grigory from the Tobolsk region." They did not meet again for months, but a link had been established, and the devotion of this authentic peasant confirmed their belief in the masses just as they feared they had lost them.

The tsar pushed for a harsh counter-revolution. Witte and the ministers "talk a lot but do little," Nicky told Mama. "I am disappointed in Witte." On 3 December, Durnovo ordered the arrest of Trotsky and the Petersburg Soviet. "Everyone is delighted that 260 important leaders of workmen's committees have been arrested," Nicholas told his mother, "all of which gives Witte courage to keep the right line of action." But on the 7th, the arrests triggered the Moscow insurgency planned by Lenin. Durnovo came to Tsarskoe Selo and urged Nicholas to launch full-scale repression.

Planned by Durnovo with Nikolasha, now promoted to commander of the Guards and commandant of Petersburg, the repression was directed by the emperor's top courtiers. The new governor-general of Moscow was Admiral Fyodor Dubasov, who had accompanied Nicky on his world tour. Using the Semyonovsky Guards, Dubasov stormed the barricades in the workers' district with artillery and machine guns. He called himself a "barn-burner" and he took no prisoners. Three thousand workers perished. "The armed rebellion in Moscow has been crushed," wrote the elated emperor. "The abscess was growing . . . now it's burst." Next, the tsar appointed another "barn-burner," his best friend General Alexander Orlov, commander of the Uhlan regiment, to reconquer the Baltics. When Orlov was not harsh enough, Nikolasha had his quartermaster explain that "Nobody on high [that is, the tsar] is going to condemn you for excessive severity but rather for the lack of

---

(Bolshevik) faction, dubbing his opponents the Minority (Mensheviks) because he had won a few unimportant votes. The Mensheviks were numerous nationally and more influential in the Petersburg Soviet. The interlinked factions fought beside one another in Moscow and Georgia, but their rivalry was increasingly vicious and the schism remained permanent.

it." Orlov shot more than a thousand and when he reported executing a group of seventy, Nicholas applauded him for "acting splendidly."

"Terror," the tsar declared to Minny, "must be met with terror." Witte briefed him that agitators were arriving from the Far East: "Are they really letting these 162 anarchists corrupt the army?" Nicky replied. "They should all be hanged." When he heard that a punitive detachment had accepted the surrender of rebellious Livonians, he insisted: "The town should have been destroyed." Arrests were celebrated with the word "Power!," while the summary execution of twenty-six rebellious railway workers earned an imperial "Bravo." Vladimir Bezobrazov, brother of Nicky's Far Eastern adviser and one of his favourite Guards officers, staged ghoulish public shows of bodies dangling on gibbets. When Commander Richter, son of Alexander's III's crony, now leading a punitive detachment in the Baltics, not only shot his prisoners but hanged the bodies afterwards, Nicholas wrote another "Bravo." Trepov informed him that Cossacks had over-used their whips. "Very well done," applauded Nicholas. When he heard of more executions, he commented, "This really tickles me."

Durnovo behaved as if he was conquering a foreign country. "I earnestly request," he commanded a Kiev subordinate, "that you order that insurgents be annihilated and their homes burned." Nicholas was impressed: "Durnovo acts superbly." Though official figures listed 1,200 executions with around 70,000 arrested, real victims are uncountable, but certainly more than 15,000 killed with 45,000 deported.*

Next, as generals retook the Caucasus, fighting house to house in Tiflis and Baku, Nikolasha proposed that two commanders start at each end of the Trans-Siberian Railway and meet in the middle, annihilating rebels "with exemplary severity" along the way. "Excellent idea," wrote the tsar, particularly if they destroyed the Jews and Poles, who had organized "the whole strike and later revolution."³³

A pogrom against the Jews begun in Odessa, where 800 were murdered, unleashed a frenzy of attacks on Jews around the empire. Nicholas justified the anti-semitism to his mother: "Nine-tenths of the

---

* Nicholas was careful with his historical reputation, ordering Witte and his ministers to return any documents recording his severity, hence few of them survived. He repeatedly refused to let terrorists off the death penalty, but when there was a miscarriage of justice he regarded it as his role as tsar to give justice. In 1908, on the night before an execution, a young aide-de-camp was convinced by the fiancée of a condemned man that he was innocent. The ADC bravely awoke the emperor at Peterhof and explained the case to the pyjamaed tsar. "I commend you for acting this way," said Nicholas. "Thank God neither of us need reproach our consciences." He went into his study and returned with a telegram that read: "Delay execution. Await further orders. Nicholas." Handing it to the ADC, he said simply: "Run!"

trouble-makers are Jews, [so] the people's whole anger turned against them. It's amazing how they took place simultaneously in all the towns of Russia and Siberia."

As the *pogromchiki* were killing 3,000 Jews from Vilna to Kishinev, two junior bureaucrats—Alexander Dubrovin and a rabble-rousing pogromist from Kishinev, Vladimir Purishkevich (the future murderer of Rasputin)—formed a Union of Russian People, a movement of noblemen, intellectuals, shopkeepers and thugs who rallied support for "Tsar, faith and fatherland" around extreme nationalism and anti-semitic violence. The Union was the political wing of rightist vigilantes, the Black Hundreds, who fought revolutionaries and slaughtered Jews. Fascists fourteen years before the word was invented in Italy, the Black Hundreds marched in the tsar's name but despised his compromises with parliamentarians. In December 1905, Nicholas welcomed Dubrovin to Tsarskoe Selo, telling him that "With your help, I and the Russian people will succeed in defeating the enemies of Russia," and accepted honorary membership of the Union, wearing its badge and financing its newspapers. By 1906, it had 300,000 members. The Hundreds shared many of his views on Jews.

Nicholas's table-talk was peppered with anti-Jewish banter, typical of many a European aristocrat of this era—telling his mother how a courtier "amused us very much with funny Jewish stories—wonderfully good at imitating Jews and even his face suddenly looks Jewish!" Alexandra herself talked of "rotten vicious Jews," often noting after a semitic name, "a real Jew for sure." But it was more than that: to Nicholas the Jews represented everything bad about the modern world. "The Englishman is a Yid," he liked to say. To him, a newspaper was a place where "some Jew or other sits . . . making it his business to stir up passions of peoples against each other." As he explained to his bodyguard commander Alexander Spiridovich, "As a Russian and as a man, knowing his history, he could not like the Jews but he did not hate them either." But actually his hatred was visceral. After reading his cousin KR's play *King of Judaea*, he wrote, in an unusually candid letter, "I was fired by a hatred of the Jews who crucified Christ."

In December 1905, an anti-semitic forgery, *The Protocols of the Elders of Zion* which blamed the Jews for the secret diabolical orchestration of world war,* was published by the Petersburg Military District press,

---

* The pamphlet was actually the result of adapting two books published in the 1860s and aimed at Napoleon III but we still do not know who created it. Produced at the turn of the century, Russian secret policemen, perhaps Rachkovsky in Paris, may have commissioned this preposterous though powerful forgery, but this is unproven. If they did, the tsar believed it to be genuine since he was still reading it after his abdication.

probably under Nikolasha. As pogroms spread, Witte discovered that the Interior Ministry was printing anti-semitic pamphlets. When he reported this to Nicholas, "His Majesty was silent and appeared familiar with all the details."[34]

Nicholas was desperate to rid himself of Witte, who is "absolutely discredited with everybody except the Jews abroad." But first the prime minister had to agree the rules of the new constitution, the Fundamental Laws, with the tsar, who insisted on preserving his autocracy*—and then negotiate a loan of 2.25 billion roubles to fund the bankrupt government. As soon as this was done, Witte resigned, declaring, "Russia is one vast madhouse." Nicholas was delighted. "He hates me as much as I hate him," said the tsar who regarded Witte as a pro-Jewish traitor. When the retired Witte started to re-emerge, "the Jewish clique sows sedition again," Nicky told Minny. Now he appointed in Witte's place his original choice, the lazy, mediocre bureaucrat Ivan Goremykin, sixty-seven years old, who was "indifferent to everything," which was what Nicholas liked.

"What's important to me," said Nicholas, "is that Goremykin will never act behind my back; I shan't be given any surprises." But the Interior Ministry mattered. When Witte's government resigned, the tsar gave the ensanguined Durnovo 200,000 roubles and Goremykin suggested that Peter Stolypin, a provincial governor, replace him as interior minister. Meeting the tsar, Stolypin refused the job—unless ordered.

"I order you," replied Nicholas, standing before an icon. "I understand your self-sacrifice. I bless you. This is for the good of Russia."

"I obey," said Stolypin, kissing the tsar's hand. Nicholas "seized me with both arms and shook me warmly," wrote Stolypin. "The die was cast."

Son of a general, this wealthy, cultured and happily married nobleman, tall, imposing and handsome with a slightly withered right arm, was a visionary leader. While governing Saratov, he had personally disarmed terrorists. "Nervousness is pardonable in ladies; in politics, there must be no nerves," he declared. He was unusually pro-semitic, regarding Russia's 6 million Jews as "not only necessary but very convenient

---

* The suffrage was broad and pivoted towards the supposedly loyal peasantry. The monarch totally controlled foreign policy and the armed forces, appointed ministers and could summon and dismiss the Duma, veto its laws and rule by decree if necessary. The result was a hybrid autocratic–parliamentary system. Like the other hybrid system in Europe, Germany's, this was still dominated by the emperor who could claw back almost absolute power if he so wished, but its problem was that the lines of authority between monarch, ministers and parliamentarians were unclear and proved even more chaotic than they had been before.

and pleasant." The remarkable Stolypin, a pragmatic monarchist determined to remake the political system, would soon dominate Russia.[35]

The night before the opening of the Duma, the tsar "couldn't sleep," wrote his sister. "He kept lying there with a feeling of sadness and melancholy." When the train arrived at Peterhof from Tsarskoe, the tsar's "only friend" General Orlov eased the tension by presenting Alexandra with a bouquet of roses. Next morning, they boarded the yacht *Alexandria*.

At 1:45 p.m. on 27 April 1906 at the Winter Palace, Nicholas, preceded by courtiers bearing the crown and regalia, followed by his wife, mother, sisters, in gowns and tiaras, and courtiers in full uniform, walked slowly into the Georgievsky Hall. To the right gathered the State Council, aristocrats in their uniforms and orders; across the room in suits and caps stood the elected Duma. Xenia stared at "several men with repulsive faces and insolent disdainful expressions! They neither crossed themselves nor bowed." As the tsar's new security chief Spiridovich put it, "One group seemed to be saying 'We've finally got what we wanted' and the other 'Don't celebrate too soon.'"

Nicholas mounted the steps of the throne, took a speech from Frederiks and briskly hailed "the great historic moment." As he finished, "a cheer broke out, the choir sang the anthem," recalled Xenia. "Mama and Alix were crying and poor Nicky was standing there in tears, his self-control finally overcome." Back at Peterhof, Nicholas "was delighted he'd at last be able to sleep properly."

Yet the Duma, meeting in Potemkin's Taurida Palace, was dominated by a liberal-leftist party of constitutional democrats, known as the "Kadets," who immediately challenged the tsar's powers, attacked the new ministry and debated confiscation of land. Trepov sensibly and secretly explored a Kadet ministry, possibly with Nicky's permission but when it was revealed, the tsar typically withdrew his favour. Trepov died soon afterwards. Nicholas and Stolypin agreed the Duma would have to go. On 5 July, Nicholas let the servile Goremykin resign and appointed the forty-four-year-old Stolypin as both prime minister and interior minister. On the 8th, flooding Petersburg with soldiers, Stolypin oversaw the dissolution of the Duma.

As Stolypin cracked down on the rebels, all the revolutionary parties, Bolsheviks and SRs as well as Georgian Federalists and Armenian Dashnaks, turned to gangsterism to fund themselves, as well as to assassination to express themselves: 3,600 officials were assassinated between October 1905 and September 1906.

At Peterhof, the tsar, accompanied by (thin Alexander) Orlov as well as Fat (Vladimir) Orlov, felt besieged by "these horrible crimes." On

12 August, Stolypin was receiving visitors at his dacha on Aptekarsky Island when three suicide bombers of the SR Maximalist faction entered the room and blew themselves up, killing twenty-seven and maiming seventy. Bleeding from the face, Stolypin carried his wounded daughter out of the ruins, followed by his three-year-old son; both gradually recovered but, at Nicholas's invitation, he moved the family into the more secure Winter Palace.

The terrorists hunted down the scourges of revolution. The next day, Min, one of the crushers of the Moscow Revolution, was assassinated. "We had to sit here, virtual prisoners," Nicky told his mother. "After killing Min, those anarchist scoundrels came here to Peterhof to hunt me, Nikolasha, Trepov, Orlov and Fat Orlov."*

That day Stolypin presided over the cabinet "as if nothing had happened." The tsar sent a personal message hailing a "divine miracle—my thoughts are with you."

"My life belongs to YOU, YOUR MAJESTY," replied Stolypin. The tsar demanded summary executions, a travesty of due process. "The emperor deigns to command," wrote War Minister Alexander Rediger to Stolypin, "that a person who commits a crime punishable by death now faces no long wait but that the sentence be decided and carried out no later than 48 hours after the crime." The indirect order of the tsar was blamed on Stolypin. The noose was henceforth nicknamed "Stolypin's necktie," and prison trains were known as "Stolypin wagons" into the reign of Stalin. The prime minister's severity dovetailed with the Okhrana's brilliant infiltration and fragmentation of the revolutionaries.

Yet tsarist repression was surprisingly gentle compared with the Soviet equivalent. If one includes junior policemen among the victims, 16,000 officials were murdered between 1905 and 1910, yet only 3,000 terrorists were hanged, while the most frequent punishment, Siberian administrative exile, was boring, cold and isolated but more like a Spartan reading-holiday than a prison camp. Stalin escaped a total of eight

---

* Admiral Dubasov was wounded in another assassination attempt. In February 1906, in the Georgian capital, General Fyodor Griazanov, who had retaken Tiflis in brutal street-fighting, was killed by Bolsheviks, a hit partly organized by young Stalin while General Alikhanov-Avarsky, a Muslim from Daghestan, who had earned the nickname "The Beast" for his reconquest of western Georgia and Baku, was murdered by Dashnaks. Hunted by these same terrorists, the tsar and his family scarcely appeared in public for the next six years. They never again lived at the Winter Palace, confined to the parks of Tsarskoe Selo and Peterhof, guarded by concentric circles of security by their Life Guards, by the Cossack Escort (under the command of their palace commandant), then by the 250 plain-clothed agents whom the tsar jokingly called "the Naturalists" because they pretended to be looking at nature, the 250 uniformed "Imperial Police," and finally by his 300-strong bodyguard commanded by General Alexander Spiridovich, who as Okhrana chief in Kiev had been wounded by a terrorist. He became a family favourite. Fat Orlov co-ordinated all of them.

times, sometimes on foot, sometimes romantically by reindeer sleigh and sometimes prosaically by catching a train. Hard labour, often in the mines, on the other hand, was brutal.

"You may say I'm fighting *against* revolution," Stolypin boasted, "but *for* reform." Modelling himself on Bismarck, he believed in a strong nationalistic monarchy backed by a parliament, but not parliamentary government. "What we want," he said, "is a Great Russia."[36] As Stolypin energetically pursued his vision, Nicky and Alix were getting to know the man who, more than any other, would come to personify their reign.

That October, Nicky and Alix received a telegram from Grigory Rasputin, "the man of God." "Little Father Tsar," it read, "having arrived in town from Siberia, I would like to bring you an icon of the Blessed St. Simon Verkhotursky the Miracle-Worker."

They had already met Rasputin twice, first with the Crows a year earlier and then for a short tea on 18 July, but now this simple telegram, Rasputin's first direct communication to them without Montenegrin intermediaries, caught their imagination. The Crows had told Rasputin that he was never to communicate with the tsars without going through them. Naturally, Rasputin, with his instincts for human nature and power play, ignored this order.

On 12 October, he arrived at the Alexander Palace to present his icon. "He made a remarkably strong impression both on Her Majesty and on myself," the tsar told Stolypin. Alexei, now aged two, was suffering a minor bleed. The parents were anxious. "Instead of five minutes, our conversation went on for more than an hour," explained the tsar, and it ended with Rasputin being taken into the nursery to meet their daughters, but above all to pray over Alexei. Rasputin must have calmed the child and the mother. He then offered to help Stolypin and his daughter, wounded in the bombing. Once he had left the palace, the tsar asked a courtier what he thought of the peasant. When the courtier suggested that he was insincere and unstable, the tsar said nothing. But, whatever happened with Alexei, Rasputin had made a greater impression than anyone yet knew. Nicky and Alix believed he was the new "man of God" prophesied by Philippe. This couple, who were morbidly suspicious of sophisticated people, welcomed him with open-armed credulity.

Grigory Rasputin, thirty-seven, born in the village of Pokrovskoe, 250 miles east of the Urals, was in his charismatic prime: he was physically striking—long dark hair centre-parted, unkempt beard, swarthy, windburned, pockmarked skin, a broken nose and deep-set staring eyes that fascinated some with their intensity and repelled others with their brazen theatricality. Rough-hewn, malodorous and coarse, he liked and

understood women, who provided most of his followers; he clearly possessed a pungent appeal.

He grew up to be a wild horse-stealing, skirt-chasing, hard-drinking
rakehell who discovered God on a pilgrimage to a local monastery. He
was unlettered but literate, and knew much of the Scriptures by heart.
He became a holy elder, a *starets*, and a wandering pilgrim, a *strannik*,
who claimed to possess mystic power to communicate directly with
God and to heal. His faith—in his religion, his mystical powers and
his destiny—was "utterly sincere," noted Grand Duchess Olga and that
belief was self-fulfilling.

Whether one believes his powers were miraculous, hypnotic or thespian, his charm was rough and simple. Siberian peasants had never
been serfs and Rasputin almost smelt of the freedom of the great open
spaces of the east. Rasputin was utterly self-possessed, and he handled
his aristocratic and royal clientele with masterful directness and fearless confidence, without a hint of servility, making even tsars feel that
they were privileged to be in his company. He insisted that Grand Duchess Militsa kiss him thrice peasant-style, and it is likely that Alexandra
kissed his hands; he called Nicky and Alix "Batushka" and "Matushka,"
addressing them with the intimate *ty*; he treated Alexei like a normal
child; and, observed Grand Duchess Olga, "he radiated gentleness and
warmth," far from the froideur of courtiers. He revelled in his feral magnetism and never concealed his sexual worldliness. On the contrary, his
sinfulness was an essential component of his holiness for he believed
that only by testing his restraint by sexual temptation and by exuberant
bouts of debauchery could he experience the elation of forgiveness and
intimacy with God. He may have been influenced by the illegal Khly-
sty sect which sought to achieve union with God by frenzied dancing,
singing and fornication, but if so, he was not a member of the sect and
denied any connection.

Both unique and typical, he was a link in the tradition of sacred wan-
derers. In the Silver Age, his rise reflected not just the fad for mystics and
séances but a febrile decadence in society and a deep disillusionment
with the Orthodox Church itself which, now no more than a government department, was filled with corrupt timeservers like the rest of
the bureaucracy. Rasputin was just the latest of a host of fashionable
healers patronized by seekers like the Crows. After wandering for many
years, marrying and fathering children in his village, then making the
pilgrimage to Mount Athos in Greece, he had arrived in Petersburg for
the first time in 1903, and was hailed by the hierarchs of the Church,
eager, like everyone else, to find gritty holiness amid so much cynical
decay, in a son of the Siberian soil.

To society ladies married to dull officers in golden epaulettes who divided their time between drilling soldiers and playing cards, this Siberian peasant with his greasy beard and wandering fingers was thrillingly real. More to the point, his insolence played on their guilt at living in palaces while the peasants starved. He was unpretentious, funny and playful, giving everyone nicknames, teasing them with earthy tales of fornicating horses while questioning them about their sex lives. His own feral sexuality, harnessed to peasant charm and mystical prestige, was irresistible to some: one woman boasted that she had fainted during the orgasm he delivered. His penis was said to be equine in scale, while (his future murderer) Felix Yusupov claimed that a fortuitously positioned wart explained his prowess. But in fact his promiscuity may be exaggerated and when later he saw prostitutes virtually every day they testified that he often just wanted to look at them and talk. Temptation and denial were the essence of his faith. Perhaps the power to shock and tempt was more satisfying than the act itself, or alcohol may have rendered him impotent. It may be that history's most notorious sex-beast—even celebrated in pop songs—was not much of a lover at all.

After he had arrived in Petersburg, his first patron Archimandrite Feofan introduced him to his first Romanov, Nikolasha, and that severe cavalryman was convinced by his holiness and introduced him to the Montenegrins. Rasputin's peasant simplicity was his essential quality for Nicky and Alix who, estranged from Petersburg society and out of touch with the countryside, craved his authenticity—"a real Russian peasant" is how Nicky described him. He was the proof, the fulfilment and the personification of the tsar and tsarina's vision of themselves and their sacred union with the peasantry. His lechery and debauchery were evidence that he was a Christ-like outsider; the repulsion he provoked from "the Pharisees" of sophisticated society proved his exceptional sanctity. To Nicky and Alix, he benefited from a holy circle: the more they revered him, the more the Pharisees hated him, which proved that he was all the holier. "He is hated," the empress often said, "because we love him."

He would never have achieved so much without the misfortune of Alexei's haemophilia. He alone could staunch the boy's bleeding either by divine healing or by his ability to calm the patient and perhaps as importantly to soothe the hysterical mother. This belongs in the realm beyond scientific explanation. Gradually he became more and more essential to the anxious parents, their trust inexplicable to a court and public that did not know Alexei's secret. But our modern hunger for family empathy has led us to neglect an equally important part of his appeal. Both the monarchs made clear that he became indispensable to them for their own needs—for Alexandra in her worsening mental condition and for Nicholas in his struggle to play the tsar. Even when Alexei was well, they needed him.

Had Nicholas kept him as a discreet family healer, and had Rasputin been content to remain one, he would still have caused a scandal. Even in a constitutional monarchy, Queen Victoria's Scottish and Indian servant-confidants John Brown and Munshi provoked outrage. In an autocracy, any royal intimate has political power but Nicholas failed to channel Rasputin away from politics. It was the promotion of Rasputin, mainly by Alix, and particularly after 1914, to the role of adviser on all matters, that helped destroy him—and his patrons.

When he met sceptics, such as Stolypin, his staring and eye-rolling, his muttered mumbo-jumbo and esoteric gestures were exposed in all their amateur hucksterism, while his petulant, vindictive anger when these tricks failed to impress, revealed a mean spirit that existed alongside his sincerity.

He was a born showman, like any evangelical preacher. He may have been unsophisticated but he was boundlessly ambitious with a sly sense of the flux of power and an instinctive feel for the psychology of courts—worldly gifts that in no way affect our judgement of whether he was a true healer or a charlatan. The fact remains that, over the years, he put himself forward as a full-service personal, religious and political *consigliere*, at the same time constantly advancing his power by threat and stealth, boasting of his connections, showing off his letters from the tsarina, raking in bribes for his powerbroking and influence-peddling, and seducing, even raping, women. Much of this was due to the weakness of tsar and tsarina and their need, indeed hunger, for Rasputin's support and validation. On Rasputin's side, it was due to his overweening vanity but also his need to guarantee his own safety by controlling the police. He was a mixture of mystical power and worldly ambition, common sense, decent intentions and unfettered egotism. His advice was often practical and humane—he was always against war and stood up for minorities like Jews—but his personnel choices were self-serving, incompetent and ultimately disastrous for the regime.

After Rasputin had prayed over Alexei, the emperor wrote to inform his prime minister that he "has a strong desire to see you and bless your injured daughter with an icon. I very much hope you will find a minute to receive him this week." Rasputin visited Stolypin and prayed over his daughter. He was not shy of the great.[37]

The Crows bathed in Rasputin's reflected glory. "Stana and Militsa came to dinner and spent the whole evening telling us about Grigory," wrote

Nicholas. Like everyone else, the Crows wanted something from the tsar. Stana Leuchtenberg wanted to divorce her husband and marry Nikolasha. The latter, who generously presented his entire palace to his jilted mistress, boasted to KR that the marriage "couldn't have been managed without the influence of Philippe from beyond." Nicky gave his permission. "Authorization can only be seen as connivance," noted KR, "due to Nikolasha's closeness to the emperor and that of Stana to the young empress." This was against the family rules, so rigorously applied in other cases, but Nicky excused himself to his mother: "I'm in such need of him." Nikolasha and Stana quietly married in Crimea. The Terrible was so happy, he was transformed, calling Stana "My Divine Salvation, Gift of God."

Just as the tsar recommended Rasputin to his prime minister, Alexandra's newest friend also needed the peasant's help. Anna Taneeva, twenty-one years old, twelve years younger than Alexandra, was the daughter and granddaughter of directors of the tsar's private chancellery. Appointed maid-of-honour, Anna nursed Alexandra's friend and lady-in-waiting Princess Sonia Orbeliani, who was dying of paralysis in the palace—but Anna ended up caring for the empress herself. "Sentimental and mystical" with the "mind of a child," this bovine, moon-faced girl, "tall and stout with a puffy, shiny face, and no charm whatsoever," was unintelligent but "extremely crafty." She fell for Alexandra with the blushing devotion of a schoolgirl passion, irresistible for the empress who "only entertained friendships in which she was quite sure of being the dominant partner."

Alexandra invited Anna on the Baltic cruise in 1905: "Dear Anna, God has sent me a friend in you." Keen to help her awkward protégée, Alexandra acted as her matchmaker with a sailor wounded at Tsushima, Alexander Vyrubov. Anna was an unstable combination of credulous mystic, galumphing romantic, cloddish narcissist and physical exhibitionist: when court doctor Eugene Botkin treated her sore throat, she insisted on being examined naked, while the guards complained of her undressing at the window.

Anna was unsure about marriage, so Alexandra asked Militsa to introduce her to Rasputin. Anna was dazzled. "I saw an elderly peasant" with "the most extraordinary eyes . . . capable of seeing into the very mind and soul." The marriage could be unhappy, he advised, but should go ahead.

Anna married Vyrubov but accused him of sexual degeneracy—and remained a virgin. She divorced him—but she became Rasputin's devoted follower, hailing him as a "saint who uttered Heaven-inspired words." Anna became the link between the Romanovs and Rasputin. "She plays an increasingly important role," noticed Xenia, "in everything."

The other perennial guest at Peterhof and on the cruises was the "emperor's unique friend" General Alexander Orlov* (no relation to Fat Orlov and his Catherinian clan), "a good-looking officer and a famous man-about-town of charming and elegant manners" who, noticed Mistress of the Robes Zizi Naryshkina, "pleased both Their Majesties."

Orlov behaved towards Alexandra like a *cavaliere servente*, bringing her bouquets and paying her compliments. He was her only male friend. "I'll admit the empress flirted with him a little," wrote Naryshkina, "and that such an indiscretion on the part of a woman as cold and proud as her, was bound to attract considerable attention . . ."[38]

Nicholas and Alexandra began to invite Rasputin frequently to the palace:[†] "At 2:30 Grigory came to see us and we received him with all the children." Even Romanovs needed appointments to see the tsar, but Rasputin just turned up. "After tea upstairs in the nursery," wrote the emperor on 29 March 1909, "I sat a while with Grigory who had come unexpectedly."

"It is an unspeakable joy that You, our beloved," the empress wrote to Rasputin on 7 February 1907,

> were here with us. How can we thank You enough for everything? . . .
> I wish only one thing: to fall asleep on Your shoulder . . . You are our all. Forgive me my teacher—I know I have sinned . . . I try to do better but I don't succeed . . . I love You and I believe in You . . . God grant us the joy of meeting soon. I kiss You warmly. Bless and forgive me—I am your Child.

Later in the year, Nicholas asked his sister Olga, unhappily married to the homosexual Peter of Oldenburg, if she would "like to see a real Russian peasant." In the nursery, "Rasputin led Alexei into the room and the three of us [Olga, tsar and tsarina] followed and we felt as if we were in church. He was praying and the child joined him in his prayer . . .

* Nicholas was no longer friends with Sandro, who had citicized him during the war and furiously resigned as a minister when the tsar conceded a constitution—he then panicked during the revolution, preparing to flee in his yacht. After 1905, the imperial couple became closer to the captain of the imperial yacht *Shtandart*, N. P. Sablin. The 420-feet yacht, named after Peter the Great's first ship and fitted with mahogany salons and 47mm guns, became a totally secure home away from home, its crew regarded as members of the extended family. (After 1917, it was converted to a minesweeper and took part in the defence of Leningrad during the Second World War, finally being scrapped in 1963.)

† At the same time, knowing that the name "Rasputin," which resembled the Russian for "debauchee," sounded vulgar, Nicholas ordered Marshal of Court Paul Benckendorff to arrange for his name to be changed to "Novi," signifying his new life and his role as the New One after the disappearance of Philippe.

conscious of his utter sincerity . . . All the children seemed to like him, completely at their ease with him."

On another visit, he put "an arm round my shoulders" and "started stroking my hand." Once, in Nicky and Alix's mauve boudoir, Rasputin openly cross-questioned Olga about her sex life: "Did I love my husband? Why didn't I have any children?"

The empress concentrated on "baby sweet" Alexei, who was escorted by two Cossack bodyguards at all times, while she treated her daughters—known by the collective acronym "OTMA" for Olga, Tatiana, Maria and Anastasia—as a single entity, dressing them in identical clothes or, when the older two could no longer wear youthful dresses, in pairs: the Big Two and Little Two. The girls shared rooms in twos, slept on hard beds and suffered cold baths every morning, so they grew up "without a trace of hauteur." Their only luxury was a single pearl and diamond for their birthday, and each had their own favourite Coty scent. The family, especially the girls, embraced photography, taking thousands of family shots with their Box Brownie cameras. Anastasia even pioneered the selfie, sitting on a chair before a mirror holding the camera at her waist.

As Alexandra and the girls did their knitting, "behind her chair, bringing into splendid relief her bright gold hair," recalled Anna, "stood a huge negro servant, gorgeous in scarlet trousers, gold-embroidered jacket and white turban." There were now just four Nubians of whom two were Americans. Their favourite was Jim Hercules, a Virginian ex-boxer, son of a slave, who went home on holiday every year and brought back guava jams beloved by the grand duchesses and a Native American tepee that stood in Alexei's playroom.

Meanwhile Alexandra was defiantly self-absorbed, chronicling her ever-mutating neurotic and physical illnesses—sciatica, headaches, backaches, leg aches, angina, grading the gravity of her enlarged heart from Number One (slight) to Number Three (severe).* Nicholas suffered too, telling Anna, "I would do anything, even going to prison, if she could only be well again." Alexandra spent most of her time lying on sofas and being pushed around in bathchairs. "She shut herself up in her own room refusing to see anyone, even the children," recalled Anna. They missed her. "My darling Mama," wrote Tatiana in broken English. "I hope you won't today be tied and that you can get up to dinner. I am always so awfully sorry when you are tied and can't get up. Perhaps I have lots of folts but please forgive me."

Her "girlies" revered Rasputin as a confessor and confidant. Olga told

---

* Dr. Eugene Botkin, son of Alexander II's physician, prescribed Veronal, a barbiturate, for her illnesses—for which she also took opium, cocaine and morphine. Botkin was criticized for caving in to Alix's demands and doling out ever more of these opiates.

Alexander II almost took Constantinople but he was foiled at the Congress of Berlin: in the centre, Prince Bismarck celebrates between the Austrian Count Andrássy (*left*) and Count Peter Shuvalov (formerly the tsar's chief minister), as the marquess of Salisbury (bearded, *far right*) talks to Ottoman delegates, while, on the left, the senile Prince Alexander Gorchakov sits overshadowed by the British prime minister, Benjamin Disraeli.

Romanov coronations were sacred-political rituals designed to bless and promote sacred autocracy: Alexander III, crowned after the assassination of his father, said his was "the happiest day of my life."

Alexander III, "the Colossus," at his main residence Gatchina, with Nicky, Xenia, Georgy, Olga and (*in front*) Michael and Kamchatka the dog.

Nicky's ballerina, "Little K."

The European royal family at the wedding in April 1894 of Ernie of Hesse and Ducky of Edinburgh in Coburg, where Nicky and Alix became engaged: Kaiser Wilhelm and Queen Victoria are seated; *Second row*: the newly engaged Nicholas and Alexandra stand behind them; her two sisters, Victoria and Irene; Miechen, wife of Grand Duke Vladimir; Alexander II's daughter, Maria, duchess of Edinburgh/Saxe-Coburg; Bertie, prince of Wales, looms behind Nicky. *Back row*: Grand Duke Paul (*second from left*), Grand Duke Sergei (*centre*, in a bowler hat); Missy of Romania is behind him; Ferdinand of Romania, Ella, Grand Duke Vladimir and, on the extreme right, Alfred, duke of Edinburgh/Saxe-Coburg.

The last court spectacular: the 1903 costume ball. *Above left* Nicky and Alix dressed as Tsar Alexei and Maria Miloslavskaya. *Above right* Moscow governor-general, the strange Uncle Sergei, with Ella, Alix's sister. *Left* Decadent Uncle Alexis, the general-admiral notorious for his "fast women, slow ships"; his mistress Zina *(below)*, duchess of Leutchenberg, "would have made her fortune on the screen as a vamp."

1. Winter Palace, St. Petersburg

2. The Cameron Gallery, Catherine Palace, Tsarskoe Selo

3. Alexander Palace, Tsarskoe Selo

4. The Little Palace, Livadia, Crimea (*left*)

5. The White Palace, Livadia, Crimea (*below left*)

6. The Lower Dacha, Peterhof

The massacre of Bloody Sunday (*above*) sparked the 1905 Revolution; Nicholas summoned Sergei Witte (*far left*) to negotiate peace with Japan in New Hampshire, with President Teddy Roosevelt (*centre*) and Japanese delegates. Nicholas conceded a constitution: opening the Duma at the ceremony in the Winter Palace (*below*)— grandees to the left, socialists to the right.

The only photograph of Rasputin with Alexandra and the children—Olga, Tatiana, Maria, Anastasia and Alexei—with their nurse Maria Vishnyakova. The girls were still wearing his amulets when they were murdered.

Rasputin's sexuality was feral—here he is with female adepts including Anna Vyrubova (*standing, third from left*), the empress's best friend and her link with Rasputin.

*Above* Nicky and the girls escort Alexandra, with Alexei on a tricycle. His haemophilia meant he could not play like other children, while Alexandra was constantly ill. She and Alexei out in their wheelchairs (*below*); Nicholas, the diligent autocrat, reads his "bothersome papers" at Alexander Palace.

*Above* At a family picnic in Crimea, a strange triangle— Alexandra watches Nicholas next to Anna Vyrubova, who played footsie with him under the table.

*Above left and left* Nicholas hiking in Crimea with key courtiers in 1908, including his best friend General ("Thin") Orlov (*centre*), the only man to flirt with Alexandra, and Prince Vladimir ("Fat") Orlov (*second from right*), who later plotted against Rasputin. With his daughters in 1914, (*from left*) Tatiana, Anastasia and Olga.

Rasputin about her first love for a young officer: "It's hard without you. I've no one to turn to about my worries . . . Here's my torment. Nikolai is driving me crazy . . . I love him . . . I want to fling myself at him." But Rasputin advised, "Be cautious." Tatiana longed to see him again: "When will you come? Without you it's so boring!"

"My little Pearl . . . I miss your simple soul," Rasputin wrote to Maria. "We will see each other soon. Big Kiss." Alexandra lectured the eldest, Olga: "Remember above all to be always a good example to the little ones, only then our Friend will be contented with you."

Nicholas appreciated Rasputin because he soothed Alexandra. "Better one Rasputin," he said, "than ten fits of hysterics every day." But it was more than that. When Nicky set off on a trip, "Grigory watches over this journey," Alix wrote to him, "and all will be well." In his quieter, less demonstrative way, Nicholas soon found Rasputin indispensable as a sort of priest-psychiatrist. "I have only survived because of his prayers," he later said.

As Rasputin's arrivals were recorded by security, Anna arranged for the emperor and empress to meet him at her bungalow, writing to the commandant of the palaces: "The elder arrived at 2 and Their Majesties wish to see him today. They think it would be better at my house." Anna's cottage, which still stands today outside the gates of Tsarskoe Selo, became what one minister would later call the "the portico of power." As Nicky recorded in his diary: "We dropped in on Anya and saw Grigory and talked with him for a long time."

In this period before his notoriety, Rasputin was a regular presence in Nicky's record of his genteel existence. There were strolls, tennis, dominoes and billiards with his children; teas with Rasputin and meetings with the prime minister: "Received Stolypin. We dined together on the balcony."[39]

"I can't tell you," Nicky told his mother on 11 October 1906, "how much I've come to like and respect Stolypin." On 20 February 1907, when the second Duma assembled, it was much more radical than the first, containing 118 socialists, in the wake of the decision by Lenin and Martov to allow their parties to participate. Stolypin and Nicholas immediately started to consider its dissolution, "but it's too early for that," the tsar told his mother; "one must let them do something manifestly stupid . . . Then slap! And they are gone!" The radicals demanded the confiscation of land, a measure which neither tsar nor premier would consider. On 6 March, Stolypin defied them in a virtuoso performance. "Such attacks aimed at paralysing the government amount to two words addressed to the authorities—'Hands Up!'" he proclaimed. "To these two words, gentlemen, the government must respond with only two words: 'Not Afraid!'" Even Nicholas was impressed.

Once they had decided to dissolve the Duma, Stolypin planned a political *coup d'état* to change the electoral law. "I waited all day long with impatience for notification from you," Nicholas wrote to Stolypin. "Things are being dragged out. The Duma must be dissolved tomorrow. No delay. Not one moment of hesitation."

On 1 June, Stolypin told the Duma to expel its extremists. When the Duma refused, he went into action. On the 3rd, police surrounded the Taurida Palace, arresting many of the Bolsheviks and Mensheviks. Holding new elections, Stolypin narrowed the suffrage (excluding non-Russians) to elect a third Duma dominated by noblemen and businessmen in which the Party of 17 October known as "Octobrists," who supported the semi-constitutional autocracy, held a majority. Yet the old convergence between Romanovs and the nobility was long since ruptured: the third Duma lasted for five years, but much of its opposition now came from the gentry. Even this "king's parliament" defied Stolypin.[40]

"Sometimes Stolypin is so high handed I get annoyed," Nicky admitted, "but it doesn't last and he is the best prime minister I've had."

The revolutionary parties were broken. While there had been 150,000 Social-Democrats in 1907, there would soon be fewer than 10,000. Many Bolsheviks quietly retired into normal life and got jobs or went into exile to fulminate and feud, like Lenin in Switzerland and Austria.* The right-wing Unionists also withered. The tsar admired his prime minister, but there were real differences between this Muscovite autocrat and this conservative modernizer. As Stolypin simultaneously cultivated nationalist right-wingers, secretly funding Unionist newspapers, he was preparing for much more liberal reforms that challenged Nicholas's deepest convictions and he started with Nicholas's fetish—the Jews.

"Isn't it abnormal to arouse and embitter a race of 5 million people?" asked Stolypin. "Clearly this is wrong." He even reflected that "the Jews

---

* Their increasingly desperate gangsterism was now hugely unpopular. When the Social-Democrats met in London in early May, the Mensheviks banned "expropriations" (bank robberies). But at the same meeting Lenin, who despised Menshevik scruples, ordered Stalin to keep robbing banks to fund the Party. The "expros" revealed unbridgeable differences between the two factions, which now became different parties. This brigandage reached its climax in Tiflis on 26 June 1907 when Bolshevik brigands, organized by Stalin, held up the State Bank stagecoach and stole 250,000 roubles, worth many millions today, killing fifty passers-by in the bomb-tossing mayhem. Afterwards, despised in his native Georgia, Stalin moved to Baku. But he was soon betrayed by double-agents, arrested and despatched into Siberian exile, where he would spend most of his time until 1917.

throw bombs" but "if I lived under such conditions, perhaps I too would throw bombs." He wanted to lift all their restrictions, but in October 1906 he proposed a "modest" improvement in Jewish rights. The appalled tsar did not answer for two months but thought about the Jewish question "night and day." Finally, on 10 December, he told Stolypin that "An inner voice keeps insisting more and more that I don't take this decision. So far my conscience has not deceived me. I intend to follow its dictates." He then explicitly declared his view of the tsar's mystical link to God: "The heart of the tsar is in God's hands. So be it."

Nicholas instinctively wished Russia to be an international power again, a role so linked to Romanov legitimacy. Both he and Stolypin agreed that Germany and Austria were the main threats, that Russia must show sympathy for the Slavs and press on to win control of the Straits. Yet Stolypin insisted, "We need peace. War in the course of the next few years would be fatal for Russia and the dynasty." Anything but a "strictly defensive policy" would be "insane." But the emperor now pursued the traditional ambition of the Romanovs in a gambit that almost led to European war.

After the Japanese peace, Nicky's new, liberal foreign minister, Alexander Izvolsky, advised a Western orientation against Germany. Izvolsky, suggested by Minny, was "obviously a vain man and he strutted on little lacquered feet," wrote Harold Nicolson, son of the British ambassador to Russia. "His clothes from Savile Row were moulded tightly upon a plump frame. He wore a pearl pin, an eye glass, white spats, a white slip to his waistcoat, his face pasty and fattening, with loose surly lips . . . and he left behind a slight scent of *violette de parme*." The British increasingly feared Germany. The foreign secretary Sir Edward Grey kept probing Russia. But the tsar remained frosty. Edward VII wrote warmly to his nephew and jovially entertained the Russian ambassador. Izvolsky argued for it. Nicky overcame the bitterness of fifty years of enmity: it made strategic sense. In August 1907, Izvolsky agreed the treaty that settled the conflicts—Persia, Afghanistan, Tibet—between the empires.* Since Russia was allied to France, which was enjoying

---

* In May 1908, Edward VII and Queen Alexandra were met at Reval by Nicholas, the family and Stolypin, on the *Shtandart*. Bertie regarded Nicky as "deplorably unsophisticated, immature and reactionary"; Nicky thought Bertie "the most dangerous intriguer." But now Bertie charmed Nicky and delighted Russian sailors by greeting them "good morning, children" in Russian. Nonetheless, prompted by his Jewish friends the Rothschilds, Bertie asked Stolypin to improve Jewish rights—and teased Alix that her children spoke English with Scottish accents. At the tsar's dinner, a British courtier found Alix weeping hysterically on deck. A year later, Nicky, the family and Stolypin sailed to the Isle of Wight for the regatta, where Olga and Tatiana were allowed the treat of a heavily guarded shopping trip to Cowes, their first public outing since the Revolution.

its Entente Cordiale with Britain, Izvolsky joined a bloc to rival that of Germany, Austria and Italy.[41]

On 16 September 1908, Izvolsky met the Austrian foreign minister Baron Alois von Aehrenthal at a Moravian castle to discuss a Balkan deal that would satisfy the dyspeptic appetites of both ailing empires and revise the 1878 Treaty of Berlin. Russia wanted the Straits opened to Russian warships and the possibility of special influence over Constantinople. Ever since 1878, Austria had "administered" the Ottoman province of Bosnia, which was populated mainly by Serbs. Aehrenthal wished to revitalize Austria by annexing Bosnia, thereby overawing Serbia, which aspired to rule not just Bosnia but all the Southern Slavs.

Nicholas had given his permission for this arrangement and, when Aehrenthal agreed, the tsar was "extraordinarily pleased." This deal creating Balkan spheres of influence could conceivably have prevented 1914, but when it went wrong, no event, until the assassination of Franz Ferdinand, did more to accelerate the world war. While Izvolsky was still winning support in foreign capitals, Aehrenthal double-crossed Russia and simply announced Bosnia's annexation. Serbia objected; the Austrian chief of staff pushed for war; Germany was ready to support Vienna.

When the news broke, the Duma, the press and Slavophile opinion attacked Izvolsky's cynical betrayal of Russia's Slavic brothers and threatened war against Austria. An enraged Stolypin assailed Izvolsky for risking European war. The tsar, who had approved this transaction, listened with "frigid reserve" and typically pretended to know much less than he did, but he agreed the deal was dead. Izvolsky called Aehrenthal (who was said to have Jewish origins) "that dirty Jew." Aehrenthal called him "a black-hearted ape." Serbia was keen to fight,* but the tsar warned that "The Balkans aren't worth the world to fight about."

Yet Austria and Russia prepared for war. On 1 March 1909, Germany presented Russia with an ultimatum: accept the annexation or Germany would intervene to back Austria. Europe was on the verge of conflict. At 6 p.m. on 6 March at Tsarskoe Selo, the emperor consulted his ministers, but the war minister, Rediger, baldly warned that "Russia lacks soldiers, artillery and fortresses! It is therefore wholly impossible to fight" Austria, let alone Germany. Besides Russia's ally France was not yet ready to be drawn into a Balkan quarrel. The tsar backed

---

* Foxy Ferdinand exploited the crisis to declare himself "Tsar of Bulgaria." Minny thought this breathtakingly impertinent and Nicholas called it "the act of a megalomaniac." But he had to recognize Foxy's title. Prince Nikola of Montenegro demanded the tsar's approval to attack Austria, backed by his daughter Stana and Nikolasha.

down bitterly. "The role Germany has played in the crisis is odious and disgusting," he told his mother.* "The form and method of Germany's action—I mean towards us—has simply been brutal and we won't forget it." Next time, Russia would be ready to fight. After this fiasco, it would have to.[42]

The emperor and his critics in the Duma were united in one thing at least—their determination to rearm Russia. The army was damaged after 1905, the navy depleted. Nicholas appointed a State Defence Council under Nikolasha to work out a military strategy but the giant cousin failed to agree such a policy and the tsar initially ordered a new fleet. The head of the Duma's defence committee, the irrepressibly unscrupulous Alexander Guchkov, an industrialist and avid duellist who had fought for the Boers against the British, proposed that the military should be run with parliamentary (that is, Guchkov's) supervision—instead of remaining the responsibility of the tsar. Stolypin backed the bill, but this touched on the emperor's control of the military. Nicholas vetoed it. Stolypin resigned. The tsar rejected it.

"That is my will," Nicholas wrote to Stolypin in the authentic voice of a reinvigorated autocrat:

> Remember that we live in Russia and not abroad, so I will not allow any thought of retirement. Of course Petersburg and Moscow will chatter but hysterical screams will soon subside. I order you to work out with war and naval ministers the necessary changes to military naval laws . . . I warn you I categorically reject a request for dismissal for you or anyone else.

Nicholas got his way. He promoted Stolypin to court steward and state secretary, but he appointed his own man, Vladimir Sukhomlinov, ex-chief of staff, as war minister to act as his military co-ordinator. Small, dapper, devious and frivolous, Sukhomlinov was an adept courtier but his Achilles heel was his sexy, pretentious wife, thirty-two years younger, who loved money and jewels. Soon loathed by the Duma on one hand and by Nikolasha on the other, he was bumptious and corrupt but more competent than he seemed. Sukhomlinov, backed by the tsar, launched a huge rearmament campaign, starting with the Little Programme straight after the Bosnian Crisis, followed by a "reorganization" in 1910 and then expanding into the Great Programme of 1913, all funded by an economy that, aided by good harvests and years of foreign investment

---

* That October, the tsar lost "his unique friend" Alexander Orlov, who died in Cairo of TB. Nicholas built him a large mausoleum where Alix often laid flowers.

and railway construction, was booming: government revenue almost doubled between 1900 and 1913–14.*

Nikolasha and the Crows now turned against Rasputin whom they saw as impertinent, ungrateful and, worse, out of their control. When the Crows confronted the *starets*, he ranted so arrogantly about "the importance of his mission" that Militsa accused him of heresy. Alexandra despised Nikolasha because he had "turned against a man of God." For his part Nikolasha regretted ever meeting the peasant: "Imagine my horror, Rasputin got to the tsar through my house."

If the tsar got his way about the military, Stolypin now dominated foreign policy, appointing his brother-in-law Sergei Sazonov as the new minister. "For the success of the Russian Revolution," Stolypin said, "war is essential. Without war, the revolutionists can do nothing."

In late 1910,† Stolypin proposed to extend the elected *zemstvo* assemblies to the Polish provinces, but conservatives in the State Council defeated the bill. Stolypin denounced them to Nicholas as "shady, smooth-tongued, mendacious reactionaries."

On 5 March 1911, weary after six years of struggle and sensing the tsar's duplicity, Stolypin again resigned. "Think of some other way out and let me hear," ordered Nicholas, but there were fundamental as well as personal differences: Nicholas believed that Stolypin's attempts to compromise with parliament were weakening the bulwarks that protected Russia from revolution. Stolypin wanted to create a new foundation for the monarchy among the lower orders, using land reforms to strengthen the peasantry and workers' welfare to win over the proletariat and concessions to win over Poles and other nationalities, but the tsar and his camarilla undermined him at every turn. He could

---

* He tried to raze many of the obsolete fortresses, to modernize artillery, to create reserves to call upon in war and update the mobilization schedules. His promotion to war minister marked the downgrading of the post of chief of staff and it was now in his interest that the holders of this post were mediocrities unable to challenge him. Yet no one trusted him. "There is something about General Sukhomlinov that makes me uneasy," Maurice Paléologue, the French ambassador, later reflected. "I know few men who inspire more distrust at first sight." He was certainly no visionary. When Sandro suggested an air force, he replied amid paroxysms of laughter: "Blériot playthings in our army?"

† On 31 October that year, Tolstoy, widely seen as Russia's other tsar, abruptly left his estate to escape his wife Sonia but fell ill on the train and had to dismount at a remote station. The world watched the ensuing drama of the dying sage. Tolstoy had long been a dangerous enemy of tsarism. In 1901, Pobedonostsev had organized his excommunication from the Church while the tsar received rude letters from the novelist (delivered by his cousin Bimbo who typically had befriended Tolstoy) telling him: "don't believe" any popular enthusiasm "is an expression of devotion for you . . . just a crowd of people who will go after any unusual spectacle." When he finally died on 7 November, it was "an event discussed a great deal too much in my opinion," Nicky told Minny, "but fortunately he was buried quietly" at his estate Yasnaya Polyana, which Stolypin shrewdly proposed to buy for the nation. Nicholas vetoed the idea.

not forgive his brilliance or insolence: "Do you suppose I liked always reading in the papers that 'The chairman of the council of ministers had done this, the chairman has done that?' " he exploded later in a rare revelation of the bitterness behind the genteel English phlegm. "Don't I count? Am I nobody?"

Stolypin named his price for staying. The tsar must send his opponents away from Petersburg, prorogue the Duma and force the bill through by decree. Mama intervened. She summoned Nicky, who wept with frustration as Stolypin passed him in the corridor outside her drawing room. "I have informed my son that you alone possess the strength and ability to save Russia," she told him. Stolypin received a sixteen-page letter from the tsar: "I don't wish to permit your departure . . ." Resenting the ultimatum but keen "to retain you at all costs," the tsar bent before Stolypin. But Stolypin's rule by decree was a mistake.

Rasputin was no longer a secret. Stolypin learned from courtiers about his frequent meetings with the monarchs, while Alexandra allowed the peasant to suggest the new ober-procurator of the Holy Synod. Guchkov, now Duma president, attacked "irresponsible influences" at court, earning Alix's undying hatred.[43]

The prime minister and tsar had more serious political differences, and Rasputin was a problem merely of the imperial household. Yet Stolypin, as an avid monarchist, regarded it as his duty to warn the tsar about the Siberian's debauchery and sectarian links. He had him followed by the Okhrana. When he presented reports of Rasputin's orgies with prostitutes in bathhouses, Nicholas answered, "I know and he preaches the Holy Scriptures there," finally telling the prime minister: "Everything you say may be true about Rasputin. In any event I can do nothing about it." The tsar suggested that the two men meet.

"Rasputin ran his pale eyes over me," Stolypin recalled. "He mumbled mysterious and inarticulate words from the Scriptures and made strange movements with his hands." The prime minister sensed "the great power of hypnosis which produced a strong impression," but, collecting himself, he threatened "this vermin" with prosecution as a sectarian unless Rasputin left the capital. Rasputin stormed out. Stolypin banned him from Petersburg for five years, challenging the tsar, who promised that he would not see Rasputin again, a promise he soon broke. Rasputin retreated to his new house in Pokrovskoe.

The empress defended "Our Friend." "Gradually," noticed Zizi Naryshkina, "everyone was judged by them according to their attitude to Rasputin. Whoever praised him was 'good'; whoever objected to him was 'bad' "—even if it was the prime minister, who Alexandra now regarded as an enemy. "He has fulfilled his role," she later said spookily, and would "retire into the background since he had nothing more to accomplish."

The battle for Rasputin was fought in the boudoirs and nurseries of the Alexander Palace. First Rasputin raped one of his earlier followers. Alexandra despatched her dim friend Anna Vyrubova and two ladies to Siberia to investigate. Naturally they found nothing untoward, but on the train, Rasputin just could not resist a captive audience: he climbed into the bunk with the maid and fondled her until she screamed.

When the Crows reported all this, Alexandra told them never to mention Rasputin again, and they realized they had been replaced in the empress's affections by Anna. They became her sworn enemies, a deepening rupture. "The family had been an undivided block with the emperor as pivot," noticed Missy, but it was "a great mistake to allow the family feeling to fall to pieces . . . Too self-centred, too exclusively interested in their own children, Nicky and Alix neglected their imperial relations, undermining their loyalty."

"You have mentioned your desire to make a pilgrimage to the Holy Land," said Nicholas to Rasputin. "This would be a good time for it." He would pay for the trip which "you've earned through your many services to the Crown." Rasputin spent Easter in Jerusalem but, on his return, was restored to favour.

"After dinner," Nicky wrote, "we had the joy of seeing Grigory after his return from Jerusalem and Athens." Alexandra had already commissioned a book, *Russian Saints Who were Holy Fools in Christ*, to explain his traditional role. But his absence had not calmed his enemies: his former supporters in the Church, Bishop Hermogen and the epileptic fool Mitka Kolyaba, lured him to a meeting and, shrieking, grabbed his penis and squeezed until he confirmed his sins. Rasputin rushed to Nicholas the next day and had Hermogen sacked and exiled.[44]

Stolypin returned from his holidays with radical—but almost fantastical—plans to create new ministries of nationality to restore the loyalty of the minorities, to remove "all restrictions on Jews" and to establish a social security system to develop health cover for workers. He would visit Washington to build an American alliance.

Needless to say, these measures would be anathema to emperor, court and police. To diminish Stolypin, Nicholas planned to take the Interior Ministry (more powerful in this strange system than the premiership because it controlled security) away from the prime minister. Amazingly the tsar asked Rasputin to travel out to Nizhny Novgorod to "gaze into the soul" of its "repulsively fat" young governor Alexei Khvostov, who might make a good interior minister. Not understanding that this peasant was the secret envoy of Nicholas II, he dismissed Rasputin, who nonetheless left with the feeling that this was a creature he could use.

At the end of August 1911, the tsar and family travelled to Kiev to unveil a statue of Alexander II. Stolypin was already there—and the tsar had invited Rasputin too. At the unveiling of the statue, Rasputin, watching the tsar and prime minister from one side, pointed at Stolypin's carriage: "Death is riding with him!"

Stolypin looked ill and gloomy. He feared either assassination (not unreasonably, since there were said to have been seventeen attempts) or death from heart attack.

He was right to worry. As the local Okhrana chief, Colonel N. N. Kuliabko, checked on any threats, one of his double-agents, a young revolutionary named Dmitri Bogrov, warned of a terrorist plot to assassinate Stolypin at the upcoming opera at Kiev's Municipal Theatre. Interviewed by Kuliabko and the tsar's chief bodyguard Spiridovich, Bogrov offered to identify "the assassin," who was staying in his apartment, if they would give him a ticket to the event. The man in charge, General Pavel Kurlov, deputy interior minister, approved this idiotic scheme.

On 1 September, the tsar and the two older grand duchesses, Olga and Tatiana, accompanied by Foxy Ferdinand's son, Crown Prince Boris of Bulgaria, a possible suitor for the girls, arrived in the imperial box for Rimsky-Korsakov's *Tale of Tsar Saltan*. The boxes were filled with Polish aristocracy in their finery, while Stolypin, wearing a white summer court uniform with gold shoulder boards, joined other ministers a few yards away in the first rows of the stalls. The policemen Kurlov, Kuliabko and Spiridovich looked for their frockcoated double-agent Bogrov, to whom they had given tickets. Kuliabko found him in the first intermission. Bogrov promised that "the assassin" had not yet left his apartment. In the second intermission, a nervous Kuliabko ordered Bogrov to go home and watch his dangerous guest. Instead Bogrov headed down towards the pit where Stolypin was chatting to Frederiks.

Nicholas, Olga and Tatiana left their box to get some tea in the foyer just as, down in the pit, the young man approached the prime minister. Stolypin "looked curiously at him as if to ask what he wanted," only for Bogrov to draw a pistol and fire two shots, one hitting his target's raised hand and the other hitting the Vladimir Cross on his chest and then penetrating his body to strike his liver. "The orchestra was playing an intermezzo," recalled Zizi Naryshkina, sitting in the imperial box next to the tsar, "when suddenly there was a metallic sound." Nicholas heard the two pops and, thinking "a pair of binoculars must have fallen on somebody's head from above," brushed aside his girls' attempt to stop him and rushed back into his box: "right there opposite me stood Stolypin," he wrote. As women screamed, "I saw a group of officers dragging someone away." Stolypin "turned slowly to face me and made the sign of the cross with his left hand. It was only then that I noticed he was very pale and had blood on the right arm of his jacket." The blood was bright on his white tunic. Stolypin touched his chest, realizing he had been hit. Then, looking at the tsar and speaking to Frederiks, he said: "Your Majesty, happy to die for the tsar." Frederiks rushed to the edge of the box to tell Nicholas, who replied: "I hope there's no reason to talk of death."

"I fear there is," said Frederiks. "The emperor was pale as death," recorded Naryshkina. "Tatiana was weeping." Members of the audience were punching the assassin as Stolypin, attended by Dr. Botkin, sank into a seat, unbuttoning his jacket. He was able to walk out of the theatre to the ambulance that rushed him to hospital, followed by the assassin who was only just rescued by the police from being lynched. Still accompanied by the two shocked girls, "who saw everything," the tsar remained in his box, "obviously distressed but showing no fear." The cast came on stage and, falling to their knees, weeping, sang the national anthem. "I left at eleven," Nicky told his mother. "You can imagine with what emotions." Back in the palace, Nicky told Alix what had happened. Accompanied by their governess Sophia Tyutcheva, who did not sleep all night, Olga "put on a brave face" while Tatiana was "very tearful." Rasputin arrived to pray with them.

"Poor Stolypin suffered a lot that night," wrote Nicholas, "and had to be given morphine." On 3 September, at the Makovski Hospital, Stolypin's wife found him chatty, but the bullet lay beside his liver. When the tsar visited, she did not allow him to talk to her husband for fear of agitating him. Sepsis set in. On the 5th, Stolypin said, "Turn out the light" and died. Next morning, Nicholas II prayed at his deathbed, repeating "Forgive me!"

The tsar immediately appointed the cautious, dapper little finance minister Vladimir Kokovtsov, whose verbosity had earned him the nickname "the Gramophone," to replace Stolypin. When it emerged that Bogrov was Jewish, Kiev's Black Hundreds called for a pogrom. Nicholas declared that he "would not allow a pogrom against the Jews on any pretext." The new prime minister rushed troops to Kiev. The emperor knew that the city was already seething with anti-semitic malice for another reason.[45]

While he was in Kiev, the city's prosecutor briefed Nicholas on a new case of the "blood libel." On 20 March 1911, the body of a boy named

Andrei Yushchinsky had been discovered in a cave outside Kiev. The Black Hundreds claimed that the body had been drained of blood by Jewish ritualists. While the boy had almost certainly been murdered on the orders of a vicious female gangster, the authorities, both to promote counter-revolutionary nationalism and to prevent anti-semitic disorders, arrested and framed an innocent Jewish brickmaker named Mendel Beilis. Even though the evidence was non-existent and the ritual itself was a myth, the justice minister, Ivan Shcheglovitov, briefed the tsar and appointed the top Kiev prosecutor to prosecute Beilis.

Now the prosecutor Grigory Chaplinsky reported to the emperor, "Your Majesty, I am happy to report that the true culprit in the murder of Yushchinsky has been found. The Yid Beilis." Nicholas should have stopped the case. Instead he crossed himself and approved.

The tsar had lost Russia's outstanding statesman due to the careless- ness and negligence, if not deliberate conspiracy, of his police. Within two days, the newspapers learned that Bogrov was a police agent: had the Okhrana, inspired by the court camarilla, arranged Stolypin's assassination? The tsar appointed a commission to investigate the dis- astrous police bungling which soon found that Kurlov and Kuliabko had been "crassly incompetent." Bogrov was hanged, but Nicky refused to try the policemen. He cut Spiridovich dead for a while but soon forgave him.

Stolypin had tried every combination to solve the riddle of how to build a conservative coalition of mass support for the autocracy while he modernized Russia, but all had failed. In the zany incoherence of Rus- sian politics, where he had to deal with bewhiskered ultra-reactionaries on one hand and steely Marxists on the other, Stolypin made enemies in all camps while losing friends with each bold innovation. A man of his time and class, Stolypin remained at the mercy of the monarch who had appointed him. Once again, the obstacle to saving the autocracy was the autocracy itself.

Nicholas's fatalism allowed him to function under unbearable pressure, but his casual callousness here is striking. Four days later, he recounted to "dear sweet Mama, the most varied impressions, both joyful and sad." After telling the story of "poor Stolypin," he spoke of the "splendid" army parade, the "glorious warm day," the "great pleasure" he'd felt in boarding the yacht again and the "truly brilliant sight" of the navy, adding, "I'm having a good rest here and sleeping a lot," while "Alix too is tired—she had a great deal to do at Kiev."

Stolypin had abdicated the right to live: "those who have offended God in the person of Our Friend," she told Grand Duke Dmitri, "may no longer count on divine protection." When a lady-in-waiting questioned their reception by marching-band at Sebastopol so soon after Stolypin's murder, Alexandra snapped, "He was only a minister, but this is the Russian emperor."

As the family settled into their new White Palace at Livadia,* the tsar and tsarina welcomed the new prime minister. After lunch, Alexandra summoned Kokovtsov for an eerie sermon from her wheelchair. When he praised Stolypin, she replied, "You seem to do too much honour to his memory . . . Believe me, one must not feel sorry for those who are no more . . . When one dies that means his role is ended and he was bound to go since his destiny was fulfilled." Warning him not to "look for support in political parties; they are of so little consequence in Russia," she concluded that "Stolypin died to make room for you and this is all for the good of Russia."⁴⁶

On 3 November, the emperor threw a ball for Olga's sixteenth birthday. The debutante wearing her hair up and a long white tulle dress with a lace bodice and sash, danced happily, surrounded by officers of the *Shtandart* and watched by the empress who did not yet know that her secret letters to Rasputin were circulating around Petersburg.⁴⁷

Rasputin had been saved by the providential ascension of Stolypin, but he knew that this scandal could destroy him. The semi-free newspapers were seething with revelations about him. "I shall never let the press free," the tsar once boasted. "The press shall write only what I want." But 1905 had changed all that, though, since the censors did not allow the press to name the peasant, they used the euphemism "Dark Forces." While the tsar encouraged his ministers to censor the papers, the dowager empress was appealing to the politicians for help against her own son. On 12 February 1912, Minny summoned Kokovtsov and, speaking with outrageous disloyalty, tearfully denounced Alexandra: "My poor daughter-in-law doesn't perceive that she is ruining both the dynasty and herself. She seriously believes in the holiness of an adventurer. We are powerless." On the very same day, Alexandra ordered Our Friend to test Kokovtsov's loyalty.

"I'm planning to leave for good," Rasputin wrote to him, "and would like to see you to exchange thoughts. Say when." Entering his office, Rasputin sat and silently fixed Kokovtsov with his deep-set grey eyes

---

* This had replaced Alexander II's wooden palaces and continued to be the scene of the annual visits of the exotic emirs of Bukhara and khans of Khiva, who brought the children generous presents. In early 1945, this was the scene of the Crimean conference of Stalin, Churchill and Roosevelt. FDR stayed in the palace itself, sleeping in the empress's boudoir; Churchill at the Vorontsov Palace; Stalin at the Yusupov Palace.

"and didn't take them off me for a long time as if he imagined he was casting some sort of hypnotic spell."

"So should I leave? They're telling tales about me."

"Yes, your place isn't here and you threaten the Sovereign."

"It's all lies. I don't insist on going to the Palace. They summon me . . . All right I shall go!" Kokovtsov had failed the test.

When the newly elected fourth Duma convened, its rotund president, Mikhail Rodzianko, a devoted monarchist, was determined to confront the tsar about Rasputin. Minny summoned him. "Don't do it," she said. "The emperor won't believe you. He's so pure in heart, he doesn't believe in evil."

"Your Majesty," replied Rodzianko, "it's a question of the dynasty."

"God bless you." Nicky's mother hurried after him. "But don't hurt him too much."

At his audience with the chain-smoking tsar, Rodzianko challenged him about "the *starets* Rasputin and the inadmissible fact of his presence at Your Majesty's court."

"Speak," said the tsar with "bowed head and averted gaze."

"The whole government from ministers to inferior ranks of the secret police is mobilized for the purpose of shielding this adventurer." The tsar gave him permission to investigate allegations against Rasputin and even presented him to the tsarevich Alexei. "I introduced myself as the fattest and biggest man in Russia," recalled Rodzianko. Alexei laughed. When Rodzianko returned with his damning report, Nicholas refused to expel Rasputin from Petersburg. He nicknamed Rodzianko "Fatso."

Alexandra's friend Princess Zinaida Yusupova, sole heiress to Russia's greatest fortune, tried to persuade her that the parliamentarian Rodzianko was a patriot, but the empress ranted at her: "Hanging is too good for men like Rodzianko." So finally Minny decided to speak out. "We had a conversation about Grigory," wrote Nicky on 15 February 1912. Alix defended Rasputin—"an exceptional man"—and denounced society as "dirty-minded gossips" and the ministers as "all cowards."

Rasputin's mischief—and the intrigues against him—now reached not just the court but the nursery: the governess Sophia Tyutcheva thought that Rasputin's visits to the girls were no longer appropriate when Olga and Tatiana were teenagers. Her views reached the newspapers. "What's going on in the nursery?" the emperor asked her. "So you don't believe in the sanctity of Grigory? And what if I told you that all these difficult years I have survived only because of his prayers?"

Tyutcheva was dismissed. Rasputin "is hated because we love him," Alexandra told Anna, adding to Dr. Botkin that "Saints are always calumniated."

Back in 1909, Rasputin had shown the empress's letters—in which she declared her devotion to the Siberian—to the demented priest Iliodor, who stole them and now gave them to a Duma member who publicized them. The new interior minister Alexander Makarov confiscated the letters and returned them to the tsar, who "turned pale, nervously took the letters from the envelope" and put them in his desk drawer. Makarov was soon dismissed. Rasputin was meant to ease the stress of ruling. Now he was magnifying it. Family was meant to be Nicholas's sanctuary from public duty. Instead it had become his torment. This time, even Alexandra turned against Rasputin. He was out.[48]

In September 1912, Nicholas and the family moved to Spała, his Polish hunting estate. Jumping into a boat, Alexei, now eight, struck his groin which swelled up. Then on 2 October, after a bumpy carriage ride through the Spała woods, Alexei, fever raging, haemorrhaging in his upper thigh and abdomen, collapsed. His screams echoed round the hunting lodge for eleven days as he prayed, "O Lord have mercy on me!," begging Alexandra, "Mama, help me!" Sometimes he felt he was dying: "When I'm dead build me a little monument of stones in the wood." Once, on seeing his pain, poor Nicky "rushed weeping bitterly to his study." The emperor "took turns with Alix to sit with Alexei"—their secret agony heartbreaking. "The poor little mite," Nicky told Minny, "suffered terribly, pains gripped him in spasms, he was delirious." On 6 October, his fever rose as he haemorrhaged into his stomach. The doctors persuaded the emperor to issue medical bulletins—without mentioning haemophilia. "When I'm dead," Alexei asked Alexandra, "it won't hurt any more will it?" On the 8th, as Nicky and Alix watched, Alexei received the last rites. The boy was dying.

Alexandra appealed to Rasputin, at home in Siberia. The next morning, 9 October, she appeared smiling. "I am not the least bit anxious myself," she said. "During the night I received a telegram from Father Grigory."

"God has seen your tears and prayers," he wrote. "The little one will not die." Alexei's fever abated. Within two days the bleeding had stopped and the swelling receded. Whether this was a miracle, the result of relaxing the mother, or the attack had already reached its climax, Rasputin was indispensable.[49]

Meanwhile Europe was on the verge of war. Keen to prepare for conflict in case it came, the emperor and Duma were raining money on the armed forces—the so-called Great Programme. Sukhomlinov was modernizing fast, building strategic new railways which meant that by 1917

Russia would be able to mobilize 100 divisions in eighteen days, just three days behind Germany. By 1914, Russia was spending more on its army than the Germans and almost as much on its navy. The German generals, watching the creation of this Russian super-army, now believed that it would be better to fight soon rather than wait for the Russians to be ready. Yet enjoying generous budgets was one thing; overcoming backwardness of training, thinking and technology was quite another. Indeed there was so much money that Sukhomlinov could not spend it all. At Livadia, the prime minister warned his sovereign, "Your army is in terrible condition," blaming Sukhomlinov.

"You're quite right," replied the tsar, "the money won't be used and our armaments won't improve."

Alexandra cut Kokovtsov dead and the court minister approached him. "The tsar," Frederiks explained, "asked me to express his displeasure at your remarks about the War Minister." As spasms of European sabre-rattling, intensified by Balkan rivalries and Ottoman decline, became more frequent, the emperor could hardly resist re-armament: "You're always right," he told the premier, "but I cannot refuse military appropriations. Heaven forbid we shan't put out the Balkan fire."[50]

The new Balkan states were bound to appeal to both Russia and Austria, but the schism after 1908 made it even easier for them to play off the two anxious, weakened empires. Both powers rightly feared war and hoped to preserve the status quo, yet both believed war was ultimately essential in the struggle for survival of the fittest. Russia remained highly suspicious of Austrian ambitions and cultivated the Slav states to prevent any more advances. This time, the spark came from Italy, a new kingdom left behind in the imperial race and keen to catch up. In October 1909, Nicholas and Izvolsky had visited Italy and agreed that, in return for future support in opening the Straits, the Italians could seize the Ottoman provinces of today's Libya in North Africa. In 1911, the Italians attacked Libya, threatening European stability and bringing the Balkans to simmering point. When the sultan temporarily closed the Straits, Russian exports were choked and Nicholas's ministers panicked, recommending the seizure of the Straits before it was too late.

The Italian conquest of Libya was the starter-pistol for war, escalating the carve-up of Ottoman Europe. The belligerent Balkan Slavs, armed with new weapons and frenzied nationalism, planned to redeem long-lost lands in an attack on the vulnerable Ottomans. The tsar and foreign minister Sazonov encouraged their appetites and co-ordinated their creation of a Balkan League around Serbia, Bulgaria, Greece and

Montenegro, hoping to control this bloc and use it as a barrier against Austro-German expansion southwards.*

Small, immaculate and slant-eyed, Sazonov was a decent Muscovite nobleman, compared by a subordinate to "the type of womanly Slav, easy and generous but soft and vague, constantly changing, resisting all sustained efforts at thinking to the logical end." A moderate Slavophile committed to the Anglo-French alliance and ultimately to the project of winning the Straits, he combined naive idealism with an emotional instability that made him unsuited to dealing with the irredentist firebrands of the Balkans. He hoped to guide the Balkan League, using his Russian veto, and, if war came, to mediate. A more sensible man might have worked to restrain the Slavs and make a deal with unstable Austria, but Sazonov was excitable and inconsistent. Foreigners soon called him "the Wobbler." Alexandra later dubbed him "Wet Chicken" or just "Pancake."

On 8 October 1912, King Nikola of Montenegro declared war. As 1.2 million soldiers on both sides took the field in the First Balkan War, the Slavic armies triumphed on all fronts over the Ottomans. Sazonov had lost control of his own monster. The Bulgarians smashed through Thrace towards Constantinople. What would Russia do if Bulgaria grabbed Tsargrad? "All right, let them," Nicky told the kaiser's brother Heinrich: they could occupy it, but only temporarily. "The occupation of Constantinople," explained Sazonov, "could compel the appearance of our entire fleet before the Turkish capital."

On the Adriatic coast, Serbia and Montenegro were swallowing the new entity of Albania. Fearing that a Serbian port would become a Russian base, Austrian generals threatened war against Serbia—which stimulated war fever in Petersburg. While Sazonov backed the preservation of Albania, Nicholas, still at Spała with the ill Alexei, had been joined by Nikolasha, that husband of a Montenegrin princess and champion of the Balkan Slavs, who encouraged him to back the Serbs. The Austrians massed their armies on Serbia's borders. Europe tottered on the edge of the precipice.

Sukhomlinov and the tsar agreed to keep 350,000 conscripts in the ranks in case they were needed. Then the war minister suggested

---

* Nicholas and Sazonov tried to turn their ungrateful, trigger-happy Slav brothers into obedient, responsible allies, but they all wanted the same territories. Serbia, guided by a powerful Russian ambassador and military aid, wanted a Greater Serbia including modern Albania, Bosnia and Macedonia. Nikola of Montenegro, promoting himself to king, aspired to the same Greater Serbia but ruled by himself. The tsar sent Nikolasha and the Crows to Nikola's coronation and gave him 600,000 roubles a year in return for Russian command of his army. Foxy Ferdinand aspired to the medieval Bulgar Empire including Macedonia and Thrace. Hoping to gain influence, Nicholas paid off Foxy's debts of 2 million francs.

mobilizing his armies on the Austrian, but not German, border—even though Austria and Germany were committed to aid each other. The insouciant Sukhomlinov planned to launch this part-mobilization—and then take his wife on holiday to the Riviera. The tsar agreed.

Meanwhile, twenty miles from Constantinople, Foxy Ferdinand was anticipating his coronation as Caesar, ordering his state coach and self-designed Byzantine royal robes.

In early October 1912, Admiral Ivan Grigorovich, navy minister, had proposed protecting Constantinople or seizing the Straits. Constantinople, said Sazonov, would grant Russia "the natural crown of her efforts and sacrifices over two centuries," giving the monarchy such prestige that it would "bring health to our internal life" and "unite government and society." Russia planned to send 5,000 troops to protect the Christians of Constantinople, followed by the entire fleet—but it was questionable whether the navy could even launch such an operation.

On 10 November, Sukhomlinov summoned Kokovtsov to the tsar's study at Tsarskoe Selo. "The tsar opening a map on the table began to explain calmly and clearly . . . it was decided to mobilize" Kiev and the Austrian borders, adding, "I wish to stress we have no intention of taking any steps against Germany." Russia had been close to going to war without telling its own prime minister.

The prime minister warned that mobilization would bring European war.

"I don't allow the thought of imminent war," answered the tsar, who still believed that his will was self-fulfilling. "We're not ready." The Wobbler, who had initiated the entire scheme, now wobbled, saying he was "overwhelmed by the approaching catastrophe." The tsar cancelled the mobilization, telling Kokovtsov graciously: "I'm even more pleased than you." Nonetheless the tsar and Sukhomlinov kept discussing these plans for another month. In the end, Sukhomlinov was allowed to bring up cavalry to the Austrian border but no partial mobilization.

Now came welcome news: the Ottomans had thrown back the Bulgarians, but Russia's other uncontrollable brothers, Serbia and Montenegro, had occupied northern Albania and its Adriatic ports. This time, Austria issued an ultimatum threatening war unless they withdrew.

"I will fight to the last goat and cartridge," threatened the king of Montenegro, who had many goats but few cartridges. Sazonov refused to back the Montenegrins who finally retreated. The real victor of the war was Foxy Ferdinand whose Bulgaria emerged almost double in size—to the fury of his erstwhile allies and Russia. The tsar turned to a more reliable protégé whom he presumed would not push Russia into a European war: Serbia.[51]

*

Alexei was recovering, but his illness triggered another crisis. Nicholas's brother Misha, nicknamed "Floppy" because he tended to fall asleep while driving, was in love with Natasha Wulfert, the "slender, dignified, sinuous and softly graceful" twice-divorced wife of a brother officer, with whom he had a son. But he promised the tsar that he would never marry her. Now, if Alexei died, he would again be heir and would never be allowed to marry Natasha. Escaping the Okhrana, who were watching him, he and Natasha eloped across Europe and married in Vienna. The tsar was incensed by his brother's use of Alexei's illness as an excuse and at a time when "everyone is talking of war." "Between him and me," said the tsar, "everything is now alas at an end," just when he was about to celebrate the dynasty's tercentenary.[52]

On 21 February 1913, a twenty-one-gun salute launched the jubilee: as Nicholas and Alexandra processed from the Winter Palace to a Te Deum in the Kazan Cathedral, Rodzianko, president of the Duma, found Rasputin sitting in his reserved seats. "I was invited here by people more highly placed than you," said Rasputin, who fell to his knees praying.

"Enough of this tomfoolery," replied Rodzianko. "If you don't clear out, I'll drag you by your beard."*

First the tsar and his family cruised down the Volga to Kostroma, where Michael Romanov had been hailed as tsar. Rasputin was there too, sitting in the front row of the cathedral.

"Everywhere I was impressed by the lack of enthusiasm and the smallness of the crowds," noticed Kokovtsov—until they reached Moscow where, on 24 May, the jubilee finally took off. Huge crowds (and of course Rasputin) greeted the monarchs.

"Now you can see what cowards the ministers are," Alexandra told Zizi Naryshkina. "They're constantly frightening the emperor with threats and forebodings of revolution, but here—as you can see for yourself—we only need show ourselves and at once their hearts are ours." To the outsider, "Tsarism was victorious," recalled Lenin, "all the revolutionary parties were smashed. Dejection, demoralization, schisms, discord, desertion and pornography took the place of politics." His Bolsheviks were riddled with police agents. The economy was booming. Nicholas, like his cousin Willy in Germany, had restored

---

* On 9 May, before the main festivities, the tsar, accompanied by Fat Orlov and Benckendorff, attended the wedding of the kaiser's daughter Victoria Louise to Ernst August of Hanover. In Berlin, he was met with "special cordiality" by his two cousins, Wilhelm II of Germany and George V of England. In their carriage, the kaiser mentioned his plan to send a German general to Constantinople; the tsar made no objection. It was the last meeting of the three emperors.

some of his prerogative power but struggled to fill the vacuum at the hollow centre. His veteran secret adviser Prince Meshchersky advised him to sack Kokovtsov, as did his most influential minister, Alexander Krivoshein, a cunning operator and ex-ally of Stolypin whose job as agriculture minister, in charge of the peasant policies, made him a key adviser. As a first step, Nicholas chose a vigorous young governor and aggressive reactionary, Nikolai Maklakov, as the new interior minister. But the monarchy was a wedding-cake of exquisitely carved icing—with no filling. This was autocracy without an autocrat.

A year earlier the shooting by troops of 150 striking workers on the Lena goldfields in north-eastern Siberia had ignited revolutionary hopes. As many as 300,000 workers went on strike. "The Lena shots broke the ice of silence," wrote an elated Stalin, recently elected to the Bolsheviks' Central Committee for the first time. "The ice is broken. It has started." But it did not start. Maklakov unleashed the Okhrana. The Silver Age poet Alexander Blok, who later investigated its files, called the Okhrana "the only properly functioning institution" in tsarist Russia. It decimated the Bolsheviks. "It's a total bacchanalia of arrests, searches and raids," observed Stalin. Lenin, in Austrian Cracow, was despairing. Revolution, he thought, "might not happen in our lifetime."

Now in Moscow, the crowds seemed to confirm Nicholas's achievement, but it was fragile. In a scene captured on film, Nicholas and Alexandra walked through Red Square surrounded by the grand dukes and courtiers, all in formal dress, epaulettes and sashes, followed by a uniformed Alexei, who, still unable to walk after his illness, was carried by a court Cossack. "I clearly heard exclamations of sorrow," recalled the prime minister, "at the sight of this poor helpless child." The crowd made signs of the cross over the boy. The atmosphere was now overshadowed by a wild foreboding. The poets, playboys, dilettantes and aesthetes of the Silver Age—Blok called them "the children of Russia's dreadful years"—sensed the coming apocalypse and reacted in a doom-laden carnival of reckless if morbid hedonism, seeking the essence of salvation, art and freedom in opium, satanism and the transformative orgasm. The Symbolist poet-novelist Andrei Belyi warned "great will be the strife, strife the likes of which has never been seen in this world. Yellow hordes of Asiatics . . . will encrimson the fields of Europe in oceans of blood," while Petersburg "will sink." As strikes spread and war-clouds darkened, Blok felt the rumblings of a volcano:

And over Russia I see a quiet
Far-spreading fire consume all.[53]

SCENE 5

# Catastrophe

# CAST

NICHOLAS II, emperor 1894–1917, "Nicky"
Alexandra Fyodorovna (née Princess Alix of Hesse), empress, "Alix,"
    "Sunny"
Olga, their eldest daughter
Tatiana, their second daughter
Maria, their third daughter
Anastasia, their youngest daughter
Alexei, caesarevich, tsarevich, their son, "Tiny," "Baby"

## THE ROMANOVS

Maria Fyodorovna, dowager empress, widow of Alexander III, "Minny"
Uncle Paul, "Pitz," married Olga Pistolkors, Princess Paley
Nikolai Nikolaievich, commander-in-chief, viceroy of Caucasus,
    "Nikolasha the Terrible," married Stana, daughter of King Nikola of
    Montenegro, one of the "Black Women," "the Crows"
Peter Nikolaievich, his brother, married Militsa, daughter of King Nikola
    of Montenegro, one of the "Black Women," "the Crows"
Nikolai Mikhailovich, "Bimbo," "White Crow"
Alexander Mikhailovich, "Sandro," his brother, married the tsar's sister
    Xenia
Dmitri Pavlovich, son of Uncle Paul, the emperor's first cousin and
    companion, murderer of Rasputin, friend of Yusupov
Marie, "Missy," queen of Romania, married to Ferdinand, first cousin
    of Nicholas II
Prince Felix Yusupov, married Irina, daughter of Sandro and Xenia,
    murderer of Rasputin

## COURTIERS: ministers etc.

Baron Vladimir Frederiks, court minister, later count
Prince Vladimir Orlov, chief of tsar's military chancellery, "Fat Orlov"

General Alexander Spiridovich, commander of the tsar's bodyguard
Vladimir Kokovtsov, prime minister, count, "Gramophone"
Nikolai Maklakov, interior minister
General Vladimir Sukhomlinov, war minister
Ivan Goremykin, prime minister, "Old Fur Coat"
Alexander Krivoshein, agriculture minister
General Nikolai Yanushkevich, chief of staff
Sergei Sazonov, foreign minister, "Wobbler"
General Mikhail Alexeev, chief of staff
Prince Mikhail Andronnikov, influence-pedlar, "ADC to the Almighty"
Alexei Khvostov, interior minister, "Tail"
Boris Stürmer, interior minister, foreign minister, prime minister
Alexander Trepov, communications minister, then prime minister
Alexander Protopopov, last interior minister
Alexander Guchkov, president of the Third Duma
Mikhail Rodzianko, president of the Fourth Duma, "Fatso"
Anna Vyrubova (née Taneeva), Alexandra's friend, "Ania," "Lovesick
    Creature," "Cow"
Countess Elizabeth Kurakina-Naryshkina, mistress of the robes, "Zizi"


## THE HIEROPHANT

Grigory Rasputin, Siberian holy man, "Our Friend"

"The tsarevich's illness and the empress's religious exaltation didn't prevent normal life," wrote Spiridovich, especially for the tsar and his daughters. After Moscow, on 9 August 1913 the family headed to Crimea. The girls had now blossomed. "Extremely pretty, with brilliant blue eyes and lovely complexion" and resembling Nicholas, Olga was the "cleverest" with a "strong will." Tatiana, tall and slender with "English manners," was a dutiful organizer like her mother but, unlike her, "She liked society and longed pathetically for friends." Open and playful, Maria was the best-looking, full lipped and yellow haired with "splendid eyes and rose-red cheeks," while Anastasia was a reckless mischief and naughty tomboy, a "very monkey for jokes," the family entertainer.

Alexandra "dreaded for her daughters the companionship of over-sophisticated" or "precocious" girls from "decadent society," so the girls mixed only with the officers from the *Shtandart* and the Cossack Escort. Olga was in love with Lieutenant Pavel Voronov of the *Shtandart*: "I love him so so much," she wrote, calling him "Sweetie pie."

As for Alexei, still protected by his two sailor-bodyguards, he was banned from playing any rough games. "Can't I have a bicycle?" he begged his parents.

"Alexei, you know you can't."

"Why can other boys have everything and I nothing?" In Romanov tradition, he adored drilling his friends from the Military School. Like every heir, he had a strong sense of his own special importance, accentuated by his secret sickness. His parents could not discipline him. KR complained about his appallingly boorish table manners: "He wouldn't sit up, ate badly, licked his plate and teased the others; the emperor often turned away while the empress rebuked her elder daughter Olga for not restraining him." The boy was touchy about his rank, loudly reprimanding a courtier who did not introduce him in full, while film footage shows him shoving a woman who turned her back on him for a second. The tsar called him "Alexei the Terrible." "Lor, he does love ragging," said Nicky in his old-fashioned English to a British officer.

On 28 September, while he was in Livadia, the emperor closely followed the "blood libel" trial of the innocent Beilis, who had languished in jail for two years as the state built its unconvincing case of ritual murder against the Jewish brickmaker. Realizing that Beilis was probably innocent, Justice Minister Shcheglovitov did not cancel a trial designed to strengthen the union of tsar and people. Instead he insured himself by dividing the indictment into two counts: first, was Beilis guilty of murder; second, had the victim been killed in a ritual murder?

An array of scientific "experts," many of them reputable professors, testified in a Kiev courtroom that draining the blood of Christian children was a Jewish tradition and that the body had been skilfully drained through thirteen wounds, thirteen being a magic Jewish number. But a brilliant defence team discredited the case. On 28 October, Beilis was found not guilty but the jury found it "proven" that the victim had indeed been ritually murdered. "I am happy Beilis was acquitted," Nicholas told Spiridovich, on hearing the news at Livadia, "because he is innocent," but "it's certain this was a case of ritual murder." Yet he had approved a fraudulent case against an innocent man and the promotion of a medieval lie.[1]

Back in Petersburg, Nicholas anxiously monitored a febrile Balkans. Bulgaria had emerged so triumphantly from the First Balkan War that its rivals, Serbia, Greece and Romania, clubbed together to steal its gains. That summer when the Second Balkan War started, the Bulgarians were defeated on all fronts, their spoils shared among the others. Even the Ottomans joined in. Nicholas called the Balkan states "well-behaved youngsters who've become stubborn hooligans," but he was now backing the most dangerous hooligan on the block. Serbia's premier Nikola Pašić came to Petersburg to confirm their alliance—for when the Austrian war came.[2]

In November, the tsar realized that a German general, Otto Liman von Sanders, had been appointed to command the Ottoman corps guarding the Straits. A junta of "three pashas" led by the young officer Ismail Enver had just seized power in Constantinople. Enver believed that only a severe combination of refreshing war and Turkic nationalism could save the empire. Once it had been protected from Russia by Britain, but even under Bismarck the Germans had started to offer themselves as a new protector. Kaiser Wilhelm had twice visited the sultan. After the Anglo-Russian alliance, Enver turned to Germany and started to rearm, ordering new battleships that would dominate the Black Sea. Russia could not risk the choking off of 50 per cent of its exports through the Straits. It had hoped to postpone any action until it was fully rearmed, but time was running out. Enver's two battleships were about to arrive. As for Liman, the Germans stepped back, agreeing a face-saving compromise.

These crises concentrated the minds of all sides. If Germany threatened France, a Balkan spark might be the only way to draw Russia in against Germany. Starting in the autumn of 1912, France, in the person of Raymond Poincaré as premier then president, confirmed that it would back Russia in a Balkan crisis. Simultaneously the scale and success of Russia's Great Programme of rearmament was alarming Berlin and Vienna. Perhaps time for them too was running out if they were to stop the Russian steamroller.

On 30 January 1914 the tsar dismissed the cautious, sensible Kokovtsov. The obvious replacement was Krivoshein, who had pushed for this change, but he slyly suggested appointing old Goremykin, "an upright corpse," as premier.* "What success can I hope for?" the "corpse" asked. "I'm like an old fur coat. Packed way for months in mothballs, I'm being taken out merely for the occasion. Then I'll be packed away till the next time." With Goremykin in charge, Nicholas had reasserted his power, but all this only added to the uneasiness in public life, the frustration that the promises of 1905 had not been honoured, the gridlock between government and Duma. Interior Minister Maklakov proposed a coup to liquidate the constitution. "I was pleasantly surprised by the content of your letter . . . which will make Mr. Rodzianko and his cronies take our bit between their teeth," wrote Nicky, who preferred to transform the Duma into a consultative body. When he discussed this plan with the other ministers, all warned against it.[3]

In February, the dowager empress gave a ball for the debut of Olga and Tatiana at the Anichkov Palace. "A stranger visiting Petersburg in 1914," wrote Sandro, "felt an irrepressible desire to settle in the brilliant capital that combined classical beauty with a passionate undertone of life, cosmopolitan but thoroughly Russian in its recklessness." At Minny's ball, the tsar found himself a stranger in society. "I don't know anyone here," he murmured, while his daughters could dance only with officers of the Cossack Escort: they did not know anyone else. But now that Olga was almost eighteen, she should marry. The tsar's first choice was the Grand Duke Dmitri Pavlovich.[4]

"Dmitri was extremely attractive, tall, elegant, well bred with deep thoughtful eyes," recalled his friend Felix Yusupov. "He was all

* The tsar considered appointing the astute Durnovo as prime minister but decided against it, most likely because he disapproved of his foreign policy. A month later, Durnovo sent Nicholas his prophetic warning against war with Germany when Russia's entente with Britain and France had somehow metamorphosed into a military obligation though no Russian interests were at stake: "In the event of defeat, social revolution in its most extreme form is inevitable." He was not alone in this view. The French and Serbian alliances were not Russia's only choice. Many believed that Germany and Austria were its natural allies. The ageing Prince Meshchersky also advised against a war on behalf of France and Serbia.

impulses, romantic and mystical," and he was "always ready for the wildest escapades." He was Nicky's first cousin, but almost a surrogate son—they enjoyed billiards, tennis and hijinks. Dmitri competed as an equestrian at the 1912 Stockholm Olympics. Inheriting the riches of both his uncles Alexis and Sergei, he lived in splendour at the latter's pink Beloselsky-Belozersky Palace. No one was so intimately irreverent: who else could joke to the emperor about masturbating over the empress? "How's the health of Her Majesty? Tell her I so often think about her that deluged in tears of powerless useless passion, I hug my pillow thinking about her." He often signed off: "I cover my aunt's arm with voluptuous kisses."

He and the tsar chuckled about Dmitri seducing the old courtiers at Livadia: "I wish I was there with you. Are you dancing in the evenings? It would be a great opportunity for me to . . . saucily press against Baroness Frederiks . . . Hee-hee-hee!" He signed himself, "I embrace my illegal mother (sorry I am her illegitimate son). Embrace the children moistly . . . Yours with heart, soul and body (except for arsehole), Dmitri." Apologizing for a long letter, he suggested, "Take this message with you when you go to shit. Time will be pleasant, ideal, and in extreme cases you can wipe your arse with it (mixing business with pleasure)."[5]

"Almost every night," Dmitri and Felix Yusupov drove to Petersburg to "have a gay time at restaurants, nightclubs and with the gypsies." Hearing of their adventures, Alexandra decided that Dmitri was not an appropriate mate for Olga; the grand duke himself had meanwhile fallen in love with another eligible Romanov, the tsar's niece Irina.

Prince Yusupov, a bisexual transvestite who was heir to a super-wealthy family,* had borrowed his mother Zinaida's dresses to flirt with officers at the fashionable Bear restaurant. After studying at Oxford, where he had joined the Bullingdon Club, Felix often played tennis at Livadia where on 11 November 1913 the tsar called him "the best tennis player in Russia. He can really teach one something." When he and his friend Dmitri both fell for Grand Duchess Irina, daughter of Sandro and Xenia, she chose Yusupov. "She was eighteen, very beautiful and very naive," says her niece, Princess Olga Romanoff. "She didn't even know what a homosexual was. Yet the marriage was very happy. She was

---

* The family had been close to the tsars since their ancestor, a Nogai princeling named Yusuf, converted to Orthodoxy. They now owned four palaces in Petersburg and three in Moscow, as well as thirty-seven estates and some Baku oilfields. Felix's father was governor of Moscow. His elder brother Nikolai had been killed in a duel by the jealous husband of his mistress, leaving Felix as heir.

a very strong character. In the Romanov family, the women are often stronger than the men." For their wedding on 9 February 1914, the tsar lent the couple a state coach and led Irina into the church.

Now Nicky and Alix had to confront the problem of Olga's marriage, which they discussed with Sazonov, the foreign minister. "I think with terror that the time draws near when I have to part with my daughters," the tsarina told him. "I could desire nothing better than that they should remain in Russia but . . . it is of course impossible."

On 15 March, Olga's suitor, cousin Carol of Romania, arrived with his parents, the glamorous Missy and the gawky Ferdinand, heir to the Romanian throne. Alexandra "managed to put an insuperable distance between her world and yours . . . The pinched unwilling patronizing smile was one of the most disheartening impressions," thought Missy. "When she talked it was almost in a whisper hardly moving her lips as if it were too much trouble." The mothers agreed that the children "must decide for themselves" and Missy "much preferred the company of the girls to their mother . . . they considered me a good sport and took me for walks." Carol failed to charm Olga. "I am a Russian and want to stay one," she told her brother's tutor Gilliard. "I don't want to leave Russia (and) papa has promised not to make me"—loving paternal sentiments except that a foreign marriage would have saved her life. After the Romanians had left, the family headed to Livadia.[6]

"We've had two very happy months," the tsar reflected after one of his Crimea hikes—but there was a fat lovesick fly in the ointment.

Since the empress was so often ill, her moon-faced friend Anna spent more time with the tsar, who, she boasted afterwards, "developed a more than ordinary desire for my companionship perhaps only because I was an entirely healthy, normal woman."

If Anna thought the tsar was in love with her, Alexandra rightly thought Anna was in love with him, deploying lovesick swoons and playing footsie under the table. "One couldn't help but notice the shocking manner she tried to flirt with the emperor," recalled Zizi Naryshkina. Nicky was embarrassed, while "The empress became mortally jealous and suspicious of every movement of her husband and myself," wrote Anna, and "said some very unkind and cruel things of me."

"My heart is heavy and sore—must one's kindness and love always be repaid thus? The Black Family [the Montenegrin sisters] and now she?" Alexandra asked Nicky. "We gave our hearts, our home to her, our private life even—and this is what we've gained. It's difficult not to become bitter." She was pleased when Nicky got away from "love scenes and rows" and "footgames." She now called Anna "the Lovesick

Creature" or just "the Cow" and declared, "I find her stomach and legs colossal (and most unappetizing)."

Just before their return, the family paid a return visit to Romania, partly with a view to a marriage, partly to win over the country in the event of war, sailing over to Constantia to meet the ancient King Carol, his heir Ferdinand and Missy. The girls were "cheerful and exceedingly sunburnt from Crimea," Alexei was "handsome but somewhat spoilt," and as for Nicky, Missy noticed "how loveable he was," but as the Romanovs left, "little did I imagine we would never meet again."

At the end of his Livadian idyll, Nicholas said to a courtier, "Let's make a pact that we all meet here again in October." Then he paused. "After all, in this life, we don't know what lies before us."[7]

On 15 June (28 June New Style), ten days after the Romanovs had returned to Tsarskoe, Archduke Franz Ferdinand of Austria was assassinated in Sarajevo.

The assassin was Gavrilo Princip, a young member of the Serbian nationalist organization Union or Death, also known as the Black Hand, who had been trained under the aegis of Colonel Dragutin Dimitrijević, codenamed Apis, chief of Serbian military intelligence. Even though the Serbian prime minister Pašić only vaguely knew of the conspiracy, it did not take long for the Austrians to discover the official link.

The Austrian chief of staff (who had advocated war against Serbia twenty-five times in 1913 alone) argued that this atrocity offered the best, perhaps last, chance to destroy the enemy and save the empire. This time the old emperor Franz Josef and his ministers agreed. But since this would provoke Russia, Austria needed German cover. In Berlin, on 22 June the kaiser gave a "blank cheque" to back Austria, the essential decision that led to war—unaware that France had promised Russia its support if Austria invaded Serbia and that Britain had secretly promised support to France. The Germans advised the Austrians to win their war fast before Russia could react. But this was a problem. On 7 July, President Poincaré of France was visiting Petersburg, so the ultimatum could only be sent when he was on his way home.

The emperor and Sazonov were now the key decision-makers: both thought war unlikely but agreed that Russia could not tolerate the destruction of Serbia. On 29 June, Alexandra consulted Rasputin, who was at his Siberian home, sending him a telegram: "It's a serious moment, they're threatening war." Just after reading it, he came out of his house and was stabbed in the stomach by a deformed woman ("Nose absent; irregularly shaped hole in its place," noted the police report), probably sent by the monk Iliodor. As he fought for his life, Nicky and Alix despatched a doctor from Petersburg—"We're deeply shaken," the empress wrote to him, "our grief beyond description"—and ordered the police to tighten Rasputin's security, then they left for a short family cruise on *Shtandart*. But contrary to the great myth of Alexandra's and Rasputin's influence, Nicholas hardly shared his predicament with his wife, let alone with Rasputin, during the entire Serbian crisis. They were irrelevant.

On 3 July Nicholas learned that Austria planned an ultimatum to Serbia. "In my view," he said, "no country can present demands to another unless it has decided to wage war."

"Horrible moments," Alix telegraphed Rasputin. "Pray for us!"

Four days later, the family moved to Peterhof to welcome Poincaré. "The complete alliance between our governments appears more necessary than ever," Nicholas told the French president, who was staying in the Great Palace. A dinner was held there that night, incandescent with "the brilliance of uniforms, superb toilettes, elaborate liveries, the whole panoply of pomp and power," with a "dazzling display of diamonds on women's shoulders," observed the urbane French ambassador Paléologue. But everyone joined Poincaré in asking: "What does Austria have in store for us?"

On 9 July, emperor and president reviewed 60,000 troops at Krasnoe Selo. At Nikolasha's banquet, the two Montenegrin Crows warned Sazonov against any wobbling and told the French that their father the king of Montenegro had told them "There's going to be war . . . There'll be nothing left of Austria . . . You're going to get back Alsace and Lorraine . . . Germany will be destroyed." The emperor flashed her a look. "I must restrain myself," Stana finished. "The emperor has his eye on me."

On the last night, 10 July, while bands played on the deck of *La France*, Poincaré told Nicholas, "This time we must hold firm." As Poincaré sailed away, in the Serbian capital Austria presented its ultimatum, designed to be unacceptable. Nicholas returned to Peterhof. He had an "aversion to telephones" and none of his studies had been fitted with them, "but now he had wires and instruments installed and spent much time in conversations with ministers." Now his foreign minister rang him for the first time on this new-fangled device to report that the ultimatum was brutal, "could not be complied with by Serbia" and was a German machination. "This means that European war," Sazonov said, was "unavoidable."

As Sazonov set off for lunch with the British and French ambassadors in Petersburg, Nicholas in Peterhof put down the phone and called in his finance minister, Peter Bark, for his weekly audience. The tsar, uncharacteristically, confided in Bark that he did not trust Sazonov who tended to exaggerate. The emperor could not believe that the kaiser would give the trigger-happy Austrians a blank cheque when he had not exploited Russia's total collapse in 1905 and when they had managed to compromise in every crisis since. Bark agreed—but many shared Sazonov's view. Meanwhile the Serbs rejected the ultimatum.

The following day, Sazonov warned the Austrian ambassador, "You're setting fire to Europe," and he told the French and British envoys that "Russia would have to mobilize." At 11 a.m. he saw Chief of Staff Nikolai Yanushkevich; at 3 p.m., he attended the Council of Ministers. If Russia "failed to fulfil her historic mission," Sazanov said, speaking first, she would become "a decadent state." No one should be under any doubt that Germany was the power behind Austria. Krivoshein, the key minister, backed him tentatively, warning that "concession was no guarantee of peace," though "no one desired war." They agreed to recommend "partial mobilization" against Austria.

Next day, at 11 a.m. on 12 July, the tsar summoned the ministers and Yanushkevich to a meeting at Krasnoe Selo, the venue for summer manoeuvres attended by the tsar every day from nearby Peterhof. There, in Nikolasha's palace, the world lurched closer to war. Nicholas entered the room with Nikolasha and then sat between the grand duke and Premier Goremykin. "Smiling but showing no emotion," the tsar turned to Sazonov, who proposed his secret "partial mobilization," against Austria only, and a preliminary stage known as "the Period Preparatory to War." The tsar was quiet; Nikolasha said nothing. Nicholas approved partial mobilization—in the event of Austria declaring war on Serbia. Afterwards the tsar and Nikolasha attended the ballet, then returned to Peterhof.

Nicholas's decision to remain closeted there is strange. Even with his new phones, he was still too removed. At the great test of his hard-won autocracy, the autocrat was barely present, leaving the initiative to Sazonov and the generals. When the generals who actually ran the mechanics of war discovered that the amateurish war minister Sukhomlinov and Yanushkevich had proposed partial mobilization, they explained that this was an administrative nonsense. If they partially mobilized against Austria, how could they then fully mobilize if necessary against Germany? There was only one appropriate plan: Plan 19A, and that was for a full mobilization.

Many of these mediocre players later blamed one another for warmongering, but the Russian generals, knowing that their mobilization would be slower than that of Germany and later than that of Austria, were terrified that France (and Serbia) would be destroyed and the war lost—if they did not hurry. And they were right to be afraid because the

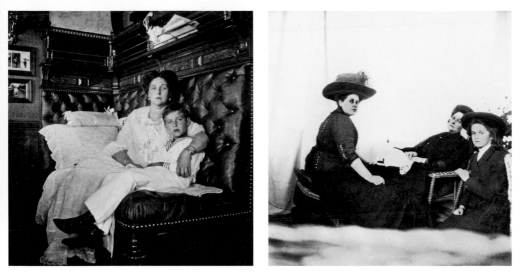

"If only she could be well," said Nicky: Alexandra's hysteria and illness were almost as stressful for the family as Alexei's haemophilia. *Above left* Alix hugs her son in the mauve boudoir, Alexander Palace; but she needed constant nursing herself by Anna Vyrubova and her daughters (*above right*).

The familiar sight of the family escorting the empress in her wheelchair, Crimea.

Encouraged by Fat Orlov, Nicholas started to collect motor cars: in Crimea in 1913, the empress arrives in a Delaunay-Belleville; Nicholas's Rolls-Royce Silver Ghost *(right)*, was one of two Rolls he owned at Livadia.

The *Shtandart* yacht was the family's favourite holiday: in June 1909 they were joined by Kaiser Wilhelm II *(top left)* who constantly canvassed Nicholas to leave the French alliance and join Germany.

*Above and below right* Livadia and the *Shtandart* were places of freedom and fun: in September 1911 the older daughters, Olga (*left*) and Tatiana, flirt with their favourite *Shtandart* officers including Pavel Voronov (with whom Olga was in love); and dance around the deck with the officers.

Summer 1912, in a secluded Finnish fjord, Nicholas, a believer in hydrotherapy, bathes naked (*below*); while down in Livadia, he lets Anastasia puff on a cigarette (*below right*).

The family entertainer, mischievous and intelligent Anastasia takes possibly the first selfie.

Alexandra, photographed in her nightgown by one of her daughters.

As Alexandra and the girls arrive at Kiev Station in 1911, Nicholas is met by his prime minister, the great statesman of his reign, Peter Stolypin, while the bewhiskered Baron Frederiks checks his medals. Alexandra believed God had withdrawn protection from Stolypin—and she was soon proved right.

Alexei (*top left*, guarding a picnic during a *Shtandart* cruise) longed to be a soldier. Father and son (*above*) in uniform at the Alexander Palace. In 1912, the family were hunting at their estate Spała in Poland (*left*), when Alexei suffered his worst attack. As his mother kept vigil (*below left*), Rasputin sent word: "The little one will not die." But the boy still could not walk and was carried at the tercentenary celebrations in Moscow, 1913 (*below*).

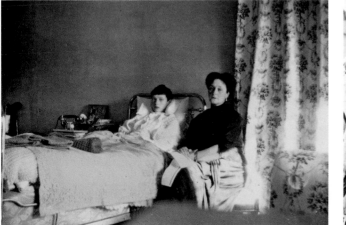

Summer 1914: at Peterhof, Tatiana, Anastasia, Maria and the tsar balance backwards (*left*), watched by Anna Vyrubova.

First World War headquarters: at Mogilev (*left*), Supreme Commander Nicholas and Alexei review their cavalry; and at Baranovichi (*below left*), Nicholas with Supreme Commander Nikolasha and Count Frederiks.

*Below right* At Tsarskoe Selo, during the war, Alix and the eldest girls served as nurses: here they enjoy a swordfight on the ward with their wounded soldiers.

Nicholas took supreme command but allowed Alexandra to run the government in Petrograd, advised by Rasputin. In May 1916, she visited him at his Mogilev headquarters to insist on sacking more minsters.

The influence of Alexandra and Rasputin outraged society: Prince Felix Yusupov (*left*), bisexual playboy married to the tsar's niece Irina, and Grand Duke Dmitri (*below*, with Alexandra) decided to kill Rasputin. Yusupov's memoirs were melodramatic but in fact Rasputin was effectively executed. When the body was found (*below left*), the fatal shot was clearly visible— point blank in the middle of the forehead.

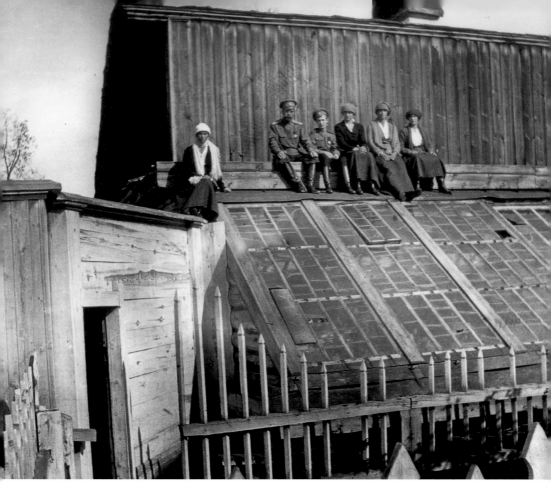

After the revolution: Nicholas in the woods at Tsarskoe Selo (*below left*); the family on the roof of the governor's house in Tobolsk (*above*); and one of the last photos ever taken of Nicky and Alix, together at Tobolsk (*below right*) before they were moved to Ekaterinburg. "A revolution without firing squads," said Lenin, "is meaningless."

German Schlieffen Plan was designed to smash through Belgium to knock out France first and then turn to obliterate Russia.

Nicholas was thinking of ways to prevent the war. On 14 July, the tsar wrote to Sazonov:

> I'll receive you tomorrow at 6. I've got an idea in my head not to lose the golden moment—I'll tell you. Should we try by agreement of France and England, then of Germany and Italy, to offer Austria to transfer its dispute with Serbia to the Hague Tribunal. So as not to lose a moment before already unavoidable events. Try to do this today . . . My hope for the world is not yet extinguished.

Spending "many hours each day in his study with Grand Duke Nikolasha and Sazonov," Nicholas was "half dazed." Country days rolled on lackadaisically at Peterhof—dominoes, tennis and swimming.

When Sukhomlinov saw him at Peterhof on 15 July (28 July New Style), the tsar seemed "serene if not indifferent to current affairs as if nothing threatened peaceful life." That was the day Austria declared war on Serbia. Nicholas telegraphed the kaiser to mediate and restrain his ally "from going too far . . . The indignation in Russia shared by me is enormous." But at 6 p.m., he received Sazonov, who asked the tsar to agree two decrees, one of general, one of partial mobilization. He approved the mobilization of the four military districts facing Austria.

On the next day, the German ambassador warned Sazonov that if Russia did not halt its measures, Germany too would mobilize: the Schlieffen schedule was incredibly tight. At Peterhof, Alexandra telegraphed Rasputin: "Terrible times. Pray for him." Rasputin's advice was clear but irrelevant. "Our Friend was always against this war," wrote Alix to Nicky later, "saying the Balkans weren't worth the world to fight about."

At the Lower Dacha, Nicky received Goremykin who was still against full mobilization. The emperor "played tennis," he recorded. "The weather was magnificent." The royal hotline between Nicky and Willy buzzed with a confusing parallel dialogue of telegrams that often contradicted that of the ministers and generals. "Your Devoted Willy" agreed to do his utmost to stop the Austrians. At 8:30 p.m. Nicky, confused by the difference between the kaiser and his ambassador, telegraphed Willy: "Thanks for your telegram conciliatory and friendly, whereas official message by your ambassador conveyed in very different tone. Beg you to explain divergency. Your Loving Nicky."

In town, at seven o'clock that night, Sazonov met the generals at the Foreign Ministry. Yanushkevich realized that partial mobilization was not enough and Sazonov was finally convinced. Russia must fully mobilize. The Austrians were shelling Belgrade. Sazonov then telephoned the tsar to explain that full mobilization would be the right answer to the German threat. The tsar agreed. Tsar and ministers signed the order that was to be sent out half an hour later at 9:30 p.m. But, minutes earlier, a telegram arrived at Peterhof from the kaiser claiming that "Russian military measures . . . would precipitate a calamity" while he was trying to mediate between Vienna and Petersburg. Nicholas must cancel the mobilization.

The tsar reached for his new-fangled telephone and called Sukhomlinov.

"I won't be responsible for a monstrous slaughter," said the tsar. "Can we stop it for a while?"

"Mobilization is not a mechanical process which one can stop at will," Sukhomlinov explained. But Nicholas overruled him. He called Yanushkevich, who phoned the director of mobilization, who in turn sent a runner to the telegraph office to halt the process. The tsar ordered Yanushkevich to return to "partial" mobilization, an order that was sent out around midnight.

Still up at Peterhof at 1:20 a.m., Nicky, trying to save the peace, let the cat out of the bag by telegraphing the kaiser to say that "Military measures which have now come into force were decided five days ago."

"That's almost a week ahead of us," said Willy. "The tsar's been mobilizing behind my back. The tsar telegraphed asking for mediation" while "in reality he's been lying to me . . . I regard my mediation as mistaken. That means I've got to mobilize as well!"

In Petersburg too, the lights were burning late as Sazonov told the German ambassador that "reversing the mobilization was no longer possible"—even though the tsar had just half reversed it.

Next morning, 17 July, "The weather was hot," wrote Nicky in his diary. "Had a delightful bathe in the sea." Grousing about the vacillating tsar, the generals met Sazonov and Krivoshein at Staff Headquarters. They recruited Rodzianko, president of the Duma, to back them. Then Sukhomlinov and Yanushkevich both phoned the tsar to say that "it was indispensable to proceed to general mobilization . . . to prepare for serious war."

"The conversation is at an end," said the emperor. They persuaded Sazonov to call. The tsar's hesitant voice, "unaccustomed to the telephone, desired to know with whom he was speaking. I told the tsar I was speaking from the chief of staff's office."

"What is it you wish?" asked Nicholas.

"I begged earnestly to see him that afternoon," his foreign minister recorded.

There was an even longer delay.

"I'll receive you at 3."

At this point, the pressure on Nicholas was punishing. "I was struck by his very exhausted appearance," wrote his son's Swiss tutor Pierre Gilliard who saw him then. But he was holding out alone against his entire military command, his civilian government and parliamentary and public opinion, which the tsar needed behind him. Given our pre-set Western view that the war was surely caused by autocrats and aristocrats, it is useful to remember that the Russian parliamentarians, from Guchkov to Rodzianko, had long been the most vociferous war-mongers calling for intervention on behalf of the Serbs.

Could Nicholas have refused to mobilize? It was nearly impossible for him to do so. It would have required the total reversal of foreign policy not just since 1905 but since 1892, to end the French and British alliances and suddenly join Germany. (Stalin, who had more power and less public opinion to worry about, did something similar in 1939 with Hitler—but that did not avoid war either.) This would have infuriated every section of society and have led to deposition, if not worse—the fate of Peter III and Paul who reversed foreign policy against univer-sal opinion. To do this, Nicholas would have had to start to reorientate Russia years if not decades earlier. It was far too late. At this stage, only German pressure on Austria to accept British mediation could have stopped the war.

Sazonov changed into court uniform and set off by train. Meanwhile, the kaiser's latest telegram repeated the threat of the day before, expos-ing the mediation as a ploy.

At 3 p.m., the "tired and anxious" emperor received Sazonov in his study, accompanied by Count Ilya Tatishchev, his military liaison with Kaiser Wilhelm whom he planned to send on a desperate mission to Berlin.

"Is it too late?"

Sazonov said it was. Nicholas showed him Willy's telegram: "He's asking the impossible . . . If I agreed, we'd find ourselves unarmed against Austria. It would be madness."

Sazonov agreed. The tsar was silent. Then: "This means sending hundreds of thousands of Russian people to their deaths. How can one help hesitating?"

"It's hard to decide," said Tatishchev.

"I will decide." Nicholas's face "betrayed a terrible inner struggle." Fi-nally, "speaking as if with difficulty," he declared: "You're right. There's nothing left but to prepare ourselves for an attack. Transmit my orders of mobilization." Sazonov called the chief of staff: "Issue your orders,

General." Yanushkevich replied that henceforth "His telephone was out of order," to prevent the tsar changing his mind again.

"Smash your telephone," said Sazonov.

The central telegraph office tapped out the first general mobilization of the Great War, triggering the movement of scarcely imaginable legions: Russia already fielded the biggest army of 1.2 million men. Five million more would be conscripted in the remaining months of 1914; 15 million during the coming war; 2 million would die.

Meanwhile Rasputin, encouraged by Alix, telegraphed Nicky: "A terrible storm hangs over Russia. Disaster, grief, murky darkness and no light . . . Let Papa not make war, for war will mean the end of Russia and yourselves." Nicholas considered arresting Rasputin for treason. Surprisingly he did not mention the mobilization to Alexandra. When Anna heard of the military preparations, she rushed back to report to the empress, whose "amazement was unbounded—she couldn't understand, she couldn't imagine under what influence the emperor had acted."

On 18 July (31 July New Style) in Berlin, the kaiser mobilized and unleashed the Schlieffen Plan to knock out France through neutral Belgium, while a token force held back the Russians in East Prussia.

Sukhomlinov was the obvious candidate for the supreme command, but, calculating that it would be a short war, he preferred to keep the War Ministry and suggested that Nicholas take it. The tsar longed to be the commander, but instead the next day he summoned Nikolasha: "I informed him of his appointment as commander-in-chief until I could join the army." Nikolasha, experiencing "an indescribable, indelible and over-exuberant feeling," accepted the tsar's "sacred will" but added that he knew nothing of operational plans. Then he asked his cousin to promise that "whatever might happen, the loss of Petersburg, Moscow, even Siberia, he would conclude no peace." Nicholas agreed, then went to vespers. In Petersburg, at 6 p.m., while Nicky was praying, the tearful German ambassador thrice asked Sazonov to stop the mobilization, then handed him a declaration of war. The two embraced. Sazonov then telephoned the court minister Count Frederiks at Peterhof.

His face showing signs of exhaustion, with pouches under the eyes, Nicholas returned with his family from vespers; they were just sitting down to dinner when Frederiks called out the tsar, who retreated with him to his study. "My conscience is clear," he told Sazonov. "I did my utmost to avoid war."

The family waited nervously. The emperor returned looking pale. Alexandra and then the four girls burst into tears. "War! And I knew nothing of it," Alexandra told Anna. "This is the end of everything."

"You can't imagine how glad I am the uncertainty is over," Nicholas told Gilliard next morning. "I've never been through so terrible a time."

The tsar should have followed Stolypin's dictum of "twenty years of peace," but it is likely his regime would not have withstood the popular outrage and prestige lost in abandoning Serbia. It was a decision of honour in an age of honour taken by a patriot steeped in the overlapping missions of Romanov autocracy, Russian nationalism and Slavophile solidarity. Then there was expediency—this might be Russia's last chance to seize the Straits.

Only a victorious super-tsar, a Peter the Great, could have stayed out—and such a tsar would have been itching to fight. Nicholas's clawback of power left him entirely exposed in 1914. He abhorred the slaughter of war but he, like most aristocrats of his time, saw it as a bracing national rite. There was no daylight between his views and those of Sazonov. After the humiliations of 1908 and 1912, retreat now would mean the end of Russia as a great power, the idea synonymous in Nicholas's mind with Romanov monarchy. Not to uphold this was as unthinkable to him as ceasing to be tsar. He was fighting for Serbia, but on a deeper level he fought to save Russia—the Romanov version. It has become fashionable to spread the guilt of the First World War liberally around Europe. If guilt is to be apportioned, the chief culprits were Austria and Germany, followed by Serbia, Russia and Britain.

That afternoon, the emperor, in field marshal's uniform, and empress sailed into Petersburg (which Nicholas now renamed "Petrograd" as sounding less German). They celebrated a Te Deum with 5,000 officials and nobles in the Nikolaievsky Hall of the Winter Palace. The sovereigns emerged on to the balcony. Twenty-five thousand people fell to their knees. Within forty-eight hours, "good news," wrote Nicholas, "England has declared war on Germany," and the day after, "Austria on Russia. Now the situation is quite clear." The Duma suspended itself in the cause of national solidarity and Nicholas basked in the "upsurge of national spirit."[8]

Russia's mobilization was a surprising success. As 4 million men rushed by railway to their units on the German and Austrian fronts, Nikolasha ordered two armies to advance into East Prussia—which was lightly defended, as Germany threw everything into its attack on France in the west.

Originally the plan had been to evacuate much of Poland and gather the main forces in the centre, with the ability to strike either Germany or Austria. But for political reasons and for the sake of the French ally, Sukhomlinov had framed Plan 19A, a compromise, committing Russia to attack Austria with four armies and East Prussia with two.

The French now begged for help. Nikolasha, a Francophile, did not hesitate, ordering both offensives simultaneously, even though neither was ready and the East Prussia operation required much greater force; instead he weakened it further. "God and St. Joan are with us," Nikolasha told the French ambassador. On 29 July, the armies under Rennenkampf and Samsonov advanced into East Prussia to encircle German forces around the Masurian Lakes, while the southern armies invaded Austrian Galicia.

On 7 August, the Russians won the first battle but Rennenkampf then managed to lose contact with the Germans. A newly appointed German command, led by General Paul von Hindenburg and Chief of Staff Erich Ludendorff, spotted the lack of co-ordination. Communications were pitiful—Nikolasha's headquarters was barely in contact with the armies, with whom they communicated by sending telegrams to the Warsaw post office which were then rushed in bundles by car to the front. On 16 August, leaving a small force to hold Rennenkampf, Hindenburg encircled Samsonov's Second Army, in the Battle of Tannenberg, capturing 100,000 prisoners. Samsonov committed suicide. A second German offensive around the Masurian Lakes ejected the Russians from East Prussia, but there was excellent news in the south where the Russians smashed into Galicia.[9]

The tsar, waiting at Tsarskoe Selo, could hardly sleep. Before he visited headquarters, he received Rasputin's blessing in Anna's villa. "Our Friend was so happy to have seen you yesterday," wrote Alexandra, but she already resented Nikolasha's prominence. Rasputin warned the tsar that "the Crows want to get him the Petrograd throne or [the new principality of] Galicia. Grigory loves you jealously and can't bear Nikolasha playing a part." The empress was beginning to interfere politically: "Now I'm bothering you with things that don't concern me."

On 19 September, the emperor arrived by train at Nikolasha's headquarters—Stavka—at Baranovichi, an oasis of railway wagons in the midst of birchwoods, where staff officers, allied military representatives and a flock of grand dukes lunched, gossiped, attended briefings. This weirdly becalmed limbo was so quiet Nikolasha called it "my hermitage" and praised his adjutant brother Peter, for being "my sleeping pill." Indeed, "It's hard to believe a great war is being waged not far from this place," mused the tsar.

Nikolasha looked and sounded the part of a Romanov warlord, but this cavalryman, now fifty-seven, had never commanded in battle and was surprisingly passive—"he avoids speaking about business and sends one to Yanushkevich," complained Guards commander Vladimir Bezobrazov—leaving his generals to argue over strategy "so as not to get in their way." The ostensible chief of staff, Yanushkevich, was no better, a military clerk overpromoted by Sukhomlinov who wanted no rival in his position. This inadequate figurehead often tried to resign. In practice, Stavka was almost a phantom headquarters. A single Hughes apparatus and sixty men ran an army of 6 million. The fronts acted more or less independently, scarcely co-ordinating and regularly delaying or ignoring Stavka orders. The tsar decorated a tearful Nikolasha in his carriage and conveyed Alexandra's request that Rasputin visit Stavka. Afterwards Nikolasha told his staff that if Rasputin showed his face, he'd hang him, a comment that soon reached the mauve boudoir.

Nikolasha was wildly confident. When his friend Fat Orlov visited Stavka a few weeks later, he concluded that "Everything is going well, morale is wonderful and soldiers fighting heroically." Nikolasha planned a thrust from eastern Poland into the heart of Germany.[10]

Back home, the tsar's girls were experiencing the terrible power of modern war. As the tsar toured the country in his train inspecting troops, the empress and her daughters became nurses at the military hospital set up in the Catherine Palace. There Alexandra, Olga and Tatiana, who were joined by Anna, cared for the broken bodies of the wounded, seeing unspeakable sights.

Alix tended a pitifully mutilated young man—"scarcely a man any more, so shot to pieces perhaps it must be cut off as so bad but hope to save it, horrible to look at. I washed and cleaned and painted with iodine" and helped apply a catheter. Even her daughters saw a patient die, but "All behaved well, none lost their head, and the girlies were brave." On 26 November, Alexandra reflected on this new and atrocious sort of war. "Well, we all knew that such a war would be the bloodiest and most awful ever known and so it has turned out."

All became attached to their wounded young men. Alix, a born nurse, was heartbroken when her favourite boy died: "Wify feels hideously sad," she told Nicky. "My poor wounded friend has gone." But there was also fun, pillow fights and love on the wards: Olga fell for a young Georgian soldier. As for Anna, Alexandra complained of her egotism. "Be nice and firm when you return," she asked the tsar, "and don't allow her footgame."

Yet Alexandra thrived in the war. Her own "illness and weakness forgotten," the empress, recalled Anna, "was at her very best."[11]

In September, Hindenburg and Ludendorff launched an offensive into southern Poland, swinging north to threaten Warsaw. The battle was a draw, but on the southern front the Russians were rolling up the Austrians. As Nikolasha prepared his invasion of Germany, the Germans on 29 October pre-empted him, attacking towards Łódź, capturing 100,000 prisoners. Nikolasha was startled. He dismissed generals and ordered a limited retreat.

On 19 November, the tsar, visiting Stavka, found a chastened Nikolasha: "he has lived through terrible moments." Shells, rifles, boots and horses were already running short: Sukhomlinov had failed to prepare for this longer war. No one had planned for a war of such infernal intensity that used up the shell reserves so fast. Rodzianko, the Duma president, visited Nikolasha to discuss the crisis. The two agreed to bypass the incompetent War Ministry and procure supplies through public organizations and private industrialists. Rodzianko asked if Nikolasha had really threatened to hang Rasputin. "The Grand Duke laughed and said, 'Well, not exactly,'" before confiding his distaste for "the fatal influence of Empress Alexandra. She was a hindrance to everything. The Grand Duke realized the empress hated him and desired his dismissal."

Now he had to cope with a third front. Enver Pasha brought the Ottoman empire into the war on the German side. On 16 October, Ottoman battleships (recently transferred from the German navy) bombarded Odessa, then in December the Ottoman vice-generalissimo launched a colossal but reckless mountain offensive across the Caucasus. The local commander panicked, ordered a retreat and fled back to Tiflis; the fear spread and the local command reported frantically to Nikolasha that they had begun to evacuate Tiflis if not "the entire Transcaucasus."

At Stavka, Nikolasha asked the British envoy to draw Ottoman troops away from the Caucasus. The request was forwarded to Secretary for War Earl Kitchener and First Lord of the Admiralty Winston Churchill, who devised an attack on the Dardanelles. But the Caucasus panic did not last long. Enver's offensive ended in total catastrophe, losing around 40,000 men, while the Russian advance continued into Austrian Galicia. Yet in London the Dardanelles planning went on.[12]

On the main front at the end of 1914, the two sides were close to where their lines had been at the start of the war—but the Russians had lost 1.8 million men in those five months and the failures had exposed such levels of incompetence and corruption that Sukhomlinov and his flashy wife were discredited. "She is a common woman, and vulgar soul," Alix told Nicky. Sukhomlinov was "in despair."

On 25 January 1915, Nikolasha and Yanushkevich ordered a "cleansing" of the entire theatre of operations through the expulsion of "all Jews and suspect individuals." Nikolasha shared the tsar's antisemitism, once telling the State Defence Council that the Jews were "an undesirable element . . . as well as their unattractive moral cast of mind, they are weak, cowardly and devoid of sense of duty." The Jews, who spoke the Germanic Yiddish, were suspected of treason. Nikolasha took Jewish hostages and executed suspects. Around 500,000 Jews were expelled in scenes of such desperate misery that even interior minister Maklakov complained, "I'm no Judaeophile but I disapprove."*

The tsar admired Nikolasha's conduct under pressure. "I must say when he is alone and when in quiet mood, he is sound—I mean he judges rightly," he told Alexandra on 26 January. But Nikolasha's view of Rasputin outraged her. Earlier that month Anna had almost been killed in a train crash that crushed her head. She was expected to die until, Anna wrote, "I opened my eyes and saw standing beside the bed the tall gaunt form of Rasputin. He looked at me fixedly and said in a calm voice: 'she will live but always be a cripple.'" The crash restored Alix's intimacy with Anna and intensified their faith in Rasputin.

These military reverses, supply shortages and cases of government ineptitude led Nikolasha to expand Stavka's almost dictatorial powers in the vast areas behind the front in a frenzy of spy-mania. "I predict in several days there'll be no shells at all," on the north-east front, warned Nikolasha, who sought to explain the setbacks by encouraging a witchhunt for German spies. But it was also a way to destroy his enemy, Sukhomlinov. On 18 February, he arrested the minister's corrupt crony Colonel Sergei Miasoedov. Nikolasha ensured he was found guilty and hanged five hours later; three of his associates, all Jews, were hanged too. When four others were found innocent, Nikolasha had them re-tried and hanged. Sukhomlinov was damaged. Nikolasha undoubtedly believed that the men were guilty, but they were almost certainly totally innocent—and he damaged the regime, never imagining that people would presume the Romanovs themselves were German agents too.[13]

The emperor, heading back to Stavka, had high hopes: "All the front is pretty well." On 6 February, Britain and France attacked the Dardanelles in a bid to break the deadlock of the western front, knock Turkey out of the war and ease the supply lines for Russia, while Sazonov negotiated to win Constantinople after the war. Alexandra was so excited by the prospects that she did her homework—"I've been rereading what Our Friend wrote when he was at Constantinople—oh what a day when Mass will be served at St. Sophia."[14]

---

* On 29 January, the empress complained to the tsar about Nikolasha's unwise orders "that only aggravate things," adding: "See that the story of the Jews is carefully done without unnecessary rows." Even the tsar was moved when he saw "masses of Jews, trains arrived with them from Courland—painful sight with all their packages and wee children." Alexandra asked Nicky to let a wounded Jewish soldier live in Petrograd—"It is difficult for a Jew who is always hampered by legislative restrictions," she wrote on 7 April 1916. "Though he is a Jew, one would like him to be justly treated." Nicky agreed.

"Just at this moment," Nicky told Alix on 9 March, "Nikolasha rushed into my carriage, out of breath and with tears in his eyes and announced the fall of Peremyshl [in Austrian Galicia]. Thank God—a sudden ray of sunshine. Oh Lovy-mine, one is so deeply happy!" Celebrating the capture of 130,000 Austrians, Nikolasha and Nicky drank champagne together. The tsar immediately planned to inspect these new conquests. Yet Rasputin sensibly wondered if it was too soon: "Our Friend would have found it better if you had gone after the war to the conquered country"—and Alexandra, now ever more suspicious of Nikolasha, added, "it's not for N to accompany you—you must be the chief one. You find me an old goose, no doubt, but if others won't think of such things, I must." Alexandra was now obsessed about the popular and majestic Nikolasha, who completely dwarfed the tsar, physically and figuratively. If he was not a great commander, he was, like Lord Kitchener in Britain, a good poster.

"Show you are the master," Alexandra told Nicholas. "Forgive me Precious One but you know you are too kind and gentle—sometimes a loud voice can do wonders and a severe look." As for Nikolasha, "you are above him." She felt she had to hector him: "You think me a meddlesome bore but a woman feels and sees things." He did not always agree with her, however.

"Darling mine, I'm not of your opinion . . . On the contrary the Commander in Chief must accompany me." While she was afraid her husband would be assassinated by a "rotten vicious Jew," she shared his joy at the conquests—"wouldn't Nicholas I have been delighted?"

On 9 April, the emperor rode into Lvov in triumph surrounded by ranks of Cossack Life Guards. Then, he wrote, "I slept in old Franz Josef's bed if you please!"[15]

Yet the glory was short lived. Berlin could not let Austria collapse. On 19 April 1915 the Germans attacked around Gorlice-Tarnów. Nikolasha retreated, losing 100,000 dead and 750,000 prisoners. On 9 June, Lvov fell, but worse was to follow as the Germans consumed Poland. The emperor tried to calm the generals at Stavka. Nikolasha, he added, "wept in my cabin and asked whether I was not thinking of replacing him with a more capable man." Russia lost 300,000 men in one month, but "the only thing that causes anxiety," admitted Nicky, "is lack of ammunition"—and 300,000 rifles. Most countries had stockpiled shells for a short war, but in Russia the ordering of new ammunition and the adapting to a war economy had been particularly slow and inept, with a reluctance to spend the sums necessary. What began as a question of supply became a public scandal. Everything was blamed on the shell shortage, which accelerated a crisis of confidence in the army and of state authority. Anti-German riots broke out in Moscow. Yet Nicholas could not see its importance. "You're always writing about public opinion," he told a journalist, "but we have no public opinion in Russia."

The blame fell on Sukhomlinov and the inspector-general of artillery, Grand Duke Sergei Mikhailovich, lover of the ballerina Little K who had made such a fortune that she had recently built an art deco mansion in Petrograd. Nikolasha and his generals joined up with Duma politicians and the press to destroy Sukhomlinov. "It is with a heavy heart I let you leave this time," wrote Alix as Nicky travelled to Stavka. "You bear all so bravely and by yourself—let me help you my Treasure. Surely there is some way a woman can be of help and use. I do so yearn to make it easier for you and the ministers all squabbling among each other . . . it makes me rage." The ministers "must learn to tremble before you—you remember Mr. Ph[ilippe] and Gr. [Rasputin] say the same thing."

Alexandra blamed Nikolasha's defeats on his rejection of Rasputin: "Would to God Nikolasha were another man and had not turned against a man of God." The tsar redoubled security around Rasputin, who returning to Petrograd, frail and shaken after his near-fatal stabbing, was keen to support the imperial couple against liberal society and Nikolasha. In March 1915, Alexandra, eager to boost his religious kudos, published Rasputin's memoirs of Jerusalem (which he had dictated and she had edited) and ordered him to pray in the Kremlin churches, a visit that led to saturnalia not saintliness. On 26 March, Rasputin cavorted with Gypsy singers at the Yar restaurant, becoming what the police called "sexually psychopathic," drunkenly boasting of his erotic exploits with the empress—"the Old Lady . . . I can make her do anything." When diners asked if he was the famous Rasputin, he proved it by dropping his breeches and brandishing his penis accompanied by the "shrieks of women, a man's curse, broken glass and the banging of doors." This was at least partly a set-up, a *provokatsia* by General Vladimir Djunkovsky, noble Guards officer and the police director, who then presented his *kompromat* to the tsar. Nicholas, as usual, coldly placed it in his drawer, demanding total secrecy. Frustrated, Djunkovsky showed his file to Rasputin's enemy Nikolasha. The knowledge that the police were plotting to destroy Our Friend encouraged Alexandra and Rasputin to look for an interior minister and police chief who would protect him.

At Stavka, as the retreat went on, Nikolasha vented his hatred of Alexandra to his chaplain: "Put her in a monastery and everything will be different and the emperor will be different. She is leading everyone to destruction." Fat Orlov, devoted to the tsar yet friends with Nikolasha, was frantically plotting. "We're living through dangerous times," he wrote to Yanushkevich on 2 June. "The terrible cloud of revolution is approaching." The tsar must sack Sukhomlinov to "throw them a bone" but "if we don't succeed, then we will have the Grand Duke [Nikolasha] in reserve." This was repeated back to Alexandra who told her husband that Fat Orlov was planning a coup.

"Everything is so serious and just now particularly painful," wrote Alix on 10 June. Nicky compromised. Three days later, at Stavka, the tsar, at Nikolasha's suggestion, sacked Sukhomlinov and Maklakov and appointed moderates in their place. In his nearby railway-wagon, Nikolasha was so exhilarated that "he quickly leapt from his place, ran to an icon, kissed it. Then just as quickly lay down on the ground and kicked his legs in the air," laughing, "I want to somersault with joy." The greater the disasters at the front, the more popular Nikolasha paradoxically became. The tsar was not even able to protect his fallen minister. Sukhomlinov had been incompetent and corrupt—but now he was also arrested for treason, the subject of a High Commission of Investigation, and facing the death penalty.

The demands for the mobilization of a modern war economy cohered with the clamour for liberal reform and the paroxysm of spy-mania. On 14 June at Stavka the tsar agreed with Nikolasha to recall the Duma and create a Special Council of Defence to co-ordinate between ministers, the volunteer organizations and the war industries. Finally, the government started to produce the required shells by spending lavishly on defence contracts.* Stimulated by this enormous expenditure, the economy was soon growing fast—but, as it did so, a series of bottlenecks in supply created a new crisis.

The Duma demanded a national government. Nicky refused, at which the parliamentarians formed a Progressive opposition bloc. Nicholas had bowed before society, and before Nikolasha, and now he bitterly resented it. "Be more autocratic my very own Sweetheart," advised Alix, who hated the new ministers. "I don't like Nikolasha having anything to do with these big sittings [of ministers]," she wrote on 17 June. "He imposes on the ministers by his loud voice and gesticulations." Nicholas needed her: "People are afraid of my influence, Grigory said, because they know I have a strong will and sooner see through them and help you being firm." She reminded him how "our first Friend [Monsieur

---

* The War Industries Committee had long lobbied for the wider distribution of war contracts. The elected provincial and district assemblies joined in, forming a volunteer Zemstvo Union led by a liberal aristocrat Prince Georgi Lvov that aimed to provide hospital services and involve private enterprise in war industry. It was popularly believed that these organizations saved the war effort—but this was a myth. It was actually the government that turned around war production.

Philippe] gave me that Image with the bell to warn against those who are not right . . . God wishes your poor wify to be your help, Grigory always says so and Mr. Philippe too." The tsar was often at the front, so now they wrote several times a day, exchanging some 1,600 letters, which reveal Alix's increasingly demented voice in its idiosyncratic English.

"Never forget what you are and must remain autocratic Emperor! We're not ready for a constitutional government." Then she came to the heart of the matter: "Nobody knows who is the emperor now—you have to run headquarters and assemble the ministers there!" As if to alleviate this bombshell, she added: "Do my long grumbling letters aggravate you, poor wee One!"

On 22 July, Warsaw fell to the Germans—and still the Russian army retreated. "It can't go on like this," Nicholas told Anna. On 4 August, when Kovno surrendered, Nikolasha was found weeping in his wagon at Stavka: "What more can one do? It's awful, awful!" But the emperor knew what to do. "You don't know how hard it's been for me to refrain from taking command of my beloved army," he confided to the Lovesick Creature, Anna. He must take command. But this command would perilously expose the monarch. When they heard of the plan, his ministers begged him not to follow that course.

Alexandra summoned Rasputin from his home in Siberia to encourage the tsar. Arriving in Petrograd on 31 July, he met Nicholas twice then returned home, sending delphic telegrams: "Firmness is a rock but wavering is death to all."

Nicholas found divine guidance: "I was standing opposite our Saviour's big picture in the big church," he later recalled, "when an interior voice seemed to tell me to make up my mind and write about my decision to Nikolasha apart from what our Friend told me."

When ministers learned that the decision was imminent, they were outraged. On 6 August, the emperor officially wrote to Nikolasha, "I have decided to take supreme command . . . I appoint you viceroy of the Caucasus." He went on, "If there were any mistakes, I forgive them." The next day the ministers begged a tense tsar, gripping a Rasputin-blessed icon given to him by Anna, not to take command. "I have heard what you have to say," he replied, "but I adhere to my decision." The ministers had no faith in his military ability, though he chose a competent general Mikhail Alexeev as chief of staff and the new Stavka was actually a considerable improvement on Nikolasha's shambolic outfit. But the tsar's job was to run the country.

The idea of the tsar taking command was not necessarily absurd. Every country at war, including Britain, was facing a similar crisis of confidence. Total war required sacrifices that demanded charismatic, legitimate leadership. The emperor could take command at Stavka and either appoint an all-powerful minister, such as Krivoshein, to solve the supply crisis or appoint a parliamentary government led by Rodzianko or a military dictator, Nikolasha perhaps. It is easy with hindsight to second-guess these decisions, but there was no obvious answer.* Instead, he took only half the essential decisions and, almost by default, he left Alexandra in charge.

Nicholas ended the meeting: "Gentlemen, in two days I leave for Stavka." He emerged "wet with perspiration."

Afterwards, the ministers met secretly and, on 22 August, ten of the thirteen signed a letter threatening to resign, the first ministerial mutiny in Romanov history. Alexandra was "shocked and horrified."[16]

That same day, Nicholas took command of the new Stavka at Mogilev— with an inspiring letter from Alexandra offering to take command of Russia:

> God is very near you more than ever. Never have they seen such firmness in you before . . . Lovy, I am here, don't laugh at silly old wify but she has "trousers" on unseen . . . Tell me what to do, use me, at such a time God will give me the strength to help you because our souls are fighting for the right against the evil . . . It's the beginning of the glory of your reign, He [Rasputin] said so and I absolutely believe it. And so you will charm all those great blunderers, cowards, blind narrowminded and dishonest false beings . . . Only get Nikolasha's nomination quicker done—no dawdling . . . Sleep well, my Sunshine, Russia's saviour.

He took Rasputin's comb with him: "Remember to comb your hair before all difficult talks and decisions, the little comb will bring its help." Possibly thanks to the Sacred Comb, the next day, 23 August, Nikolasha quietly accepted his dismissal and set off, accompanied by Fat Orlov, whom Alexandra regarded as a traitor.

"Thank God it's all over," the emperor told the empress, "and here I am with this new heavy responsibility on my shoulders. But God's will be fulfilled—I feel so calm. A sort of feeling after Holy Communion."

---

* A popular military dictator was no panacea. The evidence of Germany, where the kaiser and his civilian chancellor did hand over to military dictators Hindenburg and Ludendorff in 1916, shows that there is no guarantee this would have worked: they led the country to defeat and revolution. Nor would the Duma have proved any more competent: when the parliamentarians did form a government in 1917 under Prince Lvov, it was a poorly managed disaster. In Britain and France, however, in 1916 and 1917, Lloyd George and Clemenceau did provide fresh leadership. It is worth remembering, too, that in the different circumstances of the early defeats of the Nazi invasion of June 1941, Stalin, after a personal crisis, also assumed the post of supreme commander, a decision that could have been catastrophic but ultimately allowed him to claim credit for victory.

As supremo, existing in the isolated routine of Stavka, Nicholas seemed to achieve a sort of apotheosis. As for his chief of staff, he wrote of him, "I can't tell you how pleased I am with General Alexeev," whom he nicknamed "my squinting friend." "He does it so well." He was delighted by Alexandra's new role: "Fancy my Wify helping Huzy when he's away! What a pity you didn't perform the duty long ago or at least now during the war!"

"So Sweetheart, please forgive your little wify if in anyway I grieved or hurt and for having bored you so much these trying weeks," she wrote. "I am so touched you want my help." Days later, she and her friends Anna and Rasputin were auditioning new ministers with the help of the most disreputable band of scoundrels ever to advise a tsar. The empress possessed "a will of iron linked to not much brain and no knowledge," wrote Benckendorff, while Missy thought that Alix was "passionately ambitious and absolutely convinced her judgement was infallible." Both knew her well. Indeed she boasted that she was the first empress to receive ministers since Catherine the Great.[17]

Alexandra had spent twenty years avoiding "the miasma" of Petrograd, so when she needed to select ministers she knew no one—except Rasputin, who was despised by reputable society. As a result, in August 1915 the empress and Rasputin turned to Prince Mikhail Andronnikov, forty-one years old, an influence-pedlar who had a gift for courting the powerful with his high-camp patter—and made a fortune in war-racketeering with the help of the fallen minister Sukhomlinov. Half Georgian, half Baltic German, he was described by Witte as "a cross between a spy *con amore* and a titled hanger-on." He wittily called himself "the ADC of the Almighty," in which capacity "I have to know everything going on in Petrograd—my only way of showing my love for my country."

Holding court in an *opéra-bouffe* apartment with a bed set in a mock-Christian shrine topped with a crown of thorns, the prince (according to his servant) "had more than a thousand male conquests in my two years' service." He favoured bicycle-messengers, official couriers. Getting them drunk and seducing them under the crown of thorns, he read their messages. If they announced promotions, he would rush to congratulate the recipients before they had heard officially, claiming they owed their good fortune to the ADC of the Almighty.

This, in a contradiction beyond mere satire, was the sinister blackguard to whom a prim, self-righteous empress turned to find the ministers to rule Holy Russia. Knowing that the interior minister and police chief were about to be dismissed, Andronnikov approached Alexei Khvostov, the obese governor whom Rasputin had interviewed for interior minister in 1911, now a Duma member. If Nicholas was to reject his present ministers, Khvostov looked a plausible choice. Andronnikov proposed a triumvirate: he himself would be the fixer, Khvostov the minister, and Stepan Beletsky the police chief, a post he had held before. Andronnikov introduced the candidates to Rasputin, who accepted their compliments with the peasant's disdain for the self-abasing nobleman. Then Rasputin introduced Andronnikov to Anna Vyrubova in her little villa at Tsarskoe, where she agreed to meet Khvostov. Anna was now the gatekeeper to Alexandra.

Khvostov charmed the Lovesick Creature. She and Rasputin recommended him to the empress as the next interior minister. On 29 August, Alix reported to Nicky that Anna had met Andronnikov and Khvostov, who "made her an excellent impression. He is most devoted to you, spoke gently and well about Our Friend." Anna then introduced Khvostov to the empress, whom he buttered up royally. Khvostov "looks upon me as the one to save the situation," tsarina told tsar, "while you are away and wants to pour out his heart to tell me his ideas." Codenaming him "Tail" (*khvost* in Russian), she urged Nicholas to appoint him: "Wire to me 'Tail alright' and I'll understand."

Alexandra met the prime minister, the Old Fur Coat, every day. The Duma was out of control, booing Goremykin every time he appeared there. "I long to thrash" most of the ministers, she said, and appoint new ones who would understand that anyone who persecuted Rasputin "acts straight against us," which was "unpardonable and at such a time even criminal." On 2 September, Nicholas prorogued the Duma. One of its liberal members now compared Russia to an automobile, driven too fast by a mad chauffeur whom the passengers dare not stop for fear of killing them all.

Soon, on 7 September, Alexandra was demanding the dismissal of the ministers. As for their replacements, "Well dear here are a list of names . . . Anna got them through Andronnikov . . ." she wrote. "Please take Khvostov." Betraying her naivety, she added, "Should he be the wrong man, he can be changed—no harm in that at such times." She offered herself to Nicholas as "your Guardian Angel and helper in everything—some are afraid I'm meddling in state affairs (the ministers) and others look upon me as the one to help you (Andronnikov, Khvostov)." The Tail was "a man, no petticoats who will not let anything touch us and will do all in his power to stop attacks upon our Friend."

On 26 September the emperor appointed Tail Khvostov as Russia's minister in charge of all security. Two days later, the three scoundrels celebrated their success chez Andronnikov, where they presented

Rasputin with envelopes of cash. The Tail planned to become prime minister—and order a murder.[18]

"I'll let you have Baby," Alix promised Nicky when he became commander-in-chief. The image of tsar and tsarevich at Stavka was endearing propaganda, and the eleven-year-old Alexei, so long confined to bed and banned from boisterous play, was longing to put on a uniform and go to war. The experience would also be good training: "all his life the tsar has suffered from natural timidity and the fact he was kept too much in the background so he found himself badly prepared," Alexandra explained to the tutor Gilliard. "The tsar vowed to avoid the same mistakes in his son."

The boy, a private soon promoted to corporal, spent much of the next year at Stavka, sharing a room with the tsar in the governor's small mansion. Reporting on "Babykins," Nicky told Alix how they played and prayed together. Alexei complained of the imperial farting in the Romanov dormitory. "Baby Boy wrote today," Alix told her husband on 7 October: "Papa made smells much and long this morning. Too naughty!"

The retreat had slowed but the Germans captured Vilna and pushed into Ukraine. Alexeev planned a counter-attack against the weaker Austrians. "You must not speak of this to anyone—please do me that favour," Nicky wrote on 18 December. He meant she was not to tell Rasputin.

Meanwhile the tsar spent much time reading Alexandra's and Anna's letters*—and an English novel *The Millionaire Girl*. As the year ended with the imperial couple apart, they craved each other. On 30 December 1915 she wrote to him: "I press you tightly to my breast, kissed every sweet place, I gently press my lips to yours and try to forget everything, gazing into your lovely eyes." On 4 January 1916, he wrote back: "My dear I long for you, your kisses and caresses . . . Here away from ministers and visitors we'd talk over various questions and spend a few cosy hours together. But what can we do? Our separation is our own personal sacrifice."

She was pushing him to replace Prime Minister Goremykin: "Why don't you, now that you are free prepare all for the Old Man's change." But who would take his place?[19]

---

* Anna wrote romantic notes to the emperor. "I'm sending you a very fat letter from The Cow," wrote Alix on 6 October 1915, "the lovesick creature couldn't wait any longer, she must pour out her love otherwise she bursts." Anna called the emperor her "Lovebird"— much to Alexandra's exasperation. As for her enemies, she was unforgiving. When Montenegro faced annihilation: "well now the king, sons and Black daughters here who wished so madly for this war are paying for their sins towards you and God as they went against Our Friend. God avenges himself," she wrote to Nicky on 5 January 1916. "Only I am sorry for the people."

*

Only the most obsequious time-servers sought office in this tragi-comedy: Rasputin found the new prime minister in a retired governor of ill repute, Boris Stürmer, aged sixty-seven.

On 20 January, Nicholas appointed Stürmer as prime minister. Stürmer then met Rasputin to receive his blessing. Even Rasputin thought, "He's old but that doesn't matter—he'll do." Stürmer, however, secretly despised the peasant. When he ignored Rasputin's wishes, the peasant upbraided him, boasting: "Stürmer had better stay on his string. If he doesn't, his neck will get broken. If I say the word, they'll toss him out." But Rasputin did give some sensible advice—an imperial visit to parliament. "One must call the Duma together even for a short session," Alix argued to Nicky, "especially if you, unknown to others, turn up there it will be splendid . . . as now all are willing to try and work—one must show them a little confidence." On 9 February, Nicholas surprised everyone by appearing at the Duma, but the appointment of Stürmer, the mediocre prime minister with the German name, looked like either contempt or negligence. He was mocked, and disastrous rumours started to corrode the regime.

Pamphlets with titles like *Secrets of the Romanovs* and *The Life and Adventures of Rasputin* depicted a traitorous German pornocracy with naked lesbian hellions Alexandra and Anna in thrall to Rasputin's throbbing phallus. In a system where everything was decided secretly and ineptly, these rumours metastasized through the body politic.[20]

Stürmer's premiership infuriated Khvostov. The three scoundrels fell out among themselves. Khvostov turned on Andronnikov, denouncing him to Anna. Andronnikov avenged himself by sending a photograph of Anna and Rasputin to the dowager empress. Tail tried to bribe Rasputin to leave Petrograd, but in late January 1916 the interior minister offered Rasputin's Okhrana bodyguard Komissarov 200,000 roubles to strangle the *starets*, poison him and dump him under the ice of a frozen river. Komissarov tested the poison on Rasputin's cat. Rasputin thought that Andronnikov was trying to intimidate him and had the Almighty's ADC arrested and exiled. Tail hired another hitman, who was arrested by the third scoundrel, police chief Beletsky, who publicized this tale of pure Grand Guignol.

At first Alexandra thought this was a plot against Rasputin, "trying to drag in Khvostov with the Jews just to make a mess before the Duma." While the emperor was confiding on 13 February that he was reading an English novel *The Room of Secrets* and sniffing Alix's letter sprayed with her English perfume, Atkinson's White Rose—"the scent excites me and quite drew me to you"—she was confronting the reality. "Am so wretched that we through Gregory [Rasputin] recommended Khvostov to you," she confessed to Nicholas on 2 March 1916, "it leave me not peace—you were against it and I let myself be imposed upon." But as for her minister, "The devil got hold of him." Now Tail had to be sacked too because "I honestly am not quiet for Gregory and Ania as long as Khvostov is in power and has money and police." Such was Nicholas's fear of confrontation and self-control that he politely received even this loathsome rapscallion, dismissing him later by letter.*

"The whole story is damnable," the emperor told Alix on 5 March. But she still wanted ministers sacked—even when she could not find new ones. As for the Duma member Guchkov: "Could one not hang him?" Her mission was to protect Rasputin—and prepare the throne for Alexei. "For Baby's sake," she wrote on 17 March, "we must be firm as otherwise his inheritance will be awful as with his character he won't bow down to others but be his own master as one must in Russia while people are so uneducated—Mr. Philippe and Gregory said so too." Yet the plan to kill Rasputin only confirmed her faith. "During the evening Bible, I thought so much of Our Friend," she told Nicky during Easter on 5 April, "how the bookworms and Pharisees persecute Christ . . . yes indeed a prophet is never honoured in his own country."[21]

Just as the home front dissolved into black comedy, the army, resupplied with shells, was rejuvenated. Confidence grew. Nikolasha's Caucasian forces burst into the Ottoman heartland, taking Erzurum in February 1916 and then Trebizond in April, while a Russian cavalry force cleared pro-German forces from Persia and then galloped for Baghdad in Iraq to aid the British there.[†]

Yet the army struggled to conscript enough new recruits despite the huge pool of manpower available. Even when they did gain numerical superiority and new supplies, the Russian commanders failed to change their primitive tactics to co-ordinate infantry and artillery in order to make a breakthrough on the main front.

At Stavka, in March 1916, they planned an offensive at Lake Naroch near Vilna against the Germans who were occupied in the west at the

---

* Rasputin ran through the candidates for the job with witty fatalism: "Shcheglovitov wants it but he's a rogue; Kryshanovsky's pushing me to have dinner—but he's a swindler. And Beletsky wants it. If I haven't been murdered yet he'll be the one to do it for sure."

† This allowed Sazonov to negotiate the Sykes–Picot–Sazonov treaty in Petrograd that May, carving up the Near East, granting Palestine and Iraq to Britain, and Syria and Lebanon to France. Russia was promised not just swathes of eastern Anatolia, Armenia and Kurdistan but also, in an embarrassment of Holy Cities, a share in an internationalized Jerusalem and Constantinople.

Battle of Verdun. "Everything is ready for our offensive," Nicky told Alix
on 3 March. On the 5th, 350,000 Russians and 1,000 guns were thrown
at 50,000 Germans, who were ready for them. The muddy season invited disaster, the artillery barrage was ill planned and futile, and as
usual the co-ordination between armies hopeless. The Russians lost
another 100,000 men. "We have so few good generals," wrote Nicky.
Yet out of this debacle a new army was gradually emerging: that spring,
the tsar and Alexeev sacked the commander of the south-western
front and appointed General Alexei Brusilov in his place. Brisk, imaginative and thoughtful, Brusilov devised a new system of preparation,
reserves and concentration, to launch a modern offensive. When all the
other generals apathetically concluded that they could no longer launch
offensives, Brusilov believed he could win.

Meanwhile the romance of Nicky and Alix thrived. Both of them were
reading a soppy English tale *Little Boy Blue*, which made her muse:
"Every woman has in her the feeling of a mother too towards the man
she loves, it's nature, when it's all deep love." The emperor was moved
too: "I like it . . . I had to use my handkerchief several times," he wrote
on 31 March 1916. The tsar remembered how he had fought to marry
her "like little Boy Blue but more tenacious." Henceforth she called him
"you sweet Boy Blue." Their sexual passion was undimmed. "My sweet
love, I want you so!" he wrote on 8 April. "Please don't have Madame
Becker [her period] when I come home." She telegraphed back, on
11 April, "what a shame the engineer-mechanic came," but when he
came home, she was ready. "Your tender caresses and kisses are such
balm and such a treat—I always yearn for them," she wrote on 24 April
as he returned to Stavka. "We women long for tenderness (though I
don't ask for it or show it often)."

On 22 May, General Brusilov, using new shock tactics, broke through
the Austrian lines, heading for the Carpathians. By 12 June, he had taken
190,000 prisoners. The emperor repeatedly confided military plans to
Alexandra, adding, "I beg you not to tell anyone this." He meant the gar-
rulous Rasputin as usual, but she virtually always told him anyway: Our
Friend "begs we shouldn't yet strongly advance in the north because if
our successes continue being good in the south, they will themselves
retreat in the north," she wrote on 4 June. It is incredible that she was
sending military advice from Rasputin. Confiding that they were not
really going to attack in the north, he underlined on 5 June: "Please don't
mention this to anybody not even our Friend. Nobody must know this."

General Alexeev was worried. "I told Alexeev," the tsar wrote on the
7th, "how interested you were in military questions and about those
details you asked me. He smiled and listened silently." It was a strange

situation when the chief of staff distrusted his own sovereign and his wife. As Brusilov kept advancing, the emperor was longing for her: "How I miss your sweet kisses! Yes beloved One, you know how to give them! Oh how naughtily! Boysy hops from remembrances . . ."

Bagging 425,000 prisoners, Brusilov almost knocked Austria out of the war, one of the most successful operations of the entire conflict. The Germans, though facing the Somme offensive on the western front, rescued their ally while the timid or pessimistic Russian generals failed to support Brusilov. His last hope was the Guards, the cream of the Tsarist army: 60,000 men commanded by General Vladimir Bezobrazov, who, as Alexandra put it, was the tsar's "old comrade" from his days in the Guards. Bezobrazov declared that the Guards, which "should only be commanded by people of class" (so the tsar's Uncle Pitz, who had returned from exile in 1914, received a corps), never retreated. In late July, Bezobrazov "ordered the advance across bogs known to be impregnable," Alix told Nicky, and "his rashness . . . let the Guards be slaughtered." Thirty thousand Guardsmen were lost. Indeed Peter the Great's Guards almost ceased to exist—and the emperor lost his most loyal praetorian defenders just when he would most need them. Rasputin begged the tsar to stop "useless sacrifices, useless massacres." On 27 September, Nicholas halted the operation—but the war was going so well against the Turks that he planned to take Constantinople, forming a Tsargradsky Regiment.[22]

At the height of Brusilov's triumph, the emperor was strangely detached: "Brusilov is firm and calm. Yesterday I discovered two acacia in the garden." War is particularly corrosive in its effect on its leaders. "I felt so tired in the train yesterday," Nicky told Alix on 3 March 1916, "I remained lying down in the compartment." When Alexei was home, the sovereign was lonely. At Stavka, the ministers "persist in coming here nearly every day and take up all my time; I usually go to bed after 1:30 a.m. spending all my time in a continual rush . . . it's simply desperate." His entourage noticed that he was close to "general nervous exhaustion." Benckendorff told Dr. Botkin, "He can't continue this way much longer . . . He's no longer seriously interested in anything. He's become quite apathetic. He goes through his daily routine like an automaton paying more attention to the hour set for his meals or his walk in the garden."*

* He was taking cocaine for his colds, a usual prescription in those days, but it was said he was also taking an elixir of henbane and hashish in tea to calm his nerves, prescribed by the Buriat healer Badmaev, but these may have only increased his apathy. Badmaev, Yusupov reflected, had "such herbs that act gradually and reduce a man to complete cretinism." As

After two years of struggle, the Russians had pulled off the most successful allied operation of the war and the war economy was recovering: by the end of 1917, there would be a surplus of 18 million shells. But the morale of the home front was cracking, inflation raging, food shortages spreading. Ironically there was no shortage of grain. The harvests were plentiful, yet the peasants sold less of their grain at a moment when the cities were swollen by an extra million workers. The trains were so poorly managed that the grain was not properly collected or delivered to the cities and armies. Rasputin, who observed the food queues on Petrograd streets, offered some of his more sensible if simple ideas which Alix passed on to the emperor.

Nicky considered appointing a dictator as "master of the whole situation," but "the eternal question of supplies troubles me most of all." The tsar realized that "old Stürmer can't overcome these difficulties . . . The most damned question I ever came across. I've never been a merchant and don't understand questions of provisions."

Yet when a minister "tried to tell His Majesty in detail about the food supply . . . the emperor kept interrupting me with questions related to everyday trivia . . . the weather . . . children and flowers . . ." Watching the tsar, Benckendorff warned, "One can't rule an empire or command an army in this manner. If he doesn't realize it in time, something catastrophic is bound to happen."[23]

Back at the Alexander Palace, the empress was busily reshuffling. She could not find an interior minister so Rasputin suggested Stürmer and he was appointed. She had the efficient war minister sacked for links to the Duma and hostility to Rasputin, who rarely initiated these policies but encouraged Alexandra to sack ministers already distrusted by Nicholas—and then tried to find their replacements. The tsar no longer trusted Sazonov after his role in the ministerial mutiny and a proposal to offer Polish autonomy. Alexandra arrived at Stavka on 6 July and had "the Pancake" dismissed the next day. But she and Rasputin could not find the right foreign minister, so they appointed Stürmer. Now that cipher held the three chief ministries.

The empress thrived on the excitement, yet lived in a state of neurotic hysteria. "Feel rotten as had such pains in my tummy in the night," she reported in January 1916, and had to ring for her maid to "fill up my hot-water bottle and give me opium." She reflected on life and death. "One lives too quickly," she declared in one of her saner letters on 5 March,

---

for Alexandra, she was now "saturated" with Dr. Botkin's Veronal and other opiates, which he was too weak to refuse her. She may have been addicted but, in any case, her regular use of barbiturates, opium, cocaine and morphia can only have exacerbated her hysteria.

"impressions follow in rapid succession—machinery and money rule the world and crush all art—I wonder what will be after this great war is over." She feared for the future. "Oh darling it is difficult to be happier than we have . . . May our children be as richly blessed . . . Life is a riddle, the future hidden behind a curtain and while I look at our big Olga my heart fills with emotions and wondering what is in store for her," Alix wrote on 12 November 1915, their twenty-first wedding anniversary.

Olga was depressed. "She goes about so pale" but "must lie more—the arsenic injections will act quicker," Alix informed Nicky in October 1915. Now OTMA were less tolerant of her eccentric views. "The children with all their love rarely understand my way of looking at things," she wrote in March 1916, "the smallest even, and when I say how I was brought up they find it dull. Only when I speak quietly with Tatiana she grasps it. Olga is always most unamiable and when I am severe, sulks me."*

Yet Olga's moods were nothing compared to the rage of the Romanovs. Only Uncle Pitz remained close to Alexandra now. The dowager empress knew that Alix was simply mad and she compared Nicky's reign to the last days of Emperor Paul. She confronted her son one more time, supposedly threatening, "Rasputin or me," but in May she moved to Kiev. In Petrograd, Bimbo—Nikolai Mikhailovich—wittily mocked Alexandra "the Abominable Hessian" at the Imperial Yacht Club, calling her "the Woman Who Put Jesus Right." Alexandra called him "the White Crow"—and told Nicholas: "We've been far too weak and kind to the family."

Meanwhile Dmitri and Yusupov considered the ultimate solution to the Rasputin problem—just as Alexandra had found the perfect man to protect him. In fact she was placing a syphilitic madman in charge of imperial security.[24]

Rasputin recommended Alexander Protopopov as interior minister. He looked like the perfect minister. Elegant, multilingual and a pianist, the deputy president of the Duma was an urbane liberal conservative who

---

* Boris, decadent son of Uncle Vladimir and Miechen, asked to marry Olga, eighteen years his junior. Alix was horrified by this "well-used half-worn-out blasé young man." But there was another candidate: the Brusilov offensive had persuaded Romania to enter the war on the Allied side and Olga's marriage to Prince Carol was again seriously considered. Missy, now Romanian queen, wrote to Nicky to negotiate vast territorial gains, to which the tsar replied in English, "I must frankly own we were deeply amazed by your country's enormous demands," but if Romania joined the war, Russia would sign a treaty immediately. But the Romanians proved a military liability. The Germans took Bucharest. Missy wrote to Nicky begging for help. Meanwhile the tsar's sister Olga, unhappily married to Peter of Oldenburg, had long ago found love with Guards officer Nikolai Kulikovsky. Now she demanded permission to divorce and marry Kulikovsky, which provoked a rant from Alexandra: "What would your father have said?" The tsar approved the marriage.

had first been recommended to the tsar by Rodzianko himself. Even King George V, who met him on a visit to London, was impressed.

Nicky remembered that Rasputin had first mentioned him. "Pleased me very much," wrote Nicholas after their first meeting on 20 July 1916; "he's an ex-officer of the Cavalry Grenadiers." He was also a textile tycoon—the ideal man to solve the supply crisis. In September, Rasputin praised Protopopov to Alexandra, who started manically hectoring the emperor: "I don't know him but I believe in Our Friend's wisdom and guidance. Gregory begs you earnestly to name Protopopov there. You know him and had a good impression—happens to be a member of Duma and will know how to be with them."

"I must think that question over," Nicky replied on 9 September. "Our Friend's ideas about men are sometimes queer as you know. One must be careful, especially in nominations of high people . . . All these changes exhaust the head. I find they happen much too often." This was an understatement: during Alexandra's rule, there would be four prime ministers and five interior ministers—and his suspicions were justified.

Protopopov was "queer" indeed. There was something "peculiar" in his rolling eyes, quivering sweats, cursing outbursts and jerky conversation. Half mad, probably syphilitic, he had been cured of a disease by the doctor feelgood of Petrograd, Badmaev, Rasputin's "bosom friend" in Alix's words. Now he was said to be addicted to Badmaev's "arousing powders"—probably cocaine. In a new version of the three scoundrels, Badmaev proposed his patient as minister and his business partner General Kurlov as police chief. This was the very same Kurlov responsible for Stolypin's assassination. Tempted by power, Protopopov became an apostle of Rasputin and a convert to Alexandra's mystical autocracy. When they met, she found him "very clever, coaxing, beautiful manners."

"Please take Protopopov as interior minister," she wrote to Nicholas.

"It shall be done," Nicholas wrote back.

"God bless your new choice of Protopopov," she celebrated. "Our Friend says you have done a very wise act."

She sent Nicholas an agenda to discuss with Protopopov at their first meeting—"he should listen to Our Friend and trust his advice"; she added, "Keep my list in front of you. Our Friend begged you to speak of all these things."

Alix was proud of her new confidence: "I'm no longer the least bit shy or afraid of the ministers and speak like a waterfall in Russian. They see I'm energetic and report all to you and that I'm your wall in the rear, a very firm one. I may be of some wee use to you."

The tsar praised their arrangement: "Yes verily you ought to be my eye and my ear there near the capital while I stick here," he told her on 23 September 1916. "This is just the part for you to keep the ministers going hand in hand—you're rendering me and our country enormous use. Oh! You precious Sunny I'm so happy you've found the right work for yourself."

Stürmer and Protopopov destroyed what little remained of imperial prestige. Stürmer was suspected of probing for a separate peace with Germany—rumours that may have been correct, though there is no evidence Nicholas approved. Now known as "the German," Alexandra was widely suspected of secret German negotiations. She was certainly contacted by her German connections, but she was devoted to Russia. The babbling Protopopov boasted that he ruled with the help of Jesus Christ. "I feel I shall save Russia," he said, "I alone can save her."

In the Duma, Pavel Milyukov, the leader of the liberal Kadet Party, denounced Stürmer's ineptitude—and Alexandra's management—with the deadly question: "Is this stupidity or is this treason?"

"Both!" cried many.

On 9 November, Nicholas dismissed Stürmer and appointed a competent organizer, the ex-communications minister Alexander Trepov, as prime minister. But Alexandra and Rasputin were enraged. "Our Friend is very grieved at his nomination as He knows [Trepov] is very against him," Alexandra protested to the tsar, "and he's sad you didn't ask his advice." Sure enough, Trepov advised Nicholas to sack Protopopov and exile Rasputin.

Here was an opportunity for the tsar and he seized it, telling Alexandra on 10 November that he was dismissing Protopopov, who may be "a good honest man" but he was "not normal," jumping "from one idea to another" thanks to a "certain disease." He asked, "Please don't mix in Our Friend! It's I who carry the responsibility."

"You don't go and change Protopopov now, he'll be all right," she wrote back. "Give him the chance to get the food supply matter into his hands and all will go well." As for his supposed insanity, "He's not mad!" And Trepov should be hanged.

> I am but a woman fighting for her Master and Child . . . Darling remember, it doesn't lie in the man Protopopov or xyz but is the question of monarchy and your prestige . . . I am fighting for your reign and Baby's future . . . Don't listen to men who aren't from God but cowards. Your Wify to whom you are ALL in ALL. True unto death!

Alexandra told Rasputin about Nicky's plans and the *starets* bombarded him with telegrams. Rasputin was not acting out of megalomania: he was fighting for his life here. Drinking heavily, he had "no doubt they'll kill me. They'll kill Mama and Papa too."*

Alexandra rushed to Stavka. In a unique row, she demanded that her husband keep Protopopov and Rasputin. Nicholas exploded. "These days were indeed hard ones," Nicky apologized. "Forgive me if I've been cross or impatient, sometimes one's temper has to get through." He surrendered.

Trepov tried to bribe Rasputin to leave politics. The sovereigns were disgusted by this insult to Rasputin's sanctity. Yet the failure to remove Protopopov sealed Rasputin's fate.[25]

---

* One of those who cooked for Rasputin during the Great War was a chef at Petrograd's luxurious Astoria Hotel who went on, after the Revolution, to cook for Lenin and Stalin. He was Spiridon Putin, grandfather of President Vladimir Putin.

# Emperor Michael II

# CAST

NICHOLAS II, emperor 1894–1917, "Nicky"
Alexandra Fyodorovna (née Princess Alix of Hesse), empress, "Alix,"
   "Sunny"
Olga, their eldest daughter
Tatiana, their second daughter
Maria, their third daughter
Anastasia, their youngest daughter
Alexei, caesarevich, tsarevich, their son, "Tiny," "Baby"

## THE ROMANOVS

Maria Fyodorovna, dowager empress, widow of Alexander III, "Minny"
MICHAEL II, emperor 1917 (for one day), inspector-general of cavalry,
   "Misha," "Floppy," married Natasha, Countess Brassova
Miechen, widow of Uncle Vladimir
Ella, widow of Uncle Sergei, sister of the tsarina, abbess
Uncle Paul, "Pitz," married Olga Pistolkors, Princess Paley
Dmitri Pavlovich, son of Uncle Paul, murderer of Rasputin, friend of
   Yusupov
Nikolai Nikolaievich, viceroy of Caucasus, "Nikolasha the Terrible,"
   married Stana, daughter of King Nikola of Montenegro, one of the
   "Black Women," "the Crows"
Nikolai Mikhailovich, "Bimbo"
Alexander Mikhailovich, his brother, "Sandro," married the tsar's sister
   Xenia
Prince Felix Yusupov, married Irina, daughter of Sandro and Xenia,
   murderer of Rasputin
Marie, queen of Romania, married to King Ferdinand, Nicky's first
   cousin, "Missy"

COURTIERS: ministers etc.

Count Vladimir Frederiks, court minister
Anatoly Mordvinov, aide-de-camp to Nicholas II
Anna Vyrubova (née Taneeva), Alexandra's friend, "Ania," "Lovesick Creature," "Cow"
General Mikhail Alexeev, chief of staff
Alexander Trepov, prime minister
Alexander Protopopov, last interior minister
Prince Nikolai Golitsyn, last prime minister of imperial Russia
Mikhail Rodzianko, president of the Duma, "Fatso"
General Sergei Khabalov, military governor of Petrograd
General Nikolai Ruzsky, commander of the northern front
Vladimir Purishkevich, member of Duma, murderer of Rasputin
Prince Georgi Lvov, prime minister of the Provisional Government
Alexander Kerensky, member of Soviet Duma, justice minister in the Provisional Government, later prime minister
Alexander Guchkov, member of Duma, war minister in Provisional Government

THE HIEROPHANT

Grigory Rasputin, Siberian holy man, "Our Friend"

Romanovs, generals and parliamentarians* were all simultaneously hatching plots against the sovereign. On 7 November 1916, Nikolasha, wearing a Caucasian *cherkeska* coat, arrived at Stavka and told the tsar, "It would be more pleasant if you swore at me, chased me out of here rather than say nothing. Don't you see you will lose your crown? Install a responsible ministry." Then he said, "Aren't you ashamed to have believed that I wanted to overthrow you?" When he pointed to Alexei and said, "Take pity on him," the tsar kissed him.

Then Bimbo arrived and gave the tsar two letters, directly attacking Alexandra, Rasputin and their government. Nicholas sent them on to the tsarina. Incoherent with rage, she was "utterly disgusted," she wrote on 4 November. "Had you stopped him . . . and told him if he only once touched on that subject or me, you will send him to Siberia as it becomes next to high treason. He's always hated me since 22 years . . . He's the incarnation of all that's evil . . . grandson of a Jew!" It is hard to disagree with Missy who reflected that Alexandra "allowed hatred to enter her heart . . . behaving like tyrants of old." But Nikolasha and Bimbo failed to dislodge Alexandra. There would have to be a harsher solution. Princess Zinaida Yusupova, "whose tall slim figure, blue eyes, olive complexion and dark hair made her the most beautiful woman at court," criticized Rasputin to Alexandra, who threw her out: "I hope I never see you again."[1] Yusupova and her son Felix agreed that Rasputin had to die.

Prince Felix Yusupov had sought out Rasputin in 1909, when he was just twenty-two and back from Oxford. Rasputin was taken with the effete aristocrat, who consulted him about his own sexual ambiguity. Rasputin tried to seduce him. Yusupov was repelled. He thought that the *starets* possessed "a power you find only once in a hundred years' and concluded that only death could stop him.

---

* Guchkov plotted with the generals to capture the imperial train and crown Alexei under the regency of Misha and the direction of a responsible government. Even General Alexeev and Prince Lvov discussed the imprisonment of Alexandra and the overthrow of Nicholas, who would be replaced by Nikolasha. In November, Alexeev and Lvov asked the mayor of Tiflis, Alexander Khatisov, to propose this to Nikolasha, who rejected the plan. The coup was off—but in Kiev the dowager empress Minny (accompanied by her Georgian courtier, constant companion [and probably lover] since Alexander III's death, Prince George Shervashidze) encouraged the family to confront Nicholas. When Sandro challenged him to end his political isolation, the tsar revealingly replied coldly: "I believe only my wife."

By the winter of 1916, there was probably scarcely a salon or club in Petrograd that did not resound with such intrigues. "All classes speak" as if Rasputin's murder would be "better than the greatest Russian victory in the field," reported Lt.-Colonel Samuel Hoare, head of the British secret service in Petrograd.

The prince decided to recruit from the dynasty, from the Duma and from among Russia's allies. On 19 November he attended a Duma debate and saw Vladimir Purishkevich, a thuggish demogogue from Bessarabia, call for action against "Dark Forces." Purishkevich joined the conspiracy along with his sidekick, Dr. Stanislas Lazovert, a doctor on his medical train.

Its other leader was the debonair Grand Duke Dmitri Pavlovich, who "made no secret of the fact that [the idea of] killing Rasputin had haunted him for months." They agreed on murder, "true monarchists for the salvation of the monarchy." Dmitri's involvement was useful because, as a grand duke, he was above the law. Only the tsar could punish him. "If it hadn't been for my presence," Dmitri later told Yusupov, "you would probably have been hanged."*

Yusupov consulted the British, who were determined to keep Russia in the war. Rasputin had always opposed the war and he possessed an influence that could conceivably accelerate revolution and a separate peace. Hoare was informed of the plot by Purishkevich. But he probably already knew, since three young men on his staff, Stephen Alley, John Scale and Oswald Rayner, were close to Yusupov. Rayner had known him at Oxford. The embassy chauffeur drove Rayner to the Yusupov Palace six times between late October and mid-November, usually accompanied by Scale. The extent of British involvement may never be known, but a letter from Captain Alley to Scale, written nine days after Rasputin's killing, suggests that the British may have been party to the "plan"—"our object" being the "demise of Dark Forces."

On 20 November, Yusupov met Rasputin and asked for help with his health. When Yusupov arrived at Rasputin's apartment, he found himself mesmerized by "his enormous hypnotic power. I grew numb; my body seemed paralysed. Rasputin's eyes shone with phosphorescent light."

Yusupov wavered.

*

* The plotters remained intimate with the imperial family. Dmitri was in close contact with the tsar and tsarina, who complained about his visits to Misha's wife Natasha, with whom the young grand duke was in love. As recently as August, Yusupov and his wife Irina had gone for tea with Alexandra, who remarked how "nice and natural" they were, "she very brown and he very thin."

The emperor was back at Tsarskoe Selo. On 2 December 1916, "We spent the evening at Anna's talking to Grigory." When the tsar asked for Rasputin's blessing, the *starets* replied, "This time, it's for you to bless me," he answered, "not I you."

The next day, Ella visited her sister and Nicky and "pointed out that Rasputin was leading the dynasty to disaster. They replied Rasputin was a great man of prayer and asked me not to touch on the question."

"Perhaps it would have been better if I hadn't come," said Ella.

"Yes," said Alexandra.

"She drove me away like a dog," Ella reported to her friend Zinaida Yusupova, who, "suffocating with hatred, could not take it any longer." Both women, one a nun and future saint, sanctioned the killing: "peaceful means," Zinaida told her son, "won't change anything."

Yusupov chose the next evening when Dmitri would be in Petrograd, and invited Rasputin to meet his wife, Irina, the tsar's niece—at midnight on 16 December.[2]

On 4 December, as the emperor and Alexei returned to Stavka, Alexandra rejoiced, "I am fully convinced that great and beautiful times are coming." She asked proudly, "Why do people hate me? Because they know I have a strong will and when I am convinced of a thing being right (when besides blessed by Grigory) don't change my mind and that they can't bear."

"You are so staunch and enduring—I admire you more than I can say," Nicholas wrote from the train. He too was convinced: "The great hardship is over."

As Yusupov prepared to kill Rasputin, the *starets* was seeing the empress to advise against Prime Minister Trepov's plan for a responsible government. "My angel, we dined at Ann's with our Friend," she reported on 13 December. "He entreats you to be firm, to be the Master and not always to give in to Trepov . . . Be firm . . . Russia loves to feel the whip—it's their nature—tender love and then the iron hand." The next day, she delivered a Lady Macbeth rant: "Be Peter the Great, Ivan the Terrible, Emperor Paul—crush them all under you—now don't laugh, naughty one."

"Loving thanks for your strong reprimanding letter," replied Nicky on 14 December. "I read it with a smile because you speak like to a child." As for his prime minister, "It's a rotten business to have a man whom one dislikes and distrusts like Trepov." But the emperor had a sly plan: "First of all one must choose a new successor and kick him out after he has done the dirty business—shut up the Duma. Let all the responsibility fall on his shoulders." He signed off, "Your little huzy with no will."

On 16 December, the day set for Rasputin's murder, the tsar lunched at Stavka with "lots of foreigners" and in the evening presided over the daily briefing. In Petrograd, his daughter Olga attended a charity committee at the Winter Palace, but now even the friendliest committee members "avoided her eyes and never once smiled," reported Alexandra. "You see our girlies have learned to watch people and their faces— they have developed much interiorly through all this suffering . . . They are happily at times great ladies but have the insight of much wiser beings. As our Friend says they have passed heavy schooling." The girls and Rasputin were "full of Petrograd horrors and rage that nobody defends me."

In the mauve boudoir, the empress craved vengeance after the war: "Many will be struck off future court lists, they shall learn . . . what it was in time of war not to stand up for one's Sovereign." And she was furious with gaga Count Frederiks: "why have we got a ramolic [weak] rag as Court Minister? Only my Nicky ought to really to stick up a bit for me . . ."

In the afternoon, while Yusupov and two servants arranged a basement storeroom at the Yusupov Palace, the empress sent Anna Vyrubova to see Our Friend at his apartment. He boasted that he was off to see Irina Yusupova at midnight, an hour chosen so that Felix's parents would not learn about his visit from the servants. As Anna left he asked, "What more do you want? Already you've received all?"

A little later, at 8 p.m., Interior Minister Protopopov called at Rasputin's place to warn him: "They'll kill you. Your enemies are bent on mischief." The syphilitic minister "made me promise not to go out for the next few days," Rasputin later told Yusupov.

Anna rushed to report all this to Alexandra. "But Irina is in the Crimea and neither of the older Yusupovs are in town," said Alix. "There must be some mistake."

At the Yusupov Palace, the conspirators, supervised by Dr. Lazovert, sprinkled cyanide on to cream cakes and into wine. Dressing in uniform, Yusopov climbed into a limousine driven by Lazovert disguised as a chauffeur and headed for Rasputin's.

At 11 p.m., Rasputin washed with unusual thoroughness and, watched by his anxious daughters Maria and Varvara, dressed in a light-blue silk shirt embroidered with cornflowers, a corded belt, dark-blue velvet trousers and leather boots, sporting a gold chain with a cross and a bracelet engraved with the Romanov double-headed eagle. His fretting daughters hid his galoshes to stop him going out but just after midnight, when the police guards had gone off duty, Yusupov rang the back-entrance bell. Joking that his daughters "don't want me to go out" and that Protopopov had warned of danger, Rasputin said, "Come on, let's go," and, as Yusupov helped him don his fur coat, they set off into the night. "A feeling of great pity for the man," recorded Yusupov, "swept over me."

As Dmitri, Purishkevich and the others waited nervously upstairs, Yusupov led Rasputin into a vaulted basement decorated with a dining table, arranged to look as if a party had recently taken place. The gramophone played "Yankee Doodle." Rasputin waited for Irina to turn up—and ate the poisoned cakes. But he did not collapse, instead asking Yusupov to sing songs on his guitar. After two hours, Yusupov retired to consult the other conspirators, who agreed that Rasputin would have to be shot. Yusupov returned with Dmitri's Browning pistol.

"My head is heaving and I've a burning sensation in my stomach," complained Rasputin. "Give me another glass of wine." Rasputin suggested visiting the Gypsies and admired a crystal crucifix on an exquisite ebony cabinet.

"Grigory Efimovich," said Yusupov, "you had best look at that crucifix and say a prayer." Drawing the Browning from behind his back, he shot Rasputin in the chest. Rasputin screamed. The bullet, passing through his stomach and liver and out of his back, was not instantly fatal, found the pathologist, but would probably have killed him within twenty minutes. As he collapsed "like a broken doll," the conspirators burst in and looked down at the body with blood spreading across its blouse. Yusupov sent two of the conspirators, one dressed as his chauffeur, the other as "Rasputin," to pretend to take the *starets* home. Nervously checking on his victim in the now silent palace, Yusupov claimed he shook the body which suddenly stirred. One "greenish and snake-like" eye opened. Then the other. Foaming at the mouth, snarling furiously and oozing blood, Rasputin sprang up and seized Yusupov, ripping off an epaulette in "the ferocious struggle . . . this devil who was dying of poison, who had a bullet in his heart, must have been raised from the dead by the powers of evil. There was something appalling in his diabolical refusal to die." Rasputin collapsed again, then struggled to his feet as the prince ran screaming upstairs, "Purishkevich, shoot, shoot, he's alive! He's getting away!" Rasputin staggered out into the snowy courtyard, roaring, "Felix! Felix! I'll tell the tsarina everything!"

Purishkevich, who was drunk, drew his Sauvage pistol, ran downstairs and followed Rasputin into the courtyard. He took aim and fired twice, missed, fired again and hit his quarry. This bullet, penetrating his lower right back, passing through his right kidney, was not instantly fatal but it too might have killed him in twenty minutes.

Rasputin fell in the snow, amateurishly wounded once by Yusupov and once by Purishkevich, but still just alive. Someone, possibly Purishkevich, possibly Dmitri, or someone else with a little more professional sangfroid, a British secret agent, such as Rayner, gave Rasputin the *coup de grâce* in the middle of this forehead, so point-blank that the skin was burned. It killed him instantly. Purishkevich kicked the body in the head, but the shots had attracted some soldiers in the street. "I killed Grishka Rasputin," he cried. "Enemy of Russia and the tsar."

"Glory to God!" shouted the soldiers, kissing him and then helping him carry the body back into the palace.

A policeman had also been alerted by the shots. Purishkevich swore him to secrecy and boasted of his patriotic deed (though the policeman immediately went to report what he had heard). Yusupov hysterically attacked the body with a dumbbell and then fainted. Someone shot a dog to explain the blood-spatter. Purishkevich, Dmitri and Lazovert wrapped Rasputin in a curtain and stowed him in the grand duke's car. "Dmitri," recalled Purishkevich, "was in an almost light-hearted mood." The grand duke drove out towards the Great Petrovsky Bridge. There around 6 a.m., as Dmitri stood guard, they swung the body into a hole in the ice of the frozen Little Neva, tossing one of his galoshes after him.[3]

At his palace, the dazed Yusupov was now attended by the British secret agent Oswald Rayner, who may have been in the palace all along. Distancing himself from the crime scene, Yusupov moved to the residence of his parents-in-law, Sandro and Xenia, accompanied by Rayner: "He understands everything that has happened and is most anxious on my behalf."

Rasputin's daughters called Anna Vyrubova and then the police. Anna hurried to the empress. Protopopov called. Rasputin was still missing. The policeman reported drunken ruffians bragging about the murder. The family waited.

Dmitri and Yusupov both telephoned Alexandra asking for an audience, but Anna, manning the phone, refused: "If Felix has anything to say, let him write it to me." Her account continued: "Thoroughly aroused, the empress ordered Protopopov to investigate." When the police found Yusupov, escorted by Rayner, at Sandro's palace, he claimed that the bloodstains in his courtyard belonged to a shot dog, but he added that "my wife is a niece of the emperor" who alone could order an investigation. The police found the dead dog.

That night, Protopopov phoned Alexandra: Yusupov and Rayner were boarding a train for Crimea. The empress placed the prince under house arrest.

"We are sitting together—can you imagine our feelings," she wrote to the emperor. "Our Friend has disappeared" after "a big scandal at Yusupov's house, Dmitri, Purishkevich drunk, police heard shots, Purishkevich ran out screaming that Our Friend was killed. The police are searching." Yusupov had set "quite a paw"—a trap. "I can't and won't believe He has been killed. God have mercy. Such utter anguish (am calm and can't believe it). Kisses Sunny."

"What an awful thing!" Nicky telegraphed back overnight.

"Just took communion in home chapel," she telegraphed at 11:42 next morning, 18 December. "Searchings continue," but she now feared a coup. "There's a danger that the two boys [Dmitri and Yusupov] are organizing something still worse . . . I need your presence terribly."

"Leaving at 4:30," wrote Nicky.

"Ordered in your name to forbid Dmitri to leave his home. He is the main one involved," she reported at 3 p.m. "Body not found."

At Stavka in Mogilev, "We went on our afternoon stroll, talked about things," recalled the emperor's aide-de-camp Anatoly Mordvinov, who was with him. But Nicky had not yet read the key telegram. "Only now read your letter," wrote Nicholas at 6:38 p.m. "Anguished and horrified. Arrive tomorrow at 4."

The police found the galosh on the ice, but the cold delayed the divers. In the morning on 19 December, "They found the body in the water," she telegraphed Stavka. "Thoughts, prayers together." The children were shocked, but only the eldest Olga understood, asking, "I know he did much harm, but why did they treat him so cruelly?"

Rasputin was frozen solid. First the body was taken to hospital to thaw. Then Dr. Dmitri Kosorotov identified the three bullet wounds, but found no evidence that Rasputin had still been alive and breathing in the river. On the contrary, the shot in the forehead caused instant death.

That afternoon, the autocrat, accompanied by Uncle Pitz, arrived back at Tsarskoe. "I am filled with shame that the hands of my kinsmen are stained with the blood of a simple peasant," he said, while the dynasty, public and society celebrated Rasputin's murder.

"No! No!" cried the dowager empress. Her view was "Lord be praised for taking away Rasputin but we're in much greater trouble." Ella telegraphed Zinaida Yusupova: "God bless your dear son for his patriotic act." Her note was perlustrated by the secret police who copied it to Nicky and Alix. They must also have reported British involvement because one of the first things the emperor did was summon the ambassador Sir George Buchanan and demand to know the role of "British officers."

"Not a word of truth," replied Buchanan, apart from Yusupov's friendship with Rayner. But a week later, Captain Alley reported to Scale: "Dear Scale . . . Although matters here have not proceeded entirely to plan, our objective has clearly been achieved. Reaction to the demise of 'Dark Forces' has been well received, although a few awkward questions have already been asked about wider involvement. Rayner is attending to loose ends."

The murder of Rasputin had been an amateurish operation, "carried out," wrote Trotsky, "in the manner of a scenario designed for people of bad taste." But Yusupov's and Purishkevich's accounts, quoted above, are incomplete and melodramatic. The post-mortem found no evidence of cyanide poisoning—perhaps it had deteriorated, perhaps it had been neutralized by the wine—but none of the memoirs mentions the point-blank shot in Rasputin's forehead. Were they ashamed to have executed an unconscious peasant in cold blood—or did someone else deliver the *coup de grâce*? There is no proof that British agents were present at the murder nor that they participated, while Alley's letter, if genuine, as it seems to be, is ambiguous and proves only that the British were informed afterwards. But Rayner, whether officially or in his capacity as friend, was very close at hand; it seems the British were somehow involved.

At 8 a.m. on 21 December 1916, a police van delivered Rasputin's zinc coffin to Tsarskoe Selo's almost completed St. Seraphim of Sarov Church. The emperor and empress, together with their daughters (but not Alexei, who was poorly), arrived by limousine and the crippled Anna by sleigh—but Alexandra did not invite Rasputin's own daughters, who resented their callous exclusion. The empress gripped a white bouquet and sobbed when she saw the coffin. "My family and I witnessed a sad scene," wrote Nicholas. "The burial of the unforgettable Grigory, assassinated by monsters at the home of Yusupov." Afterwards Alexandra invited Anna to move into the Alexander Palace for her own safety, while Rasputin's daughters were brought to Tsarskoe. There Nicholas II "was very emotional and tender with us," promising "I'll try to replace your father." Alexandra gave the Rasputins 100,000 roubles and often visited Rasputin's grave. The tsar's children were unsurprisingly gloomy and fearful, asking their father's ADC, Mordvinov, to join them in their room, where they clung together on the sofa.

The killing changed little because Nicholas and Alexandra, not Rasputin, were the true authors of their own political plight. Rasputin usually just confirmed and blessed their prejudices. Far from saving the monarchy, the murder emasculated it. On 21 December, a Romanov cabal, including Uncle Pitz (Dmitri's father), Sandro (Yusupov's father-in-law) and Miechen, met to protect the killers. They sent Sandro to ask the tsar not to prosecute.

"A very nice speech, Sandro," Nicky replied to Sandro's plea. "Are you aware nobody has the right to kill, be it grand duke or peasant?" Sandro became less reasonable. "In a voice that could easily be heard in the corridor outside," wrote Anna, "he shouted that should the emperor refuse, the throne itself would fall."

Nicholas's mother asked him to close the case against Dmitri. "Prosecution immediately stopped. Embrace you. Nicky." Instead the tsar banished Yusupov to a Kursk estate and Dmitri to join the army in Persia. The murder divided the killers for ever. "That will always be a dark stain on my conscience . . . Murder will always be murder, I never speak about it," Dmitri later wrote to Yusupov. "You talk about it. You practically brag that you did it with your own hands," although "there's no nobility whatsoever in that deed." But even Alexei was appalled that his father had not really punished the murderers: "Papa, is it possible that you won't punish them? The assassins of Stolypin were hanged."

On 29 December, sixteen Romanovs, led by Miechen and Bimbo, met at the Vladimir Palace on Millionaya Street to sign a letter appealing for Dmitri not to be sent to disease-riddled Persia, which would be "the same as outright death." The tsar regarded this as a family revolt.

"No one has the right to commit murder," the tsar wrote on the letter. "I know that many are troubled by their conscience and Dmitri is not the only one implicated in this. I'm surprised by your request." He banished Bimbo and Miechen's sons to their estates.

The sovereigns must have recalled Rasputin's warning: "If I die or you desert me, you'll lose your son and your crown in six months."[4]

The day of the Romanov "revolt," the tsar sacked Trepov, premier for forty-seven days, and replaced him with Prince Nikolai Golitsyn, an old mediocrity who had served on Alexandra's charity committee—he was "soft," wrote Sandro, "he understood nothing." Protopopov, who held séances to consult Rasputin, remained the strongman. Sandro warned Nicky that "Strange as it may seem the government today is the organ that is preparing revolution." But the other Romanovs were less restrained.

Miechen summoned Rodzianko to the Vladimir Palace: "Things must be changed, removed, destroyed . . ."

"Removed?" asked Rodzianko.

"She must be annihilated."

"Who?"

"The empress."

"Your Highness, allow me to treat this conversation as if it had never happened." Even the tsar's mother now wanted Alexandra "banished. Otherwise she might go completely mad. Let her enter a convent or just disappear."

Sir George Buchanan advised the tsar that the army was now unreliable and he must regain the people's confidence.

"You tell me *I* must regain the confidence of the people. Isn't it rather for my people to regain *my* confidence?" Buchanan started to brief in favour of Nicholas's abdication. Rodzianko gave Nicholas the same advice. "Is it possible that for twenty-two years I tried to act for the best and for twenty-two years it was all a mistake?" asked the tsar.

"Yes, Your Majesty, for twenty-two years, you followed the wrong course."

Rasputin's killing gave Nicholas the political cover to remove Alexandra from politics and choose a unifying prime minister. The past could be blamed on the *starets*. But he did not take that course. His courtier Mosolov tried to warn him. "How can even you, Mosolov, talk to me about danger to the dynasty which right now everyone is trying to din into me? Can you too who have been with me during my inspections of troops also get frightened?"

Sandro made a last appeal to the couple at the Alexander Palace as Alexandra lay in bed and Nicky, wearing a *cherkesska* coat, smoked. "Please Alix, leave the cares of state to your husband," he said.

Alix "blushed. She looked at Nicky. He said nothing and continued to smoke." Sandro turned to her.

"I never said a word to you about the disgraceful goings-on in our government, better to say *your* government. I realize you're willing to perish and your husband feels the same way. But what about us? Must we suffer your blind stubbornness?"

"I refuse to continue this dispute," she said coldly. "You're exaggerating the danger. Some day when you're less excited, you'll admit I knew better."

The next day, Sandro returned with Misha to see the tsar, who once again smoked dreamily as his brother beseeched him to reform before it was too late. Misha and his wife, Natasha, both wanted a constitutional government. Misha, now inspector-general of cavalry, had been redeemed by the war, commanding the Savage Division of Caucasian troops with courage, serving under General Brusilov who praised this "absolutely honourable and upright man, taking no sides and lending himself to no intrigues; as a soldier he was an excellent leader." Before Misha left for Petrograd, Brusilov had asked him to "explain to the tsar the need for immediate drastic reforms."

"I am of no consequence," replied Misha. But he was about to find out that he was of consequence.

Nicholas called in Prime Minister Golitsyn and announced that he would appoint a new ministry. But the next day he changed his mind—though he allowed the Duma to reopen.

On 21 February 1917, Anna observed that "all his instincts warned him against leaving Tsarskoe Selo at that time." The following day, as Alexandra "prayed and Our dear Friend does so in yonder world," and as she urged him to "let them feel your fist at all times," the emperor, accompanied by old Frederiks and his trusty black American Jim Hercules, returned to the deceptive calm of Stavka.[5]

"My brain feels rested here, no ministers and no fidgety questions," he noted. But "it's so quiet in this house, no rumbling about, no excited shouts! If I'm free here I think I will turn to dominoes again," he replied, weary of his wife's nagging. "What you write about being firm—the master—is perfectly true . . . but I need not bellow at people right and left. A quiet sharp remark is enough very often to put one or the other in their place." Snowstorms had halted supplies for the troops. "Quite horribly anguishing."

On International Women's Day, 23 February, female textile workers demonstrated shouting "Give us bread." Surely Petrograd Military Governor, General Sergei Khabalov could cope with a few women? The next day, 24 February, as Olga and Alexei then Anna came down with measles, "there were rows because the poor people stormed the breadshops" in Petrograd, Alexandra reported to Nicholas. "The Cossacks were called out against them . . . but it's in Khabalov's hands." The tsar's calm was not complete madness: Protopopov had arrested all socialist leaders. While there were only 6,000 police in Petrograd, "reliable" Naval Guards strengthened the 160,000-strong garrison. Plans were made to suppress any uprising. Back in Mogilev, "I know the situation is very alarming," Nicholas told Mogilev's governor, but militarily "we are stronger than ever before. Soon in the spring will come the offensive and I believe God will give us victory and then moods will change."

On 25 February, Misha, who now featured as regent in many conspiracies, noticed "disorders on Nevsky Prospect today. Workmen were going about with red flags and throwing grenades and bottles at the police so the troops had to open fire." On Znamenskaya Square, a Cossack, traditional guardian of the Romanovs, killed a Gendarme. Protopopov reported to Alexandra that the disorders were spreading as virtually all the factories went on strike. "It's a hooligan movement, young boys and girls running about and screaming they have no bread, only to excite and then the workmen preventing others from work," she told Nicholas. If only the cold would return—the temperature had risen above freezing—the crowds would stay at home. "But this will all pass and quieten down . . . No shooting required, only order and not let them cross the bridges. That food question is maddening."

At nine o'clock that evening, Nicholas telegraphed Khabalov: "I command you tomorrow to stop the disorders in the capital."

Though coping with a house full of sick children, Alexandra had received a number of foreigners on the 25th, but lay low the next day. As many as 200,000 people were now on Petrograd's streets with cab and tram drivers on strike. Overnight, Protopopov and the ministers met with generals and Duma members at the Mariinsky Palace "to take severe measures." "I hope Khabalov will know how to stop those street rows quickly," Nicky wrote back to Alix on 26 February. "Protopopov ought to give clear instructions. Only that old Golitsyn [prime minister] doesn't lose his head!" But he was feeling the strain: "I felt an excruciating pain in the middle of my chest . . . and my forehead was covered with beads of sweat" as he prayed.

Khabalov's troops fired on the demonstrators. The protests flickered then flared again. Misha, observing the streets, noticed that "the disorders have gathered momentum. 200 killed."

At Tsarskoe, on that fine sunny day, Alexandra, wearing her Red Cross nurse's uniform, and Maria prayed at Rasputin's grave—"he died to save us"—but she reassured Nicky that "It's not like 1905. All adore you and only want bread."

Yet in Petrograd the streets were out of control and the president of the Duma, Rodzianko, was drafting a bombshell telegram informing the emperor that "Popular uprisings are taking on uncontrollable and threatening dimensions . . . Your Majesty, save Russia . . . Urgently summon a person in whom the whole country can have faith and entrust him with the formation of a government . . . Any procrastination is tantamount to death."

"Fatso Rodzianko has again written me a lot of nonsense to which I won't even give a reply," Nicholas told Count Frederiks. He ordered the dismissal of the Duma—but decided to return to Petrograd.

Overnight, the Pavlovsky Guards, followed by many other units, mutinied. The Preobrazhenskys murdered their colonel. On 27 February, the streets filled again with workers. Crowds stormed the Arsenal. Now they were armed. "The army was fraternizing with the revolt," observed Paléologue, the French ambassador. Policemen were killed. Police headquarters was set on fire. Shops were looted. Trucks and limousines were requisitioned and driven crazily through the streets. The city except for a well-defended Winter Palace was overrun by the revolution: "the beginning of anarchy," noted Misha. Khabalov appealed to Stavka: "Quickly send reliable troops from the front." When his ADC brought him the latest telegrams from Petrograd, the tsar snapped: "What's the matter, Mordvinov?" Nicholas looked at the "terrible" news for so long, the pause was "painful, excruciating."

"How happy I am at the thought of meeting you in two days," Nicholas wrote to Alix. "After the news of yesterday from town, I saw many faces here with frightened expressions. Alexeev is calm but finds an energetic man must be named to make the ministers work. That's right of course." So finally that evening the tsar, advised by the general, was ready to appoint the ministry, but first he would crush the revolution. He ordered General Nikolai Ivanov, appointed emergency commander of Petrograd, to hurry to the capital with a train of loyal forces.

At the Taurida Palace in Petrograd, Prince Golitsyn tried to dismiss the Duma, but the parliamentarians refused to go, creating a "temporary committee" under Rodzianko. When he reached the Mariinsky Palace, Khabalov admitted that the city was lost. Golitysn forced Protopopov to resign, then telegraphed his own resignation to the tsar who rejected it.

"What shall I do?" wondered Rodzianko at the Taurida Palace. "I have no desire to revolt . . . on the other hand there's no government." He appealed to the tsar—and the generals: "Sire, do not delay . . . Tomorrow may be too late." Then he summoned Misha from Gatchina.

At 5 p.m., Misha arrived on his private train and rushed to meet the prime minister and Rodzianko at the Mariinsky Palace. "By 9 p.m. shootings in the streets had begun," he recalled, "and the old rule ceased to exist." Rodzianko urged Misha to "assume dictatorship of the city," rallying the last loyal troops of the garrison. Misha refused—but at 10:30 p.m. he crossed the square to the war minister's residence to communicate with the tsar via Alexeev's Hughes apparatus. He proposed the respected Prince Lvov as prime minister. "Your Imperial Majesty may wish to authorize me to announce this."

"I will report Your Imperial Highness's telegram to his Imperial Majesty immediately," replied the chief of staff, Alexeev.

"It may be advisable to delay HM the emperor's journey to Tsarskoe Selo for several days . . . Every hour is precious."

Nicholas rejected all Misha's advice. He would not make "changes to his personal staff until his arrival in Tsarskoe Selo." At 11:25 p.m. the emperor telegraphed Golitsyn: "I personally bestow upon you all necessary powers for civil rule." But all powers had long since bled away. Golitsyn and the ministers just went home.

At 3 a.m., Misha was driven with a military escort to the Winter Palace, only just escaping revolutionaries by accelerating away. At the palace he found General Khabalov and a thousand loyal troops, but ordered them not to defend the palace. As Khabalov retreated to the Admiralty, Misha and his secretary walked through the Hermitage to emerge on Millionnaya Street. Misha knocked on the door of number 14, the apartment of his friend Prince Pavel Putiatin. "I woke with a start hearing violent knocking on my bedroom door," recalled Olga Putiatina, whose husband was at the front. "I imagined armed soldiers had burst into my apartment," but instead she welcomed a "very tired and very upset" Misha.

"Aren't you afraid, princess, of having such a dangerous guest?" he joked.

Simultaneously at Stavka, the emperor was feeling cut off. "It's a revolting sensation to be so far away and receive only scraps of bad news," he wrote. "I decided to return to Tsarskoe as soon as possible."

At 5 a.m., almost as Misha was sipping Princess Putiatina's coffee, the tsar left Mogilev in his train, taking an indirect route eastwards via Vyazma in order to leave the main line clear for Ivanov's loyal forces—but this added 200 miles and nine hours to his journey. At three o'clock that afternoon, Nicholas arrived at Vyazma, telegraphing Alexandra: "Thoughts always together. Glorious weather. Many troops sent from front."

Taking a break from nursing her children, the empress with a fur coat over her nurse's uniform, and the seventeen-year-old Maria walked around the park, greeting the troops. "They're all our friends," she said. "Devoted to us."[6]

On the Moscow–Petrograd line, Nicholas's train was just sixty miles away, but at 4 a.m. on 1 March it was stopped at Malaya Vishera. Revolutionaries blocked the line—at least that excuse halted the tsar. "Shame and dishonour," wrote Nicholas. "Impossible to get to Tsarskoe. How difficult it must be for poor Alix." After an anxious discussion, the tsar reversed his tracks, then steamed westwards to Pskov.

During the next fifteen hours of 1 March as the tsar was incommunicado, Petrograd fell to the revolution. After a firefight, the loyalists at the Admiralty surrendered. A chaotic new world was emerging in the Taurida Palace: a thousand scruffy, milling revolutionaries, ruffians and deserters of the Soviet of Workers and Soldiers vied with frockcoated gentlemen of the Temporary Committee of the Duma to rule Russia. The only link between the two was the socialist lawyer Alexander Kerensky, aged thirty-five, who was a member of both. Kyril, erratic son of Vladimir and Miechen, withdrew troops guarding Tsarskoe Selo and, waving a red flag, marched into the Taurida Palace, where Rodzianko drafted a manifesto for a constitutional monarchy—under the regency of Misha.

At 7 p.m., at Pskov, the emperor finally emerged out of the snowy wastelands, oblivious of the new world born in his absence.[7]

He found himself in the gruff grip of General Nikolai Ruzsky, sixty-three-year-old commander of the northern front. Nicholas was alone except for his devoted courtiers,* at whom Ruzsky growled: "Look what you've done . . . all your Rasputin clique. What have you got Russia into now?"

Emperor and general sat together awkwardly in the salon of the imperial train.

"I'm responsible before God and Russia for everything that's happening," declared Nicholas, still bound by his coronation oath, "regardless of whether ministers are responsible to the Duma or State Council."

"One must accept the formula 'the monarch reigns but the government rules,'" explained Ruzsky.

This, explained the emperor, was incomprehensible to him, and he would need to be differently educated, born again. He could not take decisions against his conscience. Ruzsky brusquely argued with the emperor into the night without, Nicholas complained afterwards, "leaving him one moment for reflection." Then a telegram arrived from General Alexeev revealing the widening revolution and proposing a government under Rodzianko. Nicholas, under unbearable pressure, telegraphed General Ivanov with orders "to undertake no measures before my arrival" in Petrograd. At 2 a.m., now on 2 March, Nicholas agreed to appoint Rodzianko prime minister, retaining autocratic power. Then he went to bed. Ruzsky informed Rodzianko, who replied at 3:30 a.m., "It's obvious neither His Majesty nor you realize what's going on here . . . There is no return to the past . . . The threatening demands for an abdication in favour of the son with Michael Alexandrovich as regent are becoming quite definite." In the course of that evening, the bewhiskered gents of the Duma, who wished to preserve the monarchy, and the leather-capped Marxists of the Petrograd Soviet, who wanted a republic, had compromised to form a Provisional Government—and seek Nicholas's abdication in favour of Alexei. The new premier was Prince Lvov, with Kerensky as justice minister. Now that they knew Nicholas was in Pskov, the Duma sent two members, Guchkov and Vasily Shulgin, to procure his abdication. They set off immediately.

---

* He was accompanied by the doddery but devoted court minister Count Frederiks, now seventy-nine, the count's son-in-law the sleek palace commandant General Vladimir Voeikov, the marshal of the court Prince Vasily "Valya" Dolgoruky (son-in-law of the grand marshal of the court Benckendorff and son of the one before him) and of course the African-American Jim Hercules.

Romanov power rested on the army. The generals were monarchists, but they wished to avoid civil strife in order to fight the Germans. "My conviction," telegraphed Alexeev to the emperor at 9 a.m., "is that there's no choice and abdication should take place." There was a "terrible moment of silence" as Nicholas read this. He smoked cigarettes and walked up and down the station.

At 10:15 a.m. Alexeev polled Nikolasha, Brusilov and other commanders by telegraph. In the imperial train at Pskov, lunch was agonizing. At 2:15 p.m. the chief of staff reported the unanimous decision of the generals, even Nikolasha: abdication in favour of Alexei. "There's no other way," wrote Nikolasha.

Nicholas, wearing his favourite grey Circassian coat, stood looking out of the window, thinking, "My abdication is necessary," as he recorded in his diary. Then he turned to Ruzsky: "I've decided. I shall renounce the throne." He crossed himself; so did Ruzsky.

"I agreed," he wrote, signing the telegrams to Rodzianko and Alexeev abdicating in favour of Alexei and regent Misha. The general took the telegrams, while Count Frederiks staggered out and told the adjutants in the neighbouring wagon: "*Savez-vous, l'empereur a abdiqué.*" To the anguished shouts of the adjutants, he shrugged hopelessly and then, to hide his tears, he locked himself in his carriage.

Nicholas called in the court physician Professor Sergei Fedorov, who had so often treated Alexei.

"Your Majesty," asked the doctor, "do you think Alexei will stay with you?"

"And why not?" replied Nicky. "He's still a child and must remain with the family . . . Until then Michael is regent."

"No, Your Majesty, that's unlikely to be possible."

"Tell me frankly, Sergei Petrovich," he said, "is Alexei's malady incurable?"

"Science teaches us, Sire, that it's an incurable disease. Yet those afflicted can sometimes reach old age."

"This is just what the tsarina told me." Nicholas hung his head. "Well, if that's the case and Alexei can never serve his country as I'd like him to, we have the right to keep him ourselves." He ordered General Alexeev to change the terms of the abdication.[8]

At 9:45 p.m., Frederiks escorted the two parliamentarians Guchkov and Shulgin into the salon. There they were joined by the autocrat, who was "absolutely calm and impenetrable"—but he had long hated Guchkov. "We bowed, the emperor greeted us and shook hands," wrote Shulgin. "The gesture was rather friendly." They sat at a table. Guchkov started to explain their mission until General Ruzsky came in, bowed, listened and then interrupted: "The matter has been decided."

"I've made the decision to abdicate," said Nicholas—but he would not leave the throne to Alexei. "I have come to the conclusion that, in the light of his illness, I should abdicate in my name and his simultaneously as I cannot be separated from him."

"But we had counted on the figure of little Alexei Nikolaievich to soften the effect of the transfer of power," Guchkov argued. The emperor hesitated, then added poignantly: "I hope you will understand the feelings of a father." His successor was Misha. Guchkov and Ruzsky consulted together. This was against Emperor Paul's Fundamental Laws. Misha was married to Countess Brassova: could an emperor have a morganatic wife? Yes, hadn't Alexander II married Dolgorukaya? They accepted Nicholas's plan. At 11:40 p.m., retiring to his private wagon, the ex-emperor signed the manifesto, witnessed by Frederiks—the old man "in despair," his hands trembling—backdated to 3 p.m.:

> Not wishing to be parted from Our Beloved Son, We hand over the succession to Our Brother the Grand Duke Michael Alexandrovich and bless him on his accession.*

Returning to the salon, Frederiks handed the abdication to Guchkov and Ruzsky. Nicholas was so calm, "I even wondered whether we were dealing with a normal person," recalled Guchkov. "One might expect some show of emotion but nothing of the sort." In fact Nicky was seething: "God gives me the strength to forgive all my enemies but ... I can't forgive General Ruzsky." As the ex-tsar, polite to the last, saw off Guchkov and Shulgin, his Cossack escort saluted him.

"It's time for you to take my initials off your shoulder-straps," he told them.

"Please, Your Imperial Majesty," asked one Cossack, "allow us to kill them!"

Nicholas smiled. "It's too late for that," he said ruefully.

Nicholas "renounced the throne," as an aide saw it, "as if he were turning over command of a cavalry squadron." Afterwards, as liveried servants served tea, "the tsar sat peaceful and calm," wrote his ADC Mordvinov. "He kept up conversation and only his eyes which were sad, thoughtful and staring into the distance, and his nervous movements when he took a cigarette betrayed his inner disturbance." It was agony for the courtiers. "When will this end?" wondered Mordvinov. Inside the ex-tsar was raging: "All around is betrayal, cowardice and deceit!" At that moment, Misha became Emperor Michael II.[9]

* This was compounded by two minor acts of legerdemain chicanery: Nicholas signed the appointments of Lvov as prime minister and Nikolasha as commander-in-chief, both backdated to 2 p.m.

*

As the front-line soldiers took the oath to Michael II, the new tsar was obliviously slumbering in the Millionnaya Street apartment until, at 5:55 a.m., Kerensky phoned to announce that a delegation would visit later. Misha still did not know he was tsar. At nine o'clock, the bell rang and his cousin Bimbo embraced him.

"I'm very happy to recognize you as Sovereign," said Bimbo, "since you're already tsar. Be brave and strong."

At 9:30, just after Bimbo had left, Prince Lvov, the prime minister, and his ministers including Kerensky, Rodzianko and Guchkov (just back from Pskov and now war minister) arrived. They had scarcely slept for many nights, swinging between terror of imminent slaughter to the exhilaration of living momentous history. All except Kerensky were terrified of the Soviet and most were convinced that Misha's accession would lead to "colossal bloodshed." They stood up as Michael II entered.[10]

At Tsarskoe Selo, the news of Nicholas's abdication had arrived at 3 a.m. Afraid to tell the empress, the courtiers instead told Uncle Pitz, who went to see the empress that morning. Alexandra knew that Nicky had been forced to appoint a Duma ministry. "And you who are alone, no army behind you, were caught like a mouse in a trap, what can you do? That's the lowest meanest trick, unheard of in history."

Unable to say a word, Uncle Pitz stood kissing her hand for a long time. "His heart was breaking. The empress in her simple nurse's uniform, struck him with her serenity," recorded Pitz's wife.

"Dear Alix, I wanted to be with you . . ." he said.

"What's happening with Nicky?"

"Nicky is well but you must be brave: today at one in the morning, he signed the abdication for himself and Alexei."

The ex-empress shuddered: "If Nicky did it, then it must have been necessary." Tears trickled down her cheeks. "I may no longer be empress," she said, "but I still remain a sister of mercy. As Misha will now be emperor, I'll look after the children, the hospital, we'll go to Crimea . . ."

Alix tottered towards her friend Lili Dehn. "Abdiqué!" she sobbed. "Poor darling—alone there and suffering. My God, what he must have suffered." She tried to send telegrams to Nicky but they were returned: "Address of person mentioned unknown." Now she wrote: "I fully understand your action, my own hero . . . I know that you could not sign against what you swore at your coronation. We know each other through and through—need no words." So far the five children knew nothing. Helped by Anna, Alexandra burned correspondence, but "She never recovered from the grief of destroying her youthful love letters which were more to her than the most costly jewels," wrote her daughter Olga.

When Lenin and his wife Krupskaya heard the news in Geneva, she wondered, "Perhaps it's another hoax."

"It's staggering," agreed Lenin. "It's so incredibly unexpected."

The ex-tsar steamed back to Stavka, sitting alone in the gloom, lit only by the lamp of an icon in the corner. "After all the experiences of this sad day, the emperor, always distinguished by enormous self-control, no longer had the strength to restrain himself," recalled Voeikov. "He embraced me and wept." Afterwards "I slept long and deeply," wrote Nicholas. "Talked with my people about yesterday. Read a lot about Julius Caesar." Then he remembered Misha: "To His Majesty Emperor Michael. Recent events have led me to decide irrevocably to take this extreme step. Forgive me if it grieves you and also for no warning— there was no time."[11]

In the flat on Millionnaya Street, the ministers tried to intimidate Michael into abdicating. He asked if they could guarantee his safety. "I had to answer in the negative," said Rodzianko, but Pavel Milyukov, the foreign minister, argued that this "frail craft"—the Provisional Government—would sink in "the ocean of national disorder" without the raft of the monarchy. Kerensky, the only one who could speak for the Soviet, disagreed, threatening chaos: "I can't answer for Your Highness's life."

Princess Putiatina invited them all for lunch, sitting between the emperor and the prime minister. After a day of negotiations, Michael signed his abdication: "I have taken a firm decision to assume the Supreme Power only if such be the will of our great people by universal suffrage through its representatives in the Constituent Assembly." Next day, he sent a note to his wife Natasha: "Awfully busy and extremely exhausted. Will tell you many interesting things." Among those interesting things, he had been emperor of Russia for a day—and, after 304 years, the Romanovs had fallen.[12]

SCENE 7

# Afterlife

# CAST

NICHOLAS II, ex-emperor, "Nicky"
Alexandra Fyodorovna (née Princess Alix of Hesse), ex-empress, "Alix,"
    "Sunny"
Olga, their eldest daughter
Tatiana, their second daughter
Maria, their third daughter
Anastasia, their youngest daughter
Alexei, their son, "Tiny," "Baby"


## THE ROMANOVS

Maria Fyodorovna, dowager empress, widow of Alexander III, "Minny"
MICHAEL II, ex-emperor, "Misha," "Floppy," married Countess Brassova
Miechen, widow of Uncle Vladimir
Ella, widow of Uncle Sergei, sister of the tsarina, abbess
Uncle Paul, "Pitz," married Princess Paley
Nikolai Nikolaievich, "Nikolasha the Terrible," married Stana of
    Montenegro
Peter Nikolaievich, his brother, married Militsa of Montenegro
Nikolai Mikhailovich, "Bimbo"
Alexander Mikhailovich, his brother, "Sandro," married the tsar's sister
    Xenia
Sergei Mikhailovich, their brother, lover of Little K, formerly inspector-
    general of artillery


## COURTIERS, ministers etc.

Prince Vasily Dolgoruky, marshal of the court, "Valya"
Count Ilya Tatishchev, the tsar's adjutant-general
Anna Vyrubova (née Taneeva), Alexandra's friend, "Lovesick Creature,"
    "Cow"
Countess Elizabeth Kurakina-Naryshkina, mistress of the robes, "Zizi"

Anatoly Mordvinov, aide-de-camp to Nicholas II
General Mikhail Alexeev, chief of staff
Prince Georgi Lvov, prime minister
Alexander Kerensky, justice minister then prime minister

## REVOLUTIONARIES

Filipp Goloshchekin, military commissar of the Ural Soviet Executive Committee
Vasily Yakovlev, commissar appointed to escort the imperial family
Yakov Yurovsky, member of the Urals Soviet, murderer of the imperial family
Grigory Nikulin, Yurovsky's deputy, murderer of the imperial family
Peter Ermakov, Chekist, murderer of the imperial family
Peter Voikov, member of Urals Soviet, commissar for supplies, "Intellectual"

On 3 March 1917, at Mogilev station, General Alexeev told Nicholas that the dynasty had ended. The ex-tsar was appalled that Misha's manifesto had contained "something about elections. God knows who advised him to sign something so vile." He summoned his mother but she arrived with Sandro, whose presence he found "unendurable."

"Poor Nicky," wrote Minny, "splendidly calm, collected and magnificent in this awful humiliating position. It was as if I had been hit on the head!" After dinner, "Poor Nicky opened his poor bleeding heart and we wept together."

When Sandro joined them, he found Minny "sobbing aloud" while Nicky "stood motionless looking at his feet and of course smoking."

Strolling in awkward silence with Mordvinov, the ADC tried to console him with the thought that this was the "will of the people" so let them see if they could manage better.

"A fine thing the will of the people!" Nicholas cried "suddenly with pain and walked ahead to hide his anguish." Then he told Mordvinov he would like to retire to Crimea "as a private person" or even to "Kostroma, our former fiefdom"—where it had all started with Michael Romanov.

"Your Majesty," replied Mordvinov, "go abroad as fast as possible."

"No, never," he said. "I'd never leave Russia. I love her too much."

On 7 March, the Provisional Government ordered Nicholas placed under guard and despatched to Tsarskoe so the next morning at 10:30, he addressed his staff in the hall at Stavka. Speaking in "curt, soldierly sentences, his modesty made a tremendous impression," wrote Sandro. Faced with his "heartfelt emotion, two or three fainted, many wept," recalled a dazed Mordvinov. "I don't remember what he said, I only heard the sound of his voice and the emperor didn't finish, but upset he left the room and I accompanied him." At the Governor's House, amid "total chaos of boxes and rolled-up carpets, I climbed without thinking to the top of the stairs and saw, through the open door of the study . . . the tsar was alone, near the desk, slowly and quietly collecting his things . . ."

At the station, he said goodbye to his mother, covering her face with kisses and then climbed into the train. "One of the most awful days in my life," wrote Minny, "separated from my beloved Nicky!" At 5 p.m. the train steamed away. Nicky stood in the window smiling with "an expression of infinite sadness" as Minny made the sign of the Cross and prayed, "May God hold his hands over him." She never saw him again.*

"My heart was nearly breaking," wrote Nicky.[1]

As Nicky travelled to Tsarskoe, Milyukov, the foreign minister, suggested to the British ambassador Buchanan that "the king and British government should offer His Imperial Majesty asylum in this country," noted George V's private secretary, Lord Stamfordham, at Buckingham Palace. The Provisional Government approved "the necessity of transporting . . . members of the former imperial family . . . beyond the frontiers of the Russian state."

Britain was the obvious destination. George V had been aghast at the abdication. "I fear Alicky is the cause of it all and Nicky has been weak. I am in despair," he wrote in his diary on 2 March, sending a telegram to the ex-tsar: "My thoughts are constantly with you and I shall always remain your true and devoted friend." When Stamfordham reported the plan to David Lloyd George, the prime minister, and his deputy Andrew Bonar Law, "It was generally agreed that the proposal . . . could not be refused." Next day a general arrived at Tsarskoe with an order of arrest for Nicky and Alix, but he added that they would be sent to Murmansk where a British battleship would take them into exile. Two days later, on 11 March, George V was telling the ex-tsar's long-exiled cousin Mikhail Mikhailovich about "poor Nicky coming to England." The royal family had already decided that the Romanovs, who would disembark at Scapa Flow, would go directly to Balmoral, the Scottish palace which was empty in winter.

At Tsarskoe, the children still did not know what had happened. Alix summoned Alexei's Swiss tutor Pierre Gilliard. "The tsar is coming back tomorrow," she said. "Alexei must be told everything. Will you do it? I'm telling the girls myself." The girls sobbed. "Mama cried terribly," said Tatiana. "I cried too but not more than I could help, for Mama's sake."

Gilliard told Alexei: "Your father doesn't want to be commander-in-chief any more."

Alexei was silent.

"You know your father doesn't want to be tsar any more."

"What!" said the boy in astonishment. "Why?"

---

* One Romanov had remained in high office: Nikolasha was again commander-in-chief, so respected in the army that General Alexeev asked the premier to keep him in office. But the Romanovs were hated in Petrograd. On 6 March, Lvov dismissed Nikolasha. The dowager empress returned to Kiev, then travelled to Crimea accompanied by her daughters, Olga and Xenia, and Sandro, as well as the Yusupovs. Joined by Nikolasha and his brother Peter along with the Crows, these Romanovs stayed at their Crimean estates.

"He's very tired and has had a lot of trouble."

"But won't Papa be tsar again afterwards?"

Gilliard explained that Misha had abdicated.

"But who's going to be tsar then?"

"Perhaps nobody."

Gilliard was struck by Alexei's modesty: "not a word about himself," but he was "very red and agitated."

"But if there isn't a tsar," he asked, "who's going to rule Russia?" No one knew the answer.

On 9 March, the ex-tsar arrived home.* "My God what a difference," wrote Colonel Nicholas Romanov, as the guards now called him. "I went upstairs and saw darling Alix and the dear children." Nicky set off for a walk harassed by six soldiers. "After tea," he wrote, "I unpacked my things."[2]

The next day in Tsarskoe Selo park, soldiers dug up and mutilated the body of Rasputin. "The face was totally black," a witness reported, "lumps of frozen earth were embedded in the dark long beard and hair." The soldiers took measurements of Rasputin's penis with a brick and almost certainly cut it off as a trophy. The body was displayed in Tsarskoe town hall.†

Nicky walked and worked in the gardens, the children resumed lessons and now their parents started to tutor them too. Alexandra taught religion and German, Nicky taught history. Nicky and Alexei, still wearing their military uniforms, broke the ice in front of the palace. Groups of soldiers turned up and demanded to look at Alexei. Derevenko, the burly sailor-bodyguard who had for so long carried Alexei during his illnesses, now "insolently bawled at the boy" and made him do menial tasks. Yet his other sailor Nagorny remained touchingly loyal. Nicky read Sherlock Holmes stories aloud in the evenings. Their isolation seemed almost familiar to the ex-tsar: "for have I not been a prisoner all my life?" he asked Benckendorff.

They expected to be leaving soon—for England or Crimea—but on 9 March the Soviet had vetoed the plan to send them abroad. Days later,

---

* Afterwards, Hercules the American and his fellow Nubians almost vanish from history, stranded in revolutionary Petersburg. The French ambassador Paléologue recalled that in spring 1917 "walking in the Summer Gardens I met one of the Ethiopians who had so many times let me into the emperor's study. He looks sad. We walk together 20 paces: he had tears in his eyes. I say words of comfort and shake his hand . . ." Years later, during the 1920s, an American visitor to Moscow spotted a tall black man wandering through the streets still wearing shabby imperial court dress.

† Rasputin's body was secretly removed on Kerensky's orders, quickly buried again, then dug up and burned with gasoline. His alleged penis had a longer life. Many Rasputin penises have been bought and sold, none of them genuine.

George V had "been thinking much about the government's proposal," wrote Lord Stamfordham to Arthur Balfour, foreign secretary. "The king has a strong personal friendship for the emperor and would be glad to do anything to help him . . . But His Majesty cannot help doubting, not only on account of the dangers of the voyage, but on general grounds of expediency, whether it is advisable that the imperial family take up residence in this country." George's weasel-words did not impress Lloyd George and Balfour. They replied that they did "not think unless the position changes that it is now possible to withdraw the invitation and they therefore trust the king will consent to adhere to the original invitation." But "Every day, the king is becoming more concerned," receiving as he was many letters, not least from working men, hostile to the proposal. "As you know," Stamfordham told Balfour, "from the first the king has thought the presence of the imperial family (especially the empress) would . . . be awkward for our Royal Family," and he asked the government to "make some other plan." Later that day, the king requested Balfour to tell the Russians "we must be allowed to withdraw." Four days later, "The prime minister admitted that evidently the matter was more serious than he was aware."

George V has been rightly blamed for this, but his pusillanimity made little difference. The children's measles had prevented a quick departure; that window was very small. Kerensky, the sole socialist in the government, boasted that the ex-tsar "is in my hands," but he became their protector. On 21 March, he arrived at Tsarskoe, met the tsar and arrested Anna Vyrubova, whom the press had vilified as Rasputin's mistress. As the summer came, the family planted vegetables and sunbathed. After their measles, the girls' hair fell out. In July, they shaved their heads and Alexei shaved his in solidarity. They went into the park wearing bandannas and then suddenly removed them and, laughing, took photographs.[3]

On 10 July, Kerensky, now prime minister, told Nicky that the family would soon be moved away from the "uneasy capital," ironically to protect them. "The Bolsheviks are after me," Kerensky explained, "and then will be after you." Nicky realized that "this person plays a positive role. The more power he has, the better things will be." Kerensky decided on Tobolsk, in Siberia. They packed, hiding a treasure-trove of jewellery in trunks full of letters and diaries and, to protect them, that Romanov talisman, the icon the Fyodorov Mother of God.

On 1 August, Kerensky supervised their departure from the Alexander Palace, bringing Nicky's brother Misha to say goodbye. Kerensky sat in the corner, put his hands over his ears and said, "Talk!," but the brothers were reticent. "Pleasant to meet," wrote Nicky, "but awkward to talk in front of strangers." They were "so moved and embarrassed," noted Benckendorff, "they found scarcely anything to say. The grand duke went out in tears." Meanwhile hostile crowds delayed their departure. The girls wept; Alexei, now thirteen, perched on a box holding his spaniel Joy; Nicky paced, smoking. "They had to wait until six in the morning sitting on their suitcases," wrote Zizi Naryshkina. "What a trial and humiliation. And they take it with the determination and meekness of saints."

Kerensky watched Alexandra sobbing in the corner and for the first time saw her "simply as a mother, anxious and weeping." But she wrote to Anna, who had just been released from prison, that the road to Tobolsk was eased by "our Friend" who "calls us there." The ex-empress was "glad to be going to the reaches of their Friend," wrote Naryshkina. "Nothing has changed in her mentality."

At 5:15 a.m., they left.* When they were safely in the train, emblazoned "Red Cross Mission," Kerensky shouted, "They can go!"⁴

After five days' train ride across the Urals, the family and thirty-nine retainers embarked on a steamer at Tyumen, passing Rasputin's house at Pokrovskoe. "The family gathered on deck to observe the *starets*'s house." The girls still wore lockets with Rasputin's picture. Arriving at Tobolsk the next evening, they stayed on board while the governor's two-storey mansion was prepared. When they moved into the renamed Freedom House, the family lived on the first floor, with a corner bedroom shared by the girls, a bedroom, study, salon and bathroom for the parents, and a small room shared by Alexei and Nagorny.

Time passed there with painful slowness. Nicky paced the yard ("infuriating not to be allowed to walk in the woods in such weather," he wrote on 22 August, adding that "walks in the garden are becoming increasingly tedious"). "Are they really afraid that I might run off?" Nicky, who craved exercise, asked the commissar in charge. "I'll never leave my family." They played endless games of bezique and dominoes, and the tutors Gilliard and Gibbes continued their lessons.

In Petrograd, Kerensky ruled from Alexander II's apartment in the

---

* Many of their shrinking retinue opted to accompany them, including Marshal of the Court Prince Vasily Dolgoruky and Adjutant-General Count Ilya Tatishchev, doctors Botkin and Derevenko, the Swiss tutor Gilliard and Alexei's devoted sailor Nagorny, plus Alix's ladies-in-waiting Countess Anastasia Hendrikova and Baroness Isa Buxhoeveden. The English tutor Charles Sydney Gibbes promised to join them. Frederiks, Benckendorff and Naryshkina ("Farewell darling motherly friend," Alix wrote to her, "my heart is too full to write more") were too old or too ill. And of course the family took their dogs.

Winter Palace but, undermined by military defeat and political paralysis, his power was leeching away.

Nicky corresponded with his mother and sisters in Crimea. "I'm
chopping a lot of wood," he told his mother. "The food here is excellent
and plenty of it, so that we've all settled down well in Tobolsk and have
put on 8–10 pounds." Alexandra and Anna started to exchange packages:
Anna sent clothes and Alexandra sent food since there was near-famine
in Petrograd and plenty in Siberia.

In Petrograd, on 25 October 1917, the Bolsheviks seized power. "A
second revolution," wrote Alexandra three days later. As the Germans
advanced into Russia, Lenin, the Bolshevik leader, immediately decided
to withdraw from the war which outraged Nicky: "how could these Bolshevik scoundrels have the effrontery to carry out their hidden dream
of proposing peace to the enemy?" This confirmed his belief in an international Hebraic conspiracy. "I started to read aloud Nilus's book on
the Anti-Christ to which have been added the Protocols of the Jews and
Masons (*Protocols of the Elders of Zion*)—very timely reading." Nicholas
was still blaming the evil Jews for his and Russia's fall: he was reading
this venomous anti-semitic forgery to the family. When he wrote to his
sister Xenia on 5 November, he compiled a list of revolutionaries with
their real Jewish names, claiming that Lenin was really a Tsederblium,
Trotsky a Bronshtein. While he was correct about Trotsky, Lenin was
born Ulyanov. "It's worse and more shameful," thought Nicholas, "than
the Time of Troubles."[5]

"We haven't had any significant changes in our life so far," Anastasia
wrote to a friend. "I am terribly sorry my letters turned out to be so
stupid and boring, but nothing interesting happens here." The girls
were bored. "We often sit at the windows looking at the people passing," Anastasia wrote to Anna, "and this gives us distraction." Gibbes
suggested they perform plays. "Excellent distraction," Alexandra told
Anna. "God is very near us, we are often amazed we can endure events
and separations that might once have killed us." She praised Nicholas:
"He is simply marvellous. Such meekness while all the time suffering
intensely for his country. A real marvel."

When Anna sent some dresses and perfume, the scent took the family
back to happy days. "Your perfume quite overcame us," wrote Alix. "I
went the round of our teatable and we all saw you clearly before us."

"My darling . . . your perfume reminds us so much of you," Alexei told
Anna while Alexandra reflected: "All the past is a dream. One keeps only
tears and grateful memories. One by one all earthly things slip away."

The girls started to become closer to their guards. At Christmas, they
decorated one tree for the family and another for the soldiers. "The

Grand Duchesses with that simplicity that was their charm, loved to talk to these men," wrote Gilliard, "they questioned them about their families, villages, battles in which they'd taken part."

Tatiana organized the house, Olga read quietly, while "kind-hearted, cheerful and friendly" Maria was the favourite of the guards. Anastasia's "gay and boisterous temperament . . . could dispel anyone's gloom." She starred as the male lead Mister Chugwater in the English farce *Packing Up* by Harry Grattan. When her petticoats flew up to reveal her legs in Nicky's Jaeger longjohns, "everyone collapsed in uncontrollable laughter," noted Gibbes, even Alexandra. "The last heartily unrestrained laughter the empress ever enjoyed."[6]

In February 1918 the chill of the Bolsheviks reached the family. Friendly guards were replaced by "a pack of blackguardly looking young men." Lenin's fragile regime struggled for survival. While foreign commissar Leon Trotsky negotiated peace, the kaiser's army drove deep into Russia. "The socialist fatherland is in danger," warned Lenin and must be defended to "the last drop of blood." Enemies must be "shot on the spot." The greater the crisis of the regime, the greater danger to the Romanovs.

As Nicky and Alix corresponded with friends like Anna in Petrograd and with family in Crimea, Bolshevik factions tried to storm Freedom House to kill them, while tsarist officers hatched plots to rescue them. This alarmed Lenin.

On 20 February, the Council of People's Commissars, known by the acronym Sovnarkom, chaired by Lenin, ordered that Nicholas be put on trial at a place to be decided. But Filipp Goloshchekin, an ex-dentist now military commissar of the Ural Soviet Executive Committee, suggested that the Romanovs be moved to Ekaterinburg in the Urals.

The Romanovs sensed the new peril. "Life here is nothing, eternity is everything," Alix told Anna on 2 March, "and what we are doing is preparing our souls for the Kingdom of Heaven. Thus nothing after all is terrible. If they take everything from us they cannot take our souls." All were delighted by the latest clothes from Vyrubova. "The children put on your lovely blouses. The pink jacket is far too pretty for an old woman like me but the hat is alright for my grey hair." Alexandra was only forty-five.

On 1 April, Yakov Sverdlov, chairman of the Central Executive Committee and Party secretary, Lenin's chief henchman, slight, dark, with black bouffant hair, round spectacles and a deep voice known as The Trumpet, strengthened the guards at Tobolsk and decided to bring the family to Moscow—the Bolsheviks had just moved the government back to the

Kremlin. Lenin planned to try Nicholas publicly and Trotsky proposed himself as prosecutor. Days later, Sverdlov despatched Vasily Yakovlev, a peasant's son, and experienced revolutionary, escorted by the so-called Special Purpose Detachment of 150 Red Guards, to move "Nicholas to the Urals. Our opinion is that you should settle him in Ekaterinburg for now." The Ural Bolsheviks were as divided about what to do with the former tsar as was the leadership in Moscow, but knowing that there were elements that wanted to kill him immediately, Sverdlov specified: "Yakovlev's assignment is to deliver Nicholas to Ekaterinburg alive" and hand him over to Goloshchekin, forty-two, a trusted Central Committee member appointed by Lenin and Sverdlov to run the Urals—known as "the eye of the Kremlin." Their deepest intentions are obscure. Most likely they wanted to bring Nicholas to Moscow, but, given the crisis, the Romanovs would be parked in the Bolshevik stronghold of Ekaterinburg "for now" and if in doubt, they could be killed. Lenin and Sverdlov were not afraid of bloodletting. The Nihilist Nechaev had asked, "Which member of the ruling dynasty should be destroyed? The entire ruling house." This delighted Lenin: "This is simplicity to the point of genius." He believed that "revolution is meaningless without firing squads" and had argued in a 1911 essay that "If in such a cultured country as England, it is necessary to behead one crowned criminal . . . then in Russia, it is necessary to behead at least one hundred Romanovs."

"The atmosphere around us is fairly electrified," Alix wrote to Anna on 21 March. Alexei set off a severe haemorrhage by riding down the staircase on a sled and banging his groin. "I would like to die, Mama," he cried in agony. Alexandra wrote to Anna: "Though the storm is coming nearer and nearer, our souls are at peace. Whatever happens will be through God's will."

It was her last letter. "I have come here knowing quite well that I shan't escape with my life," Count Tatishchev told Dr. Botkin. "All I ask is to be permitted to die with my emperor."

On 23 April, Yakovlev inspected Freedom House.

"Does the guard satisfy you?" Yakovlev asked.

"Very pleased," replied Nicholas, "rubbing his hands and grinning stupidly," according to Yakovlev's report.

He inspected the former tsarevich. "Alexei really did seem very ill," he reported. "The yellow-complexioned haggard boy seemed to be passing away." Yakovlev decided that the ex-tsar must leave at once. The others could follow later.

"Citizen Romanov," he told Nicholas. "I've been assigned by Sovnarkom to remove you from Tobolsk."

"Where?" asked Nicholas. "I won't go."

"What are you doing with him!" shrieked Alix. "He has an ill son. He can't go. This is too cruel! I don't believe you'll do this!"

Lenin and Trotsky had signed their peace treaty with Germany at Brest-Litovsk that ceded Ukraine and the Baltics to puppet regimes, controlled by the triumphant kaiser. "I imagine they want to force me to sign the Brest-Litovsk Treaty," Nicholas said. "But I'd rather cut off my hand."* Alexandra feared that "if he's taken alone, he'll do something stupid like he did before. Without me, they can force him to do whatever they want."

The dilemma was heartbreaking. "This is a most difficult moment for me," said Alix. "You know what my son means to me. And now I have to choose between son and husband. But I have made my choice and I have to be strong. I must leave my boy and share my life or my death with my husband." But they decided on a division of labour: Olga, Tatiana and Anastasia remained in Tobolsk—to nurse Alexei, to run the household and to "cheer everyone up" respectively; Maria would go with her parents. "We spent the evening in grief," wrote Nicholas. "Horrible suffering," noted Alix in her diary.

At tea before bed, all "did their best to hide their feelings," recalled Gilliard, knowing that "for one to give way would cause all to break down." Alexandra managed to say goodbye to Alexei calmly, but tears rolled down her cheeks. Nicky himself admitted that "To leave the rest of the children and Alexei—sick as he was—was more than difficult . . . No one slept that night."

At dawn on 26 April, Nicky, Alix and Maria, swathed in lambskin coats, climbed into carriages, followed by Prince Dolgoruky and Dr. Botkin, and galloped away. At Tyumen, "the Baggage"—the chilling Bolshevik codename for the Romanovs—got on to Special Train No. 8. "Travelling in comfort," Alexandra telegraphed Freedom House. "How is the boy? God be with you."

Unbeknown to the prisoners, the Special Purpose Detachment had just foiled an attempt by Ekaterinburg Bolshevik units to murder the

---

* The dowager empress and many of the family remained in Crimea. When the Bolsheviks signed Brest-Litovsk, the German army occupied Crimea. The kaiser ordered them to rescue Minny and the other Romanovs there. In the panic, the Yalta Soviet ordered the execution of all the Romanovs in the Crimea, so they would not fall into German hands. But they were saved by a friendly commissar who moved all of them, forty-five including servants, into Grand Duke Peter's Dulber Palace, a domed, crenellated, clifftop arabesque fantasia, which now became a comfortable Romanov prison. As Soviet troops raced to kill the Romanovs, the Romanovs prepared to defend Dulber. A firefight broke out, but the Germans saved them. They were now free. Minny moved to live at Harax, the palace of Grand Duke Georgi Mikhailovich, who was under arrest in Vologda. She lived there for eleven months, refusing the kaiser's offers of asylum and insisting on remaining in Russia. Sandro returned to his estate Ai-Todor. Nikolasha and his brother remained at Dulber.

Baggage. Yakovlev reported this to Moscow and refused to hand over the Baggage to the Urals boss, Goloshchekin: "Your detachments have the single wish of destroying the Baggage ... Do you guarantee the preservation of this Baggage?"

Yakovlev suspected a Uralite plot and, when he got to Tyumen, he pleaded for and received Sverdlov's sanction to make for Omsk while Sverdlov negotiated with the Uralites. When they gave the necessary assurances, Sverdlov ordered Yakovlev to turn around and head back: "I reached an understanding with the Uralites," he explained on 29 April. "Hand over all the Baggage in Tyumen to the chairman of the Urals regional committee; this is essential." Nicholas watched the stations passing; he realized they were retracing their steps. "Is it definitely settled we will remain in Ekaterinburg? I would have gone anywhere but the Urals. Judging by the papers, the workers there are bitterly hostile to me."

At 8:40 a.m. on 30 April, they arrived at Ekaterinburg station where a howling mob—"Hang them here!"—waited to lynch the tsar. Setting up machine guns, Yakovlev refused to hand them over. After a three-hour stand-off, Goloshchekin presided over a motorcade that took the Baggage to their new home, commandeered from a local engineer Nikolai Ipatiev, which was now designated the House of Special Purpose. Already a high fence had been built around it. On arrival they were subjected to a minute search of all their trunks. "I blew up at this," wrote Nicholas. Realizing that they were entering a dangerous new phase, Alexandra drew her talismanic sign, the swastika, on to the windowsill for luck. She would need it. At the station, Prince Valya Dolgoruky was separated from the group and later arrested, bearing maps and cash, clearly planning the family's escape.

The three girls and Alexei waited anxiously in Tobolsk. It was only on 3 May that they discovered their parents and sister had arrived not in Moscow but in Ekaterinburg, 354 miles south-west of Tobolsk.

"Here there are unpleasant surprises every day," Maria told her sisters. Nicholas added a PS for Anastasia: "I am lonesome without you, my dear. I miss you pulling funny faces at the table." The first surprise was "some sort of big fuss" in which a motley new posse, many of them Lettish workers or Hungarian prisoners-of-war from the local factories, took over as guards while there was a crackdown on fraternization with the Romanovs. Nicholas's walk was reduced to one hour a day. When he challenged this, the guards explained that this was meant to "resemble a prison regime." The next day, a housepainter arrived to whitewash all the windows.

"We suffer a great deal in our souls for you, my darlings," wrote

Tatiana to her parents. Realizing that the Ekaterinburg captivity would be harsh, the three sisters were frantically sewing their cache of jewels into their corsets, camisoles, belts and hats—an activity the family codenamed "arranging the medicines." The buttons on their summer dresses became diamonds and not only Alexei's underwear but even his army cap was woven with jewels. When the three girls pulled on this diamond-encrusted underwear, it weighed as much as four and a half pounds.

"It's difficult to write anything pleasant," replied Maria from Ekaterinburg. "There is little of that here. But on the other hand God does not abandon us, the sun shines and the birds sing . . . All that matters is to be together again soon."[7]

On 20 May the three girls and Alexei set off for Ekaterinburg, travelling by steamer and train. On the terrifying journey, the guards got drunk and tried to molest the girls to the sound of their "terrified screams." Olga was shaken, and was growing thinner and sadder. Finally arriving at Ekaterinburg, Gilliard and Gibbes, as well as the ladies-in-waiting and others, were left on the platform and told they could not accompany the family. The decision saved the lives of the tutors, who were then freed. Gilliard and Gibbes courageously stayed in the town, often walking past the house.

The family was delighted to be reunited at the Ipatiev House. The house was airless in the heat and only after complex negotiations was a tiny window opened, though first it had to be covered with a metal grille. The evenings were dreary, filled with games of bezique; Alexei was ill again; and Nicky now suffered haemorrhoids so painful he had to lie in bed, though he read *War and Peace* aloud to the family, and a biography of Emperor Paul. Olga was depressed but walked arm in arm with her father; Tatiana nursed everyone, giving the ailing Dr. Botkin morphine injections. Food and walks were rationed. Their belongings were pilfered.

Yet the commandant became increasingly kind to the family—and did not stop his guards from fraternizing with the girls. Some of the guards started to sympathize with the meek ex-tsar and they smuggled in letters, books and food from outside. The guards were mainly teenagers themselves. "They were just like all girls," recalled one of the guards, "quite lively and very friendly to us." Anastasia was "very friendly and full of fun," recalled another guard, while a third thought her "a very charming devil . . . mischievous . . . lively and fond of performing comic mimes with the dogs." The most beautiful, Maria, with her big eyes—"Maria's saucers"—was their favourite: "a girl who loved to have fun," said guard Alexander Strekotin. As time passed, "Everyone relaxed more and began to talk and laugh . . . We were especially keen to talk to the daughters, except Olga." The chats always started with the girls exclaiming things like "We're so bored . . . I know! Try to guess the name of this dog?" Soon they were "whispering flirtatiously with us, giggling as they went."

"Their personalities were fascinating to us, topics of discussion between two or three of us who passed sleepless nights," recalled a guard, "There was something especially sweet about them. They always looked good to me." Another, Ivan Kleshchev, aged twenty-one, declared that he would marry one of the girls and if her parents objected, they would elope. "All in all," Strekotin said, "we felt that we wouldn't mind so much if they were allowed to escape."

A guard named Ivan Skorokhodov started to get closer to Maria. Alix and Olga disapproved. Alix reprimanded her "in severe whispers" for flirting, and Olga, noticed Strekotin, "refused to associate with her younger sisters." On 14 June "our Maria," wrote Nicholas, "turned nineteen." After lunch, when the family celebrated in the blistering heat, Skorokhodov emerged with a birthday cake which he had smuggled in for Maria. The two flirted and disappeared together.

Already Goloshchekin was worried about security. The nascent Soviet Republic seemed to be disintegrating. A corps of ex-Austro-Hungarian prisoners-of-war trained to form a Czech Corps, mutinied against the Bolsheviks and advanced along the Trans-Siberian Railway. By June, of the major cities between the Pacific and the Volga, only Perm and Ekaterinburg remained in Bolshevik hands. Plots mushroomed around the Ipatiev House. The family began to receive secret French messages from "an officer of the Russian army" who proposed their escape. These were provocations written by a Bolshevik member of the Urals Soviet, Peter Voikov, a vain womanizer with a taste for wearing eyeshadow who, having studied in Paris, could write French. His comrades nicknamed him "The Intellectual." It would have been convenient if the family could be shot trying to escape, but the Romanovs did not fall for it. "We don't want to nor can we escape. We can only be carried off by force," answered a member of the family, probably Olga, in French.

On 13 May, Nicholas noticed a "dark-complexioned gentleman whom we took to be a doctor" examining Alexei with Dr. Derevenko (who, kept in town, was allowed to visit occasionally). In fact, this visitor was Yakov Yurovsky, a leader of the local Cheka,* and member of the Urals Soviet.

---

* Lenin's secret police was the Cheka, an acronym for the Extraordinary Commission for Combating Counter-Revolution and Sabotage.

He identified the cause of the security lapses: Anastasia, he noted, was "very attractive, rosy cheeks, a quite lovely face," while Maria "didn't behave at all like her elder sisters. Her sincere modest character was very attractive to the men and she spent most of her time flirting with her jailers." Yurovsky warned that the guards would soon be helping the girls to escape.

On the very day of Maria's birthday, as she and young Skorokhodov playfully celebrated somewhere in the house, Goloshchekin arrived to make a surprise inspection and most likely discovered Maria alone with Skorokhodov. The young man was arrested. Alexandra and Olga were furious with Maria, who "seemed closed off from most of her family." After the flirtation, Alix and Olga "treated her like an outcast."[8]

Nicky and his family were not the only Romanovs near by. The Urals Soviet was collecting Romanovs. This was unlikely to be coincidental. Lenin and Sverdlov had started rounding up Romanovs in March. By May, six other Romanovs were also being held in the Palais Royale Hotel in Ekaterinburg: Ella, Alix's sister, along with her fellow nun Sister Varvara Yakovleva, Sandro's brother Sergei Mikhailovich, three sons of KR and a son of Paul. On 20 May, they were moved to a school in Alapaevsk, north-east of Ekaterinburg.

Meanwhile Misha, the last emperor, was also in the Urals. On 7 March 1918, he had been arrested with his Anglo-Russian secretary Nicholas Johnson and brought to Bolshevik headquarters at the Smolny Institute, where amazingly his wife Natasha managed to blag her way in to see Lenin himself. "Saying it did not only depend on him," Lenin left the room. That evening, when the government met, they agreed to exile "ex-Grand Duke M. A. Romanov" to the Urals.

Misha was placed under house arrest at the Korolev Hotel in Perm, where Natasha was allowed to come for dinner. But he was now in the domain of the Urals Soviet, which had already decided to collect and exterminate the Romanovs. As the Czech Legion threatened Perm, a local Chekist, Gavril Myasnikov, aged twenty-nine, in cahoots with Goloshchekin and the Ekaterinburg comrades, recruited four ruffians who in his words "were ready to bite through someone's throat with their teeth." At midnight on 12 June, Misha and his secretary Johnson were kidnapped by the Chekists from the hotel, driven in carriages to a wood outside town and murdered with shots to the head. After Misha's silver watch had been pilfered, the bodies were burned with paraffin. Myasnikov announced that Misha had escaped and vanished; but, informed after the fact, Lenin and Sverdlov approved. Misha was the first Romanov to be killed.[9]

*

In Ekaterinburg, the Cheka picked off the ex-tsar's companions. Count Ilya Tatishchev joined Dolgoruky in Ekaterinburg prison. The sailor Nagorny, who always carried Alexei, was removed. Gilliard and Gibbes saw him driven off—before they themselves were told to leave the town. This time they obeyed. Nagorny was shot.

The Czech Legion was approaching Ekaterinburg. Two days after Goloshchekin's surprise inspection of the House of Special Purpose, he, Alexander Beloborodov, chairman of the Presidium of the Ural Soviet, and Peter "The Intellectual" Voikov met in Room 3 of the marble-floored Amerika Hotel with Yurovsky and Myasnikov, who had just murdered Misha. This committee of murderers resolved as follows:

> The Ural Regional Soviet categorically refuses to take responsibility for transferring Nicholas Romanov in the direction of Moscow and considers it necessary to liquidate him. There is grave danger Citizen Romanov will fall into the hands of Czechoslovaks and other counter-revolutionaries . . . We cannot turn away from our duty to the Revolution. Romanov's family . . . must also be liquidated.

So must Ella and their cousins. As Goloshchekin rushed to Moscow to get Lenin's approval, British, French and American troops landed in Murmansk, the start of the Western intervention in a savage civil war between the Reds—the Bolsheviks—and their enemies, the Whites. On 5–6 July, the SRs, who had been junior partners in Lenin's government, launched an uprising. Lenin crushed the rebels, but the Soviet Republic was in desperate straits: a reign of remorseless terror was seen as fully justified.

In the Kremlin, Lenin worried that the killing of the Romanov children might make a terrible impression internationally: the French Revolution, template for the Bolsheviks, had guillotined the king and queen, but spared the children. When Goloshchekin arrived, Sverdlov ordered the appointment of a commandant to liquidate the family if necessary. On 4 July, the Ural Party secretary reported to "Chairman Sverdlov for Goloshchekin" that "the matter" had been "organized according to the Centre's instructions." The Central Committee nationalized the properties of the Romanovs. It was understood that if the Romanovs should fall into enemy hands, they must be slaughtered. "We decided it here," Sverdlov later told Trotsky. "Ilich [Lenin] thought we could not leave them a living banner, especially in the present difficult circumstances." Goloshchekin's commandant was that observer of Maria's and Anastasia's flirtations: Yakov Yurovsky.[10]

*

"I came to my duty knowing I would have to take a stand on the question of liquidating the Romanovs," wrote the forty-year-old Yurovsky, an ascetic Bolshevik, bearded and husky with thick jet-black hair.* He started "disinfecting" the guards: a new team was put in place at the House on the specific orders of the Centre; the periphery was now guarded by a detachment of Bolshevik workers, the internal guard made up of local Chekists, a mix of Latvians, Hungarians, Germans, Austrians and Russians.

"Today the commandants were changed," wrote Nicholas. "The one we presumed was a doctor, Yurovsky, appointed." Yurovsky was a trained medical orderly but he had come to kill them all, not cure them. Nicky hoped he would stop the petty thefts; to restore proletarian morality, the self-righteous commissar catalogued the Romanovs' belongings. Yurovsky certainly regarded his mission with pride: "It was left to me the son of a worker to settle the Revolution's score with the Imperial House for centuries of suffering."

The family noticed Yurovsky's controlled hostility. Alexandra called him "the Ox Commandant," while Nicky noticed the hostile Latvian guards. "We like this type less and less," he wrote. Two days later on 30 June, he added: "Alexei took his first bath since Tobolsk; his knee is getting better but he can't straighten it completely yet. The weather is warm and pleasant. We have no news from the outside." This was his last diary entry.

The adults sensed death was stalking them. The vanishings of Dolgoruky, Tatishchev, Nagorny were ominous. "My voluntary confinement here is restricted less by time than by my earthly existence," wrote Dr. Botkin in a letter he never sent. "In essence I am dead but not yet buried or buried alive." On 10 July, Dolgoruky and Tatishchev were taken into the forest and shot by Grigory Nikulin, Yurovsky's twenty-three-year-old deputy commandant.

The next day, a psychopathic, long-haired Chekist, Peter Ermakov, who had once sawn off a man's head during a bank robbery, visited the nearby Koptyaki forest and selected the disused Four Brothers iron mine in which to dispose of the bodies.

On 12 July, in Room 3, Hotel Amerika, Goloshchekin told the Praesidium that Moscow had approved the execution—but with some

* It was Yurovsky who as a boy in 1891 had seen Caesarovich Nicholas passing through Tomsk on his way home from his world tour. A Jewish glazier's son, one of ten children, his father had been exiled so he was "born in prison." Trained as a watchmaker and photographer, he served as a medical orderly in the war. Once he had worshipped the tsar. Intelligent and capable, he now loathed the Romanov "bloodsuckers." He had served time in prison for murder, but was now a married father of three children living in a small apartment with his widowed mother.

reservations. Lenin still toyed with the idea of a trial yet recognized that this was now impractical. It is clear from Yurovsky's orders, received while Goloshchekin was in Moscow, that Lenin had approved the killing of the entire family in discussions with Sverdlov in the Kremlin. The timing was left to the Urals commissars because it depended on the security of Ekaterinburg. The Romanovs could not be securely moved so if the town was about to fall, the Urals Soviet was permitted to activate the order with which Golshchekin returned to Ekaterinburg. It was agreed that the Uralites would use codenames: "the trial" meant the massacre and Yurovsky's actual operation was given the prosaic codename "chimney-sweep."* Ekaterinburg was about to fall so "we decided the question on our own," recalled Voikov.

"I started to make my preparations on the 15th," recalled Yurovsky, "as everything had to be done as quickly as possible. I decided to use as many men as there were people to be shot, gathering them together . . . explaining the task. It has to be said that it's no easy matter to arrange an execution, contrary to what some people think." The factory battalion of Letts and Hungarians had already been chosen on the understanding that they would help kill the tsar. Now he had to decide the venue inside the House, selecting a cellar room, twenty-one feet by twenty-five, lit by a single bulb, half built into the hillside.

The family could feel the front getting closer: "Constantly hear artillery passing . . . Also troops marching with music," observed Alexandra. Howitzers boomed. On 14 July, a local priest, Father Ivan Storozhev, was allowed to visit and celebrate mass. He noticed that the entire family—the girls dressed in black skirts and white blouses with their growing hair now down to their shoulders—fell to their knees to pray. He was moved by the spectacle of their passion: they were believers and their ardent faith had helped them survive so far. Whatever one's view of the ex-tsar and his family, one can only admire their grace, patience, humour and dignity in the face of humiliation, stress and fear as the sky darkened and the garrotte tightened. After the mass, in a demonstration of sincere piety and immaculate manners, the girls whispered "thank you."[11]

---

* Knowing this was a deed that would scrutinized by history, Lenin and Sverdlov were both careful not to order the killing specifically in writing and Lenin himself was protected by being kept out of the correspondence completely. Sverdlov was a superb manager, Lenin made policy, and the two decided everything together. Even during the civil war, Lenin was a control freak who tried to leave as little to local comrades as possible, and it is unthinkable he would have left such a major decision to provincials. The decision to conceal and muddy these orders was deliberate and almost certainly orchestrated by Lenin. After Lenin's death, it was imperative that this saintly paterfamilias should not be tainted by the murder of innocents.

*

On 16 July, "a grey morning, later lovely sunshine," Alexei had "a slight cold," wrote Alexandra, but "all went out for half an hour." Then "Olga and I arranged our medicines"—their codename for the jewellery, suggesting they were ready for a sudden move. "The Ox Commandant [Yurovsky] comes to our rooms, at last brought eggs again for Baby."

Afterwards Yurovsky ordered a Fiat truck from the Military Garage to transport the bodies. At 5:50 p.m. Filipp Goloshchekin telegraphed Lenin and Sverdlov in Moscow, via Grigory Zinoviev, head of the Petrograd Soviet (because telegraph communications were increasingly unreliable): "Let Moscow know that for military reasons the trial agreed upon with Filipp (Goloshchekin) cannot be put off; we cannot wait. If your opinions differ then immediately notify. Goloshchekin." "Trial" was the codeword for execution; the telegram's addressees proved that the murder had been discussed at the highest level, and its tone reveals that Moscow had given Ekaterinburg the option to make the final decision. Yurovsky recalled that a telegram from the Centre gave assent—though this has never been found. Goloshchekin and Beloborodov summoned the terrifying Ermakov and told him, "You're a lucky man. You've been chosen to execute and bury them in such a way that no one ever finds their bodies."

While the Romanovs were eating supper at 8 p.m., the commandant told his senior guards: "Tonight, we'll have to shoot them all." In his office, they amassed their arsenal of fourteen guns—six pistols and eight revolvers including two Mausers. There were eleven victims and Yurovsky summoned his murder squad but "at the last minute two of the Letts backed out," refusing to kill the girls. "They didn't have what it takes." He was left with ten, or even eight, killers—himself, his deputy Nikulin, Ermakov who arrived drunk, plus two other guards and four or five others, including one who was seventeen.* Goloshchekin joined them.

After supper, Yurovsky left his office and sent away the kitchen boy Lenka Sednev, who was friendly with the family, claiming he had to meet his uncle. "Wonder whether it's true," noted Alexandra, "and we

---

* It has been a canard of anti-semites, particularly a certain type of Russian nationalist, that the murder was the work of Jews, a narrative that perfectly suited the Bolsheviks who wished to ensure Lenin was not blamed. In fact, the murder squad, except for the Jewish Yurovsky, was almost entirely ethnic Russian, though there were probably two or three who were Lettish or Austro-Hungarian. Sverdlov, Goloshchekin and Yurovsky were indeed Jews by birth though fanatical atheists, which reflects the fact that minorities—Jews, Georgians, Poles, Letts—were disproportionately represented among the Bolsheviks. They share the guilt with the overwhelming number of Russians on the Urals Soviet, the Ipatiev guards and the hit squad. But it is Lenin who bears the ultimate responsibility.

shall see the boy back again." She wrote her diary before bed: "Bezique with N. 10:30 to bed, 15 degrees."

Yurovsky waited for the truck to arrive. The lights were out in the Romanov rooms. At 1:30 a.m. on 17 July the truck arrived outside. Yurovsky knocked on Dr. Botkin's door, explaining that "Everyone had to be woken and must dress quickly. There was trouble in the city and we have to take them to a safer place," but so as not "to cause them any unnecessary pain, they had plenty of time to get dressed." Botkin awoke the family. The children carefully donned their heavy jewel-invested underwear.

Hurrying back to his office, Yurovsky assigned victims to each killer, then distributed the weapons, taking a Mauser and a Colt for himself while Ermakov "rambling drunkenly" armed himself with three Nagants, a Mauser and a bayonet: he was the only one to have two assigned victims—Alexandra and Botkin. Yurovsky ordered the squad to "shoot straight at the heart to avoid an excessive quantity of blood and get it over quickly."

At about 2:15 a.m., Nicholas emerged carrying Alexei in his arms, both dressed in military uniforms with vizored caps secretly lined with jewels, followed by Alexandra and the girls, in white blouses and dark skirts, then Dr. Botkin (dapper in suit and tie) and three servants. The three dogs remained upstairs. As they walked down, the family crossed themselves as they passed the stuffed bear on the landing out of respect for the dead. "Well, we're going to get out of this place," said Nicky. Yurovsky led them out across the courtyard into the basement, past the room where the killers waited, and through the double doors into the cellar.

"Why is there no chair here?" asked Alexandra, now thin, grey, dishevelled. "Is it forbidden to sit down?"

Yurovsky ordered two chairs brought in. Alexandra sat on one and Nicholas "gently set his son in the second in the middle of the room," then "stood in front so that he shielded him." Botkin stood behind the boy, while the steady Tatiana was directly behind her mother's chair with Anastasia behind her. Olga and Maria leaned on the wall behind. The room, thought Yurovsky, "suddenly seemed very small." Announcing he was off to fetch the truck, he left them. "The Romanovs were completely calm. No suspicions."

Outside, Ermakov told the driver to back the truck into the courtyard and gun the engines to drown out the noise of shooting. As the truck revved, Yurovsky led the executioners into the room.

Yurovsky ordered the prisoners to stand. "In view of the fact that your relatives continued their offensive against Soviet Russia," he read from a

scrap of paper, "the Praesidium of the Ural Regional Soviet has decided
to sentence you to death."

"Lord oh my God," Nicholas said. "Oh my God, what is this?"

"Oh my God! No!" came a chorus of voices.

"So we're not going to be taken anywhere?" asked Botkin.

"I can't understand you," Nicholas told Yurovsky. "Read it again
please." Yurovsky read it again. "What? What?" stuttered Nicholas.

"This!" Yurovsky drew his pistol and fired it directly into Nicholas's
chest. All ten of the killers aimed at the ex-tsar, firing repeatedly into
his chest which exploded in blood. "I shot Nicholas and everyone else
shot him too." Quivering with each shot, with vacant eyes, "Nicholas
lurched forward and toppled to the floor." The barrage hit Botkin and
the servants who collapsed, but scarcely anyone had fired at the rest of
the victims who, frozen with terror, were just screaming. It was pandemonium. Yurovsky shouted orders, but the shooting was "increasingly
disorderly," the crack of gunfire so deafening, the smoke and dust
so thick, that no one could see or hear anything. "Bullets were flying
around the room." One of the shooters was wounded in the hand. "A
bullet from one of the squad behind me flew past my head," recalled
Yurovsky, while those in front were burned.

Alexandra was crossing herself. She had always believed that she and
Nicky would be, as she wrote long before, when they were newlyweds,
"united, bound for life and when life is ended, we meet again in the
other world to remain together for all eternity." As her hand was raised,
Ermakov fired his Mauser point-blank at her head which shattered in
brain and blood. Maria ran for the double doors at the back so Ermakov
drawing a Nagant from his belt fired at her, hitting her in the thigh, but
the smoke and clouds of plaster were so dense that Yurovsky ordered a
halt and opened the door to let the shooters, coughing and spluttering,
rest as they listened to "moans, screams and low sobs" from within.
Only Nicholas and Alexandra, and two of the servants, were dead. Leading the assassins back into the room, Yurovsky found Botkin getting up
and, placing his Mauser against the doctor's head, he pulled the trigger.
Spotting Alexei still frozen in his chair, white face spattered with his
father's blood, Yurovsky and his deputy Nikulin fired repeatedly into
the thirteen-year-old, who fell but lay moaning on the ground until the
commandant called for Ermakov, who drew his bayonet.

As Ermakov stabbed frenziedly, blood squirting in an arc, poor Alexei
was still alive, protected by his diamond-armoured shirt, until Yurovsky,
drawing his Colt, shoved Ermakov out of the way and shot the boy in
the head. Olga, Tatiana and Anastasia was still untouched, huddled
together screaming. "We set about finishing them off." As Yurovsky

and Ermakov stepped over the bodies towards them, they scrambled, crouched and covered their heads. Yurovsky shot Tatiana in the back of the head, spattering Olga in a "shower of blood and brains"; next the blood-drenched Ermakov kicked her down and shot her in the jaw. But Maria, wounded in the leg, and Anastasia were still alive, crying out for help. Ermakov wheeled round to stab Maria in the chest, but again "the bayonet wouldn't pierce her bodice." He shot her. Anastasia was the last of the family moving. Slashing his bayonet through the air, Ermakov cornered her but, stabbing manically against her diamond-armoured bodice, he missed and hit the wall. She was "screaming and fighting" until he drew another pistol and shot her in the head. Now berserk with intoxicated bloodlust, Ermakov spun back to Nicholas and Alexandra, wildly stabbing first one then the other so hard that his bayonet cracked bones and pinned them to the floorboards. One of the servants, Anna Demidova, suddenly stirred: "Thank God! God has saved me!" Ermakov stabbed her until she was silent.

After this ten-minute frenzy, Yurovsky checked that the victims were all dead, then "ordered the men to start moving them." As they piled them on to the Fiat, Ortino, Tatiana's bulldog, rushed down the stairs, only to be bayoneted by one of the soldiers.* Yurovsky staggered into his office, lying on the sofa with a cold cloth on his head just as Voikov arrived to inspect the cellar: "bodies lay in an appalling jumble, eyes staring in horror, clothing covered in blood. The floor was slick and slippery as a skating rink with blood, brains and gore." As they carried out two of the girls, probably Maria and Anastasia, they started to splutter and cry, still alive. Ermakov, taking a bayoneted rifle, stabbed them again as some of the assassins vomited and fled; others pillaged watches, rings and Nicholas's diamond-studded cigarette case. Yurovsky reappeared, called the killers into his office and demanded that the looters return the valuables or be shot.

At 3 a.m., the truck swung on to the road on a halting journey to the Four Brothers mine. Out in the forest, Yurovsky encountered the drunken posse arranged by Ermakov who were pumped up to kill the family themselves. "What did you bring them to us dead for?" they complained. But the Fiat broke down and as the bodies had to be transferred to carts, the men discovered the jewels: "diamonds could be seen. The men's eyes visibly lit up." All wore amulets with tiny portraits of Rasputin. Again, Yurovsky had to draw his pistol to restore order, dismissing the

---

* The lapdog Jemmy was bayonetted too, but Alexei's adored King Charles spaniel, Joy, ran away during the murders. He returned to await his master, was adopted by a guard, then by a member of the Allied intervention forces and taken to England where he lived out his life near Windsor Castle.

extra men. It was nearly 7 a.m. The bodies were stripped naked, and the clothes were burned. Seventeen pounds of jewels were collected, to be handed over to Moscow. They threw the bodies down a mineshaft, only to discover that it was very shallow. Yurovsky started to panic. Leaving a guard and rushing back to the city, Yurovsky reported to the Praesidium at the Amerika Hotel, but admitted that he and Ermakov had failed to dispose of the bodies. Goloshchekin was furious at Ermakov's conduct but ordered Yurovsky to find another way of destroying the bodies. He rushed back and forth twice during the night, finally deciding to burn some bodies and use acid to destroy the others so "no one will ever know what happened." He asked Voikov, commissar of supplies, to procure fifteen gallons of sulphuric acid and a lot of gasoline.

"Inform Sverdlov the entire family suffered the same fate as the head," Beloborodov telegraphed to the Kremlin. Next day, the Central Executive Committee "recognizes the decision of the Ural Regional Soviet as correct."[12]

At the same session in the Amerika Hotel, the Soviet ordered the killing of the other Romanovs.*

At eleven o'clock that evening, 17 July, at the Napolnaya School in Alapaevsk, a posse of Chekists woke up Grand Duchess Ella and the others, telling them that the advance of White armies meant they had to be moved urgently. Ella, in her nun's habit, her companion Sister Varvara, three of KR's sons and Prince Vladimir Paley, son of Uncle Pitz, were tied up and blindfolded. Sergei Mikhailovich "was the only one to oppose us," recalled one of the killers, Vasily Ryabov. "He was stronger than the rest. We had to grapple with him. He told us he wasn't going anywhere as he knew they were all going to be killed. He barricaded himself behind a cupboard," until "finally I lost patience and shot him" in the arm. "He didn't resist further."

Then he joined the others as they were led out to waiting horse-drawn

---

* Many of those responsible for the murders were themselves consumed by the Revolution. In 1927, Goloshchekin approached Stalin on behalf of Yurovsky for permission to write his memoirs. "Not a word on the Romanovs," replied Stalin. Goloshchekin rose to first secretary of Kazakhstan, where he directed the forced collectivization and starvation of millions of Kazakhs. But Stalin had loathed him ever since they met in Siberian exile and had him shot in 1941. Beloborodov, who supported Trotsky, was shot in 1938. Yurovsky served as an economics official, giving interviews and occasional speeches about the murders, dying naturally in 1938. Ermakov gave lectures in schools and factories, dying in 1952. Misha's murderer, Myasnikov, went into opposition and exile, but in 1945 the Soviet secret police brought him back to Russia where he was shot. Sverdlov died of influenza in March 1919. Ekaterinburg was renamed Sverdlovsk. Lenin lies honoured in his Mausoleum; Sverdlov is buried in the Kremlin Wall. Voikov became Soviet ambassador to Warsaw where he was assassinated in 1927.

carts that set off for the woods. Unlike Nicky and Alix, they knew they were going to die. "Tell me why," said Sergei. "I've never been involved in politics. I loved sport, played billiards, was interested in numismatics."

"I reassured him as best I could," said Ryabov, but "I was myself very agitated by everything I'd been through that night."

At 1 a.m., they were made to walk towards a flooded iron mine. When Sergei again resisted, he was shot in the head. Then Ella was bludgeoned with rifle butts and thrown unconscious down the mineshaft, followed by Sister Varvara, in the hope that they would drown. But then "we heard the splashing of water and then the two women's voices," recalled Ryabov, who now began to panic, unsure what to do next. "Having no alternative," they decided to "throw in all the men as well," but "none of them drowned in the water and we were able to hear all their voices. Then I threw in a grenade. It exploded and everything was quiet." But then "we heard talking. I threw in another grenade. And what do you think? From beneath the ground we heard singing. I was seized with horror. They were singing the prayer Lord Save Your People." The murderers filled the shaft with wood and lit it. "Their hymns rose up through the thick smoke"—until there was silence.[13]

In Ekaterinburg, Yurovsky, who had not slept for two entire nights, loaded paraffin and sulphuric acid into a truck then headed back to the Four Brothers mine to retrieve the cold bodies. There was gawping at, and groping of, the naked bodies. At 4:30 a.m. on 19 July, he burned two of them, Alexei and Maria, buried their remains and moved on, seventy yards away, to a clearing in the forest where, after digging a pit, he poured acid on to the bodies and buried them. Once the grave had been smoothed over, Yurovsky gathered his men and ordered them "never to speak of what had taken place." They must "forget all they had seen."

The next day in Vologda prison, Bimbo and his two fellow grand dukes heard that Sovnarkom had announced the execution of the tsar, claiming his family had been "evacuated." The three were sent to the Peter and Paul Fortress in Petrograd where they were joined by the last son of Alexander II, the fifty-eight-year-old Pitz.

On the night of 27 January 1919,[*] Bimbo, his brother Georgi and cousin Dmitri, KR's son, were awoken in the middle of the night, ordered to strip to the waist and marched out into the courtyard in front of the cathedral. Paul was too ill to stand so he was carried out on a stretcher. In a trench before the cathedral lay thirteen dead bodies. Bimbo and the others were ordered to stand before the trench and shot. Paul was killed on his stretcher, and all were tossed into the mass grave. Eighteen Romanovs had been killed by the Bolsheviks.* But the dowager empress, wife and mother of emperors, was still in Russia.[14]

Minny and her relatives stayed at the family estates in Crimea under the kaiser's protection—until in November 1918 Germany collapsed and Wilhelm abdicated. As German troops withdrew from Crimea, civil war intensified. In December, Sandro left on a British battleship, but Minny and the others agonised over what to do. Finally, in April 1919, the British offered to rescue them all. The dowager empress, accompanied by her daughter Xenia, Nikolasha, Peter, the Crows and the Yusupovs, an entourage of fifty altogether, sailed aboard HMS *Marlborough* into exile. All were to die in the West,† where their many descendants are spread across America and Europe.

As the surviving grand dukes bickered about their legacy, sought refuge with royal relatives, and sold memoirs and jewels to maintain their fraying lifestyles,‡ the senior surviving Romanov, the unstable Kyril, son of Vladimir and Miechen, declared himself tsar.[15]

\*

* Only one Romanov was indulged by the Bolsheviks. In February 1917, Grand Duke Nikola, still thriving in his little empire in Tashkent, was, ironically, the only Romanov who was liberated by the revolution. Nikola congratulated Kerensky. In October 1917, the Bolsheviks confiscated his businesses, leaving only the cinema, and ordered him to leave the country—but he was too ill. He asked the Bolsheviks to allow his wife to become director of his palace museum, where she continued to work until the 1930s. In 1918, while the Bolsheviks were executing his cousins, this quixotic radical, scientific researcher, prolific builder, art collector, cinematic impresario and priapic romantic died at sixty-seven of pneumonia, receiving an official funeral, that was attended by thousands of ordinary people in Tashkent.
† Empress Maria Fyodorovna, known as Minny, born Princess Dagmar of Denmark, returned to Copenhagen where she died in 1928 aged eighty. Nikolasha settled in the south of France where he died in 1929, followed by his brother Peter in 1931 and wife Stana in 1935. Militsa lived on into another age. Joining her sister Queen Elena of Italy, she settled in Tuscany until the Nazi invasion in 1943, when she received asylum in the Vatican. When the Americans arrived, she rejoined Queen Elena until the end of the Italian monarchy in 1946 when she accompanied her sister and former King Victor Emmanuel III to Egypt. She died in 1951. Finally, the ballerina Mathilde Kshessinskaya, mistress of a tsar and two grand dukes, married her lover Grand Duke Andrei Vladimirovich, whose brother Kyril gave her the title Princess Romanovsky-Krasinsky. She founded a ballet school, dying in 1971.
‡ The murderers of Rasputin enjoyed a lurid notoriety. Dmitri escaped to London and Paris where he became a lover of Coco Chanel before marrying an American heiress, Audrey Emery Kyril. Dmitri died in 1932; later his son Prince Paul Romanovsky-Ilyinsky became mayor of Palm Beach. Felix Yusupov and his wife, Irina, the tsar's niece, left with

The bodies of the murdered Romanovs made their own journey. Less than a week after the murders, Ekaterinburg fell to the Whites who immediately started to investigate. Later they appointed a judge, Nikolai Sokolov, who concluded that the Romanovs had been executed even though he was unable to find the bodies.

In September 1918, Alapaevsk also fell to the Whites, who discovered the bodies of Ella and the others in their mineshaft. The coffins of the victims were placed in Alapaevsk Cathedral until July 1919, when the Bolsheviks were advancing again, and a priest transported them to Irkutsk; then, as the Reds approached once more, to Harbin in Manchuria and next on to Beijing. When Victoria Mountbatten, Marchioness of Milford Haven, elder sister of Ella and Alexandra, discovered that the nun's body was in China, she arranged for her and Sister Varvara to be transported to Jerusalem. At Port Said, the Milford Havens met them and accompanied them to Palestine. In January 1921, "two unadorned coffins were lifted from the train," wrote Lord Milford Haven, who helped carry them. "The little cavalcade wound its way, sadly, unobtrusively to the Mount of Olives. Russian peasant women, stranded pilgrims, sobbing and moaning, were almost fighting to get some part of the coffin." Ella and Sister Varvara were placed in glass-topped white sarcophagi in the very Slavic, gold-onion-domed Church of Mary Magdalene, which had been inaugurated by Sergei and Ella in 1888. In 1992 Ella was canonized.[16]

In 1977, Yuri Andropov, the chairman of the KGB, proposed that the Ipatiev House, which could become "the object of serious attention" from "anti-Soviet circles in the West," should be demolished. On Politburo orders, Boris Yeltsin, first secretary of the Sverdlovsk Communist Party, bulldozed the Ipatiev House.

In May 1979, two amateur historians, after analysing photographs taken by Yurovsky on the site of the tsar's hidden grave, began digging in the Koptyaki woods outside Sverdlovsk. They found skulls and bones, but this was the height of Leonid Brezhnev's re-Stalinized stagnation and their discovery was too early politically. They reburied the bones. The KGB had known the site all along, for their files contained Yurovsky's original report. But in 1991 the fall of the Soviet Union

---

two Rembrandts and a cache of jewels. Settling in Paris, they founded a fashion house. Felix's memoirs became an international bestseller, but he lost much of his fortune in the Wall Street Crash. He died in 1967. Irina lived on in Paris. "She always smoked French fags with a long cigarette holder," recalls her niece Princess Olga Romanoff, "always smelt lovely of Chanel No. 5, had an incredible sense of humour, a deep voice and was so elegant—never without her beautiful pearls in her ears and round the neck!"

ended Communist rule. On 11 July, an official expedition of the Russian Federation exhumed the bones, which were divided into nine skeletons. Prince Philip, duke of Edinburgh and consort of Elizabeth II, whose mother Alice was the daughter of Alexandra's sister Victoria, gave his DNA, which proved the empress's identity, while DNA from three relatives identified the tsar. But after much forensic inquiry, it was agreed that the bodies of Alexei and Maria were missing.

On 17 July 1998, the eightieth anniversary of the murders, President Boris Yeltsin attended the funeral of the emperor, his family, his doctor and the three retainers at the Peter and Paul Cathedral in Petersburg, along with thirty Romanov descendants. "It was a deeply emotional scene," recalls Prince Michael of Kent, descended from a daughter of Grand Duke Vladimir. "Very touching. A dignified occasion with a sense of finality."

"It's a historic day for Russia," declared Yeltsin. "We have long been silent about this monstrous crime . . . The Ekaterinburg massacre has become one of the most shameful episodes in our history. We want to atone for the sins of our ancestors. We are all guilty . . . Many glorious pages of Russian history are connected with the Romanovs. But this name is connected to one of the most bitter lessons." Then he drew the great moral of the terrible twentieth century: "any attempt to change life by violence is condemned to failure. This is our historic chance." After the service, the coffins were buried in the tomb of the Romanovs. The Cathedral of the Saviour of Spilled Blood was built on the site of the Ipatiev House, and smaller chapels at the site of the burials. In 2000, Nicholas and his family were canonized. "It was the closing of a chapter," thought Prince Michael. "But not the end of the story."

Far from it. The patriarch refused to participate, partly because Yeltsin's decision was so political, but also because of the incomplete line-up of the family and anxieties about identifying some of the girls' bodies.

In 2007, the partial remains of two skeletons, damaged by fire and acid, were discovered at the site of the bonfire mentioned in Yurovsky's memoirs. Most experts agreed these were the bodies of Alexei and Maria but again the Orthodox Church, keen to assert its power in modern Russia, remained unconvinced and for eight years, the bones were stored in boxes at the State Archives. In 2015, the Investigation Committee of the Interior Ministry reopened the inquiry to allow the Church a final check on the identity of all the family, using DNA provided by Nicholas and Alexandra (who were briefly exhumed), Ella (who lies in Jerusalem), Alexander II (using his bloodstained tunic in the Hermitage) and Alexander III. Finally, the Romanovs can be reunited.

# EPILOGUE

# Red Tsars/White Tsars

When Tsarevich Alexei was told that his father had abdicated, he asked, "Then who's going to rule Russia?" Marx wrote that "History repeats itself, first as tragedy, second as farce." This was witty but far from true. History is never repeated, but it borrows, steals, echoes and commandeers the past to create a hybrid, something unique out of the ingredients of past and present. No tsars were to rule Russia after 1917, yet each of Nicholas's successors, who ruled the same empire with many of the same challenges in entirely different circumstances, channelled, adapted and blended the prestige of the Romanovs with the zeitgeist of their own times.

Lenin had lost Ukraine, the Caucasus and much else at Brest-Litovsk—and without Ukraine, Russia would cease to be a great power. But ultimately Lenin shrewdly reassembled the Romanov empire, losing only Finland, Poland and the Baltics.*

Even as Stalin outmanoeuvred his rivals to succeed Lenin,† he privately believed that Russia needed a "tsar": in April 1926, he mused that, although the Party ruled, "the people understand little of this. For centuries the people in Russia were under a tsar. The Russian people are tsarist . . . accustomed to one person being at the head. And now there should be one." He studied Ivan the Terrible and Peter the Great

---

* In 1922, Lenin devised a federal structure of equal quasi-independent ethnic republics, instead of forcing them into a Russian federation. Its genius was to conserve the centralized and authoritarian Romanov empire behind the façade of a voluntary union of independent socialist peoples. Stalin devised the details and created the fifteen republics that made up the Soviet Union.

† At his death, his comrades wished to treat him like a tsar. "The tsars were embalmed just because they were tsars," argued Felix Dzerzhinsky, the founder of the Soviet secret police. "If science can preserve a human body for a long time, then why not do it?" The Romanovs were embalmed and lay in state, but were not exhibited like incorruptible Orthodox saints. Stalin, the seminarian, created a hybrid tsar–saint in Lenin, who is still exhibited in Red Square.

particularly. "The people need a tsar," he said in the 1930s, "whom they can worship and for whom they can live and work." He carefully crafted his own image to create a new template of tsar, fatherly and mysterious, industrial and urban, the leader of an internationalist mission yet the monarch of the Russians. As the Germans advanced in 1941, he studied 1812 and, in 1942–3, restored ranks, gold braid and epaulettes—and promoted tsarist heroes Kutuzov and Suvorov. Stalin's Terror allowed him to perform total reversals of policy, such as his pact with Hitler, to survive colossal self-inflicted disasters and force astonishing sacrifices from the Russians. His personal authority, homicidal brutality, Marxist-nationalistic propaganda, breakneck industrialization and command economy meant that he could deploy resources that would have been unimaginable to Nicholas. Stalin was a murderous tyrant, the Soviet experience a dystopian tragedy for the Russians, yet he out-performed the tsars, defeating Germany, leaving Russia as ruler of eastern Europe and a nuclear superpower. He always measured himself against the Romanovs. In 1945, when the US ambassador Averell Harriman congratulated him on taking Berlin, Stalin riposted: "Yes, but Alexander I made it to Paris."

In 1991, the break-up of the Soviet Union was also the disintegration of the Romanov empire that Lenin and Stalin had held on to with cunning and force. The very slyness of their fifteen-republic federation rebounded on those Marxist imperialists for the republics were never intended to become independent. But Boris Yeltsin, the new leader of the Russian Federation, used the ambitions of the republics to outmanoeuvre Soviet president Mikhail Gorbachev and dismantle the USSR. Millions of Russians now found themselves in new countries while sacred Slavic lands—Ukraine or Crimea—were lost to the Motherland. The decadent liberal West dared to push its influence into the new republics, Ukraine, Georgia, Estonia, right up against the borders of Russia.

Yeltsin created what was—apart from the elected Constituent Assembly of 1918—the first real Russian democracy, with a free press and free market. Like the tsars before Paul I, he chose his own successor, Vladimir Putin, ex-KGB colonel turned politician, to protect his family and legacy.

Putin's immediate mission was to restore Russian power at home and abroad. In 2000, his Chechen War ensured that the Russian Federation would stay together. In 2008, a war with Georgia, one of the more Westernized republics, reasserted Russian hegemony over the Caucasus. In 2014, the West's attempt to recruit Ukraine into its economic system led Putin to launch an opportunistic war that enabled him to support a war of secession in eastern Ukraine and to annex Crimea, which he saw as "our Temple Mount." His intervention in Syria in 2015 restores Russia's Middle Eastern aspirations from Catherine the Great to the Cold War.

He called his ideology "Sovereign Democracy," with the emphasis clearly on the sovereignty—Putinism blended Romanov authoritarianism, Orthodox sanctity, Russian nationalism, crony capitalism, Soviet bureaucracy and the fixtures of democracy, elections and parliaments. If there was an ideology, it was bitterness towards and contempt for America; nostalgia for the Soviet Union and the Romanov empire, but its spirit was a cult of authority and the entitlement to get rich in state service. The Slavophile mission of the Orthodox nation, superior to the West, and exceptional in its character, has replaced that of Marxist internationalism. While the Orthodox Patriarch Kyril has called Putin a "miracle of God" for Russia, the president himself sees "the Russian people as the core of a unique civilization." Peter the Great and Stalin are both treated as triumphant Russian rulers. Today's Russia is the heir of both, a fusion of imperial Stalinism and twenty-first-century digital authoritarianism—stunted and distorted by its own personal caprice, old-fashioned lawlessness, economic sclerosis and Brobdingnagian corruption, however draped in the mantle of modernity. Looking back over the four centuries covered in this book, it is curious that each of Russia's Times of Troubles—1610–13, 1917/18 and 1991–99—ended with a new version of the old autocracy, eased by the habits and traditions of its fallen predecessor, and justified by the urgent need to restore order, modernize radically and regain Russia's place as a great power. Putin rules by the Romanov compact: autocracy and the rule of a tiny clique in return for the delivery of prosperity at home and glory abroad. Alexander II's minister Count Valuev joked "there is something erotic" about adventures on exotic frontiers, and that is certainly true of Russia's televisually spectacular military exploits in the Middle East. But as the later tsars discovered, this gamble depends on economic success. Unlike them, however, Putin has the final resort of nuclear weapons.

Putin's entourage call him "the Tsar," yet it is not the great Romanovs who keep Putin awake at night but the memories of Nicholas II. One evening in his Nov-Ogaryovo Palace, his chief residence near Moscow, Putin asked his courtiers who were Russia's "greatest traitors." Before they could answer, he replied, "The greatest criminals in our history were those weaklings who threw power on the floor—Nicholas II and Mikhail Gorbachev—who allowed power to be picked up by hysterics and madmen." Putin promised, "I would never abdicate." The Romanovs are gone but the predicament of Russian autocracy lives on.[1]

# BIBLIOGRAPHY

## ARCHIVES

| | |
|---|---|
| APRF | Archive of President of Russian Federation |
| CUBA | Columbia University Bakhmeteff Archive, New York |
| GARF | State Archives of Russian Federation |
| OPI GIM | Department of Manuscripts in State Historical Museum |
| OR RNB | Department of Manuscripts in Russian National Library |
| RAS | Archive of the St. Petersburg Institute of History Russian Academy of Science |
| RGADA | Russian State Archives of Ancient Documents |
| RGIA | Russian State Historical Archives |
| RGVIA | Russian State War History Archives |

## JOURNALS

*Ab Imperio*
*AKV (Arkhiv knyazya Vorontsova)*
*American Historical Review*
*Arkhiv russkoi istorii*
*Armenian Review*
*Cahiers du Monde Russe [et Soviétique before 1994]*
*Canadian Slavic Studies*
*Canadian Slavonic Papers*
*ChOIDR (Chteniia v Imperatorskom obshchestve istorii i drevnostei rossiiskikh)*
*European Royal History Journal*
*Foreign Affairs*
*Harvard Ukrainian Studies*
*Historical Journal*
*History Today*
*Istoricheskii vestnik*
*Journal of the Royal Asiatic Society*
*KFZ (Kamer-furyerskie zhurnaly)*
*Moskovskii zhurnal*
*New York Times*
*Newsweek*
*PSZ (Polnoe sobranie zakonov)*
*RA (Russkii arkhiv)*
*RS (Russkaia starina)*
*Russian Review*
*SEER (Slavonic and East European Review)*
*SIRIO (Sbornik imperatorskogo russkogo obshchestva istorii)*

*Slovo i Delo*
*Smena*
*University of Hawaii at Hilo, HOHONU History*
*Voenno-istoricheskii zhurnal*
*Vremya*
*ZORI (Zapiski otdeleniia Russkoi i Slavyanskoi Arkheologii)*


ARTICLES

Alexander, J. T., Ivan Shuvalov and Russian Court Politics 1749–63, in A. G. Cross and G. S. Smith (eds.), *Literature, Lives and Legality in Catherine's Russia*, Nottingham, 1994

Bazarov, Alexandr, Svetleishii knyaz Alexandr Gorchakov. Iz vospominanii o nem ego dukhovnika, *RA* (1896) 1.328–50

Biron, Obstoiatelstva, prigotovivshie opalu Ernsta-Ioanna Birona, gertsoga Kurlyandskogo, *Vremya* (1861) 10.522–622

Bogatyrev, S., Ivan IV 1533–84, in M. Petrie (ed.), *The Cambridge History of Russia*, vol. 1: *From Early Rus to 1689*, Cambridge, 2006

Buchnell, J. S., Miliutin and the Balkan War—Military Reform vs Military Performance, in B. Eklof, J. Bushnell and L. Zakharova (eds.), *Russia's Great Reforms, 1855–1881*, Bloomington, Ind., 1994, 139–60

Bushkovitch, P., Shvedskie istochniki o Rossii, 1624–1626, *Arkhiv russkoy istorii* (2007) 8.359–81

Bushkovitch, P., Princes Cherkasskii or Circassian Murzas: The Kabardians in the Russian Boyar Elite 1560–1700, *Cahiers du Monde Russe* (2004) 45.1–2.9–30

Christie, I. R., Samuel Bentham and the Russian Dnieper Flotilla, *SEER* (1972) 50.119

Christie, I. R., Samuel Bentham and the Western Colony at Krichev 1784–7, *SEER* (1970) 48.111

Conlin, J., The Strange Case of the Chevalier d'Eon, *History Today* (2010) 60.4.45

Dubrovin, N. F. (ed.), Materialy i cherty k biografii imperatora Nikolaia I i k istorii ego tsarstvovaniia, *SIRIO* (1896) 98.10–14

Dvorzhitsky, A., 1 Marta 1881, *Istoricheskii vestnik* (1913) 1

Esipov, G. V., Zhizneopisanie A. D. Menshikova, *RA* (1875) 7, 9, 10, 12

Ettinger, Shmuel, Jewish Emigration in the 19th Century: Migration—Within and from Europe—as a Decisive Factor in Jewish Life,» at www.myjewishlearning .com/article/jewish-emigration-in-the-19th-century/2/

Fedosov, D., Cock of the East: A Gordon Blade Abroad, in M. Erickson and L. Erickson (eds.), *Russia: War, Peace and Diplomacy: Essays in Honour of John Erickson*, London, 2005, 1–10

Franklin, R. R., Tsar Alexander II and President Abraham Lincoln: Unlikely Bedfellows?, *University of Hawaii at Hilo, HOHONU History* (2012) 10.74–84

Gribbe, A. K., Graf Alexei Andreevich Arakcheev, 1822–1826, *RS* (1875) 12.84–124

Griffiths, D. M., The Rise and Fall of the Northern System: Court Politics in the First Half of Catherine's Reign, *Canadian Slavic Studies* (1970) 4.3.547–69

Harris, C., Succession Prospects of Grand Duchess Olga Nikolaevna, *Canadian Slavonic Papers* (2012) 54.61–84

Interview with HRH Prince Michael of Kent, *New York Times*, 18 July 1998

Ivanov O. A., Zagadka pisem Alexeia Orlova iz Ropshi, *Moskovskii zhurnal* (1995) 9

Judah, B., The President, *Newsweek*, 1 August 2014

Keep, J. L. H., The Regime of Filaret, 1619–1633, *SEER* (1959–60) 38.334–43

Klier, J., Krovavyi navet v Russkoi Pravoslavnoi traditsii, in M. V. Dmitriev (ed.), *Evrei I khristiane v pravoslavnykh obshchestvakh Vostochnoi Evropy*, Moscow, 20

Kotkin, Stephen, The Resistible Rise of Vladimir Putin: Russia's Nightmare Dressed like a Daydream, *Foreign Affairs* (March/April 2015)

Lamansky, V. (ed.), Zapiski otdeleniia Russkoi i Slavianskoi Arkheologii, 2, St. Petersburg, 1861

LeDonne, John P., Ruling Families in the Russian Political Order 1689–1825, *Cahiers du Monde Russe et Soviétique* (1987) 28.233–322

Librovich, S., Zhenskii krug Petra Velikogo, *Smena* (1993) 6.80–97

Lieven, D. C. B., Bureaucratic Authoritarianism in Late Imperial Russia: The Personality, Career, and Opinions of P. N. Durnovo, *Historical Journal* (1983) 26.2.391–402

Lincoln, W. B., The Ministers of Alexander II: A Survey of their Backgrounds and Service Careers, *Cahiers du Monde Russe et Soviétique*, (1976) 17.467–83

Lincoln, W. B., The Ministers of Nicholas I: A Brief Inquiry into their Backgrounds and their Service Careers, *Russian Review* (1975) 34.308–23

Lohr, E., The Russian Army and the Jews: Mass Deportation, Hostages, and Violence during World War I, *Russian Review* (2001) 60.404–19

Lowenson, L., The Death of Paul I and the Memoirs of Count Bennigsen, *SEER* (1950) 29.212–32

Markova, O. P., O proiskhozhdenii tak nazyvayemogo Grecheskogo Proekta, in H. Ragsdale (ed.), *Imperial Russian Foreign Policy*, Cambridge, 1993, 75–103

Menning, B., A. I. Chernyshev: A Russian Lycurgus, *Canadian Slavonic Papers* (1988) 30.2.190–219

Morozova, L. E., Dveredaktsii china venchaniia na tsarstvo Alexeia Mikhailovicha, in Morozova, L. E., Knyazevskaia, T. B., Kultura slavyan i Rus, 457–471, Moscow, 1998

Morris, P., The Russians in Central Asia, 1870–1887, *SEER* (1975) 53.521–38

Packard, L. B., Russia and the Dual Alliance, *American Historical Review* (Apr 1920) 25.3.391–410

Persen, William, The Russian Occupations of Beirut 1772–4, *Journal of the Royal Asiatic Society* (1955) 42:3–4.275–286

Podbolotov, S., Tsar i narod: populistskii natsionalizm imperatora Nikolaia II, *Ab Imperio* (2003) 3.199–223

Rieber, A. F., Interest Group Politics in the Era of the Great Reforms, in B. Eklof, J. Bushnell and L. Zakharova (eds.), *Russia's Great Reforms, 1855–1881*, Bloomington, Ind., 1994, 58–84

Ruseva, L., Oklevetannyi molvoi, *Smena* (2007) 2.96–107

Semevsky, M. I., Grigory Alexandrovich Potemkin-Tavrichesky, *RS* (1875) 3.481–523

Semevsky, M.I., Kamer-freilina Maria D. Hamilton, *Slovo i Delo* (1884) 185–1,268

Subtelny O., Mazepa, Peter I and the Question of Treason, *Harvard Ukrainian Studies* (1978) 2.158–84

Tatishchev, S. S., Imperator Nikolai I v Londone v 1844 godu, *Istoricheskii vestnik* (1886) 23.602–21

Truvorov, Askalon, Koronatsiia imperatritsy Ekateriny Vtoroi, *RS* (1893) 80.12

Ustinov, V. I., Moguchiy velikoross, *Voenno-istoricheskii zhurnal* (1991) 12.158–79

Vinogradov, V. N., The Personal Responsibility of Emperor Nicholas I for the Coming of the Crimean War: An Episode in the Diplomatic Struggle in the Eastern Question, in H. Ragsdale (ed.), *Imperial Russian Foreign Policy*, Cambridge, 1993, 159–72

Wilson, Penny, Nubian Guards, at http://forum.alexanderpalace.org/index.php?topic=348.0;wap2

Zakharova, L. G., Autocracy and the Reforms of 1861–1874 in Russia, in B. Eklof, J. Bushnell and L. Zakharova (eds.), *Russia's Great Reforms, 1855–1881*, Bloomington, Ind., 1994, 19–38

## UNPUBLISHED

Anderson, Scott P., The Administrative and Social Reforms of Russia's Military, 1861–74: Dmitri Miliutin against the Ensconced Power Elite, PhD thesis, 2010.
Klebnikov, Paul G., Agricultural Development in Russia 1906–17: Land Reform, Social Agronomy and Cooperation, January 1991, LSE, PhD thesis

## PRIMARY SOURCES

Collections of documents, memoirs, Western collections of letters and diaries: where possible, these appear under the name of the author not the editor.

*1 Marta 1881. Po neizdannym materialam*, Petrograd, 1918
Alexander I and Grand Duchess Catherine, *Scenes of Russian Court Life, Being the Correspondence of Alexander I and His Sister Catherine* (ed. Nicolai Mikhailovich), London, 1917
Alexander I, Nicholas I et al., *Romanov Relations: The Private Correspondence of Tsars Alexander I, Nicholas I and the Grand Dukes Constantine and Michael with Their Sister Queen Anna Pavlovna, 1817–1855*, S. W. Jackman (ed.), London, 1969
Alexander II, *Venchanie s Rossiei: Perepiska velikogo knyazya Alexandra Nikolaevicha s imperatorom Nikolaem I. 1837*, Zakharova, L. G. and Tyutyunnik, L. I. (eds.), Moscow, 1999
Alexander II/A. I. Bariatinsky, *The Politics of Autocracy: Letters of Alexander II to Prince A. I. Bariatinskii, 1857–1864*, A. I. Rieber (ed.), Paris, 1966
Alexander Mikhailovich, *Once a Grand Duke*, New York, 1932
Alexandra Fyodorovna, *A Czarina's Story: Being an Account of the Early Married Life of the Emperor Nicholas I of Russia Written by His Wife*, U. Pope-Hennessy (ed.), London, 1948
Alexandra Fyodorovna, *The Last Diary of Tsaritsa Alexandra*, V. Kozlov and V. Khrustalev (eds.), New Haven, 1997
Anna, Elizaveta, *Kniga zapisnaia imennym pismam i ukazam imperatrits Anny Ioannovny i Elizavety Petrovny Semyonu Andreevichu Saltykovu, 1732–1742*, Moscow, 1878
Anonymous, *The Memoirs of the Life of Prince Potemkin, comprehending original anecdotes of Catherine II and of the Russian court, translated from the German*, London, 1812 and 1813
*Arkhiv knyazya Vorontsova*, vols. 1–40, St. Petersburg, 1870–95
Asseburg, A. F. von der, *Denkwürdigkeiten*, Berlin, 1842
Buxhoeveden, Baroness Sophie, *The Life and Tragedy of Alexandra Feodorovna, Empress of Russia*, London, 1928
Bark, Peter, *Memoirs*, CUBA, New York
Bartenev, P. (ed.), *Osmnadtsatyi vek*, vols. 2–3, Moscow, 1869
Bassewitz, H-F., *Zapiski grafa Bassevicha, sluzhashchie k poiasneniiu nekotorykh sobytii iz vremi tsarstvovaniia Petra Velikogo*, RA 3 (1865) 93–274
Bergholz, F. W., *Dnevnik*, Moscow, 1902
Beskrovnyi, L. G. (ed.), *M. I. Kutuzov. Sbornik dokumentov*, vol. 4, Moscow, 1954
Bludov, D. N., *Poslednie minuty I konchina v boze pochivshego imperatora, nezabvennogo i vechnoi slavy dostoinogo Nikolaia I*, St. Petersburg, 1855

Botkin, G., *The Real Romanovs*, New York, 1931

Botkine, Tatiana, *Au Temps des Tsars*, C. Melnik (ed.), Paris, 1980

Catherine the Great, *Correspondence of Catherine the Great when Grand Duchess with Sir Charles Hanbury-Williams and Letters from Count Poniatowski*, The Earl of Ilchester and Mrs. Langford Brooke (eds.), London, 1928

Catherine II, *The Memoirs of Catherine the Great*, Cruse, M. and Hoogenboom, H. (eds.), New York, 2006

Catherine II, *The Memoirs of Catherine the Great*, ed. D. Maroger, London, 1955

Catherine II and G. A. Potemkin, *Ekaterina II i G. A. Potemkin, lichnaya perepiska 1769–1791*, V. S. Lopatin (ed.), Moscow, 1997

Catherine II and G. A. Potemkin, *Perepiska Ekaterina II i G. A. Potemkina v period vtoroy russko-turetskoy voiny (1787–1791): istochnkovedcheskiye issledovaniya*, O. I. Yeliseeva (ed.), Moscow, 1997

Catherine II, *Sochineniya imperatritsy Ekaterina II na osnovanii podlinnykh rukopsye c obyasnitelnmi primechaniyamai*, A. N. Pypin (ed.), St. Petersburg, 1901–7

Catherine II/P. V. Zavadovsky, *Pisma imp. Ekateriny II k gr. P. V. Zavadovskomu 1775–1777*, I. A. Barskov (ed.), *Russkiy istoricheskiy zhurnal* (1918)

*Chin postavleniia na tsarstvo tsarya i velikogo knyazya Alexeia Mikhailovicha*, St. Petersburg, 1882

Collins, S., *The Present State of Russia*, London, 1671

Corberon, M.-D. B., Chevalier de, *Un Diplomate français à la cour de Catherine II 1775–1780, journal intime*, Paris, 1904

Crokatt, J., *The Tryal of the Czarewitz, Alexis Petrowitz, who was Condemn'd at Petersbourg, on the 25th of June, 1718, for a Design of Rebellion and Treason*, London, 1725

Czartoryski, Adam, *Memoirs of Prince Adam Czartoryski and His Correspondence with Alexander I*, A. Gielgud (ed.), London, 1888

Dashkova, E. R., *Memoirs of Princess Dashkov*, London, 1958

*Delo 1 marta: protsess Zheliabova, Perovskoi i drugikh. Pravitelstvennyi otchet*, St. Petersburg, 1906

Derzhavin, G. R., *Sobranie sochinenii*, St. Petersburg, 1864–72

Dubrovin, N. F (ed.)., *Materialy i cherty k biografii imperatora Nikolaia I i k istorii tsarstvovaniia*, St. Petersburg, 1896

Elizaveta, *Pisma i zapiski imperatritsy Elizavety Petrovny, 1741–1761*, St. Petersburg, 1867

Elizaveta/Mavra Shepeleva, *Pisma k gosudaryne tsesarevne Elizavete Petrovne Mavry Shepelevoi*, *ChOIDR* (1864) 2.66–72

Epanchin, N. A., *Na sluzhbe tryokh imperatorov: Vospominaniia*, Moscow, 1996

Evelyn, J., *The Diary of John Evelyn*, London, 1906

Favier, Jean-Louis, *Zapiski Favie*, Vychkov, F. A. (ed.), *Istoricheskii vestnik* (1887) 29

Frederiks, M. P., *Iz vospominanii*, in S. Shokarev (ed.), *Nikolai I. Portret na fone imperii*, Moscow, 2001

Gilliard, P., *Thirteen Years at the Russian Court*, New York, 1921

Golovkine, Fyodor, *La Cour et le règne de Paul Ier*, S. Bonnet (ed.), Paris, 1905

Golovina, Varvara, *Memoirs of Countess Golovine*, London, 1910

Gordon, P., *Passages from the Diary of General Patrick Gordon of Auchleuchries*, Aberdeen, 1659

Harris, James, *Diaries and Correspondence of James Harris, 1st Earl of Malmesbury*, London, 1844

Iswolsky, Helene, *No Time to Grieve: An Autobiographical Journey*, New York, 1986

Izvolsky, A. P., *Recollections of Foreign Minister: The Memoirs of Alexander Izvolsky*, S. L. Seeger (ed.), London, 1920

Junot, L. (ed.), *Memoirs of the Duchess d'Abrantes*, London, 1833–5

*Kamer-furyerskie zhurnaly, 1696–1816*, St. Petersburg, 1853–1917

Khrapovitsky, A. V., *Dnevnik, 1782–1793*, Moscow, 1874

Kleinmichel, Countess Marie, *Memoirs of a Shipwrecked World*, London, 1923

Kokovtsov, V. N., *Out of my Past: The Memoirs of Count Kokovtsov* (ed. H. H. Fisher), Stanford, 1935

Korb, J., *Diary of an Austrian Secretary of Legation at the Court of Czar Peter the Great*, (ed. Count MacDonnell), London, 1963

Korf, M. A., Materialy i cherty k biografii Imperatora Niklaia I in N. F. Dubrovin, *Materialy i cherty k biografii imperatora Nikolaia I I k istorii tsarstvovaniia*, St. Petersburg, 1896

*Koronatsionnye torzhestva. Albom svyashchennogo koronovaniia ikh imperatorskikh velichestv gosudarya imperatora Nikolaia Alexandrovicha i gosudaryni imperatritsy Alexandry Fedorovny*, Moscow, 1896

Kuropatkin, A., *Dnevnik generala A. N. Kuropatkina*, Moscow, 2010

Langeron, Alexandre, comte de, *Mémoire sur la mort de Paul I, par le comte de Langeron*, Richelieu Collection, Mémoires de documents, MS 99, Bibliotheque de la Sorbonne, Paris, unpublished

Langeron, Alexandre, Comte de, *Journal de campagnes faites au service de Russie par le comte de Langeron: résumé de campagnes de 1787, 1788, 1789 des russes contre les turcs en Bessarabie, en Moldavie and dans le Kouban*, Archives des Affaires etrangeres, Quai d'Orsay, Paris

Lear, F., *The Romance of an American in Russia*, Brussels, 1875

Lenin, V. I., *Sochineniia*, vols. 20–1, Moscow, 1968–73

Ligne, C. J. E., Prince de, *Letters and Reflections of the Austrian Field Marshal*, Philadelphia, 1809

Ligne, C. J. E., Prince de, *Les Lettres de Catherine II au prince de Ligne, 1780–96*, Brussels/Paris, 1924

Ligne, C. J. E., Prince de, *Lettres du prince de Ligne à la marquise de Coigny pendant l'année 1787*, Paris, 1886

Ligne, C. J. E., Prince de, *Lettres et pensées*, London, 1808

Ligne, C. J. E., Prince de, *Mélanges militaires, littéraires et sentimentaires*, Dresden, 1795–1811

Ligne, C. J. E., Prince de, *Mémoires et mélanges historiques et littéraires*, Paris, 1827–9

Liria, duke of, Pisma o Rossii v Ispaniiu, in *Osmnadtsatyi vek*, P. Bartenev (ed.), Moscow, 1869

Manstein, C. H. von, *Contemporary Memoirs of Russia from 1727 to 1744*, London, 1856

Maria Fyodorovna and Anna Pavlovna, *Chère Annette: Letters from Russia 1820–1828: The Correspondence of the Empress Maria Feodorovna of Russia to Her Daughter the Grand Duchess Anna Pavlovna, the Princess of Orange*, S. W. Jackman (ed.), Dover, 1994

Marie Pavlovna, *Education of a Princess: A Memoir*, R. Lord (ed.), New York, 1931

Marie, Queen of Roumania, *Story of My Life*, London, 1934

Massa, I., *A Short History of the Beginnings and Origins of These Present Wars in Moscow: Under the Reign of Various Sovereigns Down to the Year 1610*, trans. and ed. G. E. Orchard, Toronto, 1982

Masson, C. F. P., *Secret Memoirs of the Court of Petersburg*, London, 1800

Matveev, A. A., *Zapiski Grafa Andreya Matveeva*, in N. Sakharov, *Zapiski Russkikh Lyudei. Sobytiia vremen Petra Velikogo*, St. Petersburg, 1841

Meshchersky, V. P., *Moi vospominaniia*, Moscow, 2001

Meshchersky, V. P., Some Russian Imperial Letters to Prince V. P. Meshchersky (1839–1914), Vinogradoff, I. (ed.), *Oxford Slavonic Papers* (1862) 10.105–58

Miranda, Francisco de, *Archivo del General Miranda, 1785–7*, Caracas, 1929

Miliutin, Dmitri, *Dnevnik, 1879–1881*, L. G. Zakharova (ed.), Moscow, 2010

Miliutin, Dmitri, *Dnevnik, 1873–1875*, L. G. Zakharova (ed.), Moscow, 2008

Montefiore, Moses, *Diaries of Sir Moses and Lady Montefiore*, Loewe, L. (ed.), London, 1890

Mordvinov, A. A., Otryvki iz vospominanii, *Russkaia letopis* (1923) 5

Mordvinov, A. A., *Iz perezhitogo: Vospominaniia fligel-adyutanta imperatora Nikolaia II*, ed. O. I. Barkovets, Moscow, 2014

Mossolov, A. A., *At the Court of the Last Tsar*, London, 1935

Münnich, E., *Mémoires sur la Russie de Pierre le Grand à Elisabeth I, 1720–1742*, Paris, 1997

Narishkin-Kurakin, Elizabeth, *Under Three Tsars: The Memoirs of the Lady-in-Waiting Elizabeth Narishkin-Kurakin*, Fillip-Miller (ed.), New York, 1931

Nicholas I, *Letters of Tsar Nicholas and the Empress Marie*, E. J. Bing (ed.), London, 1937

*Nikolai II i velikie knyazia*, Nevskii, V. I. (ed.), Leningrad, 1925

Nicholas II and Alexandra, *A Lifelong Passion: Nicholas and Alexandra: Their Own Story*, A. Maylunas and S. Mironenko (eds.), New York, 1997

Nicholas II and Alexandra, *The Complete Wartime Correspondence of Tsar Nicholas II and the Empress Alexandra: April 1914–March 1917*, J. T. Fuhrman (ed.), Westport, Conn., 1999

Oberkirch, Baroness d', *Memoirs of the Baroness d'Oberkirch*, Count de Montbrison (ed.), London, 1852

Olearius, Adam, *Travels of Olearius*, Stanford, Calif., 1967

Olga Nikolaevna, *Son Iunosti. Vospominaniia velikoi knyazhny Olgi Nikolaevny, 1825–1846*, in N. Azarova (ed.), *Nikolai I. Muzh. Otets. Imperator*, Moscow, 2000

Olga Alexandrovna, *25 Chapters of My Life: Memoirs of Grand Duchess Olga Alexandrovna*, Paul Kulikovsky (ed.), New Haven, 2010

*Opisanie koronatsii ee velichestva i samoderzhitsy vserossiiskoi Anny Ioannovny*, Moscow, 1730

Paléologue, Maurice, *An Ambassador's Memoirs*, London, 1923–5

Pavlenko, N. I. (ed.), *Catherine I*, Moscow, 2004

Peter the Great, *Pisma i Bumagi Imperatora Petra Velikogo*, vols. 1–13, St. Petersburg, 1887–2003

*Pisma russkikh gosudarei*, vols. 1, 4, 5, Moscow, 1848, 1862, 1896

Pobedonostsev, K. P., *Pisma Pobedonostseva k Alexandru III*, vol. 1, Moscow, 1925

Pole-Carew, R., Russian Anecdotes in the Antony Archive, CO/R/3/42, unpublished

*Polnoe sobranie zakonov Rossiiskoi Imperii*, St. Petersburg, 1830–1916

*Polnoe sobranie zakonov*, vols. 1–46, St. Petersburg, 1830

Polovtsov, A. A., *Dnevnik gosudarstvennogo sekretarya*, Moscow, 2005

Poniatowski, S. A., *Mémoires secrets et inédits*, Leipzig, 1862

Prokopovich, F., *Kratkaia povest o smerti Petra Velikogo*, St. Petersburg, 1831

Purishkevich, V. M., *The Murder of Rasputin*, Ann Arbor, 1985

Richelieu, Armand du Plessis, duc de, Journal de mon voyage en Allemagne, *SIRIO* (1886) 54.111–98

Rodzianko, M. V., *The Reign of Rasputin*, London, 1927

Rostopchin, F., *Le Dernier Jour de la vie de l'impératrice Catherine II et le premier jour du règne de l'empereur Paul*, in *Oeuvres inédites du comte Rostoptchine*, Paris, 1894

Sablukov, N. A., Reminiscences of the Court and Times of the Emperor, Paul I, up to the Period of his Death, *Fraser's Magazine for Town and Country* (1865) 72.222–241, 302–27

Samoilov, A. N., Zhizn i deiania Generala Feldmarshala Knyazya Grigoriia Alexandrovicha Potemkina-Tavricheskogo, *RA* (1867) 4, 5, 6, 7

Savinkov, B., *Memoirs of a Terrorist*, New York, 1931

Sazonov, S., *Fateful Years, 1909–1916*, London, 1928

*Sbornik dogovorov i diplomaticheskikh dokumentov po delam Dalnego Vostoka 1895–1905*, St. Petersburg, 1906

Scherer, J. B., *Anecdotes Interessantes et Secrets de la Cour de Russia*, London, 1792

Sergei Alexandrovich, *Velikii knyaz Sergei Alexandrovich Romanov: biograficheskie materialy* I. V. Plotnikova (ed.), Moscow, 2006–11

Shavelskii, G. I., *Memoirs of the Last Protopresbyter of the Russian Army and Navy*, New York, 1954

Shestakov, I. V., *Polveka obyknovennoi zhizni*, St. Petersburg, 2006

Spiridovich, A., *Les Dernières Années de la cour de Tzarskoïé-Sélo*, Paris, 1928

Stäehlin, Jacob von, Zapiski o Petre Tretiem, *ChOIDR* (1866) 4

Sukhomlinov, V. A., *Vospominaniia*, Moscow, 1926

Suvorin, A. S., *Dnevnik A. S. Suvorina*, M. Krichevsy (ed.), Moscow/Petrograd, 1923

Suvorov, A. V. *Pisma*, V. S. Lopatin (ed.), Moscow, 1986

Suvorov, A. V. *Pisma i bumagi A. V. Suvorova, G. A. Potemkina, i P. A. Rumiantseva 1787–1789, kinburn ochakovskaya operatsiya*, *SBVIM*, D. F. Maslovsky (ed.), St. Petersburg, 1893

Tokmakov, I. (ed.), *Istoricheskoe opicanie vsekh koronatsii rossiiskikh tsarei, imperatorov i imperatrits*, Moscow, 1896

Tolstoy, L. N., *Hadji Murat*, in *Great Short Works of Leo Tolstoy*, London, 2004

Tolstoya, Alexandra, *Zapiski freiliny: Pechalnyi epizod iz moei zhizni pri dvore*, N. I. Azarova (ed.), Moscow, 1996

Tyutcheva, Anna, *Vospominaniia* (ed. L. V. Gladkova), Moscow, 2004

*Vozhidanii koronatsii. Venchanie russkikh samoderzhtsev. Tserkovnyi obryad koronovaniia i podrobnoe opisanie tryokh koronatsii nyneshnego stoletiia*, St. Petersburg, 1883

Valuev, P., *Dnevnik (1877–1884)*, Petrograd, 1919

Valuev, P., *Dnevnik P. A. Valueva, ministra vnutrennikh del (1861–1876)*, Moscow, 1961

*Venchanie russkikh gosudarei na tsarstvo, nachinaia s tsarya Mikhaila Fedorovicha do imperatora Alexandra III*, St. Petersburg, 1883

Victoria, Queen, *The Letters of Queen Victoria: A Selection from Her Majesty's Correspondence between the Years 1837 and 1861*, A. C. Benson and Viscount Esher (eds.), London, 1907

Vigor, Mrs. William (Mrs. Rondeau), *Letters from a Lady who Resided Some Years in Russia, to her Friend in England*, London, 1777

Volkonskaya, Zinaida, *Lives in Letters: Princess Zinaida Volkonskaya and her Correspondence* (ed. B. Arutunova), Columbus, Ohio, 1994

Voltaire, *Oeuvres complètes de Voltaire: correspondance avec l'impératrice de Russie*, vol. 58, Paris, 1821

Vyrubova, A., *Memories of the Russian Court*, New York, 1923

Washburn, S., *On the Russian Front in World War I: Memoirs of an American War Correspondent*, New York, 1982

Weber, F. C., *The Present State of Russia*, London, 1968

Wiegel (Vigel), F. F., *Zapiski Filipa Filipovich Vigela*, Moscow 1873, 1891 and 1928; *Vospominaniya F. F. Vigela*, Moscow, 1864–6 and 1891

Witte, S., *The Memoirs of Count Witte*, New York, 1990

Yusupov, Felix, *Lost Splendour*, London, 1953

Yusupov, Felix, *Rasputin*, New York, 1927

Zhukovsky, V. A., *Dnevniki V. A. Zhukovskogo* (ed. I. A. Bychkov), St. Petersburg, 1901

Zhukovsky, V. A., Sobstvennoruchnoe chernovoe pismo V. A. Zhukovskogo ee Imperatorskomu Vel. Gos. Imp. Marii Fyodorovne, *SIRIO* (1881) 30.39

Zakharova, L. G. and Tyutyunnik, L. I. (eds.), *Perepiska imperatora Alexandra II s velikim knyazem Konstantinom Nikolaevichem. Dnevnik velikogo knyazya Konstantina Nikolaevicha. 1857–1861*, Moscow, 1994

Zhitomirskaia, S. V. (ed.), S. A. Smirnova-Rosset, *Dnevnik. Vospomimamiia*, Moscow, 1989


SECONDARY SOURCES

Alexander, J. T., *Autocratic Politics in a National Crisis: The Imperial Russian Government and Pugachev's Revolt 1773–1775*, Bloomington, Ind., 1969

Alexander, J. T., *Catherine the Great: Life and Legend*, London/New York, 1989

Alexander, J. T., *Emperor of the Cossacks: Pugachev and the Frontier Jacquerie of 1773–75*, Lawrence, Kan., 1973

Almedingen, E. M., *The Emperor Alexander II: A Study*, London, 1962

Anisimov, E. V., *Empress Elizabeth: Her Reign and her Russia, 1741–1761*, Gulf Breeze, Fla., 1995

Anisimov, E. V., *Five Empresses: Court Life in Eighteenth-Century Russia*, New York, 2004

Anisimov, E. V., *The Reforms of Peter the Great: Progress through Coercion in Russia*, New York, 1993

Aragon, L. A. C., marquis d', *Un Paladin au XVIII siècle. Le Prince Charles de Nassau-Siegen*, Paris, 1893

Ascher, A., *P. A. Stolypin: The Search for Stability in Late Imperial Russia*, Stanford, Calif., 2001

Ascher, A., *The Revolution of 1905: Authority Restored*, Stanford, Calif., 1994

Ascher, A., *The Revolution of 1905: Russia in Disarray*, Stanford, Calif., 1994

Asprey, R. B., *Frederick the Great: The Magnificent Enigma*, New York, 1986

Baddeley, J. F., *The Russian Conquest of the Caucasus*, London, 1999

Baron, Salo, *The Jews under Tsars and Soviets*, New York, 1988

Bartlett, Rosamund, *Tolstoy: A Russian Life*, London, 2010

Batalden, S. K., *Catherine II's Greek Prelate: Eugenios Voulgaris in Russia 1771–1806*, New York, 1982

Beales, D., *Joseph II: In the Shadow of Maria Theresa 1741–80*, Cambridge, 1987

Becker, S., *Russia's Protectorates in Central Asia: Bukhara and Khiva, 1865–1924*, London/New York, 2004

Beéche, Arturo, *The Grand Dukes*, East Richmond Heights, Calif., 2013

Beéche, Arturo, *The Other Grand Dukes*, East Richmond Heights, Calif., 2013

Belyakova, Z., *The Romanov Legacy: The Palaces of St Petersburg*, London, 1994

Belyakova, Z., *Velikii Knyaz Alexei Alexandrovich. Za I protiv*, St. Petersburg, 2004

Bew, John, *Castlereagh: Enlightenment, War and Tyranny*, London 2011

Bibikov, A. A., *Zapiski o zhizni i sluzhbe Alexandra Ilyicha Bibikova*, St. Petersburg, 1817

Binyon, T. J., *Pushkin: A Biography*, London, 2002

Blanch, L., *The Sabres of Paradise: Conquest and Vengeance in the Caucasus*, London, 2004

Blanning, Tim, *Joseph II and Enlightened Despotism*, London, 1970

Blanning, Tim, *Joseph II: Profiles in Power*, London, 1994

Blanning, Tim, *Frederick the Great, King of Prussia*, London, 2015

Bobroff, R. P., *Roads to Glory: Late Imperial Russia and the Turkish Straits*, London, 2006

Bogatyrev, Sergei., Ivan IV (1533–1584), in M. Perrie (ed.), *The Cambridge History of Russia*, vol. 1: *From Early Rus' to 1689*, Cambridge, 2006, 240–63

Bogatyrev, Sergei, *The Sovereign and His Counsellors: Ritualised Consultations in Muscovite Political Culture, 1350s–1570s*, Helsinki, 2000

Bolotina, N. Y., *Ties of Relationship between Prince G. A. Potemkin and the Family of the Princes Golitsyn*, Conference of Golitsyn Studies, Bolshiye vyazemy, Moscow, 1997

Bovykin, V. I., *Iz istorii vozniknoveniia pervoi mirovoi voiny*, Moscow, 1961

Brickner, A. G., *Imperator Ioann Antonovich i ego rodstvenniki*, Moscow, 1874

Bullough, Oliver, *Let Our Fame Be Great: Journeys among the Defiant People of the Caucasus*, London, 2010

Bushkovitch, P., *A Concise History of Russia*, Cambridge, 2012

Bushkovitch, P., *Peter the Great*, Cambridge, 2002, 2007

Byrnes, R. F., *Pobedonostsev: His Life and Thought*, Bloomington, Ind., 1968

Carter, Miranda, *The Three Emperors*, London, 2009

Casey, John, *Afterlives: A Guide to Heaven, Hell and Purgatory*, Oxford, 2010

Castéra, J.-H., *The Life of Catherine II, Empress of Russia*, London, 1799

Charles-Roux, F., *Alexandre II, Gortchakoff, et Napoleon III*, Paris, 1913

Charmley, J., *The Princess and the Politicians: Sex, Intrigue and Diplomacy, 1812–40*, New York, 2005

Christie, I. R., *The Benthams in Russia*, Oxford/Providence, R.I., 1993

Clark, C., *The Sleepwalkers: How Europe Went to War in 1914*, New York, 2013

Cockfield, J. H., *White Crow: The Life and Times of the Grand Duke Nicholas Mikhailovich Romanov, 1859–1919*, Westport, Conn., 2002

Connaughton, R., *Rising Sun and Tumbling Bear: Russia's War with Japan*, London, 2007

Cook, A., *To Kill Rasputin*, London, 2005

Crankshaw, E., *Maria Theresa*, London, 1969

Crawford, R. and Crawford, D., *Michael and Natasha: The Life and Love of the Last Tsar of Russia*, London/New York, 1997

Cross, A. C., *By the Banks of the Neva: Chapters from the Lives and Careers of the British in Eighteenth-Century Russia*, Cambridge, 1997

Crummey, R. O., *Aristocrats and Servitors: The Boyar Elite, 1613–89*, Princeton, 1983

Curtiss, M., *A Forgotten Empress: Anna Ivanovna and Her Era*, New York, 1974

Daly, Jonathan W., *Autocracy under Siege: Security Police and Opposition in Russia 1866–1905*, DeKalb, Ill., 1998

Daly, Jonathan.W., *The Watchful State 1906–17: Security Police and Opposition in Russia*, DeKalb, Ill., 2004

Dixon, S., *Catherine the Great*, London, 2010

Dmitriev, M. V. (ed.), *Evrei i khristiane v pravoslavnykh obshchestvakh Vostochnoi Evropy*, Moscow, 2011

Dubrovin, N. F., *Istoriia Krymskoi voiny i oborony Sevastopolya*, St. Petersburg, 1900

Dubrovin, N. F., *Istoriia voyny i vladychestva russkih na Kavkaze*, St. Petersburg, 1886

Dubrovin, N. F., *Pugachev i ego soobshchniki*, St. Petersburg, 1884

Duffy, C., *Frederick the Great: A Military Life*, London, 1985

Duffy, C., *Russia's Military Way to the West: Origins and Nature of Russian Military Power 1700–1800*, London, 1981

Dunning, C. S. L., *Russia's First Civil War*, University Park, Pa., 2001

Dyachenko, L. I., *Tavricheski Dvorets*, St. Petersburg, 1997

Ehrman, J., *The Younger Pitt*, vol. 2: *The Reluctant Transition*, London, 1983

Eklof, B., Bushnell, J. and Zakharova, L. (eds.), *Russia's Great Reforms, 1855–1881*, Bloomington, Ind., 1994

Englund, P., *The Battle That Shook Europe: Poltava and the Birth of the Russian Empire*, London, 2012

Erickson, M. and Erickson L. (eds.), *Russia: War, Peace and Diplomacy: Essays in Honour of John Erickson*, London, 2005

Fairweather, M., *Pilgrim Princess: A Life of Princess Zinaida Volkonsky*, London, 1999

Figes, O., *Crimea*, London, 2010

Figes, O., *Natasha's Dance: A Cultural History of Russia*, London, 2002

Figes, O., *A People's Tragedy: The Russian Revolution 1891–1924*, New York, 1996

Florinsky, M. T., *Russia: A History and an Interpretation*, New York, 1967

Fothergill, B., *Sir William Hamilton, Envoy Extraordinary*, London, 1969

Frank, J., *Dostoevsky: A Writer in his Time*, Princeton, 2009

Fuhrman, J. T., *Rasputin: The Untold Story*, Hoboken, N.J., 2012

Fuhrman, J. T., *Tsar Alexis: His Reign and His Russia*, DeKalb, Ill., 1981

Fuller, Jr., W. C., *The Foe Within: Fantasies of Treason and the End of Imperial Russia*, Ithaca, N.Y., 2006

Fuller, Jr., W. C., *Strategy and Power in Russia, 1600–1914*, New York, 1992

Gammer, M., *Muslim Resistance to the Tsar: Shamil and the Conquest of Chechnia and Daghestan*, London, 1994

Geyer, D., *Russian Imperialism: The Interaction of Domestic and Foreign Policy 1860–1914*, New York, 1987

Gleason, J. H., *The Genesis of Russophobia in Great Britain: A Study in the Interaction of Policy and Opinion*, Cambridge, Mass., 1950

Golombievsky, A. A., *Sotrudniki Petra Velikogo*, Moscow, 1903

Grebelsky, P. and Mirvis, A., *Dom Romanovykh*, St. Petersburg, 1992

Green, A., *Moses Montefiore: Jewish Liberator, Imperial Hero*, Cambridge, Mass., 2010

Grey, I., *Boris Godunov: The Tragic Tsar*, London, 1973

Hall, C., *Imperial Dancer: Mathilde Kschessinska and the Romanovs*, Stroud, 2005

Hall, C., *Little Mother of Russia: A Biography of the Empress Marie Feodorovna, 1847–1928*, London, 2006

Hastings, M., *Catastrophe 1914: Europe Goes to War*, New York, 2013

Hatton, R. M., *Charles XII of Sweden*, London, 1968

Hedlund, S., *Russian Path Dependence: A People with a Troubled History*, London, 2012

Hosking, G., *Russia and the Russians: A History*, London, 2001

Hosking, G., *Russia: People and Empire, 1552–1917*, Cambridge, 1997

Hosking, G., *The Russian Constitutional Experiment: Government and Duma 1907–14*, Cambridge, 1973

Hughes, L., *The Romanovs*, New York/London, 2008

Hughes, L., *Russia in the Age of Peter the Great*, New Haven, 1998

Hughes, L., *Sophia, Regent of Russia 1654–1704*, New Haven, 1990

Ignatiev, A. V., *Russko-angliiskie otnosheniia nakanune Oktyabrskoi revolutsii (Fevral–oktyabr 1917 g.)*, Moscow, 1966

Jenkins, M., *Arakcheev: Grand Vizier of the Russian Empire*, New York, 1969

Josselson, M. and Josselson, D., *The Commander: A Life of Barclay de Tolly*, Oxford, 1980

Kates, G., *Monsieur d'Eon is a Woman: A Tale of Political Intrigue and Sexual Masquerade*, New York, 1995, 2001

Kelly, L., *Diplomacy and Murder in Tehran: Alexander Griboyedov and Imperial Russia's Mission to the Shah of Persia*, New York, 2006

Kesselbrenner, G. L., *Svetleishii knyaz*, Moscow, 1998

King, G., *The Court of the Last Tsar: Pomp, Power and Pageantry in the Reign of Nicholas II*, Hoboken, N.J., 2006

King, G., *Livadia in the Reign of Alexander II*, at http://www.kingandwilson.com/AtlantisArticles/LivadiaAII.htm

King, G. and Wilson, P., *The Fate of the Romanovs*, New York, 2005

Korf, M. A., *Braunshveigskoe semeistvo*, Moscow, 1993

Korsakov, D. A., *Votsarenie Imperatritsy Anny Ioannovny*, Kazan, 1880

Kotkin, S., *Stalin*, vol. 1: *Paradoxes of Power, 1878–1928*, New York, 2014

Krylov-Tolstikevich, A. N., *Imperator Alexandr I i imperatritsa Elizaveta*, Moscow, 2005

LeDonne, John P., *Absolutism and Ruling Class: The Formation of the Russian Political Order, 1700–1825*, Oxford, 1991

LeDonne, John P., *Ruling Russia: Politics and Administration in the Age of Absolutism 1762–96*, Princeton, 1984

LeDonne, John P., *The Russian Empire and the World 1700–1917: The Geopolitics of Expansion and Containment*, Oxford, 1997

Levin, E., *A Child of Christian Blood: Murder and Conspiracy in Tsarist Russia: The Beilis Blood Libel*, New York, 2014

Lieven, D., *Nicholas II: Emperor of All the Russias*, London, 1993

Lieven, D., *Russia against Napoleon: The True Story of the Campaigns of War and Peace*, New York, 2010

Lieven, D., *Russia's Rulers under the Old Regime*, New Haven, 1989

Lieven, D., *Towards the Flame: Empire, War and the End of Tsarist Russia*, London, 2015

Lincoln, W. B., *Between Heaven and Hell: The Story of a Thousand Years of Artistic Life in Russia*, New York, 1998

Lincoln, W. B., *The Great Reforms: Autocracy, Bureaucracy, and the Politics of Change in Imperial Russia*, DeKalb, Ill., 1990

Lincoln, W. B., *In the Vanguard of Reform: Russia's Enlightened Bureaucrats*, DeKalb, Ill., 1982

Lincoln, W. B., *In War's Dark Shadow: The Russians before the Great War*, New York, 1983

Lincoln, W. B., *Nicholas I: Emperor and Autocrat of All the Russias*, London, 1978

Lincoln, W. B., *Nikolai Miliutin: An Enlightened Russian Bureaucrat of the 19th Century*, Newtonville, Mass., 1977

Lincoln, W. B., *Passage through Armageddon: The Russians in War and Revolution*, New York, 1986

Lincoln, W. B., *Red Victory: A History of the Russian Civil War*, London, 1989

Lincoln, W. B., *The Romanovs: Autocrats of All the Russias*, New York, 1981

Lincoln, W. B., *Sunlight at Midnight: St Petersburg and the Rise of Modern Russia*, Oxford, 2001

Longford, E., *Wellington: Pillar of State*, London, 1975

Longworth, P., *Alexis, Tsar of All the Russias*, London, 1984

Longworth, P., *The Art of Victory: The Life and Achievements of Field Marshal Suvorov, 1729–1800*, New York, 1965

Longworth, P., *The Three Empresses: Catherine I, Anne, and Elizabeth of Russia*, London, 1972

Lopatin, V. S., *Potemkin i Suvorov*, Moscow, 1992

Lyashchenko, L. M., *Alexandr II*, Moscow, 2002

McDonald, E. and McDonald, D., *Fanny Lear: Love and Scandal in Tsarist Russia*, Bloomington, Ind., 2011

McGrew, R. E., *Paul I of Russia, 1754–1801*, Oxford, 1992

McMeekin, S., *July 1914: Countdown to War*, London, 2014

McMeekin, S., *The Ottoman Endgame: War, Revolution and the Making of the Modern Middle East*, London, 2015

McMeekin, S., *The Russian Origins of the First World War*, Cambridge, Mass., 2011

MacMillan, M., *The War that Ended Peace: The Road to 1914*, New York, 2013

Madariaga, I. de, *Ivan the Terrible*, New Haven, 2006

Madariaga, I. de, *Russia in the Age of Catherine the Great*, New Haven, 1981

Martin, R. E., *A Bride for the Tsar: Brideshows and Marriage Politics in Early Modern Russia*, DeKalb, Ill., 2012

Marshall, Alex, *Russian General Staff 1860–1917*, London, 2006

Menning, B., *Bayonets before Bullets: The Imperial Russian Army, 1861–1914*, Bloomington, Ind., 1992

Merridale, C., *Red Fortress: The Secret Heart of Russia's History*, London, 2013

Mikaberidze, Alexander, *The Battle of Borodino: Napoleon vs Kutuzov*, London, 2010

Mikaberidze, Alexander, *The Burning of Moscow: Napoleon's Trial by Fire 1812*, London 2014

Mironenko, S., *Stranitsy tainoi istorii samoderzhaviia*, Moscow, 1990

Montefiore, Simon Sebag, *Prince of Princes: The Life of Potemkin* (now published as *Catherine the Great and Potemkin*), London, 2000

Montefiore, Simon Sebag, *Stalin: The Court of the Red Tsar*, London, 2004

Montefiore, Simon Sebag, *Young Stalin*, London/New York, 2008

Mosse, W. E., *The Rise and Fall of the Crimean System 1855–71: The Story of a Peace Settlement*, London, 1963

Muir, R., *Wellington: Waterloo and the Fortunes of Peace 1814–1852*, London, 2015

Nikolai Mikhailovich, *L'Impératrice Elisabeth, épouse d'Alexandre Ier*, vol. 1, St. Petersburg, 1909

Nikolai Mikhailovich, *L'Empereur Alexandre Ier*, vol. 1, St. Petersburg, 1912

Nosik, B. M., *Russkie tainy Parizha*, St. Petersburg, 1998

Pakula, Hannah, *Last Romantic: A Biography of Queen Marie of Romania*, London, 1984

Perrie, Maureen, *Pretenders and Popular Monarchism in Early Modern Russia: The False Tsars of the Time of Troubles*, Cambridge, 2002

Petrushevsky, A., *Generalissimus Knyazi Suvorov*, St. Petersburg, 1884

Pflaum, R., *By Influence and Desire: The True Story of Three Extraordinary Women— The Grand Duchess of Courland and her Daughters*, New York, 1984

Pflaum, R., *The Emperor's Talisman: The Life of the Duc de Morny*, New York, 1968

Pleshakov, C., *The Tsar's Last Armada: The Epic Journey to the Battle of Tsushima*, New York, 2008

Plokhy, Sergii, *The Gates of Europe: A History of Ukraine*, New York, 2015

Polievktov, M., *Nikolai I. Biografiia i obzor tsarstvovaniia*, Moscow, 1918

Poznansky, Alexander, *Tchaikovsky: The Quest for the Inner Man*, London, 1994

Price, M., *Napoleon: The End of Glory*, New York, 2014

Pushkin, A. S., The Captain's Daughter, in *The Queen of Spades and Other Stories*, London, 1958

Pushkin, A. S., *Complete Prose Fiction*, Stanford, Calif., 1983

Pushkin, A. S., *Istoriia Pugacheva*, in *Polnoe sobraniye sochinenii*, vol. 12, Moscow/ Leningrad, 1937–49

Pushkin, A. S., *Notes on Russian History of the Eighteenth Century*, Istoricheskiye Zametki, Leningrad, 1984

Radzinsky, E., *Alexander II: The Last Great Tsar*, New York, 2005

Radzinsky, E., *The Last Tsar: The Life and Death of Nicholas II*, New York, 1993

Raeff, M., *Michael Speransky, Statesman of Imperial Russia 1772–1839*, Englewood Hills, N.J., 1957

Raeff, M. (ed.), *Plans for Political Reform in Imperial Russia 1730–1905*, Englewood Cliffs, N.J., 1966

Ransel, D. L., *The Politics of Catherinian Russia: The Panin Party*, New Haven, 1975

Rappaport, H., *Ekaterinburg: The Last Days of the Romanovs*, London, 2008

Rappaport, H., *Four Sisters: The Lost Lives of the Romanov Grand Duchesses*, London, 2015

Rayfield, D., *Edge of Empires: A History of Georgia*, London, 2012

Rey, M.-P., *Alexander I: The Tsar Who Defeated Napoleon*, DeKalb, Ill., 2012

Rhinelander, A. L. H., *Prince Michael Vorontsov: Viceroy to the Tsar*, Montreal, 1990

Riasanovsky, N. V., *Nicholas I and Official Nationality in Russia, 1825–1855*, Berkeley/Los Angeles, 1959

Rich, D. A., *The Tsar's Colonels: Professionalism, Strategy, and Subversion in Late Imperial Russia*, Cambridge, Mass., 1998

Ridley, Jane, *Bertie: A Life of Edward VII*, London, 2012

Roberts, A., *Napoleon the Great*, New York, 2014

Roberts, Elizabeth, *Realm of the Black Mountain: A History of Montenegro*, London, 2007

Robinson, P., *Grand Duke Nikolai Nikolaevich: Supreme Commander of the Russian Army*, DeKalb, Ill., 2014

Röhl, J. C. G., *Wilhelm II: Into the Abyss of War and Exile, 1900–1941*, Cambridge, 2014

Röhl, J. C. G., *Wilhelm II: The Kaiser's Personal Monarchy, 1888–1900*, Cambridge, 2004

Romanov, B. A., *Ocherki diplomaticheskoi istorii Russko-Iaponskoi voiny 1895–1907*, Moscow/Leningrad, 1955

Rounding, Virginia, *Catherine the Great: Love, Sex and Power*, London, 2007

Rounding, Virginia, *Nicky and Alix*, London, 2012

*Russkiy biographicheskiy slovar* (including biographies of Varvara Golitsyna, vol. 5, 1916; Ekaterina Skavronskaya, vol. 18, 1904; I. A. Hannibal, vol. 4, 1914; P. S. and M. S. Potemkin, vol. 14, 1904), vols. 1–25, St. Petersburg, 1896–1916

Ruud, C. A. and Stepanov, S. A., *Fontanka 16*, London, 1999

Sanborn, J. A., *Imperial Apocalypse: The Great War and the Destruction of the Russian Empire*, Oxford, 2014

Service, R., *A History of Modern Russia, from Nicholas II to Putin*, London, 1998

Service, R., *A History of Twentieth-Century Russia*, London, 1997

Service, R., *The Penguin History of Modern Russia: From Tsarism to the Twenty-first Century*, London, 2009

Service, R., *The Russian Revolution, 1900–27*, London, 1999

Shchutskaya, G. K., *Palaty boyar Romanovykh*, Moscow, 2000

Shilder, N. K., *Imperator Alexandr I. Ego zhizn i tsarstvovanie*, St. Petersburg, 1897

Shilder, N. K., *Imperator Pavel I*, St. Petersburg, 1901

Soloviev, S. V., *History of Russia*, vols. 4–15, DeKalb, Ill., 1989, 1991

Steinberg, M. D. and Khrustalëv, V. M., *The Fall of the Romanovs*, New Haven, 1997

Stone, N., *Eastern Front, 1914–17*, London, 1975

Sumner, B. H., *Russia and the Balkans 1870–1880*, Hamden, Conn., 1962

Tarasov, B. N. (ed.), *Nikolai I i ego vremya*, Moscow, 2001

Tarle, E. V., *Krymskaia voina*, Moscow, 2005

Thouvenel, L., *Nicolas I et Napoléon III, préliminaires de la guerre de Crimée, 1852–1854, d'après les papiers inédits de M. Thouvenel*, Paris, 1891

Troyat, H., *Catherine the Great*, London, 1977

Tsamutali, A. S., *Nikolai I*, Moscow, 2007

Ustryalov, Nikolai, *Istoriia Tsarstvovaniia Petra Velikogo*, St. Petersburg, 1858

Van der Kiste, J. and Hall, C., *Once a Grand Duchess: Xenia, Sister of Nicholas II*, London, 2013

van der Oye, D. S., *Toward the Rising Sun: Russian Ideologies of Empire and the Path to War with Japan*, DeKalb, Ill., 2001

Vasilchikov, A. A., *Semeistvo Razumovskikh*, vol. 1, St. Petersburg, 1880

Vernadsky, G., *History of Russia*, New Haven, 1973

Verner, A. M., *The Crisis of Russian Autocracy: Nicholas II and the 1905 Revolution*, Princeton, 1990

Vitale, S., *Pushkin's Button*, New York, 1999

Waliszewski, K., *Autour d'un trône*, Paris, 1894

Warwick, C., *Ella: Princess, Saint and Martyr*, Chichester, 2006

Wcislo, F., *Tales of Imperial Russia: The Life and Times of Sergei Witte, 1849–1915*, Oxford, 2011

Welch, Frances, *The Russian Court at Sea*, London, 2010

Wheatcroft, A., *The Habsburgs*, London, 1995

Wilson, A. N., *Tolstoy*, London, 1988

Wilson, A. N., *Victoria: A Life*, London, 2015

Wortman, R. S., *Scenarios of Power: Myth and Ceremony in Russian Monarchy*, Princeton, 2006, 2013

Yeliseeva, O. I., *G. A. Potemkin's Geopolitical Projects, Associates of Catherine the Great*, lecture at conference Moscow, 22/23 September 1997, published Moscow, 1997

Zaionchkovsky, A. M., *Vostochnaia voina, 1853–1856*, St. Petersburg, 2002

Zaionchkovsky, P. A., *The Russian Autocracy in Crisis 1878–1882*, Gulf Breeze, Fla., 1979

Zaionchkovsky, P. A., *The Russian Autocracy under Alexander III*, Gulf Breeze, Fla., 1976

Zamoyski, A., *1812: Napoleon's Fatal March on Moscow*, London, 2012

Zamoyski, A., *The Last King of Poland*, London, 1992

Zamoyski, Adam, *Phantom Terror: Political Paranoia and the Creation of the Modern State 1789–1848*, London, 2015

Zamoyski, A., *Rites of Peace: The Fall of Napoleon and the Congress of Vienna*, London, 2007

Zeepvat, C., *Romanov Autumn: Stories from the Last Century of Imperial Russia*, Stroud, 2000

Zimin, I. V., *Povsednevnaia zhizn rossiiskogo imperatorskogo dvora: Detskii mir imperatorskikh rezidentsii. Byt monarkhov i ikh okruzhenie*, St. Petersburg, 2010

Zitser, E. A., *The Transfigured Kingdom: Sacred Parody and Charismatic Authority at the Court of Peter the Great*, Ithaca, 2004

# NOTES

## INTRODUCTION

1. Marx on zoology; Bismarck on Coburg as studfarm of Europe, both quoted in A. N. Wilson, *Victoria: A Life* (henceforth Wilson) 19.

## PROLOGUE: TWO BOYS IN A TIME OF TROUBLES

1. This account based on GARF 601.2.27 Yakov Yurovsky's notes 1920 and 1 February 1934 plus unpublished notes (five in total); Empress Alexandra diary, June–July 1918, stored in GARF 640.1 and published *Last Diary of Tsaritsa Alexander*, V. Kozlov and V. Khrustalev (eds.) (henceforth "Alexandra diary"). Nicholas II diary, April–June 1918, GARF 601.1.217–266 (henceforth "ND"). These sources are also quoted in Mark D. Steinberg and Vladimir M. Khrustalëv, *The Fall of the Romanovs* (henceforth Fall) 320–66. Also Greg King and Penny Wilson, *The Fate of the Romanovs* (henceforth Fate) 282–317 and Helen Rappaport, *Ekaterinburg: The Last Days of the Romanovs*, 184–202.
2. Offer of throne to Michael Romanov based on: RGADA 135.III.1.2.1–5, Gramota tsaryu Mikhailu Fedorovichu, poslannaya v Kostromu s arkhimandritom Feodoritom i boyarinym F. I. Sheremetevym 2 Marta 1613 (The Charter of the Zemsky Sobor to Tsar Mikhail Fyodorovich of his election to the throne, 2 March 1613) RGADA 135.III.1.2.28–44, March 1613, Gramota arkhiepiskopa Feodorita i F. I. Sheremeteva k Zemskomu Soboru (Formal report of the Kostroma delegates to the Zemsky Sobor on Tsar Mikhail's consent to be tsar). Sergei Soloviev, *History of Russia* (henceforth Soloviev) 16.1–15. George Vernadsky, *History of Russia* (henceforth Vernadsky) 5.1.278–83. Robert Crummey, *Aristocrats and Servitors: The Boyar Elite 1613–89* (henceforth Crummey), 1–28. Michael: Olearius, *Travels of Olearius* (henceforth Olearius) 62, 191, 262. G. E. Orchard (trans. and ed.), I. Massa, *A Short History of the Beginnings and Origins of These Present Wars in Moscow: Under the Reign of Various Sovereigns Down to the Year 1610* (henceforth Orchard), 30–4. Presence of Saltykov brothers as advisers: Russell E. Martin, *A Bride for the Tsar: Brideshows and Marriage Politics in Early Modern Russia* (henceforth Martin) 180–2.

## ACT I: THE RISE
### SCENE I: THE BRIDESHOWS

1. RGADA 135.III.1.2.28–44, March 1613, Gramota arkhiepiskopa Feodorita i F. I. Sheremeteva k Zemskomu Soboru (Formal report of the Kostroma delegates to the Zemsky Sobor on Tsar Mikhail's consent to be tsar). Soloviev 16.1–12. Vernadsky 5.1.278–83.
2. Isabel de Madariaga, *Ivan the Terrible* (henceforth Madariaga), Mongols 5–6; tsar

title 17. Ivan the Terrible, Anastasia, brideshows 50–9. Sergei Bogatyrev, Ivan IV 1533–84, in Maureen Perrie (ed.), *The Cambridge History of Russia*, vol. 1: *From Early Rus' to 1689*. Troubles: Chester Dunning, *Russia's First Civil War* (henceforth Dunning), 33–72. False Dmitris: this is based on Maureen Perrie, *Pretenders and Popular Monarchism in Early Modern Russia*. Catherine Merridale, *Red Fortress: The Secret Heart of Russia's History* (henceforth Merridale) 75–102. Martin 112–21; Romanov descent 114–15.

3. P. Grebelsky and A. Mirvis, Dom Romanovykh 1–12. G. K. Shchutskaya, *Palaty boyar Romanovykh*. W. Bruce Lincoln, *The Romanovs* (henceforth Lincoln) 26; Lindsey Hughes, *The Romanovs* (henceforth Hughes), 1–10. On Michael: Orchard, 30–4.

4. Madariaga 140–5, 295, 342, 357; effect of Ivan 371. Circassian princes/Cherkasskys: Paul Bushkovitch, "Princes Cherkasskii or Circassian Murzas: The Kabardians in the Russian boyar elite 1560–1700," *Cahiers du Monde Russe* (2004) 45.1–2.9–30. Filaret: J. L. H. Keep, Regime of Filaret, SEER (1959–60) 38.334–43 (henceforth Keep). Michael: Orchard, 30–4. Michael character: Vernadsky 5.1.308–11. RGADA 135.III.1.2. 28–44, March 1613, Gramota arkhiepiskopa Feodorita i F. I. Sheremeteva k Zemskomu Soboru (Formal report of the Kostroma delegates to the Zemsky Sobor on Tsar Mikhail's consent to be tsar).

5. Keep 334–43. Vernadsky 5.1.205–20. Dunning 50–9; serfdom 60–73. Ian Grey, *Boris Godunov* 13–14, 134–9, 159–62. Soloviev 16.44. Dunning 94–100.

6. Soloviev 15.27. Vernadsky 5.1.225–51. Dunning on uprising, 415–39. Michael in Kremlin: Soloviev 15.283. Filaret: Soloviev 15.160–231; Pozharsky and Minin 275–86. Kremlin charnel-house: Merridale 130–3. Hughes 8–12. Keep 334–43.

7. Soloviev 15.240–89, 16.1–15; Filaret's reaction 16.44–5. Vernadsky 5.1.275–83. Dunning 415–48. Hughes 12–14, 31. Richard Wortman, *Scenarios of Power* (henceforth Wortman) 9–13. Susanin: Soloviev 16.243–50. Hughes 12–13.

8. Madariaga 1–22. Dunning 28–44. Merridale 13–100.

9. Coronation: L. E. Morozova: T. B. Knyazevskaia (ed.), *Kultura slavyan i Rus*, Morozova, L. E., *Dve redaktsii China venchaniia na tsarstvo Alexeia Mikhailovicha*, 457–72. Madariaga 49–52. Wortman 10–16. Lincoln 30–3. Hughes 12–13.

10. Olearius 62, 191, 262. Orchard 30–4. Soloviev 17.92. Clocks, Merridale 140, 146. Amusements: J. T. Fuhrman, *Alexis: His Reign and His Russia* (henceforth Fuhrman) 4–6. Paul Bushkovitch, *Peter the Great* (henceforth Bushkovitch) 14–16 and 28–9.

11. Soloviev 16:16–44, 96–114. Dunning 448–59. Vernadsky 5.1.283–93. Saltykovs: Martin 180.

12. Crummey 1–28, 56, 70–82, 143, 141–2; wealth lists of boyars 108. See also: Sergei Bogatyrev, *The Sovereign and His Counsellers: Ritualised Consultations in Muscovite Political Culture, 1350s to 1570s*. Soloviev 17.85–92. Bushkovitch 14–16, 28–9. Hughes 38–9. Lincoln 82–5. Processions: Wortman 15–18. Word and deed: C. A. Ruud and S. A. Stepanov, *Fontanka* 16 (henceforth Ruud) 5–7. Terem culture: Fuhrman 38, 75–6. Pharmacy: Soloviev 25.11.

13. Martin 9–11; 20–1; 57–94; 170–1;174, 180.

14. Martin 169–85. Madariaga 50–9. Soloviev 16.165–6, 313. Lincoln 34.

15. Soloviev 16.129–50, 174–200, 17.105.

16. Filaret: *Pisma russkikh gosudarei* (henceforth PRG) 1.10–14. Soloviev 16.156–65, 17.90–3. Filaret's vanity: Vernadsky 5.1.308–11. Lykov and Filaret: Soloviev 16.222–4. Dunning 459–80. Filaret exiles boyars: Bushkovitch 49–51. Paul Bushkovitch, *Shvedskie istochniki o Rossii 1624–26*, *Arkhiv russkoi istorii* (2007) 8.359–81. Precedence: Soloviev 17.93–102; Crummey 136–40.

17. Streshneva: Soloviev 16.166. Fuhrman 1–10. Martin 186–9. Dolgorukys: Bushkovitch 32. Bushkovitch, *Shvedskie istochniki o Rossii*, 8.359–81.

18. Soloviev 16.211–25, 17.92–5. Vernadsky 5.1.345–61. Fuhrman 106–7. Bushkevich 50–1. Boyar commanders: Crummey 46–9; Fuhrman 106–7. Hughes 38–40. Philip Longworth, *Alexis, Tsar of All the Russias* (henceforth Longworth) 21.

19. Soloviev 17.83–4. Longworth 5–23. *The Domostroi/Terem*: Fuhrman 83. Bushkovitch 33. Giving birth: Lindsey Hughes, *Sophia* (henceforth, *Sophia*) 25.

20. Vernadsky 5.1.383–5. Fuhrman 7–11. Longworth 17–26. Waldemar/pretenders: Soloviev 17.55–75. Death of Michael: Soloviev 17.83–4. Fuhrman 1–4. Longworth 17–21.

## SCENE 2: THE YOUNG MONK

1. Accession/Zealots: Vernadsky 5.1.382–91. Fuhrman 9–15, 46–7. Young Alexei: Hughes, *Sophia* 5, 25. Longworth 5–11, 19–28; zealots 55–67; negro Saveli 186. Funerals: Wortman 38. Religion and ceremonies: Crummey 141. Matveev: Fuhrman 193. Coronation: *Chin postavleniia na tsarstvo tsarya i velikogo knyazya Alexeia Mikhailovicha* 38. Falconry 119; technological interests 120.

2. Kindness, tact: Longworth 69, 72, 88, 135–9; Ivan 69 and 259; fury 69–72; ducking 113–14. Hughes, *Sophia* 28. Religion: Fuhrman 32–3; Crummey 141. Pharmacy: Soloviev 25.11. Alexei's order of foreign purchases: RGADA 27.118.119–20. Kind letter to Odoevsky: V. Lamansky, *Zapiski otdeleniia Russkoi i Slavyanskoi Arkheologii* (1861) 2.702–6. Letters to steward: ZORI 2.786–8.

3. Brideshow organized: Martin 190–2. Samuel Collins *Present State of Russia* 10–12, 111–13.

4. Marriage: Fuhrman 13–15, 208–10; Martin 192–6. Hughes 30–2. *Sophia* 20. Rich boyars: Crummey 113–14; on Morozov potash 130–3. Fuhrman 116–34. Longworth 22–38; father-substitute 45. Morozov: Fuhrman 16–18. Collins 10–12, 111–13.

5. 1648 riots and Code: Olearius 203–17. Crummey 83–7. Fuhrman 16–29. Hughes, *Sophia* 34. Longworth 39–46. Law code, John P. LeDonne, *Absolutism and Ruling Class* (henceforth LeDonne) 4, 16, 212–15.

6. Fuhrman 46–7, 131–45, 155–76. Crummey 97–100. *Sophia* 35–7. Merridale 156–8.

7. Sergii Plokhy, *The Gates of Europe: A History of Ukraine* (henceforth Plokhy) 97–118. Vernadsky 5.1.463–79. Longworth 65.

8. Polish war: RGADA 27.85; notebooks RGADA 27.82; 27.86. *PRG* 5.10–12. Longworth 68–91, 161. Fuhrman 57–74, 105–16; Secret Office 104–5. Generals: Crummey 46–9.

9. Fuhrman 155–79; Crummey 102. Longworth 164–73. *Sophia* 35–7.

10. RGADA 27.337; RGADA 27.85. Bushkovitch 24–7, 225. Secret Office: Longworth 129–39 and 155. Fuhrman 81–105, 166. Crummey 28–32; 141; favourites 97; wealth 146, 113–14; generals 46–9; foreign policy leaders 56–9. Nashchokin: Fuhrman 189–92 and Crummey 97. New men: Bushkovitch 49–65. Longworth 71–2. Sex, boyars: Longworth 154. Pharmacy: Soloviev 125.11. Odoevsky/Khitrovo/Dolgoruky: Bushkovitch 21–3, 51. Miloslavsky/sex: Fuhrman 87–8. Longworth 161. Collins 110–17.

11. Copper Riot: Fuhrman 145–53. Longworth 138–53.

12. *Sophia* 38–45. Longworth 164–73, 187. Fuhrman 210–14. Crummey 97. Longworth 125–36. LeDonne 298 on tsar as sole vicar of Christ sanctifying social order. Bushkovitch 51–5.

13. Crummey 102. Fuhrman 188–95. Bushkovitch 61–78. Martin 196–202; *Artaxerxes* 204.

14. Ruud 7. Bushkovitch 49–65. *Sophia* 37–46 (description of Natalya, pleasures, palaces, dwarfs by Reutenfel). Fuhrman 195–9. Longworth 200–3. Palaces: Crum-

mey 61. Theatres: Bushkovitch 43–8; Matveev 70–9. Fuhrman 195–6. Longworth 207–8; Peter and Natalya 224. Pharmacy: 25.11–20.

15. Soloviev 25.11–17; Bushkovitch 80–7. Fuhrman 176–81, 218–19. Longworth 214.

## SCENE 3: THE MUSKETEERS

1. Tokmakov (ed.), *Istoricheskoe opisanie vsekh koronatsii rossiiskikh tsarei, imperatorov i imperatrits* (henceforth Tokmakov) 52–3. Soloviev 25.9–36; death 94–6. Bushkovitch 86–123. *Sophia* 45–8, 182. Fuhrman 219–23. Marriages: Martin 211–16; 216–19.

2. 15–26 May 1682—this account is based on the following: A. A. Matveev, *Zapiski grafa Andreya Matveeva*, in N. Sakharov (ed.), *Zapiski russkikh lyudei. Sobytiia vremen Petra Velikogo* 6–43. Count MacDonnell (ed.), Johann Georg Korb, *Diary of an Austrian Secretary of Legation at the Court of Czar Peter the Great* (henceforth Korb) 2.114–15, 250–4. *Sophia* 53–88. Bushkovitch 125–37.

3. *Sophia* 73–88; Windbag 101. Golitsyn 177. Bushkovitch 131–8.

4. *Sophia* 182–98. Bushkovitch 139. General Gordon: Dmitry Fedosov, *Cock of the East: A Gordon Blade Abroad* (henceforth *Cock*), in Mark Erickson and Ljubica Erickson (eds.), *Russia: War, Peace and Diplomacy: Essays in Honour of John Erickson* 3–11.

5. *Sophia* 221–33. Bushkovitch 142–59. Romodanovsky, Lefort, Gordon: L. Hughes, *Russia in the Age of Peter the Great* (henceforth Hughes, *Russia*) 378/9, 433. LeDonne 122–3. Korb 1.196. Friedrich Christian Weber, *The Present State of Russia* (henceforth Weber) 1.5, 137. Sigizmund Librovich, Peter Velikiy i zhenshchiny, *Smena* (1993) 6.80–97 (henceforth Librovich). Dated diary entries quoted from Patrick Gordon diary: RGVIA 846.15.1–7, published as: Patrick Gordon, *Passages from the Diary of General Patrick Gordon of Auchleuchries* ("Gordon"). *Cock* 3–11. Play regiments: Hughes, *Russia* 16–18; Peter's looks and convulsions 357–8; marriage to Eudoxia 394; Lefort 422. Marriages: Martin 219–28. Streshnev: John LeDonne, "Ruling Families in the Russian Political Order, 1689–1825: I. The Petrine leadership, 1689–1725; II. The ruling families, 1725–1825," *Cahiers du Monde Russe et Soviétique* (henceforth LeDonne, Families) 28.236.

6. *Sophia* 198–215; Shaklovity 102, 223–41, 160–9. Martin 216–23.

## SCENE 4: THE ALL-DRUNKEN SYNOD

1. This is based on Peter the Great correspondence in *Pisma i Bumagi Imperatora Petra Velikogo* (henceforth *PiB*); Hughes, *Russia*, 248–297; Ernst Zitser, *The Transfigured Kingdom* (henceforth Zitser) 157–70. Menshikov punched by Peter: Korb 2.6. Mock Synods: Korb, 1.100, 252–3. *PiB* 4.184, 7.90–1, 6.301, 11.141,11.167. Peter to Zotov quoted in Hughes, *Russia* 252, 98–9. Zotov wedding Weber 1.89–90. Anna Mons: Librovich 83–7. Royal titles "which I hate" Hughes, *Russia* 363. Time like death: *PiB* 1.444, 11.281. Death of mother: *PiB* 4.379, 22 September 1694. *Cock* 3–11. Streshnev/Musin–Pushkin: LeDonne 236–9.

2. Hughes, *Russia* 18–19. Gordon 18–25. *Cock* 3–11.

3. Hughes, *Russia* 23–6; necro–fascination 370. John Evelyn, *The Diary of John Evelyn* 3.334–5. Hughes, *Peter the Great* 101–17.

4. Beards: Korb 1.255–60. Beards decree: *Polnoe sobranie zakonov* (henceforth *PSZ*) 4.282. Cruelty *streltsy*: Korb 1.178, 187, 202, 243. Hughes, *Russia* 327. Later executions: F. W. Bergholz, *Dnevnik* (henceforth Bergholz), 10–12. Preobrazhenskoe Prikaz: LeDonne 122–3; Lopukhin opposition 159.

5. Hughes, *Russia* 26–32. Peter Englund, *The Battle That Shook Europe* (henceforth Englund).

6. Hughes, *Russia* 31, 210–12.

7. Menshikov letters to Daria Arsenieva: RA (1877) 2.239–45. Hughes, *Russia* 394–8. Peter to Catherine letters: N. I. Pavlenko, *Catherine I* (henceforth Pavlenko) 168–9. Librovich 83–90. Strength: Bergholz 1722 126–7. Prince from the Dirt: LeDonne, Families 241.

8. LeDonne 68–70. Mazeppa: Plokhy 119–130. Hughes, *Russia* 32–7; also "dumb beast" 444. O. Subtelny, Mazeppa, Peter I and the Question of Treason, *Harvard Ukrainian Studies* (1978) 2.158–84.

9. Governors: LeDonne, Families 240–2. LeDonne 68–74. Soloviev 28.82–102. Pavlenko 172–3; resurrection of Russia 27 June 1719, 230. Factional politics: Bushkovitch 255–70. Account of battle based on Englund. Hughes, *Russia* 38–45. Celebration: PiB 8.446–7, 473–5. *SIRIO* 50.291.

## ACT II: THE APOGEE
### SCENE I: THE EMPEROR

1. Weber 1.285–9. 9. Dwarfs: *PSZ* 1710 23. *PiB* 10.270–1. Alexei: Pavlenko 179–80. Senate: *PSZ* 5.2758/5.3–7/1.102. Hughes, *Russia* 102–5. Praskovia's court: Hughes, *Russia* 192; drinking 419.

2. Soloviev 28.158–80. Bushkovitch 306. Hughes, *Russia* 45–50; Shafirov 429–30. Senate: LeDonne 68–74.

3. *PiB* 7.451 and 8.20, March/July 1708, Alexei to Peter, Peter to Alexei. Hughes, *Russia* 402–7.

4. *PSZ* 1712 1–6. Peter to Menshikov: *PiB* 11.230, 496. 12 May 1711, *SIRIO* 61.142–4. Charles Whitworth despatch, 20 February 1712, PiB 12.86, 361. Hughes, *Russia* 261. Promotion: Pavlenko 188–9; pen and sword, Peter to Catherine, 2 August 1712, 180. Hughes, *Russia* 50–6; Iaguzhinsky 426. V. V. Dolgoruky: Bushkovitch 292–335. Nubians/Hannibal: I. V. Zimin, *Povsednevnaia zhizn rossiiskogo imper-atorskogo dvora: Detskii mir imperatorskikh rezidentsii. Byt monarkhov i ikh okru-zhenie* (henceforth Zimin, Negroes) 410–18.

5. Alexei, Peter's letters: Nikolay Ustryalov, *Istoriia Tsarstvovaniia Petra Velikogo* (henceforth Ustryalov) 6.345–9. Peter's second European trip inc. letters with Catherine in Paris, Amsterdam, Spa: Pavlenko 197–216. Zotov wedding: Weber 1.89–90. Hughes, *Russia* 253; Zitser, ch. 4. Alexei crisis: Bushkovitch 339–82. Collegia/senators "fishwives": LeDonne 75–80.

6. Ustryalov 6.224–6, 240, 307, 346–50, 388–444. J. Crokatt, *The Tryal of the Czare-witz Alexis Petrowitz who was Condemn'd at Petersbourg on 25 June 1718 for a Design of Rebellion and Treason.* Weber 1.229–30. Bushkovitch 383–424. Collegia: PSZ 5.3126, 11 December 1717. Zitser 160–3 Peter to I. F. Romodanovsky in Hughes, *Russia* 373; Zotov death/election 254; Rzhevskaya 252–4. Menacing hyperactivity—Lindsey Hughes's phrase—Hughes, *Russia* 459. Secret police: LeDonne 160.

7. Hughes, *Russia* 378–9. Time like death: PiB 1.444, 11.281. Assemblies: *PSZ* 5.3241.597. Etiquette, *Honourable Mirror of Youth*: Hughes, *Russia* 265; Devier 430. Drinking: *SIRIO* 40.168–9, 49.344, 60.191, Campredon despatches. Bergholz 1721 50–61. Petersburg. Defecation: *PSZ* 6.3937, quoted in Evgenii Anisimov, *The Reforms of Peter the Great: Progress through Coercion in Russia* 150. Hard labour, *katorga*/Military Code 1716: LeDonne 212–14.

8. Compulsion: *PSZ* 7.4348.152, 8 November 1723. Our people are like children: *PSZ* 7.4345.150, 5 November 1723. Savage ruler, Hughes, *Russia* 129–132; 384;

the state/common good: 387. Executions: Bergholz 1724 9–11 and 75–6. Military Code: LeDonne 212–14.

9. Evgenii Anisimov, *Five Empresses* (henceforth Anisimov) 35–9, inc. "best-looking man." Mistresses: Librovich 87–97. Mistress Eudoxia Rjevskaya, S. Bonnet (ed.), Comte Fyodor Golovkine, *La Cour et le règne de Paul Ier* (henceforth Golovkin) 9. Matrena Balk/Princess Anastasia Golitsyna: howling in *SIRIO* 1.19. Hughes, *Russia* 253. Time to go home, old man: Bergholz 1724, 67. Elizaveta: P. Bartenev (ed.), Duke of Liria, Pisma o Rossii v Ispaniiu, in *Osmnadtsatyi vek* (henceforth Liria, Pisma o Rossii).

10. Librovich 94–7. M. I. Semevsky, *Kamer-Freilina Maria Davilovna Hamilton, Slovo i Delo* (1884) 185–268. Execution: J. B. Scherer, *Anecdotes Interresantes et Secrets de la Court de Russia*, 2:272. Nyastad/Procurator: *PSZ* 6.3979, 27 April 1722. Law of succession including new title "Caesarevich": *PSZ* 6.3893. Hughes, *Russia* 97, 104–5, 273, 410–11; Iaguzhinsky, 426. Serfs ownership: LeDonne 4–6. Osterman married to Streshneva by Peter the Great: LeDonne, Families 298.

11. Soloviev 32:57–98. Bushkovitch 428–31; 376. Peter's "Heads will fly . . ." Anisimov 60. Hughes, *Russia* 57–9; exposed body 153.

12. *PRG* 4.2–54. Praskovia, Anna, Catherine: Anisimov 68–70; Soloviev 32.13–17; Mina Curtiss, *A Forgotten Empress: Anna Ivanovna and Her Era* (henceforth Curtiss) 37–45. Praskovia freaks: Bergholz 2.30. Peter and Mecklenburg: *PRG* 2.3562. Anisimov 131–3. Crams-Prick: Zitser, 167.

13. *Koronatsionnye torzhestva. Albom svyashchennogo koronovaniia ikh imperatorskikh velichestv gosudarya imperatora Nikolaia Alexandrovicha i gosudaryni imperatritsy Alexandry Fedorovny* (henceforth *Koronatsionnye torzhestva*) 6. Bergholz 1724 30–44. Soloviev 34.155. Wortman 34–9. Peter's illness/urine problems: Peter to Catherine, 4 June 1724, Pavlenko 260. Bergholz (1724) 67.

### SCENE 2: THE EMPRESSES

1. Anisimov 35–9, Mons poem. Hughes *Russia* 130. Librovich 95–7. *SIRIO* 52.358–9 Campredon, 9 December 1724. Bering Soloviev 32.149. Succession, Anna, Holstein: Anisimov 39. Mons's body: Bergholz 1724 9–11 and 75–6.

2. Bassewitz, H. F., *Zapiski grafa Bassevicha, sluzhashchie k poiasneniiu nekotorykh sobytii iz vremi tsarstvovaniia Petra Velikogo*, RA 3 (1865) 93–274 especially 173, 259. *SIRIO* 52.425–37 Campredon. VD: *SIRIO* 3.400, 454–91. Soloviev 34.155. PZh (1725) 3. Feofan Prokopovich, *Kratkaia povest o smerti Petra Velikogo* (henceforth Prokopovich) 3–4. Hughes, *Russia* 445–47; funeral 262–3. Anisimov 39–40.

3. Catherine elected: Anisimov 3–8. *SIRIO* 52.436/58.23. Ustryalov 4.135–40.

4. Wortman 38–9. Anisimov 40–2. Hugh Barnes, *Gannibal: the Moor of Petersburg* (Gannibal) 173.

5. Bergholz 1725 102. Hatred, neglect, greed: Grigorii Esipov, Zhizneopisanie A. D. Menshikova, *RA* (1875) 7–12 ("Esipov") 247. Parties: Bergholz 1725 90–4. Soloviev 10.70–5. Menshikov: Christof Herman von Manstein, *Contemporary Memoirs of Russia from 1727 to 1744* (henceforth Manstein) 1–3. Anisimov 39–51. Catherine I's drinking rules: Mrs. William Vigor (Mrs. Rondeau), *Letters from a Lady Who Resided Some Years in Russia, to her Friend in England* (henceforth Vigor). Zimin, *Negroes* 410–18. Hughes, *Russia* 397, 548; marriage of Holstein 414; Menshikov manager 432.

6. Anna, Courland: Anna to Menshikov, *PRG* 4.141–2. Curtiss 48–52.

7. Manstein 4–5. Soloviev 10.70–5. LeDonne 122–4. Philip Longworth, *The Three Empresses* (henceforth Longworth, *Empresses*) 68–72; death 75. Anisimov 51–3.

8. Vigor 26. Peter II, Menshikov: Manstein 24, 7. Menshikov to Peter II: RGADA 11.63.3v. Anisimov 72–3. Curtiss 51–4. Elizaveta: Liria, Pisma o Rossii 2.32–4, 115.

9. RGADA 11.63.3v. Manstein 4–11. Esipov, 247. Example of ingratitude—Prokopovich to Tsarevna Anna Petrovna: Aleksandr Golombievsky, *Sotrudniki Petra Velikogo* 114. Fall of Goliath, Igor Pashkov, quoted Soloviev 10.119–21. Liria, Pisma o Rossii 2.34, 115.

10. Soloviev 10.141. Liria, Pisma o Rossii 2.30–36. Manstein 12–15. Anisimov 55–7.

11. Liria, Pisma o Rossii 2.181. Manstein 22. Vigor 23–5; Blessing of Waters 29; death and smallpox 30–1; Ekaterina Dolgorukaya 34–5. Anisimov 55–60.

12. Manstein 24–37; on Biron 41–8; candidates for throne: D. A. Korsakov, *Votsarenie Imperatritsy Anny Ioannovny* 2–5, 67–70, 146–245, 265–75. M. T. Florinsky, *Russia: A History and an Interpretation* 1.440–2. Marc Raeff (ed.), *Plans for Political Reform in Imperial Russia 1730–1905*, 40–53. Anisimov 55–61.

13. Coronation of Anna: *Opisanie koronatsii ee velichestva i samoderzhitsy vserossiiskoi Anny Ioannovny* 9–10.

14. *RA* (1916) 3.257, Shakhovsky to Biron on horse; RA (1916) 4.381, Biron to Shakhovsky; giants 388. Biron killing of man: *Osmnadtsatyi vek* (1869) 3.158—letter 25 July 1725. Vigor 149–53; Osterman (Oracle nickname) 154–7; Cherkassky 158–61. talks to men like horses: Manstein 41–5. Osterman: Manstein 45; filth 333–6; character of Münnich 54–6 and 331–2. Münnich: Vigor 118–21. Osterman: LeDonne, Families 298. Comte Ernest de Münnich, *Mémoires sur la Russie de Pierre le Grand à Elizabeth I, 1720–1742* (henceforth Münnich) 125–7; jesters 126; Anna good nature 124; Anna mood and Biron 126–7. Succession: Anisimov 61, 75–84; on Biron 74–5. Anna Leopoldovna, Anton of Brunswick Brevern, Biron, Obstoiatelstva, prigotovivshie opalu Ernsta–Ioanna Birona, gertsoga Kurlyandskogo, *Vremya* (1861) 10.522–622.

15. RGADA 197.1.9.35.1, Anna to S. A. Saltykov, 20 February 1733 on tomfoolery, sent Miliutin, Golitsyn and Balakirev's wife—"Golitsyn's the best." RGADA Gosarkhiv 5.21, Anna to Saltykov, send bandura player; 89a investigate store room of Prince Odoevsky; 91 send girls; 25 wedding matchmaking; 28 send talkative girl. RGADA Gosarkhiv 18.19, send someone to replace Tatiana. RGADA Gosarkhiv 12.12a. *Kniga zapisnaia imennym pismam i ukazam imperatrits Anny Ioannovny i Elizavety Petrovny Semyonu Andreevichu Saltykovu 1732–1742* (henceforth *Kniga zapisnaia*): on taking gold off Alexei Dolgoruky, 24 January 1732, 2; take portrait from Apraxin, 25 January 1732, 3; get Volkov's letters, 22 June 1732, 35; send monkeys, 20 May 1735; send tall Turks, 10 August 1738; send false letter to Apraxina and observe how she opens it, 4 January 1739, 222; send the starling, 1 March 1739, 224. *Osmnadtsatyi vek* (1869) 3, Anna to Deputy Governor Pashkov, June 1730, on bishop talk; Anna to Osterman on Turkish war 155; describe the child as monster. Cabinet of three with ability to issue imperial orders: LeDonne 82–4. Vigor 70–2. Oginski "shared bed": Manstein 253–7; dwarves 258–60; succession 51. Zimin, *Negroes* 410–18. Osterman–LeDonne, Families 298. Security, dwarfs: Anisimov 86–100; triumvirate 100–8. Secret police: LeDonne 122–4.

16. E. V. Anisimov, *Empress Elizabeth* (henceforth Anisimov, *Elizabeth*) 9–22. Vigor 106–7. Elizaveta appeals to Empress Anna *AKV* (1870) 1.4–5, Elizaveta to Anna, 16 November 1736. Succession: Manstein 51. Heiress: Anna Leopoldovna of Mecklenburg and fiancé Ernst Biron, Obstoiatelstva 10.

17. *Osmnadtsatyi vek* (1869) 155, Empress Anna to Osterman complaining of conduct of generals. Manstein 67–88; 1735–6 Turkish war 91–134; Münnich feuds 134; 1737 campaign 148. Münnich 73–97. Anisimov 108–111. Guards at Christmas at Elizaveta: Liria, Pisma o Rossii 118–19. Mavra Shepeleva's descriptions of handsome men: ChOIDR (1864) 2:66–72, Pisma k gosydaryne tsesarevne Elizavete

Petrovne Mavry Shepelevoi. Cases against Elizaveta: *RA* (1865) 1.328–30. *SIRIO* 92.231–2 marquis de la Chétardie. Anisimov, *Elizabeth* 9–22. Vigor 106–7. Manstein 50–1.

18. Empress Anna to Osterman about d'Aderkass correspondence with Lynar: *Osmnadtsatyi vek* (1869) 3.156. Anna Leopoldovna: Vigor 106–8. D'Aderkass/Lynar: Manstein 89. Biron, Obstoiatelstva 10. Curtiss 95.

19. Anna Leopoldovna wedding Vigor 185–207. Manstein 253–4. Münnich 98. Biron on stupidity of Anton: *SIRIO* 6.100. Anna to Biron: Biron, Obstoiatelstva 100.

20. Dolgorukys: Anisimov 117–21; Münnich vanity and unpopularity 100–4. Volynsky: Manstein 267; Dolgoruky case 40; election of Biron 196–7; Münnich's luck and peace 225–47; fear of war with Sweden/treaty between Sweden and Turkey and kidnapping/murder of Sinclair 249–50. Anna's expulsion of Libman/Sanchez: Curtiss 85–7. Biron, Obstoiatelstva 10.

21. Ice wedding: Anisimov 120–4. Manstein 260–2. Curtiss 258–68.

22. Fall of Volynsky: Manstein 266–7. Münnich 111–14. Anisimov 1215.

23. Manstein 269–71. Münnich 114–22. Anisimov, *Elizabeth* 1–5.

24. Manstein 275–91. Münnich 132–43; 154–6. Biron on Anton's conspiracy: *SIRIO* 6.100. Anisimov 146.

25. Doneseniia Ed. Fincha Iordu Garringtonu, in *SIRIO* 85.243–6 (henceforth Finch). RGADA 5.1.69.2, Anna Leopoldovna to Lynar, 13 October 1741. RGADA 5.1.69.3, Anna Leopoldovna to Lynar, 17 October 1741. Münnich 139–40. Julia von Mengden and regent Anna: Manstein 295–7. *SIRIO* 96.629–30 Chétardie. Biron comments *SIRIO* 6.100 Petzold. Osterman: Münnich 154–6. Fall of Münnich: Manstein 282–8; rivalries of ministers 297; Anton best heart 328. Anna Leopoldovna as regent: Anisimov 147–53; plan to crown Anna Leopoldovna, 153. Manstein 327–8.

26. RGADA 5.1.69.2, Anna Leopoldovna to Lynar, 13 October 1741. RGADA 5.1.69.3, Anna Leopoldovna to Lynar, 17 October 1741. Manstein 324–5; Swedish war 298–314; regent to be empress 315; plot and Anna confronts Elizaveta 317–19.

## SCENE 3: RUSSIAN VENUS

1. Finch *SIRIO* 85.243–6. Chétardie *SIRIO* 92.231–2. Meetings on dark nights, Princess Joanna in *SIRIO* 92.231–3. Elizaveta and Anna Leopoldovna: *SIRIO* 96.627–30. Coup: Anisimov 171–9. Guards support: Anisimov, *Elizabeth* 21–8. Persecution of Anna Leopoldovna: Anisimov, *Elizabeth* 143–70 and Anisimov 156–70. Elizaveta orders to M. Korf on Brunswicks, threats: M. A. Korf, *Braunshveigskoe semeistvo* 108–200 and 380–3. Most trusted old friend always/trust you like myself: *AKV* (1870) 1.6–8, Elizaveta to M. Vorontsov, 3 and 21 January 1739.

2. *Pisma i zapiski imperatritsy Elizavety Petrovny, 1741–1761* 1–3, Elizaveta to Peter, 10 January 1742. Coronation Tokmakov 86–7. *AKV* (1870) 1.8, Elizaveta to Vorontsov, 30 January 1739. Foreign policy *SIRIO* 52.100. Orders Bestuzhev to examine letters of Princess Joanna *AKV* (1870) 1.10, Elizaveta to M. Vorontsov, 20 June 1745. Frederick the Great—Tim Blanning, *Frederick the Great: King of Prussia* (henceforth "Blanning") 90, Orgasm/homoerotica 64–69, Russian policy 189–207; despises female power and Elizaveta 191. Vorontsov, good manners: F. A. Vychkov (ed.), *Zapiski Favie*, *Istoricheskii vestnik* (1887) 29.389 (henceforth Favier). Vorontsov: Manstein 342. Anisimov, *Elizabeth*: Vorontsov «poor man,» eclipse and return: 211–17. Gannibal 219. Fall of Osterman: Manstein 330; Lestocq character 318–19. Bestuzhev: Mark Cruse and Hilde Hoogenboom (eds.), *Catherine II, The Memoirs of Catherine the Great* (henceforth *Catherine*) 8; Lestocq enforcer 16, black heart 8. Vorontsovs and Shuvalovs: LeDonne, Families 299–301;

Nikita Trubetskoi as minister at home 298–300 and LeDonne 90–1. Coronation: Manstein 337. Wortman 44. Prussian/French plots: Anisimov, *Elizabeth* 93–109. Fall of Chétardie: *AKV* (1871) 2.4–6, Bestuzhev to Vorontsov, 6 June 1744. Dog kennel poverty: *AKV* (1871) 2.12, Bestuzhev to Vorontsov, 2 August 1744; 33–7 Bestuzhev to Vorontsov, 18 August 1744.

3. Lopukhina case: Anisimov, *Elizabeth* 152–4. Manstein 401–2.

4. Brunswicks: Anisimov, *Elizabeth* 160–70.

5. Princess Joanna intrigues: *RA* (1904) 2.465. *AKV* (1870) 1. Elizaveta to Vorontsov, perlustration of Joanna or Catherine, 20 June 1745. John T. Alexander, *Catherine the Great: Life and Legend* (henceforth Alexander) 23–43. Catherine's life up to the coup is based on *Catherine*. Anisimov, *Elizabeth*, 230–45, Isabel de Madariaga, *Russia in the Age of Catherine the Great* (henceforth Madariaga, *Russia*) 1–30, Simon Dixon, *Catherine the Great* (henceforth Dixon) and Alexander 17–60. Aim to please: *Catherine* xlv; arrival, education, empress 8–17; popularity 26; mother intrigues 30–1; Peter smallpox 23; wedding 32; Bestuzhev 64–5. Blanning 187–200.

6. Brunswicks: *Catherine* 81, 87. Anisimov, *Elizabeth* 155–6, 160–70. Peephole incident: *Catherine* 35–9; Elizaveta irritated 198.

7. *AKV* (1870) 1.10, Elizaveta to Bestuzhev, 20 June 1745. Foreign policy *SIRIO* 52.100. Rise of Razumovsky, good nature: A. A. Vasilchikov, *Semeistvo Razumovskikh* 1.45–50. Petzold in *SIRIO* 6.616. Bestuzhev and Vorontsov use Razumovsky to petition empress: *AKV* (1871) 2.170, Bestuzhev to Vorontsov, 21 December 1752. Anisimov, *Elizabeth* 200–4. Empress beauty: Liria, Pisma o Rossii 34, 115. *Catherine* 93.Vanity: Favier 189–90, 385–95. 15,000 dresses: Jacob von Stäehlin, *Zapiski o Petre Tretiem*, ChOIDR (1866) 4.100. Loss of 4,000 dresses: *Catherine* 123. Elizaveta orders to French shops: *RA* (1778) 16.1.10–15. Expensive life: M. Vorontsov to Elizaveta, *AKV* (1871) 2.617. Vorontsov poverty: Anisimov, *Elizabeth* 216–7. Catherine debts: *Catherine* 16. Ball description: Maurice de la Messelière, *RA* (1874) 12.970–2. Nocturnal habits: Pauzie jewellery *RS* (1870) 1.76. *Catherine* 202. Morals: *Catherine* 96–7; cuckoldry bet 189; shortage of furniture 104; fires 123. Anisimov, *Elizabeth* 167–81. Collapse of Razumovsky house: *Catherine* 58–9. Dixon 65–90. Religion: Anisimov, *Elizabeth* 53. Soloviev 42.106–7.

8. Catherine/Peter *Catherine* 39; Elizaveta calls Peter monster, irritating 198; Peter as husband 35–43, 199; Chernyshevs 43; drill for Peter 47; Chernyshevs arrested 49; hounds in bedroom 53–4 and 70; Choglokova 40–7; Peter's Baturin plot 76; rat hanged 121; Madame Resource 146; wild riding 91; nephew monster: Elizaveta mocks Peter 126.

9. Serfs and masters under Elizaveta: LeDonne 84–91; serfs exiled for insolence 1760, repealed 1802: 212–14. Elizaveta and Jews: *AKV* (1871) 2.138, Bestuzhev to Vorontsov, 21 December 1745.

10. Elizaveta ageing: Favier 189–90, 385–95; rise of Shuvalovs, Ivan Shuvalov more power than minister 392; Peter Shuvalov like the Mogul 394. Ivan Shuvalov, nice looks, book, his chance: *Catherine* 75; Beketov challenge by Razumovsky 95. Anisimov, 216–8. J. T. Alexander, "Ivan Shuvalov and Russian Court Politics 1749–63," in A. G. Cross and G. S. Smith, *Literature, Lives and Legality in Catherine's Russia* ("Alexander Shuvalov") 1–13. Longworth, *Empresses* 207–8. Ivan Shuvalov, goodness personified, and Catherine the Great old friends: Varvara Golovin, *Memoirs of Countess Varvara Golovin* 44. Alexander Shuvalov terror, grimace and twitch: *Catherine* 130–1.

11. *Catherine* 72; worth the knout 174; Peter's mistresses, letters 81–3, 153; Catherine could have loved 199; Naryshkin 103; Chernyshev 105; Saltykov 109–12; sex talk

112–14; Saltykov or Naryshkin 117; Bestuzhev encourages 115; pregnant with Paul, Shuvalov 130–1; birth of Paul 133; temptation 200.

12. *Catherine* 147–50; Bestuzhev vs Shuvalov/Vorontsov 151–2; Bestuzhev's plan 191; Peter, mistress 153; Bestuzhev discredited 159; Peter hates Russia 165; damned nephew 198. This account of Seven Years War is based on Blanning, *Frederick the Great* 208–281; opium 234; Kunersdorf 239; unity of command 266. Faint of Elizaveta, Bestuzhev alarmed: *AKV* (1871) 2.211, Bestuzhev to Vorontsov, 9 September 1757. Apraxin retreat *AKV* 1.368–9, Vorontsov to Bestuzhev, 12 September and 14 October 1757. Anisimov, *Elizabeth* 113–43; Ivan Shuvalov 220–1. War run by Ivan Shuvalov: Soloviev 42.56. Shuvalov: Alexander, 7–13. Earl of Ilchester and Mrs. Langford Brook (eds.), *Correspondence of Catherine the Great when Grand Duchess with Sir Charles Hanbury-Williams and Letters from Count Poniatowski* 59–90, 165–70, 235–45. Ivan VI: Anisimov, *Elizabeth* 261–2. Alexander Brickner, *Imperator Ioann Antonovich i ego rodstvenniki* 520–34.

13. Fall of Bestuzhev, Vorontsov chancellor: Favier 389. Anisimov, *Elizabeth* 215–17, 242–6. Catherine in peril: *Catherine* 173; Catherine wins friends 179; Elizaveta faints 181; how does wife get pregnant? 182–3; Bestuzhev arrest 189; accommodating nature and looks 200; showdown with empress 202–11. *AKV* (1870) 1.6–8, Elizaveta to M. Vorontsov, 3 and 21 January 1739. *AKV* (1871) 2.211, Bestuzhev to Vorontsov, 9 September 1757.

14. Soloviev 42.21. Peter and Russia: *Catherine* 165.

15. Blanning 236–281. Anisimov, *Elizabeth* 113–43; endgame 246–8. Letter to Buturlin: Longworth 227. Prussians never beat Russians says Peter: Soloviev 42.21. *Catherine* 165; decline of Elizaveta, the plotters, pregnant, Dashkova 45–50, 74–107. Elizaveta: Favier 189–90, 385–95. Ivan Shuvalov power vanishing: *RA* (1870) 7.1396, Ivan Shuvalov to M. Vorontsov, 29 November 1761. Swollen, ailing, boils: Anisimov 235–7. Purge of Trubetskoi: LeDonne 21, 86, 90.

16. Soloviev 42.1–12; Ivan Shuvalov to Panin on succession 42.77; Dashkova's offer of coup 42.82. Catherine the Great (CtG), *Memoirs* (1955), "Last Thoughts of HIM Elisabeth Petrovna" 329–38 death of Elizaveta. Anisimov, *Elizabeth* 245–8. Longworth, *Empresses* 228–9.

17. Peter III letters to/from Frederick: *RA* (1898) 1, December 1760–March 1762 (hero, 15 March, Peter to Frederick) 7. Soloviev 42.1–12 and 22–8. *PSZ* 15.11.445, 21 February 1762; *PSZ* 15.11.444, 18 February 1762; *PSZ* 15.11.481, 21 March 1762; *PSZ* 15.11.538, 18 May 1762. Blanning 253–7—Frederick quotation "one woman dies. . . sports of fortune." The reign: Soloviev 42.79–87; Gudovich as hetman, Peter warns Dashkova 42.78–82; janissaries/Guards disbanded 42.60–8; behaviour 42.64–8; Breteuil quoted at 42.75. Anisimov, *Elizabeth* 211. Orlovs call him ugly freak, Alexei Orlov letters from Ropsha: Dixon 124–5.

18. Goltz, Schwerin letters to Frederick, Frederick's warnings to Peter III: *RA* (1898) 1.7–16, Peter III to Frederick II, 15 May 1762, I walk the streets. Soloviev 42.28–32, 60–70. Blanning 254–6. Secret police and Ivan VI: Soloviev 42.73–4. Ruud, 11. Shuvalov offers: Soloviev 42.59–61. Cadet corps: Andrei Chernyshev laughs at Ivan Shuvalov, Pisma Shuvalovu, *RA* 11 (1869) 1844. Shuvalov: Anisimov, *Elizabeth* 222. Vorontsov to Peter III: Soloviev 42.55–63.

19. Peter's threat 9 June: Soloviev 42.76–8. Gannibal 1, 228. *Elizabeth* 230–45. Madariaga, *Russia* 1–30. Alexander 17–60.

20. This account of Catherine's rise and reign is based on original research published in full in Simon Sebag Montefiore, *Prince of Princes: The Life of Potemkin* (also published as *Catherine the Great and Potemkin*) (henceforth "Montefiore") as well as biographies of Catherine by J. T. Alexander, Isabel de Madariaga and Simon

Dixon; but references for key letters are given. Alexander 1–16. Madariaga, *Russia* 21–37. E.R. Dashkova, *Memoirs of Princess Dashkova* 45–6; 74–80. Montefiore 39–47. Catherine to Stanislas Poniatowski 2 August 1762; A. N. Pypin (ed.) Catherine the Great, *Sochineniya imperatritsy Ekaterina II* 12.547. Stanislas Auguste Poniatowski, *Mémoires, secrets et inédits*, 1.377. *RA* (1898) 1.14–15.

21. *Sochineniia imperatritsy Ekaterina II* (henceforth *Sochineniia*) 12.547. *SIRIO* (1873) 12.2–4, Robert Keith to Mr. Grenville, 1 July/12 July 1762. Madariaga, *Russia* 21–37. Alexander 5–16. Montefiore, 40–4. Dashkova 74–80. Cheering Catherine: *RA* (1867) 4.482–6, Horse Guards in June 1762. Potemkin horse: Reginald Pole–Carew, Russian anecdotes in the Antony Archive, CO/R/3/92, unpublished. Peter III begs: *RA* (1911) 5:22–3, Peter III to Catherine II, 29 and 30 June 1762. Montefiore 44–5.

22. Dixon 122–139. Montefiore 48–62. *SIRIO* 7.108–20. *SIRIO* 42.475, 480. Anisimov, *Elizabeth* 245.

23. *SIRIO* 7.120–50, 1.216, 42.470–5. Soloviev 42.103–7, including Frederick the Great to comte de Ségur. Jews Soloviev 42.106. Orlov marriage? Dixon 124–5. "Our ugly freak" and Alexei Orlov letters on murder of Peter: O. A. Ivanov, Zagadka pisem Alexeia Orlova iz Ropshi, *Moskovskii zhurnal* (1995) 9.15. Ropsha: Alexandre Spiridovich, *Les Dernières Années de la cour de Tsarskoïé-Sélo* (henceforth Spiridovich) 1.231.

SCENE 4: THE GOLDEN AGE

1. Dixon 3–22. Askalon Truvorov, Koronatsiia imperatritsy Ekateriny Vtoroi, *Russkaia starina* (1893) 80.12.490–5.

2. Poland: Montefiore 46–9. Adam Zamoyski, *Last King of Poland* 61–100. *SIRIO* 7.373–4. "Northern System": Madariaga, *Russia* 33–7, 187–204. Alexander 61–76. David L. Ransel, *The Politics of Catherinian Russia: The Panin Party* (henceforth Ransel) 104–11. Prussian alliance: Blanning 283–4.

3. Montefiore 49–51. Dixon 122–155. Ransel 116–27.

4. Great Commission: Montefiore 57–9. Dixon 170–183. "Alexander 103–20; Madariaga, *Russia* 139–50.

5. Montefiore 76–93. Dixon 184–213. Voltaire, *Oeuvres complètes* 58.39, Catherine II (CII) to Voltaire, 4/15 August 1769. Christopher Duffy, *Russia's Military Way to the West* 130–6. LeDonne, *Ruling Russia* 363–4. Orlov, Chesme and Arab adventures, occupation of Beirut: *Journal of Royal Central Asian Society* 42.3–4. 275–286, William Persen, Russian Occupations of Beirut 1772–4.

6. Montefiore 60–95. Dixon 215–230 Confession: CtG, *Sochineniia* 12.697–9, CtG to Potemkin/GARF 728.1.425.1–5. Alexander 135–7; 160–1. Madariaga, *Russia* 211–13 and 258–9. Break–up with Orlov: *SIRIO* 13:270–2, 19:325.

7. Potemkin rise: Montefiore 94–161. Dixon 229–240. Pugachev is based on: A. S. Pushkin's *Istoriya Pugacheva*, his novella *The Captain's Daughter* and J. T. Alexander's two books on the subject—*Emperor of the Cossacks: Pugachev and the Frontier Jacquerie of 1773–75*, and *Autocratic Politics in a National Crisis: The Imperial Russian Government and Pugachev's Revolt 1773–1775* 1–10. Madariaga, *Russia* 239–55.

8. Roderick McGrew, *Paul I of Russia* (henceforth McGrew) 55–85.

9. Montefiore 92–105. "It's a terrible business when the prick and the cunt decide the interests of Europe": quoted in Robert B. Asprey, *Frederick the Great* 600. G.A. Potemkin ("GAP") summoned by Catherine ("CII"); RGADA 5.85.1.119, L 7, CII to GAP, 4 December 1773. GARF 728.1.425.1–5. CtG, *Sochineniia* 12.697–9, CtG to Potemkin, March 1774. "My darling, the time I spend with you is so happy . . .": RGADA 1.1/1.1.213, L 14. Talk with Orlov about *banya*: RGADA 5.85.1.213, L 14. "I

fear you might be angry with me . . .": RGADA 5.85.1.292, L 56, CII to GAP, ud. "I've withdrawn from a certain good–natured . . .": CII to Grimm, *SIRIO* 27.52.

10. Montefiore 109–135. "A woman is always a woman": Asprey, *Frederick the Great* 601–2. "Our duty is to improve on events": James Harris, *Diaries and Correspondence of James Harris, 1st Earl of Malmesbury* (henceforth Harris) 239, Harris to Stormont, 15/26 February 1780. Key letters between GAP and CII: RGADA 1.1/1.1.213, L 14. "The doors will be open": L 242. "I woke at five . . . I have given strict rules . . .": RGADA 1.1/1.54.42, L 18. "To get warm: go to the *banya*": RGADA 5.85.1.253, L 44. "My beauty, my darling, whom nothing resembles": RGADA 1.1/1.54.12, L 23. "I have masses of things to tell you . . .": RGADA 1.85.1.209, L 10. "To empower Rumiantsev and thus peace was achieved": A. V. Khrapovitsky, *Dnevnik* (henceforth Khrapovitsky), 30 May 1786. "Sweetheart, as you asked me to send you with something": RGADA 1.1/1.54.64, L 27. "General loves me?": RGADA 5.85.1.299, L 30.

11. Montefiore 122–135. Alexander 176–8. Madariaga, *Russia* 249–51.

12. Montefiore 136–184. Dixon 241–269. Rumiantsev awards/"Zadunaisky" title: RGADA 1.1/1.54.137, L 76. *SIRIO* 23.4, CII to Grimm, 3 August 1774, St. Petersburg. "I'll give you my portrait . . .": Catherine and Potemkin renegotiate/marriage? RGADA 5.85.1.362, L 72. "I'll be your humble maid": RGADA 1.1/1.54.27, L 32. "It's impossible for me to change": RGADA 1.1/1.54.255, L 17. "Cruel Tatar": RGADA 1.1/1.54.14, L 93. "I'll love you for ever in spite of yourself," "Batinka . . .": RGADA 5.85.1.160, L 53. "A sincere confession": GARF 728.1.425.1–5/CtG, *Sochineniia* 12.697–9, CII to GAP. "My darling husband . . .": RGADA 5.85.1.254, L 34. "Your wife": RGADA 5.85.1.267, L 94. Potemkin–Catherine short letters: RGADA 5.85.2.305, L 95. "The essence of our disagreement": RGADA 5.85.1.364, L 92, CII to GAP. Zavadovsky ("150 kisses shall I joyfully give you"): *Russkiy istoricheskiy zhurnal* (1918) 5.244–57, quoted in Alexander 342–52. Pisma imp. Ekateriny II k gr. P. V. Zavadovskomu 1775–1777, ed. I. A. Barskov (Zavadovsky) letters 7, 22, 30, 33, 35, 39, CII to P. V. Zavadovsky. "My Lord and Cher Epoux, Why do you want to cry?": RGADA 85.1.267, L 94, CII to GAP, Prince: RGADA 5.85.3.87, L 96, CII to GAP.

13. McGrew 70–87; rules for wife 102–3; Kurakin affair 111–38. Paul to Kurakin on Peter's dream: The Count de Montbrison (ed.), *Memoirs of the Baroness d'Oberkirch* 25. Golovkin 105–7. Marie Pierre Rey, *Alexander I: The Tsar Who Defeated Napoleon* (henceforth Rey) 13–26; Alexander education, romper suit 24–8. Catherine to Grimm on Alexander letters in *SIRIO* 23. Paul and Maria: *RA* (1876) 1.89–92, Fyodor Rostopchin to S. R. Vorontsov, 8 July 1792. Maria: N. A. Sablukov, Reminiscences of Court and Times of Emperor, Paul I, of Russia up to the Period of his Death, *Fraser's Magazine for Town and Country* (1865) (henceforth Sablukov) 1.223.

14. Catherine favourites: Montefiore 165–184. "Time belongs not to me but to the empire": O. I. Yeliseeva, *Perepiska Ekateriny II i G. A. Potemkina perioda vtoroy russkoturetskoy voyny 1787–91* 23. CtG to Zavadovsky letters 7, 22, 30, 33, 35, 39, CII to Zavadovsky. RGADA 5.85.1.296, L 114; RGADA 1.1/1.54.96, L 114, CII to GAP. "Give Senyusha the attached letters": GARF 728.1.416.51, L 115. Rimsky-Korsakov: *KFZ*, 8 May 1778. RGADA 5.85.1.141, L 124. "Thanks to you and the King of Epirus . . .": RGADA 5.85.1.59, L 125, CII to GAP, ud. "Thank you for loving me!": *RA* (1881) 3.402–3, CII to Ivan Rimsky-Korsakov. "When will I see you?": RGADA 5.85.1.59, L 125, CII to GAP. *KFZ* 1 June, 28 June 1778. *RA* (1881) 3.402–3, CII to Korsakov. *RP* 5.1.119.

15. Montefiore 215–35. Dixon 270–292. "Note on Political Affairs": *AKV* 13.223–8, A. A. Bezborodko to P. V. Zavadovsky, 17 November 1791, Jassy. O. I. Yeliseeva, *G. A. Potemkin's Geopolitical Projects, Associates of Catherine the Great* 26–31. O. P. Markova, O proiskhozhdenii tak nazyvayemogo Grecheskogo Proekta, in Hugh Rags-

dale (ed.), *Imperial Russian Foreign Policy* 75–103. *SIRIO* 23.440, CII to Baron F. M. Grimm, 19 April 1788. Meeting in Mogilev: A. A. Bezborodko, *Pisma A. A. Bezborodka* 57, Bezborodko to P. A. Rumiantsev–Zadunaisky, 4 February 1780. *SIRIO* (1878) 23.185, CII to Grimm, 7 September 1780.

16. Montefiore 223–235. "The system with Austria's court": RGADA 5.85.1.557, L 256, CII to GAP, 23 November 1787. *SIRIO* 23.145, 157–9, CII to Paul, 25 April and 7 June 1782. "The Heavy Baggage": *SIRIO* 23.621, CII to Grimm, 6 April 1795.

17. Golovkin, 138–9; practical jokes 113–16. McGrew on Maria, Nelidova and court: 169–79. Catherine on Alexander's education: Rey 26–7. Nelidova alliance with Maria: Varvara Golovina, *The Memoirs of Countess Golovine* (henceforth Golovina) 138–40. *RA* (1876) 1.89–92, Fyodor Rostopchin to S. R. Vorontsov, 8 July 1792. *RA* (1876) 1.113–18, Fyodor Rostopchin to S. R. Vorontsov, 28 May 1794. *Osmnadt-satyi vek* 3.436–446, Paul to Catherine on purity of Nelidova, "friendship holy and gentle but innocent and pure." Sablukov 1.223; Gatchina like German town 224.

18. Crimea, New Russia: Montefiore 247–260, 263–284. "Imagine Crimea is yours . . .": AVPRI 5.5/1.591.1.106, L 154, GAP to CII. "We could decide it all in half an hour . . .": RGADA 5.85.1.121, L 150, CII to GAP, 3 June 1782. "Keep your resolution, Matushka . . .": RGADA 5.85.1.440, L 162, CII to GAP. RGADA 1.1.43.61, L 163, GAP to CII, 22 April 1783. "Neither I nor anyone knows where you are": RGADA 5.85.1.461, CII to GAP. RGADA 5.85.1.504. Potemkin in Crimea, "In three days, I will congratulate you with Crimea": RGADA 11.1/1.43.86–7, L 175, GAP to CII, 10 July 1783. RGADA 1.1/1.43.67–8, L 176, GAP to CII, 16 July 1783. RGADA 1.1/1.43.69–71, L 179, GAP to CII, 29 July 1783. RGADA 1.1/1.43.74–5, L 179, GAP to CII, 29 July 1783. "Georgian business is concluded": RGADA 1.1/1.43.64, L 180, GAP to CII. "Let them jest while we do business": RGADA 5.85.1.508. *SIRIO* 27.276–80, CII to GAP. "The best harbour in the world": RGADA 1.1/1.43.80–3, L 172, GAP to CII, June 1783.

19. Montefiore 312–327. *SIRIO* 23.316–17, CII to Grimm, 25 June 1784. Potemkin returns: *SIRIO* 23.344. Potemkin lived with her day and night: *AKV* 21: letter 6, 464, E. Poliasky to Simon Vorontsov, 18 August 1784. *SIRIO* 23.317–18, CII to Grimm, 9/18 September 1784. *AKV* 31, Alexander Vorontsov to Simon Vorontsov, 21 July 1784, Riga. "Without you I feel as if I'm without hands": RGADA 5.85.4.1.524, L 186, CII to GAP. Dmitriev–Mamonov: Khrapovitsky 13. "Mr. Redcoat" RGADA 11.902, Count A. D. Mamonov to GAP, ud.

20. Montefiore 351–387. Madariaga, *Russia* 393–5. Alexander 256–7.

21. Montefiore 388–429. Madariaga, *Russia* 394–7. Alexander 262–5. "No more nails on your fingers": RGADA 1.1/1.47.5–9, L 223, CII to GAP, 24 August 1787. "I can't stand it": AVPRI 5.585.317, L 229, GAP to CII, 16 September 1787k. RGADA 5.85.2.43–8, L 233, CII to GAP, 24 September 1787. RGADA 5.85.2.49, L 235, 25 September 1787. RGADA 5.85.2.52–4, L 238, 2 October 1787. "Petersburg has the look of an armed camp . . . so my friend, I too have smelled gunpowder": *SIRIO* 27.512–13. "Nothing in the world do I desire as much as that": RGADA 5.85.2.152–3, CII to GAP, 7 November 1788. "A great hatred has risen against us": RGADA 5.85.2.150–1, L 327, CII to GAP, 27 November 1788. Mamonov: CtG, *Sochineniia* 12, 2nd half–volume, 699–701, L 355–7, June 1789. Khrapovitsky 255, 260, 11 April 1789.

22. Montefiore 422–430. Mamonov, "why didn't you tell me about it frankly?," "I felt sorry for you": CtG, *Sochineniia* 12, 2nd half–volume 699–701, L 355, CII to GAP, June 1789. RGADA 5.85.2.166–7, CII to GAP, 14 July 1789; *RS* (1876) 16.400, Garnovsky to Popov, 21 June 1789. RGADA 5.85.2.3–4, GAP to CII, 18 July 1789, Olviopol. "A sacred place": *AKV* 12.63, P. V. Zavadovsky to S. R. Vorontsov, June

1789, St. Petersburg. Catherine of Zubov, "the Child": RGADA 5.85.2.177, L 365, CII to GAP, 12 August 1789.

23. Montefiore 424–459. Catherine fell in love: RGADA 5.85.2.163, L 358, CII to GAP, 6 July 1789. "I'm fat and merry": RGADA 5.85.2.173, L 363, CII to GAP, 5 August 1789, Tsarskoe Selo; "educating young men": *RS* (1876) 16.406–7, Garnovsky to Popov. Catherine in love, Potemkin approves: RGADA 5.85.2.7, L 357, GAP to CII, ud; RGADA 5.85.2.166–7, L 319, CII to GAP, 14 July 1789; RGADA 5.85.2.163, L 358, CII to GAP, 6 July 1789; RGADA 1.1.43.42, L 362, GAP to CII, 30 July 1789. Victories over the Turks: Philip Longworth, *The Art of Victory* 156–7. "Your greatness of character": RGADA 5.85.2.204, L 383, CII to GAP, 15 November 1789. "Now we're in a crisis": Khrapovitsky, 24 December 1789. "One paw out of the mud": RGADA 5.85.2.245–6, L 425, CII to GAP, 9 August 1790. Alexander 257–92 and Madariaga, *Russia* 413–26. Robert H. Lord, *The Second Partition of Poland* (henceforth Lord) 180–5. Khrapovitsky 359, 15, 17, 22 March 1791 and 359–61, 7 and 9 April 1791; RS (1892) April 179, Memoirs of Fyodor Secretarev.

24. Montefiore 467–486 and 1–10. *SIRIO* (1878) 23.517–19, CII to Grimm, 29 April 1791. Zubov vs Potemkin: RS (1876) September 43, Knyaz Platon Alexandrovich Zubov. "Bye, my friend, I kiss you": RGADA 5.85.2.291, L 461, CII to GAP, 25 July 1791. "Your sickness upsets me utterly": RGADA 5.85.2.304, L 470, CtG to GAP. "The only escape is to leave": RGVIA 52.2.22.191, L 470, CtG to GAP, October 1791; *SIRIO* 23.561, CII to Grimm.

25. Golovina 42. RA (1876) 1.89–92, Fyodor Rostopchin to S. R. Vorontsov, 8 July 1792, and RA (1876) 1.92–7, Rostopchin to R. Vorontsov, 14 April 1793. Gielgud, A. (ed.), Adam Czartoryski, *Memoirs of Prince Adam Czartoryski and His Correspondence with Alexander I* (henceforth Czartoryski) 1.66–106, esp. Zubov in power and arrogance; hairdo 75–7; Valerian Zubov 72–5.

26. *RA* (1876) 1.92–7 Rostopchin to Vorontsov, 14 April 1793. Second Partition of Poland, Catherine clears plates: Golovina 120; Alexander marriage, Alexander character, Golovina 41; Saltykov and Alexander 42; Elizabeth beauty 53. Two angels: SIRIO 23.583, CII to Grimm, 14 May 1793. Golovina and Elizabeth: Golovina 54, 76, 86–7, 104–5. Grand Duke Nikolai Mikhailovich, *L'Impératrice Elisabeth, épouse d'Alexandre Ier* (henceforth NM, *Elisabeth*) 1.407–26, inc. Elizabeth false pregnancy 424; Alexander gives permission, 12 December 1794; Rostopchin to Vorontsov, e.g. 20 July 1794; Zubov in love 8 December 1795. Catherine old age: Czartoryski 1.85.

27. Golovina 47–8; 54, 76, 86–7,104–5. NM, *Elisabeth* 1.407–26,. Catherine to Grimm on Alexander letters in *SIRIO* 23. RA (1876) 1.92–7, Fyodor Rostopchin to S. R. Vorontsov, 14 April 1793. RA (1876) 1.113–18. Kutaisov: Sablukov 1.233. Alexander and Constantine, pride in Gatchina and Paul: Czartoryski 1.122–3; Zubov in love 88; Constantine vicious/marriage night 104.

28. Disinherit Paul: *SIRIO* 27.300–3, 23.555. Tsarevich Alexei/Peter the Great: RS (1901) 108.79. Rey 61–5. Madness: Golovkin 119–21. AKV 8.76, 93–4 Rostopchin to S. Vorontsov, 6 July 1793. RA (1876) 1.92–7, Fyodor Rostopchin to S. R. Vorontsov, 14 April 1793. RA (1876) 1.113–18, Rostopchin to Vorontsov, 28 May 1794. Catherine to Grimm on Alexander letters in *SIRIO* 23, esp. Alexander to be crowned 23.574, Catherine to Grimm, 14 August 1792. McGrew 148–69; Zubov joke 1793, plot of Nassau-Siegen, Choiseul-Gouffier on new Tiberius 184–7.

29. Dixon 305–15. Catherine approached Maria: Queen Anna of Netherlands quoted in Rey 63. Alexander refuses Catherine's offer: found in Zubov's papers quoted in N. K. Shilder, *Imperator Alexandr I* (henceforth Shilder) 1.279. Renounce throne: Alexander to Laharpe, 21 February 1796, and Alexander to Victor Kochu-

bey, 10 May 1796, both quoted in Rey 64–6. Constantine: brutality: *RA* (1876) 1.118, Rostopchin to Vorontsov, 28 May 1794. Choice of wife: Wilson 21. Lincoln quotes Custine on foot-piercing and Davydov on ugliness, hairs: Lincoln 26–7. Rats out of guns, drums, VD, cruelty to hussar reported to Catherine II by Charlotta Lieven: Golovina 98, 184–5. 1801, plans to refuse crown: Sablukov 325. S. W. Jackman (ed.), *Romanov Relations: The Private Correspondence of Tsars Alexander I, Nicholas I and Grand Dukes Constantine and Michael with Their Sister Queen Anna Pavlovna* (henceforth Jackman) 8; early loves and brutality of Constantine 26. NM, *Elisabeth* 66. Rey 309, 364, 417. Art Beech, *The Grand Dukes* (henceforth Beech) 1.21.

30. Golovin 109–21. McGrew 184–7. Constantine brutality: *RA* (1876) 1.118, Rostopchin to Vorontsov, 28 May 1794. Swedish marriage: *RA* (1876) 1.408–9, Rostopchin to Vorontsov, 11 September 1796. Michael Jenkins, *Arakcheev: Grand Vizier of the Russian Empire* (henceforth Arakcheev) 39–55.

### SCENE 5: THE CONSPIRACY

1. Fyodor Rostopchin, *Le Dernier Jour de la vie de l'impératrice Catherine II et le premier jour du règne de l'empereur Paul I, in Oeuvres inédites du comte Rostopchine* 3–38 (henceforth Rostopchin). Grand Duchess Elizabeth to mother, 29 January 1797, NM, *Elisabeth* 239–40. Czartoryski 1.140–73. Golovina 124–33. McGrew 192–243.

2. McGrew 192–243. Paul on Peter III: *PSZ* 24.17537, 9 November 1796; on military *PSZ* 1.24.17531, 7 November 1796. Rostopchin 3–38. Golovkin 123–31. Golovina 124–33.

3. McGrew 192–242. Paul's coup against ruling families and concentration of power in His Majesty's Suite, adjutants double: LeDonne 99. Order on pretty maid: Golovina 166. Grand Duchess Elizabeth to mother, 29 January 1797, NM, *Elisabeth* 239–40. Golovkin 123–31. Golovkin 123–31; Paul to Repnin on power to make marshals and most important man in empire 133; passion for ceremony 134. McGrew 192–243. New orders of dress, Alexander like Prussian, Gatchina Guards arrive: Sablukov 1.226–8; Petersburg like a German town 1.230. Paul good features 1.236–7; chivalry, humour 2.302–3; strikes officers with cane 2.306. Parade centre of all life, Paul's mixed nature: Czartoryski 1.140–73. Golovina: Nelidova–Maria faction 138–44. Kutaisov: Czartoryski 1.181–7. Kutaisov as Figaro: Sablukov 2.306. Dismissal and exile of Suvorov by Arakcheev ordered by Paul, 6 February 1797: Grand Duke Nikolai Mikhailovich, *L'Empereur Alexandre Ier* (henceforth NM, *Alexandre*) 249. Arakcheev 53–61.

4. *Koronatsionnye torzhestva* 8. Golovkin 139; Alexander and heavy crown 162. Golovina 138–59, laughter and fear; improper flowers. NM, *Elisabeth* 1.246. McGrew 233–40. Wortman 87–8. Rey 76. Romanov Family Law: *PSZ* 1.24.17908, 5 April 1797. Succession Law: *PSZ* 1.24.17906, 5 April 1797 and *PSZ* 1.24.17907, dated 1788. Caesarevich: *PSZ* 1.24.6, November 1796–1797, no. 17910 577–9. Lopukhina: Sablukov 1.222–41 and 2:302–27. Arakcheev 64.

5. *Osmnadtsatyi vek* 3.428, Nelidova to Paul, 12 December 1796; brings Paul and Maria together 14 May 1797 430 and 432; as grumbler 433, like sister 436; advises moderation 439; 449; Maria and Paul to Nelidova, August 1797, 456. Ruckus with Nelidova, dancing, humour: Sablukov 2.303. Family life of Paul Maria and children: GARF 728.1.1394.4–31, Notes of Nicholas I on playing with Paul and fun/fear.

6. McGrew 244–271. Golovina 171–85. Golovkin 169–85; rule of three women 185–7; rise of Rostopchin 188. NM, *Elisabeth* 2.155, 28 April 1805. Marriage of Lopukhina: McGrew 269–70. Suvorov and Lopukhina: Golovina 184. Rey 79–83. Kutaisov:

Lothario, escapes with Paul, never hurt anyone: Sablukov 1.234; Paul single combat with Napoleon 2.306; rise of Lopukhina, generosity, "beside himself," makes Lopukhin prince, house for Gagarina, joins Kutaisov on visits 306–10. Rise of Kutaisov, Lopukhina plot/Rostopchin chief role: Czartoryski 181–4. Family life: GARF 728.1.1394.4–31, Notes of Nicholas I.

7. Paul foreign policy—alliance with Austria/GB, war with France: Longworth, *Art of Victory* 236–98. Malta and alliance: McGrew 271–300. On Napoleon: Andrew Roberts, *Napoleon the Great* (henceforth Roberts) 185, 285–6. Knights of Malta, marriage of Litta/Scavronskaya: Golovkin 179.

8. McGrew 289–300. Roberts on Napoleon/Paul invasion plans 286. Paul and Georgia: Donald Rayfield, *Edge of Empires: A History of Georgia* (henceforth Rayfield), 256–7.

9. McGrew 282–312. Sacking of Lopukhin: *RA* (1876) 2.90, Rostopchin to Vorontsov, 22 December 1798, and *RA* (1876) 3.76–92, 12 June 1799 and 10 July 1799. Appointment of Obolyaninov, lack of suspicion: Sablukov 1.234; Arakcheev "the Ape" 1.235; Alexander and Constantine terrified, tremble 1.234. Sacking of Arakcheev and relationship with Alexander: Arakcheev 61–68. Alexander, Elizabeth and Constantine, Alexander unhappy, liberal feelings, orders Czartoryski to draft manifesto of reform and abdication: Czartoryski 1.161–8. Paul locks Demidora in room with Alexander: Golovina 186.

10. Changes of alliance and early Panin conspiracy: McGrew 312–341.

11. This account of the conspiracy and assassination is based on Comte de Langeron, *Memoire sur la mort de Paul I, par le comte de Langeron*, Richelieu Collection, Mémoires de documents, MS 99, Bibliothèque de la Sorbonne, Paris, the unpublished memorandum of Langeron who interviewed Pahlen and most of the conspirators. McGrew 341–355. Shilder 1.291, Paul to Pahlen, 26 February 1797; Paul suspicions 1.302, Paul to N. I. Saltykov, 29 January 1801. Kutaisov never known to injure anyone 1.233; Obolyaninov as procurator: Sablukov 1.234; three officers struck with cane for which Paul paid dearly 2.306; Gagarina into Mikhailovsky Palace 2.311; Pahlen "the brave man acts," exile of Rostopchin/Arakcheev, Alexander and Constantine under arrest, retake the oath, Sablukov dismissed, the murder 2.311–20. Leo Lowenson, *The Death of Paul I and the Memoirs of Count Bennigsen*, *SEER* (1950) 29.212–32. Golovina 227–38; Pahlen tells Paul of conspiracy of Maria and sons 227. Napoleon alliance: Roberts 286–7. Czartoryski 1.187; Alexander's view, regrets and plans for Paul after deposition; Bennigsen, view of Constantine, Nikolai Zubov Herculean, informs Alexander, Maria, I am Empress 1.222–46. On Prince General Vladimir Yashvili struck by cane: S. L. Seeger (ed.), Alexander Izvolsky, *Recollections of a Foreign Minister: Memoirs of Alexander Izvolsky* (henceforth Izvolsky) 39–40. NM, *Elisabeth* 273, Empress Elizabeth to her mother, 13 March 1801, Maria hysterical, Alexander damaged, mad joy. Pushkin sees Skariatin at balls in 1834: Tim Binyon, *Pushkin* (henceforth Binyon) 440. Paul's illegitimate daughter Moussine Yuriev: NM, *Elisabeth* 2.111, Empress Elizabeth to mother, 10/22 October 1803; 2.336, Empress Elizabeth to mother, 3/15 August 1809; death of Princess Gagarina, Paul's mistress 2.155, to mother, 28 April/10 May 1805. NM, *Alexandre* on plot 7–8, inc. description of Alexander, on 12 March by Lt Sanglin. The night of the conspiracy, Michael "I bury my father" etc: GARF 728.1.1394.4–31, Notes of Nicholas I. Arakcheev—dismissed twice and summoned: 69–80.

12. Pahlen treacherous, Alexander I and Grand Duchess Catherine, *Scenes of Russian Court Life, Being the Correspondence of Alexander I with His Sister Catherine*, Grand Duke Nikolai Mikhailovich (ed.) (henceforth Catiche) 112–18, Alexander to Grand Duchess Catherine, 18 September 1812. Czartoryski 1.223–55, Alexander

summons Czartoryski, Alexander's view of conspiracy, get rid of a fly (Pahlen), forgiveness of Valerian Zubov, plans for Paul to garden 267–8; "court of exaggerated simplicity" 327. NM, *Alexandre* 10–15; ability to hide feelings by Baron Korff 21. GARF 728.1.1394.4–31, Notes of Nicholas I. Napoleon's rage at killing of Paul: Roberts 295.

### SCENE 6: THE DUEL

1. Alexander character Roberts 295. Caulaincourt quoted in Price 37. Carnival: NM, *Elisabeth* 2.43–50, Elizabeth to mother, 6/18 September, 9/21 September; 24 September/6 October 1801. Liberalism: Rey 87–130. Czartoryski 1.257–70; change in foreign policy 271–9; coronation increased sadness 278; meeting with king of Prussia 1802 283; Kamenny Ostrov 290; ministries 297–304; universities 307. Memel Prussian meeting, 29 May 1802: NM, *Alexandre* 25–6; reforms and Secret Committee 26–32. Serfdom: LeDonne 84–91; serfs exiled for insolence 1760, repealed 1802, 212–14. Alexander liberal view of Russian blood libel: John Klier, *Krovavyi navet v Russkoi provoslavnoi traditsii*, in M. Dmitriev (ed.), *Evrei I khristiane v pravoslavnykh obshchestvakh vostochnoi evropy* (henceforth Klier) 191–2. Abolition of Secret Expedition and its replacement by interior ministry under Kochubey and later under Petersburg governor-generals plus interior, justice and war ministries: LeDonne 125–7; Arakcheev returns as artillery inspector 102–3; new ministries, Council of State, Alexander's distrust of grandees 105–12. Arakcheev 84–109.

2. Maria Naryshkina: NM, *Elisabeth* 2.131, 10 June 1804; 2.145 death of Naryshkina's child, Elizabeth to mother, 21 November/3 December 1804; 253 Catiche behaviour, Elizabeth to mother, 29 August/10 September 1807; 278 death of Lisinka Alexandrovna, 2/14 May 1808. Catiche 27–31: Alexander's passionate letters to her 15, 19, 20, 24 September 1805; 84 my little family, Alexander to Catiche, 18 January 1812; 82 my happiness in my little household, 24 December 1811; 67 take interest in my children, 25 April 1811; 72 thanks for kindnesses to my little family, 5 July 1811. Binyon 560: Vigel quote. Naryshkina dress, Choiseul-Gouffier quoted in Golovina 55; Naryshkins 191. B. Arutunova (ed.), *Lives in Letters: Fifteen Letters from Tsar Alexander I to Princess Z. A. Volkonskaya* (henceforth *Lives in Letters*) 97. Alexander feelings of eclipse by Napoleon: Czartoryski 1.331–5. Catiche 83: Napoleon as infernal, 24 December 1811; 112–18 Napoleon as talent, 18 September 1812.

3. NM, *Alexander* 34–9. NM, *Elisabeth* 2.175, Alexander at Austerlitz, Elizabeth to mother, 11/23 December 1805. Dominic Lieven, *Russia against Napoleon* (henceforth Lieven) 43–7. Rey 158–174. Napoleon/Austerlitz: Roberts 357–90, inc. quotes from Napoleon on Dolgoruky's arrogance; letter to Josephine on Russian destruction; on Alexander as fickle and weak 359; Francis makes love to one woman 392. Czartoryski as Russian minister 268; Alexander eclipsed by Napoleon, hostility to Czartoryski of Dolgoruky, Alexander mocks Chancellor Vorontsov 331–5.

4. Roberts 390; Eylau 442–5; Friedland 449–55. Lieven 43–7. Rey 174–178. NM, *Alexandre* 41–5. NM, *Elisabeth* 2.240, Elizabeth to mother, 16 March 1807.

5. Tilsit: Roberts 456–63, inc. 459–60 Napoleon chattered; Alexander I on Napoleon's grey eyes to Sophie de Tisenhaus, later comtesse de Choiseul-Gouffier, quoted Roberts 635; Alexander duplicity 29. Rey 178–186. Lieven 46–56. NM, *Alexandre*, inscrutability, Korff 21; Napoleon on Alexander missing something; Finland war Petersburg beauties 65. NM, *Elisabeth* on disloyalty of family, Dowager Empress and Constantine and Catiche, Elizabeth to mother, 29 August/10 September 1807. Catiche to Alexander on Napoleon and marriages to stupid and

clever princes, bad joke letters from 26 April, 5 May, 13 May, on Tilsit 25 June 1807, 33-42; 43 Alexander to Catiche on laughing longest 1808; on possible Catiche marriages to Emperor Francis, Napoleon, Oldenburg 292, Empress Maria to Alexander, 11 May 1807, and Napoleon rumours on Catiche and Catiche offered herself as bride to Napoleon if state demanded it 297, Maria to Catiche, 23 December 1809, and refusal of Napoleon suit, Catiche to Maria, 26 December 1809.

6. Lieven 70-85. Erfurt conference: Roberts 488-93, inc. Napoleon letters. Rey 186-211. Arakcheev 110-138. Arakcheev The Vampire: NM, *Alexandre* 266. LeDonne 102-5, 112. Speransky: NM, *Alexandre* 58-63, inc. Arakcheev quote; Council of State and general jealousy 68-71; contrasts by Batenkov between Speransky and Arakcheev 71-2. Elizabeth embarrassed by Savary and French alliance: NM, *Elizabeth* 2.199, Elizabeth to mother, 23 August 1807. Talleyrand: Rosalynd Pflaum, *By Influence and Desire* (henceforth Pflaum) 61-101. Swedish war: Michael Josselson and Diana Josselson, *The Commander: A Life of Barclay de Tolly* (henceforth *Barclay*) 46-72; reforms as war minister 73-90. Alexander slipperiness: Roberts 295; Price 37.

7. Swedish war: *Barclay* 46-72. Arakcheev 114-26. Peace; appointment of Rumiantsev: NM, *Elisabeth* 2.344, Elizabeth to mother, 7/19 September 1809.

8. Roberts 295, 517, 537-41. Catiche 48: Napoleon marriage to Anna, Alexander to Catiche, 23 December 1809; Napoleon marriage 297, Maria to Catiche, 23 December 1809.

9. Gruzino and Minkina: Arakcheev 84-110. Description of Arakcheev and Minkina grenadier figure: A. K. Gribbe, Graf Alexei Andreevich Arakcheev, v 1822-1826, *RS* (1875) 12.84-124. *Catiche* 52, Alexander on Gruzino, 7 June 1810. Barclay reforms as war minister: *Barclay* 73-90. LeDonne 101-5. End of relationship with Maria Naryshkina: NM, *Alexandre* 71. A. N. Krylov-Tolstikevich, *Imperator Alexandr I i imperatritsa Elizaveta* (henceforth Krylov-Tolstikevich) 163.

10. Rey 212-232. Arakcheev 138-150. Declining Russo-French alliance: Lieven 60-101, preparations by Arakcheev and Barclay 100-37; intelligence gathering by Chernyshev and Nesselrode 79-85, Continental System 78-80; Alexander offensive plans 92-3, Polish probes 123-132; Russian reforms and preparations 102-36. Roberts on Alexander offensive plans; Continental System 548-50; Russian preparations 562-7; Napoleon-Alexander letters 563-4. Alexander's creation of police ministry: LeDonne 127-30. NM, *Alexandre* 83-91. Alexander and Barclay reform army: *Barclay* 91-146. Catiche 54: blood will flow, 26 December 1810; 57 my family are at your feet, 19 January 1811; 67, 25 April 1811; 72 What can be hoped of Napoleon? Speransky reform, 5 July 1811; 78 "a dog's life," 10 November 1811. On tension and preparations: Adam Zamoyski, 1812: *Napoleon's Fatal March on Moscow* (henceforth Zamoyski, 1812). On Chernyshev: Bruce Menning, A. I. Chernyshev: A Russian Lycurgus, *Canadian Slavonic Papers* (1988) 30.2 (henceforth Menning) 190-219. Warnings to Napoleon: Caulaincourt report to Champagny, duc de Cadore, foreign minister, 19 September 1810, quoted in Price 37.

11. This is based on Lieven, Roberts, Zamoyski, *1812*, and Rey; personal decisions based on Alexander's correspondence with Catiche; and Prince Golitsyn. Alexander's and Rostopchin's key correspondence with Kutuzov is from L. G. Beskrovnyi (ed.), *M. I. Kutuzov. Sbornik dokumentov* 4. Fall of Speransky, rise of Rostopchin: NM, *Alexandre* 91-119; religious revelations and relationship with Prince Alexander Golitsyn 160-7 and Koshelov 175-6. Oligarchy of grandees/families limits tsar, "They took away Speransky, who was my right hand": LeDonne 105-12. Lieven 85-90; diplomatic manoeuvres with Austria 91-4; Kutuzov and Ottoman war 95. Rey 233-257. Catiche 81: sentry duty, no foot-kissing, 21 November 1811; 83 infernal being, 24 December 1811; 84 horizon darkening, 18 January 1812. Re-

lations deteriorate, Roberts 557–64, Napoleon, size of army, leaves Paris, bids for Ottoman support: Roberts 564–79. Georgia: Rayfield 259–71.

12. Lieven 138–73. Roberts 567: Caulaincourt's warnings and Napoleon's answer; Napoleon's strategy and deployments 569–70; leaves Paris 575; numbers of Grand Army 576–9, "largest invasion force"; crosses Niemen 580; splits in Russian command 581.

13. Retreat: Lieven 138–73. Roberts 580–99, Balashov bon mot and Napoleon's letters to Alexander I 586; Napoleon follows Barclay 594; Smolensk "at last I have them/bodies sweet" quotation 596–7. Recriminations in high command and Alexander's mysticism: Bagration to Arakcheev and Yermolov, from Vilna to Moscow: NM, *Alexandre* 91–119; religious revelations and relationship with Prince Alexander Golitsyn 160–7 and Koshelov 175–6. Kutuzov, imposed on Alexander by oligarchs, families: LeDonne 108. Catiche 98: Constantine hopeless, why you had to leave the army, June 1812; 102 Alexander to Catiche, my coming to Moscow not in vain, it made me cry like a child, 12 July 1812; 104 the blame is yours, 5 August 1812; 308, Prince George of Oldenburg on possible commanders, 5 August 1812; 105 Alexander to Catiche, 8 August 1812, choosing Kutuzov; 112–18 Alexander's explanation, 18 September 1812. GARF 679.1.6.2–3, Alexander appoints Kutuzov, 8 August 1812. RGVIA 1/L 1.3574.III.56, Kutuzov to Rostopchin, 17 August 1812.

14. Borodino and after: Lieven 174–214. No one is sure of the exact size of the armies: these figures are Lieven's; Roberts computes Napoleon 103,000, Kutuzov 120,000. Roberts 600–6: bloodiest battle till Marne, casualty figures 604, 607. RGIA 1409.1.710.1.234, Kutuzov reports on Borodino to Alexander, bloodiest of battles, withdrawal, 29 August 1812. RGVIA 1/L. 1.1.3574.IV.22, Kutuzov abandonment of Moscow to Rostopchin, 1 September 1812. RGIA 1409.1.710.1.230, Kutuzov tells Alexander not the fall of Russia. RGVIA fond VUA.453.19, Alexander to Kutuzov, shock 7 September 1812. GARF 679.1.8.1, Alexander to Kutuzov, 17 September 1812. RGVIA, fond VUA.453.20–2, Alexander to Kutuzov, 2 October 1812. Colonel Michaud's interviews with Alexander quoted in Shilder 3.124, 509–10.

15. Lieven 215–41. Roberts 609–19. Catiche 108, Catiche to Alexander, 3 September 1812; 108 "You are loudly accused," 6 September 1812; 109 Alexander to Catiche, my determination; 109 Catiche to Alexander, "Bagration died yesterday," 13 September 1812; 112–18. "Those fatal four miles poisoned all delight," 18 September 1812; Catiche to Alexander, 23 September 1812; 123 Alexander to Catiche, Bagration paper "my commission is fulfilled," 24 September 1812. Burning of Moscow and Rostopchin: see Alexander Mikaberidze, *The Burning of Moscow: Napoleon's Trial by Fire 1812*.

16. Lieven 241–84. Catiche 129, Alexander to Catiche, "God has done everything," 2 November 1812; 136 Catiche to Alexander, "Delight is general," 25 November 1812; 142 death of Prince George, Catiche to Alexander, 15 December 1812. After Borodino, *Barclay* 145–6. Retreat: Roberts 634–5 and quotes Alexander I to Tisenhaus, later Countess Choiseul-Gouffier on Napoleon, "What a career he's ruined."

17. This is based on the following: Lieven chapters 9–14. Price chapters 3–7; Rey 258–270. Roberts 642–60. Alexander's letters in NM, *Alexandre*, Elizabeth's letters in NM, *Elisabeth*. Arakcheev 158–70. Barclay 166–204. Price: Metternich profile, Stendhal quote 40–1; Lützen and Bautzen 61–75; Reichenbach negotiations 79–88; Prague congress 101–9; Schwarzenberg 115; tsar's court 116, letter to his wife; defeat at Dresden 119–27; Kulm 127–34. Volkonskaya: *Lives in Letters* 92–132. Maria Fairweather, *Pilgrim Princess* (henceforth Fairweather) 57–71. Alexander I to confidant Alexander Golitsyn, Alexander to Golitsyn and negotiations with allies, description by Golitsyn, NM *Alexandre*, 119–43. Catiche 164, Alexander at

Kalisch with Prussian alliance, 23 February 1813; 174–85 Catiche in Prague and Teplitz from 28 April 1813; 185 Alexander, Lützen, Bautzen and after 14 May 1813; 190 truce, 28 May 1813; 193 Catiche bribes Metternich, 20 July 1813. On Nesselrode, background: W. Bruce Lincoln, The Ministers of Nicholas I: A Brief Inquiry into Their Backgrounds and Service Careers, Russian Review (July 1975) 34.308–23 (henceforth Lincoln, Nicholas I Ministers) 314.

18. Rey 261–77. Roberts on Leipzig 660–86; invasion of France 687–99. Price on Battle of Nations, Alexander threatened by cavalry 135–52; Frankfurt 161; Alexander's plan for a French republic 117 (General Moreau); crossing into France 168–70; Châtillon Congress, Castlereagh 187–90, Schwarzenberg on Alexander's buffoonery 190; Alexander vs Bourbons 191; republic or kingdom 198; Blücher pregnancy with elephant, advance 217. On the road to Paris with ministers: Adam Zamoyski, Rites of Peace: The Fall of Napoleon and Congress of Vienna (henceforth Zamoyski, Rites), Metternich quote 108; Metternich tells off Alexander 116–17; middle-class mistress Catiche arrives 123; evenings with Alexander 132. Catiche 196: Alexander "dog's life" at Teplitz, 5 October 1813; 198 doleful on Switzerland, 15 December 1813. Castlereagh with Alexander: John Bew, Castlereagh (henceforth Bew) 335–51. Arakcheev 166–70. Barclay 166–86.

19. The entry to Paris: Price 224–8. Arakcheev 166–7. Barclay 200–1.

20. Talleyrand "gold mixed with shit": Price 161; notes to Marie-Louise 217; Talleyrand wants Marie-Louise regency 222–6; Alexander at Talleyrand's house, Senate deposes Bonapartes 227–36; mission of Caulaincourt, Elba 237–44. Roberts 700–16. Arakcheev 167–70. Barclay 194–2004. Zamoyski, Rites 180–5. Catiche 224, 8 April 1814; 228 Alexander on Napoleon's abdication, 20 April 1814.

21. Catiche 217–30. Charmley 7, 10, 18–34. Rey 277–8.

22. Zamoyski, Rites—Nesselrode 68; Wilhelmina 79; Madame Schwartz 302; Constantine as Angry Hyena; tsar flirts with Auersperg, called oaf 313; threats to Saxony 325; blackmails Metternich through Sagan 330–1; Constantine hits Windischgrätz 340; Alexander chat–up, Countess Szechenyi bon mot, tsar's big bottom 350–2; Czartoryski and Elizabeth 353; Beethoven 376; Razumovsky fire 384; Saxon settlement, Alexander rude to wife 410; dictator of alliance 461; Chernyshev pimps harlots, Volkonsky mistress and Bethmann letter 476; Czartoryski heartbreak 483. NM, Alexandre 143–55, on Naryshkina, Holy Alliance, Alexander to Koshelev 175; and Alexander to Golitsyn, 8–15 February 1821, inc. anti-Christian revolutionary conspiracy and idea of Holy Alliance coming to Alexander at Vienna, only prevented by return of Napoleon 221–31; change of government, rise of Arakcheev and Golitsyn in Petersburg 165–6. Elizabeth in Vienna: NM, Elisabeth 2.584–6, Elizabeth to mother, 2 October and 11 November 1814. Arakcheev 166–73. Fairweather 101–18. Bew 373–89. Courland sisters: Pflaum 208–60. Zamoyski, Rites 510–12. Rise of Krüdener: Rey 278–86. Paris after 100 Days/promotion to prince: Barclay 200–3.

23. Zamoyski Rites 510–12. Krüdener: Rey 278–86. Barclay 200–3. Alexander to Catiche on Virginia, 3 June 1815. NM, Alexander—Krüdener, Stourzdza, Golitsyn and Koshelev 155–71; Holy Alliance and Alexander's description in letter to Count Lieven, 16 March 1816, quoted 169–77.

24. NM, Alexandre on mystical seer Tatariov and Arakcheev vs Golitsyn 180–7; reform plans for Poland and Russia 188–90 and 205–8; Speransky decrees 193 and 207. Rey 310–20. Conversation with Borstell: GARF 728.1.633. Military colonies and different attitudes to Russian and other peasants: NM, Alexandre 208–17; Metternich quote on Alexander changes 209; revolution and Semyonovsky mutiny, Alexander to Golitsyn, 8–15 February 1821, inc. anti–Christian revolutionary conspiracy. Empress Alexandra (Mouffy) on military colonies: Una Pope-Hennessy,

*A Czarina's Story: Being an Account of the Early Married Life of Emperor Nicholas I of Russia Written by His Wife* (henceforth Pope) 9–20. Arakcheev 171–203. Alexander travels, Rey 347–50. Congresses, Aix, Alexander's Spanish plan and Holy Alliance: Adam Zamoyski, *Phantom Terror: Political Paranoia and the Creation of the Modern State 1789–1848* (henceforth Zamoyski, *Phantom*) 183–91.

25. Arakcheev 188–96; secret societies and Semyonovsky mutiny 210–12. Zamoyski, *Phantom* 326–30. Rey 327–42; Caucasus 328–9; colonies 321–6. British view of Congress system: Rory Muir, *Wellington: Waterloo and the Fortunes of Peace 1814–1852* (henceforth Muir) 172–4. Alexander and Borstell: GARF 728.1.633. Aix Congress: Charmley 40–45 on Countess Lieven, Metternich; on Nesselrode 56–7; Troppau and Laibach 65–79. Bew 505–6. Secret police: Ruud 16. Police ministry abolished 1819, replaced by three agencies run by Arakcheev, Petersburg governor-general Milodorovich and interior minister: LeDonne 128–30. Objections to military colonies by Barclay 206. Pushkin and fat-bottomed despot: Binyon 55, 100–4.

26. Constantine *RA* (1876) 1.118, Rostopchin to Vorontsov, 28 May 1794. Wilson 21. Custine on foot–piercing and Davydov on ugliness: Lincoln 26–7. Golovina 98 and 184–5. Plans to refuse crown: Sablukov 325. Jackman 8, 26 Maria disapproves of mistress then approves marriage, Maria to Anna, 17 July 1820, and 59, 7 February 1821; 136 Petersburg as prison, Constantine to Anna, 12 June 1827. Amiable lover to Lieven: Charmley 10–11. NM, *Elisabeth* 66. Rey 309, 364, 417. Beech 1.21.

27. Nicholas: GARF 728.1.1394.4–31, Notes of Nicholas I. NM, *Elisabeth* 2.647, marriage of Nicholas and Alexandra, Elizabeth to mother, 27 June/9 July 1817. Youth: W. Bruce Lincoln, *Nicholas I* (henceforth Lincoln, *Nicholas*) 48–50; marriage 48–72. Romance/marriage with Nicholas: Pope 9–47. Beech 1.47. Nicholas virgin at marriage, syphilis visit: M. A. Korf, Materialy i cherty k biografii Imperatora Niklaia I in N. F. Dubrovin, *Materialy i cherty k biografii imperatora Nikolaia I k istorii tsarstvovaniia*, 98–100. Hatred of Poles and Jews: Dubrovin Materialy i cherty k biografii imperatora Nikolaia I i k istorii ego tsarstvovaniia, *SIRIO* (1896) 98.10–14. M. Polievktov, *Nikolai I. Biografia i obzor tsarstvovania* 3, Rey 308–10. GARF 728.1.1210, Constantine to Alexander, 14 January 1822; GARF 728.1.1167, Alexander to Constantine, 2 February 1822; succession manifesto by Alexander, 16 August 1823. GARF 679.1.68.

28. Rey 342–6; secret societies 357–63. "Synagogues of Satan," Alexander complains of Comité Central and trap to Constantine, Zamoyski, *Phantom* 267–275; surrounded by assassins 330; Verona 302–6; Wellington and street sex quoted by Chateaubriand. Muir 193–7. Societies: Lincoln, *Nicholas* 32–4. Secret police: Ruud 16. Verona Congress: Charmley 81–93; Greek question 124–6.

29. NM, *Alexandre* 241–328. Arakcheev 204–38; Minkina murder 239–62; fall of Golitsyn, Volkonsky, no right to be severe 222–36; Sherwood 252. Arakcheevschina/ fall of Golitsyn: Rey 352–7 and 363–6.

30. Rey, account of Countess Choiseul–Gouffier 351–3; Michaud to see Pope 367. Sophia and sin: Golitsyn to Alexander, GARF 728.1.120. Taganrog: Alexander to Elizabeth, GARF 658.1.96, 5 September 1825. Alexander orders investigations and arrests by Dibich and Chernyshev; death: GARF 728.1.1394.4–31, Notes of Nicholas I. Taganrog, letters of Alexander to Elizabeth, Elizabeth letters to her mother on honeymoon idyll and then Alexander's decline and death, told in letters to mother: NM, *Alexandre* 241–328. Alexander visits Vorontsov Crimea and Alupka: Anthony L. H. Rhinelander, *Prince Michael Vorontsov: Viceroy to the Tsar* (henceforth Rhinelander) 77–9. Departure to Taganrog and death: Rey 366–85; retire with Volkonsky as librarian 376; Kuzmich myth and medical reports 381–5.

Fairweather 159–62; last meeting and letters with Alexander 177; death and funeral cortège, Ilya the coachman 181–4.

## ACT III: THE DECLINE
### SCENE I: JUPITER

1. GARF 728.1.1394.4–31, Notes of Nicholas I. Nicholas's impulse to take throne: S. V. Mironenko, *Stranitsy tainoi istorii samoderzhaviia* 89–90. S. W. Jackman (ed.), *Chère Annette: Letters from Russia 1820–1828: The Correspondence of the Empress Maria Feodorovna of Russia to Her Daughter the Grand Duchess Anna Pavlovna, the Princess of Orange* (henceforth Annette) 100–1; Maria Fyodorovna on Emperor Constantine, dreadful position, hears cannonfire: Maria to Annette, 1, 2, 5 and 15 December 1825. Lincoln, *Nicholas* 18–47, 70–85. Jackman 115–16, Anna of Orange to Constantine, 27 December 1825. Wortman 131–3.

2. Wortman 130–1. Elizabeth Longford, *Wellington: Pillar of State* (henceforth Longford) 162–3. Muir 233–7. Annette 112–13, Maria to Annette, 18, 19 February and 19 March 1826. Eastern Question and Nicholas as his own foreign minister: Lincoln, *Nicholas* 110–12, 117–19.

3. OR RNB 380.479.1, Nicholas to A. N. Golitsyn, 13 July 1826. Nicholas's instructions on executions: OR RNB 738.37.15, Nicholas to Count P. V. Golenischev-Kutuzov, 1826. "No less reason to complain": RAS 198.13.2.18, Nicholas to Paul's mistress Nelidova, 4 April 1826. Nicholas "system": Lincoln, *Nicholas* Ministers, 308–23; army, all is order, Nicholas to Mouffy quoted 312. Chernyshev: Menning 190–219. Jonathan W. Daly, *Autocracy under Siege: Security Police and Opposition in Russia 1866–1905* (Daly 1) 12–17. Perlustration and surveillance: Binyon 449–5. Empress Alexandra on Benckendorff: Pope 46. Benckendorff and actress: Lieven 248–9. Lincoln, *Nicholas* 89–90. Ruud 18–21. Inspections with Benckendorff "to astound Moscow," Benckendorff diaries quoted in Lincoln, *Nicholas* 171; reform commissions 99; new ministers 99. Yermolov tainted, interrogation of Griboyedov: Laurence Kelly, *Diplomacy and Murder in Tehran: Alexander Griboyedov and Imperial Russia's Mission to the Shah of Persia* ("Kelly") 131–40.

4. Wortman 135–9. Annette 116, Maria to Annette, 13, 25 July 1826. Binyon 240–5; Benckendorff 244–51. Young Tsarevich Alexander: E. Radzinsky, *Alexander II: The Last Great Tsar* (Radzinsky) 53.

5. Persia: Lincoln, *Nicholas* 110, 113–15. Nicholas suspects Yermolov : RS (1880) 29.619–25, Nicholas to Dibich, 10 and 27 March 1827. Rayfield 277–80. Kelly 128–43; rise of Paskevich 143; ar 143–62; embassy 179–94.

6. Ottomans: Lincoln, *Nicholas* 115–30. Nicholas to Grand Duke Michael on siege of Brailov, 8 June 1828 quoted in A. S. Tsamutali, *Nikolai I* 346; Nicholas to Michael on death of Maria, "we have orphans," 24 October 1828. Varna/Menshikov wound: Lyubov Ruseva, Oklevetannyi molvoi, *Smena* (2007) 2.96–107. Death of Maria: *Annette* 162, Alexandra to Annette, 24 October 1828. Death of Griboyedov: Kelly 195–204.

7. Lincoln, *Nicholas* 130–48. RGIA 706.1.71, Nicholas to Michael on "scoundrel" Metternich, 24 April 1843. Fear of assassination: RA (1897) 1.16, Nicholas to Paskevich, 30 June 1835.

8. Wortman 145. Lincoln, *Nicholas* 275. "smile of a condescending Jupiter," Anna Tyutcheva, *Vospominaniia* 44. Home life, schedule and advisers: Lincoln, *Nicholas* 154–66. Mouffy "in a golden cage": Anna Tyutcheva, *Vospominaniia*, Moscow, 2004, 51, 55. Mouffy: Lincoln, *Nicholas* 60, 115 and 364. Wholesome image: Wortman 126–7. Mouffy: Binyon 443. Dancing and learning of political plots: Pope

41–3; Nicholas on family happiness 31, Nicholas to Annette, 28 February 1846; our peaceful cottage, Peterhof, 28 July 1837 222; "our favourite corner" 190.

9. Children: Jackman 185, children "dearer than any conquest," Nicholas to Annette, 19 September 1829; 145 my boys, "angelic" soul of young Alexander, 16 February 1828; 83 "little fellow a soldier," Nicholas to Annette, 16 July 1820; 98 absent-minded boy. Nicholas drills family, Grand Dukes NN and MN: Beéche 1.79–80. "Play regiments": Wortman 148. Young Alexander: tearful, emotional, military instincts: Zapiski K. K. Merder, *Novyi zhurnal* (1995) 3. Zapiski K. K. Merder, *RS* (1885) 45.347–8, 538–29; 46.488–90; 47.227–8 (henceforth Zapiski K. K. Merder). "Keen to ensure son feels like me": *RA* (1897) 1.6, Nicholas to Paskevich, 22 May 1832. Lack of enthusiasm for military/soldier in soul: Alfred Rieber (ed.), *The Politics of Autocracy: Letters of Alexander II to Prince A. I. Bariatinskii 1857–1864* (henceforth Rieber) 22, Nicholas to Merdera; secretive nature, Merdera reports 32; wish never to be tsarevich 19. Court life: Wortman 148, 151. "I like people having fun": Jackman 190. Nubians 1810, first Americans, costumes, darkness of skin and regular position, reduction in cost of Nubians in 1851, just eight Negroes: Zimin, *Negroes* 410–18.

10. Nicholas's sex life: Annette 24 on Nicholas's libido and abstinence, Maria Fyodorovna to Annette, 7 July 1820. Leo Tolstoy, *Hadji Murat*, in *Great Short Works of Leo Tolstoy*, 616. Varenka Nelidova, secrecy: M. P. Frederiks, *Iz Vospominanii. Portret na fone imperii* (henceforth M. P. Frederiks) 54–5. On Nicholas's friendship of seventeen years with Nelidova: Grand Duchess Olga Nikolaevna, *Son Iunosti. Vospominaniia velikoi knyazhny Olgi Nikolaevny 1825–1846*, in N. Azarova (ed.), *Nikolai I. Muzh. Otets. Imperator* (henceforth Grand Duchess Olga Nikolaevna, *Son Iunosti*) 248–9; on Amalia Krüdener, 235–6. Krüdener and Buturlina on Nicholas I as strange man: S. V. Zhitomirskaia (ed.), S. A. Smirnova–Rosset, *Dnevnik. Vospominaniia* 8–9, 10 March 1845; on timing of visits to Nelidova 7, 5 March 1845. Binyon 381; on flirting with Pushkina and harem of actresses 529; Krüdener and Buturlina 567; on "dangling" after Natalya Pushkina, driving past window 566.

11. Binyon 244–62; 437–9; 442; 449–52. Uvarov and nationalism: Lincoln 237–52. Binyon 480–5 on Uvarov against Pushkin, Nicholas on reviews 316–17. Pushkin and Elise Vorontsova: Rhinelander 75–7.

12. Binyon 524–99; d'Anthes marriage to Ekaterina 609–10; duel and death 611–27; 639–50; November 1836, Nicholas advises Natalya to pay attention to virtue; Nesselrode 149; funeral 296; Zhukovsky complains of harassment to Benckendorff 311.

13. This is based on Moshe Gammer, *Muslim Resistance to the Tsar: Shamil and the Conquest of the Chechnia and Dagestan*; John F. Baddeley, *The Russian Conquest of the Caucasus*; Rayfield, *Edge of Empires*; Lesley Blanch, *The Sabres of Paradise*. *RA* (1897) 1.22, Nicholas to Paskevich, 21 October 1837.

14. Zapiski K. K. Merder; "I wish I'd never been born a tsarevich" *RS* 45.528; Nicholas to Alexander II, I can forgive anything except except lack of a sense of duty, *RS* 47.41; Nicholas notices little zeal for military science *RS* 48.514; secretive nature *RS* 47.430. Alexander education and youth: Sobstvennoruchnoe chernovoe pismo V. A. Zhukovskogo ee Imperatorskomu Vel. Gos. Imp. Marii Fyordorovne 1828, *SIRIO* (1881) 30.39. Wortman 169–80; marriage 180–5. Rieber 32; secretive nature, Merder reports 32; Nicholas as more than father 19–22. Cossacks: Menning 190–219. Alexander reverie, Kalinovskaya, a trip: GARF 672.1.340.10, Nicholas to Gen. Toll, 8 August 1838. Alexander parades, October 1839: I. A. Bychkov (ed.), V. A. Zhukovsky, *Dnevniki V. A. Zhukovskogo* 509. Tsamutali, Nicholas questions Marie relationship and then delighted with Marie: Nicholas to Toll, 12 October 1839 and 21 April 1840. Syphilis visit: Korff, *Materialy* 98–100. Tour: Lincoln 215. Dutch visit to Annette: Jackman 281, Annette to Nicholas, 1 March 1839. London: A. C.

Benson and Viscount Esher (eds.), *The Letters of Queen Victoria: A Selection from Her Majesty's Correspondence between the Years 1837 and 1861* (henceforth *Queen Victoria's Letters*), diary entries May 1839. Bariatinsky takes message to Marie: Rieber 60–1. Nicholas correspondence with young Alexander on life and marriage with Marie: L. G. Zakharova and L. I. Tyutyunnik (eds.), *Venchanie s Rossiei: Perepiska velikogo knyazya Alexandra Nikolaevicha s imperatotom Nikolaem I. 1837;* 143 Nicholas to Alexander, 24 June 1837; 81 Alexander to Nicholas, 3 July 1837. Jackman 300, Alexander to Darmstadt to propose, Nicholas to Annette, 7 January 1840. Birth of children, Nikolai Alexandrovich: Jackman 313, Nicholas to Annette, 3 October 1843.

15. Rhinelander 123–59; Nicholas initial distrust of Vorontsov 101–6; love life and lifestyle 160–7; Nicholas pomposity on thanks 142–3; Caucasus in 1830s and appointment of Vorontsov 280–92. Winter Palace burned down: RA (1897) I.22, Nicholas to Paskevich, 3 January 1838.

16. S. Tatishchev, *Imperator Nikolai I v Londone v 1844 godu, Istoricheskii vestnik* (February 1886) 23.3.602–4. *Queen Victoria's Letters* 2.16–17. Orlando Figes, *Crimea* (henceforth Figes) 61–70. Lincoln 221–4; J. H. Gleason, *The Genesis of Russophobia in Great Britain* (henceforth Gleason) 35–45. They want to kill me: RA (1897) I.16, Nicholas to Paskevich, 30 June 1835.

17. Lincoln 180–95. Geoffrey Hosking, *Russia: People and Empire* 144–9, inc. quote on evil of serfdom, and 367–97; Samarin and Nicholas 382. Uvarov: Binyon 480–5. Lincoln 237–52. On contradictions of nationalism and empire: Dominic Lieven, *Towards the Flame* (henceforth Lieven, *Flame*) 46–57.

18. Velizh "blood libel" case: Klier 192–5. Vorontsov on ludicrous persecutions: Rhinelander 87–8, 108. L. Loewe (ed.), Moses Montefiore, *Diaries of Sir Moses and Lady Montefiore* 329–35. Abigail Green, *Moses Montefiore: Jewish Liberator, Imperial Hero* 181–94; on status of in Russia 174–80. Edmund Levin, *A Child of Christian Blood: Murder and Conspiracy in Tsarist Russia: The Beilis Blood Libel* (henceforth Levin) 39. Hatred of Poles and Jews: Dubrovin 10–14. Also: Polievktov 3. See: N. Riasanovsky, *Nicholas I and Official Nationality in Russia, 1825–1855.*

19. Lincoln 156–9. Death of Alexandra (Adini) in July 1844: Jackman 312, Nicholas to Annette, 2 September 1844. Nicholas and his daughters' marriages, "Your old friend, papa, on Ollie, Tarasov, 1.178, Nicholas to Olga, 26 December 1845. Marriage of Olga: Jackman 314, Nicholas to Annette, 26 September 1846. Benckendorff and Amalia Krüdener, Nicholas's reaction and adoption of baby/marriage to N. Adlerberg: Grand Duchess Olga Nikolaevna, *Son Iunosti*, 235–6. Death of Benckendorff: RA (1897) I.32, Nicholas to Paskevich, 18 September 1844.

20. No mercy: RA (1897) I.32, Nicholas to Paskevich, 18 September 1844. Lincoln 269–90; speech to nobles on danger of household servants, 21 March 1848; on anniversary of Decembrists in 1850 speech to Preobrazhensky Guards; family belongs to you as you belong to me 251; fear of rumours of German rule among the masses 91. Death of Michael: Jackman 331, Annette to Nicholas I, 15 September 1849. Messianic tone on visit to Moscow: Wortman 162, Nicholas I, 14 March 1848, manifesto on visit to dedicate Thon's new Great Kremlin Palace.

21. Lincoln 303–11. Joseph Frank, *Dostoevsky: A Writer in his Time* 163–83. Radzinsky 89–94.

22. Lincoln, *Nicholas I* Ministers 321–3. No changes necessary whatsoever advises Chernyshev: W. Bruce Lincoln, *The Great Reforms: Autocracy, Bureaucracy, and the Politics of Change in Imperial Russia* (henceforth Lincoln, *Reforms*) 149. Rhinelander 115–18: Vorontsov urges railways and coal-driven steamers for Black Sea. Kostia urges steamers for navy: Radzinsky 73; average age of ministers 65. Withdrawal from court life: Jackman 334, Nicholas I to Annette, 23 December 1851. Build-up to the Crimean War: this is based on Figes 90–164. V. Vinogra-

dov, The Personal Responsibility of Emperor Nicholas I in the Coming of the Crimean War: An Episode in the Diplomatic Struggle in the Eastern Question, in H. Ragsdale (ed.), *Imperial Russian Foreign Policy* 159–70. Varna/Menshikov wound: Ruseva 96–107. Rise of Napoleon III: Serena Vitale, *Pushkin's Button* 324, Nicholas receives Baron George d'Anthes/Heekeren as Napoleon envoy, 10 May 1852. Decline of Nicholas: L. Thouvenel, *Nicolas I et Napoléon III, préliminaires de la guerre de Crimée, 1852–1854, d'après les papiers inédits de M. Thouvenel*, 217–19, 250–1, 331–3, marquis de Castelbajac to M. Thouvenal. Pomposity: Rhinelander 143. Anna Tyutcheva, *Vospominaniia* (henceforth Tyutcheva) 174, arrogant, cruel expression, 22 July 1854. Pressure on Nicholas: war is imminent 337, Nicholas I to Annette, 20 May 1853; 340 "war, I don't look for it but I don't flee from it," Nicholas to Annette, 7 October 1853. Rhinelander on Vorontsov opposed war 191–2; his nephew British secretary for war 191–2.

23. This is based on N. F. Dubrovin, *Istoriia Krymskoi voiny i oborony Sevastopolya* (henceforth Dubrovin, *Istoriia*), Figes; Lincoln, *Nicholas*; A. Zaionchkovsky, *Vostochnaia voina 1853–1856*; E. V. Tarle, *Krymskaia voina*; Jackman. Rhinelander 191–2. Holy vocation, overcome with cares: Jackman 341, Nicholas I to Annette, 3 February 1854; 341 God and 1812, Nicholas I to Annette, 3 February 1854; 342 Nicholas, no inclination for entertainments, Grand Duchess Elena Pavlovna to Annette, 16 February 1854; 344 Tsarevich Alexander ready to welcome Royal Navy and visible from the Cottage, Alexander to Annette, 29 April 1854 and 2 July 1854; 346 the ingratitude of Emperor of Austria, will attack us, Nicholas to Annette, 13 July 1854. Nicholas correspondence with Menshikov and Gorchakov: Dubrovin, *Istoriia* 2.31, Nicholas I to Menshikov, 30 September 1854, "Don't give up," 1812; 4 truthful reports, Nicholas I to Menshikov, 3 October 1854; 5 not decent, Nicholas to Menshikov, 10 October 1854; 114 maintain honour, Nicholas to Menshikov, 16 October 1854; 256 "Cheer up," Nicholas to Menshikov, 31 October 1854; 31 are we still not the same Russians, Nicholas to Prince M. Gorchakov, 30 September 1854; 253–6 Menshikov depressed, Nicholas to Gorchakov, 1 November 1854. Nicholas declines at court: Tyutcheva 182, heartbreaking, weeping, 19 October 1854; 188 Gatchina dark unbending oak, tsar in socks 24 November 1854; 192 feeding child, 7 December 1854. Shamyl and kidnap of Georgian princesses, June 1854, Jemal interview with Nicholas, and swap with Jemal-Eddin, March 1855, swap on day of Nicholas funeral: Blanch 316–21, 359–88.

24. This is based on the unpublished letter of Grand Duchess Alexandra Iosifovna, wife of Constantine Nikolaievich, to the duchesse de Berry, 7/19 April 1855 (from private collection of Countess Stefania Calice). Death: Tyutcheva 194–203, 10–19 February 1855. Nicholas attended wedding of Alexandra Kleinmikhel: M. P. Frederiks 87. RGVIA 846.16.5450; RGVIA 846.16.5452; Dr. Mandt o polednikh nedelyakh imperatora Nikolaia Pavlovicha, *RA* (1905) 2.480; Nekotorye pobrobnosti o konchine imperatora Nikolaia Pavlovicha, *RA* (1906) 3.9.143–5; Noch c 17–18 fevralia 1855: rasskaz doktora Mandta, RA (1884) 1.194. D. N. Bludov, *Poslednie minuty i konchina v boze pochivshego imperatora, nezabvennogo i vechnoi slavy dostoinogo Nikolaia I* 4–6; Figes 321–3; Lincoln 348–50; Radzinsky 97–9. Alexander takes command, "sovereign not feeling well, he asks me to give you the following orders," orders to General M. Gorchakov: *RS* (1881) 32.9–12, Alexander II to Gorchakov, 14 February 1855.

### SCENE 2: LIBERATOR

1. *RS* (1883) 37.1–3, Alexander II to M. Gorchakov, on fears of Austrian intervention, Vienna negotiations, Sebastopol bombardment; 4 June 1855, not all is lost; 11 Au-

gust 1855, loss of glorious troops; 3 September 1855, "don't lose heart. Sebastopol is not Moscow." Rieber 18–19. François Charles Roux, *Alexandre II, Gortchakoff et Napoleon III* (henceforth Roux) 1–40. W. E. Mosse, *The Rise and Fall of the Crimean System* (henceforth Mosse) 12–25. Figes 324–410.

2. Roux 41–108; on Morny mission 109–207. Mosse 12–52. Figes 411–65. On Morny: Rosalyn Pflaum, *The Emperor's Talisman: The Life of the Duc de Morny* (henceforth Pflaum, *Morny*). W. Bruce Lincoln, The Ministers of Alexander II: A Survey of their Backgrounds and Service Careers, *Cahiers du Monde Russe et Soviétique* (1976) 17.467–83 (henceforth Lincoln, Alexander II Ministers). Alexandr Bazarov, *Svetleishii knyaz. Alexandr Gorchakov, Iz vospomin o nem ego dukhovnika, RA* (1896) 1.328–31. G. L. Kesselbrenner, *Svetleishii knyaz.* On Gorchakov diplomacy: Rieber 73. Gorchakov mission and French alliance, Russia "collecting herself": Mosse 55–104. French diplomacy of Kostia: L. G. Zakharova and L. I. Tyutyunnik (eds.), *Perepiska imperatora Alexandra II s velikim knyazem Konstantinom Nikolaevichem. Dnevnik velikogo knyazya Konstantina Nikolaevicha. 1857–1861* (henceforth Zakharova), 17, Alexander to Kostia, 20 January 1857, letter from Napoleon suggesting friendship; 22–29 March 1857, warns Kostia meeting with Napoleon—take care in your conversations, esp. with Napoleon himself, "Listen, don't compromise yourself pushing your own ideas"; 46 Kostia to Alexander, 4 May 1857, Napoleon never lies but never tells whole truth; 63 Alexander to Kostia, 15 September 1857, I met Napoleon, wonderful, frank, but see what happens in practice.

3. Rieber 73; 103 Gorchakov on restraint in Asia, Alexander II to Bariatinsky (henceforth "A to B"), 2 May 1857; on Caucasus war, Rieber 60–70; 103 "embrace you," A to B, 2 May 1857; 142–4 A to B, 7 May 1861, wishes he could talk to Bariatinsky, and 25 April 1861 needs Bariatinsky here. Rieber 72–82, Indian Mutiny chance to profit, A to B, 28 September 1857, on Gorchakov memo, 28 April 1858, probes into Central Asia; 79–82 role of Bariatinsky and Nikolai Ignatiev—opportunity for trade and threat to Britain; 73 Bariatinsky sees chance to destroy British army in Central Asia. Bariatinsky love life and courage: Blanch, *Sabres of Paradise* 392–5.

4. Coronation: *Vozhidanii koronatsii. Venchanie russkikh samoderzhtsev. Tserkovnyi obryad koronovaniia i podrobnoe opisanie tryokh koronatsii nyneshnego stoletiia* 129. Roux on Morny, 150. Pflaum, *Morny*, 172–5. Wortman 196–209.

5. This is based on the correspondences of Alexander II with Kostia and Bariatinsky; on W. Bruce Lincoln, *The Great Reforms: Autocracy, Bureaucracy and the Politics of Change in Imperial Russia* (Lincoln, *Reforms*): Kostia 44–6; character of Rostovtsev 76–8; working of Editing Commission 80–5. W. Bruce Lincoln, *Nikolai Miliutin: An Enlightened Russian Bureaucrat of the 19th Century* (henceforth Lincoln, *Miliutin*); on bureaucratic infighting, support by Elena, feud with Rostovtsev and Editing Commission 48–62. Ben Eklof, John Bushnell and Larissa Zakharova (eds.), *Russia's Great Reforms 1855–1881* (henceforth Eklof): Larissa Zakharova, Autocracy and the Reforms of 1861–74 in Russia 19–38; on Alexander 21–22; on Rostovtsev 27. Kostia character, the brothers correspond on serf issue, Zakharova 65, Alexander touched by crowds (and beauties), Alexander to Kostia, 16 August 1858; Kostia encourages Alexander 66, Kostia to Alexander, 19 August 1858; 88 great excitement, Alexander to Kostia, 1 February 1859; 98 Kostia to Alexander, 11 March 1859, solution is land plus government guarantees; 122 Kostia to Alexander, committee meeting for final review and I as chairman, heated debate, 10 October 1860. GARF 722.1.684, Alexander to Kostia, 19 October 1863, I appreciate you. Zakharova 270–309: diary of Kostia on battle against the Retrogrades, on appointment to chair main committee and heated discussions, 29 September 1860 to 5 March 1861. Roles of Elena Pavlovna and Bariatinsky: Rieber 48–9; on

connection between military reform and serf reform, the road to emancipation 28–54; letters to Bariatinsky on serfdom—108 A to B, 2 November 1857, great excitement on liberation of peasants; 110 A to B, 22 November 1857, Nazimov rescript. Elena, fun Thursdays: R. Fillip-Miller (ed.), Elizabeth Narishkin-Kurakin, *Under Three Tsars* (henceforth *Naryshkin*) 34.

6. 1858, success vs Shamyl: Rieber 106–26, A to B, 14 January 1858, veritable joy; 19 May, new and brilliant result; 30 August 1858, Shamyl, what a famous fellow, and two great results in Far East on Amur by N. N. Muraviev-Amursky; 18 September 1858, brilliant success. Rieber 126–33, 20 April 1859, the most beautiful present; 28 July 1859, taking Dargo; 10 August 1859, heart filled with joy; 11 September 1859, Shamyl captured; 7 December 1859, Bariatinsky marshal.

7. Shamyl captured: Rieber 126–33, A to B, 20 April 1859, the most beautiful present; 28 July 1859, taking Dargo; 10 August 1859, heart filled with joy; 11 September 1859, Shamyl captured; 7 December 1859, Bariatinsky marshal; 49 on Bariatinsky later career—resign or not from viceroy, appoint Mikhail as successor and delicate private question, 26 November 1862. On tragedy of Circassians see Oliver Bullough, *Let Our Fame Be Great*. Meets Katya Dolgorukaya: GARF 678.2.389.1–2, memoirs of Princess Yurievskaya.

8. Zakharova 98, Kostia to Alexander, 11 March 1859, solution; 122 Kostia to Alexander, final review. GARF 722.1.684, Alexander to Kostia, 19 October 1863, 270–309, Kostia vs Retrogrades, 29 September 1860 to 5 March 1861; 1 January 1861, most important era in millennial existence of Russia; tsar's speech to State Council, 28 January 1861; day of signing, 19 February 1861; announcement, 5 March 1861. Rieber 7 March 1861, signed. Lincoln *Reforms*: signing of decree 86; legal and local government reforms 99–143. Eklof 19–38: see essay Zakharova, Autocracy and the Reforms of 1861–74 in Russia; on Alexander 21–2; autocracy from Alexander to Bismarck 35.

9. Tyutcheva 26–7; 40–2 Alexandra Dolgorukaya "Tigress"; 170 fun, 27 June 1854; 304 faint, 20 November 1855. Marie refuses to undress: C. Melnik (ed.), Tatiana Botkine, *Au Temps des Tsars* 31–2. News of Nixa: GARF 641.1.16, Alexander II to Marie, 19 August 1863. Secret code between AII and Marie: GARF 677.1.4.5–6, A. Adlerberg to Alexander Alexandrovich, 15 August 1880. Alexander mistresses Dolgorukaya, Labunskaya, Makova, Makarova, Korazzi: L. Lyashchenko, *Alexandr II*, 131–2. Bismarck favoured by Romanovs and boxes full of pretty women: Jonathan Steinberg, *Bismarck: A life* (henceforth Steinberg) 150–7—at ballet 156. Daniel Home séances 10 July 1858; 5 November 1858; 5 January 1859 in Tyutcheva 396–97; 433–5; and 443–5. See also John Casey, *Afterlives: A Guide to Heaven, Hell and Purgatory* 373–74. The daily walk, intense look: Fanny Lear, *Romance of an American in Russia*, 58. "Managerial tsar": Eklof 75–8—see essay Alfred J. Rieber, Interest Group Politics in the Era of the Great Reforms 58–84. Alexander character: K. K. Merder—secretive RS 47.430. Rieber 126, in my position a good dose of calm and philosophy, A to B, 14 December 1858; 104, 20 May 1857, each minister responsible to me for their own duty; so-called progress and suspicion of journalists/writers 117, A to B, 6 March 1858; 120, A to B, 7 July 1858, autocratic link between Sovereign and God gives us our strength. GARF 678.2.283.15, obligations of my position imposed duties that I cannot neglect, 17 May 1872. GARF 678.2.283.20, Alexander explains how he rules as collegiate autocrat to Katya Dolgorukaya, 23 February 1874. Robert R. Franklin, Tsar Alexander II and President Abraham Lincoln: Unlikely Bedfellows? *University of Hawaii at Hilo, HOHONU History* (2012) 10.74–84.

10. Rieber 117, A to B, 6 May 1858, severe vigilance, never a fan of *littérateurs*. Polish/Italian revolts: Rieber 84–6, and A to B on Italian revolutions, 23 July 1860; Na-

poleon's intrigues in Italy, 12 September 1860; feebleness of Gorchakov and need to talk to Bariatinsky, 7 March 1861; Polish revolt and need for your ideas, 25 April 1861; search for new viceroy, 5 July 1861; imagine coming to terms with such a government, Napoleon, A to B, 12 September 1860. Diplomacy, Italian crisis and Polish revolt: Mosse 116–30. France, Italy, Poland: Roux 266–325.

11. GARF 641.1.15, letters on Nixa's tours: Alexander to Marie, 19 August–6 September 1863, and Nixa to Empress Marie, June 1862. Pobedonostsev: Robert F. Byrnes, *Pobedonostsev: His Life and Thought* (henceforth Byrnes) 33. Too stupid/ pillow-fight: Tyutcheva 223, 7 March 1856.

12. Portrait of Bismarck is based on Steinberg 4–6 and his time as ambassador in Petersburg 147–153; on intimate friendship with Mouffy 151–2; lays out full plan to Disraeli 174; Schleswig-Holstein crisis 210–227.

13. Minny to her father and letter of Queen Louise to Queen Victoria quoted in Coryne Hall, *Little Mother of Russia: A Biography of the Empress Marie Feodorovna, 1847–1928* (henceforth Hall) 17–26. GARF 641.1.16, Alexander II to Marie, 19 August 1863.

14. Alexander Alexandrovich and marriage to Princess Dagmar, Grand Duchess Maria Fyodorovna (henceforth called Alexander III or Sasha and Minny in Notes): Empress Marie letter, 17 September 1867, quoted in Greg King, *Livadia in the Reign of Alexander II*. Alexander III: Wortman 250–7, on Alexander III to tutor, change of courtiers. Importance of Nixa in Alexander III's life and new responsibilities: AIII to Maria Fyodorovna, 22 May 1884 and 11 April 1892. Alexander II and Meshcherskaya: Hall 27–9.

15. Assassination: Ruud 31. Guardian angel, 4 April 1866: GARF 678.2.129, Alexander II (A) to Dolgorukaya (D or Katya in Notes), 4 April 1880. Katya first meetings with Alexander and conversation on day of assassination. GARF 678.2.289.1–5, Princess Yurievskaya (Katya Dolgorukaya) unpublished memoirs (henceforth "Katya memoirs"). Alexander looks in 1865: Théophile Gautier quoted in E. M. Almedingen, *The Emperor Alexander II* 205.

16. Assassination attempt, 1865: Ruud 31. Dominance of Shuvalov, GARF 678.2.277.20, Alexander II, Dnevnik, 24 August 1871. Ruud 31–9. L. G. Zakharova (ed.), Dmitrii Miliutin, *Dnevnik, 1873–1875* (henceforth Miliutin), 75, 31 December 1873, and downfall 1 January 1875. Lincoln, *Reforms* 76–8. Rieber 50–1 Shuvalov resistance to serfdom reform. Shuvalov in power, ambition to be Bismarck, Tolstoy classic education, administrative control, Pahlen fights independent judiciary: Eklof 75–8—see essay Rieber, Interest Group Politics in the Era of the Great Reforms. Shuvalov Third Section and Gendarmes: Ruud 29–31. Trepov created tsar's forty-man bodyguard; and first security bureaux Okrannoe otdelenie, dismissal of Shuvalov, you prefer it in London don't you?: Daly 1. 17–23. Meshchersky on character of Shuvalov: Knyaz' Vladimir Petrovich Meshchersky, *Moi vospominaniia* (henceforth Meshchersky) 119–336.

17. Marriage, problems with Minny, drinking, birth of Nicholas II: Hall 41–53–7. Wortman 250–7: Beéche 1.101. Marriage, problems with Minny, drinking, birth of Nicholas II: Hall 53–7.

18. Joseph Frank, Dostoevsky 244–82; 372–405; 601–616. Rosamund Bartlett, *Tolstoy: A Russian Life*, 118–79. Geoffrey Hocking, *Russia and Russians*, 306–352. Orlando Figes, *Natasha's Dance* on Dostoevsky on peasantry 221; on soul 331; on Slavic nation 335, 338, view of corrupt Europe 65. Policing: Daly 1. 20–22. Ruud 27–31.

19. Katya Dolgorukaya, memory of 1 July 1866: GARF 6782.283.30, A to D, 1, 2 and 3 July 1877. Alexander and Marie, sad anniversaries: GARF 641.1.32, Alexander II to Marie, 20 October 1879. "*Bingerles*," happiest day: GARF 678.2.283,

A to D, 1 January 1871. Private collection, pleasure like a mad thing: D to A, 13 November 1871; immense pleasure, 11 November 1871. "First tête-à-tête": GARF 678.2.289.3–5, Katya memoirs.

20. Paris: GARF 678.2.283.32, A to D, 7 July 1879. Mad for each other, nothing else existed: GARF 678.2.120, A to D, 23 February 1878. Assassination, guardian: GARF 678.2.129, A to D, 4 April 1880. Tsarevich Alexander to Meshchersky, 7 June 1867 and 10 September 1868. Napoleon III caused Nicholas I's death: GARF 678.2.289.23, Alexander diary on death of Napoleon III, 28 December 1872. Shuvalov's account of the Paris escapade, told to Tolstoya: N. I. Azarova (ed.), Alexandra Tolstoya, *Zapiski freiliny: Pechalnyi epizod iz moei zhizni pri dvore* (henceforth Tolstoya) 97–100. Paris bliss and prayer: private collection, A to D, 29 January 1868. Paris arranged to meet/into each other's arms/running away to America: GARF 678.2.289.8–10, Katya memoirs.

21. GARF 678.2.289.23, Alexander diary on death of Napoleon III, 28 December 1872. Prussia 1870s, Prussia will never forget/new Prussian uniform/stone oppressing me: GARF 678.2.277.4, Alexander diary, 26 February, 27 February, 2 March 1871. Powerful neighbour: GARF 678.2.278.18, Alexander diary, 2 September 1872. Uncle Wilhelm and the ballerinas, best friend of Prussia: GARF 678.2.279.5, Alexander diary, 15–25 April 1873. Franco–Prussian War and renouncing of Paris Treaty: Steinberg 286–311. Russia rolls back Treaty of Paris: Mosse 158–83. Roux 465–98. Prussian pigs: Igor Vinogradoff (ed.), Some Russian Imperial Letters to Prince V. P. Meshchersky (1839–1914), *Oxford Slavonic Papers* (1862) 10.110–18 (henceforth Meshchersky Letters), Alexander III to Meshchersky, 9 August 1870. Military reform: Lincoln *Reforms* 143–58. Military reforms and rivalry of Miliutin and Bariatinsky: Eklof 139–58—John S. Buchnell, Miliutin and the Balkan War— Military Reform vs Military Performance. GARF 722.1.104.55, Kostia diary on military reform, 21 April 1873, battles "gave me a headache"; 17 December 1873, Pobedonostsev tirade against Jewish equality, 21 April. Miliutin, *Dnevnik* 21–9, 8 April 1873 to 2 May 1873 and 58–80 process of reform, 3 December 1873 to 1 January 1874. Scott P. Anderson, *The Administrative and Social Reforms of Russia's Military, 1861–74: Dmitri Miliutin against the Esconced Power Elite*, PhD thesis, 2010.

22. Letters from Alexander II (A) to Princess Ekaterina Dolgorukaya (D or Katya) and unless stated all GARF 678/ citing dates: GARF 678.2. 283.8, "we did it four times, you're very passionate and totally unreasonable, I need a rest," 9 February 1871. Hate to interrupt our *bingerle*: Private Collection (PC), A to D, 6 January 1868. Love you passionately want *bingerle*, PC, 1 February 1868 11 a.m. Want you my minx, angel, 30 January 1868 9:30 a.m. Trembling with anticipation thinking of tonight and *bingerle*, 29 January 1868 10:30 a.m. What pleasure our *bingerle*/ you shared by frenzied joy, 1 February 1868 4 p.m. D to A, dream husband, I take pleasure in frenzy, overwhelmed my immense pleasure I received, can't wait for more, 11 November 1871. D to A, immersed, bewitched, filled with one feeling . . . *Bingerle* was magical . . . I pressed against you and took my pleasure like a mad thing . . . Drenched by you, dined with great appetite, want to be in your arms, I can't wait till two, 13 November 1871. D to A, we tire ourselves out, all in me trembles, I can't wait till 4.45 to see you, 14 November 1871. D to A, that good hour was intoxicating and I took pleasure like mad thing, this darling special despot, 14 November 1871. A to D: I want to admire the treasure and long to be inside your *coquille*, oh I'm not ashamed, it's natural, 1 January 1870. Naughty minx, we throw ourselves on each other like cats and come to delirium, 2 January 1870. Delight to dip into you again, darling bobinka, 5 January 1870. I'm impregnated

with *bingerles* on the bed where you move on me and glue yourself to me and then on the sofa where it's my turn, I love to see you without knickers, 1 December 1870. We grip each other like cats without even having time to undress and then put on our favourite costume [naked] until delirium, 12 January 1870. You glued yourself to me and sat on me and I entered your *coquille*, we become one, rejuvenated. Sex four times, very passionate and very unreasonable, 9 February 1871. What fever your husband entered your *coquille* in all the positions possible, I drove into the darling little thing when she held her legs in the air, 9 April 1871. Sex on sofa, table and bed, 5 May 1871. I can't think without laughing of costume I wore when Vava came in oh what horror, 16 September 1872. Sex to madness, 17 May 1871. Sex three times how mad we are, 8 May 1873. Can't resist your adorable *coquille*, 7 November 1871. I enjoy the *bingerles* until delirium and I felt with happiness your fountain water me several times which redoubled my pleasure, 9 May 1874. All the positions possible, 11 August 1875. Livadia, Crimea, sex was delicious, 15 September 1875. Your body so appetizing, Vava sucks on *bingerle* like a leech, 14 May 1876. My *bingerle* makes compliments to Vava and has become fully armed, 17 June 1877. Memories of first love-making and taking off knickers, 1 July 1877. Katya's memoirs on their life together: GARF 678.2.289.11, his mean family and his grace; GARF 678.2.289.12, I followed him everywhere, saw no one; GARF 678.2.289.13, illness, doctors suggest children, I trembled for him, no one else thought of him, baby George born; GARF 678.2.289.14, soft bed, new uniforms, tricking him. Alexander II's drawing of naked Katya: B. M. Nosik, *Russkie tainy Parizha*, 58. Kostia: Beéche 1.51–63; Nikolai 1:69–73; Mikhail 2.171. Mossolov 74. On Mikhail Nikolaievich: Grand Duke Alexander Mikhailovich (Sandro), *Once a Grand Duke* (henceforth Sandro) 37.

23. Alexis: letters from Alexis's travels in GARF 641.1.18. Beéche 1.123–5.
24. This is based on Fanny's memoirs in Eva and Daniel McDonald, *Fanny Lear: Love and Scandal in Tsarist Russia* (henceforth McDonald, *Fanny*) 34–127.
25. This account of the Khiva and Central Asian wars is based on: Seymour Becker, *Russia's Protectorates in Central Asia*; Dietrich Geyer, *Russian Imperialism: The Interaction of Domestic and Foreign Policy 1860–1914* (henceforth Geyer) 86–9; and Peter Morris, The Russians in Central Asia, 1870–1887, *SEER* (1975) 53.521–38. Khiva: GARF 678.2.278.24, Alexander diary, 11 February 1873. Letters to Nikola (Nikolai Konstantinovich) Fanny 127–59. Rieber 72–82; Indian Mutiny opportunity A to B, 28 September 1857. Gorchakov memo, 28 April 1858, probes into Central Asia; 79–82 Bariatinsky and Nikolai Ignatiev opportunity; 73 destroy British army? Miliutin, *Dnevnik* 36–8, inc. conquest of Khiva report by Kaufman, 16 June 1873. Eroticism of imperial adventures: Petr Valuev, *Dnevnik P. A. Valueva, ministra vnutrennikh del (1861–1876)* (henceforth Valuev, *Dnevnik*) 2.60, 20 July 1865.
26. GARF 772.1.106.53–60, Kostia diary, 10–19 April 1874; Miliutin diary, 17 and 18 April 1874. Fanny 188–269; US diplomats quoted in McDonald, *Fanny Lear* 271–99. Maria and Alfred, old fool Victoria: GARF 678.2.279.9, Alexander diary, 5 July 1873. Heavy heart: GARF 678.2.279.8, Alexander diary, 29 June 1873. *Queen Victoria's Letters* 2.328–39. Fanny 181–4. Unpleasant inmate/murder is out: Wilson 358–61. Maria as tsar's helper and duchess of Edinburgh: Hannak Pakula, *The Last Romantic: A Biography of Queen Marie of Roumania* (henceforth Pakula) 25–34. Life at Clarence House: Marie queen of Roumania, *Story of My Life* ("Marie Roumania") 3–88.
27. Shuvalov vs Miliutin, "fly to you on horseback" for sex: GARF 678.2.283.17, A to D, 27 October 1873. Darling Gogo: GARF 678.2.283.18, A to D, 14 December 1873. Narodniki: Ruud 38–40. Daly 1.22–25. Frank, *Dostoevsky* 687–693. Figes, *Nata-*

*sha's Dance* 220–236. Fall of Shuvalov: Miliutin, *Dnevnik* 75, 31 December 1873 and downfall 1 January 1875. You prefer it in London, don't you?: Daly 1.23. Eklof 75–8: see essay Rieber, Interest Group Politics in the Era of the Great Reforms; fall of Shuvalov 78.

28. Wortman 229; Sasha to Minny quoted 257. Geyer 68–776. Miliutin, *Dnevnik* 19 January 1876 and 8 February 1876; things go badly for Serbs, 31 March 1876; 14 June, Alexander counts on League of Three Emperors; 15 July, Alexander on reproaches for our passive stances, he seems calm, inside turmoil; 27 July, allows officers to Serbia; 30 July, tsar remembers thirty years earlier/plan for education of Nicholas; 1 October meetings with Alexander, Miliutin and Ignatiev, how to get out of trap; 11 October, Alexander considers commander-in-chief Nikolai or Totleben; 16 November, Serbia in dire straits; 8 February 1877, need to rely on military. Sasha and Pobedonestsev criticize Alexander: Byrnes 142–4. Fear and stress to Katya: GARF 678.2.105, A to D, 14, 20, 23 August 1876 (to Livadia, rides to see her, Turkey no allies, Prussia, Austria could join us), GARF 678.2.106/107, A to D, 23 September; GARF 678.2.107, A to D, 6, 11 October 1876. Nicky on Alexander II's calm: Charlotte Zeepvat, *Romanov Autumn* 16.

29. This account of war is based on Eklof 139–58, John S. Buchnell, Miliutin and the Balkan War—Military Reform vs Military Performance; B. H. Sumner, *Russia and the Balkans*; and Alexander diary/letters. GARF 678.2.279.17, Alexander diary, 1 January 1877, God help me. *Bingerle* armed: GARF 678.2.283.29, A to D, 17 June 1877. GARF 678.2.279.8, Alexander diary, Bismarck to prevent anti-Russian coalition, 20 January 1877. GARF 678.2.280.2, Alexander diary, infamous England, 16 March 1877. GARF 678.2.280.7, Alexander diary, our ally Carol of Romania 20 May 1877. GARF 678.2.280.11, Alexander diary, 14 and 15 June 1877, magnificent panorama. GARF 678.2.280.12, Alexander diary, 17 June 1877, Disraeli. GARF 678.2.280.15.16, Alexander diary, 25 June 1877, thinks of father. GARF 678.2.280.16, Alexander diary, 28 June 1877, Mikhail retreats. Katya memoirs: GARF 678.2.289.17–19, stupidity of Nikolai furious at unpardonable defeatism, tired. Miliutin, 4 July 1877; Adlerberg advises return home, 8 July; 10 July, Nikolai sobered; 12 July, bad news at Plevna; 14 July, Nikolai doesn't realize problem. GARF 678.2.280.21, Alexander diary, 9 July 1877, first Plevna. GARF 678.2.280.25, Alexander diary, 19 July 1877, more Plevna.

30. GARF 678.2.280.30, Alexander diary, 29 July 1877, heart hurts. Miliutin, *Dnevnik* 6 August 1877, faints/unimpressed with commanders. GARF 678.2.280.32, Alexander diary, 2 August 1877, life with courtiers, bad news from Plevna. GARF 678.2.280.35, 7 August 1877, Nikolai more attacks on Plevna. GARF 678.2.280.46, Alexander diary, 26, 29, 31 August 1877, tsar watches Plevna attack/casualties. Miliutin intervenes 29–31 August 1877; happy nature of tsar, 3 September 1877. Deaths GARF 678.2.280.50, Alexander diary, 5 September 1877. GARF 678.2.280.54, Alexander diary, 15 September 1877, Victoria "tramp," mad. GARF 678.2.280.63, Alexander diary, 27 September 1877, Sasha letter. GARF 678.2.280.67, Alexander diary, 6 October 1877, Nikolai and ballerina lose trust. Sasha's view of "stupid" commander Nikolai: RGIA 919.2454.61, Alexander Alexandrovich 21 December 1877. Tsar confides re Plevna to Katya: *bingerle* sends compliments: GARF 678.2.283.29, A to Katya, 17 June 1877. GARF 678.2.114115, A to D, 13, 18, 20, 21 July 1877, sad, Nikolai ignores superiority, summons Guards. GARF 678.2.114–15, A to D, 13, 14, 18, 24, 30 July 1877. Waiting for fall of Plevna: GARF 678.2.117, A to D, 4, 27 October 1877, sex dreams, Totleben tactics, mobilize Guards, Nikolai lost confidence, marriage one thing we lack. GARF 678.2.117–18, A to D, 16, 18, 20, 24, 28, 29 November 1877. Alexander undermines Nikolai: Miliutin 8 October 1877; capture of Kars, 6 November; 15 November depression; tsar

"younger," thanks Miliutin. GARF 678.2.280.99, Alexander diary, 28 November 1877, fall of Plevna. Grand dukes—Nikolai commander: Miliutin, *Dnevnik* 11 October 1877, Totleben or Nikolai? Alexis to war: GARF 678.2.280, Alexander diary, 9 June 1877. Mikhail at war: Loris in Peter Zaionchkovsky, *Russian Autocracy under Alexander III* (henceforth Zaionchkovsky 2) 22. Sandro 27–47. Radzinsky 258–73. Nikolai: Beéche 1.74–5. Alexander weeps at list of Guards' deaths: Lincoln, *Reforms* 155.

31. GARF 678.2.119, A to D, 11 December 1877, sweet sex; children happy to see Papasha, A to D, 29 December 1977, share victory, children tender. GARF 678.2.119, A to D, 7 and 9 January 1878, joy of victories, peace worth, Adrianople news, when we are together, arrival of British fleet. GARF 678.2.119, A to D, 13 and 14 January 1878, await news from Berlin, cavalry to Constantinople, oh how I enjoyed *bingerle*. GARF 678.2.119, A to D, 21 January 1878, armistice pleasure, bad news from Vienna and London. GARF 678.2.119, A to D, 27 January 1878, wonderful *bingerle* before dinner, English fleet to Constantinople. GARF 678.2.119, A to D, 1 February 1878, love to wake up with you. GARF 678.2.119, A to D, 3 February 1878, nothing from my brother yet; news agitates me, old fool of queen. GARF 678.2.119, A to D, 6 February 1878, more calm if I know we occupy Constantinople. GARF 678.2.119, A to D, 21 February 1878, *bingerle* wanted it and cried "Yes yes." GARF 678.2.119, A to D, 11 March 1878, anguish, bad night. GARF 678.2.120, A to D, 18 March 1878, children make me happy amid tribulations. GARF 678.2.120, A to D, 20 March 1878, Turks more afraid of British than us; I'll join you at 3.30. Dilemma of Prince Alfred, duke of Edinburgh on HMS *Sultan*, Byzantine throne, shows letters to Maria and Empress Marie's letter to Prince Alexander of Hesse on fishwife Victoria: Wilson 376–85. Alexander diaries: GARF 678.2.7. 93, return to Petersburg, 8 December 1877; Ignatiev count, 12 December 1877; 24 December, Sofia taken. GARF 678.2.7.2, Nikolai no confidence, 11 January 1878; GARF 678.2.7.3, Nikolai occupation inevitable/Ignatiev negotiates/ near city, 12 January 1878. GARF 678.2.7.4, Nikolai close to city, success turns head, 13 January 1878. GARF 678.2.7.7, war, five days an eternity, 19 January 1878. GARF 678.2.7.7, Bismarck will mock us/history condemn me, 20 January 1878. GARF 678.2.7.9, war against Britain/enemy Beaconsfield, 26 January 1878. GARF 678.2.7.11, threat to occupy city, 29 and 30 January 1878. GARF 678.2.7.11, orders to take city, 30 January and 1 February 1878. GARF 678.2.7.23, we forgot Bismarck advice/Constantinople gone for ever, 29 March 1878. GARF 678.2.7.25, Nikolai sacked, 15 April 1878. GARF 678.2.8.5, if I had a Bismarck, 5 March 1879. GARF 678.2.8.4, Three Emperors doesn't exist, 6 February 1879. Advance so fast surpassed our wildest assumptions: Miliutin, 12 January 1878; 28 January 1878, excited tsar orders occupation of city; 11 February 1878, now Nikolai hesitates reasonably saving us from catastrophe; 19 February 1878, peace, jubilation.

32. Account of Congress based on Sumner, *Russia and the Balkans*; Geyer 78–80; Steinberg 368–373; Steinberg quotes Disraeli on Gorchakov and the dog 367. Gorchakov vs Disraeli: Salo Baron, *The Jews under Tsars and Soviets* 48. GARF 678.2.120, A to D, 30 April 1878, happy with marshalate; 16 March 1878, sex; 26 May, she reads despatches to him. Berlin: GARF 678.2.122, A to D, 3 June 1878, I fear Congress will end in war; 12 June, slept well after *bingerles*; 17 June, a veritable coalition against us at Berlin; 20 June, *bingerles*, Batumi essential; 22 June, we would fight for Batumi; 27 June, all Europe under genius Bismarck. GARF 641.1.32 Alexander to Marie 10 August 1878: Bismarck plots vs Russia with Austria. Miliutin 2 June to 22 July 1878, negotiations at Berlin and public opinion hostile to government, emperor humiliated; Gorchakov situation beyond powers, 3 April 1876; totally senile, 6 November 1877; tsar loses temper with Gorchakov,

11 October 1877. Bulgaria: medieval size at San Stefano; smaller version at Berlin; new prince Battenberg: Stephen Constant, *Foxy Ferdinand, Tsar of Bulgaria* (henceforth *Ferdinand*) 18–25.

33. Zaionchkovsky 32–91. Daly 1.24–5. Mezentsov assassination attempt: GARF 678.2.122, A to D, 22 May 1878, God bless your pregnancy. GARF 678.2.122, A to D, 4 July 1878, shame of partition of Bulgaria. GARF 678.2.122, A to D, 13 July 1878, delicious Moushka. GARF 678.2.122, A to D, 4 August 1878, Mezentsov killed, "charming century." Crimea: GARF 678.2.122, A to D, 27 August 1878, nervous on police; 4 September 1878, what it costs to leave you; 3 September 1878, birth of baby Ekaterina. To Petersburg: GARF 678.2.122, A to D, 25 September 1878, *bingerles*; 26 September 1878, bleeding from sex?; 8 October 1878, must not get pregnant; 28 October 1878, need to be inside you. Alexander diary: GARF 678.2.7.8, trial of 193 *narodniki* and shooting of Trepov, 24 and 25 January 1878. GARF 678.2.7.34, Mezentsov killed, 4 August 1878; invisible hand, 26 September 1878. GARF 678.2.7.41, gives 10,000 roubles to D, 25 October 1878. GARF 678.2.7.47, my serenity of character not lost, 22 December 1878. GARF 678.2.8.5, Kropotkin killed, 22 February 1879. GARF 678.126, A to D, 1 January 1878, happy new year. Kabul 1878: GARF 641.1.32, Alexander to Marie, 26 August 1878. Ruud 39–42. Daly 1. 24–26

34. GARF 678.2.8.6–8, Alexander diary, miraculously saved/governor-generals, 2–5 April 1879. GARF 678.2.289.22, Katya informed of April 1879 attempt, he weeps, saved me for you. Assassination; Valuev suggests governor-generals: Zaionchkovsky 52–60, inc. Loris-Melikov plan against sedition 56–7; Valuev "half-ruined sovereign"; 78–91 Alexander discusses reform with Valuev, Kostia; 89 Sasha opposes 23 January 1880. Tsar hunted like hare: Tolstoya 26. Marie health: GARF 641.1.31, Serge to Marie, 29 April 1879. GARF 641.1.31, Alexander to Marie, sorry you're unwell, 6 May 1879. GARF 641.1.29, Alexander to Marie, wedding anniversary and reunited soon. GARF 641.1.32, Alexander to Marie, 1, 2 and 4 August 1879, new resources of health, at manoeuvres, glad your health better. GARF 641.1.32, Alexander to Marie, 8 September 1879, memories of Nixa. GARF 641.1.32, Alexander to Marie, 10 August 1878, three executions, Bismarck plots against us with Austria. GARF 641.1.32, Alexander to Marie, 18 August 1879, Marshal Manteuffel arrives with letter from Kaiser Wilhelm dictated by Bismarck listing what Germany has done for us and paid its debts. Move into Winter Palace: Miliutin, 13 May 1881, recounts Adlerberg's version. Alexander and Dolgorukaya: GARF 678.2.129, A to D, 11 March 1880, doubly enjoyed *bingerles*; 19 March 1880, you shared crazy pleasure, the sacred cult of us. GARF 678.2.130, A to D, 10 and 23 April 1880, good to cry out, our good rooms, my real life concentrated in the good moments together. Awkwardness of Katya hidden from children, esp. Sergei and Paul, and Grand Duchess Maria: Beéche 1.120. GARF 678.2.7.26, creates title Yurievsky for son, 24 April 1878. Alexander diary: GARF 678.2.8.10, 10 May 1879, like a novel. GARF 678.2.8.22, 30 August 1879, like a hunted wolf.

35. GARF 678.2.8.26, train bomb 20 November 1879. Miliutin, *Dnevnik* 20 November 1879. GARF 678.2.8.27–8, Alexander diary, threatening letter on desk, 3 December 1879, and news of plan of Winter Palace by terrorists, 4 December 1879. Palace bombing, Khalturin: Tolstoya 34–5. Katya's fears and suspicions of explosives plot: GARF 678.2.289.25–9. Negligence and in Winter Palace tsar very pale, Sasha in panic, Empress Marie hears nothing, she wept: Tolstoya 29–41. Reform: Zaionchkovsky 80–91. Alexander diary: GARF 678.2.8.29, reform and Valuev/Marie won't live long, 1 January 1880; exiles Hendrikova, 14 January 1880. Valuev, *Dnevnik* 47, 9 January 1880, Alexander discussed his 1863 plan. Show Russia a

sign of his trust—Alexander sees Kostia, 13 January 1880, quote from diary of
E. A. Peretts quoted in Zaionchkevsky 84. Winter Palace bomb: GARF 678.2.9.6,
Alexander diary, palace bomb, 5 February 1880. Miliutin, *Dnevnik* 5 February
1880. Sasha diary, 5 February 1880, GARF 677.1.307.319–20. Prince Alexander
of Hesse diary/notes quoted in Lyashchenko, *Alexandr II*, 288. Naryshkin 62–3.
Katya's account: GARF 678.2.289.30–3.

36. Zaionchkovsky 92–3, quotes Kostia. Sandro 57–60. GARF 678.2.9.7, Alexander
diary, Sasha proposes commission, refused, then tsar appoints Loris, 8, 9, 10 February 1880; menace to children, what a nightmare, 16 February 1880. GARF
678.2.9.9, Loris attempt, 20 February 1880. GARF 678.2.9.10, Gogo and execution, 21 February 1880. GARF 678.2.9.10, "poor liberty," 23 February 1880. GARF
678.2.9.13, Katya worries about Gogo's future, 9 March 1880. GARF 678.2.9.13,
Katya: "hang terrorists," 16 March 1880. GARF 678.2.9. 14, Loris unites police, sacks Drenteln, Loris same powers as me, 22 March and 24 March 1880.
Cherevin Jewish memo: Zaionchevsky 338. Sasha and Loris relations: GARF
677.1.307/308. Rieber 104. Zaionchkovsky 92–116, Kostia on Petersburg panic,
Valuev aplomb and arrogance of "Michael I," Saltykov-Schedrin charisma; 330
Loris works with Sasha; 7–14 Loris takes control, "united command"; Loris and
Sasha, 340 Pobedonostsev to E. F. Tyutcheva on Loris's two patrons and third
supporter in a certain woman; 11 April memo, 129–44; appointment of Pobedon-
ostsev 146. Meshchersky on Loris as agile, clever 420–37; sacking of Tolstoy and
Drenteln 439–44. Loris eastern mind, sly eyes, "the Juggler": Naryshkin 63. The
Great Dictator: Sandro 65–6. Miliutin on dictator Loris: Miliutin, *Dnevnik* 10 Feb-
ruary 1880. Police organization: Ruud 48–55. Daly 1.26–31. GARF 678.2.9.18,
Alexander diary, Marie dies, double life ends, Katya demands marriage, Adlerberg warns, 22, 23, 24 May 1880. GARF 678.2.9.19, Alexander diary, coronation,
constitution, then retirement, 25, 26, 27 May 1880. GARF 678.2.9.19, Sasha and
Alexander talk, 30 May 1880. GARF 678.2.9.22–3, Bazhenov archpriest refuses,
Katya advises confide in Sasha, marriage, 28 June, 3, 4 and 6 July 1880. Sasha's
view of his mother's death, Alexander's remarriage, the scum sacred influence of
his mother/Nixa: GARF 642.1.709.13–16, Alexander III (Sasha) to Minny, 22 May
1884. Katya memoirs: GARF 678.2.289.34, if not threat of assassination, we
wouldn't have married during mourning; the wedding, GARF 678.2.289.35–6.
Adlerberg warns against marriage: Miliutin, *Dnevnik* 4.78–9, 18 August 1879.
Adlerberg says tsar in hands of Dolgorukaya, influence increases, Dolgorukaya
sassy, stupid and immature: Miliutin, *Dnevnik* 4.337, 13 May 1881.

37. Byrnes 140–5, Alexander on Pobedonostsev, Pharisee, fanatic; 147–9 Pobedonostsev says I'm a believer against idols; view of Alexander II in 143 letters to Sasha
criticising decisions in 1877–8; in letters to E. Tyutcheva 143–4; and Dostoevsky
93–109. Pobedonostsev on Loris: Byrnes 140. Frank, *Dostoevsky*, works with Meshchersky 617–19, 671, 679 (Meshchersky, Prince Full-stop); friendship with
Pobedonostsev, reveres tsardom 678–9 and 801–7; despises Yids 745; hatred of
Jews 836; meets Romanovs Sergei, Paul, Konstantin Konstantinovich 767, dinner
with Sergei 781; received by Sasha 914.

38. Loris and Katya: Zaionchkovsky 145–7; Katya thinks Loris outstanding; 340 Pobedonostsev to E. F. Tyutcheva on Loris's two patrons and after death of empress,
third supporter in Yurievskaya. Alexander diary, Loris interior minister: GARF
678.2.9.24, Loris—order restored, 6 August 1880. Livadia: GARF 678.2.9.25,
Katya, 16 August 1880. GARF 678.2.9.26, letter to Sasha, money for Katya,
11 September 1880. GARF 678.2.9.29, Yurievsky name close to Romanov, 4 December 1880. Miliutin 22 August 1880; introduced to Katya in Livadia, 26 August

1880; Katya appearance, 4 October 1880; tension with Sasha, 11 October 1880. Alexander II on Sasha: diary 24 January 1881.

39. GARF 678.2.8.5 discusses our States–General/Sasha aggressive/we're very different men, 24 January 1880. Tolstoya 119–21 on Daria Tyutcheva resignation, Alexander II reaction, and Katya curse/criminal affair. Crimea, Katya shares life and death, spite of daughters-in-law, gracious and Loris/Katya alliance: Katya memoirs, GARF 678.2.28.36–42. Zaionchkovsky 174–89, inc. 176 Pobedonostsev to E. F. Tyutcheva on wild insipid illiterate education plan, monstrous absurdity of plan, disgusting meeting; Polovstev diary on heir angry with Loris; and 340 Pobedonostsev to E. F. Tyutcheva on Loris's two patrons and third supporter in a certain woman/it sickens me to look at him. Confrontations with Minny and Sasha, Minny tricked: Naryshkin 64–71. Katya memoirs on family monsters, Sasha incapable of ruling, if only I had someone to succeed me, family dinner on return, how I conducted myself, he acclaims her beauty and female jealousy, Dolgorukys older than Romanovs, Sanny (Grand Duchess Constantine) asks if Katya empress, no wish to be empress, he tells Gogo he loves him, GARF 678.2.289.43–8. I. V. Plotnikova (ed.), *Velikii knyaz Sergei Alexandrovich Romanov: biograficheskie materialy* (henceforth Plotnikova) 3.189, 245–6, Sergei to Alexander Alexandrovich, 19 July 1880, and Alexander Alexandrovich to Sergei, 6 December 1880; Sergei/ Paul discover the news about Alexander II's marriage: 201 Sergei to Maria Fyodorovna, 5 January 1881. Conflict with family over Katya, Alexander at sixty-four like eighteen-year-old, Romanovs meet Katya: Sandro 60–6. Resentment of Loris and Katya; You have no heart, tsar to Minny: Naryshkin 69–71. Ministers meet Katya: Byrnes, Pobedonostsev disgusted "wench" Katya 144.

40. Alexander diary: GARF 678.2.9.31, discusses constitution unlike Europe with Loris and plans Editing Commission, 4 January 1881; Skobolev takes Denguil Tepe, 13 January 1881. GARF 678.2.8.2, second letter warns of Malaya Sadova Street shop, 25 January 1881. GARF 678.2.8.4, special commission to debate reform; Sasha opposes the reform but thanks to Loris, Nabokov and Kostia accepted; I signed; to be read at Council of Ministers on 2 March, 17 February 1881. GARF 678.2.8.4, happiest day of my life, anniversary of serf liberation, 19 February 1881. GARF 678.2.8.4, arrests and search for revolutionaries inc. Perovskaya, 20 February 1881; Loris asks if guards are loyal, 22 February 1881. GARF 678.2.8.5, warning given to Katya's brother Prince A. Dolgoruky, 23 February 1881. GARF 678.2.8.5, Miliutin backs reforms to save dynasty, 25 February 1881. GARF 678.2.8.6, Loris to publish *ukaz* on coronation and constitution on same day, 26 February 1881; Zhelyabov arrested; 27 February 1881; Valuev advises avoid Malaya Sadova, 28 February 1881. Daly 1.31. Abaza, throne can't rest on a million bayonets, quoted in Orlando Figes, *People's Tragedy* (henceforth Figes, *PT*) 41. Retire to America: GARF 678.289.10, Katya. Zaionchkovsky 174–89; 28 January 1881 Loris memo 179–81; Lenin's view 182. Meetings on constitution, Loris excludes Pobedonostsev: Byrnes 147–150. GARF 678.2.8.2, Alexander diary, someone near me who counts left to live (e.g. Sasha), 24 January 1881.

41. GARF 678.2.8.8, tsar writes diary at 8 a.m. on Loris optimism, reforms, coronation then retirement, decision to ignore all warnings, inc. that of Katya. Last *bingerles* with Katya: Dr. Botkin to A. S. Suvorin, *Dnevnik A.S. Suvorina* 66, diary entry 14 September 1893. Sandro 70–4. Adrian Dvorzhitsky, 1 Marta 1881, *Istorichesskii vestnik* (1913) 1. Details of conspiracy: *1 Marta 1881 goda. Po neizdannym materialam; Delo 1 Marta: protsess Zheliabova, Perovskoi i dr pravitelsvennyi otchet.* Tsar very good mood, at Manège, at deathbed, Sasha and Katya hold head: Miliutin, *Dnevnik* 1/2 March 1881, 272–5. Andrei Maylunas and Sergei Mironenko (eds.), *A Lifelong Passion: Nicholas and Alexandra: Their Own Story* (henceforth *LP*), Bill

of Indictment, 1 March 1881 1–4. Sasha's view of his mother's death, Alexander's remarriage, "the scum burst out" leading to 1 March: GARF 642.1.709.13–16, Alexander III (Sasha) to Minny 22 May 1884. Fear of bombers en route to Sunday parades, Loris warns of attacks: Katya memoirs, GARF 678.2.289.54. Tolstoya 191–7: Nelidova runs in to tell Tolstoya, the scene at deathbed, Sasha sobbing on chest of father then embraces Yurievskaya, bloodstained tunic, children enter with Shebeko.

42. Zaionchkovsky 203–38; on Baranov 349; on Gatchina security 197; 8 March Council 206–7; 211–15 Ignatiev memo, 12 March; 217 tsar lost in indecision, Pobedonostsev; 222 "living with madmen and they think I am an idiot not from nineteenth century but from sixteenth," Pobedonostsev to Tyutcheva, 10 April 1881; 227–39 the 21 April Council and Alexander's Manifesto, inc. 235 AIII to Pobedonostsev approving Manifesto, 27 April 1881. Pobedonostsev letters to Alexander III and Tyutcheva in Byrnes 150–64. Escape to Gatchina, skunks and first days in power: Sandro 75–9. Gatchina fortress and Baranov: Miliutin, *Dnevnik* 4.45–51. The correspondence of Pobedonostsev and Alexander III is published in *Pisma Pobedonostseva k Alexandru III*, vol. 1. Comedy: Valuev, *Dnevnik 1877–1884*, 23 March 1881. 8 March Council: diaries of Miliutin, Valuev and Perretts. 27 April Council meeting and 28–29 April meeting at Loris house and shock of Manifesto: Miliutin diary. Vorontsov-Dashkov (VD) warns of attacks: GARF 677.1.741.96, VD to AIII, 3 March 1881. Alexander III exhilarated by sacking Loris: Plotnikova 3.248, AIII to Sergei Alexandrovich. On atmosphere on accession: I. A. Shestakov, *Polveka obyknovennoi zhizni* (henceforth Shestakov, *Polveka*) 738–40, accession of Alexander III, sacking of Kostia, appointment of Alexis after emperor constantly "repeated that grand dukes should not head departments . . . sudden impulse," a saturnalia of autocracy, honest people sacked, my soul aches. Incapacity of Alexander III in Katya memoirs: GARF 678.2.289.43. Tsar makes settlement with Katya Yurievskaya via Loris and Adlerberg: GARF 677.1.4.43, Adlerberg to AIII, 10 April 1881. GARF 677.1.519, Loris to AIII, 10 April 1881. Grand Duke Sergei visits Katya Yurievskaya, disgusting: Plotnikova 3.214, Sergei to Konstantin Konstantinovich (KR), 17 September 1881. Sacking of Kostia: Beéche 1.62–4. Sacking of Nikolai Nikolaievich and sex mania: Paul Robinson, *Grand Duke Nikolai Nikolaevich: Supreme Commander of the Russian Army* (henceforth Robinson) 36. Beéche 1.77. Nikolai begs Alexander III for nobility and titles for illegitimate children: RGIA 919.2.2454.88, AIII to 22 November 1882. Zaionchkovsky 2.21–23.

### SCENE 3: COLOSSUS

1. Sacred influence on AIII of his mother and Nixa: GARF 642.1.709.13–16, Alexander III (Sasha) to Minny, 22 May 1884. Sweet Minny, missing you: GARF 642.1.709.19–22, AIII to Maria Fyodorovna (Minny), 9 May and 12 May 1884. Dinner with Nicky and Georgy, GARF 642.1.608.11–17, AIII to Minny, 13 May 1884. GARF 642.1.709, Minny to AIII, 21 May 1884, pleased you missed me. How not to behave, Bertie prince of Wales's baccarat scandal: GARF 642.1.709.117, AIII to Minny, 2 June 1891. Zaionchkovsky 2.14–19. Russian brutality necessary in a Russian tsar: A. A. Mossolov, *At the Court of the Last Tsar* (Mossolov) 3–5. Witte 28–30: Alexander III straight-talking, not unintelligent, worry about fatness; 37–41 limited education, gifted with broad sympathetic understanding which in ruler more important than rational brilliancy; doused Misha with hose and Misha soaked him back. Edward W. Wcislo, *Tales of Imperial Russia: The Life and Times of Sergei Witte* (Wcislo) on Alexander III: imposing, bear-like, husky and fat, in appearance "an absolute lout like a big Russian peasant" but enormous

character, words never differed from his actions 130–33. AIII anti-social, at ball he hides, empress dances: Shestakov diary, 2 February 1887, quoted in Zoia Belyakova, *Velikii Knyaz Alexei Alexandrovich. Za i protiv* (henceforth Belyakova) 153. Hall 117–31: Minny's style and sociability. Children at Gatchina: John Van der Kiste and Coryne Hall, *Once a Grand Duchess: Xenia, Sister of Nicholas II* (henceforth *Xenia*) 10–12, inc. Minny dislike of Gatchina and Sasha happy. Paul Kulikovsky, Karen Roth-Nicholls and Sue Woolmans (eds.), *25 Chapters of my Life: The Memoirs of Grand Duchess Olga Alexandrovna* (henceforth *Olga*) 31–44. Family games: Edward J. Bing (ed.), *Letters of Tsar Nicholas and the Empress Marie* (henceforth Bing) 28, Nicky to Minny, 15 May 1884. Sasha's humorous eyes: Sandro 139. Papa turned on the hose: Nicholas II diary is at GARF 601.1.217–266 (henceforth ND with date)—ND 7 June 1884. Papa so dear and kind to me: *LP*, Nicky to Alexandra of Hesse, 8 May 1894. Sandro 161 on Nicky and two brothers: Georgy the cleverest of the three, Misha simplicity of manner, favourite. Hall 117–31 Cherevin best friend, Cherevin character refined courtier mixed with primeval savage, sees world in two halves, despise Vladimir, Romanovs accuse Cherevin of drunkenness, AIII when cross "like a gloomy bear," AIII backed Cherevin, AIII lying on back drinking, 1880s doctors ban drink, watched by Minny, Cherevin and AIII hide drink in boots, Mother of Invention: P. N. Lebedev, *Cherevin i Alexandr III*, *Golos minuvshego* (1917) 5/6.96–101. Zaionchkovsky 2.338 quoting Mossolov; ego big, drunk, Witte quoted 225.

2. Alexis as admiral: Shestakov, *Polveka* 738–40, accession of Alexander III, sacking of Kostia; appointment of Alexis. I. A. Shestakov, diary: RGA VMF 26.1.1–7, Alexis indifferent to everything, 24 April 1882; how lazy my Grand Duke, 2 May 1882; does not think about right things, 26 December 1883; infuriates me, 27 June 1884. Alexis and Zina: Marie queen of Romania, *Story of My Life* (henceforth "Marie of Romania"), 1.92. Laziness of Alexis: Belyakova 161–7, Sandro on Alexis "Beau" Brummel best looking, only interested in "love-making, food and liquor," fast women, slow ships 188–9 and pagan Zina 171–2. On grand dukes in politics: Zaionchkovsky 2.21–3. Family Law changed: Hall 119, stop playing the tsar 116.

3. Zaionchkovsky 263–6; Alexander comment on Gospel 364. Alexander hatred of Jews and on Tolstoy, Sergei and Durnovo policies: Zaionchkovsky 2.72–7. Anti-semitism of Alexander and Sergei 328 and 377 Alexander's special hatred of Jews: Polovtsov diary, 18 April 1890. "Rotten Jew": Bruce Lincoln, *In War's Dark Shadow*, 30. Baron 45–50 and 356. Pobedonostsev—third of Jews must disappear: Hall 142. Anti-semitism of AIII and entourage: Cherevin Jewish memo: Zaionchkovsky 338. Marie Kleinmichel, *Memories of a Shipwrecked World* 129. Pobedonostsev anti-semitism: Byrnes 205 letter to Dostoevsky on Jews as ulcer. Frank, *Dostoevsky*, novelist shares views on Jews with Pobedonostsev, reveres tsardom 678–9 and 801–7; despises Yids 745; hatred of Jews 836. GARF 677.1.741.104–9, Vorontsov-Dashkov to AIII, 2 May 1882, warns against anti-semitic policies. New security: Daly 1.32–41. Emigration of Jews to America: figures from Shmuel Ettinger, Jewish Emigration in the 19th Century: Migration—Within and from Europe—as a Decisive Factor in Jewish Life (at www.myjewishlearning.com/article/jewish-emigration-in-the-19th-century/2/).

4. Zaionchkovsky 241–303; Zemsky Sobor 287–98. Anti-semitic policies: Zaionchkovsky 2.72–7. On schemes to sell Jews by Ignatiev: Baron 356. Naryshkin 86: Ignatiev Mentir Pasha. GARF 677.1.741.104–9, Vorontsov-Dashkov to AIII, 2 May 1882, Ignatiev's lies. Ignatiev had mentioned the Zemsky Sobor idea when he talked to Alexander Alexandrovich at Livadia in 1870; Ignatiev memoirs, GARF 730.1.161.5. Alexander III on literature: Byrnes, Pobedonostsev view of Leo Tolstoy as dangerous lunatic 256–7. Rosamund Bartlett, *Tolstoy*, tsar sees him as

"godless nihilist" 252; Tolstoy asks for mercy for Alexander II assassins—"Our Christ not your Christ," replied Pobedonostsev; AIII receives Sonia Tolstoy and permits *Kreutzer Sonata* publication 331. Zaionchkovsky 2:176: Alexander III censors Tolstoy.

5. Zaionchkovsky 252–5; Cherevin bid to take control of Police Department and Gendarmes defeated by Ignatiev 253. Daly 1:32–48: Sacred Retinue, emergency laws, new security forces under Ignatiev and Tolstoy, Sudeikin, Rachkovsky, Degaev. P. N. Durnovo: Abraham Ascher, *P. A. Stolypin: The Search for Stability in Late Imperial Russia* (henceforth *Stolypin*), 48. Founding of Sacred Retinue: Sergei Witte, *The Memoirs of Count Witte* (henceforth Witte) 22–5.

6. Zaionchkovsky 2.276: AIII drunk with power—Lamsdorf; Peter without the cudgel—Vannovsky. AIII bureaucrat obliteration: Figes, PT 7. AIII, long relationship with VD: GARF 677.741.1, VD to Tsarevich Alexander Alexandrovich, 28 July 1866; advice on military appointments during 1877 war, GARF 677.1.741.6, VD to Alexander Alexandrovich, 9 December 1877; advises move to Winter Palace for security, GARF 677.1.741.96, VD to AIII, 3 March 1881; on famine, cut the balls and banquets as contribution to committee for food, it would make decent impression, GARF 677.1.741.138, VD to AIII, 27 August 1891. Spała article and resignation of Vorontsov-Dashkov and AIII reply: AIII to VD (end of September/ beginning of October 1890): RGIA 919.2.1166.2; VD to AIII about his resignation (4 October 1890): GARF 677.1.741.117; AIII to VD, in which tsar refuses resignation, calls VD friend and assistant (5 October 1890): RGIA 919.2.1214.253–4; the article on AII in *Spala: Pravitelstvenny vestnik* in 1890, nos. 212, 214 and 215. On digest of memoranda, on triumvirate of Vorontsov, Richter and Cherevin: N. A. Yepanchin, *Na sluzhbe tyrokh imperatorov* 165–7. Relations with ministers: Sandro 75–86. AIII and Pobedonostsev: Zaionchkovsky 2. 23–29; AIII and Dmitri Tolstoy 29–31.

7. Coronation: GARF 642.1.608.25, AIII to Minny, 16 May 1884. Sandro 86–91. Wortman 270–9. Hall 101–6. Alexander III personally supervises Khodynka Field: Sandro 192.

8. Foreign policy. Three Emperors League: Steinberg 384–7; 423–4. Afghanistan and near war with Britain: Geyer 113–15; Bulgaria and Three Emperors, Montenegro: 115–21. Tensions with Austria over Bulgaria, AIII view of Ferdinand of Coburg: *Ferdinand* 52–5, 103–14. Toast to Montenegro: Sandro 80. Montenegrin marriages and King Nikola: Elizabeth Roberts, *Realm of the Black Mountain: A History of Montenegro* (*Montenegro*) 261–7. Christopher Clark, *The Sleepwalkers: How Europe Went to War in 1914* (henceforth Clark) 91–2. AIII on public opinion to Giers: Dominic Lieven, *Nicholas II* (henceforth Lieven, *NII*) 92. Arbiters of public opinion Katkov and Meshchersky, Dmitri Tolstoy: Zaionchkovsky 2.29–31; on Katkov 31–7; on Meshchersky 37–41. Meshchersky 420–45. Frank, *Dostoevsky*, works with Meshchersky 617–9, 671, 679 (Meshchersky, Prince Full-stop). Katkov on foreign policy: Geyer 111.

9. Noise followed by a jolt, *Olga* 22. Nicky's account: Plotnikova 3.211, Nicholas Alexandrovich to Sergei, 17 December 1889. Awful event: Bing 40, Nicky to Minny, 20 October 1889. Hall 137. Witte 28–36: meets Alexander III, Jewish railway, that blunt fellow, appointment to government. Wcislo 133–4: AIII, "my travel is forbidden because it's a Yid line"; Witte character 135, a certain "lack of restraint and brazenness of speech part of my character." Rise of Witte: Geyer 130–45. On Vladimir: Beéche 1.113, Vladimir, CO the Guards, arts and Diaghilev; Sandro 156–7. Nationalities: 1897 census quoted in Stephen Kotkin, *Stalin*, vol. 1: *Paradoxes of Power, 1878–1928* (henceforth Kotkin) 56. Statistics on nationalities: Figes, PT 79–81; Lenin worse the better quoted 129; SRs founded 163. David Shim-

melpenninck van der Oye, *Toward the Rising Sun: Russian Ideologies of Empire and the Path to War with Japan* (henceforth Oye) 61–81: Witte, character, vision economic growth and Far Eastern railway. Witte on possibilities of Asia to Alexander III, quoted in Geoffrey Hosking, *Russia and the Russians* 329. On Stalin and seminary, see Simon Sebag Montefiore, *Young Stalin*. Kotkin 11–12. Famine: GARF 677.1.741.138, VD to AIII, 27 August 1891.

10. Sandro 158–60: "flaunted his many peculiarities"; Ella "ravishing beauty, rare intelligence, delightful sense of humour." Marie of Romania on Serge, Ella 1.93–97. Grand dukes in politics: Zaionchkovsky 2.21–3. Sergei Moscow governorship: Zaionchkovsky 2.22–3, 38, 72–6, 97. Wortman 311–12. Witte 380: Sergei and Durnovo anti-semitism to please, "Jew-baiting at court very predominant." Sergei buggering chaplain: John Röhl, *Wilhelm II: the Kaiser's Personal Monarchy* ("Rohl 1")123. Sergei sad to leave regiment and cries, funny sad, the job doesn't scare me, it interests me very much: Plotnikova 3.356, Sergei to Nicky, 30 May 1891. Jewish emigration—111,000 in 1892, 137,000 in 1892: figures from Ettinger, Jewish Emigration in the 19th Century. On marriage and character: Beéche 1.136–44. Sergei and Ella marriage: Christopher Warwick, *Ella: Princess, Saint and Martyr* (henceforth *Ella*) 82–4; Sergei character 85–93; Jerusalem 93–7; Guards 98; arrival of Ella 101–4; sex 130–3; Ella Jerusalem revelation 144–6; marriage of Grand Duke Paul and Princess Alexandra of Greece (Grand Duchess Alexandra Georgievna) 151; Moscow pogrom 165. Sergei and Ella: *LP* 256–7 quoting from Marie Pavlovna's memoirs; 265 Ella to Nicky, 26 February 1904, "He loved order."

11. Germany and France: Alexander to Giers, August 1885: *American Historical Journal*, 25.3 (Apr 1920), 394; 391–40, L. B. Packard, "Russia and the Dual Alliance." Geyer 157–60, 172–7. Steinberg 436–7; on decision to discontinue Reinsurance 450, 460. Röhl 1.31–7: Willy "visit to Petersburg 1888 and tsar" view of Willy; visit to Germany 1889 218–25; on Willy's health and sanity 298–9 and 334; Reinsurance Treaty 335–47; French at Kronstadt 364–5; relations with Willy 473–8. AIII literally nauseated by boy monkey Wilhelm: Lebedev 96–101.

12. Nicky never laughed, rarely cried, loved army: Sandro 186–7. Witte 179: inexperienced but rather intelligent, well mannered, good breeding concealed shortcomings; views Englishman as a Jew 189. Wcislo 139, Alexander III to Witte—Nicky a boy and uninterested in state affairs. Cherevin, AIII's favourite child Georgy/ unimpressed by NII: Lebedev 96–101. Nicky distance, imperial mist—Marie Romania 2.65 and 2.326. Zaionchkovsky 2.19–21, inc. Lamsdorf half-boy half-man quote; wild parties in Guards; influence of Pobedonostsev and Meshchersky; 29 funny Jewish stories, Nicky to Minny, 5 September 1884. Polovtsov, *Dnevnik* 26 January 1892. *LP* 67: "You don't know how sly I can be," Nicky to Alix, 2 June 1894. Sandro 186—thin education but with excellent English. Lieven, *NII* 106, tells Pobedonostsev "I always agree with everyone and then do things in my way." Lieven, *NII* 28–43, inc. quotes from Olga, on being childish, quotes from Vladimir Ollongren on Alexander calling Nicky "girly"; influence of Heath, reading habits, self-control, intelligence, preparation to rule. On Nicky's view of newspapers as a Jew sitting there: Röhl 1.758, Nicholas to Helmuth von Moltke 1895. Limited horizons, sailor suits: Hirsch 161. Jews horsedealers, Hirsh at Sandringham: Bing 84, Nicky to Minny, June 1894. Alexander Orlov, Nicky's only unique friend: Spiridovich 1.285–6. Patrimonial views of tsardom Census of 1897: "Khozyain Zemli Russkoy/Khozyayka Zemli Russkoy": GARF, F.601. Inv. 1. File 2. Fol. 2, 28 January 1897. Figes, *PT* 6–7. Robinson on Nicky's fear of Nikolasha 35. Correspondence between Nicky and Sergei: Plotnikova 3. First meeting with Kshessinskaya: Coryne Hall, *Imperial Dancer: Mathilde Kschessinska and the Romanovs* (henceforth *Dancer*) 13–15; recommendations for Nicky from Cherevin

and Pobedonostsev 18; first meetings 20–1. Nicky in town all the time, Alexander alone at Gatchina: GARF 642.1.710.54–7, Alexander III (Sasha) to Minny, 16 April 1892. Training for tsar: childishness: ND 24 January 1894, hide and seek like little children. Preparations for rule: Nicky helping with English in letters to Queen Victoria: GARF 642.1.709.19–22, AIII to Minny, 12 May 1884. ND 17 December 1893: went to Council of State, wormed out of Committee of Ministers; 17 January 1894, visited regiment and Council of State; at Papa's request read report from defence minister; 24 January 1894 read papers of Siberian Committee. Nicky's fun upbringing with his father, games with donkeys: Bing 28, Nicky to Minny, 15 May 1884. Alexander II's calm: Zeepvat, *Romanov Autumn* 16. Meeting with Alix: ND 27 May 1884; 19 November 1884.

13. Alix. Golden hair/look: Anna Vyrubova, *Memories of the Russian Court* (henceforth Vyrubova) 3. Queen Victoria, your very loving, grateful and dutiful child: *LP* 28, Alix to Victoria, 26 December 1893; 52 my sweet Alicky, watch over her, Alix's nerves, 22 April 1894; 64 Alix's nerves, treatment, her father's death, anxiety over brother, Victoria to Nicky, 25 May 1894. Benckendorff on Alexandra, "a will of iron linked to not much brain and no knowledge," Lieven, *NII* 227. Pierre Gilliard, *Thirteen Years at the Russian Court* (henceforth Gilliard) 16. Alexandra— Ernest of Hesse on her strength, need for superior will to bridle, tsar an angel but doesn't know how to treat her: Naryshkin 204. Meets Nicky, mentions in ND: 27 May 1884; 19 November 1884; 31 January 1889 to 27 February 1889 on Alix's visit 1889.

14. World tour: Oye 15–23. Minny's advice and anxiety about Georgy illness, Nicky behaviour, assassination attempt: Bing 43, Minny to Nicky on Georgy illness; 46 Minny to Nicky, 16 January 1891, 59, "Papa and I at the end of our strength; second time God's saved you, like Borki," Minny to Nicky, 6 May 1891. Hall 144–7. NII. Sandro 189. World tour: Oye 219. Willy's views of sex on tour, and hidden jewels: Röhl 1.125.

15. ND: talked about marriage with Papa, "my dream to marry Alix"; only obstacle religion; Eddy withdrawn, 21 December 1891; Minny hints about Hélène, daughter of comte de Paris, 29 January 1892; two loves coexist, Alix and K, 29 January 1892; once loved Princess Olga Dolgorukaya, ND 1 April 1892; permission to start finding out about Alix, 10 January 1893. Ella to Nicky on prayers in Jerusalem: *LP*, Ella to Nicky, 19 June 1889. Ella role in romance: Ella 150–3, 174–6. Minny on Nicky–Alix romance: Hall 150–3. Nicky and Little K: *Dancer* 23–44. Little K: ND, dashed to see my MK, 29 January 1893; London wedding no attractive women, 18 June 1893; round ball on legs, Queen Victoria, 19 June; everyone finds great resemblance between me and Georgy, 20 June. Alix cannot be untrue to faith: *LP* 24, Alix to Xenia, 8 November 1893; 25 Alix to Nicky, can't do it against conscience. Sergei and Ella as intermediaries: Sergei's diary, GARF 648.1.29:286, 9 October 1893; 290, 13 October 1893; total reprimand from Sergei, to Nicky, GARF 601.1.1340.81–2, 14 October 1893; Alix invites Nicky—Grand Duchess Ella to Nicky—GARF 601.1.1253.42, 18 October 1893. Everything is over: ND 18 November 1893. *LP* 26, Nicky to Alix, 17 December 1893, the depth of our religion. Looks: Vyrubova 3. Nicky social life in Guards, four-day binge: ND 26 November 1893; parties at Vorontsovs', Trubetskois', card games, macao with Uncle Alexei; 12 January 1894, Uncle Vladimir to club, tipsy; 24 January, hide and seek like little children; 26 January, best ladies at Montebello party; 27 February, dancing for nine hours with Sandro; 8 March, soirée at Aunt Miechen's, seventy gypsies, fun and chatted to Pototsky; 25 March, to gypsies with Sandro and Konstantin Konstantinovich (KR). Hide-and-seek: Polovstov, *Dnevnik* 26 January 1894. Nicky's life in the Guards: Zaionchkovsky 2.20. Nicky delight in Guards life: *LP* 13, Nicky

to Alix, 23 May 1889. Childishness: ND 24 January 1894. Attends ministers: ND 17 December 1893; 17 January 1894, v regiment and Council of State; 24 January 1894, Siberian Committee. Alexander's first illness: ND 17 January 1894. Departure for Coburg: ND 2 April 1894. LP 36, KR diary, 3 April 1894—Minny advises ask Queen Victoria. Coburg: ND 5 April 1894, Alix sad, arrival of Victoria in pomp, talked for hours; 6 April, Willy arrives; 7 April, wedding; 8 April, wonderful day, my betrothal; 9–15 April, reactions, excitement, tea with Victoria. LP 40, Nicky to Minny, 10 April 1894; 42 Minny to Nicky, 10 April; Minny to Nicky, 14 April; AIII to Nicky, 14 April; 50 all my life belonged to you, Nicky to Alix, 20 April; 52 my sweet Alicky, watch over her most anxiously, Alix's nerves, "I am the only person answerable for her," an orphan, no one but me, your devoted Grandmama, 22 April; 61 Victoria as old belly woman, Nicky to Georgy, 9 May; 61 Alix in Harrogate/public/bathchair, Alix to Nicky and Nicky to Alix, 10, 13, 16 May; 64 Alix's nerves, treatment, her father's death, anxiety over brother etc., Queen Victoria to Nicky, 25 May; 65 Alix on "new position," Alix to Victoria, 28 May. Bing 73: Minny's delight, 10 April 1894; Nicky's account of engagement, Nicky to Minny, 10 April. Nicky in England, locked in lavatory: ND 14 June 1894; Sandringham ND 17, 26 June, with Bertie, Franz Ferdinand, Empress Eugénie. Part of English family, too hot, in tailcoat: LP 72, Nicky to Georgie, 29 June 1894. Jewish horsedealers, Hirsch at Sandringham: Bing 84, Nicky to Minny, June 1894. LP 75, Alix to Nicky, 10 July 1894, passion burning; 81 Nicky to Alix, 22 July, you've got me entirely. Little K anon letters to Alix: Dancer 44–5; and K's new protectors Sergei Mikhailovich and Andrei Vladimirovich 66–83. Nicky confession and Alix forgiveness: ND 8 July 1894. Wedding of Xenia and Sandro: Olga 45–6. LP 61, Nicky to Georgy, 9 May 1894 improper kissing; Georgy to Nicky, 9 June, sexy gymnastics of Xenia and Sandro. Sandro wedding: Sandro 150–4. Hall 150–3.

16. Bing 86, Papa tired and insomnia on cruise on yacht Tsarevna, Minny to Nicky, 27 June 1894; after illness starts, Cherevin drinking: Zaionchkovsky 2.19. Illness: ND 11 August and 15 September 1894. LP 84–9, Nicky to Alix, 11 August 1894; 11 September, enchantress, I'm gelatine; 15 September, to Livadia. Alix comment and Alexander death: ND 10–20 October 1894. Olga 47–8, inc. Nicky unhappy at burden; wedding to Alix 48. Sandro 190. Charlotte Zeepvat, Romanov Autumn, 146–7. Ella on the death scene to Queen Victoria: Ella 178. Minny's breakdown: Hall 155–64. Accession Nicholas II: ND 20–30 October 1894. Olga 47–8. Death of Colossus and Nicky's crisis: Sandro 190–1. Arrangements of funeral, role of prince of Wales: Hall 164–7.

17. ND 20 October–1 November. On Yanishev asking AIII re preparation of heir: KR, 7 December 1894. Greg King, The Court of the Last Tsar: Pomp, Power and Pageantry in the Reign of Nicholas II (henceforth King) 325–42; Olga Alexandrovna quotes.

### SCENE 4: MASTER OF THE LAND

1. ND 1, 2, 3 November 1894. Black face of AIII: KR 3 November 1894. This account of the funeral is based on King 325–42. Too little of Alix: ND 1, 2, 36, 7 November 1894. KR on funeral: 7 November.

2. ND, 8, 9, 14, 15, 17 November 1894. LP 104, Duke of York to Queen Victoria, 16 November 1894; 100 Georgy to Nicky, 9 November, missing wedding; 108 Nicky to Georgy, 19 November, strength not to break down. KR 15 November 1894. King 343–57.

3. New life starts: Nicky to Georgie 19 November—LP 114. KR 10 November 1894,

on better to sacrifice one uncle; 14 November 1894 on uncles try to influence; Minny aggrieved; 15 November 1894, wedding and sacrifice; N overloaded with work; in his study 18 November. Nicky "gentle, dwarfed by giant" uncles: Marie of Romania 2.65. Uncles: Sandro 155–160 and 194–5. No real secretariat/chancellery: Lieven NII 11–121. Sealing envelopes/distrust of secretaries: Mossolov, 10–12.

4. ND 17 January 1895, senseless dreams. "Father never once mentioned responsibilities that awaited him" and AIII's comment to Yanishev: KR 7 December 1894. Sergei vs Vorontsov on coronation and threat to resign: Naryshkin 146.

5. Nicky's daily life, micro-managing, horse and carriage for Alix: GARF 553.1.6.5, NII to Benckendorff, 1896; Easter eggs GARF 553.1.6.47, NII to Benckendorff, 20 March 1915. Love life, whistle: Vyrubova 4; Alexandra to Countess Rantzau quoted 12; unable to order cakes 27; Court, black Nubian Guards: this is based on the research of Penny Wilson—see http://forum.alexanderpalace.org/index .php?topic=348.0;wap2. Joseph T. Fuhrman (ed.), *The Complete Wartime Correspondence of Tsar Nicholas II and the Empress Alexandra* (henceforth F): we make one, F 41, Alexandra (A) to Nicholas (N), 17 November 1914; thanks for happiness/life as riddle, F 300, A to N, 12 November 1915; nicknames Lovebird etc., F 55, A to N, 26 November 1914; I want you so, Madame B, F 447, N to A, 8 April 1916; Oh Pussy, F 450, A to N, 10 April 1916; F 424, I kiss with tenderness/your shyness, A to N, 26 March 1916; "tell boysy that lady," F 374, A to N, 1 February 1916; your sweet lips, F 373, A to N, 13 January 1916; F 380, girly kisses, A to N, 4 February 1916; F 366, "burn with impatience to see," A to N, 13 January 1916; couldn't have endured burden without you, my shyness, F 339, N to A, 31 December 1915; always doing it, F 324, A to N, 12 December 1915; F 506, Boysy hops, 16 June 1916. Interior decoration: GARF 553.1.6.4, NII to Benckendorf, 1895. Alix pregnant? KR 11 December 1894.

6. ND 25, 26, 27 November 1894; 28 September 1895, on mauve room sofa; 1 January 1896, ceremonials; 28 March 1896, Easter kissing 1600. KR 14 November 1896, on Vladimir vs Minny. Coronation preparations: GARF 644.1.204.97–8, Sergei to Pavel, 15 April 1894. Sergei vs Vorontsov on coronation and threat to resign: Naryshkin 146. Immersed in preparations, discussion with Nicholas over details of coronation ceremonies: GARF 601.1.1340.114, Nicholas to Sergei, undated. *LP* 108, Nicky to Georgy, 19 November 1894; 120 Willy to Nicky, 14 September and 13 October 1894; 124 Nicky to Georgy, 18 December 1895; 130 Ella to Nicky, 20 April 1896. Sandro 195 on uncles.

7. *Koronatsionnye torzhestva*, 89. KR 8, 9 14 necklace broke, May 1895; 18 May, bodies seen by KR's brother Dmitri; 29 May, blames Sergei, photograph; 29 May, Pahlen appointment and Sergei threat. *LP* 138–9, Xenia diary, 18, 19 May; Olga memoirs; 144–5 Nicky to Georgy, 29 July 1896; Georgy to Nicky, 5 August 1896. ND 9, 17, 18 May 1896. Sandro 191–4: coronation, warning about Khodynka, the Montebello ball. Jewels dropped in ceremony, 3,000 dead, findings of Pahlen: S. L. Seeger (ed.), Alexander Izvolsky, *Recollections of a Foreign Minister: The Memoirs of Alexander Izvolsky* (henceforth Izvolsky) 69–70. Joyless Alix: Marie Roumania 2.65–79. Coronation, Zizi becomes lady-in-waiting, Khodynka, Sergei vs Vorontsov on coronation and threat to resign, wagons of corpses: Naryshkin 146–50. Hall 181–2. King 357–88. Nicky's view of tsar and God, dangerous to stop halfway/my terrible responsibility before my Maker: Bing 166, Nicky to Minny, 20 October 1902. Court officials/statistics: King 97–109.

8. Nicky on family vs national diplomacy: *LP* 145, Nicky to Victoria, 10 October 1896. Ottoman crisis: Geyer 192. Byrnes 131. Witte 186–7. Sean McMeekin, *The Russian Origins of the First World War* (henceforth McMeekin) 144. Far Eastern

policy 1894–1900: Geyer 187–205. Oye 5–15; world tour 15–23; Nicky's vision 49–53; Witte's *pénétration pacifique* 61–81. Germany: Röhl 1.749–60, 929–31; Kiaochow 954–61. Kaiser visit: Bing 128–9, Nicky to Minny, 23 July and 1 August 1897. Railway, Chinese Eastern Railway and annexation of Port Arthur: Witte 82–104. Eastern policy: Lobanov-Rostovsky, French mistress, Jewish books: Dominic Lieven, *Russia's Rulers under the Old Regime* (henceforth Lieven, *RR*) 198–9. Alexandra's personality: correspondence with Queen Victoria quoted in Figes, *PT* 26–8. Marie of Romania 2. 67. Death of Lobanov on train: Naryshkin 152. Priggish Alix and Hamlet: Beéche 2.119. Silver Age: Bruce Lincoln, *In War's Dark Shadow*, 349–88.

9. Oye on Kuropatkin 86–91; Kaiser and Far East 146–58. Izvolsky 70 on Muraviev sycophancy. Bing 137, Nicky to Minny, 18 March 1898. Witte to Alexander III on Russian domination of Asia: Geoffrey Hosking, *Russia and the Russians* 329.

10. Oye on Ukhtomsky 42–59; on Kuropatkin and warning to Nicholas 86–97. Alexei Kuropatkin, *Dnevnik generala A. N. Kuropatkina* (henceforth Kuropatkin), 7 April 1898 and 22 September 1899.

11. *LP* 172, Georgy to Nicky, 15 June 1899; Georgy funeral 176—Xenia diary, 14 July 1899. ND 14 June 1899. KR 14 June 1899.

12. Oye on Boxers 159–71; Manchuria 172–86; Lamsdorf 167; Manchuria, Korea, comments to Prince Heinrich of Prussia 182–5. Bing 137–4, Nicky to Minny on Port Arthur, 18 March 1898; Beijing, 11 August 1900; Boer War, 9 November 1900; taking Mukden, 23 September 1900. Witte 107–14 on Nicholas's thirst for conquest, Kuropatkin seizing Manchuria, Kuropatkin flightiness, courtier charms empress. Believe in myself: Meshchersky Letters, Nicky to Meshchersky, 28 February 1903. Geyer 206–12. 100 per cent Byzantine, Witte quoted in Figes, *PT* 21.

13. Illness in Livadia: Witte 194–5. LP, Xenia diary, 26 October to 13 November 1900. Alix inadequacy in politics: Mosolov 1.32–4. Birth of Anastasia: ND 5 June 1900. KR 6 June 1900. *LP* 189; death of Queen Victoria and Nicky to Edward VII, 22 May 1901. Moscow enchantment: *LP* 181, Nicky to Xenia, 5 April 1900. Meetings with Philippe "Our Friend": ND 10, 11, 13, 17, 19, 20, 21 July. *LP* 193, Alix on Mr. P, "one comfort to me," 27 August 1900; 194 interor ministry police report on Philippe. Bing 144: such ecstasy, Nicky to Minny, 5 April 1900. Vyrubova: definition of communion with God and prophets but dislike of table-tipping and spiritualism 67–9. Witte 195–204: craze of occultism, Montenegrins nurse Alix, rise of Philippe. Supernatural faith of Nikolai Nikolaevich (Nikolasha) quote by his chaplain Father Georgi Shavelskii in Robinson 14 and known as Terrible Uncle (Diadia Groznyi) 3. Bond of religious ecstasy and links between Montenegrins and Alexandra: Naryshkina 163; Dr. Philippe's prophecy of Far East 174.

14. B. A. Romanov, *Ocherki diplomaticheskoi istorii Russko–Iaponskoi voiny 1895–1907* 111–12. Oye on Bezobrazov 187–95 and quotes on bayonets and treaties 199. Braggart, half-mad adventurer, Nicky liked fantastic schemes: Izvolsky 71. On Nicholas's ambitions in East: Kuropatkin, 16 February 1903; on Bezobrazov, 24 July 1903; Nicholas on Bezobrazov as inspiration and policy correction, 19 August 1903. Geyer 206–19. Dr. Philippe's Far East policy: Naryshkin 174.

15. Nicholas on Russia as landed estate—Master of the Land in census 1897: "Khozyain Zemli Russkoy/Khozyayka Zemli Russkoy": GARF 601.1.2.2, 28 January 1897. Sipiagin: Wortman 350–4; the balls 353–4. Sipiagin and Tsar Alexei, banquets, frivolity: Izvolsky 70. Sipiagin "deep wound in my heart," Nicky feeling strong: Meshchersky Letters, 2 and 5 April 1902, Nicky to Meshchersky. *LP* 200 on Sipiagin killing, Ella to Nicky, 3 April 1902. Police limitations and Zubatov proposals, Daly 1.124–7. KR 20, 22, 25 August 1902. Baku working class/Stalin

and Trotsky quotes in Montefiore, *Young Stalin* 66, 196. Working class, highest death rates in Petersburg, excrement, cholera: Figes, *PT* 108–13. Zubatov's new police methods: Daly 1.72–123.

16. GARF 586.1.950.2, NII to Plehve, 7 April 1902; I'm not a fan . . . smug, arrogant scoundrel, GARF 586.1.950.9, NII to Plehve, 8 July 1902; crack down suddenly and hard, GARF 586.1.950.11, NII to Plehve, 1 January 1904. Sandro 199: Pobedonostsev recommends scoundrel Plehve. Plehve and pogroms: Ruud 235–6; Azev and Plehve 125–51; too clever 152–8. Witte 380–1: Plehve, leading spirit of anti-Jewish policy. Plehve on danger of Jews to Kireev quoted in Lieven, *RR* 343. Plehve changing beliefs: Alexander III quoted in Zaionchkovsky 85–6. Plehve promotes Zubatov to Petersburg: Daly 1.124–38; 138–9 pogrom. Lenin and Chernyshevsky, quoted in Figes, *PT* 131.

17. *LP* 202–10: removal of Philippe, Alix to Nicky, 23 July 1902, on Ella warning and lie about remedy; Xenia letter, 19 August 1902 on Minny warns Nicky and 20 August 1902 on pregnancy and 31 August 1902 on power of suggestion; 209 Nicky to Alix, 1 September 1902, naughty; Alix to Nicky, 3 September 1902, sweet eyes; 211 Nicky to Minny, 20 October 1902; Minny to Nicky, 23 October 1902, on Grand Duke Paul marriage. Naryshkin 170–1. Bing 168–70, Nicky to Minny, 20 October 1902 (*LP* 211). On Misha: *LP* 227.

18. Sandro "last spectacular ball in the empire" 235–6. King 405–18.

19. Daly 1.140–8. John Röhl, *Wilhelm II: Into the Abyss of War and Exile, 1900–1941* (henceforth Röhl 2) 176–85: Reval meeting. Useful war, Kuropatkin 206: war to avoid revolution, 11 December 1903; 85 Nicholas distrusts ministers, 28 November 1903; 115 tsar is right, better understands glory than ministers, 16 February 1903; 141 tsar would trust me better if not a minister, that's true, 4 August 1903.

20. St. Seraphim: *LP* 203, Alexandra to Nicholas, 23 July 1902, on Alexandra ordering Pobedonostsev to canonize Seraphim. ND 17, 18, 19 July 1903. Japan: Oye 172–95: Geyer 187–205. KR 5 September 1903. Sandro 201: Nicholas dismisses Witte who tells Sandro: "Oriental full blooded Byzantine"; Kuropatkin Japanese army "joke" 237–8. Helen Rappaport, *Four Sisters: The Lost Lives of the Romanov Grand Duchesses* (henceforth Rappaport): attitude of imperial children to Japanese 72. Plehve's Odessa strikes, multiplying opposition, fall of Zubatov: Daly 1.140–8. Kuropatkin on Plehve's methods and coming bloodshed and dissatisfaction, 24 July 1903. War: Sandro, warning to N 239–40. Kaiser encourages war against Japan: Röhl 2.188–9; meeting Wiesbaden 264–70.

21. Crackdown GARF 586.1.950.11, NII to Plehve, 1 January 1904. Revolution gathering, war coming: Sandro 237. NII as ruler: Lieven, *NII* 106, "agree with everyone," Pobedonostsev; 109 Plehve on nature of autocracy to Kuropatkin; 136 Princess Svyatopolk-Mirsky on NII: most false man in the world. Witte: fullblooded Byzantine—Sandro 201. Witte 179, 189. Zaionchkovsky 2.19–21, half-boy half-man. Polovstov, *Dnevnik* 26 January 1892. *LP* 67: "You don't know how sly I can be," Nicky to Alix, 2 June 1894. Lieven, *NII* 28–43 Marie Romania—imperial mist 2.327.

22. GARF 568.1.661.16, Nicholas to Alexeev, 3 January 1904, possibility of rupture. *Sbornik dogovorov i diplomaticheskikh dokumentov po delam Dalnego Vostoka 1895–1905* 40–50, Nicholas to Alexeev, 14, 16, 28 January on allowing Japanese to land in South Korea. *LP* 230, Xenia diary, 31 March 1904. Constantine Pleshakov, *The Tsar's Last Armada* (henceforth Pleshakov) 3–6, 32–3. Richard Connaughton, *Rising Sun and Tumbling Bear* (henceforth Connaughton). Kaiser: Röhl 2.264–83. Alexei and mistress booed at theatre: L. A. Tikhomirov quoted in Zaionchkovsky 271. Beéche 1.129.

23. KR sins, 19 September 1903; "best man in Russia," 19 November; constant war

with my conscience, 15 December; bad thoughts in church, 21 December; secret vice, 28 December; depraved, 9 January 1904; back to bathhouse on Moika,
20 January; beautiful wife, 14 January; predilection for simple men, 19 April;
overwhelmed by sin 21 May; Sergei and brother, 23 June; waiting for birth of
Nicholas and Alexandra's child, 24 July; back to bathhouse like a squirrel on a
wheel, 26 July. KR birth of Alexei, 30 July; visit baby Peterhof, 2 August 1904.

24. Appointment of liberal Mirsky: Daly 1.148–51. Minny begs in tears: Paul Benckendorff quoted in Lieven, *NII* 134. On political policy, dangers of U-turns: dangerous
to stop halfway / my terrible responsibility before my Maker: Bing 166, Nicky to
Minny, 20 October 1902. Nicky letters to Militsa quoted in Zimin, *Negroes* 28–31.
Alexei: *LP* 243–46. ND 30 July 1904. KR birth of Alexei, 30 July; visit baby Peterhof, 2 August 1904. Haemophilia: account of Roman, son of Peter and Militsa,
is quoted in Rappaport 77–81. English disease: *LP* 228, Grand Duchess Xenia,
13 February 1904; 239 Alix to Nicky, 15 September 1904. ND 30 July 1904, 8 September 1904. KR 2 August 1904: Misha delighted. On Olga's prospects: Caro-
lyn Harris, Succession Prospects of Grand Duchess Olga Nikolaevna, *Canadian
Slavonic Papers* (2012) 54:61–84. Haemophilia origins; Queen Victoria suffering
as parent of Leopold: Wilson, 30–1, 272, 320.

25. Figes, *People's Tragedy* 168–173. Lieven, *NII* 104–40. Andrew Verner, *The Crisis
of Russian Autocracy* 100–37. Sandro 243–8. Lack of will: KR 18 November 1903
Pleshakov 60–89. German help to fleet: Röhl 2.285–93.

26. December 1904 unrest spreads: KR 18 November, 4, 21, 28, 30 December 1904.
Verner 100–37.

27. Daly 1.150–2. Verner, *Crisis of Russian Autocracy* 137–67. Lieven, *NII* 139–40. ND
8 January 1905.

28. Ruud 158–9. Daly 1.154–6. Lieven, *NII* 140–1. Figes, *PT* 173–181. ND 8 January
1905. KR 9 January and 11 January 1905. Alexandra to Princess Victoria of Battenberg 11 January 1905: Sophie Buxhoeveden, *The Life and Tragedy of Alexandra
Feodorovna, Empress of Russia* (henceforth Buxhoeveden) 108–10. Robert Massie,
*Nicholas and Alexandra* 97–100.

29. Daly 1.156–7. *LP* 245–64. Boris Savinkov, *Memoirs of a Terrorist*; Marie Pavlovna,
*Education of a Princess: A Memoir*; Ivan Kalyaev testimony (including Ella's claim
that Sergei retired out of fear of murder); Grand Duchess Xenia, 4 February 1905:
all quoted in LR 250–64. KR 4, 5, 6, 9 February 1905. ND 4 February 1905. Peasant revolt: Figes, *PT* 188–91. Caucasus revolution, Stalin in Chiatura: Montefiore,
*Young Stalin* 132–8.

30. Tsushima: Pleshakov 261–279; fall of Alexis 311–315. ND 1 November 1908. Revolution spreads; assembly concession 184–88. Lieven, *NII* 144–6. Sandro: Russia
on fire 249; 14 May 1905 picnic at Gatchina, news of Tsushima arrives, N "said
nothing as usual" 248. KR 20 June 1905. ND 17 August, 14 September 1905.
Witte to America: Witte 135–61; meeting on *Shtandart*, 14 September 1905. Views
and appointment of Nikolasha: Robinson 62–3. ND 17 August, 14 September
1905. Björkö: Röhl 2.368–71, 379–80.

31. Björkö: Röhl 2.368–71, 379–80.

32. ND 12, 17 October 1905. GARF 543.1.232.1–4, Trepov to Nicholas, 16 October
1905; GARF 595.45.6–7, Nicholas to Trepov, 16 October. On Nikolasha as Terrible Uncle, stupidity (Minny), temper and hysteria, killing borzoi dog, mysticism,
view of tsar as divine: Robinson 4, 14–16; mistresses, mysticism and Stana 51–5;
Nikolasha summoned; Kireev and Mosolov stories of Nikolasha's threats, Nikolasha's fault 67–70; Nikolasha happy to jump out of window (1916 account of
General V. M. Bezobrazov) 290. Kyril impudence: *LP* 277–8, Nicky to Minny,
5 October 1905. Bing 185–8, Nicholas to Minny, 19 October 1905; 192 Minny to

Nicky, 1 November, on supporting Witte, Trepov admirable conduct and Niko-lasha soldier at heart. This account is based also on Verner 225–45. Abraham Ascher, *The Revolution of 1905: Authority Restored* (henceforth Ascher, 1905) 10–15. Witte 237–50. Caucasus: Montefiore, *Young Stalin* 138–53. Nicky attitude to Witte, evil days, wrong path: Naryshkin 189.

33. Witte under pressure; crackdown by Durnovo: Verner 260–80; examples of Nicholas's brutality 272; Witte crackdown 274–80. Crackdown in Moscow, arrest of Soviet: Witte 273–84; brutality of weak men 286–92; undermined by Trepov 315; warns Nicholas like ship in storm 317; Durnovo liberal, energetic, compe-tent, love affairs and love letters to Spanish ambassador 321–3; Trepov character 326–31; pogroms Trepov 327; and anti-semitic campaign by Kommisarov and Ra-chkovsky 331; reports conspiracy to tsar who didn't intend to punish the captain 332. Nicholas on Cossack whips: *Stolypin* 71. Durnovo crackdown, 15,000 killed and wounded: Figes, *PT* 200–2. Alex Marshall, *Russian General Staff 1860–1917,* on Alikhanov-Avarsky/ Griazanov 64. Bezobrazov, Orlov and Richter brutalities: Ascher, 1905, 333–4. Approval of brutalities by Orlov etc. in letters to Minny: Bing 194, Nicky to Minny, 10 November 1905, council of ministers talk a lot, disap-pointed in Witte; 195 Nicky to Minny, 17 November, peasant disturbances, not enough troops; 196 Nicky to Minny, 1 December, Witte deals with revolution-ary movement energetically; 200–2 Nicky to Minny, 8 December, old heedless Liberals now clamouring for decisive action, army likes Nikolasha and has con-fidence in him; 202 Nicky to Minny, 15 December, Semyonovsky Regiment to Moscow yesterday, Dubasov in Moscow, Orlov to Livland; 205 Nicky to Minny, 22 December, armed rebellion in Moscow crushed, Vorontsov ill; 207 Nicky to Minny, 29 December, Dubasov in Moscow; Baltics Orlov, Richter good work, ter-ror must be met by terror; 210 Nicky to Minny, 12 January 1906, Orlov splendid work, Nikolasha excellent idea, Meller-Zakomelsky Siberia; Durnovo splendid, Trepov indispensable. Nikolasha plans the crackdown and orders quartermaster to insist on Orlov severity (1,170 killed): Robinson 70–5. "Tickles me": Lincoln, *In War's Dark Shadow* 310. Nicholas delays execution on recommendation of ADC: Spiridovich 1.72–3. Rasputin: Nikolasha meets Rasputin first, account of Prince Roman Petrovich (Militsa's son) quoted in Robinson 70. First Nicky/Alix meet-ing: ND 1 November 1905.

34. Jewish jokes and Nicholas's attitude to Jews (and later to Beilis case) Spiridovich 1.393–4, 2.142, 446–7. Alexandra on Jews: F 115, A to N, 13 April 1915; F 242, A to N, 17 September 1915. Röhl 1.758, Nicholas to Helmuth von Moltke 1895. Elders of Zion: Ruud 204–18. Daly 2.123–30. On Black Hundreds and Dubrovin meet-ing: Witte 192; Mosolov 143. Jewish imitations: Bing 30, N to Minny, 5 September 1884. Jewish attitudes, "English man is Yid": Witte 190. Fired by hatred of Jews: Nicholas to KR—Beéche 2.120.On Black Hundreds: Kotkin, *Stalin* 99–101. Figes, *PT* 197. Reconquest of Caucasus: Montefiore, *Young Stalin* 152–4.

35. Witte, Nicholas hates him: Naryshkin 197. Stolypin, background: *Stolypin* 1–33; disarms revolutionaries 60; nerves 60; MVD 88–9; law and Duma 100–5. Gore-mykin: H. H. Fisher (ed.), V. N. Kokovtsov, *Out of my Past: The Memoirs of Count Kokovtsov* (henceforth Kokovtsov) 123–9. On Goremykin: Gerasimov quoted in Ascher, *Revolution of 1905* 63–70. Witte and Jewish clique: Bing 221, Nicky to Minny November 1906.

36. Opening of Duma *LP* 286, Xenia diary, 27 April 1906. KR 27 April 1906. Spiri-dovich 1. 59–64. Nikolasha proposes Stolypin as premier: Robinson 89. Stolypin, MVD and premier; bombing, and first dismissal of Duma: *Stolypin* 97–182. Bing 215–17, Nicky to Minny, 16 and 30 August 1905. Child blowing up nanny, 16,000 officials killed—quoted in Kotkin, *Stalin* 104; decline of parties 118. Figes, *PT*

233–4. Tsar demands immediate executions, martial law, his view passed on by War Minister A. F. Rediger to Interior Minister Stolypin, 1 July 1906: RGIA 1276.1.92.11, Rediger to Stolypin. Alex Marshall, *Russian General Staff 1860–1917*, on Alikhanov-Avarsky/Griazanov 64. Tsarist oppression: Ascher, *1905*, 333–4. Imperial security: King 110–1; Spiridovich 1.271/284–7.

37. Rasputin: James T. Fuhrman, *Rasputin: The Untold Story* (henceforth *Rasputin*): background and character 15–30; arrival 40–8. A Russian peasant: Olga Alexandrova quoted in Massie, *Nicholas* 189. Penile wart, female orgasm: Figes, *PT* 32. Rasputin meets Nikolasha first then the Crows: Prince Roman Petrovich quoted in Robinson 71; Vyrubova 67–70.

38. King 107; *Rasputin* 46–8; Vyrubova 1–67. Orlov: Naryshkin 188.

39. Alix lying in bed all day: Vyrubova 20; anything if she was well 24; driving fast 21; one friend 33; OTMA upbringing, younger two etc. 36–7; Tsar orders cinema: GARF 553.16.32, NII to Benckendorff, 13 February 1913. Gilliard 28 on Vyrubova, sentimental mystical, Alix only dominant friendship. Vyrubova's friendship for Alex, mania and mystic superstition: Naryshkin 186. Nicholas only survived due to his prayers: Sophia Tyutcheva quoted in Rappaport 162. *Rasputin* 39–48; Alix and daughters' letters to Rasputin 94–5. ND 18 July, 12 October, 9 December 1906; Stolypin, 27 May 1907; 6 November, 27 December 1908, on visits to Anna to see Rasputin; 4, 29 February, 29 March, 26 April, 15 August 1909. KR 6 and 10 November 1906, on Nikolasha and Stana. Nikolasha's divorce: Robinson 97–101. Vyrubova 69. *LP* 290, Nicky to Stolypin, 16 October 1906; 297, Alix to Nicky, 17 July 1907; 304, Xenia diary, 7 September 1908; 306 Olga memoirs; 308–10 Alix to Olga, 1 and 11 January 1909 on "girlies" and Our Friend; Tatiana to Alix, 17 January 1909. Olga Alexandrovna, *25 Chapters of My Life*, 98–101. Bing 227, Nicky to Minny, 22 March 1907, on Nikolasha's marrage. Hercules: Zimin, *Negroes* 409–10 and 415–18, quoting Vyrubova and Maurice Paléologue. Hercules and Nubian Guards: this is based on the research of Penny Wilson—see http://forum.alexanderpalace.org/index.php?topic=348.0;wap2. Veronal and other opiates: Rappaport, *Ekaterinburg*, 55, 60; girls' luxuries 74–75.

40. *Stolypin* 115–49; Jewish reform 169–2; second Duma, 174–6; coup and third Duma, 202–15; Vorontsov, Caucasus 237–9. Jewish reform: *Krasnyi arkhiv* (1925) 5.13, Nicholas II to Stolypin, 10 December 1906. Hatred of Jews: *LP* 340, Nicky to KR, 14 September 1912. Bing 220, Nicky to Minny, 11 October 1906, like and respect Stolypin; 228, 29 March 1907, on Duma, "slap! and they are gone." Figes, *PT* 225–8.

41. Military reforms: Lieven, *Flame* 146–8. Norman Stone, *Eastern Front* (henceforth Stone) 24–6. Robinson: 88–104. Stolypin reforms; on Jewish and other reforms 1906–7: *Stolypin* 150–206. SD memberships: Kotkin, *Stalin* 118. Izvolsky: Lieven, *Flame* 192–7.

42. *Stolypin* 251–60; 279 meeting with Edward VII at Reval. Lieven, *Flame* 148–50, 197–203; 208–24. Geyer 277–80. Clark 185–90. Geyer 276–8. Margaret MacMillan, *The War that Ended Peace: The Road to 1914* (henceforth MacMillan) 391–422. Stone 24–6. 11 August 1907, calm at home, Izvolsky, British triumph, *Stolypin* 253; 1908 crisis 257–9; war fatal for dynasty 259. Figes, *PT* 225–9. Robinson 88–129. Edward VII at Reval: *Stolypin* 279. Reval/Cowes: Mossolov 210–12; Spiridovich 1:170–5. Miranda Carter, *The Three Emperors* 352–4; Cowes 374–6. Jane Ridley, *Bertie: The Life of Edward VII* 398–422. Rappaport 124–8. King 426–32. 1908 crisis, key ministerial meeting: AVPRI 340.787.7.162–6. Izvolsky portrait: Harold Nicolson, *Lord Carnock* 216. Bulgaria, Ferdinand as tsar, Izvolsky calls Aehrenthal "ce sale juif," NII says act of megalomaniac but accepts Ferdinand as king on Petersburg visit: *Ferdinand* 214–34. Minny outraged at Ferdinand: Bing, Minny to

Nicky 12 March 1909. Montenegro demands wars: *Montenegro* 264. Friendship and death of General A. A. Orlov, 4 October 1908, in Cairo: Spiridovich 1.271, 285–6. Alexander Orlov unique role: Naryshkin 188.

43. *Stolypin* 327–62. Kokovtsov 263–70; don't I count for something 282. Rappaport 149–52: Sophia Tyutcheva on girls at assassination and visit of Rasputin. Stolypin on war and revolution: Serge Sazonov, *Fateful Years, 1909–1916* (henceforth Sazonov) 232. Stolypin in decline: Figes, *PT* 226–31. War and military policy, fortress razing and creation of reserve Sukhomlinov reforms, Little and Great Programmes, economic data: Stone 19–33. Lieven, *Flame* 225–6. Sukhomlinov: V. A. Sukhomlinov, *Vospominaniia* (henceforth Sukhomlinov) goal to clear out grand dukes 191; and to create army equal to Germany 210; to tsar I was primarily a servant 214 or technician 233; 25 July, tsar completely calm with Nikolasha, megalomania of Nikolasha, all powerful 243; Nikolasha looked like Ivan the Terrible with his fits of rage 244. Sukhomlinov visits Livadia 1909, pretty wife loved beautiful toilettes, loathed by society: Spiridovich 1.1385. Incredible friovolity: Kokovtsov 310–35. Laughed at aeroplanes: Sandro 264. Geyer 288–92. MacMillan 353–5. William C. Fuller, Jr., *Strategy and Power in Russia* 425–33. William C. Fuller, Jr., *The Foe Within* 45–8. Maurice Paléologue, *An Ambassador's Memoirs* 1.83. Fall of Nikolasha, failure of his reforms: Robinson 104–8; the Crows row with Rasputin (memoirs of Prince Roman Petrovich: Roman Petrovich Romanov, *Am Hof des Letzten Zaren*) 108; Alexandra on Nikolasha vs man of God and Nikolasha's regret (memoirs of his First World War chaplin G. Shavelskii) 108–9. Death of Tolstoy: Bing 260 N to Minny 11 November 1910; Bartlett, *Tolstoy* 386–7; 412–9.

44. Rasputin vs Stolypin and church leaders: *Rasputin* 49–85. Whoever praised him was good: Naryshkin 196–7. Sukhomlinov 191–3, manoeuvres, evil one, weak one. Stolypin, late crises. military naval laws, crisis of reforms: *Stolypin* 250–326. Tsar rejects Stolypin's resignation, vetoes naval bill: GARF 601.1.1125.4–5, Nicholas II to Stolypin, 24 April 1909.

45. Stolypin assassination: *Stolypin* 363–88. End of Stolypin, no party: Figes, *PT* 230–1. Stolypin gloomy, tsar schedule, shooting, appointment as PM: Kokovtsov 271–8; *Rasputin* 87–91. Bing 264–7, Nicky to Minny, 1 September 1911. Rappaport 149–51, quoting Sophia Tyutcheva. Ruud 173–200. *LP* 331, M. P. Bok, Stolypin's daughter. Naryshkin 199. Mistake of family feuds: Marie Romania 2. 223

46. Beilis, Kokovtsov, loss of Stolypin: *Stolypin* 363–88. Kokovtsov 271–8; not Khvostov 276 and 292; new PM conversation with Alexandra on Stolypin and fate 283. *Rasputin* 87–91. Bing 264–7, Nicky to Minny, 1 September 1911. Rappaport 149–51, quoting Sophia Tyutcheva. Ruud 173–200. *LP* 331, M. P. Bok, Stolypin's daughter. Naryshkin 199. Mendel Beilis case, Chaplinsky reports in Kiev, anti-Jewish law on trade in Siberia: Levin 116–24.

47. Olga's ball: Rappaport 156–7. Vyrubova 22.

48. Kokovtsov 291–300. Rasputin crisis: M. V. Rodzianko, *The Reign of Rasputin* (henceforth Rodzianko) 36–9, audience with Minny; 40–57 audience with tsar and Yusupova report on Alexandra's wish to hang. *LP* 337, Rodzianko memoirs; Xenia diary, 25 January, 16 February, 16 March 1912, on Minny, Xenia, Yusopova talks. ND 15 February 1912. Vyrubova 30: Tyutcheva rebuked severely. Better one Rasputin than ten hysterics: Nicholas quoted in Figes, *PT* 33. Borodino: *LP* 340, Nicky to KR, 14 September 1912. King 316–17. Wortman 379–82.

49. Illness of Alexei in Nicholas's words: Bing 276, Nicky to Minny, 20 October 1912. Alexei's illness: Vyrubova 42–3, build me a monument, Nicky rushes out, Rasputin message. *LP* 342, 343–8, Nicky to Minny, 20 October 1912. ND 5–13 October 1912. Gilliard 8–12.

50. Kokovtsov 313–429. Sukhomlinov 191–3, manoeuvres, evil one, weak one. Rob-

inson 108–29: rise of Sukhomlinov, rivalry with Nikolasha, Nikolasha's return to favour, cancels war minister's manoeuvres. Sukhomlinov in Livadia: Spiridovich 1.1385. Attempt to sack Sukhomlinov: Kokovtsov 310–35. Sazanov: MacMillan 458–61; Sazonov womanly 461. "Sad wobbler" quote in *Ferdinand* 257. Pancake: F 226, 11 September 1915; 421, 17 March 1916; 537, 17 July 1916. Sazonov 90–7. Clark 340–2 on 1912 crisis and plans. Geyer 288–92. MacMillan 353–5. *Ferdinand* 242–7, inc. 2 million francs for Ferdinand from NII. Montenegro coronation: *Montenegro* 276–28. Military policy: Fuller, *Strategy and Power in Russia* 425–33. Fuller, *The Foe Within* 45–8. Paléologue, *Ambassador's Memoirs* 1.83.

51. Balkan wars: Lieven, *Flame*, portrait of Sazonov 232–4; the First Balkan War 241–72, inc. tsar leans towards Serbs 258, against autonomous Albania; revision of Kokovtsov version 267–9. MacMillan 448–80. Sazonov 90–7. Clark 281–90, 340–2. McMeekin 20–7. German and Austrian roles: Röhl 2.880–6, 917–32. Bulgaria in First Balkan War, advance towards Byzantium, attitude of Sazonov and Nicholas II towards Balkan League and Bulgarian success, Sazanov wobbling, *Ferdinand* 245–74. *Montenegro* 279–301. Sazonov 68–78. Hunting calms nerves: *LP* 346, Nicky to Minny, 20 October 1912. Military doctrine what I order: D. A. Rich, *The Tsar's Colonels: Professionalism, Strategy, and Subversion in Late Imperial Russia* 221. Sukhomlinov 152: blames Sazonov for Slavophile war policies; Nicholas 1911 wanted command army 191. Stana and Militsa as Montenegro supporters, Nikolasha neutral: Robinson 128. Kokovtsov on Sukhomlinov, Alix: 301–19; extra military budget 342–4; partial mobilization crisis 344–51; Militsa canvasses Kokovtsov 357. Sazonov to Kokovtsov, 12 November 1912, quoted in Ronald P. Bobroff, *Roads to Glory* 55. V. I. Bovykin, *Iz istorii vozniknoveniia pervoi mirovoi voiny* 125–7; Nicholas, 23 November 1912. Naval plan: KA 6.51–2, Grigorevich to Nicholas, 25–26 October 1912. Sazonov memorandum to Kokovtsov quoted in McMeekin 25.

52. Rosemary and Donald Crawford, *Michael and Natasha: The Life and Love of the Last Tsar of Russia* (henceforth *Michael*). Beéche 1.194–5. *LP* 349–51, Minny to Nicky, 4 November 1912; Nicky to Minny, 7 November; Okhrana agent report 17 December.

53. Tercentenary: Kokovtsov 360–2. Spiridovich 2.337–45; Berlin wedding 321. Rodzianko 74–7. On ministers: Naryshkin 206. Wortman 383–94. King 389–401. Sex, Blok, Belyi and Silver Age: Lincoln *In War's Dark Shadow* 349–88. Alexander Blok quoted in Figes, *PT* 14. Lena and Stalin: see Montefiore, *Young Stalin* 256–7. Kotkin, *Stalin* on Blok quote on Okhrana 130; on Marxism and Nationalities 133; on Lenin quote "tsarism victorious" 135. Worse better: Figes, *PT* 129. Meshchersky, Maklakov, Krivoshein: Lieven, *Flame* 293–5.

### SCENE 5: CATASTROPHE

1. Spiridovich 2.360–402; on Beilis verdict 2.447. Beilis trial: Levin 205–91. Figes, *PT* 240–3. On Alexei: KR 18 March 1912. On Alexei and character of girls: Vyrubova 37–9. Gilliard 24–5. Rappaport 165–170. Rappaport, *Ekaterinburg* 90 (Alexei) and 73–85 (girls).

2. Balkan League fallout, Bulgaria falls out with Russia in *Ferdinand* 270–9; Second Balkan War 279–87. *Montenegro* 279–301. MacMillan 458–61. Clark 340–2. Sazonov 90–7. McMeekin 25. Montenegro, end of Russian closeness: *Montenegro* 279–301.

3. Second Balkan War: Lieven, *Flame* 272–90; Poincaré gives blank cheque on support to Russia 240; Liman crisis 284–7. Sazonov 97–103. Nicholas quoted by Sa-

zonov in Clark 275. Kokovtsov 313–429; on Turks and Liman 389–93. Goremykin: Sandro 252, corpse. Liman: Sazonov 117–25; 117 Nicky tells Sazonov of Kaiser conversation in Berlin; February 1914 conference, 126 offensive against Constantinople inevitable in European war. Kokovtsov decline in power then dismissal, Goremykin as "old fur coat": Kokovtsov 439. Fall of Kokovtsov, appointment of Maklakov, discussion of dismissal of Duma or conversion into merely consultative chambers, influence of Krivoshein and Meshchersky: Lieven, *Flame* 294–7. Durnovo possible premiership: Dominic Lieven, Bureaucratic Authoritarianism in Late Imperial Russia: The Personality, Career, and Opinions of P. N. Durnovo, *Historical Journal* (1983) 26.2.391–402. Lieven, *NII* 17; Durnovo memorandum 195–7. Geyer 285–7, 310–21. MacMillan 29–37. Nicholas plans abolition or reduction of Duma powers with Maklakov: GARF 601.1.1119.1–2, NII to N. Maklakov, 18 October 1913. Malinovsky, Lenin quote and Stalin: Montefiore, *Young Stalin* 280–325. On Poincaré, French generals' visits and French commitment to include possibility of Balkan crisis: Clark 294–308; Liman von Sanders crisis 335; meeting at Prussian wedding 339; January–February conferences 341–8; machismo 360. Liman crisis and special conference: McMeekin 30–5. Hall 248–9.

4. Daughters OTMA in love: this is based on Rappaport 191–206.
5. V. I. Nevsky, *Nikolai II i velikie knyaza*, Leningrad, 1925: 45 how do you live, embrace "aunt's arm with voluptuous kisses." Dmitri Pavlovich (DP) to Nicholas II, 29 September 1911; 46 "heart, soul and body except (for arsehole), DP to NII, 16 October 1911; 48 chance to dance with Zizi or Baroness Frederiks, DP to NII, 17 November 1911; 50 "wipe your arse," "hug my pillow thinking about empress," DP to NII, 19 March 1914.
6. Last season and girls in love: Rappaport 207–222; Olga's suitors 212. Romanian marriage possible for Olga, description of OTMA girls and visit: Marie Roumania 2.327–331. Olga marriage—Gilliard 32 Olga says papa promises not to make me leave Russia, I'm Russian. On Anichkov ball: Helene Iswolsky, *No Time to Grieve*, 83–5. Yusupov: ND 8 October, 11 November 1913. *LP* 372, Xenia diary, 8 October 1913; 380, Xenia diary, 9 February 1914. ND 9 February 1914. Author interview with niece of Grand Duchess Irina, Princess Olga Romanoff.
7. Pašić in Petersburg quoted in Clark 280. Crimea, Anna's betrayal: F 73–6, Alix to Nicky, 28 April 1914, 26 January 1914, 26–27 October, 19 November 1914, 27 January 1915; 3 November 1915. Crimea: Spiridovich 2.450–60; Anna in love with Nicholas 450–2. Vyrubova 158. *Naryshkina* 206. Romanian visit, sunburnt girls, loveable Nicky: Marie Romania 2.336–338. Last Crimean trip, Romanian visits, Olga to stay in Russia: Rappaport 214–21, quoting 217, Nicholas to Agnes de Stoeckl. Olga on staying in Russia: Gilliard 32. Romania possible marriage, Sazonov 103–15; conversation with Alexandra about fear of parting with daughters 110.
8. The July–August crisis, Poincaré visit and road to war: Sazonov 150–60, 177–216; mobilization cancellation crisis 193–205; declaration of war 212; Stolypin irreplaceable 232. Sukhomlinov on 20–30 July 1914: blames Nikolasha 221–8; blames Sazonov for war policies 152; Nicholas always said he would command army 191; Russia never so prepared as in 1914, mobilization like clockwork 245. Rodzianko 106–8. Hague mediation: OPI GIM 180.82280, Nicholas II to Sazonov, 14 July 1914. Rasputin against this war: F 283, A to N, 1 November 1915. Nikolasha moved by offer of supreme command and Te Deum at Winter Palace: Robinson 134. Sukhomlinov refuses command: Stone 51–2. Te Deum at Winter Palace, Nicholas in tears: Rodzianko 110–11. Lieven, *Flame* 313–42. Nicholas's version of the Sazonov call and likelihood of war, 24 July 1914, and ministers meeting that after-

noon: Peter Bark, *Memoirs* 7.1–4, 7–26. Gilliard 36–40: declaration of war. Dazed Nicky, meetings, new telephones, Alix uninformed: Vyrubova 479. Geyer 312–20. Nicky–Willy telegrams: Röhl 2.1065–70. McMeekin 53–75. MacMillan 551–602. Sean McMeekin, *July 1914*, 260–305. Lieven, *NII* 197–204. Kotkin, *Stalin* 156: mobilization, conscription statistics.

9. August–September, the first battles: Stone 45–69. Robinson 157–69.

10. Stavka and Nikolasha: Robinson 142–90; Nikolasha "my hermitage" 202. Stone 51–3.

11. Wounded soldier dies: F 86, A to N, 2 March 1915; F 83, 28 February 1915. Alexandra needs to be bridled: Ernest of Hesse quoted in Naryshkin 204. Nursing Alexandra best: Vyrubova 9; invigorated 49; train crash 55. Rappaport 227–54.

12. Stone 70–91. Robinson 170–206. 13 September 1916, Rodzianko, visit to Stavka, conversation with Nikolasha on Rasputin hanging 118–19. Enver offensive and defeat: Sean McMeekin, *Ottoman Endgame* 146–53.

13. Nikolasha dominates ministers: F 153, A to N, 17 June 1915. Spy mania, Jewish repression F 125, A to N, 4 May 1915; F 128, N to A, 8 May 1915. Robinson 100 and 207–9. Jewish deportations: Eric Lohr, The Russian Army and the Jews: Mass Deportation, Hostages, and Violence during World War I, *Russian Review* (2001) 60.404–19. Miasoedov case innocence: Fuller, *The Foe Within* 132. Nikolasha spy mania: Robinson 216–18; 217 "I predict no shells at all," Nikolasha to N, 24 February 1915.

14. F 89, N to A, 2 March 1915; F 102, A to N, 5 April 1915. Robinson 221 on Nikolasha and Dardanelles. McMeekin, *Ottoman Endgame* 163–221.

15. F 99, N to A, 9 March 1915; F 100, A to N, 4 April; F 104, A to N, 6 April; F 107, N to A, 7 April; Jew, F 115, A to N, 13 April.

16. Stone 122–43; shell shortage 144–64; retreat 165–93; the sections on the war materials and economic crisis are based on Stone 194–211. Robinson 231–44: Nikolasha complains to NII of lack of ammunition 240; Orlov letter to Yanushkevich, 2 June 1915 245; sacking of Sukhomlinov, Maklkov, Nikolasha's apogee, kicks legs up (Shavelsky), Nikolasha weeps, plans to constrain Alexandra (Shavelsky), nerves shot (Polivanov), Alexander and Nicholas sack Nikolasha 245–59. Rodzianko 128–47. Trial of Sukhomlinov: F 397, A to N, 4 March 1916.

17. Stone 187–93. Robinson 240–60. Rasputin and Bark: F 131, A to N, 11 May 1915. Panic, N weeps: F 131, N to A, 11 May 1915. Rasputin from God: F 135–7, A to N, 10, 11 June 1915. Nikolasha vs Man of God: F 138, A to N, 12 June 1915. More autocratic/spy at HQ: F 145, 14 June 1915. No faith in Nikolasha/the bell/a woman's instinct: F 147, A to N, 16 June 1915. Goremykin/period/Khvostov: F 156, A to N, 18 June 1915; F 160, A to N, 22 June, Djunkovsky report on Rasputin. Sergei Mikhailovich and Kshessinskaya mixed up: F 169, A to N, 25 June 1915. Dismissal of Nikolasha, wify's trousers unseen, no dawdling: F 171, A to N, 22 August 1915. Orlov out: F 174, A to N, 23 August 1915. Ministers' letter, Sazonov called them together: F 177, A to N, 24 August 1915. Robinson 191: Nikolasha—put Alix in monastery, quoted from Shavelsky his chaplain. Vyrubova 57–9: row with dowager empress, Nicholas shocked by Warsaw, hard not to command, given icon, tells ministers, sweating. Lieven, *NII* 227. Minny on Nicholas's mistake: diary quoted in Hall 264–5. No public opinion: Stanley Washburn, On the Russian Front in World War I: Memoirs of an American War Correspondent, quoted in Joshua A. Sanborn, *Imperial Apocalypse: The Great War and the Destruction of the Russian Empire* (henceforth Sanborn) 101. Alexei education at headquarters: Gilliard 62. Alix ambitious and infallible: Marie Romania 3.351–2.

18. *Rasputin* 155–66. Rasputin advises on church appointments: F 160–2, A to N, 22 June 1915. Have signed military nominations: F 179, N to A, 24 August 1915.

Trousers needed at HQ: F 180, A to N, 25 August 1915. Thank God it's over/ Fancy Wify helping Huzy: F 181–2, N to A, 25 August 1915; keep autocracy/Khvostov, F 171–3, A to N, 22 August; denounces Sazonov and Polivanov/smell the letter, F 177, A to N, 24 August; Andronnikov consulted, F 191, A to N, 29 August 1915; get rid of Guchkov, F 193, A to N, 30 August; hang Guchkov?, F 200, A to N, 2 September; sack Sazonov and Khrivoshein, don't see Rodzianko, names to replace Samarin, Andronnikov praises Khvostov with Rasputin etc., F 212, A to N, 7 September; Sazonov Pancake, appoint Khvostov, Andronnikov recommends, Goremykin struggling, all for Baby, F 225–8, A to N, 11 September; Khvostov plans, F 242, A to N, 17 September; Khvostov/Tail, a man, no petticoats, F 247, A to N, 17 September; sees Rasputin to discuss Tail, F 261, A to N, 4 October. Benckendorff on Alexandra, Lieven, *NII* 227.

19. Stone 208–14. Railway crisis: F 197, N to A, 31 August 1915. Alexei at Mogilev: F 265–8, N to A, 6, 7 October 1915; F 281, N to A, 31 October, and A to N, 1 November. Andronnikov and Rasputin urge changes: F 284–9, A to N, 2–3 November 1915.

20. Goremykin, hissed in Duma: F 292, A to N, 6 November 1915; Rasputin dream of Constantinople, F 295, A to N, 8 November; Rasputin with Goremykin, F 316–17, A to N, 29 November; receives Khvostov/reads *Millionaire Girl*, F 339, N to A, 31 December; new PM candidates, consults Khvostov on Stürmer, F 349, N to A, 5 January 1916; appoint Stürmer PM, Khvostov hoped to be PM himself, F 352, A to N, 7 January; advance to Erzurum, F 354, N to A, 7 January; sack Dzunkovsky and Drenteln and Orlov who planned "monastery for me," F 356, A to N, 8 January.

21. *Rasputin* 164–6. F 384–402: 384, A to N, 10 February 1916–6 March 1916; F 388, A to N, 13 February 1916, A rejects Boris and Dmitri plans to marry Olga; sacks War Minister Polivanov and successor, F 409, N to A, 10 March; apples from Rasputin to N, F 413, A to N, 13 March.

22. Naroch, Brusilov offensives. Stone 232–63; description of V. Bezobrazov 225, especially 261 Stone's phrase "pantomime machismo." N appoints Brusilov, F 415, N to A, 14 March 1916; kiss every sweet place, F 419, A to N, 15 March; Philippe and Rasputin advise be masterful, F 421, A to N, 17 March; Boy Blue, F 429, N to A, 13 March; Pharisees' wickedness against Rasputin, F 437, A to N, 5 April; Fleet occupied Trebizond, F 439, N to A, 5 April, and landings there, F 473, N to A, 23 May; my Boy Blue, F 447, A to N, 8 April, and F 463, 1 May; troubles with minister of interior, F 459, A to N, 28 April; don't mention offensive plans to anyone/Brusilov offensive, F 491, N to A, 5 June; remembers Walton on Thames, F 495, N to A, 8 June; Stürmer honest and supply crisis, F 500, N to A, 11 June. (N's earlier request to keep military secrets: F 196, N to A, 31 August 1915.) Many POWs captured: F 537, A to N, 17 July 1916; Alix at Stavka, F 547, A to N, 3 August, and N misses her calm, 3 August; despair about Bezobrazov "ordered advance where bogs known to be impregnable, let Guards be slaughtered," F 548, A to N, 4 August; N sacks Bezobrazov, F 564, N to A, 16 August. Rasputin advises against losses, F 553, A to N, 8 August 1916; A's period spoils everything—nuisance, F 568, A to N, 20 August; faith in Rasputin's wisdom for country, F 569, A to N, 4 September; A sees Stürmer then Rasputin, F 573, A to N, 7 September. Sanborn 108–29; Kazakh rebellion 177–8; F 495 and F 593 Rasputin: food supply advice, 9 June and 20 September 1916. Brusilov and surplus of shells: Kotkin, *Stalin* 162–4. Russian advance into Anatolia and expeditions into Persia and Iraq: Robinson 263–87. Tsargrad expedition: F 582, N to A, 13 September 1916. Russian advance to Erzurum, Trebizond and expeditions to Persia and Iraq: McMeekin, *Ottoman Endgame* 270–84; April 1916, Sazanov negotiates huge territorial gains

for Russia with Sykes-Picot in Petrograd 284–6; February–April 1916, Baratov expedition Persia and towards Baghdad in Iraq, 289–90; Tsargradsky Regiment 312–21.

23. Nicky's exhaustion: Alexander Naumov agriculture minister, Benckendorff, Fabritsky quoted in Lieven, *NII* 220–27. Benckendorff quoted in Gleb Botkin, *The Real Romanovs* 125. Paléologue on Badmaiev elixir: *Ambassador's Memoirs*, 6 November 1916. N lonely: F 205, N to A, 4 September 1915. Alexandra takes opium: F 366, A to N, 14 January 1916; N takes cocaine, F 303, N to A, 12 November 1915. *LP* 541, Yusupov to Bimbo, 14 February 1917. Grain and railway crisis: this is based on Stone 283–301. Supply crisis: F 505, N to A, 15 June 1916; Rasputin advice on prices, F 505, A to N, 16 June; Sazonov long nose, F 537, A to N, 17 July. Idea of military dictator suggested by Krivoshein/problems with Stürmer: F 560, N to A, 14 August 1916; Alexeev calls for military authorities to replace Stürmer, A to N, 14 August. Stürmer cannot overcome this difficulty/supply/most damned question ever come across: F 593, N to A, 20 September 1916. N and A's drugs: Rappaport *Ekaterinburg* 55 and 60.

24. Romanov conspiracies: Dmitri and Boris: F 387, A to N, 13 February and 10 March 1916; F 429, A to N, 26 March, on family and Olga/Kulikovsky; the Club and Nikolai Mikhailovich, F 655, A to N, 4 December. Nikolai Mikhailovich bad person, grandson of Jew, my greatest enemies in family: F 641, A to N, 4 November 1916; F 300, A to N, 12 November 1915. Ruin of Dmitri going to that lady, Brasova: F 556, A to N, 11 August 1916. Plots of Guchkov and Aleexev: F 591, A to N, 19 September 1916. On Dmitri and Brassova: Beéche 2.52. Sandro at Kiev: 297–302. Dmitri tells gossip: Vyrubova 66.

25. N mentions Protopopov, recommended by Rasputin: F 520, N to A, 25 June 1916. Alexandra urges Protopopov: F 574–80, 7, 22, 23, 27 September 1916; N praises A political role, 23 September. Appoints Protopopov: F 596, A to N, 21 September 1916. Protopopov urges freeing of Sukhomlinov, appointment of Kurlov: F 606, A to N, 26 September 1916; list for N to discuss with Protopopov suggested by Rasputin, Badmaev treats Protopopov, Rasputin is Badmaev "bosom friend" and Protopopov cured by him, F 609, A to N, 27 September 1916; F 623, A to N, 16 October. A tells Rasputin about Protopopov crisis/urges Stürmer to give food supply to Protopopov and N agrees: F 631, A to N, 30 October 1916, and N to A, 30 October. Protopopov not normal, "peculiar" and eye-rolling: Rodzianko 218–19. Stürmer and Protopopov, inc. ruling with Christ and Gendarme uniform: Figes, *PT* 285–7. Stürmer dictator; Protopopov I shall save Russia: Rodzianko 219. Secret talks with Germans: Kotkin, *Stalin* 199. Anatolii Ignatiev, *Russko-angliiskie otnosheniia nakanune Oktyabrskoi revolutsii (Fevral-oktyabr 1917 g.)* 41–52.

### SCENE 6: EMPEROR MICHAEL II

1. Romanovs confront tsar: Nikolai Mikhailovich (Bimbo) letters and my enemies in the family, bad person, Jew: F 642, A to N, 4 November 1916, and letters F 642–5, N to A, 4 November 1916; N apologies for not reading them, 5 November. Sandro confronts Nicky: Sandro 305; I believe no one but wife 305. Robinson 288–90 quoting Grand Duke Andrei Vladimirovich and Shavelsky's accounts of Nikolasha's conversations with tsar; the Lvov–Khatisov coup 288–9. *Armenian Review* 3 (1950) 112–13. Sandro on Zinaida Yusupova 236. Trepov PM and crisis of almost sacking Protopopov: F 648–57, A to N, 10 November 1916; don't change Protopopov, A to N, 10, 13 November, 4, 5 December; sacked Trepov not Protopopov, F 664, A to N, 9 December; Rasputin lives for Russia and you/entreats you to be firm/only not a responsible cabinet/horrible Trepov/give strong country for

Baby, F 671, A to N, 13 December; "Be Peter the Great, John the Terrible, Emperor Paul—crush them all under you—now don't laugh, don't be naughty," F 674, A to N, 14 December. Hatred of Alexandra: Marie Romania 3. 152.

2. Yusupov conspiracy: Irina and Felix Yusupov to tea with Alexander, F 560, 14 August 1916: "both nice and natural, she very brown and he very thin." Zinaida and Ella confront Alix. *Rasputin* 197–205.

3. Killing of Rasputin: *Rasputin* 197–213, 225–31. The accounts of Felix Yusupov including Felix Yusupov, *Rasputin* 155–63 and V. M. Purishkevich, *Murder of Rasputin* especially 69–95. Possibility of English conspiracy: see Andrew Cook, *To Kill Rasputin*, esp. Stephen Alley letter 217. Vyrubova 80–2.

4. The fall-out—sequence of letters between A and N: see F 680, A to N, 16 December 1916, N to A, 16 December; finding Rasputin's body, F 686, A to N, 19 December. Nicky on day of Rasputin's vanishing: A. A. Mordvinov, *Iz perezhitogo: Vospominaniia fligel–adyutanta imperatora Nikolaia II* (henceforth Mordvinov) 2.530–1; reaction of the children 532. Reaction to Rasputin's death: *Rasputin* 215–24, 233–8. Ella to Zinaida on Rasputin's death: *Ella* 286; Dmitri to Yusupov, dark stain 287. Minny "no!," Sandro 308–9. Alexei, papa won't you punish them: Vyrubova 39. F686–7 19 December 1916–22 February 1917.

5. Sacking of Trepov *Rasputin* 182; family conspiracy 221–3. Empress to be annihilated, conversation with Maria Pavlovna (Miechen): Rodzianko 246; reception with tsar, wants to thrash Protopopov 252–4. Sandro interview with Nicky and Alix—"nobody has right to kill" 309–310; new premier Golitsyn "soft . . . understood nothing, knew nothing" 311; back to Alexander Palace with Misha and without Misha: 312–316. Nicky to Mossolov—no danger to dynasty, Lieven, *NII* 230–1. Vyrubova on Sandro's visit: 88; Misha visit 90; Nicholas knows centre of intrigue is British embassy 91; N upset and A feels return to Stavka dangerous 91. Nicholas to Stavka and A encourages strength: great firmness needed, you look weary, feel my lips tenderly on yours F 686 A to N 22 Feb 1917; measles F 688 A to N 23 February 1917; "my solitude, What you write about being firm, the master, is true" F 687 N to A 23 February 1917. Jim Hercules: Zimin, *Negroes* 409–11, 415–18. Penny Wilson, at http://forum.alexanderpalace.org/index. php?topic=348.0;wap2.

6. Revolution: F 686–95, A to N, 22 February 1917; disorders in town, A to N, 26 February, and N to A, 23 and 24 February. Mark D. Steinberg and Vladimir M. Khrustalëv, *The Fall of the Romanovs* (henceforth *Fall*) 46–56; 76 text of Rodzianko telegram, 26 February 1917; 81 "totally calm," War Minister Mikhail Beliaev to Alexeev, 27 February; 81 civil rule, NII to Nikolai Golitsyn, 27 February. Garrison figures: Kotkin, *Stalin* 168; Michael (Misha) diary quotes and role in Petrograd 256–78. Vyrubova 91–3. Figes, *PT* 307–16. Presence of Jim Hercules at Stavka and last sight of Moscow/Paléologue sees weeping court Negro, quoted in Zimin, *Negroes* 417–18. Penny Wilson, at http://forum.alexanderpalace.org/index .php?topic=348.0;wap2. ND 27 February–3 March 1917. *Michael* 255–265.

7. *Fall* 57–9; 88 grand ducal manifesto. Mordvinov on telegrams: 27 February 1917, Mordvinov 1.53–6. *Michael* 265–75. F 696–701, N and A letters and telegrams, 28 February–2 March 1917. ND 27 February–3 March 1917.

8. Showdown with Ruzsky: F 696–701, N and A letters and telegrams, 28 February–2 March 1917. *Fall* 58–63, 88–93: on Rodzianko ministry, Alexeev to NII, 1 March 1917, and telegrams from Nikolasha and Brusilov and other commanders. Mordvinov 1.56–95, inc. Fredericks announces abdication conversation with Professor Fedorov. ND 1–3 March 1917. Figes, *PT* 316–18. Lieven, *NII* 232–3—N "responsible before God and Russia for everything."

9. *LP* 573, Benckendorff, 9 March 1917. Guchkov mission: *Fall* 96–100, protocol

of talks between Guchkov, Shulgin and NII, 2 March 1917. Figes, *PT* 339–43. *Michael* 288–91. Tsar peaceful but secretly agonized/can't forgive Ruzsky: A. A. Mordvinov, Otryvki iz vospominanii, *Russkaia letopis* (1923) 5.112–13; see also Mordvinov 1.95–139. ND 1–8 March 1917. Kill them, ask Cossacks; too late says N: Vyrubova 96.

10. *Michael* 295–301.

11. ND 3–7 March 1917. *LP* 561, Olga Paley on Grand Duke Paul informs Alexandra, 3 March 1917. *Michael* 295–301, 308, NII to Misha. Tears, reaction of daughters, Alix burns love letters, Vyrubova 93–95. Letter of Olga to Anna.

12. *Michael* 302–15.


SCENE 7: AFTERLIFE

1. Walking with Nicholas—go to Kostroma or abroad: Mordvinov 1.145–6; last speech and collects things not hastily on 8 March 1917, 192–3. Hall 282–5, inc. Minny's diary. ND 3, 4 March 1917; 8 March, last day in Mogilev, heartbreaking. Sandro 319–24. Sight of Sandro unendurable to Nicky—Vyrubova 96–7.

2. Gilliard 80–2. Vyrubova 94–7. *LP* 568, George V to NII, 6 March 1917; 569–72 Benckendorff memoirs, 8 March, Kornilov visit. ND 7 March 1917. Balmoral plan: author interview with Prince Michael of Kent.

3. Tsarskoe: Vyrubova 95–9. Rappaport 306–21: 313 Anastasia letter, 20 May 1917; 313 Anastasia, 4 July 1917; 315 Olga Nikolaevna to Olga Alexandrovna, 21 June 1917. *Rasputin* 238–40. Rasputin-cucumber: Lars Tharp, *Antiques Roadshow— How to Spot, a Fake*, 12. Nicholas as prisoner for life: Rappaport, *Ekaterinburg*, 27.

4. ND 9 March 1917, first walk with Dolgoruky; 21 March, Kerensky visit; 23 March, walks with Olga and Tatiana; 2–3 April, break ice/gapers; 8 April, guards from Soviet; 18 April, reading; 23 April, family in gardens; 14 May, gardening; 3 June, Kerensky/crisis with Alexei's gun; 9 June, sitting here like prisoners; 26 June, Montecristo; 5 July, July days, root of all evil in Petrograd and not in Russia itself; 8 July, Kerensky PM—"the more power he has, the better" 28 July, Conan Doyle/ Livadia or where?; 31 July, the last day at Tsarskoe/meeting with Misha. *Fall* 153, Olga to P. Petrov, 19 June 1917; 154 Olga to Olga Alexandrovna, 21 June; 166 Alix to Anna, 1 August; 168 Elizaveta Naryshkina, 1 August. Departure for east: Rappaport 318–25; Alix to Naryshkina 320; Anastasia to Gibbes 321. Vyrubova 96–100. Gilliard 210–30. ND 9, 21 March 1917, on arrest by Kerensky of Anna. *LP* 575, Lord Stamfordham note, 9 March 1917; 578 George V diary, 11 March; 578 Stamfordham to A. J. Balfour, 17 March; 580 Balfour to Stamfordham, 20 March; 853–7 Stamfordham to Balfour, 21, 24 March (two letters); 588 Stamfordham note, 28 March (Lloyd George more serious than he was aware). The departure and Misha: *LP* 600–4, Benckendorff. Jewellery: Greg King and Penny Wilson, *The Fate of the Romanovs* (henceforth *Fate*) 70.

5. ND 29 September, 6, 20 October (AIII anniversary), more disgraceful than Troubles, 17 November 1917; on *Elders of Zion*, 27 March 1917. *LP* 611, Olga to P. Petrov, 10 October 1917. Vyrubova 133–5, letters from Alexandra. *Fall* 201–2, Nicky to Xenia, 5 November 1917.

6. Tobolsk: the girls Rappaport 339–55. Correspondence: Vyrubova 130–145 including A to V 14 and 21 October 1917; Alexei to V 24 November 1917; 8 December 1917 A to V I know the past is all done; Tatiana to V 9 December 1917; Alexei to V 10 December 1917; Anastasia to V we sit at the windows looking at people; A to V your perfume overcame us, it went the round . . . Nicholas a real marvel; all the past is a dream; A to V 2 March 1918 eternity is everything. Gilliard 235–262

7. ND 12 April 1918, Yakovlev to take me away/more than difficult; no one slept.

Vyrubova 154–6 A to V a new commissar has arrived, Yakovlev . . . Sunbeam is ill; 21 March we feel a storm approaching; late March A to V storm coming nearer, souls at peace. ND 17/30 April–30 June/13 July 1918, arrival in Ekaterinburg, tension between locals and our commissars, drive to Ipatiev, Dolgoruky not allowed in, Ukraintsev, prison regime, whitewashing. *Fate* 79–102, 112–13: policy of Centre, transfer to Ekaterinburg, crisis at Tiumen station, arrival at Ipatiev; diamonds hidden in corsets quoting Alexandra Teglev 136. *Fall* 239, Alexandra's diary, 23–25 April 1918, on visit of Yakovlev, Alexei illness, her "horrible suffering" of choice; 245 Yakovlev to Goloshchekin, 27 April; Sverdlov to Yakovlev, 27 April; 251 Sverdlov to Yakovlev, 29 April, hand over to Ekaterinburg; 255 interview with Yakovlev in *Izvestia*, 16 May; 278 arrest of Dolgoruky. Rappaport 364–6: letters of Olga, Anastasia and Tatiana to parents, May 1917. Tatishchev's fatalism: Botkin 192. Gilliard not wanted and free, walk past Ipatiev 269–72. Lenin on Romanovs: V. I. Lenin, *Sochineniia* 20.166–7, 21.16–17. Goloshchekin, Sverdlov characters: *Fate*, 253–95. For Goloshchekin and Sverdlov relations with Stalin in exile, see Montefiore, *Young Stalin* 259–60. Rappaport, *Ekaterinburg*, 128–34; new regime/jewels/codename/Alexei 171–83, 191.

8. GARF 601.2.27 Yakov Yurovsky's notes 1920 and 1 February 1934 plus unpublished notes (five in total) including most detailed, note of 1922 in APRF 3.58.280, cited in *Fate of the Romanovs*; Pavel Medvedev's note 21–22 February 1919, Sokolov Archive, Houghton Library, Harvard University, Kilgour Collection 35.2.86; and Peter Voikov interview in Gregory Bessedowsky, *Im Dienste Der Sowjets* (Leipzig 1930). Alexandra diary, June–July 1918 GARF 640.1; *Last Diary of Tsaritsa Alexander* (eds. V. Kozlov and V. Khrustalev). ND April–June 1918: GARF 601.1.217–266 *Fall* 277–85; Yurovsky 285; the decisions to kill, review of evidence leaning towards a decision by the Urals Soviet 287–94; Lenin and Sovnarkom approve transfer of family to Ekaterinburg, 2 May 1918; 310 army officer escape plan, 19 June, and reply, 21–23 June 1918; life in Ekaterinburg, testimony of Medvedev 346–8 ND 17/30 April–30 June/13 July 1918, Ekaterinburg, tension between locals and our commissars, drive to Ipatiev, Dolgoruky not allowed in, pop-eyed enemy, prison regime. *Fate* 140–2, 146–7: the molestation of girls on journey to Ekaterinburg and betrayal by Buxhoeveden, arrival and separation of Gilliard and Gibbes; the sympathies of guards for prisoners and flirtation with girls especially Alexander Strekotin. Appointment and inspections of Yuri Yurovsky, Peter Ermakov 233–45; Goloshchekin 245–7.

9. LP 665–6, testimony of killer A. V. Markov. *Fate* 200–11. *Michael* 349–63.

10. Lenin and Goloshchekin in Moscow: *Fall* 290–345. *Fate* 282–295. Peter Voikov, Bessedowsky 203–205. Rappaport, *Ekaterinburg*, 129–43.

11. Yurovsky preparations. *Fate*: 297–302. *Fall* 346–64. Rappaport, *Ekaterinburg*, 28–43; decision 129–443. Character of Goloshchekin/Ermakov and others: *Fate* 268–80; Goloshchekin in Moscow 113–15. LP 674–7, A. G. Belodorodov to N. P. Gorbunov, Sovnarkom, 4 July 1918; Protocol of Presidium of Central Executive Committee, 5 July; Sovnarkom protocol, 5 July.

12. ND 12/26 May–30 June/13 July 1918. ND 27 November 1894 written by Alexandra. This is based on the various published memoirs of Yurovsky, Medvedev and unpublished full account of Yurovsky in AVPRI and also that Strekotin, both cited in *Fate*. *Fall* 346–64. *Fall* 333: Goloshchekin to Sverdlov and Lenin, 16 July 1918. *Fate*, 268–80 Letts and killing squad; 297–331 the killing and burial. Alexandra diary, 11–16 July 1918. Arrival of Voikov and girls still alive: Bessedowsky 208–211. Rappaport, *Ekaterinburg*, 184–202; burial 203–6; dog 207, 214. After the murders, lives of Goloshchekin, Yurovsky etc: *Fate* 509–14.

13. Death of Ella and Grand Duke Sergei Mikhailovich: *Ella* 299–307. Beéche 2.218–19.

14. Burial: *Fate* 316–331, Rappaport, *Ekaterinburg*, 203–6. James Cockfield, *The White Crow: The Life and Times of the Grand Duke Nicholas Mikhailovich Romanov, 1859–1919* 242. Beéche 1.165, 2.200–2, 181–3.

15. Crimea and after: Hall 288–352. For their escape: Frances Welch, *The Russian Court at Sea: The Last Days of A Great Dynasty: The Romanov's Voyage into Exile* (London 2010). On later lives of Romanovs: see Arturo Beéche, *Grand Dukes* and *The Other Grand Dukes*.

16. Ella burial: *Ella* 306–12. Simon Sebag Montefiore, *Jerusalem: The Biography* 444.

## EPILOGUE: RED TSARS/WHITE TSARS

1. Embalming Lenin: Dzerzhinsky quoted in Kotkin, *Stalin* 543; "Russian people are tsarist" Leningrad, April 1926, quoted 586; creation of the USSR, 475–81, 485–6. Stalin to Maria Svanidze on tsar, Ivan the Terrible teacher quoted in Simon Sebag Montefiore, *Stalin: The Court of the Red Tsar* 182–3; new empire 524; when he presented new official history textbooks, tsars and Bolsheviks blended into one another: Nicholas I combined "economic modernization with authoritarian methods"; Alexander II increased Russian power and territory; Alexander III achieved "politically conservative stabilization," while the modernization undertaken by Stalin, "one of the greatest Soviet leaders," whose Terror is scarcely mentioned, resembled "the reforms of Peter the Great"; Putin, the story of his grandfather 118 and 300. See Vladimir Putin, *First Person* (N.Y. 2000). On history and Putin: Vladimir Shapentokh, Anna Arutunyan, *Freedom, Repression and Private Property in Russia* 51–5, inc. quotes from Patriarch Kyril on miracle of God. Textbooks: Alexander Filippov (ed.), *Noveishaia istoriia Rossii 1945–2006* 87–8. Russian core civilization: *Nezavisimaia gazeta*, 23 January 2012, interview with V. Putin. This account of personal style of Putin, inc. story of traitors/weaklings like Nicholas II, is based on: *Newsweek*, 1 August 2014, The President by Ben Judah, inc. Putin's assertion: "Never abdicate." Thanks to Ben Judah for sharing unpublished details of this story.

# INDEX

## A NOTE ABOUT THE AUTHOR

Dr. Simon Sebag Montefiore is a historian of Russia and the Middle East. *Potemkin: Catherine the Great's Imperial Partner* was short-listed for the Samuel Johnson Prize. *Stalin: The Court of the Red Tsar* won the History Book of the Year Prize at the British Book Awards. *Young Stalin* won the Los Angeles Times Book Prize for Biography, the Costa Biography Award, and le Grande Prix de la biographie politique. *Jerusalem: The Biography* was a worldwide best seller. Montefiore's books are published in more than forty languages. He is the author of the novels *Sashenka* and *One Night in Winter,* which won the Paddy Power Political Fiction Book of the Year Award in 2014. A Fellow of the Royal Society of Literature, Montefiore graduated from Cambridge University, where he received his PhD. He lives in London.

A NOTE ON THE TYPE

This book was set in Scala, a typeface designed by the Dutch designer Martin Majoor (b. 1960) in 1988 and released by the FontFont foundry in 1990. While designed as a fully modern family of fonts containing both a serif and a sans serif alphabet, Scala retains many refinements normally associated with traditional fonts.

Composed by North Market Street Graphics, Lancaster, Pennsylvania
Printed and bound by Berryville Graphics, Berryville, Virginia

—